✧ Tools for Your Journey into Self-Discovery ✧

The experience of interpreting your birth chart can help you to re-discover yourself in a very direct way. On a deep level, we all want to be free of our personal traps. Many elements of character shown in the birth chart can be repressed, pushed into the unconscious mind as a way of surviving or adapting, and these often control conscious actions, invisibly, from the background. When you find it impossible to break through personal "blocks," an accurate chart interpretation can pinpoint exactly what is stopping you and what you need to do to find your way through it. By resurrecting your repressed elements, you can restore yourself to your own true, original personality with healing effects.

Also located in your birth chart is the whole pattern and sequence of types of experiences in your life, along with their changes through time. In some ways, the pattern of events that occur in a life, and the precise times at which they happen, are predetermined; yet every individual, when not reacting from conditioned habit, has free choice of how to respond to any experience. We create our own limits. We can also create our own freedom.

By finding and interpreting the planetary positions at your birth, you chart a course into your inner space and begin a process of knowing and awakening yourself as never before; plus you begin to recognize that you have choices and can choose the pathways you want your life to take. And that is the purpose of this book. To give you the tools for your own journey into self-knowledge and self-awakening.

Bon Voyage.

About the Author

Dennis Oakland was born in Derby, England, in 1939. His career has included work in science and administration, including seven years with the British Civil Service. His studies of Buddhist teachings and other disciplines took him to Scotland and then Canada, where he became a professional astrologer in 1970. He has practiced in Toronto, Vancouver, and Edmonton, Canada; Sidney, Australia; and currently throughout New Zealand.

His major interests include eastern religion and philosophy, western sciences, and psychology, particularly paths of integration and awakening. He has appeared on radio and television, gives lectures and workshops, and also does individual interpretations. Writing has been an outgrowth of his teaching experiences, and he is currently working on a new book.

To Write to the Author

If you wish to contact the author or would like more informaiton about this book, please write to the author in care of Llewellyn Worldwide, and we will forward your request. Both the author and the publisher appreciate hearing from you and learning of your enjoyment of this book and how it has helped you. Llewellyn Worldwide cannot guarantee that every letter written to the author can be answered, but all will be forwarded. Please write to:

Dennis Oakland
c/o Llewellyn Worldwide
P.O. Box 64383-594, St. Paul, MN 55164-0383, U.S.A.
Please enclose a self-addressed, stamped envelope for reply, or $1.00 to cover costs.
If outside U.S.A., enclose international postal reply coupon.

Free Catalog from Llewellyn Worldwide

For more than 90 years, Llewellyn has brought readers knowledge in the fields of metaphysics and human potential. Learn about the newest books in spiritual guidance, natural healing, astrology, occult philosophy, and more. Enjoy book reviews, new age articles, a calendar of events, plus current advertised products and services. To get your free copy of *The Llewellyn's New Worlds of Mind and Spirit*, send your name and address to:
Llewellyn's New Worlds of Mind and Spirit
P.O. Box 64383–594, St. Paul, MN 55164–0383, U.S.A.

The Llewellyn Modern Astrology Library

Your PLANETARY PERSONALITY

Everything You Need
To Make Sense of Your Horoscope

Dennis Oakland

1995
Llewellyn Publications
St. Paul, Minnesota, 55164-0383, U.S.A.

FIRST EDITION
Second Printing, 1995

Library of Congress Cataloging-in-Publication Data:
   Oakland, Dennis.
        Your planetary personality : everything you need to make sense of your
horoscope / by
      Dennis Oakland.
           p.   cm.—(Llewellyn modern astrology library series)
   Includes bibliographical references.
      ISBN 0-87542-594-1
      1. Natal Astrology. 2. Horoscopes. 3. Astrology.   I. Title.   II. Series.
   BF1719.035   1991   91-47574
   133.5′4—dc20   CIP

Llewellyn Publications
A Division of Llewellyn Worldwide, Ltd.
P.O. Box 64383, St. Paul, MN 55164-0383

✧ **Dedication** ✧

This book is dedicated to the Archetypes of Astrology
and to all those who have helped me along the way (especially Ed,
for the ephemeris, and many hours of help with computing).

May it benefit all living beings!

THE LLEWELLYN MODERN ASTROLOGY LIBRARY

This series contains books for the *Leading Edge* of practical and applied astrology as we move toward the culmination of the 20th century.

This is not speculative astrology, nor astrology so esoteric as to have little practical application in meeting the needs of people in these critical times. Yet, these books go far beyond the meaning of "practicality" as seen prior to the 1980s. Our needs are spiritual as well as mundane, planetary as well as particular, evolutionary as well as progressive. Astrology grows with the times, and our times make heavy demands upon Intelligence and Wisdom.

The authors are all professional astrologers drawing from their own practice and knowledge of historical persons and events, demonstrating proof of their conclusions with the horoscopes of real people in real situations.

Modern Astrology relates the individual person to the Universe in which he/she lives, not as a passive victim of alien forces but as an active participant in an environment expanded to the breadth, *and depth*, of the Cosmos. We are not alone, and our responsibilities are infinite.

The horoscope is both a measure, and a guide, to personal movement—seeing every act undertaken, every decision made, every event, as *time dynamic*: with effects that move through the many dimensions of space and levels of consciousness in fulfillment of Will and Purpose. Every act becomes an act of Will, for we extend our awareness to consequences reaching to the ends of time and space.

This is astrology supremely important to this unique period in human history, when Pluto transits through Scorpio and Neptune through Capricorn, and the books in this series are intended to provide insight into the critical needs and the critical decisions that must be made.

These books, too, are "active agents," bringing to the reader knowledge which will liberate the higher forces inside each person to the end that we may fulfill that for which we were intended.

Carl Llewellyn Weschcke

✧ Contents ✧

✧ Introduction ✧

Why Study Astrology?

In the summer of 1970, during my first year as an astrologer, Rab Wilkie (an astrologer friend) and I looked after a stall in the Canadian National Exhibition in Toronto. The stall belonged to a friend who ran the Studio of the Joyous Brush. It was in a place where we could see all the activity in the exhibition hall, but badly placed to attract attention, so we had lots of spare time on our hands.

To fill some of this time, we calculated the astrological chart for each day, on the day (this can be done for any moment in time, for any place on Earth, and is known to depict the thrust of events happening there and then). We then updated the chart from minute to minute, paying particular attention to every point through the day when any planet crossed the local horizon (rose in the East or set in the West) or crossed the vertical meridian (above or below), these being the most active points in any chart. We found to our delight that when no planet was transiting any of these "angles," most people in the hall were clustered attentively around the exhibits, but as soon as any planet hit any of those four "cardinal points" there was a rush of activity as people flooded from place to place.

Though any planet would do to stir a flow of people, we found that whenever the planet Uranus (astrologically connected with independent individualism) crossed an angle we were visited by an eccentric musician from the other side of the hall, coming over for a "rave." We came to expect his visits at those times.

Apart from this general "flow-pattern," the current planetary aspects (angular geometric relationships between planets) deeply affected the mood of the time and the activity. If Mars was involved, people moved with a directed energy; if Venus, they ambled around, usually eating as they went; if Saturn, crowds were smaller, enthusiasm and involvement less, except where serious business interests were involved; if Jupiter, enthusiasm was high, and the babble of sound was pronounced; and so it went.

A few years later, I was driving in the South Island of New Zealand with a friend, a new astrologer. We decided to do the same thing, to calculate the precise times of planets crossing the angles. Since we were on the move south we had to take our changing latitude into account. We noticed that the planet Neptune (associated particularly with water) was culminating, or coming to the "midheaven," the highest point in the local sky. Having calculated its precise moment of crossing the meridian, we did a count-down; 5..4..3..2..1.. and the first drops of rain hit the windshield.

Over the years of my career as an astrologer, I have taught many people the basic elements of astrology. One technique I use is to put on the blackboard a list of the current transit planetary aspects, then ask class members about the quality and type of their experiences during the past week. I then point out what could be expected from the present aspect pattern (without attempting to force experience to fit theory), and people suddenly discover strong common streams in their experiences. I use this method to demonstrate that every person is directly aware of the effects of planetary aspects, even though they do not know that such aspects are happening. Over the years I discovered that I could guess very accurately which planets were currently aspecting each other, simply from the nature of my experience at the time. Not only could I guess what aspects were happening, but I usually looked in an ephemeris to check what was happening within ten minutes of their culmination (becoming precise).

From these examples, you can see that astrology is something that can be experienced and observed directly. Anyone who takes the trouble to look into it will find that it works, that the effects described by astrologers in books are not a matter of imagination or wishful thinking, but are real. As an astrologer, I object to all the public statements against astrology by otherwise rational scientists, since it can be guaranteed that they have never taken the trouble to explore astrology in its own terms. Anyone who does so finds that it works, and works with great precision. But what has this approach to do with newspaper astrology? Practically nothing. The type of so-called astrology that you find in newspaper horoscope columns is the result of media pressure on astrologers to produce something for the entertainment of the public, even though the astrologers know, and publicly state, that it is the weakest possible way of using astrology. We cannot predict with any kind of accuracy what will be happening to one-twelfth of the human race (any one sun sign), at any one time. Astrology can be very precise when used individually, but loses power by becoming randomized when used collectively.

You may be looking for reasons to help you to decide whether to enter the exploration of astrology, for facts and figures or whatever to convince you that the study is worthwhile. Such things come to you in the form of experiences as you explore the subject. Nothing that anyone tells you about it can have the same impact as your own personal experience. Remember that anything you are told, or taught, by others, is their experience, not yours. Real knowledge does not come to you by your absorbing supposed facts related to you by someone else, but only comes to you through your own direct experience.

Having said that, why should you read this book? Perhaps if I tell you about the steps that led me into astrology, that will help you to gain an idea of its potential value to you, and encourage you to take the first few steps yourself.

My contact with astrology began in the form of a friendship. In 1961 I left my parental home near Nottingham, England, and moved to London, to enter the Civil Service at the age of 21. Experiences during my childhood had left me emotionally unsettled and confused, and wanting to understand the whys and wherefores of human suffering, wanting to understand why I hurt, and how to undo it. Though I didn't realize it at this time, I also wanted to uncover the causes of war, having been born just at the start of World War II. To pursue this, I joined the Buddhist Society when I arrived in London. (Basic tenets of Buddhism that led me in: There is suffering; it has causes; anything arising from causes is temporary; therefore there are ways to end suffering.)

Lance Cousins was a member of the Cambridge University Buddhist Society, and visited London regularly to attend meetings of the London Buddhist Society. Being of a similar age, we and the other young members clustered together.

Astrological elements, talk of "sun-signs" and such, cropped up in Lance's conversation. This puzzled me, since I held the common superstition, that astrology and such things are occult nonsense, and I wondered why this "big-brain" from Cambridge would pay any attention to them.

There matters rested for several years, except for my noticing that Lance's astrological comments had a certain aptness, that they weren't very wide of the mark.

During that time I dived into meditation to start exploring my own inner world, and read voraciously in psychology and philosophies to try to encompass all the various viewpoints on how mankind ticks. Of particular value to me were Vipassana, or Insight meditation, and Buddhist psychology. My mind began to open up, and I let it take me where it would, into space sciences (following my teen-age fascination with flight, and curiosity about the stars), into physics (to understand the physical universe), into physiology to understand the human body—and so on. My curiosity had been unlocked.

I began to understand that man's mind is very sensitive and is easily marked, forced into restricted patterns, conditioned. Even our understanding of what is real in the Universe around us is conditioned by the views of the family and culture in which we grow up. Whatever we believe to be real, we hold equally strong (and possibly equally false) views about what is not or cannot be real, and these views are only beliefs.

I began to understand that those views are all very relative, and that they predetermine the way we see ourselves and the world around us, not letting us even perceive things that we hold to be unreal, even if they actually exist (like scientists with astrology).

The strongest part of the building or conditioning of our views and attitudes comes from hurtful experiences. As living creatures we are designed to survive, and to learn how to survive against many kinds of potential danger. Our bodies, when experiencing threatening situations, switch on to very intense levels of functioning (fear, fight, flight), and imprint very deeply any response learned in and to such situations.

Any threat of withdrawal of love, or any show of disapproval or anger from our parents, teachers and other elders, is terrifying to us when we are young (this doesn't change as we age, we simply become accustomed to dealing with it). Having to adapt to the adult world is traumatic, having to learn to lie, to lose our innocence and our idealism, and adopt adult neuroses, is the most difficult thing we ever do in our lives. Conditioning comes from often repeated experiences, as we come to respond to them habitually.

All forms of conditioning in us can be undone, since they are simply acquired habits; we weren't born with them (unless we take reincarnation into account, and even past-life experience is still conditioning). Suffering comes from responding to our surroundings and the people in them as though they are still threatening, either to take away things and experiences that we need, or to impose on us those that we don't want. It also comes from not feeling able to be, or to express freely, who we really are inside ourselves. Liberation from suffering comes from undoing such conditioned habits, leaving us free to respond to the world from the depths of our basically healthy being (and if we weren't fundamentally healthy, the human race would never have survived this long). Remaining locked in our own conflicts, we pass them on to all around us, creating the society and the world we live in. If you want to understand more of this, I recommend you read *The Continuum Concept* by Jean Liedloff (on natural childhood needs) and *The Primal Scream* by Arthur Janov (on dealing with repressed hurts).

All of us are distinctly individual beings, and none of us have the right to take such individual identity away from any other person, or in any way to override his or her own true being. Unfortunately, as parents we believe we have to "civilize the little brute" and place restraints on our children (different kinds in different countries). Our children then grow up conditioned to expect control from above, and continue to create and support societies in which this happens, giving them little true control over the directions of their own lives.

Here I speak to those who believe that we have to be controlled to restrain our antisocial tendencies; there are no criminals or psychotics or even antisocial types among us when we have been given the real loving recognition as ourselves that we need from birth onwards, for, whatever we have been given, we tend to return that favor. If we have been given rejection, we throw it back at those who we feel reject us.

From our own true inner identity springs our own true sense of purpose and direction in life; in fact our identity and purpose are one and the same thing. Living our own lives and carrying out our own purposes are identical when we know who we are, and cannot happen at all if we are still being who we have been told to be, or not being who we have been taught not to be. When whole cultures bring up their children to submit to outer ideas of who and what they should be, you can guarantee that there will be little happiness there, and that people will turn to substitutes for real living, such as materialism, and entertainment, to fill the inner void.

All this gradually crystallized in my mind over the next few years as I came to understand the processes that had affected my own life. I saw that they were the same for all of us. I began to see the need for an accurate way of diagnosing what kinds of conditioning any individual had been through in life, and found it in astrology.

Meditation led me into a ten-month retreat period in 1966-67 (I later recognized this as the time of the Uranus-Pluto conjunction, the major influence on the idealistic 1960s and the Space-Race; the dark face of this aspect triggered the Vietnam War and the Arab-Israeli Six-day War when it culminated). This retreat was spent largely at what became Samye Ling Tibetan monastery in Scotland, when Chogyam Trungpa Rinpoche, Akong Rinpoche and Sherab Palden Beru came to take over my teacher's meditation community center. Toward the end of that retreat, I became aware of my need for more and deeper instruction, and decided to follow my teacher to Canada, his homeland, to which he had returned a year or so earlier.

On returning to London and re-joining the Civil Service (I was by this time an Executive Officer in the Science Research Council), I lived with a friend of Lance's while preparing to emigrate. This friend, Glynn Davies, was a wild, whiskered Welshman, director of his own company, and an astrologer.

Glynn demonstrated astrology to me by drawing up the birth chart of a close friend of mine who he hadn't met. His interpretation of her character through her chart had enough resemblance to my experience of her to convince me that there was something quite deep and accurate there. However, I was distracted by approaching emigration, and said to myself "If I dive into that, it looks quite large enough to drown in," and decided not to pursue it.

In July 1968 I flew to Toronto, where I found a very active Dharma group. One member ran a bookshop, and since he was an astrologer, his shop had a very good astrological section. I was hooked, and spent every available minute (including spare moments at my job as a computer programmer for the Ontario Provincial Government) learning to calculate and interpret birth charts. (Astrologically speaking, my progressed Ascendant was going from Capricorn into Aquarius at that time; I was moving from an orthodox view of myself and my life toward a more individualistic and holistic one, and Aquarius is *the* astrological sign. In 1989, my Ascendant moved from Aquarius into Pisces, the oceanic, and I finally took up scuba diving.)

I found quite enough in astrology to satisfy myself that it did work, but did not find enough depth or coherence to satisfy the perfectionist in me. So I began to explore beyond what was taught in the books, using everything I had learned from physics, psychology, and other studies. I learned by asking people whether the book interpretations were accurate, and if not, how not. Since I was living among people who were all working to increase the depth of their self-knowledge, I had an excellent early grounding in exploring astrology. This was enhanced by further meditation practice under a good teacher and by active exploration of my own mind and life, and those of others, through explorative psychotherapy of an eclectic nature.

I gradually found that the whole pattern and sequence of experiences in people's lives could be found in their birth charts, and in their chart progressions or changes through time. I also found that every individual always has free choice of how to respond to any experience, when not reacting from conditioned habit. We create our own limits. In some ways, the pattern of types of event that occur in a life, and the precise times at which they happen, are absolutely set, predetermined; what is not completely predetermined is how we respond to the events of our lives. Since our response decides the path we take, each major decision involving a choice of direction, our individual astrological event-pattern actually covers a multitude of possible lives, or ways of living.

In psychotherapy I discovered that many elements of character shown in the birth chart could be repressed, pushed into the unconscious mind as a way of surviving or adapting, and would then control conscious actions invisibly from the background. I also found that those repressed elements could be resurrected, restoring the person to their own true original personality, with healing effects. I now believe that this is the death and resurrection and the being born again to life more abundant intended in true Christianity, the crucifixion being the impaling of the true being on the cross of convention and conditioning, the transfiguration being "ye shall know the truth and the truth shall make you free," enabling us to find the kingdom of Heaven within.

I recognized that in interpreting someone's birth chart (including my own) I could help them to re-discover themselves in a more direct and deeper way than by using any other tool, excepting their own direct self-exploration through meditation or psychotherapy. If anyone finds it impossible to break through personal blocks, an accurate chart interpretation by a skilled and knowledgeable astrologer can pinpoint exactly what is stopping them, and help them to find their way through it, if they want to know, to find out. If they don't want to know, nothing will release them—but usually on some deep level we all want to be free of our personal traps.

I spent a year working in a stockbroker's office after the O.P.G. cut back staff, then left to start practicing as an astrologer full-time, telling myself that I would take the study as far as I found it to work, and stop when I found its limits.

That was twenty years ago, and I am still going, knowing now that there are no limits, except my own. Along the way, the study has taken me further into all sorts of psychology and methods of awakening (from which the interpretations in this book have sprung), into symbolism and archetypes, into deep levels of physics. The view that I have formed of astrology during that time is this: what we call astrology is the same thing as space-time geometry.

That may sound complicated, but is not. We live in three dimensions of space linked inseparably to one of time. This four dimensional matrix has some basic geometrical properties, abilities to produce certain kinds of form and to put those forms through certain kinds of changes. This is all that we ever experience in our world or ourselves, form—going through changes. These universal tendencies towards forming and changing are what we think of as laws, whether of physics, biology, psychology, or any other sciences. The Universe has one fundamental pattern, which produces all things. Apparent differences are just that, apparent, not finally real.

Our Solar System

The generally accepted image of astrology is that it is the study of the rhythms of movements (changes) in the solar system, of the ongoing movements of the planets, acting as local focuses for laws of form and change, which affect Earth.

Think of it this way: Our solar system coalesced from a huge cloud of hydrogen, enriched by small amounts of heavier elements which came from earlier supernovas (which is all we are made of—of star-stuff). As the system formed, it did so as a complex whole. Gravity first drew hydrogen, the lightest, and therefore the most mobile element, to the center, where the squeeze of gravity heated it to thermonuclear incandescence. The Sun was born.

Heavier elements were drawn toward the center, spiraling inward and flattening into a spinning plane. After a while, radiation pressure, light from the Sun, blew a "wind" outward. The heavy elements condensed into lumps, which first stuck together electromagnetically, then grew by gravitational attraction. The heavy inner planets formed from a mixture of rock and metals. The remaining lighter elements, gases, were blown outward, eventually to draw together as the gas-giant outer planets.

The solar system is a complex whole, formed from simple laws. Each planet in the system has been going around its own orbit since the system formed 4.5 billion years ago. All those orbital motions (including changes in the orbits themselves) are the most massive changing element in the system, and anything that develops inside the system—such as the very thin, delicate film of life and climate on Earth, or the weather pouring out from the Sun—has been subjected to those rhythms for the whole of its existence.

Protoplasmic life is sensitive to changes in its environment, and adapts strongly to any regularity in those changes, building responses appropriate to them, and ways of life around them. It is not just life that is sensitive to such rhythms, but any system or complex whole that is delicately balanced, or in dynamic equilibrium (which covers everything). Any such system simply needs an input of a regular or rhythmic kind to begin swinging in harmony with that input; this is called rhythm entrainment. If a system is unstably balanced, a push can lead to catastrophe.

Anyone who plays a stringed instrument can tell you about resonance. Briefly, rhythm is contagious. A string of particular length, thickness and tension, if struck or plucked will make a similar string nearby begin to vibrate, even with no obvious physical connection between them. Of course there is a connection; vibrations are set up in the air surrounding the first string, and move through the air to shake the second.

Not only will any similar string respond, but also any that can vibrate at any harmonic of the tone of the plucked string. A harmonic is any simple fractional or multiple relationship between two vibrations. Since vibrations or frequencies are counted in oscillations or cycles per unit of time (for example a second), a harmonic can be described as a vibration of a half, a third, a quarter, a fifth, and so on (or twice, three times, four times, etc.), of the same number of cycles per second. The range of possible harmonics is very large, being all simple numerical and fractional relationships between frequencies.

Also, if two oscillating or cyclic systems have rhythms that are close to the same frequency, the smaller will be pulled into line, into unison with the larger. The planetary rhythms of our solar system are the largest and strongest local vibrations.

Think of the planets in motion around the Sun, and moons moving around their planets, as being vibrating strings, as an harmonic system. Their vibrations are counted in years per cycle rather than cycles per second, but the principle is exactly the same. In continual motion at their different rates (from one orbit per month for our Moon, to one per 247.7 years for Pluto), the planets evolve through all possible geometric harmonic relationships with each other. It takes them some 40 million years before they begin to repeat the pattern. These changing relationships constitute the process of time that we experience, its changing waves and pressures swaying the ebb and flow of processes here on Earth, from evolution, through climate, through history to momentary individual experience.

Nothing else exists except processes. We think (falsely) in terms of events, being materialistically conditioned to think of *things*, and being too short-sighted in time to be able to perceive everything as a dynamic flow of processes. Every "thing" or object is actually a cross section of one or many processes going on through time.

A human being is a complex of many processes happening on many levels, some physical, some emotional, some mental, some social, and so on. Most, if not all, processes are wave-like, varying in their levels of activity between limits. We sleep and wake; our energies vary; our attention wanders over many things, returning again and again to familiar paths; our experiences wander through a variety of (mostly familiar) spaces, often very regularly. Wave-like processes are easily entrained or locked into any stronger local rhythms that have a wave-length or a harmonic close to their own natural frequencies.

Some scientists object that planetary forces are too small to have any effect on us. They forget that our eyes and our brains have cells that are capable of responding to single quanta of energy—the smallest amount of energy in the universe. Ten percent of the brain has this ultimate sensitivity. Information is often far more important to living systems than is sheer force, and information can be carried by very tiny energies. Our eyes take in less energy than we feel from the planets, but we can hardly call our eyesight or the information that we gain through it insignificant in our lives. No one yet knows how or why astrology works; no one yet knows how or why gravity or electro-magnetism work either, but that doesn't stop us from basing all our living experience on these forces.

Enough introduction; we'll now go on to an overview of what a birth chart is, and then look at how to draw up a birth chart.

✧ 1 ✧

How to Work Out
Your Own Chart

THE OVERVIEW

This part of the book is to help you to understand *what* you are doing in drawing up a birth chart. If you want to leave this, you can skim on to the method in the next chapter which tells you *how* to do it.

A birth chart is a diagram or map of the exact positions of all the planets in our solar system, as they were at a particular instant of time (the birth moment), as seen from a specific place on Earth (the birthplace). We call such maps birth charts simply because we usually draw them up for the births of human beings, though they can be drawn up for the starting moment of any event or process (the "birth" of a business, of a town or a country, of an idea, of a relationship . . .). Thus, a birth chart is a kind of snapshot, capturing the activity of one moment (in space-time). Traditionally, such a chart is called a horoscope, which means literally "an observation (or view) of the hour (or time)."

Why do we take the birth moment as the significant time? Astrology is the study of processes. Every process has a moment of beginning, a focal point from which it exists as an independent entity separate from its preconditions. Think this way: when a seed is cast out from a plant, it lies dormant for some time. It may have the potential for life, the potential to grow into a living, experiencing plant, but that potential has not yet been activated. Only when the conditions are right does the germination begin, and the new plant take an active role in its world. For humans, the womb-period is experientially a relatively dormant one (although womb-experience does affect the child). By using a chart of the birth moment, we are focusing particularly on the developing process of the active involvement of the individual in the world, on the combination of personality and life-experience (in scientific terms, on the interplay between nature and nurture). Also, we have no accurate way of finding out the moment of conception, which is the one other important beginning-point for any individual.

So that you can get a glimpse of the full physical nature of what a birth chart depicts, let us take a small journey through space-time.

1

The Zodiac

Here you are, at present sitting in a particular place, and at a particular point in time. In your imagination, float up from where you are, rise steadily above the ground, watch it recede from you, seeing ever more of it come into view. The higher you rise, the more curved the horizon becomes until you can see that the Earth is a sphere turning beneath you. The sky turns from blue to black, and the stars appear.

Now look all around. The most obvious objects in the blackness of interplanetary space around you are the Earth itself, blue-white and beautiful, and the only visible living thing, then the brilliant Sun around which the Earth is moving, and the white Moon circling the Earth. If you have risen above the northern hemisphere you will see the Earth spinning counterclockwise both on itself and around the Sun. If you are above the southern hemisphere you will see both the eastward turning of Earth and its orbital motion as being clockwise.

Surrounding you in all directions are billions of stars, a few close and/or bright, the rest forming vast misty clouds in the distance. These star-clouds are flattened into a broad milky path running right around the Earth and Sun at enormous distance, which is our view of the swirling spiral of our galaxy from inside its disc. Regions of the galaxy, particularly toward its center, are obscured by huge dark clouds of dust, remnants from exploded stars, just like the cloud from which our solar system and ourselves were born. The dust-clouds are breeding grounds for new stars and planets. Beyond our galaxy are billions of others, the closest appearing as small misty spirals; the more distant are seen in giant clusters splashed out through apparently infinite space.

The light from the very closest star takes over four years to get here; from the most distant star in our galaxy it takes some 70,000 years, while the light from the most distant galaxy takes several billion years to arrive. By comparison, light from our own Sun takes just over eight minutes to get to Earth.

If you look carefully at the closest stars, you can see that they do not appear to move at all (they actually do, but very slowly indeed). Against the backdrop of the universe, we can see a few spots of colored light that crawl along, and if we look very closely, we can see them as spheres. These are the planets in our own solar system, the Earth's closest neighbors in space. Again they appear to be strung out along a line that circles the Earth, since they all move around the central Sun in near-circular orbital paths, all of which are very nearly in the same flat plane. This plane is tilted about sixty degrees off the plane of our galaxy.[1]

Let us speed the passing of time so that we can see the planets' movements better. Our attention is attracted first to a tiny point of light very near the Sun. This is the planet Mercury. We notice it first because it is moving around the Sun faster than any of the other planets. In fact, it races around a little over four times as the Earth circles the Sun but once. The second noticeable thing about Mercury is that as it circles the Sun, it dips in toward it and swoops out away from it in a regular wave-like motion. As it does this, we can see that it turns on its own axis (spins on itself) precisely twice for every three times it orbits the Sun. (In astrology we find that where Mercury is involved, there is usually a pattern of "two-to-three," whether of events in a sequence, points in a journey, or stages in whatever is developing).

Looking outward from the Sun and Mercury, we can see that the rest of the planets are all moving around the Sun at different speeds, spread out in the near-flat plane of the

---

1. Erlewine, M. and M. *Astrophysical Directions*. Heart Center Publ., 1977.

solar system, like racers in the various but very unequal lanes of a broad race track. The closer to the Sun in the center a planet is, the faster it moves; the further away, the slower, out to cold, tiny, distant Pluto, around 39 times as far from the Sun as is the Earth, and taking almost 248 times as long to circle around it, forever being "lapped" by the other, faster planets.

Let us use one of Pluto's years as the measure or yardstick and time the circling of all the other planets. Moving inward from Pluto's orbit we come first to Neptune, which goes around its path one-and-a-half times to Pluto's once. To be accurate, Pluto's orbit is such that it actually overlaps Neptune's, allowing Pluto to come in closer to the Sun than Neptune; Pluto is on that inside track now. Next in is eccentric Uranus, spinning around its orbit on its side, rolling around the Sun nearly three times per Pluto year; then comes Saturn with bright rings and family of moons, circling the Sun nearly eight-and-a-half times; then vast turbulent Jupiter, largest of our planets, pouring more energy out through its own lunar family than it gets from the Sun, which it orbits nearly 21 times; Mars is next, small, ruddy and dusty, completing nearly 132 orbits; then comes our Earth ticking off almost 248 orbits or years; Venus completes over 402 laps around the solar center, while fast Mercury traces its own path 1,028 times.

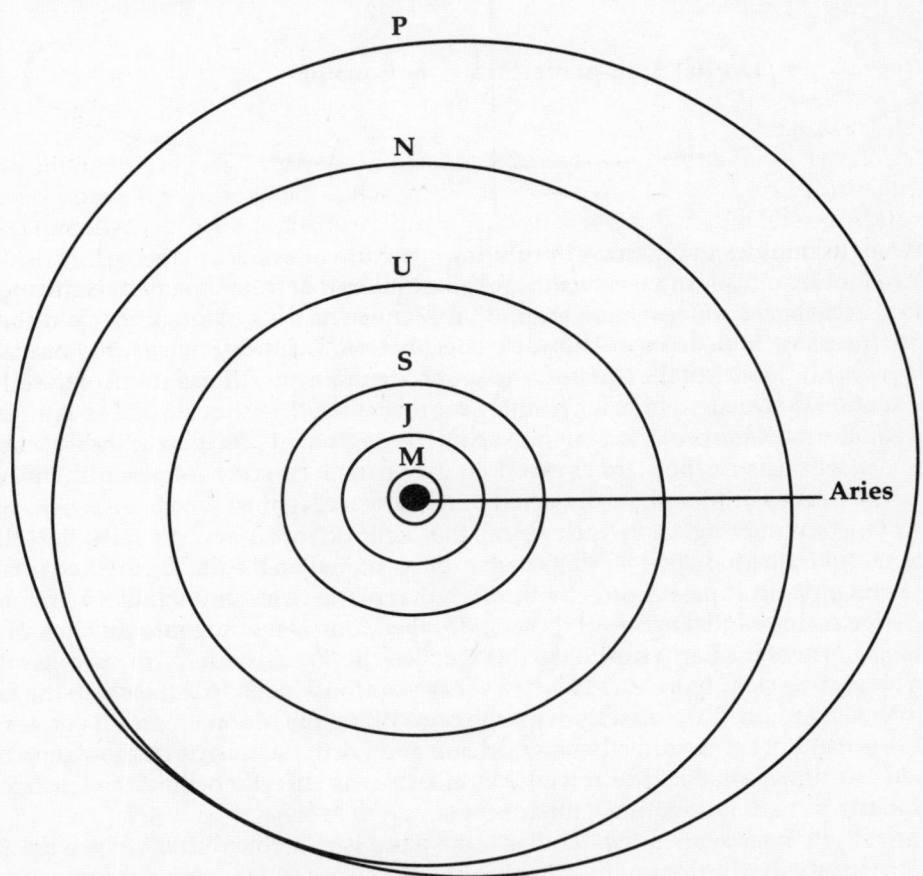

The Orbits of our Solar System

Since we see the rest of the planets from the point of view of Earth, which is itself circling the Sun, we see our own orbital motion added to theirs. If the Earth is overtaking an outer planet ("passing it on the inside track"), or being overtaken by an inner one, we may see the other planet as moving backward against the stellar background; we call this apparent reverse motion retrograde. If a planet was retrograde at the time of someone's birth, its effects are usually far more personal and inward-turned.

If we want to measure the planets' movements accurately, or just to describe or pin-point their positions at any one time, we need some framework or co-ordinate system within which to assess and describe them. Since we must measure planetary movements in three dimensions of space plus one of time, we need a base-line that can be used to describe all four dimensions. As earthlings, the handiest and most meaningful yardstick we have is the Earth itself, and particularly its plane of movement around the Sun.

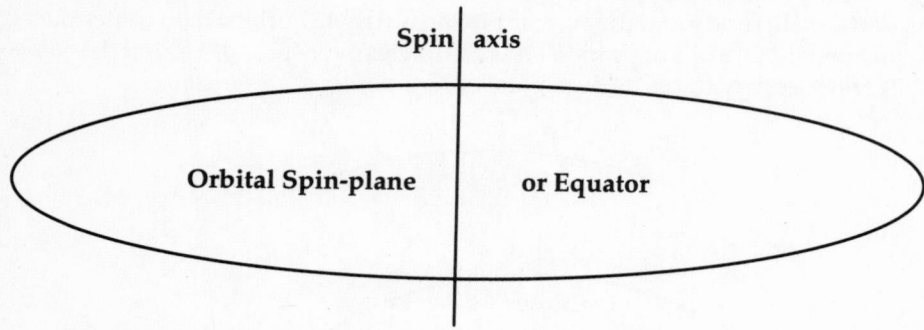

When we look at any rotating or orbiting structure or system in three dimensional space, we find that it has an axis of spin, and an equatorial or orbital plane at right angles to that axis. Distances are measured around the plane in degrees of longitude, and above or below the plane in degrees of latitude or declination. Latitude is measured on Earth running north and south of the equator, and in space running north and south of the ecliptic. Declination is measured in space running north and south of the celestial equator (the Earth's equatorial plane projected out into space). A degree is 1/360 part of the full circle.

In fact, we measure the planet's positions in two main co-ordinate systems. The first is that of the Earth's orbital plane projected out into space, against which we see the Sun and the planets as moving, and which we call the "Ecliptic" or zodiac. We call it the ecliptic since, as our own Moon traces out its own orbit, centered on the Earth but tilted off the Earth's orbital plane, it passes directly through that plane twice on each of its circlings, that is, twice each month. On one of these nodes the Moon is moving into that half of its path that is north of the Earth's orbit (so this is called the "north node"), on the other it is moving south (the "south node"). Twice in every year those nodal points where the two orbits intersect are lined up directly with the Sun. When the Moon crosses its nodes at these times, it either comes directly between Sun and Earth, casting its shadow onto the Earth and creating a solar eclipse at New Moon, or passes directly behind the Earth and through Earth's shadow, creating a lunar eclipse at Full Moon.

The ecliptic is also called the "Zodiac" (the word is related to "Zoo"), since the ancients labeled its sub-divisions with animal names descriptive of the characteristic effects felt from those parts of the zodiac.

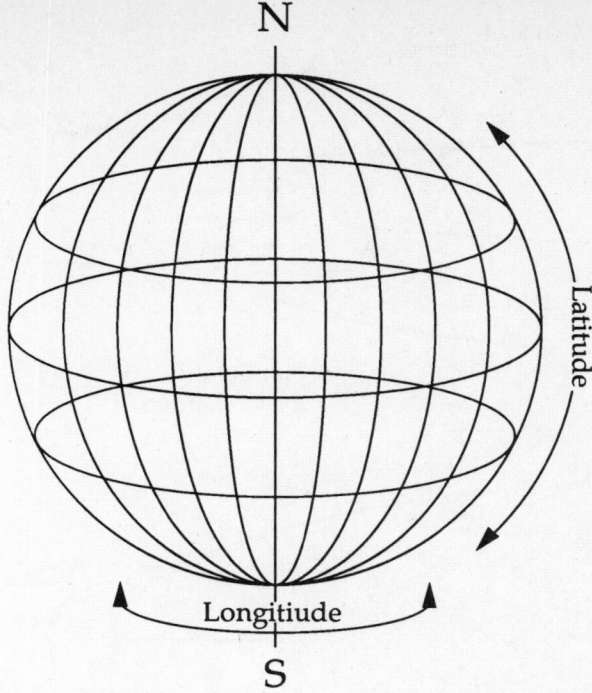

Latitude and Longitude

Since we divide any circular space into 360 equal divisions we call degrees, we do this with the Sun's apparent track around the Earth. We also divide this whole into 12 equal sectors of 30 degrees each, which we call "signs" of the zodiac.

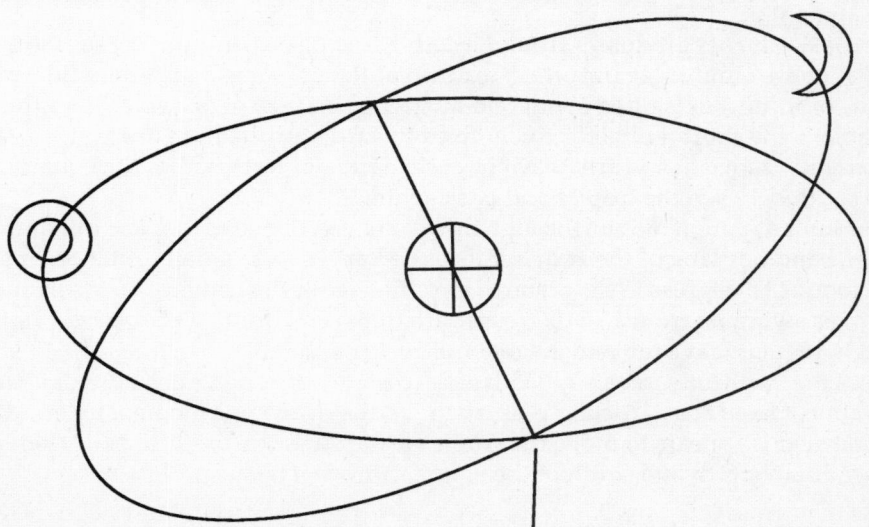

Nodal axis, where orbits intersect.

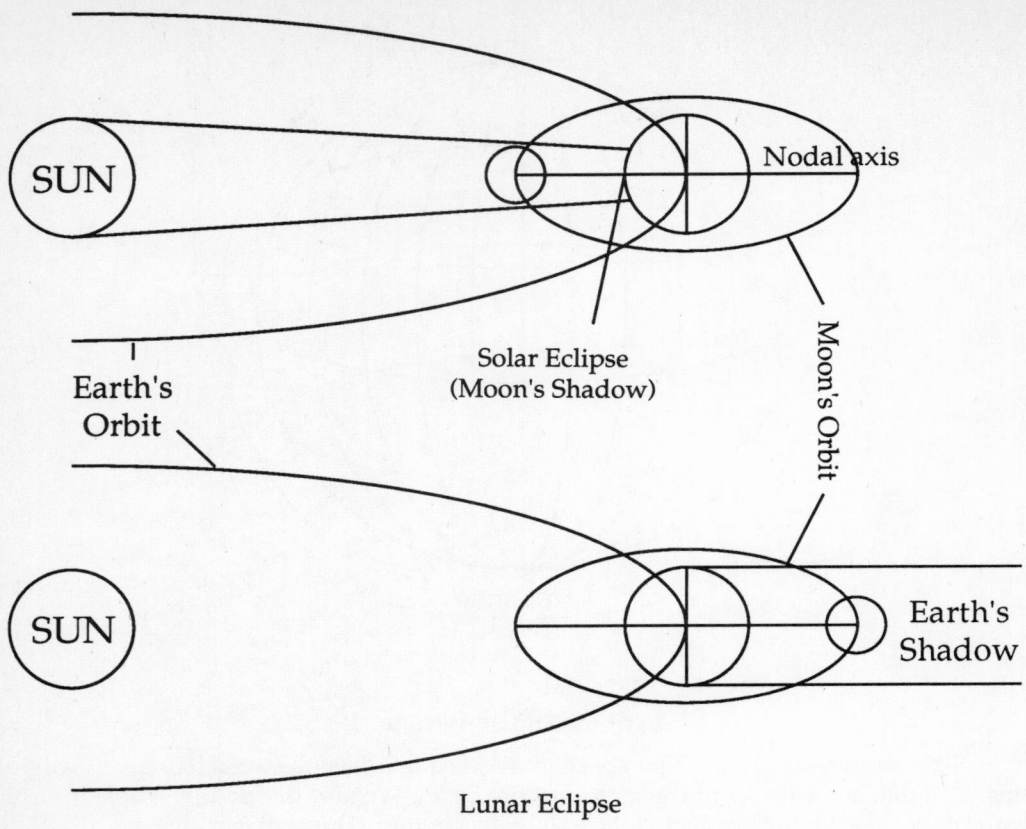

Lunar Eclipse

As the Earth goes gradually around its orbit, tracing out the year, we see the Sun apparently move around us against the backdrop of the universe. Earth does not spin upright in its orbiting, but is tilted about one-quarter of the way to one side. Since this tilt is fairly stable in the short term, effectively fixed toward one direction in space, we see the Sun apparently move in a yearly wave or cycle back and forth across the equator, from north to south between the tropics and back again.

The Sun's apparent motion through the year (as Earth circles it) traces out the central line of the band or plane of the zodiac. Since the Earth's axis of daily rotation or spin is tilted at about 23.5 degrees to the plane of its orbit, we see the zodiacal belt (surrounding the Earth) as swinging from 23.5 degrees north of the equator to 23.5 degrees south in a completely regular wave movement, one full cycle per day.

Since the Earth only moves 1/365th of the distance around its orbit in a day, the Sun appears almost fixed at a particular point in the zodiac at any one moment in time. Over a period of a year it appears to move the whole way around the zodiacal belt. Therefore it moves gradually north and south of the equator through the year.

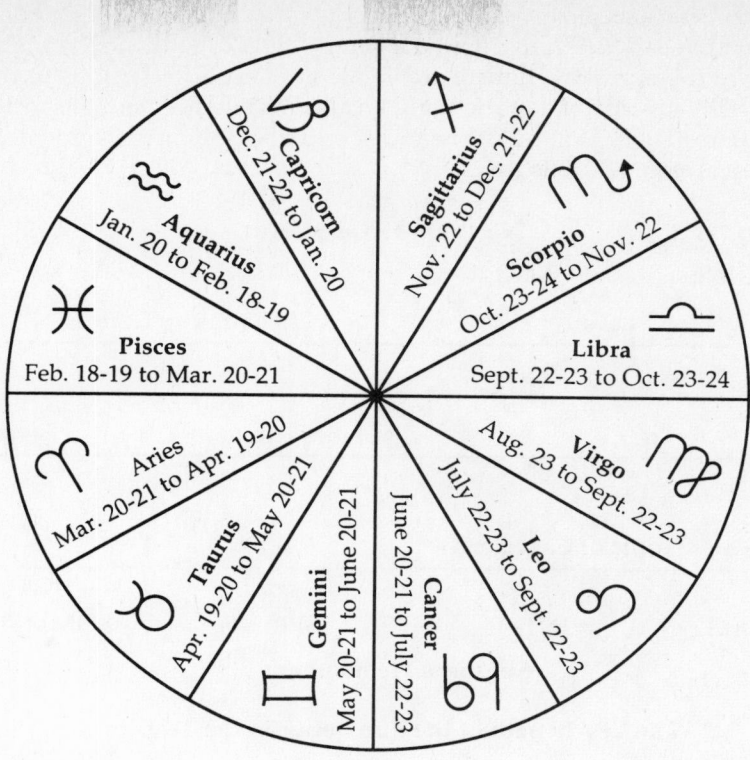

The Zodiac, or Solar Year-Circle.

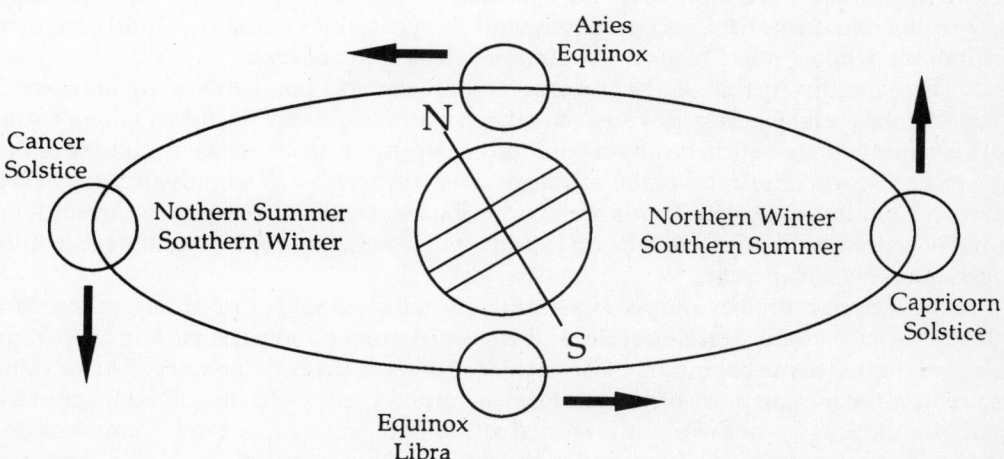

The apparent yearly path of the Sun.

When the Sun is seen overhead at the equator and moving north, day and night are equal in length over all the Earth since both hemispheres are equally illuminated. Spring is beginning in the northern hemisphere, while autumn or fall begins in the southern hemisphere. This equality of day and night is called an equinox, and the northern spring or vernal equinox (about March 21) is regarded as the beginning of the zodiac, and begins the first zodiacal sign, which is Aries.

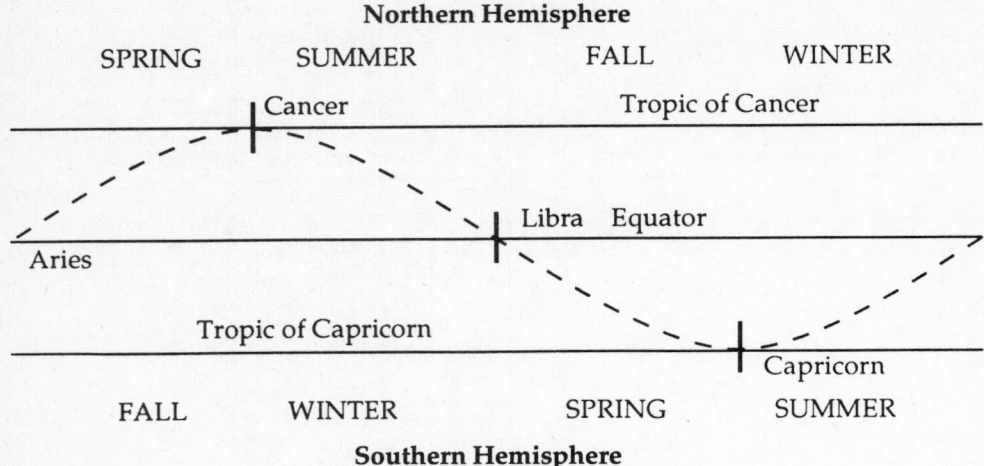

The Yearly path of the Sun between the Tropics.

When the Earth has moved 90 degrees around its orbit three months later, the Sun reaches its northernmost position, overhead at the Tropic of Cancer. Day is at its longest in the north, night in the south, and it is summer in the northern hemisphere, winter in the southern. This seasonal solar extreme is called a solstice, and this particular solstice (around June 21-22) marks the beginning of the zodiacal sign of Cancer.

Add another three months (to the 23rd-24th of September) and the Sun has swung back to the equator for the second equinox of the year, the middle or counter-balance point of the whole cycle. This is the beginning of the sign of Libra.

Three months further on the Sun is at its southernmost point, this being the second solstice of the cycle. The Sun is overhead at the tropic of Capricorn (bringing winter to the north, summer to the south) on about the 22nd of December, marking the beginning of the sign of Capricorn. (The dates of the equinoxes and solstices "slip" slightly through a day or so over a four year period. This is because the Earth takes 365.256 days to go around the Sun. The extra quarter-day we save up to add on to the year as a full day once every four years—making a leap-year).

These two equinoxes and solstices mark out the cardinal points of the zodiac. Our calendar is based totally on this cycle, and was once properly aligned with it, New Year being celebrated at the beginning of Aries (March = Mars, the ruling planet of Aries). Unfortunately the human pride of various Roman emperors chopped the calendar about by changing the lengths of the months named after them, and William the Conqueror decreed that the year begin on January 1st, the date of his coronation.[2]

2. De Vore, Nicholas. *Encyclopedia of Astrology*. Totowa, NJ: Rowman, 1976.

In between the equinoxes and solstices the quarters of the zodiac are further divided, making three signs in each quarter, each a month long, being roughly the active, passive, and mediating elements of that quarter. Four quarters of three signs gives us the twelve signs of the zodiac.

Why twelve rather than any other number? The foundation of astrology is geometric resonance in space and time. Resonances are always regular equal subdivisions of a whole. If we consider the quarters of the zodiac, we can see that they are composed of two divisions of the whole circle into halves, each half being itself divided precisely in half. The one-fourth harmonic contains the one-half as well as the whole. There are some resonances that are very rich in internal harmonics. The one-twelfth, or twelve-fold division of the whole is extremely rich, containing as it does the one-twelfth, one-sixth, one-fourth, one-third, one-half and the whole as harmonics (it can be divided by 12, 6, 4, 3, 2 and 1).

We could say that there are actually an infinite number of zodiacs, one for every possible subdivision of the full circle of the Earth's orbit, but that they have a natural order of power. The twelvefold zodiac is strongest because it has the most powerful internal resonances. Some years ago a science-fiction writer wrote a spoof book claiming to have discovered a thirteenth sign of the zodiac and many people believed him, demonstrating both his own ignorance and theirs of the nature of astrology.

The Houses

I mentioned that there are two co-ordinate systems that we use to describe the positions of the planets. The second one is more Earth-based than the first (the zodiac), so let us return to the surface of our planet to look at it.

Wherever you are on the face of the Earth, you have a certain local perspective on its turning, and on what that turning does to the apparent positions of the planets and the stars at any one moment. The Earth "rolls over on itself" in 24 hours, making everything we see in the sky seem to revolve around us once in that time, like the park as seen by children on a roundabout (merry-go-round). The movement of the planets around their orbits (or through the zodiac) in one day is quite small—a maximum of about two degrees in the case of Mercury, excepting the Moon—which moves between roughly 12 and 15 degrees in a day.

We see everything around us in relation to a certain natural framework of space, that of the horizon (and the surface that we live on that spreads from horizon to horizon) and the vertical line, running from above us to below us, made noticeable by gravity. This is again the "plane and polar axis" co-ordinate system; distance around the horizon is called "azimuth," and above and below the horizon is called "altitude"; the pole overhead is the "zenith" while the one beneath your feet is called the "nadir."

From wherever we are on Earth, we can see the belt of the zodiac apparently swinging around us as our planet turns. It comes up over the eastern horizon, swings through the sky to set in the west. Since the zodiac goes around us once in a day, and the planets move through it far more slowly, we see them carried around with it, rising and setting.

The Angles

At any one moment in time a particular degree of the zodiac (called the Ascendant) will be rising on the eastern horizon, and the opposite degree, the Descendant, setting on the western horizon. Another degree, between the two, will be at the highest point that the zodiac reaches in the local sky, on the midheaven, or MC for the Latin *Medium Coeli* (on the longitudinal line that runs overhead from due north to due south). Its opposite point, the IC (Latin *Imum Coeli*, or lowest heaven) will be under the Earth, at the lowest point of the zodiac, somewhere beneath your feet.

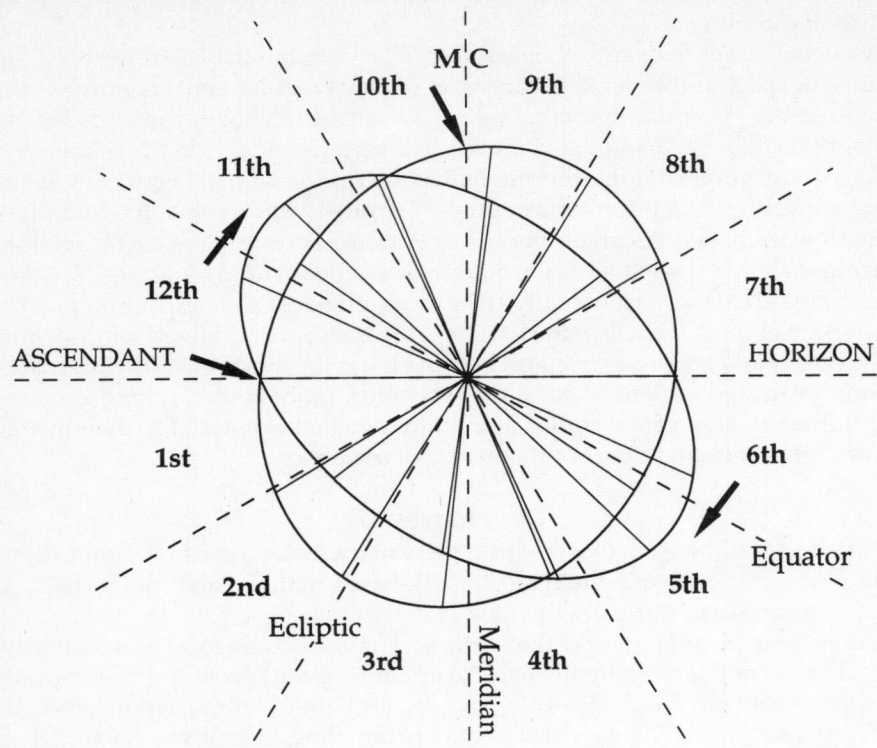

These four points (east-west, above-below) are the cardinal points of the relationship between local space and the zodiac. They are exactly like the zodiacal cardinal signs in nature, but where the signs are more like universal principles, laws or archetypes, the local points act as elements of personal real experience in the world. We call these cardinal points the angles.

The Twelve Houses

Just as the zodiacal quarters are each divided into three to make the twelve signs, so are the local quadrants, making what we call the twelve mundane houses. Instead of giving the houses names as we do with the zodiacal signs, we simply number them from one to twelve, starting at the eastern horizon, going below the earth to the western horizon for the first six, then up from the west, overhead and down to the east for the houses from seven to twelve.

The Local Viewpoint (House Tables)

Our view of the zodiac and of the planets in it depends on our latitude on Earth, our position north or south of the equator, as well as on our longitude, or position around the Earth, from east to west. The further from the equator we are, the closer to our horizon the zodiac will appear to be, and the more aslant we will see it (in the tropics—we see the zodiac as swinging overhead during the day). Since the zodiac is tilted by 23.5 degrees to the equator, during one day, one turn of the Earth, it appears to rock backward and forward from north to south, and back again.

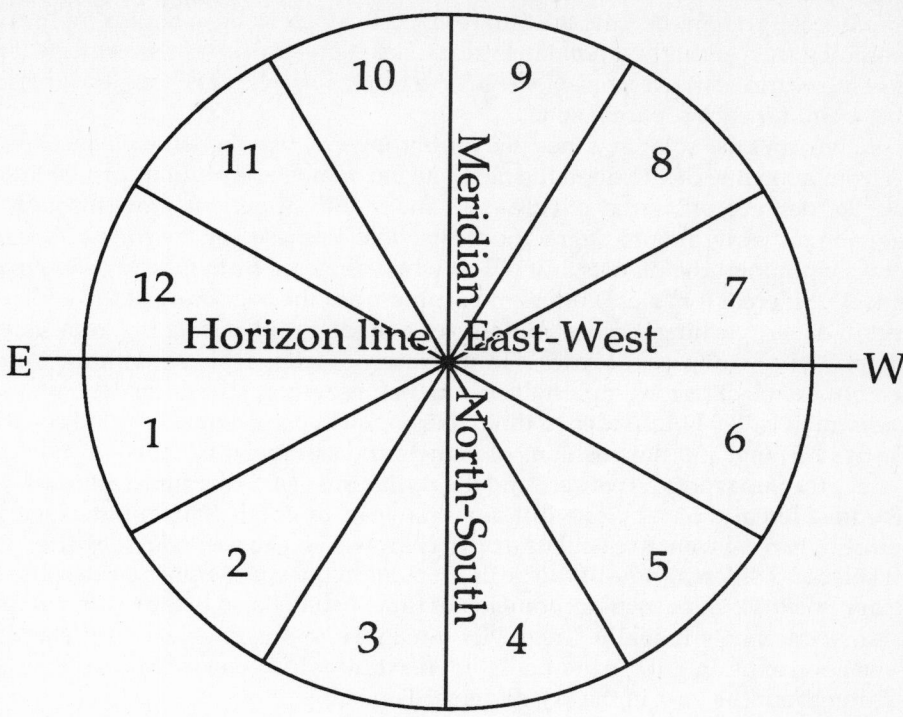

The Circle of the Mundane Houses

Because of this slant, or perspective distortion created by the relationship between our latitude on Earth and the tilt of the zodiac, the amount of the zodiac (on average thirty degrees) seen within any of the houses varies depending on *where* you are on Earth, as well as *when* you are, at what point in the daily zodiacal circling. For this reason, we have to have house tables showing the points in the zodiac that coincide with the "cusps" or border points of the houses, and we have to have these house tables calculated for the viewpoint we get from different degrees of latitude, and for every moment through the (sidereal) day.

When working out a birth chart, the information we need is the position of the birth in space-time; this includes the birth moment or position in time (time of day, day, month, year), and the position in space (longitude and latitude of the birthplace).

Time

In order to know where any of the planets may be relative to our place on Earth, we first have to know where they are in the zodiac (which we can look up in an ephemeris, or list of planetary positions through time), then where their zodiacal places are, relative to where we are. Since the zodiac is effectively immoveable in space (in the short term; over long periods of time it does precess, or move around), but the Earth turns, we need to know which way the Earth is pointing at any moment of time, relative to the zodiac.

When we measure time here on Earth, we normally use the position of the Sun as the basic reference point. Before we instituted time-zones within the past century, time was measured locally, from the time the Sun reached the local noon-point (or midheaven in astrological terms), its highest point in the local sky. Nowadays we measure time for large slices of the world, using a *standard meridian*, a particular degree of longitude, as the beginning point for each separate zone.

But we can't use solar or zone-time for finding exactly where the planets are, for as we go from noon one day to noon the next, the Earth moves around its orbit a little (one 365th of 360 degrees, or one day out of a year) and the Sun appears to move through space, through the zodiac by about a degree. So we need a clock based on the zodiac itself to help us not only pinpoint the planets, but tell us where they are from here (or were from the birthplace). Sidereal (or "star") time is measured from the beginning of the zodiac (zero degrees of Aries) reaching the local midheaven or noon-point. If it is zero hours local sidereal time, then zero degrees of Aries is immediately overhead. Sidereal time is measured using a 24-hour clock; for example half an hour before zero Aries culminates (comes to the mid-heaven) it is 23.5 hours sidereal time. Astronomers use sidereal time to keep track of the Earth's turning, and the positions of planets and stars relative to it.

Since the Sun works its way around the zodiac in a year, solar time continually shifts relative to sidereal time—by one full day in a year, or about four minutes every day. Therefore, when we want to calculate a birth chart we have to work out the difference between solar and sidereal time at the birth moment in question. Ephemerides, listings of planetary positions at particular moments of time, usually also list the sidereal time for those same moments (usually Greenwich Mean Time—used as a world standard of time—at noon or midnight). In this book, sidereal time is linked to the Sun's ongoing positions throughout the year in the Sun-Sidereal Time table.

But we are not all born at Greenwich, nor are we born at the longitudes used as our zone-time markers, so we have some adjustments to make for the position of our birthplace on Earth when calculating our sidereal time.

Time and space are interchangeable. One sidereal day is one full rotation of the Earth (360 degrees of turning), so our 360 degrees of longitude measured around the world are also measurements of time. Therefore, 180 degrees is 12 hours worth of turning, 90 degrees is 6 hours, 15 degrees is 1 hour, and so on.

Since we use the Greenwich meridian as the world time-standard, we have first to convert the birth (or event) time into Greenwich time terms, then to work out the sidereal time at Greenwich at that moment in the year, then go back to the birthplace by working out the longitudinal time difference (how far around the world it is from Greenwich).

Once we have the local sidereal time, we have done the most complex part of our birth chart calculations. Knowing the sidereal time, we can simply look up the orientation of the zodiac to that place and time in the tables of houses, or in this book, on the house graph for the closest latitude to the birthplace (or if you want to be more precise, work between two latitudes and split the difference in proportion to the exact birth latitude).

As you may imagine, the perspective view of the zodiac as seen from one hemisphere on Earth is not the same as is seen from the other hemisphere. In fact it is precisely opposite, which means that we can use the same house tables or graphs to find the local house cusps (edges or borders), but have to reverse them; with the graphs in this book this is done simply by reading the graphs from the left and bottom labels for the northern hemisphere, or from the right and top labels for the southern hemisphere.

HOW TO WORK OUT YOUR BIRTH CHART

I have developed a reasonably simple method of calculating both Sidereal Time and the House cusps for any chart. You need these to work out which planets were in which houses at the given birth time. We will assume for now that you want to draw up your own chart, but to give you a practical numerical example, I will use my own birth data to draw up my own chart. Simply substitute your own data and follow the sequence of steps given to erect your own chart, or use someone else's birth data to erect their chart. If you have accurate birth data, you can draw up, cast, or erect any chart you want to study.

While I call this method reasonably simple, I know how daunting the process of drawing up an astrological chart seems to those who have never done it before. Don't rush it, take it easy, do it step-by-step and check the steps you do. There is plenty of room to make mistakes with such an unfamiliar procedure, so try to understand what you are doing with each step.

Great accuracy is not needed for the purposes of finding which houses your planets are in, in this book. You can work with approximations and estimates. I have described the process with exact examples just so you can check what you are doing against them if you need to. At least make sure your estimates are about right, and in the right direction.

The sequence is this:

You need to know three things: (1) your birthdate (day, month, and year); (2) your birth time (in hours and minutes. Was it A.M.—before noon—or P.M.—after noon? Was it during Daylight Saving Time? and what Time Zone were you born in?); (3) your birthplace (look it up in an atlas or a gazetteer to find its co-ordinates of longitude and latitude—in degrees and minutes, or try to work these out approximately if the place is not listed in an atlas or gazetteer); note all these things down. (I was born at 12h:53m:18s p.m. British Summer Time (Greenwich Time Zone), 24th October 1939, in Derby, England, 52N55, 1W30.)

Remember throughout that you are dealing with time (with hours of 60 minutes, and minutes of 60 seconds) and with space (with degrees of 60 minutes of arc each), so you must remember to calculate in sixties where necessary, not in tens.

The first step is to work out the exact position of your Sun (and all the other planets, if you wish) from your birthdate and time. To do this, look at the page of the ephemeris (listing of planetary positions through time) dealing with your birth year. Note which column contains the Sun's positions, and look down it to find your birthday. (For my birth, I look at 1939, look for October, look for the 24th.)

Since the ephemeris is calculated for Greenwich or Universal Time (at noon), you will have to convert your own birth time into Universal Time terms to be able to find the exact positions of the Sun, Moon and planets. In the method used in this book, you need the exact position of the Sun to be able to work out your Sidereal Time to find your house cusps.

Here you need to know two things; which time zone were you born in? and were you born during a local observance of Daylight Saving Time? If you were born during Daylight Saving Time, you must first subtract the amount of DST from your birth time, to turn it into pure zone standard time terms. The amount of daylight saving time is usually one hour, though Great Britain has sometimes used "double summer time" of two added hours, and New Zealand has used "summer time" of half an hour, and there are a few other odd examples around the world. Note that if you were born before 1 a.m. and you have to subtract DST you will be put back into the day before your birthday.

If you were not born during DST, simply use your birth time as given, and add or subtract your zone difference from Greenwich to convert it to GMT. Use the Zone Table to do this. (It is often an astrologer's greatest problem to find zone time information and data on summer or daylight saving times for all the various places in the world. There are excellent publications to help you here by Doris Chase Doane, of the American Federation of Astrologers, on time changes in the U.S.A., in Canada and Mexico, and in the World.)

If you were born to the west of the Greenwich meridian, add your birth-place Zone Time to your birth time to arrive at the Universal or Greenwich Time at your birth. If you were born east of Greenwich, subtract the zone time from your birth time to obtain your birth GMT (or UT). Write it down (label it as GMT). Again, you may be put back into the day before, or put forward into the day after your birthday. Make sure you know which GMT day you end up in. (In my case, I was born in England, in the Greenwich Time Zone, and there was British Summer Time until November 19th that year; so my GMT of birth is actually 11:53:18 a.m.)

To find your Sun position (and eventually those of all your planets), you will have to interpolate—or work between two dates and positions. The Sun's positions are given in the ephemeris once every five days. You need to calculate exactly how far between the two dates you were born, say 3 days, 15 hours or 3-5/8 days; divide this by 5 to turn it into a proportional part of the 5-day period (29/40), then multiply this figure by the actual movement of the Sun during the period (say 5 degrees, which gives 3 degrees 37.5 minutes' movement). Add the Sun's movement to its position at the beginning of the period to get its actual position at the moment of your birth. This is fairly easy, since the Sun moves almost exactly one degree per day.

To review, note how far your birth moment was between the two Sun ephemeris dates (the one prior to your birth and the one following it), stated in GMT terms. Divide this figure by five. Then take the difference between the two Sun positions listed and multiply it by the (fractional) result. This gives you the exact position of your Sun. In my case, I was born on October 24, 1939, and that date is listed. I was born almost at GMT noon, and interpolating between the 19th and 24th of October does not even make one minute of arc's difference, so my Sun position is 0 degrees 10 minutes of arc of Scorpio as shown in the ephemeris.

Look up your calculated Sun position in the Sun-Sidereal Time table to find your solar sidereal time. If you want to be accurate, note that the sidereal times are stated for precise degrees of the Sun's position, and that at your birth the Sun was somewhere between two exact degrees. Again you can work between the two to find your exact solar-sidereal time.

My Sun was at 0 degrees 10 minutes of Scorpio, so my solar-sidereal time (SST) was 10/60ths (10 minutes of arc into a degree of 60 minutes of arc) or 1/6th of the difference between the sidereal time for 0 Scorpio (14h:07m:15s) and the sidereal time for 1 Scorpio (14h:11m:10s). The difference between the two sidereal times is 3 minutes 55 seconds. One-sixth of this is 39 seconds. Adding this (elapsed time) to the earlier figure, 14h:07m:15s plus 39 seconds is 14h:07m:54s.

To this SST you must also add the difference between your birth time and noon. If you were born before noon, the difference will be negative, so you will be subtracting. If you were born after noon, the difference will be positive, so you will be adding it. I was born at 11:53:18 a.m. GMT, so I have to subtract 7 minutes and 42 seconds from the SST, (14:07:54) giving 14h:00m:12s. Unless you are absolutely certain of your birth time, you will probably be working with a rounded-off time stated as an exact hour or half-hour. If so, don't worry about accuracy since you have no accurate starting point. Also, if you find the figure you end up with is over 24 hours, just subtract the excess 24 hours to keep your answer within one day. Or if you end up subtracting a figure that is larger than your SST, just add 24 hours to the SST before subtracting. This doesn't change anything, it simply keeps the final figure positive and within a 24-hour day.

These two figures (noon sidereal time and your birth time difference from noon) give you the sidereal time at the moment of your birth for your time zone. But you were probably not born exactly on your zone time longitude, so you have to correct for the difference between your birthplace and your zone longitude. Remember that time and space are linked, that 360 degrees around the world is equal to 24 hours. (Usually you will have been born less than 15 degrees from your zone longitude, or less than an hour). Since 15 degrees = 1 hour, 1 degree = 4 minutes. Therefore, multiply the difference between your birth longitude and zone longitude by 4 to work out how many minutes that distance represents in sidereal time (called the "longitude-equivalent").

If you were born to the west of your time zone longitude (earlier in sidereal time than your zone longitude), subtract your birth-place longitude-equivalent time from your time-zone sidereal time. For example, if you were born in Calgary, Alberta at 114W10, this is west of your Mountain Standard Time zone longitude of 105 degrees west. The difference between the two is 9 degrees and 10 minutes of arc (114:10—105:00 = 9:10). 9:10 multiplied by 4 (minutes time per degree longitude) gives you a longitude-equivalent time of 36 minutes and 40 seconds, which you would subtract from your zone sidereal time. Another general example: if you were born anywhere in New Zealand (between 166 degrees east and 179 degrees east), you were born west of your zone longitude (180 degrees east).

If you were born to the east of your time zone longitude (later than your zone longitude), you will have to add the time difference for the actual longitude of your birth-place to your birth time sidereal time. For example, if you were born in Chicago your zone longitude is 90 degrees west, for Central Standard Time, but your birth longitude is 87W45,[3] so you were born to the east of your zone longitude by 2 degrees 15 minutes. Then you add this longitude-equivalent time (2.25 degrees multiplied by 4 = 9 minutes exactly) to your zone sidereal time.

The result you get is the exact sidereal time of your birth (assuming your birth time to have been exactly right in the first place) at your place of birth. From here you simply need to look up this sidereal time on the house graph for the latitude nearest your birth latitude, to find the local house cusps at your birth.

For example, I was born at 1W30, a degree and a half west of the Greenwich meridian (zero degrees longitude). 1.5 multiplied by 4 is 6 minutes. Since I was born to the west of the zone meridian or longitude (0 degrees), I was born earlier in sidereal time relative to it, so I must subtract my longitude difference from the zone sidereal time, which gives an answer of 13h:54m:12s as my sidereal time of birth at my birthplace.

---

3. Collins Atlas.

Let's tabulate these steps:

1. Birth date and time =   /   /19   .   h   m (a.m. or p.m.?). DST? Y/N
        Refer to Ephemeris (Sun to Mars) for your birth date, and take:

2. a) Sun's position prior to birth date   =   :

   b) Sun's position after birth date   =   :

                 difference   =   :

(If the second figure is less than the first, note that the Sun has gone from one zodiac sign to the next. Deal with it by adding 30 degrees to the second figure to calculate the difference between the two.)

3. Birth time converted to Greenwich terms   =   h   m (a.m. or p.m.?) (Save this figure. You will need it to work out your planetary positions.)

   plus number of days to prior Sun position   =   d   h   m

                 divide by 5   =

   multiply by Sun's movement (difference)   =

(This answer is how far the Sun moved from it's position prior to your birth time, up to your birth. It must be added to that prior position to find the Sun's position at your birth.)

4. Position of the Sun at your birth (Sun) =   :

   Refer to Sun-Sidereal Time table to find: h   m   s

5. a) Sidereal time given for degree before Sun   =   :   :

   b) Sidereal time given for degree after Sun   =   :   :

                 difference   =   00:0   :

   Minutes of arc of Sun's position divided by 60   =

   multiplied by Sidereal Time difference   =

   added to Sidereal Time for degree before Sun   =   :   :

This answer is the Solar Noon Sidereal Time at your birth-moment. Now to refine this to your birth time and place:

6. How far is your local birth time from noon? (Put – if before noon, + if after noon)

                 =   :   :

(Add this to your solar noon sidereal time if + , subtract if -). The answer is your birth sidereal time for your time zone.   =   :   :

7. How far (degrees and minutes of longitude) were you born from your zone longitude? To find this, subtract your zone longitude from your birthplace longitude.

                 =   d   m

   Multiply this by 4 to turn it into minutes of time.   =   m   s.

   Add this to your time zone sidereal time if you were born east of your zone longitude, subtract it if you were born to the west of it.   =   h: m: s.

This is the Sidereal Time at your place and time of birth, which you now use to find your house cusps.

Finding the House Cusps

Firstly, if you want to increase the accuracy of the house graphs, get the particular ones you want, such as the one(s) for the degree of latitude closest to your birth-place, enlarged at your local copy-shop. You will be able to estimate the sidereal times and the positions of your house-cusps more accurately on a larger graph.

House Cusps for the Southern Hemisphere.

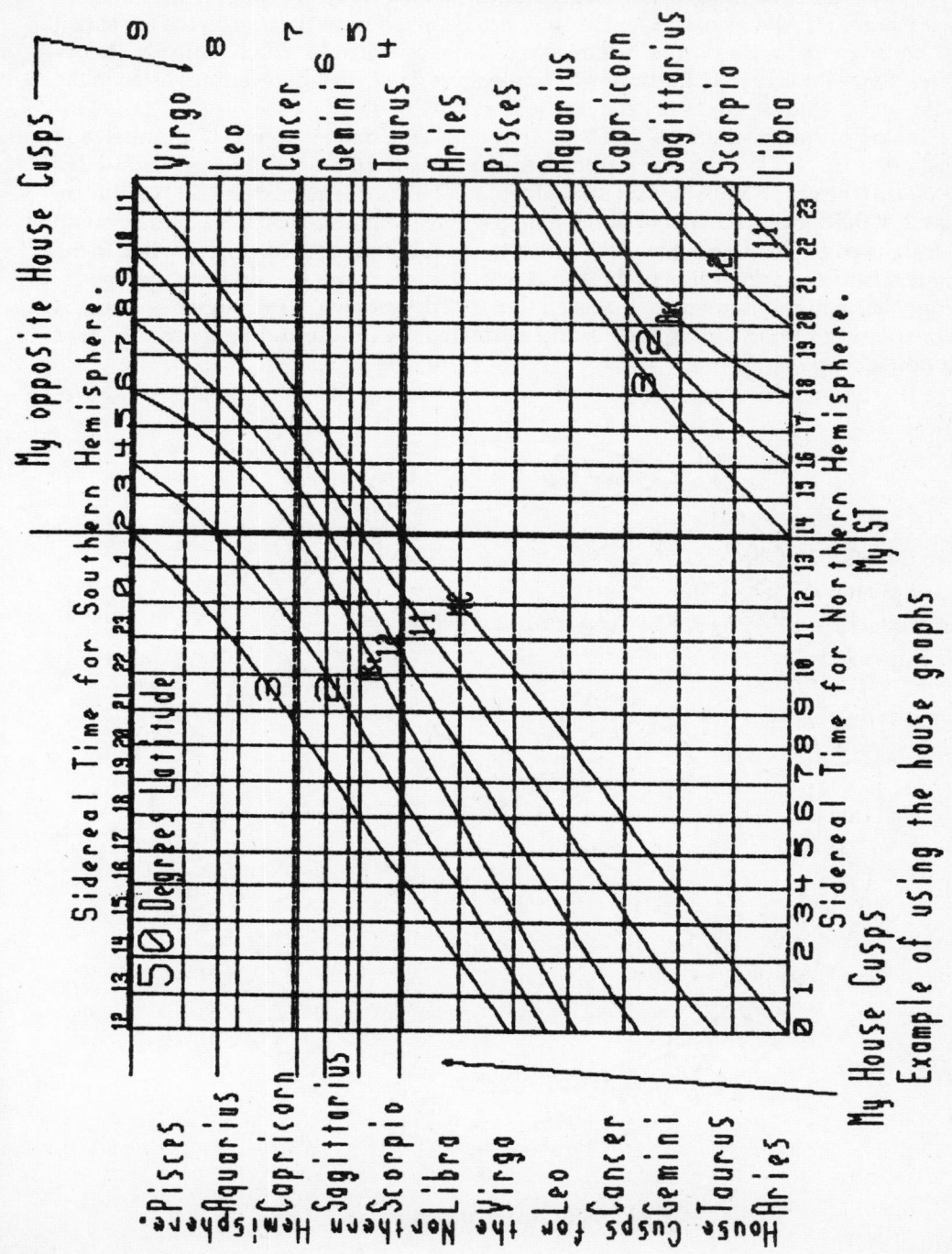

My opposite House Cusps

Sidereal Time for Southern Hemisphere.

50 Degrees Latitude

Virgo 9
Leo 8
Cancer 7
Gemini 6
Taurus +
Aries
Pisces
Aquarius
Capricorn
Sagittarius
Scorpio
Libra

House Cusps for the Northern Hemisphere.

Pisces
Aquarius
Capricorn
Sagittarius
Scorpio
Libra
Virgo
Leo
Cancer
Gemini
Taurus
Aries

My House Cusps

Sidereal Time for Northern Hemisphere. My ST

Example of using the house graphs

My birth latitude was 52N55 (Derby, U.K.), so I look on the house graph for 50 degrees. You will look at the graph for the latitude nearest your own birth latitude. If you were born halfway between two of the latitudes used, you may use both graphs and split the difference.

You will see that the sides of the graphs are labeled "sidereal time for the northern hemisphere" at the bottom, and for the southern hemisphere at the top; on the left side it says "house cusps for the northern hemisphere," and on the right "for the southern hemisphere." Since I was born in the northern hemisphere, I use the sidereal times listed at the bottom, and the house cusps listed at the left.

Taking my sidereal time of 13h 54m, (remembering that an hour is 60 minutes, so I am 54/60ths or 11/12 of the way through the 13th hour) I place a ruler or straight-edge *vertically* up the graph from that sidereal time, 11/12 of the distance from "13" to "14" on the scale at the bottom; I then look at the points where the house-cusp lines intersect with the straight-edge. Looking *horizontally* across the graph from each intersecting line to the left side, I can read which sign of the zodiac each house cusp is in, and roughly how far through that sign it is. Remember that each sign is 30 degrees wide, each sign beginning at 0 degrees and running through to 30, and estimate how far through that space each of your house cusps is.

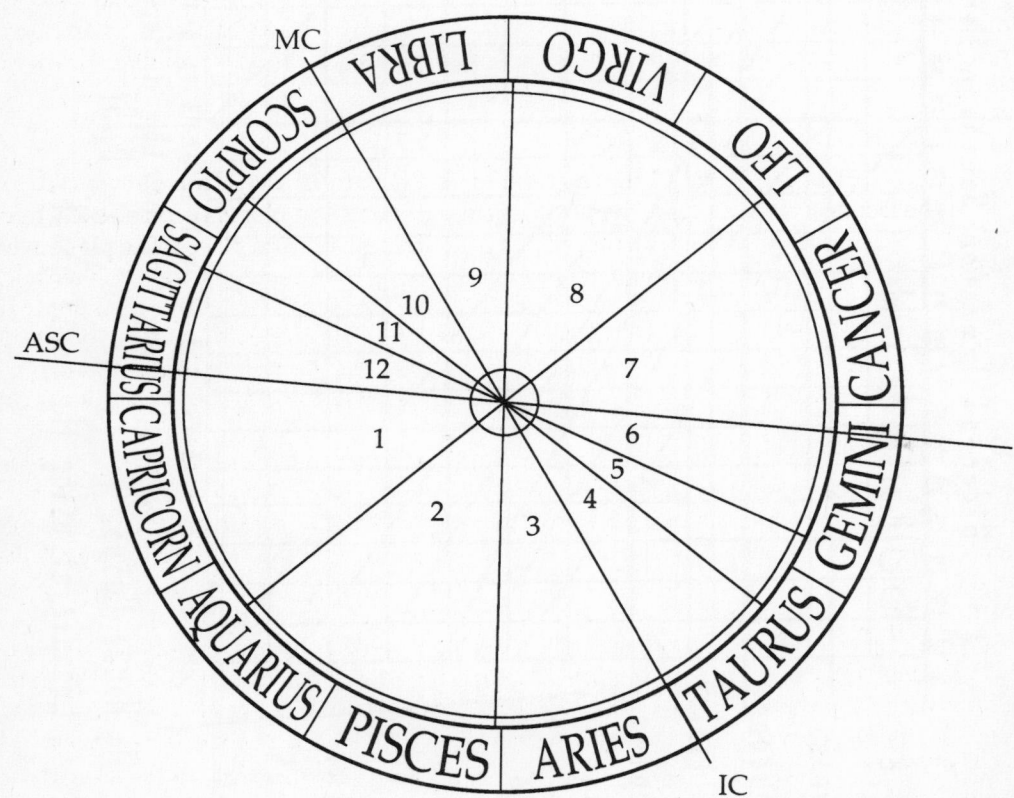

My House Cusps drawn in.

The illustration shows this process for my chart. Follow the sidereal time line (at 13 hours 54 minutes) up to the line marked MC (mid-heaven). You can see that it hits that line very close to the point where it crosses over from Libra into Scorpio. In fact my MC is at 0 degrees 53 minutes of Scorpio. Similarly my 11th House cusp, where the sidereal time line crosses the line marked 11, is about 2/3 of the way through Scorpio, actually at 22 degrees plus. My 12th House cusp (on the line marked 12) shows about 1/3rd through Sagittarius, actually being at 9 degrees plus. My ascendant appears to be near the end of Sagittarius, being in fact at 24.5 degrees. My 2nd House is 1/3rd through Aquarius (actually 9 degrees plus), and my 3rd very late in Pisces (in fact 28.5 degrees).

Though the graph only lists six house cusps, the other six are precisely opposite to them in the zodiac, so you can use the same graph lines but reversing the signs. The 7th is opposite the ascendant, 8th opposite 2nd, 9th opposite 3rd, 10th (or MC) opposing 4th, 11th opposite 5th, 12th opposite 6th. You can see these relationships on the illustration showing the circle of the mundane houses.

You can read the zodiacal sign positions of the other six houses of your chart by looking to the index for the opposite hemisphere to your birth at the other side of the graph. The degree positions are exactly the same, only the signs are 180 degrees, or half-way, around the zodiac.

When you have your house cusps worked out, you can draw them on the chart form provided, though if you want to do charts for others you may prefer to make photo-copies of the chart form and use those. Again, remember that a sign is 30 degrees wide, beginning at zero and ending at 30, and the sequence goes around the chart counterclockwise.

Finding Your Planets and Placing Them in the Houses

The last task is to calculate the positions of the Moon and planets (you already have it for the Sun), and to put them all on your chart in the appropriate places. The planets are listed in the ephemeris (beginning on page 361) beside the calendar date, at Greenwich Noon. Their positions in the zodiacal signs are shown by the three letters between their degrees and their minutes, as in 27 (degrees) CAN(cer) 43 (minutes) shown as 27CAN43. Refer to either the list of planets, or the chart form, for the full names of the signs.

The ephemeris for the Moon shows its positions every two days, so you will need to work out where your birth moment is (in Greenwich Time terms, remember!) within those two days, and calculate the precise position of the Moon at that time. Since the Moon moves the best part of a sign in two days, you will have to take care, noting which sign it was in on each of the two days either side of your birth, calculating its movement, adding it to the earlier position, and making sure you end up with it in the right sign. Consult the list of the signs for their sequence, or look at the Moon's two positions on the chart form and work out visually where it should be in between the two.

The Moon and the Sun are the only planets for which any accuracy is really necessary for the purposes of this book. Note that the Sun, Mercury, Venus and Mars are listed every five days; Jupiter, Saturn, Uranus, Neptune and Pluto are listed every 15 days; and the Moon's North Node is listed once every three months. You can easily see where the planets and node are to within a degree or two, just by taking an estimate between the dates listed. Note particularly where any of your planets are changing signs, where the three-letter name-tag changes from before your birthday to after it. Where this happens, make sure which sign it is actually in at your birth moment—was it still in the last part of the previous sign, or the first part of the next? Read the appropriate interpretation. Mostly, a "guesstimate" of your planetary positions will be accurate enough to work with in this book, though if you think you may explore astrology further, I advise you to cultivate a habit of precision, and learn a proper method of calculating the chart.

Before using this table, remember to check whether the birth time in question occurred during local Daylight Saving Time or Summer Time. If it did, then subtract the appropriate amount of time from the birth time (usually one hour) to give your Zone or Standard Time. Then go on to this table to help you calculate how far the birthplace is from the local Standard Time meridian. If you were born west of the Greenwich meridian, you will have to add your zone time to your birth time to gain Greenwich or Universal Time. The number of hours you have to add are noted in the "To get to GMT" column. If you were born east of Greenwich, the figure in that column will be negative, so you must subtract that number of hours from your birth time to find Greenwich Mean Time.

STANDARD TIME ZONES OF THE WORLD

Name of Zone or Standard Time;	Meridian;	To get to GMT;
Universal, or Greenwich Mean Time or Western Europe Time	0W00	
Central or Middle European Time	15E00	−1 Hour
Eastern European Time	30E00	−2 Hours
Baghdad Time	45E00	−3
USSR Zone 3	60E00	−4
USSR Zone 4	75E00	−5
Indian Standard Time	82E30	−5.5
North Sumatra Time	97E30	−6.5
South Sumatra Time	105E00	−7
Java Time	112E30	−7.5
China Coast Time	120E00	−8
Japan Standard Time	135E00	−9
South Australia Standard Time	142E30	−9.5
Guam Standard Time	150E00	−10
New Zealand Time (pre 1946)	172E30	−11.5
International Date Line, and New Zealand Time since 1946	180E00	−12
Bering Standard Time, Nome Time	165W00	+11
Hawaiian Standard Time(to 8th June 1947)	157W30	+10.5
Alaska–Hawaii Standard Time	150W00	+10
Yukon Standard Time	135W00	+9
Pacific Standard Time	120W00	+8
Mountain Standard Time	105W00	+7
Central Standard Time	90W00	+6
Eastern Standard Time	75W00	+5
Atlantic Standard Time	60W00	+4
Newfoundland Standard Time	52W30	+3.5
Brazil Zone 2	45W00	+3
Azores Time	30W00	+2
West Africa Time	15W00	+1

TABLE OF SIDEREAL TIMES FOR THE SUN
AT EACH DEGREE OF THE ZODIAC

Deg:	h :m :s	Deg:	h :m :s	Deg:	h :m :s	Deg:	h :m :s
A 0	23:52:30	T 0	01:52:40	G 0	03:54:50	C 0	05:58:25
R		A		E		A	
I 1	23:56:30	U 1	01:56:44	M 1	03:58:57	N 1	06:02:33
E 2	00:00:31	R 2	02:00:49	I 2	04:03:04	C 2	06:06:41
S		U		N		E	
3	00:04:31	S 3	02:04:53	I 3	04:07:11	R 3	06:10:49
4	00:08:31	4	02:08:57	4	04:11:19	4	06:14:57
5	00:12:32	5	02:13:02	5	04:15:26	5	06:19:05
6	00:16:32	6	02:17:06	6	04:19:33	6	06:23:13
7	00:20:32	7	02:21:10	7	04:23:40	7	06:27:21
8	00:24:33	8	02:25:15	8	04:27:47	8	06:31:29
9	00:28:33	9	02:29:19	9	04:31:54	9	06:35:37
10	00:32:33	10	02:33:23	10	04:36:02	10	06:39:45
11	00:36:34	11	02:37:28	11	04:40:09	11	06:43:53
12	00:40:34	12	02:41:32	12	04:44:16	12	06:48:01
13	00:44:34	13	02:45:36	13	04:48:23	13	06:52:09
14	00:48:35	14	02:49:41	14	04:52:30	14	06:56:17
15	00:52:35	15	02:53:45	15	04:56:37	15	07:00:25
16	00:56:35	16	02:57:49	16	05:00:45	16	07:04:33
17	01:00:36	17	03:01:54	17	05:04:52	17	07:08:41
18	01:04:36	18	03:05:58	18	05:08:59	18	07:12:49
19	01:08:36	19	03:10:02	19	05:13:06	19	07:16:57
20	01:12:37	20	03:14:07	20	05:17:13	20	07:21:05
21	01:16:37	21	03:18:11	21	05:21:20	21	07:25:13
22	01:20:37	22	03:22:15	22	05:25:28	22	07:29:21
23	01:24:38	23	03:26:20	23	05:29:35	23	07:33:29
24	01:28:38	24	03:30:24	24	05:33:42	24	07:37:37
25	01:32:38	25	03:34:28	25	05:37:49	25	07:41:45
26	01:36:39	26	03:38:33	26	05:41:56	26	07:45:53
27	01:40:39	27	03:42:37	27	05:46:03	27	07:50:01
28	01:44:39	28	03:46:41	28	05:50:11	28	07:54:09
29	01:48:40	29	03:50:46	29	05:54:18	29	07:58:17

Deg:	h :m :s	Deg:	h :m :s	Deg:	h :m :s	Deg:	h :m :s
L E O		**V I R G O**		**L I B R A**		**S C O R P I O**	
0	08:02:25	0	10:05:45	0	12:07:30	0	14:07:15
1	08:06:32	1	10:09:48	1	12:11:29	1	14:11:10
2	08:10:38	2	10:13:52	2	12:15:29	2	14:15:06
3	08:14:45	3	10:17:55	3	12:19:28	3	14:19:01
4	08:18:52	4	10:21:59	4	12:23:28	4	14:22:57
5	08:22:58	5	10:26:02	5	12:27:27	5	14:26:52
6	08:27:05	6	10:30:06	6	12:31:27	6	14:30:48
7	08:31:12	7	10:34:09	7	12:35:26	7	14:34:43
8	08:35:18	8	10:38:13	8	12:39:26	8	14:38:39
9	08:39:25	9	10:42:16	9	12:43:25	9	14:42:34
10	08:43:32	10	10:46:20	10	12:47:25	10	14:46:30
11	08:47:38	11	10:50:23	11	12:51:24	11	14:50:25
12	08:51:45	12	10:54:27	12	12:55:24	12	14:54:21
13	08:55:52	13	10:58:30	13	12:59:23	13	14:58:16
14	08:59:58	14	11:02:34	14	13:03:23	14	15:02:12
15	09:04:05	15	11:06:37	15	13:07:22	15	15:06:07
16	09:08:12	16	11:10:41	16	13:11:22	16	15:10:03
17	09:12:18	17	11:14:44	17	13:15:21	17	15:13:58
18	09:16:25	18	11:18:48	18	13:19:21	18	15:17:54
19	09:20:32	19	11:22:51	19	13:23:20	19	15:21:49
20	09:24:38	20	11:26:55	20	13:27:20	20	15:25:45
21	09:28:45	21	11:30:58	21	13:31:19	21	15:29:40
22	09:32:52	22	11:35:02	22	13:35:19	22	15:33:36
23	09:36:58	23	11:39:05	23	13:39:18	23	15:37:31
24	09:41:05	24	11:43:09	24	13:43:18	24	15:41:27
25	09:45:12	25	11:47:12	25	13:47:17	25	15:45:22
26	09:49:18	26	11:51:16	26	13:51:17	26	15:49:18
27	09:53:25	27	11:55:19	27	13:55:16	27	15:53:13
28	09:57:32	28	11:59:23	28	13:59:16	28	15:57:09
29	10:01:38	29	12:03:26	29	14:03:15	29	16:01:04

Deg:		h :m :s	Deg:		h :m :s	Deg:		h :m :s	Deg:		h :m :s
S	0	16:05:00	C	0	18:01:30	A	0	19:57:35	P	0	21:54:20
A			A			Q			I		
G	1	16:08:53	P	1	18:05:22	U	1	20:01:28	S	1	21:58:16
I	2	16:12:46	R	2	18:09:14	A	2	20:05:22	C	2	22:02:13
T			I			R			E		
T	3	16:16:39	C	3	18:13:06	I	3	20:09:15	S	3	22:06:09
A	4	16:20:32	O	4	18:16:59	U	4	20:13:09		4	22:10:05
R			R			S					
I	5	16:24:25	N	5	18:20:51		5	20:17:02		5	22:14:02
U	6	16:28:18		6	18:24:43		6	20:20:56		6	22:17:58
S											
	7	16:32:11		7	18:28:35		7	20:24:49		7	22:21:54
	8	16:36:04		8	18:32:27		8	20:28:43		8	22:25:51
	9	16:39:57		9	18:36:19		9	20:32:36		9	22:29:47
	10	16:43:50		10	18:40:12		10	20:36:30		10	22:33:43
	11	16:47:43		11	18:44:04		11	20:40:23		11	22:37:40
	12	16:51:36		12	18:47:56		12	20:44:17		12	22:41:36
	13	16:55:29		13	18:51:48		13	20:48:10		13	22:45:32
	14	16:59:22		14	18:55:40		14	20:52:04		14	22:49:29
	15	17:03:15		15	18:59:32		15	20:55:57		15	22:53:25
	16	17:07:08		16	19:03:25		16	20:59:51		16	22:57:21
	17	17:11:01		17	19:07:17		17	21:03:44		17	23:01:18
	18	17:14:54		18	19:11:09		18	21:07:38		18	23:05:14
	19	17:18:47		19	19:15:01		19	21:11:31		19	23:09:10
	20	17:22:40		20	19:18:53		20	21:15:25		20	23:13:07
	21	17:26:33		21	19:22:45		21	21:19:18		21	23:17:03
	22	17:30:26		22	19:26:38		22	21:23:12		22	23:20:59
	23	17:34:19		23	19:30:30		23	21:27:05		23	23:24:56
	24	17:38:12		24	19:34:22		24	21:30:59		24	23:28:52
	25	17:42:05		25	19:38:14		25	21:34:52		25	23:32:48
	26	17:45:58		26	19:42:06		26	21:38:46		26	23:36:45
	27	17:49:51		27	19:45:58		27	21:42:39		27	23:40:41
	28	17:53:44		28	19:49:50		28	21:46:33		28	23:44:37
	29	17:57:37		29	19:53:43		29	21:50:26		29	23:48:34

House Cusps for the Southern Hemisphere.

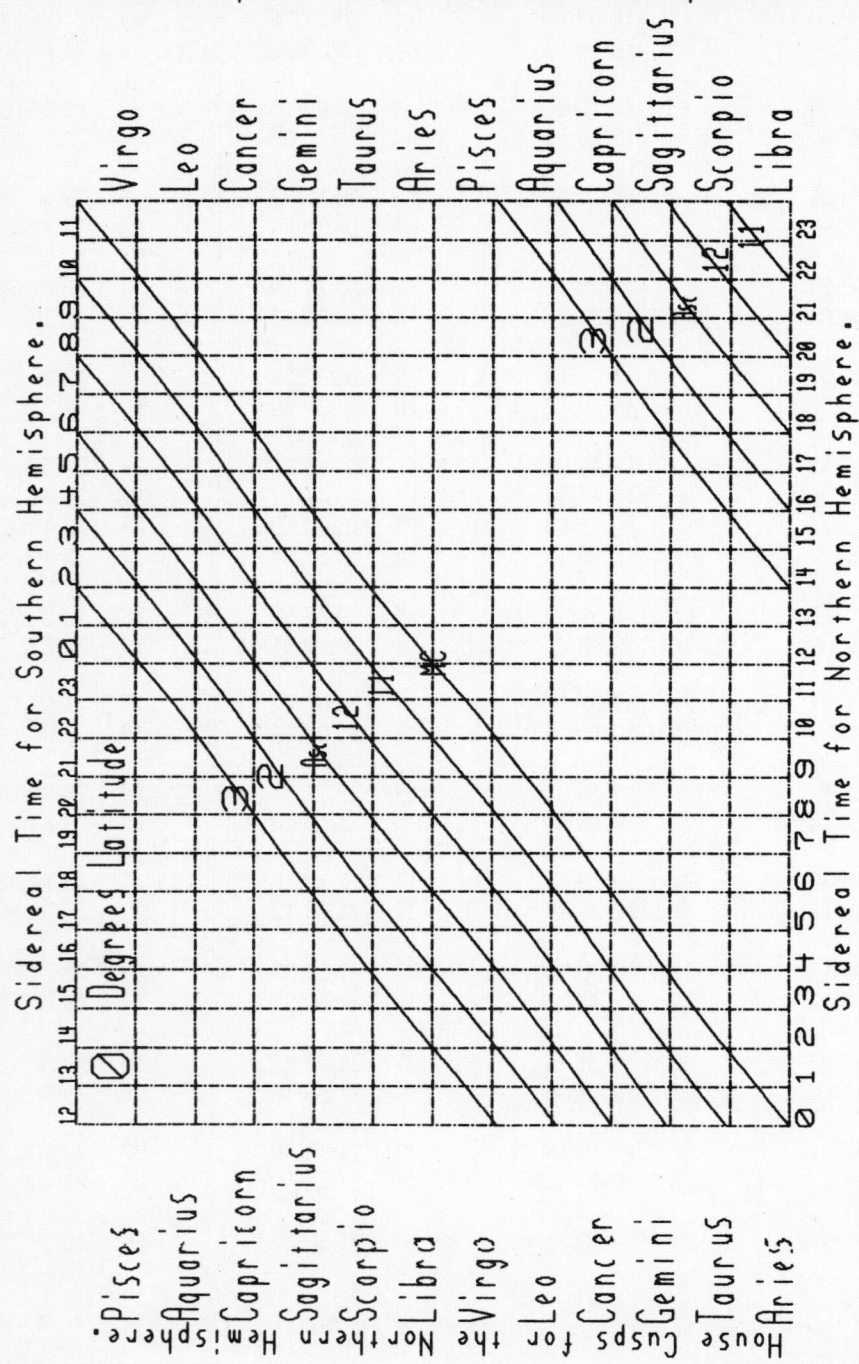

House Cusps for the Southern Hemisphere.

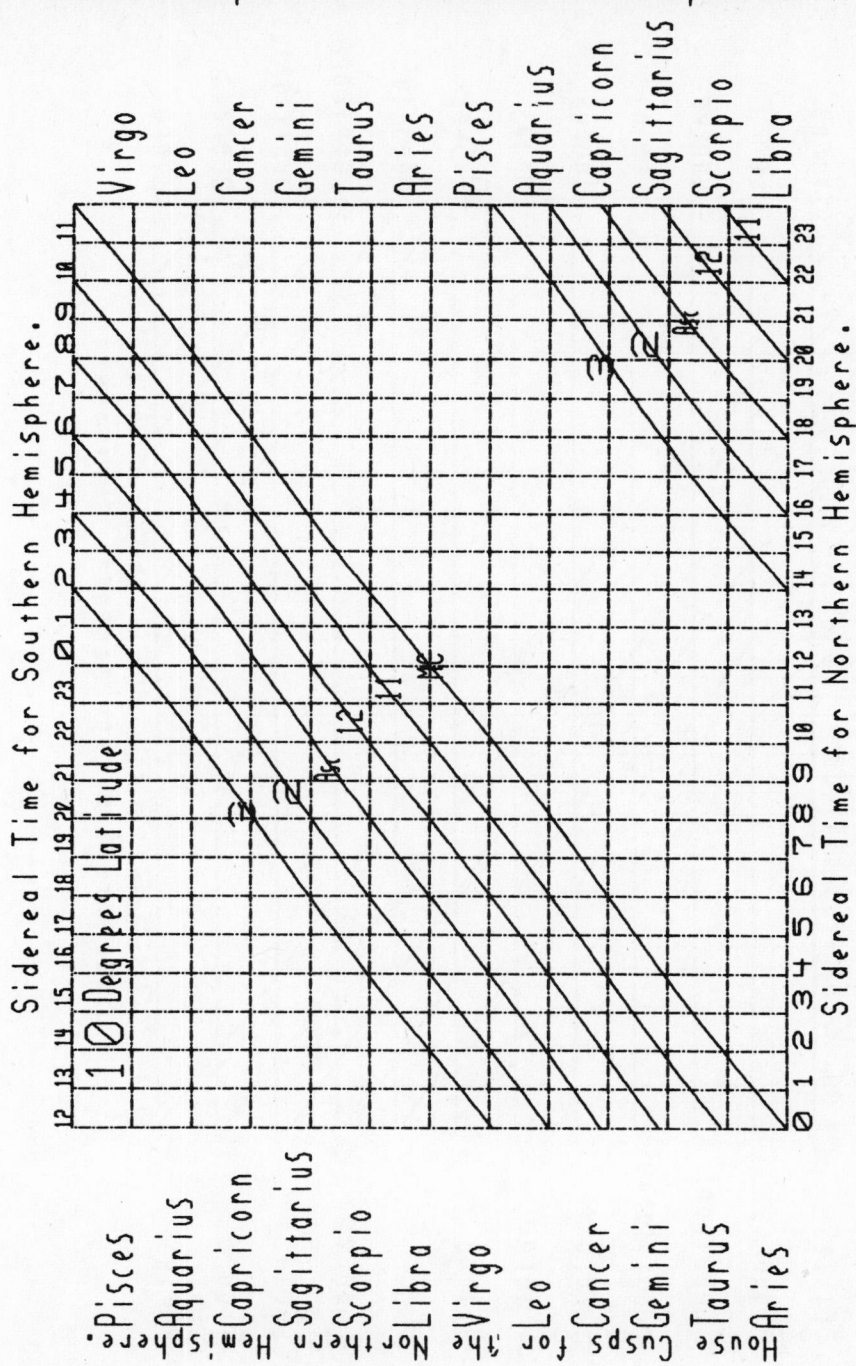

House Cusps for the Southern Hemisphere.

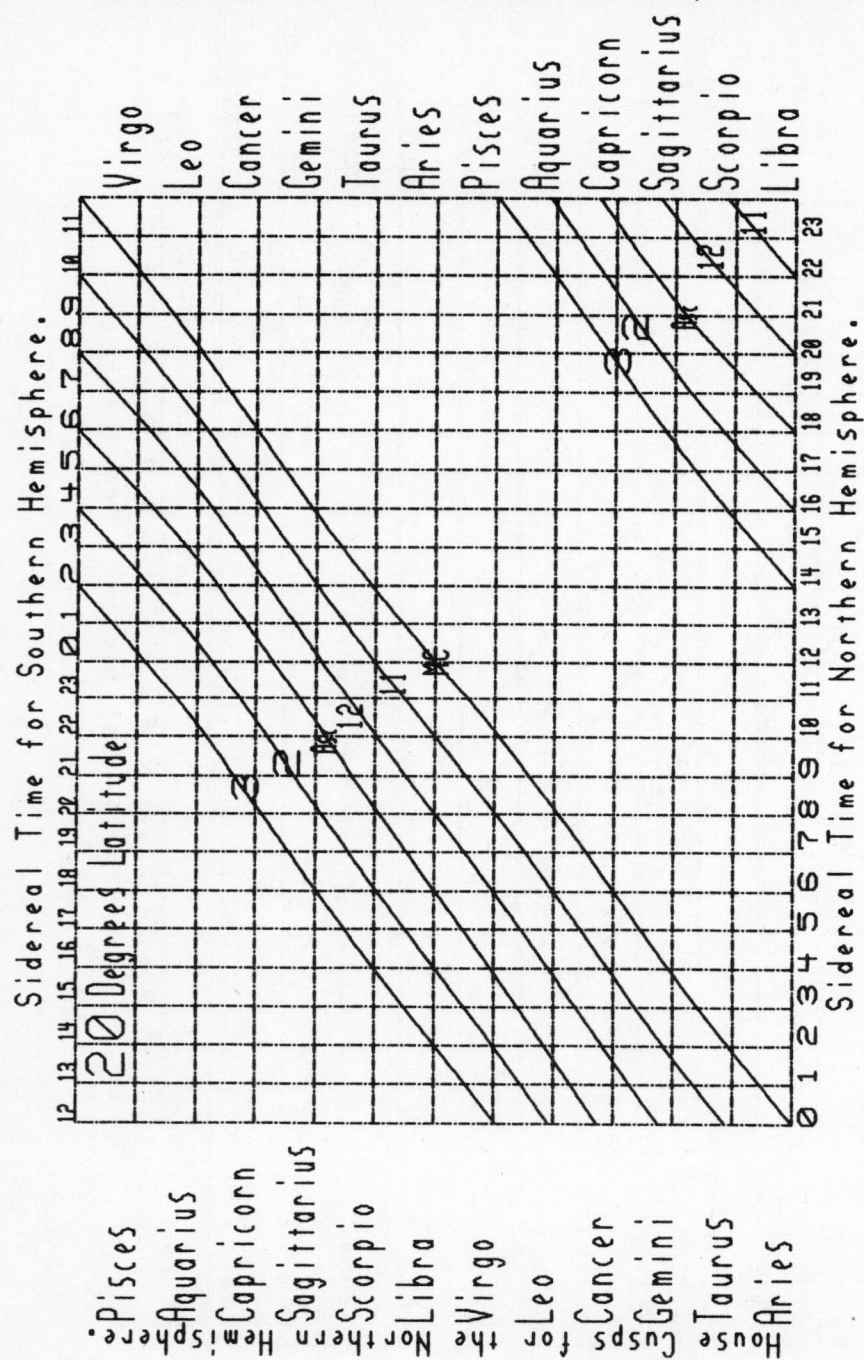

House Cusps for the Southern Hemisphere.

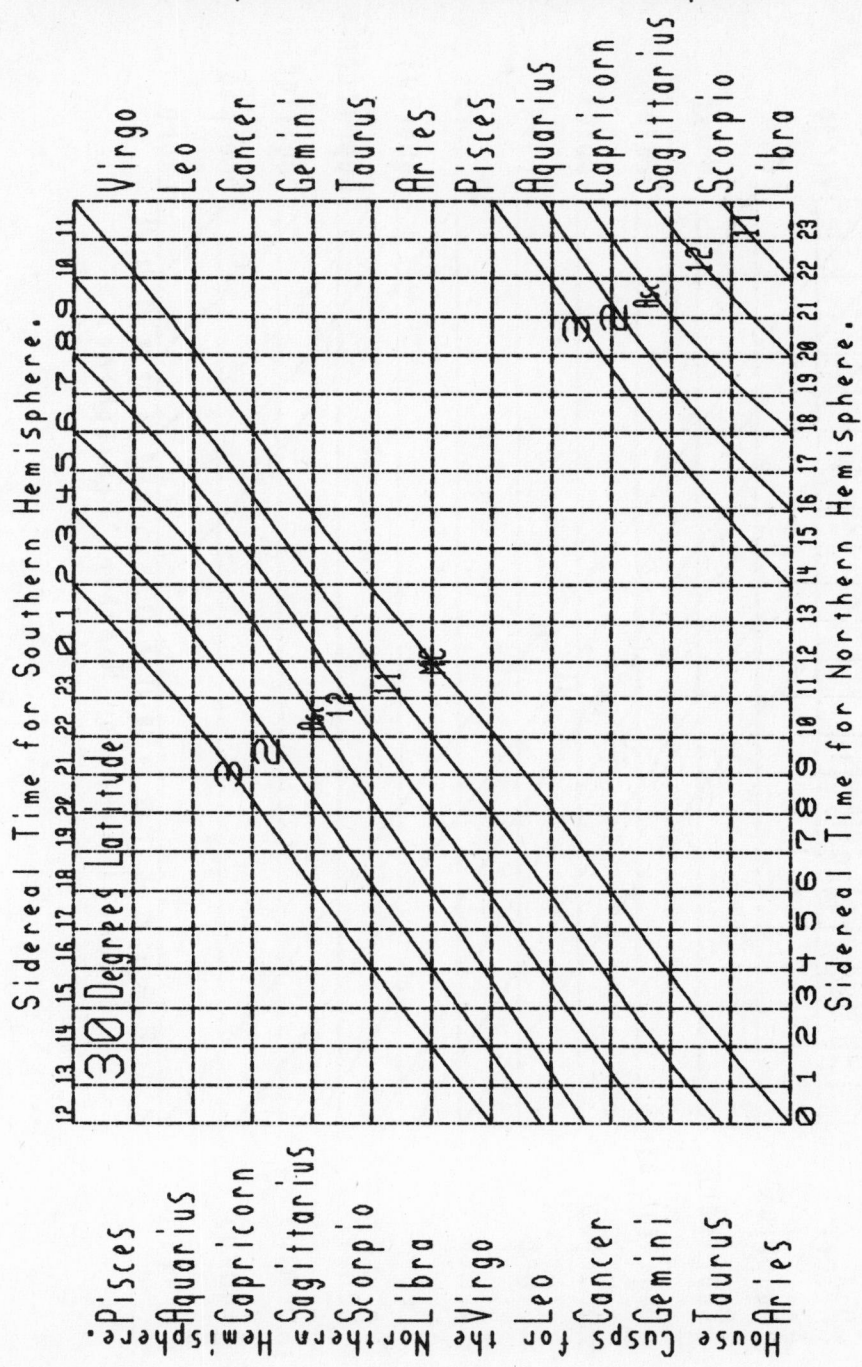

House Cusps for the Southern Hemisphere.

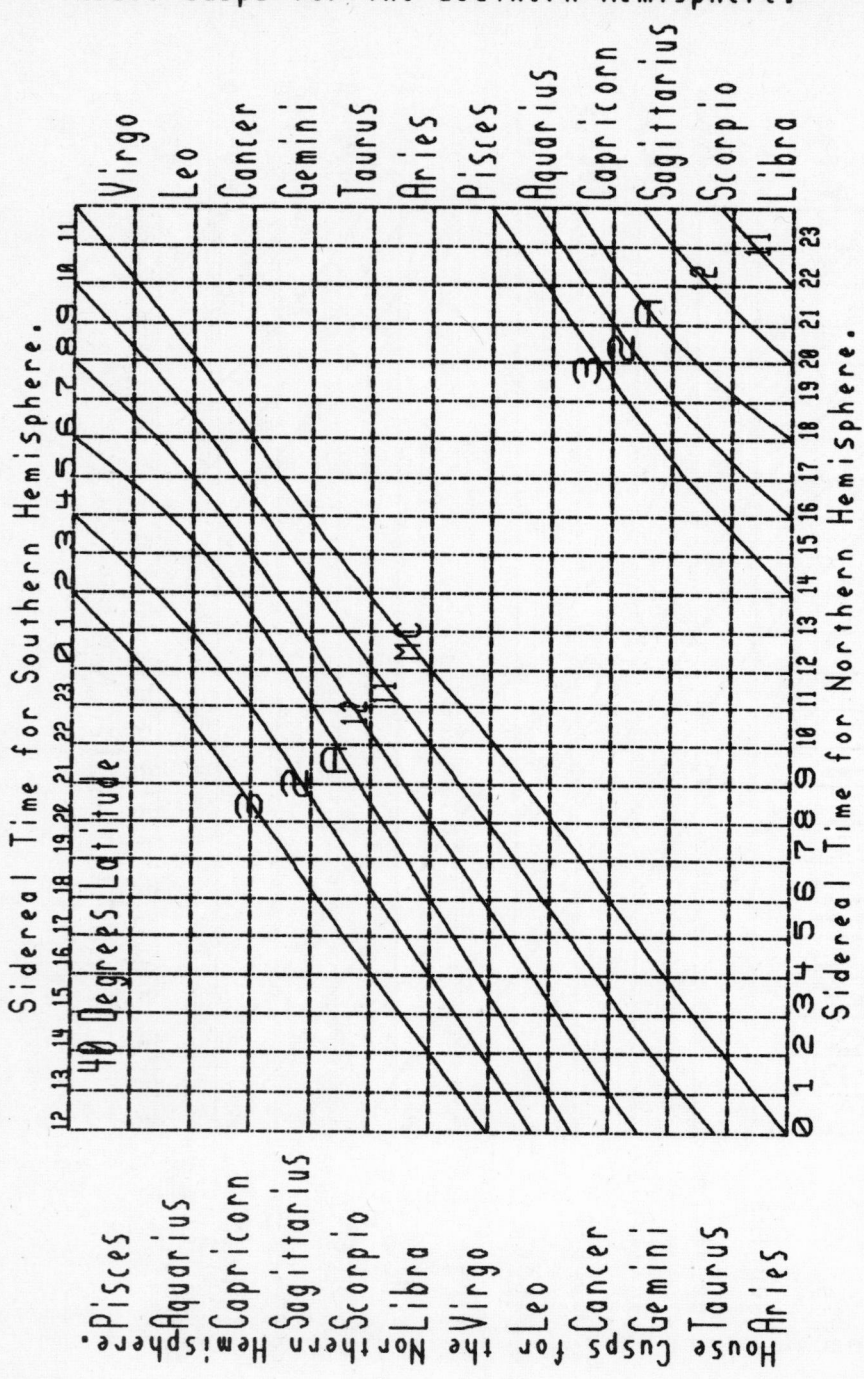

House Cusps for the Southern Hemisphere.

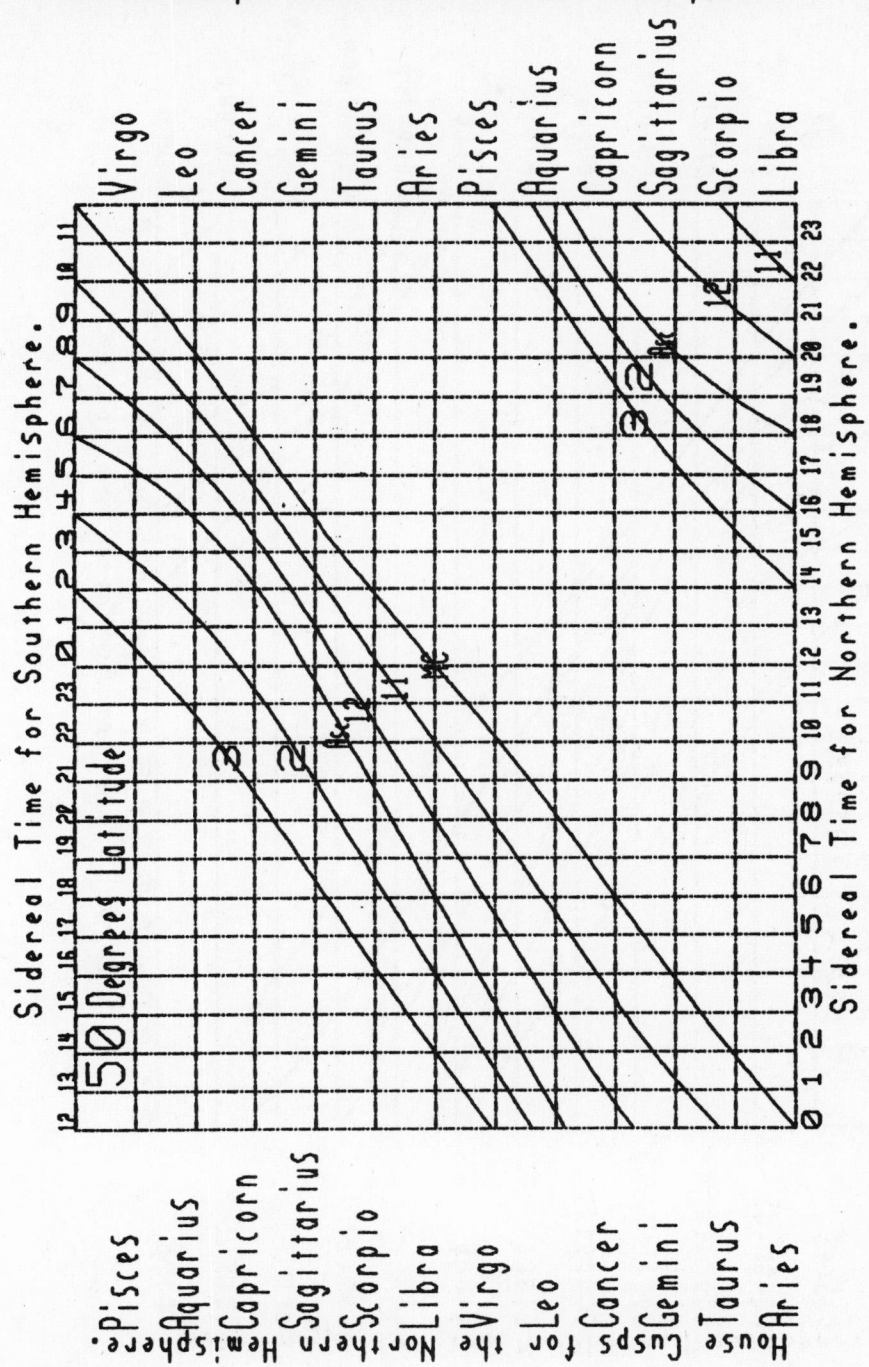

House Cusps for the Southern Hemisphere.

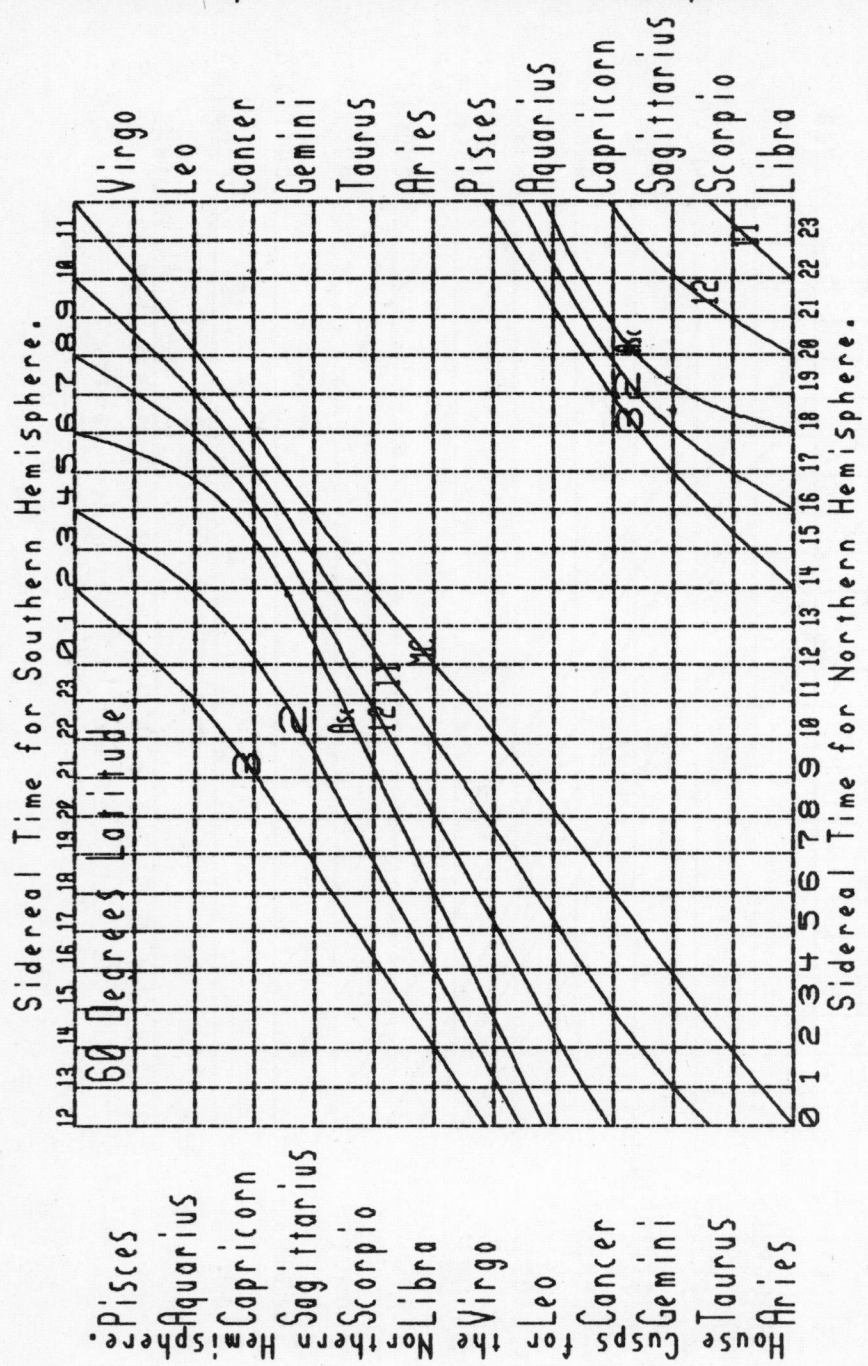

Chart Form

The house graphs only give you an approximate idea of where your house cusps are, and therefore of which houses your planets are in, if they are close to a house cusp. Taking my chart as an example, all the planets are fairly well within their houses, excepting the Sun, actually just on the 9th House side of the midheaven; Jupiter, just into the 3rd House; Saturn, at the end of the 3rd House; and Uranus close to the end of the 4th.

If you do find that a planet is very close to a house cusp, read the interpretations for that planet in both of the houses. There are many possible house systems. The one used in this book, Placidus, is a good compromise system or average between all the others, so a borderline planet may easily have effects in both of the houses separated by any cusp. A house is a part of an overall process (the whole chart), rather than a thing-in-itself. A house-cusp is a point where one stage of the process changes into the next stage, so a planet near a cusp will always affect such a point of change.

Now we go on to the interpretation of your chart.

✧ 2 ✧

Introduction to the Interpretations

Astrology is the study of how resonances in local space-time (patterns of movements in our solar system) affect the local course of events. It has largely become concerned with the events that make up the lives of individuals, though it can be used to follow the development of any activity, so long as its starting point in space and time can be defined accurately, as with the birth of a baby.

A human being (as any other being or thing in existence) is a process that is spread out through time. To trace that process through its stages of unfolding, we require a tool that gives us a time-lapse or time-compressed view of the shifts and changes of a lifetime. Astrology is that tool.

Astrologers recognize that the laws of our reality are symbolic and archetypal (acting as prime root forms from which realities spring). They also recognize the geometric foundations of those laws, or that space-time has basic forms and patterns that spring directly from them.

We live in a universe of four fundamental dimensions, three of space and one of time. In it, objects having form undergo changes. Form itself evolves, having both the capacity to maintain itself and to change. Change may be constructive or destructive, bringing improvements or erosion, birth or death. Between these poles run an apparent multiplicity of threads of experience, which we find are connected by certain constants, such as our continuing awareness of ourselves as centers of experience.

In all that we experience, the one constant is change, yet change that alternates between limits in cyclic fashion. As humans we first became aware of such change in the cycles of day and night, of the waxing and waning of the Moon, of the seasons of the year. In everything that we have learned since the same lesson of cyclicity can be found, from the spinning of atomic particles both on themselves and around orbits, to the spinning and orbiting of moons around planets, planets around stars, stars around galaxies, and galaxies around each other.

The prime law is of cyclicity. The prime cycle for the Earth is its orbit around the Sun, known as the *Zodiac* or the *ecliptic*.

Though the archetypal cycle is a whole in itself we can distinguish parts, and break whole processes down into elements that have different qualities. This is all that science ever does, in ever-increasing detail.

The first step in breaking down the whole cycle of the Earth's orbit is to note the tilt between orbit and equator, and to see that it makes the Sun appear to move in a cycle from overhead in the northern hemisphere to overhead in the south, and back again, through the course of a year. The extreme north and south points are the solstices, or the peaks of summer and winter, and the times when the Sun is over the equator are the equinoxes (times when day and night are equal in length). The equinoxes, being on the equator, are part of it as a nodal, mean or average line about which the Sun's position varies, and they divide its cycle in two. The solstices as extremes act as peak and trough, summer and winter, giving us a hierarchical axis, and, together with the equinoxes, divide the whole cycle into four equal parts.

These four quadrants of the year are our seasons. They are also a two-to-three dimensional "cross-section" through four-dimensional space-time, each quadrant bearing a relationship to the universe seen as a developing series of dimensions: one, two, three, and four. As archetypes, they are a pattern or blueprint of developing form or structure, and each quadrant contains its own development from the simplest beginning, toward its full stretch (which includes its own opposite), and then swinging through all the possible variations between. We can call these thesis, antithesis and synthesis, but the usual astrological labels are *cardinal*, *fixed* and *mutable*.

The three phases or parts of each of four quadrants make up what we know as the twelve signs of the zodiac (and on a local level, the mundane houses). This is not the place to elaborate on the four-dimensional zodiac. That I am doing in a book (or perhaps a series of books) in preparation, called *The Four Dimensional Mandala*.

For now it is enough to say that the signs are patterns for all the parts of a complete cycle of development through time (thus a cycle of experience, growth, unfolding), and of complete development in space (*e.g.*, as a body). You may gain some idea of the full cyclic pattern in human experience through life from the introductions to each chapter.

The "houses" are the other main element in this book. They are a similar division of space to the signs, but are based on the birthplace of a person or other "process." Their major divisions are the eastern and western horizons (or where the zodiac crosses them) as the horizontal or balance line, and the meridian or noon-point above and its opposite immediately below as the vertical or hierarchical line. The same subdivision of the quarters into processes of forming, extending or opposing, and oscillating—or cardinal, fixed, and mutable—make up the twelve.

The difference between signs and houses is that the signs are universal patterns, laws in themselves, while the houses show those laws being put into action in the various arenas of the world, indeed indicating the arenas themselves.

Thus while Aries, as the first sign of the zodiac, may be the archetype of initiative and energy, it is the first house of the birth chart through which a person focuses these qualities into the world. Since the Earth is continually rotating, the signs of the zodiac move in order past each and every point of the local houses during a day. Therefore, the moment of birth is the decisive factor which "fixes" the coincidence between signs and houses for the person born at that time, placing a particular degree of one of the twelve signs along the direction of each house cusp or border, showing exactly what orientation to the total pattern of law, of order, the individual has, at what point they enter the universal process.

A house is an entry, a doorway into a basic area of human or life experience. The sign on its cusp shows the psychological faculty and attitude that the person uses to approach that area, and through those attitudes what directions of experience they choose out of a world full of possibilities.

The planets of our system move around their orbits, each at its own rate, the closer to the Sun the faster (Mercury, the closest, speeding around it in 88 days), the further out the slower (Pluto, furthest, taking nearly 248 years for one cycle). Each planet has connections with one or two of the signs, the pattern running symmetrically from the cusp between Cancer and Leo to that between Capricorn and Aquarius. Moon and Sun are associated with Cancer and Leo respectively, then moving out from the Sun, Mercury with Gemini and Virgo, Venus with Taurus and Libra, Mars (and Pluto) with Aries (and Scorpio), Jupiter (and Neptune) with Sagittarius (and Pisces), and Saturn (and Uranus) with Capricorn (and Aquarius). Each planet outside Earth's orbit is associated with two signs, one of which it "rules" at a conscious level, the other as an unconscious counterpoint to the conscious ruler.

SIGNS	PLANETARY RULERS
ARIES	ruled by MARS (and PLUTO)
TAURUS	ruled by VENUS (and TRANSPLUTO, when found)
GEMINI	ruled by MERCURY
CANCER	ruled by THE MOON
LEO	ruled by THE SUN
VIRGO	ruled by MERCURY
LIBRA	ruled by VENUS (and TRANSPLUTO)
SCORPIO	ruled by PLUTO (and MARS)
SAGITTARIUS	ruled by JUPITER (and NEPTUNE)
CAPRICORN	ruled by SATURN (and URANUS)
AQUARIUS	ruled by URANUS (and SATURN)
PISCES	ruled by NEPTUNE (and JUPITER)

Traditionally, the signs are subdivided in three basic frameworks, those of polarity (positive and negative), modality (cardinal, fixed, mutable), and element (earth, water, fire, air) as follows:

SIGN	POLARITY	MODE	ELEMENT
Aries	Positive	Cardinal	Fire
Taurus	Negative	Fixed	Earth
Gemini	Positive	Mutable	Air
Cancer	Negative	Cardinal	Water
Leo	Positive	Fixed	Fire
Virgo	Negative	Mutable	Earth
Libra	Positive	Cardinal	Air
Scorpio	Negative	Fixed	Water
Sagittarius	Positive	Mutable	Fire
Capricorn	Negative	Cardinal	Earth
Aquarius	Positive	Fixed	Air
Pisces	Negative	Mutable	Water

Positive and negative are not moral judgments, rather they indicate activity and passivity or receptivity, extroversion and introversion. Cardinal implies initiating, able to start things, having a sense of what form or order ought to be. Fixed means stable, tending to perpetuate things, to carry them out. Mutable infers changeable or adaptable, able to move on from one thing to another, and to change to suit circumstances. The elements are more or less the Jungian functions: Earth being the sensing, physical or practical type, Water the feeling or emotional and psychic type, Air the intellectual or thinking and mobile type, and Fire the energetic, conscious or intuitive type.

How to Interpret the Planetary Positions.

The planet connected with a sign is called its "ruler," and is basically its mobile principle; the sign is an archetype or law, the planet in its continual motions and relationships shows how that law is operating in practice at the time. Since each house cusp falls into a particular sign, the planet "ruling" the sign is considered to "rule" the house. Thus if the 4th House cusp is in Sagittarius, Jupiter will be its ruler, wherever it happens to be in the zodiac at the time. Therefore when you want to explore a particular house in your chart (or anyone else's), first note which sign the house cusp is in (and read the introductions to that sign and that house if you want to explore them in depth), then which planet rules that sign, then where (in which sign, and in which house) that planet is placed—and read those interpretations.

The sign that a planet occupies, being more universally "archetypal" than the house it is in, shows faculties and parts of personality that already exist in the new-born individual before any are conditioned or trained by experience. Thus they indicate factors of personality that are innate, whether this means that they arise from the individual's genetic makeup, or spring from past lives, however these factors may be modified, trained, or conditioned in this life (through the houses).

The houses, as areas of experience in this life, show the conditioning of the personality by outer circumstance, or at least the mesh of interaction between the two.

While the sign on the cusp of a house shows the inner or psychological principles that will be put into that area of experience of the world by the individual, the position of its ruling planet adds complexity, detail, focus, and activity to that general view, as do the aspects to that planet, which are not covered in this book.

Aspects are simple geometric relationships between planetary positions. If two planets are in the same few degrees of the sky, they are in conjunction; if separated by a sixth of the full circle, sextile; by one quarter, square; by a third, trine; by a half, opposing. The number of aspects is infinite since they are numerical or geometric harmonic parts of the whole circle of the zodiac, and it can be subdivided forever; but in modern practice only the most major harmonics are used, even though this means that astrologers miss a lot of detail that way.

The aspects are generally divided into easy and difficult, or harmonious and stressful. Easy aspects allow us, the real inner being, to develop within the areas of operation of the particular planets (and the signs/houses that they rule) without frustration, thus indicating "talents." Difficult aspects block and re-channel our development, forcing us to adjust in more painful ways. They show experiences in our lives that we take as being painful, and around which we usually build neurotic stumbling-blocks into our make-up. Difficult aspects to the ruler of any house often show a) the way we mishandle our experiences in that area of life, and b) the way we inwardly feel we deviate from the culturally accepted "norm" in that area (and probably how we cover our deviation). They show how the inner being has difficulty meshing with the outer world.

But this book does not deal with aspects. Its concern is with the placing of planets in both signs and houses.

Timing

Precise positions of planets in houses show the timing of events in life (on many different time-scales). The nature of the event depends on aspects to the planet and particularly on the houses ruled by the connected planets. You can use the life development schema outlined in the chapter introductions to trace this major pattern of development through life. (For example, if you have Saturn in the 8th house, you will have experienced Saturnine effects during your puberty—the precise time depending on how far Saturn is through that house). With an accurate birth chart, you can rotate it to read a major pattern of development through life.

To begin the interpretation of a chart, first you need an accurately drawn chart. Then you need to begin by choosing an area of life to examine, a house to start from. The usual choice is to begin from the first house since it indicates a person's surface of personality, their immediate attack on, or focus in, the world (and, in fact, indicates birth as the beginning of the life).

Whichever house you begin from, I advise you always to remain aware that the chart is a whole. If you start from the first house, all the others bear a relationship to it as parts of it as a whole. The same is true for any other house, though the subsidiary meanings of all the other houses will shift to fit the theme of the one you are looking at. For example, if you are looking at the 4th House as being your mother, or the mother of the one whose chart you are examining, then the 5th House, next after it, is her 2nd House, indicating her ability to touch, her values, attitudes to money and possessions etc. The 6th House will then become her 3rd, showing her intellect, rational or logical abilities, ability to communicate (the way she spoke and what she said), education, and so on. The whole chart is a hologram, meaning that every part contains the whole, though from its own point of view.

This "holographic" method of reading the chart bears rich fruit. The lives of parents, of brothers and sisters can be read as easily as that of the individual concerned, as can details of every part of his/her interactions with any area of life. It means that each planet is in every possible house for the individual, specific houses for specific life arenas. And never forget that the whole chart is the individual, whatever point of view you are reading it from.

While the average family balance as emerging from the birthchart has mother as the 4th House (and the rest, read from there) and father as the 10th (etc.), in some families this pattern is reversed. If you find the parental interpretations "off the mark," please try reversing mother for father and father for mother.

Details of the principles of signs and houses are given as introductions to each chapter (or house area). They are given as discursive examinations of life periods involved, faculties that are trained or conditioned during those times, and ways in which such trained faculties move out into action in the world. I have tried to describe the processes operating in each region, to give you an understanding of what is involved, rather than intellectual knowledge, or a set of "keywords," which I consider a very lazy way of using astrology and not conducive to developing understanding. I have not discriminated between signs and houses in the introductions; I leave it to you to consider how inner drives will differ from outer manifestations of such drives in areas not always appropriate to them.

Thus the 1st House introduction talks equally about Aries, the 2nd about Taurus and so on. If you start exploring aspects, in looking at difficult aspects to house rulers, remember that any basic need not satisfied at the appropriate developmental time of life halts our psychophysical and emotional development at that stage, or at least fixes it around unsatisfied need, from which we then respond to the world.

For convenience, the interpretations of the ascendant will be placed in the chapter on the 1st House, even though these interpretations also carry something of the 7th House in them. Likewise the interpretations for the 10th House or Midheaven will be found in the 10th House chapter, even though they include comments on the 4th House too.

Rule: Don't believe that in this book, or in any other information you find about anything, you have the whole picture. You only get fragments of the whole (barring total omniscience, a rare thing!), and always filtered through the limited viewpoint of the individual (and we are all biased one way or another). Please do not impose your (or my) theories onto others. Find out what *is* so from them, you'll learn more that way.

To review: consider zodiacal signs as archetypal principles; the inner nature of the being, including their chosen outer stamping grounds, perhaps as developed in past lives, perhaps being their personal genetic mix; latent, already built.

Consider houses as normal avenues of experience, as showing our learning of responses in and to those areas, our personality becoming conditioned by circumstances. Each house is thus the beginning of the experience of a particular complex function of body-mind-personality-experience, and shows the training of that function from that beginning in this lifetime. As a beginning or 1st House of a particular region, it shows the personality of that function—which grows and changes through all later houses.

Look to the sign and house position of the planet *ruling* the sign on the cusp of the house as your first indicator. A planet in a house tends to be a superimposition on the functioning of that area rather than absolutely fundamental to it, and will be a displacement of drives from the house that the planet rules. It may show how the person had to hide part of themselves (the ruling planet), and what they hid it behind (the "occupying" planet).

Wherever the planet may be, it carries the whole theme of its own sign with it, though that will be modified by the sign and house that it occupies. If you want to explore more of the nature of each sign, look at the interpretations of its ruling planet through all the signs and houses, as well as at the introduction to that sign/house.

If you want to develop your abilities in astrology, I suggest that, as a continuing exercise, you take the introductions to each sign-house chapter and go "around the houses"; take a house as a starting point or theme and relate all the others to it from its point of view. If you chose the 5th for example, then the 6th would be its own "2nd" or value framework, the 7th its 3rd, or conceptual adaptability, communications, and so on. In this way you will round out and deepen your knowledge, gain flexibility in interpreting, and build a foundation for a rich and complex knowledge of humans and of astrology. Then integrate into it everything you know about psychology, philosophy, sociology—whatever interests you. Use the house-sign framework as your filing system and symbolic computer. Pour experience into it, take it out again totally interwoven. Do the same with every chart you interpret. Good luck!

✦ 3 ✦

Aries
and the 1st House

The Ascendant, or cusp, of the 1st House is the birth moment on our astrological clock, and shows, or in astrological thinking *is*, the first moment of experience of the new-born baby. This moment, for any baby born in western cultures, usually includes some degree of birth trauma, pain or shock (imposed by modern birthing methods, or by the mother's anxieties). The trauma leaves its traces in the attitudes of the baby to new experiences in this world—attitudes shown by the whole birth chart pattern, but responded to from the ascendant. A birth trauma leaves us with our own particular objects of fear, types of fear and consequent defensive aggression (active or passive) as we try to fight against them, even though we rarely, if ever, remember what we are fighting against.

Even at birth (or rather, especially at birth) we are very sensitive to what the world does to us, and very capable of imprinting expectations about life in general from the little experience we have. These expectations will be non-verbal and non-rational since we have not as yet developed either verbal or rational abilities.

Our very first impressions of the new world, since they are our first impressions about anything in a very impressionable mind, easily imprint deeply to become a foundation for so-called "innate" attitudes toward the world, life and experience. We learn our first lesson in responding to new beginnings, ways of acting or reacting at the start of anything new. Since all experiences develop from what are initially new ones (and we can only experience in the present moment, which is always new), these become ways of dealing with experience in general. These learned responses to experience become known as personality. In the terms of Jungian psychology this is more properly called persona, meaning "a (theatrical) player's mask." Our own kind of readiness to respond to experience, and our methods of responding are all that other people ever really see of us.

The 1st House, following on from the ascendant, involves the cradle period in the life of the individual. A baby learns that it is a distinct point, or center, in space and time. Its mind rests entirely in the present moment, since it has yet to learn to focus on anything else, even to conceive of the existence of past or future, which then do not exist for it. Its intensity of experience is total since entirely unfiltered. It has all its instincts available, all its faculties (though undeveloped as yet), all of its being, since none of these things have yet been restrained in any way (unless in response to intrauterine experiences). The baby is whole and responds to every experience as a whole, with everything it has.

A baby's first task in life is to learn to focus its attention through its senses (initially its eyes and ears) onto the surrounding world, and to track objects of interest. It gradually gains the sense of being an individual (a single focus of experience) through being the controller of its own point of focus of attention, *i.e.*, of being the "attender," the one who is looking out through its senses. As it learns to focus its attention, it begins to learn which impressions it gets from its world are of particular interest to it (initially mother's face above all else, later other faces in general). These it begins to select in preference to other stimuli. As primary focuses of attention they are what is sought out, "hunted," focused upon, and desired from the world. These become primary aims in life. This is the process of building a personal sense of direction, basic viewpoint, aim, of picking things and experiences to act toward when action becomes possible.

The second task of a baby in the cradle is to kick and struggle, to exercise its muscles so as to become able to tackle its world, to act toward it and within it. Its energy is effectively an enormous potential to become. It only begins to become something as it acts, as it uses its initiative, and its first step is simply to become able to move itself at all. Every one of us has a need to act, to prove ourselves, to find out and show what we can do, whether to ourselves or to others. Frustrations in the cradle, such as being tucked in to the point of being tied down, or being left in isolation, become blocks on free action and response later in life.

The 1st House shows our ability to take the initiative and act, our degree of singleness of focus and of purpose, our point of expansion out into the world. We could think of this as being the development of the warrior, learning to handle life, to become effective, the pioneer tackling new territory. In modern scientific symbolism, this is the explosion of the whole potential of the universe from the single point of the big bang, and its outward thrust to become a manifest universe.

Pain makes us learn to be cautious in our approach to things, to be ready to defend ourselves against whatever may hurt us. This can hold back the free flow of our initiative into life and experience. In our personalities, when involved with others, this defensive caution becomes a mask, or a series of masks, shields behind which the real personality hides, often with weapons drawn in case of a need for further defense. (This is the Plutonic face of Aries, or the sword and shield of Mars).

Physiologically, the 1st House shows the conditioning of our energy, of our muscles, of the adrenal hormones that prepare our senses for perceiving and our muscles for acting (*i.e.*, our activating systems, drives, desires); it shows the training of our eyes and sense of vision as our primary focusing sense, but also the head as the prime carrier of senses with the brain as the initiator of action; it also includes our surface defenses against the impacts of experience, such as dead surface skin, nails, and hair, particularly on over-sensitive sensory receptor cells, plus their psychological parallels; the defended surface covering over the vulnerable inner personality, including the building of "scar tissue," if wounded. In the cycle of digestion, the 1st House indicates the front teeth, the incisors, which take the first bite when eating.

In the process of perceiving, this is where "sensory energy" comes into contact with the surface of our bodies, and mechanically works its way through toward the sensory cells. For example, light entering the eye through the lens, being focused onto the cells of the retina; sound entering the channel of the ear, shaking the eardrum, and the tiny bones of the inner ear, before reaching the cells of the cochlea.

ASCENDANT IN ARIES
Ruled by Mars

You have a strong drive to be first, whether in competition, in your opinion of yourself, or in any area of life that interests you. The new fascinates you (you probably can't be bothered with the old) and you need constant fresh experience to keep you alive. If nothing new is developing, you are very likely to start something yourself, plunging ahead, pioneering, or carving new pathways. Your awareness tends to be single-pointed and focused entirely on the present moment and its necessary actions, but not necessarily ranging much further than that.

You like expending your energy, and find value in any form of tool or weapon (concrete or abstract) that helps you apply it exactly where you want it, and, if you can't find the right tools, then you may make them yourself. Do-it-yourself could easily be a way of life for you, although while you start plenty of projects you are not necessarily very good at finishing them (once they lose their newness, why then they are boring old stuff, aren't they?). This does not apply to lifelong goals, for your very single-mindedness should bring rapid success when you do not let the pull of other new developments divert you.

Your energy and competitive drive thrust you toward the top in your chosen field(s), whether sports, business, the armed forces, or others (characteristic Aries sports are target sports, *e.g.*, shooting). Your head-first drive can get you there, but often with accidents to the head along the way (got any scars there?). Other people often find you too direct, too aggressive, too pointed in your approach to them, even interfering, for your surface opinion of yourself is usually pretty good. From your own side, you can't relate easily to anyone unless you can respect them, at least as an equal, and you do not like to admit to anyone being superior to you, which can leave you as a lone wolf.

Depending on other factors in your chart, your intense self-awareness could actually make you go in the opposite direction from the headlong outer thrust described, because any experience you enter into, you enter intensely; if any drove you to become more withdrawn, or shy, then you would become so intensely too! Mars' sign and house position in your chart will define your most likely directions. The problem is that you lack perspective by being self-aware but not particularly aware of others, thus you can't see how similar your experience is to theirs. This is the quality that you need most for complete balance, and not simply awareness of others, but to be able to see things from their point of view. Normally this will come to you through your major relationships, and through any circumstances that show you that your energy is really designed to help others; in fact it is incomplete without them.

Anyway, you prefer to be causative, to make your own way in life, to make your own first contacts, to lead yourself. You need to define your long-range goals and develop persistence in pursuing them, organizing yourself so that you are acting on them here and now. The realization that every moment is a new beginning can help you to see that you are always starting afresh, even when continuing on the same track. Recognize that you have a warrior's approach to life.

ASCENDANT IN TAURUS
Ruled by Venus

In outer personality and general approach to your world you are stable, persistent and enduring, aiming for and reaching out to those things in which you find value. These may be material possessions, since you have an earthy feeling for financial and material stability, and for enjoyment of the good things of the earth. You approach the world through your senses, and seek out things to appreciate through them and to satisfy them. Thus you can have quite a sensual involvement in life, tending at the extreme to over-indulgence. Your appreciation of things can develop into a fine sense of beauty, quality and value, whether natural, artificial or abstract, your appreciation being a major facet of your tendency to measure, taste and evaluate everything. You are quick to find out what you like, but also to reject what you dislike, and refuse to be involved with it. You can be extremely stubborn in sticking to the values that you have formed, thus keeping your life in a single-minded pursuit of what pleases you, avoiding what you believe to be unpleasant, and thus never dealing with it.

You are persistent in pursuit of your goals, usually never varying your aims or direction, an excellent quality that can eventually achieve anything. Therefore, it is essential for you to have clearly defined goals whose pursuit will develop the best qualities of your being—otherwise you will be strengthening the negative in you by continual exercise. You dislike change and have difficulty making decisions that may affect the direction of your life, your gentleness being carried to the point of indecisiveness, brooding over whatever problems there may be. In forming judgments, you prefer to penetrate to the essential heart of the matter to avoid waste of time and effort, but irresoluteness in the face of problems can leave you drifting to and fro, since you won't back off, but sometimes can't see how to go forwards. A resolute and even military decisiveness can help you to cut through after you have thoroughly pondered the matter, not allowing fresh doubts and scruples to arise—which would only make you feel humiliated by your inability to act, and you can curse yourself soundly for that.

Your peaceable approach to life often leads to problems in dealing with others who you feel are intractable and difficult. Since you mostly bury your own aggression it seems to you that others are more aggressive. You repress it in yourself because you don't like it, so you judge others who show it, being inwardly intolerant towards them—which does not help you to relate to them. In dealing with them, and with your own unconscious aggression, you need to drop all prejudice and allow the mind of the other to act freely upon you. Thus you can establish a true contact with, and come to understand them—the only way to have any personal control within the relationship, or to heal the split in yourself between peaceful and warlike sides. You can make a strong moral impression upon the other by non-judgmental acceptance while still keeping your own values. You lose inner peace and independence if you rely too heavily on others, swinging from joy to sorrow, mainly because of the powerfully jealous possessiveness that you can pin upon your partner. You fix your attitudes too strongly, both for and against others and yourself.

ASCENDANT IN GEMINI
Ruled by Mercury

Your outer personality and approach to your world is actively intellectual, variable and questioning. At your best your curiosity leads you to study and explore a wide variety of subjects, seeking understanding in the form of information, developing your intellect. You need open communication with others, and tend to adapt yourself readily to people and circumstances around you, which can make you something of a chameleon, changing color to match your surroundings. So you can be inconsistent and inconstant, being different things to different people. You like being involved in everything, leaving you with problems in deciding between mutually exclusive alternatives, since you want the best of both worlds. Or, you split your attitudes to new experiences, both wanting to be involved and not, at one and the same time, showing one reaction on the surface while holding the other within.

This split comes from a fixation during the period when you were learning to talk and first began to understand your parents' words. It probably springs from learning their ideas of good and bad, being made to be a good child in ways that they wanted but you didn't, and/or being called a bad child if you were yourself (and you are sensitive to the implications in the names and labels that are used towards you). You are divided between a desire for recognition from others and a need to be yourself which you probably feel to be totally incompatible, so you have learned to display your different faces as circumstances permit. You may have learned to use questioning or talking as a defense, leading conversations where you want them to go, knowing that others can't get at you if you are directing the flow of their minds. (Some Gemini types become teachers.)

Your "good-child/bad-child" swing may make you refuse to accept the basic reasons for morality. You may be caught at the point in your youth when you first recognized that you were growing up; if you remained a baby, you could get away with anything and be loved for it, but if you grew up, you would have to become moral and responsible. Again you wanted the best of both worlds, so part of you decided never to grow up. You want to be recognized as an adult without having all the frustrations and duties, so you are likely to look for short-cuts and easy ways of doing things. You would also like your opinions and ideas to carry some weight with others, to have influence and power, but don't always recognize that they can only do so if your words are supported by your entire conduct, only firm and consistent conduct making any real impression on others.

In making decisions, split aims can make you spread your hopes very widely, so that if any of them don't come off, you can change horses in midstream to gallop off in a different direction. Or, your developed intellect surveys the possibilities with a broad overview, optimistically choosing the best route for your long-term growth and education. You can be light-hearted and gregarious in relating. One of your natural relationships is one in which you are the student and your partner is the teacher (or negatively, judges your morals). If your dualism is uppermost you run away from relationships that become oppressive, with a nervous, highly-strung reaction.

ASCENDANT IN CANCER
Ruled by the Moon

You approach your world receptively and reflectively, absorbing it directly through your emotions and being easily swayed by environmental influences. Your variable feelings leave you with a need for security and constancy around you, particularly in relationships, since you feel that it isn't there inside you. You absorb many influences from your surroundings, and reflect them immediately, which makes your outer personality a patchwork of pieces. You look for things and people to identify with to give yourself a more consistent personality, first in your family and especially with your mother, since your longest and most secure roots are there, whatever the actual relationship was like. You absorb attitudes and demands of other people readily, feeling pressures to conform, and, being impressionable, you feel guilty if you don't—though you may resent this.

You want recognition from others and adapt your responses to reflect what you feel they want, while often keeping your own personality hidden inside you, as though you look out from behind a one-way mirror. This springs from an early fixing point in your life, when you felt that you had to be what your parents wanted of you to keep their affection, and not to disappoint them. You felt that your security was outside you rather than inside, the opposite of what you needed. Your powerful protective instincts defend anything or anyone that you identify with, as well as protecting your own inner security, but as long as you feel safe in your protective shell you will go along with others. One major "shell" is your moods, which you use as an emotional barrier wall to keep others out and yourself in. You feel that others will disapprove of and minimize what you want to do, so you approach your objectives in a sideways manner so that you don't appear to be going in that direction. Yet in pursuit of those objectives you can be extremely tenacious, recognizing your needs and seeking to fulfill them, and if you don't succeed at first, returning again and again until you do.

You may replay your childhood with your parents in your relationships, either remaining a child yourself, wanting others to take responsibility for looking after you, or turning it around and becoming the parent yourself, taking on the obligations of nurturing them. Either way your relationships may have an inferiority/superiority split, though you may see it as a matter of security and responsibility. You can let your partners dominate with yourself swinging in gravitational orbit around them, or do the opposite.

In making decisions, you either use your reflective mind to look for the order and rules of the situation, organizing carefully and conservatively from there toward your goal; or you let your doubts dominate you, expecting the worst from your choices, being pessimistic about your prospects. Since the whole direction of your life depends on your decisions, you will either climb steadily to success, considering your tenacity, or will wallow in self-pity if you stick with your negative feelings. Where you do evaluate the order in any situation and respond readily and consciously to it, rather than instinctively, you can gain a great clarity in your own being, putting yourself in order.

ASCENDANT IN LEO
Ruled by the Sun

You approach your world with pride, honor, passion and playfulness, seeing it as an opportunity for testing your talents and for enjoying to the hilt. You hate to feel that you are not the master of any situation and capable of creatively organizing it to your own designs. You probably have a love of self-display and an inventive mind that finds plenty of opportunities for putting on a flourishing show. Your playful creativity, if well established, can give you major talents, whatever your favorite area of operation, since you enjoy pouring yourself out into it and have a fixed stability of purpose that can see even major projects through to completion.

If your self-respect is stable and adequate you give others as much respect, recognition and friendship as you give to yourself, but if it is not then you overreact by emphasizing all your differences from other people, making yourself the conceited center of attention and not caring much about them. Since you do generally maintain a good opinion of yourself, you are very able to be of help to the many around you that don't approve of themselves, helping to highlight their uniquenesses, their special qualities as individuals; in this way you can be very humanitarian in your relationships, always being approachable, and as ready to listen to useful advice as to give it. If you have become stuck in your own pride, however, you tend to look down on others, feeling that you should be in command over them, keeping yourself detached from them while feeling that you have every right to manipulate them as you please, becoming tense and wary in an effort to avoid being trapped by those that you consider inferior to you; you are then quite unable to take any advice from others since you think that you know everything better than anyone else, so they soon give up any attempt to influence you, leaving you alone.

You are rather susceptible to love affairs, or at least to wanting to have the great love of a lifetime. So long as your motives are honorable, all goes well. You do not go out to seek a partner but allow your character to have its effect on those around you, and the ones who are receptive to you respond readily. To attract others you must place yourself beneath them, being receptive to them and thus allowing them to flow toward you. But if you impose your will, and seek out who you want to relate to, drawing them into your net, your range is limited to those that you choose, and you have already established your superiority and their inferiority, which will never turn out well, at the very least because they will sense your attitude and resent it.

In making decisions you fix your mind firmly onto the pursuit and attainment of your ideals, wanting nothing less. You prefer, if possible, to pursue a unique course through your life, not being traditional or conventional in what you aim for. Naturally you can strike problems if you are not treading a known path, but you are generally ready to seek the aid and advice of friends of like mind and to allow someone fully equal to the situation to lead. In the face of major difficulties you seek out the error in your own viewpoint, turning the obstacles into an occasion for self-education and inner enrichment. If you are of the superior type, you find someone else to blame for the whole thing.

ASCENDANT IN VIRGO
Ruled by Mercury

You approach your world in a reserved, discriminating and analytical manner, keeping control by meticulous attention to detail. Critical of yourself and of everything that you deal with, you seek perfection in all that you do. Your discrimination may look for and therefore find imperfection instead. Perfectionism is your tool to fight impurity, illness, chaos, decay and dissolution in your life, or anything that arouses your anxiety, struggling to support life against the things that threaten it. Your confidence is at its best when you have everything efficiently ordered, but is not particularly good the rest of the time, worry thrusting you into a flurry of scattered activity to get everything done, and you can find more to do than most.

Your underlying character is sensitive, vulnerable and very responsive to others. At best you are compassionately giving, and ready to be of service to others' needs, to work for their support, against their problems and difficulties. Your focus may be more on animals or plants than on people, a Virgo ascendant sometimes being the mark of a farmer, veterinarian, or biochemist (Virgo represents life-chemistry). Inwardly you may dream of the perfect romance (and refuse, or criticize anything less—unfortunately your partners are all human), of living a rich, exotic life in a fairy tale world, building perfection in your fantasies, perhaps finding fault with the world around you because it isn't what you want. In making decisions, you pursue your visions of perfection, but may feel that they are unrealizable, or will dissolve if you reach out to them, or that making them real mars their beauty by making them mundane, and therefore faulty. You set up an image of perfection to pursue, and work hard to accomplish it where you trust that it is attainable (when you put your suspicions aside), but you need to realize that it is ultimately a perfection in yourself that you seek. Whatever you want to achieve, investigate the facts exactly, for you can become slipshod and confused in your judgments (sometimes through attending to too much detail rather than considering the whole picture), keeping the appearance of perfectionism for the outer world.

Your mother worked at taking on responsibility. She wanted her world ordered and under precise control. She used her authority to criticize everything that wasn't as she wanted it to be (including you). She wanted to present a meticulous social image, to be beyond criticism herself. Emotionally, she was deeply sensitive, possibly readily dissolving into tears, and was either quite giving, charitably pouring herself out to the protection of her family, or vulnerable and tending to mope about the "martyrdom" of motherhood. If the latter, she was insecure and emotionally chaotic, tending to crumble easily. Your father was either gentle in his authority to the point of it being nonexistent, or was overbearing to an extreme degree. It is probable that he did not take responsibility very well, either evading it completely and being rather directionless, or grasping at it with overpowering strength because of his fears of loss of standing or of control. He was emotionally reserved, either quietly cautious and holding worries in check, or critical—demanding perfect order around the home.

ASCENDANT IN LIBRA
Ruled by Venus

Your outer personality is charming, pleasant, poised and harmonious, designed to avoid conflict and contention, to keep your life and your relationships balanced and peaceful, since your first desire is to be liked by others. You dislike rough, dirty or unpleasant circumstances or people, your fastidiousness preferring to relate to the beautiful in everything. You are very aware of relationships and of your role within them, and you are in your element acting as mediator, peace-maker and diplomat. You calm turbulence and build bridges between differences of opinion, since you can usually see merits in all viewpoints (preferring to be impartial in your judgments, neither for nor against anything or anyone). You are egalitarian, believing in fairness and justice for all, and that all people should have equal rights—this is the face that you prefer others to see.

Naturally one of your main problems is indecisiveness; if you see all things as equal, how can you decide between them? If they are equal, why bother to do anything? This may leave you lazily inert. Your impartiality can be indifference, not caring one way or the other, and your dislike of the rougher aspects of the world can make you avoid it to keep the gentle life that you prefer. Trying to keep everything nice, you evade trouble instead of meeting it and dealing with it, and thus resolving it. You would often rather look at other people's problems (from a detached distance, of course) than admit to your own, finding it easier to deal with the objective than with the subjective, but you would really rather see no problems at all.

Indifference and inertia lead to stagnation, and problems do not disappear by being ignored, both of which require you to use the side of your character that you avoid, namely decisiveness and energy, to remove the cause of your indifference. You perceive in terms of cause and effect, and may avoid action to avoid causing things and states that you don't like; remember that it goes both ways, that you can also cause what you do like, by acting. You cause your own life's pattern, you cannot blame it onto others, not with honesty, and not without wrecking your relationships. The wise person turns his attention onto himself to discover where he was at fault in difficult situations, thus educating himself and remaking his character.

Your father was probably vigorous and direct, if not attacking, in use of his authority, seeing only his own point of view when he laid down the law. His restless energy aimed at achievement, and may have leaped from project to project without truly completing any. Your mother's authority was more equable and reasonable, encouraging you to be aware of others, to be tactful and defer to them. she may have been judgmental where she thought that you weren't being nice.

Your intellectual creativity and balanced judgment, when exercised, can develop great refinement of mind, able to see from many viewpoints and make rounded assessments of any situation, associating the Libran ascendant with the legal profession, and the arts. Libran professions include accounting, journalism, literature, dancing, design, counseling, mediation, public relations and being a personal representative.

ASCENDANT IN SCORPIO
Ruled by Pluto

You have intense drive and fixed purpose when you find what you feel worthwhile doing. You have to feel useful, competent, capable, that you are not wasting yourself, time, effort or resources, since waste of potential appalls you. You immediately break problems down into their fundamentals, their essential elements, discarding the rest as being useless. You feel that problems contain their own solutions, and would rather deal with causes than with symptoms. As a child you probably took your toys apart to find out how they worked, and may still do so, being dissatisfied with surface appearances in anything. You want to know how and why things are done, built, made, put together in their particular way, and you admire efficiency of function, simplicity and directness. Naturally this trait sometimes makes engineers, or detectives, or psychiatrists, being valuable wherever it is necessary to find the root of a problem, deal effectively with it, and restore proper function.

On the human level, your awareness of pain is high, be it physical, emotional or psychological. For example, you are intensely aware of anything in others' attitudes that seems to reject you, and have built defenses against being hurt. One defense is not to show your feelings, keeping an immobile face that doesn't show pain or weakness, overriding and suppressing such feelings if they are there. Another is to use intense silent watchfulness, being constantly aware of the emotional bias of every situation and being ready to react in self-defense—though your idea of self-defense is to strike fast and hard to make sure that they never try anything against you again. You have your survival instincts right at the surface. Filtering your world through them makes you see threats where there may be none. You don't like people prying into your affairs, often because your intense conscience doesn't approve of things that you have done or been, so you sometimes lash out through conscience problems, venting your anger at yourself on the other person.

Your conscience is a face of your sense of pain. Knowing what hurts you, you know what hurts others. It can help you to deal with others' problems, neither seeking them out nor interfering (unless you are an arrogant and overbearing type) but being willing to use your "surgeon's compassion" to cut to the heart of the matter and help heal it. You will probably find others using you as a good firm shoulder to cry upon, knowing that you won't dissolve into tears yourself nor be sloppily sympathetic, but will offer directly practical advice from your perspicacious observations of human nature. At your best, the tougher the situation the better you deal with it, being able to draw upon those survival instincts for power and capability, and never avoiding a difficult situation.

At worst, you focus so entirely on your own problems as to be unaware that others also have them. You hang obsessionally onto the fact that *you* have been hurt, and strike out at those around you with barbed words and barbed actions, driven by vengeful feelings. Or you believe that whoever hurt you was right, and have an appallingly poor self-image, believing that you deserve the rejection you feel you get. In general you are likely to master any such problems by sheer persistence of drive toward healing and health.

ASCENDANT IN SAGITTARIUS
Ruled by Jupiter

Your outer personality is cheerful, open, and outgoing, facing life with optimism and enthusiasm. You prefer to focus on the broader issues in everything you deal with, gaining
an overview of any subject that interests you, a view from the heights, developing broad-
mindedness in the intellectual sense if not in all others. You explore, ranging freely over
wide territories, whether traveling, studying, or in your probable involvement in philosophy or religion. You seek to draw an inner nourishment from the inexhaustible well-
springs of life through discovery of the truth in the laws of growth, development and evolution, to know what the most positive potentials are and what future they lead to. In
seeking the truth you are honest, knowing that you must be true to yourself in order to
know what truth is, and you can be fearlessly outspoken, not seeing why the truth should
ever be hidden. You aim for wisdom, and freely pass on your experience to others, being
likely to teach in some way, not necessarily orthodox, since you have little respect for the
strictures of the classroom situation, recognizing that enthusiasm for the subject matters
more than formality.

If egotism has taken charge in you, you will be more superior and overbearing, your
"view from the heights" being a looking down upon others, and your search for truth a
belief that you know it all and others ought to hear about it and take your word for it. You
override others' views and opinions, *knowing* that yours are better, putting yourself on an
invisible pedestal separating you from the mass of people. Your confidence can be arrogance, yet isn't stable, being able to fluctuate wildly, as can your aims and hopes in the
world. You set up one hopeful aim after another, sometimes several at once, seeking opportunities but being ready to drop them and move on if they don't come off easily. In
making decisions you can be split, looking for the best possibilities but being uncertain
where they lie, so setting up alternatives and being ready to change your mind. The same
applies to relationships; you accept substitutes for love; you like to be involved but also
like your freedom, so you remain in two minds about them, ready to run away (one of
your main defenses) if it doesn't work out as you wish. Thus you can be irresponsible,
though you hate to admit it, because this reduces your good opinion of yourself. Some
with Sagittarius rising lean toward the manic-depressive, swinging up into wild enthusiasms followed by a crash into depression, hopes rising and then crumbling.

Gentleness breaks up and dissolves divisive egotism, together with recognition of
the common ground and origin of all beings, consciousness that the creative driving force
of life is greater than any creature. Only those free of selfish ulterior considerations who
persevere in being honest and just are able to dissolve their egotism and free that vital
creative power within themselves. Your teaching pattern helps by enabling you to give
away to others all that you gather for yourself, breaking down personal barriers. The
more you give to others, the more you have to give. Your great search can become awe in
the face of infinity (when you are not the largest thing in your own awareness), and lead
you to become involved in great ventures for the promotion of the welfare of mankind, or
of all living creatures.

ASCENDANT IN CAPRICORN
Ruled by Saturn

You have a conservative, orderly and orthodox approach to life, leaning toward being serious and self-controlled. Economical, practical and industrious, you are aware of the structured order of the material world and of how to deal with it. You recognize laws, rules, and patterns of order and form in all that you meet, particularly in human society and relationships, and probably feel it right and proper to maintain them, acting with reserve, dignity and decorum. You are aware of the hierarchies of power and position, the "pecking orders" within groups, patterns of dominance and submission between people, perhaps desiring to rise to the top of the heap, being more comfortable there than further down and under somebody else's thumb. You may be ambitious, driving to achieve and succeed, perhaps in a profession, to gain an ultimate goal in life or standing and recognition in society. Always older than your years, you take responsibility readily, seeing it as a part of adulthood and as leading to the recognition that you seek.

Your orderly nature may make you a stickler for the letter of the law, capable of narrow-minded judgment of those who are more liberal than yourself. Your awareness of the rules and restraints demanded by the conservative society can leave you with little spontaneity, and with guilt if you transgress them, or ready to make others feel guilty if they do. You can be cautious and doubtful to the point of fear, wanting a well-protected security in your life and ready to hold firmly to what you have, perhaps making your life and yourself rigid and inflexible. Knowing the psychological rules, and needing to have things under control, you may manipulate others to serve your own ends (whether openly or covertly). If so, you do not recognize their rights as free individuals, assuming personal superiority over them (in counterbalance to your inferiority feelings). Or your doubts may lead you to take a pessimistic view of everything, looking for the negative in all that you meet—and naturally finding it—leading to grumbling and moaning.

If you want any authority or responsibility over others, even within your family, you will do best by learning how to serve first, for only then do you gain the respect and assent of willing followers. If you try to do it by manipulation, force of position, or cunning, you will invariably arouse resistance, since no one likes to be used. It also helps if you are ready to adapt to the demands of the time and circumstances rather than imposing your own view of order, which may not be appropriate; you should not wear yourself out by resisting the "flow" that is available. If you are aiming to achieve, you need to allow yourself periods of rest, relaxation, refreshment and recuperation, otherwise you become stale, which can depress any living organism.

How much of your surface personality was built in response to your mother's authority (which was probably strict and controlling)? She was conservative in social views, possibly a pillar of society, and maybe ambitious, wanting public recognition for achievements. The security of home and family would have been of prime importance to her. Some facets of your persona may have developed as reactions to your father's emotional coolness and reserve, tendency towards depression, or instinctive manipulation.

ASCENDANT IN AQUARIUS
Ruled by Uranus

You are an independent individualist, approaching life with an eager and open mind, seeking freedom and awakening. Your active and inventive intellect questions everything to understand how it all fits together—not through orthodox views, for you are not concerned with maintaining tradition, but stretching your understanding no matter what strangeness it discovers. You move rapidly from fact to fact, seeking links and connections, speeding over whole logical sequences or groups of connected concepts in a flash. This may make you over-complex in dealing with things, forgetting that tasks are easy if attended to simply. You may have mental "fusion reactions" when an integrated picture suddenly emerges from the information mass. Integration is what you seek, not only through intellect but in all facets of your life, psychological and social.

At best you are a humanitarian, a utopian dreamer seeking the ideal social structure to bring growth and happiness to all, perhaps as a practical social worker struggling to even out the imbalances and injustices of the system. You see the need for change in the social order to help change the nature of humanity—to bring out its best instead of its worst. You want to see the ideals that you identify so strongly with become real. Sometimes this means that the ordinary world does not satisfy you, has too little stimulus to keep you interested, and you seek it in things beyond the usual and normal, and may live in a science-fiction world of your own invention.

At worst you are a tense, rebellious individualist who refuses to conform, a breakaway from the system. You don't want to be labeled, categorized or pigeonholed, or made into anything that you don't want to be, desiring to be a free individual in your own right. Fair enough, but sometimes you take it to extremes of reaction against others' views and attitudes, not so much being what you want as being what they don't want. You may want to blow up the system, promoting anarchistic revolution against authority. You fear being trapped, being ready to react fast to get out of restrictions; yet being a rebel ties you absolutely to what you rebel against. You blame your own condition onto others, instead of seeing that you alone are responsible. You don't want to be one of the masses, preferring to be an utter individualist, emphasizing all of your differences from others (having to invent some along the way). You use detachment as a defense, saying "I am not involved" or "I don't care," standing back and being the dispassionate observer.

Being different is a form of superiority that makes you react against or away from others, and sets you apart on an isolated peak. The law is that what is high shall be worn down, and what is low will be filled up. An open being has neither separative pride nor need to be different, finding satisfaction in being fully human (knowing that each and every one is unique), and thus essentially modest. Aquarius deals with differences, and the leveling of them, in the individual and in the mass, (overcoming all bias against self, others or society), seeking social justice from the ironing out of extreme conditions (wealth and poverty, for example). If this is your ideal, make sure that your ideas, words and actions all match.

ASCENDANT IN PISCES
Ruled by Neptune

You carried much of the womb state into life with you, a dreamy inward drift, beginning life as an innocent romantic dreamer living in a fairy-tale world. When very young you found it impossible to distinguish the real from the imagined or dreamed. You were a long time becoming aware of the boundaries between inner and outer, and used your inner world as a safe, beautiful, secluded retreat from difficult outer life. You probably still do so to some extent. Emotionally open and sensitive, you can feel other people's feelings as powerfully as you feel your own.

Positively, you have a deep compassion for the sufferings of others and a desire to help heal them. Negatively, you are vulnerable to others' attitudes, particularly to criticism, and anxious to avoid being pinned down. To protect yourself, you act out the roles that others seem to want of you, building a camouflage to hide behind, using your subtle impressionability to take on the local color. You can be a chameleon, actor or actress, since you pick up tiny hints from others and react with delicately pitched responses.

You notice how situations, relationships, and things decay and dissolve. At best this helps you live your life with love, without clinging, giving you the wisdom of knowing that all things must end and dissolve back into the Universe. At worst you fear loss to the point of being paranoid, then hide your fears and avoid anything that arouses them. You build a cotton-wool cocoon, an inner sanctuary that covers fears over, fogs them out using drink, drugs, or any other smoke screen, including living in your daydreams, creating unreality to avoid reality. So you may be vague, dithering, and indecisive, and thus need to relate to a complementary type of character, precise, practical and perfectionistic. But such people are also usually critical, and you take on your martyr or "doormat" persona. You bemoan the sadnesses and decay of the beautiful in the world, especially where it affects you, finding martyrdom an easy role to play.

Your early tendencies to imagine yourself as the hero or heroine of any tale give you a rich, dramatic inner theater and an often unconscious tendency to play out many of those imaginative roles in later life, not even realizing that you are doing it. The satisfying roles are often those with much drama, or with pathos and deep hurts nobly suffered, but they are still roles being played out.

You may be a nature mystic, able to lose your separateness, your personal boundaries, to blend with natural surroundings, feeling with great depth all the life around you. Beautiful and peaceful moments are likely to come in such circumstances where you can avoid the confusing complications of the usual human relationships; the Piscean character can be quite a loner, a monastic individual preferring to contemplate the universe, rather than entering into all of it's hurly-burly.

Your desire to be of service to others can make you hospitable to the point of self-sacrifice. The best outlet for this characteristic is in hospital or charity work; otherwise your aesthetic sensitivity could lead you into fine arts, particularly music, painting, or theater, photography and films, or fashion.

SUN IN ARIES
✧ The Warrior ✧ Pioneer ✧ Tool User ✧

The astrological age of Aries extended from about 2000 B.C. to 0 A.D., the age of the Greek heroes, adventuring around the known world, battling monsters and men, often murdering their own kin through sheer impulse of temper. Hercules is the human, and Ares the god archetype.

The Ram is used as the symbol for the head first, head down, headlong forward charge of the full Aries type. Aries is that part of the full human personality that focuses upon action in the immediate moment. You are aware of your world from your point of view only, and of what you can do with it right *now*. You are ardent, active and energetic in pursuit of immediate goals (the only kind of goals that you like), tending towards a reckless impulsiveness. Your enthusiasms frequently verge upon the fanatical and you are ready to fight your way through to the prize. You love the battle so much that you don't always mind which side you're fighting for, just so long as you can hack your way through the fray. You hold your opinions with equal energy just because they are yours, right or wrong, and can needle others into a debate for the sake of having an opponent. You only respect those who stand up for themselves and stand up to you. You prefer to have complete control over your own actions and dislike having anyone in immediate command over you, being self-starting and self-directing.

Constancy is not normally one of your virtues and you find it difficult to maintain your impetus toward a goal that is too far ahead or takes too long for you to attain. Thus you can change your aims and ideas with as much energy as you take them up with initially. Your desire for immediate results can cause you to take short-cuts, innocently forgetting or ignoring moral and legal issues in the process and occasionally building a complete muddle. Refusing to admit to failure, you would rather "cut the Gordian Knot" by further incisive, but perhaps equally misdirected, action, or simply abandon the tangle. By such action you can arouse fierce opposition from others, including those that think you their friend, and your love of battle does not heal these issues at all.

You are competitive and like being first, whether in sports, business, or whatever field you choose. You don't compete just for the sake of the game, but in order to win and to live with intensity. The desire to be first can lead you into research, pathfinding or pioneering in any arena of life. For some the newer the field the better, for others that doesn't matter, so long as they are hacking out new territory within it. It is the process of hunting for the new experience that you like, of coming upon the fresh discovery, be it inward or outward. You can't tolerate inaction.

The Aries head-first attitude usually leads to scars on the head.

While this describes the classic Aries personality, you will no doubt vary from it in many ways. Your own most major differences will be shown by the house placement and aspects of the Sun, and by the sign and house placement and aspects of Mars.

MOON IN ARIES

You are rather emotionally one-pointed, tending to fix your feelings upon fresh focal aims, whether these be a new relationship, a new goal, or any other new experience. You are rather self-aware, having been encouraged to stand on your own feet by your early life-experiences. You understand that your security depends on your own actions, and you have a drive toward achievement through action, to accomplish and to be first in your field, whether this be family or profession. At best, this means that your style will be quite individualistic, since you won't follow anyone else's ways, and that you are capable of being a pioneer, of creating new avenues in your field. At worst, it means that you are only aware of your own viewpoint and can impose it rather aggressively on others, not recognizing that their views and feelings are as important to them as your own are to you.

The Moon represents the emotions and emotional "armoring." Your emotions are vigorous and direct, and your armor is to defend your own ground alone, isolating yourself and attacking the enemy in a direct frontal assault (the best defense is a good attack). *Aggress* originally meant "to walk toward," and you are aggressive, meaning thoroughly capable of directing yourself at any new experience and being ready to act, to enjoy, to attack, or to defend yourself as the need may arise. You are candidly honest, frequently excessively so, tending toward emotional exaggeration by stating things with more energy than they deserve. You tend to follow your own track in life without paying any attention to the effect it has on others (unless it is deliberately intended to have an effect on them), automatically assuming that everyone else is as self-reliant as you are. In relationships of any kind, you must respect the other person before you relate to them in any depth, and if you don't respect them, then you have no time for them at all.

You may, in fact, not perceive these things about yourself, but instead relate to persons showing the same qualities of initiative and self-awareness, using them as a mirror to see yourself in. Your decidedness about yourself or anything that is important to you may be a way of ensuring that you see things solely the way you want to, excluding the very possibility of them being any other way.

You may love active adventure or the sporting life, or any activity to expend energy, or to cover new ground. You tend to do what you want to do when you want to do it, not often being aware of the consequences, leaping without looking, and having to deal with the results afterward. In chess, or any other game, your initial attack would be excellent, but your end-game probably poor.

In being precipitate and wanting to accomplish too much at once, you may end by succeeding in nothing. You need to control your inner fire to avoid excess, or at least to realize that its power tends to cause turbulence and disruption from time to time, as your moods swing, and they swing with vigor. You are only aware of the mood that you are in right now, and only remember the same moods of the past, forgetting your other moods and the views that go with them.

MERCURY IN ARIES

You have a mind that is forceful and combative, that attacks ideas like a warrior in battle, not necessarily with delicacy or subtlety, but certainly with direct energy. You don't like logical tangles or conceptual complexities, but cut your way through them by the shortest route. You probably prefer your ideas to lead straight into action, to be practically concerned with things that can be done immediately, not being very interested in pure abstractions, unless they open new territories of thought. (Albert Einstein had Mercury in Aries).

You pounce upon new ideas and fresh information with enthusiasm, but unless Mercury has good supporting aspects, you don't generally connect together all that you learn into a complete body of knowledge, leaving it all as a set of isolated facts. Similarly, your mind is not very interested in past or future, being much more involved in what is going on right now. You are very capable of questioning energetically and of pursuing information singlemindedly yourself, pathfinding in new areas of knowledge, doing your own research for just as long as your interest is maintained, which, with your impulsiveness, is not necessarily very long (unless Saturn aspects Mercury, in which case you will hunt your mental quarry steadily for a long time).

You are intellectually, or at least verbally, aggressive and competitive, enjoying argument and debate, the challenge and vigorous stimulation of mental combat. Your blind spot is that you find it difficult to see points of view that may differ from your own, since your thoughts tend solely to involve yourself and your own position. You are also usually too impulsive to think things out carefully, being impatient to get on with it, to move into action, and thus often go off "half-cocked." You find it more interesting to begin things than to continue or complete them.

Your language will generally be direct, simple and straight to the point, though you are capable of making your statements with a rousing vigor. You do not mince words, except those of your opponent in a debate. Whether you are honest or not depends on how strongly you feel about the subject, since you are capable of exaggeration and overstatement in defense of your cause, though not deliberately intending to lie. You hate being caught in dilemmas and will hack your way out of them, not always resolving them, but sometimes destroying the situation that produces them. If you do not express your more aggressive thoughts to the people that they concern, (if Mercury is in a very retentive house or aspects) those thoughts are capable of having their own battle within you—and with your difficulty in seeing others' points of view, they become ever more deeply embedded, until you can get things out into the open and off your chest.

You certainly think for yourself, seeing no reason why you should have to accept anyone else's ideas as gospel, being ready at least in your own mind to challenge them and do battle with them. You pursue what you understand to be true through your own discovery.

VENUS IN ARIES

Well able to start your own relationships, enjoying the "hunt" and final capture, the beginning of your relationships is the most important point for you. You need to be very aware of the attitudes you form toward your partner right at the start, for you will find that they determine how the whole relationship develops.

You can be very direct in relating and in your general outreach to others. Your attention, when you give it, is single-pointedly focused upon its object, whether this be a partner or other person, or anything else that you value or feel for. You demand a lot of attention, definitely wanting your partner to know that you are there, though your own affections run in bursts. When you are not giving your attention to anything outside your own being it is focused upon yourself alone, all other or all self, with nothing in between.

You relate in the present moment, past and future being irrelevant to what you are sharing now. This means that the current state of your relationships is all that you see, losing sight of there ever having been (or that there may possibly be) anything else between you. You also feel compelled to act to keep the relationship going, feeling that if nothing is happening right now, then nothing is happening at all.

You are competitive in relating, fighting to be first in your partner's affections, whether against human rivals or their other interests, perhaps to the point of creating opponents to battle with.

Self-centered and headstrong in relating, you are very aware of what you want. You defend your values vigorously, and may provoke some fighting in your relationships as you do so, even if your partner isn't attacking you. Many of your choices are designed to give yourself esteem as a self-directing being, and you do not want to be deflected or diverted by others' preferences, being ready to pull out if you feel that you are being imposed upon. You can be concerned about what others think or feel toward you, but do not want to be trapped in their relationship habits, neuroses or projections, nor in their negative self-evaluations, since you may have enough of your own. You also need to respect your partner, and require the same in return.

You are impulsive and immediate in forming values, quick and direct in your judgments, including those that you form toward yourself. Very aware of your own aims, drives and desires, you are not always aware enough of those of others. Thus you are quite able to dislike yourself, some of your conflicts with others being only an outward projection of your inner battles. Where you have formed a distaste for yourself, you distract yourself from it by turning outward into action, finding things to do so that you won't have to look at yourself too closely. Thus you often need someone else to value you to counterbalance your lack of self-value. Over-developed self-concern can change only when you learn to love yourself wholesomely, to have a real respect for your own being, and only then does it become possible for you to have the same depth of feeling and concern fully for another.

If you have had to bury your own attitudes here, you will relate to people who show all the qualities mentioned, instead of showing them yourself, living them through someone else.

MARS IN ARIES

You have a headlong, uncontainable, impulsive energy that is always searching for something fresh to do, or to accomplish, being easily bored if nothing is happening. You dive into vigorous action simply for the sake of being in action, and are motivated by the first thought that comes into your head, rarely wasting time on second thoughts, and often not wasting too much on the first. This can naturally lead to blind, and therefore dangerous, actions. You drive to get things done, but lose interest rapidly when the first impulse has worn off. This means that you can start many projects but are not very good at continuing or completing them, unless you have worked hard on self-discipline and consistency (astrologically, if Mars has good aspects to Saturn, which will cool, stabilize and direct your energies). Your headstrong independence and fascination with anything new makes you a natural pioneer or pathfinder into unknown territories, where any discovery is made for the first time. You will generally leave the methodical exploration of the areas that you open up to others, however, since you generally do not have the patience to go over the same ground more than once, nor the desire to waste time when there is still new ground ahead.

This reflects your desire to be first in anything you enter into, your competitive drive to succeed against all competition or opposition, and to act alone without interference from others. Essentially these are ways of separating yourself from the crowd (you are rather a "lone wolf"), and gaining self-esteem, of isolating your own individuality. It involves an unconscious fear of being made to feel inferior by others, and of having your own desires, drives and initiative overridden or taken away from you, a fear that you face down by direct confrontation in the effort to reassure yourself of your own worth, strength and courage, and to remain in sole control over yourself. This fear focuses almost all your attention onto yourself and your own drives and aims, making you very subjective and self-centered. You refuse to be made to feel inferior, and even if nothing threatens you, will be looking for battles to fight in order to establish yourself in your own eyes. This makes it difficult for you to respect others if you feel they interfere with you or negate you in any way, and you are ready to use your explosive temper to fight all those that you interpret as being opponents.

Your vigorous competitive energy is well used in sports, where your desire to be first can be expressed in a healthy and direct way, with no harm done to anyone. Your own forcefulness gives you an interest in applied force or power, often leading to involvement in engineering (engines and production of motive power), and tool using (energy applied to shape things, paralleling initiative-energy applied to shape events), and sometimes weaponry, if your aggression is a little out of hand. The headlong nature of your energy usually leads to accidents to, and scars on, the head.

JUPITER IN ARIES

You have energy, enthusiasm and optimism combined together in a restless search for personal growth and wider experience. You are ready to sample anything new that comes your way if you feel that it will contribute to further self-opening and understanding. You dive readily into new pursuits, elaborate upon them rapidly and enthusiastically, seeing great possibilities, but sometimes without taking enough care, being too superficial. You want to explore the further reaches of human growth and spiritual understanding (whatever your personal philosophy), and if possible to be a pioneer and researcher, developing new tools and techniques and maybe testing their effects upon yourself, though sometimes too hastily and naively. You could become active in improving spiritual (or otherwise educational) teaching and methodology for all, but you are first and foremost concerned with your own development, striving for enhanced self-understanding.

If Jupiter is aspected badly you may be more than a little opinionated about your own understandings or philosophical acumen, being ready to judge others and their teachings from a superior position, though you will usually be at least outwardly tolerant toward other individuals that you believe to be searching. You are capable of being self-important, overbearing, and rather morally conceited, having no false modesty but exaggerating your claims to experience and understanding. You also have a rather flaring temper, ready to fire broadsides at any opponent, producing a shotgun scatter of self-righteous judgment. You dive too impulsively into fresh areas and don't really follow any one through to completion, your enthusiasms collapsing after the initial burst, being likely to make many fresh starts in your lifetime. It is unlikely that there is much actual malice in you, for you want to become a representative of whatever you believe to be truth, and you are able to climb down from any superior position that you adopt if you realize that you are in error. Your difficulty may lie in admitting that you could be wrong.

You prefer to have the simple self-confidence and trust, should we say faith, of a child. You may elaborate that faith into a main tool for self-development, knowing that trust applied single-mindedly is able to achieve miracles. If your trust has been damaged in your growth, then your self-confidence may have suffered, but will resurrect itself eventually, and be more conscious and therefore stronger than before. In the long term you are likely to stick to a single, though very large, aim, but you may scatter yourself all over the spectrum within it, finding it difficult to apply yourself consistently to a single track of method, while not losing sight of the eventual goal. Your energetic enthusiasm is likely to become a crusading zeal when fully aroused, and your single-pointed fervor can carry others along with you, turning you into a leader, or sustaining you alone in your fight toward your goal.

SATURN IN ARIES

You will be resourceful when it comes to thinking up new ways to put yourself down. Your self-doubts make you rather cautiously self-defensive, leaving you stiff and re-served in reacting to new situations. You doubt your ability and your right to fight for your own existence and survival, which, in reaction, may make you overdo it. In competi-tive situations you are slow and cautious, finding it difficult to express your inner being to the outer world, though perhaps you tend to attack people first, through fear of being at-tacked yourself. Your doubts make you slow to enter into new experiences, but only new experiences lead on further, thus leaving you frustrated with your scope in the world. You would love to have the status of being first and best in something, (inferiority feelings make you want to prove your superiority) and you may fight long and hard, largely within yourself, to achieve that aim. You would love to flow freely and spontaneously out into fresh experiences, but undermine your own efforts through self-doubt. There is no need to be on the defensive all the time and people are not always opposed to your point of view, or your desires.

You do not like to feel uncertain, powerless or out-of-control. Thus, a long-range aim in your life is likely to be to find order in yourself as much as in all else, so to research into laws, structures and patterns of form. You will find this much easier as you cease to inhibit yourself so much. You are capable of initiating new methods in whatever you do, through your tendency to be aware of, or to research, new frameworks of order, or to re-build the old ones (wanting to strip down the old and rigid and squeeze new freedoms out of the law). When you set your aims you are capable of getting stuck in, and staying with it, until the job is done. Yet in organizing things, slowness in accomplishing it is frus-trating, and a newer impulse or interest tends to take over and override earlier drives and desires.

There is a danger, under affliction, of falls affecting the head area. You may have the feeling of banging your head against a brick wall when you try to fulfill your long-term aims. You notice every delay and frustration, feeling that you cannot move as freely or as immediately as you want to, that life thwarts you. This is because you feel that you are not supposed to aim for, or ask for what you want, because you are not supposed to be selfish (often this pattern is set by a dominating parent). This can leave you with a lot of pent-up aggressive resentment, which in adulthood may emerge as a self-willed, or self-controlled thrust to get what you want no matter what (or who) stands in the way, or to feel justified in being pessimistic about any new possibility in your lifetime.

This may be tangled by your not wanting to be disciplined, ruled or controlled by anyone but yourself, and if you built any strong resistance against being pushed by any-one, you may equally resist being pushed by yourself. It is certain that you will not be happy until you use your self-discipline and active organizing ability to fulfill your goals, finding along the way that no one but yourself has been stopping you.

URANUS IN ARIES

During the seven years that Uranus was last in Aries, television signals were first transmitted across the Atlantic ocean and color television was demonstrated; the first East-West Atlantic flights occurred and the Graf Zeppelin flew around the world; Einstein published his unified field theory, Byrd flew over the South pole, and color film was developed; there were the beginnings of many new social reforms; perspex was invented, as was the flash bulb; Amy Johnson flew from London to Australia, and a British Arctic Air Route was pioneered; the Empire State building was built, the atom smasher developed, the BBC took over the development of television, and radio astronomy began. This was a time of pioneering the use of newly developing technologies that have proved to be central to the modern world.

Where you use your Uranian side, you are highly individualistic, impatient and impulsive, head-down and full speed ahead, seeking excitement and stimulus in your life. You tend not to be a traditionalist in any way, preferring not to be hamstrung by the past, but to break new ground wherever possible, to blaze new trails. You may seek new regions in which to adventure, or new types of adventure to experience. You insist on having freedom to act in your own right, neither diverted nor directed by any other person, group or authority, rebelling immediately at any restrictions, fighting against anything that you see or feel to be a trap, and breaking deliberately through barriers and limitations, wanting to prove that no one or nothing can bind you. (Roger Bannister, the first man to run a mile in under four minutes, was born in this period and had his Sun conjunct Uranus). You want to stretch the limits of human abilities, and to prove that they are not limits at all, that further evolution and new futures are available to those that seek them. You can be very directly outspoken, not seeing any reason why you shouldn't speak your mind, ready to experiment with new opinions or views and to test them in argument.

You may, where Uranus has difficult aspects, be extremely impulsive, leaping so rapidly from one new stimulus to another that you never truly explore any of them, never mind staying stably in contact with, or finishing, any involvement. Thus you can be a dilettante as you skip very lightly from interest to interest, skimming the surface of each. Your independence may be explosive and abrupt, your temper violently unrestrained, or able to erupt at a moment's notice. You want things to happen right *now*, any delay being intolerable to your impatience, and you prefer to change track without warning, wanting never to be trapped by the past. You see the past as dead weight to be rejected, discarded and left behind, refusing any form of restriction, demanding revolutionary change and being ready to fight for an absolute kind of personal freedom—and perhaps political freedom too, since your views here can be fanatical. Many leaders of modern liberation or terrorist movements will have Uranus in Aries.

ARIES NORTH NODE—LIBRA SOUTH NODE

You have a powerful tendency to be indecisive; feeling that all things are equal you vacil-late from one side to the other, from one view to its opposite. You don't like conflict, yet you set yourself an internal battle every time you try to make a choice. You are aware that for every action there is an equal and opposite reaction, psychologically as well as physi-cally, and that for every view there is a polar opposite, as well as a thousand shades of difference. You avoid offending others since you want to be liked by them, so you con-tinually adapt and adjust, flexibly accommodating your personality to theirs. In fact you tend to live in and through others, making you very responsive to their attention, suscep-tible to flattery to the point of gullibility, and resentful if they don't notice what you do or reward you for it. If conflict looms you become the mediator—diplomatically trying to heal the breach and reconcile the opposites, going out of your way to please and to smooth out the ripples. Your dislike of friction shows in your hatred of coarseness, the other face of your love of beauty and refinement, the Arts being your natural stamping ground.

You have not truly learned to be an individual in your own right with your need to gain identity through others. You must recognize that acting for yourself is not selfish and is a necessity to becoming self-directing. Developing your own initiative and the ability to see simple promise in your own self-development in all new situations is essential to mas-tering your own life. Asserting yourself will never offend others since your diplomatic abilities are developed enough not to be lost. Splitting yourself between your own inter-ests and those of others makes it impossible for you to be sure of what your own interests are and creates dithering. Your best interest lies in learning to leap joyfully head-first into new experience, not in sitting on the fence or teetering on the brink.

SUN IN THE 1st HOUSE

You want to be creative and causative, to show your abilities in action and strive for what you believe in. You approach your life with your sense of honor up front, building your self-respect, or pride, through what you can accomplish. You prefer to be in the forefront of new developments, leading the way, acting as a coordinating center. Your pride in yourself shows in your readiness to pour forth effort, to work for what you think is right, to take the center stage, to be the center of attention. Your sense of honor would usually not allow you to dominate, though you do tend to take charge in any situation that allows it, often overshadowing others in the process. Where most people use masks to hide their inner being from the world, you tend not to do so, facing the world in a direct, open, and sometimes passionate way, putting your whole being and attention onto the present moment. You are generally able to face down anything that you fear, dealing with it directly and never backing away from difficulties. Sometimes this can make your force of personality difficult for others to handle.

You need to be aware of exactly what passions are driving you, for you may let the more negative side of your pride predominate, reacting too strongly to anything that hurts your pride or overrides your creative efforts. In cases like this, you can be contentious, argumentative and overbearing to the point of being arrogant. You can also let your libidinous, hedonistic and pleasure-loving side take over, letting the rest of the world go to the devil while you indulge in whatever pleases you, particularly your love affairs. You may still remain involved in the vanguard of developments, but your motives will be distorted by conceit and self-exaltation, while your drive to be the center of attention takes over completely, taking the limelight away from everyone else. In this state you would brook no opposition from others, losing your sense of honor and acting dishonorably to maintain your position, and using it to ride roughshod over anyone who looked remotely like taking center-stage away from you. This side of you is like a spoiled child, having tantrums in order to get its own way.

Your mother was dominant, forceful in the way that she laid down the law, which was whatever she thought it was. She was possibly overbearing in the way that she ruled the roost. She took the top status in the household for herself and probably made sure that she kept it by overruling others. Her pride depended on her social standing, possibly on her gaining public recognition. She was an organizer of no small proportions, able and efficient if she was directing everything. Negatively, she was capable of using the laws and rules for her own purposes, or of disregarding them if she felt like it. She was probably interested, if not directly involved, in politics.

Your father was quieter, probably reflective, and a family man. He identified closely with his own family, particularly his mother. He was deeply emotional, though keeping up a certain proud reserve as a protective barrier, and he could cling intensely to anyone or anything that he identified with. His parental, protective and territorial instincts could be fierce, he being ready to attack anyone who threatened his family or his security.

MOON IN THE 1st HOUSE

You approach every new moment of your life directly through your feelings. They color your vision, your response to, and your interpretation of every experience. Your moods dominate your actions so that as your moods swing, the direction and power of, and the intention behind, your actions change between positive and negative. You can go around in circles as you advance and withdraw, swinging with how secure you feel at any one moment. You are tied to your needs, and feel impelled to act to fulfill them; one of those needs is for an emotional defense which will include you (a) building a personality shield to hide behind, rather like a one-way mirror—where you can see out, but others can't see in, and (b) going sideways toward your objectives so that others don't know what they are until you reach them. You act to build your security, and to nourish yourself with whatever you need in the way of experience, food, safety, a secure territory (home), support and recognition—or at least response—from others, and fulfilling your instinctual drives, *i.e.*, self-satisfaction.

You are perhaps aware of everything solely through the filter of your needs, seeing the world only for its potential to supply them, and not being truly aware of others and their needs, except in that light. If so, you need a personal revolution to break free of the hold of your needs, and it can come from deliberate awareness of their regular swings, enabling you to adjust to the demands of different times. With more awareness, you also recognize that others' needs are similar to your own, and must equally be met. Reaching out to nurture or "mother" others (even if you are male) becomes natural, as you realize that just seeking the satisfaction of your own needs keeps you in a baby-like position. If you recognize this, then you drop your emotional barriers and personal boundaries and are receptive to everything around you, responding to environments and people to the point of taking on the local color very accurately, mirroring it all. You know that you are highly impressionable, but you are ready to flow freely into events, realizing that your security lies within yourself, not in anything attainable out in the world. Your emotional shield then becomes a completely open response to everything, with nothing hidden away behind it.

Your mother's authority was very protective, trying to keep you within safe boundaries, tending solicitously to your needs and hurts, and above all else, hanging on to you. Her rules drew definite limits beyond which you were not to go, and she enforced them emotionally, using her position as parent, and your love for her, to back them up. Your emotional bonds to her ruled you more effectively than anything else could, even though you would sulk in disappointment. You learned to split your identity between the response that you showed on the surface, and the one inside.

Your father was very much a family man, domestic security being highly important to him, the safety and protection of his family coming first. He may have set tighter boundary limits for you than your mother did. He had strong ties to his own mother, positive or negative, and came from a close-knit family. He was rather emotional, his moods affecting you directly as you were caught up in their swings.

MERCURY IN THE 1st HOUSE

You have a mercurial approach to life, meaning active, changeable, volatile. You like to be on the move, getting about, making contacts. You adapt rapidly to new circumstances, quickly learning the attitudes and responses that will get you by, using your wits to find out what to do before going into action. It could be said that you live by your wits, being likely to be quick-witted, ever-ready with a fast retort to cap the conversation.

You face the world with constant questioning, seeing alternatives in everything, trying to sort out which way to go with every fresh experience. You are usually uncertainly nervous about meeting the new, even though your curiosity is bound to be aroused, so you set up alternatives for yourself as escape routes, just in case. Thus you can always be found to have at least two directions to choose between at any moment, and you vacillate between them before making a choice, which may be predetermined by habit. You don't know which, of two or more different personalities that you have (perhaps formed through a split in your family), that you want to be, so they alternate in choosing directions to go. You choose what viewpoint to hold by rejecting alternatives, which ones depending upon which part of you is dominant at the time. So you are quite capable of changing your mind later, or of doing two or three things at once. You use your experiences to question who and what you actually are, not realizing that this depends on what you let yourself become by developing, and consistent development is impossible if you keep changing direction. With consistency you can become expert in varied branches of any one subject.

Your habit of seeing alternatives shows a polar split in you. You actually want to live from both ends of this split, which seem mutually incompatible to you, yet you are the person who has set those two ends apart. You divide yourself, which may scatter your energies to the point of them becoming ineffective. You will probably find that your split depends either on an idea that you hold about yourself, or that you never chose whether or not to grow up.

You are likely to be the perennial student, forever chasing new knowledge, fresh information. You don't necessarily do much with it when you have it, just filing it away and chasing after more. You may be a "media junkie," feeling a need to read all the papers, listen to the radio, and watch television to find out what's going on, identifying with the flow of information that the world produces at every moment, even collecting pens.

You mother probably wanted to impress others with her mental competence, but was uncertain what the results would be and so held back. In her authority she was an explainer of the laws and rules, not always consistent in applying them, so you were unsure what you could and couldn't get away with, which part of yourself you could allow to act. Your father's moods were changeable and fluctuating, and it is likely that his emotions were rather immature, caught between being childlike and adult. His need for recognition from other members of the family varied from day to day in an emotional push and pull of opening and closing emotional boundaries, which may also have included a swing between dominance and submissiveness.

VENUS IN THE 1st HOUSE

One of your prime aims in life is to be loved and accepted by others; you want to be valued by them. To this end you act with charm and pleasantness, not pushing yourself or rocking the boat, not acting in any way that would disturb or disrupt others, unless it can be done with such charm as to be forgiven, trying to make yourself attractive. You can absorb quite a lot in the way of "heated" attitudes from others before you feel that it is necessary to react, or you may simply choose to ignore them, allowing them to flow through you, preferring to keep the peace. You look for your own version of beauty, harmony, pleasure and peace in situations, being put off by grossness, ugliness and unpleasantness. In other words, you judge all that you meet by your own particular set of standards and don't want to relate to anything that doesn't match them. If you don't like it, you avoid it. Thus you are very selective and evaluating. You may have an artist's eye for balance and proportion in line and shape, and a well-developed sense of touch and taste—your tastes should be refining as you use them. Your sense of beauty will probably focus mainly on song and dance.

You don't always see any point in expending your energies or exerting yourself, leaning toward being lazy and loving leisure and pleasure, though if Venus is in a particularly active sign your pleasures may be vigorous. You would rather judge whether an action is really necessary, evaluating its merits and the possible value arising from it, before deciding whether to act on it or not. You are likely to have a browsing and sampling approach to life, tasting a little here, feeling the quality there, as though you are in a store full of goodies. If Venus has particularly difficult aspects you may use all this as a shield, a defense system to avoid strife and struggle in life, probably projecting onto others and saying that they are responsible for any difficulties that you have.

Approval from others is particularly important to you and you are likely to go out of your way to get it, either earning it naturally by being pleasant and loving yourself, or wrapping them around your little finger with charm, or using attractiveness. You can be very adept in using these tactics, whether in playing a game, or simply relating to someone, since you are able to put yourself in their position and see things from their viewpoint when you try. You do need to be aware that no one likes to be used, this being the negative side of your talent.

Your mother wanted social acceptance, though probably did not like to go out to get it. She was sensitive to the needs of those around her and felt obligated to try to fulfill them. Not necessarily authoritative, she more likely used charm and pleasantness or reason to get you to respond, though she did tend to judge you by society's standards, perhaps monetary ones. Your father needed somebody to lean on, gaining security from his relationships, particularly with women. He needed to feel wanted but probably had difficulty in showing his likes or loves to anyone not very close to him.

MARS IN THE 1st HOUSE

You focus your awareness on yourself, your own interests, your own immediate life, and not on too much else. Even when with others you remain single and singular. You are a warrior, seeing life as a battle where the one rule is to win. Thus you may see threats and competition around you against which you have to struggle, fight, and resist. You can be too competitive, pushy and aggressive, invading others' space without invitation, trespassing on their preserves. Consider: those who are ready to fight must think that they have adversaries or outright enemies; those who think that way are insecure; those who are insecure would do well to deal directly with their own inner insecurities, instead of projecting them out and causing strife for others. The more difficult the aspects to your natal Mars, the more aggressive you will be, whether or not it comes right out into the open.

Naturally this could become contentiousness, quarrelsomeness, readiness for fights and arguments. If this is the case, you should recognize that even if you are in the right, to push an argument is to create enemies; if you are clear-headed and strong, you will be able to meet your opponent half-way. If you find this difficult, then let a person who is clear-headed and neutral arbitrate between you.

In action you are direct and vigorous, preferring to attack life with energy, to approach it head-on, to go out and do battle with it. You don't see any reason to beat about the bush in any situation, focusing immediately on the issue at hand. Your attention is mainly on the present moment, on what is arising *now*, and you want to act to make things happen now. You prefer to initiate events, rather than to let them happen to you; thus you are a self starting, self-directing person, and you don't like anyone else to direct or to rule immediately over you. Since you do not think much about the future, you usually don't stop to consider the results but simply act, diving in head first. Thus you may be too impulsive and often act uselessly, trying to "push the river" of your life instead of letting it flow by itself. Therefore you need more deliberation and caution.

You are interested in anything new and modern; you probably pursue fresh developments yourself, doing your own research. Your competitive drive to be first could make you a pioneer and innovator in your fields of interest. Sometimes this placing of Mars arouses an interest in sports, weaponry or the martial arts, the weapons, or tools, usually being those with sharp points and edges, or requiring accurate aiming. It also usually indicates scars on the head.

Your mother is likely to have been aggressive and perhaps martial in her discipline, vigorous in laying down the law, tending to provoke arguments. Since she pushed, you pushed back. She was equally pushy as an organizer, demanding action from you, though delaying if acting for herself. She aimed for achievement, even if that achievement was yours. Your father was given to aggressive rumblings of mood, especially if anyone trespassed on his territory, needing his own well-defined space. He would have preferred to depend on himself, but tended to be dependent on others, needing to be pushed into action; he would be crabby if his needs were not fulfilled.

JUPITER IN THE 1st HOUSE

You have a cheerful and optimistic approach to life, facing new experiences with hope and enthusiasm, expecting everything to develop well toward the future. You have an explorative nature that will lead you into many fields of activity, a restlessness that keeps you on the move, leaping from one thing to another, covering ground. Like an explorer with a map, or perhaps like a walker on a high hillside, you prefer to be able to take a broad overview of any territory that you are involved with, a wide view of the land below. This is an accurate simile since you are likely to love the wide open spaces, preferring to be bounded only by the horizon. For some this is more true in a mental sense, their territory of exploration being the world of the mind, usually in philosophy or religion.

Your travels are in pursuit of your prime aim of personal growth; you do not believe in standing still in life, but in evolving yourself; you do not necessarily believe that there is a particular goal to achieve, since if you have not reached it you can't understand it, and you may feel that it is better to travel than to arrive. You realize that any new experience may open up a new world and that there are boundless worlds to explore. In pursuit of *truth* you may practice a high level of ethics, valuing honesty above all things, knowing that unless you are "true" you can't see the truth.

It is difficult for you to stick to one aim or activity for any great length of time since you keep finding fresh enthusiasms, new areas to dive into, each as interesting as the last (unless Jupiter is in a fixed sign and under stable aspects, or the rest of your chart is predominantly fixed). If Jupiter has any difficult aspects you may be using this scattered side of you as a personal defense, maintaining your level of enthusiasm to hide something else; keeping your hopes for future developments high because things are unsatisfactory in the present. You may be unconsciously expecting your hopes to be dashed, and so keep changing their focus. Your explorations then take on the character of running away, which you do quite readily—and if caught in a position where you can't run, you can put on a huge display of temper, with thunderbolts of righteous wrath—display being the operative word. You won't admit to loss of confidence, or to being in the wrong, and in this you can be quite conceited. Your honesty then becomes more of a bluff, a confidence trickster's job that you do upon yourself as much as for others' benefit. You may be thoroughly irresponsible, being just as ready to walk out of relationships as to walk into them. It is also possible that your roving is actually a greed for experience, working on the principle that more is better, even though you do nothing with what you experience but just leap ahead to the next involvement. Another problem which you may have is blowing things up until they are completely out of proportion, whether in telling your own tall stories or in exaggerating your difficulties.

Remember that the more honest you are, especially with yourself, the deeper your penetration will be into the mysteries of living.

SATURN IN THE 1st HOUSE

Your whole approach to life is serious, seeing it as a challenge, a long climb toward your goal of self-development. You look for order in everything and thus impose much order on yourself, perhaps hemming yourself in with restrictions. You may see restriction all around you, yet feel that to act responsibly you must submit to it, or even impose it upon yourself. You want to gain control over your own life and to gain status and recognition for your actions and achievements, or simply for yourself as a person.

Probably shy, stiff and awkward as a child, self-doubt, caution and fear in new situations made you slow to act or be outgoing. The habit of doubting new circumstances may still be with you, together with your self-control. You find it nearly impossible to be frivolous, spontaneous or abandoned, though you may have learned to wear a mask that seems to show these qualities. Whatever mask you have developed, you should beware allowing it to be a rigid prison that allows no expression of your inner personality.

Your birth was probably difficult, the birth-canal not letting go easily—leaving you with a sense of banging your head against a brick wall. Your early impression of the outside world was that it was cold, hard, and perhaps manipulating. You were probably tucked tightly into your bed, strapped down, leaving you feeling that you can't, or shouldn't, be active or move freely.

Your mother's authority was strict and dominant, her rules appearing at times more important to her than you were, and demanding from you conformity and self-restraint. You probably had to act under orders and felt guilty if you did not do what was wanted of you, or in seeking recognition, what you required of yourself. In wanting to act for yourself you became aware of opposition, frustration and delay, or irresponsible (childlike) action was simply not allowed. All this left you with a sense of inferiority, perhaps feelings of resentment, and a desire for more positive kinds of recognition, though the tools that you use to achieve it now are very likely the same ones that were used on you, which keeps you in the same old controlled state.

If you felt very inferior then you may still expect your world to treat you the same way; fearing the worst, you tend to see the worst. You may marry a partner who will exert the same control over you, even to the point of putting you in bondage. In other words you actually (though unconsciously) seek out self-restricting experiences.

If you fought such feelings and control from others, then you most likely take direct charge of your own life, allowing no interference from anyone else, but actually manipulating them rather aggressively (though underneath you still have the same doubts). Your drive is then for the achievement of your own material ambitions, feeling that since you couldn't have what you wanted as a child you are going to make sure that you get it as an adult.

You tend not to be very trusting of yourself or of others, your reserve acting as a wall that neither allows you to reach out to them, nor allows them to get close to you. You need most to dissolve your self-protective wall, to relax your cautious self-limiting attitudes and allow yourself the freedom that is all around you. You need to be more trusting.

URANUS IN THE 1st HOUSE

You have little or no interest in following the rules and traditions of society, preferring at all cost to remain a free individual. You hate being trapped by anyone or anything, being capable of a tense wariness if you feel threatened, ready to move on at a moment's notice. You are normally friendly and easy going in the extreme, as well as being active and independent. A prime aim in your life is to keep and enhance your independence, and to this end you practice detachment. You can be extremely alive and alert, needing a lot of stimulus, utterly interested in any fresh developments in the world; for some, particularly in science (electronics, communications technology, data processing, space sciences, and lasers), for others in whatever represents the independent viewpoint, such as alternate society views and philosophies. You love to move fast and so can be thoroughly impatient, wanting things to happen *now*, if not yesterday, and can get bored easily if nothing interesting is happening.

Your nervous temperament absorbs stresses from all around you, and your need to be aware of yourself as an individual requires that you have time entirely alone, to sort yourself out and take stock. You probably value your time spent in isolation since it helps you to understand who you are, to integrate yourself. Your view of the world is multi-level; you learn in many different directions and spend time weaving together what you have learned into a unique web of ideas, cross-connected in all directions. Some of your learning is likely to be in the borderline science region, whether UFOs, Bermuda triangle disappearances, the Philadelphia experiment and so forth. Whatever the case, you identify easily with the rare and unusual, and may be highly intelligent.

If you have difficult aspects to Uranus, your independence will be rebellion against anything normal as you drive yourself to not be like others. You will tend to alienate yourself as an individual, refusing to be a member of anybody's society but your own. You will be very unpredictable as you constantly change your aims, your views, and your actions. You will use your detachment as a barrier that will not allow anyone to get close to you, thus you are a poor risk in marriage—or other relationships. Your restless impatience is unlikely to allow you to settle at anything for long; when you get bored, you go. You are quite likely to have been hyperactive as a child, and may be no different as an adult.

You will either identify with the modern space age society, and be fascinated by the prospect of travel to the stars, as well as with other technological prospects; or with the alternate society, going back to grass roots and building a life style that depends on no one else but yourself, or be a humanitarian, active in support of human growth and awakening. Whatever the case, your direction in life will be subject to periodic review (sometimes fairly unconscious) and occasional total revolution as you break out of one whole lifestyle and set of ideals straight into another. Your capacity for this kind of complete change is large, and you may make several thorough shifts in a lifetime. The shifts are likely to be in pursuit of integration, each period being designed to complete a part of your being, and leaning toward interweaving and fusing every part together to produce liberation—total personal freedom.

NEPTUNE IN THE 1st HOUSE

There are two distinct types here. The first is the thorough innocent who believes in magic and mystery, that the universe is filled with wonder, and is fused into a single living whole. If this is you, you dissolve into beauty very easily, are very receptive to any new experiences, are intensely sensitive, though you may have learned to live with it, and probably quite seclusive—preferring to be alone most of the time. Your inner life may be much richer than your outer, your imagination or your visionary sense supplying you with the stimulus that you need, perhaps too much since it may become a substitute for actual experience and action. Or it can give you a vision to pursue, perhaps to fulfill in your own being, becoming the image that you desire. The negative side of this is that you may (perhaps unconsciously) act out a fantasy role in your life.

Your awareness of the world around you may be quite vague if you live within yourself too much; however much reading you do, it does not replace direct experience. You are probably a great reader, your imagination involving you totally, as well as being musically inclined and generally involved in the arts. Vulnerable, you can be a chameleon in your own defense, taking on the color of your surroundings, acting out the personality that protects you most. Where you are outgoing, you will be involved in mystery and meditation, music and magic, theater and illusion, charity and service to others.

The second type are those who were so vulnerable at an early age that they learned to hide within themselves completely, leaving a camouflage personality at the surface, and using it to deflect anything that might even remotely be likely to hurt them. This makes them thoroughly deceptive, elusive and evasive, unable to admit to their true feelings or true personality at all, building smoke screens so thick that not even they really know what is behind them. They lean toward misery and martyrdom, complaining that life does not give them what they want, the living that it owes them. For stimulus, and for an extra smoke screen to blur things out, they turn to drink, drugs and total self-indulgence, putting their inner chaos into their outer life and probably wondering why things do not turn out the way they want them. Naturally they are very lonely, since they do not give themselves to anyone else. Some will live out their own illusions about themselves completely, acting out some self-justifying or even self-exalting role, interpreting all their experiences to match their beliefs.

The two types are not different except in their ability to admit their sensitivity to themselves, or to others. The second is capable of becoming the first when they realize that their problems are of their own making, that it is only their view that the world is against them, the truth being that they have been against their world.

The fully open type has a full, rich sensitivity to all things that can take them into the mystic's fusion with the universe. They are able to allow their awareness of themselves to dissolve into their surroundings, becoming completely absorbed into nature and the cosmos, into a total identification with life that has a boundless depth to it. They become the most gentle, loving, compassionate people, utterly giving.

PLUTO IN THE 1st HOUSE

You face life with intensity, and take everything very personally, particularly the painful experiences that you meet. You were probably hurt while being born, or taken away from your mother for a while, and left feeling utterly rejected and unwanted, feeling that life was going to hurt or reject you, expecting pain in any new situation. Anything that you look for you can find, then rationalizing it to make it seem understandable; you have looked (not entirely consciously) for reasons why you should be hurt, rejected, or unwanted. You possibly found good reasons for seeing your life this way. Your personality may have taken various paths. One is to have become painfully shy, backing away from the world into your hurt feelings (a likely stage in any case). Another is to fight back intensely against what hurts you, having tantrums as a child and being prone to rages as an adult. Yet another is to have learned not to show hurt, hiding behind an impassive face as part of an impregnable defense, repressing your pains so that you are no longer directly aware of them.

You don't like letting others know what's going on inside you since it seems much safer that way, which can leave you extremely self-reliant, not to say secretive and alone. Naturally you need outlets for all that you bottle up, and sometimes can allow yourself to get very close to someone who you feel understands your hurts and won't use them against you, and then you can let it all out. When you have opened your heart completely to anyone you are capable of total commitment to them, allowing them into your inmost core (so it is devastating to you to be betrayed by one you love, and you can be fiercely, passionately jealous). Where you don't find such an outlet you can bury pain for years, which may eventually do a lot of damage to your system, perhaps erupting in degenerative disease. You seek acceptance in sex; its intense closeness helps you feel that you are wanted, and even then you may find it hard to believe ("they must be mad, or have some ulterior motive," "just want me for sex"). If you don't accept yourself, how can you see anyone else as doing so? You feel functional rather than decorative, meaning that where you feel that people don't want you (sometimes expressed as believing that you are ugly), you have learned to look after yourself, to become competent and capable as a survivor.

If your self-view and view of your actions and motives is positive, you have all the energy, capability and enthusiasm that you need to accomplish your aims. If your self-view is negative, including as self-blame all the blame that you have ever received, your regenerative and general energies will be low and accomplishment seem painful or impossible.

You will drive yourself toward personal transformation once you understand that you are self-obsessive. Your world-view will change when you realize that you have been clinging to pain and hating yourself (even if you have buried that under an apparent self-love). You have a tunnel-vision concentration that makes it seem that the world is only what you focus upon; so you need to select your focal points very carefully, looking for beauty at least as much as ugliness, and recognizing that you are no more good or bad than anyone else. (Think back to the way that your mother imposed her authority, and the way that your father expressed his feelings).

NORTH NODE, 1st HOUSE—-SOUTH NODE, 7th HOUSE

You tend to live a lot through other people, submerging yourself in their lives, trying to please them and to be liked by being flexible and accommodating. By diplomatically giving way to them and allowing them to lead and act, you frustrate and defer your own potential for leadership and selfhood. Being very receptive to their views of you and allowing them to influence you, you lose in self-awareness and self-understanding. Docile acquiescence and charm allows others to take advantage of you, where you actually need to be able to act for yourself, to know your own preferred directions and move vigorously toward them.

You may find, as you use your own initiative for yourself, a tendency to become an extremist. You want to get on with the job, to live intensely, not to be frustrated by others at all in establishing your own identity and pursuing your objectives. While this is essential to you, a certain balance is valuable in the long run; balancing your ability to relate and your own enterprise so that you end up neither submissive nor dominant, but in either case, involved.

✧ 4 ✧

Taurus
and the 2nd House

The 2nd House at its simplest shows our capacity for outreach from ourselves toward making contact with the "other," or contrarily, our dislike of, and movement away from, the other. Implicit in this house is the polarity running between self as an abstract (mental) observer, and the concrete world of experience. Our tools here are our senses and the depth and intensity of our perceptions through them; our abilities to sense, taste, touch, measure, and evaluate are all yardsticks by which we assess our experience or "taste" our lives. They are our capacity to take in and to appreciate the qualities (and quantities) of the world. They are expressions of our need for contact (*e.g.*, touch), whether with other people or with the rest of our world.

As we taste life, we find its tastes to be varied; some are sweet, some bitter, some sour. We learn here whether we can appreciate the bitter along with the sweet, the pains and frustrations in life along with the pleasures, or whether we would rather shut out what we don't like. We may focus mostly on the bitter, believing that pain and conflict are going to be normal in our lives. If we accept all tastes without clinging to any, we remain in touch, and the world makes sense to us (to mix metaphors). If we become out of touch, the world ceases to make any sense. Take these analogies as far as you can.

In our development through life, the 2nd House deals with the crawling period in babyhood, when we open our senses by plastering them over everything available, grabbing things, putting them in our mouths, learning the qualities of the world through touch, taste, smell and so forth. Freudian psychologists call this the "oral" period. It is during this time that we learn that the objects in our world are or can be permanent (continuing to exist even when we are not looking at them), which we did not know before. This teaches us that we can return to experiences that we come to like, or must learn how to keep on avoiding the ones we don't like.

As we experience, we learn what we appreciate or want, what we consider pleasing, and what we do not want, or feel to be unpleasant. We select what we prefer from the whole range of experience available in our world; thus we build our frameworks of personal values or tastes, which define the objects and objectives that attract us. We move toward what we prefer, making it our target or goal, and we move away from what we dislike. If we pursue our preferences with persistence, our pursuit will open up definite avenues of experience in and through life. Our choices predetermine our direction.

When we pursue particular goals, we frequently must repeat the actions needed to gain them. We are shaped or molded by our own repeated actions; thus our tastes and preferences predetermine what we become, though they themselves are predetermined by what we choose to focus on (1st House) in the first place. Mathematically, this would be called a vector of force—meaning a certain amount of power of motion thrusting in a chosen direction. This thrust has a range, a spectrum, which runs from "static inertia"—perhaps appreciating everything and finding no reason to pursue anything with vigor, or having no special interests, or perhaps believing that no objective can be gained —to "dynamic inertia," thrusting powerfully and persistently towards a narrow objective. You can see that this range includes relaxation (or perhaps hopelessness) at one end, and dynamic tension (perhaps aggression) at the other.

We also learn, while crawling and exploring (depending on our family or home circumstances), whether we will be allowed to attain the objectives we pursue, and how, and with what results. We learn whether we are going to be stopped from reaching out to and holding what we want, or separated from it by obstacles, or have it snatched out of our hands, or be frightened off by others' anger, or diverted from our aim by substitutes or bribes, or made to accept what we don't want simply because they want us to have it, or whatever. In this we learn whether the objects/objectives we want to pursue (and our very pursuit of them) are accepted by others. If they are, we know that we can belong, becoming respectable (acceptable) members of society. If they are not, we begin to become outsiders who pursue values differing from those of the mainstream. We also learn whether we are capable of persisting in getting to what we want despite obstacles, and achieving our "forbidden fruit." We learn to be either winners or losers.

This (the crawling period) is also the time when we determine if we feel wanted, demonstrated by being held, cuddled, carried, touched, or snuggled by others. Societies that give lots of cuddles, holding babies and carrying them often, usually have great sexual freedom in adulthood, and are the least prone to interpersonal violence and sexual crimes of all societies.

The less we get, the less we feel capable of giving, which leaves only our alternative defense against the other—violence. Not being held also leads to a grasping possessiveness, an addictive attempt to squeeze what is needed, or what is felt to be lacking, from objects. Things replace people as sources of pleasure. Possessing becomes thoroughly confused with belonging. Here are the psychological roots of the "consumer, armed defense" society.

Our historically recent (6,000 years, since agriculture began) tendency to want ownership over or to possess objects or people, is a desire that springs from the insecurity of lacking the love and contact we need in babyhood (ever since parents began to spend time away from us, focused on work), and it has built our capitalist society. Yet here in the 2nd House we also have our capacity for giving, for generosity, something natural to humans when we recognize that the world gives everything to us, but which we tend to lose (or not to want to use) when we feel we aren't getting what we need.

The full range of the 2nd House runs between total openness of values (appreciating everything in our experience, and thus having every choice, together with feeling we have almost everything we need, and being able to give easily to others); it develops when we interpret or evaluate objects and objectives on the bias of personal needs; and it may end in total closedness, appreciating nothing, being hostile to everything, allowing ourselves no healthy choice, and becoming mean and grasping, feeling that we are in poverty. In Western cultures the general public choice is usually to grasp at money and goods, rather than to pursue truly human values. (The sum total of all our personal 2nd House values is the foundation of the social value system, symbolized by the 11th House).

The 2nd House also shows how the physiology of our parathyroid glands has been affected by our conditioning. The parathyroids control our bodies' ability to store energy resources as calcium in bone tissue, or to draw upon it to raise muscle tone for effort (relaxation-exertion). Muscle tone rises when effort is required, either to pursue what is wanted or to escape what is not (or to fight it). Muscle tone relaxes (or should be able to, though this is increasingly difficult in our high-tension era) when there is no reason for effort or when goals have been achieved.

The 2nd House shows the effects of conditioning on our senses, including whether they have been put under any form of psychological-emotional strain which could lead to failure of function. It equally shows how the senses can be opened further by practice, leading to richer experiences.

It also deals with the mouth; the molars or grinding teeth; the tongue and the sense of taste; the throat, the vocal chords, and the voice (particularly its tones and range); the neck; the sensory layer of the skin immediately beneath the protective dead surface. In the cycle of digestion, the 2nd House indicates chewing (using the back teeth) and tasting the food.

In perceiving, here is where incoming energy impinges directly onto our sensory cells. These cells "store" the energy, measuring it before reaching a threshold potential and beginning to send a signal to the nervous system.

SUN IN TAURUS
✧ The Measurer ✧

You approach your world through your senses, particularly of touch and taste, and what you receive through them you evaluate into likes and dislikes, into systems of value and taste. Your values may be the basic ones of peace, stability, love of nature and beauty, or the supposedly civilized ones of money and material possessions (usually substitutes for love). Whichever they are, you will pursue them with steady persistence until they are reached, no matter how long that may take. The dynamic of Taurus is a straight-ahead motion, from the near-standstill of the cud-chewing cow to the powerhouse of the charging bull; the basic principle being that of inertia, or mass in steady motion, from zero to full tilt. This pattern gives you a steadiness of attitude toward your world, a preference once your values are fixed not to change them at all. While this can be steadfastness, perseverance or faithfulness, it can also be stubbornness and obstinacy.

Your attitude toward money is that while having it is nice, it only represents what it can be exchanged for. You enjoy the process of exchange, for example, with gifts. You are honest with money, hating to be in debt. While you are not necessarily an original thinker, your reflectiveness and tenacious pursuit of ideas can ultimately make you quite philosophical. Your security depends upon your pride and sense of honor, particularly toward your family, to whom you can be fiercely protective; you prefer a certain opulent display in your home. Your creativity largely focuses upon the basics of life-support, food, clothing and household, where meticulousness expresses developed and refined tastes, and self-criticism an aspect of perfectionistic pride. Your discrimination is basically tolerant and uncritical, preferring things to be nice and pleasant, accepting the views of others as equal to your own unless they clash fiercely—then you can be implacably judgmental.

In occupation you prefer to work directly with others in pleasant, attractive surroundings, in work which promotes beauty, deals with the creation of material goods, or with finance; for example, accountancy or banking. In relationships you are intense, fixed and faithful but inclined to be jealous. You prefer plenty of close physical contact with your partner though if any hostility arises you are then untouchable. Some Taureans marry for money. Sexually you are open, honest and enthusiastic, though sometimes preferring quantity to quality. In philosophy, religion or morals you are conservative, either belonging to an old established system or being skeptically doubtful. You prefer your beliefs to be well-structured and ordered, evolving into a system of laws which you prefer others to adhere to also. When traveling you like to go slowly, in order to appreciate the form of the countryside. Politically and socially you have fixed ideas, disliking change unless it is to promote an ideal humanitarian system. In friendship you can be sensitive and giving, to the point of experiencing your friends' feelings as strongly as your own.

While this describes the classic Taurus personality, you will vary from it in many ways. Your most major differences will be shown by the house placement of the Sun and by the sign and house placement of Venus.

MOON IN TAURUS

Your emotional security depends upon having and maintaining whatever you value, whether this be material possessions or far more abstract systems of values. Much of your basic personality is founded on your ability to appreciate; whether through your senses—natural beauty, comfort, and material quality; through your feelings—peace, harmony, and connectedness; through your intellect—proportion and measurable order. You have a well-developed feeling for quality, and your life will involve the steady, persistent pursuit of those things that gratify this feeling. This could make you an out-and-out materialist, or one who must create a feeling of being of substantial value, or who finds the real value in all things around you.

You may use your values as a self-protective wall to keep out whatever makes you insecure, meaning that they will then be self-centered and exclusive. Otherwise you will hold values that create fellowship with others by emphasizing wholesome and inspiring mutual goals, bringing people into contact and uniting them in common causes.

Your type of emotional armor is to stick stubbornly to your attitudes, resisting any pressure and refusing to be moved. If the pressure becomes intolerable (and only then), you are capable of exploding, but this will be rare since you prefer at least the appearance of peace. Otherwise you are capable of diving into sensual self-indulgence, pursuing pleasure because your objective seems unobtainable.

You have a natural, uncomplicated common-sense practical attitude, except where you set yourself against those things that you dislike, when sheer stubbornness can keep you obstinately narrow-minded and even intolerant, refusing to consider alternative views. In such cases you should simply retreat from the situation without introducing conflict. Where you are too set upon your own values you can keep yourself from progressing or developing, from opening to fresh experience, by not even seeing that other ways are possible. You have a very straight-line view of your life, setting up goals and moving very steadily toward them, allowing nothing to divert you from your path. You resist change unless it is a change that you are aiming for, preferring stability and constancy to all else (especially in relationships where any inconstancy in your partner, or hint of a rival, can arouse a fierce jealousy).

Your love of nature is probably well-developed, a tended garden or a beautiful sunset giving you the peace that you love. If your tastes are more abstract, the arts will bring you much satisfaction. With your natural feeling for materials you surround yourself with good, comfortable furnishings and fine clothes in the best of taste, unless this sense is inhibited, for example by feeling that there isn't enough money to afford them. Under some difficult aspects you may be niggardly and over-cautious, not realizing that everything is available in life to those who are willing to reach out with confidence toward it, and give of themselves at the same time. Under other types of difficulty you might be extravagant, spending money over-freely to try to make yourself feel good when you don't.

MERCURY IN TAURUS

Much of your thinking and the general way that your mind works will be based on attitudes formed before you learned to talk. Then, naturally, your thinking had to be sensory, using the images brought by your senses, and memories of them, as the raw material for thought. This means that your thinking may not be particularly verbal and thus abstract, but rather sensory and concrete. So much of it may be about material things, or distinctly realistic, common-sense, in touch with concrete reality and not split off into abstractions. Another focal point in your mental development is likely to be your values or evaluations. You may develop your ideas about your tastes, values, preferences and aversions, likes and dislikes, until your tastes become quite discriminating, and may then be applied in arts, fashion, and dealing with materials. Or your mind may have focused early on number or measure, leading you to explore mathematics, physical science, or any other area that requires strict measurement or a linear accounting, such as money and business exchange or surveying.

Your mind works in a distinctly linear fashion, moving in a straight line from start to finish and not deviating off onto side-tracks (unless Mercury is at the end of Taurus). When you set yourself a goal in your mind, you are capable of pursuing it with a stubborn undeviating determination which may be slow and plodding, or like a charging bull, but with considerable force behind it since it is all channeled into the one track. This can give you tremendous applied concentration that ignores all else but its goal. Otherwise, if you have no particular mental aims or interests, you browse along, sampling and tasting whatever crosses your path, but not going out of your way to use or apply your intellect, being somewhat lazy in your thinking. The end results of your thoughts may be predetermined by your values, your reason supporting your preferences since you don't like changing them, your intellectual values thus becoming very fixed. This can make you obstinate in your opinions in the face of opposition, refusing to question them back to their roots or to consider alternatives. This position is one which eventually demands that you turn around and reconsider all your intellectual opinions and values, and will lead you to reverse a number of them, changing like to dislike and vice-versa; the same reversal may also happen in your materialistic attitudes.

Your persistent pondering may focus on questions such as: "What is true value?" "In what does it lie?" "Is it in material things?"; in which case life should be a matter of gathering money and possessions of value and feeding your senses with what you enjoy. Or does it lie in human attitudes towards life and each other? If so, then life should be a development of humanity, of mutual support and affection, affirming people rather than things at all times; or in nature, then working in cooperation with natural laws and living things. So your reversal of attitudes will be from feeding desires that are never satisfied, toward giving the affection that you would like to get.

VENUS IN TAURUS

Your affections are likely to be firmly fixed on one romantic partner for a very long time. Once you have formed an attachment, or a like or dislike, you tend not to change it, sticking possessively to the same preferences and involvements from then on, being capable of plenty of quiet jealousy if your attachments are challenged. Your steadfastness is something that you use to give yourself stability, continuity and permanence, often stubbornly excluding fresh new experience in order to live in a comfortably unchanging world. You avoid those things that you do not like or appreciate, simply shutting them out, and seek a peacefully uncomplicated life of reaching out to and living with who and what you value most.

You are a sensory and sensual individual, your senses of touch and taste probably being particularly well-developed, and you delight in feeding them, loving good food, fine materials, luxurious conditions, and if you have remained in touch with the depths of your own being, in particular loving green and growing places, having a special affinity for plants. If, however, you have lost touch with yourself you could be quite a materialist, pursuing money and possessions instead of love and experience. Basically you want to feel that you have a solid self-worth and absolute security, whether at the bank, or in your own eyes, or in relationships with your loved ones. You are well aware of material values and of quality, a fact that usually shows in the gifts that you probably love giving. This actually shows your capacity for appreciating beauty or quality in anything—nature coming first, civilized values second in a healthy being.

You love to be closely in touch, both physically and metaphorically, with nature, with loved ones, with everything that you appreciate. Touching and being touched is extremely important to you, and you would tend to shrivel up if not touched often. It is probably for this reason, among others, that your personal attractiveness is important to you, since in love you generally prefer to attract your partners than to pursue them, being given to a certain placid passivity, a habit that probably developed in your earlier, shier years. If trouble looms, your general reaction is to be quietly reserved, patient and lasting it out with dogged persistence, keeping the peace that you value at all costs. You hate to let go of anything that you value (unless given as a gift), a fact that can stubbornly entrench you against whatever may threaten your safe and secure world. In this way you may let a large part of life pass you by as you protect your small personal part of it.

When you fix your values, you also fix your sights on attaining the goals that they define. Then you are capable of pursuing what you want for a lifetime, perhaps becoming so fixed on the goal that you forget to give it up once attained. You also find it difficult to change both values and aims, even when all evidence in your experience shows you that you need to, further showing your difficulty in throwing anything away.

MARS IN TAURUS

You are slow, steady, stable, and persistent in applying your energies, which will probably be aimed at attaining material goals. Your attention is firmly fixed on the pursuit of the things that you value most, on feeding and fulfilling your personal tastes, or to achieve what concrete targets you aim for. Thus you have a certain tunnel vision narrowness, being unable to see beyond what *you* want, and being determined to get it. You are slow to formulate goals, and to begin acting upon them, but when you do you are persistent, consistent, and stubbornly immovable from your aim, with one-track single-mindedness of purpose. Naturally you can be very slow to change your views and values, or to accept changes into your life. You are likely to continually recreate the same old conditions, habits, attitudes, and patterns in your life in general, and in your own being in particular. One reason for this is that you measure yourself and your actions against your own standards, and you want to measure up by being completely consistent in your own eyes. Another reason is that you can be very possessive of whatever you want, and determined to hang on to it when you have got it, be it a material object, another person in a relationship, or a way of life.

Your determination in hanging on to what you want is equaled by your resistance to what you don't want. It is likely that both reflect a fear of loss, or of not being able to have what you want or need when you want it. Also you identify yourself very strongly with your needs—effectively saying "if you don't let me have what I want, you are rejecting me." Such fear can make you hang on doggedly to what you want or have, yet can also make you angry with the object of your desires for the frustration that it arouses in you. Your drive to reach out to grasp who or what you want is strong, but can also be held back by confused and unexpressed anger. Your anger is very slow to arouse, being used as a defense only in extreme situations, but when it surfaces it has all the force and impact of a charging bull. Whatever defenses you have learned to use against loss, you stick to them with your usual stubbornness and resistance to change.

You want a peaceful life of suiting yourself and feeding your tastes, encouraging you to pursue money as an objective, or helping you to learn to make things for yourself (you have the potential to be a fine craftsman or artisan—having a feeling for good materials and tools). You enjoy using your abilities to shape the world around you, making things to your tastes. Those tastes are sensual and sexual, and you are passionate, not particularly subtle, jealous and possessive. In your willingness to fight for what you want you would probably enjoy the haggling over prices in Arab market places, where personal qualities are measured by bargaining abilities.

Since your fixity of purpose can be both creative and destructive, you need to point your desires at fully wholesome goals, for example at understanding both yourself and others, and at promoting the well-being and the best interests of everyone around you, including yourself. Then you will find that you have what you need as a whole human being.

JUPITER IN TAURUS

During this lifetime you are going through a growth of personal values. You want to feel that you represent something large and substantial, which may be a philosophy or religion, or may involve personal material and financial growth. Either way you identify your own values with the larger scale of things, wanting to reach out to and be involved with the greatest worth that you feel you can attain. Your growth toward such achievement will be slow, steady, and probably undeviatingly direct, since you have a rather stubborn persistence in your hopes for the future. In other words you are usually looking for something more that you can have, or be, or become, wanting to gain more of what you like or appreciate the most. In doing this you elaborate upon your values, your likes and dislikes, building on your earlier preferences and expanding them until they become a rationalized philosophical system that justifies you in your pursuit; be it of money, experience, or religious faith.

If Jupiter has difficult aspects, this outreach can become greedy and unbalanced as you continually want more of whatever you value. Materially, this leads to great possessiveness, over-indulgence in food and other material pleasures, and extravagant tastes, with a likelihood of becoming financially over-extended. If you don't feel that you can get what you want, your material discontents are likely to be projected through your hopes for the future into a Micawber-like attitude of "well something is bound to turn up," while actually doing little about it. If you have over-elaborated your sense of personal worth, then you are likely to judge others as being of lesser value than yourself, boosting your conceit and self-righteousness. Your greed may be for educational attainment, collecting degrees or other qualifications to boost your self-esteem; or for philosophical or religious experience, always chasing after more tangible proofs of your beliefs, perhaps stretching and elaborating your interpretations of your experiences to prove your preferred system.

Since happiness depends on contentment with oneself, pursuing more demonstrates inner discontent, and no matter how much one gains it is never enough. With this position much contentment can be found in the appreciation of natural simplicity, and in the free sharing with others of everything that is of value. Receiving without giving is unbalanced, personal material growth without generosity showing a top-heavy conceit and self-exaltation at others' expense. The same applies to the acquisition of spiritual growth without continually giving it away to others.

You should be very capable of attracting the good things of life, of understanding where and how growth and development are to be found, and you have the patient steadfastness and perseverance to reach any goal you set for yourself. You probably value truth and honesty above all else, if you have not become too acquisitive, and also enjoy solid, natural things, having a deep feeling for the countryside, as well as its products. Your values are likely to be basically tolerant and accepting, finding qualities to appreciate in everything and everyone that you meet.

SATURN IN TAURUS

You have an earthy reserve and caution which shows in your desire to have your world stable, ordered and consistent. You evaluate everything that you meet against your rather traditional and conservative (and perhaps snobbish) set of values in a search for permanence and security. You are capable of forming deep, long-term, serious attachments to anything and anyone that you appreciate, and equally deep and persistent aversions to whatever you dislike. Once your values are fixed, they are very difficult to change. You are likely to have long-range material ambitions, using steady patience, persistence, and caution in your outreach toward them, doubting that things will come easily without such control, organizing yourself in a measured, paced manner as you slowly build toward your goals. You probably fear poverty and the loss that could lead to it, fearing deprivation or destitution, or losing personal worth. You feel that your status depends on how much you have (whether of possessions and money, or of more abstract values), and that you have to struggle long, hard, and slow to earn it. Your fears could easily lead to avarice and greed, to the point of miserliness; to being overburdened with material responsibilities, allowing no freedom or spontaneity into your life; and also possibly directly to the loss that you expect, since you would point yourself straight at it by the persistent doubtful focusing of your mind upon it.

Otherwise you may believe that material values are evil and deny yourself any sensory, sensual, or financial fulfillment, leaning toward the austere and judgmental in your attitudes toward the physical world. You will judge others against your standards as severely as you judge yourself, seeing only your own very conservative viewpoint, and believing that what you feel to be right for yourself must be right for all. Basically you are intolerant of what you feel to be greed within yourself and others, the basic "greed" turning out to be a need for a warm loving and giving interaction with other people and with the world. Somewhere along your road you have come to feel that you are guilty and that you don't deserve to have what you want most, so if you can't have it—and that causes you pain and frustration, you call it evil and think that no one else should have it either.

You either feel the need to be sure of your material safety, perhaps to the point of clinging to it, or feel that you can't have it. There is the middle way of non-attachment, the recognition that true value lies only in yourself, that it is you who gives things value. The better potentials here include: discipline and development of your senses so that they are trained and enriched in their ability to perceive, particularly to see structure and order in everything; enjoyment of sensory and material things without attachment, but with a highly developed feel for textures, tastes, qualities—and a corresponding creative ability with such things; a disciplined and conscious forming of tolerant and open personal value systems, able to accept all things by understanding their place in the order of things.

URANUS IN TAURUS

Uranus was in Taurus between mid-1934 and mid-1942, during which period radio broadcasting wavelengths were standardized, the BBC began its television service, the first regular airmail service began, as did a regular trans-pacific air service, BOAC was established, and the first regular U.S.-Europe passenger service was begun by Pan American; a Russian balloon went 13 miles up, a French bathyscaphe went 3,000 feet down; radar was invented, as was the jet engine, and atomic transmutation began. Other inventions were: polyethylene, 35mm film, nylon stockings, the ballpoint pen, polythene, penicillin, and terylene; labor regulation laws were established in Germany, social security legislation and minimum wages and maximum working week in the U.S., comprehensive labor agreements and a week's holiday with pay in the U.K., plus various economic theories and research institutions were founded. In other words, the modern technological era was being established, along with the changes that it brought to society.

You belong to a generation that has grown up with changing values, established values breaking down in new social circumstances and having to be replaced by fresh attitudes. In your personal values, you are likely to be split between desiring a stable, placid, material security and a free, mobile, liberated independence. Your ideal probably includes wanting to be financially independent, free of economic ties and restrictions, not to have to bother with chasing money and goods. But you have an awareness that money and materialism is not the right foundation for awakening and integrating your own being. You tend toward a frequent re-evaluation of the stream of your life, where you have come from and where you are going to, attempting to understand and tie together the varied layers of experience that comprise you—to understand the interconnectedness of your life on many levels. You are capable of an utterly unswerving persistent drive toward any goal, and of applying complex, multilevel inventive thought to practical aims— in fact you are unlikely to use such thought unless you can see a practical outcome from it.

In your split values you may well hang on both to traditional and radical views, to security and freedom, to being greedy while believing that you don't care for material things. Behind this may be a stubborn refusal to change, a desire for things to be absolutely permanent while partially recognizing that everything is subject to continual change. Thus you are likely to keep on repeating life patterns from the past, maintaining old values despite their trapping you in uncomfortable old states of mind, while believing that you are making efforts toward change—the changes often proving to be variations on an old theme. The security-oriented side of you does not allow the liberating, adaptive side the freedom that it needs to relinquish the traps of your past. If you are directly aware whenever you restrict yourself from further growth and opening that is available to you, you can learn from the situation exactly how those parts of you work, and turn it into a lesson in self-liberation. This cannot happen if you use the situation to blame others for the traps that you feel.

TAURUS NORTH NODE—SCORPIO SOUTH NODE

You have in you a hidden intensity of raw instinctive power, an awareness of where your survival lies and a readiness to destroy anything that threatens it. This may show in jealousy, since your sexual drive is potent and your possessive and self-gratifying attachment is intense; it may emerge in the pursuit of revenge for hurts received, real or imagined, a revenge that can take years to mature; or perhaps secret internal scheming to be ready for the next battle well in advance. Your awareness of pain is well-developed, too well-developed in fact, since it can distort your view of the world beyond reason, making you fight conflict where none exists, creating unnecessary crisis and emergency. You feel the pain of rejection strongly, yet can practice it on others. You hate being blamed for anything, but are ready to blame others. You would hate to be treated as a sex-object for another's gratification, but can put others in that position. You feel hurts powerfully, but the hurt lies in the way that you interpret your relationship with the world around you, through your defensiveness.

Your conscience is also powerful when you acknowledge it and is quite ready to help you to destroy the negative facets of your life. Each time that you are repelled by something you need to see why you reject it. Whenever your intolerance arises recognize why you won't tolerate things. No one but you is responsible for your feelings, and for the actions and attitudes that arise from them. You are in the process of transforming your values from harsh to tolerant, from embattled to peaceful, from rejection to acceptance, and are transforming your own world in the same action. You are working toward simple acceptance on all levels, acceptance of yourself, then acceptance of others. Leave aside the feeling of personal valuelessness that doesn't let you have anything, and recognize that you are as valuable as all life. You are learning how to release the volcano of your feelings to fertilize the soil of your life.

SUN IN THE 2ND HOUSE

You identify strongly with your own values. Your self-esteem is based on the value-system that you have developed, upon maintaining it and achieving the goals that it sets you. Your values are essentially your idea of honor, even of nobility as a person, and you are stubborn in pursuit of them, hating to deviate from your set course, or to be diverted from it by anyone else. Any goal that you set yourself, you make yourself achieve, because to fail would be to lose self-respect, to suffer a loss of pride. Sometimes maintaining your pride may make you deliberately follow a course that others see as disastrous or foolish or stubbornly misguided, in deliberate opposition to others' values; nevertheless you will pursue your juggernaut course to the end.

Where you reach out to life motivated by honor and generosity your conduct is firm and consistent, your heart free from prejudices and therefore open to truth. Your perceptions are then clear and conscious, and the values that you form from them are substantial and enduring. This stability of inner truth tends to influence others in very wholesome ways.

You are very aware of material values and of your ability to be creative with them, whether with money or with the physical raw materials of the world. Your abilities here depend upon whether your pride disdains anything outside yourself, or your consciousness extends out to enrich your senses and awareness of the physical world. (You can test this by looking at your tastes; if they are undeveloped, you have isolated your pride inside you; if you are richly aware of the flavors and textures of things, you are extending yourself out to incorporate more than just yourself and can enjoy creating with them.) You should beware of being too subjective, and thus too self-centered. Positively, you love giving gifts and can be quite extravagant with them; negatively, your extravagances would be poured upon yourself. Your gifts are, in a way, a part of your own identity—you give yourself.

You are likely to be very conscious of money and what can be done with it. You may be very capable of managing it, of being able to make whatever you need when you need it. Your material creativity should make you an excellent business person. Your greatest riches come when you are earning for someone else, sharing your abilities. At your best, money is a means to an end rather than an end in itself; it will reflect the way your pride works. You either flow with giving and receiving, things, experiences, people passing through your being and being enjoyed while they are there, not clung to; or you do cling, striving to get what you want, feeding your own arrogance and losing humanity in the process. If your happiness depends on attachment, whether to people or things, you will be tossed about between joy and sorrow.

Among others, you express your feelings in either a cheerful, sunny, open and accepting way, or in a prideful and overbearing way, depending on how self-centered you are. You appreciate sunlight and leisure, play-time and playfulness, love affairs, children, self-enrichment. Or you love gold, position, yourself, fame, superiority. The choice is yours, as it always is.

MOON IN THE 2ND HOUSE

You are aware of boundary limits on your ability to reach your objectives, which will have come from parental restrictions on what you could have as a small child. In your early life you alternated between feeling that you could and could not have what you wanted. This alternation is built into your ability to gain your material objectives, producing a cyclic rise and fall in the amount that you earn and own, and a regular swing in your aims, and in whether you feel that you can gain them. At times you have goals, plus the determination and persistence to reach them, and can gather all that you want. At other times it is as though a glass wall stands between you and your goals, or you simply ignore them and prefer to amble along and browse your way through life, plodding along in a domestic rut, sticking to very habitual tastes.

So you are tenacious but cyclic in pursuit of your goals, returning over and over again to laying the foundation for your ideals and preferred lifestyle, though perhaps getting stuck at the foundation level, especially as your moods go into withdrawal. You need to feel that you are in charge of the material creation of your own security, able to turn a dream or vision of emotional fulfillment into reality. If dissatisfied, you feel that all your involvements are limited to the commonplace, whether you like it or not; that you can only have what is ordinary and everyday, just fulfilling your basic needs (as a child, when your parents gave you clothes or other necessities as presents), or that everything that you aim for and create becomes ordinary in the process, no matter how extraordinary it may have seemed to begin with. If secure in yourself, your tastes are simple, enjoying the natural basics necessary for living, and you feel that you can have what you want. You value your home life, and prefer your home to have pleasing sensory qualities, suggestive of security.

Your experiencing of your world is cyclic as your mood changes; you alternately go out to it and withdraw into your shell. You are moody if you are involved in anything that you don't like. Your moods dominated your early friendships, for when you were confident you could relate to your group easily, but when your mood was low you isolated yourself emotionally and would not be involved, a pattern that set definite, though periodic, limits on your social abilities.

After meeting new experiences you become very reflective in your evaluations of them, being aided by an excellent sensory memory; you continue reflecting by periodically elaborating your analysis of your past experience, reviewing or running it through your mind again. Where you develop this reflectiveness consciously it can become a refined philosophical discrimination, and be applied in contemplative philosophical work.

Your mother's social values were fairly ordinary, her ideals were of home and family security and her social contacts were mainly with family, this placing unconscious limitations on the range of your own socializing. Your father was quite protective of children and left you with a self-limiting caution. He may have identified with you so strongly as to feel that you were just a reflection of him as a parent, in a kind of take-over bid. He had plenty of potential for creativity, but may only have fulfilled it in domestic ways.

MERCURY IN THE 2ND HOUSE

During your life, your values, likes and dislikes, will move from an initial attitude to very nearly the opposite, and eventually back again. You question your reasons for valuing anything, and what values to pursue in life between alternatives. Your intellect becomes involved in simple matters of appreciation, and possibly confuses the issue, for from an intellectual point of view there are few reasons for having any preferences. Different sides of your personality form their own preferences, so that your values change depending on which part of you is dominant at the time. You are likely to change direction as you pursue first what one side wants, then the other, ending up uncertain about exactly what you do want. Sometimes this split of values is a vertical one, one side being unconscious and the other conscious; then you will stick stubbornly and single-mindedly to one set of preferences, half-knowing that there are very valid alternatives for you, which you need to work from in order to be more complete as a person, but refusing to admit that you recognize them.

Your mind is likely to focus strongly on your material life of money and possessions, perhaps to the point of an education in business affairs or economics. You value knowledge, ideas, education, also communication, change, and mobility. As your likes and dislikes change, so you acquire and dispose of your possessions. Money, gifts, and goods you see as exchange in the abstract sense (*e.g.*, the thought behind the gift is important to you), you see them as give and take, back and forth. You like acquiring small things, collecting books, and when shopping will often find that you buy pairs of items. You appreciate handicrafts and may practice two or three different ones, moving from one to another as time goes on. Crafts that may appeal to you are knitting, macrame, matchstick models, weaving or basket weaving. You may also appreciate literature and do some writing yourself. Your changeability in values may show in your having two distinctly different groups of friends and lifestyles that you relate to. This may be a reflection of a split in your ideals, which you very likely inherited from your mother.

Your mother was an intellectual idealist, often disagreeing with society's ways from a detached viewpoint, liking to exercise her mind in questioning what alternatives were possible. Mentally she was looking for connections between all facets of life and society. She wanted mental freedom to pursue her original thoughts, even if she never applied any of them, and needed personal freedom of movement to lead her own social life, though she was often a loner. Her detachment would leave her seeming to be cool, indifferent, and impersonal.

Your father is likely to have been manually or intellectually creative, with a flood of ideas and projects bubbling in his mind. A part of him didn't want to grow up and be an adult, so many of his leisure pursuits may have had a childlike flavor to them, including some of his tastes in reading. Thus he probably related well to children and young people. His self-respect may have been split, so he both liked and disliked himself, and his attitude to you would have varied in the same cycle.

VENUS IN THE 2ND HOUSE

Your values, tastes, and preferences are quite important to you, including their opposite face, your dislikes and aversions. From your childhood on you have been given to a simple, direct outreach to whatever you appreciate, feel to be pleasant, attractive, or valuable, building your system of values in the process. You have a well-rooted desire to reach for experience, take it in, absorb and assimilate it, effectively tasting the qualities of your world as you go along, in the same way as tasting and eating food. This may develop your tastes to a high degree, refining your ability to measure and evaluate your experiences, rather like counting your money, or adding up the value and amount of your possessions. You are likely to prefer peace, harmony, beauty, and proportion in all your experiences, liking a life of pleasure and leisure rather than struggle and strife. You may also like singing, dancing, fine clothes and materials, and the pleasures of food and drink. It may also be that you value your relationships with others; if so you are likely to be a bridge builder between yourself and others, able to reach out and touch physically with ease as well as to make real contact on an emotional level.

On the most positive side, you are very simply accepting of all experience, able to find value in it, and thus to enjoy and be at peace with it, being as able to give as to receive. The negative side, Venus having difficult aspects that you have not resolved, goes more to a judgmental dissatisfaction with your experience. In this case, you grasp after your preferences, which are likely to be materialistic, having a greed for sensation, ownership, and exclusive possession of goods or experiences, feeling that you never quite have enough, always wanting more. Conversely, you become more negatively discriminating, finding more and more things to dislike and avoid, closing off to many avenues of experience, actually making your world of experience smaller. Mythologically, this is the eating of the fruit of the Tree of Knowledge of Good and Evil; before the moment in which discrimination began, all was accepted, all was perfect; immediately afterwards things were labeled as good or evil, the one to be pursued, the other to be avoided or rejected, the judgments being almost entirely personal preference and aversion. In the legend not only did dissatisfaction begin, but death also began. Greed and attachment brings loss. Simple appreciation of all things means that you can never lose anything, for you don't (can't) own anything.

Your mother is likely to have been socially gay, pleasure-loving, and charming, relating with flexibility and ease to others, and loving variety of experience. Negatively, she may have leaned toward social pretensions and vanity, and judged others socially by their possessions and tastes. Your father, in identifying closely with his own values, and having to maintain a high sense of his own worth, could not tolerate rejection by others, acting to create in himself a personality that would avoid it, perhaps developing a certain vanity. Yet he would judge others readily as not measuring up to his own standards, particularly if he felt imminent rejection from them. He may have been able to relate easily and with affection to children.

MARS IN THE 2ND HOUSE

You have a single-minded approach to your goals in life and tend only to see what is straight in front of you. Thus you may lose awareness that alternatives are possible and not expect any. You are able to hold a single aim or viewpoint for a long time. Also you have strong desires: you want what you want, when you want it, and can be quite angry if your aims are frustrated. Though your anger may have a long fuse, it still carries a lot of weight behind it. You like to enter into life with vigor and to be causative. You have a strong flow of energy and like to expend it, rather than sitting around and doing nothing, placing value on direct action.

You have decided likes and dislikes, impulsive and immediate evaluations, and are usually quite clear about why your preferences are formed as they are. Things that you value include energy, initiative, directness, capability and efficiency. You like science, engineering and machinery; lean, spare, and functional design; tool using and craftsmanship, and are likely to keep all your tools (even kitchen knives) very sharp. You appreciate the new and modern, research and path-finding, and may make it a life-long aim to discover, develop or produce something totally new. Being competitive (at least in your evaluation of your own productions and efforts) you want to be first in something practical. You like adventurous exertion, do-it-yourself, and hot and sharp tastes in food. Hypocrisy, indecision, fuzziness, sentimentality, confusion, unproductive effort, laziness and faint-heartedness all repel you.

Your strong flow of energy means that your muscle tone is likely to be high, particularly in the neck, giving you what is known medically as a military neck. This means that you could be called stiff-necked. You may spend some time on developing your muscles or strength, whether for sports, or to deter the opposition. You are ready to fight in your own defense, though generally preferring to keep the peace.

You perceive sharply (for example your visual focus should be clear and your sensitivity to radiated heat quite high). You prefer to penetrate surface appearances in anything, looking for new ways of seeing on which to build new values. You can visualize your ideas clearly, and hold them with energy.

In work you like to keep your energies free, active, and explorative, looking for new ground to explore or new territory to conquer, but may find it hard to keep a single aim, and may become stale and dissatisfied if you have to keep on doing the same old thing. You prefer new ground to old.

In relationships you like direct, straightforward, and energetic sexuality in a partner, and are likely to relate to people with strong survival drives, though perhaps hidden and entrenched.

Your mother was either a social loner, or liked vigorous social activity with others, perhaps sports. She may have been strongly individualistic, maintaining her own independence, fighting anything that she saw as trapping her. Your father may have been rather egocentric, aware of himself and his own drives, to the exclusion of others. He may have seen himself as having to battle his way through life. He is likely to have been very direct with children, encouraging them to exercise their energy and initiative.

JUPITER IN THE 2ND HOUSE

Your outreach to your world is confident and enthusiastic and you are generally optimistic about your continued involvement with any part of it, expecting positive experiences that lead to growth and to wholesome developments. This applies to your experience in most areas, but particularly to your financial and material life. Your cheerfully trusting attitude hopes for the best prospects, therefore looks for them, and therefore generally finds them. This attitude began in your first year of life when you were crawling around exploring everything, and I do mean *everything*, for you restlessly moved from one object to another, enjoying them all. If the door or gate were open, you headed through it. Few obstacles were put in your way so you felt that many things were available to experience, that there was plenty of space to explore, and you wanted to explore it all. You were directly given many things, and cheerfully learned to give in return. Your behavior toward gaining experience and getting what you wanted was formed then and will have remained broadly the same, so that your optimism will have encouraged your exploration of the various fields of experience opened to you in your early life.

As your experience grows, so does your ability to appreciate and evaluate it, and the value systems that you build from this. Your values will be positive, open-minded and generous toward most things, supporting your readiness to reach out to experience more in life, and you are likely to develop a philosophical framework by which to measure your experience. Thus things that you value will include travel, widening your experience and learning. You are likely to be confident and easy-going about the material side of your life, honest and generous with money and gifts. Your material affairs could easily go through quite an expansion if your mind turns that way, since you are capable of seeing just where the best growth opportunities lie and of reaching for them.

If Jupiter has difficult aspects, then you may be lavish with money, something of a spendthrift, feeling that there is no reason why you can't have *more*. You may pursue a restless, greedy, and self-indulgent search for experience; for more expensive possessions, more money, richer food and drink, for bigger and better everything, continually changing your goals and inflating them when what you have turns out to be unsatisfactory. You feel that you haven't got enough. You need to find out what it actually is that you don't have enough of, because nothing else will satisfy you.

Your mother was either (positive) socially gregarious and outgoing, having many friends and acquaintances; holding tolerant and liberal social views, and probably being involved in large organizations—perhaps of a philosophical or religious nature, or involving open-air pursuits; or (negative) she went out to enjoy herself, gambling, drinking, racing, having a good time despite the effect on others.

Your father was either (positive) a cheerful, easy-going man, liking to spend his leisure in outdoor pursuits, enjoying enthusiastic play with children, or he was (negative) rather bombastic and overbearing, having an inflated sense of self-importance, a large conceit.

SATURN IN THE 2ND HOUSE

You can be cautious and conservative in your values and tastes, preferring to identify with traditional orthodox views, methods and goods in your life-style, with "meat and potatoes," though your tastes may develop slowly, particularly for such things as antiques. You are slow in evaluating your experiences, testing them against what you already have or know, not being ready to accept the new or let go of the old, resistant to change. Your outreach to the world is methodical, maybe even fearful; the goals that you set for yourself are either long-range and ambitious but slow to mature (perhaps through doubting that you can reach them, though you have enormous perseverance when you use it), goals of status, position, recognition—as well as of material success; or you set your sights low, feeling that you can't have (maybe even don't deserve) what you would like to have. For example, in your occupation you either set your aim for the eventual achievement of a high position, or you expect little or no growth.

At your worst you have a depressed view of your personal worth, and thus of what you can have as your own in life; this may make you afraid of poverty (you would hate to be at the bottom of the material "ladder"), stingy, or at least frugal in your strict control of money and possessions. You might even be selfish, avaricious or greedy, though you would probably rather starve than owe anything to anyone. You may even fear the responsibility of ownership, knowing the pain of loss, and the greater this fear the more likely you are to make the loss happen.

As a child in the crawling stage, in your first year, you may have been aware of frustration and blockage when you wanted to reach objects to explore them, perhaps having a playpen limit your scope, or a parent who strictly controlled what you could and could not have to touch and hold. Some experience in that time also made you careful about what you grabbed hold of, and may have involved a fall. You may not have been allowed to put things into your mouth (needing to explore the tastes and textures of your world), leaving you with a need to feed your tastes or use your mouth that can't be satisfied, together with the feeling that whatever you get, it isn't enough.

Or you may have formed a steady, constant pursuit of what you wanted early in life, biding your time, never deviating from your aim even if its attainment takes you a lifetime.

Your mother's social values were conservative, she fearing censure from severe public opinion and requiring of you a stiff, formal self-restraint in public, (you were supposed to be good, meaning not to reach out to anything or anyone). She was not active socially, save in formal ways, having few friends—perhaps one or two long-term ones. Your father was aware of his dignity with children and did not unbend or play easily; he may instead have been rather controlling, or curiously formal with you. Most probably he had little leisure time to spend with you, or felt that he had to use it for constructive purposes, not play.

URANUS IN THE 2ND HOUSE

Your major values are more likely to be your ideals of personal freedom and independence than anything else. You prefer to be free and unfettered in your outreach to life, ready to sample anything that does not trap you, seeking contact with those things and situations that will keep you awake and alive. You are very fast in your evaluation of new events and circumstances in your life. You welcome involvement with the unusual, the unorthodox, the stimulating, and abhor boredom and sameness in your life. You are ready to change your values, and thus your general direction, in pursuit of what you value, so long as you can see the change opening up fresh avenues of freedom and growth as an individual; otherwise you stick to the pursuit of your ideals without deviation from your track. You will either not care much for material things, feeling that experience is more essential, or be very much a member of the consumer society.

This all assumes that Uranus had no difficult aspects at your birth. If it had some, then your independence of values will be more a stubborn drive to be different from others, your fast evaluation will be a tense avoidance of traps, a refusal to follow the same path as anyone else; the freedom that you require being a rebellion against being restricted by anything, a fear of commitment. You are likely to pursue one stimulus after another, perhaps changing your goals erratically, or never setting any up; or you will persist in wild and willful courses to the bitter end. You are also likely to be a thoroughgoing materialist, pursuing money and possessions rather than more human values. Money is unlikely to stay with you, as you hang onto it for a little while and then blow it all. Similarly with possessions, you will find that few things remain with you for very long.

The two types outlined above differ in their experiences during their first year of life (and what followed from there). The first was allowed to crawl around freely and explore everything available without hindrance, many healthy stimuli being in the environment. This left the feeling that everything in the world was available, and could thus become a part of the person's lifestyle and experience. The second is likely to have had things snatched away by a tense and impatient parent, leaving the feeling that nothing in the world would remain within their grasp for long. The first can be friendly and sharing with possessions since nothing depends on the issue but the pleasure of sharing; the second is more ready to share other people's goods than their own. Sometimes they have a "sour grapes" reaction, claiming that they have no interest in material goods ("I don't care"), because they feel that they can't have them anyway, but as soon as the possibility of gaining appears—dropping that mask and diving in whole-heartedly.

Your tastes will be individualistic, liking things that have special qualities of their own, being rare and unusual, perhaps individually produced rather than mass-produced. You appreciate inventive qualities and integrated design. You are likely to be interested in clever gadgetry, in computers and calculators, in stereos and television, in the technological productions of modern science, and the more unusual the better; perhaps an interest in astronomy helps you to appreciate telescopes.

NEPTUNE IN THE 2ND HOUSE

There are two possibilities with this placing. The first is that your senses were enriched in your infancy by exploring many tastes, textures and qualities; in so doing they became capable of a rich sensitivity, a subtlety of perception of sensation beyond the ordinary (perhaps including a psychometric sense, an ability to feel the past history of any object that you hold). This makes your awareness of your world quite deep and refined, building an appreciation of beauty, quality, and refinement in all things, material and otherwise. The values that you build on this foundation are sensitive and subtle, your depth of appreciation allowing you to give to your world as richly as you feel it has given to you. Thus you would be charitably giving, generous to a fault, accepting all things, averse to nothing. You appreciate music and the fine arts, refinement of taste in food and drink, and beauty in nature.

The second possibility is that your senses were deprived of stimulus in your first year, giving them no food for growth. This will apply to your senses of touch and taste in particular, leaving you with a need for oral stimulation, and a feeling of unfillable emptiness. Sometimes this produces alcoholism, or other addictions. Your tastes will be undeveloped, your sensory awareness of your world relatively vague, making you live more inwardly. You may also have been left alone with the same results. As a baby you may have had things taken away from you, or were left in a very empty space, leaving you feeling that you could not have anything, or be in contact with anything, or that you would lose anything that you managed to grasp. This can make you try to hold onto what you have, but not very hard, knowing that it won't last, and you may have lost hope that you could ever have what you wanted. Your values will be confused, not knowing what to value, or why, and your aims in life vague. They may also be caught by image, things being valued for their illusory qualities or their appearance, with little awareness of true worth. If you were not touched much as a baby, your body image will be foggy and your social abilities to reach out and contact others will be undeveloped.

You will either pursue a vision of human compassion and love, a mystic's fusion with the universe, a dissolution of all sense of separation from everything, or you will tend to chase fantasies, setting up illusory goals, most likely with the end result of losing them or becoming disillusioned by them if you chase them, for you are just as capable of simply dreaming about them, without doing anything to gain your aims.

PLUTO IN THE 2ND HOUSE

In early childhood your determination to have what you wanted, to pursue and grasp experiences that interested you, was intense. Your dislikes were equally intense, and you hated being forced to have anything you didn't like. You identified so strongly with what you wanted that you felt personally rejected if you could not have it. You felt that any obstacle in your way prevented you from being yourself, discovering and appreciating your world in your own personal way.

If you were faced with obstacles (such as parental disapproval of what you wanted) you first felt very hurt by their lack of understanding of your needs, then angry at being rejected while stubbornly chasing what you wanted (very stubbornly, since you felt such moments as fights for personal survival). If you were totally blocked you felt shattered, and may have given up hope of getting what you really wanted. Later, you probably built a set of substitute aims or desires, but with no real depth of interest in them, nor real desire to attain them. If so, you evaluate your experiences in life as being painful, or dry and meaningless, or as being worthless, finding no value in anything. Perhaps your values are cynical, angry, designed to prevent you from being hurt further, though they don't, they simply keep your experience narrow by excluding you from life.

You may have decided that you were going to get what you wanted, even against disapproval, so you either had to fight rejection or blame to get there, or keep your goals secret. In this case you habitually hide your aims and evaluations from others. It may be that your aims and attitudes won't bear openness, that you are hiding stubborn hostility and negativity that others would reject in self-defense if they knew it was there. They may be doing so, while you interpret that rejection personally, judging them harshly, refusing to recognize that your own hard values cause it by their very intolerance.

If you didn't feel that your values and desires were rejected, you will have kept single-mindedly to the long-term goals formed early in life. You evaluate everything in terms of usefulness to your goals, appreciating efficient use of time, resources, money, and effort. You love tools that perform well, admiring capability and effectiveness. Your own efficiency is such that, if you need a fortune to accomplish your aims, you are capable of making it. But remember, being able to love brings happiness; money doesn't.

You evaluate your life-experience intensely, tasting it in depth and not minding the occasional hot or bitter tastes, penetrating each experience to the core. In fact, you like intensity of experience generally. You probably recognize that life can lead to pain, or it can lead to healing and transformation. Pain follows when your values are in any way harsh, intolerant, or biased. Healing comes when pain is dissolved by filling it with awareness and understanding. Transformation comes when all faces of life and self are accepted equally, without preference or aversion.

Whatever the reasons, some allow their material affairs to fall into chaos, having no sense of value, spending money as though it were water. Some practice financial deceptions, others are deceived. Some feel that what should be solid and dependable in their world just dissolves away. Some set themselves impossible illusory goals to achieve, and many feel that their life has no particular direction; and then some achieve their visions.

NORTH NODE, 2ND HOUSE—SOUTH NODE, 8TH HOUSE

You live strongly in your emotional survival instincts, which made you aware of death, and of the pain of rejection from others rather early in your life. Rejection made you feel that you could not have the love, possessions or other things that you wanted, so you focused your intense emotional drives on getting them by hook or by crook, whether you deserved them or not. Where you feel that you are rejectable (and your conscience says so) you keep much of yourself secret, hidden from the eyes of others. When you feel the need for love, you have learned to overwhelm others with sexual intensity and draw them to you, proving to yourself that you can divert them from their path and make them want you whether or not they wanted to, which still doesn't make you feel wanted. You are jealous if their attention wanders since you need it for reassurance, even if you don't admit that to yourself. The same applies to possessions; you feel that they *can* have and you *can't*, so you seek after the same things they have.

You need to realize that the feelings of rejection that make you act this way are entirely your own, and from the past, not relevant or true now, even though you hang on to them in self-justification. You need to purge yourself of them to be able to form simple basic values of your own, that can state what you need, where you want to go, and lead you to attain it openly. Your fear that what you want will be taken away causes that to happen again and again, and the only way to stop it is to stop fearing.

✧ 5 ✧

Gemini
and the 3rd House

Life-stage: somewhere after the age of 13 months and up to two to three years, we find the child learning to walk and talk. Walking involves learning to use the limbs with increasing coordination, not only the legs but also the hands. This stage begins when the nervous system is finally fully sheathed in myelin, an insulating and amplifying fatty substance, associated with Sagittarius or the 9th House. When sheathed, it becomes capable of handling and imprinting precise signals. The child can now begin to explore, to get hands and mind into everything, its curiosity now having use of the tools of both mobility and manual dexterity. It is during this period that a child begins to use one hand in preference to the other.

Taking curiosity as being the capacity for questioning, language is also its tool. While a child may be told many things by its parents, it only begins to find out what it wants to know by asking its own questions. The process of learning to talk is initially one of retention by repetition; that is, of hearing something frequently, then copying or mimicking it. Then as the child begins to understand how words are used, it absorbs words about things and words as labels for things, from parents and others. The most interesting words are about self ("what they say I am") and about those elements of the world that the child finds personally interesting ("what they say things are"). The child begins to absorb given beliefs or abstract concepts from others, and to recognize that others do not approve of the child believing or thinking differently from them. A process of education or brainwashing has begun.

For example, the ideas that a child is given about itself and its world by its parents and others are rarely objective; as a child ceases to be a baby its parents begin to "civilize" it, to teach it to speak, think, and act as they wish, and not from instincts or motives of its own of which they don't approve. From these the child forms both self-affirming and self-denying concepts (good child and bad child), around which it begins to structure its personality. This is often thought of as learning right and wrong, but is rather learning what is and is not allowed, what can and cannot be talked (or thought) about (which defines what future areas of exploration and experience of the world are allowable), what it can and cannot do or be and still have approval. It also learns to say *no*, and finds out whether that is allowed, whether its autonomy as a person is left intact, or denied, not allowing it to be itself at all.

In all of these, the child learns and builds allowable responses to the world. These responses, as they become habitual reflexes, form a personality, which is often a substitute or cover for its own original being. I call this the "splitting period," and the loss of innocence or fall from grace. It is usually during this time that the child realizes that mother isn't going to do or be everything that it wants of her, and its innocent belief in her as an all-loving, all-protective, all-giving goddess is shattered. Often this is triggered by the birth of the next child in the family. The elder child then has to adjust to being second in mother's attention. It may decide at that time that growing up is useless if the baby gets all the attention, so it is better to remain a baby (in personality). It may decide this even if no other child comes along, if parental pressures on it to grow up are strong. Whatever happens, most children have to bury something of themselves, which begins the building of an unconscious personality. This personality is added to every time the being has to restrain any natural reaction, to hide any response, to adapt to emotional pressures. In this way we become liars.

We learn to communicate, to use concepts, to use words and language, to convey ideas to others. This includes the ability to interpret, to understand concepts received, to understand others' language, meaning, or intentions. Eventually we go to school, where language is used as the basis, practically the only element, of our instruction in "facts," to prepare us for the limited range of experience allowed to us in the modern world. We get no instruction in living as humans, or in the breadth of the range of human (and other) realities. Nor do we receive any instruction to educate the right hemispheres of our brains.

The background to our capacity to learn is the short-term memory. This is our ability to take or imprint a pattern from current experience, at least for a short time, like remembering a phone number. As we learn to hold onto impressions, we start building associations, links between experience and concept, and between concepts. We are trying to integrate our experience, what we are currently learning, with what we have already learned, comparing present experience with that of the past. What we learn or are taught to recognize in any part of our experience becomes what we can consciously remember about it, an abstraction from reality that holds onto only a very small part of anything, turning it into an idea, a concept. In this way our thinking comes to deal with only small elements of the whole reality around us, which elements we then believe are the whole.

The full pattern of the 3rd House can be called input-processing-output. This includes our ability to respond to stimulus, to react, and the rule is the same as in computing; "garbage in—garbage out." Whatever we are taught, that is what we reiterate. Here we build reflex reactions and automatic associations. We begin talking and thinking by learning to focus on the specifics pointed out by words, names; and then we learn to generalize from concepts gained (using the methods we are taught as being rational), and eventually this also becomes an automatic reflex. But here we get our feedback from experience as we continue to perceive our world and act within it. From this feedback comes our adaptability, as we learn how to respond. This interchange between world and mind, between concrete and abstract, continues as we form concepts or plans from our experience, or act from mental plans or schemes, thus imposing our concepts onto our experience. We learn and we apply what we learn. We learn to interpret the nature of the world through seeing similarities and differences between objects, situations, or elements of our experience.

As we learn, we understand the relationship between our actions and the reactions we get from them. We learn to assess what the probabilities are. We have a drive to influence or cause change to our circumstances when they aren't what we want them to be. We learn to coordinate both inner and outer change, by adjusting one side to the other, whether self to world, or world to self. Naturally on major issues, at crucial times, such adjustments become branches, turning points in life, changes of direction. (Hermes, Mercury, ruler of Gemini, was God of Crossroads, particularly of forks in the path.)

Physiologically, the 3rd House covers the arms, hands, fingers; the bronchi and the ability to take in and put out air; the sensory and motor sides of the nervous system, and its ability to carry and to exchange information. Some of the nerves in the brain are kept at an extremely sensitive threshold, being able to react to single quanta of energy (the smallest possible bit of energy in this universe). This means that we couldn't be any more sensitive, being capable of responding to the most absolutely minimal change in our environment. Since pairs of quanta can be directly and instantaneously connected across vast distances, it also means that we have a physical foundation for certain psychic abilities.

The 3rd House gland is the thyroid, which controls our basal metabolic rate, being the rate at which our bodies can produce energy for use. This rate has its own natural cycle, moving up and down between limits, gearing us up for activity, extroversion, dealing with our world, and down for introversion, rest, relaxation, reflection, and recuperation. We could call this the alternation between doing and not-doing. These alternations of energy form the basis of mood-swing.

In the digestive process, the 3rd House includes swallowing, and the peristaltic action of the esophagus that carries food down to the stomach. It also includes the ability to vomit, to return or reject food. Parallel to this is the cough reflex, designed to eject unwanted material from the lungs and breathing passages.

In perception, after any sensory cells have stored or measured enough incoming energy impinging on them, they trigger a chemical change that leaps the synaptic gap between them and their associated nerves. The nerves are stimulated to change their level of electric charge, which change travels along the fibers of the nerves towards the brain, thus carrying information about conditions at the surface of the body.

SUN IN GEMINI
✧ The Communicator ✧ The Yo-Yo ✧

Gemini represents the nervous system with its two-way flow; information streaming from senses to brain, and impulses to action flowing from brain to muscles. The nervous system builds reflexes whether physical (snatching hand away from hot stove, playing an instrument) or mental (from associating names with objects to being able to lecture on a complex subject).

As a Gemini, in your very early years you were sensitive to the names used toward you, particularly those that said "you are a good child if you do what *we* want," or "you are a bad child if you do what *you* want!" You learned to bury the side of your personality that did not get attention or was threatened. If called a bad child you most likely became a bad child because they noticed you for it. Where approved of for being good you buried your bad child side—your independent contrariness—your ability to say "no." Splitting your personality in half, you still respond with both sides, but now they are in conflict, splitting your attitude toward all things of any personal importance, so that you change your mind continually about them. Each side of you wants different things, frequently complete opposites, and you hate chasing one for fear of losing the other. You can be morally dualistic, perhaps being very respectable in your banking job, and continually thinking of all the ways to rob the place (never actually intending to do so); or you go the other way—thieving and lying, perhaps with skill, while being a complete innocent inwardly. Your split being can make you aware of being a liar, for anything that you say will only be true for the part of you that is speaking and quite untrue for your other faces.

You need diversity and change to satisfy your various natures, your adaptability and flexibility in varying circumstances, your ability to show different parts of yourself to different people. You may have two different jobs or professions in your need to be mobile and active, being the communicating link between places, people and ideas. You have difficulty in staying on one track for any length of time, and you hunt for alternative methods and solutions to any problem.

Your likes and dislikes vary with your moods, which can be tense and nervous, leaning to worry where security is concerned. You can work with great intensity in short bursts, but if you decide not to like working, nothing can persuade you to put any effort into it. In your leisure you like relating to others, being gregarious and enthusiastic, and like quantity and variety in your relationships. Your major survival defense is to use caution, doubt, and restraint which can drive manipulativeness, or build into wariness and readiness to sprint away from trouble. In philosophy or religion you prefer to make up your own mind, linking ideas from varied sources into a personal system (though some Geminians have rigidly fixed ideas here). You are sensitively receptive to public opinion, ready to act out appropriate attitudes to satisfy it, whatever the truth beneath.

While this describes the classic Geminian personality, you will vary from it in many ways. Your major differences will be shown by the house placement of the Sun and by the sign and house placement of Mercury.

MOON IN GEMINI

Your emotional security depends upon your ability to communicate effectively, it being likely that your safe times as a child included sessions of chattering away with mother; and you prefer to avoid being pinned down. Emotionally you are changeable and restless, not holding the same feelings toward anything (or anyone) for any great length of time, unless you have two or three different feelings toward them and simply swing between them. You sense opposites in everything and either want both sides, want neither, or one but not the other. Where you want both sides and feel them to be mutually incompatible, you tend to alternate, first pursuing one until difficulty or frustration arises, then pursuing the other. If you want neither, you spend your time in running back and forth, avoiding both. If you want one of a linked or similar pair of things, you chase the wanted and avoid the unwanted, alternating. You should realize that the opposites are in yourself, in your way of feeling about things, like and dislike alternating, and pulling you this way and that.

Your changeability may make it difficult for you to feel deeply about anything, and often you substitute thinking for feeling, since ideas seem more clear-cut than split feelings, but remember that your feelings supply your thoughts with direction so that your ideas become just as inconstant as the feelings behind them. You appreciate the world of ideas, whether in education, literature, or light-hearted conversation. You like to feel that you are logical, and you are capable of a fast and light-hearted wit, particularly enjoying playing with words. Mobility delights you and you can often be found running around seeing people, doing errands, or making contacts.

Much of your personality is built around your ability to make connections, whether intellectually in concepts, emotionally in linking people together, or physically moving and connecting places together, for you like to be a link or a messenger. What you are probably trying to connect are your own separate facets, for your emotional defense system or armoring is to set things apart, intellect from feeling, one side of the personality from another, threatening concepts from their connections, until you feel as though you are two (or more) different people. Then you are abstract and logical about feelings to keep yourself separate from them. This is where the roots of your inconstancy lie ("lie" is the right word when your feelings change so much that no one thing you could say about them would be finally true).

Safety for you is not to be trapped in any one point of view, attitude, or situation, but always to have an alternative lined up to move on to. Or if you maintain any constancy on the surface, your inner safety lies in knowing that you also hold other feelings about the situation.

You gain a sense of personal identity, more self-awareness, in relating to people who are literary, intellectual, studious, mobile and adaptable, seeing yourself in them as in a mirror.

MERCURY IN GEMINI

Your mind is alert, active, and probably very much alive, since your nervous system is constantly on the go. You are a little like a busy street, with perceptions, thoughts and connections continually on the move and intermingling. Like a busy street, the traffic flows two ways, perceptions coming in and reactions going out; and with your continual questioning of everything current, your mind itself alternates from question to answer to question, back and forth. Your nervous system floods with information, always giving you a variety of impressions to sort out and deal with at any moment, so you have to scan and select rapidly, and with mental agility, in order to keep up with everything. Since you are curious about everything you don't want to leave anything out, which can, at your worst, leave you split and scattered all over the place, spreading yourself very thinly, and undecided about everything. At the worst you can become utterly split in your views, so that you are caught in dilemmas of choice in which neither side is wrong, or neither side is right; where you want neither or both, but can only take one choice. Your curiosity will dive into anything handy, wanting to know what it is all about, the questions often seeming to be more important than the answers, but leaving you at least mildly knowledgeable in many areas.

In your early learning you became fascinated by the use of words to represent things, by the whole process of abstraction and labeling; and then by connectives: this *and* that, *from* here *to* there, for example; such words in describing processes, motion and connections show the way that your mind works, and the things that you focus upon. You are aware of connection, process, and interplay between things, events, and people, and like to be involved in whatever is going on. Thus you can be very adaptable with your readiness to adjust to any situation. Your adaptability in part springs from your tendency to separate your inner and outer responses, so that you can have two attitudes or streams of thought running concurrently. Naturally this may mean that you can be superficial, thoroughly dualistic, or even two-faced, yet on the positive side you are capable of building excellent reasoning and logical abilities.

If you apply your abilities, you can have an active interest in the range of human thought, in the whole field of communications, in education and teaching, or any other area of the transfer of knowledge or information. If you are more concretely oriented, your interests may lie in such things as transportation, traffic and transit systems, or other areas of local travel. You may be particularly involved in looking at the connections between mind and matter, between ideas and things, between abstract and concrete on any level at all.

This position is best symbolized by two opposed points, linked together by a third which bounces back and forth between them. The two points represent any polarity of opposites; good and evil, right and wrong, black and white, real and unreal, concrete and abstract, etc. The third and moving point then connects them together, yet continually changes its own polarity from one to the other and back again, resting nowhere, remaining undecided; or bridging the gap.

VENUS IN GEMINI

Your values, your likes and dislikes, your preferences and aversions, are quite flexible and varied, which enables you to adapt to a variety of people and circumstances. You are probably capable of both liking and disliking the one person or thing equally strongly for different reasons, or of appreciating equally things that appear to be opposed and mutually exclusive. This is likely to be because your values are intellectually based, because you value things more for an idea or set of concepts that you associate with them, than for any other kind of value they may have. You can easily adjust your values to match those of any partner or person in a close relationship with you, being able to agree equally well with two people whose values may be utterly at odds with each other. In fact you are quite capable of having more than one relationship at a time, and at best you can love them all equally well, though at worst you are simply flirtatious, fickle, and insincere.

You have many ideas about love, which you redefine and modify with each experience you have, and so can easily become entangled in concepts about what it should be. You would like it to be close to an intellectually abstract and romantic ideal that you hold, and may be put off by strongly physical relationships. Your affection tends to be impersonal and intellectual, and you feel a strong need for open communication with your partner(s), needing to talk freely with them, as much to satisfy your curiosity about them as for any other reason, though you probably want to get a verbal expression of their feelings from them, and prefer to show your own feelings verbally rather than in other ways.

If you feel that you are being tied down, you pull away with an almost reflex withdrawal, going into the alternate side of your dual feelings about your partner, yet you are very likely to bounce right back again. If being tied down satisfies your concepts about love, you are more likely to accept it without a quibble. The majority with Venus in Gemini are not inclined to settle in one permanent relationship, considering their need for, and love of, varied experience, but conservative social attitudes which look down on such taste for variety as being fickleness tend to demand a more consistently one-to-one approach, and can cramp your style.

You take pleasure in language and communication, perhaps on the simple level of liking to chatter, maybe playing with words, witty and joking, maybe loving learning (though often identifying with it through intellectual and learned individuals that you meet). Your feeling for words may incline you toward poetry, or other forms of creative and aesthetic language, though perhaps you just read romantic novels. You like to explore other people's ideas (in particular the ones that concern you, and in which you can gain a view of yourself from the outside), and to undertake studies with others where free intellectual exchange stimulates your mind more than you can manage alone. You like to be mobile, to get around with others in your local area, indulging yourselves in the variety of pleasures that are available.

MARS IN GEMINI

You have a restless and variable nervous and intellectual energy expressing itself in many questions and an active lifestyle. At school you probably drove to achieve, to be first in class, but dropped out of the competition if anyone else beat you. You love exercising yourself in learning, but don't like anyone teaching you or accepting anyone else's word for anything, unless it fits in with your own ideas. You are intellectually sharp and analytical, curious about anything new that you encounter, and keenly interested in any type of fresh experience. You are always ready to move about energetically under your own steam in pursuit of experience. You may be outwardly argumentative, loving debate and intellectual contests, or you may keep all your arguments inward, involving different sides of your personality in battles. When preparing to act, you will generally have to decide which part of yourself to act from, usually being split between alternatives of adult responsibility and pure childlike enjoyment, though your own personal split may be between different, but mutually exclusive, opposites.

In action you are changeable, adapting rapidly to circumstances, adjusting to which way the wind is blowing, usually ready to turn around with a reflex withdrawal and go in the opposite direction if things don't suit you. In this way you can avoid deep commitments and passionate involvements, while you still keep your options open to do the other. You can appear to be unconcerned while actually being serious and responsible, and can act as though responsible when you are not involved. This is because you have a fear of commitment, of being inescapably tied down to anything, particularly to any one strong and unvarying principle, or to any person in a relationship, no matter how strongly you actually feel about them. Your mind, like everyone else's, is split between child and adult parts, and between good child and bad child elements formed by your parents' attitudes to you; you don't want to commit yourself finally to being any one of them, for if you want to be all that you are, but have a problem combining your different facets. Your original nature was, and is, innately good, but your impulses may not always follow that nature, thus losing truth and innocence. Yet if you act from it, your motivations are pure and you act with certainty and without thoughts of personal advantage. Without this an unreflectingly instinctual way of acting can bring only misfortune. Beyond this you also have a fear of emptiness, of having nothing happening, nothing to do to distract yourself from the probable conflict between your different parts.

You like to be practical, learning how to do various things, yet often don't do, or don't complete, truly essential jobs. You can decide definitely to do something, and then change your mind, and often don't bother to inform the other people involved. Your ingenuity and resourcefulness lead you to try many things, perhaps many jobs in your lifetime; certainly your changeability leads to many changes and turning points.

JUPITER IN GEMINI

You have a restless curiosity that likes to roam around over a variety of subjects, gaining smatterings of information and conceptual knowledge in all. Your nervous impulsiveness keeps you on the move, both physically in traveling around and about, and mentally in picking up other people's ideas and philosophies from here, there, and everywhere. You seek to know and to understand, but often just collect abstract information without ever learning anything deeply by direct personal experience. You then like to pass on what you have learned, taking the ideas that you have acquired as your own, transmitting them to others and teaching them. All too often you may be imposing ideas that you don't really understand, but simply like to identify with, tending to force others to adopt them in your belief that you know best, that your ideas are right for them.

If Jupiter has difficult aspects, you are uncertain in yourself, being rather split in your attitudes and your hopes about most things, your confidence going through a yo-yo swing between optimism and pessimism, between being kind, cheerful and happy, and being a grouch with all the cares of the world on your shoulders. Often your confidence is a pretense, and if anyone comes close to penetrating it you can erupt into rage in a mistaken self-defense. You feel that by asserting confidence, even when you don't feel it, you will make things be all right, will make your superficial factual knowledge into truth to give you the certainty that you lack. You try to find truths outside yourself and become confused when they don't give you any greater feeling of being true within yourself, which is why you feel the need to have others adopt them as being true, to give your faith some support. We can call it faith since it is a placing of confidence in something actually unknown by yourself, an assertion of trust with little or no experience to back it up. You can be mentally scattered, changeable and undecided, never really making your mind up fully about anything, and thus tending to dabble in everything that arouses your interest. Thus you may be a dilettante, having broad but superficial knowledge in many areas. You may be a perpetual student, juvenile in attitudes, never finally learning anything in depth, or by direct experience.

Otherwise if you are selective and consistent in your learning, your wide curiosity can lead to much intellectual growth. Your breadth of interest is likely to include religion and philosophy, education and law, and ideas on the evolution and development of mankind, or of life itself; your preference for taking an overview may lead you to apply the lessons of the past to the future, making projections from history to forecast the shape of coming trends. You may apply your studies in teaching or lecturing, in writing, journalism and commentary, in broadcasting or information services. You may have a drive to turn great but abstract ideas into realities, or to popularize areas of higher knowledge that the public usually do not meet face to face. You do need to make sure that your knowledge has a strong foundation, that it isn't a top-heavy superficial structure, an empty pretense.

SATURN IN GEMINI

You are likely to have a serious, ordered mind that looks for pattern and structure in everything that it examines, that classifies and organizes by logical concepts, by strict laws and forms. At best you have a mental discipline and concentration that pursues themes over a long period, slowly building rational systems of thought, carefully linking ideas together until they crystallize into perfect order. Your potential for rigorous reasoning may make you a brilliant scholar if you have aimed for the attainment of knowledge or for academic status, though this will normally come through plodding, careful application and slow, orderly review. You seek intellectual certainty because you have doubts, and perhaps use your doubts as a tool to stimulate questions, where you do not let them get in your way and obscure your thinking.

When your doubts dominate, your mind is more suspicious, narrow, cautious and conservative. You may then fear the new, the unexplored, or the apparently irrational, and attempt to control, manipulate, and dominate circumstances that arouse such fears in you. You are quite aware of any limitations in your educational status and may make efforts to improve it, or at least to maintain it in others eyes, not wanting to be thought uneducated, silly or stupid (though some with this placing are deliberately silly to avoid seriousness and to control situations). The same effort keeps you serious and controlled in your communications with others, so you find it difficult to be spontaneous or free flowing in conversation, and may have no abilities in small talk or light-hearted chatter (while the silly types produce an endless flood, to prevent real depth from being reached). With difficult aspects to Saturn you may have been denied education, or have had a narrow schooling in which achievement was more important than the awakening of your curiosity. Or you may have assimilated many narrow, earth-bound and negative ideas that have come to control your mind, ideas perhaps of law and order, rules and regulations, fate, predestination, guilt and retribution.

You are intellectually sensitive to rules and regulations, and as a child would have been very aware of any hints from your elders that you were thought of as a bad child. You wanted to gain recognition for being good, and would have controlled your behavior for that purpose, but if you were called bad, you will have judged yourself strictly by their standards—and have found many things wrong with yourself, building your self-doubts. Through resentment you may later have reacted against such guilt-making judgments, but since you had already swallowed the system of rules this would simply have proven to you that you were bad and have developed an internal conflict. So what you are actually guilty of is self-judgment, and you may of course project this onto others and say "they are the bad ones, they deserve the punishment."

This position symbolizes caution and control over input and output; in learning, being restrained about taking in fresh ideas, and about making any outward response to them; in breathing, slowing and controlling inspiration and expiration so that your breath is shallow; in any situation, slowly mulling over what you perceive and putting your thoughts into order before responding; in traveling around, finding reasons not to, or delaying going out.

URANUS IN GEMINI

Uranus is the planet of the unexpected—of sudden upheavals, or of abrupt changes in circumstances, such as accidents; the forces of electrical energy and the high-speed communication and transportation of the modern world; of computers and aviation; of radio and television. As this planet takes seven years to pass through one zodiac sign it is in the same sign for all those born at the same time as yourself and tends to be one of the "Generation Markers." Therefore its house position is more important to you as an individual than its zodiac sign position, which puts its trademark on every person for the whole period.

From 1942 to 1949, Uranus was in the sign Gemini. During this period there were many new technological advances, particularly in aviation, the jet engine and the first supersonic flight, automated flight, rocketry—the V2, electronics, and radar. The atom was split, leading directly to the atomic bomb; the first computer was built, magnetic tape and the transistor invented; the first cyclotron was built. Also the war brought with it a flourishing black market.

This placement gave us a generation with a whole new way of looking at things, a generation that learned to question early, and to support its own independence by learning how to say "no" as one of its first words. A free-thinking philosophy developed about this time, and a restless, changing atmosphere prevailed, particular attention being given to the education system, increased mobility, and industrial change. There was also an increasing alienation of modern man from his deeper natural roots.

You are not prepared to accept things the way they are without questioning the validity of all arguments, and whether or not they should be kept that way. If you find things to be outdated you have no hesitation whatever in changing them, but perhaps have second thoughts afterwards, being uncertain whether the change is actually in the right direction. You are also ready to leap at opportunities, especially for further personal independence, occasionally at the expense of clear-cut morality.

From this period travel became very much taken for granted as being a part of everyday life, and no big thing as it had been to earlier generations, growing up with motor vehicles becoming common. You probably enjoy a lot of short trips and running around for all kinds of reasons. Having grown up with ever-increasing levels of nervous stimulus, more radio, television, learning to handle cars and other machines, learning ever more complex sets of nerve reflexes, you tend to need a fair amount of change to keep you happy.

You may be an original thinker; since you grew up seeing more and more complex ideas developing around you, you learned that it is possible to fit many concepts together into inventive new forms. Boredom need never be a part of your life, but remember that exploring many different directions at once can amount to disunity, therefore concentrate your ideas to see one thing through before rushing off on another tangent, or you may develop an inconsistency and avoidance and get frustrated by it, not to mention the unsettling effect this buzzing about can have on the more peaceful types around you.

GEMINI NORTH NODE—SAGITTARIUS SOUTH NODE

You are highly strung, having a wild, restless energy that wants to be free to roam, have adventures, and explore. The wild horse of your mind prefers to stampede over the spaces of the world without limitation or frustration, exploring the empty lands under a wide and open sky without regard for the limiting aspects of society. Sometimes this simply means that you run away from responsibility into scattered activity, taking liberties rather than being at liberty. You are probably outspoken and prone to put your foot in it, lacking in tact, too ready to teach and not enough to learn from others. Your desire to be involved in the big things of life leaves you believing that many ordinary things are beneath your notice. A certain know-it-all conceit is a facet of something that could be called arrogance, or a kind of moral superiority. Perhaps we could call it bluff, both hearty, hail-fellow-well-met bluffness and the confidence trickster's bluff. Your over-enthusiastic energy leads you into excessive, even though well-intended, behavior.

You need to develop your awareness that in dealing with others a certain give-and-take is essential; that in order to teach, learning is necessary; that in holding conversations, listening is just as much a part as is talking. Your wildness of mind needs to be trained toward clarity and logic of thinking, toward sequential straight-line connections rather than firing off in all directions. To this end you should educate yourself properly. Your freedom of action should be tempered by the realization that it is pointless to offend others' concepts of right and wrong if you are going to live with them. This does not mean that you should be dishonest but simply that you should be adaptable to the ways and ideas of others, and take your delight in flexibility of response. You may find great delight in using your breadth of view to open the curiosity and understanding of others from their basic education to a wider vision of the world.

SUN IN THE 3RD HOUSE

You are lively and alert, active, mobile, and curious about many things. You pursue ideas with enthusiastic creativity, turning abstract concepts into concrete realities. Being mercurial, you inquire into many different areas, building a wide variety of interests. You learn readily and identify closely with what you learn, and with your ability to learn. Thus your intellect is well-nourished, keeping it healthy and open, a state which is likely to continue through your lifetime. Your ability to communicate with others is equally important to you, and you may talk a lot, or develop abilities in public speaking or oratory, or write freely and creatively—to pass on your flourishing ideas, or to be the center of attention. You may be involved in creativity in literature or the realm of ideas. In speech you are cheerful and sunny, probably with a well developed wit, perhaps liking to tell stories. You gain pride and self-respect through the response you get from others, and from identifying yourself with what you regard as best in the human mind.

Your flexible changeability can make you "all things to all men," identifying equally well with very different types of people, and adapting your response to fit them. Your pride goes through a bounce pattern, swinging up and down, your self-view being split between approval and disapproval. When you approve of yourself you are happy and your creativity flourishes; when you are down on yourself you may be equally down on others, pouring your discontent onto them in overbearing, even arrogant attitudes in speech. Your sense of honor may make you back down later. You may at many times be reacting to situations on two levels at once, from stable pride and downtrodden pride, flickering from moment to moment in choosing which to act from. The negative side comes from your childhood when you hated any implication that you were a bad child, the pride that you took in the whole of your personal world toppling at such times. Your responses to those things that were labeled bad then split between avoiding them, acting solely from personal honor, and going ahead into them despite other people's opinions. You may be very conscious of the whole moralistic split between good and evil.

Your mother probably had a sense of refinement and a sensitivity to beauty in all things, particularly the expressive arts—especially music. She is likely to have been charitable, compassionate and hospitable. If more negative, she would have been private and self-secluding behind a barrier of camouflage; highly imaginative—particularly prone to self-exalting fantasies; and somewhat vulnerable, reacting strongly if she felt that anyone was attacking her or putting her down. Thus she was complex, elusive, and difficult to deal with. She may have focused particularly on everything that dissolved her self-respect or negated her pride.

Your father was a perfectionist in many of his attitudes. If he applied this to work he was highly creative, particularly in organizing and coordinating capacities, and may have worked for himself. It is also possible that he was lazy as far as work was concerned. He may have been interested in health. His discrimination, if used negatively, would have made him critical of others, building his own pride and sense of superiority at their expense by finding fault with them.

MOON IN THE 3RD HOUSE

Your intellect is reflective, receptive and retentive. If you use it well then you feed yourself with a lot of information on a subject, mull it over, reflecting and reviewing the connections that you perceived, imprinting it well into your memory in so doing. Then if questions or further themes rise to consciousness, you ponder them until you can't go any further, put them aside—until they arise again, possibly with more material out of your voluminous storehouse of facts, develop a little more, are put away again, ultimately coming to a rounded completion. This cyclic pattern of thinking can gradually build a philosophical mind capable of a great depth and breadth of thought. It often builds its structures from ordinary domestic material; for example some people with Moon in 3rd develop an understanding of family psychology from observing their own family, or other people with their children. You probably work by taking observations and checking them against theories, and vice-versa, back and forth. You don't necessarily believe that you understand anything until you can see ideas and events matching over and over again.

Your feelings strongly affect your thoughts, coloring and diverting them so that you cannot think clearly where your emotions are involved. Then your reflectivity is moodiness as your thoughts are hooked by memories, usually of events where you are uncertain, and can't tell right from wrong. Your emotions regarding your family, particularly your mother, may have been thoroughly split at some past time, leaving you not knowing exactly what you feel, love or hate, attraction or repulsion. You also don't know whether you want to grow up emotionally, or to remain a child. To avoid this ambivalence you have learned to live more in your intellect than in your feelings, finding more safety in facts and abstractions than in close human contact. Your thinking, and thus your interpretation of your experience, varies with your moods, making only negative logical connections and interpretations when you are down, only positive ones when you are up.

You may use wit as an emotional defense, or turn conversations around, pointing them back where they came from to avoid letting anyone in through your shell. You also reflect others' attitudes back in conversation, like a mirror, keeping your own opinions hidden behind it. This can be a talent, since it can make you a very good listener, when you are not caught up solely in reflection upon your own thoughts.

Your mother could be imaginative, sensitive, sympathetic and charitably giving, able to feel others' feelings as strongly as her own. She probably appreciated music and theater. Her feelings could be very sentimental, yet also quite private. She may have tended toward martyred moods, acting out a role in which she was highly put-upon, and nobody really cared for her at all.

Your father had a reflectively analytical tendency, and a very practical approach to domestic living necessities. He may have had critical, finicky, and fault-finding moods, finding nothing to his satisfaction, picking on little domestic details of food, tidiness and cleanliness. He tended to worry fretfully in his low moods, though he didn't necessarily show it.

MERCURY IN THE 3RD HOUSE

You are mentally active, lively and changeable, frequently switching the direction of your thoughts, questioning down one avenue after another in pursuit of ideas and connections. Curiosity has always been your strong point and you learned early how to ask questions, or how to find answers for yourself. You also learned how to make the right responses to people, how to match their attitudes, expressing yourself in ways that would be accepted by them. This began when you were learning to talk and began to understand from your parent's words what they required of you. You learned that you got a nicer response if you did what they wanted, doing what they didn't approve of when they weren't there, dividing your actions between doing what was acceptable to others and what you had to do alone, the first being the "good child," the second the "bad child." Thus your personality developed a "moral" division which depended on other people's ideas of right and wrong, reflecting one outwardly but keeping the other inwardly. Your views about yourself are also likely to be divided, but you probably give the alternative sides of yourself equal time.

You can be very adaptable, agreeing with someone at one moment, turning around and doing the opposite of what you just agreed with the next. At its worst extreme, in some people this trait becomes lying and sheer two-facedness, and may go along with a lack of respect for the property rights of others—coming from childhood curiosity, exploring what it wanted to, whether it belonged to anyone else or not. You have a well-developed ability to copy, whether this is others' attitudes or anything else. Words, concepts, ideas, labels, and names are important to you, and you can be fascinated by the connection between such abstractions and the real thing that they represent. Some of the earliest words that you learned fixed in your mind to become a foundation for your attitudes toward yourself and your world. You have probably been known by a nickname or a shortened version of your own name, or even by two or three different names.

Your father had a very discriminating mind, rather analytical and perhaps picky; he would have been precise and perfectionistic about words, language and ideas. His ability to be critical is likely to have caused you some problems as you had to adjust to avoid falling foul of it. He would have been a good worker, being able to deal with masses of detail and keep it all precisely ordered, and his work would have been the major focus of his mind.

Your mother's mind was more sensitive, imaginative and accepting, and she was interested in the subtle and mysterious aspects of the universe. She probably read widely, absorbing what she read to the point that if asked a question on any subject, she is likely to have had an answer—even if she didn't know where it came from. Music and arts may have been among her studies. She is very likely to have needed periods of seclusion, to be alone with nature. Much of your flexibility of adjustment to others is likely to have come from her since she was sensitive to others' minds and attitudes. She probably had a well-developed, whimsical wit.

VENUS IN THE 3RD HOUSE

Verbally you tend to be charming and tactful, having other people in mind, judging your words and attitudes to match the circumstances, not saying anything which might offend others or provoke hostility or rejection. To this end you think tactically, measuring the effects of your words and ideas on those receiving them, diplomatically adjusting them to the reactions of the listener. In this you develop a grace of expression, also probably loving the textures and qualities of words, the flow of language, the well-rounded phrase. Your intellect, if not lazy, is judgmental and evaluating, taking pleasure in abstract thought, in weighing and measuring the logical pros and cons of any set of ideas, particularly of the connections between concepts or groups of concepts. Your speech, as well as your thought, is likely to be smooth and unhurried, expressive of your love of ideas, language, and the pleasures of communication. This liking for language could easily lead you into writing, at least for your own benefit and pleasure, if not to contribute to the realm of literature, in which you may want to gain merit and value.

In your relationships you are very aware of the processes of give and take, and whichever your partner is doing, you tend to do the opposite—presumably in an effort to balance. You can also be of two minds as to exactly how you feel about them (judgmental intellect finding reasons for both liking and disliking), this making you vary in your response from being attracted to being repelled, from approaching to retreating. Naturally this can make you appear to be a flirt. You try to be fair-minded, but this often means simply that you try to find exactly as many points against anything or anyone as for them. In other words your logic may be strictly two-valued; yes or no, for or against, black or white, with no shades in between, which confuses you in a world where everything actually *is* in between. You know what your likes and dislikes are, then you try to rationalize them, to find logical reasons for having those opinions—your intellect making a take-over bid for your preferences. Since you can't find logical reasons for any view, it makes you consider the opposite, and change your mind—and reverse it for the same reason. This may be a short cycle or a very long one, but your values will change as your opinions change.

Your mother had a dreamy romantic side that lived in past loves or lost loves, her tender feelings usually kept camouflaged and secluded from further pain, which made others feel that it was not right to reach out to her, or to impose on her. She was often happiest left alone. She may have had a tendency to play the martyr in relationships, or simply to submerge herself in service to others.

Your father had a judgmental and discriminating side that readily found fault with others, and with all the basic aspects of his life. He wanted to be surrounded by niceness, pleasantness and perfection, then kept himself reserved from the faults and imperfections that he found. His responses were cool and ordered, he reacted to others meticulously in what he considered to be the right and proper ways.

MARS IN THE 3RD HOUSE

Your thinking can be vigorous, incisive and direct. Intellectually you are interested in the developments of the moment, whether they be your own new ideas or the latest thoughts to emerge on the public scene. You may be particularly interested in new methods and tools in communications, in new understanding of the mind (*e.g.*, in psychology), or in the direct communication of new or innovative ideas. If you pursue these interests you are likely to enter your own lines of study and research, your curiosity being energetic, active and explorative. If Mars had no very difficult aspects, you were probably first at school, or in direct competition for first place. If you couldn't be first, you may have refused to compete. Under difficulties, you are likely to have had fights and battles at school, or on the way there and back, whether with schoolmates or teachers, perhaps through being verbally aggressive and argumentative. Your verbal fighting tendencies could make you a good debater, being straight to the point, making points clearly and energetically, getting your point across. You are capable of using words and ideas as weapons, and will do so unless there is a direct Scorpio or Pluto contact with your 3rd House.

You may think of yourself as a fighter, and you have either been told to stand up for yourself, or told off for doing so while growing up. Whatever the case, you have probably been left in two minds about it, either using your own energy directly on others, or being on the receiving end, but turning what should be a two-way flow into a one-way street. If not, you enjoy verbal contention.

Apart from this side, you are likely to be a tool-user, with a practical mind that needs to know how to do things for yourself, fixing your own car, for instance. You may prefer to make things from scratch, from plan or blueprint through to final product, or you will work in reverse, making plans from actual objects; from the abstract to the concrete or vice-versa. You may spend time doing things that train your manual dexterity and reflexes, or hand-eye coordination, or manual strength. You may tend to repeat actions two or three times. You are likely to be flexible in your aims, setting up two or three alternative routes to a goal, or two or three ways of doing the one task, ready to switch from one to another if the need arises.

Your father was eminently practical in his working life, whether as a tool-user, or as a self-directing and aggressive go-getter. He may have spent time in the armed forces. He is also likely to have been cuttingly critical, vigorously analytical and perfectionistic. He was capable of finding fault with anything, usually on a utilitarian basis.

Your mother most probably gave way in fights, for the sake of peace, but she felt vulnerable to them and was capable of fighting back if cornered, though she may have talked her way out first. Many of her fights existed only in her own imagination. She was probably well able to direct the course of conversation for her own ends. If well-balanced, she was very able to visualize a course of action, and then pursue it directly and simply. Her envisioning may have included much intuition.

JUPITER IN THE 3RD HOUSE

You have a restlessly energetic mind that fires off in a multitude of directions and tangents, questioning absolutely everything, and you have difficulty settling on any one area of exploration at any time. For example, you are likely to be widely read and may have half a dozen books going at once. Being an intellectual map-maker, you are a generalist rather than a specialist, preferring to have an overview across a field of knowledge, rather than to dwell on detail. Continual elaboration of ideas may evolve into large and complex, possibly philosophical, structures of thought.

You are likely to have an interest in psychology and may extend this on to studying the broad range of human thought from literature to religion. You will be tolerant of many viewpoints and are likely to see knowledge, philosophy, and religions as growth devices, though your interest is more likely to be objectively intellectual than practical. If religious, you may tend towards pantheism, or some view that takes into account the evolution of Man's religious attitudes. You may belong to a creative group for the expanding of consciousness.

You feel that your faith is a matter of personal choice, and are likely to change your direction fully at some stage in your life, though this may finally include a return to your original faith. This alternation of faith may instead involve your loss of an original state of full confidence in yourself, but ultimate regaining of it through broad experience, or through confidence in knowledge gained.

You could be a story-teller and like to write books and articles on a variety of subjects. You can be free with comment and opinion, but sometimes exaggerate, overstate, and be verbally pompous, outspoken and eruptive. You like long words, dictionaries, encyclopedias, atlases, and may study etymology. Being candid and honestly outspoken, you can also be rather tactless and prone to "foot-in-mouth disease." You are likely to use these qualities in teaching, tending toward higher education.

Your working life may involve at least one major change of direction, but is likely to be generally restless, sometimes involving travel. You are capable of large scale organizational work, dealing with reams of information, though you can become confused because of your easy-going attitude to such things. Thus you are not always good in detailed organizing. Work in schools, bookshops, or broadcasting of information is possible, or in lecturing, teaching, or any form of education. You may instead end up as a writer, having a mind capable of covering a lot of ground, or of exploring the broader ramifications of the subjects that you choose, together with the desire to pass on what you have learned, perhaps directed to opening others to a higher mental awareness or to a cosmic view.

You are socially liberal, conscious of broad issues, of positive growth potential in society, and you can be outspokenly critical of government or politicians, or of systems of rule and control. You prefer your view of the world to be as wide as is possible, not liking to limit your mind, your intellect, or your imagination to a narrow scope in anything.

SATURN IN THE 3RD HOUSE

You have a serious, orderly mind that tries to find structure in every bit of information learned, and to fit it all together into an overall system. You also doubt that you have understood any idea immediately. This can make you a slow student since you will not move on to new facts until the ones you have are properly organized. You may have been judged to be slow at school and developed doubts about your ability to learn because you did not keep up with the rest. The problem here lies in the educational system not taking account of pupils' varied natural learning speeds, judging faster students to be better than careful ones. Your education may have been narrowly disciplinarian, cut short, or denied.

Your habit is to test each new fact against an old framework of knowledge to see where it fits, perhaps to your detriment, since the field of knowledge is continually expanding, new understanding overthrowing the old in revolutionary ways. Testing all against your system you pre-program the answers to all your questions; "if they don't fit, they are not answers." Your caution will make you ultimately profound and philosophical where you allow yourself flexibility; or narrow and rigid if you do not.

Some with this placement will be narrow, rigid, dogmatic and skeptical, actually fearing being thought silly, sticking to status knowledge, limiting the reach of their minds to the point of making themselves stupid. Their thinking is extremely cautious, their testing system being ultra-conservative public opinion. New thoughts cannot enter their minds, extreme doubt being used to exclude them. Yet others are talkative, controlling and manipulating conversation, dominating it completely—usually to avoid talking about anything close to home, but making sure that others listen.

Many have difficulty communicating on any but a serious level, having no small talk and not believing that others want to listen to them. For some, the difficulty arises in the time lag between input and output, before they can organize a reply the conversation passes on to fresh topics. This may result from being called slow as a small child; taking your explorations seriously you would spend time on them, and when very young would have dawdled along, perhaps to the frustration of your parents. For some it is a result of having no one to talk to while growing up—and not forming the habit.

This type of slow concentration is frequently paralleled with slow, rather inert breathing—a symbol of slow intake and output. This leaves little available oxygen in your system, allowing only small energy production which depresses your metabolic rate. This reflects your caution of intake and output in all things, particularly mentally in communication between your conscious and unconscious levels. You may be restricting the flow between the two, perhaps out of fear of the irrational. You may need a discipline such as Yoga breathing to re-establish a deeper natural breath.

Your mind absorbs scientific concepts easily, particularly basic physics—and any discipline that has a rigorously ordered (perhaps mathematical/geometrical) framework. You are quite likely to apply this ability in your work. It may lead you to the ambition to understand the connection between abstract and concrete, between natural law and what it produces, between creator and creation.

URANUS IN THE 3RD HOUSE

Your mind is fast and active, tending to jump around in every possible direction, leaping ahead from one connection to another that is not necessarily directly linked at all, but that takes you down any one of a thousand alternative side tracks. Your words are likely to spill out of you rapidly, leaping along. In your haste to catch up with your ideas you may not finish what you were saying but drop it and jump to the next idea. This can make you very difficult to follow, especially since you prefer to pursue the more unusual tracks of connections—and have probably been thinking about some of them for years, building concept frameworks like jungle gyms and learning to swing around them fast. If you have learned to use your mind well, then you could be highly intelligent, not caring for orthodoxy in your ideas but using the mistrustful, wary side of your mind to check every point, thus learning what to trust and what not to trust.

You keep a friendly, easy-going detachment on the surface, whatever tensions may lie beneath, though you are ready to cut off and move away instantly should the need arise. Your escape reflexes are fast. Your nervous system moves from trust to mistrust very rapidly. This may have developed from a parent's tense wariness for you when you were learning to walk, their readiness for instant action to avert accidents being imprinted into you; or it may have developed from your parents' early approval of your independence ("you little rebel"—with chuckles) turning into disapproval—after you had learned that being rebellious was all right. You learned to say no for yourself quite early.

If you have learned to handle the activity of your nervous system, then your education should have gone very well indeed, your curiosity being endless and your ability to connect facts almost instantaneous. If not, then you would have been hyperactive, scattered, would have made endless mistakes from jumping to conclusions too quickly, and have formed some very peculiar ideas early, when you didn't know any better. Your mind would then need a conscious and deliberate discipline to keep it rigorously to a single track, to check everything, so that your potentially high intelligence can develop with the proper tools.

You are likely to accept the unusual in information more readily than most, such as flying saucers, the Bermuda triangle, chariots of the gods, and any other borderline science area; otherwise your studies may include electronics, computing (particularly programming), automobiles, aviation, astronomy or any high level technology, sociological or humanitarian subjects, and your reading is likely to include science fiction.

Your readiness to change, to adapt to fresh circumstances, may be admirable, but your problem would be to maintain consistent attitudes long enough for you to develop anything to the full; though this may be no problem if you have any persistence, since then you will pursue chains of ideas ever further into fresh territory until they lead you back to your starting point, where you start again at a higher level.

Early independence may have made you rebel against accepting your parents' view of the world, or of yourself, demanding that you work things out for yourself, probably coming up with distinctly different answers to the usual. Also perhaps broken schooling may have made for difficulties in your education.

NEPTUNE IN THE 3RD HOUSE

If Neptune had positive aspects, your imagination draws you toward archetypal frameworks of thought expressed in symbolic languages of deep subtlety (mathematics, archetypal psychology, Tarot, Cabbala, I Ching, mythology, mystical philosophies, poetry). You assume that there is a simple background order, that all things are interrelated, and study to understand or describe the links, which you assume are rich, diverse, complex and multi-level. Early in life you were fascinated by ideas such as infinity and eternity, by the boundless nature of the universe. You want to know everything, and to this end you read widely. Your mind may be encyclopedic, able to fish up information on almost any subject.

Sensitive to the implications of words, you may study their origins, history, and development through time. You may be sensitive to the meanings of names and take on personality coloring from them (being known by another name than you were given, or choosing one for occult reasons). You may have been taught the names of colors or musical notes very early, having your sensitivities opened to them, making them primary facts in your world. You respond with innocent openness to your world, and it responds by giving you all that you need.

If Neptune had difficult aspects, you connect your ideas with fantasy instead of fact, the result being chaos. You felt that you were victimized at school, and would drift from the subject at hand into your fantasies and emotions. Your ability to communicate may have been affected by difficulties with coordination in your nervous system, perhaps through a switch from left to right-handedness, leading to confused words and language. For you, the dividing line between fact and fiction is thin, and may not exist at all (you learned to tell stories quite early), and you may think that the truth is whatever you believe it to be, or use lies as a camouflage, a smoke screen to hide your vulnerability. You can imagine saying something, and believe that you have actually said it, and become embroiled in confusion about what has or has not been said. You may have been confused by your parents giving confusing or nonsense answers to innocent questions, or by changing their responses to you in arbitrary ways. You are confused about what others mean by what they say.

In your mental fantasy world you "write the dialogue" of your interaction with others. Being confused, vulnerable, potentially paranoid, considering others as threats, believing their motives to be hostile (and camouflaged), expecting to be used, to be martyred, you are defensively devious. Reacting to these negative fantasies, you pour confusion into your relationships. You may say you "have to play two parts, yourself on one side, and playing their game on the other, putting on all the necessary veneers and camouflages to get along (in the alienated world). You are not allowed any *real* communication in that world. You have to believe that what you are doing is right, otherwise you're going to be very lonely." But in believing in your own paranoia, you are bound to become lonely.

PLUTO IN THE 3RD HOUSE

If we are called something often enough as children, we start believing it; this is called programming. You would have fought such programming strongly, yet fixed it through brooding on names and words used toward you, especially any that said you were a bad child. For example, if you were called a liar, you resented it thoroughly, but may have become one as a form of revenge. Your thoughts may dwell on hurts received, yet you may make them invisible to yourself if your conscience pricks you. You may fluctuate from hostile thoughts turned toward others, then back in on yourself in self-punishment, then out again, since you feel that you receive so much harsh judgment.

Early in life you used words as a defense, speaking strongly for your own rights, but probably found that adult rules would not allow such language from children. Thoughts become stuck in your mind, angry thoughts gaining in pressure through being repeated over and over again, probably from being shut-up as a child. If such thoughts are held in too long they can brew up into a violent inner turmoil which eventually must explode, and often does so, at least in swearing. You tend more toward silence than being a chatterbox, unless you learned a defense of talking continually to deflect others' attention.

You are a broodingly intense thinker, with definite opinions of your own. You may tend to stick to narrow and intolerant views, or to ideas of tolerance and healing, and perhaps to both in alternation. Your mind is penetrating, if you decide to use it, and would be of great use in such things as research work. Sciences and occult subjects may particularly attract your attention, but no matter what you go into you have the makings of an excellent detective. You have an intense curiosity about secrets, and feel impelled to find out about anything that is hidden (*e.g.*, during your childhood, things kept behind locked doors or hidden in drawers).

You have a potentially powerful drive for knowledge but may have been rejected in your quest for it during childhood. You would have asked penetrating questions, but were aware of every time that others were made uncomfortable by those questions (they possibly involved personal secrets, sex and/or death), and would have learned to keep your mouth shut to avoid censure or rejection for your questioning. You learned to keep your thoughts to yourself, possibly now believing that they are no one else's business, or that they don't want to know what you think anyway.

Your intellect is practical, and you learn easily when you can see the purpose of the knowledge. Otherwise for you there is no purpose to it, so no reason to expend effort in learning. If it is useful to you then you will learn, if it isn't, you won't. School will have been difficult for you, maybe because you want to get right to the roots of anything that you learn (when you want to learn); also because your first experiences there were probably painful. Thus you may have blotted out any desire to know. Otherwise you could have a good engineering mind, knowing how to deal with machinery or combustion engines, appreciating the functional efficiency of such systems. Your appreciation of efficiency may have come from your father, a hard and capable worker; your silence may also have developed from relating to his sharp-edged and intolerant criticisms.

NORTH NODE, 3RD HOUSE—SOUTH NODE, 9TH HOUSE

Your greatest need is to bring your ideas down from their broad, restless wandering through realms of future hopes of freedom into rationalized logical concepts that you can turn into realities. You like to think widely, but often without checking your basic framework for facts, or giving yourself the education that would enable you to do so. Your mind fires off in all directions, elaborating and enlarging on themes, not liking to be stuck in any of them; this is a facet of a certain irresponsibility of mind that also produces a readiness to run away from any situation that promises to ruin your hopes. Your early religious education or ethical training could have left you with rather self-exalting ideas that need to be tied down to reality to remove unnecessary conceit from them.

You need to learn to communicate simply and directly, always using the exact truth, and understanding the connection between concrete things and the concepts and labels used to describe them, cutting out exaggeration, overstatement and over-generalizing. To gain the facts that you need, you should extend your education with a careful course of study.

✧ 6 ✧

Cancer
and the 4th House

Meaning only exists for us in any experience if we can attach memories of previous similar experiences to it, together with what we learned from them. The groups of perceptions and ideas/feelings about past experience that we link together in the 3rd House here become the foundation of our acquired reality. This we maintain by a continual inner repetition of definitions, associations and memories, kept carefully within our acquired rational rules for reality. That reality includes ourselves as we build similar clusters of associated ideas and feelings about ourselves from our experience and from the attitudes of others toward us. Our sense of identity is being fed and coming toward its first coalescence, building consistencies from the commonplaces in our experience.

Where we receive and absorb the rhythms and repetitions of our experiences (all experience being basically cyclic), we form not only concepts, but whole groups of associated concepts; we not only imprint experiences, but connect together whole groups of associated experiences, and ways of responding to them. These make up our own local personal reality, large parts of which are built around our needs for security, and for continued acceptance from our parents. This is the patchwork quilt of conditioned personality.

Repeated experience imprints and becomes memory; repeated action or reaction becomes habit; repeated response to constants in experience imprints and becomes personality of the conditioned or behavioral kind. In living, we need to form a repository of experience from which to interpret new events and experiences, to fit them into the matrix of the familiar. We use this ability continually, so it becomes habitual and unconscious. The more insecure we are, the more we rely on our habits, being steady and familiar, and try to turn any new event into a familiar, commonplace, and therefore secure thing—avoiding its new possibilities since they may be dangerous; or we reject it and exclude it from our boundaries. The unfamiliar, beyond the boundaries of the known, is only fascinating to us when we are secure in ourselves, unless it becomes a way to escape from ourselves.

Between the ages of two and four to five years (later for slow developers) a child learns to recognize increasingly complex patterns and rhythms in its existence. It does so by noting what is common to its experiences, within the rational range defined by its elders, and registering that in its memory, and so structuring its memory and its sense of familiarity or continuation. The mind records every facet of experience, but we train recall to be rational, to work from the brain's left hemisphere, which deals with adaptation-by-action. This type of recall will leave out the irrational elements of the experience, and things that the conscious mind does not want to acknowledge. Thus we can have a normal recallable memory of any event, and an unconscious (or right-brain-holistic) but complete memory of the same event, not rationalized and so possibly quite different, and with a different recall system.

For example, children who remember past lifetimes (and there are many who do so in their early years) often find that their parents will not accept such things as being real. The child knows that its memories are real, after all, they *are* its own being, but feels the fear the parents feel when their own world-view is threatened. To keep its relationship with them comfortable the child usually has to deny what it knows in itself and accept the parents' view that such things are impossible, silly, wrong, evil, threatening, pure imagination, or whatever. Eventually it masters the art of forgetting, while learning to remember only what is allowable as being real. Similarly with absolutely anything that does not fit in with the parents' (or society's) view of what is real or permissible, and there are many such things in a child. Thus the child loses its own reality, forgets its own being, and becomes a member of its local culture.

The child is learning from its parents (and others) how they interpret the world. The need for security forces the child to learn to interpret the world in the same way, even if this conflicts with its own perceptions and experience. Rationalizations (ideas) built about the nature of the world become established as safety devices, and after a while, anything alien to them is excluded. Everything within the allowed boundaries is the safe territory of the known, while what is beyond them becomes the fearful ground of the unknown. We accept the implicit definition that the known (or rather, the labeled) is *all* that exists, that nothing else is real. Our rationalizations then become our only available way of interpreting, and thus seeing, the world.

The child establishes boundaries, not only of allowed behavior (and these not without a struggle), and thus of personality, but also of interpretation of reality. The two become one and the same to the child. Elements of the child's natural personality submerge, and along with them all ways of seeing the world that are outside the allowed range. Psychological territorial borders begin to be erected to exclude from our experience those things that we do not want to be hurt by (which may at the same time be the very things that are most wanted). These defensive "walls" being erected against what threatens us are always directly in contact with such threats (in our own minds).

The child becomes a reflecting mirror of the parents, effectively saying "I need you to give me existence, to tell me what I must be in order to gain your love, approval or at least recognition." Mother is naturally associated with love, security, breast, food, stomach, (the easy and natural intake of needed experience from the world) peace, relaxation and many other positive things. But then (usually) a split occurs in which mother apparently becomes alien and by comparison with the initial experience, hostile. The child becomes confused about its own change of status, about mother's apparent change, and is split between the need for its original stress-free state—and all that went with it—and the need to defend itself against emotional hurt, as well as the need to grow up. It may want to remain a baby so that it can keep mother as a satellite, or find that it can turn mother's protectiveness on by acting as a baby, "I can't do it, you do it for me." Alternatively it may grow to feel that being dependent is a trap that must be avoided, and thus cut away from home and family as early as possible.

The boundaries of the child's world depend on how protective its parents are toward it. If highly protective the child will be allowed to do little, to experience little, and will grow up insecure. If parents are easy-going, the child will move out as freely as it wishes into exploration of the environment, gaining confidence as it goes.

If not split, the child remains in love with its world and its parents, as they are with it, and is secure and single in that unquestioned knowledge. Independence will be encouraged, or rather never discouraged, so the child takes as much as it needs at any time, knowing that the parents are there if needed. It sees the parents as good patterns for its own future being, and happily includes parenthood into its future through enjoyment of the parent-child relationship (*e.g.*, playing "mothers and fathers," though this game can also be used to act out stress).

Developing awareness of the environment and its rhythms becomes a deepening identity with nature (impossible in cities), as the child comes to recognize the patterns of life and to understand that they apply to it in equal measure with all other life. So the child's own boundaries are the boundaries of the world within its experience, and constantly growing. The child then learns deep lessons of living quite early, by never being shielded from them; learns of birth, life and death, and accepts them as natural, must do so since they occur within its own experience. That is, the child learns both light and dark faces of the Great Mother, without making distinctions.

The child's experience varies between poles or extremes; positive experience, including praise, recognition and affection from parents encourages a positive up-welling of feeling, an enthusiastic and energetic response to life; negative experience, especially censure, blame, restriction, and lack of recognition of basic needs from the parents tends to put the child more into states of resentment, inertia and depression. Since parental and environmental forces are usually cyclic, an oscillation of basic mood or character is set up, becoming tied to the metabolic cycle of the thyroid gland. If the forces that mold it are frequent or relatively constant, the cycle of mood-swing or set of mood is also made constant, and can become a biochemical prison. Then the moment-to-moment mood of the individual may be shifted into one of its set patterns by the merest reference to one of the forces that formed the personal cycle, so that the whole environment becomes filled with emotional triggers.

This mood-swing cycle becomes an alternation in the ability of the developing individual to take in experience directly from the environment. On the metabolic upswing the individual is more confident, relaxed and open to experiences; on the down-swing he becomes more defensive and less able to accept his experience, splitting himself away from it. Memory becomes streamed into layers associated with our various emotional states; when happy we cannot remember our low states very well; when depressed we find it hard to remember that we are sometimes happy; thus each state and each area or range of experience gradually builds its own personality level.

The 4th House includes territorial regions, personal physical and psychological spaces from the intimate to the public. The most powerful instinct in nature is the need to have secure personal space, a defined and defendable territory that can be held against all outside threats. Such territories in nature are also nurturing grounds from which food can be gathered (originally hunting and gathering regions), and on which families can be bred and raised safely. Thus the 4th deals with security regions and their boundaries, real estate, home, domesticity, the breast, the dining room and mealtimes, boundedness, self-imposed limits, parenthood, family bonds; "identification with" becoming "identity."

Physiologically, it includes the sense of smell, which is directly connected to the endocrine glandular system. We inhale the hormones that others breathe out, and they trigger our own glands to produce the same hormones, to put us into the same mood. The first use of this system is at birth when mother and baby imprint on each other through smell, turning on mother's maternal instinct and child's security in her. Later uses keep us in the same emotional state as our parents, or others sharing our space. Nature's logic here is that if they are afraid, we need to be; if they are relaxed, we can afford to be. This connection also pulls women's menstrual cycles into unison if they spend much time together, and creates the mob psychology of the football crowd, political rally, or riot.

The sense of smell in nature is used to mark territories, to identify members of the herd, to mark trails so that groups can find each other, to distinguish strangers.

The glandular system itself prepares the body for experiencing. Glands are nurturers, preparing us for complete involvement in and response to the current activity of the world and beings around us. Our glandular or emotional range is itself a limiting factor on our experiencing. If we cannot feel with an experience, it remains outside our experiential boundaries, outside ourselves. If, for example, we are incapable of ecstasy and euphoria, we cannot blend fully with the objects of experience, and are limited to lower and more anxiety-biased ranges of involvement. Defendedness (adrenalin, fight or flight) works against euphoric acceptance and keeps us separate. Modern western cultures have lost most of their capacity for euphoria, for blending with nature.

The sympathetic nervous system is concerned with all those facets of the body that are involved with stimulus, excitement and exertion, while the parasympathetic side leans towards calm, contentment and relaxation, which matches and is connected to the thyroid cycle of activity and rest. These parts of the nervous system are not normally under conscious control, thus coming into the realm of the unconscious personality in their conditioned or association-reflex patterning. Their most obvious effect in Cancerian or 4th House terms is in mood-swing, the normal alternation of functioning between the two extremes involving all the glandular, and thus emotional, changes that are necessary for the balanced cycling of the being between activity and rest, and through all appropriate responses to changing levels of stimulus from the environment.

Unfortunately these up and down swings become directly affected by any split or conflict in personality, ceasing to be a simple alternation of energy and relaxation and becoming an anxiety-centered phenomenon. Then activity becomes more aggressively defensive, or perhaps manic in breaking away from restraint, and passivity ceases to be restful since personal uncertainty and insecurity disturb it. Being at the low energy end of the normal energy cycle simply makes a threatened individual feel less capable of effective action, more threatened and more desirous of safety and security, therefore more likely to use all the protective methods and devices that have been learned.

Another 4th House connection is food. Feeding is one of the battlegrounds of independence for a child (the others are toilet training—8th House, and bedtime—12th House); in digestion, the 4th House includes the break-down of the tissues of the food by hydrochloric acid and enzymes in the stomach. Further physiological associations include the cerebellum or instinctual, body-controlling and nurturing part of the brain; the lymphatic system, which circulates a lubricating and cleansing fluid around the body's tissues; the pancreas and control over the sugar levels in the bloodstream; the breasts and the capacity to nurture; the alveoli, which are the membranous sacs at the ends of the bronchi in the lungs, and are the place where air is absorbed into the bloodstream, thus fulfilling a nurturing function.

In perception, this is where incoming data begins to be matched to memory, where our bodies try to make sense out of what is coming in through our senses by comparing it with past experience.

SUN IN CANCER
✧ The Mirror ✧

You are extremely receptive to all environmental and emotional influences, taking them in and reacting immediately and energetically to them. Since the strongest early influences in your life are home, family and mother, this is where your responses are most powerful, and since you reflect their attitudes right back, you come to copy them habitually, out of your need for security in their acceptance. You want emotional response from others since you are dependent upon them and can control and manipulate in relationships in order to get it, knowing exactly which mood to use to gain the reaction you want. You may be prepared to do anything to gain sympathy and maternal protectiveness from another, for example in ill-health—exaggerating the symptoms of a minor ailment until it looks like a major disease. Your outspoken complaining is a facet of your very actively critical, fault-finding mind which blows things up out of proportion.

You are very territorial, needing personal space to identify yourself with for security and safety, whether in your home or elsewhere, and you will defend that territory absolutely, to the death if necessary. Your pride is quite intense though you keep it secret and you are very sensitive to rejection, blame, ridicule, or humiliation being torture to you. You are capable of blotting such hurts from your mind, though they still continue to affect your moods. Frequently you are self-rejecting when you do anything against your conscience. You are very aware of all your instinctive needs and are continually impelled to satisfy them, your ideal state being complete material security and full, close, sensitive, physical contact with others. You use your memory as a resource for security, remembering closeness in relationships and pleasant and peaceful states. You also use your moods as an emotional fortress in order to keep others out and remain secure.

Since you respond so completely to everything that you meet, your personality can incorporate all of it, so that you become a storehouse of attitudes, abilities and impressions. You are capable of mastering them all and drawing upon them at will, projecting your moods by playing upon them like a musical instrument and calling forth from others a wide range of emotion. Many fine entertainers are Cancerians, displaying this ability to draw response from their audience, and their well developed mimicry. Cancerians value their creative abilities and the widely ranging sensitivities which enable them to play many roles.

Your worst problems grow from clinging to security, from being dependent on others, continually acting the role of a child wanting to be looked after. This can make you overly cautious when making decisions—pessimistic about where they will lead rather than serious, mature, and orderly about developing them. You should decide by planning for the longer range developments and implementing your decisions actively and with imagination, rather than tensely and with confusion.

While this describes the classic Cancerian personality, you will vary from it in many ways. Your major differences will be shown by the house placement of the Sun and by the sign and house placement of the Moon.

MOON IN CANCER

Your security lies in your close identification with your home and family, with land or property, or with the things that you use as an outer support for your identity. You are very aware of your emotional needs and tend to cling to anything that means security to you, and you can be tenaciously defensive of those things if you feel them to be threatened. You are a very territorial person, extremely aware of the boundaries of any personal territory, building safety within them and keeping all threats outside. You do this emotionally also, keeping a wall of defensive reserve raised that only a few special people are allowed through. This wall is like a one-way mirror since you can see out through it but you reflect other people's attitudes and feelings right back at them. Reflective is the appropriate word for you, since you take in every influence from your environment and from other people and reflect them all straight back, taking on their attitudes, accents and personalities. This makes you an excellent mimic.

You are sensitive to your own biochemistry, to your every glandular variation, meaning that you are moody and emotionally changeable (though over a repeating cycle). When your energy is high so is your mood, and nothing can go wrong for you, but when your energy is down so are you—then you can't see anything as going right, and perhaps can't remember that they ever have been right. You would benefit from a close study of your moods, noting the basic patterns and your shifts of attitude through the cycle, so that you are not completely dominated by them, or submerged in them. You will find that being by water always helps to calm, clear, and invigorate your mood.

Your need for an adequate defense makes you indirect in your approach to things that matter a lot to you, in fact you tend to approach your emotional objectives sideways, trying to appear as though you aren't going in that direction at all. These objectives are likely to involve your relationships with others since your security generally lies with them. You use the indirect approach to protect your "soft and squishy" feelings from hurt and to give yourself time to entrench yourself into an impregnable position. You have the self-protectiveness of an oyster, letting the surrounding ocean flow through you, but being ready to close your shell if threatened.

Your security depends on being surrounded by familiar things, so you often limit yourself to the commonplace and domestic areas, not allowing yourself growth into new things, though this gives you the right qualities for parenthood, for small children need the security of familiar and stable conditions. You should be an excellent parent, knowing the needs of children and loving to supply them. All your emotional sensitivity can be poured into raising a young family and creating a home around them. If you had difficulties with your mother, you will have to work to avoid creating the same difficulties with your own children. Often the security of hanging onto the familiar makes you cling to habits for a long time, which can make much of your emotional life repetitious. Only direct awareness of these patterns will help you to undo them. In other words, don't hang onto the wrong things.

MERCURY IN CANCER

You have a reflective and retentive mind which absorbs knowledge by taking in lots of information, then looking for pattern, agreement, and repetition within it. Where human learning is concerned you like the security of feeling that everybody agrees on it. To boost your sense of identity, you subscribe to certain areas of knowledge just in order to feel that you belong to something outside yourself. Your mind focuses on those facets of your own experience that are cyclically repetitive, building you a good memory for the commonplace basics of life. Your intellect keeps up the security of your knowledge and of your personality by reviewing and rebuilding your past from moment to moment. You recreate your childhood for example, and reinforce your image of who you are by re-imprinting what you have been and have experienced. Thus you find it difficult to let go of, or be free of, the past. While the reflectiveness of your mind can return to themes over and over again, deepening your thinking until it may become profound, you may also be on a treadmill of habitual thought. Your thoughts and feelings are tied together so that whatever sways your feelings, your logic and reason are bent around to support them. You think about your feelings and about feeling situations, perhaps analyzing them too much and becoming caught in traps of circular thinking; "if this, then that. If that, then this." Your feelings can make it difficult for your mind to move straight toward any goal in thinking, redirecting it so that it takes long and circuitous routes, often returning to where you began. You may be emotionally sensitive, but switch your feelings on and off at will, shifting from using your heart to using your head. You are capable of using your intellect as a defensive wall around your emotions, an armored barrier that opens and closes depending on the state of your security.

All thinking that goes beyond the immediate situation produces stress, at least by not allowing your mind any peace. To find yourself, the original self that was innocent and in harmony with the world, you need to bring your mind to rest. To regain the ability to see things as they really are, you need to cease telling yourself how they are supposed to be, and in silence just let them be.

Your need to depend upon others varies with your moods, like a small child who runs away from mother, only to run back for food and comfort, then runs away again. You cling, then break away, then cling again, back and forth. You may never have made a decision to grow up and be independent, yet always want the alternative that you don't have between being looked after and standing on your own feet. When you feel safe and secure, you can go out and face the world, but the feeling doesn't last and you need to return to a safe harbor.

Your intellect enables you to work well within such areas as real estate, property, domestic maintenance, food service transportation and supply, customs, ocean freight terminals, area information services, local transportation systems, maintenance or management of sports grounds and small parks or other properties, and many more.

VENUS IN CANCER

You have a very receptive and reflective emotional response to others in your relationships, meaning that their attitudes to you arouse an equal response from you. You need a close, nurturing security in your love-life, and can cling to it very strongly when you find it, making deep emotional bonds. In doing this you seek to recreate a feeling of love, affection, and warmth from your early life, filling a need that you may feel was never properly fulfilled within your family. If it was, then you still hang on to that need, keeping yourself in the position of a child, dependent on a parent figure for affection. You may recreate your early circumstances in that way, or by reversing the roles and playing out the part of the parent yourself, putting your partner into the child's role, in either case acting a little like a child playing "mothers and fathers." Naturally you lean strongly toward marriage and the creation of a home, a family, and domestic bliss, though often what you create is a mirror image of your own early home life, including conflicts and all.

You keep your own world together by hanging onto everything that you identify with, and excluding all that you don't like, pushing it outside your safe, secure territorial boundaries. You create nests of security (reflecting your love of home, family and domesticity), your personal territories involving everything that gave you a feeling of safety and protection as a child, and including those people with whom you feel safe. If you feel very insecure, you may keep everyone else outside your shell, ending up feeling empty within; yet you have a strong need to gain a reflection of yourself, an emotional confirmation that you exist and are worth knowing and loving through others' response to you in your relationships. You want love to be shown to you, so that you can feel secure in it, and so you can be emotionally moody and demanding. Your very receptivity to others, plus your needs, can make you easily hurt, and then you become moody and sulky. In this, as in many other things, you can be overly retentive.

Through your ability to cling, you can be very persistent in pursuing a partner, though your methods are usually indirect, perhaps simply finding ways of being in the same place at the same time, and hoping that familiarity will do the rest. You have an instinctive understanding of how to create security for your partner, by feeding and looking after them, by responding directly to their likes and dislikes, assuming that you are not too much concerned with your own needs. You usually prefer to do your relating and romancing at home, over a good meal for example (and you probably like to cook), making your partner comfortable and talking about things and experiences that you have in common, creating a bond of identity. You find it easy to become sentimental about those people, things, and places that you identify with, having ones that you like to return to over and over again, and your idea of true love is likely to include sharing them all with your partner.

MARS IN CANCER

As small children we all have to learn to see the world around us as our parents and elders see it, to fit in with them. You have learned to act along the line of least resistance, using your initiative to maintain what you have learned to understand as being the real nature of your own world of experience.

You act to build security for yourself, and probably for your family. You can work hard to build a secure home and to maintain it as you want it, but be frustrated and resentful if you feel that others are not doing their share, or are undoing your work. You have a definite desire to own your own place, to build or modify it to your own ideas. Your ideas here may run to spare, functional and efficient design—leaving out frills and overdecoration. You effectively want to rebuild your personal world to your specifications, to fulfill your own needs, probably designing it to be as you would prefer your early family life to have been. Thus you can close your personal world in around yourself, building protective barriers against whatever you feel to be threatening.

You act to keep your contacts with your family, though probably feel like an isolated individual within it. Being over-receptive to conflict and hostility, you build emotional fortress walls to keep it out, excluding yourself from deep involvement as you do so, thus building your own isolation. You tenaciously cling to old arguments within yourself, replaying them over and over again, long after they are dead and gone as far as others are concerned. Thus, you keep recreating old patterns rather than entering into new experiences. You usually avoid expressing your anger directly to prevent domestic discord, preferring passive resistance by entrenching yourself in a defensive position. But on occasion you will come out of your shell and fight, recalling every frustration and resentment that you have stored away, and bringing it out as ammunition.

Your fight is to retain security in your own being, since you fear not being safe and secure. You build your emotional wall not only to protect yourself from family discord, but also to keep some of your selfhood, inwardly fighting the demand to conform or belong. Outwardly you act as you feel others (originally your parents) want you to so that you can gain recognition from them, having your existence affirmed and approved. Yet in doing this you do not act for yourself, and feel that you lose part of yourself, and resent it—keeping hold of what you can inside you, building a boundary line between the selfless on the outside and the selfish on the inside. If nobody recognizes what you do for them, you become moody and emotionally frustrated, and probably store that away as ammunition for later use. You inwardly demand recognition from parent figures, but don't go out of your way to get it—beyond doing a certain amount of what they want—then fume if they don't give it. This of course enters into your relationships, as you adjust to your partner, then being angry if he/she doesn't praise you for it. The positive face of this lies in your capacity for firm determination within yourself, and gentleness and adaptability in your relations with others.

JUPITER IN CANCER

You are deeply and perhaps highly emotional, your feelings and your mood swings being both large and active. On the wholesome side, you have broad, rich feelings for your family and are loyal and devoted to them, and to anyone else with whom you identify. You have a deep attachment to your home ground, to the places and people that you knew while growing up, and that were part of the experience that built your identity, and you gain in security within yourself by roaming among them in your memory. You replenish yourself by re-enacting inwardly the experiences of your past, deepening your foundations by keeping and constantly rebuilding a close familiarity with your roots. This gives you a good, grounded sense of reality, a feeling of having an identity that stretches far beyond the limits of your own body and the present moment, and leaves you with a secure confidence in yourself that you are then ready to share with others; appreciating what it is like to be well nurtured by the world, you are prepared to give yourself out in nurturing others.

If Jupiter has difficult aspects, then your dependency needs are large and you cling moodily to the past, exaggerating memories both of incidents that threatened your security and broke your trust (fueling your anger), and of those times to which you cling for indulgent self-nurturing. You hold onto attitudes of childhood innocence and trust, not wanting to grow up into the complexities of adulthood, whatever your age, keeping up an emotional barrier against fresh experience by surrounding yourself with the past. Your emotions lean toward the maudlin and overly sentimental as you indulge yourself in elaborating them out of proportion to the circumstances. Sometimes you protect an inner emptiness by overwhelming others with a gush of feeling, or try to pump security feelings or self-justification from a well that you have already pumped dry. If this is the case, you need to replenish that well by giving yourself freely to others instead of demanding that your own needs be met.

You will probably seek to establish a good home where you can relive the joys of your childhood through your own children. You may turn your feelings for your local region into an interest in property, land, real estate, farming, or gardening; and your love of domestic nurturing into food production, cooking (you may be a gourmet or a gourmand), or involvement in hotels and restaurants, and other such "nurturing grounds." Some with Jupiter in Cancer have a deep feeling for the ocean, and become sailors and fishermen, some being world travelers, expanding the boundaries of their experience and coming to feel at home anywhere in the world.

SATURN IN CANCER

As a child you were very aware of a need to copy or conform exactly to the requirements that you felt other people imposed on you, so that you could have the safety and security of acceptance from them. This went so far as to make you accept their view of what reality is, discounting or ignoring your own perceptions. You worked hard to fit in and to stay within any kind of boundaries that were set for you. So you now tend to stay strictly within the known.

Whether you felt your mother to be cold and authoritarian, or sympathized with the difficulties of her life, your relationship with her colored your emotions deeply. You are likely to have been left with a deep need for security which you find difficult to express emotionally. In self-protection you probably hold a strong wall of reserve around you, a caution which may not allow any spontaneous or intimate closeness to others. You perhaps felt that security in the form of respect from family or mother was denied to you. It may have left you in a long depression, or with a tenacious ambition to gain the kind of domestic or emotional security that you need. Since this need is likely to run deep it will drive you toward achieving it eventually.

Your sense of emotional isolation may make you doubt that you will find the nurturing closeness you want with another person, but if you become very aware of your restraint in emotional intimacy you may be able to dissolve your reserve. If you do this you may also need to undo a tendency to cling. Beyond these feelings you will find a deep and abiding seriousness of affection with a powerful nurturing drive. You will still need to feel that you have respect from your family, and will take on domestic responsibility to give security to others, rather than to take it.

You are emotionally sensitive in that you take everything deeply and seriously, especially where home and family are concerned. Your need for approval can make you identify with any system or organization which gives it to you, however cold and impersonal it may be. Your upbringing probably left you with many self-doubts, and you wish that others would take them away from you, but fear that expressing your feelings would lead to disapproval. In some people, this need turns to clinging to material possessions, which represent security. In others, the strong emotional defense becomes the house which may be felt as being a fortress, symbolizing both protection from attack from outside and withholding of feeling inside.

Hopefully you have avoided one difficult result of this position, that of estrangement from members of your family. Whatever the case may be you need to be sure not to crystallize your most negative feelings into an immovable attitude, not to let depressed emotional views color your view of life to the point of making you see everything as being worse than it is.

People with Saturn in Cancer are often attracted to caves and underground places since the solid, womb-like security of them can satisfy an inner need. In its most positive form, this can bring an ability to draw upon the deep nurturing resources of the Earth itself, through farming or other earth-contact.

URANUS IN CANCER

Uranus was in Cancer between mid-1949 and mid-1956, during which time the world was beginning to be aware of some dangers of the modern technological era, and was starting to seek some security against them. For example: concern was growing at the dangers to health and heredity from nuclear radiation, and the public attention was first drawn to the connection between cigarette smoking and lung cancer. Protectives developed at this time included the first contraceptive tablet and the polio vaccine, legislation for the security of tenants, and a UNESCO symposium on human rights. Developments included: the opening of the trans-atlantic telephone service, the invention of solar batteries capable of storing the sun's power in electrical form, and vertical take-off aircraft. Oceanic exploration was active, a nuclear submarine was built and Thor Heyerdahl sailed the Kon-Tiki across the Pacific ocean to Easter Island. (Cancer is connected with security, heredity, the home and family, the lungs, and the ocean).

You were born into a changing set of attitudes regarding security, with conflict growing between the desire for explorative material progress and the safety of the individual. Most people of your generation have a struggle between wanting to be completely independent as an individual and wanting to have a close, warm contact with home and family, often showing in a break away from the family with security needs submerged under a "who needs that?" attitude. At the one extreme, we find a complete rebellion against any family ties whatsoever, and at the other, staying at home but feeling trapped by it. You would like to be close and to cling but are afraid of being trapped by others, and will pull away abruptly if you feel that you are; you would love to be completely independent but feel the need for support from outside yourself, perhaps turning your friends into an extended family. Naturally you can be subject to a certain amount of emotional whiplash as your feelings switch from one mode to the other, and you probably end up feeling insecure whatever the outer state of your security is. You are wary about putting roots down too deep, no matter how much you may want to, for fear that you will have to suffer the hurts of cutting them off to regain or retain your freedom.

Your moods can swing very abruptly from one extreme to another, even though you may practice detachment from them; likewise your social abilities will cycle up and down. You are able to bridge the gap between yourself and others some of the time, opening your personal boundaries to them, and needing to be alone in your own space at other times, refusing to let anyone else in for any reason. You can change from one to the other at a moment's notice, using your ability to assume an emotional detachment as your prime emotional barrier defense, appearing to be light, easy-going, relaxed in feeling—even playing the fool while not letting your guard down or letting anyone get too close to you. Yet you need a bunch of people to identify with, a group that gives you a sense of who you are, an identity beyond your own skin. The question obviously is, "why do you feel the need to keep yourself separate from others while wanting to be a part of them?"

NEPTUNE IN CANCER

Neptune was in the sign of Cancer from 1901 to 1916, so its effects in the sign apply to the whole generation born at that time, while its house placing is more completely personal.

During its passage through Cancer: hormones were first discovered (Cancer deals with the glandular system); William James published *The Varieties of Religious Experience* (Neptune represents our connectedness to the collective unconscious or the mystical face of reality), Australia gave women the vote, Mrs. Pankhurst founded the Women's Social and Political Union, night shift work was forbidden for women (Cancer is the archetypal woman as in the "Great Mother"); social protections began to emerge against unscrupulous business practices, as in the American Pure Food and Drugs Act, and investigations of massive business frauds (Cancer is the nurturing and protective sign).

During the whole of this period, Neptune and Uranus were in opposition, shown in the turbulent changing and dissolving of national boundaries, frequent revolutions of subject peoples, increasing vulnerability of nations leading to World War I and the Russian Revolution, both of which marked the world that emerged from this era; as did the scientific advances of the time, for Einstein published his special theory of relativity in 1905 and the general theory in 1915, which have changed our understanding of the nature of this universe, and have irrevocably changed our lives (nuclear fission, the atomic bomb, nuclear fusion, the hydrogen bomb).

Where your character has been particularly marked by Neptune's position, you may have a deep-rooted love of the people and environments with which you identify, with a boundless desire to nurture them, to protect and enfold them against any harsh invading conditions. But you also feel that your special territories are very vulnerable to forces of change from outside, that their (your?) protective boundary limits are fragile and easily eroded away. The major attacking force is that of change—social and political change at least—possibly more personal kinds of change. If you have resisted it, you may have excluded the changing world around you and live in an isolated dreamland, keeping the uncomfortable outside your safe ground; if you haven't resisted it, you have feared the loss of your security and of the outer ground of your identity, fearing being swept away in the flood.

You may have protected yourself against such fears by assuming a mask of indifference, of "I don't care," preferring the loss of feeling that attitude demands, to admitting to the turbulence of having to react to a very changing world. Or you may have kept the most positive face of this pattern open, and be able to admit to how much you care about the people and the places of your world, giving out your sympathy and compassion to them in healthy and fully humanitarian ways. If you have done this, your receptivities are enormous, giving you a sizable psychic potential.

PLUTO IN CANCER

Pluto was in Cancer from 1914 to 1939. Its move into this sign marked the outbreak of World War I, and the form of fighting involved showed very Cancerian characteristics. Cancer rules the home and family, and the war was between the "Fatherland" and the "Mother country." If you think of the symbol of Cancer, the Crab, living in or by water, with its defensive tenacity and the way it moves with a sideways progress, this can be seen in the action in the muddy trenches of Europe, with very slow forward progress and much side-stepping movement. Cancer is associated with the alveoli of the lungs, the part attacked by the poison gases. Tanks were used for the first time, being the shell of the Crab; it is known as a water sign, and Pluto deals with the depths, and submarine warfare began.

This period included times of great hardship, first the war with the consequent breakup of families and loss of young men, followed by the depression with years of starvation level living, the Fascist era of dictators and political bigotry, in the United States the gangster era, and then the build-up of tension prior to World War II. Your years of growing up will have been marked by these things to some degree.

The psychology involved is of defense of boundaries, whether national borders or personal physical or psychological territories. The fight is to maintain security within and keep perhaps deadly threat out. You keep your security by hanging on to the familiar (*e.g.*, family) and excluding the unfamiliar. You cling to commonplaces of the reality absorbed from your parents in your early life, deploring changes which erode that pattern of life away (that life included a powerful but invisible demand for everyone to conform to an unstated set of social rules, with automatic rejection for those who transgressed them). You fight tenaciously to hold your own ground, perhaps using intensity of moods to deflect unwanted approaches from others. You may hang on to memories of how much better everything was in "the good old days," thereby excluding the new and the here-and-now. Or you may simply have been trapped in the conformity pressures of your time, having to keep your real being invisible to defend yourself against rejection.

But Pluto has a habit of shattering the status quo, and in this time many old boundaries (national and social, political and economic) disappeared or were penetrated. Old securities were lost as the reality of the world was transformed. The foundation of society and of science changed, partly through increasing industrialization and mass-production. The period also marked the development of women's movements toward freedoms undreamed of by previous generations as they fought their traditional roles in a patriarchal or male-dominated society. Those women born after this time are unlikely to be confined again in the way their predecessors were. Women the world over began to emerge into many fields in which they had never before been involved, with professional women intruding into the previously secure male domains of power.

As Pluto remains in any sign for such a long time, there is little purely individual significance about the sign placement. It sets the survival patterns for the whole generation. A study of the house Pluto is found in will give you more personal information.

CANCER NORTH NODE—CAPRICORN SOUTH NODE

You have quite a strong need for recognition by others and aim for prestige and dignity. You may even marry to achieve social status and recognition. You are capable of burdening yourself with responsibilities and obligations in order to gain this recognition, often making your work harder that it actually is to this purpose. Needing recognition, you find it very hard to tolerate failure in yourself, and have a rather reserved form of morality. You can be self-righteous and condemn the actions of others—though you can keep this to yourself—for you would not like others to know that you have been secretly judging them in order to maintain your own superiority.

Fear of being inadequate or being found to be inadequate makes you build a wall around yourself. If anyone tries to break in you build the wall higher. You can be ambitious, calculating, and manipulative of self and others in your pursuit of a goal, and allow no personal weakness to prevent you from achieving it. You have learned to manipulate the laws to your own advantage in order to prove your own capabilities. Now your need is to develop a deep regard for others, using the responsibilities you know how to gain to nurture them. This often means that you may assume very strong family burdens, enabling you to help others along.

You will now find that there is more security in being honest and open about your emotions, in not clinging to materialistic goals but to family relationships that can allow you to express your need to be close to others. You will find that you are changing from appreciating power, position and prestige, to appreciating closeness and warmth. The more you are able to give to others, the more you will find that you will overcome the depression of a self-imposed separation from them.

SUN IN THE 4TH HOUSE

You are strongly attached to your home and family, particularly your mother, gaining personal identity, security and self-respect from their approval and recognition, and losing pride if you don't get it. You strengthen your sense of identity in a daily self-renewal by reviewing your memories, telling yourself and others the story of your life. You identify with and store up the past to strengthen your character. Where your pride is negative, you reinforce it by remembering personal hurts with resentment; if positive, by remembering the good times, the love, attention, and personal boosts that you received. Whichever the case, you cherish and nurture your pride inside a modest guardian defense, storing firmness, even tenacity and determination within an outer gentleness and adaptability. Your territorial instincts are fierce and you can roar out in defending whatever you identify with, again—particularly your family. You do not allow anyone to invade your borders or to get inside you, though you may be magnanimous in opening your doors to them, when you want to. In fact you have a great deal of sometimes tyrannical instinctual power held in restraint, kept civilized and ordered by a framework of habit.

You need recognition and reactions from others, and you know how to get them to react to you in the way that you want, by talking a lot, for example. Needing to identify yourself with others, you tend to cling to them, allowing them at least part way inside your personal territorial boundaries, turning them into your extended family. You love your home life, and (male or female) may be a good cook, or domestically creative in other ways, becoming the nurturing parent yourself, caring for and nourishing—giving your family or yourself what your mother gave you to make you feel secure. You may also be very self-indulgent, perhaps feeding unsatisfied childhood needs, for the breast (food and drink), for comfort, or for attention. You can also be quite moody, especially when you don't get what you want.

Your mother had a strong personality, proud, autocratic, and rather dominant, normally being the center of attention, and taking the lead in most circumstances. Generally sunny and cheerful, she had a sense of honor and rightness and usually acted from it, preferring to be causative and creative, to make things happen. At worst she may have been overbearing, forceful, and arrogant, overriding everyone else in keeping her position as number one. She could lose sight of others' rights, ignoring them in getting her own way. She ruled herself, and if anyone else tried to rule her, without her consent, they would have had trouble on their hands.

Your father's pride entered directly into his relationships, and if positive, he promoted the welfare of others as much as he did his own, recognizing them as equals. He was capable of great charm and diplomacy, tactfully deferring to others, no matter what their status. If negative, his relationships were pride battles as he tried to gain superiority by putting others down. Instead of tact, he used tactics to end up in the position that he wanted to have relative to his opponents.

MOON IN THE 4TH HOUSE

You have a powerful need for security, for deep roots, for a sense of belonging to someone or something outside yourself. You identify with people and places as a support for your own sense of identity. This is probably because your mother was very protective toward you, acting to keep you safe from what she regarded as harmful environmental influences. Your dependency on her left you ill at ease without someone else to look after you, to act as a mirror to you, telling you who and what you are and reassuring you.

Your feeling for, and need for home, family, mother, and the familiar ground of stable domestic circumstances runs very deep indeed. Much of this pattern grew from your own deep receptivity to all the influences that surround you, and your powerful emotional responses to them, which show themselves as strongly variable moods, your endocrine system being quite active.

You will find that your sense of smell is well-developed and that passing aromas readily trigger your memory and your emotions, recalling situations long past. You recall the past frequently as a method of reaffirming your sense of identity. The sense of smell is particularly sensitive to the hormonal traces put out by people and is directly linked to the whole glandular system, triggering it to respond with similar secretions. A whiff of adrenalin from someone, for example, triggers your adrenal glands to produce, putting you into their mood. This is a part of the herd instinct, which is designed to keep groups of creatures all in the same emotional state, relative to their environment. You respond very readily to such environmental influences, present or past. The present circumstances encouraging you into the local group mood. Past influences, such as intense feelings once held within a particular room, will also bring a strong response from you so that you have an almost psychic sense of what has occurred in the places that you visit.

Your territorial instinct is strong, demonstrating itself in your need to have the boundaries of your personal space (whether around your body, your own home, or whatever space you identify with) well-defined and probably well-protected. Your personal boundary limits may extend out to include the whole country, producing quite a patriotic attitude in you.

Your receptivity and need to reflect the attitudes of others has probably made you into a natural mimic, conscious or unconscious. If conscious, you can probably copy others' mannerisms very well indeed; if unconscious, you will automatically take on the accents, attitudes, and gestures of those around you. Since you are very retentive you do not easily let go of attitudes or possessions which you gain; thus your personality could become a clutter of various acquired elements and your home full to overflowing with your collections.

Your emotional responsiveness and strong protective instincts can make you a natural parent. You like to nourish and protect others just as you like to be looked after by others. Your moods cause difficulties as they swing, for you build emotional barriers around you in self-defense, keeping others out when you do not feel secure, entrenching yourself deeply. To you, as your mood changes, the whole world seems to change to match.

MERCURY IN THE 4TH HOUSE

You tend to swing strongly between security and insecurity, and between needing security and pulling away from it. Sometimes you know that you want to depend on others, and at other times you want to depend on yourself alone. In this your moods change quite rapidly, often returning to feel the needs you had as a child, which can hold you back from developing emotionally. You may turn this around, thinking that it is the needs of others in your family that hold you back. You get "butterflies" through uncertainty about whether things are going to turn out all right, as you are pulled between hope and the possibility of disappointment.

Your mind keeps replaying the past, at least in ideas, rerunning everything that taught you how to be who you are now, your parents' child. In talking you are likely to recycle memories, sharing them in conversation to give you a common bond, or reminding those in the family of shared experience. One of your major needs is for open communication, to talk and to be understood by others. This may have begun when you were two to five years old, and had trouble getting your words in order and making others understand you. You need to feel that others will listen to you, becoming more secure if you are communicating well, but you worry about being misunderstood. You feel insecure if no one is talking, particularly if you are left feeling that you are not worth talking to.

You mentally review what you are about to say, rehearsing and rearranging the words to say it the right way, and then perhaps say it in the same fashion, expressing it in two or three different ways. Your habits of thinking are similar; you recycle your thoughts, bringing themes back again and again; your logic can go around in a circle of "if this, then that—if that, then this." You also tend to replay past conversations, worrying about whether you were understood, "what did they think when I said that?" With your uncertainty in self-expression, you are quite ready to give way to others' ideas, being modest about your own, at least on the surface, but hanging onto them inwardly.

Other things that frequently occur with Mercury in the 4th House are: living for at least a short period in your childhood with other people, or between two homes—not making for a strong territorial security; leaving home eventually as an adult, and returning more than once, thus shifting from independence to dependency, back and forth. Using talking (a lot?) as your territorial defense, to define your own personal space, or to divert others if they approach private territory of any kind.

Your mother was a nervously active person, getting around a lot, making connections and visiting people. She tended to say one thing and then do another, feeling that what she said was the more important, then backing down or changing her mind. Thus she was inconsistent, and possibly quite split in her directions or her personality. Your father appreciated light intellectual relationships and the exchange of ideas, though he may not really have known whether or not he wanted to be involved. He would go back and forth between being talkative and silent, between thinking of others and thinking of himself.

VENUS IN THE 4TH HOUSE

You felt, for part of your childhood at least, that your family was a loving, supporting, and protecting one, and that you could depend quite happily upon them. If things remained this way you will still be closely involved with them, your relationships being close and nurturing. If not, then you have made the difficult decision along the way not to keep your close ties with them. You prefer a peaceful domestic life in which you can have your (preferably pleasant and harmonious) relationships and your pleasures happily at home, finding that you have to make a distinct effort to go out. Secure boundaries are important to you, within which to hold all that you treasure, beyond which to keep all friction and unpleasantness. These are emotional boundaries too; being very receptive to every influence from others, you have to get to know them quite well before they will be allowed inside and you can show them what you like and value most. You maintain your territorial security by keeping others on the other side of a barrier of charm and pleasantness, until you love them enough to let them inside. The same was probably true throughout your family. You move from fear of others to free acceptance. You need support and affection from others to feel secure, very much needing to be liked or loved, but it must be stable affection; otherwise it makes you more insecure, and your moods then swing exactly in time with the swings of your relationships.

To keep yourself happy, you will cast your memory back to the better times of the past, recalling how much enjoyment and affection there was then. If that doesn't work, then you forget the past and instead feed yourself with your special pleasures, with those foods and experiences that have come to mean security and love to you, or you try to re-create that love in whatever other way has become normal to you. You may have been, or perhaps still are, the darling of the family, or of one parent in particular; so in your relations with others you have a special relationship to try to recreate. Even if you have become quite independent in other ways, you are in danger of clinging to others for a past security that has nothing to do with them.

Your mother herself probably needed a lot of attention from others, while she actually gave as much or as little affection as she felt like giving, in spite of the circumstances rather than because of them. She preferred to keep everything in the family pleasant, avoiding disharmony and disruption and becoming very uncomfortable if they occurred. While she wanted to lead her own life, she could cling to others for fear of being left alone.

Your father's feelings and reactions were easily swayed by the world and the people around him, and he would rather do things with others than on his own. He would try to please others and be agreeable, charming and diplomatic, wanting to be thought well of by them, yet could swing to the opposite extreme and deliberately be annoying and argumentative. These may have been his public and private faces, or both have been seen within your family. Thus relating to him was a push-pull affair of continual readiness to adjust to his swings.

MARS IN THE 4TH HOUSE

Your energy levels and ability to act in your own interests vary in a cycle along with your moods. On the upswing you can use your initiative fairly directly to pursue and fulfill your needs, while on the downswing you would rather have others act for you while you go into a moodily aggressive withdrawal.

While you were a child your mother held the initiative, being energetic and direct (perhaps thoroughly argumentative), usually acting for you—thus taking your initiative away from you. Since she was probably pushy she may have shoved you into action when you didn't feel like it, and would have preferred to hang onto her for security. One way or another your actions depended on her. This may have been frustrating, leading to battles of will between you, conflicts of interest and of direction, leaving you feeling that if you wanted your own way you would have to approach it indirectly to avoid being stopped or diverted. You learned to sidle towards your objectives, which you cling to with great persistence on your upswing, losing energy and interest on your downswings. Your father's example, of going along with what mother wanted, probably didn't help you much.

As an adult you probably still expect others to push you into action, or encourage you to get on with things, thus getting mother's love for you, and keeping you in the position of a dependent child, battles and all. You may want to depend on yourself but are dependent on others, preferring that they have the responsibility for your actions. Your initiative is driven by your feelings and instincts, especially your need for acceptance, instead of being under conscious control, and you tend to use aggression as an emotional shield, a personal territorial defense, matching the aggression in your early home life. You don't like anyone trespassing on your territory, being ready to fight them off. Thus your own parental instincts can be strong and fierce, children being your territory. For women, the child becomes the prime focus of attention, while men are likely to resent attention being taken away from them; otherwise their fighting instincts to protect home and family are aroused.

You are likely to take either a parent or a child role in relationships, tending to make ties with those either much younger or much older than yourself. In the first case you can take the lead yourself, in the second you depend on the other to take the initiative. You are also likely to need family approval for your actions, or are at least directly aware of the nature of your family's opinion of what you do (some battle with their families, becoming isolated from them, while others act almost solely within the family circle). Since the aim of your actions is toward personal security, you are likely to work to own your own home, and may well prefer to build it yourself, to have it exactly as you want it.

You have a problem in starting anything new, usually acting to maintain the past to keep familiar things and states perpetuated, yet when you actually do begin a new endeavor you are capable of great tenacity in pursuing it, in so doing often being able to rebuild the foundation of your own life, so that it actually does depend on yourself and not on anyone else for security.

JUPITER IN THE 4TH HOUSE

You have a tendency both to build emotional walls to protect the confidence that you need for security, and to keep breaking them down as you need more room to move and grow. This varies with your mood swing as your trust goes from high to low levels. On the low end, you hold onto memories of the good times in the past—in your early life—when you were fully approved of, the center of positive attention. Then you seek that kind of appreciation from others to boost your well-being, needing recognition from them to restore your confidence. Or you become very angry at all the injustices that you felt were done to you. In these states you can be over-emotional, though you don't always show this on the surface, preferring to display positive feelings. On the high end of your moods you want to go out, to stretch your personal boundaries and experience more of the world around you, to explore fresh territory. At these times your security depends more on the future or growth prospects that you can see developing not being frustrated by outer circumstances, knocking your confidence back.

As a child you needed your home and family as a safe base from which to roam, and to which to return to store up confidence. You did not like narrow limits being placed on you, fighting them if they were, and for the most part you had freedom to move. When emotions flared in your home, you would often run away, preferring to escape rather than face them, even when you were the cause. In memory you may be clinging to what you consider to be past injustices, actually blowing them up out of proportion to the actual events; that is, you expand your subjective view of life, putting yourself under the microscope, until you see your standpoint in exaggerated perspective rather than as it was, your awareness being almost purely focused within yourself. If this negative side of you is strong you will be given to wild mood swings; your hopes and enthusiasms soaring high, then collapsing into depressions in which you exaggerate your personal needs and desire to be looked after.

On the positive side, your restless nature may to lead you to travel, this position of Jupiter frequently indicating living in foreign countries for a time. Less restlessness and you would be more inclined to move your home to another part of the country, or to live out in the country or in large houses where you have room to move. Another alternative is living on a hillside where the view is wide enough and the air fresh enough to satisfy you. You are likely to prefer to live in large, open homes with plenty of trees around them.

Your mother was probably an outspoken person, having either a frank, extroverted and gregariously cheerful nature, or a morally overbearing one in which she would not have admitted to being wrong. She would have been quite free with her advice, most likely encouraging you to stand up for yourself and trying to pass on some of (at least what she considered to be) her broad experience, perhaps over-forcefully.

Much of your father's confidence would have depended on how his relationships with others were going, and he may have expended a lot of effort on being genially agreeable. He would have been capable of flaring up if he felt that others were not being open and honest with him, didn't like him, or he was being suppressed, yet his attitudes to them may have included a certain amount of bluff.

SATURN IN THE 4TH HOUSE

As a child you may have been required to help rather a lot in the home, having rather strict parents with firm beliefs in your need to learn the essentials of discipline and self-control.

You probably felt somewhat restricted in your early life, as if the weight of the world was resting on your shoulders. As a youngster you were no doubt rather grown-up for your age, your family requiring conformity to their expectations, and being capable of making you feel quite guilty if they didn't get it. Their coolness of self-expression may have made you feel unworthy or inferior, instead of your simply seeing it as a quality of their personalities. Your home would probably have been marked by regularity, for example in timing of meals, and meal times may have been an ordeal, with total propriety and discipline being expected of you. If you were often in a state of fear at the table, your digestion will have cut off, and you may now have the physiological habit of a slow digestion if you still retain some of the old fear.

Your need for security would demand that you own a home of your own. You would be very discontented in rented homes, and don't feel that you belong unless you own something. This is a reflection of a need to be in complete control of your own security base so that no one else can dominate you by being in control of it.

You would be very careful about your plans for your old age security, as you would dislike very much to be a burden to others as you age. You feel that maturity demands you depend upon yourself, not on others. However you should try not to cut yourself off from your family as you grow old because this would make them, as well as you, very unhappy. You do have a tendency to wall yourself off in conservatism because of your lack of self-worth and feeling that others won't like you (a very self-proving attitude).

You are instinctively conservative, cautious and doubtful, holding back on the expression of your feelings. You control your actions by restraint, and control what you receive from others by an unconscious manipulation of their responses, probably learned from a self-controlling mother. Somewhat reserved, you tend to be very aware of the implied rules and regulations in any circumstances, *e.g.,* whose place it is, what rights you may have there (usually taking a self-limiting view), who has precedence over you and others.

You can cling to negative views for a long time, these views emerging from your inferiority feelings, making you feel that you are worthless and undeserving; the longer you continue to be self-denying, the greater your depression will become. Your greatest need is for order in you life, for security of a solid and tangible kind, and for recognition from your family. You particularly need to be without guilt, to overcome the feeling that you have fallen from grace. You need to be able to broaden your horizons, not to keep yourself within narrow limits.

You may take an interest in genealogy or other forms of family history because you like to feel that your roots go a long way back into the past, especially if you can find any noble connections with your family, since some elements of your family are likely to have an element of snobbery or an awareness of social status.

URANUS IN THE 4TH HOUSE

Your attitude toward your security is an independent one. You prefer not to depend on anyone else to supply your needs, valuing your freedom to look after yourself. Many things that others regard as essential to security—a stable home, regular meals, someone to look after them, ties with the past—you may feel you can do without, saying "I don't need them." You were probably the same during your childhood, not letting anyone do things for you that you could do yourself, and liking to roam independently in your home area (on your bicycle?), not liking any limits placed on your territorial boundaries. In fact you feel trapped if any such limits are made and are likely to break out of them quite rapidly.

If Uranus has difficult aspects, your independence is a tense, mistrustful withdrawal from depending on support from home, family, mother; wariness of being trapped in situations that erode your freedom, or that once broke your trust. You have a deep need for support, and probably can't admit to having that need. The need surfaces in abrupt, cranky mood changes—swinging instantly from apparent detachment to tense rebellious anxiety—and in a rapid jumping from one security (or mother) substitute to another, short bursts of clinging followed by pulling away (the moth and the flame), if Uranus is in a mutable sign.

Your wariness of being trapped may come from your personal space being invaded as a child, maybe by a dominant parent, perhaps by having to share your room. If so you probably assumed an indifference or detachment to it. The breaking of your trust of your mother may have happened through her having to be away from you when you were very young, when you had to repress your deep need for her because it hurt too much to feel it.

Your early home life may have been active and bustling with many people passing through (security for you = being surrounded by activity and people); or isolated (security = being entirely alone); or an aloof and detached atmosphere, family members being isolated individuals (security = maintaining your separation); or your family broke up (security = being warily independent). Your security feelings depended on your mother's personality which was either friendly, idealistic, active, and independent; detached; or abrupt, rebellious and impatient—and perhaps a mixture. Your moods will reflect whichever she was. Often Uranus in the 4th House shows that the endocrine system "smell bond," usually built at birth between mother and child, was not established, leaving your mother with her maternal instinct switched off; and you grew up feeling the lack.

The style of your own home will be either modern electrical/electronic with plenty of gadgets and definitely room for a car or two; or alternative society/idealistic, back to nature and independent of outside power and resources; or your own very individualistic design, maybe mobile; or perhaps "I don't care," if you can't admit to security needs.

Your awareness of your environment is either very alert, rapidly scanning all facets of it and interested in all, or is detached—rather cut off, leaving you isolated in yourself. Your basic understanding of the nature of the reality around you, and of your relationship to it, is quite likely to go through some changes.

NEPTUNE IN THE 4TH HOUSE

Your life as a baby with your mother may have been fairy-tale ideal, close, sensitive, loving. Breast euphoria left you drifting in reflective reverie, floating in a meditative dream state, losing personal boundaries totally. This left you able to empathize with and nurture any living creature, sensitive to their moods and security needs, compassionately ready to fulfill them. Or mother left you alone a lot, making you very vulnerable and insecure, empty and alone, confused about what you ought to be to belong, given to chaotic mood swings—pulled by any passing tide!

Your mother had images of what she preferred her life to be and noticed every time that it was not, possibly covering things over, camouflaging them to keep up appearances, feeling martyred by events. Even her personality may have been an act, a camouflage defense, and thus unreal. As a child you were directly aware of this but confused by it, but you naturally absorbed and may use the same tendencies yourself as an emotional defense. "What mother does in self-defense is safe(ty) for me." Thus you can be be emotionally evasive, confusing, ever changeable, and inconsistent. Your mother's personality left you emotionally soft, whether for good or ill.

Your home was either peacefully empty and secluded, a place of warm hospitality, or thoroughly chaotic, with no system, pattern, or order. You may dream about the ideal home, the perfect living circumstances, and you could want to create gracious living to express the beauty that you feel so much, within your own home, or be compassionately hospitable. You are likely to live by water, or in an institutional home at some time, whether orphanage, monastery, sanitarium, boarding school, or whatever.

Your memory could be photographic (and probably was, early in your life), capable of bringing back all the emotional tones of a past time in depth, especially the euphoric times; for example, those times when you blended in completely with nature, or recollecting your intense response to color (*e.g.,* blue bottle glass in sunlight). Your memory is extremely responsive to your sense of smell, a vagrant whiff re-evoking a whole past time in full emotional flavor. Or it may have become confused by your imagination, taking memories and playing with them, perhaps to recreate the past as you would have preferred it to be, or it has been confused by others contradicting your memories, or you may remember selectively in terms of the martyrdoms that you feel you have suffered.

Your moods are subtle, ranging from dissolution into nature (misty mornings in autumn, light on water) including great tenderness, the soul of the poet or mystic; to a vague abstraction, drifting and losing awareness of your surroundings to the point of easily getting lost; to being vulnerable and lonely, becoming paranoid at the very worst; to a boundless vague discontent. Being by water helps you to balance yourself, keeping you fully in touch with your feelings, whether you appreciate them or not.

Your personal reality may be something of a fairy-tale, gentle, romantic, imaginative, being your feeling of how life should be. You also have a fragile territorial defense, a feeling of helplessness at having your personal space invaded by others.

PLUTO IN THE 4TH HOUSE

You keep your feelings extremely well hidden, but they are very powerful and even obsessional. You hide them because of your deep receptivity to pain, particularly the pain of rejection, which you are likely to have felt from your mother while growing up, or the pain of being possessed by her to the point of not being allowed a personality of your own, or perhaps from a tragedy in the home. You contain your pain, keeping it to yourself, building strong protective emotional boundaries around any suffering that you feel, effectively around yourself, maybe growing up thinking that no one wanted you. (Stomach ulcers can develop if you suppress this pain for too long.) You either brood on the past, remembering the worst parts of it, or slam your mental doors upon it, refusing to acknowledge that it is there; whichever the case you probably still have your feelings fixed around it. You will either be clinging to the past, however painful, for some form of security, or will have cut off all roots and connections with it. Real transformation of your feelings and your life will come when you can truly let go of the past.

You like to hide things—even your house could be hidden from public view behind trees or high fences, for example. You like secret places and need a lot of total privacy. Tunnels or underground caverns could appeal to you. All of these are symbolic expressions of your need to hide your feelings from view—effectively hiding your real self. You hide rage, bottling it up and never letting it out, thus building up a tremendous pressure inside which can eventually wreak havoc upon your body if not released. You hide your most intense needs from others and quite possibly from yourself, afraid that you will be hurt or rejected if you show them, but becoming agonizingly frustrated and self-pitying when they aren't met, and resentful that others don't see them and rescue you. You have a dissatisfied child inside you, and you probably don't like that part of yourself, leading to still more frustration and self-rejection. Your attitudes here were trained by your mother, being copies of, or reactions to, her personality.

She was a strong and capable person, efficient but not soft, intolerant of many things. Her personality was, in part, a defensive system designed to protect herself from rejection, so she could not show weakness or admit to being vulnerable. She could be hard and cutting, attacking before she was attacked, or keep up a silent emotional barrier that allowed no one within hurting distance of her. Naturally you needed closeness and warmth from her, but the strength of her feelings and their rejecting edge hurt you. So you felt that if you were to get the love that you needed, you would have to be hurt first; or felt that such hurt was love. You may have buried all your feelings about her, or your security needs, and so not understand what I am saying.

Beyond all that, you may like to dig into family secrets, or research family trees. There are likely to be dramatic transformations in your home situation over the years, perhaps meaning deaths in the family, or constant alterations of the home; it could be a transformation of your feelings changing your whole response to, and relationships with, your family (forgiving them?). You are likely to have an interest in matters pertaining to ecology, or earth sciences, and could become a very good gardener, given the right incentives.

NORTH NODE, 4TH HOUSE—SOUTH NODE, 10TH HOUSE

You seek security in recognition by others, being depressed and unhappy if such recognition is lacking. You want to be up toward the peak of any hierarchy you enter, representing solid social values, taking on responsibility for others and being in control. You become so concerned with maintaining the dignity of your assumed role that you do not display the real person underneath it, feeling that the achievement you are aiming for is more important than maintaining close emotional roots with others.

This drive for the power of position often hides an unadmitted desire for parental affection, (perhaps especially from one demanding parent) changed into the need for the adulation and approval of society. Any recognition gained or status achieved is usually not enough since it never brings that simple security of affection from loved ones. Your maturity begins with the recognition of this need and develops with your ability to climb down from your lonely mountain peak to join with ordinary people in domestic love. You are moving from dominating your world to simply accepting it, from taking control of everything to just letting it be. Instead of being an authority among authorities, you are becoming a person among people.

✧ 7 ✧

Leo
and the 5th House

Roughly between the ages of four and seven years (earlier for fast developers, later for slow), children experience a surge of energy. Their egos are forming as they learn what is and isn't secure in life, and what they themselves can and cannot be according to the reality allowed them by their parents and culture. Having built the habits or basic personality that will handle their security, they then use what free energy is left to continue the exploration of world and self through play.

The archetypal game at this time is "I'm the King of the Castle (hill, mountain, whatever), and you're the dirty rascal." The child is establishing who and what he/she is, partly by making distinctions between self and other, and by building a defense of selfhood, a set of personal boundaries excluding the other; partly also by practicing a consistent response to circumstances. Many games are played at this time which both explore possible personal roles, helping the child to grow into and build useful personal identities within the varied areas of experience in life, and help in dealing with anxieties, in learning to defend the inner self if it is embattled in any way.

The games include "doctors and nurses" (for children who have had personal contact with the medical profession, usually difficult), "mothers and fathers" (for most), "cowboys and Indians" (to establish territorial dominance, and identify with winners in life), and many others as exercises in designing personal identities from culturally available material. In the games (and generally) we give identity to everything we experience, not just to ourselves; we apply single labels (such as "I") to clusters of experience.

Some of the child's activities are designed to attract attention by performing, "Look at me, look at me, look at what I can do!" The child needs attention as a plant needs sunlight, and will wither without it. This need may make the child try to overshadow others, vying for its parent's attention against its brothers and sisters, perhaps being resentful of those who take the needed attention away from it. The need only becomes strong and self-centered if the child has not been given the affirming attention, the love, that it needs.

In the process of learning to become a conscious self, we create in our minds boundaries of separation from the other, definitions of personal territory. We do so by the tagging of those things that we recognize as "Ours" as being *self*, and "Theirs" or "Not-Self" as *other*. The ego, or consciousness of selfhood, itself grows and fixes at boundaries between self and other, between inner and outer, as we learn to define which is which. These boundaries may be narrow or wide, from "I am nothing" to "I am everything," which often springs directly from an earlier sense of self-value ("I am worth nothing/ everything"). However they are set, they are expressions of the amount and kind of self-respect that the individual has. Life cannot be lived effectively with poor self-respect. Where it is healthy, the individual does not expect rejection, but rather expects acceptance, since this is what he/she has already received. It is rejection (whatever the kind) from parents and others that damages our self-respect, and may impel us to try to gain acceptance from others, *e.g.*, lovers—perhaps having lost the belief that others will ever love us. We may feel impelled to seek love because of feeling the lack of it, otherwise we will let the lover into our heart through total acceptance.

The capacity for love of both self and others grows with love well-given and well-received in parental nurturing, or friendship. We can call it the capacity for "heart." The full heart extends out beyond the self to the world; the empty heart is isolated within the self, through lack of love given and received. Self-respect depends on your capacity to give warmly and honestly *of* yourself, including *to* yourself.

A healthy sense of selfhood allows us to put ourselves into anything that interests us, to let our sense of play, our creativity run free. ("I enjoy doing this, expressing myself this way, therefore I do it often.") A healthy ego also includes a sense of honor; if our self-respect is intact we won't act in any way that gives us a poor opinion of ourselves. But if our pride has been damaged and self-respect shattered, we may feel worthless and undeserving, forming our sense of self around the feeling, and may not feel like extending ourselves or our creative drives at all. Or we may fight against the damage and boost our pride back aggressively in overcompensating self-inflation, perhaps becoming destructive rather than creative in the process. We may then feel "how much can I get away with?" and ignore honor, rather than "what more can I explore?"

If happy in ourselves, we keep extending our boundaries of experience into all that interests us, so we keep on growing as people. Then we will either choose a personal ground of growth and pursue it intently (many major performers, musicians, and dancers began their training during this period of life), or take as our task the exploration of many areas of experience, being a nomad rather than a householder. If our self-view has been hurt, we either passively retire into ourselves to shut the world out, but then feel hemmed in; or we actively push ourselves onto the world, extending our personal territories (security boundaries) outwards, sometimes riding over those of others in spates of empire-building. In this we may be expressing our desire for others to orbit around ourselves, instead of our having to orbit around them.

Remember that we lay the foundation for and begin establishing all these ego attitudes between four and seven years of age. Children are frequently held within the personal ego-boundaries (empires) of parents as extensions of themselves, or simply protected within their nurturing outreach, the area covered by their parenting instinct. This is the 2nd or potentially possessive house from the 4th, the parental instinct.

The ego forms at psychological and physical boundaries, at places of definition of the difference between self and other. These boundaries are places where the traffic passes in and out, where the world pours in, and self pours out. They are also filters, for we decide (not always consciously) what we want to let in or out, what we want to show of ourselves, and to receive from others. This ego-boundary pattern is why the immune system (fully personalized only by the age of seven when the ego is structured) works by sampling the surface membranes or boundaries of our cells, for they are where our personal molecular identity coding is formed by that age. And it is why personal identity is felt strongly at the body's surface (its most conscious region), though it can extend to things deeper inside, or further outside self.

The physiology of the 5th House includes the heart, and the blood type, plus the thymus—the gland that provides general immunity until the personal immune system is formed, and may be involved in forming that system. The spine bears a relationship to our pride; if our pride is healthy, our posture is erect and unforced; if damaged, we slump; if we fight the loss, we stiffen our backs, often damaging them.

The thalamus in the center of the brain is the major coordinating and rerouting center for all data coming in from the senses. It is involved in emotion, personality, personal drives, and perception and interpretation of pain. It is capable of acting as a filter—and can be programmed to allow only chosen material through to the pre-frontal cortex and consciousness. But before any data is sent to the cortex it is refined by other lobes of the brain, a 6th House function. The brain organizes all incoming sensory data, for example light and color within retinal areas, touch within areas of skin, area mapping the sensory cells onto a body-surface map or image, making a full sensory self-image.

SUN IN LEO
✧ The Monarch ✧

Individuals born with the Sun in Leo have a strong personality fixing-point in their life between five and seven years of age when the play urge is at its strongest, and when their personal ego is crystallizing. They usually retain their playfulness as creativity and their ego as pride, self-respect or self-approval, all essential to a Leo's well-being.

As a Leo you need to feel that you are a creative center, a coordinating focus for all that goes on around you. Do you remember playing "I'm the King of the Castle" and recall all the ways in which you learned to draw attention to yourself (or tried to)—"Look at me, look at me, look at what I can do?" You must feel that your creative drives belong to you alone. If you are not very creative as an adult, can you remember being stopped in your youth from doing things that you really put your heart into and identified with very strongly; or remember someone else interfering, whether taking over your game, trying to discipline or direct you, taking the credit for it ("my child"), or otherwise spoiling your enjoyment of your special area? If so, can you also remember your stubborn pride refusing to have any more to do with it, thus making it untouchable?

If your self-respect is simple and healthy, then you will respect others as much as you respect yourself. If your pride has been damaged in any way, then you will probably have rebuilt it with some rigidity and exclusiveness—and tend to assume an egotistical, perhaps pompous and patronizing superiority over other people. Healthy pride gives you a sense of honor and a nobility of character, since it is based on a deep personal conscience that allows you to do nothing against it—certainly not to harm others in any way. You have a rather fierce parental protective instinct which you may extend magnanimously as a cloak of protection to those around you, or negatively use it to dominate them and take them over, seeing them only as extensions of yourself. Damaged pride makes you like a wounded cat, ready to lash out at anyone close, your ferocious territorial instinct ready to defend yourself at any cost (to them).

Your feelings run deep and strong; you prefer to enter life with some passion, whether in dramatic self-display (you may like to shine in public), or in love-affairs (which can happen in great bursts of enthusiasm), or the passion of creativity. Any repression of your depth and intensity of feeling puts these drives out of reach, leaving you more indolent and lazy, though your passion can then flare up in roaring anger. An uninhibited Leo is a sunny and extravagant character in all senses of the word; colorful, theatrical, naturally the center of attention, and usually in the center, if not in charge of everything that is going on. An inhibited Leo usually works more on groundless conceit, fixed and unrealistic opinions about themselves, and anything that they identify with or against.

You have a need to expand your area of coverage, your spread of personal interests and involvements, the things in life with which you identify, like a monarch expanding the kingdom. Your life should be one of gaining personal ground or territory.

MOON IN LEO

Leos love to shine, but the Moon shines by reflected light, depending upon something outside itself for its radiance. Your emotional radiance depends perhaps on the attention that you get from others, or on your being open to the wholesome forces of the world around you. Whatever your fuel, with it you shine, without it you burn out. If it depends on others' attention, your happiness is very conditional, unfree.

Your particular emotional armor is to build your pride as a defensive barrier that no one can penetrate, creating a sense of personal superiority, attempting to be beyond reproach or above attack. Thus you may have difficulty admitting to being wrong, or in taking personal advice. If you don't put yourself on a pedestal you are a very warm-hearted person, sunny, giving, and as generous as they come, ready to fight other people's battles for them, and to be fiercely protective of those who need it.

You are strongly territorial, either fiercely defending your own ground against others, keeping them outside your boundaries, (making yourself an exclusive person) or you generously open your borders to others, including them in your own being as much as in your space. You then like to share your territory with others, enjoying company in the comfort of your own surroundings.

Beware becoming self-centered and unaware of the needs of those around you, putting your own needs first. You are able to demand what you want from others, sometimes making them resent having to give it. Usually you are unaware of being selfish, feeling that you are simply positive about your needs while others are less sure of themselves, so that you have every right to go ahead as you wish. The Leo drive to be the center of attention is behind this, but it can be much more humane to use your sense of honor, and give to others all the rights and the respect that you want from them.

Drama is a part of your emotional life, and you may enjoy stage work of some sort, or anything that expresses your abilities in self-display, giving yourself an outlet for your flourishing creativity, and enabling you to enjoy the mundane everyday activities that you might otherwise feel to be boring, lacking the drama that you need. This dramatic flair is an expression of personal pride, meaning that if you pour yourself into anything, you feel it is worth doing with flair, vigor, and color. You can turn the ordinary into full-fledged drama to fulfill this need.

You have excellent qualities for the raising of children, the Moon providing the maternal element, while Leo has the talents necessary to lead children into creative, full and useful lives. You like to spend a lot of time with them, helping with their creative projects or homework, playing your favorite games, giving them the things that you enjoyed or wanted most in your own childhood, to give them a happy emotional foundation for life. You love lazing around, your leisure giving you the emotional refreshment that you need. You are naturally creative and probably spend time making things for your home, children, or for others, and many good dressmakers, interior decorators, or carpenters and other skilled workers, have this placement.

MERCURY IN LEO

Your mind is likely to have a certain playful quality to it, liking to take ideas and explore them creatively to see what can be made out of them. Since your pride enters into your intellectual workings, you like to think in ever bigger terms, perhaps to the point of building up grandiose structures in your mind, and not being particularly concerned with details or smaller concerns.

Since you identify closely with your ideas, your concepts and opinions become fixed around your view of yourself, therefore you polish your concepts up until they shine and are generally not shy about producing them for the benefit and entertainment of others (unless you have lost self-respect along the way). In so doing you may perhaps exaggerate, or become intellectually arrogant, overbearing, dramatic and forceful in speech and expression, though usually you will retain your dignity of expression whatever the circumstances.

You can radiate an appearance of authoritative knowledge, being conscious of what you do know and taking pride in it, though you may become very fixed and self-important, dogmatic or bigoted in your thinking with Mercury under difficult aspects. You could have a dramatic flair with words and ideas, but this trend may show more inwardly in your preferring to think honorable or noble thoughts, or liking to read about heroic and edifying adventure, or considering the achievements of the human spirit, using these things to try to lift yourself above a world that may seem humdrum, into one more to your liking.

Considering what humans are capable of, both good and bad, should set you to examining yourself, to considering what motivates you and whether you measure up to your high intellectual opinions of how you should be. If not, you will deliberately set out to put your own life in order, that is to fit yourself in with the natural order, not to oppose it and create conflict.

You should have a flourishing intellectual creativity, and take pleasure in playing with words or ideas. You probably like to play games of various kinds, especially those that require some thought, logic, or analysis, whether board games, card games or crosswords and other word play. You may have a special appreciation of territorial games, such as chess, Go, war games, and others. If you prefer more active play, it will normally be of the back-and-forth kind, such as tennis, cricket, or games having a continual interplay between two opposed points. On the work front, your creative mind will generally move toward the organizational or managerial level, being of great value in coordinating and planning the efforts and productions of yourself and others into a well-synthesized whole.

You will find your best outlets in areas that take ideas and create concrete realities from them, particularly ones that will affect the larger areas of your environment, or that use your playfulness, such as in teaching children—especially in awakening and encouraging their mental development, keeping their playful curiosity as alive as your own.

VENUS IN LEO

In your relationships with others you are ardent, passionate and proud. You fix the direction of your affections easily, and can be lavish in displaying them, in fact loving a certain amount of theatrical self-display in any relationship. You love play, pleasure, entertainment and enjoyment shared with others, and will probably create extravagant parties and social affairs at which your dramatic flair can show itself at its best, and you can be in the spotlight. You love having your creations and yourself admired and complimented by others, and at worst you may be vain, overly proud and self centered, while at best you are warm-hearted, sunny and outgoing, loving and giving. You love to create beauty, comfort, pleasure, and richness of effect to be shared, particularly in romancing, and you take delight in creating and entering into the more glamorous facets of love affairs.

Since among your values is a preference for honor and perhaps even nobility in your own being, and in your relationships, you enter into them quite passionately, giving most of yourself freely and openly. There is a reserve inside you that watches others to judge the honor and wholeness of their motives, and maybe evaluates yourself against them, or judges them against your values, usually maintaining or boosting your own pride in the process. You can test others to find out whether they are worth relating to, which often means whether you think they are worthy of you. You may choose a partner to relate to on the basis of their social display value, on the power or drama of the effect that you can create as a couple, or how many glamorous trappings you bring together. Otherwise you may like to relate to artistic, or other kinds of creative people, enjoying the feeling of sharing in their talents, and perhaps of sharing your own with them.

Your fixity, passion and pride combine to give you a desire for the *grand amour*, the once in a lifetime great romance into which you can pour the whole of your being. It may be that your love of dramatic display will encourage you to play out the more tragic type of romance, for the theatrical value that it has, and for the supposed nobility of the role that you can play. The motivations for such playing out can be quite unconscious, and will derive from early romantic reading, plays seen, or whatever source—so long as you identified deeply with it at the time. Thus your expressions of feeling and methods of relating may be demanded by the role. Unfortunately your display of power or passion of feeling can frighten away the more conservative and reserved types, or not allow them to get close to you.

At worst you may play out your relationships to gain superiority at your partner's cost, casting them into inferior roles, or inwardly judging them with the same result. Or you see them as extensions of yourself, worth fighting for if necessary, but not recognizing their own need for independent existence, which can make slaves of them, and a mockery of your honor.

MARS IN LEO

Your high-spirited energy and initiative are poured into maintaining your pride, self-respect, and creativity. You have a strong sense of identity that you defend against loss or erosion at all times and under all circumstances, and you can be passionately determined in doing so. It is useful to question whether the self that you defend is truly your own being, or simply who you have learned that you are from early life experience within your family. There is a sizable difference. If you are your own being, your creative energies will simply flow freely without conflict. If you defend your conditioned ego, part of you fights to survive against surrounding armies, part identifies with the invaders in an entrenched territorial struggle. Some of that struggle is for recognition, to act in such ways as to become the center of attention; some is to retain what pride you have left, vigorously, perhaps extending it over wider ground in a kind of empire-building.

Your pride leads you to build large aims in your life in which you seek complete personal fulfillment, since you don't want to be concerned or connected with anything that you judge to be small, mean, or weak, though sometimes being unrealistic in what amounts to an effort at self-glorification. It also makes you prefer to be fair and honorable in all that you do, though you may have a problem at times in avoiding being superior, arrogant, and overbearing. Your desires are passionate and fixed, and in love you can be ardent and fiery, though possibly also jealous and possessive.

You tend to have fixed beliefs and opinions in your effort to stand for firm principles, and you will fight for anything that you identify with, often arousing friction and opposition from others by coming on too strongly, by being too imperious. Because of your effort to keep your pride and the consequent firmness of your opinions, you can't take advice easily from others or admit to being wrong, which leads you at times to act as though you believe you are infallible. Your confident strength in yourself gives you good abilities for leadership, though in a position of command you would probably have a struggle with your internal sense of superiority or desire for dominion over others. The more combative side of your pride can make you set up situations where you are in direct competition with others, even when they aren't competing with you, though you don't readily tolerate losing—even losing ground or losing face.

Obviously your abilities can be fine indeed where you are working from your strong creative drives and from your sense of honor. What you do need to beware is being driven by a fear of loss of self-worth, pride and personal prestige, which can make you self-focused, overly subjective, and possibly selfish. You need to use your persistence and determination to put aside any arrogance and develop an unselfish modesty, realizing that every other person ultimately has the same potentials as yourself. Your creative abilities can be applied with single-mindedness when you are not impelled to compete with others for a supreme position, which, after all, is a form of envy.

JUPITER IN LEO

You have an optimistic and enthusiastic zest for life matched by few, and you can enjoy things in a big way. You like to identify yourself with the larger arenas of action in life, not being interested in anything small, or that you believe to be petty. You prefer to approach everything with a sense of honor and even nobility, keeping the best of good moral intentions for the sake of your own self-respect, and giving of yourself with a flourishingly benevolent generosity. You can be lavish in your pleasures, leaping into things with huge enjoyment and plenty of laughter, loving your leisure and playtime, and probably drawing on large reserves of creative abilities to bring things off with a certain opulent display. Naturally you have a certain affinity for children, since you still retain all of your childhood enjoyment of play yourself, and you probably like to help them open up to and explore their world, giving them as much breadth and richness of experience as you can. You can be kind-hearted, warm, and affectionate.

Where Jupiter has particularly difficult aspects, you are capable of a potentially huge self-inflation, building pride, arrogance, and egotistical superiority. Thus you may be overbearing, often in a moralistic way, imposing your own views on others, cutting across and overriding them in conversation, in your perhaps unstated belief that you know best for yourself and for them, and that they are not worth listening to. You think that you are never wrong, which leads you to jump to conclusions in a lazy and over-general way, perhaps believing that, because you identify yourself with a particular answer, it must therefore be right. If you are ever actually proven to be wrong by someone else, you are likely to blow up in their face, being given to rather extravagantly unrestrained displays of rage—huge, overblown, childlike tantrums. You still dive into things with zest, but seeking self-expansion, gambling and speculating in a spendthrift way, often being quite careless about the possible results. The same pattern is found in your love affairs, which may be remarkable for their numbers as you seek self-gratification through the use of others. If your top-heavy pride is on weak foundations it is bound to fall down. Only when the inflated frog-skin bubble of your arrogance bursts will we find out if there is really a prince inside it.

The most wholesome aspects of this position produce a steady, stable honesty; a quiet self-confidence which needs no outer support; a radiance of faith or trust that is contented with a simple life, riches being found in the giving of one's own being to others. You have a fair potential for leadership through your steadfastness and reliability, your ability to take a large and creative overview in any situation, and your readiness to enter the bigger arenas of life with confidence and self-reliance. You could be capable of organizing on a large, even opulent scale, but are probably at your best where economy is not required.

SATURN IN LEO

On the negative side, you are slow to form a true sense of identity, to realize who you are in any depth, because of persistent self-doubts. Your doubts cause you to need and to seek respect and recognition from others, to gain a better sense of personal importance. Doubting yourself, you find it hard to believe that others like, respect, or love you, which makes your struggle to gain respect (inappropriately) from them particularly difficult, and makes your need all the larger. You have a sense of personal inadequacy and insignificance which you find hard to tolerate (and perhaps to admit to), and may be jealous of all those with more public success than yourself. Resenting those who gain more recognition than you could drive you on toward achievement, so that you can come to feel important, admired and respected, by yourself as much as by others, since your self-respect is low. You need to feel important, powerful and dominant in compensation, which could lead you to be dictatorial and domineering, controlling and commanding (and be puzzled when others don't love you), or to be negative about others in important positions.

You find it hard to show your real self (which you neither know well, nor like much), so you can be stiff and formal socially, or at least controlled, seeking popularity and becoming depressed if not accepted. You can make strenuous efforts at being superior, while actually being shy, both over-inflating and underrating yourself. You build a variety of ego trappings, things that you can display as examples of what you can do, of how creative you are, like a child saying "Look at me, look at what I can do," seeking approval, a pat on the head or a medal. Yet your inner lack of self respect blocks the full flowering of your creativity, which will tend to be formal and rigid, and therefore not fulfilling—working from rules to gain status instead of from playful enjoyment of self-discovery. You find it difficult to relax and play simply, freely and spontaneously, having a stiff sense of your own dignity in an effort to reserve your fragile pride. You may have yourself and your life thoroughly under control so that your pride is protected and doesn't feel fragile, imposing an inner dominance and dictatorship, but it shows up in your need for love, and difficulty in ever feeling that it is there.

You have difficulty expressing affection openly without being certain that it will be returned, and you are never really sure about that. You can take a lot of loving and never be satisfied since you don't feel loved, yet you feel that you can't afford to be ignored. And if you are actually rejected, you may be heart-broken. This may have begun in your early life when you were only given recognition for your formal achievements, for performing, or for how well you met rigid social requirements, and not for yourself as a human being, making any recognition that you got extremely important to you, actually being trained to *be* the social roles that you had to fill, and thus never really identifying with yourself.

Positively, you have the potential for a deep self-respect based on your knowledge of yourself as a responsible and honorable being, with a readiness to aid any other being to find their own self-respect. You are more interested in mastering yourself than anything else, in realizing your full consciousness, and opening your heart to the world.

URANUS IN LEO

Uranus was in Leo between mid-1956 and mid-1962, during which time the world was entering a major creative period of the emerging technological society. The period began with the first satellite launching (Sputnik 1) and ended with Russian cosmonaut Yuri Gagarin (first), and then two American astronauts in space. The first satellite explorations of the Moon and of Venus commenced, and the International Geophysical Year brought the exploration of our own planet into sharp focus. New radio telescopes were exploring the heavens, while the first nuclear submarine traveled under the Arctic ice (the Russians launched a nuclear ice-breaker, and the Americans a nuclear passenger cargo ship). The advances were flamboyant—DNA molecular structure was determined, the first artificial heart pacemaker developed, and chlorophyll synthesized. Nor were the arts left out, with the development of stereophonic recording, the lifting of censorship restrictions in Britain and the United States (*Lolita* and *Lady Chatterly's Lover*), the design and building of Brasilia, and the design and beginning of the Sydney Opera House.

Being born in this period, you insist on being in independently creative command of your own life, as far as is possible, and if it doesn't seem possible, you will make very sure that it becomes so. You won't be overridden by anyone else on anything that concerns you, your self-respect depending upon keeping your full independence and individuality in all circumstances, including, and despite, those times that you defer to others (from your own free decision, of course). You do not permit others to lead you or to direct you, not as superiors anyway, since you do not admit to others ever being superior to you. You may give your respect to someone whom you consider to have accomplished something creatively original in their own right, but you still do not assume that this makes them any better than yourself. You take pride in your independence, in being different—and if you aren't different, you will make yourself become so, "because being the same as everyone else is boring."

You want to become more completely conscious of yourself as a person, to understand who, what and why you are as you are, but your refusal of help from anyone else and insistence on seeing things entirely your own way can easily leave you stuck in a set of attitudes that trap you, stubbornly refusing to consider alternatives, or to be shown anything by anybody else, then blaming your problems onto others. This is particularly so if Uranus had difficult aspects when you were born. You don't like being questioned by others about your own ideas because you hate having to explain yourself to anyone, particularly if there is a chance that you have made a mistake somewhere. You hate to be accountable to any other person for who and what you are, and to be sure that you are who you want to be, you will create all your own standards on anything important to you, and ignore those of society if they diverge from your path, not even really admitting that they exist. In other words you can be thoroughly stubborn in your insistence on having your own way in everything relating to yourself. You keep your personal territorial boundaries well protected against invasion by others.

NEPTUNE IN LEO

Neptune was in Leo from late 1914 to mid 1929, the early part of this period being the changing of fashions from the Victorian-Edwardian era toward the modern style. Fashions became decorative and imaginative, tending toward extravagant display. The arts were in a phase of flourishing creativity with a profusion of new styles and kinds of expression developing, including Dada, Surrealism and Jazz as early forerunners. The movies went through the greatest part of their early growth during this time, ending with the first sound films, and full color. In other words this was the silent, black and white era. Other entertainment developments were the night-club and the cocktail. This was also the period during which C. G. Jung's psychological studies became public knowledge, and a new interest in the archetypal levels of the mind emerged. Jung was a Leo with a strong Neptune.

Being born during this period, your imagination is likely to be highly creative, where you have used and developed it, tending toward a certain extravagance of expression and feeling for dramatic statement, though this may have developed into an ever-refining subtlety of expression. If consciously developed, you use your imagination as a creative tool, building clear images of the end result that you desire, then creatively making it real by following your blueprint. If you live in your imagination at all, you live in a highly colored, vivid and theatrical world, in which you are most probably the main character, playing out the roles that you identify with most strongly, recreating your personality in chameleon-like fashion for the purpose. You have a romantic streak that seeks the one true love in your life, being capable of great and genuine devotion to loved ones. If you use the more developed side of Neptune, you have a generous charitableness, a boundless sense of honor that seeks to promote the best welfare of all beings, pouring yourself out into organized service to others, recognizing that your own being has no final boundaries but actually includes everything and everyone.

If Neptune was under difficult aspects, you may have a rather inflated self-image, fantasy feeding your ego as you enlarge upon all your best qualities. You may boost this fantasy pride by entering upon love-affairs and seeking adoration from your lovers, unconsciously playing out your image of the great romance, or by showing off your creativity and insisting to yourself that you are talented (or by simply dreaming of these things). You may strive for the appearance of success, pride requiring that you out-display everyone else. You may be extravagant in pursuit of pleasure. You may have an inverse conceit, seeing yourself as a noble martyr downtrodden by others, suffering the slings and arrows of outrageous fortune, but of course bearing it with courage and fortitude, in your own eyes. Of course if you have been building self-exalting images you probably won't be aware of the fact, since you would have camouflaged it over in order to make the images more real—more believable by yourself.

Remember that the fullest level of self-acceptance is one that accepts all others equally.

PLUTO IN LEO

Pluto deals with survival instincts, with the mental and physical repression and elimination functions. It also involves the pain sense, and major healing and regeneration elements such as the leucocyte (white corpuscle) system of the body, repression release and consequent transformation of personality. Its motion from one zodiacal sign to another releases repressed, and therefore raw, instinctual, and often hate-charged emotions.

Pluto was in Leo from 1939 to 1957. Its move into this sign marked the outbreak of World War II, and the form of this war is indicative of Leo dramatics. The Thousand Year Reich attempted to purify the world by destroying the "Chosen People," setting out to conquer the whole world, opposed by the Empire; stagecraft and propaganda; Nazi troops and their patriotic indulgence of their self-appointed leader. All that goose-stepping, saluting and display was no help in the fight to conquer the world, but it did make them think that they were unbeatable, a common Leo misconception. The Allies were not free of this grand pageantry either. All sides indulged in extravagant displays of glory, self-justification, and self-gratification, rather along the lines of a major Hollywood movie production. The whole display led up to the development and use of the atomic bomb.

The beginning of this period was marked by great hardship, caused by the war following so closely after the Depression. However, Leo creativity moved into action to rebuild industries, the ensuing time being one of continual growth. This was a time of huge increases in mass production. Once the war was over, the new industrial patterns that were set up continued to extend further.

Public understanding of psychology, of ego development, of repressions and how they work, of the potentially transformative power of the unconscious, became more general, as did psychotherapy. This whole generation is aiming at a conscious transcendence of self-limiting egotism as it grows, and thus wrestling with the serpent of raw instinctual drives, sometimes losing and being swallowed up.

Personally, you have an intense pride which you use as a survival defense. If it is damaged (if Pluto had difficult aspects), you stiffen your pride to become rigid around the point of pain, even if this cramps you into uncomfortably limited personality postures. You are capable of being arrogant, of using an explosive temper (roaring like a lion), of satisfying your ego with sexual games. In self-defense you feel it necessary to push your own boundaries outward, rampaging into other people's spaces (physical or psychological), putting them on the defensive. If your self-respect is undamaged then you are creatively inclined, liking to exercise your competence in constructive ways. You will have a powerful protective feeling for the underdog, and a conscience which incorporates a sense of honor and nobility. You strive to gain greater self-awareness.

These traits will be strong only if Pluto is very strongly placed, or is a personal ruler. Pluto's house placing shows far more personal effects.

LEO NORTH NODE—AQUARIUS SOUTH NODE

You have tended to make yourself into a relatively isolated individual, detached and aloof from the mass of people, in order to develop your differences—your full sense of individuality. You think your own thoughts with little reference to the mainstream of knowledge, except for material to act as a starting-point and stimulus for your unique trains of logic. Creating your own life separately from others, you become aware of your isolation, of a certain loneliness created by your independence. While the inventive aspects of your mind can thus flourish unchecked, your need for human society may be unfulfilled, and harder to fulfill as you become harder to understand by others. Also, the longer you are alone the harder it is for you to be disciplined as you move rapidly from idea to idea in search of inner stimulus, until you become the only one who can understand your own connections. You care little for the rules and traditions of society, preferring to make up your own.

While you work on your ideals in your own mind they may be hard to make concrete and objective, and you need to develop your creativity to realize them. Your inventiveness can become a rich resource for self-recreation and your idealism lead you on to rich achievement. You need others of similar mind so that you can be a coordinating center to develop the utopia that you desire, turning your detachment into full-fledged self-respect and helping others to overcome their feelings of self-limitation. Your idealism is developing into a sense of honor and nobility where fair-play can overcome the competitive struggles of society and allow all individuals the right of self realization. You need recognition for your efforts, and should never allow yourself to say you don't care.

SUN IN THE 5TH HOUSE

Your creative abilities are at least potentially great. You identify very closely with your creativity, this showing first in your play as a child. You played *your* games in *your* way, and loved gaining approval or attention in doing so, but hated anyone trying to dominate your play, horn-in on the act, change your games, or otherwise spoil or take away what you were doing. If this happened, your pride made you capable of never wanting to go back to that game or creative pursuit, or of denying that you ever liked it in the first place. Thus you may have blocked many avenues of creativity. If you have left them open and not gone overboard in building pride then the possibilities are wide, and it is all a matter of choice. You may take a hobby and turn it into a business, profession, or lifestyle; or work on your artistic talents, developing yourself toward greatness in your field; or in your developing consciousness of yourself you may work on personal awakening. You could bring greatness and abundance into your life through your qualities of leadership, and through your will being honorably directed toward large endeavors.

Your worst problem is your pride, for you can encourage it to grow beyond bounds, becoming domineering, overbearing, and arrogant in the process. You may still strive for the heights, but climb beyond your powers, and thus set yourself up for a fall; or never make the attempt, being lazily satisfied with pride alone, founded on nothing but your view of yourself. The rule here is that you must use your sense of honor in all that you do, seeking your own happiness and that of others by persisting only in what you know to be right, throwing out everything that you know is degrading. Otherwise your blown-up pride will either be easily deflated by circumstances that show it to be based on very little, or it will make you live in an illusion. There is nothing but personal effort in pursuing the good standing between the negative path and the positive. When you are centered in healthy self-respect and self-awareness, you know your own potentials and what you have done about developing them, and can respect the same things in others, not needing to overcompensate for personal lacks, and thus never being swung around by circumstances.

Your mother's values were probably based on her sense of honor, her inner truth, and she identified closely with them. For example, to her, giving gifts was giving of herself. She was money conscious, capable and creative with it, as well as with materials, and her tastes leaned toward the rich, and perhaps toward effect and display. She may have felt that her happiness depended on her attachments, to things or people, and have been swung between joy and sorrow by circumstances. She may have been stubborn and immovable in her ways, and at the worst, grasping.

Your father was a survivor, likely to have been intensely practical and competent, perhaps fighting back at anything that he felt to be attack or rejection, and making sure that he won the battles. He was creatively capable, both at building up, or repairing, and at tearing down, or eliminating. He could be quite secretive, certainly never showing if he felt hurt, and probably not showing his deeper or more intense feelings.

MOON IN THE 5TH HOUSE

You have learned how to become a creative, and self-creating person; how to take an image of what you want to become, to create of yourself, your circumstances, your life—and how to turn that image into a reality. You probably learned by copying or mimicking others first, then became more individualistic in your attempts, ultimately realizing that you had no problem in being an original person yourself. You learned early how to gain attention by your efforts, and that much security lay in the recognition that you received for showing what you could do. You blossomed under the warm regard given to your successes. Thus you gained enough pride, or self-respect—if not more than enough, for it is possible that you have gone toward a great outward display of ability, or even of magnificence—but at that extreme are lacking in inner seriousness.

If your pride is overdeveloped, even though you have potentially great abilities with eventual success seeming to be a matter of mere details, you are likely to relax, becoming lazily indifferent and letting things take their own course—leading to decay. This position is a combination of water (Moon) and fire (5th House) or of emotion and energy, and the right balance must be kept if the "water" is not to put out the "fire," or the "fire" to dry out the "water." When the right balance is found, lots of motive power is produced. Too much outward shining dissipates this energy and too much moodiness makes you irresolute. This is a combination of modesty and pride; modesty should be the outer container for pride, maintaining on the surface a certain caution and reserve, not annoying others by flamboyant and inconsiderate behavior, or being too emotionally forceful and direct. Much depends on just where your awareness is placed, for if it is solely on yourself then your view as a whole is blocked and limited, some with this position relating more easily in their vanity to a mirror than to other people. If you use your receptivity to become more conscious of what you are perceiving of your world, and how, then you could become a very conscious individual indeed. The potential is there, the problem is not to waste it.

To be secure in yourself, you need to play and to create. If you are on the modest side you may have learned to be domestically creative and make this your only play, baking for example; but you probably need more of an outlet for pure self-expression to feel complete. You identify very strongly with your family, taking pride in their achievements, and being annoyed by their pitfalls.

Your mother is likely to have been very tenacious in holding onto what she valued, including secure boundaries for her family, and domestic bliss. She may also have been very retentive with money and possessions, though her financial affairs had their ups and downs, being rather cyclic. This matched the way that her values varied with her moods, as did her ability to reach out to experience, or her feeling that she could have what she wanted.

Your father's deeper feelings would have been hidden from view, much of his security depending on his not feeling rejected by others. If he did feel rejected, he would shut himself off from further contact rather firmly. He could bottle up hurts that he felt for quite a long time, defensively not showing that he felt hurt at all.

MERCURY IN THE 5TH HOUSE

Your view of yourself is probably split, your self-respect varying up and down, from having pride to disliking yourself. It is probable that during your childhood you became uncertain whether you wanted to be the child that your parents required, or to be yourself, even if then they wouldn't accept you. In your uncertainty you veer back-and-forth between being both, putting yourself down if you are what others want of you, losing closeness with them if being your own person.

Much of this comes from your self-view being formed around a period when you were at the turning point of deciding whether you wanted to grow up or remain a baby. If you decided to stay a baby, then you could always play at being an adult. This can cause problems in your relationships with children since, though part of you can love them easily as an adult and a parent, the other half—your child side—feels that it should be in their place and resents taking on adult responsibilities. In part you don't want to know yourself better since a half of your self-view is negative—feeling that you could be pretty horrible beneath the surface, even though the other half feels that you are fine. It may show in uncertainty about your sexual status, "am I wanted or not?" being the same as "do I like me or not?" You also use dualism to protect yourself, saying "I don't know," rather than being found to be wrong.

You are likely to have many creative ideas, but may identify yourself with the ideas rather than doing anything about them. You may have difficulty making up your mind exactly what you want to do, switching between different possibilities as your view of yourself changes. It changes as you question just who you are, never being sure of your own identity as your self-respect bounces up and down. When your self-respect rises you can accomplish things, when it falls you become self-attacking and find it hard to do anything. So you swing like a yo-yo as you support your pride and then knock it down. If you feel adequate in yourself, then you don't need to do anything but enjoy what you do. If you don't feel adequate, however, your creativity disappears.

Your manual creativity could be well-developed as you like to dabble in everything. You may be skilled at crafts if you maintain your interests in them, consistency being your main problem. Otherwise you could be very creative with words and language, with pen, pencil, and paper, having potentials in creative writing and in drawing.

Your mother's values were dualistic and inconstant, whether about money and goods (saying "money's not everything" and then chasing after it), or about what she wanted to aim for in life. Her tastes, preferences, likes, and dislikes could reverse themselves completely over a period of time. She could give, and then take away again, or promise something and then not deliver. She valued education and communication.

Your father had an intense mind, and tended to keep many of his thoughts to himself, unless they came out in temper. He was unsure whether he was accepted or rejected in his relationships, and whether he wanted to remain involved or to get out, though he would have kept this hidden, except for his reactions to rejection. He is likely to have been a penetrating thinker in practical matters, preferring to work things out for himself, rather than accepting anyone else's word for anything.

VENUS IN THE 5TH HOUSE

Much of your self-respect depends upon the kind of response you feel you are getting, or are able to arouse, in others. You are quite self-judging and spend much effort trying to live up to your own expectations. You try to be attractive, perhaps to the point of being vain about your looks or other qualities, assessing just how far you measure up to your image. You then act out this attractive role with others, being rather self-conscious, remaining cheerful and pleasant in order to gain their attention and win their affection, sometimes also using your creative abilities to achieve this end. You can enter into love affairs for this purpose, being able to create the right romantic feeling and setting to start them off. Yet in evaluating yourself you tend to use others for comparison, sometimes finding it necessary to judge them negatively in order that you can be superior to them, particularly if you feel that they may reject you. You would find it hard to admit to this, for you prefer to see yourself as having a sense of fair play. Actually you do, but it depends on whether you feel that your pride is at stake.

You are likely to be generally creative, in decorative arts and with materials, particularly fabrics, yarns, threads, string and such (fashions or furnishings); also perhaps in song, dance, writing, or design. You may like tactical games, such as chess, and generally prefer lazy or peaceful pleasures, having a love of leisure and pleasure. You relate easily to children, finding pleasure in their company, and enjoy helping them by smoothing their way for them. You are likely to treat them as equals, rather than being superior to them in the usual adult way. That is, unless Venus was in difficult aspects at your birth, in which case you could be quite judgmental with them, requiring them to reflect your ideas and attitudes, demanding charm and tact from them, whatever you give.

You probably have a good sense of value in land and property, and may make money by investing in such areas, or perhaps build up your own little empire by extending your own property.

Your father was capable of storing up his more intolerant and judgmental feelings for some time and then bringing them all out in angry bursts, hiding it all behind charm beforehand. He could hurt others easily yet make you feel bad by acting hurt if you returned the smallest part of his accusations. He did not like to admit to the darker side of himself. In the public eye he was charming and pleasant, not allowing others to see into his intense feelings—saving them for those close to him; in other words he was a "Jekyll and Hyde" type, blaming others for his own bad conscience.

Your mother was capable of a good deal of patience, preferring to avoid the ugly and the unpleasant, trying to maintain peace, harmony and comfort. She needed her pleasures, such as gardening, to keep herself in a pleasant state. She would express her affection by giving gifts, and perhaps by being close and touching. She was also quite aware of money and value, being a rather evaluating person.

MARS IN THE 5TH HOUSE

You see yourself as a fighter, something of a warrior, battling your way through life to create each new moment and development of your life by yourself. Your ability to act vigorously and creatively is important to your self-respect and to maintaining an adequate self-image. You act in order to be yourself, so your pride depends on what you can *do*, what fresh endeavors and projects you can start, or what new developments you can identify with—in being one of the initiators, though you would probably prefer to be *the* initiator. Your drive toward personal accomplishment is likely to make your leisure time active as you thrust yourself forward to do things, to start, develop and direct practical projects, preferring to do something rather than sit and do nothing. A lot of your creativity is likely to be with tools, in making things. In your youth, and perhaps in your adult life, this energy may have taken you toward sports, and, depending on the aspects to Mars, either into directly competitive activities where your pride depended on being first, or in individual pursuits where you competed directly with yourself—developing your own skill, strength, speed, and coordination. You applied and built upon your abilities to be self-directing in aiming for achievement. You prefer to be a single and singular person, not to have your initiative taken away from you by anyone else.

You either tend to defend whatever you regard to be your own territory very well indeed, being entrenched as in a fortress, or to extend it vigorously, breaking through old boundaries and into new ground, though if it belongs to anyone else, that could cause battles—so you may be an empire-builder.

In love affairs you are also energetic and direct, most probably being the initiator. Your loves would not be mild ones, but more passionate, often involving fights; for some the tendency is to fix intensely on one love of your life, while for others it is the new conquest or fresh involvement that holds their interest. With children you may have too much of your ego invested, for you are likely to be too pushy with them, tending to direct their actions instead of allowing them to act for themselves, frequently leading to battles of will. This is likely to carry on a family tradition since your parents would have been more stubbornly aggressive than otherwise.

Your mother was very aware of her own values, not particularly aware of alternatives or of others' views, and wanted things her way. If things were not to her taste, then fights were possible. She was vigorous and direct in the tone of her self-expression, at times having a martial quality and strength to her voice. When she wanted anything she went after it with a single-minded directness that you also exhibit.

Your father had a number of intense drives that he kept hidden, together with a tendency to act in secret, keeping his motives invisible. In relating he could be direct and forceful, possibly turning his partnerships into battles, otherwise into effective working units. He is likely to have been energetic, capable and competent, a survivor who was ready to fight if threatened and was otherwise quietly watchful.

JUPITER IN THE 5TH HOUSE

You have a very expansive attitude toward yourself and your creative abilities, being optimistic about your potential, what you are capable of tackling. You prefer to see yourself as a creative explorer, going beyond the limits set by others into fresh territory; thus you set yourself distant goals to achieve—and are unlikely to admit it to anyone if you find that you can't fulfill them. In other words you keep your pride or self-respect at a high level, and do not like it to be reduced by anything or anyone. At the best you have a sense of honor and justice that would allow you to do nothing that was wrong in your own eyes. Your breadth of vision would enable you to tackle very large undertakings, having the ability to see yourself and your world on a huge scale—together with a drive for broad and varied experience. You want to expand your experience because your self-respect depends on your need to see yourself as evolving, growing, pushing your boundaries further all the time. You hate to feel that you are static, or that you have reached, or ever will reach, your final limit of growth.

If Jupiter had any very difficult aspects to it, you could be pushy to the point of an overbearing, domineering conceit. You prefer to see yourself as outstripping all others, and live on the inflation of your pride to ever larger levels. Thus you would have little regard for others' individual rights or merits and may boost yourself by climbing on their shoulders, though you wouldn't admit to needing to do so. You lean towards being an empire-builder, expanding your own territory (of whatever kind) by encroaching on, and taking over, that of others, which means, for example, that you would take credit for other people's efforts. You hate being proven wrong or embarrassed in others' eyes and would rather run away, but your pride won't allow you to be seen to do that, so you have to make it look like something else, a flurry of creativity, a fresh display of abilities acting as a con-man's bluff, new projects urgently requiring your attention. Expanding the boundaries of your ego simply means that you have more space in which to be alone, though you will arrogantly deny needing anyone else, while still pursuing any number of affairs.

Either way you are something of a gambler in your attitude to life; you are prepared to pour a lot of yourself into whatever fresh prospects are arising, living on hope and expectations of developments in the future. You probably like to spend your leisure time outdoors, perhaps tramping, jogging, perhaps practicing archery, a specifically Jovian sport, or with horses; or you may like to use your leisure to broaden your mind, or to pursue any of a variety of hobbies; your restlessness and creative impulsiveness is unlikely to let you stick to only one track for any great length of time.

Your mother's values were either based on honesty, optimism, and pursuit of excellence (with a religious or philosophical foundation), or on a spendthrift, restless chasing after experience, feeling that she was not getting enough out of life, no matter how much she had.

Your father didn't show his true colors, hiding his deeper self from the world. If he felt that he was under attack, or that anyone was getting too close for comfort, he could erupt in a great display of rage, and devastate his opponent by telling home truths in the most cutting way.

SATURN IN THE 5TH HOUSE

You take yourself seriously, judging yourself by a strict set of rules to see whether you measure up. You are very conscious of your status in others' eyes as well as in your own, wanting recognition from them in order to build self-respect. Aware of your dignity, you are slow to let go, to relax and play, feeling that you must be doing something responsible with your leisure for which you can gain recognition. The rules by which you judge yourself were originally your mother's values, orthodox standards of duty, responsibility, self-discipline and restraint, and respect for elders. When you failed to measure up to them you felt guilty, inferior and depressed, your pride diminished. You were either left that way, still now feeling belittled, or more likely swore to regain self-respect and status (resenting the put-down if Saturn is under difficult aspects, though resentment would conflict with your serious code of honor). If you let depression take over, it darkened your consciousness, diminishing your sensory awareness, making your world seem grayer and colder, leaving you feeling that brightness and beauty were gone. If you drove to regain your pride you set up long-range, though perhaps unconscious, ambitions to prove yourself. Perhaps unconscious because your fear of failing again will be high, and it is easier not to admit to your need to prove yourself than to do so and lose.

Your mother was cautious and controlling with her possessions, and while you were in the crawling stage (during your first year of life) she set definite limits on what you were allowed to reach out to, to touch, and to hold. These bounds were not to be broken (she may have used a playpen), leaving you the habitual feeling that there would always be narrow limits on what you can have for yourself, deserve, or aim for and gain in your world. This may have left you envious of the possessions of others. Also in toilet training you realized that she would only give approval if you were very self-restraining, bottling yourself up. You feared her disapproval for she could become quite cold toward you. She was probably not a touching person, tending rather to give only formally appropriate kinds of physical affection, for example if you had been very good or achieved something. Thus you learned to be controlled by the kind of attention that others give you, to seek for approval while doubting that you will get any. You unconsciously limit yourself socially, being cautious and reserved in your response to others, which may leave you having only a few friendships or social avenues, or solely formal ones connected with your status.

You felt like an unloved child, inadequate and insignificant. Since such feelings are intolerable, one of your reactions was probably for you to boost your pride, pushing yourself toward a counterbalancing sense of superiority, unstable, having a poor foundation. This would start an alternation of ups and downs, of superiority and inferiority, self-inflation and self-contraction—though these mood-swings may be very long ones.

As a child you liked to build your own play-structures; as an adult, where you develop your creativity it will be constructive, or concerned with three-dimensional form. This may include interests such as architecture, pottery, sculpture, or geometry, crystallography, geology, history. Your creative development may be slow, but if begun, steadily develop towards fulfillment of your aims, mastery of your interests.

URANUS IN THE 5TH HOUSE

Your self-awareness should be high. Your consciousness scans rapidly and can assemble a multitude of bits of information into a complex whole. Your ego, as one of the wholes, is a compound of various self views that you have woven into your unique individualism. Your ego will develop and change as your self-awareness increases; in other words you are aware of being a process of change—rather than a static, fixed entity. You are aware of being different from the average, and value that difference. You refuse to be caught in the traps of conformity—preferring to be free and independent above all things, and taking pride in it. You identify yourself closely with an idealized self-image, and your self-respect depends upon how far you manage to fulfill your humanitarian ideals in contributing to your own awakening and integration as a person, and to that of others.

You prefer your creativity to be unbounded, changing between different areas of hobbies, pursuits, leisure pastimes, feeling that there is no reason why any being should not tackle anything. You like to exercise your intelligence and apply it to creative problems, enjoying using your inventive abilities in your own special areas of interest. You may also like a lot of stimulus in high-speed activity in your leisure time, such as squash or tennis, skiing, driving fast; and maybe flying, gliding, hang gliding or sky diving (a childhood hobby may have been making model airplanes). Or you may spend your leisure catching up on technological and scientific developments in the modern world. You identify with all the developing space age awareness of mankind.

Your independence does not lean you toward marriage, but rather to living with another individual as two equal and free friends.

Your attitude to children is friendly, idealistic, and perhaps impersonal, but certainly not superior, and you like to encourage their intelligence to develop and their views of their world to remain open.

Where Uranus has difficult aspects, you are more likely to be impatient and abrupt with children, expecting your fixed ideas to be followed as though there are no other opinions, not allowing the child to build its necessary independence of mind. Yet you let them run wild until they irritate you. You may also be separated from your first child. You are likely to feel that having children traps you, holds you down. You stay detached toward them, remaining personally uninvolved so that your feelings cannot be trapped by love for them; the same applies to your attitude toward yourself. Your independence is a self-isolating and alienating separation from others, boosted by your ideas about your differences from them. You refuse to be trapped by others, but you have trapped yourself rather well. You lean toward having rather detached and short-lived affairs, short because of your lack of deep personal involvement and wariness of traps.

You would have been a rebel against authority in your puberty years, against rigid rules, refusing to be dictated to (though not necessarily openly).

Your mother's values were either idealistic and humanitarian, encouraging your independence as she valued her own; or alienated from natural things and money hungry, expressing little or no warmth of affection to you, and rigid in her requirements.

NEPTUNE IN THE 5TH HOUSE

If Neptune is under difficult aspects, you are likely to hold many subtle illusions about yourself. Your imagination is the core of your self-view, and has been exercised deeply in your childhood by your love of acting out in play your favorite roles—whatever they were, or of *becoming* the hero/heroine of any and every book that you read. You dreamed in detail what it would be like to be your hero, (who may have been a religious figure—Jesus, saint or martyr) and live out their life. The most intense side of this tendency may have faded, but you will have been left with many traces—maintaining your pride by self-exalting fantasies, loving to read, drift and dream, perhaps being involved in theater as an adult, or protecting yourself from harsh reality by building a smoke-screen of drink, drugs or delusion, or using others to fill roles in your self-created theater of life. Your senses are sometimes limited in their full contact with the world by your living inwardly in your fantasies.

There is little malice in you, for you tend to hang onto your innocence. You can be very generous indeed, putting no limits on your giving. You idealize charity, thinking charitably of others on a subtle level, and so you find it difficult to hang onto your possessions, tending to give them away, or just let them go. This is frequently a problem when you have a lot of pseudo-friends who are ever-ready to borrow from you, forgetting about paying you back. You are ready to give to anyone you call a friend, and to befriend anyone who pays you any attention, being rather lonely, and having a boundless need for affection. This need gives you the desire for an ideal union—a perfect fusion with another, which can leave you susceptible to very confusing romantic affairs, even though you also tend towards self-isolation and celibacy. These and many other things you hide from public view, camouflaging and covering over your secrets since you are intensely vulnerable to public opinion, feeling that it lacks tolerance and compassion.

On the positive side, your sensitively receptive consciousness and whimsically imaginative playfulness can make you very creative indeed. Your special areas may include music, painting, photography, theatre, anywhere that creativity with images is of value. You may also appreciate sailing and being alone with nature, though you may also like to be involved in large public gatherings where you can be swept up in the intensity of mass-feeling. The fulfillment of your personal dreams is very important to you; for you to be able to create the world that you want you will continually refine your tastes and values, holding a creative image of your aims as a blueprint to work from. The more consciously clear this image is—the closer it will become to being actual. You will also find that you make exactly the right social contacts to achieve your aims, without trying.

Your mother's values were sensitive and imaginative, perhaps sentimental, or very refined. She could be tender, sympathetic, generous, charitable and compassionate and easy to touch. Your father hid his sensitivities away, keeping them secret from others. Whenever he was generous, he would also complain about receiving little in return.

PLUTO IN THE 5TH HOUSE

Your pride is powerful but you tend to keep it hidden away, invisible to others. Your view of yourself is intense, may be very good or very bad, and possibly both at once. If bad, you are ultra-aware of past rejections which hurt your pride, and have been stuck in brooding resentment about them, being self-obsessed. Your self-view is that you have had the dirty trick done to you, and are the rejected and hurt one. In retaliation, you reject many things in your life, including other people, simply excluding them from your awareness to the point that it is now automatic and invisible to you. You enclose your fierce pride inside a barrier that no one can get through, to protect it from further harm, but in doing this you isolate yourself so that others are aware that you don't want them to come close, and they stay away, thus proving that you are rejected. In truth you reject and resent yourself, intense conscience prickings making you feel that you are unacceptable.

If your self-view is positive, you take pride in your competence and capability, your practicality in handling things, even your strength and power as a survivor, perhaps displayed in learning survival in the wild, hunting, or in martial arts such as Karate. You may be interested in motor-bikes or other machinery, or in stripping things apart to understand how they work, wanting to know the driving force within everything. You identify with your sexuality, taking pride in your passion, and are likely to have become sexually aware at an early age, some of your childhood play being purely sexual exploration. (Occasionally 5th House Pluto implies sexual interference by others as a child, or rape). If your self-respect is strong, your sense of honor will be absolute, and you will never break your own moral code, being a fierce judge of yourself and your motives.

You have an intense creativity, but want it to be entirely your own; if as a child someone criticized or rejected what you did, or took over to show you how it was done, you would have rejected that area since it had been spoiled for you. In this way you may have chopped off many avenues of development, feeling an intense loss that you may have rejected from consciousness, now avoiding such areas to avoid further loss. If this is the case, transformation awaits you in re-awakening your creativity, and you will find that your whole personality will become more intensely alive as you let your passionate playfulness re-emerge.

Your mother's values were powerful, her likes and dislikes black and white. If self-rejecting, she felt that she could never have what she wanted, and actively condemned many things that she would otherwise have liked because they were beyond her reach. She may have been fiercely possessive, never letting go of what she valued, protecting such things against being taken from her. She may also have been very materialistic.

Your father had intense instinctive drives, either openly responding to everything around him with passion, or being actively rejecting and intolerant. His survival drives were powerful, and he would find things to fight where no one else could. He would either face the hidden sides of life, such as sex and death, directly—never avoiding them or covering them over, or would do the opposite—refusing to admit to their existence.

NORTH NODE, 5TH HOUSE—SOUTH NODE, 11TH HOUSE

Your mind can be very inventive indeed. You enjoy taking ideas and knitting them together, combining multitudes of ideas into complex and integrated whole systems. You can be ingenious in the connections that you make, and frequently you interweave your ideals with your ideas, organizing your networks of connections to prove that your ideals are right. You are very capable of using these complex ideas as a way of proving your individual differences from other people, of making yourself into an independent and unusual person, but much of this process is in ideas only, completely abstract, and bears little relationship to concrete reality. You need to use your ideas creatively, to learn how to apply them more concretely and to realize them so that your intellectual individualism is put fully into action. As they are expressed by your creativity they should flourish into conscious self-understanding. Effectively your ideals are wishes and these are an expression directly of yourself, and of the world that you want to live in.

You will find as you wish for things that they do come true, but you will have to be careful about what you wish for, simply because they come true. In turning your inventiveness and idealism into concrete creation and turning your wishes into realities, you will be changing yourself from an abstract person into a far more concrete, real, and alive being. You need to use your multi-level mind in self-awareness and self-integration.

As you develop your creativity you are likely to find yourself involved with children, using it to stimulate their awareness of the complex world around them, to awaken and involve their curiosity, to encourage them to become self-aware.

❖ 8 ❖

Virgo
and the 6th House

A child between the ages of (very roughly) six or seven to eight or ten years is in the process of adding detail to its picture of both world and self. What was a playful involvement with life becomes more oriented to learning how to deal with its practicalities. I think of this as the time of "what's mom doing in the kitchen? baking a cake? I want to learn how to do that," and "my dad is a carpenter, and I'm going to be one when I grow up." The child's experiential boundaries are growing ever outwards, and begin to overlap those of others, and if open-hearted, the child's capacity for full sharing in everything to do with space, food, effort, and all else needed for living is awakening.

A child, in order to become a capable adult, has much to learn in handling the basic problems of living. Supporting one's life once involved knowing how and where to find food (the skills of hunting and gathering, and what constitutes nourishing food); how to prepare it for eating; how to find shelter, and keep it in good condition for living; how to make functional clothing if necessary, and keep it in good order; how to remain healthy, or to deal with illness. Those were and still are the basics of how to keep our bodies, and thus our lives, in good shape, and they used to take us just a couple of hours a day to look after, all raw materials being supplied free by nature, until "progress" took over. Now we have to work for a third of the day to earn a living, to gain the money to buy everything we need from others who control the resources. Meanwhile, many of the most basic living skills have been lost to individuals through leaving them to specialists.

Knowing how to handle the support of life involves learning massive amounts of detail about the multitude of things in our environment, their properties and potential uses, plus learning the skills of handling them, methods and techniques that help us to do the job most effectively. It also involves learning about several, perhaps many different environments, and if they are shared with other living creatures (human, animal, plant), what is readily available to us, what we can and cannot do or use in these environments. Building this capability for knowing environments (ecological regions) in detail is essential, for without it our life suffers, its quality diminishes, the likelihood of our remaining healthy and comfortable disappears. For full support of our own life, it is also essential to develop the self-awareness to know what is going on in our own being, body and mind, to diagnose the problem if any; currently this is a lost art.

The 6th House shows our capacity for handling this kind of analytical detail, our primary focuses of interest and special skills. It includes our development of analytical abilities of mind capable of handling the multitude of details of living, of sorting them all into categories or groups, each one of which is associated with a particular area of experience, and of calling on that organized storehouse of knowledge at will. This storehouse is continually available just below our consciousness, supplying us with every detail of knowledge we have gained about everything we can currently perceive in our immediate environment. We tap this storehouse whenever we focus on anything specific and require information about it, what use it has, and how to handle it. Frequently the most important focus is on overlapping areas, such as between our knowledge of our own current needs, our awareness of what is available in our environment, and our competence at adapting it to our needs. The practical skills, methods and techniques that we develop to apply this knowledge or analytical capacity then become our methods of working with our world, and they point us toward certain avenues of work and working areas.

The 6th House also demonstrates where we are particularly aware of any lack, any unfulfilled needs in ourselves, which leave us prone to anxieties. It thus also indicates how (and whether) we act to deal with anxieties, worries, or tensions (or perhaps still expect a parent to do it for us, as we do in modern cultures, employing specialists to do the jobs). Nervous stress, *i.e.*, anxiety, is the primary cause of illness. Multitudes of bacteria and viruses are constantly in our environment, and in our bodies, but we generally remain healthy. When under stress, our resistance drops and we become more vulnerable to such outside agents of disease. (Here is where our boundaries are open and vulnerable to invasion). The 6th House describes the particular parts of the body and the bodily functions that are the most vulnerable to illness.

Since mind and body are inseparable, bodily and mental functions run in exact parallel; this is why a mental (emotional) struggle will produce a physical ailment. Just as physical health is total only if all dietary needs are supplied, psychological health is maintained only if all our mental and emotional needs are met, including the need to learn, to expand our experience. We often go to work in areas that allow us to try to fulfill those unsatisfied needs, which also often means in areas where we are, at least initially, ineffective, or are worried about our effectiveness and trying to prove or develop it.

The 6th (as the variable 3rd House from the endocrine 4th) indicates the interweave of our various glandular cycles, which produce complex variations in our mood swings. Overall they move between periods of balance as our basic, natural, unconditioned being surfaces, and periods of unbalanced swings between high and low as the tensions of our conditioning dominate. In high energy periods we feel able to handle the problems of living, but may overcompensate for personal problems and stresses. In the low energy times we don't feel able to handle things, so anxiety rises as our sense of self-worth diminishes and the world weighs us down.

Physiologically, the 6th House deals with the small intestine and its functioning. The small intestine has the task of breaking down long chain molecules in foodstuffs so that the remaining molecules will be small enough to pass through the intestinal wall and into the bloodstream. This is the actual bodily work of maintaining life by providing its necessities. If our diet (or our life experience) is lacking something essential, our being will become anxious until it is supplied. Note the parallel with the analytical ability of mind and the capacity for abstracting useful, or personally meaningful, detail from experience. What it leaves out becomes trash, material for which we can find no personal use or meaning. Just as the enzyme reactions in the gut include complex molecular buildup as well as breakdown, so the mind organizes the elements of our experience into categories, into a personal filing system of pigeonholes, as well as analyzing their contents into details.

Information from the senses, coordinated together by the thalamus, is rerouted to various lobes of the brain for interpretation. For example, visual data goes to the visual cortex at the back of the brain, and is built into a complete picture, not only of what is there before us, but which also has added to it a multitude of details about everything within the range of our vision, in case any of the information is needed. These sensory pictures from every sense are then routed toward the cortex, ready to come to consciousness.

SUN IN VIRGO
✧ The Critic ✧

The sign Virgo represents that part of the whole human being that analyses, sifts, categorizes and classifies by breaking things down into basic elements in order to assimilate or understand them, and builds up from these basics to fulfill life. It deals with the breaking down of large molecules of foodstuffs in the small intestine into glucoses to be absorbed into the blood stream through the intestinal wall. This analysis or breakdown provides the raw materials for the support and continuation of bodily living.

As a Virgo you are likely to be critical and perfectionistic, fastidious and fussy about those things that you feel to be most important to maintaining yourself. For most these will be occupation, food, clothing, shelter, and health, all of which have to be continually tended to prevent the forces of entropy, chaos, decay, or dissolution from taking over. You will either have mastered these areas, delighting in becoming more creative, precise, and refined in the way that you handle them, or struggle with them, anxious and worried that your continual juggling act will eventually drop something important and the whole thing will fall apart, or you have already given up and let everything drop into chaos, confusion, and neglect. You may feel that life is a fight against invisible monsters that threaten the survival of self, family, or lifestyle. Most of these anxieties arise from your sharp critical awareness, seeing fault, failure, and imperfection in everything, (including other people). Just remember that every time you judge anything or anyone as imperfect you are adding more imperfection to your world, and if you are totally critical you will never see anything but imperfection everywhere. Also remember the main drives behind your criticism, (a) fear, (b) desiring to seem more perfect yourself by comparison. Your critical abilities are of value only when balanced by respect, sympathy, and compassion for others, and depth of feeling for and with life.

When you are relaxed and confident you are one of the most capable workers around, able to understand complex systems of order and organization, frameworks of laws and rules, and to handle masses of detailed material or information without error. You are a perfectionist and your work will show how far this trait has or hasn't developed. Your work may deal with living systems, in biochemistry, working on farms or with animals, or connected with diet and health. Highly developed Virgoans prefer to be of service to others, catering to, and looking after their needs and for this reason are frequently found in medical or healing professions. Otherwise your work is likely to involve keeping complex systems in order, maintaining standards of purity, perfection, and precision, or supplying services that will do the same. Generally preferring not to be in charge, you are found more in the supporting roles in life, the ones without which everything would collapse. Your greatest consciousness is of the amount of order in your life, and of your own central role in maintaining that order.

While this describes the classic Virgo personality, you will differ from it in many ways. For information on your main differences see the house position of the Sun, and the sign and house placement of Mercury.

MOON IN VIRGO

Your security depends on your having things the precise way you want them. This may mean that you have your home totally neat and tidy, with a place for everything and everything in its place, or that you find fault with things that are not as you want them to be. This applies equally to your judgments of what goes on inside you. You worry when unsettled, your feelings jumping around irregularly, anxiety about your inability to keep life running smoothly sometimes building to a high pitch. You are nervous about being contaminated by unwanted influences, things that threaten to invade your life or your being and disrupt it, and try by your criticism to exclude them or cut them down to size. You prefer keeping your life in an orderly state to prevent things falling into disorder and decay.

Where you fight chaos, you should realize that the chaos is in you, being your anxieties themselves, your insecurity about handling the material world. Part of you feels weak and uncertain, and would still rather have Mother do it all for you. Where you seek perfection outwardly, you really want to be perfect yourself, to be beyond criticism and anxiety, to exclude the imperfections inside you that threaten you the most. Some with the Moon in Virgo found security in childhood by being helpful around the home and gaining approval for it; these people keep their desire to help and be of service to others, some building it into compassion that may be expressed through work in healing, particularly dietary control. Whatever the case, you are likely to be personally involved with illness, in yourself or your family, through your life. You can develop a sizable awareness of what life needs for its support and maintenance, and give these things in nurturing others. You grow as a person by becoming more responsible, by caring for others—or for any living thing—industriously and modestly, by being an excellent support and a good provider.

Since you need to feel that you are effective in the material world, you work to create and control material order. You can be one of the most efficient people around, able to handle masses of precise detail that would swamp others, a concise and organized worker. Your reflective analytical mind can develop an ever-widening clarity and precision. On an emotional level, you have no desire for fame and fortune, or for being in the limelight, preferring simplicity of life to any form of grandeur, a well-tended, even well-pruned existence, rather than opulence.

In relationships you need to avoid being critical of your partner, for if you seek purity and perfection you will not find it by looking for faults. You use your perfectionism as an emotional armor to keep others out, to give yourself emotional safety. You are emotionally cool to things or people that do not meet your precise standards, using meticulous reserve as an antiseptic barrier. If you do want perfection, then you should acknowledge the natural perfection that already exists in all things in abundance, for a critical eye can only see imperfection, beauty being in the eye of the beholder.

MERCURY IN VIRGO

You are likely to have a logical, analytical mind, focused upon the minute details and practicalities of every idea that you use. You are a practical thinker, needing to understand the use or function and boundaries or limitations of every concept and item of knowledge that you absorb, so needing to be well informed, methodical and precise. Learning should come easily to you, if you don't scatter your mind with anxieties, and your analytical nature may prefer scientific subjects (particularly the life-sciences; biology, botany, medical, or veterinary subjects) where precision is needed in the foreground and imagination is required to hold all the details together. You should have an ability in mathematics, or in health and dietetics, and work well in service organizations. Much of your mentality was formed while you were learning to be of practical use at home, in housework, neatness, tidying up after yourself, learning the details of basic life-support work. You probably vary between being neat (most of the time), and sloppy (when you can't be bothered keeping all the necessities under control) though this trait may only emerge over a long period.

You search for perfection of intellectual understanding, thus you try to define every concept precisely by its contexts and its relationships, try to understand every logical or grammatical connection in detail. You want it perfect, or you don't want it at all. But you will find that the more precisely you try to focus, the more aware of imprecision you are. Eventually you will tire and let go, and become more aware of the subtle, general, and indefinable connections between things. For example, in the relationship between particle and field, or figure and ground, the Virgoan usually notices the particle and the figure, not the field or ground—but needs to learn to perceive the opposite. You may find that you have been keeping everything highly defined in order to keep chaos or disorder at bay, but the disorder that you keep at bay can sometimes be life itself.

One negative trait which you should avoid is that of becoming over-critical and unsympathetic, a real nitpicker; you may defend yourself from things/people that you fear by finding fault with them, making them inferior to yourself and thus not worth relating to. Another difficulty to overcome is the tendency to worry, being so analytical you can worry things to pieces, and you can build quite a charge of anxiety which can take its toll of your nervous and digestive systems, capable of producing ill-health in the long run. But you should not worry about this either. The best support for your health is to be relaxed.

You work well where a meticulous sense of detail is needed, including secretarial and general office work; medicine (including veterinarian); hygiene; dietary control; in science, where precise recording and analysis of results is required; and technology or engineering, for the same reasons. Normally Virgoan types are ideal people to keep all the gears meshing smoothly.

VENUS IN VIRGO

In love you give yourself in many practical ways, since you like to be of service, simply and sincerely, to those you love. You are meticulous in keeping your relationships running smoothly by taking worries away from your partner, by working for them and being a helpmate, a support for their life, tending their physical needs. Yet you often find it difficult to express your feelings. Your tendency toward precise social propriety does not make for closeness, and may be a form of shyness, or a way of avoiding what you feel is unwelcome contamination from others, not wanting anyone to invade your borders, unless you allow them in.

In your love life you may tend to withdraw slightly, feeling that any display of emotion is not quite proper. Your greatest problem is a tendency to analyze every relationship, to the point where there is nothing left for pure feelings to develop. You want perfection in your partnerships and tend, in early life, to project that desired perfection onto your partners, not seeing them as they are but as you prefer to have them be. Then you notice that they are not what you think and criticize them, which is unfair since it does not allow the others to be themselves and sets you in a superior position. You may be used to having relationships that are mutually critical (what were your parents like?) and find it hard to stop the habit. Your evaluations are finicky in general, since you desire perfection in all things. You especially seek a rather unrealistic perfection in your love life. You are not always outwardly critical, but may reserve your judgment inwardly on those things and people that do not meet your standards. However when you do fall in love you are a very faithful partner.

If you have a feeling for art, it will be of the very precise and analytical, or critical type. You are not one for great abstractions or surrealism, but should be more at home among such things as technical drawings, depictive, or pictorial art which require detail. You may not allow yourself to understand art deeply through approaching it too analytically, where allowing yourself to flow into the feeling of it aids absorption in depth (you cannot appreciate a rose by pulling it apart).

Your working situation is likely to be a pleasant one, since this is where you can use charm and social ability very well. You are capable of making the work area attractive and aesthetic, soothing to the senses. Your desire to be beyond criticism, and to be liked, can make you try hard, and your need to be of pleasant service is of value in many occupations, particularly where you deal with others as individuals, such as being a personal secretary or representative, receptionist, or in any medical auxiliary role. Precision in aesthetics could be your working focus, whether in fashion, design, or furnishings, or meticulousness or analysis in relationships, such as helping others heal, physically or mentally, or dealing with their living problems. Otherwise you may simply deal with living things, plants, or animals.

MARS IN VIRGO

You are meticulous, careful and methodical in action, and prefer your actions to lead to perfection of some kind. You work best when you have a clear and precise aim in mind when you begin anything and are capable of working hard toward your goals, though you do tend to allow your energies to be scattered along the way, especially when struggling with your inner tyrant. You are cautious and practical in the use of your initiative, and your tendency to be sharply analytical enables you to get jobs done cleanly and with a minimum waste of effort, unless you let your eye for detail mislead you.

There is probably a struggle going on in you between the desire for order and uncivilized nature which you feel to be chaotic; if so, the chaos is actually your nature as a living creature, and the order is the requirements of the surrounding society in which you are a member. The first we can symbolize by a wild deer, the second by a machine, without heart. You may be acting as an accomplice in keeping your own full feeling for and contact with life under attack, threatened and vulnerable.

You can be fussy and highly critical, which can make you argumentative about little things. You allow your energies to become dispersed by having too many things to do at once, starting the next thing without finishing the first. Desiring to be perfect, you would like everything that you do to be done perfectly, but if you see fault in what you do then you want to move on to something new and start afresh (to avoid criticism from either yourself, or from others). Your desire to do it right can make you leave things undone. If you allow yourself more reasonable or relaxed standards, plus allowing yourself time to learn how to do things well, then you will have an easy but efficient routine in which things fall precisely into place like a well maintained machine.

Your physical nervous energy can run high, but is most likely to fluctuate in a complex cycle, periods of balance alternating with ones of scattered and variable imbalance. When you overwork you will have times of exhaustion; a steady and even routine is the only way to avoid these, one which on encountering obstructions seeks out the suitable path on which advance and retreat are possible. Your adrenal glands are affected by worry, producing fitful bursts of energy, which in turn vary your viewpoint on life as well as your general level of health. When your energies are low, so is your optimism, and you see fault in everything; when your energy is high, so is your mood and things seem more nearly as perfect as you wish them to be.

Your precision of view is valuable in technical fields, for example in dealing with fine tools or precise machinery. Your analytical perception is useful in science, particularly in research—definitely where an ever finer clarity of understanding of physical laws is needed (*i.e.,* your perception tends towards the microscopic). Medicine may appeal, particularly surgery, where precision and the eye for detail is essential. Fine and detailed craft-work may also attract you, and the more minute the detail the better.

JUPITER IN VIRGO

The main problem with this position is that of being unable to see the wood for the trees, the whole for the parts. Jupiter amplifies and elaborates, whereas Virgo concentrates on every precise detail. Within this lifetime your analytical abilities will be growing and are likely to lead to a highly developed critical faculty. Your wish for perfection will be imposed on everything. You will demand integrity in every detail of your world whether from yourself, others, or from conditions that you meet. You are likely to have a fairly precisely defined philosophy of life that will value purity, seek perfection, and demand practical work.

Although often quiet rather than bombastic, you are still capable of a very outspoken form of criticism, particularly if anyone transgresses your idea of moral rectitude. You are capable of making mountains out of molehills, though through your discriminating abilities you may see that others have viewpoints that are as valid to them as yours are to you. Your analytical refinement and ability to take a critical overview could be applied to areas such as theater or literature, *e.g.,* in becoming a critic.

You may have analytical interests in geography, botany, philosophies, higher education or religion, particularly in practical applied work in such areas. Thus you may work in charitable areas related to physical and mental health, or in educational organizations. Or you may keep track of all the details involved in areas of warehousing, distribution, exporting, importing or advertising of goods. Your meticulousness about truth, morals and religion may be taken to extremes. You want detailed perfection in a big way. You are likely to hold philosophical attitudes to daily life-support and work and will aim for honesty and integrity meticulously maintained in employment. You will like cleanliness, order, and precision in dress and housekeeping.

You may tend to amplify your worries, and your confidence is not the best, timidity being quite possible. Wide swings between confidence and worry are likely at times. Your analytical mind may be overactive, and not able to complete one train of thought without scattering onto another, and another set of details. Fritz Perls, a psychotherapist, said for people like you, "don't push the river, it will flow by itself." In other words, do not let your overactive nervous system take you over. It is possible that you have gone to the opposite extreme if Jupiter is under difficult aspects, and may be more Bohemian and sloppy in your life, and careless about details.

You will develop a lot in and through work throughout your life and will find that confidence about your potentials here will lead you straight toward the best opportunities. Worry will do the opposite since you are predicting that things will go wrong and events not work to your benefit. You will be able to work best when you can use both your abilities to take account of details, and your capacity to put them into an overview.

SATURN IN VIRGO

Let us look at the undeveloped type first: You are aware of the load of duties, responsibilities, frustrations, and anxieties in supporting your life, whether in occupation, housework, health maintenance, or other areas. You feel impelled to keep everything strictly ordered and controlled since you feel that if you don't maintain order it will all fall into chaos and confusion (the confusion is within you); in keeping order you become detached from the softer and more irrational aspects of your humanity that could throw you into chaos (meaning feelings), and become intellectually dispassionate towards them. Disorder and disorganization make you anxious, being aware of how easily things can crumble and get out of hand, and you become depressed by the constant effort that seems to be demanded of you. You become discontented with and resentful of the material world that requires such effort. You fight against dirt and disease, decay and disintegration outwardly, or against their inward psychological counterparts, feeling that you must build a barrier of caution and reserve against imperfection. You have your own rather orthodox and conservative idea of perfection, imposing it onto your world and judging everything (yourself included) against it, but it can be a rather darkly negative, critical and materialistic judgment which finds fault in all things. You are over-concerned with details in your effort to structure, define and control your world, trying to organize all of its parts into a rigidly concrete world-view.

In work, you can be meticulously organized by keeping all the rules and regulations, yet if you are pushed you can ignore important areas and over-focus on small details—in other words, having a civil or public servant's mentality. You probably aim for long-term security in your occupation, and may stick to it through all kinds of frustration, dislike, and resentment that you may feel toward it, feeling that you should be dutiful and responsible—even when you become gloomy and depressed by the whole area. Your work development may be slow or restricted through lack of skills and training, or through self-doubt, and while you may enter service occupations, being in a subservient position and doing menial work for others, you will probably resent being a servant.

On the more positive or developed side, you will have worked in some depth to understand the basic structural frameworks of life. You will have sought perfection in nature, to understand it and to serve it, possibly in the medical field, studying the basic biological and physiological laws, working to conserve and promote proper and healthy development. Instead of imposing your own view of what you think that perfection ought to be, you strive to understand the perfect order that exists in things as they are, and to align yourself with that order, recognizing and accepting that perfection exists in yourself as much as in anything else. You understand that you don't have to hold your world together, that it will do so itself. You assimilate all that you learn slowly and carefully, organizing it into a detailed framework of order, a well-arranged structure, which, if your mind is not agitated, crystallizes into a direct awareness of the living world at work. Naturally this can lead to major abilities, in healing or in organizing, and to a sense of the integration of your own life with the world around you.

URANUS IN VIRGO

Uranus was in Virgo from mid-1962 to mid-1969, during which time the space era was being established, with much basic work being done following the dramatic upthrust into space in the previous seven years. Space medicine was emerging as a new science, and some feedback from the space program was filtering through to industry, changing methods and materials. Telstar, the first communications satellite, was launched, as were further research probes to Mars and Venus, gathering data. As is usual with any focus on Virgo, health matters were in the public eye, with the British Royal College of Physicians and the American Surgeon General both reporting on the connection between smoking and lung cancer, and the thalidomide scare started the period, so the world began to recognize dangers from biochemical technology. Many new sub-atomic particles were discovered, anti-matter ones among them. Computer technology began to be applied in the workplace. Technological work prospects created the "brain drain" of scientists from the U.K. to the United States, and the Beatles reigned supreme. Uranus was in conjunction with Pluto for the greater part of this transit through Virgo, so the majority born at that time will have that aspect.

Being born at this time would give you the foundation of a very fast analytical mind, capable of taking details from a variety of sources and weaving them together inventively into a practical, usable whole. You may have a fascination with chains and networks of connections of a practical or technical nature, and be able to rapidly analyze the possibilities for change involved in making minor modifications to natural processes. For example, Virgo deals with life chemistry, and a major field emerging from the late 1960's is that of recombinant DNA technology, biological engineering, and genetic manipulation. Your potential speed of both analysis and synthesis is high, and you have an ideal of perfection in everything that you do, if you haven't become a rebel.

If Uranus has difficult aspects, your speed of analysis may be used to pick apart what others say to you, looking for anything that appears to be criticism, and being ready to react against them with an uncaring attitude. You have your own criticisms ready to retaliate, as evidenced by the Punk generation, part of their rebellion being against all the neatness and tidiness requested by their parents (Virgo's special area), and against their own biological limitations, testing their bodies to the limit. You have a high charge of nervous energy, much of it stimulated by the stresses and tensions increasing in the world that you were born into. Your mind is potentially faster and clearer than those of earlier generations, where not used to criticize your circumstances destructively—for that only means that you train yourself to see the worst in everything and become unable to see how to make anything good out of it—or to want to try. You may refuse to apply yourself to learning anything in detail, becoming bored quickly since you probably grew up with a high level of stimulus around you, television in particular. You jump to conclusions, being too scattered and impatient to do anything well or to carry things through to completion. You want to be perfect and to find perfection without having to do the work involved in developing yourself.

NEPTUNE IN VIRGO

Neptune was in Virgo from mid-1929 to mid-1943, the early part of this period introducing sound and color movies, and the wider screen. Technical advances were made in color films, and in development of plastics and synthetics. Paperback books were introduced, and the ball-point pen invented. Fashions changed from the flamboyance of the twenties to a more conservative and modest style, the same being true in film and theatrical presentations.

Being born during this era, your imagination tends towards the detailed and the perfectionistic. You seek for some ultimate kind of perfection, which you may feel is outside you; a part of you wants to blend back into the universe, but you are also aware of being a discreetly separate part of it. You grew up through a period in which anxieties were rife, absorbing many of them into your system without realizing it, giving you a vague, perhaps invisible background level of worry. This will focus upon every point where you recognize that you do not live up to your inmost images of a perfected you, as you subtly find fault with yourself by comparing yourself with those images. Simple trust in the wholeness of your own being is broken down by an overly analytical tendency, supported by being brought up in a period when the public had become aware of such things as bacteria or germs, and being given by your training a feeling that you have to keep yourself pure against threatening and invisible impurities in the world around you, or within yourself. Naturally this goes on at a totally unspoken and unconscious level of your mind.

We can call this a problem of focus. One ability of the mind is for it to accept everything without question, giving a feeling of completeness, of being part of it all. The counterbalancing mental ability is its focus on all the separate details in order to know their functions, and what you can do with them. This part has to know the dangers of the everyday world so that it can avoid them or deal with them. Neptune in Virgo introduces a struggle between these two parts, between all-encompassing vision and minute analysis, between total innocent trust and constant practical worry, introducing a tendency to wander into vagueness and fantasy when faced with necessary work, and to fish up anxieties when you should be fully relaxed. You would like to see a perfect you in a perfect world, but your imagination dreams up imperfections which you then believe to be real. Often these are projected out onto the world around you, so that you can always see where things depart from the perfect; or it is focused on practicalities, on how pure, or impure your food is (preservatives, additives etc.); or on the people around you, how far they depart from the ideal that you would like to relate to, and so on.

The cure for this tendency is to train yourself to see the natural perfection in everything around you, in every living thing (including bacteria) and in every process of natural law; to regain a simple trust instead of feeling threatened, however subtly, by the ordinary world; and to realize that you don't have to be perfect, that you make a martyr of yourself that way, or make yourself act out a perfection that you don't feel within you. What you are already is basically perfect.

PLUTO IN VIRGO

Pluto was in Virgo from 1957 to 1972, this period beginning with the Middle East war, the Suez crisis, the Hungarian revolution, labor riots in Poland, and terrorist strife in Cyprus—all relatively little wars, rather than the global wars fought under Cancer (1914) or Leo (1939). The world seemed to be constantly bickering. CND or ban the bomb marches began, and German atomic physicists refused to contribute to design or testing of nuclear weapons. Britain exploded megaton bombs.

This era saw a change in attitudes toward work. People moved away from the Victorian protestant work ethic idea that to be useful work had to be hard, and began to accept that automated machinery would eventually replace man in many jobs. This Pluto influence brought massive developments in the health area. We saw incredible new treatments given for many diseases which previously had very little help available. New analytical methods enabled science to discover strains of virus and bacteria which were previously unknown, and by identification to work on cures for them. In nuclear science a multitude of sub-atomic particles were discovered; in fact a flood of detail was emerging in every field of knowledge. This transit also saw changes in attitudes to sex and its various moral issues with the introduction of new birth control methods. The old standards were no longer valid, and the "New Morality" developed rapidly.

Many of this generation will be technological geniuses, many will be subject to intense anxieties, many will develop healing abilities beyond the normal, including psychic healing. Being born during this era, your mind is capable of handling much detail when applied to the task. You grew up with complex technology available, and with an increasingly analytical mind-state being used by your parents. This analysis can come naturally to you, but can also easily turn into an intense criticism of all that you do not like, and anxiety (usually repressed) about the disasters that the world faces. With jobs being far less available you may feel socially rejected and useless, and relieve your frustrations by reacting against society in various ways. The Punk generation shows its feelings by identifying with junk (the rejected) in everything; music, fashion, jewelry and so on, turning against parental standards, such as neatness, in the usual teen-age rebellion (and in the process showing no self-respect).

Your generation's main method of defense is to ignore details that you don't want to be concerned with, thus possibly building up a very incomplete view of the world that you live in; also critically attacking whatever bothers you, finding supposedly good reasons for blaming and rejecting something else as a cause for your own state; building intolerance against supposed impurities and imperfections in your life. Your main route to self-transformation is to learn to be of deep service to others, working for the health, welfare and survival of all (shown by the intense growth of alternative healing methods and groups in recent years).

Examination of the house position of Pluto is much more relevant to the individual than the sign position, which is the same for everyone born in this extended period.

VIRGO NORTH NODE—PISCES SOUTH NODE

Your past tendencies are to a kindness and compassion to others, to an inner sensitivity of feeling that can experience their sorrows and sufferings, always ready to give and to be of service to them. Unfortunately this is also a tendency to fall for sob-stories which catch your sentimentality, since you can identify with the doormat or victim in anyone. Your understanding of persecution and of martyrdom is a personal one, even if only real within your imagination, which can be vivid. Your emotional sensitivity and romanticism encourages you on the path of renunciation—often meaning letting go and allowing yourself to drift where you do not want to face things. This can produce a dreamy lack of attention to detail that automatically leads to confusion as you are faced with the difference between your dreams of the way things could be and the way they actually are. You can escape from reality into self-built illusion all too easily.

You need to develop (and may already have developed) your analytical awareness, your discriminating abilities, your drive to the practical creation of purity and perfection in your mundane life. The greater the development of these abilities, the more you will be able to fulfill your desire to be of service in a practical way, and the more aware you will be of who actually needs your help and who is wallowing in self-pity as you could. You can then also work on making real your dreams and visions, seeing clearly which are truly possible and which are sheer wish-fulfillment and unnecessary. Your drifting then turns into a precision in dealing with everyday realities that has no problem with life-support (work and housework, the daily maintaining of life) and finds perfection in that. In a sense the whole process is one of focus, coming out of a dream into being clearly and practically aware of all the details of the world around you.

SUN IN THE 6TH HOUSE

You seek perfection, you want to be perfect, and therefore want all that you do to be perfect. Discriminating and conscious of detail, you are aware of what you believe are imperfections in your world and in yourself, and you either worry about them or hide them by putting on a display of your better points. You hate others to see fault in you because you see too much yourself, for example being aware of every detail (or flaw) of your own appearance because you look too closely and critically.

Because you see imperfection, you become anxious about your life-support, *e.g.*, your health—aware of how fragile life can be and what can go wrong with it; you may be hypochondriacal about your health, imagining imperfections in your physical state. In housework you prefer to have the house tidy, the pantry stocked, your diet worked out (a lush and luxurious one possibly), and your clothes clean and neatly pressed as a matter of personal pride. You feel that untidiness reflects badly upon you, but if your self-respect was ever shattered you may be lazy and untidy. You are probably more critical of yourself than anyone else could be, yet will react even to self-criticism by boosting your pride—or resurrecting it since your criticism knocks it down. And if anyone else criticizes you, well, that's just the last straw!

You are strongly work-oriented (assuming undamaged self-respect) and prefer creative and leading roles in your occupation. You do not like being subservient to others, preferring to work for yourself if possible (and you are capable of making it possible). You may have pride battles with the boss (maybe just in your mind) saying "well, he/she is no better than I." You take pride in your work, wanting to shine and be recognized for it, and work well where creative display and meticulous details are needed. You may use your orderly and meticulous qualities in such areas as mathematics where perfectionism is rewarded and error can be analyzed away. You prefer organizing and telling others what to do rather than doing the donkey-work yourself. Work should become creative play for you, for example you would enjoy working with children as a play-director or such, but you must avoid spoiling your work area by using it as a negative pride-prop, such as saying "My work is much more perfect, creative, better than theirs."

Your mother was intellectually or manually creative, with a lively and wide-ranging curiosity. She could turn abstract ideas into concrete actualities fairly easily, and perhaps create systems of abstract thought from her experience. She was direct and outspoken and when she spoke you had to take notice. Yet she was not totally consistent, being quite adaptable to a variety of people and circumstances, and quite capable of changing her mind (becoming as fixed in her second attitude as she was in her first).

Your father preferred a wide scope, whether he was a restless rover, an open-air person, or broad-mindedly philosophical in an easy-going way. He gave outspoken advice freely and openly, passing on his experience for your education. He was cheerful and confident, yet he had a temper that could throw thunderbolts. He was capable of running away if things didn't suit him. Appearing to be open and honest, he could use his honesty selectively to bluff others with, telling parts of the truth and allowing others to make their own judgments biased by that partiality.

MOON IN THE 6TH HOUSE

You are capable of being industrious and methodical as a worker in a supporting position, being receptive to detailed and precise methods of working, doing well in any position in which you can give service to others. You work best in areas that have a nurturing element to them, perhaps that provide for the feeding or sheltering of others, for example in food supply, baking, real estate, or building—out of many possibilities. You tend to work best as part of a group in which you collect, pool and then distribute whatever you deal with, usually on the basis of supplying the needs of public demand. In work you behave with modesty, decorum, and pleasant manners, generally being content to be of service, to be good at your job, and to behave with simplicity. In the long run you are likely to become a key figure by your constancy and consistency as a worker, gaining the respect of those around you (though your moods can disturb that consistency).

By contrast, some with this position become greedily dissatisfied with modest circumstances. They develop a rather restless ambition, not to become or to do anything special, but merely to escape from what they consider to be a lowly position. They are very aware of all their appetites and seek to gratify them more than enough, becoming greedy and luxury-loving. The basic desire to be of service is focused entirely upon themselves, not on others, and they build on their critical side to become arrogant. They may also use illness as a way of making themselves dependent on others and claiming their attention.

For most with the Moon in the 6th House; your analytical mind will develop through your tendency to reflect on details of your day-to-day living, since your security depends on you having them in your grasp. Anxiety arises if you do not, and you then tend to criticize the problem area. Your abilities to be critical can be fed by your moods to become an emotional complaining, usually about the imperfections of your circumstances, how other people mess things up etc. for example moaning about the mess made, and the amount of work to do when members of the family visit. You tend to find security in neatness, tidiness, cleanliness, and to become insecure and anxious if conditions are not kept this way. You are capable of bringing pet worries back up over and over again, fretting about little things. In your childhood you gained attention, and thus security, by complaining about your worries, thus feeding and establishing the habit. You also gained attention for being helpful and useful about the house.

Your mother had a reflective mind, perhaps not developed in any special way, but deep in the sense that she would return again and again to the same themes, deepening them a little each time around. There were times when she could be a very good listener, acting as a mirror to those she talked to, and responding with sympathetic concern. There were also probably times when she didn't listen at all, when she was entirely concerned with her own thoughts, and she used this state as her emotional defense.

Your father's basic mood was probably cheerful and outgoing, kindly and tolerant, and he liked to be outdoors, the wider the spaces the better. He was honest and probably outspoken, though restless and a little highly strung, and ready to run off if trouble loomed.

MERCURY IN THE 6TH HOUSE

Your mind has an analytical or critical turn that you use on everything, yourself included. You learn the practical aspects of all that you deal with, noting the function and use of everything around you, and what you can do with it. You can be a capable and efficient worker at anything requiring analysis or meticulous attention to details, or needing your ability to link together various available resources and methods to satisfy the needs of the system within which you work. You are good at finding out just what those needs are and working to satisfy them, whether in work or any other area of your life-support, or your dealings with others. You have an intellectual interest in perfection, be this in personal neatness, cleanliness and work, or in more abstract areas, and imperfection can disturb you, producing anxiety and tension. You feel that if every detail of your life isn't organized and under control, then it will fall into chaos; therefore you have to work at it continually, and if you stop to rest then you fall back and will have to catch up again, final perfect completion remaining unattainably ahead of you.

This position deals with the way that you responded to household duties as a child; there are two distinct possibilities. One is stated above, the result of willingly taking on duties, wanting to perform them well to prove yourself, yet feeling not quite capable. The other reaction is to have turned away from all those duties, deciding to remain a child for as long as possible, letting your parents do the household work. In this case you find it hard to arouse interest in making a living, feeling that the world should support you; you also have little interest in tidiness and cleanliness, that being your mother's job, not yours. Naturally you become anxious about your life-support, if no one is looking after it. Sometimes we find the intermediate, the person who makes the effort, then collapses, then struggles back again. It all depends on your response to house-training.

Where you use your critical mind on yourself, you boost your worries by picking yourself apart. You may be seeking to be perfect, to be beyond criticism by others, which makes you anxious, and never be free from your self-criticism, leaving you equally anxious. Anxiety and tension lead to ill-health. In some cases an individual can unconsciously bring on ill-health as a convenient way of dropping worries and responsibilities. In general, with Mercury in the 6th House, you will have to deal with poor health in your life, whether your own or someone else's.

Your mother had an active questioning mind, in pursuit of knowledge or information. She was logical and thought things out even when feeling was a more appropriate tool. She was rather ambivalent about many matters, changing her mind quite freely as the balance of her thinking tipped one way and the other.

Your father probably had an intellectual interest in philosophy, religion, or higher education, or in communication over wider regions. He also tended to apply his intellect a little inappropriately in regions where a mental synthesis was needed. His mind was restless and ranged widely as he tried to gain understanding, which he then tried to pass on, possibly by lecturing.

VENUS IN THE 6TH HOUSE

Your value judgments are analytical, critical and meticulous, and through them you are seeking perfection. Thus you judge things against your standards of perfection. Naturally many things and many people are going to fall short. Since you prefer not to relate to imperfection, to disorder or unpleasantness, you try to keep yourself uncontaminated by any of them, in a kind of spotless purity. You try to maintain your perfection in the way that you relate to others, analyzing what should be the right and proper response to them, the correct attitude to hold, and so forth, putting each prepared response into its appropriate place at the appropriate time. As your relationships develop your discernment begins to find faults to occupy its attention. Then you become anxious and uncertain since things are not to your liking and you begin to pull out, but in a state of chaos (what you are trying to avoid) because you know that there is no right response when you have cut someone else down.

You find imperfection as a way of maintaining your own self-respect, or pride. If you see other things or people as less perfect than you, the judge, then you must be more perfect than them. But your judgments have no real bearing on whether or not something is perfect in its own right, and ultimately all things are, as expressions of their own intrinsic nature. You cannot seek happiness by looking for your own idea of perfection, but only by recognizing that perfection is already there. If you do so, you have a love of all life that is ready to put itself to the service of that life, working to fulfill its needs, acting as a partner to Nature. You have at least the raw material of compassion, and you work to put things together rather than to pull them apart. In work you prefer to deal directly with people, in areas where tact, charm, and diplomacy are important; where beauty, comfort, taste, and value are being promoted; where refined evaluation and judgment are necessary; in finances, for example banking or accountancy; or with plants or animals; or perhaps fabrics, fashions, or foodstuffs.

Your mother may have been quite tactful and pleasant in speech, in general preferring harmony in her communications with others. She had a judgmental mind but tried to remain fair and open, though her habit of weighing up the pros and cons often left her undecided about things, or ready to change her mind as she considered other aspects of the subject she was examining. In her better moods she would allow you, as a child, to get away with a lot, and then pull you up short on very small things as her mood changed; so she swung from calling you a good child to calling you a bad child, though in general she preferred the former.

Your father could be a very cheerful, open, freedom loving person, whose ethics were based on peace and pleasantness, and on a flexible and generous sense of proportion. It is quite possible that he may have flared into a judgmental temper if anyone transgressed his rather abstract moral standards, but he may also have run away, getting out of the home in order to keep the peace. He probably found value in higher studies and philosophy, and sought his peace in the great outdoors, or simply in the open air.

MARS IN THE 6TH HOUSE

You are energetic in pursuit of perfection in your actions and your work. Your analytical mind seeks clarity and precision, developing a cutting edge to attack imperfection or sloppiness, whether in yourself or in others. You tend to attack and dissect things, stripping them apart in your effort to make them perfect. Thus you can be sharply aggressive in your criticisms of things, situations or people, actually making yourself suspicious in your desire to have things right. You can be too sharply focused on details to be able to see the validity or perfection of the whole, whether of the results of your own actions, or of the state of the world around you. You feel that getting on with the basics of daily living is a battle; if Mars has no difficult aspects you enjoy the battle and intend to win it. Under difficulties you see it as a struggle that has to be maintained, a continuing effort against erosion to keep life safe and in order, in which case you worry energetically, attacking your problems head-on, turning them into a fight, and enlarging them by your close intense focus, like looking at them through a microscope.

You are a hard and energetic worker, preferring to be self-starting and self-directing. You want to act to accomplish things on your own account, and don't like being made to, or continually asked to. Thus you prefer working alone and not having anyone else directing you or interfering with you—and particularly not criticizing you, for if they do you will fight back, being quite capable of criticizing your own actions yourself. You usually prefer to be working on something new, or making fresh contacts rather than going over old ground. For some, this is the mark of the tool user or tool maker, particularly dealing with sharp instruments; symbolically it deals with sharp or focused energy applied to a multitude of single point details. You are energetic in all facets of your life-support, including basics such as housework and shopping, and probably get into a fretful and critical temper if things are not in order.

In health, a main problem will be of energy; for example fatigue from overwork, muscular strain, adrenal stress, hemoglobin problems; otherwise such things as headaches and eyestrain and difficulties that develop from pushing yourself too hard. You are unlikely to focus much attention onto your health, expecting your body to do its job efficiently; those that do focus on health usually enter the medical profession—normally on the surgical side.

Your mother is likely to have been direct and vigorous in her thoughts and speech, not beating about the bush but coming straight to the point. She was also quite possibly argumentative, entering disputes and debates with daggers drawn and intending to win. She held her opinions energetically (even if she held the opposite opinion just as energetically the next day). Your father was more of a lone traveler, putting his energies into his own explorations and pursuit of opportunities, and not really wanting anyone else along with him. He was capable of a sharp, and perhaps aggressive, focus on moral issues. His temper would have made quite a display when it blew, though he would usually have been easy-going.

JUPITER IN THE 6TH HOUSE

You have a perfectionist streak that prefers to relate to the best in everything, to see all things changed for the better, but because of this you tend to find fault with it all. You elaborate on your ideas of perfection, picking on small details and putting them under your critical microscope, thus blowing them up out of proportion to their actual size. You are not particularly consistent in this, tending to jump from detail to detail, producing a kind of shotgun scatter pattern of generalized criticism. You don't actually see the big picture very well. You can be quite moralistic, often assuming a superior attitude toward the imperfections that you find, though you may be quite humorous about them where they don't really matter to you. Your dissecting mind will focus largely on your life-support areas; work—you being pro-justice and fairness in working conditions and ready to crusade for them, producing the odd explosive situation; health—being finicky about your diet, cleanliness and exercise, though some are too self-indulgent in this area.

In work you are cheerful, honest and easygoing on the surface, but you have a problem in becoming distracted and scattered by details, unable to maintain an overview. You may also be rather restless in your general working life, this position often indicating the varied career of a person who moves on from hope to hope, from prospect to prospect, moving on as each hope fails or collapses under your critical gaze. You can be stable in an occupation if it satisfies your restlessness and need for breadth of coverage, for example if it involves plenty of traveling, whether in your work, moving from one place to another— or in driving for a living. Common occupations with Jupiter in the 6th are: forestry and other outdoor growing concerns; carpentry, building, construction; traveling salesman, company representative; travel agent; import/export; work in bookstores, universities, information services; teaching; journalism, particularly as a columnist or foreign correspondent; advertising. This is by no means all; work for large corporations, publishing houses, in the law, with horses or other large animals, as a tour guide, are also common. In other words, any occupation that covers a wide ground, is concerned with distant places, with the great outdoors, with growth and expansion, or with developing any process between plan and completion.

In health matters, your greatest sensitivities lie in your blood pressure (if high, this comes from a suppressed desire to run away from problems and can be countered by jogging); over-rich diet leading to obesity problems or cholesterol difficulties, *e.g.*, arteriosclerosis (also caused by stress over a long period of time); liver detoxification problems. Most of your difficulties here will be avoided if you use your preference for honest, natural food, and get enough outdoor exercise.

You mother was an outspoken person, not afraid to put forth her ideas and opinions on most subjects. She probably suffered from "cat out of the bag" or "foot in mouth" disease, not being aware of or not caring about the consequences of what she said. Your father was, in general, easy-going, and rather restless. He may have had a broadly philosophical or religious tendency, open-minded and tolerant; or may have been a rover.

SATURN IN THE 6TH HOUSE

The analytical side of your mind is slow and cautious, a certain element of fear making you careful to order your thoughts within strict boundaries of doubt. You have a tendency toward a serious or depressed emotional tone to your thinking, a slow deep worry about your responsibilities in the basic daily running of your own life, which makes you want to have total control over it. You try to organize your life, your work, your home, for safety and security. This ordered organization could be something of a fetish with you, since you recognize everything in life that is not under your control. You think about your security very seriously, and rather without optimism. Your doubts can make you negatively discriminating, skeptical, and self-critical, evaluating yourself against very orthodox (and perhaps narrow-minded) standards. You may be critical to the point of complaining about anything that is not to your liking.

This tendency will focus particularly on your work. While you are capable of being very organized and responsible, taking any job seriously and sticking to it, you still may feel that your status is not what you would like it to be, being very aware of your place in the hierarchy of power and wanting recognition for your efforts. You prefer, if possible, to be in control, in a planning position. You would be a slow, cautious worker, best employed in an area where the rules are clear-cut and require meticulous application, for example the Civil Service; in an area where strict scientific analysis is needed, particularly medicine (physiological analysis); laying roads, earth moving or construction; or building life-support basics in food, clothing, or shelter. If the aspects to Saturn are good you should reach the top of your chosen field in the long run, and be respected for your organizing ability, conscientiousness, and professionalism. However if the aspects are negative, you expect a rough deal out of the work arena; if this is so then you need to deal with your pessimistic expectations and whatever resentments you hold, and realize that you get what you expect, and that working to rule doesn't get you very far.

Periodic doubt and depression can affect your health, making you particularly prone to colds and flu, and if excessive may lead to chronic ailments, long and debilitating, though not necessarily severe. Some will suffer arthritic complaints and others from maladies that affect the bones, frequently a reflection of a stiffening of the mind. Some with Saturn in the 6th House tend to be hypochondriacs, brooding about every minor (and perhaps imaginary) ailment, while others use their illnesses to exert control over their family.

Your mother's mind was also serious, holding ideas of duty and obligation; her words were capable of making you feel guilty and immature (bad child), and tended to build the strict, orthodox and self-controlling aspects of your ideas of good and bad. With her, words were probably enough to control you. Your father may have been religiously strict, or a skeptic (atheist or agnostic) but he also held strong ideals of ethical responsibility, though he may not have imposed them on you, except at certain times of lecturing.

URANUS IN THE 6TH HOUSE

Your nervous system is capable of a rapid mixing and cross connecting of reflexes, of streams of information received, of awareness of levels of need in your being and of what must to be done to fulfill them. This gives you a fast analytical mind, able to connect and assess multitudes of facts and details, integrating them into a coordinated system. Thus you can learn quickly in your work and can tackle a high information flow; this also means that you need a lot of stimulus, and that after learning to do a job you can quickly become bored unless it interests you enough to keep you awake. If your interest is not held you can feel trapped, and seeing no reason to suffer that, you move on. So you may change jobs many times, doing something different each time, until you find work stimulating enough to keep you involved. You are a fast and independent worker, unless you are a rebel.

You may find interest in working with business machines, computers, data processing; with electronics; radio/TV, communications and media; aviation, aero-space industries; transportation systems, traffic control; auto maintenance, rental, racing etc.; astronomy, astrology; social work. To boil it down—coordinating and integrating many streams of information; dealing with systems of high speed communication or transportation.

You prefer to be highly independent in your own life-support, not depending on anyone else for it. In the daily running of your life you arrange things for speed (shopping, cooking, or cleaning) and may do several jobs at once, coordinating them so that you are able to switch from one to another as necessary. You probably appreciate all the household gadgets and machines. Your attitudes here were mainly formed between your seventh and tenth years; you preferred to be able to offer your help independently in your home, but if anyone tried to force you to help—then you rebelled and refused. If you rebelled, then your working life has its difficulties as you refuse to be pushed around or dictated to by anyone, being too independent to be a good worker. You may tend to do your jobs in your own way, disregarding the laid-down rules and methods, finding short-cuts, or you may rebel and "goof-off," saying "I don't care."

In health matters your main problem is nervous tension through over-active worrying (though you may say "I don't care" on the surface) and perhaps intestinal gas problems. Your tensions are likely to be in the solar plexus and abdominal regions (anxiety centers). You may develop an active interest in alternative methods of healing and experimental dietary systems. If interested in this area, you are likely to link together several techniques of healing into an unusual format, or use highly developed integrated systems such as Yoga, acupuncture, or radiesthesia.

Verbally, your mother was either rather abstract and detached, or rapid fire—talking fast and not always finishing her sentences before moving on to the next—leaving you with the task of filling in the missing links. Your father was probably highly independent, particularly in his ethics and his philosophy of life, believing that people should be allowed to go their own way without interference and make their own discoveries.

NEPTUNE IN THE 6TH HOUSE

There are two distinct types with this placing: (a) Clear or developed; and (b) confused or undeveloped. I will refer to them as (a) or (b). The two types are not finally separate but run in a line of development from (b) to (a), or in a line of decay from (a) to (b).

Your analytical mind is capable of (a) fine detailed discrimination and unusually subtle analysis using your intuition; or (b) vague and confused discrimination, being unable to see what details are relevant or important, allowing your analysis of circumstances to be done by your imagination thus producing unreal results. Your approach to daily life-support (such as housework), is (a) to use a smooth, unruffled flow of effort that keeps everything at its best, producing gracious living, a naturally harmonious and beautiful life style; or (b) sloppy, chaotic and untidy, letting things drift, letting food go moldy and dirty clothes pile up on the floor. This is a reflection of (a) a trust of life, being in harmony with it, feeling that daily living has its own perfection and purity; (b) an anxious fretting about life, feeling that imperfection and impurity is everywhere and that you are vulnerable to it, that there is nothing you can do about it, and if it is going to crumble then you will crumble with it. (A) finds little fault in anything, trusting the stream of life to flow in the right direction of its own accord, while (b) finds imaginary faults in nearly everything, does not trust life to flow in any good direction and so has a free-floating anxiety with no specific focus.

(B)'s anxiety produces imaginary, hysterical, and undiagnosable health problems, while if (a) has any ailments they are often a bodily dissolution of old psychological patterns, freeing, releasing and opening both body and mind. Both are physiologically highly sensitive to drugs and should use far smaller doses than are normally advised though some of type (b) use drugs very haphazardly, others show remarkable resistance to the effects of drugs or anesthetics, use large doses, and end up with liver problems. General sensitivities are to bacterial or fungal infections; hypothalamus-related ailments, *e.g.*, insomnia or other sleep problems, body fluid balance difficulties, extreme appetite or total lack, heat/cold sensitivity problems; meningeal ailments; problems with the feet.

Type (a) may spend time in a hospital ministering to others, giving compassionate service to those in need, being capable of some subtle kinds of healing and often interested in occult or spiritual methods, or in subtleties of diet and biochemistry, particularly vitamin therapy. (B) at the worst may spend time in hospital simply to be looked after, producing imaginary complaints to gain attention. Where (a) is capable of great service, (b) often feels like the doormat at work; he/she may want to be helpful, but allows things to get into a chaotic state out of sheer confusion; or just lets things drift and fall apart.

Likely areas of work for you are in hospitals, museums, libraries, art galleries or any large public institutions; hotels, restaurants, pubs, clubs, cocktail lounges, theaters or other public entertainment or hospitality areas; in the oil, chemical, photographic industries; or in any area where image is important, such as fashion or films; fishing, shipping or other oceanic connections; dealing with ecclesiastical properties.

PLUTO IN THE 6TH HOUSE

You need to feel that you are effective, capable, competent in your work, for if you don't you will pile up stress and inner irritation until it affects your health. You are capable of working extremely hard, or of hating work and refusing to work at all, one or the other. If you are hard-working, you don't mind the dirtiest, roughest and hardest of conditions, or the most back-breaking of jobs, and can apply yourself with total effort and effect. You can tackle what many feel to be the intolerable aspects of life, such as crime, disease, garbage and sewage, recognizing that somebody has to do it. This is a pattern for police and detective work, nursing and medical work, psychology and psychotherapy, cleaning, waste and sewage disposal, repairing ecological damage, undertaking, power production, atomic energy, forges, furnaces and kilns, mass-production, armaments, mechanics, engines and engineering, and repair work. Those who go in for clean work may be employed in the mass-money area, financing, mortgages, loans, investments, wills and trusts, or economics.

You have an intensely discriminating mind, efficient, intolerant of wastage, practical and shrewd, oriented toward dealing with the raw materials and basic essentials of living. You must fulfill all your personal needs, be they physical, emotional, intellectual, or spiritual, since any left unfulfilled will arouse stress and anxiety—although you may not admit this consciously in your need to appear competent. You see work and health maintenance as survival matters, and may be very aware of life-support essentials— or have ignored these areas entirely. This will show in your diet, which you will either carefully design for health, perhaps being fussy and particular, eliminating everything harmful, including all essentials; or you lean toward junk foods and careless cooking, and probably a high meat intake to satisfy your carnivorous instincts.

Your mother was either very sharp tongued, or silent about things that bothered her deeply. Where she spoke out, this made you anxious, perhaps feeling that you weren't wanted, that she wouldn't look after you. Since this was a survival threat, your survival instincts made you look after yourself—unless you made your mother look after you, by acting helpless, for example. But that wouldn't take away anxiety, which you tried to bury, perhaps under an attitude that everything is all right. It may surface in your moods of intense criticism toward things in yourself or in others that you see as a threat, or that your mother complained about. If buried deeply it will surface in migraines or other headaches, or odd illnesses that may lead to blackouts—trying to avoid seeing what is surfacing in your mind, for example hatred or fears. These can be cured by facing them. Otherwise you may, by an act of will, reject illness, or even become a psychic healer.

Some stress may have come from your father, whose temper may have been explosive, or whose moralism may have been absolutely black and white, particularly where sex was concerned. His religious or philosophical attitudes were either fanatical and fundamentalist, or nonexistent. He may have shut out anything he didn't like by running away from it, or he may have been intensely gregarious, or a teacher of deep knowledge of life.

NORTH NODE—6TH HOUSE, SOUTH NODE—12TH HOUSE

You are a sensitive and vulnerable person who tends to live in the private realm of your own imagination. You drift in reflective reverie, building a safer and more perfect world within than you feel the real world to be. Your outward confidence is low and you can be fearfully suspicious and critical of those around you, particularly when they do not match your dream of perfection, finding them imperfect by comparison. Watching both your own inner world and gazing on others from your seclusion, you can come to believe that others are watching you. Combine this with your sensitivity to others' feelings (feeling them as strongly as your own) and tendency to automatically give way to them; add to this your capacity for endless fretful and vague fear, plus rich imagination, and you end up with a strong potential for paranoia, or at least feelings of martyrdom. Your fears leave you with no confidence in the future while your drifting with the tide doesn't build one.

You need to build up your faith, and your analytical awareness of how to affect events by applied effort. Efforts made to become fully competent in handling all details of life-support, dealing with basic human needs, and making life comfortable and safe should be of great value to you. Your sensitivity gives you the ability to be compassionately helpful to others, and you have a natural ability to heal, using your own unusual methods. It is likely that you will spend time dealing with illness as well as dealing with, or working in, hospitals or other large public institutions. You will come to recognize that most illness is based on fear, tension or anxiety and that when the cause is removed, the effect—the ailment—disappears. Every problem in life can be seen as an ailment from this viewpoint.

✦ 9 ✦

Libra
and the 7th House

Here we have awareness of the present moment as the point of balance between past and future, in the form of our awareness of the current relationship between ourselves as the central experiencing subject and the environment as surrounding object. This includes our awareness of the relationship between cause and effect generally, including our ability to be causative in our own lives through our decisions and actions, and of the effect we have on the environment and it has on us. Therefore it is the point of potential for change as we make fresh decisions on current needs. This awareness includes recognition of our current personal needs, of imbalances of any kind, whether physical, emotional, mental, or spiritual, in ourselves or our lives, and recognition of the need to correct any imbalance. It includes the drive toward balance, together with an awareness of what is needed as counterbalance.

Our current state of awareness is the mirror of the local environment, the picture that we hold in our minds of the present state of both self and other. It includes awareness of the relationship between ourselves as subject and the object, whether that is a situation, a thing, or a person. Our right-brain awareness holds together the whole picture of our current world, our left-brain awareness moves from point to point within that picture, from self to other, from one focus of interest to the next. This is our conscious relationship between self and surroundings, between ourselves as the center and everything around us as the surface of our sphere of sensory awareness. Here we relate the other to self, to our own needs, views, and preferences. In relating self to the other we make the beginnings of bonds of relationship, whether positive or negative, whether of attraction or repulsion. We all have a fundamental need for peaceful, satisfying, and preferably beautiful relationships between self and whole. We also need, if we can't have peace, to be able to redress excesses, whether to minimize conflict, or to return blow for blow.

We make discriminating choices of what to focus on, what to be aware of and then move into, out of all possible available experiences. Our choice of what to be aware of separates our personal universe (small) from the impersonal (vast). Projection of our own viewpoint onto the world—seeing things from where we are—means that what we see in the world is the image in the mirror, the reflection of our own choice of focus. The discriminating use of our tastes and our creative intellect, while it can bring fruitful results, also implies our rejection of what we don't appreciate, or at least, our refusal to be

199

involved with it. The 7th is the area where we begin to filter out signal from noise, to make our choice of figure from ground, to distinguish between what we regard as part of our reality and what does not belong to it. This includes whatever parts of our own personalities we don't want to deal with, to face in the mirror. We can only be aware of, and correct, imbalances that we can admit to. What we leave out we either refuse to be aware of at all, or it becomes the irritants in our world, usually projected onto others.

The 7th House includes our inner awareness of the relationship between conscious and unconscious elements of mind, between surface and center of being, of the angelic or civilized and demonic or uncivilized instinctual faces of our personalities. If this relationship is unresolved or unaccepted in us, projection of the shadow or dark side onto the other, whether person or situation, is the most likely result, and that creates conflict between us and our world. If we accept everything that we are, the relationship is a fount of power, of instinctual, creative, and regenerative energy rising from the depths.

The relationship between the two (conscious and unconscious, self and world) is determined by the *filter* we place between them. The filter functions in the same way as a radio tuner, allowing only our chosen station through, only the reality we choose to see (inner and outer). If very selective, what we allow ourselves to see of ourselves is narrow, rejecting much—and we equally reject the same things in others around us, thus building a tight, defensive, and uncomfortable life, seeing many things around us that we do not consider to be nice. If our self-acceptance is high, we allow far more through to consciousness, our view of the world is richer, wider, and deeper, and we find little to reject—building an open, warm, accepting life. What we reject in ourselves remains in the unconscious, suffering under the harsh judge which is the filter (except where projected onto others and attacked in them). This predetermines our level of blending with the other, of defended individuality at one extreme, or of ability to relate in such depth as to be able to fuse with others at the opposite extreme.

Here lies our capacity for perceiving from different points of view and thus gaining depth perception, exactly as we do using two eyes for binocular vision. This obviously includes our capacity for interacting with others generally, the opposite sex or chosen partners in particular. Learning to see from others' points of view as well as our own teaches us far more than we'll ever see alone. It teaches us tolerance and understanding at least. If we don't have those, we use various kinds of charm and tactics to get along with others, or to hide from them our inner faults. Our need to use tactics increases the less tolerant or more defended we are, since we then see others as at least potential enemies; battle requires at the minimum giving back as good as you get, but preferably knowing how to stop or to destroy your enemy. Tactical awareness also involves seeing from the other's point of view, but using it to figure out their likely actions or decisions in advance, to use against them.

The Libran or 7th House life-period lies between eight or nine years old and 12 to 13. During this time a child feels the need to begin making its own major decisions. It has built the analytical ability and knowledge of detail about the local world that are essential for effective decision-making.

There are many and varied motives behind our decisions; the motives that we admit to are frequently a civilized veneer that we superimpose on less conscious or admissible ones. Yet most decisions are made to gain a tactical advantage in life, even if that advantage is simply correcting an imbalance. But we also have here a *governor* on our decisions and actions, which tones down the extremes to which we might otherwise go. It is our need for the approval of others (beginning with our parents), our desire to to be liked by them. Obviously this governor ceases to work if we decide we no longer want their approval.

The growing child is very aware of impending adulthood, and no longer wants to be treated as a child, but more as an equal. It is beginning to transfer its main focus in relating from parents to others outside the family, and from friends of the same sex to those of the opposite sex. (Much of what the youngster will be able to put into the relationships he/she makes throughout life will spring directly from the imprints into their being of the relationship they perceive between their parents). This is usually a period of idealism, of wanting everything in life to be nice. The uncivilized youngster is becoming a civilized adult.

Physiology

The center to surface pattern is also at work in the relationship between the nucleus of any cell and the rest of the cell, including the surface membrane. The nucleus actively dictates the processes that go on throughout the cell, being in total all the processes of life itself, and these processes obviously have to be kept in balance. Since the cell does not exist in isolation, it has needs that it must supply from the outer world, the surrounding nurturing fluid. Every cell in the body has a surface skin or membrane, which is permeable, actively capable of taking in essential nutrients from the surrounding fluids, and of putting out manufactured proteins and other products for general use, as well as of eliminating wastes. The cell membrane acts by choice, depending on inner needs, and on the balance of inner and outer states.

In digestion, the small sugar molecules resulting from intestinal digestion (6th House) are here absorbed through the permeable membrane of the intestinal wall and into the bloodstream for circulation as fuel for the whole body. What remains in the intestine is now waste, and it is passed down into the colon for elimination. The kidneys are constantly filtering all the fluids of the body, actively choosing from knowledge of the body's current needs what materials are to be retained and what to be eliminated.

The 7th also covers the sense of balance, and the ovaries and female reproductive organs. The female organs are specially designed to welcome and contain a particular part of the outer world, in the form of the male organ, then to contain and nurture newly conceived beings until they are ready to emerge into the outer world. The eggs released by the ovaries are single large cells, and have the full ability to choose which sperm (out of the multitude) they will allow to unite with them, to penetrate their membrane and fertilize them.

SUN IN LIBRA
✧ The See-Saw ✧

General principle of Le Chatelier: When any system in equilibrium is disturbed, it always reacts in such a manner as to oppose the force which upset the balance. Or, for every action there is an equal and opposite reaction.

Mentally and physically Libra represents all elements of every being that work to achieve a state of balance. These include the kidneys with their function of balancing the chemicals, fluids, and electrolytes of the body to its exact needs; the inner ear and the center of gravity coordinating together to maintain physical balance; and subject-object awareness, the clear knowing of the relationship between self and other in the world with which you are involved.

You want to achieve a state of peaceful harmony in life, even if it means going through war to reach it. Some Librans avoid conflict at all costs, showing the classical diplomat face of the sign, being flexible and accommodating, tactful and conciliatory, doing anything to avoid rocking the boat. They continually adjust to other people's attitudes and actions, never showing any preferences of their own. This is one way of balancing a relationship, allowing the other to lead the dance with the Libran continually following, forgetting that for balance and equality two people with all their preferences and aversions must be involved, not just one and a mirror. These Librans hate ugliness with a passion and will do anything to avoid it, bury it, deny that it exists, maintaining a fairy tale fantasy image of life, and relating to those who play out well-developed images in fashion, lifestyle and personality.

On the other hand are those who use their awareness of others' motivations to keep a tactical balance, being able to put themselves in the others' place, seeing situations from their viewpoint, adjusting their tactics to counter-balance their opponents. These are the generals and the chess players. They will usually take an opposing viewpoint in a discussion or argument, whatever their own views happen to be, and if the opponent switches viewpoint so does the Libran.

You have the ability to see things from various points of view and you know that they are all valid, which may make it appallingly difficult for you to make a simple decision on anything. Besides, using a balanced viewpoint all things are equal, so how can you affirm or deny any of them. Indecision is your greatest bugbear; even decisive Librans often undo their decisions—changing their mind or counter-balancing previous actions.

You are at least potentially very intellectually objective and aware. Your intellect, if developed, is capable of balanced reasoning and judgment, which some Librans use in the law, others in literature or the arts, especially dance. The average Libran uses his/her judgment to keep up personal poise, taste, and attractiveness, outdoing all others in care and attention paid to dress and appearance.

While this describes the classic Libran personality, you will vary from it in many ways. Your most major differences will be shown by the house placement of the Sun and by the sign and house position of Venus.

MOON IN LIBRA

Your emotional security depends upon keeping everything in your life harmonious, balanced, in proportion, in fact generally nice. You have a feeling for beauty, which you would like to pervade your whole existence, keeping ugliness and discord at bay. You use charm in your relationships to stay in control and keep the peace, to ensure that you are liked, and you use subtle tactics to gain this end, being capable of flattery, diplomacy, and tact. If you find it impossible to keep the peace you are capable of using your tactical instinct to keep the balance in battle, being aware of the strengths, qualities, and mentality of the opposition and using this knowledge to stay one step ahead by thinking from their viewpoint.

Beware discriminating against that which you feel to be unpleasant simply because it offends you (rough or crude individuals, for example), and use your ability to see from the opposite point of view, in order to extend your understanding of all facets of life, to be perfectly fair and just to all.

Equality is a prime need in you, even when you gracefully give way to others. At best you recognize that everyone has their own point of view, however varied these may be, but may enjoy taking an opposing position in a discussion for sheer intellectual exercise. At worst, you may twist others' words to suit your own argument. This mental flexibility can make it difficult for you to make clear, simple decisions, complicating things by seeing too many alternatives and being unable to decide between them, since to you they all appear equal. Your indecisiveness and your detached intellectual judgment are your emotional armor, keeping the unpleasant at a safe distance, avoiding the cruder, muddier side of life (to the point of making it invisible to you). You see your whole relationship to your world as either peace (with everything flowing pleasantly) or war (being involved in struggle with your experiences). You tend to lean on others for assistance when the world seems too rough for you, sometimes becoming obligated to them and losing your autonomy, your freedom of decision. At the worst times you feel like giving up completely.

You need relationships because you feel incomplete without someone else to reflect you back. This is a psychological need to complete your own being by uniting with your other half, your unconscious side. You tend to project your innermost being onto any partner and relate to that rather than to the person themselves. Where you are in conflict with the other, it is in fact yourself that you battle with, seeing yourself reflected in them as in a mirror (seeing in them what you refuse to recognize in yourself). Your preference for relating only to the pleasant can make you relate only to image, style, and flair in others, as you display the same surface values. Or you may show a well-developed discrimination, which, if positively used, produces a clear and balanced judgment. This is of enormous value to lawyers, writers, artists and designers (and may also involve a well-developed physical balance of use in dancing, which you are very likely to appreciate).

MERCURY IN LIBRA

Your mind is rational and evaluating, possibly judgmental, focusing strongly on your relationships with others, and on their thoughts, attitudes, and motivations. When you consider anything, you usually try to reach a balanced opinion by considering several alternative viewpoints (or at least two opposed ones), assessing their relative merits and the probable outcome of pursuing each to its conclusion. You are frequently undecided about which path to take, since you can usually see equal possibilities or equal problems in all, and want all, or none. Thus it can be difficult for you to make a final decision about anything that is important to you.

Your dualism comes partly from your awareness swinging between subjective and objective, between being focused entirely on yourself, then completely on the other, be that a person or any other circumstance. So you move back and forth between seeing your own point of view and seeing theirs.

In communicating with others you will usually tactfully or diplomatically defer to their opinions in order to keep your contacts open and pleasant, and to gain reflections of, or alternatives to, your own point of view. On the other hand you can also deliberately take an opposing viewpoint to argue from, whatever your own opinions are, in order to stimulate a vigorous discussion, knowing that ideas can only be highlighted by contrasting them with their opposites. Thus your own opinions are flexible, and you may not believe the truth to be a single thing, but that it includes all possible shades of viewpoint. This gives you reasons for being totally contrary if you feel like it, and in the long run you are likely to alternate between agreement and disagreement, even where the same topic is concerned throughout. A lot depends on how much security you feel within yourself, because if you need the approval of others very much, then you will tend to adjust your own views to match theirs. Whatever happens, you will usually avoid uncouthness of manner, and unfairness of attitude both in yourself and in others, preferring to remain pleasant at all costs.

In relationships you probably lean toward a continual back and forth pattern, moving toward your partner if they are moving away, and backing off if they seem to be clinging. One way you achieve a balance is to swing first one way and then the other, while holding the middle as an ideal. You think like a dancer, having to counterbalance all your partner's (or opponent's) moves perfectly if the dance is to flow properly. Since you are able to think from other people's positions you are capable of well-developed tactical thought, allowing you to plot move and countermove, a talent useful in battle, chess, or diplomacy.

Your interest in the motives of others may lead you into such fields as: psychology, counseling, public relations, negotiation, arbitration; in being a personal representative or mouthpiece for another. Your feeling for words and ideas fits you for journalism, creative writing, or information services. Both traits together, combined with your intellectual dislike for unfairness and desire to redress balances, suit you for the law.

VENUS IN LIBRA

You work on the principle of balance in all things, in your relationships, values, and your general life. This theme encourages you to seek harmony and proportion in all that you do, and makes you very responsive to others, balancing or counterbalancing them in all respects. This position often produces good dancers, and dancing is a perfect symbol for its main effects, with its need to adjust every movement precisely to those of the partner— to avoid being out of step. You can be romantic and affectionate, acting with charm, tact, and consideration in deference to others, seeking out their needs and requirements, and responding directly to them. You look for companionable and harmonious personal relationships, not feeling complete in yourself unless you are involved with another. You desire to please and to keep things pleasant, disliking coarseness, bad manners, and uncouthness, and will usually avoid open conflict.

Your preference for balance also gives you a highly developed feeling for equality, and you are likely to believe that anything less than equal rights for all is unjust. Thus, if anyone acts against you, you are quite capable of retaliating, though usually using your tactical thinking ability , and in seeing from the other person's point of view to redress the balance exactly, usually without hostility but with a fine sense of justice. You may be deliberately contrary, emphasizing exactly opposed points of view in order to keep a balance by contrast, always taking the other side of a discussion, whatever your own viewpoint may be. This may be patterned on your aesthetic preferences, which are capable of being highly developed, since you probably realize that pure harmony and balance can be artistically dull without some contrast, a certain well-judged and precisely placed discord, or juxtaposition of complementary elements adding interest. Or you may prefer to compromise on all points of conflict, this sometimes being taken to extremes of constantly giving way to others, thus losing all equality in the interest of a rather repressed form of harmony or supposed peace.

Psychologically this position represents the projection of the unconscious personality, or anima, onto the partner. This unconscious side contains all that you do not want to admit to being. As an essential part of your complete personality, it needs to be expressed and integrated with the conscious side. Where you cannot consciously accept it, it is unconsciously projected or thrown onto others that you meet, negatively by judging them to be what you dislike (in yourself, of course), and positively by feeling them to be what you need to become complete, both being subjectively true at one and the same time. Your relationships with others (all others) will show you very directly the nature of the relationship between your own opposed, conscious, and unconscious personalities. It is only when such projections have been overcome by acceptance of your alternate side that you can ever see another person clearly for what they are in their own right, and thus avoid all relationship games. Equally, it is only then that you can know exactly what you do want in a relationship, without indecision and struggles of adjustment.

MARS IN LIBRA

In action, you are responsive to the others around you, being involved in their aims and interests to the point of having difficulty in identifying exactly what your own are. A part of you would like to be selfish, but you hold back your own drives and desires because you want to fit in, yet can inwardly resent having to give way, feeling it to be unfair that they do what they want while you don't. You want approval from others, to be noticed, appreciated and recognized as an equal, and are offended if anyone treats you as anything else.

Much of your awareness of yourself comes from the response that you stimulate or provoke in others, and you have probably developed great skill in directing their reactions exactly where you want them to go, having a fine sense of tactics. Thus you are in charge of your relationships, while appearing to be tactfully responsive to the other person. You give them your own motives, making it appear as though they were theirs.

You have a strong sense of justice and dislike any treatment of yourself or of others that you see as being unfair, and can very actively judge those that hand out such treatment. Inwardly you judge, while outwardly remaining fair, yet you hate being judged by anyone else, feeling that that is decidedly unfair. While your effort at being fair helps your relationships, your feelings about the unfairness of the other person can leave you feeling justified in judging them, particularly when you tend not to stand up for yourself outwardly, allowing things to get to such a pitch that the relationship ends (though you may fight sometimes, just to be able to "kiss and make up"). Then when left alone, your judgments are pointed at yourself, and you need someone else around to take your awareness off yourself. Often the motives and intentions that you feel others have toward you are only your own, projected out onto them, seeing yourself in and through them.

You make comparisons between yourself and others, being easy and friendly with them, yet also being competitive. You can take ideas from them, or feed them your own, then say "Let's try this, and we'll see who can do best." You want to appear to be equal, yet win at the same time, or to be seen to win, then graciously and outwardly give credit to your opponent in fairness and sportsmanship. In your depths you have a fight going on between self-centered attitudes and all-inclusive ones, between darkness and light, which is unconsciously played out in your relationships, with you being uncertain as to who is on which side. You probably see yourself as being on the opposite end of a see-saw from others; "They are the aggressors, I am the mild, reasonable peace-maker who diplomatically de-fuses or prevents the fights," "I do things to keep the relationship going, so should they," "If I'm in the right, they are in the wrong"; or when self-judging "They are right and I'm wrong," though when you are truly fair, neither is wrong. You need to find common undertakings with others in which to affirm the pursuit of wholeness and integration, to dissolve any divisive egotism.

JUPITER IN LIBRA

You are tolerant, open and gregarious in relating to others, finding happiness and stimulation for your most cheerful and easy-going side in their company. You pour out enthusiasm with others and enjoy giving freely of yourself to them. You adapt readily to their views, attitudes, and drives, considering any other viewpoint however divergent from your own, and openmindedly exploring its wider ramifications and developments. Your creative intellect grows in breadth and tolerance, and works on themes of justice and equality for all, considering such ideas in the abstract and then applying them in your own relating. You are offended by injustice, and spend time mentally weighing and evaluating the broader moral issues in law and in life, looking for where individual and social rights lie—and questioning what constitutes justice and equity. Such objective thinking on large issues develops your philosophical mentality, capable of far-seeing judgment—considering all alternative viewpoints along the way. In communication with others, your consideration makes you diplomatic while still speaking your mind, adjusting your attitudes not to give offense.

If Jupiter has difficult aspects, your tactful restraint may make you take on too much of others' ideas, attitudes, and problems. Seeing from too many points of view leaves you undecided about everything, swinging restlessly between many alternatives, thoroughly scattered when making decisions. You elaborate upon attitudes that spring from ambivalence about yourself and the directions that you want to explore in life. You want to make decisions involving the larger issues in life, perhaps on a philosophical, legal, moral, or religious basis, but are pulled from one alternative to another, seeing potential paths of personal growth and development in each. In swinging around you may never decide to commit yourself to fulfilling any of them, or you may decide enthusiastically to jump into the biggest and best, but without laying a proper foundation or doing the necessary groundwork. You are overly generalized in your judgment, not taking specifics and details into account, being lazy and somewhat superior in your thinking. You can produce a wide spectrum of creative ideas without ever truly developing any of them.

You may also leap into relationships with irresponsible enthusiasm, responding readily to other people's desires, as well as to your own. By being whatever the other wants, possibly promising more than you are ready to give through misplaced charm or tact, you can lose the respect that others may have for you—and probably your self-respect also. You may hold many high and fine opinions regarding morality in life and in relationships, perhaps at times using them to judge others—thus gaining in superiority yourself, but never acting upon those opinions, becoming hypocritical in the process. If any other person turns and judges you, you will be ready to erupt, then run away.

Your talents in dealing with people can suit you for teaching and counseling, psychology and mediation, public relations and direct contact forms of advertising, while your preference for justice suits you for ombudsman-type positions, the law, or dealing with complaints. You may also have a talent for journalistic or literary writing.

SATURN IN LIBRA

You recognize any requirement for order, control, dutifulness, or conformity in your relationships, whether with individuals or with the world in general; and need to give or to receive respect, recognition, and commitment with partners. You are responsible with others, keeping peace and harmony by working toward mutually beneficial compromise. You are aware of the social rules, regulations, and restraints (including the unspoken ones) required to stabilize relationships, and readily adjust your role to achieve that end, adapting to obstacles by bending flexibly around them. Thus you can be serious and formal with others, aware of and ready to respond to their needs. Your seriousness in relating encourages stable, long-term partnerships, avoiding the short-term or superficial, since you require commitment and responsibility from others as you do from yourself. You believe that people are equal, so that you cannot impose yourself onto them, or overrule or manipulate them, nor do they have any right to do so to you, unless it is absolutely mutual. Being egalitarian you have a strong feeling for justice and equity, this being a classic position for lawyers, though you should beware emphasizing the letter of the law at the expense of the spirit.

If Saturn has difficult aspects, you may be brusque, and pay little attention to form, not fitting in with your environment, drawing strict and self-isolating limits in the relationship between yourself and the other. Your relationships may be utterly dependent, dutiful, cautious and reserved, bound and restricted, responsibly persevering, or depressing liabilities, authoritarian, possessive and demanding, or to an older or very serious person. You feel either inferior or superior relative to others (actually both, one conscious, the other unconscious)and may resent them, silently judging them and blaming them for your feelings. Or you may expect your relationships to go downhill, becoming cold and unresponsive with little depth of feeling, contributing to this with your own reserve. Or your idea of duty may be totally projected onto others, demanding and exacting what you want from them, restricting them, being judgmental and manipulative toward them. In this case you are projecting your own feelings of inferiority onto them in an effort to feel superior within yourself.

This position has shades from inferiority to superiority, from modesty to conceit, and may swing from one to the other, with mutual respect and recognition at the center. Difficulties arise in your effort to control your subject-object relationships, instead of allowing them to be open and natural. The negative views you hold toward others are guaranteed to spring directly from your own unconscious personality, what you do not like or accept in yourself being seen as belonging to them. You need to heal the breach between the conscious and unconscious aspects of your personality, to overcome judgment of one by the other.

The I Ching says "high mountains are worn down, and valleys filled up. Fate undermines what is full and prospers the modest. Man can shape his own fate as his behavior exposes him to benevolent or destructive forces."

URANUS IN LIBRA

Uranus was in Libra from mid-1969 to late 1975, during which time relationships began to change their nature rather radically, as evidenced by changes in the divorce laws. Earth began to realize that it was not alone in space as men landed on the Moon and Voyager probes were sent out to Jupiter and beyond. The alternate generation went through one of its more peaceful stages with the Flower Children, while student idealism was high—and the Kent State university shootings occurred, a demonstration of the sheer size of the generation gap, the split between youthful ideals and conservative fears. The air transport age went a step further with the Concorde flying at twice the speed of sound. The nature of justice came into question as the Watergate scandal was before the courts.

Those born in this generation will want their relationships to be free, liberal and open, with neither partner trapping the other into anything that they don't enter willingly. You are likely to have a great deal of respect for the rights of all individuals, your own included, desiring equality and the greatest freedom for all. Your awareness of human rights is thus likely to be well developed, and you will be pro-justice, whether or not that justice is written into the laws of the country. Your awareness of others is fast and should be friendly, with you being ready to treat anyone as a friend unless they prove themselves to be otherwise, when you will simply cut them off, not refusing to relate to them but refusing to be at all close. You have a talent for relating to others in very human ways, not feeling that you have to be stiff and formal at all, but adapting readily to their abilities to relate—delightfully able to play the fool with them if they can take it. Your creative mental abilities should be very much alive, your mind being able to take a variety of themes and knit them together inventively into quite unusual results. You have a capacity to develop distinctively individual literary talents.

If Uranus had difficult aspects, you are likely to have a powerful conflict between the need to be liked by others (which can make you very quick to adapt to their ways) and the need to have your own freedom, ending in you feeling trapped by the relationship, while actually being trapped by your own split. You may be very wary of being trapped by the attitudes of anyone else, being ready to step out of any relationship abruptly if they seem to be trying to tie you down. If you are in a long-term relationship you may still keep your independence by being detached in attitude toward your partner, or feel that both of you should be free to relate to others at the same time. You don't want to be forced into being linked with any particular thing, person, or point of view, preferring to be detached from them all, at least in theory ready to consider any, but wary of being labeled by your associations. In trying to make up your mind when making decisions, you will either jump to a decision very rapidly and impulsively, without considering where it may lead you, or do the opposite, considering every possible alternative, tensely looking for traps to avoid, and you may swing from one to the other.

NEPTUNE IN LIBRA

The Neptunian principle is that of the collective unconscious mind, reflected in a society's images of itself (in theater, literature, films and fashion) and in the individual's imagination (images of self). It colors all the dreams, images, the compassion, and most sensitive faculties of the whole population, including their religious tendencies (feeling of belonging to the whole). Dealing with the deepest sensitivities, it also deals with protective coloration (camouflage). Neptune takes 14 years to move through a sign of the zodiac so it belongs to a whole generation.

Apart from a brief revisit to Virgo in 1942, Neptune was in Libra from 1941 to 1956. During this period Aldous Huxley's *Perennial Philosophy* and Carl Jung's *Psychology and Religion* appeared (both 1941), the Dead Sea scrolls were discovered, the World Council of Churches was formed, all indications of an awakening intellectual interest in philosophy/religion, and of a dissolution of old barriers of thought. To put it simply, there was an opening of public awareness to the possibility of Transcendence. The period ended with Billy Graham's mammoth evangelistic meetings. On the popular front we had the emergence of the crooners, (the first teen-age pop idol, Frank Sinatra) the long-playing record, Cinerama and Cinemascope, and Tolkien's *The Lord of the Rings*.

Personally, you will have in your make-up a great deal of sensitivity to relationships (including your whole relationship to your world) involving a fairly high romantic idealism. On its most positive side this can produce a great deal of compassion towards others including a tendency towards empathy, feeling their feelings as strongly as your own. Under difficult aspects it can project the romantic ideal onto others without regard for who they actually are, and also use charm as a protective camouflage—wanting to be liked, and to keep relationships peaceful and pleasant. Your sensitivity to others can allow you to be influenced quite unconsciously by the most subtle pressures, including psychic ones. In relationships you need to be clearly aware of what drives you, to avoid the confusion, chaos, and possible disillusionment that can occur when you find that you have been living out an imaginative play, scripted by yourself. You should also beware of camouflaging your true feelings and intentions, because this can lead to much deception and confusion.

In decision-making you need to develop the use of your imagination as a blueprinting tool, to fix a clear image of your objective to aid you towards realizing it, to overcome potential confusion. If you don't form your aims clearly you are capable of drifting, letting vagrant fantasy images pull you this way and that. Be sure that your dreams are clear and realistic ones, not just pleasant fantasies to keep the world at bay.

If other elements of your chart show artistic tendencies this placing shows a potentially great depth of aesthetic refinement, its special areas being dance and literature. In Neptune's own areas of music and fine arts the tendency is toward abstract expression.

PLUTO IN LIBRA

Pluto was in Libra from 1972 to 1984, this period of history being the diplomacy era, with more international efforts being made to resolve wars and conflicts than ever before. The passage of this planet through the sign takes so many years that examination of the house position is much more relevant to the individual than the sign position, which is the same for everyone born in this extended period.

Those born during this period are very aware of injustices and inequalities around them. They do not, in general, want to be regarded as different than their fellows, wanting to be treated as equals. They can and will work to keep relationships as they want them to be, preferring them to be pleasant and peaceful with no turmoil, yet they are very ready to react intensely and intolerantly to rejection—even to slight hints of it. They don't want anyone else to rock the boat but can give it a good shaking themselves. With the development of tolerance they can be extremely and exactly just, willing to look at any situation from all points of view involved, and to take all into account in making their judgments. Many will not tolerate anything else but absolute directness and honesty in relationships, hiding nothing, while the more defensive and insecure ones will be constantly judging what they have to hide to avoid rejection by others. Those who do repress parts of themselves will have a fairly intense tendency to project the reasons for their problems onto others and blame them—a very normal habit, but they will do it more strongly than other generations.

As this generation reaches adulthood and enters positions of power, we will see some transformations in the legal systems and in the concept of justice itself; on the positive side with human rights being defended more strongly, with the principle of equality for all being affirmed; on the negative side the judicial system being used by powerful and secret vested interests to maintain their own positions, as usual but more so. In a few year's time we will see some great legal battles that will affect the nature of the subsequent society.

A psychological peculiarity with this generation is their tendency to be all-or-nothing in their subject-object awareness, their attention being focused entirely on others or outer objects of attention on the one hand, and being entirely subjective and internal on the other—shutting everything else out. Their greatest problem is to balance the subjective and the objective, the internal and the external. Many will become extremely abstract thinkers, using an intellectual detachment as a defense against harshness in their world, but enjoying breaking problems down to their basic essentials and building their creative thinking up from there into efficient analytical judgment. Their worst tendency will be to avoid stress and pain, ignoring it in the hope that it will go away, thus not resolving problems.

They may come to understand the nature of the relationship between subject and object, and left and right hemispheres of the brain, in great depth. If so, they will find that mankind has a natural fusion with the universe, which has been broken since the dawn of agriculture. They will work toward re-establishing that balance, which will make cosmic vision once more a commonplace, available to all.

LIBRA NORTH NODE—ARIES SOUTH NODE

You tend to jump head-first into new experience; any new experience attracts you for you like to be in the vanguard, ahead of the crowd. Your impulsive energy keeps you on the move so that constancy is not normally one of your virtues. Your competitive drive thrusts you to be first in whatever you tackle, though you are not interested in what you have achieved but more in what you are about to achieve. Your drive for progress tends to keep you alone even when you are with others, for you are usually more aware of yourself and your own interests than of them and theirs. Your sense of identity is strong and can be seen as self-centeredness or even vanity. Since you choose and prefer your own point of view you can be highly opinionated, this emerging in actions where you persist in your own way even when the circumstances are quite inappropriate. Yet you find that every goal, once reached, is not a goal at all, but is a new balance point at which to take stock and decide on fresh directions.

Your biggest mistake lies in not being aware enough of others, of their attitudes and needs. You need to understand that you are not alone but actually have companions on the path. You may be unused to sharing things, experiences, or yourself with others, but it is your very great need. You want what they have got, but strangely the only way to get it is to give them what you have. As you learn to share you find that everything that you have pioneered is of mutual use and benefit, and that they can help you as much as you can help them. You need to level out your separative ego to be able to realize that there are multitudes of different points of view, all completely right from their own standpoint, and that your own is simply a part of the whole balanced network, just as you are a part of the whole.

SUN IN THE 7TH HOUSE

You use your relationships with others as a support for your sense of identity, your self-respect having come to depend on the response you get from your partners and the way your relationships develop. Although you have always been aware of other people, originally your involvements with them were innocent and open, guileless and natural. At some time in your growth it is probable that you fell afoul of undeserved reactions from another, damaging your sense of honor and your pride. Your most probable response is to have learned to mistrust others, building mental reservations about them, armoring yourself against attack in advance, seeking a tactical advantage in case of trouble. Since you do this yourself you suspect others of doing the same thing, and warily try to ferret out their wiles and intentions, while probably keeping tactful and diplomatic relations with them on the surface. This does not build any trust in you, nor allow the possibility of true closeness in relating, but rather leaves you lying in wait, planning a secret ambush for the other.

Whenever you consciously plan ahead with guile you have lost simple innocence of purpose, and make it difficult for yourself to see what the truth of the situation actually is, and to respond to others with pure motives. Your interpretations of your experience are filtered directly through, and therefore strongly colored by, your pride, only allowing you to perceive circumstances clearly if your pride is entirely honorable. Whenever you accept that others' motives may be pure, and respond to them from this view while still adapting to the demands of the time, you return to a simplicity that allows you to do the right things with instinctive certainty, with no thought of personal advantage.

When you act from innocence your natural drive is to care for and further the interests of others. You use your consciousness of them to help them find their own directions, being a natural counselor. Also your decision-making ability is no longer clouded by self-guarding motives, taking away ambivalence, indecision and judgmental attitudes. Your awareness of the other in your life, whether people or situations, becomes wholehearted and uncomplicated, and your respect for self and other become equal.

Your mother was a strongly territorial and fiercely protective person who identified deeply with her family and with her role as a mother. She could talk a lot in her need to hold others' attention, in order to get a reflection of herself back from them. She may have been outwardly gentle and modest, but a powerhouse of instinctual determination within. Quite emotional, she could cling to those she felt close to, being highly offended if they turned away from her in any way. She would maintain her sense of identity by reviewing and reiterating the past, reminding herself of who she was.

Your father was ambitious and rather dominant, his self-respect depending on his achievement of professional or public status; for example he may have been interested in politics and power. He was authoritative and possibly overbearing, allowing no opposition to the laws that he laid down, though he may occasionally have felt himself to be above the law. He was a good organizer, particularly when directing others.

MOON IN THE 7TH HOUSE

In relationships with others you seek security, safety, and domesticity. You see marriage as a safe harbor, a state for the creation of home and family, for the protection and nurturing of the young and you choose your partner for his/her abilities as a help-mate in this direction. It can take you a long time to involve yourself deeply with a partner, since you raise emotionally self-protective barriers that you do not lower easily, protecting yourself against losing affection, as well as relating to people who do similarly. But once you have begun a relationship you can work tenaciously to keep it going, including your partner protectively in your own territory. You may believe that your partner clings more than you do, but may be projecting this, seeing your own clinging in him/her. You will sometimes have long swings of mood between self-protection and open relating.

You know in an instinctive way how to reflect others' attitudes to be accepted by them, returning their expressions, responding to their actions but often no more, playing a fairly passive role with others. You also tend to use them as a mirror in which to see your own reflection, gaining a needed security in your own being from their interest in you—perhaps even using them as a parental prop or a crutch to lean on—definitely shining by their reflected light. You may want to depend fully on them but find it difficult to give yourself entirely, feeling an invisible barrier between you. You place strong limits on your responses to others and will not go beyond them. You want the safety of finding needs in common with your partner. Even then you may test your security by strong mood swings toward your partner—a continual push-pull alternation as your own feeling of security within the relationship varies (whatever your partner does).

These attitudes were probably established in your early home life, particularly by your relationship with your mother. The likelihood is that she was very protective of you, perhaps too much so, acting as a safety fence around you to protect you from the world, being ever-ready to heed and look after you. In doing so she may have made you too dependent upon her. If you are a male, you will find it difficult to replace her, and this is exactly what you are likely to attempt, in marriage either putting yourself back into the role of being a dependent child or taking over your father's role, and losing yourself in the process. If a female, you may feel impelled to become as nurturing and protective yourself, practically allowing your mother's personality to take you over so that you live out a carbon copy of her life instead of creating your own. If your dependency on her was very strong all this may make no sense to you because this is exactly what you would like. But it means that your own personality may in part be submerged, latent, undeveloped. If so, then instinctive clinging will be the main characteristic of your relationships; otherwise your ability to nurture others, to give of your own being, will be very well developed, with you seeking nothing better in life than to do just this, though in doing so you may place too narrow a set of limitations upon yourself.

In making decisions you often seek to recreate the past, remembering how things used to be and trying to perpetuate them, or you emulate someone that you want to be like, copying their attitudes, actions and aims.

MERCURY IN THE 7TH HOUSE

You appreciate light intellectual relationships in which you can communicate and exchange ideas freely. You use your ability to be charming in speech, to be flexible and adaptable, to initiate relationships. You are attracted by people who are active, mobile, curious, questioning, flexible, and changeable. In other words you like Mercurial characters. Becoming involved with changeable individuals and capable of changing your own mind quite frequently, your relationships tend to be in a constant state of flux as you swing between like and dislike, attraction and repulsion, toward and away from your partners. Your flexibility in relationships is of a type that can flirt fairly readily, can relate easily to more than one other person at a time, and with any psychological complications can play push-pull games (for example "you don't want me, I want you!" "you want me, I don't want you!"), or be involved in triangular relationships.

Your awareness swings from outer to inner, from awareness of the other to awareness of self, your likes and dislikes alternating at the same time. If you don't like yourself you need them to like you, if you like yourself you don't need them at all. In your intellectual approach to relationships (remaining detached in self-defense?) you may not recognize that feeling is more appropriate, and you can cause havoc for others when you change your mind.

Your conscious cortical thinking, decision-making for example, is analytical and abstract, setting up alternative view points on any subject. For example "If I do this, then this will result; If I do that, then the other will result." Then you become dualistic, "but if I chose this—then I can't have that," and vice-versa. Even if presented with a simple yes/no decision you can introduce unnecessary complications, dilemmas, and paradoxes. You logically rehearse the possible outcome, looking for branching points leading to alternative endings, and then can't make up your mind which you prefer. This is why you reserve the right to change your mind, even at the last minute, and why you develop your ability to think in tactical terms—like a chess player. You may play both ends against the middle just to see what will happen, as an experiment.

Verbally creative, you work well in any communications area, especially communicating one-to-one, as in reporting or counseling. You enjoy the use of language and like to play with words and ideas, and prefer to keep them pleasant since you dislike argument, (unless Mercury is in an aggressive sign).

Your father's authority was verbal and perhaps inconsistent. His intellectual abilities were probably well developed, though formally and conservatively. He may have worked in offices, or in basic transport, communications, or business, but is likely to have changed professional directions at least two or three times.

Your mother's moods were changeable and probably unsettling to you since they would change her personality fairly strongly; she could be two different people at opposite ends of her mood swing. Her attitudes to motherhood may have changed at the same time, and if you do create push-pull problems in relationships you may have inherited them from your relationship with her.

VENUS IN THE 7TH HOUSE

You prefer your relationship with life and with others to be peaceful, harmonious and pleasant, and you are capable of using much charm, diplomacy, tact, and tactical thinking to achieve this end. You judge people as potential partners on their attractiveness of appearance, pleasantness of manner, charm, and responsiveness, on their qualities as social escorts, and in general on their aesthetic qualities. This is part of your preference to see and relate only to the pleasant and beautiful in everything, preferring to avoid the ugly and unpleasant at any cost. While this can show well-developed tastes and artistic awareness it can, if you avoid the harsher aspects of reality, cause you to be superficial, never dealing with intensity or depth in anything. Your diplomacy, for example, may sometimes stifle conflicts of opinion or viewpoints that need to be brought into the open in order to be resolved. In keeping the peace you may just hide the fact that a war exists rather than actually ending it.

Assuming that you do not hide from reality, your ability to understand many viewpoints, to see the various sides of any question or subject, can give you a well-balanced, well-rounded judgment (this pattern is often found in the charts of lawyers). You will use your judgment for the promotion of peace and harmony, for the resolution of conflict, whether in law-courts, on the battlefield (tactical awareness), in the arts, particularly dance and literature, or in making the everyday decisions necessary to bring about a strife-free future. But seeing everything as being equal can make it difficult for you to decide at all, and laziness can make you postpone deciding.

Frequently, in order to keep peace with others, you will give way to them, letting them have their way, deferring to their tastes and judgment even when you do not actually appreciate them at all. You may be acting from a highly developed idea of equality, allowing them their independent right to their choice, but where you give way you leave the situation unequal. Diplomacy is not a field recognized for producing honesty, and one dictionary translates tact as meaning insincerity. Wanting your relationships to be happy and at peace in order to protect you from harshness in life, you can submerge yourself altogether, not letting your partner know how you feel in depth, perhaps in avoiding conflict not even letting yourself know. This does not build true and deep relationships. It is very much like the dancing that you can enjoy so much, where each partner is adjusting continually to the movements of the other; it helps tremendously if one partner is actually leading, and for equality's sake that each partner can take the lead periodically.

Your father's authority was reasonable and equable though still judgmental—he ruled in order to have peace and quiet. His law was that you get along with others and give way to them. He probably used his aesthetic judgment or his diplomatic abilities in his work.

Your mother also preferred harmony and beauty in the home and responded instinctively and readily to those around her, finding pleasure in being a mother. She may have felt that relating to others was more important than housework, an attitude that would satisfy her occasionally indolent and pleasure-loving moods—she used pleasantness as her shield from unpleasant feelings.

MARS IN THE 7TH HOUSE

You like relating to direct, stimulating, vigorous individuals; aggressive, competitive and often sporting types with plenty of initiative to act for themselves; enthusiasts with a strong sense of their own (current) directions, good at starting things, but not always so good at continuing or finishing them. You like to be actively doing things in your relationships, otherwise you can become bored with the lack of stimulation; in fact you are capable of starting arguments when things are too quiet for you, just to stir things up. You enjoy the fights for their ability to bring things out in the open and clear them up, also preferring to use direct, straightforward methods. You and your partner may alternate in being the aggressor, but you prefer your arguments to be between equals—you do not like to be dominated by others (though you may welcome a certain playful domination in your relationships).

When you are confident, you are capable of starting your own relationships quite directly, acting as a hunter in pursuit of prey. Once you decide that you want to get to know someone, you allow little to get in your way as you drive through to your objective. You are capable of taking the lead and getting other people moving. When you are not confident, you allow others to take the lead rather than to take it yourself. Even if you put forward your own ideas, you would rather let someone else begin to act and follow them. Sometimes you are too lazy to make the effort to start, so you let others decide on the direction to go in, being happy to go along with them, though you become frustrated and angry if others take the initiative all the time without considering you. For you to be happy, they must respect what you want to do; you don't mind giving in to them just as long as you can be what you want, and do what you want.

If you feel that your partner is not giving you your just and equal rights you will fight for justice, and when you decide to fight you mean it. You can be a good tactician, knowing where and when to apply force to get the results you want, being able to put yourself in your opponent's place and figure out their strategy, thus having your own retaliation prepared in advance, or a way of blocking their attack.

In making decisions you are not very interested in where your actions will lead you in the future, you decide right now to act right now on something immediate and definite (though you may bring up alternative options, or let others do so, making deciding more difficult).

Your father's authority was dominant and aggressive, he being the boss and cracking the whip, starting arguments and then overriding everyone else's views. He may have been a tool-user and metal-worker, was probably self-employed and certainly self-directing, competitive and vigorous in work. He wanted to be first and best. Your mother's protective instincts were strong. She would pounce angrily upon you if you were doing anything that she felt was unsafe, bursting out with sudden tempers, sometimes on the tribulations of being a mother. She fought tenaciously when under attack, and in protection of home and family. She would have wanted her own house built or changed exactly to her desires.

JUPITER IN THE 7TH HOUSE

You prefer open and honest relationships to people who are expansive, confident and outspoken, or having a larger perspective or overview on life. Some may be outdoor types, horse-folk, travelers, religiously inclined or involved in higher education. With Jupiter in difficult aspects they may be gamblers, con-artists, irresponsible and escapist, or arrogant and overbearing.

You enter relationships with ease, enthusiasm, and lots of charm, being hopefully optimistic about the many opportunities and potentials in partnerships and wanting to make the best out of them. You prefer your relationships to grow in mutual exploration and learning. You like long, open-air walks with your mate, on hills, for example, where you can share the view of widespread countryside, and far-reaching ideas, and a great deal of laughter.

You pour energy and enthusiasm into your relationships, so they can be fiery and eruptive. With psychological difficulties here, you can be arrogant and overbearing, boosting your conceit at the expense of your partner, as well as being ready to escape, to run from one relationship to another. Here your irresponsibility rules supreme; you are an opportunist, both in relating and making decisions. You hope for a future that is better than what you have now, but then spoil what you have by looking down on it, considering yourself superior to it, so it is never good enough. You jump randomly from one opportunity to another, keeping hope ahead of you, boosting your own superiority at the expense of each circumstance, leaving a trail of unfulfilled hopes behind you (both your own and others).

Without such difficulties, you are hopeful for the future, confident of the outcome of your decisions, including the bigger ones. You are tolerant about the outcome, so any developments are entered into happily. You realize that there are many alternative routes through a lifetime, so you give yourself alternatives when deciding, so that you can choose as opportunities arise. You tend to decide on things ahead of time as your restless intellect explores the future. Some major decisions in your lifetime will concern personal growth, travel, higher education, philosophical or spiritual development; effectively the expansion of personal boundaries to incorporate larger territories.

Your judgment is broad-minded, liberal and balanced, tolerant of others and generously egalitarian. As your awareness of principles of law, social or natural, develops, particularly your awareness of cause and effect, you like to pass on your broadening knowledge and teach other individuals. Your intellectual creativity develops and expands over the long term, perhaps in journalism, literature, or philosophy.

Your mother's moods included an easy-going tolerant confidence, cheerful and outspoken (unless under stress when she could erupt in anger). She did not like tight and confining limits, preferring space to explore, freedom to move. Your father's authority was either cheerfully tolerant, or the "wrath of Zeus," throwing thunderbolts, small things being exaggerated out of proportion. His professional development was either a growth pattern, spreading across ever-widening horizons, or a restless, opportunist dissatisfaction that leaped from one thing to another.

SATURN IN THE 7TH HOUSE

You are serious, cautious, and deliberate in relationships, being formal and reserved, maybe shy, or at least self-controlled. You may stick to the rules and limits of propriety, the right and proper things to do and ways to act and react with others. You probably feel guilty or inferior if you do not do the right thing, so you may lack spontaneity in your responses. You want recognition in their eyes, preferring approval to disapproval, so you remain self-controlled and therefore cool in response to them.

You grew up feeling that if you were not adult and responsible in relations with others, dutiful and obedient, then you were guilty of breaking the law and worthy of condemnation. This theme may have been implicit or explicit, mild or strong, and your potential response is quite varied. You may perhaps expect the same propriety from others and thus relate only to orthodox, status-conscious, and reserved individuals, requiring that all the formalities, rules, and rituals be maintained between you, that they act responsibly and dutifully towards you.

If you felt humiliated and inferior in your youth you will either expect to be humiliated by others again and again, unconsciously choosing a partner to do it to you (a dismal prospect which may make you cautious about entering relationships at all). Or you will turn the tables and humiliate your partner, making them feel inferior and imposing your control over them to the point of total dominance or bondage. Much manipulation can enter into your relationships, often unconscious or hidden control, a jockeying for superiority turning the whole partnership into one of dominance and submission.

Your best prospects are for a stable and serious marriage with mutual trust and responsibility, slowly deepening respect and affection developing as you mature together into a crystalline understanding of the perfect order of the world around you. You may marry later than most of your friends, delaying it for career concerns. You can work well in partnership because your sense of responsibility toward others makes you pull your weight in any venture. You can be the one who gives a partnership its stability and organization. You will inevitably make relationships that do entail responsibilities.

Your thinking is ordered and well-formulated (where not skeptical or doubting). You prefer order in your dealings with your world, often meaning that you impose your own order upon it rather than seeing the inherent structure. In making decisions you plan for long-range goals, not fearing commitment to responsibilities (unless you are neurotic) to gain an ultimate aim in self-development or profession.

Your father's authority was strict and you had to know your place under it. He could judge you severely if you broke his rules or transgressed his idea of proper social conduct. He was probably ambitious, aiming for the top in his work; he was socially formal, reserved and conservative. You wanted his recognition and approval. Your mother's cautious protective instincts set strict local limits beyond which you were not to go. She did not express her feelings freely, her mood being serious, perhaps depressed, otherwise dominant and controlling. She may have come from an old, established family, taking an interest in its history or genealogy, or simply being aware of long roots. She had responsibilities and obligations to them.

URANUS IN THE 7TH HOUSE

You are impulsive when starting new relationships, ready to jump in spontaneously on a moment's notice. You like the electric charge of nervous energy that builds as you get close to someone else, the rapid, immediate attractions that can happen, the excitement of new stimulus as you explore the differences of other personalities. You prefer relating to lively, intelligent people, unorthodox in their approach to life, perhaps alternate culture types, with some eccentric and rather revolutionary. In relating you prefer to be able to keep your independence, for you do not like being trapped by others. You hate losing your freedom, and would rather escape the relationship than be tied down. For many this means separation/divorce. You are ultimately seeking the ideal relationship, deep friendship shared in freedom, intense mutual awareness developing to the point of telepathy, rather than any ordinary pattern of relating, which may mean that you do not allow yourself simple ordinary human relationships.

Under difficult aspects you will be wary of others, nervous when first meeting them, tensely watchful and mistrustful of their motives. You will keep up a barrier of detachment, alienating yourself from them, ready to cut out of the relationship at the drop of a hat. You will be prepared to say you don't care when you actually do. You seek your own independence by trying to find it in others and are not always prepared for it if they are very independent of you. You must be able to allow both them and yourself freedom.

You can be impulsive in making decisions, rapidly coordinating a multitude of elements, scanning varieties of possibilities, hunting for the quickest route to your idealized aims. Your major decisions will promote personal independence, breaking out of old ruts, the development of your individuality and personal integration. Under difficulties you feel that you face rigid attitudes from others that try to trap you into being what you are not, tensely recognizing where such traps may lie in wait for you, organizing your tactics to avoid them.

Intellectually you can be inventively creative, looking for alternative possibilities to ordinary views and methods, capable of linking ideas, where others do not see connections, into unusually fresh concepts. You may restlessly explore new ideas in orthodox science or alternate science. You prefer your world to be active and exciting, maybe driving fast for relaxation, certainly preferring mobility and change in your leisure time.

Your father's authority was either liberal and friendly, promoting your independence; or irritable, impatient and rigid, requiring immediate action from you; or very detached and unconcerned. His work may have been connected with modern communications or transportation, and may have gone through some major changes of direction. Socially he was either an idealist and anti-authoritarian, at extremes communistic or anarchistic, or an isolated individual.

Your mother probably had modern or experimental ideas about motherhood, or was totally detached about the whole affair, or felt trapped by it and isolated at home. Her moods went through abrupt changes, bursts of impatience interspersed with the detachment that she used as an emotional defense. She came from a home that was either quite isolated, or incredibly active.

NEPTUNE IN THE 7TH HOUSE

Unless Neptune has no difficult aspects to it, your relationships could be a mass of confusion. You are sensitive to others and you seek the perfectly gentle, dream-like, and non-stressful relationship. You have a romantic image of what this relationship should be like—possibly not a single image, but an ever-changing vision of your ideal partner. You may have absorbed many romances from movies or from reading, and part of you constantly seeks your dream-lover in everyone you meet or pass in the street. Even when you don't get to know someone, you imagine what a relationship with them would be like. The stronger this image, the closer it is to becoming real; then, in your early years at least, you actually meet them and may blush, stammer, and back away in confusion and shyness. You may learn to be less vulnerable and perhaps put away many dreams, but they still exist as potentials waiting to be fulfilled. Then you meet someone and they seem right, romance develops, and perhaps you marry, becoming confused when they are not what you expected; or you work hard to keep the romantic image of your relationship but may never let it be real, or allow your partner to be a person in his or her own right rather than an actor/actress playing the secondary role to your lead in your theatrical romance (and you may specialize in the tragic ending).

You are very capable of using camouflage, acting out roles, adapting subtly to others, and you are attracted to others of a gentle, dream-like nature, quiet and shy, deceptive people, or those who project an elaborated image of their favorite role. There can be much unreality in your relationships. You may perhaps relate to animals more easily than you do to people since they are more emotionally responsive and less likely to hurt you. If you use your sensitivity to others with clarity then you will respond compassionately to them, recognizing their vulnerabilities, seeing where they keep up illusions in self-defense against the world, where their sensitivities let things drift and crumble around them, fulfilling their expectations of martyrdom. You relate to them with gentleness, understanding, and the desire to heal. Your ideal relationship is one in which you can be with your partner, opening and sharing your most subtle feelings about life and the mysterious universe, being involved in a meditative mysticism together, or applying your energies in charitable areas, or within the fine arts.

You have a creative imagination, best used in visualizing the developments of your decisions, blueprinting the outline of the future, sketching out your plan of action and then following it; otherwise you may simply dream about what you would like to happen and never do anything to make it real. Major life decisions will involve the pursuit of a personal vision, perhaps in the arts, perhaps including the development of refinement, compassion, charity, and universal love. A large part of your life is likely to be secluded from the eyes of others for you value your privacy. You value delicacy and refinement in your possessions and could be a connoisseur of arts, fine foods, and wines.

Your mother was probably an emotionally gentle being, loving privacy in her home life, rather reflectively dreamy and infinitely protective. She liked her home to reflect her idea of gracious living. Your father's authority was either very gentle indeed, loving and compassionate or exactly the opposite, hard, stern, and unbending.

PLUTO IN THE 7TH HOUSE

You have intense attractions and repulsions towards others. You judge their competence or incompetence relative to yourself, and your relationships as essential or inessential. Fearing rejection, you have your defenses ready to reject others first. You judge others, suspecting hidden hostile motives on their part, projecting your own defensiveness onto them and expecting the same in return. You hide your intolerance, perhaps behind charm, being silent and secretive in relating, but this self-built barrier separates you from others and makes you want to tear it down, to penetrate and uncover their secrets, to lose your separateness in total fusion with your partner. This shows most obviously in sex, a powerful drive when you begin a relationship. You see potential partners as sex-objects, but your defense against rejection, despite your physical passion and intensity in relating, does not bring closeness. You don't express deep feelings, even to yourself, assuming that what you don't admit to can't be hurt. But then your partner can't know that you care, and may end the relationship, so your feelings create what they wanted to avoid. Deep hurts and conscience problems related to the death of a loved one, perhaps a grandparent, may have begun this pattern—fearing loss of love, you find it hard to admit to loving.

You hate dominance and rejection from others, and when you fight you mean business! Years of old hurt feelings can explode when triggered by another. In a quarrel you intend to annihilate the opposition. You need to understand these old feelings, boiling over through a new pressure, looking closely to find their original cause, and releasing them without harming anyone, using your rage as a road to self-knowledge.

You brood agonizingly when making decisions, feeling that your survival depends on them. You may avoid painful decisions altogether, burying them, making them invisible. Where deep feelings aren't involved you decide upon the practicality, economy and utility of the goal, eliminating inessentials. You are critical of the usefulness, efficiency, even necessity of material goods, for example machines, but you appreciate the best. You find difficulty turning creative ideas into concrete realities since your image of your own competence is at stake. A major life-decision that you will make is for self-transformation, to reunite the conscious and unconscious aspects of your mind. Your conscience is a powerful guide here: if you consciously accept all self-shaming, conscience-prone views of yourself, without self-blame—until you discover what lies behind them—you will come to understand yourself in great depth. Obsessional self-analysis does not work, since it can drive you to project it onto others in self-defense. You need to learn to perceive without defensive critical analysis, without judgment, seeing objects and people around you without attraction or repulsion, without acceptance or rejection, without desire or aversion.

Your mother's emotional defenses were silently powerful. Her protective instincts focused on pain, so you felt you had to be hurt to be loved. She could react with rage if you overstepped her limits, making you fear going too far. She wasn't tolerant of motherhood. Your father's authority may have been silent and invisible, or have hammered away at you, occasionally erupting in violence. His practical competence and efficiency were important in his work and he would have been known as a hard and capable worker.

NORTH NODE—7TH HOUSE, SOUTH NODE—1ST HOUSE

Much of your personal security has been based on using your initiative to direct your own life, on being accountable solely to yourself. You are first in your own awareness and prefer to be first in all things, hating to be beaten or surpassed, or to feel that you have failed. Always ready to fight your own battles, you dislike being tied down by any other being, preferring to be a lone wolf. In the exhilaration of action others would encumber you, so you do not cooperate easily. Incisive and decisive, you do not usually have second thoughts about anything, not liking to have to stop and consider the outcome of your actions.

In balancing your personality you need to learn courtesy and cooperation, learning to relate to others as equals rather than as competitors. When you do, you will find that you have much to give, your personal strength being applied to understanding the other and capable of giving to them the power of self-direction that you have built in yourself. You may never depend on others but you do need to be able to share with them and may find that your life actually becomes dedicated to their welfare, and the development of tact, courtesy, and the ability to make decisions including their welfare will be of enormous value to you.

✧ 10 ✧

Scorpio
and the 8th House

The 8th House is concerned with the intensity and polarity of our relationships, meaning how much energy is passing between ourselves and the other in our lives, and whether it is motivated and directed positively or negatively. This includes how much depth we can get into in any interaction between self as subject and the other as object (whether situations or people), and whether we have any staying power. It is where our outreach from personal values or needs touches the other in our lives, where we may look to the other to fulfill our desires (or fight it if we feel threatened). The outreach or the defense will be obsessional if we are fixed around unfulfilled childhood needs, clinging to security. It will become a using of the other (thing or person) rather than free, open involvement.

The psychological conditioning shown by the 8th House comes from our family's ego, from their combined sense of selfhood, of self-respect. These things include the boundaries that they erect to define their selfhood, and separate it from the rest of the world. Those boundaries manifest in their attitudes towards their children, whether they gave us love, whether they really acknowledged our existence as people in our own right, whether they owned us, or rejected us. The attitudes we felt from them become the emotional and security foundations for our own sense of selfhood and personal pride, including the defensive boundary limits that we have learned to build around them in self-protection. Our ego mood-swings are built in response to this background. The security needs of our ego or inner personality depend on which of those needs were fulfilled, and which were left unfulfilled in our childhoods. Such needs manifest in our relationships with others, through the values we expect others to place upon us, and that we (perhaps unconsciously) place upon them. These then predetermine the way that our relationships develop.

To be able to deal with our world, we must build abilities to handle the whole variety of situations in which we may find ourselves. These abilities may be competence and capability of physical kinds, emotional, or psychological, but all come under the general heading of survival abilities. If nothing threatens us, we need to be able to enter into experience with some intensity if we are going to gain much from it (and if we felt loved as children, we know no reason not to be fully open to experience). At the peak of our abilities to relate, we can focus so totally on an object, say a tree, that we lose our self-boundaries and become the tree, penetrating deeply into its nature. Most of us have put up too many psychological barriers to be able to do that readily, barriers to defend against any further erosion of what remains of our selfhood after our upbringing. These barriers are the defensive face of the same abilities, involving toning down our interactions, putting a protective partition between self and world.

Between thalamus and cortex in the brain runs a channel that can carry all the information that is at any moment flooding through our senses from the world, and from every level of our own current inner states, including all the remembering and processing that is fitting our whole current picture of the world together. That channel can carry it all, but for efficiency and simplicity in dealing with our world we cut out all the unessentials, all awareness of the processing, and much about ourselves, to leave us clearly and undistractedly aware of our environment. The channel has a built-in dimmer switch on intensity of experience, which includes in its province the pain threshold. In a sense it prevents us from being penetrated by more than we can handle, and will at extreme moments shut everything out, making us unconscious.

We choose what to shut out. We decide, initially consciously—often at moments of extreme emotion—what we want to be aware of, and more importantly what we don't want to know, what we can't tolerate. Every time we have been faced with anything we found too painful to face, we have buried the intolerable thing out of sight. As we grow, so usually does the pool of unconscious pain, the hell below our awareness. (Implicit here is our bravery or cowardice in facing things.) What has been made invisible usually includes moments of total shame, instants when we really hated someone, or when we lost belief in our own honor and goodness. We still know that those things are there inside us, we simply refuse to recognize them.

When we relate to others, if they begin to come really close to us, we believe that they may discover our guilty secrets, those parts of us that we believe to be utterly undesirable, so we may have to keep other people at a certain distance, or cut off from them. If our consciences are whole and unstained, or have been healed by facing the inner monsters, we can let others come as close as they like, and can accept them, value them, love them as deeply as we love ourselves. Then our capacity for sharing is an open bridge from self to other, bringing peace. If we value the other, we promote his/her/its welfare with care and love. If we do not, we will misuse it. Each reflects the way we treat ourselves.

If we value our experience of our world, we enter it with acceptance and intensity, bonding strongly with it. Such deep experiencing builds our body of experience (ultimately all that we have of life) rapidly. If we refuse such intensity of experience, we remain relatively empty (and know it in our depths). We could say that we are experiential capacitors, storing the charge of experience, storing power. What experiences we allow ourselves to enter upon depend on where we place our values as we continually select our personal reality from everything available (usually we choose what we have been taught to believe is real). But here is our ability to affect and to be affected by the other in our lives, the flow of energy exchange between subject and object, up to and including magic as the full power of focus of receptive attention and active intention onto the other.

When we reach puberty (from our early teens, until about 20), our desire for acceptance, to be truly and deeply wanted by someone else, becomes very powerful indeed. If we have actually been accepted as individuals up to that point, then puberty will be easy, but frequently it is not. If the 2nd House outreach has been satisfied (if we were touched, held, cuddled as a child), sexuality will come easily. If we were not given confirmation of love and acceptance as children, violence is far more likely to come easily to us. We know how much physical love is given to children in our culture by the amount of violence in it.

We have a need, as teen-agers, to be accepted as adult (and many cultures initiate young people into adulthood very deliberately), but our (western) culture still regards us as children—largely because the need for extended education keeps us dependent on our parents. We are trying at that time to build our initial adult personality, but the process is hampered by parental reactions. Frequently the Freudian monster of incest raises its head, not always to become a conscious factor, but often unconsciously, to attract and be attracted to, the parent of the opposite sex—who then usually fights such attraction by attacking its cause in the form of the child. The parent of the same sex often responds to the new rivalry by attack. The child then frequently becomes the scapegoat for all the parent's problems, real or imaginary, the screen onto which their own shadows are projected.

Often the child starts to reap the results of "nice boys/girls don't touch that" in babyhood, when discovering the pleasures of their own bodies. This either forces them to become secretive and perhaps ashamed of themselves, or to repress powerful feelings and suffer consequent obsessional tendencies and bigotry, or perhaps to become disobedient and rebellious in claiming their own experience of life. These qualities become a part of the forming adult personality. Or the child may trip over its early toilet training. Toilet training is one of the battlegrounds of independence for a child, in which it may resist coercive efforts. But one of the frequent results is to build in the mind the anal-genital connection that sex is dirty, which at puberty means "I am dirty and no one will want me."

Also of importance here is the timing of puberty. If it happens at the same age as most others, this allows the young person to become one of the crowd in sharing experiences, to be accepted as a member of the society as an adult, to be mainstream. If puberty turns on early, it may do so before the repolarizing toward the opposite sex has happened, leaving members of the same sex as the most likely partners, creating homosexuals. If puberty turns on late, the young person is left out of all the earlier shuffling for partners, has no contemporaries to share that process with, and so is left as something of a lonely outsider, usually for life. (For males, the timing is with the onset of testosterone production, for women, of estrogen).

There are many possible patterns here, and in our culture many of them are traumatic, filled with pain. Obviously this does not have to be the case. There are many cultures which raise their children very healthily where sex is concerned. Much depends on how close parents will let themselves be to their children; the emerging young adult will generally be able to be just that close with others. In modern western cultures that's often not very close.

Physiologically we have here the combustion chamber of life; blood sugars in circulation are oxidized, burned together with oxygen, providing energy for muscles (activity) and brain (direction). The two together give whatever intensity we have in both strength and awareness. The process produces wastes (carbon dioxide and water) which are then eliminated via the bloodstream. Wastes from the digestive process are temporarily stored in the bowel and large intestine, and then discarded. The overall process is that of using the useful (taking in what enhances life), eliminating the useless (rejecting what adds nothing to life), and includes the capacity of cells, of body, and of mind to take in nutrients and incorporate them, and to separate the now useless and excrete wastes. I call it storage and discharge. The emotional boundaries of the psychological filter act in the same way, placing limits on self-consciousness, excluding what we would rather have outside our sense of self, though actually invisibly storing it by encapsulating it inside us, not truly eliminating it (a foundation for cancers).

The immune system, in attacking and eliminating the "not-self" in the body is a major element in our ability to survive. The immune system of a baby is strengthened when it is cuddled by its parents, and that of adults when loved by a partner. The pain threshold has been mentioned, as have the survival instincts, one of which is sex (including reproduction).

SUN IN SCORPIO
✧ The Survivor ✧ The Eliminator ✧ The Volcano ✧

The sign of Scorpio represents all physical and psychological systems in any living creature that promote survival of the individual or the group, eliminate the unwanted and regenerate damaged elements back to complete health. Examples are the auto-immune and antibody systems which destroy and eliminate any foreign material in the body; sex, a force for the survival of the race, and the regeneration of the individual; berserk rage, a force to fight for life when it is threatened; repression, an ability to elimi-nate from consciousness that which threatens ego survival, and the sense of pain, the warning that damage is being done.

As a Scorpio you can be pragmatic, efficient, and if necessary, ruthless. You hate waste, whether of materials, effort, or of human potentials. On the negative side you are aware of anything that smacks of personal rejection and are ready to fight against it, using every kind of defense including rage, sarcasm, revenge and rejection of the other, in retali-ation. You are capable of ferreting out your opponents' weakest spots and of hitting directly at them, knowing exactly what will hurt them the most. You use silence and secrecy, being able to bottle things up for years, obsessionally storing and brooding on your hurts, building up your intolerance toward those that hurt you until you can strike back in the most devastating way at your disposal. You need to be aware that the same things hurt everyone and that your actions simply add to the sum total of human suffer-ing, which includes your own. All beings face death, which is a far more final retaliation than any you can devise.

On the positive side, where you recognize that pain in others, it gives you a deep conscience that will never harm another deliberately, and will work with the compassion of a surgeon to eliminate the causes of pain. You work for the healing of ills, for the regen-eration of what has been damaged, back to full health. You want to transform yourself, and through yourself, the world; eliminating war, conflict, intolerance, and bigotry; and you have the competence, efficiency, and ability to work with total energy and concentra-tion in order to do it. Where you see something to be necessary, nothing will stop you from achieving it. Where you see something to be unnecessary, you eliminate it. If it has to be done it will be done. You have a drive to penetrate behind the surface of things to understand the essential basics. You are not interested in frills and decorations but in why and how things work, and you will take them apart and put them back together again until you know how they work and can repair them. Then you work out how to do as much as possible in the shortest possible time with the least waste of energy.

The most sexual sign of the zodiac, you pour as much intensity into it as you do into everything else, though it is often a problem area. One main problem is often the feeling of not having had an adequate initiation into adulthood during your adolescence.

While this describes the classic Scorpio personality, you will vary from it in many ways. Your most major differences will be shown by the house placement of the Sun and by the sign and house placement of Pluto.

MOON IN SCORPIO

You are intensely emotional, but don't show it to anyone, unless they are very close indeed. Your emotions are passionate, both positively and negatively. You hate half-measures in anything, and commit your feelings to their object with a fierce intensity. You are not particularly tolerant, feeling that mercy and gentleness are overrated virtues, but build powerful likes and dislikes which you hold on to stubbornly. You take emotional hurts very deeply indeed, but may refuse to show that you have been hurt, bottling it up, building an apparently impenetrable armor-plated emotional shell. The feelings that you store eventually reach the last straw point, and erupt in a volcanic explosion which can (and may be intended to) devastate those around you. If you are of the more negative kind, you plot revenge for ages and take fierce delight in seeing your opponents bite the dust as your revenge comes to maturity. Remember that others also feel pain; they simply don't hold onto it as obsessively as you do.

More positively, your understanding of suffering can make you an emotional healer, a good shoulder to cry on. You won't feel sorry for the cryer, but will feel their pain with them, and will dig out and help them to see exactly what they did wrong, how they made the situation that hurt them—and how they can hope to resolve it. If they can't, you will advise them to drop it and be rid of it. Much depends on whether you have resolved your own old hurts, for if you are still clinging to them, you won't want anyone else's problems piled onto you. If you have, then you are one of the world's natural nurses, doctors, or psychotherapists, able to understand and identify completely with the sufferings and needs of the other person.

You appreciate practicality and efficiency, and can't tolerate waste—whether of time, effort, or human potential. Sometimes this shows in an inability to throw out old things, including bodily elimination problems, extreme possessiveness, and jealousy, reflections of hanging on either to security (to what you feel is *yours*), or to your old bottled-up feelings. Either way you will find that an occasional purge of your clinging tendencies will be very beneficial and cleansing. Some Moon Scorpio people go to the opposite extreme and trash everything (and everybody), a reflection of intolerance and rejection, so you just can't win, can you? Much of your practicality springs from your feeling that your security depends on your own survival abilities, that no one else is going to look after you (or you won't let them), so you have to look after yourself, whether you like it or not. You may find it hard to admit that anyone else can be efficient, and keep up a certain invisible level of rejection of most people so that you won't be hurt by getting too close to them. Otherwise if you do open your feelings to let others in, you let them right in with nothing held back, which can be a frightening and transforming experience for all concerned.

There is a connection with the occult in this position of the Moon, particularly with witchcraft. The secret lies in the intensity of directed feeling. Warning: this is dangerous to the user if used with intent to harm, but beneficial if directed for other's good.

MERCURY IN SCORPIO

Your stubborn and penetrating mentality, when properly used, is capable of getting to the practicalities at the root of any problem and transforming any area of knowledge. You do not allow your thinking to be swayed by others' opinions, tradition, authority, or anything but the goal you want to reach. This total focus on the pursuit creates incredible concentration. Your concentration effectively puts pressure on your unconscious mind, which then uses its massive resources to find an answer. You may enjoy mystery, detective, and spy stories, and should enjoy the mental exercise of solving them, and could enjoy the real thing just as much. Detective games are a part of your make-up in that you refuse to be beaten by any problem that needs deductive or investigative thinking, unless you have shut your mind off by rejecting such things as unnecessary, in which case you don't think very much at all.

You are capable of learning with intense depth and focus if you believe the study to be useful, otherwise you can't see the point in applying yourself. You prefer your studies to be of direct practical use rather than purely theoretical, and in this sense you think like an engineer. Your approach is to eliminate everything that is unessential to the subject at hand, to find what is absolutely essential, building on that basis. Under difficult aspects this gives a very intolerant edge to your mind, cutting out everything that you consider to be junk. You appreciate efficiency, power, and a cutting sharpness in intellect, demonstrated by your not wasting words and ability in sarcasm.

You keep a close guard on your tongue, saying no more than you feel is necessary on any topic (and you feel that the bare minimum is needed). You don't spread secrets entrusted to you, and definitely not your own. You may be confided in by many through your knack of being able to "psych out" their problems. By discussing them with you they find solutions which they could not find alone.

Should someone cross you, they will have good cause to regret it. You are adept at cutting your enemies down with a minimum of words, a maximum of sharpness and sarcasm, each word aimed to hit the mark and devastate. You probably experienced your fair share of arguments while growing up, or brooded over what you should have said, sharpening this verbal weaponry. You brood on verbal hurts for a long time, your thinking becoming obsessional, angry, and frequently very divided, your conscience doing battle with your resentments and/or jealousies. You have intense ideas of right and wrong but don't always apply them equally between yourself and others, forgetting or making invisible to yourself the worst that you have done to others.

Your studies may include plumbing, garbage disposal, sewage, recycling; physics, especially nuclear; psychotherapy or other forms of mental healing; vulcanology; sex, reproduction (including xerography); surgery, pathology, and physical healing systems; secret intelligence work, detective work; the sub-stratum of power in any area; survival instincts and unconscious drives.

VENUS IN SCORPIO

Your attitudes in relationships are intense, passionate, and fixed, yet you are probably rather silent, finding it very difficult to express or even admit to the depth, power, and full range of your feelings. Your problem is your sensitivity to rejection by others, and to all pain and loss in relating, and you keep up your guard against being hurt by any of it. Yet you have the desire to enter into a total relationship, in which you can strip away all secrecy and defensive barriers, and plunge into a complete fusion with your partner. But you are afraid that if you come even remotely near such depth, something will go wrong and it will bring great pain.

You feel that love and hate, attraction and repulsion, pleasure and pain, beauty and ugliness are inseparable, and whatever you feel on the surface, you feel something of the opposite inside. This makes it difficult for you to feel fulfilled, and can drive you to want to take any relationship you have to greater depths, then being afraid that your partner won't like what they find inside you (as you don't like what you find inside yourself), and building your defenses against rejection higher still, sometimes reacting to others as though they were rejecting you, even when they are not.

This problem is in your feelings of self-worth. You have a self-judging conscience that doesn't tolerate the more instinctual drives and defenses that you use in relating, and can become very self-attacking. It is the opposite side of the coin to the instincts themselves, and increase in strength on one side is balanced by a corresponding increase on the other, creating a very highly charged and embattled situation within you. That internal battle can be made to erupt outwardly by judgment from others, that being the last straw, with you perhaps reacting by going in the opposite direction, doing what they judged you for. You do not like admitting what your conscience contains, and may try to bury it, making it unconscious, though it may still be obvious in your judgments of others, since you don't tolerate in them what you hate in yourself. You know that there is a transformation that you have to go through, but may not realize that it lies in learning to love yourself, to let go of harsh, uncomfortable self-judgment, in learning to drop the barriers that you have had to erect to protect yourself against your own attack upon yourself.

So in the usual run of things, you need to prove that you are lovable by others, and can thus be intense and fixed in relating, and very jealous if your position is threatened. Some may not be able to accept that anyone can love them, and will use sex as a substitute or replacement. Sex is an important part of your relationships, as an avenue of expression for your passionate feelings, and as a way of feeling that you are accepted in depth by another.

Beyond this conflict, you make deep and faithful bonds with others, and explore the heights of human experience in relating, being capable of healing both self and other through love. The major healing is within, in learning to love your own being, your own depths.

MARS IN SCORPIO

Your aims, drives, and desires are intense and powerful, and when you have set up a goal for yourself you will allow nothing and no one to get in the way of your attaining it. Your drives are linked directly to your survival instincts, giving you the ability to draw upon deep reserves of energy, determination, and resourcefulness, together with the capacity to focus all of your powers undeviatingly upon your aims. It also gives you the type of courage that will face the greatest difficulties, including death, if necessary, in pursuit of your goals. You can thrust through all obstacles and overcome all opposition by sheer drive and perseverance, thoroughness and efficiency. You know how not to waste energy, and how to apply it exactly where it is needed, though at times you are capable of overdoing it and using more force than the job requires, leading to damage. You may have, or will develop, a talent in engineering or mechanics. You will work to be totally self-sufficient, not wanting to have to depend on anyone else in achieving your ends, preferring to know how to do everything yourself by using your own initiative.

Naturally such drives, used badly, can be ruthless, and if aimed against others in retaliation for real or imagined offenses—you could carry grudges for years, building anger, fury, and internal arguments to a high pressure until finally taking revenge. This pattern of storage and discharge will be there one way or another, whether in your working inwardly on projects until you are certain that they have been planned, or felt through fully, then going into intense activity to complete them; or in storing grudges for ages until you take revenge; or in repressing your initiative or aggression until it erupts somehow. In the latter case, in your childhood you may have had to deal with what you felt to be overpowering hostility from another toward yourself or your actions; you tried to fight back but found that it brought more pain, so you bottled it all up in silence and in secrecy about what you wanted to do, or felt; you would have repressed some feelings completely from consciousness, making them totally invisible to yourself, such as hatred for the person or situation that hurt you. Thus you may be carrying invisible grudges that you have to hide from yourself, building up unconscious emotional pressure, which either eventually surfaces as ill-health—the body breaking down from the emotional stress that it is forced to carry with no relief, or it emerges in intense anger toward people or situations that are similar to the early one(s), but is inappropriate in aim and intensity. Sometimes such buried anger is turned upon oneself destructively, self-hatred substituting for the original focus.

If your drives are motivated by pure intentions, you are capable of reaching spiritual heights of development beyond the usual, with your one-pointedness of mind and all or nothing attitude. If used negatively, you will be capable of cruelty and destructiveness, and personal moral degradation, seeing no reason why you shouldn't go to hell in your own way. Either way you are likely to have to face temptations, for your powerful desires seek intensity of experience, and in action you want to break through all normal limitations into whatever lies beyond.

JUPITER IN SCORPIO

On the positive side, you have a powerful conscience which knows directly that what hurts you can hurt others, and works to prevent and undo pain. You will be almost painfully honest, knowing that to be whole in yourself, you cannot afford to be otherwise. You fight intensely for things that you know to be right and true, having a crusading sense of justice, knowing that the foundations of law and morality have to be the prevention, healing, and alleviation of suffering. While you may fight human problems, perhaps striving for the rights of repressed minorities and underdogs of any kind, you may also focus on the environment, working against wastage of resources, pollution, and ecological rape.

Your focus may be inward; you may be an explorer of the unknown realms of the psyche, a map-maker of the psychological underworld, opening up the closed-off regions of the unconscious mind, struggling to understand and rise above the lower instinctual aspects of your being. You are likely to drive toward a great transformation, of yourself or of your world, taking an intense, uncompromising stand on central principles of life, not that you believe to be true, but that you know by direct experience. Your desire to penetrate the barriers of reality may show in an interest in what lies beyond death, wanting to break through to experience and explore the hidden worlds that are normally beyond reach. Whatever the direction of your interests, you are ready to face and enjoy tough conditions with an enthusiastic expenditure of energy, possibly in intense outdoor activity, for example learning to develop broad-ranging abilities as a survivor in the wild. You may have the rampaging energy of a freebooting adventurer.

If Jupiter had difficult aspects, you are likely to feel a lot of pain and to exaggerate it out of proportion to its cause. You make mountains out of molehills by brooding on them, looking for the worst in others in reaction to hurts. You may see them as being angry and superior toward you, which is a projection of your self-judgments out onto them. You are intolerant toward yourself, but don't want to admit to being wrong in any way to anybody—especially to yourself, saying "it's them, it's all their fault, they are wrong, not me." You may become superior, arrogant, overbearing, self-inflating, and sarcastically outspoken, freely throwing blame around. In other words you can be unmerciful in your judgments, taking your flaring conscience battles out on yourself or others, magnifying what you decide are their faults, and probably making bitter enemies in the process. You repress what you don't like about yourself, yet you are still honest and can't quite bury it, so it erupts, surfacing again to trigger another explosion. Your effort to deny what is right in front of you makes your attention become superficial where essentials are concerned, so your understanding of vital matters may be overly generalized. Your compulsive, enthusiastic upsurges of interest are followed by scattered attention and collapse as you have to face realities or difficulties. Where your conscience makes you feel unwanted (by yourself), you try to regain feelings of being desirable by seeking sexual activity, but if you are arrogant toward your partner(s) you compound your difficulties, for you will blame yourself, feel bad, try to bury it, seek solace, and repeat the whole pattern again . . . .

SATURN IN SCORPIO

You tend to hide deep within yourself whatever you feel to be inferior, burying passions in your heart. Since they are there, they still govern your thoughts and actions, even if from the background. Passion obscures reason and so must be fought, no compromise being possible. Instinctual drives that cause evil must be openly discredited and not glossed over. A direct onslaught does not work since the fight strengthens both sides, and our faults continue victorious. What is needed is (1) working to establish the good; (2) reducing the inner conscience battle by recognizing that the passion has some reason for being, some form of validity—such as it being a natural, though unsocial, instinct. Your shadow exists, accept it. Simply don't feed it.

You have held back feelings like water behind a dam or pressure inside a volcano. This pressure (which can be used as a driving force) may burst forth, either fruitfully or to cause havoc. The cause of the pressure is your own retentiveness. Accumulation without dispersion leads eventually to overload and collapse.

You can feel bitter resentment toward anyone who hurts you, and harbor a grudge for many years before you get the revenge you desire. However this does nothing to improve the state of your emotional health and could give you quite a bad time, even when buried out of sight.

You may have grown up under a martinet's discipline, and had to keep your mouth shut and take it, no matter how bad you felt, or how much you wanted to fight back or speak in your own defense. You were most probably subjected to strong, even severe, parental discipline in puberty. This may have left you with doubts about your adequacy as an emerging adult, but with an intense drive to prove yourself within the system in the long run. This may cover resentment and frustration which would like to blow up the system, or at least transform it from the inside.

Your attitudes toward sex are either rather Victorian, seeing it as an evil (meaning feeling guilty about it), or you enter into it in a very earthy fashion. In the first case your self-control is extreme, while in the second a tendency to manipulate to get what you want must be avoided, allowing the natural seriousness of your feelings to be expressed openly rather than bottling them up. Your involvements with others' money also displays your unconscious feelings; whether you manipulate to get it, feel that you can't have anything from them, or are simply aware of the reasonable social rules and restraints here. You may deal with other people's money through your work, in legal matters or legacies.

Basically you are cautious or fearful in evaluating your relationship to the other, whether that be the world, people you relate to, or your own unconscious mind. Fear creates reserve and suspicion which drives a wedge between the two. This restrains the natural human desire to have full close contact with the other, restricting enthusiastic movement toward contact. Full maturity enables you to stand alone unconcerned, if need be, or to relate in depth and seriousness.

URANUS IN SCORPIO

Uranus was in Scorpio from the end of 1974 to the end of 1981, during which time there were many strong revolutionary and liberation forces at work in the world, fighting for a transformation from the old order toward a new one. The general mood of letting it all hang out was becoming established in the minds of a generation, and we had women's lib, gay lib, and the yippies. The space program was working toward economical ways of getting into space with the shuttle being developed, and the auto industry was turning toward economy too, part of the alternate mood of not wasting any more. Electronic technology moved fully into the micro-chip era, and home computers, calculators and video games became common, and cheaper every year. The computer era had finally arrived, with systems being installed in offices, stores, and supermarkets, among others.

Being born during this period, and if you use your full potential, you will have a powerful interest in such things as technological efficiency, micro-engineering, and in doing things with a maximum of speed and a minimum of wasted time, effort, materials, and money. Your mind is capable of delving deep into the roots of how things work, and you will be interested in gaining a core understanding of essential principles, knowing the absolute basics in depth and inventively putting them together to produce radical new technologies, or fresh in-depth understanding in your areas of interest, whatever they may be. Many born during this period will want to delve into the mind to know how it works, and will work on themselves to break through their own internal barriers to understand it from the inside. Some will do it by linking modern knowledge with yoga and other deep traditional techniques, not keeping useless frills and rituals, but finding what works and how it works. You will be capable of dredging information and knowledge from your unconscious mind by focusing intensely on a problem, continually questioning—thus stimulating your mind to solve it at a deep level, eventually bringing the complete answer up to the surface in a surprise burst of insight.

On the more difficult side, you can be too intensely impatient, too impulsive, and have far too strong and quick a temper, not tolerating anything that you feel to be a trap to your independence, and being very ready to fight for your freedom. You may store up this kind of fight for years, hiding the intensity of your feelings, and then burst out with it all in an uncontrolled and maybe violent rush. (Where you have grown up seeing a lot of violence on television, you must recognize that this is not everyday reality.) A part of your rebellion may be to refuse to learn, which is self-destructive and self-defeating, meaning that you then can't build the necessary knowledge to be able to deal with your world—you deliberately turn yourself into a loser. If you feel the need to rebel intensely, to blow up or change the world, start with yourself—transform your own nature first. Learn to recognize how much you react from highly-charged instinct, warily seeking out everything that could possibly be seen as a trap in order to fight it or avoid it, instead of looking at your world through more friendly and tolerant eyes.

NEPTUNE IN SCORPIO

Neptune was in Scorpio between December 1955 and November 1970. During this time society's self-image went through a transformation starting with Rock and Roll, the "Angry Young Men," and kitchen sink drama, ban the bomb marches, the cold war, sputniks, beatniks, and brainwashing. This was the drug era, begun by the beatniks and continued by one youthful generation after another, with some deep and mystical delving done into the nature of mind, and a lot of human potential wasted. Scorpio deals with puberty and initiations into adulthood, whether given by friends or by parents, and Neptune with drugs and altered states of consciousness. This is the first generation to grow up with the birth-control pill, dissolving the old fears that once existed between the sexes, liberating sexual activity. Scorpio also involves the repression and release threshold of the mind, and what is beyond it, being all that humans do not want to face about themselves. Much erupted from the mass unconscious during that period as shown by the entertainment media; increasing violence in movies and literature (the James Bond era) increasing focus on sex in all the media, continuing with full frontal nudity on stage and explicit sex in films. What was once daring or shocking is now boring, and much of what was buried is now open.

Born in this period, you have a tremendous range of potential in your being, from plumbing the instinctual depths of sexual and survival drives, feeling an intense vulnerability that needs a powerful and impenetrable defense to protect it, covering what you don't want to see in your own being with a self-deluding camouflage, and using the same camouflage in deceptive self-defense against others; to having a deeply sensitive knowledge of how human beings work, understanding their fears, pains, and vulnerabilities from the inside and having compassion for them, using practical compassion in the healing of others. On the one hand you could be paranoid, reacting from every fear in your being, seeing imaginary threats all around you and defending yourself continually against them by the most subtle, devious, and perhaps violent means possible; and on the other have an intense innocence that is all accepting—to the point of a total psychic openness and great spiritual depth. Naturally you are likely to be somewhere between these extremes.

One defense will be silent privacy, a refusal to let others penetrate into your secret areas, keeping parts of you safe from hurt. Yet you are very receptive to the same hidden parts of others, and may be either deeply sympathetic or quite intolerant toward them (depending on how you feel about your own). If you can't tolerate your own deeper sensitivities you will cover them with camouflage, deceiving yourself, whether by drink, drugs, fantasy, or confusion. If you accept them, then you also accept that others feel the same way, your sensitive conscience refusing to hurt others under any circumstances, unless it will help to heal them. Your intense imagination has nothing at all barred from its imagery, your mind being capable of considering things that other generations cannot admit exist, providing an avenue for intuitions to arise from the unconscious, potentially helping to dissolve the barriers between levels of your mind; unless you are repressing things, and struggling not to have certain images arise.

PLUTO IN SCORPIO

Pluto is in Scorpio from 1983 to 1995. Scorpio is its home, and its effects will be felt with full force. During this period relationships of all kinds, whether between individuals, groups, or nations, will be very intense. On the negative side, those who do not want to admit to their own motives in the way they deal with others will, as usual, project their own motives onto their opposite number. This usually leads to more conflict, and on the international front, may lead to war. When Pluto approached the center of Scorpio in 1990, Iraq invaded Kuwait, and when Pluto reached the center of Scorpio in 1991, the new Western and Middle East Alliance responded in full force.

But now the other party may no longer play that game by reacting to accusations or other provocation, but may see through it, and try to get their opponent to become aware of what they are doing (a difficult task since such awareness is repressed in the first place because it is too uncomfortable to accept, because of buried conscience problems). One major example is South Africa. The whites project their own shadows onto the blacks, and believe themselves justified in their actions, and can't understand why the rest of the world doesn't approve. Naturally the blacks fight back against such bigotry, giving the whites cause to continue repressing them. Again 1991 found blacks and whites beginning to dismantle Apartheid.

We all have things that we refuse to recognize in the way we interpret our worlds and react to them. Those invisible elements are normally pains, traumas that we prefer to ignore, to keep the pain away. Yet our survival instincts are impelled to do battle with what we feel threatens us, and look for the same threatening pain in many situations (and anything we look for with any intensity, we will find), so our outer lives contain the conflicts that we don't want inside us. Then it all seems to be someone else's fault.

Only when we acknowledge that we have been refusing parts of our own experience, cutting ourselves apart to hide pain, can we begin to heal that pain. Only when we accept everything about ourselves that we have rejected in the past can we come to any inner peace and wholeness. And when we come to that our outer world also becomes peaceful, for we no longer fight invisible dragons.

During this historical era such therapeutic awareness is very available, which means simply that old pains are close to the surface (which can make it a very touchy time)—and the inner drive to heal the breach is strong. Whether the governments of the world will be able to make use of the healing potential is another matter; they are notoriously close to the dinosaurs in instinctual nature, usually embroiled in whatever survival struggles they can find to fight. It may be up to the individuals of good-will in the world to heal themselves, then help to heal others, starting a chain-reaction of health and mutual acceptance.

SCORPIO NORTH NODE—TAURUS SOUTH NODE

You have a stubborn and complacent streak in the core of your being that can make you repeat old attitudes and habits endlessly, even when you know that they are of no value to you. You have learned what pleases you and how to obtain it, your determination becomes immovable when set toward a goal and remains so long after the goal has lost its appeal. You do not like to change your ambitions because they are ideals to you, and to change them would be to change your whole world-view. If you do change your values or tastes it is usually by substituting one thing for another, rather than any complete change. You acquire more than you need in the world until you are carrying too heavy a load, whether of goods, knowledge, habits, or attitudes. You also want to acquire more qualities and facets of your own being and become depressed when you are belittled, rejected, passed over or devalued in any way.

Your greatest need is to know what to eliminate from your life and how to do it in order to transform your own being. You have a personality death and rebirth to go through to burn away old values and reduce your life to fundamentals. The unconscious drives behind earlier attitudes must become conscious so that you are no longer driven. These drives come from survival attitudes fixed around painful feelings that have been repressed so that making them conscious is usually painful, conscience building and self-liberating. The image is that of a snake discarding its old skin in order to be able to grow.

SUN IN THE 8TH HOUSE

Negatively, you are quite aware of the possibility of being blamed, shamed, or rejected by either yourself or others, how it hurts, and the damage that it does to your pride. Therefore you keep your hurt pride and much of your real self secretly hidden away from the world, invisible and protected, and possibly resentful, since no one can actually know who you are, or appreciate the real you. Your stored pride becomes intense and concentrated but split apart; on one side a secret judge rejects and blames yourself or others, (either the sun shines out of them and you are rotten, or vice-versa); and your other side is hurt by every judgment you make against yourself, splitting yourself into judge and judged, angel and devil, light and shadow. The state of your self-respect interprets, filters and constantly evaluates every part of your relatedness to your world, actively choosing and rejecting how to see it. If you judge yourself to be bad, everything that you experience seems bad. If unsplit, you have a penetrating clarity of perception of situations and people. It may not be rejection that bothers you most, but danger and difficulty in your life. You may feel that you are fighting to survive, and your feeling of competence in handling everything that fate throws at you depends on your self-respect, and vice-versa. Where this has become a part of your self-image, you have to find difficulties and perhaps disasters to struggle with, prove yourself against, or to punish yourself with, even if you do so unconsciously and automatically. Where you are faced with difficulties you need to stop and look for the error in your view of the situation, in yourself.

You are quite ready to delve into the areas of repressed, unconscious, painful emotions in your being in order to become conscious of, and thus resolve them, instead of being driven by them. Your pride and your self-judgment are antagonists, even when one is conscious and the other isn't. Regarding inner accumulation of pride, remember the law of Nature, one facet of the law of balance: that the high will be ground down, and the low will be filled up.

More positively, you are capable of great efficiency, and dislike waste of time, effort, and materials; you are good at eliminating inessentials, paring things down to bare essentials. You should be equally capable in building up and repairing as in tearing down and eliminating. This comes from your fascination with how things work; as a child you probably took things apart to find out what made them work, and then had to learn how to put them back together again.

Your mother was proud, perhaps arrogant and wanting to be the center of attention. She had great creative potential, and could have been talented and accomplished at anything that she applied herself to, though may have been lazy and *laissez-faire*. She would either have played readily with children, or have been commanding and organizing with them, regarding them as extensions of her own ego.

Your father was either an open-minded, independent individualist, friendly and sociable in his manner though remaining unattached, or was rigid in thoughts and attitudes. He liked his solitude as much as his social life, if not more, perhaps being self-isolating. He was probably interested in the rare or unusual in life, and in current attitudes and developments in human society, and was most likely a humanist.

MOON IN THE 8TH HOUSE

Your feelings are intense and you keep many of them hidden from the view of others, because you fear rejection if they know what your feelings are. Since much of your security depends on the stability of your relationships, you cling to your partner(s), hiding your emotions from view, or being unable to say what you feel. You become possessive, and jealousy is one of your more common feelings, with the pain, hurt, and fury of feeling rejected by the one you need, even if they don't actually reject you but simply show interest in things or people other than yourself. You store up all the small rejections that you decide you have had, until eventually one more little rejection becomes the last straw. When you feel rejected you don't forgive easily, hanging onto your hurts for ages, brooding resentfully and possibly plotting revenge. If you decide to fight, you can keep it up for a lifetime, even if your opponent doesn't want to fight. You may also deny that you have these feelings at all, keeping them invisible to yourself in self-defense, since if you admitted to the worst of the way you feel, you would lose self-respect.

You are passionate in everything you feel, even if you never show any of this to the world. Your passion can be creative or destructive, depending on whether you feel wanted or not. Because you take everything intensely you may have had to repress your feelings at, or immediately after, the most intense moments of your life. If this is so, you will have memories with no feelings attached, or no memories at all of those events. This may deaden your later responses to similar circumstances, or leave you reacting passionately without knowing why, Some people use this emotional intensity to find out how their unconscious drives work, becoming natural psychotherapists and emotional healers. Others use it in pursuit of occult power, knowing that an obsessional focusing of feelings on a desired goal can psychically make it happen. Unfortunately such goals are often instinctual and negative, causing harm to all concerned, particularly if they are aimed at eliminating things that you refuse to tolerate.

Your problem is to point your emotional drives in positive directions, eliminating clinging, hostility, and other such behavior by getting them out of your system—not by burying and thus intensifying them. You have to use your constructive feelings and de-fuse the destructive ones, no longer using your moods and your ability to bounce others' feelings back at them as an emotional defense.

Your mother's attitude to children was powerfully protective, being aware of their needs for security, and meeting them. She identified strongly with them, taking pride in their achievements and being annoyed with their shortcomings. She was also quite creative, perhaps using her abilities mostly in domestic directions, baking for example. She knew how to gain attention from others for excelling in what she did, her pride depending on getting approval. She was emotionally cheerful, direct, and rather forceful.

Your father was more emotionally detached, though probably friendly and sociable. His independence was important to him, and he hated being trapped by anyone or anything. He needed his friendships and social contacts (largely within his family) for security.

MERCURY IN THE 8TH HOUSE

You have a mental intensity capable of brooding on any subject that attracts your attention until you have broken it down into essentials, stripping it of unnecessary garbage, working to find the core essence, the central meaning of the thing. Then you file away what you have learned in shorthand form, ready to recall whenever connections or situations arise that need that knowledge. If you see any knowledge as being essential, you are capable of demanding it from your own unconscious mind, whether in the form of memory of things already learned, or as new connections, fused together from slim evidence, hints, and small clues—the answers erupting into consciousness after the problem has been brewing on the back burner for a while. Otherwise, if you can't see knowledge or learning as being essential, then you can't be bothered with it. You keep many of your ideas secret since you feel that others will laugh at, ridicule, or reject the connections and ideas that are important to you. You will only produce them for public consumption when you are entirely sure of yourself, remaining silent until that time.

You have learned to think using the survival centers of the brain. This produces problems, such as your mind becoming obsessionally stuck on hostile thoughts whenever you think that others have turned against you. You are then capable of playing push-pull and double games in your relationships, attracting the other into relating with you until you can turn around and reject them in revenge. This may be quite unconscious, and spring from hurts that happened long ago, but your intensity can replay your wish to have revenge with people who had nothing to do with the original hurt, saying "you don't want me? I want you, you want me? I don't want you!" Since this can become an automatic reflex, you may be confused by your own duality in carrying on relationships, and in sex, only knowing that your feelings run between attraction and repulsion, usually in opposite phase to your partner's feelings. This pattern may repel you as your conscience arises and you recognize how you can hurt others, particularly with cutting language—pent-up frustrations emerging in scathing attacks, yet you may find it hard to recognize what you do since you don't let your right hand know what your left hand is doing.

You keep your thoughts running on two levels, those that you will admit to having to others, and those that you won't, perhaps even to yourself. You keep your most intense feelings under mental control, often distracting your attention away from deep feelings as a way of avoiding and repressing them. Yet they do come to the surface in your ideas about yourself and others. If you study your own mind closely and come to understand just what drives it, then letting go of your obsessions, you are capable of being a natural psychologist or psychotherapist, able to ferret out what buried feelings motivate others too. But you will find that intellect is not the right tool to use in this exploration since you use it as a form of defense; only by going directly to the feelings that you have covered over can you understand them in depth. To want to do so, you have to stop blaming both yourself and others before you can begin this detective work. Otherwise you will be stuck in a futile inner argument in which you are both antagonists.

VENUS IN THE 8TH HOUSE

You are likely to have two quite different faces; one is charming and pleasant, apparently accepting and tolerant—and you use this face for public consumption, as your defense against being rejected by others. The other is judgmental and intolerant, ferreting out those facets of others that don't measure up to your standards, storing them up as a potential weapon to use against those that show the slightest hint of rejecting you, then bringing them all out in a blasting attack. You don't want to be hurt, so you hide your intense feelings and values—not wanting others to know what they are so they can't attack you. In hiding them, you are actually rejecting yourself, not allowing those important parts of yourself any expression, and therefore any acceptance by others. You feel that they are already rejecting you without them having done anything, projecting your self-rejection onto them. So you fight those closest to you out of a hurt that you don't even let them know exists, and that they most probably have nothing to do with. In swinging from charm to attack you become a Dr. Jekyll and Mr. Hyde.

Effectively, you have a very self-judging conscience, one that makes it nearly impossible for you to admit to feeling, thinking, or acting in any way that you judge is no good. So you have to hide from your own judgments whenever you follow your instincts into action, particularly in sexual matters. When your conscience nags you have little interest in sex, but your self-rejection makes you need strong acceptance from others, closeness, contact, and warmth. This need is stored up until it is intense enough to break loose, reach out, and make contact. But then you feel wrong and back off because you have actually shown your feelings; then you feel that it is the other rejecting you, not yourself. You find it very difficult to admit to needing anyone else, partly because the sexual side involves a Freudian clinging to the parent of the opposite sex; partly because your need is intense, and because you know just how much you can be hurt. So you can hurt others in order to avoid being hurt yourself. Also, any judgment from others is the last straw, the slightest little thing from them can hurt you, and make you counter-attack powerfully.

Your mother's self-respect depended on how others accepted her. She had to be attractive to them, and used charm to make sure that she was. She also preferred to feel superior to them and judged them against her standards, particularly if she felt that there was a possibility of them rejecting her. She was fairly creative, either with materials such as fabrics, yarn, string, or wool, or in song or dance. With children she could be closely involved, tending to relate to them as equals and liking to smooth their path for them.

Your father liked his social life as an expression of his independence. He was capable of being socially charming, and pursued his tastes and pleasures out with friends. His values may have been basically humanitarian, and his expression of feeling detached, though perhaps subject to abrupt changes. He did not like to be trapped by his relationships, and may have assumed an attitude of not caring about them to avoid such a trap.

MARS IN THE 8TH HOUSE

You have very intense drives, both for personal survival and in sex, which you keep hidden away from view. The survival drives would have shown strongly during your puberty, when your aggression level was high; your readiness to fight, or simply to go your own way alone, was strong. At that time a young person needs an initiation or acceptance into adulthood in recognition of their own changing status. You were probably left to your own devices then and had to initiate yourself, so you learned to stand on your own feet and fight your own battles, but effectively were left feeling like a child. Thus you have to keep proving yourself, proving your abilities to act for yourself, to fight for and direct your life.

You can be overly aggressive within yourself, seeing the possibilities of being attacked or rejected by others and having your defenses ready for action, though kept out of sight until the moment comes. Some with this position enter the martial arts to improve their fighting abilities. Others, more intensely uncertain, hide any aggression—even from themselves—until they feel deeply threatened, when they can fight very powerfully indeed, and keep the battle raging long beyond what is necessary—if any of it is necessary at all. In other words, you may be looking for threats to defend yourself against, and anyone looking for anything with any persistence is guaranteed to find what they seek; even if it doesn't exist, they'll make it exist. The positive side of this is the competence in various directions that it makes you build, the drive to becoming able.

You feel that your actions and directions are strongly affected by the preferences and aversions of others, that they are not going to want what you do, so you act alone. Even when involved in a close relationship you still act alone, playing your cards close to your chest. Your fear of rejection makes you forget to lower your barriers, thus keeping a separation from others that you do not finally want. The main rejection that you actually experience is from yourself. You may also feel that it is left entirely up to you to keep your relationships going, that without your actions they would fall apart. At these times you thrust yourself upon your partner more and more strongly, not realizing that this may be pushing him/her backwards, that it takes balanced cooperation to make it work.

Your sexual drives are strong, or you focus directly upon them, identifying yourself closely with them. Your first experience was a strong fixation point for you, stronger than the average, and at the time you may have wanted your partner to be the only one ever. You may be caught between a passionately intense focus on your partner and holding yourself back to avoid the hurt of rejection in case it happens.

Your mother's attitude toward children is likely to have been vigorous, active, and probably aggressive. She knew what she wanted them to do, and pushed. Her ego was strong and tended to invade other people, including you. She kept herself busily active on projects of her own besides looking after children. Your father was a social lone wolf, preferring to act independently, often out by himself. His idea of society was probably all male—out with the boys, in a sports team, or other all-male society.

JUPITER IN THE 8TH HOUSE

You are reluctant to show your true colors, to display your deeper self openly and honestly to the world. You feel that if you do you will be rejected—and you fight against that happening. The first step of the fight is secrecy, not to let others know what is going on inside you. The second is to be ready to use a great display of rage, to erupt in a big way and deflect others entirely—a form of bluff, also using bombastically outspoken and cutting language, telling the truth in the most devastating way. The third defense you use is to run away, normally after the explosions, needing to escape and leave the conflict behind you, though you usually carry it with you, fuming and blowing it up out of proportion. For some extreme types the running away takes on a rather absolute character, going toward suicide as they exaggerate the magnitude of their pains. Thus your relationships probably do not develop in a particularly stable way. You would prefer that they could, but have difficulty in opening yourself to others with confidence. You may also keep your defenses up by judging others against your expectations of them, effectively making them fall short by doing so—and making yourself secretly superior by comparison.

Sexually, you tend to be active and restless, perhaps more concerned with the amount of experience that you get, rather than its type, though some with this position will be looking for the biggest and best and will react sexually in a big way. In this you are future oriented, looking to the next time, how it is going to be, rather than how it actually is, projecting your sexual hopes onto the future. Some are sexual rovers, liking to go adventuring, exploring the breadth of the range of experience available to them; most will be honest, open, and aboveboard within sex, able to be more frank then than at any other time. This in itself causes some problems of trust, as secrets displayed then become a point of vulnerability, something on which you may be attacked or rejected, or which might be revealed by your partner. Thus your battling side would be triggered again.

There is a side of you that wants to discover the truth behind death. This may relate to a specific death in your experience (why did it happen? how could things go that far? how could anyone suffer so much?) or to the whole theme of death and what is beyond it. If so, you want to know plenty, not being satisfied with snippets of information, perhaps becoming an explorer of this vast region.

Your mother was either a confident and reasonably extroverted person with a healthy self-respect, or was more arrogant, overbearing, and bombastic, and grabbed the limelight. Toward children she was easygoing, probably outspoken, could be quite happily and openly involved, but could become explosive if she felt that things went too far. She may have liked horse-racing. Your father was probably actively independent, socially gregarious, and tolerant, liking to enjoy himself with his friends—wherever he could enjoy good-humored company. Or he may have been a philosophical humanitarian, wanting the best development for society, or for the whole human race.

SATURN IN THE 8TH HOUSE

You are cautious and controlled in expression of your deepest feelings, often not expressing them at all for fear of the results. You take attitudes of blame or rejection from others very seriously and hold your deeper self strictly reserved to avoid that kind of censure. When you feel threatened by anything you slow down into a deep and doubtful reserve, controlling yourself and the situation as firmly as you can. This control may be secretive, hiding your own motivations from others, manipulating circumstances and making sure that you are not found out. You take other people's values seriously, but may doubt that they mean you any good; for example you may feel that authority figures plot behind your back and may intend to stab you in it. Your doubt and caution, sometimes intense, make you plan for the long range in any survival battle, a facet of your character that could lead you into protracted legal battles. You fight for the survival of your status or your dignity.

You are not exactly optimistic about the development of your relationships, expecting them to go downhill, which you encourage by your growing self-protective reserve as time goes by. You may, instead, develop a deepening seriousness, an increasing sense of responsibility to your partner. This responsibility could transform you where you can accept it as a sign of maturity and adulthood. You may have a problem here if you were under strict discipline during your teen-age years, since you felt that it kept you as a child, not recognizing you as a developing adult, leaving you with (perhaps unconscious) doubts about your status as an adult, and resentful about that. Also you may have been stiff and awkward in your first approaches to the opposite sex, possibly reserved and shy in your seriousness, perhaps ending up feeling guilty. Yet you were also aware of the social status and recognition gained by having a partner, and may have played the status game, learning to do the right and appropriate things, and may have become skillful but too self-controlled in that area.

You may feel that you won't survive unless you are in complete control, showing a deep clinging to security, a facet of a fear of death. This survival caution may be financial and material as well as physical, showing in investment in property, usually involving commitment to heavy responsibilities in mortgages or long-term loans, perhaps with doubts about your ability to sustain them, though these doubts diminish with time.

Your mother's attitude to children was that she had to be in control, she had to organize them and keep them in order. She probably felt that she didn't have time for frivolities or for play with you, her time being better used for practical, responsible, and constructive things (this limited your own playfulness as a child and as an adult). Conscious of her dignity and status in others' eyes, she was slow to relax.

Your father's social values were conservative; he was aware of social stratification, of the caste system of status and position, and may have belonged to a professional society or a group in which he held a responsible position, though he had few long-term friends.

URANUS IN THE 8TH HOUSE

You probably prefer to be sexually liberated, free, friendly, and open. You think that it should be good fun without anyone being hurt by it, and may experiment freely during your independent teen-age years. You have an ideal of not trapping your partner sexually, or being trapped yourself—very likely because you have experienced just such a trap and know how it hurts. The trap probably happened with you fixing your feelings onto a partner as an ideal, putting the other person on a pedestal, normally an uncomfortable and confining position to be in. Your relationship being intense, he/she being extremely special to you, you felt that you could not live without him/her. Then it ended abruptly (as the pedestal crumbled) and you pulled your feelings away very sharply, possibly swearing never to let it happen again, to keep your feelings more detached in the future. But when you do that, although it feels necessary as a survival defense, you can never enjoy sex in the same way. So you actually store your feelings up while being detached (saying "I don't care, I am not involved," and then they tend to erupt again quite rapidly. Thus your sexual cycle moves from no interest to high interest.

The same detached defense then comes out in other areas as you feel it to be inappropriate to put your intense feelings into the situation though they will emerge as a wary, tense avoidance of traps, a readiness to escape at a moment's notice, and sometimes in destructive ways, with a hair-trigger rage ready to erupt unpredictably. Thus your relationships can end sharply. You do not repress feelings for very long without them boiling back up to the surface again in a highly charged release. You rebel against repression, whether self-caused or from others, unless you keep yourself very repressed, having buried all independence at some past traumatic time.

You do not follow tradition or society's repressed attitudes in sex, being capable of equally strong feelings for either sex—not necessarily physical feelings, though some may act these out. Some with Uranus in the 8th House hold unusually liberated ideas concerning sex, while others go to bizarre extremes (which is which may depend simply on who is doing the labeling); some may switch sexual polarities completely. Yet others will have rather neurotic and tense sexual attitudes, the tension being also physical in nervous fear clenches in the anal-genital musculature, reducing pleasure vastly and sometimes leading to hysterical complaints. These often develop from anxieties in the toilet training period, which probably included a rebellious fight against impatient and rigid training, a child's own preference being to train itself independently. These tensions may be confirmed by the first sexual experience being a disaster, tense, definitely not together, and probably over much too quickly. You may now regard sex itself as being something that can trap you.

You are possibly very wary of borrowing money on loans, again fearing traps and preferring to be as financially independent as possible; alternatively you may have over-liberal ideas of how to use credit or borrowed finance, or simply use credit very actively, ridding yourself of loans early so as not to be tied down.

NEPTUNE IN THE 8TH HOUSE

During the first few months of your life your mother's relationship with you was very tender indeed, and your reaction to it was euphoric, blissful, and wide-open. You started your life by giving every ounce of your love to her without reserve, holding nothing back. Things did not last that way, since this left you vulnerably open and sensitive, particularly to other people's values, or your imagined version of their evaluation of you. The slightest hint of rejection, blame, or censure hurt you very deeply and you had to build yourself a defense against the pain, otherwise you would not survive out in the world. Initially your defense was an inward, shy reserve, a readiness to back away into seclusion, particularly during your teen-age years. Though shy, your need for love may have made you flow easily into sexual encounters, though your pure ideal of love leans toward celibacy. You have covered your social sensitivity by hiding behind a camouflage of acted out roles. You may even have become successful socially, though still be shy and lonely underneath. There is often an intense loneliness with this position, an on-going, usually unconscious, recognition of the loss of the perfect relationship (with mother), even if it was you who withdrew. The camouflage building may be long in the past, you may have forgotten that you needed it, but your need still shows in your relationships. You want them to develop past their starting point into the ideal giving, euphoric state of total mutual openness, to continue forever in bliss . . . but are probably still too vulnerable to be able to admit to your depth of feeling, even to yourself (take your sensitive ability to dissolve into sex, into the drifting dream state).

So your relationships develop into a confusion of acted out roles and projected romantic fantasies, your need to be a baby in conflict with your need to hide yourself. They may dissolve away from under you (as you back into seclusion for safety, maybe just letting things slide). You fear the loss of the perfect relationship, so you do not let any develop that far; or you play out the martyr, constantly giving way to your partner and hiding within yourself, not rejecting them, knowing how much it hurts, but then perhaps they reject you. You are very lucky or very open if it does develop into the mutually compassionate empathy that you want.

You may have ceased to admit to yourself just how sensitively you used to feel, repressing even the memory in self-defense. Remember how music used to make you feel? There is a deep romanticism in you that you keep secret. It emerges when you make decisions. After you have first looked at a possible decision and started to weigh it up, your mind takes you on an imaginative journey to what might happen, and often leaves it at that because you might fail, or get hurt, or . . . If you have learned to use your imaginative faculty consciously you simply visualize the development of your actions and then follow that track, allowing of course for the vagaries of the world.

You need to admit to your depth, to yourself and to others. Once you allow it to surface, your world can be far closer to the way that you want it. Your psychic faculties can also emerge instead of being held down or denied. Your awareness of the deeper mysteries of life is powerful then, and develops daily into greater depth and subtlety; and the relationship that you want becomes totally possible.

PLUTO IN THE 8TH HOUSE

You are powerfully emotional, and you either admit to this or you don't. If you do, then the sheer intensity you put into every situation can sometimes frighten others, or wear them out. You take everything very personally indeed, and things that others do or say (that other people might completely ignore) you take as personal rejection, as blame or attack, which you hate and will fight against. You have an intense conscience, when you admit to it being there, which doesn't let you get away with anything, plus powerful survival instincts which drive you to fight whatever you feel to be a threat. These come from a highly developed awareness of pain—physical, emotional and social—which you feel impelled to struggle against and overcome. You use secrecy, hiding everything of yourself that you don't want others to know about, protecting it from harm. You defend yourself with explosive rage, physically in lashing out, and verbally in sarcasm, biting language designed to devastate. You may brood over revenge for ages, obsessionally clinging to wrongs done to you, until you have found the perfect destructive retaliation, taking your victim by surprise. You may be a master of war games and tactics, *e.g.*, chess; always aiming to win, preferably in a devastating way, since you do not like to lose.

If you have buried your intense feelings and can't admit to having them, you will find yourself faced with situations that keep bringing them up. You hate horror movies and mention of death or of massive pain, avoiding such things as far as is possible. You live inwardly, folding a protective psychological shield around yourself to keep others out, refusing to open yourself to anything in case it might hurt you. You brood on your hurts but hide this from yourself, not admitting to your feelings in case you have to face them. You feel that you have been rejected and hurt badly, but you now reject yourself by your isolation. You desperately need to feel that others really want you, and this may emerge in sex—since you have powerful drives, whether you admit to them or not—but you can't believe that they do want you, your opinion of yourself being very poor, so you suspect them of ulterior motives in relating to you, and this ruins your relationships, as does your silence. Simply, you have a problem in eliminating the garbage from your being, probably physically as much as emotionally.

You are capable of completely transforming yourself by admitting to and accepting those things that you have rejected about yourself. You can be very unforgiving—and need to forgive yourself on a deep level. Your greatest crime is likely to be hatred, which you can't let go of without recognizing it. Your conscience may make you hate yourself for hating—a vicious circle that must be broken.

We could blame your parents for some of this, but you need less blame in your life, not more. So instead we'll say that your intensity can take you anywhere in human explorations that you want to go, when it is free of entanglement. You want to break through— or break out of—your world into a different one, and you can do it, once your volcano has blown, once your repressions have surfaced and been cleared out. Your conscience is your best guide; what hurts you also hurts others. Aim not to hurt but to heal, for you have magnificent healing powers.

NORTH NODE—8TH HOUSE, SOUTH NODE—2ND HOUSE

You are very fixed in pursuit of those things that you value, maintaining a straight-line track toward your goals, finding security in money and physical possessions. Often your preference is for a placid, even existence in which you can feed your senses with pleasures and have all that you want, but you become enmeshed in material concerns and possessiveness, losing sight of other goals in life. Jealous possessiveness can lead you into battles with others where they have what you believe to be yours and you *want* it. You can be totally stubborn and immovable when change is really needed in your being, refusing to alter your values or to consider alternatives, falling into a lazy inert perpetuation of the same old states. Where change ceases, death already exists.

You must become aware that physical things are for use, and that it isn't necessary to carry more than you actually need at the time. This also applies to all your attitudes in life, for you need to purge yourself of the useless and unnecessary in order to lighten your load. Your pursuit of pleasure covers a rejection of pain, but it is only when you admit to what hurts you that you can heal those hurts. One key: material goods are usually a substitute for love, and sex frequently is also. You will transform yourself by intense examination of everything that you value, coming to understand which values are real, natural and worthwhile, and which involve clinging to crutches and distractions for the sake of security.

❖ 11 ❖

Sagittarius
and the 9th House

In the 9th House, our outreach to the other in our lives reaches its greatest intensity, but is also polarized and may alternate between going out into wider experience and retiring away from it. Here we live through the links or bridges of communication that we have built between ourselves and the wider world, whether to us that world consists of things, people, places, and ideas, or spiritual search. We seek to understand our relationship to the whole (even if the particular whole is simply a whole subject at university, or one whole viewpoint on the world), and to re-unify ourselves with the whole where we have lost contact, or to find the reasons for that loss of contact and understand it.

Where our own consciences judge us and find us lacking, or we have buried within us things that we feel are unacceptable to others, we find it difficult to extend ourselves out to others with confidence, to feel that the other will find us acceptable. In our past history we humans (mostly our prophets) have elaborated such self-judgments into philosophies, religions, legal and ethical codes, in which we have imposed the same judgments onto everyone. Then we have tried either to live up to them, or to make others live up to them. If we are honest, we try to improve ourselves, usually according to some acquired outer standard, rather than returning to the integrity of our own being; if dishonest, we bombastically judge others for their failure, establishing our own hypocritical superiority to them in the process, while camouflaging our own faults and deceiving both self and other. Then we may become the religious type who sees everyone else's sins, but suffers frequent crises of faith if we catch sight of our own arrogance through our filter.

If we are not entangled in self-judgment, our desire to know our relationship to the whole will be pure enthusiastic exploration, a confident extension of self out into wide-ranging experience. The natural life-period for the 9th House is between about 20 and 30 years of age. Young adults going out into the world have a need to explore it, and in the same action to explore their own abilities, to understand what they really appreciate in their life in the world, and how they most enjoy expressing that appreciation.

In the early stages, given freedom of choice, a young person must dabble in many things, sampling widely, pursuing their enthusiasms. Only by following their noses do they come to understand what they appreciate, and through that, who they are, using the world as a mirror. Then when they come to the 10th House they can choose a life-track that is truly theirs, not one imposed by others. But if they have had to hide behind masks, their masks determine the direction they must take, and they may be confused at their lack of enthusiasm for going the "right" way.

Physiologically, young adults are usually at their peak of health, strength, clarity of mind, and sexual fertility, all designed to help them scatter their seeds in the world for future growth. Much of the continued maintenance and energizing of the body falls onto the liver. It both stores short-term energy resources and detoxifies the blood. If it is functioning well, the confidence of the individual can be high, since health and strength are available. The 9th House is partly concerned with how we feel about the possibilities of the future, whether we are optimistic about where we are going, or troubled in any way. Here is where we demonstrate our faith in what has not yet happened, where we may gamble our lives by trusting to our luck. Luck is a combination of whole-hearted trust in outcomes, and the world's (karmic) response to generosity of spirit.

In our interaction with the world, we are capable of absorbing enormous amounts of experience. Then we have to understand that experience, to interpret it, to draw abstract lessons, knowledge, and wisdom from it. If our interpretations are narrow, the knowledge gained will be narrow and so will the track we take. If we assume we already understand, we will learn nothing new. If we really want to learn, we will recognize that we know little or nothing as yet, but are capable of learning, and will try to understand our experience as it is, without imposing any personal biases onto it. We only grow by going into the unknown, by free, open acceptance of the other into our lives. When we accept the other deeply, we grow beyond our old limits into much wider experience.

Throughout our lives we meet many people, many situations, make many kinds of relationship, have to learn how to handle them, and move on from them. Where we meet the other with acceptance we learn. Here lies our capacity for sharing views, for honest communication with others, for accepting advice or genuine teaching from them (which will depend on what we believe to be true). Here we may eventually give out what we have learned for the benefit of others, at the best, teaching our wisdom.

If we have no confidence, we will feel vulnerable to possible (often imaginary) threats from around us. And if we do, we will have no time to spare for philosophies other than the paranoid. We can then either run away, or turn and fight. If vulnerable, we may try to convince both ourselves and others that we are strong, fierce, unbeatable—and hope that this confidence trick will work. The same applies to our competence in dealing with the world in general.

Otherwise the 9th is simply our involvement in the broad arena of public communication and dissemination of information and goods. This includes publishing, advertising, warehousing and sales, distribution and communication networks, plus all the traffic that flows along them. Instead of honest communication we may get the salesman's pitch, public relations hype, the con-artist's ploys, the missionary's efforts to convert us, all efforts to convince us that what they have is right for us. All are methods of using others to satisfy personal motives, without truly caring at all for the other.

Further physiological themes here are: storage of fats as long-term fuel reserves (if famine is expected), thus obesity; the arteries and their ability to contract to raise blood pressure in situations of fight or flight to fuel exertion, thus high blood-pressure and arteriosclerosis; and the control of the pituitaries over adrenalin and arousal.

SUN IN SAGITTARIUS
✧ The Traveler ✧ The Explorer ✧ The Philosopher ✧

Your classic time of life is from age 20 to 30; everyone goes through a Sagittarian phase at that time, being the time of peak physical health, intellectual clarity and curiosity, and peak fertility; all these aid what should be a time of flourishing exploration of your world, of diving into everything with enthusiasm to test yourself, to extend your range, to discover what rouses your deepest interest and enthusiasm, and to fertilize or be fertilized by your experience.

Everyone is changed by their experience. If tackled with openness, it opens you; the broader and deeper your involvement in the world, the broader and deeper your character becomes. At best you pursue truth, around you and inside you, never satisfied with less, your long-range aim being to expand and evolve yourself, perhaps to the point of regaining total union with your universe (through philosophical or religious pursuits), perhaps being satisfied with gregarious contacts with others, or with much learning spread widely, focused on the largest subjects.

You alternate between subjective and objective, between focusing in on yourself, and out onto others or the world. Your need is to bring the two together, which may manifest as studying, then teaching; or as relating, then running away when you feel your freedom being eroded away, but coming back to fulfill the relationship; or as diving into your own mind, then applying what you have learned about yourself to your understanding of everyone.

Your energies, and with them your confidence, faith, or trust are variable. When high you charge out into fresh enthusiasms with vigorous enjoyment, never expecting anything to go wrong, and it won't. But when your energies drop, you lose confidence; if you feel threatened then you are capable of exploding in a big way, pouring out a volcanic temper designed to devastate. Yet your confidence is often low enough to make you then run away. You normally need to go for a long walk in fresh air to calm down after an explosion. This cool-down is when you start to admit to where you were wrong, where you were projecting blame onto the other party, when you realize that you have something to apologize for. If you don't get this far, your temper remains high, but is really directed at yourself for not being entirely honest.

You tend to rush forward into the future; at least the future is probably more important to you than the past or present. This may be because there are more discoveries and explorations to be made, or it may be a running away from the past or an uncomfortable present moment. Whether you are running, or standing and exploding, it will be because of ethical problems, difficulties with your own morals. You originally were entirely honest and above-board. You either have, or believe that you have, broken your trust in yourself, in your honesty and honor. If they are intact, you do not run, and you honor everyone else, feeling happily equal to all. If you judge that you are not fully ethical (consciously or unconsciously) you will try to shift blame, becoming morally superior in the process, then subject to your own hypocrisy, inwardly finding yourself lacking.

MOON IN SAGITTARIUS

Your emotional nature is restless, optimistic, and expansive, and generally cheerful and gregarious. The restlessness shows physically since you are a little high-strung, having an excess of energy and finding it difficult to sit still for long. Your feelings are continually bubbling, your optimism always looking to the more hopeful developments or opportunities of the future as you instinctively search out the path of best growth or widest experience. You gain security in yourself by feeling that you are identified with the larger order of things, with the right teaching or faith, or the right moral structure, though you initially choose this on emotional grounds or follow your family pattern, rather than having conscious reasons for involvement; or your wider scope may be the great outdoors or foreign lands. Whatever your choice, you do not usually stick to a single aim for long, your restlessness moving you on to greener pastures and new involvements as you search for the end of the rainbow.

You have bursts of confidence, taking you out into activity for a while, but then it fades. The low end of your mood-swing is tied to the flight side of your fight or flight reflex, and when you are down you are ready to run away from whatever offends you or makes you feel insecure. As your confidence rises, so do your hopes, and you build them up, pinning them on your new enthusiasm, perhaps to the point of glorifying or idealizing it; but then your confidence and enthusiasm fade, and to you it seems that the object of your interest has lost its appeal. You may become angry with it as another lost hope and run away toward the next. If you have stopped chasing outer objectives, having given up hope that they will work out, you may have pulled all your expansiveness into yourself, becoming conceited, egotistical, and superior on the upswing, and angry with yourself for not being what you feel you should be on the downswing (which you probably project out onto others, finding reasons to be angry with them).

Apart from this you will be honest and open but perhaps use the truth selectively as a defense, not telling lies but misdirecting as a bluff, or use emotional openness as a form of self-protection, knowing that people are unlikely to question what is behind it; the salesman's cheerfully gregarious charm, for example. Emotionally, you do need to trust your own honesty, so you need to question how far it goes. When you do trust it absolutely, you know that it will navigate you in the right directions for you, and that you can trust whatever comes. Any strong swings of feeling that you have are usually problems of trust, faith, or confidence, as is any need to run away.

Your openness to the broader ranges of experience could easily take you traveling around the world, the Sagittarian Moon being a common factor in charts of travelers, outdoorsmen, and explorers, as well as perennial students, teachers, philosophers, and religious people (and salesmen and con-artists). It can indicate living in foreign countries.

MERCURY IN SAGITTARIUS

Your mind prefers to focus on large issues and explore broad themes, to cover whole territories in a single bound. You are intellectually restless and have wide-ranging views and many ideas on many large subjects, and you are generally prepared to talk about them or lecture on them at the drop of a hat. You are something of a perpetual student in your itch to learn, and probably in your sense of humor too, though both may be a little broad. You like to cover such large areas that you are not always concerned with details or with strict facts, usually preferring to gain a general overview of a subject, and may become lost in the vastness of knowledge, becoming superficial, scattered, and confused. Your restlessness can cause you to keep on moving from one theme to another without ever really finalizing your knowledge in any of them, though you may believe that you will never reach the end of learning. Any one fact or idea tends to bring up a whole chain of branching and proliferating connections and associations, and if it doesn't then you work on it, evolving fresh networks as you go along.

You like to study how things grow, whether natural growth, or the evolution of a species, or a language. You want to understand how things develop and proliferate through time, how a philosophy or any other structure of ideas develops, or the growth and codification of a body of law. You may, with any Aries in you, become involved in the exploration and development of new bodies of information, or new areas of study and research. Or with a more inward orientation, you will work at opening communication between your conscious and unconscious sides, perhaps through dreams, knowing that to bring the two together is to become whole in yourself, and to be able to tap the inward root of all knowledge.

Your main aim is likely to be to discover the truth, and you prefer to be truthful yourself, though you sometimes use what you believe to be true, rather than strict fact. Your tendency to exaggerate can lead you astray, overstating and enlarging on things, or getting them out of proportion. You are certainly likely to be outspoken, not failing to have opinions on most subjects. You may be much concerned with justice, ethics and morals, philosophy or religion, being interested in structures of thought and belief, and may be given to a certain pedantic, moral sermonizing. At least you are likely to like telling others what it's all about, perhaps in actual lecturing or teaching. You could be a good teacher, since your own enthusiasm for your subject(s) will arouse enthusiasm in your students, and your inclination toward hopeful, optimistic, and humorous views would ease the path of learning.

Other areas of study and perhaps work include: geography and map-making, exploration, climatic studies, the overlap of ecological zones, forestry, evolution; foreign languages, language development, philosophy, religions, education; the travel and hotel industries, import/export; advertising, broadcasting, journalism, publishing, bookshops, or universities.

VENUS IN SAGITTARIUS

In relating to others you tend to be free, frank, and open, friendly and outgoing. In your life in general you like plenty of wide experience, and it is the same in relating too, as you value the personal growth that you can find in being involved with a wide variety of people and circumstances. You like exploring experiences with others, sharing things that broaden your views and open your perspectives, and you do not generally hang back, being ready to go openly into fresh possibilities with full hopes that they will turn out well for all concerned. Your love of variety and breadth does not make you seek out stability as you are in no hurry to be tied down, and this can leave you free to explore the wide spectrum of relationships. You don't necessarily run around from one to another, but you do have a restless streak here that doesn't want to be limited to a narrow or confined pattern.

You prefer to be honest, open, and outspoken with others, though if Venus has any difficult aspects you may use this as a bluff to disarm opposition. On the same grounds, your relationships may have their tempestuous side as you do not hold back your reactions, but can flare up if anything goes contrary to your preferences, also being ready to run away afterwards, preferring open movement to being bottled up at any time. This can combine with your hopeful nature to become an impulsive search for the "gold at the end of the rainbow," as you leave any relationship or situation that doesn't appear to fulfill those hopes, then projecting them on to the next...and the next...You don't always involve yourself deeply in relating to others, probably feeling that to do so may block your growth, may cut out those wider avenues that you value so much, which sometimes leaves you simply pleasure seeking, joining in while it is fun, but no longer than that.

If particularly negative, you will use your relationships as a way of gaining a certain moral superiority over the other person, judging them in such a way as to find them lacking, effectively gaining stature yourself by climbing on their back.

Particular experiences that you like to share, or will find yourself sharing, include exploring the wide-open spaces of the world in travel, (and you may do it on horseback sometime), feeling out its cultural and artistic developments in study, or its mental and spiritual aspects through philosophy and religion. You may only fully enjoy a relationship if it keeps your contacts with the wider range of experience open by including such avenues. Your restlessness is best given its head in any such arena of exploration, which will probably help you to be more settled in more purely person-to-person affairs. Your taste in the arts is likely to be toward the more flourishing and flamboyant types of expression, such as the baroque and rococo periods in painting and music (try Beethoven), symphonic music, religious art forms, and landscapes, but the most important element here is your own enthusiasm.

MARS IN SAGITTARIUS

You have a highly restless and impulsive energy that wants to experience and explore everything, but may find it difficult to stick to any one avenue of experience. You would like to go adventuring, spreading yourself across the horizon in all directions at once, chasing after everything that you identify yourself with, which is rather a lot. Thus you have difficulty in being consistent in your aims for any length of time, as you chase energetically from one possible goal to another, without necessarily ever reaching any. You are usually far more interested in the opportunities of the future, in what you are going to do, than in what you are doing now. However much you do, it is never enough to satisfy the very breadth of your aims. Therefore you often end up being dissatisfied with the present moment because it is not good enough, or big enough, or interesting enough for you, so you project more hopes onto the future instead of dealing with them right now. You have a certain offhand attitude which could be interpreted as being easy-going, but may have become sloppiness, which can be wasteful of money, materials, and energy; half finishing a job and then restlessly moving on to something fresh.

You can be argumentative, querulous, and vigorously outspoken in what you may believe to be your effort to reach the truth, and you can hold your opinions with a morally superior attitude, ignoring or overriding the views of others. Your temper is capable of dramatically noisy flare-ups and great displays of destructive rage, but usually doesn't do any ultimate harm except in shattering the confidence of those around you. You also have a strong escape mechanism, saying your piece and then storming out, or running away, before you have to listen to the other point(s) of view. We could look upon this as an expression of your drive for freedom at any cost, or as an evasion of any backlash that might penetrate your bluff and show you that, while you tell others what you think is wrong with them, you don't look at what you yourself are doing. Essentially you have a fear of being picked at, criticized and negated by others, of being made to feel small.

Your restless energy is well expressed in outdoor pursuits, such as camping, hiking, and hunting, all of which give you the wider scope and freedom that you desire. Given the full expression of this side of your being, you would be an explorer of wild, untouched lands, pioneering the opening of new territories, living off the land and drawing your maps as you go. You may express this in explorations of a more intellectual or spiritual nature, opening territories that are new to you; or a dissatisfied search for stimulus may lead you into gambling and sexual profligacy, taking the chances that excite you in a way that involves no physical effort or danger to yourself. You can be very fair and open in your attitudes, treating life as a game that should be played according to the rules, even though you will bend those rules as far as they will go in your own direction. You can be friendly and egalitarian with children, acting like an overgrown child yourself, and being a big brother to them.

JUPITER IN SAGITTARIUS

You have a restless and free-ranging enthusiasm that prefers to be involved in the wider areas of life-experience, and goes out to explore the variety and richness of the world. Your major avenues of experience are likely to be: physical, in travel—entering into a variety of cultures; mental, in higher education—gaining a broad overview of large areas of knowledge; spiritual, in philosophy or religion—seeking to understand the place of man in the universe. You will be largely concerned with morality and ethics, attempting within your own being to represent the truths that you have found, and to maintain high standards of honesty—knowing that in order to find the truth, you have to be true within yourself. Whatever the case, you seek an all-inclusive viewpoint, like a walker on a hilltop, trying to expand your mind to encompass all that you meet in life. Your need for freedom and scope may turn you into a natural outdoorsman, your restless energy and desire to cover ground being well expressed in hiking, hill walking, or horseback riding. You probably see your life as being a journey of discovery for the development of wisdom, the gaining of universal knowledge for the benefit of all, and you are very likely to give out what you have learned, perhaps in orthodox teaching and lecturing, perhaps in other ways. You would make a fine teacher because of the enthusiasm that you bring to your studies and can impart to your students, awakening in them the joy of discovery.

Your difficulties involve too great a breadth of coverage, a restless and impulsive scattering of your mind over too wide a field, a perennial youthful irresponsibility that never settles down to anything in depth. While you are capable of discovering general principles within specific experiences, you often have a tendency to exaggerate in your enthusiasm, or in your desire to represent the biggest and the best, blowing what you know up out of all proportion to the facts. You may feel that if you have found the truth, that it must be true for all others, and that they must therefore accept it—whether they want to or not. Thus you could become a narrow-minded proselytizer of your religion or creed, being morally self-righteous and overbearing, creating for yourself a sense of superiority in being the representative of the one true faith. In this state you are unlikely ever to listen to the views and opinions of others, "knowing" that you are right.

Obviously this is self-inflation and has nothing to do with truth. Those who feel the need to create a sense of superiority usually build it to cover over a weak foundation, using it as a bluff to prevent themselves and others from seeing how empty it is. Genuine inner truth is never ashamed of simplicity and humility, for it realizes that truth is far greater that any individual can ever know. Naturally if anyone challenges your superiority you are in a shaky position, and will normally first erupt in angry self-defense, and then run away so that neither they, nor yourself, can penetrate your bluff. You will probably be very good at running away, making it look as though you are running toward the hopes and possibilities of the future, of which you will build many—wherever the present moment, or your present self, is not satisfying to you.

SATURN IN SAGITTARIUS

You may have a deeply serious moral or ethical code for which you are willing to renounce the world, to give up anything, even life itself, so that the good and the right may prevail. In interacting with your world and the people in it you are serious, orderly, and perhaps profound. You see the gaining of maturity as learning the laws of the world and cooperating with them, thus you are likely to hold a deep respect for teachers, philosophers, and perhaps for religion and religious men. You accept the law as revealed through them, as it brings understanding and enlightenment. You nurture your spirit by feeding it with fuel, feeling that life must grow beyond the visible into the invisible. You aspire toward the transcendental.

Since you keep yourself open to the beneficent forces of the world around you, returning as much as you receive, your energy should be continually refreshed and enduring, capable of putting forth long hours of effort.

On the contrary side, if Saturn was in difficult aspects your aspiration may be more of a snobbery, with you cultivating the right connections, looking for alliances with people in powerful or high positions. This will be unbalanced in that you will also avoid those less well-placed than yourself, keeping yourself on the bottom rung of the ladder by chopping off those below you. If you are religious you should learn to think very carefully before you attempt to convert another person to your particular following, as an element of self-righteousness in your attitude can cost you very dearly in friends over a period of time.

Your energies are also likely to be restricted or extremely slow to renew themselves, your reserves small and easily exhausted, which may indicate a liver problem.

One of the problems with Saturn here is the tendency to set high hopes, but to believe that they are always likely to be dashed, or are not going to come off in the way you want them to. You tend to allow your doubts to grow, to elaborate, to blow up out of proportion. This may have been because you grew up with parents whose attitude toward responsibility and discipline was rather easy-going, and thus not always consistent (though probably sometimes rather eruptive). For example, as a child you may have been promised something, say a trip to the circus; then your parents changed the plans at the last minute, thus shattering all the excitement that you had built up as the time approached. We can call this a loss of faith, and it can occur for you in the religious area as much as in any other. It occurs partly because you hang very serious expectations upon the future, and partly because you have a tendency to make large and rather absolute rules for both yourself and others (including God), and if anyone breaks them you find it hard to forgive and to re-establish your own trust or confidence.

If you have a need for intellectual recognition, this can be achieved by taking extra educational courses at an adult level, once you have established yourself in life. At this time you have the depth of concentration necessary to see it all through to its conclusion.

URANUS IN SAGITTARIUS

Uranus was in Sagittarius from late 1981 to late 1988. In this time we saw growth in the drive out into space, with the shuttles showing their value, the Voyager missions bringing the outer planets to our doorstep, and Halley's comet attracting much attention in space as well as on the ground. Russian space stations were manned on a regular basis, and much scientific experimentation went on in space, producing new knowledge, new materials, and a much wider understanding of the universe. There were changes in higher education, with crossovers of different disciplines and subjects, bridging knowledge across the gaps, particularly through the use of computers. The same applied to philosophy and religion, with various teachings (shamanism, Wicca) gaining more attention, with further exploration of the common links between teachings, and new hybrids arising. Advances in communications technology put all parts of the world into much closer and faster communication, and satellite television brought us nearer to a full global broadcasting system. Sociological views became broader with efforts to understand the effects of all levels of society on each other, and of various different cultures in interaction.

Those born in this time have minds capable of taking many streams of information and seeing the common factors, then blending them by cross-connecting everything that is mutual to all. They are capable of forming fresh and unusual overviews, and of triggering revolutions in the fields of advanced knowledge, whether academic or holistic. Their attitudes toward morality will tend to be individualistic, liberal, and tolerant, of the "nothing is wrong if it harms no one" type, believing that it is everyone's prerogative to form their own moral views, independent of any particular philosophy or religion. Their curiosity about philosophies is intense, and they will probably explore a variety of options, not fixing upon any as the final truth but building their own understanding of the common ground of all, pursuing their own individual paths. They will be freedom-oriented, believing that personal liberty is everyone's right, and will tolerate no restrictions being placed upon them. They will be rovers, mentally and physically, never being content with confinement to narrow horizons in anything. Some will be rovers in space.

Being restless, they may become bored very quickly when they do not receive enough stimulus, and will rapidly move on to something or somewhere else. Thus they are capable of being highly mobile, but not always stable or consistent in the long term. The need for stimulus may scatter their minds and enthusiasms too widely to allow them to enter into any one thing in depth. Some will be great generalizers, others attempting to appear profound by producing scattered snippets of wisdom, disconnected fragments of all that they absorb. Marriage will be more difficult for this generation with their high need for freedom to move and hatred of being tied down too finally by anything. Some will be explosive rebels, refusing ties of any kind and ready to run away from them.

Nevertheless, they are capable of high ideals of honesty and integrity, and if allowed to develop freely by following their own curiosity will not go very far wrong. They need to learn how to discipline their interests and enthusiasms to keep them in focus, and if given a view of the vastness of the universe, this is likely to arouse deep interest, and may provide them with a path of study for life.

NEPTUNE IN SAGITTARIUS

Neptune was in Sagittarius between November 1970 and November 1984, during which time there was a marked religious and philosophical resurgence among young people as eastern teachings and other philosophies became fashionable; scientists became more aware of the marked similarities, if not identities, between science and eastern philosophies (shown in books such as the Tao of Physics, and the Dancing Wu Li Masters); fashions in films embraced huge themes, developing toward epic adventures, with a marked increase of foreign films into domestic markets. People traveled in greater numbers than ever before (to the point that in Greece, in 1979, the tourist population outnumbered the Greek people, and the country ran out of food).

Being born during this period, you will have a restless searching nature that will not be satisfied with the small in anything. Whether your search takes you around the world in travel, seeking to understand the natures of the various lands and peoples, or into higher education—trying to look beyond the boundaries of the knowledge taught there toward the boundless, or into a spiritual exploration aiming for the infinite, your mind is potentially capable of visualizing and absorbing things on a grand scale. You will want to range over the widest horizons available to you, to expand your own being as far as you can. Naturally you may have a problem in spreading your attention too widely and diffusely, of being too general in the way that you learn, of finding it difficult to pin yourself down to specific facts or places or attitudes. If you train your imagination to become a visualizing tool, learning how to hold clear and well-built images of whatever you want to learn or absorb, you will find that it will help your mind to expand its scope tremendously. You will probably want to know everything, or at least to have a big overview, to know how all things fit together, if not to expand out from this world completely in space travel or in cosmic consciousness, so the sooner you train your mind in that direction the closer you will be to achieving your aim.

In your ethical or moral attitudes you will either have a clear and simple compassion for all, including yourself, recognizing that good lies in not harming anyone; or you will be confused, probably by the motives that drive others and cause harm. You may act from unethical motives and try to hide the fact from others, and perhaps from yourself too. If this is the case you will be very sensitive to any implication that you do wrong, acting to give the impression of being morally superior while actually being a fraud.

Some subjects that you might like to study to help you to build your overview or to cut through any confusion are: geography, anthropology, ethics, symbolism (including Jungian psychology), mysticism and comparative religions, cosmic consciousness, and meditation, or cosmology.

SAGITTARIUS NORTH NODE—GEMINI SOUTH NODE

You are split in your attitudes to most things, not knowing what you want, wanting both opposite possibilities, or neither. It is difficult for you to hold a single view, idea, or attitude toward anything, for you fear that if you adopt one then you will lose out on the possibilities of the others. You are afraid of losing what you hope for so you never truly commit yourself to it, always being ready to change horses in midstream. This naturally leads to the loss that you fear, thus proving that you were right not to pin your hopes down, and right to set up alternatives. Put in other words, you are very adaptable but not very consistent, your mind being naturally rather restless.

You need to recognize that only by affirming what you believe in, what you know to be truth, can you ever come close to it. Only by admitting whole-heartedly to your true hopes and wider aspirations can they ever be realized. Only by trusting the information that you store away can you use it as a map, a guide for your own direct exploration of the territory that it depicts. Instead of running back and forth over the same old ground you need to go and keep on going, over ever-wider horizons. You should leave behind your need to have others give you identity by reacting to you, and go out into the immensity of the world alone. Your quest for information becomes a search for truth, your inconsistency becomes honesty in all things, and your light intellectual wit becomes a deep belly-laugh of genuine appreciation of the world.

SUN IN THE 9TH HOUSE

You have a restlessly explorative nature that aims to discover the truth by ranging through the broad regions of knowledge or wisdom. Your explorations may make you a traveler or outdoors person, a perennial student, philosophically or religiously inclined. You gain in a sense of identity and self-respect by allying yourself with high principles and broadening your tolerance through your voyages of discovery. Your general aim is to grow, to evolve, to awaken your entire being toward some ultimate goal. To do this you know that your aims must be clear, convincing, and inspiring to you, and that you have to have the strength to carry them out, which is where problems arise since, although you display confidence, it is actually rather uneven. You have a problem of faith, probably both within yourself and with your aims, or with the tools used to achieve them.

When you lose confidence mistrust arises. Where you cease to trust, you start to run away, like a highly strung horse. Your discrimination is highly developed. Where it seeks perfection in all things, it finds it. Where it looks for imperfection, it also finds it, and exaggerates it, blowing it up out of proportion. You then pull away because that is not what you want (often exploding first, at having your trust broken—again). You seek further for what you want, find something wrong with it, move on . . . The "perfect" is always in the future, instead of here and now. When you have pulled away from many facets of yourself, mistrusting them, you scatter and fragment yourself, particularly when you cease to trust your own honor and integrity.

You began life with a simple, natural sense of morality and rightness within yourself and toward the world, trusting everything. Loss of trust drives you to try to regain it in something, but doesn't always let you trust enough to do it. You need to realize that you still have in you the simple innocence and trust that you began with, and that it is your conscious mind and your pride that have covered it with complexities in trying to find a truth that you actually *are* in yourself.

You have such a profusion of impulses in you, a teeming multitude of things struggling to take form, that you can be chaotic, firing off in all directions. Inner pressure builds to the point that it bursts forth as an emotional thunderstorm, clearing the air. To order your chaos, you need guidance from mature and experienced teachers, to learn what to renounce and what to pursue.

Your mother was a discriminating person, probably critical and fault-finding with those around her. She didn't like finding fault in herself, or for anyone else to do so either, but felt justified in picking at the faults that she found in others. She was a good worker where her self-respect depended on it, particularly in organizing or controlling others, yet she could be a lazy housekeeper.

Your father was in some ways vulnerable and retiring, allowing circumstances to ride over him, leaning toward being the martyr, doormat or victim. He was basically gentle and giving, liked his privacy, his books and his music, but would use a personality camouflage to hide behind to keep stress out.

MOON IN THE 9TH HOUSE

Emotionally you can be easy-going, tolerant and gregarious, very fond of your freedom and of having plenty of room to move, preferably out in the open air. You gain in feelings of security by having wide-open territories to live in, and to identify with, for you don't like having close boundary limits around you. You are emotionally hopeful, liking to have things to look forward to, opportunities ahead of you, again gaining security by feeling that things are developing positively in the right directions. You have a natural philosophical or religious tendency, not necessarily thought out, but rather felt, and not requiring you to belong to any organization, unless you keep up a family tradition here. The same quality gives you a basic feeling for morality, a sense of right and wrong that needs no rules or commandments to maintain it, but simply identifies with the needs of life in general. (Unless you keep yourself on track by avoiding what your mother would have criticized).

You also tend to be emotionally restless and a little highly strung. Your confidence is cyclic, swinging with your moods, waxing and waning. When it is high, little can go wrong for you, or, even if it does, you approach it optimistically and take it in your stride; but when your confidence is low your restlessness increases to the point where you want to run away and leave everything behind, heading for the hills and freedom. In between, you sometimes assume a mask of confidence as a bluff, an emotional defense that, through going outwards positively, doesn't always allow others in. At your best, you aim to absorb knowledge, understanding, wisdom, and can become something of a sage, giving out all that you have learned for the nurturing and growth of others, and for some this leads to writing or teaching. At your worst, you have a greed for experience that feeds itself on everything it can find, restlessly moving on from one thing to another without absorbing anything in depth, the rule being "more is better, whatever it is." On this side, the more you experience, the greater becomes your craving for experience.

Your major need is probably to identify closely with a teacher or teaching that can point the way to expanding your consciousness, showing you how to stretch the boundaries of your personal reality to open to the wider universe. In this you can feed your hunger for experience with spiritual food. Some spiritual development is likely to occur by your becoming more conscious of, and in, your dreams; also by a discipline of meditation or contemplation.

Your mother had a critical and perfectionistic edge to her feelings, showing in tidiness and upsets about people messing things up. She tended to worry about the family and about life-support in general, giving herself in service to others, liking to do things for them, even if she complained.

Your father leaned toward rather private and withdrawn moods, closeting himself away from the family. He tended to feel martyred by others, an expression of his rather sensitive and vulnerable feelings. At his best he would be charitably giving and compassionate, identifying with others' feelings as strongly as with his own, having a deep feeling for nature, and a sizable imaginative streak.

MERCURY IN THE 9TH HOUSE

Your mind likes to travel over broad spans of thought and knowledge, exploring the range of ideas in various areas (especially higher education, philosophy and religion). Or you may just pay lip-service to such things and avoid deep involvement, pursuing them for a short time and then pulling away. Mentally, you like to feel that you can soar to the heights, and bring what you have discovered down to earth, like Prometheus. You want to be a messenger and disseminator of higher truths, pouring out and maybe lecturing on what you have learned, yet you may tend to reduce your truths to a formula—a set of concepts that can be understood by the average intellect, which can turn them into trivia. Or you may do the opposite, making trivial thoughts into profound philosophy. Or you may simply want to communicate widely and freely, perhaps finding work that will let you do so; radio, television, advertising, or teaching, or in an area where your restless nervous energy can be expressed in motion, by driving or traveling, particularly by doing a lot of running around in your local area.

You may be morally dualistic, having different rules for yourself and for others, "it's wrong if they do it but it's all right if I do it," and you can be thoroughly outspoken to anyone who does anything "wrong" against you. You are capable of using the truth to tell lies with, slanting it carefully to give just the impression that you want others to get. Your confidence may fluctuate up and down, leaving you chasing the opportunities that interest you for a while, then turning around and running away. Your faith in religion or philosophy, or even in life itself, follows the same path, as do your relationships, which often do not come to a distinct end, but resurrect themselves as you change your mind, restarting, then pulling apart again, then starting up ... You want personal freedom, yet don't want to lose anything else by having it, wanting the best of both worlds. You may never quite trust that your hopes will be fulfilled, believing for a little while and reaching out, then ceasing to trust and backing off, over and over, and also shifting between at least two mutually incompatible sets of hopes. In other words you have never made up your mind which future you actually want to have, so you don't build a solid one. It is possible that you may keep returning to the past, for example when first leaving home, going back to live there more than once.

This is a symptom of a split between your conscious and unconscious personalities, each wanting something different. You need to discover what your less conscious side needs (perhaps by studying your dreams to open communication), and work to fulfill those needs.

Your mother's mind was rather analytical, somewhat perfectionistic, perhaps criticizing or nagging about what was wrong or out of place, instead of noticing what was right with things. She could be nervous and worrisome, especially about getting all of her work done, and probably wasn't consistent about doing it. Your father was more of a dreamer, his mind drifting in his own private world, perhaps in pursuit of knowledge, perhaps as a camouflage to protect himself from the harsher aspects of reality. He would back away into seclusion at times, needing personal privacy. He may have had a delightfully whimsical and imaginative wit.

VENUS IN THE 9TH HOUSE

You can display a great deal of gregarious and humorous charm, with a confident outspokenness which may cover something quite different underneath. If Venus has difficult aspects, you appear honest, open, and easy-going, yet can make direct moral judgments on other people, giving yourself an apparent moral superiority. You like to be the judge in the high seat sometimes, looking down on lesser mortals, and, like the Gods, the truth is sometimes what you make it, rather than what it is. You can show broad, high, ethical values to others, and be lazy about maintaining them, inflating your position by comparing yourself with others. Much of this is bluff—and judging them before they can judge you, which they probably aren't doing. Your confidence is variable, so you need to boost it, but sometimes do it by building conceit instead.

You are capable of pinning high hopes onto your relationships, that the *big* love that you want will come (and you are capable of absorbing a lot of love). But at least one of your big hopes is likely to have crashed in the past, so you repeat the pattern—hoping that the next one, or the one after that, is going to be *it*, and being prepared to pull out and run away if it isn't (again), perhaps with an explosion or so before that happens. You make relationships easily when your confidence is high, and can unmake them fairly easily too, when it drops.

If Venus had few difficulties, you will have a love of truth and honesty, a belief in fairness and equality for all, and will judge no one. You will very likely also have a love of religion or philosophy, and some will have, or have had, the desire to be a channel or a bridge for their particular teaching, a priest or some other type of go-between. This may still be a reflection of the desire for the great love, of pinning your hopes onto the beyond, rather than the here and now—for you do tend to place your values into what will be, rather than what is. For others, being the go-between or mouthpiece may mean going into radio, television, advertising, or other large-scale areas of communication, where you can tell others what it's all about; some become famous writers. You want to communicate widely, one way or another, and may have relationships with people in the communications field, or with travelers—finding in them channels to involvement in wider spheres. For some the wide-open spaces are wider spheres enough, great delight and peace being found in the hillsides and the wide perspectives.

Your mother is likely to have had a well-developed, discriminating mind, being able to see imperfection in almost anything, and wanting to relate to perfection. Her self-expression is likely to have had a calculated quality to it, as she tried to relate to others in the way she judged proper. Some of her values were for practicality, cleanliness, precision, leaning toward the finicky. She may not have been able to express her love very well, except by doing practical things for you.

Your father hid away some of his more sensitive and romantically imaginative feelings and values. He very likely valued his privacy and seclusion, in which he could dream of the ideal relationship, not necessarily being able to achieve it in his outer life.

MARS IN THE 9TH HOUSE

Your restlessly explorative energy likes to rove over wide horizons, whether physical, mental, or spiritual (meaning travel, higher education, or further learning, and philosophy, religion, or spiritual growth studies). You would rather cover broad and preferably new ground in anything that you do, than stick to narrow, known, or familiar territory. Your aim is upward and outward, and you would love to be able to fly like an arrow to gain an overview of those regions that interest you. You want to expand your awareness, your understanding, your being, like a young adult going out into the world alone for the first time with it spread out before him/her, awaiting exploration. Every new contact for you is a potential, an opportunity for personal growth into a whole new area, new lands to discover or conquer. (Some of your childhood interest is likely to have been in tales of exploration, discovery, and conquest.)

Your problems will include variability of energy; with so much ground to cover and only being able to go in one direction at a time, you may spread your interests over too wide a spectrum, and move restlessly from one to another, being given to fitful bursts of enthusiasm and variation of direction. If you can keep yourself strictly aimed in one direction, you are then capable of such energetic enthusiasms as to be in danger of becoming a fanatic. This side can be courageous and reckless, while the variable side is the person who explodes fairly easily and then runs away from the fight. You may use the explorative facets of your being as a way of evading the present by running toward the future. Your desire for personal freedom of spirit does not help your relationships to be stable or support marriage, nor does your leaning toward being sharply and vigorously outspoken in relationships, and your readiness to attack others' ideas.

You may want to be your own teacher in life, to pioneer and open new ground in higher thought or spiritual endeavor by and for yourself, and you may need to remember the saying, "he who has himself as a teacher has a fool for a student." Your ethics will be decidedly self-made and their nature will depend upon how much anger you carry, how much you desire to fight for your rights. You are likely to appreciate the warrior's approach to philosophy and religion, such as the Sikh teachings, the history of the Muhammadan Jihad, or the Crusades, the Samurai code of Bushido, or the teachings of Don Juan. Even if your interests in these wider areas have not yet developed, your energies will still be restlessly searching. Your temper should be honest, direct, and straight-forward, and under little restraint; being allowed expression easily it would not build much pressure, though if you lean toward arrogance it could be decidedly volcanic.

Your mother had a sharp cutting edge to her analytical mind. She was either aggressively critical, or had a sharp clarity of focus that dealt with problems vigorously, not letting what she saw as imperfections survive for long. She was an energetic worker and didn't like anyone directing her—preferring to be in charge of her own efforts. Your father, on the other hand, had an impractical side to him; he is likely to have chased dreams, or to have imagined all the things that he would like to do—and not have done them. He would camouflage many of his actions because he felt vulnerable to attack.

JUPITER IN THE 9TH HOUSE

You prefer to be involved in the wider sphere of things, to approach life in such a way as to cover the broadest ground and gain the greatest overview. You seek a breadth of knowledge that will give you a complete coverage of your particular territory, a view from the heights that may allow you to glimpse the lands beyond. In a sense you have a geographer's mind, an explorer's and map-maker's vision of your world, whatever your preferred sphere of operation, though certain areas will be most natural for you. These include geography, the law, politics, journalism, the military and acting professions, plus higher education, philosophy, and religion. You search for knowledge, for truths, laws, or general principles that you may then be able to disseminate in a kind of broadcasting of seeds for future growth. You are a futurist, more concerned with what is developing and evolving—perhaps over the very long term—than with things of the moment or of the past, unless they point the way to the future. You like to try to see the world as a whole, together with the possible developments of the mass of humanity, which is where your philosophical or religious tendencies may show most strongly.

In order to cover such wide ground you must keep moving, exploring restlessly, a nomad freely roaming the world (whether the physical world, or that of ideas) unfettered by boundaries. Your search for wider horizons frequently makes it difficult for you to commit yourself to long-term involvements since you don't like carrying excess baggage, and your preference for personal freedom is very well-developed. In the more negative type this may be used as the escape route, running away—from the present into the future—from commitment into irresponsibility. This evasion would be unlikely to last since the drive toward honesty is very strong here; the need to pursue and discover the truth, to identify personally with it, and to broadcast it and make it widely known (this is a common position in the charts of lecturers and teachers of higher education). The readiness to run is the mark of a highly strung personality, like a wild horse refusing to be caught or tamed. Major symbols for this position are the nomadic horseman and the centaur.

Your tolerance should be one of your most marked characteristics, your willingness to recognize that there are many viewpoints, many frameworks of understanding, and that all are true as seen from from their own position. You may be ready to assimilate many views in your effort to come to the truth, to structure your own knowledge; unless Jupiter had very difficult aspects, in which case you could have very conceited attitudes in morality, philosophy or religion, believing that you have the truth as your personal possession, that it is your duty to teach that truth to others, whether they want to hear it or not.

Your mother is likely to have had a broadly discriminating mind, a meticulousness of honesty that was critical of untruth, and a nervous restlessness of mood that brought wide variations into her approach to the daily running of life. Your father's imagination was well-developed, and his world-view broad and tolerant, but probably rather general. He may have been a charitable person, though perhaps his confidence was fragile, leading him to like his seclusion, or being alone with nature.

SATURN IN THE 9TH HOUSE

Your attitude toward the future probably swings between an optimistic hope for ultimate achievement and a depressive and guilty feeling that you'll never make it. Your pursuit of opportunities is cautious and controlled, and either very organized or very doubting, actually closing the doors instead of going through them.

Religion or philosophy is likely to be important to you. You may have been brought up in a traditional religious framework, or have entered one along the way. This faith may have emphasized law, guilt, submission to authority and to the will of God. In your seriousness, you may have questioned it to the point of losing your faith, your doubts about the orthodox attitudes developing into skepticism. You may be an agnostic or atheist out of disillusionment, some experience making you lose hope or faith, leaving you feeling that the future will not bring what you want, expanding and elaborating your doubts. Partly this is in your way of thinking, since you very seriously question any object of thought. You use doubt as a way of being objective about it, never accepting anything on face value (unless you were taught not to question in your faith, when you will remain quiet about your doubts—which will grow inside you). In other words, you have a serious, reflective, analytical mind with a fair degree of caution, which should not be elaborated into skeptical doubt, for the sake of your intellectual health.

In the long run, you will redevelop faith or philosophy through your need to understand the larger framework of laws in which your life exists. You assume that the universe is ordered and organized—in fact your awareness of order is growing—and you need to feel that you know that order, know that it is benign, not harsh; and to know your place in its hierarchies—hopefully to climb to the top, to a peak experience of understanding. A late university career may be a reflection of this climb (likely areas of study, science, medicine, philosophy, orthodox psychology—behavioral or Freudian—political science, history, geology, archaeology, architecture) to gain a disciplined and crystallized overview. You should beware rigidifying your beliefs or knowledge into a dead system of laws, of letting the organized framework become more important than the spirit, since your seriousness could lead you into fanaticism.

You have a highly developed sense of responsibility, though you vastly prefer that it is tempered with personal freedom, and you find it hard to accept any other authority than yourself—becoming easily disillusioned with them (another facet of your loss of hopes). There are times when you would like to run away from responsibility and your strict ethical code will not allow it, your sense of justice being finely tuned; then you are likely to flare up if anyone touches on your guilt.

Your mother was probably capable of a rather dogmatic and judgmental criticism; she certainly had a perfectionistic sense of duty and responsibility, being in strict and organized control of her work. She may have tended toward states of depressed worry, perhaps caused by your father's occasional lack of responsibility. He may have been given to imaginative but impractical schemes, or have been rather depressive and vulnerable.

URANUS IN THE 9TH HOUSE

Your attitudes to religion and philosophy change during your life as you experiment and explore. Your approach to them is intellectual, idealistic, liberal, and tolerant, believing what proves true in your experience and letting others do the same for themselves, never imposing your ideas onto them; unless you have taken the rigid way, and believe that your teaching is the only true one, that all must believe. You may try various teachings, but won't stick to any single one unless it includes all your personal beliefs, preferring to mix your own individual blend from elements gathered from all. You bow to no supreme authority, believing that each person has the right to their own opinion, that religious authority takes away independence. You believe in fairness and will not accept the idea of a god or universe that is unfair; that there is a place for everybody and no one is a misfit. Highly independent yourself, you want others to have the same right. Fair and open-minded, you believe that people should do what they want if they harm no one else, and you follow that liberal rule in your own morality.

You believe that independence leads to wider knowledge and vice versa; that all beings need freedom to explore what is out there in the universe (including travel to the stars); that all is interconnected, so that it doesn't matter what individual path one follows since they all lead to the same end. The path you feel lies in increasing awareness of all that exists, and you seek integration to develop and ultimately to bring together all facets of your own being. To this end, you may study and practice yoga or some other practical spiritual disciplines, and astrology or other multi-level intellectual studies.

This is all highly positive. Under difficult aspects to Uranus you will be highly rebellious, pursuing personal freedom and avoiding being trapped or tied down by anything. This causes abrupt breaks in your relationships as you run away from ties. Thus you can be irresponsible, your idea of moral freedom being avoidance of commitment. Some with Uranus here develop fixed and self-exalting ideas about their religious or philosophical standing or attainments, believing themselves special or unusual. Some have telepathic messages from higher sources, or space beings from flying saucers that explain unusual philosophies and give special messages to mankind. Or they may be of the "chosen few."

In higher education you may study sciences, particularly electronics and data processing; electrical engineering; transportation technology; astronomy, space studies; media communications; sociology/psychology; or any study involving the multi-level interconnection of several disciplines.

You will develop a broad overview, based on the interweaving of all that you learn. You tend not to use single viewpoints, but complex, integrated sets of ideas that link in every direction, incorporating all that you come across, justifying each concept by the number of links that it has with every other concept. You don't mind including ideas that others consider wild or impossible if you can find supporting proofs. The negative type does not care if there is no proof, so long as the ideas are well out of the ordinary,

You are likely to travel actively during your lifetime. Some experience space travel dreams or astral journeys. Your dream symbolism tends to be modern, electrical, and have abrupt changes of context.

NEPTUNE IN THE 9TH HOUSE

Your understanding of the subtleties of life is growing during this lifetime; it either has led or will lead you into the study and pursuit of a mystical religion or philosophy, or of some teaching that opens boundless perspectives to you. You have, at least at times, a deep feeling for the endless nature of this universe, and a desire to dissolve the limits of your being out into it, into the mystic's union with the transcendental. To this end you are likely to contact teachings that involve such things as meditation as paths of personal evolution, teachings that give beautiful and subtle images of the path, or that involve deep knowledge of the archetypal facets of mind and universe. You may feel that if you cannot enter this state of union then you are utterly separate and alone (maybe lonely).

You may have gone through a crumbling of your faith in religions, becoming confused and uncertain, a crumbling that would have affected you very deeply, since your faith or trust was originally boundless and innocent. Your trust may now be rather fragile, a facet of the crumbling of your views of conventional order in your world. These views will be gradually replaced by a more subtle and fluid overview as your trust redevelops with direct experience, becoming a confidence founded on knowledge, we hope, because it is possible for you to develop self-exalting delusions, if Neptune is under particularly difficult aspects. If so, you are capable of letting such fantasies grow and elaborate into a complex self-justifying structure. Not wanting any narrow boundaries, you push your imagination out into the "wild blue yonder" and take its fancies as truth. You will then think that the truth is whatever you believe it to be, a state that does not encourage sanity.

Your ability to navigate into the future depends on how you handle this side of yourself. If your trust is undamaged, or has been resurrected, you will find that you flow easily and naturally into exactly the circumstances and conditions that you need for your further growth, magically so at times, and sometimes you may have clear visions of your future. If you do not trust, you fantasize about possible developments in your life, but don't follow them through, using your imagination as wish-fulfillment alone.

Your ethics are either clear and simple, with compassion and gentleness growing (in the image of Christ or Buddha); or are chaotic as you dissolve normal moral limits. If you justify self-deception, you will also justify yourself in deceiving others. The positive type tends to have intensely clear senses and vivid dreams, often precognitive and in color, and including astral travel. You are likely to have had an experience of out-of-body travel at the moment of birth.

In higher education, you may study anthropology; cosmology; myths, legends, and symbols; microbiology or biochemistry; oceanography; religious studies; music or other fine arts; psychology, particularly Jungian; or any study that subtly blends all areas of scientific knowledge. You may not lean toward orthodox higher education at all, but become involved in religious or occult studies. Spiritualism is likely to attract you at some point in your life, or perhaps Theosophy, or esoteric aspects of religion or philosophy. In fact anything that opens up boundless perspectives, vast and all-encompassing overviews, will attract you.

PLUTO IN THE 9TH HOUSE

Where religion, philosophy and ethics are concerned, you either have intense opinions on the matter, or none at all. If the former, you believe that having a faith or religious practice is essential, and pour tremendous energy into it, possibly being a fundamentalist, holding strict, rigid, black and white views on morality, or holding the bare essential views—belief in God, obeying commandments and so forth. Or you may explore to discover what are the essential facets of a religion or philosophy, then discarding everything else as junk, retaining only the core and working with that. You view a philosophy as a working tool, neither more nor less, valuable solely in terms of the human transformation that it produces when applied. You might look toward teachings of great power, particularly those that open contact with the unconscious, liberating energy from your depths by taking you through all your fears and defenses. Specific teachings here include Tibetan or Indian Tantra, Kundalini yoga, "warrior" philosophies, or active, practical psychotherapy.

If you are a fundamentalist (you are unlikely to be reading this), you should beware making your moral views overly rigid since you have a "hellfire and brimstone" conscience. You may be incapable of admitting to being wrong yourself, and will be morally intolerant of others instead, projecting your own sins onto them, becoming a hypocrite. If you take a strong stand against hypocrisy, check to see if you keep yourself unaware of your own, for it is very likely. You may not be religious but still "do unto others as they do unto you," usually meaning taking revenge for what they do to you, and preferably twice as much—not "an eye for an eye" but "two eyes for an eye" instead. You have an intense idea of justice, or perhaps of injustice, being ready to fight for your rights. If you are generous, you will crusade for the underdog, fighting for human rights for the repressed and rejected peoples of the world; but if less generous, you will use your ferocious temper to drive others into the ground, believing that you have a perfect moral right to do so, and not seeing that you are adding to the total of human suffering, including your own. You will use your sharp-edged outspokenness freely on others when you are in a bad mood. You use humor as a pain defense, laughing at hurtful things to release tension. If you are not narrow-minded your sense of humor will have a distinctly bawdy side to it.

Your mother was probably hard-working, practical, efficient, and capable. She would not tolerate dirt, junk, or messiness and would attack it with vigor, wanting total cleanliness in her home and family, or she would just let the dirt and mess pile up. She was capable as a nurse or in dealing with illness, since she was prepared to tackle those sides of life that others can't tolerate. Her analytical mind was extremely sharp, though she would have needed to see good reasons to use it, and she could be clinical, critical, and perfectionistic, her criticisms being cuttingly sharp and probably nagging.

Your father would have been more easy-going, but rather private, needing seclusion and putting up barriers and defenses emotionally in order to get it. He was intensely vulnerable but used a camouflage of capability and toughness, or used a psychic defense creating curtains of protection around himself. If his vulnerabilities were hurt (and he took criticism from others very deeply), he may have believed that everyone was against him, or that the world was very painful.

NORTH NODE—9TH HOUSE, SOUTH NODE—3RD HOUSE

You want to know everything, and may continually chase after more information, facts, or knowledge with insatiable curiosity. This can scatter your mind over wide reaches of restless rambling after understanding, filling you with an encyclopedia full of details. It can also give you material for endless conversations, chewing over the hows, whys, and wherefores of the various faces of the world. You probably feel that you need more education to answer your multitudinous questions, perhaps to overcome your uncertainties about yourself and life.

You need to recognize that knowledge and wisdom are not the same thing, that use of intellect doesn't necessarily involve the spiritual perspectives of the higher mind. You tend to be uncertain through all your questioning, since every answer leads you on to several more questions; thus you need trust in your path, the faith that you are heading toward the universal goal. Your morality is based on ideas given to you as a child as to what constitutes good and evil behavior, but you need to examine the foundations of ethics and morality. More than anything else you need to *know*, to discover the real truth through your own experience, not just the authorized version ("Ye shall know the truth and the truth shall set you free"), and then to pass on what you know. This may lead you into teaching, but probably not the usual kind, for you are too restless for that form of repetition, as much as for organizing and codifying your material. You should demonstrate what you know by living it, and since you know that there is always more to explore, you never make your mind up finally about anything. Your dualism and uncertainty are your worst points; never being finally sure about anything can disrupt all areas of your life.

✧ 12 ✧

Capricorn
and the 10th House

Around the age of 30 the desire becomes strong to settle down, to dig in and build a home and family, and/or to master something in life. Though modern western cultures encourage this stage to happen earlier, this is its natural time. We could call it taking responsibility for the direction of our lives, we could say it is the culmination of the previous exploration—the discovery of what we want to devote our adult lives to. Or it is when we objectify our need for security by carving a place in our culture, a personal niche chosen because the particular forms in that social arena give us a secure feeling, perhaps by identifying us with a particular history or tradition, or by giving us a chance to achieve something we value or want.

The 10th House is where we build our understanding of the laws, forms, governing principles, both natural and cultural, that we meet in our lives, and learn to use it. Our first instinctive understanding of natural laws comes from our physical interaction with the world as babies, in which we learn that we have mass, that to move it we must understand the proper leverage of bones and muscles, the correct amount of force to use and in what direction; that the world has properties that require correct handling. We also learn how we are ourselves handled by our parents, physically, emotionally, psychologically— what kind of emotional and psychological leverage they use on us. This leverage will be in the range between loving involvement and coercive authority, between being accepted fully as a person and being treated as a thing, and through it we learn our first methods of how to rule ourselves and others.

We are given direction as to how to live by parental rules and imposed limits (and it is usually the father who lays them down). If their direction is given with love, it will give us our independence, and we'll learn to enjoy fitting in with their needs of our own independent desire. We will become good and responsible people who respect the opinions of elders and those in responsible positions, and who largely conform to them as reasonable, though we are not tied to them or by them. If we feel their authority to be controlling, we realize that we are not being recognized for what we are as individuals, but are being squeezed to fit into a shape not our own. Then we have the choice of either conforming, and repressing our frustrations, mutiny, and real individual selves out of sight, or of rebelling, and perhaps getting ourselves into trouble with the law, while keeping some individuality. If we are male, this is where we have our instinctual struggle for dominance against the "old bull," our hierarchical drive to gain leadership of (at least part of) the herd, and control of the females in it.

As children we need recognition from others to know that we are all right, or acceptable. Whatever we are given recognition for, that becomes the path we are most likely to take to seek reward, and becomes a role-model for our independent lives as adults. This may become an ambition to achieve, to demonstrate our prowess, to gain status in others' attention, to be recognized. If we are given no recognition as children, we may end up without direction, or hopefully try one track after another (but with no actual inner hope of success). If we are subject to rejecting authority we grow up feeling that we will end up being judged and condemned, and may feel like planting a bomb under the judge, or may become lawyers so as to be in charge of the law. We may end up feeling guilty according to the law, with consequent depression.

The pattern that we grew up with becomes the most probable way that we will deal with our wider life as adults. If we react to life from the habits we formed as children (which is very likely, unless we fight to build our own awareness), our way of taking responsibility for our own life is predetermined, as is our attitude toward authority of any kind, including that of society's expectations of conformity. These last we may take as defining our way of belonging to society. If we do the right thing, we will be accepted as respectable people (even though the cost may be the loss of large parts of our individuality). The overriding judge of conservatism, whether inward or social, is called "superego" by Sigmund Freud and "senex" by Carl Gustav Jung.

Our capacity for understanding laws and rules is primarily natural, designed to comprehend the regularities of the workings of nature, then to understand how to use them or respond to them. For those who grow up in cities this faculty is starved, apart from it observing human interactions, and understanding that their world is totally under human control, of human making. The understanding of laws that grows then is very abstract and psychological. For those who have grown up with nature, the laws have an organic reality; they recognize that they are meshed with, and part of, laws larger than themselves, and can cooperate with them, help them to fruition. For those who have a strong contact with the deep resources of their own being, natural laws have a rich, magical quality. Pursuit of this kind of understanding could take them into farming, horticulture, naturalism, or a philosophy that takes them toward mastery of self-in-nature. It could take them well beyond the bounds of the commonly known and into the unknown.

The city-bred may try to understand nature through the sciences, imposing the constraints of rationality onto something which is far larger than the rational mind. They may prefer to use science to feel that they are in direct, manipulative control of the uncontrollable, masters of nature. They may enter business to gain power or status, and use the natural world as a tool, resource, or plaything in the process, with no regard for its needs. This attitude is responsible for much damage to our world, including the people in it.

Here lies our sense of responsibility, our capacity for giving security to the other. As children we are either allowed to take responsibility for ourselves, thus learning how to handle it; or we are not, being thus told that we have no right to control of our own being. In the second case we will then either learn to submit to others (government, bosses, police, bureaucrats) in life, swallowing all our frustrations and anger; or we may learn to return the favor given, and impose our own harsh and uncaring authority on others. Or, we may recognize that we are entirely responsible for our own actions, and for their results—all of them. In which case, if we have any heart we will decide not to do damage to the world around us, but rather promote its interests, if we can understand them.

The physiology of the 10th House includes the skeletal system, the natural scaffolding of bony levers that helps us master gravity. The most specific bodily part connected with Capricorn is the knees, known by mountaineers as the most important part of the body. If your knees are bad, you can't climb, and can't reach the peaks. The anterior pituitary gland controls the stages of our aging, of our physical growth, of puberty, and of maturing. It is also concerned with the development of our secondary sexual characteristics at puberty, and with preparing the body for childbirth.

MIDHEAVEN IN ARIES

Your father had a direct energy that would leap into new projects and experiences, perhaps without necessary second thoughts. He made his own way in life, depending on no-one else, being something of a lone wolf. His headlong nature could be exciting if you were going along with him, but hard to take if pushily directed at you. Similarly his focus on his own viewpoint and readiness to do battle with anyone else's was infuriating if you were on the receiving end. His vigor may have taken him into sports, the armed forces, or executive positions.

You have (inherited from him?) a drive to do your own thing in life, to achieve your own goals using your own energies and skills. You want to be first in your field, and are ready to compete with all comers for that position. You think that the social order depends on the actions of strong individuals, and that to achieve you have to become such an individual by developing your own initiative. Desire for new experiences may lead you to change goals frequently. Professionally and socially you do not want to be under anyone else's rule, preferring self-government and self-direction, so you prefer to work alone and make your own decisions without interference from above, or better still to be self-employed. If you do have to deal with any authority over you, you see them through the filter of your own personality so that they appear to have the same narrow focus of energy.

Your mother could be charming and poised, being pleasant in order to keep the peace. She avoided conflict, using tact and diplomacy to smooth things over, to keep everything nice. She was aware of others, and could accept their views and attitudes as equal to her own. She could consider many different views, so she found it difficult to make clear-cut decisions. To avoid unpleasantness she would sometimes hide her own views and feelings entirely and would not act in her own interests, not wanting to be the cause of trouble. She was also capable of being intellectually judgmental toward anything that offended her sense of justice.

Your conditioned emotional nature is founded upon her character. You want to be liked so you keep things emotionally pleasant, since your security depends on the state of your relationships. If they flow well then you are happy, if they go badly you are uneasy and off-balance. You use charm as a defense to help your relationships along and you automatically adjust your attitudes to match, or to balance and complement those of others around you. In your low moods you are indecisive, not knowing which way you feel about things, becoming uncertain.

For balance in your own being, you need to combine the two parts of yourself, your self-directedness and receptivity to others. One way is to become an intermediary between leaders and followers, management and workers, for example; acting as a disinterested channel open in both directions. You are able to learn the lesson that to rule is also to serve. Where you see things in others that you want in yourself you will imitate the good in them, making it your own, and eliminating all but innocent motives within yourself.

MIDHEAVEN IN TAURUS

Your father had a stable personality and preferred the routine and arranged order of his life to remain static, placid and unchanging. In attitudes stubborn, with fixed views and values, his values were of special importance to him. He had an earthy quality, probably enjoying the pleasures of the senses, the table, and the countryside, though he may have been more a materialist focused on money and possessions. Solid, and maybe stolid, he did not seek excitement and change, generally sticking to the established order, and once he aimed at a goal it was impossible to divert him from it.

Your attitudes to ambition, authority, profession, and self-development have been molded by your relationship with your father, and will have similarities to his character. Socially you are fairly conservative, relating to the stable and secure elements of society, supporting solid public values. Your aims may be materialistic, and you see society as a hierarchy of wealth. Your ambitions may be to gain in possessions and other forms of value, to be recognized as being worth something, to reach a material peak. Or you may care little about ambition, so long as you can go your own unruffled way through the world, perhaps still with determination to attain some personal goal. You believe that aging includes being able to have what you want.

Your mother's character was sharp, competent and capable, probably aggressive in a cutting manner. She would not show her deeper feelings readily, keeping them hidden from view, feeling that they were no one else's business—yet she could probe into others and ferret out their secrets with skill. These she would either use against them, defending herself from hurt by attacking (being oversensitive to rejection), or she would help them to understand and heal their own problems, showing deep understanding of the hidden sides of human nature.

Your feelings were shaped by her so you probably don't show them readily, keeping emotional security by hiding their intensity from others and maybe from yourself too. For you, security is learning to survive emotionally against all the knocks, conflicts, and crises. You feel pain and rejection easily, and use an emotional armor to hide hurts, having survival defenses ready to use if you feel that you are under attack—rage, for example. If you felt rejected by your mother's attitudes you are insecure, though you will probably have reacted by proving your competence in looking after yourself. Or you may seek security and acceptance through sex, but find it difficult to let down your emotional barriers enough to allow another to be really close to you.

Your more stubborn, authoritarian side may judge your emotional intensity and reject it, arbitrarily imposing order in your being by imposing peace, increasing your rejection feelings. If you feel rejected you feel that your value is low, and you cannot change that by seeking public recognition, for to do so would only increase your conflict. Or your emotions may take over and disrupt the stability of your life, in which case you need a mixture of hardness and clarity to judge what is right and impose order.

MIDHEAVEN IN GEMINI

Your father was probably alert, changeable, communicative, and questioning, adapting readily to the people around him, to the point that he may have seemed all things to all men. He either wanted to be involved in everything, having a problem in making up his mind between opposite possibilities, or he didn't want to be stuck in anything, being inconstant and inconsistent. At best he was a student of everything, a fund of information on a variety of subjects, always ready to explore the field of knowledge. At worst he was juvenile, never sticking to anything for long. (There is a possibility that you had at least two father-figures.)

Your long-term aims in life may have the same changeability as your father as you set up mutually incompatible goals to satisfy different sides of your being, and switch from one to another. You may be uncertain about your goals, seeing as much, or as little, reason for going one way as another. You may be divided in your views about laws, authority, society, and politics, running back and forth between the radical and the conservative, between avoiding the laws or using them for your own ends, or accepting them freely and supporting them as a good citizen; or you tend to be a student and theoretician in such areas. In professional directions you may lean toward the media, communications fields, teaching, basic business, or transportation, with a likelihood of at least one complete change of profession in your lifetime, perhaps eventually reverting to your original direction.

Your mother showed a cheerful, outspoken, and confident face to the world. She may have been interested in religion or philosophy, certainly having wide-ranging views or being interested in the bigger things in life. She was either completely honest, maintaining high moral standards herself, or rather overbearing in her effort to be morally superior to others. She was restless and perhaps highly-strung, not necessarily sticking to one path or pursuit for long, but covering many in her explorations. One of her attitudes may have been that more is better.

Your feelings have something of her nature, trained by experience. Your security depends on your confidence, on how your hopes develop, and on how much space you have to roam around in. You don't like confinement, needing plenty of elbow room, and defend your territorial rights with explosions. Your feelings are generally cheerful or you use cheerfulness as a protective emotional barrier. Your feelings are restless and variable, given to bursts of enthusiasm and optimism, perhaps followed by depressions, with spurts of volcanic anger in between. If you feel that the future holds promise, you are high and happy, but if not you are ready to run away from the situation (as you may have run away from home). The more is better attitude may make you build a lavish and splendid home life.

You are best advised to retain honesty, honor, and modesty. If you lean toward instinctual arrogance and social duplicity, scheming to get your own way, you will alienate those close to you.

MIDHEAVEN IN CANCER

Your father had a personality that was reflective, receptive, and emotional. He would have been self-protective in a moody way, and you may have seen his protectiveness toward you as being moods, clinging, or control. He was a family man, needing the security of a stable home environment, wanting safe and familiar circumstances as a support for his own, probably rather insecure, personality. He would often simply act as a mirror to others, reflecting back their attitudes rather than showing any of his own, hiding himself inside a protective shell. When he went after anything he could be very tenacious indeed, though he would often be indirect in his approach. He wanted his needs to be recognized and accepted, if not met, by others.

In your drive toward achievement and recognition you will have tended to follow in his footsteps, needing the encouragement of others in support of your own insecurities, and not always having the independence to feel that you are master of the situation. Where you work toward professional status or public recognition you will be valuable in supporting positions where your own tenacity and protectiveness aid those you serve. Your most natural professional directions will be those in which you act for the support and nurturing of others, providing for their needs of security, food, or shelter; or work connected with the ocean, such as fishing. Where you work for your own ends, you should beware fulfilling your own needs (or filling your own pockets) at the expense of others or in ways that you dare not show openly.

Your mother was cool, controlled, rule-oriented, and organizing, rather conservative and very much aware of her own status. She probably had the household well disciplined, meals on time, things run to schedule, but in doing so probably made you feel guilty or inferior if you didn't fit in with her framework or rules and regulations—perhaps done silently through her expressions of disapproval. She leaned toward controlling herself and others, perhaps in manipulative ways, demanding that duty and responsibility be fulfilled. Mealtimes may have been an ordeal, with strictly proper behavior expected, until you had mastered it, but leaving you with your digestion slowed down by fear of the reactions that you would get.

To gain security with her you had to become self-controlling, trying to gain recognition for being adult, building emotional reserve that responded only with formally appropriate reactions, perhaps becoming inhibited and depressed in the process. Your emotions have become serious and controlled, cautious and reserved, and perhaps resentful and frustrated; your need for security is absolute, and you may hang on to the material symbols of security in possessions, property, and position, as substitutes for the affection that you need, but that you might find difficult to accept if it was forthcoming now. Or you may have had the recognition that you needed from her, and responded with filial duty, being happy to take on responsibility. In this case, your feelings will run deep and serious, and being responsible and having security will run hand-in-hand for you.

MIDHEAVEN IN LEO

Your father had a personality that was proud, dominant, perhaps honorable, and perhaps flamboyant with a well-developed sense of play, but certainly self-expressive. He was either cheerful and responsive, being easy to get along with, or self-centered and only aware of his own point of view—which he imposed on others in a superior fashion. If you got along well with him, feeling that you had the best of his attention, then you will feel that it is fairly easy for you to gain public recognition and prominence, finding creative self-expression in the effort. If he was more arrogant, then you will feel that authorities and bosses are overbearing and self-centered, either suffering under their dominance while trying to maintain self-respect, or showing them by doing better than they do. Whichever, you originally wanted to shine for your father, and to bask in his approval. Working toward mastering a profession will be one of your best avenues for self-knowledge and self-development, since you will identify yourself very closely with such a pursuit. What you will need to watch is that it doesn't become a way for you to become conceited, too proud and arrogant yourself.

Your mother would have been something of an individualist, either an active one pursuing her own free curiosity into whatever strange areas it led her—being an open-minded idealist, or a self-isolating one, wary of being trapped into what others wanted her to be and keeping up a barrier of detachment between herself and the world. If the first, security for you would be freely following your interests without any feeling that you have to be confined to the conventional, and your home environment will reflect the breadth and variety of your pursuits. If your mother was wary and detached then you are likely to be insecure, your own feelings having been trained into a tense wariness. It may be that your mother was impatient, and that you had to speed up to suit her at an early age, now going full speed ahead (but maybe not realizing why). You most probably feel that security is having independence, that you do not want to be emotionally tied down or trapped by anything. Your prime emotional defense is detachment, standing back from whatever is going on and just observing. So you either have a great deal of emotional freedom, or feel tense, uncertain, and anxious.

There are various possibilities arising from the combination of the two sides: You may take everything carelessly and playfully through inexperience, needing to be shown the seriousness of life, and to learn a measure of discipline in order to amount to something. You may be weak, wanting to be powerful, and lose your individuality by slavish imitation of strong personalities in higher positions, or simply entangle yourself in empty imaginings. You may have an inner strength that enables you to be tolerant and kind toward human folly, giving you qualities that would enable you to take on responsibility. Or if you are entirely free from inner conflicts, you can let your full creative power come forth in the leading of great enterprises, being a born ruler of men, and a dynamic and far-seeing organizer.

MIDHEAVEN IN VIRGO

Your security depends upon you realizing your imaginative or visionary views in your domestic life. Emotionally sensitive, in childhood you lived in an innocent Garden of Eden in which your dreamy receptivity dissolved the boundaries between you and all else, and your imagination would take you deep into anything you observed. When hurt you would retire in confusion into a private space of your own for safety, often in your imagination, in private dreams of a more perfect world.

As an adult you will return to at least the feeling of these images for emotional security, and probably act them out, though they will have evolved, now being a part of your background personality. Your home will reflect these self-images, whether they be of country gentleperson, art-conscious sophisticate, worldly-wise traveler, or whatever your version is. Your home will probably be secluded or enable privacy to be attained, or will reflect your idea of gracious living; or it may be chaotic and jumbled, reflecting your emotional upheaval. You will most likely live or have lived at some time in a monastery, hospital, or other type of institution.

Your emotional defense is camouflage and flexible adjustment to others' feelings; you are emotionally able to change color like a chameleon. This confuses you as to what your own feelings really are. At best you have a very compassionate nurturing tendency, not liking to see anything or anyone hurt. Your relationship to animals in your early home life may have formed some of these feelings.

You use solitude, reading, drifting, and dreaming, both as resources to feel secure and to avoid the chaotic facets of your emotional life, and you use busyness to avoid emptiness and loneliness. Your need for emotional camouflage takes you into states of dullness at the bottom of your mood swing, using sleep, drink, drugs, fantasy, or other self-suggestion to put a layer of cotton-wool around your sensitivities. At the top of your moods you are clear and sharply focused, perhaps critical of your periods of self-indulgence. You are vulnerable to criticism by authorities, and should avoid becoming a critical and perfectionistic authority yourself. You aim for moral purity, to avoid being criticized by your super-ego or moral censor.

You aim to achieve perfection of some kind. Your problem here is that it may be an imaginary and idealistic form of perfection that you seek, perhaps set way out of reach, dreaming the impossible dream, wanting purity of an inhuman kind. If your innocent and compassionate side predominates, it will be for spiritual perfection. Your sensitivity to the order of things enables you to see the structure of nature's laws with precision.

Your sensitive feelings help you to identify with all of life, and these qualities will be used in your self-development and your profession. Your high-road to self-development is through service to others, genuine service, not used to make you seem more perfect than they are by comparison. You should develop your analytical mind as far as is possible, while remaining aware of the need for synthesis.

MIDHEAVEN IN LIBRA

Your father was charming, courteous, and tactful, and worked to maintain harmony and avoid conflict in relationships, mediating to iron out differences of opinion. He may have seen all viewpoints as being equal, and thus have been indecisive, leaning toward indifference and inertia. Or he may have been judgmental of those who act without consideration for others, having a strict view of justice and equality, being offended by selfishness in action.

Thus you had to learn to consider others, at least in public or in your father's eyes, learning social standards of politeness, deference, charm, tact, and how to relate correctly to others. If your relationship with your father was good, you find it easy to relate to the authorities in your life, being aided in your development by them, being ready and able to work in partnership with them. If it was not so good, then you seek the relationship that you wanted with him through others, controlling yourself in order to make it work, but not really expecting it to. Your persistence in this may be admirable, but unless you seek the right thing in the right place, you cannot find it. Your general upward direction will have been affected by him; if he was indecisive, you may be unable to decide what life-style or profession to pursue, or may start on one and change your mind—becoming inconstant, or have decided not to be like him by becoming firm in your aims. If the last (the best of the choices), beware of rigidity, which will not allow you to adapt to the needs of the time. What does need to be unswerving is the inner law which determines your general direction.

Your mother was a strong individual, active, energetic, with plenty of initiative, not necessarily sticking to one aim for long as she moved from one new direction to another. She poured her energy aggressively into every moment, which could have been exhilarating for you as a child caught up in the action, or disturbing since you would get little peace with her. It is possible that she made battles out of things that didn't need to be so, perhaps stirring up opposition for the sake of debate. It is also possible that your father had to balance out the effects of your mother's personality.

Your emotions and security needs were shaped in your relationship with her, so your feelings may be active and seek to exercise themselves on the world, finding avenues for action, looking for what you can do with every situation. If your mother often took over and acted for you, security may be having someone else do it all for you, or will lie in getting your own initiative back by acting for yourself, even if you didn't learn how as a child. Where your mother saw her own point of view first, so do your emotions. Thus you may be in conflict between what your feelings want, and what your social training says is reasonable, between self-centered drives and consideration for others, the balance of the fight depending on how the balance of power was between your parents.

MIDHEAVEN IN SCORPIO

Your security depends on your being able to gain your objectives simply, without complications. In childhood, it depended on what you could have, or were given of what you wanted, love being expressed by presents or by "you have been good, you can have . . . "— this possibly being bribery on occasion. Insecurity was aroused by your being refused what you wanted. Your sense of your own value was built by these experiences, positive and negative, and as an adult you want to feel that you are of substantial value, whether this is in material terms or more abstract personal worth.

Since you are emotionally a sensory/sensual person you also needed reassurance by touch, by being held and cuddled. Much of your adult emotional security depends on whether you got it, and how you responded to it. You also needed, and still do, peace and harmony at home, a placid, unruffled existence in surroundings having pleasing sensory qualities, stability, and perhaps natural beauty. The further you are from this state, the more we can guarantee that you had problems with your mother, as a child.

You try to gain security, real or imagined, from entrenching yourself firmly in a rut of stable, repetitive habit, becoming stubbornly immovable. (You bellow like a bull if you feel that your territory is being encroached upon.) The best use of this quality is in the persistent pursuit of all that you feel to be most worth having, but must realize that all you need is within your own being.

Your Scorpio Midheaven shows that, being rooted in your own values, you will notice when society's values do not match yours. You may want to transform society (secretly, from the inside) toward better values. It could make you implacably opposed to authority, be it the boss or the government, feeling it to be intolerant or very harsh and unfeeling. There is a sexual basis for this feeling, like a young buck in a herd knowing that to grow up he has to fight the old bull for supremacy. This fight against authority may be so well hidden as to be invisible even to you, but will show in a reflex way, such as if you achieve any high position, you will find yourself under attack.

Your ambitions may be so powerfully important to you that you dare not fully admit to yourself what they are, for fear of absolute failure. Your ultimate goal is self-transformation; the gaining of personal power toward the death of your old nature and the rebirth of your spirit. Consciously this shows in a very strong super-ego conscience that attacks you for every wrong that you judge you have done, probably to be buried by you to avoid potent self-condemnation (which hurts). Remember when you use this condemnation on others that it properly belongs to you, and your transformation will begin. In healthy people this is an intense social conscience, with the desire to heal social ills.

You either feel subject to the powers that be (feeling that *they* are crooks or power-seekers), or want to be powerful (probably meaning wealthy) yourself, or you understand the psychology of power and are not interested, only wanting to reduce the amount of pain in the world, to contribute to the end of suffering.

MIDHEAVEN IN SAGITTARIUS

Your father was either cheerful and open, explorative and extrovert, or was moralistic and overbearing, setting himself up as a superior example. He liked relating to the larger things in life, having a general overview of them, perhaps through traveling, learning, philosophy, or religion, and he may have cheerfully passed his experience on to you, teaching you what he knew and encouraging your optimism about your growth in life. Or he may have had quite a temper, flaring into displays of rage if you transgressed his principles. He was not necessarily constant, perhaps optimistically leaping into a variety of aims, spreading himself over too wide a ground, or being an opportunist—too ready to change horses in midstream.

Your aims in life, your ambitions toward self-development, were affected by your relationship with your father. If he was a good example, you seek an overview of life, to understand its governing principles and align yourself with them. You will go through a large development of confidence or faith, keeping yourself on the right track by deep self-examination, looking at the effects that you produce and knowing that when they are good, you are free of mistakes. If you did not relate well to him, your views on life and yourself are more narrowly egocentric, lacking breadth of vision, seeing your world from a self-defended point of view, and you will need to seek self-knowledge by looking at the effects that you create.

Your mother was either questioning and intellectually alert, or scattered and inconsistent. If the former she kept her mind alive by interest in a variety of subjects, being a fund of information and stimulating your curiosity in the process. If the latter then she was dualistic, holding no set opinion on anything, adapting herself flexibly to others at one moment, and speaking against them when their backs were turned the next. Your relationship with her was a push-pull affair. If positive, you ran to her for affection and then ran away to explore, security for you now being having the best of both worlds, a good home base plus mobility and exploration. If negative, she alternately clung to you and pushed you away, leaving you feeling insecure both ways so that you generally want the opposite of what you have, closeness, warmth, and security with another if you don't have it, and freedom and independence if you do. Thus your feelings and needs may be split and scattered, leading eventually to inertia and indifference.

If you ended up in an internal tangle, it can be resolved by first knowing the causes of your state, and then taking hold energetically to redirect your being; then develop an objective overview, not colored or distorted by your subjective state, and you deliberately develop the best in you, not feeding states of confusion or duality by not allowing yourself to settle into them.

If you are free of inner conflicts, then your path is probably one of contemplating the workings of the universe, seeking truth in natural law, and acting as a channel for it, that it may work at its best and produce the best for mankind. You may be a professional explorer/teacher.

MIDHEAVEN IN CAPRICORN

Your father was cool, orderly, orthodox, and possibly austere. He kept himself and his world under conservative control, wanting security and stability in his life, preferring all to be well regulated. He was status-aware, wanting recognition for his achievements, but may have been pessimistic about getting it. He is likely to have been authoritative, laying down the law and perhaps making you feel guilty if you broke it, requiring as much duty and responsibility from you as he did from himself. He made you aware of the hierarchy of authority in society, and either seek recognition from it yourself—wanting power, position and the fulfillment of your own ambitions, or resent any system that can make you feel inferior by judging you by its own standards. He may also have led you to be aware of the kind of order that structures the world that we know, such as natural law or history. If so, then you have learned to appreciate the regularity and consistency of the world, and desire to know exactly where you fit into it, perhaps to develop yourself to master it by understanding the laws.

Your mother was protective and perhaps clinging, setting definite boundaries for you to keep you safe from harm. She was emotional, perhaps moody—erecting emotional barriers to hide behind while reflecting back the attitudes of those around her. She was a family person, home security being very important to her, making sure that everyone was well fed and looked after, and probably in keeping up her contacts with her own family, her mother in particular.

Your feelings and security needs as formed in your relationship with her will reflect her personality, being based on needing a secure and well-protected home life, and on fulfilling the needs that she provided for. Your emotions will go through a definite mood swing, reflecting the changes in her personality as her own moods changed. If she clung to you, you may have felt it necessary to break away to gain independence, and in this case you find it difficult to admit to needing plain, straightforward home security—leaving the need unfulfilled and yourself insecure.

If your father ruled the household rigidly, you have probably absorbed such rule into yourself, inwardly ordering yourself to respond, and probably overriding your own feelings. This would arouse as much resentment in you now as it did when you were a child, leaving you feeling frustrated. If this is so, you need to recognize that the only worthwhile rule is that which is acceptable to the ruled, in this case your feelings—you should accept their needs and rights and rule yourself accordingly. You may have been left feeling inferior, and have tried to adjust by boasting of whatever kind of powerful or high connections you have, or by assuming a form of superiority that you cannot truly claim as your own. If you feared your father, you may strive to achieve a high position in order to "show him," having to face and overcome your fears in the process. Or if your life was happy, or you have resolved early difficulties, you face life with a profound inner seriousness that is self-aware and self-examining, searching your heart and setting your life in order.

MIDHEAVEN IN AQUARIUS

Your father was independent and individualistic, hating to be held in check or trapped by anyone or anything. He may have had an alert and questioning mind, delving into anything that interested him and not being stuck in tradition or orthodoxy, bigotry or bias, but pursuing his own ingenious and probably humanitarian track. Or he may have been a wary person, using detachment as a defense to prevent others from coming too close to him. Another possibility is that he had extremely fixed ideas (bigotry and bias) and would not tolerate differences of opinion. Your relationship with him may have been active and stimulating, awakening your mind to the strangenesses in the order of the universe; or perhaps you had little real contact with him, idolizing him from a distance to begin with, then losing hope for any closeness with him (and probably saying "I don't care"); or you became stuck with his rigidities as your rule system and tend to be narrow-minded yourself; or you rebelled against his rigidity and against all other authority, refusing to submit to anyone's rule, becoming mentally fixed in the opposite direction.

Your mother was proud, preferring to keep her self-respect, come what may. She may also have been creative, able to pour herself into playful activity, and honorable—able to respect others as much as she did herself, in which case she was quite openly loving and giving. She liked to be the center of attention and could probably put on an elaborate show of self-display, having a dramatic flair. She could also organize well, particularly when it came to organizing others. She may have had a rather domineering streak, feeling that she had the right to take command and rule in the home, seeing her own point of view only and overruling others as she pleased. She is likely to have been fiercely protective of her own rights and interests.

Your feelings and security needs will have been strongly colored by her. On the positive side, she would have supported your self-respect and natural pride, giving you a sunny disposition since you felt loved, and had the approval that you needed. On the negative side, if she was overbearing, you struggled to retain pride against her; if you wanted her love—or at least her attention, you would have had to submit to her take-over bids, losing self-respect; if you struggled against her, you thrust against your own love for her, losing self-respect; the end result being that you had to try to resurrect it, leading to a mood swing of personal pride, up and down. Your security now depends on how stable your pride is; if healthy and wholesome, then it is stable and not egotistical; if it has been damaged and rebuilt then it probably is unstable, being easily knocked down, though perhaps well-armored.

If you have ended up with a vacillating inner arrogance then you may seek success but not have the consistent strength to fulfill it, or may turn away from it saying "who needs that anyway?"; being satisfied with inner conceits. Or if your self-respect is real, you will tend toward modesty and unpretentiousness, being satisfied with being a real person, a full human being—and thus not needing mundane success, in fact being on the side of the lowly.

MIDHEAVEN IN PISCES

Your father was probably rather gentle and retiring, a private person who needed his time alone. He may have been shy and vulnerable, and have used a camouflage personality to hide behind, disguising his true nature, and keeping himself in the background. (If he was very vulnerable, he may even have used an extremely aggressive outer persona). On the positive side, he may have been sympathetic and compassionate with a love of living things, especially animals, or have appreciated fine arts and music, and refinement in all things. More negatively, he may have been a suspicious person—expecting the worst from others, often just giving way to them without a fight, making himself a doormat and feeling like a martyr. He may also have had a vivid imagination.

If your relationship with him was good, then it was probably very good indeed, since he would have encouraged you to open your receptivities to understand and appreciate the subtle order that pervades all life, or to appreciate the products of human culture. You would now be able to work in areas that require charity or compassion, or in cultural or artistic fields. If your relationship with him was poor, it may have been nearly non-existent, with you feeling that he was impossible to reach, and maybe giving up the effort—but being left feeling rather sad and empty about it all. In this case, you would probably feel rather directionless in life, either having no ambition, or a confused set of images of what you want to become in the world.

Your mother would have had a more discriminating personality, probably precise and perfectionistic, possibly very critical and picky. She would have been quite concerned with keeping things going, running the household, getting all the work done for life-support, all the cooking, cleaning, and tidying, and on the move most of the time. She may have done it all from a love of being of service to others, or from a fear that everything would crumble if she didn't. In the first case, you will feel secure in yourself and will be able to give of yourself in helping others; in the second, you will be more tense and anxious, worried that things are not stable, and actively (though perhaps silently) self-critical, making yourself more insecure. Your own emotional nature will either appreciate perfection in everything around you, or will actively find fault with it all.

If your critical side is strong, you probably keep yourself socially isolated by finding fault with self and others, refusing congenial contacts and remaining alone. If this is the case, your world-view is probably a little sour, and you tend to pile drudgery upon yourself by finding fault needlessly, and feeling obliged to deal with all the faults that you thus make. (You use criticism as your territorial defense, to hold what you feel is a safe ground, excluding what you don't want). You then need to look at the world with greater acceptance and find joy in it, thus becoming happy about anything that you do, and relieving your load. If you are not so much critical as perfectionistic you will aim for perfection automatically in everything; you may need to be sure that the perfection that you seek is humanly attainable, and not just a fairy-tale image.

SUN IN CAPRICORN
✧ The Achiever ✧ The Judge ✧

Capricorn represents those facets of any creature that are aware of pattern and order in its being, its life and its society, and that maintain that order. It also deals with the evaluation of order in any being, by the slow, steady, long-term crystallization of attitudes and habits into fixed patterns, and by the organization of experience into mature understanding.

As a Capricorn, you are aware of law and order in your world, whether it be the order of the laws of science, describing the regulated workings of all aspects of the universe, or the laws of society, requiring conformity and obedience. As a child you recognized the power and authority of your parents, and would have been obedient to their rules, wanting recognition from them for your responsible and adult attitudes. You were aware that the best place to be, where the law is concerned, is on top of it—in charge, rather than being dominated by it. You learned about dominance and submission early. You learned that breaking the rules brought censure and guilt, while keeping them perhaps brought recognition and improved status. This left you either recognizing your place in the order of things and prepared to maintain it, or feeling guilty and inferior with no self-respect, or prepared to work your way to the top of the system, master it and take charge of it yourself (politics may appeal to you). In order to do the latter, you built your ambitions, set your long-range goals, planned out your approach, and committed yourself to taking on the responsibilities that your path required. If of a negative disposition, you would manipulate the rules and the people around you to achieve your ends, knowing exactly what conformity pressures to apply and how to apply them, what buttons to push or strings to pull.

On reaching the peak, you will administer the law with as much wisdom and compassion as you have gained along the way, being master of your field, administrator of your territory, but perhaps rather too inclined to apply the letter of the law and not the spirit, for you are rather cautious and conservative. But you will then have the standing and recognition that you need, together with the mastery and control over your own affairs; after all, this is where your ultimate security lies, isn't it?

Capricornians of a philosophical disposition, as many are—being serious and methodical—will try to understand the higher spiritual laws and find their place within them, submitting themselves to the transcendental order. They work to overcome their doubts and to explore the architecture of the universe through science or religion, and where they strive to achieve mastery it is over themselves.

Doubt, developing into skepticism, and depression are your worst problems, along with guilt and the building of attitudes that are too cautious and rigid. The latter plays a part in the development of typical Capricornian ailments, rheumatism, and arthritis, for example, rigidity of body springing from rigidity of mind.

While this describes the pure Capricornian personality, you will vary from it in many ways. Your major differences will be shown by the house placement of the Sun and by the sign and house placement of Saturn.

MOON IN CAPRICORN

You can be very self-doubting, and your emotional security depends on your knowing that other people approve of you, and that you approve of yourself when judged against your own set of rather conservative and orthodox standards. You have to feel that you have adequate status of whatever kind, otherwise you get depressed, because either they, or you, yourself, do not approve of you, or because, according to judgmental standards, you are guilty of not measuring up. You hate being shamed or otherwise losing status, since it makes you feel shut out in the cold and the dark, and you need approval to warm you and make you feel all right. You probably feel that you have been deprived of the respect and recognition that you need by a cold, hard world. Emotionally you can be cool, reserved, and cautious, when you are unsure of what response you will get; or you may have mastered emotional self-control so that you can always make the appropriate response when required. If you have, then you manipulate your feelings to be what others seem to want them to be, or will get you what you need, probably automatically by now, since this started in your childhood.

You feel the emotional strictures around you, the unspoken do's and don'ts, and the stiffened, rigid withdrawal of some people, if you overstep the bounds of emotional propriety. This is your awareness, what you look for, at least as much as it is their reaction. You try to keep your dignity and decorum, giving you difficulty in being spontaneous, unless it is demanded as proper in your social circle, and then your spontaneity is likely to be under control. The emotion behind it is fear, fear of rejection by the group, whether that group is the family or other social elements. Need for approval may make you seek acceptance by achievement, being responsible and respectable, doing what they will approve of. And if your drive to success was to gain approval, and it doesn't last, then what do you do? You may have fixed your feelings onto a personal goal for your own reasons. A major underlying reason is likely to be material security, since you would hate to be poor and at the bottom of the social strata.

You can be very insecure about your own worth, yet the seriousness of your feelings can lead you to become a person of considerable depth, assuming that you are fully conscious of all your more instinctive drives. Your feeling for natural laws and ability to identify with them can give you a deep certainty about the rightness of the natural order that can outstrip the faith of many religious people. Your hunger to know that order and your place in it can be profound, leading you to a lifelong crystallization of understanding, and a depth of maturity reached by few. But you don't get there by being bothered about your status in others' eyes.

The Moon in early Capricorn goes charging into ambitions and projects full of enthusiasm, but not knowing the rules; in the middle it is well aware of the rules and feels bound to maintain them; toward the end it realizes that all frameworks of rules are traps and begins to desire to be free.

MERCURY IN CAPRICORN

Your mind is serious, orderly, and thinks in a structured fashion, using orthodox rational methods. Slow and cautious in thought, you carefully place each point of information in an ordered framework of knowledge before incorporating more. A practical and perhaps materialistic thinker, you consider the ultimate goal in any study (usually being in personal, professional or social self-development), and organize your areas and methods of learning to attain that goal. Intellectually aware of frameworks of law, order, organization, and pattern, you may specifically study them, learning to think rationally within their defined limits. You tend to uphold their laws, being concerned with consistency, in your own mind and in its objects, and are thus not necessarily original, experimental (except within the rigorous limits of scientific method), or radical.

You want an orderly world and disapprove of disruption of that order, which can make you slow to accept changes. It also makes you think in terms of discipline, restriction and control, which you probably think of as being responsibility, and you use such controls both on yourself and on others under your authority, thus allowing little independence or spontaneity. So you can be manipulative, using your understanding of the rules, and of the way that things and people work, to make them respond as you want them to. Since you respect the rules, customs, and restraints of orthodox conservative society, you will generally not allow yourself or those under your control to act against the rules, even unspoken ones. Thus you tend to remain proper and dignified in speech and expression, and avoid frivolity, preferring to talk about serious matters or things of deeper meaning, except where your sense of the incongruous makes light fun of things that are out of place.

It is likely that you will eventually question and reconsider your attachment to orthodoxy, and begin to think originally for yourself. When you do, with your serious mind, you are able to become profound and philosophical, working toward a deep understanding of natural order. You then break out of dependency on socially approved systems of thought, a dependency that limits you to accepting only what everyone knows to be true, an attitude which, if universal, would have kept mankind living in trees.

If Mercury has particularly stressful aspects, you tend toward rigid and suspicious doubts, perhaps of your own mental abilities, perhaps of things outside yourself. Your doubts may swing from one to the other, your skepticism not allowing you to trust, reserve and caution not allowing understanding to grow. In some cases the doubts will encourage curiosity and exploration, thus eventually wiping out the doubt.

You are suited to such studies as: history, archaeology, geology, (studies that involve time), agriculture, mathematics (especially geometry), physics, physiology, law, government, politics, social organization, management, systems and procedures, or law enforcement. Any of these could become occupations or professions.

VENUS IN CAPRICORN

In relationships you are cool, reserved, and self-controlled; aware of form and propriety—of socially correct behavior. You would hate to be shamed in the eyes of others or judged against their standards, so you retain your dignity and decorum, perhaps at the expense of spontaneity, making yourself old before your time. You judge yourself, your relationships, and your possessions, and probably most other things in your life, against standards of status and position, of whether they improve your social standing or enhance your prestige. Your sensitivity to judgment by peers and superiors is a reflection of the fact that you believe their social hierarchy to be a valid one, and cling to your own need for recognition, or at least acceptance, within it. This often indicates an unresolved need for recognition from your parents and elders, or more positively, that you had such recognition and felt it to be love, and so pursue it. So your attitudes may be to seek material and social gain, or you may simply be serious and responsible in your affections, seeking security and stability in your love life. You dislike open public display of feelings, and may also restrain yourself in private too, feeling that such control makes you superior, though you are capable of an earthy sensuality, if this is not the case.

Your reserve will enable you to relate more easily to older people than to younger ones, this position often indicating marriage to one older than yourself, marriage relatively late in life, or at least to one of a serious and conservative disposition. Marriage will appeal to you, rather than freer or looser relationships, simply because of the orthodox, secure stability that it represents. On the negative side, you may marry for position, wealth, and power; or, as you are well aware of the laws and rules in relating, you may be something of a manipulator, knowing exactly what to do to elicit exactly the kind of response that you want from others; or, your self-doubts in relating may make you seek reassurance from your partner, or make you very cautious about relating in the first place, leaving you sad and alone. Positively, your affections can be totally serious and enduring, fully capable of taking on all responsibilities required by relating, and when you commit yourself to another your love can last for a lifetime.

Your tastes go through a long, slow formation, and will be likely to lean toward the formal and traditional. You will probably appreciate antiques and antiquities, traditional arts and crafts, classical music, and may be interested in the history of art. Capricorn itself leans toward solid art forms such as sculpture, architecture, bonsai, and landscaping, and may express its interest in gemmology. Your early tastes and values may simply be taken directly from your elders, your own being slow to develop, taking shape gradually like a crystal forming from a solution. When they have finally formed, they are likely to be almost immovably solid, so you need to consider very clearly just what type of values you want to live with for a lifetime.

MARS IN CAPRICORN

You point your energies and initiative toward distinct goals of worldly achievement, and pursue those goals with discipline, order, and organization. You have the ambition to reach the peak of whatever you apply yourself to, the consistency of long-term focus to set up an ultimate goal and to use everything at your disposal to move toward it. This may involve the desire to gain a final goal of power, position, and control, or of personal status and recognition by society, or of development of your own abilities and potential as a person toward completion. Whatever your final aim, you use self-control, awareness of principles of order, and material practicality in your pursuit, plus the taking on of any and all responsibilities that will get you there. The seriousness of your approach to life makes you act older than your years, normally giving you the ability to relate well to your elders and superiors, to whom your approach is likely to be direct and forthright, with no submissiveness, though with cool reserve and the ability to take orders responsibly.

You may be very materialistic, recognizing value in the orthodox hierarchies of goods and power, that "it is better to be at the top of the pile than at the bottom." If so, you are fairly likely to be a runner in the rat-race, gathering to yourself all the strings of power that you can, and using any position that you achieve for the manipulation of others toward your own ends of gaining power and control. You know how to use all the rules, social, business, ethical, and interpersonal, to help yourself along your way. You can be coldly calculating, disregarding the human values and rights of others and seeing them only as tools to be used. This attitude is the opposite side of the coin to a fear of being powerless, of being at the bottom of the heap, of being under everyone else's control, having to respond to their whims, without dignity, respect, or personal rights.

The more stable and humane type has certain fears too, notably of social censure and loss of respect or recognition by others, and may take great pains not to lose them, taking no chances and working hard to be worthy of respect. Thus they work hard and responsibly within the system, upholding its attitudes and values, being offended by and scornful of ways of life other than their own. Having identified closely with a certain society or world-view, any rejection of it or opposition to it is taken as a personal affront. Essentially this is a matter of effort being expended to maintain the order of the world that you know, of learning its laws, and either researching them further in order to understand them better (to master them), or of identifying yourself with them and acting to enforce them—which gives this placing an affinity with the armed forces and with the police force (among other conservative and rule-oriented organizations). On the research side, this can be an excellent placing for a scientist, particularly in physics, physiology, structural engineering (particularly exploring material stress and fatigue), and any form of systems research.

JUPITER IN CAPRICORN

You may have a problem with your hopes, feeling that they are always going to be dashed, that anything you look forward to will turn out badly. Your optimism is cautiously held in check by your pessimism, so that every time you want to grow, to go out joyfully to experience, you allow your doubts to stop you, so things can't develop the way that you want them to. You let your doubts get out of hand, elaborating on them and blowing them up out of proportion, interpreting situations as being worse than they actually are by looking for their worst aspects. If this is the case, then you can fall into big depressions and wallow in negativity. You may also restrain your enthusiasms by adhering to all the rules of social restraint and propriety, all the "thou shalt not's" of orthodox public opinion, though struggling and flaring inwardly against the restrictions upon you that those attitudes represent. Yet you work at being all that they want you to be, at being dignified and sober, at being the good child or citizen, out of your need for respect and recognition by your elders, betters, and peers. Seeking status in others' eyes, you try to overcome feelings of inferiority, which you hate; yet you exaggerate upon every incident that arouses such feelings in a morbid kind of negative self-justification. Similarly you hate to feel guilty, being very aware of the rules, and either berate yourself for every incident where you broke them, or project all that feeling out onto others in a self-righteously superior moral indignation.

You may have an ambitious drive toward a social and material position of superiority, to counterbalance your inferiority feelings, seeking dignity and recognition to fill the lack that you feel. You may become a representative of the conservative and traditional establishment, upholding all of its principles and laws—perhaps more strictly than its other members—in an effort to gain moral superiority. You may have a great concern with law and with maintaining it, being either an example of great personal integrity, or of hypocrisy, depending upon how honest you are within yourself. You tend to maintain your dignity and self-control, and possibly your self-importance, in most circumstances, being prudent and cautious, perhaps to excess. If you seek public life, you may expend so much time and effort upon it that your private and family life suffers in consequence, but your organizational abilities are likely to lead you to high office. Your sense of duty and responsibility is likely to be highly developed, even though you may sometimes be frustrated by the inhibitions that it places upon your freedom, unless you see power and responsibility as being a kind of freedom.

You have the potential to gain an excellent overview of principles of law, whether natural, in the sciences; social, in government, the legal profession, or the police; moral and spiritual, via a religion or philosophy. It may show in large scale organizational abilities, or in spiritual work to fulfill the law. If the latter, you will have a quiet, stable faith in the rightness of all things, and apply yourself with steady determination to crystallizing your own being into perfect clarity and order.

SATURN IN CAPRICORN

Saturn is in its home here and works with its full range of expression. You have a cautious, orderly, and orthodox streak a mile wide, which will probably be aimed at some form of complete personal achievement in your lifetime, or at being a coordinating center of influence, to gather and organize people around you. You are in no hurry since you recognize the value of time, of developing things slowly and carefully so that they form properly and perfectly, and are done at the right time. You have to have aims and goals to achieve, to feel that there is something that you are going to attain to or become, gaining mastery, whether in the material world or in self-development. You prefer not to begin anything until you have an image of the final completed goal, not stepping onto the path unless the end is in sight. You seek an ordered certainty, a feeling that the laws and rules of whatever you are dealing with are consistent, and that you can therefore use them to get to your goal. Thus you are practical and organized, consistent, persistent, and completely responsible where your ambitions are concerned. You are able to filter out distractions, knowing how to keep your awareness within the strict boundaries dictated by your aim, blocking any interference which might deviate you from it.

Your ambitions may be for worldly power and status, for recognition from the authorities in whatever area you identify yourself with, wanting recognition as a master of your field, establishment as an authority among authorities. Or your drives may be to develop your own being to a crystalline clarity, to complete psychological and psychic order, to a great depth of understanding of the laws of nature, and a mastery of both yourself and them. Whichever the case, you have a deep awareness of systems of order, hierarchies of power, whether in the mundane and material world or in universal law, and a tendency to judge yourself according to your position in the hierarchy. Your drive to achieve will possibly be to compensate for a lack of the recognition that you wanted and needed as a child from your parents or peers, or alternatively it may be to gain control of what seems like an uncertain world. Essentially you impose control over your world, keeping it in a manageable state so that you can feel secure and in charge. What you do with that control depends on your sense of honor; you may keep honesty, humanity and integrity in all that you do, and acceptance of the social order and of the need for it, or you may manipulate all the rules and laws to your own advantage, showing respect for nothing, not even yourself.

You may seek the limelight, needing to be important, or shun it, perhaps fearing humiliation. Whatever the truth, it is extremely likely that you will believe that there is an order or authority above and beyond yourself, perhaps to be challenged and achieved in your own right, perhaps to be submitted to and respected. The truth may be that you yourself dictate your own vision of order to your world, structuring it according to your belief of what it should be. There certainly is order in all things, the question is whether human beings can actually know the true ultimate nature of that order.

URANUS IN CAPRICORN

The planet Uranus was in the sign of Capricorn from December 1904 to November 1912. During this period Einstein's special theory of relativity was publicly stated, the Automobile Association and the Austin Motor Company were founded, and motor buses began running in London. Labor reforms acted to undo excessively harsh laboring conditions, Minkowski's four-dimensional geometry (the mathematics of relativity) emerged, subway lines were opened in London and New York. The Model T Ford was produced, Bleriot flew across the English channel, and cinema was emerging as a medium of entertainment. The roller bearing was invented, the first railway was electrified, and labor laws required a half-day holiday for employees. The GPO took over British telephone systems, the Royal Flying Corps was established, the first regular air service began—in rigid airships—between Berlin and Friedrichshaven, and the Titanic was lost on its maiden voyage.

Obviously, the old world was ending and a new one coming into being, attended by all of the excitement and all of the problems of massive social change. Being born during this era, you have grown with ever-accelerating change going on around you. You have either reacted by learning to accept it, and coming to enjoy the greater freedoms and flexibilities that the new age has brought to every individual, learning to adjust your picture of the world as fresh knowledge becomes public; or you have become insecure about change and have tried to stick rigidly to what you know as being stable (traditional) and secure, in the process making your mind static by refusing to change your ideas.

If you have adapted, your understanding of the frameworks of order that hold the world together has become complex and very much interwoven, your understanding of law in all facets of the world, physical and social, becoming alive and active. You have seen older ideas of class structure break down, with avenues for all to set their sights on high and unusual ambitions and achieve them being ever more available. You may have done your part in helping these changes along, being ready to reorganize both your world and your understanding of it, and possibly aiming to make it closer to a human ideal than before. Many in your generation have a deeply scientific leaning with a readiness to open themselves to alternatives to the established order.

If you have been more traditional, it is likely that you have resisted change, keeping your ideas in the old mold quite firmly. You have tried to remain unchanging in a changing world and have probably become tense and frustrated in the process. You probably prefer to identify yourself with relatively strict and stern values and conservative political views, feeling that to do so gives you a kind of special status. You will deplore the loss of the old social order, since it has eroded the position that you would prefer to have had within it, wishing that society was still compartmentalized into nice, neat categories of rank and privilege. In order to keep some status, you may have kept yourself separate from society, isolating yourself into a backwater where you feel that you can retain the individuality that your position gives you, keeping the past intact from the flood of the emerging future.

NEPTUNE IN CAPRICORN

Neptune entered Capricorn in 1984, a significant year in that much of the English-speaking world was watching to see if George Orwell's vision of things (of totalitarian dictatorship, of brain-washing and utter conformity) came to pass. In some ways he was right, in that those at the peaks of hierarchies have been entrenching their right-wing political positions, often by very deceitful methods (Ronald Reagan and the Nicaraguan/Iranian arms deals, for instance). The rich have been withdrawing resources from the lower, working, levels of society, leaving a greater gap between rich and poor, which has been emphasized at the upper end in status-conscious fashions, and in increasingly conservative public morals, such as anti-crime drives, while at the lower social levels an increase in compassion has brought massive charitable aid to the famine stricken areas of the world.

The psychology of this position is one of sensitivity to social structures and status, including the polarity between the "haves and the have-nots," wealth and poverty, fearful retention of safe social positions, versus generosity to all who are in need. As can be seen, there is either a tendency to build defensive barriers to protect personal vulnerability from whatever is feared—erosion by the forces of chaos—which also often includes a display of social rank, of wealth, power, privilege (burglar alarms and security devices installed in all wealthy homes); or a tendency to identify with the underprivileged, with the hungry, the needy, the unemployed, feeling a personal responsibility to ease, if not to overcome, suffering (an open door to all).

The innate sense of responsibility to others either encourages responsible social action, or—when the positive path is not taken—a subtle and probably deeply buried sense of guilt. Such guilt can cause extreme touchiness where the (often imagined) judgments of others are involved, or can bring depression, since their own consciences make such judgments about themselves (though these may be deliberately silenced).

The wholesome personality not only identifies in depth with human beings, but with nature as a whole, having a deep receptivity to natural forces, a grounded yet subtle feeling for life and for patterns of order and organization in time. These people may be able to understand that the apparent hierarchy of universal laws is in fact a mutual interdependence, within which every member of humankind plays a role, responsible or irresponsible, through his or her own choice.

The main point here is that if individuals born at this time take full and compassionate responsibility for their own actions, they will discover that the whole human race is their family, and all life their friend. If they do not, they will feel isolated and alone, and may feel that everyone is against them.

CAPRICORN NORTH NODE—CANCER SOUTH NODE

You are all too aware of your own needs, and like a child you look for someone else to satisfy them for you. When they are not met you can become cranky, moody and resentful. You also want the status of having the attention of others, even if you only use it to complain to them about your miseries. You would usually rather be dependent on them than independently adult yourself. You are very retentive of anything that represents security to you, whether it be memories, mementos, collections or people; you are insecure, remembering the irrational fears of childhood, the unfulfilled needs, and the fear of parental judgment. You need a secure territory of your own, but are very aware of the pecking order or power hierarchy, of the likelihood of being dominated by others within shared space, and still feeling yourself to be a child you give in to them, submit and become depressed. You feel that you need more practice to become adult, and may be in search of a father figure.

You need to turn the tables by taking on responsibility, first for yourself, then for others; becoming the parent instead of the child. Then you can set up your own aims for self-fulfillment and organize yourself to achieve them in the long run, instead of waiting for anyone else to do it for you. Your clinging to the past becomes an appreciation of history and tradition, of feeling secure with the background forces in life; your need for family turns into an identification with the stability of society; and your desire for attention transforms into the ambition to gain the standing appropriate to your value as a responsible being. The more you are parent to yourself and in full responsible command of your own life, rather than letting others be responsible for you, the less you will experience your depressed moods and fears, and the closer you will come to full achievement.

SUN IN THE 10TH HOUSE

You are very aware of the hierarchies of order, of status and position in your life, and of your place within them. Your self-respect depends on you feeling that you have good standing in the eyes of others, recognition for your achievements, and approval by your peers. You should be an able organizer, capable of planning for the long term, particularly to achieve your own goals, which you identify with strongly, not feeling fulfilled unless you have accomplished them, and risen to the top of your field. You do this by becoming conscious of, then creatively mastering, the whole framework of laws or principles of your chosen area, and probably rising to an administrative position. You use your sense of honor and of propriety to maintain your dignity in whatever you do, and probably make sure that you do your best, not only for yourself, but for all others concerned, this position being excellent for the building of a very real sense of responsibility.

Your need for recognition began in your relationship with your father. If he gave you recognition for your abilities and accomplishments, your pride became focused on that and you learned to become an achiever. If he did not, then you felt the need for his approval and tried to gain it, experiencing a struggle for recognition from an uncaring world. It is possible that he was very focused upon himself and the effects of his own actions, and he gained pride through being creatively involved in fresh developments. In this he may have been a hard act to follow. He may perhaps have been dominant, over-bearing and arrogant, making your need for positive approval more intense, and creating in you a desire to show him, to beat him in his own game. Whatever the case, the end result will be visible in your developed attitude toward authority, including your own, and in the whole pattern of your search for achievement and recognition.

On the more negative side, you may be forceful, dominant, and overbearing in authoritative positions (and the rest of the time), boosting your ego by the position that you hold, and perhaps manipulating the rules for your own advantage. In this case your desire for power could be boundless, not having enough, however much you gain. On the other hand you could be lazy and uncaring about personal accomplishment, being satisfied to blame the system for your lack of position.

Your mother was very conscious of her relationships with others, and either innocently direct, or rather wary of them. If the second, then she prepared her tactical position to take her opponent by surprise. In doing so she suspected similar ulterior motives on their part and that they were plotting an attack, actually projecting her own motives onto them. In this case, she would not have been easy to relate to. Otherwise, she may have been very open, cheerful, and honorable toward others, naturally egalitarian, and a good warm-hearted counselor.

MOON IN 10TH HOUSE

You are emotionally receptive to patterns of power, authority, and social status, to law, rules, and regulations, and to your own position inside such structures; for example, you are sensitive to general social and cultural attitudes, and tend to reflect them and respond to them automatically, using them as a set of personal boundary limitations, as a public persona. This sensitivity reflects your need for recognition and public approval, to have your own established public or social status. At the extreme, this may become a hunger for power, position, and fame, wanting recognition or power for its own sake. Those who feel this extreme need will do anything to gain attention in the public eye, going beyond the usual bounds of public decorum, simply to have others' attention focused upon them. Basically, this is a matter of gaining feelings of security by attracting attention or recognition, and the majority will work toward it by using dignity, decorum, and the taking on of responsibility, preferring respectability to being shamed in the estimation of the public. Where this need is strong, it goes back to an unfulfilled need for attention and recognition from a parent, usually father, in early years, wanting to be noticed with approval by him, or simply noticed.

If this drive is not extreme, you have a well-developed receptivity to the needs of others, and a willingness to take on even very heavy responsibilities in fulfilling those needs. You would make a good parent, or a professional in some nurturing or caring type of field, providing protection, help, nourishment, or support to those requiring it. In professional areas your receptivity to others' needs would enable you to work well in groups, having support from, and being in support of, others. In pursuing your aims, you need their support, and work to draw to you the right people and conditions to further those aims. You are tenacious in pursuit of your goals, personal or professional, which would enable you to take on large and difficult labors, though your persistence may vary cyclically with your moods. This placing is a common one for those who work in direct contact with the public within fairly orthodox frameworks.

Your father was a receptive man, most probably strongly focused on his family, acting directly to protect and provide security for them. He was also moody and emotional, though hiding some of his feelings behind a protective shield and simply reflecting back the feelings of others. His aims would generally have been reasonably ordinary, and probably varied with his moods, though he persisted in them in the long run, often approaching them indirectly. He may have had a strong feeling for the land, for his own property, or for his territorial rights.

Your mother had a need for others and could cling to them in relationships, to the security of their support. She could reflect and respond to their attitudes with sensitivity, acting like a mirror to them—and perhaps hiding herself behind the mirror. Or she needed them as mirrors to herself, in which she could gain a sense of her own identity, and see her own needs reflected. She wanted security in her relationships, and could test that security by a push and pull of feelings, though never going beyond strict emotional bounds—and often also keeping her deeper feelings behind a conventional barrier.

MERCURY IN THE 10TH HOUSE

You have a serious, orderly, cautious mentality, approaching fresh information with a certain reserve. You don't believe that you have understood anything unless you can fit it into a whole system of concepts, placing each item of information into the ordered whole. You are interested in systems of order, hierarchies of law or control, whether in nature, physical sciences, or political or social areas, though you may be ambivalent about them. You are interested in the connections between abstract law and its concrete manifestations; in how things, people, and events develop their forms and processes through time; thus you like to see how ideas develop into realities. You may impose your idea of order onto your world, perhaps not liking the order that exists, being somewhat conservative and resisting change, perpetuating the patterns that you have come to believe are right; yet you may turn around and change all that. You probably began by copying many of the public views of what constitutes social standing and learned how to assume the correct attitudes in manners, etiquette, and dress, but are likely to turn away from their attitudes toward your own in the course of your life.

Your intellectual standing is important to you, and you measure it against the system, whatever that is to you, whether educational qualifications, I. Q. ratings, personal wisdom, or other standards. You may put yourself into positions (*e.g.*, professional) where you can impress others with your knowledge, gaining status or superiority from it, and at the extreme could be an intellectual snob, though you began by being shy and diffident about your abilities. You are uncertain about whether you can reach the goals that you set for yourself, underrating your potential and undermining your persistence by doing so, and you set up alternative directions so that you can change track if it seems that you will fail. Your self-discipline is inconsistent. In fact, you live with divided views about what your ultimate goals in life are. Whichever one you pursue, you can feel guilty for not fulfilling the other(s). Your split of aims could be between the spiritual and the material. If so, you have difficulty deciding which world-order to affirm, or to pursue.

Your relationship with your father probably went through a turnaround early in your life. To begin with, you had him on a pedestal as an ideal to be adored and attained; then something made him topple off in your eyes, and you turned away. Thus you lost your first goal, and have been uncertain about whether it is worth pursuing goals at all, as well as about people in positions of authority or superiority, questioning their credentials to be in such positions. Your status in your own eyes will have gone through the same early soaring, followed by a crash, which leaves you (unconsciously at least) uncertain whether you want to gain the heights—if you might then fall from them, like Icarus.

Your father had a rather dualistic personality, swinging in a volatile way from positive to negative and back. He may have been lively, alert, vocal, and questioning, and liked to be quite mobile. Your mother liked light, intellectual relationships, but was uncertain within them whether or not to like her partner. She could vary between thinking exclusively of others and thinking solely of herself.

VENUS IN THE 10TH HOUSE

You are very aware of the rules in social situations, and of how other people can use them to judge you, and you want to be accepted socially. You want very much to be able to measure up to those standards, not wanting to be judged as lacking in social standing, grace, poise, or know-how, and have probably worked at some time to master those standards and values. You would like to be looked up to by those to whom you have looked up in the past, possibly wanting to be superior to those who judged you inferior. Yet you can be shy, conservative, or slow in pursuing that aim, for fear of being judged again. You may decide to pursue a profession in order to gain that kind of standing, or to gain superiority, at least in your own eyes if not in theirs, or you may be a snob about the famous or influential people that you have met. Many values that you set for yourself are judgmental, bringing you a likelihood of continual doubt as to whether you actually do measure up, however well you are doing. You may turn the tables by projecting your doubts out onto others, minimizing their achievements to gain stature yourself by comparison, but this does not resolve your own doubts. This may make you keep on re-evaluating whether you want to stay in the track that you have chosen.

Much of this is a reflection of your well-developed sense of form, developed by judging and evaluating patterns of order of some kind, perhaps in being responsible for money, or in developing beauty in form or design. You have an aesthetic appreciation of perfect order which may show in liking architecture, or geometry, or crystals, or any other kind of well-structured form. Perhaps it shows in an appreciation of law, or government or corporation structure, or the patterns and mores of society. Whatever it may be, you like to be related to an ordered system, and may be, or want to be, a representative, spokesperson, or mouthpiece for it, interpreting the system for others, like a priest. Or you may have a desire to relate directly to figures of authority and status, gaining kudos, standing, or position yourself in the act.

You are also directly aware of others' feelings, and may feel a demand to respond to them, to react, and perhaps a responsibility to try to balance them out and fulfill them. You will either defer to them easily, flowing along with their needs, or override them, trying to replace their feelings with your own values, depending on your relative status, turning relationships into situations of dominance and submission. Much of this may come from your early relationship with your mother. She was probably publicly charming and privately quite judgmental, sometimes deliberately annoying others in the family for the sake of provoking a response. Above all, she wanted others to relate to her, and made sure that they did, one way or the other.

Your father wanted to live his life peacefully in pursuit of his own values and pleasures. He could be charming and pleasant to know, since he wanted others to think well of him, which they probably did, yet actually be a little impenetrable and difficult to reach. You probably felt that his love was there, but was not necessarily constant, or enough. You probably wanted more of a relationship with him than you had, and set him up as the standard for your own values, and perhaps felt that you failed by comparison.

MARS IN THE 10TH HOUSE

You are strongly oriented toward achievement, focusing your energies on self-development toward professional goals or long-range ambitions. In your work, at least, you prefer to be number one, not particularly liking to have anyone in immediate authority over you, wanting to be in sole charge of your own area—to the point of wanting to be your own boss. The pyramid of power you may see as something to climb, to fight your way to the top, or to avoid entirely, to do without competition. To this kind of end, you use your energies in a constructive and organized way, disciplining yourself to be persistent, to develop your skills, both in working and in managing, so that you become a master of your field.

Your aim is both security and establishment, and you may want to become a force to be reckoned with in society, a prime mover. You have a certain conservatism, and either identify with the established order and its history, or want to be your own social order. You may want to build a new order of things in your own life, or in society, or both. Whatever you want you will achieve by your own efforts, rather than being supported by others, and you want to do it to prove yourself to yourself, perhaps not being interested in the recognition and approval of others, though some will make this a prime aim.

Particular skills that you may have or develop involve an awareness of both organizational structure and the power or energy that drives it. For example, engineering or mechanics; politics and the power of the law; science or other research into the driving forces of the universe. Mountaineering is a skill that may interest you, with your drive to climb to the top.

If Mars has difficult aspects you are more likely to be in a head-on conflict with authority through your life, ready to do battle with those who are in any superior position to you, feeling that they block your actions or put brick walls in your way for you to bang your head against. You may want to prove to them just who is best (you, of course) and struggle your way to the head of the pecking order. You may be a rat-race achiever, seeing this as being the actual social order of your world, a competitive struggle for supremacy among the strong. If so, look back to your relationship with your father and remember when you decided to show him who was best, to outdo him.

In general, your father is likely to have been a go-getter, a person of considerable initiative and decisiveness, who was ready to act in pursuit of his own aims at a moment's notice. He was not necessarily consistent in his aims or views, the fresh impulse of the moment often carrying him away. With difficult aspects, he may have been too aggressive, forceful, argumentative, too sharply focused and attacking for your comfort, and too variable in his impulsiveness.

Your mother was ready to let your father take the lead, though she did not like having her own initiative taken away from her. She would rather let others decide what to do just so long as they considered her, and would probably start a fight if they didn't. If she fought she was probably a capable tactician, knowing her opponent's motives and adjusting her strategy to win through.

JUPITER IN THE 10TH HOUSE

Your social views may be general, tolerant, and easygoing, because you would prefer to live in a society that would deal with you that way. You would rather be optimistic about your potential to grow and gain position within society, to deal with big things, yet may see its rules, regulations, and restrictions as inhibiting your own freedom of growth. You are capable of setting yourself high, broad aims for personal growth and self-development, but allow your enthusiasms to be dampened, your hopes to be dashed, by the slowness with which things actually develop. Therefore you tend to keep changing your aims, as one seems to be blocked—moving on to another. In other words, where you do want to achieve something you are often not persistent or disciplined enough to take it to completion, as you oscillate between optimism and pessimism, leaving yourself disordered and disorganized. You would like to gain wide recognition for your achievements, acknowledgment by society for something major, but may not entirely believe that it can happen. You want to develop on into a good future but allow yourself to get bogged down in the past.

As you develop persistence and self-discipline you are capable of dealing with and achieving great things, since you then have the ability to plan for the long term. This comes from your general interest in systems, whether systems of law, social or natural, philosophical or religious frameworks of organization, or any other kind. You tend to be interested in how such things evolve, in the historical perspective of their growth. If you have not yet pursued an interest in such areas, you will find that it will come naturally to you and be of benefit to fulfilling your directions in life. You may, for example, focus on politics, on the making of the laws that govern society, the philosophy behind them, or their application in justice, and their continuing evolution within the courts.

You will need to be certain that your tendencies to set your sights too high and fall short, and to spread your aims over too wide a field, do not lead you astray. If you are too impatient in your aims your pattern is likely to be that of a rapid (probably over-inflated) growth followed by a collapse; where you practice a patient persistence your growth should be long, slow, and steady toward the peak that you desire. This is assuming that you are not so easygoing that you have no such desire. The range of this position is wide, from the get-rich-quick entrepreneurs—ready to stretch and manipulate the law as far as it will go, to honorable men in high position—working for the best growth of society at large.

Your professional directions may be in the fields of: law, politics, religion, hotels, travel, shipping, import/export, journalism, higher education, bookstores or information services, horses, racing, forestry; basically any area that covers a very wide ground, in very large organizations, or ones concerned with growth, expansion, outdoor pursuits, broad horizons; or broadcasting of information, such as teaching.

Your father was either a cheerful and optimistic person with many enthusiasms, tolerant and outgoing, perhaps with a philosophical or studious approach to life in general; or a more bombastic, conceited, and overbearing type, moralistically self-expanding at others' cost, with a fiery temper that would burst out in great displays.

SATURN IN THE 10TH HOUSE

You are very aware of the laws in your life, whether these are laws of society made by the government, conservative social opinion and morality, laws of nature as described by science, spiritual laws, or whatever. You take the law seriously, whether you appreciate it or resent it, and are aware of your own status within the system that you identify with. You are either submissive— knowing your place and fulfilling it responsibly, or see the system as a mountain to climb to a position of authority, respect, and recognition, or of power, control, manipulation, and domination. This is an awareness of hierarchies of control, pyramids of power, organizational frameworks, of who is at the top and laying down the law, who in the middle administering it, and who at the bottom dictated to by it.

　　You were aware in this way from an early age, recognizing the position of advantage that your parents, elders, teachers, and superiors held in making and imposing rules on the younger ones. You were particularly responsive to the influence of your father. He was either strict, conformist and self-controlled; or negative and pessimistic—a "Scrooge" in his attitudes to life; or of little use in giving you a sense of responsibility and direction, perhaps from not being there at all. You either wanted his respect and recognition because it was worth something, or resented his influence (or lack of it) over you, perhaps having no respect whatsoever for him and feeling superior to him. Whatever your relationship was, it formed your attitudes to authority, position, and responsibility in your own life. The more your identity was suppressed under the rules and by emotional deprivation, the greater your ambitious drive to take over control and gain power for yourself. (Napoleon and Hitler both had Saturn in their 10th houses; Hitler's father was domineering.)

　　If you aim for achievement you are very likely to succeed, being responsible, organized, aware of how to use the laws to your advantage, and thoroughly persistent in any climb to the top. You are capable of planning for the very long term by applying all your knowledge of organization, management, discipline, and control, perhaps imposing all your own ideas of right and wrong on those under your rule. Much depends on the nature of those ideas, whether they are the *Code Napole;on* or the Hitler pogrom, but they are likely to involve concepts of discipline, control, and restraint, rather than freedom, growth, and exploration. In other words, you can be narrow-minded about what you think to be right in society. If you have gone the negative way, you may use a position of authority   to manipulate the law to your own ends, to maneuver others, delighting in the power and position that it gives you. Examples involve the worst elements of the civil service, the police force, and the government.

　　You may also be very sensitive to public opinion. Self-consciousness about your public image and fear of failure or humiliation may leave you very cautious about stepping out of line, never mind reaching for the heights; and if you do—your fear can lead you straight to the failure that you expect (remember Napoleon and Hitler); it is a fear of falling from a height.

URANUS IN THE 10TH HOUSE

As a youngster you probably idealized your father for his friendliness and independence, among other qualities, or may (if Uranus has difficult aspects) have rebelled against his arbitrary changes. Whatever the case, your relationship with him has had a strong effect in forming your attitudes toward society, authority and responsibility. On the positive side, you are likely to have ambitions to fulfill or attain an ideal, to reach for a star; *Per Ardua ad Astra* may be your personal motto (by effort, or by climbing the heights, to the stars). You feel that the freedom and independence you aim for can only be achieved by seriously taking on the responsibility to do so, a complex—though light—self-discipline being your road to maturity.

Your understanding of the order of the world around you is multi-level; you perceive a variety of different systems of order, or of law, in operation and you are capable of weaving them all together quite rapidly into a complex whole. You tend to be a generalist rather than a specialist, since any professional speciality that you pursue will lead you on to integrating it with all closely related areas. These are likely to be in the fields of modern communications (such as media work, radio, or television) or transportation (road, rail, aviation, space-flight), data processing or computing, electrical engineering or electronics, social work, or something completely unusual and individualistic.

Your relationships with authority tend to be friendly and democratic; you prefer to be involved in governing systems that allow completely creative involvement and free expression by all people at all levels, round-table systems that allow all points of view to be aired and integrated rather than vertical hierarchies in which each person has the law imposed by the one above them and impose themselves on the one below. Your political attitudes are the same, being in favor of the protection of the free rights of the individual, and against their erosion by law (laws reduce personal freedom by defining it, they never increase it). You will very likely work from the inside to change society more toward the ideal, by action or by personal example.

Where difficult planetary aspects enter the picture you are more likely to have problems with authority. You may see the system as being arbitrary and unjust, tyrannical in its imposition of law and order, utterly uncaring about the individual. You may think that society is going toward totalitarian rule; and you may rebel against the system that you live in and advocate tearing it down, to be replaced by your idea of the right way. You do not think that anyone has any right to tell you what to do, because you hate to be trapped in that position. You won't have anyone reducing your status in your own eyes, and you claim not to care what your status is in their eyes—blatantly untrue since you really want to have special standing and recognition from others, simply for being yourself, but feel that you have lost it in the past, have fallen from a high peak, perhaps into a black hole. You may feel that you stand entirely alone, in isolation.

A possible opposite face of this placing is that you may be entirely rigid-minded in imposing your own authority onto others, neither seeing nor admitting to there being any other valid points of view.

NEPTUNE IN THE 10TH HOUSE

In youth you may have projected your faultless hero ideal onto your father—seeing him as having all the good qualities that you want in yourself, but don't feel that you have. If so, you seek the perfect world order, but may think that it is outside yourself and unattainable (frequently the case if your father wasn't present while you were growing up). You have ideals of a peaceful and compassionate society in which you can do what you want. You want authority to be tolerant, and you extend the same easy-going tolerance to others.

You may have projected your fantasies, sensitivities, or confusion onto your father, perhaps seeing him as having the faults that you don't admit to having. Then you rejected his authority, and probably replaced it with your fantasy idea of perfect authority. You may seek the perfect father in religion or some kind of absolute law. You want to identify with the "True Law," to be absolutely right so that others can see it. You think that if you can see that the law is right, then why can't everyone else? You think that other viewpoints are wrong, being narrow-minded in your views. You may be paranoid about being wrong in others' eyes. You may also feel responsible for everyone else—taking on boundless authority. You think that they should do what you want them to do, which is a way of taking total control. If you can't do this openly, then you will manipulate subtly and deviously. You don't want to submit to God, you want to be God. You do not see what the natural order is, you impose the order that you believe in.

If your father was strict, or absent, then you may be a law unto yourself, breaking all rules and limits. You do as you please, yet really want someone to control you, to give you orders; you fight your own social conscience, yet in your depths would really rather be the good child. You have an overwhelming need for recognition, to have others' approval on a huge scale, but may just fantasize about it—being enormously vulnerable to public opinion (some may act to gain recognition, such as becoming a movie star or notorious criminal, and some boast, with nothing real behind it.).

In self-developmental or professional directions, you may be confused and unable to make any clear choice; may set unattainable dream goals; may choose a profession for its image; may work in charitable or other public institutions, or the hospitality industry—hospitals, hotels, theaters, restaurants and such, or with the arts, or the ocean, or in oil, chemical, or biological industries.

Your own authority may be gentle or vulnerable—your control dissolving easily, or you may let things dissolve into chaos. You may be utterly submissive to higher authority. You may feel that you are a victim or a martyr to authority, having to submit to injustices, perhaps seeing them as being the hand of God or fate. Your relationship with your boss may simply crumble for no apparent reason.

If you overcome confused attitudes toward authority or higher laws you can achieve depth and subtlety in self-mastery, developing understanding of universal principles to a crystalline clarity. Your own authority then becomes compassion; your self-discipline dissolves away because it is no longer needed. A meditation discipline would be of value to you.

PLUTO IN THE 10TH HOUSE

Your attitudes toward authority are very much concerned with the inequalities of the system, from one side or the other. You either believe that might is right or that the workers are downtrodden, and more likely the second. Assuming this, you feel that the masses are being exploited to produce wealth for the few, and that this is completely unjust. You feel that those in authority are self-seeking, demanding, and intolerant, not caring for those who work for them and acting in support of the manipulating power clique to keep you, the underdog, down. You feel that the system is a rat-race, dog-eat-dog, ruled by the law of the jungle, and you would like to transform it to bring true equality for all, or would just like to blow the whole thing up. You hate being judged according to a class structure, or being thought of as higher or lower. In other words, you have a furious resentment of anyone in any position of power over you.

Alternatively you may identify with the system, seeing no reason why you shouldn't gain as much money and power as you can, subscribing to the free enterprise system, and believing that those who do not make it to the top are left behind because they don't work, or are lazy. You believe that only the strong survive, and that any method you use to gain your intense ambitions and keep your position is justified. You may opt out of the whole thing, believing that those in power are all self-seeking, have vested interests and ulterior motives, that politicians, for example, are a bunch of crooks chasing power for its own sake. You may have resolved all your emotional frustrations with your father and see that efficiency in disciplining and directing your own life is simply essential to survival as a person, and work toward your own transformation to become complete master of yourself. You need, most of all, to become gentler in your self-rule, relaxing the rigid authority that you impose on yourself from the inside.

Your father was an intense person who had to be competent and capable in his own eyes, if not in those of others. He was not open in expressing his feelings, excepting rage, keeping the rest silently hidden away to defend himself against hurt and rejection. Unfortunately, his defenses had the effect of rejecting others—for example his drive for efficiency would make him point out where others went wrong in what they were doing, or officiously taking over to show them how to do it, thus making them out to be incompetent, rarely complimenting them for what they did right. He was not particularly tolerant. Your reaction to him was to shield yourself from his temper, to lose hope of being thought capable or efficient by him, and possibly ending up resenting or hating him. You probably got into furious battles with him where all your most intense feelings erupted. Or you were afraid to face him and had to bottle yourself up. All your attitudes to authority and power spring from here.

Your potential professional directions include: any mass production area; engineering and mechanics; cleaning, garbage and junk businesses; plumbing, drain-laying, sewage (anything involving disposal and elimination, including the Mafia); high finance, loans, investments; dealing with the affairs of the dead such as wills and trusts; science, particularly atomic physics and medicine (including surgery and nursing, or any form of healing); or police, detective, or spy work.

NORTH NODE—10TH HOUSE, SOUTH NODE—4TH HOUSE

You have a very basic need for emotional security, a need to be able to depend on those close to you, whether family or other individuals, for trust, safety, and support. You need it because you didn't feel that you had as much as you wanted of it, and this can make you cling. Whether you felt a lack of support or plenty of support from your mother, you may now try to give yourself that support, keeping yourself in a dependent state by playing both mother and child roles, including transferring this need onto your own children, or you may feel that you will never have the security that you need. You may be caught up in the needs of others in your family, in emotionally responding to them, perhaps becoming their support. If you have to look after them when you want to be looked after yourself, you will feel thoroughly unappreciated.

Your long-term need is to become thoroughly responsible in and for yourself, in command of your own affairs, gaining in mature control of your life. This is likely to lead you away from family matters into pursuit of your own professional directions or your own self-development, substituting status and recognition in society for emotional security from those close to you. You develop from feeling the restrictions of boundaries around you to climbing beyond them all, being master of them, not slave to them. Balance eventually comes in being master of your own home security, coming full circle.

✧ 13 ✧

Aquarius
and the 11th House

In the 11th House we recognize our relationship with the world we identify with in its context within the whole. We see that we are each individuals in our own right, having absolutely individual lives—and no one sees or experiences the world in quite the same way as anyone else; yet at the same time we are simply human beings, members of the mass, indeed of life itself. Here the boundaries of our sense of selfhood adjoin those of others, like property boundaries.

Our social range runs from needing isolation from others in order to know ourselves, to needing the company of others to confirm that we exist and are acceptable. If our 11th House faculties are fully opened we come to understand our own humanity in depth, and through it that of all others. In fact, if our personality boundaries, the boundaries of our consciousness, are wide open, we may find ourselves merged with the telepathic group-mind, or further, with the world, the universe as a whole, and know for a certainty that we are part of the whole. In order for this to happen we have to be prepared to go beyond ourselves, beyond self-centered concerns.

Think of it this way. Every cell in our bodies has exactly the same genetic coding; none has any inner way of knowing whether it is to be a liver cell, a cone in the retina, a nerve in the brain, or whatever. Yet each is differentiated into playing its special role as part of the organ it occupies. It appears likely that it is ultra-violet radiation from dividing cells that radiates through the whole body, telling each part where it is within the whole, and therefore what role it should be playing. The nervous system also coordinates every organ and ability of the body together into a complex living whole. Every role played is essential to the whole. A cell or organ that decides to go its own independent way, consuming nutrients while not contributing to the whole, is tumorous, paralleling the tendency of some humans and groups to grab resources and power for their own benefit rather than for that of the community as a whole.

Our human society has many integrating signals flowing through its various layers (just like all the radio and television signals, all the telephone messages, all the road, rail, or air traffic). All of these are interpreted or used differently by each different social "tribe" or group, yet all are used to define where they are within the whole. The conservatives try to maintain and use the structure of the whole; the radicals know that it has to adapt and change; the revolutionaries want to blow it up; the nihilists mourn for the death

311

of humanity. All the extreme social views have some validity, all serve functions and provide essential elements, including checks and balances against each other, and society would be incomplete if all did not exist.

The 11th, as the objective side of the 5th House, is where we externalize our egos, our sense of selfhood, into the social or otherwise outer areas of experience that interest us as unique individuals (where we seek the stimulus we prefer). We choose our tribes or social groups as extensions of ourselves, as outer statements of who we are. These social arenas are where we spend our more public leisure time. Where we are creative, here our creative play is objectified into active inventiveness, usually shared with others, bringing together elements of our environment and possibly people in new and exciting ways (look at our street theater as the Aquarian era approaches).

All that most individuals usually know is that their own personal society consists of their chosen friends and contacts, plus all that constitutes their chosen lifestyle, clubs, bars, video game parlors, or other elements of their social circuit, as chosen outer territories. Some people stick firmly to the territories they know; some move around and sample; few discover any really new ground or go beyond the known and into the unknown, though many like to identify with areas that seem to do so (ancient astronauts, UFOs, Don Juan), a way of "going beyond by proxy."

Together with the territory go ideas about how it should all be run. In early life these views are ideals about how life should be, how humans should treat each other and all life, held with all the passionate idealism and innocence of youth. Many lose their idealism, at least temporarily, in growing up or learning to deal with the world the way most others do (often becoming cynically detached or alienated in the process). In later life we can resurrect our lost idealism as we go through the mid-life crisis or transition, laying down the burdens of (conformity to) the requirements of creating the home, bringing up families, and generating the resources to do it all.

People in their middle years, usually from between 40-45 until about 60, or retirement age, find that the world does not require the same things of them. They have brought up their children, who have probably now left home, so that responsibility has vanished. They have probably achieved their set professional goals, done their empire-building, or if not there is now doubt as to whether they ever will. Ambition becomes very dry when you find that achievement does not automatically bring happiness with it. For those working at a basic level, life stretches on with no sign of changing its low evaluation of them. Inwardly, old, unsatisfied parts of personality are trying to struggle up to the surface to gain expression. If these buried parts are given their way, life changes—sometimes radically. If these buried needs are not allowed expression, often something in the individual just gives up hope, becomes depressed, or otherwise feels finally trapped.

The whole personality is trying to come to an integrated state. The major rebalancing at this time of life is along four axes; four basic attitudes may need to change. One is toward age; in the early 40s we inwardly feel little different than we did as teen-agers, yet we are now one of the "old fogies" that we may not have respected as kids, so we have to adjust our views (frequently difficult since we are growing older, and our culture has no real place for the old). A second area is our social concern; if we have gone our ways as individuals with little involvement in our culture we will now find a need to contribute something of value to the human race. If we have generally been contributing members of society, we will need more separate independence to discover ourselves. The third axis is our creativity; if we have generally built rather than destroyed, we will now need to tear down some of our structures. If we have hacked at life, we will now need to affirm it and become creative. The last parameter is sexual; in their middle years men need to learn to work more from their feminine side, their capacity for feeling, for nurturing, for responding to others. Women find that they can now become more self-assertive, use their initiative to pursue their own aims, discover their power.

This period of life is given concrete expression in the Hindu culture as the time of leaving the householder's life (after having fulfilled it), and becoming a sannyasin, a holy wanderer in search of enlightenment.

More functionally, the 11th is the region where our bodies and minds coordinate together as a complex multi-faceted unit, as a whole. This is also true for our experience through time, through our lives. This is where we see the common threads of our individuality weave together through time, come to understand our own make-up, if we give ourselves that chance; and to understand how our individuality has led us to our personal common patterns of life experience within the whole, our personal myth within the great myth.

SUN IN AQUARIUS
✧ Space Age Man ✧

Aquarius represents those elements of a complete being or system that are designed to tie it all together into a complex, interrelated, multilevel whole, coordinated to handle all kinds of change and information within its environment. For example: in man the sympathetic nervous system; or in man's world, the computer, electronics, communications and transportation systems.

As an Aquarian you have a mind that will take up a theme and pursue it endlessly, bringing in information from a wide variety of sources to tie together into your own special network of ideas. Any new idea that you meet will be tested against your network to find out *where* it fits, not *if* it fits, since you assume that all things are interrelated. You need a high level of stimulus to avoid boredom so the more exciting your ideas the better you like it, whether they are from science/technology (particularly space and speed—transportation and communication) or alternate society philosophies and New Age thought, human awakening, UFOs and telepathy. You are more interested in the links between different areas of thinking than in the specialist ideas themselves, so inventiveness is your strong point.

You have a high ideal of personal freedom and independence, and do not like to be trapped by anyone or anything. This, plus your high level of activity, makes you need to detach yourself from others and spend time alone to sort yourself out. Although Aquarius is the sign of human society, friends, and groups, the average Aquarian is often an isolated individual who dislikes crowds. You hate domination from anyone and distrust power groups of any kind, and your humanitarian idealism would prefer to see social and personal freedom for all, desiring to transform society from the inside. You see the need for change both socially and in yourself, and while you stick to your attitudes and ideas for long periods, you store up potential and then make total and abrupt changes.

Unless your fixity of mind has made you one of the rigid, narrow, and dogmatic Aquarians, you are tolerant of the views and lifestyles of others, no matter how different from your own, since you realize that there are infinitely many viewpoints and, you never know, they may be right. You either are rigidly orthodox, or you feel vulnerable to rigid orthodoxy and may deliberately rebel against it to emphasize your own individuality. The negative Aquarian can be the mad inventor or scientist whose wild ideas diverge completely from the usual, have apparently little foundation in fact, and lead them to believe that the system is out to get them because they are different. This happens when the Aquarian mind works in complete isolation and thus gets out of touch with reality. Mistrust, wariness, and self-isolation are your defenses and, when taken too far, remaining fixed for too long, they can turn into paranoia.

Aquarian themes: aviation and space travel; astronomy; astrology; radio/television; high electronic technology—computers, computer games, space invaders; space and time travel; flying saucers; the Bermuda triangle; teleportation; science fiction; and borderline sciences.

MOON IN AQUARIUS

Your security lies in your independence, and your emotions are founded on this need, especially your unattached friendliness. You are wary of being trapped by anyone or anything, ready to pull away at any moment in a tense, abrupt withdrawal if that seems likely to happen. Your feelings can change instantly at even small hints of anyone clinging to you, or trying to make you react in ways that you don't want to. If you take this to the extreme you are a very independent but isolated individual. Emotionally a humanitarian idealist, you would prefer to live in a world where everyone is allowed freedom to be themselves entirely, to go their own way without interference, without having to conform to the expectations of others. Thus you may find it difficult to maintain close emotional relationships, other than friendships, keeping a certain distance or detachment so as not to be tied down. You prefer to relate to yourself as an individual, and to humanity as a whole, rather than to anything in between, and you identify closely with those changes in society (particularly in the alternate culture?) that promote the rights and freedoms of all people.

One of your main emotional defenses is your tendency to say "I don't care," or "I am not involved," about things that do affect you deeply, a form of quiet rebellion in which you will deny even your own needs. You don't even want to be trapped by them, and can separate yourself from them—finding a multitude of interests and stimuli to keep you actively involved while avoiding them. But eventually they build to the point that you can't ignore them any more, and you make abrupt changes in your life, your lifestyle, and your general attitudes, as you turn to fulfilling the parts of you that have been left unfulfilled. The more rebellious your feelings have become, the longer this takes, since you only rebel against things that concern you deeply, finding an opposed alternative, even if it doesn't actually suit you.

Your humanitarian instincts may turn to interests in society, social work, social movements and alternatives, liberation movements, and such. Or you may lean toward the more technological side of modern developments, identifying with the aerospace and global communications era, or with the more science fiction-like aspects of modern times, such as UFOs, the Bermuda triangle, ancient astronauts. You prefer your world to be stimulating, unusual, and decidedly different, as you want to be yourself, not identifying with the mainstream in anything. You would either like to live in an isolated "back to nature" paradise (and you do need time spent entirely alone); or your home may be a busy meeting point for radicals and intellectuals, or interest groups of whatever kind. Some with the Moon in Aquarius are thorough-going materialists with a hunger for all the luxuries produced in the modern world, particularly elaborate stereo, and other electronic systems, and definitely automobiles, mobility and communication being very important to you. They use the external and concrete aspects of Aquarius, while the humanitarian idealists and utopians work from the internal and idealistic ones.

MERCURY IN AQUARIUS

Your mind needs a lot of stimulus and activity; it scans quickly over a multitude of areas looking for fresh interests and connections. Though this can make you a mental butterfly, if you follow your interests thoroughly you'll find that you do the Grand Tour, following chains of connections on and on from subject to subject until you return to your starting point, several levels higher.

The unusual is likely to interest you, whether it be flying saucers, yoga, electronics, aviation, space flight, astronomy, astrology, in fact anything that takes your mind into areas of vast abstraction, multi-level thinking, unusual connections; or can give it wings. The more totally connected the subject is with mankind, humanity, and its prospects and possibilities, the better.

You are capable of pursuing a train of thought for very long periods, tracing connections until you are well outside known territory. Because you care little for intellectual tradition, you are capable of great inventive originality. You want to understand how the universe is linked together. Unless, that is, you have taken the rigid and narrow path and stick solely to what you have been taught, never changing your mind or really thinking for yourself; though in the course of your life you may initially go in this direction, ultimately turning around toward openness and mental flexibility, and discovering the delights that you had missed.

Because of your powerful tendency toward abstraction, you can become too detached, living in a world of your own mental construction which may be a long way from the reality of the others around you. You need to maintain your connections with humanity and can do this by pondering on the nature of society and applying your thoughts to creating more ideal conditions for humans (allowing them to express and develop all facets of their humanity). Then your idealism needs to be brought down to earth and made practical.

You may benefit from being aware that the individual mind is ultimately not separate from the universal mind; this fact may help you to understand telepathic experience, or how something can be invented in several places at one time. You yourself can be directly aware of the telepathic network. Or you may simply find yourself interested in modern high speed communications, whether radio, television, telephones, data processing, or transportation.

You may find that you fall into the trap of using scientific, technological, or other jargonese, and become impossible to understand; or find that your thoughts speed so fast that you forget to finish sentences (presumably hoping that your listener will telepathically understand what you mean), or finish other people's sentences for them in your hurry to get on to the next topic.

You prefer the liberal and unorthodox in education, whether experimental schools or complete independence in following your own nose. You may be interested in promoting and developing intelligence, or in mental integration or liberation. You can be intellectually humanitarian, egalitarian, and quite without pride or prejudice.

VENUS IN AQUARIUS

Your values are aimed at keeping your freedom and independence as an individual, and your relationships go the same way. You are friendly, but may be detached and impersonal, in order to keep a certain separation between yourself and others, to avoid being trapped into any relationship that will inhibit you, or narrow your choices. You can be lively, effervescent, and liberal in your relating, and do not feel any need to follow tradition or to stick to conservative convention, preferring to be spontaneous and unconventional in your responses. Your reactions to others are fast and can lead to your relationships beginning very suddenly, with your need for freedom keeping them casual; and since all phenomena are cyclic, they may end as abruptly as they began. You tend to keep your affections on an intellectual level, allowing you to change them as rapidly as you can change your mind, though a part of you would prefer a stable and enduring partnership.

You poured a lot of idealism into your early relationships, but circumstances may have wrenched you away from those that you loved, leaving you not wanting to invest any depth of emotion in others if you were going to lose them and be hurt. Or, alternatively, it may be that one you idealized fell off the pedestal that you had put them on, and you ceased to trust so deeply. This type of withdrawal may leave you very independent, but also isolated and lonely. You may not admit to this, defensively saying "well, who needs other people anyway." The truth is that you do, having a deep feeling for humanity generally, and wanting to find the ideal partnership with another in a depth of friendship and mutual awakening. But if you protect yourself from loss by being detached, you recreate the loss that you don't want, pushing you further into your "who cares" defense.

You do not want to be stuck in a conventional stereotyped and unintelligent relationship, bringing up children in front of a television set; and if you are, then you tend to withdraw further into detached self-isolation. You need relationships that continually deepen in friendship, where you both open up, admit to and pursue your ideals, crossbreeding your understandings of the world and the human situation, and working for personal and social integration. You want to bring all parts of yourself into play in relating, so that they may grow and flourish until you can reach your full potential as a being, and you want a partner who is going the same way, so that you can help each other along the path.

Your unconventional tastes can take you into unconventional relationships, as you are ready to experiment with the unusual in partners and in forms of relating, also disliking jealousy and possessiveness. Your tastes will be very much formed by yourself, not pursuing orthodox opinion, but tying together all the strands of your own experience and preferences. You may like modern electronic and abstract forms in art and music, especially those that have a thrilling and stimulating effect upon the nervous system, such as laser light shows; or lean toward ancient, medieval music for example; or to alternative culture forms, like protest songs.

MARS IN AQUARIUS

Your energy and initiative is aimed at developing and keeping your own free independence. You want to be unfettered by convention, orthodoxy, or anything else that you feel may undercut your individual liberation. You are stubbornly set on being your own person, not going along with the herd and thus losing autonomy, ready to rebel against anything that you see as trapping you into being anything that you don't want to be for yourself. You would rather be entirely in charge of your own life, believing that every individual has that right and should stand up for it. You may also be ready to fight for the rights of others, even to the point of supporting political revolution, though you may simply support other individuals in their own struggle, not believing that anyone has the right to dominate, interfere with, or redirect any other being—without their total permission. You probably keep your freedoms by remaining detached from all that may limit them, not entering struggles but standing aloof, and thus being a lone wolf, an isolated individual in a society of one.

Your impatient energy drives you to move fast and do everything now, to aim for the freedom that you seek in experiencing beyond the ordinary. Your field of action is intellect, knowledge, and information, and perhaps society and humanitarianism, and you are ready to race down any avenue that stimulates your interest. In conversation you tend to leap from topic to topic as your mind freely cross-associates ideas, or as you become bored with pursuing one theme for long. You are attracted by rare and original knowledge or ideas, and can be a researcher of fresh and unusual connections between apparently unconnected areas, being fascinated by the interweaving of systems. This reflects a personal interest in integration, whether of your own being toward complete self-development, or of the universe around you—wanting to know how it all fits together. Modern technological developments may interest you, or fringe sciences, such as UFOs. You are likely to be fascinated by the inventive science-fiction possibilities of the future, and may itch to live there yourself, to make it happen now—to zoom off and explore the space-time universe, feeling frustrated by the limitations of the ordinary world around you. Your mind needs a lot of stimulus to keep it alive—and unless you explore the things that fascinate you, you can end up being bored with life.

You have a fear of being trapped, which can make you very wary of giving others anything to hang onto, or to use against you. Outwardly you are friendly but detached, keeping your individualistic differences to yourself, thinking that they aren't anyone else's business. You are very wary of committing yourself to anything where your trust has been broken in the past, which shows in being ever-ready to change direction, alter plans, switch ideas and reasons for acting or for being involved, all on an instant's notice. Your need to stand on your own feet may lead you into being a materialist, pursuing money and goods for their own sake. If so, technological gadgets will probably interest you, vehicles and stereos, television and video recorders, for example.

JUPITER IN AQUARIUS

You are friendly, free, frank, and open, and intend to live a life of question and search for understanding without being tied to orthodox ways. You want to explore all the realms of possibility and probability, to dive enthusiastically into experiencing what others hardly conceive of as existing, stretching your awareness of the more unusual facets of reality. You want to know how everything is interrelated, not with the deliberately cautious approach of scientific method—which excludes many things from the range of its investigations, but seeking to know how all patterns, principles, viewpoints and laws interweave into an integrated whole. You don't care what you consider, so long as it holds truth within it, for you seek a total overview within which all things fit, wanting to know how the universe fits together as a whole, despite the apparent multiplicity of its parts. You would enjoy being able to leap into the future and watch it develop and blossom, to know how the story of the universe turns out in the end.

You have a big, restless drive for personal freedom, refusing to be restrained or held in check by anything. You have to feel free to explore and to grow in your own way without interference, against which you would rebel. You feel more comfortable in giving help and advice to others than in taking it yourself, which could oblige you to accept others' views as your own, and you feel that would undermine your own free independence. You are willing to consider a wide variety of viewpoints as long as you have full free choice as to which to adopt. Through your life your independence will be expanding, particularly via mental, philosophical, and spiritual directions, and you will blend your own personal mixture from all that you explore.

In your search, your humanitarian feelings grow, and you would like to be able to reach out to help everybody. You have huge hopes for the well-being and betterment of humankind, even if your view of its current condition is pessimistic. You would like to believe in, or to promote, human growth toward an ideal state, whether political or spiritual, a Utopia that would encourage the full flowering of all human potentials. Toward this end you leap into humanitarian studies, considering the state of humankind from many angles, perhaps from unorthodox, alternative society, or holistic views. You may join organizations which aim to uplift mankind, or to promote social reform, or become involved in revolutionary groups and activities.

On the negative side, your restless changeability may leave you unable to settle down to anything for long, or commit yourself to anything, since that could limit your freedom. You may be undisciplined, irresponsible, and rebellious. You find it difficult to keep to a single track, impulse impelling you to go in every direction at once, and to overstep the bounds of social restraint to prove how independent you are of them (actually proving your rebellion to be tied to those things that it opposes). You hate being restrained, limited, or inhibited by anything, this occasionally producing claustrophobia, and you are ever-ready to run away impulsively and escape from such situations. Otherwise you will put on a superior detachment, observing everything from a high and self-isolating position, refusing to be involved.

SATURN IN AQUARIUS

You have a long-range desire to understand the order in all things, to know how every different system of order in the world and in humanity fits together and interweaves into a complex whole. You may work with historical and traditional views, or scientific and technological ones, or unusual alternative attitudes, or blend them all together in your search for the pattern of objective truth. You are particularly likely to be interested in the patterned processes of time and change, maybe in the physicist's sense as the four-dimensional space-time continuum, or maybe as fate and predestination, seeking the great plan of the universe. Your interests may also include astronomy and other space subjects, and perhaps in cross-breeding time and space, astrology. You build your own unconventional rules and traditions from what you piece together through persistent and serious pondering, which itself deepens your mind and your perception of form and order.

You see patterns of orthodoxy around you in the conservative restraints placed upon the individual in society, and although you want to belong, to identify with humanity in the mass, you refuse to be limited or categorized by belonging—preferring being alone to having your independence taken away. In fact you can be socially aloof, a loner, making a virtue out of your differences from others, your uniqueness. You can feel like an outsider and have difficulty in making light, casual friendships, no matter how much you would like to feel like a member of the group. It is possible that you are socially self-conscious, aware of your social standing, too stiffly formal or socially inept, over-cautiously slow, drawing back through fear of not being accepted or of public shame, doubting and mistrusting others. You then practice a cool detachment, emphasizing your isolated individuality, and saying "well who needs other people anyway?" Alternatively, you may have learned how to use the social rules to your own advantage, pulling all the strings to gain your admission to those levels of society that you want to be identified with, and naturally not the lower ones. In doing this you lose your independence and become a follower, pulled by your own strings. Your social awareness may be humanitarian, not discriminating but identifying with all levels of mankind; or it may be hierarchical, seeing society as a pyramid to be climbed to the top, to gain a kind of superiority to counterbalance your inferiority feelings.

Whatever framework you identify with, social or intellectual, or both, you should beware of letting your search for order rigidify your life. Intellectually you may turn every fresh point of understanding into just another dead part of your formalized pattern, squeezing everything to fit your pre-shaped conceptual boxes, turning the new and unusual into the old and stale. Alternatively, you may so doubt and mistrust all information received that you can never put it together into a framework, an incipient world-view, so that to you the world appears dangerously random in its workings. Or again, you may be stuck in a fixed interpretation of your experience, using a rigidly ordered viewpoint for security, no matter how many times you may glimpse that it is wrong; or you are socially materialistic, desiring to reach the peak of the well-to-do society.

URANUS IN AQUARIUS

Uranus was in Aquarius from early 1912 to early 1920, in which time Einstein's theory of general relativity was published and its first major proofs emerged. Science went through a revolution and was being integrated into society, with demand for greater awareness of it in schools and universities, the establishing of groups of scientific societies to promote application of science for the national benefit, and the establishment of the DSIR (Britain). World War I stimulated the development of aviation and scientific research, the first fighter and bomber aircraft being built. There were many social reforms including social insurance and benefits for the aged, and child labor was phased out. Astronomy was entering a period of great development, the structure of the universe being explored as it had never been before. C. G. Jung's book, *The Unconscious*, began a revolution in psychology, and was in part the origin of surrealist art. Jazz music emerged on the public scene, and to cap it all, the Russian revolution occurred, and the Nazi party was formed.

Being born during this period, you are likely to have developed, or at least absorbed, a social and humanitarian awareness, and perhaps an interest in scientific and technological things. Your mind is capable of pursuing trains of thought of an original kind for long periods, developing your own independent ideas on any subject that interests you, and it should be able to accept that you live in an ever more rapidly changing world. You can absorb and work with radically new ideas, and particularly cross-connect and interweave them, seeing where apparently unconnected facts fit together. You probably never feel that you have to follow tradition on anything, preferring to test truths out for yourself, rather than taking anyone else's opinion for gospel. You most likely recognize the need of every human being for their own free independence, their right to pursue their own course of growth and integration in their own way, without interference from any authority, while also seeing society's responsibility to protect and act in the best interests of the individual. At your best, you are highly humanitarian, and will be working for the promotion of social changes that will lead to the ideal society.

If Uranus had difficult aspects, you will be either revolutionary and rebellious, or rigid in your views. If the first, you see no reason to have to conform to, or be trapped by, anyone else's ideas, refusing to follow the crowd in anything, being a compulsive individualist, wary of everything that might reduce your freedom. You can be thoroughly impatient, hating to be slowed down by any circumstances in your speedy path through life and becoming bored if nothing is happening. You may isolate yourself as an independent individual, refusing to be tied down, preferring being alone to socializing. If you are of the more rigid type, you stick to your fixed ideas in everything, refusing to consider other points of view. You may support your stand by believing that you are special or different, perhaps identifying with a cult or group that sees itself as having the "One Truth," and that must therefore become the masters or the pattern of a new world order (like the Communists, Nazis, or fundamentalist Christians).

AQUARIUS NORTH NODE—LEO SOUTH NODE

Your pride sets you apart from others by making differences between you that are ultimately unreal. You prefer to feel superior, to be the center of your own universe and to dominate it, together with the people in it. You want to be the hero, applauded for your magnificent accomplishments; you hate to be commonplace or to have your pride diminished, your dignity assaulted, or your self-respect reduced. Your idea of honor and nobility turns easily into sheer snobbery, and when your views are not appreciated or not allowed to override those of others, you isolate yourself from people—pulling away from contact and saying you don't care. While you can be fiercely protective of those close to you, all too often it is because you regard them as extensions of your own being, rather than as individuals in their own right. You don't allow them the selfhood that you protect so fiercely in yourself.

You are in the process of becoming more humanitarian, of recognizing that all beings should be accorded full human rights and recognized for their individual qualities, no matter what your opinion of them may be. You are but one individual in the multitude, having all of the potentials that any of them have, no more and no less. Any self-development is ultimately a development of the human race, any personal integration contributes to the integration of the whole world. Where pride separates you from others and can dominate your mind to the point of making it into a totalitarian dictatorship, a fascination with the range of human achievement and identification with it pulls down personal barriers and breeds tolerance for all. Losing personal pride is not to lose self, but to gain identification with the universe.

SUN IN THE 11TH HOUSE

You are independently individualistic in all that you do, valuing your freedom and your differences from others. Your self-respect depends on pursuing your ideals through to fulfillment. These will include personal development and awakening, and be based on your efforts to understand the human condition, its relationship to this universe, and how it all hangs together. You identify yourself with your knowledge, which itself is multi-level—since you work at interweaving everything that you have learned into a whole. You don't mind how odd the information you use may be, or what the results are, so long as you can find the truth. In doing this you can go way off the beaten track into unknown territory, and find that you are alone and isolated, with few links to society or mankind as a whole. If this has happened, then your learning is likely to be ponderous and one-sided, becoming oppressive, since it receives no refreshment from outside.

You need the company of your own kind, so that you can share the study and practice of the truths that you have found, and find more lightness, humor, and joy than you can by yourself, replenishing and restimulating your interest. Remaining alone in your search you can become exhausted, sinking into a gloomy, isolated detachment with no roots in society, without nourishment and so dry and withered. You may originally have chosen to be alone because your pride was once damaged by so-called friends; or because you had to leave behind people that you loved—and don't want to experience that loss again. On the other hand, you may have remained thoroughly sociable, being the center of attention, the life and soul of the party, your ego depending on the feedback that you get from others. In this case you are well able to play the fool, feeling few inhibitions, playing everything for laughs.

Your drive for freedom can make you react against anything that seems like a trap, becoming highly charged and using the full force of your personality to break out. At these times you are wary and mistrustful, abrupt and impatient, and ready to slash at ties that may not bind you.

Your mother was an intense person, aggressive and intolerant at times, particularly if she ever felt that she was being rejected. She drove herself to be capable and efficient, and hated wasting her own time and effort on what she felt to be worthless. She was well aware of pain and knew either how to heal it, or how to inflict it onto others by stinging attacks. She didn't show her own hurts or her areas of incompetence to anyone.

Your father was more placid, preferring a peaceful life in which he could enjoy what he liked, indulging his tastes. He may have been money conscious, certainly conscious of where value lay, and he was probably creative in a material way. He was very stubborn in pursuit of the goals that he set, plodding away until he reached them. He would have been sunny and cheerful in self-expression, and in his way of interpreting his experiences.

MOON IN THE 11TH HOUSE

Emotionally you are lively and alert, liking plenty of stimulus and change, and being ready to respond to anything fresh and different. You are curious about the unusual, receptive to things that are out of the ordinary, and you gain a sense of security by identifying yourself with them. You don't want to be ordinary, you want to be different and unusual. Your love of stimulus probably shows in a love of speed and activity, a need—as your moods rise—to have something happening. You like your freedom and hate to be tied down or trapped by anything or anyone, preferring independence to limitations any time, and are sociably ready to relate to a variety of people who represent active and independent qualities to you. Despite this your main social circle is your family, or any group becomes a larger family to you. Yet you are also rather a loner, enjoying your free time by yourself when you can reflect upon your own ideals, and upon the more unusual elements of the world that you live in.

You garner your independence, hoarding all those facets of your life which give you personal freedom, keeping things that will tie you down outside the borders of your psychological and emotional territory. This can make you rather self-isolating in your nervous and tense wariness of traps and abrupt switches of mood, which do nothing to promote or help you develop toward your ideal of domestic bliss. Despite your independence, you have an ideal of being part of a close and warm family unit, but may raise that ideal beyond the humanly attainable, rejecting those people or states that do not measure up by keeping your detachment and "I don't care, I am not involved," attitude. You can be friendly while keeping your emotional distance, and are emotionally liberated enough to be able to play the fool and turn convention on its head, not being at all concerned with maintaining dignity or formal social display.

You may, at your best, turn your feelings toward the welfare of humanity as a whole rather than being concerned with individuals, except as representatives of the whole. You are capable of developing a strong streak of humanitarianism that may take you into areas of society in which you can nurture the needs of the masses, promoting their welfare, protecting and providing in ways that people cannot do for themselves—without ever taking away any of their independence. In this you will find the truly human family you need, and the wider sense of personal identity you seek.

Your mother was intensely emotional but kept many of her feelings secret, hiding them away from others. She was particularly receptive to pain, whether physical, emotional, or social, and she would either fight moodily against what she interpreted as personal rejection or attack, or respond to the difficulties of others, helping them to heal their problems and hurts with the nurturing instinct of a psychotherapist or a surgeon.

Your father preferred a placid domestic existence surrounded by things that he valued, perhaps in material goods, or in contacts with nature. His values and aims shifted with his mood swings. When he decided to attain a goal, nothing would move him from that aim, but if he had no particular goal he was content to plod along peacefully, and didn't like being disturbed from his rut.

MERCURY IN THE 11TH HOUSE

Intellectually you are something of a universal seeker, ready to consider any ideas, ready to learn in any area of thought, in pursuit of integrated knowledge. You are not so interested in individual items of information as in where they link in with everything else, since you believe all things to be interconnected. You secretly want to believe in everything, and in doing so to return to a primal innocence. Some of your knowledge will relate to, or be applied to, the study of mankind, of society, and of human awakening toward ideal goals. You can theorize a lot and become quite heated about the radical changes that you see are needed in society and in human nature. You don't like to place any limits on your thinking and you are wary of becoming trapped into any stereotyped ideas, yet you also know what ultimate general goals you want your thinking to arrive at, and program it to get there, using your ideals as guidelines. You need a lot of mental stimulation and you are also ready to stimulate others, challenging their minds into alternative ways of thinking, disseminating fresh, inspired, and usually humanitarian ideas.

Socially you tend to be a loner, having had friendships earlier in your life which you either lost, or which brought problems that left you mistrustful about getting too close to anyone. Your need for closeness and trust with others, and difficulty in reaching out to it, leave you building ideals of human relationships which remain abstractions as you refuse to be trapped into situations where your trust could be broken again. If you are alone, you want to be involved; if involved, you want your privacy. You remain detached and impersonal to avoid being trapped, particularly in communication in intimate relationships, though you may use your quick wit to play the fool or the eccentric to fend off those who come too close. Thus, though you can offer ideas for the healing of the human condition, you don't apply your ideas to resolve your own state. Your mind, in developing in isolation, leans toward originality, and possibly high intelligence, rather like the forced growth of a hothouse plant.

A part of you would love to stay with the orthodox society of your youth, another wants to relate to a society of people of like—and independent—mind, leaning toward the liberal, radical, or alternative type; in the long run you are likely to move from the first to the second, and eventually move at least part of the way back again. Thesis, antithesis, and synthesis; it is also possible that you could spontaneously break out into a totally different direction, in a quantum leap of personal change.

Your mother was sensitive to rejection by others but didn't want them to know it; therefore kept many of her thoughts and feelings secret, storing up pressure which would then come out in a powerful verbal attack. She tended, perhaps unconsciously, to play a push and pull game in her relationships, effectively saying "you don't want me? I want you"; "you want me? I don't want you." This is one of the roots of your wariness in relationships.

Your father's values were rather dualistic, for example he may have said, or implied, that money didn't interest him, and chased after it. He was inconsistent, perhaps sometimes tentative, in his outreach to those around him, and to his general goals in life.

VENUS IN THE 11TH HOUSE

You tend to be an idealist, seeking freedom. Your values are for personal independence and liberation, and you do not like to be trapped, caught, limited or inhibited by anything or anyone. You usually express a detached, quirky, idiosyncratic kind of friendliness, which changes very abruptly to mistrustful wariness if you feel trapped. Your ideals extend to your ideas on relationships. You have set up in your mind, at some time past, an image of an ideal relationship, probably one in which the barriers of alienation between individuals dissolve away into boundless mutual trust and understanding, as two free individuals develop together along a path of awakening to the universe. Naturally you may find ordinary, mundane relationships rather frustrating, particularly if you don't measure up to your own idealistic image in them. You keep your detachment in relating because it is easier to step out and let go if you have not invested yourself deeply, and you may play the fool so that it looks as if it doesn't matter to you, to avoid being hurt. You probably learned to do this after a relationship that you thought was going well came to a very abrupt end. You may set love up as an intellectual ideal, trying to figure out what would be the perfect kind of relationship, sometimes fixing your ideas on one view that you pursue with intensity for a while. These views are likely to be unorthodox, and for some will include themes such as group marriage.

Your mind works well with abstractions, being able to scan rapidly over and evaluate the relationships between different systems of thought or groups of ideas. You seek to understand the network of links between all things, the patterns that hold everything together. You are able to work with various viewpoints at once, perhaps blending them into one multi-level point of view. As you do this during your life, your values are naturally going to change, and it is quite possible that since you seek integration you will find it, but it is integration of being that you want, not simply of intellect. You may become too enmeshed in patterns of ideas. You are likely to have developed a love of the starry sky, the boundless universe, and a yearning to experience more of it.

Your mother had a "Jekyll and Hyde" facet to her personality, being charming in public, and capable of being very judgmental in private. She was very sensitive to any hint of rejection from others, being unable to stand being hurt by them, but could lash out and hurt others with little restraint. She actually had a powerful conscience that nagged her, and if she wasn't living up to it, she had to bury it—to make it unconscious, but she couldn't remove the feelings of self-rejection that went with it, so she projected them all onto someone else, blaming whoever was handiest at the time. She found it difficult to give of herself. Perhaps you can see where your wariness of traps in relating comes from?

Your father wanted a peaceful and placid life, a basic stability and security. He had an appreciation of materials and could handle them well, together with a well-developed measuring or evaluating ability. He most probably liked singing. Your parents are very likely to have had disagreements about money and values, your father having the values, your mother doing the disagreeing.

MARS IN THE 11TH HOUSE

You are energetic in pursuit of your own independence. You don't want to be tied down or trapped by anything, so you tend to be a lone wolf. You focus readily on the more futuristic ideas that abound today, and may have ideals of living in a science fiction world, or an alternative society paradise. You live in and through your ideals, pursuing the more unusual, but definitely individualistic, possibilities in your own being, having little interest in the commonplace. You may like to be in the forefront of new developments in society or social attitudes. You follow your own nose in forming your views on society and what it should be, never following the crowd but always being out in front. You do not like to be made to be anything that you don't want to be, or to live any lifestyle that you do not create for yourself.

Your lone wolf side may make you spend much time alone, probably trying to fuse all your various facets into an integrated whole, cross-linking to interweave everything that you are, but perhaps scattering yourself further in the process. You are interested in the connections between all things, assuming that every single thing must relate to everything else, and where you don't know the connections you may do the research for yourself, pioneering new conceptual bridges, cutting new paths of thought. The problem here is that you may end up as a dilettante, a "butterfly" of ideas, flitting too rapidly from one to another to gain full benefit from any, particularly since you don't like to cross the same ground twice. If you are not so much of a loner then you probably leap with energy into social groups in pursuit of your ideals, always looking for and enjoying the new contacts, but probably losing interest as the newness fades.

Some with this placing go in for team sports, enjoying the social energy, the speedily coordinated activity and the involvement with the group as a competitive entity; or they may focus on sporting heroes as their ideals. Others who like sports prefer solo efforts, needing high speed and fast reflexes, particularly gravity drop sports such as skiing, hang gliding, or skydiving. You may need such outlets to satisfy your nervous energy and need for stimulus. Some are very socially active, making most of their own first contacts, feeling that the initiation of friendships depends on them alone, sometimes being too pushy in this way.

Your father had a single-minded approach to his goals, persisting in one aim for a long time. His outreach after them was energetic, though probably stable. His values were self-made and he appreciated new things and ideas, as long as they didn't go against his preconceptions, which he held vigorously. He liked practicality and efficiency and couldn't stand fuzziness or sentimentality. He probably valued his own physical strength, and may have been stiff-necked with personal pride. When angry, his voice had a martial quality to it.

Your mother had intense drives which she tended to hide. For example she often acted in secret, not wanting others to know what she was doing, or why—assuming that others would get the wrong idea and reject her if they knew. She also felt that it was up to her to keep her relationships going, that they might fail without her efforts—so she was sometimes pushy, not realizing that she could be pushing others away.

JUPITER IN THE 11TH HOUSE

You are an independent character, preferring plenty of freedom and social room to move. You have a thirst for wide knowledge and experience, and ideals of growing toward understanding life on a broad scale, perhaps to understand humanity as a whole. Not necessarily serious or consistent in this, you take your enthusiasms as they come, as bursts of interests in diverse areas—which you knit together gradually in an integrated overview. Generally broad-minded and tolerant in your social views (depending on Jupiter's sign), you have a lively awareness of society's developments, of how and in what regions it is growing and where it is going. You have ideals here too, for justice and honesty, for a healthy, open growth for all individuals into a positive future. You are probably enthusiastic about the growth of technology, of better communications and more available travel, identifying with the growth society.

If Jupiter is well-aspected and in a positive sign, you get along easily with people, readily making friends among a wide cross-section of society—including travelers and foreigners, or rovers and free spirits of any kind. You join in with enthusiasm, expressing your opinions openly, ready to speculate, to philosophize, to be socially honest and outspoken. You may belong to religious, philosophical, or educational groups, and your readiness to be involved may easily lead you into the upper echelons. Your sense of social justice may fight for the protection of the rights of free individuals against erosion.

If Jupiter has particularly difficult aspects you may fight furiously for revolution, to explode social restrictions; or you refuse to be trapped by anything, maintaining a superior detachment, ready to explode or run away at any time. You may never fully commit yourself to anything—or may use your socializing as an escape route, a direction to run in if things get tough.

You like stretching your mind over wide ground, however unorthodox some of that ground is. You could be very interested in the broad reaches of the universe, both physically and in ideas, and can incorporate these things into your future-oriented ideals— perhaps pushing them beyond the bounds of current human possibility. This could be another face of your rebellion against limitations.

Some with Jupiter here are the life and soul of a party, liking pubs and clubs, going out on the town, to the races, loving a lot of laughs, and perhaps being socially wild. Others prefer spending much of their time alone, gaining perspective on the outside world from personal isolation, enjoying the view from a figurative hill. This view may be literal, in love of the hilltops, the fresh air and winds, the wide perspectives and exalted viewpoint. Many move between the two.

Your mother was either easygoing and tolerant, with intense enthusiasms toward life and open attitudes towards sex; or did not like to show her true colors, building secret superiority by silent judgment, hiding much of herself to avoid rejection, and ready to blow up and/or run away if anyone came too close to her emotionally. Your father's values were probably generous and open, perhaps philosophical, and his evaluation of his experience positive and honest; or he was moralistic, superior, and bombastic, and capable of blowing up and going on a crusade if he felt that anyone had overstepped the mark.

SATURN IN THE 11TH HOUSE

You are aware of hierarchy, rank, and privilege in society, and of the advantages of being up rather than down. You understand that it is a caste system of the individual's amount of power, wealth, or status, with total power/wealth at the top and poverty/submission at the bottom. You have your own ideas of why this should be so, possibly preferring to live in an ordered society subject to law, with rewards and punishments, and recognitions of personal worth.

Your social values and life style are probably conservative, orthodox, and traditional, whatever your personal brand of orthodoxy may be (most likely modern scientific materialism). You see personal freedom and independence as only proper within a defined system of rules and limitations, and probably assume that this should be so for everyone. You may define this as "no independence without responsibility," seeing the two as being equal. You may doubt your own ability to be completely independent, or may have a long-range ambition for total personal independence (however you define that, probably financially). Thus you may be a social climber; or be depressed about your position at the bottom of the heap; or if you are one of the fortunate few—recognize the advantages that you have, perhaps using them to manipulate society, either for your own ends or for its benefit, depending on your morality.

Socially you are reserved, having very few old friends. In your younger years at least, you were probably shy, stiff, and awkward among others, very aware of your status and dignity, or of what the neighbors might think, wanting social recognition and respect, and afraid of censure. On the other hand, you may have been a snob, aware of your superior social standing, of belonging to the right crowd, or being a member of the establishment. Either way you are particularly sensitive to social humiliation, to falling from your position, to the judgment of the crowd, or to simply not being accepted. Thus you remain a loner, an isolated and perhaps lonely individual.

There are alternative types; one who takes on responsible positions in social groups, professional associations, lodges and clubs, the committee member; a frivolous manipulator for social attention, the butterfly; one who seeks to belong to the ultimate social order or spiritual hierarchy, the utopian or seeker after the masters. Most are afraid of change in society, cautious about accepting new elements into their world, yet who would benefit enormously from accepting that many lifestyles are possible, all valid for those who pursue them. This reluctance to change often brings much frustration in later life, since sticking to the main social stream, being responsible, means that your direction in life is dictated by outside forces and you cannot do what you want, cannot pursue your own ideals to self-fulfillment, and thus end up feeling trapped by circumstances.

Your father's values were probably conservative. He valued old fashioned virtues, order, discipline, and restraint. He is unlikely to have been a demonstrative person, only giving physical affection or approval to you at formally appropriate times and for good reasons, if at all. Your mother, if she felt threatened by anything, would become cautious, reserved and controlling, her doubts becoming intense. They probably had problems with money, either over control of it or lack of it.

URANUS IN THE 11TH HOUSE

You are one of the world's idealists, your most major ideals being for the freedom of the individual, for human rights for all. You are likely to believe that individuals should be allowed to go their own way, to pursue the development of their own ideals and the lifestyle that goes with them without being diverted from their path or otherwise interfered with by others. For this reason you probably do not tend to identify with particular social groupings, cliques, or clubs, unless they happen to aid you in the fulfillment of your own direction, because the group has a mind of its own which dominates its members. You are aware of the herd instinct in mankind, of the mass mind at work, and you do not want to be trapped by it into subscribing to any views that you have not developed purely in and for yourself. Thus socially you tend to remain a loner, accepting the freely given friendship of other individuals as being of more value to you than any recognition given by a group simply for being one of its members. Yet your social awareness can give you a commitment to helping society or humanity to change toward the ideal.

You may also be rather a revolutionary, feeling that freedom from any kind of oppression or coercion by society, or any group, is the right of every individual; and that if that freedom is not specifically given—as in a code of human rights, then it is usually taken away by imposed laws, and that one must fight to regain or retain it. Sometimes rather than fight, particularly when you feel that they also have a right to their—often oppressive—opinions, you simply opt out, detaching yourself from their society and leaving them behind. Though your detachment is frequently purely mental, a retreating within yourself; you have a need for that detachment on a physical level too, a need to be totally by yourself for periods of time, emptying yourself of the jangle of others and discovering who and what you are as a being in your own right—seeking pure personal integration.

Your individualism is likely to be mental too; you prefer to develop your own framework of ideas on everything, trusting what you yourself learn or feel to be true, rather than ever depending on others' idea of the truth. Since you are likely to spend much time living in your ideas and constantly developing them, they are likely to cover unknown territory, or at the least, known territory from an unusual angle. No one will ever be able to claim that your ideas belong to anyone else but you.

Some Uranians dive into anything to do with space, UFOs, the strangenesses that hover at, or beyond, the edge of the known, wanting there to be no final limits on the nature of the reality that they live in.

If Uranus had any difficult aspects at the time of your birth you are more likely to be a rebel and revolutionary, ready to tear down society because you feel that it is dictatorial, dominant, and constricting; or you reject it and its ways completely, refusing to subject yourself to any of its rules for any reason at all, going your iconoclastic way by yourself. You are probably deliberately looking for fault in society at all times, continually rejustifying your stand to give you fresh reasons not to take any responsibility for anything but yourself. You make yourself isolated and refuse friendship, warily trusting no one and nothing. Your preferred political viewpoint is anarchy.

NEPTUNE IN THE 11TH HOUSE

Socially you can be a romantic, imaginative idealist. You would like to live in a happy and peaceful, green and natural society, not noisy, harsh, or bustling. You identify with those who work for the betterment of mankind, with the peace movement, with charitable lodges, with ideals of compassion and charity extended to all. You don't believe it to be fair for discrimination to exist in society, for limits of any kind to be placed on anyone. You have a problem defining exactly what you want out of an infinite range of possibilities, for ultimately you want the whole boundless universe at your doorstep. You wish for the impossible, while feeling that everything is possible, perhaps feeling that if a thing is possible then it is too ordinary and not good enough. If you can't have your imagined perfection you lose interest and drift, you can't be bothered, particularly with your own creativity in work or leisure.

You can't imagine being fully satisfied with anything; for example you imagine buying, owning, or achieving something, how beautiful it will be to have it, then are disappointed when you attain it and you don't feel any better. For example sexually, though your moods are frequently celibate and your needs disappear, when you feel the need it is an emptiness which never can be filled.

You spread and universalize your ideas until they expand out to infinity and dissolve into the void or fade into nothingness. This includes your religious ideas, where you found early ones confusing, though your imagination was caught by stories and pictures. You identify with the "innocents" and you would prefer to remain innocent. Wanting innocent perfection you notice all that is not innocent and perfect, though you may sometimes prefer to delude yourself. Socially you may notice crumbling and decay in the places and people around you, meeting drifters and drunks, and members of the drug culture, people that you feel are not living in the real world—even when you enter their world yourself. You feel compassion for them and would like to help them, since you prefer not to discriminate morally, to differentiate between good and evil, though you may belong to a society of people who live entirely in images, camouflaging their humanness.

Those that you relate to are likely to include people in the arts, theater, music, photography; or perhaps surfing and sailing. Close friends or lovers may be whimsical and imaginative, acting out fantasy roles and projecting their well-developed ego images. Some of them will be self-exalting, believing themselves to be important figures in religion or history. You may meet with genuine mystics or those of truly refined self-development, true "Christ-types."

You may not feel that you have many friends, being socially self-secluding; or you may have the illusion of having many friends. While you can feel much affection for others, you never feel truly close to them, or feel yourself to be part of society. You feel that you cannot impose upon others.

Your mother hid her tenderness and sensitivity, her vulnerability producing secrecy. She could give in money or affection, but complained that she never received enough in return; whereas your father could be sensitive and not mind showing it, being affectionate and easy to touch, generous and charitable.

PLUTO IN THE 11TH HOUSE

You should have an intense independence, refusing to depend on anyone or anything outside of yourself. In friendships and social contacts you recognize the possibility of being rejected by intolerant and bigoted social attitudes, the ones that refuse to accept or relate to anyone outside the group. You feel strongly about the underdog, identifying with the repressed minorities of the world, and probably want to see society transformed (perhaps quietly, from the inside, perhaps by violent revolution), so that equality, justice, and human rights are available to all, regardless of race, color, or creed. You do not mind who you relate to, and are probably personally familiar with ghetto situations and urban poverty, being open toward those that the narrow-minded would regard as the dregs of society. You are intensely against repressive authoritarian systems, police states, apartheid and such, including anything which erodes the independence of the individual—taxes for example—preferring complete command over your own life with absolutely no interference from anyone else.

Desiring utter self-sufficiency, you can be very practically inventive. You prefer a lifestyle in which you depend on your own resources, growing your own food, generating your own power, recycling everything for economy and efficiency. You may be interested in generating methane gas from wastes for fuel, using solar- or wind-generated power, in living in a remote place in natural circumstances and on natural foods, disturbing the local ecological cycle as little as possible. You may believe that society is breaking down, or that a disaster will destroy it, and you aim to survive if it does. You separate yourself from society as a survival defense, personally and in lifestyle, using total detachment to avoid hurt in case you lose friends, or they turn against you (this being an unconscious origin of your feeling that society may break down). You may intensely emphasize your differences from others to account for why you feel unwanted by them, why you do not feel like a member of society.

Alternatively, feeling the pressures of social intolerance, you may have fitted in, hiding personal differences from the group and agreeing with them totally, holding the same blind prejudices as the rest so that you are not rejected by them. Fear of rejection makes you lose your individuality by keeping it secret; by being one of the bunch you cease to be yourself. In this case you will hate certain social minorities, projecting all the intolerance that your own conscience holds for yourself onto them, blaming them for all society's ills (like the Nazis with the Jews).

Your father valued efficiency and self-sufficiency, and may have taught you to be the same. His values were practical and utilitarian, perhaps black and white with many intolerances. If so he was not generous—and had invisible strings attached to anything he gave you, so you may have learned not to accept things from him, becoming suspicious of his motives. Your mother was emotionally intense and secretive, taking things very personally, seeing rejection where none was intended, fighting back with sarcasm and possibly taking revenge. Alternatively, she was a self-repressing person, secretive, burying her feelings and refusing to admit that they existed, avoiding dealing with pain, hating the mention of death.

NORTH NODE—11TH HOUSE, SOUTH NODE—5TH HOUSE

You are prone to having love affairs as a boost to your ego, finding a kind of security in the appearance of love that they give and in their bolstering your pride. You want to be the center of attention so you like the approval that your lovers give you, needing feedback to support your self-respect, and you would like others to approve of your loves and your creativity, yet may despair of gaining that respect. You usually have to give yourself the approval that you need instead, creating a rather self-centered pride in substitution. You are inventively creative, but find it hard to believe others will ever be truly interested in your creations, and may abandon many of them, losing interest yourself. While your playfulness enables you to relate very well to children, you may lose contact with your own first child. (The psychology here seems to spring from difficulties in the development of your relationship with your mother.)

You need friendship in equality with other individuals of your own kind, and will blossom within a group that enables you to drop your negative pride which blocks your growth. You will come to recognize yourself more as an example of human potential emerging, and value the growth of all that potential, in others as much as in yourself. You are moving your center of personality away from your ego and toward fully individuated selfhood, which means that you need to explore your own humanity in depth. You are growing in detachment and universal idealism as your personal pride diminishes.

✧ 14 ✧

Pisces
and the 12th House

The 12th House begins, at its deepest foundation, as the innate knowledge that nothing in this universe is ultimately separate from anything else. Whether we call this the collective mind (unconscious), universal mind, cosmic consciousness, God, "no man is an island," "It's All One," the primordial unmanifest, the Void—no matter what the label—here is where we blend into the Whole.

Any blending of this nature, to a being who also has awareness of a separate existence as an individual, of being in a distinct place at a distinct time, is felt (whether consciously or unconsciously) as an interplay between self and universe. If the individual is very vulnerable and defensive, this interplay will be felt as threatening rather than enlightening. The prime threat is that, because all things continually change, we have to expend effort just to live, just to stay in the same place. If we do nothing, we die of starvation. If we do nothing, we lose ground, things then fall apart, crumble and decay. Thus it is up to each of us to hold ourselves together against erosion. To do this we have to create separative, isolating boundaries between self and other, thus losing the feeling of connectedness to the whole, at least temporarily. Alternatively, we sometimes use inaction to let things drift and dissolve, when we don't want them to continue—or when we don't want to invest any effort.

The time of life connected with the 12th House is the last part of life; in western cultures this is from retirement to death. If an individual has led a richly fulfilling life, full of real human experience, this time is one of blending of all experiences into wisdom, and of giving freely to others, being able to empathize with their problems and frailties. Then death comes as a final fulfillment, without fear.

If the life has not been fulfilling, if the being has generally submerged their own needs beneath those of others, rather than "loving thy neighbor *as* thyself," then old age is more of a crumbling, seeing death ahead as the final, unwanted experience, the final indignity.

The 12th House is the final repository of everything in life, the storehouse of all images: of self, of personal contexts and experience within them, of the society around ourselves in all its values and activities, of humankind and where it is going, of life, of the world with its past, present and future, of the extent of our awareness of the universe.

The 12th is input-output or mutability in four dimensions. It is where we make abstractions or build concepts (though more usually, images) from the totality of our world-experience through time, and act from them. Our experience includes both that gained through the physical senses and that from the psychic range of mind alone. For example, this is the place in which all the sensory computing in our brains comes together, and our fully detailed and colored picture of our personal world of experience is finally complete, including all our knowledge of our interaction and interpenetration with it, as apparently objective fact.

This area is concerned with our experience through time, with the patterns we perceive in life, repeated processes, scripts or roles we see, or rather interpret, ourselves as playing. We play the roles that we believe are ours, writing fresh experiences from the scripts, writing fresh scripts from our experience, playing our parts on the stage of the world (what we can see of it). We can write them positively, with enthusiastic interest in the outcome; or we can write them negatively, from fear and paranoia, seeing nothing good emerging from our lives.

The interpretations that we have learned to use to understand experience, the personal filters that place things in personally meaningful contexts, here become the final arbiter on all experience, on our very being and all of its mesh in the world. The images of selfhood that we end up with are all definitions that we have learned to apply to ourselves, ways of perceiving and of labeling ourselves (verbally or otherwise), personally held images or illusions. The same applies to our awareness of the world as a whole.

If our awareness of self and world is wide open, freely accepting, flexible, so is our feeling of meshing with the world. In this case we can allow that the universe is vast, mysterious, magical, and so are we, being inseparable from it. Our experience will then include the magical and mysterious from time to time, since we will not block it out. Stated in other terms, our connection with the psychically potent collective unconscious is open, and archetypal experiences can come into our consciousness. Obviously this requires that we accept things that others reject, be open where others are defensive, skeptical, hostile, even though in their terms this makes us innocent or naive. This is also where we can work with that connection to the unconscious, using visualization, imagination, symbolism, meditation, tarot or any other tool that speaks the language of the right brain (holistic unconscious). Such work is to reconnect conscious and unconscious, self and totality, once and for all. The work may be carried on in monasteries, meditation centers, schools of mystical philosophy, or lodges such as the Masonic (when they have not been taken over by the conservative establishment and turned to support its viewpoint).

A strong 12th House type (one who has the Sun, or several planets in the 12th) is continually receiving input from the surrounding world (both inner and outer) on a multitude of levels, some very subtle indeed. Such a person may never recognize this consciously, only knowing that they are beset by continually changing moods, feelings, and attitudes as the tides of the world swing this way and that. Or they may know what they are receiving, and be able to interpret the current flux of the world (perhaps generally, perhaps in specifics). If they have learned to perceive archetypal forces, whether they interpret them as symbolic or real, as abstractions from reality or reality itself (*e.g.*, in the form of spirits), their world will be populated by, and affected by, such things. Thus their range may appear to be from the disturbed to the psychic, their view of the world being somewhere between the paranoid and the cosmic.

Modern western mankind is taught intense separation from the cradle onward, so this is not his best area of operation, his most comfortable place to be. Separation experienced through the 12th House is felt to be somewhat ultimate, to be isolation from the universe, imprisonment, martyrdom, or the judgment of God. Forms of hypochondria can develop here for precisely opposite reasons; early psychic experience, if not accepted by parents or peers, can leave one feeling wrong, so connectedness is wrong; losing feelings of connectedness—when these are basically natural to us—leaves us empty, isolated, alone, lonely—thus not fitting in, misfit. So you're wrong if you do, wrong if you don't.

This is the region where the social hierarchies become very mobile, where people rise and fall along them. (I have known of several cases of people born in some old aristocracy—with their Suns conjunct Neptune—who, during their lives, saw their old lives crumble away, and were left in relative poverty). When the hierarchy was purely Christian, during the Piscean era, the rising and falling was seen as being the rising of the saintly to heaven and the falling of the sinners to hell. Now it would be the rising of the winners to fame and fortune, and the falling of the losers into obscurity and poverty. Here we have, in the theater of our own minds, perhaps played out in the world, the winning roles of rock star, millionaire, great discoverer, astronaut and so on, as well as losers such as victim, patient, prisoner, welfare or charity recipient, addict, asylum inmate, the one with the terrible problem. Each role requires others to play complementary roles; for example saviors absolutely require sinners and addicts to play opposite them, and may make others play out such roles, even if they don't actually fit. I emphasize that these are learned *roles*. At their best they will be the playing out of our personal, chosen, wholesome myths.

As the storehouse of images, the 12th House is the home of imagination. This is where our fantasies emerge, whether built consciously as visualizations, or arising spontaneously from the depths. In them we see the process of the mind writing scripts by taking elements of past experience and putting them together into something new. We may also see unfulfilled parts of ourselves expressing their needs in wish-fulfillment fantasies. Also, psychic experiences, or repressed elements, that cannot be allowed as contents of consciousness in direct form, are frequently transformed into acceptable fantasy images.

The practical side of this is that fantasy serves us first as an avenue of communication with our own depths, a royal road to self-knowledge; second as the drawing board on which we sketch out potential future experience, to be acted on in the 1st House. We also blend in past experience by reviewing it, and possibly changing it in image to suit ourselves better, beginning to rewrite the script. Since this is where we have awareness of time as a whole, including precognition (awareness of future events, since here the larger mind is not limited by time), it can be a potent navigation tool, being used to first design, then sense, the future that we want, and aim us straight toward it. Negatively, if we are obsessed by images of doom and disaster we are perfectly capable of aiming ourselves directly at the catastrophe we fear—so as to fulfill our ego-image of martyrdom, even though we may never consciously acknowledge what we are doing.

The psychological side shows in our spontaneous fantasies, sent up from the unconscious. The depth of the mind has direct knowledge of everything that we have ever been, of all our unresolved stresses, fears, and conflicts, of all our strengths and potentials; of everything we have been, are, and could become. It has the ability to tap all the knowledge available within our genetic memories (the whole of human potential) and everything that can be perceived through psychic connectedness with the universe. Some would call this the voice and hand of God. I would say that this is part of what Jesus meant by "Ye are Gods." Opening our contact with this storehouse can allow all our natural inner wisdom to surface, all the drive of our total being toward health and transcendence, toward knowing our fusion with the universe.

A being with a fully conscious 12th House would be able to slip from one kind of reality to another—where few are even aware that reality has many faces. Such a one would be continually in flow with the currents of time, always resonating to synchronicities, things always magically or miraculously falling into place in their lives. At the height of development their awareness would be able to move into past, present, future; move out into the universe or down into the atom. Here we have the full, unbounded range of mind, of Vision (which to the orthodox of our day, including the church, is insanity).

By comparison with that potential, most of us are in prison, knowing somewhere in the back of our minds that we are not what we could be. Since our surrounding psychic reality comes from the mass-mind of our culture, they are the reason we are so limited, they are all plotting against us, to do us harm (actually the reason is that we have erected the same defenses as everyone else, behind which we hide). Since some of our world does operate on conservative and suspicious defensiveness (*e.g.*, politics, the military) the world of the paranoid has some truth in it.

The bodily side of the 12th House includes the hypothalamus, the master gland in the brain. Its functions include control over our levels of consciousness and their cycles, from deep, dreamless sleep through dreaming, waking, and mystical states, toward cosmic consciousness. It integrates the functions of the endocrine (glandular or emotional) and nervous (mental) systems. It is linked directly to the cerebral cortex (conscious mind), to the pituitary glands (overall bodily control), and can take over direct control of hormone levels (body preparedness for experience, plus emotion). It is extremely sensitive to stress, and is connected with emotions of vulnerability. It also controls the fluid balance of the body, and through that, its ability to handle heat or cold. It continually samples the bloodstream, and turns on the appetite if blood-sugars are low.

Traditionally, Pisces rules the feet, once the part of the body that carried us through life, and the part that, if damaged, could make us most vulnerable.

SUN IN PISCES
✧ The Actor ✧ The Mystic ✧

You belong to the most sensitive and impressionable sign of the zodiac. In your early life you probably lived in your own dream-world, having elements of a fairy tale fantasy into which you blended all your feeling-impressions about everything around you. Often alone, or preferring to be alone, you did not have to build up any strong emotional defense against others, and could let your feelings flow out into complete identification with your environment. In dealing with others, this helped you to feel their feelings as strongly as your own, so that you could feel deeply with them and for them. Where you experienced any harsh conditions, you had no defense and would retire into your seclusion— perhaps to cry things out, certainly to feel very vulnerable, confused and very hard-done-by. Then you would turn to your dream world for solace, finding in it the perfection that you desired. Perhaps you added your imagination and hurt feelings together to produce a sense of martyrdom, feeling that the worst just *had* to happen to you, but that you would suffer it with noble resignation. There is something of the doormat or victim in you.

Martyrdom is one of many Piscean roles. You are a chameleon, capable of changing color to suit the circumstances. Your impressionable imagination can soak up images, whether story-lines from literature, fairy tales, myth and legend, or from religion; in fact from anywhere, and you can easily imagine yourself in the central role—inwardly living it out. Where you fixed on a role early in life, you may have later forgotten about it but still be playing it out quite unconsciously. Thus you are capable of becoming anything at all; or of imagining yourself to be anything, retiring into yourself and letting your affairs slide because you have what you want inside. You use camouflage, confusion, role-playing, and seclusion as your prime personal defenses, perhaps including the inward camouflage of drugs and drink to keep things hidden from yourself.

When you face the world around you, you are one of the finest people, capable of deeply compassionate service to others through your ability to identify totally with their problems, understanding what they feel like, and knowing how to dissolve them. Your sensitivity can develop into a deep refinement of being, dissolving your own personal boundaries into a close identification with life, and with the whole universe. You do not believe that there are any final boundaries, often subscribing to mystical philosophies, or entering occult studies (particularly where images are concerned: dreams, archetypes, Tarot, symbolism). Meditation is one of your most direct routes to opening your own depths.

In the world, your qualities are used at their best in music, the fine arts (especially painting but also photography), cinema, theater (image again), in the sciences of anthropology and biochemistry, or hydrocarbon chemistry, but ultimately anywhere that your imagination can be put to use, which includes practically everything. Albert Einstein was a Piscean, using his imagination to visualize the nature of space-time, and to change the world we live in.

MOON IN PISCES

You are emotionally sensitive and you tend to withdraw into yourself to protect your feelings, which can easily be hurt. This shyness can be neurotic if not kept in check, because your very receptivity can leave you feeling that you have no emotional defenses. In fact you have, those defenses being the use of privacy and the enjoyment of pleasant natural surroundings for relief, the use of emotional camouflage and acting to divert others, and the enjoyment of your own private inner world whether in reading or in pure imagination. This may also mean that you cling to your illusions for security, deluding yourself.

You are generally kind and giving to others, as you know how it feels to be hurt, and would not willingly cause pain to anyone unless you feel overwhelmingly threatened. Being very receptive to how others feel, and often sharing in their pain, you tend toward compassion, when not defensive. You keep much of the innocent imaginativeness of the child and would love to live in an ideal world, far from the difficulties of real life. Being sensitive, as a child you would have been a "cry-baby," knowing full well that it helped you to dissolve away hurts, but you may also feel imposed upon as you have something of the martyr or victim in you.

Your imagination is vivid and a great resource, nothing being beyond your reach if you use it to visualize your goals and blueprint your actions. Your worst failing here is to use it only as an escape route, avoiding actualizing your dreams because you already have them inside, feeling that to attempt to make them real is to expose them to being crumpled or spoiled by reality. You instinctively believe that everything is interconnected, that nothing is separate from anything else, and you may have a strong psychic ability. You tend to be a nature mystic and also have a very romantic nature, and can feel very hurt if the little thoughtful actions you are so capable of go unappreciated.

Your biggest problem is inconsistency, changing direction as your vagrant moods swing across the spectrum, yet in a strange way it can be a great strength. Neurologists and mystics both tell us that we live each in our own world, created by our interpretation of the raw material that pours in through our senses and backed up by the consensus of opinion of our society as to what reality is. You have the ability to dissolve old interpretations, thus dissolving the framework of your reality, coming closer to the true "ground of being," a path described by Carlos Castaneda in his books about his sorcerer's apprenticeship, with Don Juan Matus.

Some form of mystical or meditative path should interest you and be of great benefit to you; you have a hermit's tendencies already and time spent in a monastery, or meditation center, would put you more fully in touch with your deeper being. The use of visualization techniques in contemplation will open contact with the archetypal unconscious, opening the roots of your personality to your dissolving and remaking.

MERCURY IN PISCES

You have an imaginative mind which, at best, has a photographic imprint and recall of anything that you learn. You are able to use your imagination as an intellectual tool, visualizing the subject under consideration, and working within the image to test out ideas. You blend together everything learned into complex whole impressions, rather than remembering individual facts, which may sometimes leave you rather vague and general, but can also build you an encyclopedic mind. When your curiosity and imagination combine, you are capable of absorbing enormous amounts of information—rather like blotting-paper, probably with the feeling that you are not learning something new, but are re-awakening something already latent in you. You have a boundless sense of innocent wonder when you are learning, but if you have lost that, or have not awakened it, then you find it difficult to arouse any interest in learning at all.

Your mind blends together all that you know at an unconscious level, plus being able to dredge knowledge out of thin air in psychic fashion, and is capable of becoming very subtle and intuitive. You lean toward knowing by feeling, by subtle sensing of the universal principles that are involved, almost invoking them when you think about them, learning how they work by observing them in everything around you, checking your image against reality and reality against your image.

You are a romantic and a cosmic idealist, though you may not admit this to anyone, being sensitive to their responses to your ideas, and perhaps shy about showing them to anyone. You know that there are vast unknown realms to be understood, not all accessible to the intellect, and that perhaps some of the subtleties of this universe can never be known, unless by mystical methods. You may perhaps feel that you are confused and lost in a vast mystery or emptiness.

If Mercury has difficult aspects, your receptivity of mind can make you too easily influenced, and your ability to soak up all viewpoints can leave you confused, with a chaotically fragmented view of reality. If you lost interest in learning then you drift in a vague daydream, a mental landscape empty but for fantasies and wistful wishful thinking. Your use of your imagination on your experiences becomes entangled with your vulnerabilities. This, at its worst, builds paranoid thinking, ideas of martyrdom and persecution developing from the swing of your self-view between submissive self-abnegation, and self-exaltation. When your thinking is caught around personal illusions, it is necessarily chaotic and confused, usually arising from backing away from the world into yourself, and losing touch with concrete reality. It is likely that you have a conflict between desires to retire away from the world, and to enter more completely into it.

Your imaginative mind is of value in theater, music, painting, photography, poetry, imaginative writing; in scientific areas such as: biology and the life sciences; anthropology and cultural studies, particularly into the mythic and archetypal level of the mind of a culture; myths, legends, symbolism, archetypal psychology, going further in mysticism, tarot, I Ching, Cabbala, and others; and mathematics, most particularly in relativity and curved space geometry.

VENUS IN PISCES

Your attitudes toward other people in relationships are gentle, romantic, and rather imaginative, and you have a desire to experience the perfect, exalted, unselfish love. You are highly impressionable, and recognize and respond to other people's feelings as readily as you recognize your own, which can either lead you toward being compassionate toward them, or to retire away in order to protect your own vulnerable openness. In the first case you can reach out to others readily and sympathetically, making close bonds of affection (that do not have to be sexual, though you may be very susceptible), and finding or making something close to the ideal in love. In the second case you find it extremely difficult to open your feelings fully to others, having to hide them away behind a camouflage defense to prevent yourself from being hurt. Thus relating can be very difficult for you, and you may retire into an inner world of romantic dreams where you can find, at least in illusion, the great love that you want. Or you may displace it and look for a mystical love, a divine marriage of some kind that doesn't have to involve other human beings—or maybe you simply find it easier to love animals. Again, you may instead pour all of your feeling into the arts, especially music, painting, theater, and ballet.

Your sensitivity to hurt can easily lead you to feel that you are being picked on, and with your imaginative attitude to relationships you can elaborate this into an element of martyrdom, feeling that you are a victim. If you believe your own imagination in this, then you may fall into all sorts of delusions about your involvements with others. You can all too easily play a doormat role, deferring to others when it is not really necessary; or you may be the sponge, soaking up everyone else's feelings and losing yourself in the soggy mess. It is very possible that your early feeling for romantic or mythical story-lines leads you to store away inside you one or two complete romances as scripts, which you then unconsciously play out as an adult, without realizing that you are only acting something out—and are not actually involved in a real love. You may cling to your illusory loves because they are far more beautiful than real life, preventing yourself from finding true closeness with another. Remember that soap operas tend to lack substance.

Either way, you have a depth of feeling that brings you to identify with all of life, which may be easy or difficult for you to express. Your artistic tastes are likely to lean toward the delicate and imaginative in expression, the nebulous and the subtle. Your tastes may be very refined, or be very sentimental and over-effusive, lacking in discrimination. Whichever they may be, you would benefit from working on personal artistic abilities, in order to be able to express some of the feelings that you can express in no other way. Music, with its ability to depict the finest shades of feeling, should be a natural means of self-expression; as also should painting—for its capacity to give form to your imaginary internal world; or opera, for its dramatic story-lines.

MARS IN PISCES

Your energies are probably rather low-key, and you are likely to drift along with no particular focus or direction, unless you have a vision of some ultimate goal in mind. You are likely to be rather self-secluding, living a quietly private life of withdrawal from general society, not usually having the self-confidence to deal very directly or vigorously with the world. Your inner world of imagination is where you will have most of your adventures, dreaming of action as a substitute for doing things, perhaps reading of other people's adventures and going along in fantasy, looking at others' lifestyles and imagining what it would be like to be them. If you have more confidence than this position alone shows, you might aim to sail around the world single-handed, or paddle up the Amazon in a canoe, adventuring off into exotic places and braving the elements alone. But usually these things remain dreams as you give way to others through life, serving them in compassion, or never doing what you want in playing out a role of martyrdom. If the last is true, then you will store up inner frustrations and resentments, feeling abused in a kind of inverse self-justification, and may act with guile and cunning to get what you want.

You can be highly emotional, leaning toward tears easily, but also toward ecstasies when you are alone with nature. Your very sensitivity toward others leaves you confused as to whether you should go their way, doing only what they want of you (or what you imagine they want) and denying your own desires, or whether you should go your own way by yourself—feeling that there is no middle ground. Often you won't fight for your own beliefs, letting them slide into oblivion in your misdirected effort not to go against others, adding to your load of frustration. You never actually enjoy anything that you do in this way, becoming more sour and martyred as time goes on, and only because you do it to yourself. Continual helpfulness and giving way to others can leave you feeling that you have absolutely nothing of your own, and you then naturally feel very vulnerable indeed, and it is at this point that you finally fight back, against the next person that seems to demand anything of you, or to take something away. Since it is a last ditch stand, it takes on the power of a fight for your life—against someone who has done nothing. You yourself do the giving way, no one makes you do it, it is you that feels vulnerable and confuses your own motives, not treating yourself as being equal with others, though maybe counterbalancing with self-exalting fantasies.

You may have given up this whole battle and decided to lead your life alone, so as not to disrupt either yourself or others. If so, do you do the things that you want to? Or do you still drift and dream about them instead? You do need to act out some of your visions to fulfill yourself, to make them real so that you can find out who you really are. But you also need to find that point of balance where you can do what you want to, without feeling that you should be the doormat to others, while still being able to be of service to them, given freely and without obligation by yourself.

JUPITER IN PISCES

Your emotional depth and sensitivity is great, with tolerance and compassion for all life. You can be charitably generous and giving, without judgment or discrimination against others, knowing that all things are utterly interconnected, with no final boundaries or barriers between them. You can feel a huge reverence for and trust of the universe, believing, or knowing intuitively, that there is an all-encompassing evolutionary thrust toward complete spiritual development. Your faith may be simple and innocent, trusting everything to work toward the best interests of everyone, feeling that there is no reason to fear anything. Your imagination is rich and broad and you may use it in contemplation or meditation, visualizing and thus arousing in yourself direct understanding of, and identification with, universal principles or archetypes. You would benefit from a study of symbolism, archetypes, analytical psychology, or anthropology.

These drives may take you into mystical teachings and philosophies, perhaps pursued on occasion in retreats, ashrams or monastic settings. You will feel the need for periods of complete seclusion to turn inward and explore the realms of the mind, and work on returning to the cosmic origins of being. You prefer to hold a huge world-view that can include all other views, of an all-encompassing spiritual, mystical, psychic universe. You may be attracted by eastern philosophies, particularly those that see all things created as illusory, a play of the divine imagination, or a vast, theatrical magic show without real substance. In this case you desire to re-enter the creative void behind all manifestation. You may have a struggle between the desire to be of deep service to others, in healing or spiritual teaching work, and the need to pursue your own private and secluded development.

If Jupiter had difficult aspects, you may be very vulnerable and use seclusion as a means of running away, a thorough-going escapist finding many ways of hiding from stresses that you fear; in fantasy, in dissolution into drink and/or drugs, in building camouflage personalities that deceive others and deflect their interest from the real you. You use smoke-screens within yourself to hide a huge feeling of loneliness, possibly being socially gregarious in pubs and parties, where you can find at least an illusion of being wanted. Your trust is vulnerable, taken advantage of and misused by others in your desire for their acceptance. Your charity is an indiscriminate giving with no recognition of real needs. Where spiritually inclined, you are taken in by show and ceremony, deceived by false teachers, confused by vast, complex, and shaky philosophies. In your feeling that there are no boundaries, you are capable of leading a chaotic life with no final aim or purpose, adrift without a rudder.

Your natural involvements in life include: the theatrical and cinematic world; the fine arts, galleries and concert halls; hospitals and healing institutions; restaurants, bars, hotels—the hospitality industry; church properties, monasteries, and retreat centers. Your "oceanic" tendencies could take you into shipping, sailing, oceanography, or marine biology. In some sense your life will be a "mapping of the trackless waters," an exploration of an uncharted ocean.

SATURN IN PISCES

There are three basic stages within this position. The first is the person who is extremely vulnerable and fearful. If this is you, you allow all your fears and doubts to become boundless, feeding them with your imagination, dwelling upon all of your sorrows. You become a tragic romantic, writing for your inner theater scripts in which everything goes wrong, turns out badly, all becomes doom, bleakness, and sorrow; and nobody "lives happily ever after." You feel that all of the order in your life is going to dissolve and fall into chaos, that anything that can be trusted or relied upon will break down or turn against you, that you have no control over your own life. You have a vague, subtle, generalized sense of guilt and obligation which leads you to submit all too readily to outside control, sacrificing yourself through a feeling of indebtedness or in an act of penance, for example, to the long-term responsibilities of looking after an aging parent, or other elderly people. You may feel responsible for everyone and everything, including the state of the world. You feel that restriction is going to be imposed on you one way or another, that you are going to lose—and in timidity and fear you give up too easily. You see order and dominance in the world and feel that you are at the bottom of the heap, and you may find outer ways to express it, in imprisonment, hospitalization, or self-imposed isolation, adding to your emotional suffering and depression, your feelings of loneliness and powerlessness. Your withdrawal may be by blotting the world out through drugs, drink or any other handy fog. Essentially you have a rather paranoid doormat side that acts out the role of the martyr or victim.

The second type fights all this. If this is you, you impose order very rigidly in your life, against your fears and against allowing things to fall into chaos, to crumble and decay. You refuse to be ruled by anything beyond yourself because you feel that it is dangerous to submit, that to do so would be to allow your very self to be eroded away. You struggle to prevent yourself from falling into an inner abyss of emptiness and loneliness, yet the severity and caution that you impose on your life causes that very feeling by shutting out warmth. You trust very little, if at all, and strive to prove your mastery over your life, perhaps creating delusions of personal power in order to compensate for inner feelings of ultimate inferiority. You have to admit to being vulnerable before any deep change can occur in your life. In both types, you imagine your burdens to be far larger and heavier than they are, and tend toward the feeling that everyone is against you, perhaps unspoken, but an expression of your all-pervasive doubts.

The third type retains, or regains, trust in the workings of the universe. If this is you, then you have a deep, subtle sense of universal laws and principles behind all life, and a boundless, simple belief that all is in perfect order. You probably perceive this order as being archetypal and spiritual, both formed and formless at one and the same time. You may see your world as a blossoming and decaying of forms through time, of images forming and dissolving, but ever growing toward an ultimate end. You tend to relax all personal control over your life and let the universal powers direct you, recognizing that if your own being is to dissolve, it is to lose yourself into the infinite, to return to your source.

URANUS IN PISCES

Uranus was in Pisces from early 1919 to early 1927, during which period the old world-order was crumbling as a new one emerged. Alcock and Brown flew the Atlantic and Ross Smith flew from London to Australia. Airships were developed, the first helicopter flew and the first motor scooter was invented. Talking pictures began, the first color feature film was made and jazz was becoming popular. Television was first demonstrated by John Logie Baird, the first public radio broadcasting station was opened and the BBC was founded. Prohibition became the law in the U.S. Those born during this period include: Margot Fonteyn, Sir Edmund Hillary, Kingsley Amis, Maria Callas, and Peter Sellers.

This was an era when people were dissolving the limitations of the past and the feeling was that anything goes, amply demonstrated by the Roaring Twenties. The public image or general world-view was one of great social freedom and of unlimited potentials being open. Russia was in the early and openly experimental stages of the new communist order, the people were still in charge. Those born during this era have a sense of a potentially unbounded freedom, that the possibilities of the individual are unlimited. Thus many have become interested in eastern philosophies and mysticism, in meditation and yoga—and other forms of discipline for the awakening of the individual to the infinite, as well as simply trying to extend themselves beyond anything that humans had done before.

You have a combination of imagination and idealism that could have taken you into a rare and unusual exploration of the mind, perhaps into interests in depth (archetypal) psychology, social anthropology, psychicism, or to the ways in which the vast variety of psychological world-views are linked together in your own experience and that of humanity as a whole. You will have benefited greatly if you have studied symbolic, mythological, and psychological systems, and have puzzled over the nature of the mind itself, and you may have been led to search for avenues of liberation, seeking for a spiritual transcendence. Or you may have been more practically oriented and have used your open feelings for humanity in charitable work for the cultural opening and development of others, or have used your active imagination and vivid sensitivities in the sciences or the arts.

If Uranus had difficult aspects, you may have been impractically idealistic, letting your dreams run away with you, not wanting them to be tied down to the merely mundane, but spinning fresh ones that soar off into the wild blue yonder. You may have used a detached and active independence as your defense for your vulnerabilities, isolating yourself rapidly from threats, becoming very wary of probably rather imaginary traps and being ever-ready to change direction to avoid them, which from an outside point of view would make you quite unreliable. Since your imagination is capable of taking almost random elements and of putting them together into a (to you) meaningful picture, you may have built many false views of your own world and your circumstances, living in your own invented fantasy realm. If so, you may have shut out large parts of the real world, isolating yourself to keep your illusions intact, privacy and separation being a major defense.

PISCES NORTH NODE—VIRGO SOUTH NODE

You work to maintain the purity of your own being against an impure world, or you think that it is impure. You are sensitive to the attitudes of others and become meticulously self-controlled to avoid critical censure. You know what others require you to be if you are to be accepted by them, and fear losing that acceptance. You are also instinctively aware of all that goes into keeping you alive and together, and develop anxieties (particularly tensions in the solar plexus) about organizing it all. Desiring to keep chaos at bay, you develop a critical mind and eye that analyses every moment and tries to keep it all in line. Naturally the more picky you become the more impurity you see and the tighter your grip on everything has to become, until you are busy all the time. Sex naturally falls easily into the class of impurities, as finally does life itself.

You have forgotten the innocent trust of childhood that accepts all things as wholesome and pure, that leaves your world as a unified whole rather than pulling it apart into millions of fragments. You need to move from analysis to synthesis, from criticism to acceptance, from anxiety to whole-hearted trust. Now, instead of counting all the individual leaves, twigs, and branches—you need to enjoy and appreciate the forest as a whole living entity and to feel the life in it, rather than figuring it out. Your analysis is a way of retaining your separation from everything, of hanging onto loneliness, rather than accepting everything and blending into it. You will know when you are blending since your intuition will begin to open, demonstrating directly how totally connected to the universe you are.

SUN IN THE 12TH HOUSE

You are sensitive and imaginative, your imagination about yourself and your possibilities being richly creative. This can take you into a great personal cultural development, since those sensitivities refine your awareness of beauty, whether in arts or in nature; probably in the arts, since your creative drives are involved, and because you identify with the highly developed productions of human culture. You are a private person, enjoying the richness of your inner world, protecting your vulnerabilities from the outer. You may be shy, retiring, and lonely, your self-respect being particularly vulnerable, dissolving easily, often to be resurrected by your fantasies about yourself. Since you fluctuate between an innocent enthusiastic involvement in whatever flourishes around you, and a falling back into vulnerable confusion if it doesn't flow perfectly smoothly, things do not usually end very well for you, crumbling into disorder as you back out and let them drift.

Your flair for drama, plus receptivity to criticism from others, can over-dramatize what you feel from them, and play it up inwardly as though you were being martyred, perhaps even believing it yourself. You feel, consciously or unconsciously, that the role of noble martyr suits you, yet hate being the doormat to anyone. Your martyred feeling arise even when faced with quite small obstacles, because you are basically gentle and hate to force yourself against resistance. The weaker types use obstacles to put blame onto others and bewail their fate, becoming paranoid, preferring to believe that others are against them rather than cut through their own ego illusions, compounding their confusion; the stronger ones use such times to see where they go wrong, learning the workings of their own minds, enriching themselves in the process. You need to be aware of your vulnerable and illusion-building tendencies at all times, so that you are prepared to deal firmly with them in advance.

Your identification with all life and charitable and compassionate nature may show in a love of animals, or be used for the healing and helping of others. This could take you into hospitals and institutions of physical or mental healing, service to others being one of your "high roads" to fulfillment. You may explore the reaches of your own mind, particularly the collective unconscious, through psychology, or through occult or symbolic means. You are capable of consciousness of the deeper workings of the mind, especially of the areas where the personal dissolves into the universal; most of your problems and your talents arising from the fact that your personality boundaries are rather thin; compassion to others is your only worthwhile defense.

Your mother was outspoken, probably morally honorable and interested in philosophical, religious, or higher educational areas. She took a broad overview of everything, and taught you by passing on her experience, perhaps being morally superior and condescending, with flashes of fiery temper when others didn't think her way.

Your father's flourishing curiosity would dabble in everything, building many interests. He was probably intellectually or manually creative, liking to make things from plans, or to build mental abstractions from experience. He adjusted easily to others, perhaps becoming "all things to all men," his adaptability seeming two-faced. He may have been intellectually arrogant or overbearing.

MOON IN THE 12TH HOUSE

Emotionally you are highly sensitive and receptive, responding to slight shifts in the feelings of those around you. Your feelings are easily swept away by beauty in nature, art and music, toward subtle and perhaps ecstatic heights. You feel the feelings of other people, or any living creature, as strongly as your own, and at best you feel a deeply compassionate response to them, putting your feelings aside in order to see to their needs. You feel an identity with all life, and with the universe as a whole, and tend to marvel at its mysteries—and you want to dissolve yourself into it, losing personal boundaries entirely. Your imagination is caught by glimpses of the boundless nature of all things, of universal principles, or the infinite creation springing from its source. You would love to return to that source. It may not only be your imagination that responds, for this position indicates a psychic receptivity, the boundaries of the personal mind being open to the collective unconscious.

At your worst your sensitivities are vulnerabilities, swept around too easily by every influence, until you don't know who and what you are anymore. You need seclusion to protect yourself from the grosser influences of the world, loving privacy, yet ending up very lonely if you shut yourself away too much. This becomes worse when you feel that you are at the mercy of everything, unable to protect yourself, building feelings of martyrdom, of being attacked and hurt by all that you can't handle. You then retire away into weepy and confused states, your imagination magnifying the confusion by building self-justifying and perhaps self-exalting views and reasons around what are often imaginary hurts. You use emotional camouflage as a defense against others, sometimes being taken in yourself by the acts that you put on, making your confusion worse. You drift and dream in your own isolated world, letting things slide into chaos as you pull your privacy screens and your fog-bank of illusions around you like a cloak. Your view of reality is that it is only what your feelings and instincts project onto it. You are capable of clinging to and perpetuating your illusory views for a long time.

When you break through those views your charitable and compassionate side is able to awaken and develop toward its peak. You may then give yourself into healing work, losing concern for yourself in empathy for others. Your privacy becomes less of a need, and you will extend open hospitality freely to others. You may study, absorb, and work with occult or mystical systems designed to do the great work of purifying the individual until they can dissolve back into their source.

Your mother had a restless emotional nature, cheerful and outspoken sometimes, then flaring into argumentative moods, perhaps not expressing them openly but running away from such scenes. She needed plenty of space and probably loved being outdoors. She may have been philosophical or religious, either genuinely so, or just following her family habit, and was probably quite moralistic. Your father's emotions were active and inconsistent, changing with his changes of mind. He tended not to trust feelings much and overrode them with his intellect, thinking things out where a feeling response was more appropriate.

MERCURY IN THE 12TH HOUSE

Your mind is romantically receptive and imaginative and swings between drifting and dreaming, and applying itself to practicalities. Your imagination gives form to the formless, seeing shapes in the clouds, interpreting future possibilities from romantic myth; and turns the formed into the formless, thinking about events that are past and finished, imagining how they could have been if . . . , rewriting scripts, turning the real into a fairy tale. Thus you live in two worlds, the actual and the might-have-been. At any moment in dealing with everyday events you probably have another channel running, reinterpreting everything from an imaginative viewpoint, leaving you finally uncertain about how anything actually *is*. Your interpretations swing (perhaps through your life) from being charitable toward others but not to yourself, and being kind to yourself but hard on others; relax your defensive discrimination and realize that you are the same as them. You may have moments of utter mental abstractedness, losing awareness of the world around you, of who you are, what day it is—losing your way on familiar streets. At the opposite extreme you can be sensitively in touch with everything.

Watching your imagination, you should be able to see how your mind brings things and events into being, first building an image of something desired, needed, or feared, then elaborating the image and drawing the reality into being by focusing attention on it. You are likely to experience precognition, thinking about something, then having it happen afterwards. Part of your mind is continually functioning on a psychic level, but your awareness of this depends on whether your world-view accepts such things as being real; if it doesn't then you edit them out of your consciousness so they don't exist. If you accept psychic possibilities it could lead you into an interest in mysticism or the occult, though your interests vary with the openness and closedness of your mind, running through a spectrum from total involvement to complete lack of interest. Your intellectual interests may include music and fine arts, photography, drugs and altered states of mind, mysticism and symbolism, and perhaps Jungian psychology. If you use your full mental potential your mind is encyclopedic, reading and pondering many things so that you have information and connections on every subject filed away and available to be drawn upon at any moment.

Your mother may have been interested in the higher mind, whether in education, philosophy or religion, but her interest may have been lightweight. She could philosophize or moralize about trivial things, and her morality was split-level, censuring things in others that she would actually do herself, "do as I say, not as I do." She could be outspoken, and though apparently honest, could bend the truth to suit herself.

Your father was mentally and physically active, his mind moving constantly from one thing to another, bubbling with ideas and possibly with wit. He was curious and could usually see two sides to any question, not necessarily making his mind up between them. He related as easily to younger people as to older ones. He was probably good with his hands, particularly in turning ideas into realities.

VENUS IN THE 12TH HOUSE

You may not show it to the world, but you are a romantic. In your likes and dislikes, particularly where relationships are concerned, you are imaginative and sensitive to the point of being vulnerable. Your sensitivities to other people can run so deep as to be empathy or compassion, feeling their feelings as strongly as your own and being swept up by them, though for some this is only sentimentality. Naturally, being this way, you don't like arguments, contention, or even differences of opinion, preferring to be left in peace. Of course you want, or may feel that you have had, the perfect love—a sensitive, boundless depth of mutual sympathy, understanding, and self-sacrifice, transcending the grossness of the world. If you feel that you had that love, then it is extremely likely that you lost it, and have been dreaming about it ever since, aching over the loss, swimming in self-pity, a martyr to true love. You prefer your dreams of true love to the reality of a relationship with another human being because you want perfection and, well, humans aren't perfect. So for much of the time you would rather be alone, or perhaps make do with wining and dining and such, so long as it can be kept pleasant. You probably relate to animals more easily than to people.

You focus strongly on the endings of your loves, and of anything else that you value, becoming a martyr to the loss. You are quite aware of the dramatic potential of such times, having a natural feel for theater, for what the script should say next, and you play them for all they are worth—not necessarily very consciously, but in your imagination, and you may rerun them like old movies, always worth a tear or two. Many people need their illusions to protect themselves from reality, except that in the relationships you do have you actually attract a good deal of criticism from your partner(s). You choose perfectionists of one sort or another, perhaps not dreaming that their discriminating tendencies may actually find fault with you. Your uncritically innocent imagination needs that counterbalance, but you need it in yourself rather than from someone else.

You value the boundless mystery of life, taking interest in the psychic, possibly showing psychic tendencies yourself. Things such as the Tarot, or other symbolic channels for psychic ability and the collective unconscious, attract you. Either they, or your imagination itself, or a meditation discipline, will open for you direct communication with those parts of your being that are boundless, but you do need to know what you are doing, and not let your romanticism sweep you away again.

Your mother tended to build great hopes for her relationships, but was prone to her hopes being dashed, so she would just project them off into the future again. She probably valued philosophy or religion, but may have used them to create a certain moral superiority over others, being capable of some outspoken judgments. She preferred her values to be a broad overview, and a basically tolerant one.

Your father's values were intellectual, and could change and reverse themselves quite readily, particularly to gain acceptance from others. His judgment on basic moral issues would vary with his mood, from the tolerant to the more severe. Thus he could be quite inconsistent.

MARS IN THE 12TH HOUSE

You have a strong need for personal privacy, which includes keeping many of your motives, desires, aims, and actions hidden from the eyes of others (though some will act very much in the public eye). You may prefer to act entirely alone, feeling that if you are with others you must defer to their wishes or give up your own. You have many private dreams of things that you want to do or to achieve, which may go beyond the bounds of the ordinary—whether to break records, transcend limitations, or to be first into realms that others may not know exist. These dreams are constructed by an imagination that focuses on action, on doing, on going beyond by your own efforts. You have visions of your actions having great power. You understand, at least intuitively, that in order to achieve the impossible, or even the unlikely, you need to hold a clear strong image of your goal, and to keep on affirming it energetically. To this end you mentally keep your ultimate aim in view and organize your thoughts toward it. Much depends on the strength of your trust or faith, for if you don't really believe that you can attain what you want, this enters your vision and makes it crumble. If your belief is absolute then it is unlikely anything would stop you from getting there, where you are the only person to consider, and you are the centerpiece of your own imagination.

As a child your imagination was probably caught up by tales of heroes, warriors, or adventurers; of those who won through against impossible odds to glorious achievement. Perhaps your heroes were sportsmen—champions only, of course—or pioneers into unknown territory, leaders of voyages of discovery. You may use your imagination as a refuge from a dull world that, for you, lacks vividness and drama, a place of retreat where you can be a hero yourself, keeping your adventures inward and private—protected from erosion by reality. Some images may be of what you would do if faced with a fight, being vulnerable to aggression. You may hold scripts that program disaster for you, tales of heroic martyrdom, of striving for the heights and failing nobly, or being destroyed by others. You may use your images as the spur to achievement, the blueprint for your future, knowing that you can become what you visualize. Whatever the image held, it attracts its counterpart in real life, whether by automatically turning your mind in the right direction, or by psychic attraction.

This is the self-programming imagination, which writes the scripts that may be acted out. For its programming powers to work well, the scripts must be clear-cut, with no doubts or ambivalence written in, the visions kept straightforward and perfectly aimed, and action must be taken upon them or you divide yourself into real and unreal parts. They should also include the best interests of others, or you build self-centeredness.

Your father's mind was probably incisive, vigorous and straightforward. He liked debate, perhaps being argumentative, verbally cutting and pushy. He had an intellectual approval of energy and action, though most likely for his own actions. Your mother was probably interested in the broader ranges of human initiative, in the pioneering and adventuring spirit and the explorations that it can make, the ground that it can cover.

JUPITER IN THE 12TH HOUSE

You have a broad and active imagination which is capable of taking any theme and elaborating it into a major production, building on any basic story line to produce a complex dramatic development, generally with hope and optimism. This is a facet of a wide-ranging sensitivity and a sometimes fragile confidence that boosts itself by inwardly playing out your hopes, dreams, and wishes in inner theater. You may write yourself many such scripts, and those that you imagine most often are those most likely to come true in your life. Some of your story-lines may come from wide reading of classics and adventures.

Your confidence may be fragile because you are too aware of your vulnerability, perhaps blowing it up out of proportion within yourself, though using an elaborate camouflage to conceal it from others. If you do this a lot then your inner life is rather divorced from the outer world, and this can sometimes make you feel that people don't care much for you, but actually means that you don't let them know who you are, behind your acts. You are also likely to feel that you have to face a lot of endings in your life, and you expect some of them to be big and explosive. If you let your imagination play with this theme, then you are actually programming them to happen.

Your elaborate daydreams show a desire to go beyond all normal bounds, perhaps to be utterly without limits, to dissolve all separation between yourself and the universe. You may lean toward mysticism and pursue a vision of transcendence, perhaps through a meditative way, (some with Jupiter here being monastically inclined), or within the occult paths of symbolism and ritual. Your feelings are capable of being empathic, compassionate and charitable, actively giving yourself in service to those in need, perhaps in hospitals, institutions, or in charitable organizations. It is hard to define any single path for you since you outline so many for yourself, and it depends on what your confidence allows you to choose. You may choose the theater and acting, playing many roles on stage for others, and for the applause necessary to your well-being; or choose journalism to be involved directly with the drama of the wider world. You may project your dreams out onto the political stage, or into an adventuring life, the rule being: the bigger the stage the better. Your mind can be very broad and philosophical, liking to build concepts into wide and elaborate frameworks of ideas that attempt to include everything.

You may enter into the more elaborate social affairs, wining and dining, among others, with enthusiasm, though you are also likely to gain great enjoyment from seclusion. Your reclusive side may lead you to want to get away from it all into remote areas, in the wilds, by the ocean perhaps, or for the total romantics, onto a desert island.

Your father is likely to have had an open and active mind, liking to range freely over many broad and general ideas, and would have been outspoken and honest. Your mother may have been more philosophically inclined, perhaps being religious, but certainly strongly focused on ethics, but may have used them to gain moral superiority. She preferred to face her world with trust, confidence or faith, with a wide overview, and may have been a teacher or educator.

SATURN IN THE 12TH HOUSE

Your worst problem with Saturn here is that you allow your doubts to dominate your imagination, and through that, all your thinking. You let your doubts become boundless, leading you into very depressed views of yourself in your world. Some of these came from your father's strict or negative ideas, from his words being cool and commanding, from his reserve in self-expression; some from your mother's conservative moral rules, she perhaps being from a strict religious background, but capable of making you feel guilty (a miserable sinner, perhaps); some from strict authority in your early schooling, or your own slowness in being able to structure your ideas; some from discipline consisting of being sent to bed, to be alone and depressed, imprisoned in your room.

Whatever the case, you may have developed the feeling, generalized and apparently without a source, that you are somehow guilty and deserve the worst; a vague fear that something is out to crush or control you; a feeling that you have a penance to fulfill, a recompense to make to the world. You are very sensitive to ideas of responsibility and duty, perhaps ending up looking after an aging parent—or feeling guilty if you don't, feeling that you will have to submit to restriction and authority. You assume that others are negatively critical and judgmental of you, thus building imaginary fears; just another aspect of your depressed and fretful worrying.

You will need periods of solitude to sort out your feelings, but should take care not to become too secluded from the realities of the world, because this is the time that mental disturbances can develop, accelerated by depression and isolation. You may feel it to be difficult to achieve your more ambitious aims, and may prefer doing something behind the scenes, as it is less likely to cause you distress. You may feel powerless to control your life, doubtful about your abilities to deal with the mundane realities of life-support, including your occupation, and so need to realize fully that no one else is in charge of you but yourself. You tend to allow the disciplined structures of your life to crumble and dissolve, not maintaining them, just letting things drift.

A good path of development for you is to discipline your imagination to hold only images of the life that you would most like to lead, not allowing doubts and negative story-lines to take over; imagination is the mind's tool for drawing up blueprints of the future, and any image held is an instruction to the unconscious mind to navigate toward fulfilling it. Thus depressing images take you into a depressing life and wholesome ones lead to a wholesome life. There is a fundamental rule here: that what you visualize be as much for others' benefit as for your own, otherwise you are increasing self-centeredness at a deep level of the mind.

Take care of your feet, for the bones and cartilage can give health problems with this placement, or you may be subject to foot cramps as you try to grip the ground for security, feeling that it is not stable—a projected image of your feeling about life in general.

URANUS IN THE 12TH HOUSE

Your imagination is actively multilevel, interweaving varieties of themes and streams of facts into complex cross-connected structures. You organize abstract ideas into original forms, experimenting with them to see what patterns emerge, and your receptivity to current, modern, or alternative thought is high. You do not like limits being placed on the way that you think, preferring independence of mind to discipline being imposed from outside you (either because the authorities in your schooling were liberal, or because they were rigid and keeping your independence of thought was a means of rebelling). Thus your intelligence is likely to develop. Your feeling that all things are interconnected is particularly meaningful since your mind is rather open to the telepathic network, the level of mind where no separation exists between individuals. This means that many of the ideas that you pick out of the air are not yours at all, but come to you from elsewhere. Your need for privacy is high because you need to disentangle yourself from intense social input, and from other people's telepathic noise, just to find yourself.

Since your individuality is vulnerable this leaves you with a choice: whether to separate yourself out as an individual, or whether to dissolve into the pool of the mass mind by using a spiritual discipline, losing all personal boundaries into the mystic's fusion with the universe. For those who feel vulnerable about losing their individuality this is a threat. They feel, usually unconsciously, the pressure of all the other minds around them, and may connect this feeling with their mistrust of their own deeper unconscious mind, producing paranoia of the telepathic invasion or control type, (and you hate the idea of your mind being dominated by anyone else). As this position also indicates abrupt changes from one state of consciousness to another (a peculiarity in the functioning of the hypothalamus, a gland in the center of the brain, controlling awareness levels, often triggered by an intense focus on imagination), their mental control by others' paranoia has some real experience to build upon.

Your receptivity to developments in scientific or fringe science areas, possibly arising from your father's interest in such matters, can, when explored with your multi-level mental organization, enable you to become a leader in such fields, or in those involving the occult or UFOs. Your ability to organize instantly is well-developed; if you see something that needs to be done, you don't wait for others to decide about it, you simply leap in and do it; you also dislike orders being passed down the chain of command to you, preferring to be told first-hand if anyone wants you to do something. You also like independent cooperation and so does the partner that you choose, being ready to take on any role in the household, whether male or female. Your social opinions are liberal and independent; you believe that everyone has a right to his own opinion and lifestyle, that every person's fate is in their own hands. You lean toward a detached, compassionate idealism. It is also likely that your social opinions and your world-view will go through several distinct and even revolutionary changes in the course of your life, from relatively limited fixed ideas to very liberal ones.

NEPTUNE IN THE 12TH HOUSE

A lady with Neptune in her 12th House once told me that she had little imagination, then five minutes later looked at the shoots, each with twin leaves, in a potted plant on her windowsill, and said, "Look at those whales diving into the sea." You are sensitive and imaginative and have a strong need for personal privacy to protect your vulnerabilities. You feel that the world is held together by very subtle forces, probably psychic in nature, and ultimately mysterious and unknowable. You probably study these forces in some way, perhaps in archetypal psychology, tarot, through spiritualism, freemasonry, or other symbolic mystical systems. If your security level is high, you are fascinated by the boundless wonder of the universe and would love to be able to dissolve yourself out into it, to explore it fully. You have a deep faith in the ultimate rightness of everything, a tolerance that accepts all and can reach out to others with compassion and full-fledged charity, an ability to give yourself to others in service to their needs, which may take you into hospitals or institutions. You are capable of wholesomely taking on responsibilities for others.

You may be a connoisseur of the fine arts, particularly music, painting, and theater, and/or gracious living, or at least wining and dining, appreciating refinement in all things. Your life may be lived very publicly, very privately, or a mixture of both.

If your security level is low, your vulnerability invades your imagination, feeding it with suspicions. To you the mysteries become plots that are going on behind your back. You project your anxieties out onto the world, believing that everything that you worry about is real, your imagination blowing them up to huge proportions. You use your privacy to protect yourself from a world you feel is hostile, and in backing away from it you tend to lose touch with reality. The border between your imagination and the real world is a thin one, and may dissolve completely, leading to delusions.

If negative, your mind has a very subtle level of criticism that finds fault with everything, including yourself—though you may not admit to this. Thus your world is not good enough, and you feel that you are under attack from an invisible direction. Since you also tend to focus strongly on endings, the decay, dissolution, and crumbling of things in your life, and feel incapable of doing anything about it, you may add it all together into the paranoid feeling that the whole world is out to "get you." If you have little that you value in life beyond your dreams, you may inflate them into believing yourself to be something special, and let your mind mix this in to give a reason why "they" are against you. Or you may simply feel like a martyr, that you are a doormat or victim to everyone. You need to realize that you are causing all your own problems, however much you want to blame them onto mythical others. At the extreme, you could let the order of your life dissolve into chaos, and be institutionalized, or become the recipient of charity yourself. You find being responsible for yourself hard to handle.

This is stated strongly; naturally there are many shades and mixtures in between the very open type and the total paranoid and you must judge for yourself just how much you have of each, realizing that you can go whichever way you choose.

PLUTO IN THE 12TH HOUSE

You can be intensely vulnerable, your imagination playing with what you fear, such as visualizing what you would do if, for instance, you were attacked in a dark alley and had to fight for your life. Sex (*e.g.*, rape) and violence will be the usual themes. In self-defense you become intensely private, hiding yourself away, and, wanting to be invisible, pulling psychic veils around yourself to the point that others are aware of them. Your problem is that your imagination is intense and broods on your deepest fears, and on your most intense desires, especially ones that you can't consciously admit to having, which can actually make you feel that such things have happened, or that they are bound to happen. Where most people can bury or repress anything that deeply disturbs them, in you these things keep bubbling up to the surface, and your usual way of dealing with them is to camouflage them, trying to make them look different. You may be fighting to hold your own personal reality together, fearing that it is going to break down and crumble into insane chaos.

You believe, whether consciously or unconsciously, that there is a lot more to reality than most people know, and what is beyond the normal may both fascinate and terrify you. If it terrifies you, you are over-sensitive to your fears, feeling very vulnerable to attack, or even to simple criticism from others. The more you avoid dealing with your fears the worse they get, leaving you feeling that the whole world is hostile and may be out to get you. The way to stop this is to face those fears directly, and you will then find that they are almost all illusory. You need to overcome your fears since they leave you feeling alien and alone, and you have the ability to destroy your illusions by penetrating them with direct awareness.

If the "beyond" fascinates you, you probably understand that reality is the opinion held by the majority about what is real, that our minds hold together the world that we know, giving it a shape acceptable to us. Outside our framework of reality anything is possible. If you have gone through your fears, then you are capable of opening yourself to further realities, of undergoing a psychic transformation that will show you that your mind is boundless, reaching to infinity. To go beyond you must transcend your own world-view. You have probably already experienced clairvoyance or precognition as a preview of what lies beyond, and have an intense curiosity about it, questioning everything without exception.

Your father had an intense mind, probably thoroughly practical and knowledgeable about anything that interested him, but only interested in what was useful. He was able to work problems out like a detective, curious about the hidden—and about how everything worked. Or he may have refused to learn, not seeing any point in it. He could be silent, and also very sharp-tongued, being able to carve people up unmercifully with words, and probably with bad language, possibly being very heavy-handed too. Your mother was either deeply philosophical or religious, or couldn't be bothered with it. If the first, she was either an intense fundamentalist with rigid and overbearing moral attitudes; or she saw philosophies as working tools to transform people, and her morality was tolerant, being against causing, and toward healing, pain.

NORTH NODE—12TH HOUSE, SOUTH NODE—6TH HOUSE

You are subject to anxieties about your security that make you pay meticulous attention to the details of living in order not to be swept into chaos. You feel a need to rush into activity to organize your daily living, nervously making sure that every detail is accounted for, fighting against chaos. This can exhaust you, but also gives you the excuse for self-pity or for resentment. Your analytical tendency develops to the point where you are critical of every imagined imperfection that you see in your world and in other people. You perhaps use this to make yourself feel more perfect by comparison. You divide your world into small, categorized compartments which become smaller and more numerous as time goes on, trying to understand the functions of all things by splitting them into their component parts. In doing this you do not allow yourself to be aware that the world is also an integrated whole, fused together in a subtle and mysterious way.

As you develop a more holistic awareness you will find that your worries drop away, your simple trust in the universe develops, your nervousness vanishes. You become more aware of life as flowing in and through everything including yourself, learning to lose the personal boundaries set up by analysis. You may have been trying to avoid contamination by life, but your newer view sees perfection in all, including such things as bacteria and decay. From buzzing activity you move to loving your privacy and contemplative times, as you also go from the flurry of maintaining your own life to a compassionate helpfulness in that of others.

✧ 15 ✧

Where to Go From Here

If you find that your interest in astrology is strong, and you want to learn more about it and develop your skills in calculating charts and interpreting them, what do you do next?

There are a large number of books on the market that can help you to learn to cast a chart, while also teaching you more of the traditional fundamentals of astrology than I have included in this book (my personal approach is more experimental and explorative than traditional).

Among these books are short and reasonably simple ones, such as Ronald C. Davison's *Astrology*, and Jeff Mayo's *Teach Yourself Astrology*, as well as many books containing more detail. These include *The New Waite's Compendium of Natal Astrology*, which has been around since 1917, though currently out of print, and which contains a condensed ephemeris for a hundred years, house tables covering many degrees of latitude, and a fully detailed approach to calculating charts; another major introduction to astrology is found in Llewellyn George's *A to Z Horoscope Maker and Delineator*.

Many people find it easier to study astrology through classes, at which they can ask questions, and get their own work checked by an expert instructor. There are usually classes available in any city, some run within the normal night schools, some by local astrological associations.

What more do you need to know? Well, the approach taken in this book is designed for ease and simplicity, not for full inclusion of all facets of astrology. First, you would need to learn the conventional approach to calculating sidereal time; then the use of accurate house tables to calculate house cusps to the degree and minute of arc; next the use of an accurate daily ephemeris to pinpoint the planetary positions. The material in this book is fully adequate to teach you about the general meanings or effects of the positions of planets in signs and houses, though you would need to know the astrological theories that stand behind them. From there you would need to learn about planetary aspects, which have not been included in this book, but which constitute possibly the most major part of astrology. Unfortunately, I know of no books that I personally consider to give a deep or fully accurate view of the mundane houses or of planetary aspects; though modern astrology is developing, it has a long way to go before it fulfills its potential. I intend to do what I can to produce such books over the next few years.

I would recommend that while you are learning astrology, you try from the beginning to integrate within that new knowledge subjects with which you are already familiar. My own previous studies included several approaches to psychology studied as aids to understanding eastern philosophies of human awakening. Along with these, I found several approaches to understanding symbolism and mythology and the nature of archetypes invaluable. My preferences there included the Tarot and the Cabala, and Jung's writings on archetypal psychology, and the Greek myths of the planetary deities. Think of it this way: the mathematical side of astrology requires the use of your left brain hemisphere's abilities in analysis, mathematics, and precision. Any development of those will help you to construct and to analyze charts, and to progress them. The symbolic side of astrology needs your right brain's abilities in understanding symbolism, its holistic talents to sift through and blend the relationships between the archetypal elements of the chart (planets, signs, houses, aspects). Here is where your richest growth in exploring the deep layers of meaning in astrology will come from.

For myself, I was also interested in physics, which I found useful in understanding the foundation of natural laws and processes; in solar system astronomy, which helped me to place everything I did in astrology into its wider context; in weather and climate, which helped me in observing the continual flow of current planetary aspects and what they were doing to our weather. But these are of very broad use; what I perhaps found most useful was to erect charts for friends, and then to interpret the chart with them, and to ask them whether this was how it worked, was this the way they experienced themselves and their own lives? In this way you can get direct feedback as you learn, everybody becomes your teacher (though I would also say that few people know themselves in great depth, at least early in their lives; the older they are, the better the chance that they have learned to know themselves).

I have tried to give you some clues to understanding the standard pattern of human development in the introductions to the signs and houses. You can, if you begin with an accurate chart, use these to explore the life development of each individual, by turning the whole chart around to "where they are now"; for instance, if in their 20s, to the 9th House; if from 30 to 45, to the 10th House; 45 to 60, to their 11th House, and so forth; and read the chart from there as being their current experience of life, their 9th—or whatever—House as being their current 1st House, with all the remainder of the houses rotated to match (10th becomes 2nd; 11th becomes 3rd . . .). In this way, their current house framework, and house rulerships, change through time, matching their growing experience. Their natal pattern of aspects shifts its meanings as the rulerships change, changing the whole emphasis of how they use or respond to them, as well as changing their house placing in the rotated chart.

This technique can bear great fruit when learned early in your use of astrology and developed over time. There are many other such methods, not all currently known, as this one wasn't until I found it through exploring and experimenting. Whatever you do, don't ever just take any *authority's* word for what works and what doesn't in astrology, or anything else for that matter. If you do, you will have learned a set of opinions, and little else. Find out for yourself, and in so doing help your own abilities to learn, to explore, and to understand to grow and flourish. May you find as great an interest and enjoyment in astrology as I have. May your mind awaken beyond all limits.

✧ Appendix ✧

EPHEMERIS TABLES

Sun, Mercury, Venus, and Mars

Jupiter, Saturn, Uranus, Neptune, and Pluto

The Nodes

The Moon

Ephemeris Tables for Sun, Mercury, Venus and Mars

00Date	Sun	Mercury	Venus	Mars
01/01/1900	10Cap39	19Sag38	07Aqu00	14Cap15
01/06/1900	15Cap45	26Sag21	13Aqu12	18Cap07
01/11/1900	20Cap51	03Cap28	19Aqu24	21Cap59
01/16/1900	25Cap57	10Cap52	25Aqu36	25Cap52
01/21/1900	01Aqu02	18Cap31	01Pis46	29Cap46
01/26/1900	06Aqu07	26Cap25	07Pis55	03Aqu41
01/31/1900	11Aqu12	04Aqu35	14Pis04	07Aqu37
02/05/1900	16Aqu16	13Aqu03	20Pis10	11Aqu32
02/10/1900	21Aqu19	21Aqu49	26Pis16	15Aqu28
02/15/1900	26Aqu23	00Pis56	02Ari18	19Aqu25
02/20/1900	01Pis26	10Pis14	08Ari20	23Aqu21
02/25/1900	06Pis28	19Pis27	14Ari19	27Aqu18
03/02/1900	11Pis29	27Pis55	20Ari16	01Pis15
03/07/1900	16Pis29	04Ari37	26Ari10	05Pis12
03/12/1900	21Pis29	08Ari30	02Tau02	09Pis08
03/17/1900	26Pis28	08Ari54	07Tau50	13Pis04
03/22/1900	01Ari25	06Ari12	13Tau34	17Pis00
03/27/1900	06Ari22	01Ari58	19Tau15	20Pis55
04/01/1900	11Ari18	28Pis19	24Tau50	24Pis49
04/ 6/1900	16Ari13	26Pis36	00Gem21	28Pis43
04/11/1900	21Ari08	27Pis07	05Gem45	02Ari36
04/16/1900	26Ari02	29Pis37	11Gem03	06Ari28
04/21/1900	00Tau55	03Ari42	16Gem14	10Ari19
04/26/1900	05Tau47	09Ari03	21Gem15	14Ari10
05/01/1900	10Tau38	15Ari25	26Gem06	17Ari59
05/ 6/1900	15Tau29	22Ari42	00Can45	21Ari48
05/11/1900	20Tau19	00Tau50	05Can10	25Ari35
05/16/1900	25Tau08	09Tau48	09Can18	29Ari21
05/21/1900	29Tau57	19Tau36	13Can06	03Tau06
05/26/1900	04Gem45	00Gem07	16Can28	06Tau49
05/31/1900	09Gem33	11Gem03	19Can21	10Tau31
06/05/1900	14Gem20	21Gem55	21Can39	14Tau12
06/10/1900	19Gem07	02Can13	23Can13	17Tau51
06/15/1900	23Gem53	11Can38	23Can57	21Tau28
06/20/1900	28Gem40	20Can04	23Can45	25Tau05
06/25/1900	03Can25	27Can29	22Can33	28Tau39
06/30/1900	08Can12	03Leo49	20Can25	02Gem13
07/05/1900	12Can58	08Leo58	17Can37	05Gem44
07/10/1900	17Can44	12Leo45	14Can30	09Gem14
07/15/1900	22Can30	14Leo52	11Can36	12Gem42
07/20/1900	27Can16	15Leo06	09Can18	16Gem09
07/25/1900	02Leo03	13Leo18	07Can54	19Gem34
07/30/1900	06Leo49	09Leo59	07Can30	22Gem57
08/04/1900	11Leo36	06Leo21	08Can02	26Gem19
08/ 9/1900	16Leo24	04Leo03	09Can25	29Gem38
08/14/1900	21Leo12	04Leo17	11Can34	02Can56
08/19/1900	26Leo01	07Leo30	14Can19	06Can12
08/24/1900	00Vir50	13Leo30	17Can34	09Can25
08/29/1900	05Vir39	21Leo37	21Can16	12Can37
09/03/1900	10Vir30	00Vir55	25Can19	15Can47
09/08/1900	15Vir21	10Vir33	29Can40	18Can55
09/13/1900	20Vir13	20Vir03	04Leo16	22Can00
09/18/1900	25Vir06	29Vir10	09Leo04	25Can03
09/23/1900	29Vir59	07Lib52	14Leo04	28Can04
09/28/1900	04Lib54	16Lib11	19Leo13	01Leo01

Date	Sun	Mercury	Venus	Mars
10/03/1900	09Lib49	24Lib07	24Leo31	03Leo57
10/08/1900	14Lib45	01Sco43	29Leo55	06Leo49
10/13/1900	19Lib42	09Sco00	05Vir27	09Leo37
10/18/1900	24Lib39	15Sco54	11Vir04	12Leo23
10/23/1900	29Lib37	22Sco22	16Vir45	15Leo04
10/28/1900	04Sco37	28Sco10	22Vir31	17Leo42
11/02/1900	09Sco37	02Sag55	28Vir22	20Leo16
11/07/1900	14Sco38	05Sag51	04Lib15	22Leo45
11/12/1900	19Sco40	05Sag47	10Lib12	25Leo08
11/17/1900	24Sco42	01Sag42	16Lib11	27Leo26
11/22/1900	29Sco45	25Sco07	22Lib13	29Leo37
11/27/1900	04Sag49	20Sco39	28Lib16	01Vir42
12/02/1900	09Sag53	20Sco40	04Sco22	03Vir39
12/07/1900	14Sag57	24Sco16	10Sco30	05Vir27
12/12/1900	20Sag02	29Sco51	16Sco38	07Vir06
12/17/1900	25Sag07	06Sag25	22Sco48	08Vir34
12/22/1900	00Cap13	13Sag31	28Sco58	09Vir50
12/27/1900	05Cap19	20Sag53	05Sag10	10Vir53
01/01/1901	10Cap25	28Sag27	11Sag22	11Vir42
01/06/1901	15Cap30	06Cap09	17Sag35	12Vir15
01/11/1901	20Cap36	14Cap02	23Sag48	12Vir30
01/16/1901	25Cap42	22Cap06	00Cap01	12Vir28
01/21/1901	00Aqu47	00Aqu23	06Cap15	12Vir05
01/26/1901	05Aqu52	08Aqu55	12Cap29	11Vir23
01/31/1901	10Aqu57	17Aqu40	18Cap43	10Vir21
02/05/1901	16Aqu01	26Aqu34	24Cap57	09Vir01
02/10/1901	21Aqu05	05Pis18	01Aqu11	07Vir24
02/15/1901	26Aqu08	13Pis14	07Aqu25	05Vir35
02/20/1901	01Pis11	19Pis14	13Aqu39	03Vir38
02/25/1901	06Pis13	22Pis01	19Aqu53	01Vir39
03/02/1901	11Pis14	20Pis51	26Aqu07	29Leo43
03/07/1901	16Pis15	16Pis40	02Pis21	27Leo56
03/12/1901	21Pis14	11Pis52	08Pis34	26Leo22
03/17/1901	26Pis13	08Pis47	14Pis48	25Leo04
03/22/1901	01Ari10	08Pis13	21Pis00	24Leo05
03/27/1901	06Ari07	09Pis57	27Pis13	23Leo25
04/01/1901	11Ari04	13Pis29	03Ari24	23Leo06
04/06/1901	15Ari59	18Pis22	09Ari36	23Leo04
04/11/1901	20Ari54	24Pis19	15Ari48	23Leo21
04/16/1901	25Ari48	01Ari07	21Ari59	23Leo55
04/21/1901	00Tau40	08Ari42	28Ari10	24Leo43
04/26/1901	05Tau33	17Ari00	04Tau21	25Leo46
05/01/1901	10Tau24	26Ari01	10Tau31	27Leo01
05/06/1901	15Tau15	05Tau48	16Tau41	28Leo27
05/11/1901	20Tau04	16Tau13	22Tau51	00Vir04
05/16/1901	24Tau54	27Tau05	29Tau00	1Vir50
05/21/1901	29Tau43	07Gem55	05Gem09	03Vir44
05/26/1901	04Gem31	18Gem10	11Gem18	05Vir46
05/31/1901	09Gem19	27Gem28	17Gem27	07Vir54
06/05/1901	14Gem06	05Can37	23Gem35	10Vir09
06/10/1901	18Gem53	12Can35	29Gem43	12Vir29
06/15/1901	23Gem39	18Can16	05Can51	14Vir55
06/20/1901	28Gem25	22Can32	11Can59	17Vir25
06/25/1901	03Can12	25Can10	18Can06	20Vir00
06/30/1901	07Can58	25Can59	24Can13	22Vir38

Ephemeris Tables for Sun, Mercury, Venus and Mars

00Date	Sun	Mercury	Venus	Mars
07/05/1901	12Can44	24Can55	00Leo21	25Vir21
07/10/1901	17Can30	22Can18	06Leo27	28Vir07
07/15/1901	22Can16	19Can05	12Leo34	00Lib57
07/20/1901	27Can02	16Can37	18Leo40	03Lib49
07/25/1901	01Leo49	16Can00	24Leo46	06Lib45
07/30/1901	06Leo36	17Can50	00Vir51	09Lib44
08/04/1901	11Leo22	22Can12	06Vir56	12Lib45
08/09/1901	16Leo10	28Can54	13Vir01	15Lib49
08/14/1901	20Leo58	07Leo28	19Vir05	18Lib56
08/19/1901	25Leo46	17Leo08	25Vir08	22Lib06
08/24/1901	00Vir36	27Leo09	01Lib11	25Lib17
08/29/1901	05Vir25	06Vir59	07Lib13	28Lib31
09/03/1901	10Vir16	16Vir23	13Lib15	01Sco48
09/08/1901	15Vir07	25Vir18	19Lib15	05Sco06
09/13/1901	19Vir59	03Lib43	25Lib15	08Sco27
09/18/1901	24Vir51	11Lib42	01Sco13	11Sco50
09/23/1901	29Vir45	19Lib15	07Sco11	15Sco15
09/28/1901	04Lib39	26Lib22	13Sco07	18Sco42
10/03/1901	09Lib34	03Sco01	19Sco03	22Sco12
10/ 8/1901	14Lib30	09Sco04	24Sco57	25Sco43
10/13/1901	19Lib27	14Sco20	00Sag49	29Sco16
10/18/1901	24Lib25	18Sco20	06Sag40	02Sag51
10/23/1901	29Lib23	20Sco20	12Sag28	06Sag27
10/28/1901	04Sco22	19Sco15	18Sag15	10Sag50
11/02/1901	09Sco22	14Sco31	23Sag58	13Sag46
11/07/1901	14Sco24	08Sco11	29Sag39	17Sag28
11/12/1901	19Sco25	04Sco36	05Cap16	21Sag11
11/17/1901	24Sco27	05Sco36	10Cap49	24Sag56
11/22/1901	29Sco30	10Sco00	16Cap16	28Sag43
11/27/1901	04Sag34	16Sco14	21Cap37	02Cap30
12/02/1901	09Sag38	23Sco19	26Cap52	06Cap19
12/07/1901	14Sag43	00Sag47	01Aqu57	10Cap10
12/12/1901	19Sag48	08Sag24	06Aqu52	14Cap01
12/17/1901	24Sag53	16Sag07	11Aqu34	17Cap54
12/22/1901	29Sag58	23Sag53	16Aqu01	21Cap47
12/27/1901	05Cap04	01Cap45	20Aqu09	25Cap42
01/01/1902	10Cap10	09Cap43	23Aqu54	29Cap36
01/06/1902	15Cap16	17Cap51	27Aqu10	03Aqu32
01/11/1902	20Cap21	26Cap07	29Aqu54	07Aqu28
01/16/1902	25Cap27	04Aqu32	01Pis54	11Aqu25
01/21/1902	00Aqu32	13Aqu00	03Pis05	15Aqu22
01/26/1902	05Aqu37	21Aqu13	03Pis19	19Aqu19
01/31/1902	10Aqu42	28Aqu33	02Pis31	23Aqu16
02/05/1902	15Aqu46	03Pis47	00Pis42	27Aqu14
02/10/1902	20Aqu50	05Pis27	28Aqu04	01Pis12
02/15/1902	25Aqu54	02Pis49	25Aqu00	05Pis09
02/20/1902	00Pis57	27Aqu31	22Aqu00	09Pis06
02/25/1902	05Pis58	22Aqu45	19Aqu35	13Pis02
03/02/1902	11Pis00	20Aqu34	18Aqu03	16Pis58
03/07/1902	16Pis00	21Aqu10	17Aqu31	20Pis53
03/12/1902	21Pis00	23Aqu58	18Aqu00	24Pis48
03/17/1902	25Pis58	03Pis49	19Aqu22	28Pis42
03/22/1902	00Ari56	03Pis49	21Aqu30	02Ari34
03/27/1902	05Ari53	10Pis12	24Aqu16	06Ari26

00Date	Sun	Mercury	Venus	Mars
04/01/1902	10Ari49	17Pis18	27Aqu34	10Ari18
04/06/1902	15Ari45	25Pis03	01Pis18	14Ari07
04/11/1902	20Ari40	03Ari25	05Pis22	17Ari57
04/16/1902	25Ari33	12Ari27	09Pis45	21Ari45
04/21/1902	00Tau27	22Ari07	14Pis20	25Ari31
04/26/1902	05Tau19	02Tau24	19Pis08	29Ari17
05/01/1902	10Tau10	13Tau06	24Pis06	03Tau01
05/06/1902	15Tau01	23Tau48	29Pis11	06Tau45
05/11/1902	19Tau51	03Gem57	04Ari23	10Tau27
05/16/1902	24Tau40	13Gem01	09Ari42	14Tau07
05/21/1902	29Tau29	20Gem46	15Ari06	17Tau46
05/26/1902	04Gem17	27Gem05	20Ari34	21Tau24
05/31/1902	09Gem05	01Can51	26Ari06	25Tau00
06/05/1902	13Gem52	04Can54	01Tau41	28Tau36
06/10/1902	18Gem39	06Can07	07Tau19	02Gem09
06/15/1902	23Gem25	05Can27	13Tau00	05Gem42
06/20/1902	28Gem12	03Can16	18Tau43	09Gem13
06/25/1902	02Can58	00Can25	24Tau28	12Gem42
06/30/1902	07Can44	28Gem03	00Gem16	16Gem10
07/05/1902	12Can30	27Gem10	06Gem06	19Gem37
07/10/1902	17Can16	28Gem20	11Gem57	23Gem03
07/15/1902	22Can02	01Can39	17Gem49	26Gem27
07/20/1902	26Can48	07Can03	23Gem43	29Gem51
07/25/1902	01Leo35	14Can22	29Gem39	03Can12
07/30/1902	06Leo22	23Can18	05Can37	06Can33
08/04/1902	11Leo09	03Leo18	11Can36	09Can51
08/09/1902	15Leo56	13Leo38	17Can36	13Can09
08/14/1902	20Leo44	23Leo46	23Can37	16Can25
08/19/1902	25Leo33	03Vir26	29Can40	19Can40
08/24/1902	00Vir22	12Vir32	05Leo45	22Can54
08/29/1902	05Vir12	21Vir04	11Leo51	26Can06
09/03/1902	10Vir02	29Vir04	17Leo57	29Can18
09/08/1902	14Vir53	06Lib33	24Leo05	02Leo27
09/13/1902	19Vir45	13Lib30	00Vir15	05Leo35
09/18/1902	24Vir37	19Lib52	06Vir25	08Leo42
09/23/1902	29Vir31	25Lib30	12Vir36	11Leo48
09/28/1902	04Lib25	00Sco09	18Vir48	14Leo51
10/03/1902	09Lib20	03Sco21	25Vir01	17Leo53
10/08/1902	14Lib16	04Sco20	01Lib15	20Leo54
10/13/1902	19Lib13	02Sco16	07Lib29	23Leo52
10/18/1902	24Lib10	27Lib04	13Lib43	26Leo49
10/23/1902	29Lib09	21Lib18	19Lib59	29Leo44
10/28/1902	04Sco08	18Lib43	26Lib15	02Vir37
11/02/1902	09Sco08	20Lib39	02Sco31	05Vir27
11/07/1902	14Sco09	25Lib49	08Sco48	08Vir16
11/12/1902	19Sco10	02Sco42	15Sco04	11Vir01
11/17/1902	24Sco13	10Sco16	21Sco21	13Vir44
11/22/1902	29Sco16	18Sco06	27Sco39	16Vir24
11/27/1902	04Sag19	25Sco58	03Sag56	19Vir01
12/02/1902	09Sag23	03Sag51	10Sag13	21Vir34
12/07/1902	14Sag28	11Sag41	16Sag31	24Vir03
12/12/1902	19Sag33	19Sag33	22Sag48	26Vir27
12/17/1902	24Sag38	27Sag26	29Sag06	28Vir48
12/22/1902	29Sag43	05Cap23	05Cap22	01Lib02
12/27/1902	04Cap49	13Cap25	11Cap40	03Lib11

Ephemeris Tables for Sun, Mercury, Venus and Mars

00Date	Sun	Mercury	Venus	Mars
01/01/1903	09Cap55	21Cap29	17Cap57	05Lib13
01/06/1903	15Cap01	29Cap31	24Cap14	07Lib09
01/11/1903	20Cap06	07Aqu11	00Aqu31	08Lib56
01/16/1903	25Cap12	13Aqu51	06Aqu48	10Lib34
01/21/1903	00Aqu18	18Aqu16	13Aqu04	12Lib03
01/26/1903	05Aqu22	18Aqu49	19Aqu20	13Lib20
01/31/1903	10Aqu27	14Aqu56	25Aqu36	14Lib25
02/05/1903	15Aqu31	08Aqu58	01Pis51	15Lib16
02/10/1903	20Aqu36	04Aqu38	08Pis06	15Lib52
02/15/1903	25Aqu39	03Aqu31	14Pis19	16Lib12
02/20/1903	00Pis42	05Aqu13	20Pis33	16Lib15
02/25/1903	05Pis44	08Aqu53	26Pis46	15Lib58
03/02/1903	10Pis45	13Aqu54	02Ari57	15Lib22
03/07/1903	15Pis46	19Aqu52	09Ari07	14Lib27
03/12/1903	20Pis45	26Aqu33	15Ari18	13Lib13
03/17/1903	25Pis44	03Pis52	21Ari26	11Lib43
03/22/1903	00Ari42	11Pis43	27Ari34	09Lib59
03/27/1903	05Ari39	20Pis06	03Tau40	08Lib07
04/01/1903	10Ari35	29Pis03	09Tau46	06Lib10
04/06/1903	15Ari31	08Ari34	15Tau49	04Lib16
04/11/1903	20Ari25	18Ari39	21Tau52	02Lib29
04/16/1903	25Ari19	29Ari09	27Tau52	00Lib54
04/21/1903	00Tau12	09Tau39	03Gem51	29Vir34
04/26/1903	05Tau04	19Tau34	09Gem48	28Vir33
05/01/1903	09Tau56	28Tau19	15Gem43	27Vir51
05/ 6/1903	14Tau46	05Gem31	21Gem37	27Vir28
05/11/1903	19Tau37	10Gem57	27Gem28	27Vir26
05/16/1903	24Tau26	14Gem29	03Can16	27Vir42
05/21/1903	29Tau15	16Gem01	09Can01	28Vir16
05/26/1903	04Gem03	15Gem34	14Can44	29Vir06
05/31/1903	08Gem51	13Gem33	20Can23	00Lib10
06/05/1903	13Gem38	10Gem49	25Can58	01Lib28
06/10/1903	18Gem25	08Gem30	01Leo30	02Lib58
06/15/1903	23Gem12	07Gem32	06Leo57	04Lib40
06/20/1903	27Gem58	08Gem24	12Leo18	06Lib31
06/25/1903	02Can44	11Gem11	17Leo33	08Lib31
06/30/1903	07Can30	15Gem47	22Leo41	10Lib40
07/05/1903	12Can16	22Gem04	27Leo41	12Lib57
07/10/1903	17Can02	29Gem55	02Vir32	15Lib20
07/15/1903	21Can48	09Can10	07Vir11	17Lib50
07/20/1903	26Can34	19Can23	11Vir37	20Lib25
07/25/1903	01Leo21	00Leo00	15Vir48	23Lib06
07/30/1903	06Leo08	10Leo24	19Vir40	25Lib52
08/04/1903	10Leo55	20Leo18	23Vir09	28Lib43
08/ 9/1903	15Leo42	29Leo34	26Vir12	01Sco39
08/14/1903	20Leo30	08Vir12	28Vir40	04Sco38
08/19/1903	25Leo19	16Vir12	00Lib30	07Sco41
08/24/1903	00Vir08	23Vir36	01Lib31	10Sco48
08/29/1903	04Vir57	00Lib21	01Lib39	13Sco58
09/03/1903	09Vir48	06Lib22	00Lib49	17Sco12
09/08/1903	14Vir39	11Lib31	29Vir00	20Sco30
09/13/1903	19Vir31	15Lib28	26Vir25	23Sco49
09/18/1903	24Vir23	17Lib45	23Vir24	27Sco12
09/23/1903	29Vir16	17Lib41	20Vir25	00Sag38
09/28/1903	04Lib10	14Lib42	17Vir56	04Sag06
10/03/1903	09Lib06	09Lib21	16Vir18	07Sag37
10/08/1903	14Lib01	04Lib24	15Vir40	11Sag10
10/13/1903	18Lib58	02Lib58	16Vir01	14Sag45
10/18/1903	23Lib56	05Lib49	17Vir17	18Sag23
10/23/1903	28Lib54	11Lib42	19Vir21	22Sag03
10/28/1903	03Sco54	19Lib09	22Vir04	25Sag44
11/02/1903	08Sco54	27Lib13	25Vir22	29Sag27
11/07/1903	13Sco54	05Sco24	29Vir07	03Cap12
11/12/1903	18Sco56	13Sco33	03Lib15	06Cap59
11/17/1903	23Sco58	21Sco36	07Lib42	10Cap47
11/22/1903	29Sco01	29Sco31	12Lib24	14Cap36
11/27/1903	04Sag04	07Sag23	17Lib20	18Cap27
12/02/1903	09Sag09	15Sag12	22Lib27	22Cap18
12/07/1903	14Sag13	23Sag00	27Lib44	26Cap11
12/12/1903	19Sag18	00Cap46	03Sco09	00Aqu04
12/17/1903	24Sag23	08Cap30	08Sco40	03Aqu58
12/22/1903	29Sag28	16Cap04	14Sco17	07Aqu53
12/27/1903	04Cap34	23Cap10	19Sco59	11Aqu48
01/01/1904	09Cap40	29Cap09	25Sco45	15Aqu44
01/06/1904	14Cap46	02Aqu42	01Sag34	19Aqu40
01/11/1904	19Cap52	02Aqu12	07Sag27	23Aqu36
01/16/1904	24Cap57	27Cap15	13Sag20	27Aqu31
01/21/1904	00Aqu03	21Cap01	19Sag20	01Pis28
01/26/1904	05Aqu08	17Cap25	25Sag19	05Pis23
01/31/1904	10Aqu13	17Cap24	01Cap20	09Pis18
02/05/1904	15Aqu17	20Cap04	07Cap22	13Pis13
02/10/1904	20Aqu21	24Cap30	13Cap25	17Pis07
02/15/1904	25Aqu24	00Aqu03	19Cap30	21Pis00
02/20/1904	00Pis27	06Aqu24	25Cap35	24Pis53
02/25/1904	05Pis29	13Aqu19	01Aqu40	28Pis45
03/01/1904	10Pis30	20Aqu45	07Aqu46	02Ari36
03/06/1904	15Pis31	28Aqu39	13Aqu53	06Ari26
03/11/1904	20Pis31	07Pis00	20Aqu00	10Ari15
03/16/1904	25Pis30	15Pis51	26Aqu07	14Ari03
03/21/1904	00Ari27	25Pis12	02Pis15	17Ari50
03/26/1904	05Ari24	05Ari01	08Pis23	21Ari36
03/31/1904	10Ari21	15Ari13	14Pis31	25Ari21
04/05/1904	15Ari16	25Ari27	20Pis39	29Ari04
04/10/1904	20Ari11	05Tau06	6Pis46	02Tau46
04/15/1904	25Ari05	13Tau25	02Ari54	06Tau28
04/20/1904	29Ari58	19Tau54	09Ari01	10Tau07
04/25/1904	04Tau51	24Tau13	15Ari09	13Tau46
04/30/1904	09Tau42	26Tau14	21Ari17	17Tau23
05/05/1904	14Tau33	26Tau00	27Ari24	20Tau59
05/10/1904	19Tau22	23Tau57	03Tau32	24Tau34
05/15/1904	24Tau12	21Tau03	09Tau40	28Tau07
05/20/1904	29Tau01	18Tau31	15Tau47	01Gem40
05/25/1904	03Gem49	17Tau23	21Tau55	05Gem10
05/30/1904	08Gem37	18Tau03	28Tau03	08Gem40
06/04/1904	13Gem24	20Tau31	04Gem10	12Gem09
06/09/1904	18Gem11	24Tau40	10Gem18	15Gem36
06/14/1904	22Gem58	00Gem18	16Gem26	19Gem03
06/19/1904	27Gem44	07Gem17	22Gem34	22Gem28
06/24/1904	02Can30	15Gem35	28Gem42	25Gem52
06/29/1904	07Can16	25Gem03	04Can51	29Gem15

Ephemeris Tables for Sun, Mercury, Venus and Mars

00Date	Sun	Mercury	Venus	Mars	00Date	Sun	Mercury	Venus	Mars
07/04/1904	12Can03	05Can27	10Can59	02Can37	04/05/1905	15Ari02	03Tau59	14Tau42	25Sco01
07/09/1904	16Can48	16Can15	17Can08	05Can57	04/10/1905	19Ari57	06Tau58	14Tau19	24Sco42
07/14/1904	21Can34	26Can52	23Can17	09Can18	04/15/1905	24Ari51	07Tau15	12Tau55	24Sco04
07/19/1904	26Can21	06Leo58	29Can27	12Can36	04/20/1905	29Ari44	05Tau12	10Tau37	23Sco06
07/24/1904	01Leo07	16Leo22	05Leo36	15Can54	04/25/1905	04Tau36	01Tau57	07Tau40	21Sco52
07/29/1904	05Leo54	25Leo03	11Leo46	19Can11	04/30/1905	09Tau28	28Ari55	04Tau32	20Sco22
08/03/1904	10Leo41	03Vir01	17Leo56	22Can27	05/05/1905	14Tau19	27Ari19	01Tau43	18Sco40
08/08/1904	15Leo28	10Vir16	24Leo06	25Can42	05/10/1905	19Tau09	27Ari37	29Ari38	16Sco53
08/13/1904	20Leo16	16Vir45	00Vir16	28Can57	05/15/1905	23Tau58	29Ari48	28Ari29	15Sco04
08/18/1904	25Leo05	22Vir22	06Vir27	02Leo10	05/20/1905	28Tau47	03Tau36	28Ari21	13Sco21
08/23/1904	29Leo54	26Vir55	12Vir37	05Leo23	05/25/1905	03Gem35	08Tau48	29Ari08	11Sco46
08/28/1904	04Vir43	00Lib04	18Vir48	08Leo34	05/30/1905	08Gem23	15Tau13	0Tau45	10Sco27
09/02/1904	09Vir34	01Lib21	24Vir58	11Leo46	06/04/1905	13Gem10	22Tau45	03Tau04	09Sco25
09/07/1904	14Vir25	00Lib11	01Lib09	14Leo56	06/09/1905	17Gem57	01Gem22	05Tau59	08Sco42
09/12/1904	19Vir16	26Vir27	07Lib19	18Leo05	06/14/1905	22Gem44	11Gem00	09Tau22	08Sco20
09/17/1904	24Vir09	21Vir21	13Lib30	21Leo13	06/19/1905	27Gem30	21Gem29	13Tau08	08Sco19
09/22/1904	29Vir02	17Vir31	19Lib40	24Leo21	06/24/1905	02Can16	02Can24	17Tau14	08Sco37
09/27/1904	03Lib57	17Vir18	25Lib51	27Leo28	06/29/1905	07Can03	13Can12	21Tau36	09Sco15
10/02/1904	08Lib51	21Vir01	02Sco01	00Vir34	07/04/1905	11Can49	23Can26	26Tau12	10Sco10
10/07/1904	13Lib47	27Vir35	08Sco10	03Vir40	07/09/1905	16Can34	02Leo55	00Gem58	11Sco22
10/12/1904	18Lib44	05Lib36	14Sco20	06Vir45	07/14/1905	21Can21	11Leo36	05Gem55	12Sco48
10/17/1904	23Lib42	14Lib07	20Sco30	09Vir48	07/19/1905	26Can07	19Leo27	11Gem00	14Sco28
10/22/1904	28Lib40	22Lib41	26Sco39	12Vir51	07/24/1905	00Leo54	26Leo28	16Gem12	16Sco20
10/27/1904	03Sco39	01Sco06	02Sag48	15Vir52	07/29/1905	05Leo40	02Vir36	21Gem30	18Sco24
11/01/1904	08Sco39	09Sco19	08Sag56	18Vir52	08/03/1905	10Leo27	7Vir42	26Gem54	20Sco37
11/06/1904	13Sco40	17Sco21	15Sag04	21Vir52	08/08/1905	15Leo15	11Vir30	02Can22	23Sco00
11/11/1904	18Sco41	25Sco14	21Sag12	24Vir51	08/13/1905	20Leo03	13Vir42	07Can55	25Sco31
11/16/1904	23Sco43	02Sag59	27Sag19	27Vir48	08/18/1905	24Leo51	13Vir51	13Can33	28Sco09
11/21/1900	28Sco46	10Sag37	03Cap26	00Lib43	08/23/1905	29Leo40	11Vir39	19Can14	00Sag55
11/26/1904	03Sag50	18Sag10	09Cap32	03Lib38	08/28/1905	04Vir30	07Vir32	24Can58	03Sag47
12/01/1904	08Sag54	25Sag34	15Cap37	06Lib31	09/02/1905	09Vir19	03Vir06	00Leo46	06Sag45
12/06/1904	13Sag58	02Cap40	21Cap41	09Lib22	09/07/1905	14Vir10	00Vir40	06Leo37	09Sag48
12/11/1904	19Sag03	09Cap10	27Cap44	12Lib11	09/12/1905	19Vir02	01Vir42	12Leo30	12Sag56
12/16/1904	24Sag08	14Cap24	03Aqu46	14Lib58	09/17/1905	23Vir55	06Vir17	18Leo25	16Sag09
12/21/1904	29Sag14	17Cap03	09Aqu45	17Lib44	09/22/1905	28Vir48	13Vir27	24Leo24	19Sag25
12/26/1904	04Cap19	15Cap31	15Aqu43	20Lib27	09/27/1905	03Lib42	21Vir59	00Vir24	22Sag46
12/31/1904	09Cap25	09Cap47	21Aqu39	23Lib07					
					10/02/1905	08Lib37	00Lib58	06Vir27	26Sag10
01/05/1905	14Cap31	03Cap39	27Aqu32	25Lib45	10/07/1905	13Lib33	09Lib54	12Vir31	29Sag38
01/10/1905	19Cap37	00Cap56	03Pis22	28Lib19	10/12/1905	18Lib30	18Lib36	18Vir37	03Cap08
01/15/1905	24Cap42	01Cap57	09Pis09	00Sco50	10/17/1905	23Lib27	27Lib01	24Vir45	06Cap41
01/20/1905	29Cap48	05Cap30	14Pis51	03Sco18	10/22/1905	28Lib25	05Sco09	00Lib54	10Cap17
01/25/1905	04Aqu53	10Cap35	20Pis28	05Sco40	10/27/1905	03Sco24	13Sco03	07Lib05	13Cap55
01/30/1905	09Aqu58	16Cap37	26Pis00	07Sco59					
					11/01/1905	08Sco24	20Sco45	13Lib16	17Cap34
02/04/1905	15Aqu02	23Cap16	01Ari24	10Sco12	11/06/1905	13Sco25	28Sco15	19Lib29	21Cap16
02/09/1905	20Aqu06	00Aqu24	06Ari41	12Sco19	11/11/1905	18Sco27	05Sag34	25Lib43	24Cap59
02/14/1905	25Aqu09	07Aqu55	11Ari49	14Sco21	11/16/1905	23Sco29	12Sag37	01Sco57	28Cap44
02/19/1905	00Pis13	15Aqu49	16Ari46	16Sco15	11/21/1905	28Sco31	19Sag15	08Sco12	02Aqu30
02/24/1905	05Pis15	24Aqu06	21Ari31	18Sco00	11/26/1905	03Sag35	25Sag08	14Sco27	06Aqu16
03/01/1905	10Pis16	02Pis49	26Ari01	19Sco37	12/01/1905	08Sag39	29Sag34	20Sco43	10Aqu04
03/06/1905	15Pis16	11Pis57	00Tau13	21Sco04	12/06/1905	13Sag43	01Cap16	27Sco00	13Aqu52
03/11/1905	20Pis16	21Pis30	04Tau04	22Sco19	12/11/1905	18Sag48	28Sag46	03Sag16	17Aqu42
03/16/1905	25Pis15	01Ari22	07Tau28	23Sco22	12/16/1905	23Sag54	22Sag31	09Sag33	21Aqu31
03/21/1905	00Ari13	11Ari16	10Tau21	24Sco11	12/21/1905	28Sag59	16Sag46	15Sag51	25Aqu21
03/26/1905	05Ari10	20Ari32	12Tau36	24Sco45	12/26/1905	04Cap04	15Sag00	22Sag07	29Aqu11
03/31/1905	10Ari07	28Ari21	14Tau06	25Sco02	12/31/1905	09Cap10	16Sag59	28Sag25	03Pis01

Ephemeris Tables for Sun, Mercury, Venus and Mars

00Date	Sun	Mercury	Venus	Mars
01/05/1906	14Cap16	21Sag20	04Cap42	06Pis50
01/10/1906	19Cap22	27Sag01	10Cap59	10Pis40
01/15/1906	24Cap28	03Cap28	17Cap16	14Pis28
01/20/1906	29Cap33	10Cap25	23Cap33	18Pis17
01/25/1906	04Aqu38	17Cap43	29Cap51	22Pis05
01/30/1906	09Aqu43	25Cap18	06Aqu07	25Pis52
02/04/1906	14Aqu48	03Aqu12	12Aqu24	29Pis39
02/09/1906	19Aqu51	11Aqu24	18Aqu40	03Ari24
02/14/1906	24Aqu55	19Aqu56	24Aqu56	07Ari09
02/19/1906	29Aqu58	28Aqu51	01Pis13	10Ari52
02/24/1906	05Pis00	08Pis06	07Pis28	14Ari36
03/01/1906	10Pis01	17Pis37	13Pis43	18Ari18
03/06/1906	15Pis02	27Pis06	19Pis58	21Ari58
03/11/1906	20Pis02	05Ari55	26Pis12	25Ari38
03/16/1906	25Pis01	13Ari09	02Ari25	29Ari17
03/21/1906	29Pis59	17Ari49	08Ari38	02Tau55
03/26/1906	04Ari55	19Ari19	14Ari51	06Tau31
03/31/1906	09Ari52	17Ari47	21Ari03	10Tau07
04/05/1906	14Ari48	14Ari14	27Ari14	13Tau41
04/10/1906	19Ari43	10Ari27	03Tau25	17Tau14
04/15/1906	24Ari37	08Ari02	09Tau34	20Tau46
04/20/1906	29Ari30	07Ari40	15Tau44	24Tau17
04/25/1906	04Tau22	09Ari22	21Tau53	27Tau46
04/30/1906	09Tau13	12Ari47	28Tau01	01Gem15
05/05/1906	14Tau04	17Ari36	04Gem08	04Gem43
05/10/1906	18Tau55	23Ari34	10Gem15	08Gem09
05/15/1906	23Tau44	00Tau34	16Gem20	11Gem35
05/20/1906	28Tau33	08Tau29	22Gem25	15Gem00
05/25/1906	03Gem21	17Tau19	28Gem29	18Gem23
05/30/1906	08Gem09	27Tau03	04Can32	21Gem45
06/04/1906	12Gem57	07Gem32	10Can34	25Gem07
06/09/1906	17Gem43	18Gem29	16Can36	28Gem28
06/14/1906	22Gem30	29Gem22	22Can36	01Can48
06/19/1906	27Gem16	09Can41	28Can35	05Can07
06/24/1906	02Can03	19Can12	04Leo33	08Can25
06/29/1906	06Can49	27Can47	10Leo30	11Can43
07/04/1906	11Can35	05Leo26	16Leo25	15Can00
07/09/1906	16Can21	12Leo07	22Leo19	18Can16
07/14/1906	21Can07	17Leo43	28Leo11	21Can31
07/19/1906	25Can53	22Leo06	04Vir01	24Can46
07/24/1906	00Leo39	25Leo00	09Vir50	28Can01
07/29/1906	05Leo26	26Leo03	15Vir36	01Leo15
08/03/1906	10Leo13	25Leo01	21Vir20	04Leo28
08/08/1906	15Leo01	22Leo02	27Vir01	07Leo40
08/13/1906	19Leo48	18Leo02	02Lib39	10Leo53
08/18/1906	24Leo37	14Leo45	08Lib15	14Leo05
08/23/1906	29Leo26	13Leo52	13Lib45	17Leo16
08/28/1906	04Vir15	16Leo12	19Lib12	20Leo28
09/02/1906	09Vir06	21Leo35	24Lib34	23Leo39
09/07/1906	13Vir57	29Leo18	29Lib51	26Leo49
09/12/1906	18Vir48	08Vir18	05Sco01	29Leo59
09/17/1906	23Vir40	17Vir43	10Sco03	03Vir09
09/22/1906	28Vir34	27Vir01	14Sco57	06Vir19
09/27/1906	03Lib28	06Lib00	19Sco40	09Vir28

00Date	Sun	Mercury	Venus	Mars
10/02/1906	08Lib23	14Lib37	24Sco10	12Vir37
10/07/1906	13Lib18	22Lib52	28Sco26	15Vir46
10/12/1906	18Lib15	00Sco49	02Sag22	18Vir55
10/17/1906	23Lib12	08Sco28	05Sag57	22Vir04
10/22/1906	28Lib11	15Sco50	09Sag04	25Vir12
10/27/1906	03Sco10	22Sco54	11Sag37	28Vir20
11/01/1906	08Sco10	29Sco36	13Sag30	01Lib28
11/06/1906	13Sco10	05Sag45	14Sag33	04Lib35
11/11/1906	18Sco12	10Sag58	14Sag40	07Lib42
11/16/1906	23Sco14	14Sag34	13Sag48	10Lib49
11/21/1906	28Sco17	15Sag18	11Sag57	13Lib56
11/26/1906	03Sag20	11Sag55	09Sag19	17Lib03
12/01/1906	08Sag24	05Sag24	06Sag19	20Lib09
12/06/1906	13Sag28	00Sag15	03Sag27	23Lib14
12/11/1906	18Sag33	29Sco27	01Sag10	26Lib19
12/16/1906	23Sag39	02Sag22	29Sco48	29Lib24
12/21/1906	28Sag44	07Sag27	29Sco27	02Sco28
12/26/1906	03Cap50	13Sag41	00Sag06	05Sco31
12/31/1906	08Cap55	20Sag32	01Sag39	08Sco34
01/05/1907	14Cap01	27Sag45	03Sag58	11Sco36
01/10/1907	19Cap07	05Cap12	06Sag55	14Sco37
01/15/1907	24Cap13	12Cap51	10Sag24	17Sco38
01/20/1907	29Cap18	20Cap44	14Sag18	20Sco37
01/25/1907	04Aqu24	28Cap51	18Sag33	23Sco36
01/30/1907	09Aqu28	07Aqu13	23Sag05	26Sco33
02/04/1907	14Aqu33	15Aqu52	27Sag51	29Sco29
02/09/1907	19Aqu36	24Aqu48	02Cap49	02Sag24
02/14/1907	24Aqu40	03Pis57	07Cap57	05Sag16
02/19/1907	29Aqu43	12Pis58	13Cap13	08Sag08
02/24/1907	04Pis45	21Pis18	18Cap35	10Sag57
03/01/1907	09Pis46	27Pis52	24Cap03	13Sag44
03/06/1907	14Pis48	01Ari29	29Cap36	16Sag28
03/11/1907	19Pis47	01Ari27	05Aqu13	19Sag10
03/16/1907	24Pis46	28Pis13	10Aqu54	21Sag49
03/21/1907	29Pis45	23Pis41	16Aqu37	24Sag25
03/26/1907	04Ari41	20Pis06	22Aqu23	26Sag56
03/31/1907	09Ari38	18Pis42	28Aqu12	29Sag24
04/05/1907	14Ari34	19Pis37	4Pis02	01Cap46
04/10/1907	19Ari28	22Pis30	09Pis54	04Cap03
04/15/1907	24Ari22	26Pis52	15Pis47	06Cap15
04/20/1907	29Ari16	02Ari25	21Pis42	08Cap19
04/25/1907	04Tau08	08Ari56	27Pis37	10Cap16
04/30/1907	09Tau00	16Ari19	03Ari33	12Cap04
05/05/1907	13Tau51	24Ari29	09Ari30	13Cap42
05/10/1907	18Tau40	03Tau26	15Ari28	15Cap09
05/15/1907	23Tau30	13Tau10	21Ari27	16Cap24
05/20/1907	28Tau19	23Tau37	27Ari27	17Cap25
05/25/1907	03Gem07	04Gem31	03Tau27	18Cap11
05/30/1907	07Gem55	15Gem25	09Tau27	18Cap41
06/04/1907	12Gem43	25Gem45	15Tau28	18Cap52
06/09/1907	17Gem30	05Can11	21Tau30	18Cap46
06/14/1907	22Gem16	13Can35	27Tau31	18Cap21
06/19/1907	27Gem03	20Can54	03Gem34	17Cap37
06/24/1907	01Can49	27Can04	09Gem37	16Cap37
06/29/1907	06Can35	01Leo57	15Gem41	15Cap23

Ephemeris Tables for Sun, Mercury, Venus and Mars

00Date	Sun	Mercury	Venus	Mars
07/04/1907	11Can21	05Leo23	21Gem45	13Cap59
07/09/1907	16Can07	07Leo06	27Gem51	12Cap31
07/14/1907	20Can53	06Leo53	03Can56	11Cap04
07/19/1907	25Can39	04Leo48	10Can02	09Cap44
07/24/1907	00Leo25	01Leo28	16Can09	08Cap36
07/29/1907	05Leo12	28Can13	22Can16	07Cap44
08/03/1907	10Leo00	26Can28	28Can25	07Cap10
08/08/1907	14Leo47	27Can13	04Leo34	06Cap58
08/13/1907	19Leo34	00Leo46	10Leo43	07Cap06
08/18/1907	24Leo23	06Leo55	16Leo54	07Cap34
08/23/1907	29Leo12	15Leo08	23Leo04	08Cap22
08/28/1907	04Vir01	24Leo33	29Leo16	09Cap29
09/02/1907	08Vir52	04Vir21	05Vir28	10Cap52
09/07/1907	13Vir42	14Vir01	11Vir40	12Cap31
09/12/1907	18Vir34	23Vir17	17Vir53	14Cap25
09/17/1907	23Vir27	02Lib06	24Vir06	16Cap30
09/22/1907	28Vir19	10Lib30	00Lib20	18Cap46
09/27/1907	03Lib13	18Lib28	06Lib34	21Cap13
10/02/1907	08Lib09	26Lib04	12Lib48	23Cap48
10/07/1907	13Lib04	3Sco18	19Lib03	26Cap31
10/12/1907	18Lib01	10Sco08	25Lib17	29Cap21
10/17/1907	22Lib58	16Sco28	01Sco31	02Aqu16
10/22/1907	27Lib56	22Sco06	07Sco46	05Aqu18
10/27/1907	02Sco55	26Sco37	14Sco01	08Aqu24
11/01/1907	07Sco55	29Sco19	20Sco16	11Aqu33
11/06/1907	12Sco56	29Sco03	26Sco31	14Aqu47
11/11/1907	17Sco57	24Sco53	02Sag46	18Aqu04
11/16/1907	23Sco00	18Sco24	09Sag01	21Aqu23
11/21/1907	28Sco02	14Sco01	15Sag16	24Aqu45
11/26/1907	03Sag06	14Sco11	21Sag31	28Aqu09
12/01/1907	08Sag09	17Sco58	27Sag45	01Pis34
12/06/1907	13Sag14	23Sco45	04Cap00	05Pis01
12/11/1907	18Sag19	00Sag30	10Cap15	08Pis30
12/16/1907	23Sag24	07Sag44	16Cap28	11Pis58
12/21/1907	28Sag29	15Sag12	22Cap42	15Pis28
12/26/1907	03Cap35	22Sag48	28Cap56	18Pis58
12/31/1907	08Cap40	00Cap32	05Aqu09	22Pis29
01/05/1908	13Cap46	8Cap24	11Aqu22	26Pis00
01/10/1908	18Cap52	16Cap25	17Aqu33	29Pis30
01/15/1908	23Cap58	24Cap37	23Aqu45	03Ari01
01/20/1908	29Cap03	03Aqu01	29Aqu55	06Ari31
01/25/1908	04Aqu09	11Aqu38	06Pis05	10Ari02
01/30/1908	09Aqu13	20Aqu21	12Pis13	13Ari32
02/04/1908	14Aqu18	28Aqu54	18Pis19	17Ari02
02/09/1908	19Aqu22	06Pis39	24Pis25	20Ari31
02/14/1908	24Aqu25	12Pis30	00Ari28	24Ari00
02/19/1908	29Aqu28	15Pis03	06Ari30	27Ari28
02/24/1908	04Pis31	13Pis30	12Ari29	00Tau56
02/29/1908	09Pis32	08Pis53	18Ari26	04Tau23
03/05/1908	14Pis33	03Pis58	24Ari20	07Tau49
03/10/1908	19Pis33	01Pis04	00Tau12	11Tau15
03/15/1908	24Pis32	00Pis51	06Tau00	14Tau40
03/20/1908	29Pis30	02Pis56	11Tau44	18Tau04
03/25/1908	04Ari27	06Pis45	17Tau24	21Tau27
03/30/1908	09Ari24	11Pis51	23Tau00	24Tau50

00Date	Sun	Mercury	Venus	Mars
04/04/1908	14Ari19	17Pis56	28Tau30	28Tau12
04/09/1908	19Ari14	24Pis50	03Gem55	01Gem34
04/14/1908	24Ari08	02Ari27	09Gem13	04Gem54
04/19/1908	29Ari01	10Ari45	14Gem23	08Gem14
04/24/1908	03Tau54	19Ari45	19Gem24	11Gem33
04/29/1908	08Tau45	29Ari25	24Gem15	14Gem52
05/04/1908	13Tau36	09Tau46	28Gem53	18Gem10
05/09/1908	18Tau27	20Tau33	03Can17	21Gem27
05/14/1908	23Tau16	01Gem21	07Can24	24Gem43
05/19/1908	28Tau05	11Gem37	11Can10	28Gem00
05/24/1908	02Gem54	20Gem54	14Can31	01Can15
05/29/1908	07Gem42	29Gem00	17Can22	04Can30
06/03/1908	12Gem29	05Can47	19Can37	07Can44
06/08/1908	17Gem16	11Can12	21Can09	10Can58
06/13/1908	22Gem03	15Can06	21Can49	14Can12
06/18/1908	26Gem49	17Can16	21Can34	17Can25
06/23/1908	01Can35	17Can36	20Can18	20Can37
06/28/1908	06Can21	16Can06	18Can07	23Can49
07/03/1908	11Can07	13Can21	15Can16	27Can01
07/08/1908	15Can53	10Can22	12Can10	00Leo13
07/13/1908	20Can39	08Can27	09Can17	03Leo25
07/18/1908	25Can25	08Can27	07Can03	06Leo36
07/23/1908	00Leo12	10Can48	05Can42	09Leo48
07/28/1908	04Leo58	15Can28	05Can21	12Leo58
08/02/1908	09Leo45	22Can19	05Can57	16Leo09
08/07/1908	14Leo33	00Leo57	07Can24	19Leo20
08/12/1908	19Leo21	10Leo43	09Can34	22Leo31
08/17/1908	24Leo09	20Leo53	12Can21	25Leo42
08/22/1908	28Leo58	00Vir52	15Can39	28Leo52
08/27/1908	03Vir48	10Vir25	19Can22	02Vir04
09/01/1908	08Vir37	19Vir27	23Can25	05Vir15
09/06/1908	13Vir28	27Vir57	27Can47	08Vir25
09/11/1908	18Vir20	05Lib58	02Leo24	11Vir37
09/16/1908	23Vir12	13Lib31	07Leo13	14Vir48
09/21/1908	28Vir06	20Lib36	12Leo13	18Vir00
09/26/1908	03Lib00	27Lib10	17Leo22	21Vir12
10/01/1908	07Lib54	03Sco06	22Leo40	24Vir24
10/06/1908	12Lib50	08Sco10	28Leo04	27Vir36
10/11/1908	17Lib46	11Sco57	03Vir36	00Lib49
10/16/1908	22Lib43	13Sco40	09Vir12	04Lib02
10/21/1908	27Lib42	12Sco23	14Vir54	07Lib15
10/26/1908	02Sco41	07Sco37	20Vir40	10Lib28
10/31/1908	07Sco40	01Sco26	26Vir30	13Lib42
11/05/1908	12Sco41	27Lib59	02Lib24	16Lib57
11/10/1908	17Sco43	29Lib07	08Lib20	20Lib11
11/15/1908	22Sco45	03Sco42	14Lib19	23Lib26
11/20/1908	27Sco48	10Sco08	20Lib21	26Lib42
11/25/1908	02Sag51	17Sco24	26Lib25	29Lib57
11/30/1908	07Sag55	25Sco00	02Sco31	03Sco13
12/05/1908	12Sag59	02Sag43	08Sco38	06Sco30
12/10/1908	18Sag04	10Sag30	14Sco46	09Sco46
12/15/1908	23Sag09	18Sag11	20Sco57	13Sco04
12/20/1908	28Sag15	26Sag09	27Sco07	16Sco21
12/25/1908	03Cap20	04Cap05	03Sag19	19Sco39
12/30/1908	08Cap26	12Cap07	09Sag31	22Sco57

Ephemeris Tables for Sun, Mercury, Venus and Mars

00Date	Sun	Mercury	Venus	Mars
01/04/1909	13Cap31	20Cap17	15Sag43	26Sco16
01/09/1909	18Cap37	28Cap33	21Sag57	29Sco35
01/14/1909	23Cap43	06Aqu51	28Sag10	02Sag54
01/19/1909	28Cap49	14Aqu52	04Cap24	06Sag13
01/24/1909	03Aqu54	22Aqu00	10Cap39	09Sag33
01/29/1909	08Aqu58	27Aqu04	16Cap52	12Sag54
02/03/1909	14Aqu03	28Aqu32	23Cap07	16Sag14
02/08/1909	19Aqu07	25Aqu35	29Cap21	19Sag34
02/13/1909	24Aqu10	20Aqu00	05Aqu35	22Sag55
02/18/1909	29Aqu14	15Aqu14	11Aqu49	26Sag16
02/23/1909	04Pis16	13Aqu18	18Aqu03	29Sag37
02/28/1909	09Pis18	14Aqu14	24Aqu17	02Cap59
03/05/1909	14Pis18	17Aqu18	00Pis31	06Cap20
03/10/1909	19Pis18	21Aqu52	06Pis45	09Cap42
03/15/1909	24Pis17	27Aqu32	12Pis58	13Cap03
03/20/1909	29Pis16	04Pis01	19Pis12	16Cap24
03/25/1909	04Ari12	11Pis10	25Pis24	19Cap45
03/30/1909	09Ari09	18Pis56	01Ari36	23Cap06
04/04/1909	14Ari05	27Pis18	07Ari48	26Cap27
04/09/1909	19Ari00	06Ari15	14Ari00	29Cap48
04/14/1909	23Ari54	15Ari49	20Ari12	03Aqu07
04/19/1909	28Ari47	25Ari59	26Ari22	06Aqu26
04/24/1909	03Tau40	06Tau36	02Tau33	09Aqu45
04/29/1909	08Tau31	17Tau14	08Tau43	13Aqu02
05/04/1909	13Tau22	27Tau21	14Tau54	16Aqu18
05/09/1909	18Tau13	06Gem22	21Tau04	19Aqu33
05/14/1909	23Tau02	14Gem00	27Tau13	22Aqu46
05/19/1909	27Tau51	20Gem04	03Gem22	25Aqu58
05/24/1909	02Gem39	24Gem27	09Gem31	29Aqu07
05/29/1909	07Gem27	27Gem01	15Gem40	02Pis14
06/03/1909	12Gem15	27Gem40	21Gem48	05Pis18
06/08/1909	17Gem02	26Gem30	27Gem56	08Pis18
06/13/1909	21Gem49	24Gem03	04Can04	11Pis14
06/18/1909	26Gem35	21Gem18	10Can12	14Pis06
06/23/1909	01Can21	19Gem24	16Can19	16Pis52
06/28/1909	06Can07	19Gem09	22Can27	19Pis33
07/03/1909	10Can54	20Gem54	28Can34	22Pis06
07/08/1909	15Can39	24Gem39	04Leo40	24Pis32
07/13/1909	20Can25	00Can20	10Leo46	26Pis48
07/18/1909	25Can12	07Can48	16Leo53	28Pis55
07/23/1909	29Can58	16Can47	22Leo58	00Ari49
07/28/1909	04Leo45	26Can50	29Leo04	02Ari31
08/02/1909	09Leo31	07Leo18	05Vir09	03Ari58
08/07/1909	14Leo19	17Leo35	11Vir13	05Ari09
08/12/1909	19Leo07	27Leo23	17Vir17	06Ari02
08/17/1909	23Leo55	06Vir36	23Vir20	06Ari36
08/22/1909	28Leo44	15Vir12	29Vir22	06Ari49
08/27/1909	03Vir33	23Vir15	05Lib24	06Ari42
09/01/1909	08Vir24	00Lib43	11Lib25	06Ari13
09/06/1909	13Vir14	07Lib39	17Lib26	05Ari25
09/11/1909	18Vir06	13Lib55	23Lib25	04Ari19
09/16/1909	22Vir58	19Lib24	29Lib24	03Ari01
09/21/1909	27Vir51	23Lib51	05Sco21	01Ari36
09/26/1909	02Lib45	26Lib46	11Sco17	00Ari09

00Date	Sun	Mercury	Venus	Mars
10/01/1909	07Lib40	27Lib30	17Sco12	28Pis46
10/06/1909	12Lib36	25Lib13	23Sco06	27Pis33
10/11/1909	17Lib32	20Lib03	28Sco58	26Pis34
10/16/1909	22Lib29	14Lib28	04Sag48	25Pis54
10/21/1909	27Lib27	12Lib06	10Sag36	25Pis32
10/26/1909	02Sco27	14Lib10	16Sag22	25Pis30
10/31/1909	07Sco26	19Lib31	22Sag05	25Pis49
11/05/1909	12Sco27	26Lib34	27Sag45	26Pis25
11/10/1909	17Sco28	04Sco19	03Cap21	27Pis19
11/15/1909	22Sco30	12Sco18	08Cap53	28Pis30
11/20/1909	27Sco33	20Sco18	14Cap19	29Pis54
11/25/1909	02Sag36	28Sco14	19Cap40	01Ari31
11/30/1909	07Sag40	06Sag07	24Cap53	03Ari20
12/05/1909	12Sag44	13Sag58	29Cap58	05Ari19
12/10/1909	17Sag49	21Sag50	04Aqu51	07Ari26
12/15/1909	22Sag54	29Sag43	09Aqu32	09Ari42
12/20/1909	28Sag00	07Cap38	13Aqu57	12Ari04
12/25/1909	03Cap05	15Cap34	18Aqu03	14Ari31
12/30/1909	08Cap11	23Cap24	21Aqu46	17Ari05
01/04/1910	13Cap17	00Aqu52	25Aqu00	19Ari43
01/09/1910	18Cap22	07Aqu21	27Aqu39	22Ari24
01/14/1910	23Cap28	14Aqu36	29Aqu37	25Ari09
01/19/1910	28Cap34	11Aqu59	00Pis44	27Ari58
01/24/1910	03Aqu39	07Aqu51	00Pis52	00Tau49
01/29/1910	08Aqu44	01Aqu43	29Aqu59	03Tau42
02/03/1910	13Aqu48	27Cap28	28Aqu06	06Tau37
02/08/1910	18Aqu52	26Cap37	25Aqu24	09Tau34
02/13/1910	23Aqu55	28Cap35	22Aqu19	12Tau32
02/18/1910	28Aqu59	02Aqu30	19Aqu22	15Tau32
02/23/1910	04Pis01	07Aqu42	17Aqu01	18Tau33
02/28/1910	09Pis03	13Aqu47	15Aqu34	21Tau34
03/05/1910	14Pis04	20Aqu33	15Aqu08	24Tau37
03/10/1910	19Pis04	27Aqu52	15Aqu42	27Tau40
03/15/1910	24Pis03	05Pis43	17Aqu09	00Gem44
03/20/1910	29Pis01	14Pis04	19Aqu21	03Gem48
03/25/1910	03Ari58	22Pis57	22Aqu10	06Gem53
03/30/1910	08Ari55	02Ari21	25Aqu31	09Gem58
04/04/1910	13Ari51	12Ari18	29Aqu18	13Gem03
04/09/1910	18Ari46	22Ari40	03Pis24	16Gem09
04/14/1910	23Ari40	03Tau04	07Pis47	19Gem14
04/19/1910	28Ari33	12Tau57	12Pis24	22Gem20
04/24/1910	03Tau25	21Tau37	17Pis13	25Gem26
04/29/1910	08Tau17	28Tau39	22Pis12	28Gem32
05/04/1910	13Tau08	03Gem45	27Pis19	01Can38
05/09/1910	17Tau58	06Gem48	02Ari31	04Can44
05/14/1910	22Tau48	07Gem44	07Ari51	07Can51
05/19/1910	27Tau37	06Gem42	13Ari15	10Can57
05/24/1910	02Gem25	04Gem16	18Ari44	14Can03
05/29/1910	07Gem13	01Gem30	24Ari16	17Can09
06/03/1910	12Gem01	29Tau33	29Ari52	20Can16
06/08/1910	16Gem48	29Tau10	05Tau31	23Can22
06/13/1910	21Gem35	00Gem38	11Tau12	26Can29
06/18/1910	26Gem21	03Gem55	16Tau55	29Can36
06/23/1910	01Can07	08Gem53	22Tau41	02Leo43
06/28/1910	05Can54	15Gem24	28Tau29	05Leo50

Ephemeris Tables for Sun, Mercury, Venus and Mars

00Date	Sun	Mercury	Venus	Mars	00Date	Sun	Mercury	Venus	Mars
07/03/1910	10Can40	23Gem22	04Gem18	08Leo57	04/01/1911	13Ari36	28Ari27	14Tau01	15Aqu58
07/08/1910	15Can25	2Can39	10Gem09	12Leo05	04/09/1911	18Ari31	06Tau40	20Tau03	19Aqu42
07/13/1910	20Can12	12Can54	16Gem02	15Leo12	04/14/1911	23Ari25	12Tau57	26Tau04	23Aqu25
07/18/1910	24Can58	23Can35	21Gem57	18Leo21	04/19/1911	28Ari19	16Tau52	02Gem03	27Aqu09
07/23/1910	29Can44	04Leo07	27Gem52	21Leo29	04/24/1911	03Tau12	18Tau19	08Gem00	00Pis53
07/28/1910	04Leo31	14Leo09	03Can50	24Leo37	04/29/1911	08Tau03	17Tau26	13Gem55	04Pis37
08/02/1910	09Leo18	23Leo31	09Can49	27Leo46	05/04/1911	12Tau54	14Tau52	19Gem49	08Pis20
08/07/1910	14Leo05	02Vir13	15Can49	00Vir55	05/09/1911	17Tau45	11Tau48	25Gem39	12Pis03
08/12/1910	18Leo53	10Vir15	21Can50	04Vir05	05/14/1911	22Tau34	09Tau31	01Can28	15Pis46
08/17/1910	23Leo41	17Vir38	27Can53	07Vir15	05/19/1911	27Tau23	08Tau52	07Can13	19Pis28
08/22/1910	28Leo30	24Vir19	03Leo57	10Vir26	05/24/1911	02Gem12	10Tau05	12Can56	23Pis09
08/27/1910	03Vir19	00Lib15	10Leo03	13Vir37	05/29/1911	07Gem00	13Tau04	18Can35	26Pis49
09/01/1910	08Vir09	05Lib13	16Leo10	16Vir49	06/03/1911	11Gem47	17Tau36	24Can10	00Ari27
09/06/1910	13Vir00	08Lib57	22Leo18	20Vir01	06/08/1911	16Gem34	23Tau31	29Can41	04Ari05
09/11/1910	17Vir52	10Lib56	28Leo27	23Vir13	06/13/1911	21Gem21	00Gem41	05Leo07	07Ari41
09/16/1910	22Vir44	10Lib34	04Vir36	26Vir27	06/18/1911	26Gem07	09Gem03	10Leo28	11Ari16
09/21/1910	27Vir37	07Lib24	10Vir48	29Vir40	06/23/1911	00Can54	18Gem33	15Leo43	14Ari48
09/26/1910	02Lib31	02Lib10	16Vir59	02Lib55	06/28/1911	05Can40	28Gem57	20Leo51	18Ari19
10/01/1910	07Lib25	27Vir31	23Vir12	06Lib10	07/03/1911	10Can25	09Can47	25Leo50	21Ari47
10/06/1910	12Lib21	26Vir19	29Vir25	09Lib26	07/08/1911	15Can12	20Can31	00Vir40	25Ari12
10/11/1910	17Lib18	29Vir19	05Lib40	12Lib43	07/13/1911	19Can58	00Leo43	05Vir18	28Ari35
10/16/1910	22Lib15	05Lib21	11Lib54	16Lib00	07/18/1911	24Can44	10Leo13	09Vir43	01Tau54
10/21/1910	27Lib13	12Lib59	18Lib10	19Lib18	07/23/1911	29Can30	18Leo57	13Vir53	05Tau09
10/26/1910	02Sco12	21Lib14	24Lib25	22Lib37	07/28/1911	04Leo17	26Leo55	17Vir43	08Tau21
10/31/1910	07Sco12	29Lib35	00Sco42	25Lib57					
					08/02/1911	09Leo04	04Vir08	21Vir10	11Tau28
11/05/1910	12Sco12	07Sco51	06Sco58	29Lib18	08/07/1911	13Leo51	10Vir33	24Vir10	14Tau30
11/10/1910	17Sco13	15Sco58	13Sco15	02Sco39	08/12/1911	18Leo39	16Vir01	26Vir36	17Tau27
11/15/1910	22Sco15	23Sco57	19Sco31	06Sco01	08/17/1911	23Leo27	20Vir21	28Vir22	20Tau17
11/20/1910	27Sco18	01Sag49	25Sco49	09Sco24	08/22/1911	28Leo16	23Vir13	29Vir19	23Tau01
11/25/1910	02Sag21	09Sag37	02Sag06	12Sco48	08/27/1911	03Vir05	24Vir10	29Vir22	25Tau37
11/30/1910	07Sag25	17Sag21	08Sag23	16Sco12					
					09/01/1911	07Vir55	22Vir42	28Vir27	28Tau06
12/05/1910	12Sag30	25Sag02	14Sag40	19Sco38	09/06/1911	12Vir46	18Vir53	26Vir34	00Gem25
12/10/1910	17Sag34	02Cap38	20Sag58	23Sco04	09/11/1911	17Vir37	14Vir00	23Vir56	02Gem34
12/15/1910	22Sag39	10Cap01	27Sag15	26Sco32	09/16/1911	22Vir30	10Vir33	20Vir54	04Gem31
12/20/1910	27Sag45	16Cap55	03Cap33	00Sag00	09/21/1911	27Vir23	10Vir37	17Vir55	06Gem16
12/25/1910	02Cap51	22Cap40	09Cap49	03Sag29	09/26/1911	02Lib16	14Vir30	15Vir30	07Gem47
12/30/1910	07Cap56	26Cap04	16Cap07	06Sag59					
					10/01/1911	07Lib11	21Vir12	13Vir57	09Gem02
01/04/1911	13Cap02	25Cap24	22Cap24	10Sag30	10/06/1911	12Lib07	29Vir22	13Vir22	10Gem00
01/09/1911	18Cap08	20Cap18	28Cap40	14Sag02	10/11/1911	17Lib03	08Lib05	13Vir48	10Gem39
01/14/1911	23Cap13	14Cap00	04Aqu57	17Sag34	10/16/1911	22Lib00	16Lib49	15Vir07	10Gem58
01/19/1911	28Cap19	10Cap31	11Aqu13	21Sag08	10/21/1911	26Lib58	25Lib22	17Vir14	10Gem55
01/24/1911	03Aqu24	10Cap44	17Aqu30	24Sag42	10/26/1911	01Sco57	03Sco41	20Vir00	10Gem30
01/29/1911	08Aqu29	13Cap39	23Aqu45	28Sag17	10/31/1911	06Sco57	11Sco46	23Vir19	09Gem43
02/03/1911	13Aqu33	18Cap18	00Pis01	01Cap53	11/05/1911	11Sco57	19Sco40	27Vir06	08Gem35
02/08/1911	18Aqu37	24Cap01	06Pis16	05Cap30	11/10/1911	16Sco59	27Sco24	00Lib55	07Gem09
02/13/1911	23Aqu41	00Aqu27	12Pis30	09Cap07	11/15/1911	22Sco01	05Sag00	05Lib43	05Gem28
02/18/1911	28Aqu45	07Aqu27	18Pis43	12Cap46	11/20/1911	27Sco03	12Sag27	10Lib27	03Gem37
02/23/1911	03Pis46	14Aqu53	24Pis56	16Cap25	11/25/1911	02Sag07	19Sag43	15Lib23	01Gem45
02/28/1911	08Pis48	22Aqu45	01Ari07	20Cap04	11/30/1911	07Sag10	26Sag39	20Lib31	29Tau55
03/05/1911	13Pis49	01Pis04	07Ari18	23Cap45	12/05/1911	12Sag15	02Cap57	25Lib48	28Tau16
03/10/1911	18Pis49	09Pis49	13Ari28	27Cap25	12/10/1911	17Sag19	07Cap57	01Sco13	26Tau50
03/15/1911	23Pis48	19Pis03	19Ari37	01Aqu07	12/15/1911	22Sag24	10Cap25	06Sco45	25Tau42
03/20/1911	28Pis47	28Pis45	25Ari45	04Aqu49	12/20/1911	27Sag30	08Cap46	12Sco22	24Tau54
03/25/1911	03Ari44	08Ari48	01Tau52	08Aqu32	12/25/1911	02Cap36	02Cap57	18Sco04	24Tau27
03/30/1911	08Ari40	18Ari54	07Tau57	12Aqu15	12/30/1911	07Cap41	26Sag48	23Sco51	24Tau20

Ephemeris Tables for Sun, Mercury, Venus and Mars

00Date	Sun	Mercury	Venus	Mars
01/04/1912	12Cap47	24Sag13	29Sco41	24Tau33
01/09/1912	17Cap53	25Sag27	05Sag34	25Tau03
01/14/1912	22Cap58	29Sag14	11Sag29	25Tau50
01/19/1912	28Cap04	04Cap31	17Sag27	26Tau52
01/24/1912	03Aqu09	10Cap41	23Sag27	28Tau07
01/29/1912	08Aqu14	17Cap26	29Sag28	29Tau35
02/03/1912	13Aqu19	24Cap37	05Cap30	01Gem13
02/08/1912	18Aqu23	02Aqu09	11Cap34	03Gem00
02/13/1912	23Aqu26	10Aqu01	17Cap38	04Gem55
02/18/1912	28Aqu30	18Aqu15	23Cap43	06Gem58
02/23/1912	03Pis32	26Aqu52	29Cap49	09Gem07
02/28/1912	08Pis34	05Pis53	05Aqu56	11Gem21
03/04/1912	13Pis34	15Pis18	12Aqu03	13Gem41
03/09/1912	18Pis34	25Pis00	18Aqu10	16Gem05
03/14/1912	23Pis34	04Ari44	24Aqu18	18Gem33
03/19/1912	28Pis32	13Ari54	00Pis26	21Gem04
03/24/1912	03Ari30	21Ari36	06Pis34	23Gem39
03/29/1912	08Ari26	26Ari59	12Pis42	26Gem16
04/03/1912	13Ari22	29Ari33	18Pis49	28Gem56
04/08/1912	18Ari17	29Ari12	24Pis58	01Can39
04/13/1912	23Ari11	26Ari34	01Ari05	04Can22
04/18/1912	28Ari04	23Ari00	07Ari13	07Can09
04/23/1912	02Tau57	20Ari05	13Ari21	09Can56
04/28/1912	07Tau49	18Ari52	19Ari29	12Can45
05/03/1912	12Tau40	19Ari40	25Ari37	15Can36
05/08/1912	17Tau30	22Ari18	01Tau45	18Can27
05/03/1912	22Tau20	26Ari28	07Tau52	21Can20
05/18/1912	27Tau09	01Tau58	14Tau00	24Can15
05/23/1912	01Gem58	08Tau35	20Tau08	27Can09
05/28/1912	06Gem46	16Tau14	26Tau16	00Leo06
06/02/1912	11Gem33	24Tau54	02Gem24	03Leo03
06/07/1912	16Gem20	04Gem31	08Gem31	06Leo01
06/12/1912	21Gem07	14Gem58	14Gem39	09Leo00
06/17/1912	25Gem54	25Gem54	20Gem48	11Leo59
06/22/1912	00Can40	06Can46	26Gem55	15Leo00
06/27/1912	05Can26	17Can06	03Can04	18Leo01
07/02/1912	10Can12	26Can39	09Can13	21Leo03
07/07/1912	14Can58	05Leo21	12Can21	24Leo06
07/12/1912	19Can44	13Leo11	20Can30	27Leo10
07/17/1912	24Can30	20Leo09	27Can40	00Vir15
07/22/1912	29Can16	26Leo08	03Leo49	03Vir20
07/27/1912	04Leo03	01Vir01	09Leo59	06Vir26
08/01/1912	08Leo50	04Vir34	16Leo09	09Vir33
08/06/1912	13Leo37	06Vir25	22Leo19	12Vir41
08/11/1912	18Leo25	06Vir12	28Leo29	15Vir50
08/16/1912	23Leo13	03Vir45	04Vir39	19Vir00
08/21/1912	28Leo02	29Leo40	10Vir49	22Vir10
08/26/1912	02Vir51	25Leo36	17Vir00	25Vir22
08/31/1912	07Vir41	23Leo37	23Vir10	28Vir35
09/05/1912	12Vir32	25Leo00	29Vir21	01Lib48
09/10/1912	17Vir24	29Leo44	05Lib31	05Lib03
09/15/1912	22Vir16	07Vir01	11Lib42	08Lib19
09/20/1912	27Vir09	15Vir43	17Lib52	11Lib35
09/25/1912	02Lib03	24Vir52	24Lib01	14Lib53
09/30/1912	06Lib57	03Lib58	00Sco12	18Lib12

00Date	Sun	Mercury	Venus	Mars
10/05/1912	11Lib52	12Lib49	06Sco21	21Lib31
10/10/1912	16Lib49	21Lib20	12Sco31	24Lib52
10/15/1912	21Lib46	29Lib33	18Sco40	28Lib15
10/20/1912	26Lib44	07Sco28	24Sco49	01Sco37
10/25/1912	01Sco43	15Sco10	00Sag57	05Sco02
10/30/1912	06Sco42	22Sco37	07Sag06	08Sco27
11/04/1912	11Sco43	29Sco51	13Sag13	11Sco54
11/09/1912	16Sco44	06Sag46	19Sag21	15Sco22
11/14/1912	21Sco46	13Sag14	25Sag28	18Sco51
11/19/1912	26Sco49	18Sag55	01Cap34	22Sco21
11/24/1912	01Sag52	23Sag07	07Cap40	25Sco53
11/29/1912	06Sag55	24Sag38	13Cap45	29Sco25
12/04/1912	12Sag00	22Sag02	19Cap49	2Sag59
12/09/1912	17Sag04	15Sag45	25Cap52	06Sag34
12/14/1912	22Sag10	10Sag01	00Aqu53	10Sag10
12/19/1912	27Sag15	08Sag24	07Aqu53	13Sag48
12/24/1912	02Cap21	10Sag36	13Aqu51	17Sag26
12/29/1912	07Cap27	15Sag10	19Aqu46	21Sag06
01/03/1913	12Cap32	21Sag01	25Aqu39	24Sag46
01/08/1913	17Cap38	27Sag37	01Pis29	28Sag28
01/13/1913	22Cap43	04Cap39	07Pis15	02Cap10
01/18/1913	27Cap49	12Cap00	12Pis57	05Cap54
01/23/1913	02Aqu54	19Cap37	18Pis34	09Cap39
01/28/1913	08Aqu00	27Cap28	24Pis06	13Cap25
02/02/1913	13Aqu04	05Aqu37	29Pis30	17Cap12
02/07/1913	18Aqu08	14Aqu04	04Ari46	20Cap59
02/12/1913	23Aqu12	22Aqu51	09Ari54	24Cap47
02/17/1913	28Aqu15	01Pis57	14Ari51	28Cap36
02/22/1913	03Pis18	11Pis18	19Ari35	02Aqu25
02/27/1913	08Pis19	20Pis37	24Ari04	06Aqu16
03/04/1913	13Pis20	29Pis18	28Ari15	10Aqu06
03/09/1913	18Pis20	06Ari24	02Tau04	13Aqu58
03/14/1913	23Pis19	10Ari49	05Tau27	17Aqu49
03/19/1913	28Pis18	11Ari53	08Tau18	21Aqu41
03/24/1913	03Ari15	09Ari46	10Tau31	25Aqu33
03/29/1913	08Ari12	05Ari46	11Tau57	29Aqu26
04/03/1913	13Ari07	01Ari55	12Tau30	03Pis18
04/08/1913	18Ari03	29Pis47	12Tau03	07Pis10
04/13/1913	22Ari57	29Pis51	10Tau35	11Pis03
04/18/1913	27Ari51	01Ari56	08Tau13	14Pis55
04/23/1913	02Tau43	05Ari42	05Tau15	18Pis46
04/28/1913	07Tau35	10Ari47	02Tau07	22Pis37
05/03/1913	12Tau26	16Ari58	29Ari21	26Pis28
05/08/1913	17Tau16	24Ari04	27Ari19	00Ari18
05/13/1913	22Tau06	02Tau04	26Ari14	04Ari07
05/18/1913	26Tau55	10Tau54	26Ari10	07Ari55
05/23/1913	01Gem44	20Tau36	27Ari01	11Ari42
05/28/1913	06Gem32	01Gem03	28Ari42	15Ari28
06/02/1913	11Gem19	11Gem58	01Tau04	19Ari14
06/07/1913	16Gem06	22Gem52	04Tau01	22Ari58
06/12/1913	20Gem53	03Can15	07Tau25	26Ari40
06/17/1913	25Gem40	12Can48	11Tau13	00Tau21
06/22/1913	00Can26	21Can23	15Tau21	04Tau01
06/27/1913	05Can12	28Can58	19Tau44	07Tau39

Ephemeris Tables for Sun, Mercury, Venus and Mars

00Date	Sun	Mercury	Venus	Mars	00Date	Sun	Mercury	Venus	Mars
07/02/1913	09Can58	05Leo31	24Tau20	11Tau14	04/03/1914	12Ari54	15Pis31	25Ari26	17Can15
07/07/1913	14Can44	10Leo57	29Tau08	14Tau48	04/08/1914	17Ari48	20Pis09	01Tau37	19Can18
07/12/1913	19Can30	15Leo03	04Gem05	18Tau20	04/13/1914	22Ari43	25Pis54	07Tau47	21Can27
07/17/1913	24Can16	17Leo34	09Gem10	21Tau49	04/18/1914	27Ari36	02Ari32	13Tau57	23Can40
07/22/1913	29Can03	18Leo13	14Gem22	25Tau17	04/23/1914	02Tau29	09Ari58	20Tau05	25Can59
07/27/1913	03Leo49	16Leo51	19Gem41	28Tau42	04/28/1914	07Tau21	18Ari10	26Tau13	28Can22
08/01/1913	08Leo36	13Leo43	25Gem06	02Gem04	05/03/1914	12Tau12	27Ari06	02Gem21	00Leo49
08/06/1913	13Leo24	09Leo57	00Can34	05Gem24	05/08/1914	17Tau03	06Tau47	08Gem27	03Leo19
08/11/1913	18Leo11	07Leo10	06Can07	08Gem40	05/13/1914	21Tau52	17Tau09	14Gem33	05Leo52
08/16/1913	22Leo59	06Leo48	11Can45	11Gem53	05/18/1914	26Tau41	28Tau00	20Gem37	08Leo29
08/21/1913	27Leo48	09Leo27	17Can26	15Gem03	05/23/1914	01Gem30	08Gem52	26Gem42	11Leo09
08/26/1913	02Vir37	15Leo01	23Can10	18Gem10	05/28/1914	06Gem18	19Gem14	02Can45	13Leo50
08/31/1913	07Vir27	22Leo50	28Can58	21Gem12					
					06/02/1914	11Gem06	28Gem41	08Can47	16Leo34
09/05/1913	12Vir18	01Vir58	04Leo48	24Gem10	06/07/1914	15Gem52	07Can03	14Can48	19Leo21
09/10/1913	17Vir09	11Vir33	10Leo42	27Gem04	06/12/1914	20Gem39	14Can14	20Can49	22Leo09
09/15/1913	22Vir01	21Vir01	16Leo37	29Gem53	06/17/1914	25Gem26	20Can12	26Can48	24Leo59
09/20/1913	26Vir54	00Lib09	22Leo35	02Can37	06/22/1914	00Can12	24Can47	02Leo46	27Leo51
09/25/1913	01Lib48	08Lib53	28Leo36	05Can15	06/27/1914	04Can58	27Can49	08Leo42	00Vir45
09/30/1913	06Lib43	17Lib13	04Vir38	07Can47					
					07/02/1914	09Can44	29Can05	14Leo37	03Vir41
10/05/1913	11Lib38	25Lib12	10Vir42	10Can12	07/07/1914	14Can30	28Can26	20Leo31	06Vir39
10/10/1913	16Lib34	02Sco51	16Vir48	12Can29	07/12/1914	19Can16	26Can04	26Leo24	09Vir37
10/15/1913	21Lib31	10Sco10	22Vir55	14Can37	07/17/1914	24Can03	22Can49	02Vir13	12Vir38
10/20/1913	26Lib30	17Sco10	29Vir04	16Can37	07/22/1914	28Can49	20Can00	08Vir01	15Vir40
10/25/1913	01Sco28	23Sco45	05Lib15	18Can26	07/27/1914	03Leo36	18Can51	13Vir48	18Vir43
10/30/1913	06Sco28	29Sco43	11Lib27	20Can04					
					08/01/1914	08Leo22	20Can08	19Vir31	21Vir49
11/04/1913	11Sco28	04Sag44	17Lib39	21Can28	08/06/1914	13Leo09	24Can01	25Vir12	24Vir55
11/09/1913	16Sco30	08Sag05	23Lib52	22Can39	08/11/1914	17Leo57	00Leo21	00Lib49	28Vir03
11/14/1913	21Sco31	08Sag37	00Sco07	23Can34	08/16/1914	22Leo45	08Leo38	06Lib24	01Lib12
11/19/1913	26Sco34	05Sag09	06Sco22	24Can13	08/21/1914	27Leo34	18Leo10	11Lib55	04Lib24
11/24/1913	01Sag37	28Sco40	12Sco37	24Can32	08/26/1914	02Vir23	28Leo07	17Lib21	07Lib36
11/29/1913	06Sag41	23Sco35	18Sco53	24Can32	08/31/1914	07Vir13	07Vir57	22Lib42	10Lib49
12/04/1913	11Sag45	22Sco55	25Sco09	24Can10	09/05/1914	12Vir04	17Vir22	27Lib58	14Lib05
12/09/1913	16Sag50	26Sco02	01Sag26	23Can28	09/10/1914	16Vir55	26Vir18	03Sco07	17Lib21
12/14/1913	21Sag55	01Sag19	07Sag43	22Can24	09/15/1914	21Vir47	04Lib46	08Sco08	20Lib40
12/19/1913	27Sag00	07Sag45	14Sag00	21Can01	09/20/1914	26Vir40	12Lib47	13Sco01	23Lib59
12/24/1913	02Cap06	14Sag43	20Sag17	19Can22	09/25/1914	01Lib34	20Lib24	17Sco42	27Lib21
12/29/1913	07Cap12	22Sag02	26Sag34	17Can31	09/30/1914	06Lib28	27Lib36	22Sco11	00Sco43
01/03/1914	12Cap18	29Sag32	02Cap52	15Can33	10/05/1914	11Lib24	04Sco20	26Sco24	04Sco07
01/08/1914	17Cap23	07Cap13	09Cap09	13Can33	10/10/1914	16Lib20	10Sco33	00Sag19	07Sco33
01/13/1914	22Cap29	15Cap04	15Cap26	11Can39	10/15/1914	21Lib17	16Sco00	03Sag50	11Sco00
01/18/1914	27Cap34	23Cap08	21Cap43	09Can55	10/20/1914	26Lib15	20Sco18	06Sag54	14Sco28
01/23/1914	02Aqu40	01Aqu25	28Cap00	08Can26	10/25/1914	01Sco14	22Sco45	09Sag23	17Sco58
01/28/1914	07Aqu45	09Aqu57	04Aqu17	07Can15	10/30/1914	06Sco13	22Sco16	11Sag10	21Sco29
02/02/1914	12Aqu49	18Aqu44	10Aqu34	06Can24	11/04/1914	11Sco14	18Sco03	12Sag09	25Sco02
02/07/1914	17Aqu53	27Aqu41	16Aqu51	05Can52	11/09/1914	16Sco15	11Sco39	12Sag10	28Sco36
02/12/1914	22Aqu57	06Pis32	23Aqu07	05Can41	11/14/1914	21Sco17	07Sco24	11Sag12	02Sag12
02/17/1914	28Aqu00	14Pis42	29Aqu23	05Can48	11/19/1914	26Sco19	07Sco42	09Sag15	05Sag49
02/22/1914	03Pis03	21Pis07	05Pis39	06Can13	11/24/1914	01Sag22	11Sco39	06Sag34	09Sag28
02/27/1914	08Pis04	24Pis31	11Pis54	06Can54	11/29/1914	06Sag26	17Sco38	03Sag34	13Sag07
03/04/1914	13Pis06	24Pis04	18Pis09	07Can50	12/04/1914	11Sag30	24Sco34	00Sag44	16Sag49
03/09/1914	18Pis08	20Pis21	24Pis23	08Can58	12/09/1914	16Sag35	01Sag57	28Sco32	20Sag31
03/14/1914	23Pis05	15Pis33	00Ari36	10Can19	12/14/1914	21Sag40	09Sag31	27Sco15	24Sag15
03/19/1914	28Pis03	12Pis04	06Ari49	11Can50	12/19/1914	26Sag45	17Sag11	27Sco00	28Sag00
03/24/1914	03Ari00	11Pis01	13Ari02	13Can31	12/24/1914	01Cap51	24Sag56	27Sco45	01Cap46
03/29/1914	07Ari57	12Pis19	19Ari14	15Can19	12/29/1914	06Cap57	02Cap47	29Sco22	05Cap34

Ephemeris Tables for Sun, Mercury, Venus and Mars

Date	Sun	Mercury	Venus	Mars
01/03/1915	12Cap03	10Cap45	01Sag45	09Cap22
01/08/1915	17Cap09	18Cap52	04Sag45	13Cap12
01/13/1915	22Cap14	27Cap10	08Sag16	17Cap02
01/18/1915	27Cap19	05Aqu37	12Sag13	20Cap53
01/23/1915	02Aqu25	14Aqu09	16Sag30	24Cap45
01/28/1915	07Aqu30	22Aqu30	21Sag04	28Cap38
02/02/1915	12Aqu34	00Pis06	25Sag52	02Aqu32
02/07/1915	17Aqu39	05Pis47	00Cap51	06Aqu26
02/12/1915	22Aqu42	08Pis07	06Cap00	10Aqu21
02/17/1915	27Aqu46	06Pis13	11Cap16	14Aqu16
02/22/1915	02Pis48	01Pis14	16Cap39	18Aqu11
02/27/1915	07Pis50	26Aqu13	22Cap08	22Aqu07
03/04/1915	12Pis51	23Aqu32	27Cap42	26Aqu03
03/09/1915	17Pis51	23Aqu39	03Aqu19	29Aqu59
03/14/1915	22Pis51	26Aqu03	09Aqu01	3Pis55
03/19/1915	27Pis49	00Pis08	14Aqu45	07Pis51
03/24/1915	02Ari46	05Pis25	20Aqu31	11Pis46
03/29/1915	07Ari43	11Pis38	26Aqu20	15Pis41
04/03/1915	12Ari39	18Pis37	02Pis12	19Pis36
04/08/1915	17Ari34	26Pis16	08Pis04	23Pis30
04/13/1915	22Ari28	04Ari33	13Pis57	27Pis24
04/18/1915	27Ari22	13Ari30	19Pis52	01Ari16
04/23/1915	02Tau15	23Ari06	25Pis48	05Ari09
04/28/1915	07Tau07	03Tau20	01Ari44	09Ari00
05/03/1915	11Tau58	14Tau02	07Ari42	12Ari50
05/08/1915	16Tau48	24Tau48	13Ari40	16Ari40
05/13/1915	21Tau38	5Gem03	19Ari39	20Ari28
05/18/1915	26Tau27	14Gem19	25Ari39	24Ari15
05/23/1915	01Gem16	22Gem19	01Tau39	28Ari01
05/28/1915	06Gem04	28Gem55	7Tau40	01Tau46
06/02/1915	10Gem52	04Can01	13Tau41	05Tau30
06/07/1915	15Gem39	07Can30	19Tau43	09Tau12
06/12/1915	20Gem25	09Can10	25Tau45	12Tau52
06/17/1915	25Gem12	08Can58	01Gem48	16Tau31
06/22/1915	29Gem58	07Can06	07Gem51	20Tau09
06/27/1915	04Can45	04Can16	13Gem55	23Tau45
07/02/1915	09Can30	01Can37	19Gem59	27Tau19
07/07/1915	14Can16	00Can16	26Gem04	00Gem52
07/12/1915	19Can03	00Can54	02Can09	04Gem23
07/17/1915	23Can49	03Can44	08Can16	07Gem52
07/22/1915	28Can35	08Can44	14Can22	11Gem19
07/27/1915	03Leo21	15Can44	20Can30	14Gem45
08/01/1915	08Leo09	24Can26	26Can38	18Gem09
08/06/1915	12Leo55	04Leo17	02Leo46	21Gem30
08/11/1915	17Leo43	14Leo34	08Leo56	24Gem19
08/16/1915	22Leo31	24Leo43	15Leo06	28Gem07
08/21/1915	27Leo20	4Vir24	21Leo17	01Can22
08/26/1915	02Vir09	13Vir33	27Leo28	04Can35
08/31/1915	06Vir59	22Vir08	03Vir40	07Can45
09/05/1915	11Vir49	00Lib12	09Vir52	10Can54
09/10/1915	16Vir41	07Lib45	16Vir05	13Can59
09/15/1915	21Vir33	14Lib48	22Vir18	17Can01
09/20/1915	26Vir26	21Lib17	28Vir31	20Can01
09/25/1915	01Lib19	27Lib06	04Lib45	22Can58
09/30/1915	06Lib14	10Sco58	10Lib59	25Can51
10/05/1915	11Lib09	05Sco30	17Lib13	28Can41
10/10/1915	16Lib06	06Sco58	23Lib28	01Leo27
10/15/1915	21Lib03	05Sco28	29Lib42	04Leo09
10/20/1915	26Lib01	00Sco39	05Sco57	06Leo46
10/25/1915	00Sco59	24Lib39	12Sco12	09Leo18
10/30/1915	05Sco59	21Lib22	18Sco27	11Leo46
11/04/1915	10Sco59	22Lib38	24Sco42	14Leo07
11/09/1915	16Sco00	27Lib23	00Sag56	16Leo22
11/14/1915	21Sco02	04Sco00	07Sag11	18Leo30
11/19/1915	26Sco04	11Sco27	13Sag26	20Leo30
11/24/1915	01Sag07	19Sco13	19Sag40	22Leo22
11/29/1915	06Sag12	27Sco03	25Sag55	24Leo04
12/04/1915	11Sag16	04Sag53	02Cap09	25Leo35
12/09/1915	16Sag20	12Sag43	08Cap24	26Leo55
12/14/1915	21Sag25	20Sag34	14Cap38	28Leo01
12/19/1915	26Sag31	28Sag28	20Cap52	28Leo52
12/24/1915	01Cap36	06Cap26	27Cap05	29Leo28
12/29/1915	06Cap42	14Cap29	03Aqu18	29Leo46
01/03/1916	11Cap48	22Cap37	09Aqu31	29Leo46
01/08/1916	16Cap54	00Aqu43	15Aqu43	29Leo26
01/13/1916	21Cap59	08Aqu32	21Aqu54	28Leo46
01/18/1916	27Cap04	15Aqu29	28Aqu04	27Leo46
01/23/1916	02Aqu10	20Aqu24	04Pis14	26Leo26
01/28/1916	07Aqu15	21Aqu40	10Pis22	24Leo51
02/02/1916	12Aqu19	18Aqu27	16Pis29	23Leo01
02/07/1916	17Aqu24	12Aqu36	22Pis34	21Leo04
02/12/1916	22Aqu27	07Aqu52	28Pis38	19Leo05
02/17/1916	27Aqu30	06Aqu11	04Ari39	17Leo08
02/22/1916	02Pis33	07Aqu25	10Ari38	15Leo20
02/27/1916	07Pis35	10Aqu45	16Ari36	13Leo45
03/03/1916	12Pis36	15Aqu32	22Ari30	12Leo25
03/08/1916	17Pis36	21Aqu20	28Ari21	11Leo25
03/13/1916	22Pis36	27Aqu54	04Tau09	10Leo44
03/18/1916	27Pis34	05Pis06	09Tau54	10Leo22
03/23/1916	02Ari31	12Pis52	15Tau34	10Leo21
03/28/1916	07Ari28	21Pis12	21Tau10	10Leo36
04/02/1916	12Ari25	00Ari05	26Tau40	11Leo08
04/07/1916	17Ari20	09Ari34	02Gem04	11Leo56
04/12/1916	22Ari15	19Ari37	07Gem22	12Leo57
04/17/1916	27Ari08	00Tau06	12Gem32	14Leo11
04/22/1916	02Tau01	10Tau40	17Gem33	15Leo36
04/27/1916	06Tau52	20Tau44	22Gem23	17Leo11
05/02/1916	11Tau44	29Tau43	27Gem01	18Leo55
05/07/1916	16Tau34	07Gem12	01Can24	20Leo48
05/12/1916	21Tau24	13Gem00	05Can30	22Leo48
05/17/1916	26Tau13	16Gem58	09Can15	24Leo54
05/22/1916	01Gem02	19Gem00	12Can34	27Leo06
05/27/1916	05Gem50	19Gem03	15Can24	29Leo24
06/01/1916	10Gem37	17Gem23	17Can36	01Vir46
06/06/1916	15Gem25	14Gem43	19Can04	04Vir13
06/11/1916	20Gem12	12Gem11	19Can42	06Vir45
06/16/1916	24Gem08	10Gem48	19Can22	09Vir21
06/21/1916	29Gem45	11Gem10	18Can03	12Vir00
06/26/1916	04Can31	13Gem29	15Can49	14Vir42

Ephemeris Tables for Sun, Mercury, Venus and Mars

Date	Sun	Mercury	Venus	Mars
07/01/1916	09Can16	17Gem40	12Can56	17Vir27
07/06/1916	14Can03	23Gem37	09Can50	20Vir16
07/11/1916	18Can49	01Can13	06Can59	23Vir07
07/16/1916	23Can35	10Can15	04Can48	26Vir01
07/21/1916	28Can21	20Can21	03Can31	28Vir58
07/26/1916	03Leo07	00Leo55	03Can13	01Lib57
07/31/1916	07Leo54	11Leo21	03Can52	04Lib59
08/05/1916	12Leo42	21Leo16	05Can22	08Lib03
08/10/1916	17Leo29	00Vir36	07Can35	11Lib09
08/15/1916	22Leo18	09Vir18	10Can24	14Lib17
08/20/1916	27Leo06	17Vir22	13Can43	17Lib27
08/25/1916	01Vir55	24Vir53	17Can27	20Lib40
08/30/1916	06Vir45	01Lib43	21Can33	23Lib55
09/04/1916	11Vir36	07Lib54	25Can55	27Lib11
09/09/1916	16Vir27	13Lib15	00Leo31	00Sco30
09/14/1916	21Vir19	17Lib28	05Leo21	03Sco51
09/19/1916	26Vir12	20Lib08	10Leo22	07Sco13
09/24/1916	01Lib06	20Lib33	15Leo31	10Sco37
09/29/1916	06Lib00	18Lib04	20Leo49	14Sco04
10/04/1916	10Lib55	12Lib57	26Leo13	17Sco31
10/09/1916	15Lib51	07Lib37	01Vir45	21Sco01
10/14/1916	20Lib48	05Lib28	07Vir21	24Sco33
10/19/1916	25Lib46	07Lib41	13Vir03	28Sco07
10/24/1916	00Sco45	13Lib10	18Vir49	01Sag42
10/29/1916	05Sco44	20Lib24	24Vir39	05Sag19
11/03/1916	10Sco45	28Lib21	00Lib33	08Sag58
11/08/1916	15Sco46	06Sco29	06Lib29	12Sag38
11/13/1916	20Sco48	14Sco36	12Lib28	16Sag19
11/18/1916	25Sco50	22Sco37	18Lib30	20Sag03
11/23/1916	00Sag53	00Sag33	24Lib34	23Sag48
11/28/1916	05Sag57	08Sag25	00Sco39	27Sag33
12/03/1916	11Sag01	16Sag15	06Sco46	01Cap21
12/08/1916	16Sag06	24Sag03	12Sco55	05Cap10
12/13/1916	21Sag10	01Cap52	19Sco05	09Cap00
12/18/1916	26Sag16	09Cap40	25Sco16	12Cap51
12/23/1916	01Cap21	17Cap21	01Sag27	16Cap43
12/28/1916	06Cap27	24Cap37	07Sag40	20Cap36
01/02/1917	11Cap33	00Aqu52	13Sag52	24Cap30
01/07/1917	16Cap39	04Aqu57	20Sag06	28Cap24
01/12/1917	21Cap45	05Aqu10	26Sag19	02Aqu19
01/17/1917	26Cap50	00Aqu51	02Cap33	06Aqu15
01/22/1917	01Aqu55	24Cap33	08Cap48	10Aqu12
01/27/1917	07Aqu00	20Cap24	15Cap02	14Aqu08
02/01/1917	12Aqu05	19Cap48	21Cap16	18Aqu05
02/06/1917	17Aqu09	22Cap03	27Cap31	22Aqu03
02/11/1917	22Aqu13	26Cap11	03Aqu45	26Aqu00
02/16/1917	27Aqu16	01Aqu33	10Aqu00	29Aqu58
02/21/1917	02Pis19	07Aqu45	16Aqu13	03Pis55
02/26/1917	07Pis21	14Aqu35	22Aqu28	07Pis52
03/03/1917	11Pis22	21Aqu56	28Aqu42	11Pis48
03/08/1917	17Pis22	29Aqu46	04Pis56	15Pis45
03/13/1917	22Pis21	08Pis04	11Pis09	19Pis40
03/18/1917	27Pis20	16Pis52	17Pis22	23Pis35
03/23/1917	02Ari17	26Pis11	23Pis36	27Pis30
03/28/1917	07Ari14	06Ari00	29Pis48	01Ari22

Date	Sun	Mercury	Venus	Mars
04/02/1917	12Ari10	16Ari12	06Ari00	05Ari15
04/07/1917	17Ari06	26Ari30	12Ari12	09Ari07
04/12/1917	22Ari00	06Tau18	18Ari24	12Ari58
04/17/1917	26Ari54	14Tau54	24Ari35	16Ari48
04/22/1917	01Tau46	21Tau45	00Tau46	20Ari37
04/27/1917	06Tau39	26Tau31	06Tau56	24Ari24
05/02/1917	11Tau30	29Tau03	13Tau06	28Ari11
05/07/1917	16Tau21	29Tau21	19Tau16	01Tau56
05/12/1917	21Tau10	27Tau43	25Tau26	05Tau40
05/17/1917	26Tau00	24Tau58	01Gem35	09Tau22
05/22/1917	00Gem48	22Tau16	07Gem44	13Tau04
05/27/1917	05Gem36	20Tau43	13Gem53	16Tau44
06/01/1917	10Gem24	20Tau55	20Gem01	20Tau22
06/06/1917	15Gem11	22Tau57	26Gem09	24Tau00
06/11/1917	19Gem58	26Tau42	02Can18	27Tau36
06/16/1917	24Gem45	02Gem01	08Can25	01Gem10
06/21/1917	29Gem31	08Gem45	14Can33	04Gem43
06/26/1917	04Can16	16Gem49	20Can40	08Gem14
07/01/1917	09Can03	26Gem07	26Can46	11Gem45
07/06/1917	13Can49	06Can24	02Leo53	15Gem13
07/11/1917	18Can35	17Can09	09Leo00	18Gem40
07/16/1917	23Can21	27Can48	15Leo06	22Gem06
07/21/1917	28Can07	07Leo57	21Leo11	25Gem30
07/26/1917	02Leo54	17Leo25	27Leo16	28Gem53
07/31/1917	07Leo40	26Leo11	03Vir21	02Can14
08/05/1917	12Leo28	04Vir15	09Vir25	05Can34
08/10/1917	17Leo15	11Vir37	15Vir29	08Can52
08/15/1917	22Leo03	18Vir15	21Vir32	12Can09
08/20/1917	26Leo52	24Vir03	27Vir34	15Can24
08/25/1917	01Vir41	28Vir50	03Lib36	18Can38
08/30/1917	06Vir31	02Lib18	09Lib37	21Can50
09/04/1917	11Vir22	04Lib00	15Lib37	25Can00
09/09/1917	16Vir13	03Lib19	21Lib36	28Can09
09/14/1917	21Vir05	00Lib00	27Lib34	01Leo16
09/19/1917	25Vir58	24Vir54	03Sco31	04Leo22
09/24/1917	00Lib51	20Vir34	09Sco27	07Leo25
09/29/1917	05Lib46	19Vir39	15Sco21	10Leo27
10/04/1917	10Lib41	22Vir48	21Sco15	13Leo26
10/09/1917	15Lib37	28Vir58	27Sco06	16Leo24
10/14/1917	20Lib34	06Lib47	02Sag56	19Leo19
10/19/1917	25Lib31	15Lib13	08Sag43	22Leo12
10/24/1917	00Sco30	23Lib44	14Sag28	25Leo02
10/29/1917	05Sco30	2Sco08	20Sag11	27Leo49
11/03/1917	10Sco30	10Sco21	25Sag51	00Vir34
11/08/1917	15Sco31	18Sco23	01Cap26	03Vir15
11/13/1917	20Sco33	26Sco16	06Cap57	05Vir54
11/18/1917	25Sco35	04Sag02	12Cap23	08Vir28
11/23/1917	00Sag38	11Sag43	17Cap43	10Vir58
11/28/1917	05Sag42	19Sag18	22Cap55	13Vir24
12/03/1917	10Sag46	26Sag46	27Cap58	15Vir45
12/08/1917	15Sag51	04Cap00	02Aqu51	18Vir00
12/13/1917	20Sag55	10Cap42	07Aqu30	20Vir09
12/18/1917	26Sag01	16Cap14	11Aqu54	22Vir12
12/23/1917	01Cap06	19Cap27	15Aqu58	24Vir07
12/28/1917	06Cap12	18Cap39	19Aqu38	25Vir54

Ephemeris Tables for Sun, Mercury, Venus and Mars

Date	Sun	Mercury	Venus	Mars
01/02/1918	11Cap18	13Cap25	22Aqu49	27Vir32
01/07/1918	16Cap24	07Cap03	25Aqu25	29Vir00
01/12/1918	21Cap30	03Cap41	27Aqu19	00Lib16
01/17/1918	26Cap35	04Cap08	28Aqu21	01Lib19
01/22/1918	01Aqu40	07Cap18	28Aqu25	02Lib09
01/27/1918	06Aqu45	12Cap09	27Aqu25	02Lib44
02/01/1918	11Aqu50	18Cap01	25Aqu27	03Lib01
02/06/1918	16Aqu54	24Cap33	22Aqu43	03Lib01
02/11/1918	21Aqu58	01Aqu36	19Aqu39	02Lib42
02/16/1918	27Aqu01	09Aqu04	16Aqu44	02Lib03
02/21/1918	02Pis04	16Aqu55	14Aqu27	01Lib05
02/26/1918	07Pis06	25Aqu09	13Aqu05	29Vir48
03/03/1918	12Pis07	03Pis50	12Aqu45	28Vir15
03/08/1918	17Pis07	12Pis57	13Aqu24	26Vir29
03/13/1918	22Pis07	22Pis30	14Aqu55	24Vir34
03/18/1918	27Pis06	02Ari23	17Aqu12	22Vir37
03/23/1918	05Ari11	12Ari21	20Aqu05	20Vir42
03/28/1918	07Ari00	21Ari48	23Aqu28	18Vir54
04/02/1918	11Ari56	29Ari56	27Aqu16	17Vir19
04/07/1918	16Ari51	05Tau59	01Pis25	16Vir00
04/12/1918	21Ari46	09Tau31	05Pis50	14Vir58
04/17/1918	26Ari39	10Tau23	10Pis29	14Vir17
04/22/1918	01Tau33	08Tau51	15Pis19	13Vir55
04/27/1918	06Tau24	05Tau50	20Pis18	13Vir52
05/02/1918	11Tau16	02Tau42	25Pis26	14Vir07
05/07/1918	16Tau06	00Tau43	00Ari40	14Vir40
05/12/1918	20Tau56	00Tau33	06Ari00	15Vir28
05/17/1918	25Tau45	02Tau18	11Ari25	16Vir31
05/22/1918	00Gem34	05Tau43	16Ari54	17Vir48
05/27/1918	05Gem22	10Tau37	22Ari27	19Vir15
06/01/1918	10Gem10	16Tau47	28Ari03	20Vir54
06/06/1918	14Gem57	24Tau07	03Tau42	22Vir42
06/11/1918	19Gem44	02Gem33	09Tau24	24Vir39
06/16/1918	24Gem30	12Gem03	15Tau07	26Vir44
06/21/1918	29Gem17	22Gem25	20Tau54	28Vir57
06/26/1918	04Can03	03Can18	26Tau42	01Lib15
07/01/1918	08Can49	14Can07	02Gem31	03Lib40
07/06/1918	13Can35	24Can25	08Gem22	06Lib11
07/11/1918	18Can21	04Leo00	14Gem15	08Lib47
07/16/1918	23Can07	12Leo47	20Gem10	11Lib28
07/21/1918	27Can54	20Leo46	26Gem06	14Lib13
07/26/1918	02Leo40	27Leo56	02Can03	17Lib02
07/31/1918	07Leo27	04Vir14	08Can01	19Lib55
08/05/1918	12Leo14	09Vir33	14Can02	22Lib52
08/10/1918	17Leo01	13Vir39	20Can03	25Lib53
08/15/1918	21Leo49	16Vir13	26Can06	28Lib57
08/20/1918	26Leo38	16Vir49	02Leo10	02Sco04
08/25/1918	01Vir27	15Vir04	08Leo15	05Sco15
08/30/1918	06Vir17	11Vir11	14Leo22	08Sco28
09/04/1918	11Vir07	06Vir33	20Leo30	11Sco44
09/09/1918	15Vir58	03Vir32	26Leo39	15Sco03
09/14/1918	20Vir51	03Vir55	02Vir48	18Sco24
09/19/1918	25Vir43	07Vir58	08Vir59	21Sco48
09/24/1918	00Lib37	14Vir47	15Vir11	25Sco15
09/29/1918	05Lib31	23Vir07	21Vir23	28Sco43

Date	Sun	Mercury	Venus	Mars
10/04/1918	10Lib27	02Lib01	27Vir37	02Sag14
10/09/1918	15Lib22	10Lib55	03Lib51	05Sag47
10/14/1918	20Lib19	19Lib36	10Lib05	09Sag22
10/19/1918	25Lib17	28Lib01	16Lib21	13Sag00
10/24/1918	00Sco16	06Sco10	22Lib36	16Sag39
10/29/1918	05Sco15	14Sco06	28Lib52	20Sag20
11/03/1918	10Sco15	21Sco49	5Sco08	24Sag03
11/08/1918	15Sco16	29Sco22	11Sco25	27Sag47
11/13/1918	20Sco18	06Sag45	17Sco42	01Cap33
11/18/1918	25Sco21	13Sag52	23Sco59	05Cap21
11/23/1918	00Sag24	20Sag39	00Sag16	09Cap10
11/28/1918	05Sag27	26Sag45	06Sag33	13Cap00
12/03/1918	10Sag31	01Cap31	12Sag50	16Cap51
12/08/1918	15Sag36	03Cap49	19Sag07	20Cap43
12/13/1918	20Sag41	02Cap02	25Sag25	24Cap37
12/18/1918	25Sag46	26Sag09	01Cap42	28Cap31
12/23/1918	00Cap52	20Sag00	08Cap00	02Aqu26
12/28/1918	05Cap57	17Sag33	14Cap16	06Aqu21
01/02/1919	11Cap03	19Sag00	20Cap34	10Aqu18
01/07/1919	16Cap09	23Sag00	26Cap51	14Aqu14
01/12/1919	21Cap15	28Sag28	03Aqu07	18Aqu10
01/17/1919	26Cap20	04Cap47	09Aqu24	22Aqu07
01/22/1919	01Aqu25	11Cap38	15Aqu39	26Aqu04
01/27/1919	06Aqu31	18Cap52	21Aqu55	00Pis01
02/01/1919	11Aqu35	26Cap25	28Aqu11	03Pis58
02/06/1919	16Aqu39	04Aqu16	04Pis26	07Pis54
02/11/1919	21Aqu43	12Aqu26	10Pis40	11Pis50
02/16/1919	26Aqu46	20Aqu57	16Pis54	15Pis45
02/21/1919	01Pis49	29Aqu51	23Pis06	19Pis40
02/26/1919	06Pis51	09Pis07	29Pis18	23Pis34
03/03/1919	11Pis52	18Pis40	05Ari29	27Pis27
03/08/1919	16Pis53	28Pis15	11Ari39	01Ari19
03/13/1919	21Pis52	07Ari15	17Ari48	05Ari11
03/18/1919	26Pis51	14Ari50	23Ari56	09Ari01
03/23/1919	01Ari48	20Ari00	00Tau03	12Ari51
03/28/1919	06Ari45	22Ari08	06Tau08	16Ari40
04/02/1919	11Ari42	21Ari12	12Tau12	20Ari27
04/07/1919	16Ari37	18Ari01	18Tau15	24Ari13
04/12/1919	21Ari31	14Ari13	24Tau16	27Ari58
04/17/1919	26Ari25	11Ari28	00Gem15	01Tau42
04/22/1919	01Tau18	10Ari39	06Gem12	05Tau25
04/27/1919	06Tau10	11Ari54	12Gem07	09Tau06
05/02/1919	11Tau01	14Ari57	18Gem01	12Tau46
05/07/1919	15Tau52	19Ari28	23Gem51	16Tau25
05/1/1919	20Tau42	25Ari13	29Gem40	20Tau02
05/17/1919	25Tau31	02Tau00	05Can25	23Tau39
05/22/1919	00Gem20	09Tau45	11Can07	27Tau13
05/27/1919	05Gem08	18Tau27	16Can46	00Gem47
06/01/1919	09Gem56	28Tau03	22Can22	04Gem19
06/06/1919	14Gem43	08Gem28	27Can52	07Gem50
06/11/1919	19Gem30	19Gem24	03Leo18	11Gem19
06/16/1919	24Gem16	00Can18	08Leo39	14Gem48
06/21/1919	29Gem03	10Can42	13Leo53	18Gem15
06/26/1919	03Can49	20Can19	19Leo00	21Gem42

Ephemeris Tables for Sun, Mercury, Venus and Mars

Date	Sun	Mercury	Venus	Mars
07/01/1919	08Can35	29Can02	23Leo59	25Gem06
07/06/1919	13Can21	06Leo51	28Leo48	28Gem30
07/11/1919	18Can07	13Leo42	03Vir25	01Can52
07/16/1919	22Can53	19Leo33	07Vir49	05Can14
07/21/1919	27Can39	24Leo13	11Vir58	08Can34
07/26/1919	02Leo26	27Leo27	15Vir46	11Can53
07/33/1919	07Leo13	28Leo56	19Vir12	15Can12
08/05/1919	12Leo00	28Leo21	22Vir09	18Can28
08/10/1919	16Leo48	25Leo41	24Vir31	21Can45
08/15/1919	21Leo36	21Leo41	26Vir13	25Can00
08/20/1919	26Leo24	18Leo01	27Vir07	28Can13
08/25/1919	01Vir13	16Leo33	27Vir06	01Leo26
08/30/1919	06Vir03	18Leo15	26Vir05	4Leo38
09/04/1919	10Vir54	23Leo10	24Vir09	07Leo49
09/09/1919	15Vir45	00Vir34	21Vir27	10Leo59
09/14/1919	20Vir36	09Vir24	18Vir24	14Leo07
09/19/1919	25Vir29	18Vir44	15Vir28	17Leo15
09/24/1919	00Lib23	28Vir00	13Vir06	20Leo22
09/29/1919	05Lib17	07Lib00	11Vir36	23Leo28
10/04/1919	10Lib12	15Lib37	11Vir06	26Leo33
10/09/1919	15Lib08	23Lib54	11Vir36	29Leo36
10/14/1919	20Lib05	01Sco52	12Vir59	02Vir38
10/19/1919	25Lib03	09Sco34	15Vir08	05Vir39
10/24/1919	00Sco01	16Sco59	17Vir57	08Vir39
10/29/1919	05Sco01	24Sco07	21Vir18	11Vir37
11/03/1919	10Sco01	00Sag56	25Vir06	14Vir34
11/08/1919	15Sco02	07Sag14	29Vir16	17Vir30
11/13/1919	20Sco03	12Sag42	03Lib45	20Vir23
11/18/1919	25Sco06	16Sag40	08Lib29	23Vir15
11/23/1919	00Sag09	18Sag00	13Lib27	26Vir05
11/28/1919	05Sag12	15Sag17	18Lib34	28Vir53
12/03/1919	10Sag16	09Sag00	23Lib52	01Lib39
12/08/1919	15Sag21	03Sag19	29Lib18	04Lib22
12/13/1919	20Sag26	01Sco49	04Sco49	07Lib03
12/18/1919	25Sag31	04Sag13	10Sco27	09Lib41
12/23/1919	00Cap37	09Sag00	16Sco10	12Lib15
12/28/1919	05Cap42	15Sag03	21Sco57	14Lib47
01/02/1920	10Cap48	21Sag47	27Sco47	17Lib14
01/07/1920	15Cap54	28Sag55	03Sag40	19Lib37
01/12/1920	21Cap00	06Cap19	09Sag36	21Lib56
01/17/1920	26Cap06	13Cap57	15Sag34	24Lib09
01/22/1920	01Aqu11	21Cap47	21Sag34	26Lib16
01/27/1920	06Aqu16	29Cap52	27Sag35	28Lib18
02/01/1920	11Aqu21	08Aqu14	03Cap38	00Sco12
02/06/1920	16Aqu25	16Aqu54	9Cap42	01Sco58
02/11/1920	21Aqu28	25Aqu51	15Cap46	03Sco34
02/16/1920	26Aqu31	05Pis01	21Cap52	05Sco01
02/21/1920	01Pis35	14Pis10	27Cap58	06Sco18
02/26/1920	06Pis37	22Pis42	04Aqu05	07Sco21
03/02/1920	11Pis38	29Pis39	10Aqu12	08Sco10
03/07/1920	16Pis38	03Ari51	16Aqu20	08Sco45
03/12/1920	21Pis38	04Ari29	22Aqu28	09Sco04
03/17/1920	26Pis37	01Ari49	28Aqu36	09Sco04
03/22/1920	01Ari34	27Pis27	04Pis44	08Sco46
03/27/1920	06Ari31	23Pis36	10Pis52	08Sco08

Date	Sun	Mercury	Venus	Mars
04/01/1920	11Ari27	21Pis45	17Pis01	07Sco12
04/06/1920	16Ari23	22Pis13	23Pis09	05Sco57
04/11/1920	21Ari17	24Pis42	29Pis17	04Sco27
04/16/1920	26Ari11	28Pis46	05Ari25	02Sco45
04/21/1920	01Tau04	04Ari06	11Ari33	00Sco54
04/26/1920	05Tau56	10Ari26	17Ari41	29Lib01
05/01/1920	10Tau48	17Ari39	23Ari49	27Lib12
05/06/1920	15Tau38	25Ari41	29Ari57	25Lib31
05/11/1920	20Tau28	04Tau32	06Tau05	24Lib03
05/16/1920	25Tau18	14Tau10	12Tau13	22Lib52
05/21/1920	00Gem06	24Tau33	18Tau21	21Lib59
05/26/1920	04Gem54	05Gem26	24Tau29	21Lib27
05/31/1920	09Gem42	16Gem21	00Gem37	21Lib15
06/05/1920	14Gem29	26Gem48	6Gem45	21Lib23
06/10/1920	19Gem16	06Can22	12Gem52	21Lib50
06/15/1920	24Gem03	14Can56	19Gem01	22Lib34
06/20/1920	28Gem49	22Can27	25Gem09	23Lib35
06/25/1920	03Can35	28Can50	01Can17	24Lib51
06/30/1920	08Can21	04Leo01	07Can26	26Lib20
07/05/1920	13Can07	07Leo48	13Can34	28Lib01
07/10/1920	17Can53	09Leo55	19Can43	29Lib54
07/15/1920	22Can39	10Leo09	25Can53	01Sco57
07/20/1920	27Can25	08Leo26	02Leo02	04Sco10
07/25/1920	02Leo12	05Leo13	08Leo12	06Sco30
07/30/1920	06Leo59	01Leo45	14Leo21	08Sco59
08/04/1920	11Leo46	29Can31	20Leo31	11Sco34
08/09/1920	16Leo34	29Can40	26Leo42	14Sco16
08/14/1920	21Leo22	02Leo41	02Vir57	17Sco05
08/19/1920	26Leo10	08Leo25	09Vir02	19Sco58
08/24/1920	00Vir59	16Leo21	15Vir12	22Sco57
08/29/1920	05Vir49	25Leo36	21Vir22	26Sco01
09/03/1920	10Vir39	5Vir21	27Vir33	29Sco09
09/08/1920	15Vir30	14Vir59	03Lib43	02Sag21
09/13/1920	20Vir22	24Vir16	09Lib53	05Sag37
09/18/1920	25Vir15	03Lib06	16Lib03	08Sag57
09/23/1920	00Lib09	11Lib31	22Lib13	12Sag19
09/28/1920	05Lib03	19Lib33	28Lib22	15Sag46
10/03/1920	09Lib58	27Lib12	04Sco32	19Sag15
10/08/1920	14Lib54	04Sco30	10Sco41	22Sag46
10/13/1920	19Lib51	11Sco25	16Sco50	26Sag21
10/18/1920	24Lib48	17Sco52	22Sco59	29Sag58
10/23/1920	29Lib47	23Sco40	29Sco07	03Cap37
10/28/1920	04Sco46	28Sco28	05Sag15	07Cap18
11/02/1920	09Sco46	01Sag36	11Sag23	11Cap01
11/07/1920	14Sco47	01Sag54	17Sag30	14Cap45
11/12/1920	19Sco49	28Sco21	23Sag37	18Cap31
11/17/1920	24Sco51	21Sco55	29Sag43	22Cap19
11/22/1920	29Sco54	16Sco57	05Cap49	26Cap07
11/27/1920	04Sag58	16Sco25	11Cap54	29Cap57
12/02/1920	10Sag02	19Sco42	17Cap57	03Aqu48
12/07/1920	15Sag06	25Sco12	24Cap00	07Aqu39
12/12/1920	20Sag11	01Sag48	00Aqu01	11Aqu31
12/17/1920	25Sag16	08Sag55	06Aqu00	15Aqu23
12/22/1920	00Cap22	16Sag19	11Aqu58	19Aqu16
12/27/1920	05Cap28	23Sag54	17Aqu53	23Aqu09

Ephemeris Tables for Sun, Mercury, Venus and Mars

Date	Sun	Mercury	Venus	Mars
01/01/1921	10Cap33	01Cap36	23Aqu46	27Aqu02
01/06/1921	15Cap39	09Cap27	29Aqu36	00Pis55
01/11/1921	20Cap45	17Cap27	05Pis22	04Pis48
01/16/1921	25Cap51	25Cap39	11Pis03	08Pis41
01/21/1921	00Aqu56	04Aqu04	16Pis40	12Pis33
01/26/1921	06Aqu01	12Aqu42	22Pis11	16Pis24
01/31/1921	11Aqu06	21Aqu28	27Pis36	20Pis15
02/05/1921	16Aqu10	00Pis09	02Ari51	24Pis06
02/10/1921	21Aqu14	08Pis08	07Ari58	27Pis55
02/15/1921	26Aqu17	14Pis24	12Ari55	01Ari43
02/20/1921	01Pis20	17Pis34	17Ari39	05Ari31
02/25/1921	06Pis22	16Pis45	22Ari07	09Ari18
03/02/1921	11Pis23	12Pis35	26Ari17	13Ari04
03/07/1921	16Pis24	07Pis35	00Tau04	16Ari49
03/12/1921	21Pis24	04Pis15	03Tau26	20Ari33
03/17/1921	26Pis22	03Pis32	06Tau15	24Ari16
03/22/1921	01Ari19	05Pis12	08Tau24	27Ari57
03/27/1921	06Ari17	08Pis42	09Tau48	01Tau38
04/01/1921	11Ari13	13Pis33	10Tau16	05Tau17
04/06/1921	16Ari09	19Pis27	09Tau46	08Tau55
04/11/1921	21Ari03	26Pis13	08Tau14	12Tau31
04/16/1921	25Ari57	03Ari42	05Tau49	16Tau07
04/21/1921	00Tau50	11Ari54	02Tau48	19Tau42
04/26/1921	05Tau42	20Ari49	29Ari42	23Tau15
05/01/1921	10Tau33	00Tau25	26Ari58	26Tau47
05/06/1921	15Tau24	10Tau42	25Ari00	00Gem18
05/11/1921	20Tau14	21Tau28	24Ari00	03Gem47
05/16/1921	25Tau03	02Gem19	23Ari59	07Gem16
05/21/1921	29Tau52	12Gem42	24Ari54	10Gem43
05/26/1921	04Gem40	22Gem09	26Ari39	14Gem10
05/31/1921	09Gem28	00Can27	29Ari03	17Gem35
06/05/1921	14Gem15	07Can30	02Tau02	20Gem59
06/10/1921	19Gem02	13Can12	05Tau29	24Gem22
06/15/1921	23Gem49	17Can28	09Tau19	27Gem45
06/20/1921	28Gem35	20Can04	13Tau27	01Can06
06/25/1921	03Can21	20Can51	17Tau52	04Can26
06/30/1921	08Can07	19Can45	22Tau29	07Can46
07/05/1921	12Can54	17Can11	27Tau18	11Can04
07/10/1921	17Can39	14Can05	02Gem15	14Can22
07/15/1921	22Can25	11Can45	07Gem21	17Can39
07/20/1921	27Can12	11Can13	12Gem34	20Can55
07/25/1921	01Leo58	13Can01	17Gem53	24Can11
07/30/1921	06Leo45	17Can15	23Gem17	27Can26
08/04/1921	11Leo32	23Can45	28Gem46	00Leo40
08/09/1921	16Leo19	02Leo07	04Can19	03Leo54
08/14/1921	21Leo07	11Leo45	09Can57	07Leo07
08/19/1921	25Leo56	21Leo51	15Can38	10Leo19
08/24/1921	00Vir45	01Vir49	21Can22	13Leo31
08/29/1921	05Vir35	11Vir24	27Can10	16Leo42
09/03/1921	10Vir25	20Vir27	03Leo00	19Leo53
09/08/1921	15Vir16	29Vir00	08Leo53	23Leo03
09/13/1921	20Vir08	07Lib04	14Leo49	26Leo13
09/18/1921	25Vir01	14Lib41	20Leo46	29Leo22
09/23/1921	29Vir54	21Lib51	26Leo47	02Vir31
09/28/1921	04Lib48	28Lib31	02Vir49	05Vir40

Date	Sun0	Mercury	Venus	Mars
10/03/1921	09Lib43	04Sco36	08Vir53	08Vir48
10/08/1921	14Lib39	09Sco53	14Vir59	11Vir55
10/13/1921	19Lib36	13Sco58	21Vir06	15Vir03
10/18/1921	24Lib34	16Sco09	27Vir15	18Vir09
10/23/1921	29Lib32	15Sco26	03Lib25	21Vir15
10/28/1921	04Sco31	11Sco09	09Lib37	24Vir21
11/02/1921	09Sco31	04Sco52	15Lib49	27Vir25
11/07/1921	14Sco33	00Sco46	22Lib02	00Lib30
11/12/1921	19Sco34	01Sco12	28Lib16	03Lib34
11/17/1921	24Sco36	05Sco20	4Sco31	06Lib37
11/22/1921	29Sco39	11Sco30	10Sco47	09Lib40
11/27/1921	04Sag43	18Sco37	17Sco03	12Lib42
12/02/1921	09Sag47	26Sco09	23Sco19	15Lib43
12/07/1921	14Sag51	3Sag49	29Sco36	18Lib43
12/12/1921	19Sag57	11Sag34	05Sag52	21Lib43
12/17/1921	25Sag01	19Sag21	12Sag09	24Lib42
12/22/1921	00Cap07	27Sag12	18Sag27	27Lib39
12/27/1921	05Cap13	05Cap07	24Sag44	00Sco35
01/01/1922	10Cap19	13Cap10	01Cap01	03Sco30
01/06/1922	15Cap24	21Cap21	07Cap19	06Sco24
01/11/1922	20Cap30	29Cap39	13Cap36	09Sco16
01/16/1922	25Cap36	08Aqu01	19Cap53	12Sco06
01/21/1922	00Aqu41	16Aqu10	26Cap10	14Sco55
01/26/1922	05Aqu46	23Aqu33	02Aqu27	17Sco41
01/31/1922	10Aqu51	29Aqu06	08Aqu44	20Sco25
02/05/1922	15Aqu55	01Pis14	15Aqu01	23Sco07
02/10/1922	20Aqu59	29Aqu00	21Aqu17	25Sco46
02/15/1922	26Aqu02	23Aqu42	27Aqu33	28Sco22
02/20/1922	01Pis06	18Aqu37	03Pis49	00Sag55
02/25/1922	06Pis07	16Aqu10	10Pis04	03Sag24
03/02/1922	11Pis09	16Aqu37	16Pis19	05Sag48
03/07/1922	16Pis09	19Aqu19	22Pis34	08Sag08
03/12/1922	21Pis09	23Aqu37	28Pis48	10Sag23
03/17/1922	26Pis07	29Aqu05	05Ari01	12Sag32
03/22/1922	01Ari05	05Pis25	11Ari13	14Sag34
03/27/1922	06Ari03	12Pis27	17Ari26	16Sag30
04/01/1922	10Ari59	20Pis08	23Ari37	18Sag16
04/06/1922	15Ari54	28Pis24	29Ari49	19Sag54
04/11/1922	20Ari49	07Ari17	05Tau59	21Sag21
04/16/1922	25Ari43	16Ari48	12Tau09	22Sag36
04/21/1922	00Tau36	26Ari56	18Tau18	23Sag39
04/26/1922	05Tau28	07Tau31	24Tau25	24Sag27
05/01/1922	10Tau19	18Tau14	00Gem33	25Sag00
05/06/1922	15Tau10	28Tau28	06Gem40	25Sag15
05/11/1922	20Tau00	07Gem42	12Gem45	25Sag12
05/16/1922	24Tau49	15Gem35	18Gem51	24Sag50
05/21/1922	29Tau38	21Gem58	24Gem55	24Sag10
05/26/1922	04Gem27	26Gem44	00Can58	23Sag11
05/31/1922	09Gem14	29Gem45	07Can00	21Sag57
06/05/1922	14Gem01	00Can52	13Can01	20Sag30
06/10/1922	01Gem48	00Can09	19Can01	18Sag54
06/15/1922	23Gem35	27Gem55	25Can00	17Sag16
06/20/1922	28Gem21	25Gem07	00Leo58	15Sag40
06/25/1922	03Can07	22Gem52	06Leo55	14Sag13
06/30/1922	07Can54	22Gem08	12Leo50	12Sag58

Ephemeris Tables for Sun, Mercury, Venus and Mars

Date	Sun	Mercury	Venus	Mars
07/05/1922	12Can40	23Gem22	18Leo43	12Sag01
07/10/1922	17Can25	26Gem41	24Leo36	11Sag24
07/15/1922	22Can12	01Can59	00Vir25	11Sag06
07/20/1922	26Can58	09Can09	06Vir13	11Sag10
07/25/1922	01Leo45	17Can55	11Vir59	11Sag35
07/30/1922	06Leo31	27Can49	17Vir42	12Sag19
08/04/1922	11Leo18	08Leo13	23Vir22	13Sag22
08/09/1922	16Leo06	18Leo06	29Vir00	14Sag42
08/14/1922	20Leo54	28Leo21	04Lib34	16Sag17
08/19/1922	25Leo42	07Vir36	10Lib04	18Sag06
08/24/1922	00Vir31	16Vir16	15Lib30	20Sag08
08/29/1922	05Vir21	24Vir23	20Lib50	22Sag21
09/03/1922	10Vir11	01Lib57	26Lib05	24Sag45
09/08/1922	15Vir02	08Lib57	01Sco13	27Sag18
09/13/1922	19Vir54	15Lib22	06Sco13	29Sag58
09/18/1922	24Vir46	21Lib02	11Sco04	02Cap47
09/23/1922	29Vir40	25Lib43	15Sco45	05Cap42
09/28/1922	04Lib34	29Lib00	20Sco12	08Cap43
10/03/1922	09Lib29	0Sco11	24Sco22	11Cap50
10/08/1922	14Lib25	28Lib27	28Sco15	15Cap01
10/13/1922	19Lib22	23Lib38	01Sag43	18Cap17
10/18/1922	24Lib19	17Lib49	04Sag43	21Cap37
10/23/1922	29Lib18	14Lib44	07Sag09	25Cap00
10/28/1922	04Sco17	16Lib09	08Sag51	28Cap25
11/02/1922	09Sco17	21Lib03	09Sag44	01Aqu54
11/07/1922	14Sco18	27Lib52	09Sag40	05Aqu25
11/12/1922	19Sco19	05Sco30	08Sag36	08Aqu57
11/17/1922	24Sco22	13Sco24	06Sag34	12Aqu32
11/22/1922	29Sco25	21Sco21	03Sag50	16Aqu08
11/27/1922	04Sag28	29Sco16	00Sag48	19Aqu45
12/02/1922	09Sag32	07Sag09	28Sco01	23Aqu24
12/07/1922	14Sag37	15Sag01	25Sco54	27Aqu03
12/12/1922	19Sag42	22Sag52	24Sco43	00Pis43
12/17/1922	24Sag46	00Cap46	24Sco33	04Pis23
12/22/1922	29Sag52	08Cap43	25Sco24	08Pis03
12/27/1922	04Cap58	16Cap42	27Sco06	11Pis44
01/01/1923	10Cap04	24Cap38	29Sco33	15Pis24
01/06/1923	15Cap10	02Aqu15	2Sag36	19Pis05
01/11/1923	20Cap15	09Aqu00	06Sag10	22Pis45
01/16/1923	25Cap21	13Aqu45	10Sag09	26Pis25
01/21/1923	00Aqu26	14Aqu50	14Sag27	00Ari04
01/26/1923	05Aqu31	11Aqu22	19Sag03	03Ari43
01/31/1923	10Aqu36	05Aqu19	23Sag52	07Ari21
02/05/1923	15Aqu40	00Aqu37	28Sag52	10Ari58
02/10/1923	20Aqu44	29Cap12	04Cap02	14Ari35
02/15/1923	25Aqu48	00Aqu43	09Cap19	18Ari12
02/20/1923	00Pis51	04Aqu18	14Cap44	21Ari47
02/25/1923	05Pis53	09Aqu16	20Cap13	25Ari21
03/02/1923	10Pis54	15Aqu12	25Cap48	28Ari55
03/07/1923	15Pis55	21Aqu51	01Aqu26	02Tau28
03/12/1923	20Pis54	29Aqu06	07Aqu08	06Tau00
03/17/1923	25Pis53	06Pis52	12Aqu52	09Tau30
03/22/1923	00Ari51	15Pis09	18Aqu40	13Tau00
03/27/1923	05Ari48	23Pis58	24Aqu29	16Tau29

Date	Sun	Mercury	Venus	Mars
04/01/1923	10Ari45	03Ari21	00Pis21	19Tau57
04/06/1923	15Ari40	13Ari16	06Pis13	23Tau24
04/11/1923	20Ari34	23Ari37	12Pis07	26Tau50
04/16/1923	25Ari28	04Tau06	18Pis03	00Gem16
04/21/1923	00Tau21	14Tau07	23Pis58	03Gem40
04/26/1923	05Tau14	23Tau01	29Pis56	07Gem03
05/01/1923	10Tau05	00Gem22	05Ari53	10Gem26
05/06/1923	14Tau56	05Gem52	11Ari52	13Gem48
05/11/1923	19Tau46	09Gem24	17Ari51	17Gem09
05/16/1923	24Tau36	10Gem51	23Ari51	20Gem28
05/21/1923	29Tau24	10Gem17	29Ari51	23Gem48
05/26/1923	04Gem13	08Gem09	05Tau52	27Gem06
05/31/1923	09Gem00	05Gem23	11Tau54	00Can24
06/05/1923	13Gem48	03Gem08	17Tau55	03Can41
06/10/1923	18Gem34	02Gem18	23Tau58	06Can58
06/15/1923	23Gem21	03Gem16	00Gem01	10Can14
06/20/1923	28Gem07	06Gem07	06Gem04	13Can29
06/25/1923	02Can54	10Gem43	12Gem08	16Can44
06/30/1923	07Can40	16Gem55	18Gem12	19Can58
07/05/1923	12Can26	24Gem39	24Gem17	23Can12
07/10/1923	17Can12	03Can44	00Can23	26Can25
07/15/1923	21Can58	13Can52	06Can29	29Can39
07/20/1923	26Can44	24Can30	12Can36	02Leo51
07/25/1923	01Leo31	05Leo03	18Can43	06Leo03
07/30/1923	06Leo18	15Leo07	24Can51	09Leo15
08/04/1923	11Leo04	24Leo33	01Leo00	12Leo27
08/09/1923	15Leo52	03Vir19	07Leo09	15Leo39
08/14/1923	20Leo40	11Vir27	13Leo19	18Leo50
08/19/1923	25Leo28	18Vir55	19Leo30	22Leo01
08/24/1923	00Vir17	25Vir44	25Leo40	25Leo12
08/29/1923	05Vir07	01Lib49	01Vir52	28Leo23
09/03/1923	09Vir57	7Lib00	08Vir04	01Vir34
09/08/1923	14Vir48	11Lib01	14Vir17	04Vir45
09/13/1923	19Vir40	13Lib24	20Vir30	07Vir55
09/18/1923	24Vir33	13Lib31	26Vir43	11Vir06
09/23/1923	29Vir26	10Lib50	02Lib57	14Vir17
09/28/1923	04Lib20	05Lib46	09Lib10	17Vir28
10/03/1923	09Lib15	0Lib42	15Lib25	20Vir39
10/08/1923	14Lib11	28Vir48	21Lib39	23Vir50
10/13/1923	19Lib07	01Lib10	27Lib53	27Vir01
10/18/1923	24Lib05	06Lib48	04Sco08	00Lib12
10/23/1923	29Lib03	14Lib13	10Sco22	03Lib24
10/28/1923	04Sco03	22Lib21	16Sco37	06Lib35
11/02/1923	09Sco03	00Sco39	22Sco52	09Lib47
11/07/1923	14Sco03	08Sco53	29Sco06	12Lib58
11/12/1923	19Sco05	17Sco00	05Sag21	16Lib10
11/17/1923	24Sco07	24Sco59	11Sag36	19Lib22
11/22/1923	29Sco10	02Sag52	17Sag50	22Lib34
11/27/1923	04Sag13	10Sag40	24Sag04	25Lib46
12/02/1923	09Sag18	18Sag25	00Cap19	28Lib59
12/07/1923	14Sag22	26Sag09	06Cap33	02Sco12
12/12/1923	19Sag27	03Cap48	12Cap47	05Sco24
12/17/1923	24Sag32	11Cap18	19Cap01	08Sco37
12/22/1923	29Sag37	18Cap22	25Cap14	11Sco49
12/27/1923	04Cap43	24Cap26	01Aqu27	15Sco02

Ephemeris Tables for Sun, Mercury, Venus and Mars

Date	Sun	Mercury	Venus	Mars
01/01/1924	09Cap49	28Cap20	07Aqu40	18Sco15
01/06/1924	14Cap55	28Cap24	13Aqu52	21Sco28
01/11/1924	20Cap00	23Cap54	20Aqu03	24Sco40
01/16/1924	25Cap06	17Cap30	26Aqu13	27Sco53
01/21/1924	00Aqu12	13Cap26	02Pis23	01Sag06
01/26/1924	05Aqu16	13Cap04	08Pis31	04Sag18
01/31/1924	10Aqu21	15Cap35	14Pis38	07Sag31
02/05/1924	15Aqu25	19Cap57	20Pis43	10Sag43
02/10/1924	20Aqu30	25Cap28	26Pis47	13Sag55
02/15/1924	25Aqu33	01Aqu47	02Ari48	17Sag06
02/20/1924	00Pis36	08Aqu40	08Ari48	20Sag18
02/25/1924	05Pis38	16Aqu03	14Ari45	23Sag28
03/01/1924	10Pis39	23Aqu52	20Ari39	26Sag39
03/06/1924	15Pis40	02Pis07	26Ari31	29Sag49
03/11/1924	20Pis40	10Pis51	02Tau19	02Cap58
03/16/1924	25Pis39	20Pis03	08Tau03	06Cap06
03/21/1924	00Ari36	29Pis43	13Tau44	09Cap14
03/26/1924	05Ari34	09Ari47	19Tau19	12Cap21
03/31/1924	10Ari30	19Ari57	24Tau49	15Cap26
04/05/1924	15Ari25	29Ari40	00Gem14	18Cap30
04/10/1924	20Ari21	08Tau10	05Gem31	21Cap33
04/15/1924	25Ari14	14Tau49	10Gem41	24Cap33
04/20/1924	00Tau07	19Tau15	15Gem41	27Cap33
04/25/1924	05Tau00	21Tau15	20Gem31	00Aqu29
04/30/1924	09Tau51	20Tau54	25Gem08	03Aqu23
05/05/1924	14Tau42	18Tau42	29Gem31	06Aqu15
05/10/1924	19Tau32	15Tau42	03Can36	09Aqu02
05/15/1924	24Tau21	13Tau09	07Can19	11Aqu46
05/20/1924	29Tau10	12Tau04	10Can37	14Aqu26
05/25/1924	03Gem58	12Tau49	13Can24	17Aqu01
05/30/1924	08Gem46	15Tau23	15Can34	19Aqu30
06/04/1924	13Gem34	19Tau34	17Can00	21Aqu52
06/09/1924	18Gem21	25Tau11	17Can34	24Aqu07
06/14/1924	23Gem07	02Gem07	17Can10	26Aqu13
06/19/1924	27Gem54	10Gem16	15Can48	28Aqu10
06/24/1924	02Can40	19Gem36	13Can30	29Aqu57
06/29/1924	07Can26	29Gem54	10Can36	01Pis30
07/04/1924	12Can12	10Can42	07Can29	02Pis49
07/09/1924	16Can58	21Can27	04Can40	03Pis53
07/14/1924	21Can44	01Leo42	02Can32	04Pis40
07/19/1924	26Can30	11Leo16	01Can19	05Pis09
07/24/1924	01Leo16	20Leo06	01Can06	05Pis18
07/29/1924	06Leo03	28Leo10	01Can48	05Pis09
08/03/1924	10Leo51	05Vir31	03Can21	04Pis39
08/08/1924	15Leo38	12Vir04	05Can36	03Pis52
08/13/1924	20Leo26	17Vir45	08Can27	02Pis49
08/18/1924	25Leo14	22Vir20	11Can48	01Pis37
08/23/1924	00Vir03	25Vir33	15Can33	00Pis18
08/28/1924	04Vir53	26Vir55	19Can39	29Aqu00
09/02/1924	09Vir43	25Vir56	24Can02	27Aqu46
09/07/1924	14Vir34	22Vir28	28Can40	26Aqu44
09/12/1924	19Vir26	17Vir31	03Leo30	25Aqu57
09/17/1924	24Vir18	13Vir34	08Leo30	25Aqu28
09/22/1924	29Vir12	12Vir57	13Leo40	25Aqu19
09/27/1924	04Lib06	16Vir15	18Leo58	25Aqu30
10/02/1924	09Lib01	22Vir34	24Leo23	26Aqu00
10/07/1924	13Lib57	00Lib33	29Leo54	26Aqu49
10/12/1924	18Lib53	09Lib10	05Vir31	27Aqu56
10/17/1924	23Lib51	17Lib51	11Vir12	29Aqu18
10/22/1924	28Lib49	26Lib23	16Vir58	00Pis55
10/27/1924	03Sco48	04Sco42	22Vir48	02Pis43
11/01/1924	08Sco48	12Sco48	28Vir41	04Pis44
11/06/1924	13Sco49	20Sco42	04Lib37	06Pis54
11/11/1924	18Sco50	28Sco28	10Lib37	09Pis13
11/16/1924	23Sco52	06Sag06	16Lib39	11Pis40
11/21/1924	28Sco55	13Sag36	22Lib42	14Pis13
11/26/1924	03Sag58	20Sag56	28Lib48	16Pis52
12/01/1924	09Sag03	28Sag00	04Sco55	19Pis37
12/06/1924	14Sag07	04Cap29	11Sco03	22Pis26
12/11/1924	19Sag12	09Cap49	17Sco13	25Pis19
12/16/1924	24Sag17	12Cap50	23Sco24	28Pis15
12/21/1924	29Sag22	11Cap54	29Sco36	01Ari13
12/26/1924	04Cap28	06Cap34	05Sag48	04Ari15
12/31/1924	09Cap34	00Cap10	12Sag01	07Ari19
01/05/1925	14Cap40	26Sag55	18Sag15	10Ari25
01/10/1925	19Cap46	27Sag36	24Sag28	13Ari32
01/15/1925	24Cap51	01Cap00	00Cap42	16Ari41
01/20/1925	29Cap57	06Cap02	06Cap57	19Ari51
01/25/1925	05Aqu02	12Cap03	13Cap12	23Ari01
01/30/1925	10Aqu07	18Cap42	19Cap26	26Ari13
02/04/1925	15Aqu11	25Cap48	25Cap40	29Ari25
02/09/1925	20Aqu15	03Aqu16	01Aqu55	02Tau37
02/14/1925	25Aqu18	11Aqu06	08Aqu09	05Tau50
02/19/1925	00Pis21	19Aqu18	14Aqu24	09Tau03
02/24/1925	05Pis24	27Aqu54	20Aqu38	12Tau16
03/01/1925	10Pis25	06Pis53	26Aqu52	15Tau30
03/06/1925	15Pis25	16Pis18	03Pis07	18Tau43
03/11/1925	20Pis25	26Pis01	09Pis20	21Tau57
03/16/1925	25Pis24	05Ari50	15Pis34	25Tau10
03/21/1925	00Ari22	15Ari10	21Pis47	28Tau23
03/26/1925	05Ari19	23Ari11	28Pis00	01Gem36
03/31/1925	10Ari16	29Ari02	04Ari12	04Gem49
04/05/1925	15Ari11	02Tau10	10Ari24	08Gem01
04/10/1925	20Ari06	02Tau26	16Ari36	11Gem13
04/15/1925	25Ari00	00Tau17	22Ari47	14Gem25
04/20/1925	29Ari53	26Ari52	28Ari58	17Gem37
04/25/1925	04Tau45	23Ari45	05Tau09	20Gem49
04/30/1925	09Tau37	22Ari22	11Tau19	24Gem00
05/05/1925	14Tau28	22Ari27	17Tau29	27Gem11
05/10/1925	19Tau18	24Ari40	23Tau39	00Can21
05/15/1925	24Tau07	28Ari31	29Tau48	03Can32
05/20/1925	28Tau57	03Tau43	05Gem57	06Can42
05/25/1925	03Gem45	10Tau06	12Gem06	09Can52
05/30/1925	08Gem33	17Tau34	18Gem15	13Can02
06/04/1925	13Gem20	26Tau04	24Gem22	16Can12
06/09/1925	18Gem07	05Gem33	00Can31	19Can21
06/14/1925	22Gem54	15Gem55	06Can38	22Can31
06/19/1925	27Gem40	26Gem48	12Can46	25Can41
06/24/1925	02Can26	07Can42	18Can53	28Can49
06/29/1925	07Can12	18Can05	25Can00	01Leo58

Ephemeris Tables for Sun, Mercury, Venus and Mars

Date	Sun	Mercury	Venus	Mars
07/04/1925	11Can58	27Can44	01Leo06	05Leo07
07/09/1925	16Can44	06Leo33	07Leo12	08Leo16
07/14/1925	21Can30	14Leo31	13Leo18	11Leo26
07/19/1925	26Can16	21Leo38	19Leo24	14Leo35
07/24/1925	01Leo03	27Leo49	25Leo29	17Leo45
07/29/1925	05Leo49	02Vir57	01Vir33	20Leo54
08/03/1925	10Leo37	06Vir49	07Vir37	24Leo04
08/08/1925	15Leo24	09Vir03	13Vir41	27Leo13
08/13/1925	20Leo12	09Vir18	19Vir44	00Vir24
08/18/1925	25Leo00	07Vir16	25Vir46	03Vir34
08/23/1925	29Leo49	03Vir20	01Lib48	06Vir45
08/28/1925	04Vir39	29Leo01	07Lib48	09Vir56
09/02/1925	09Vir29	26Leo27	13Lib48	13Vir07
09/07/1925	14Vir20	27Leo10	19Lib46	16Vir19
09/12/1925	19Vir12	01Vir24	25Lib45	19Vir31
09/17/1925	24Vir04	08Vir20	01Sco41	22Vir43
09/22/1925	28Vir57	16Vir50	07Sco37	25Vir57
09/27/1925	03Lib51	25Vir54	13Sco31	29Vir10
10/02/1925	08Lib46	04Lib59	19Sco24	02Lib24
10/07/1925	13Lib42	13Lib49	25Sco15	05Lib39
10/12/1925	18Lib39	22Lib20	01Sag04	08Lib54
10/17/1925	23Lib36	00Sco34	06Sag51	12Lib10
10/22/1925	28Lib34	08Sco31	12Sag36	15Lib26
10/27/1925	03Sco34	16Sco15	18Sag18	18Lib43
11/01/1925	08Sco33	23Sco45	23Sag56	22Lib00
11/06/1925	13Sco34	01Sag02	29Sag31	25Lib19
11/11/1925	18Sco36	08Sag03	05Cap01	28Lib37
11/16/1925	23Sco37	14Sag39	10Cap27	01Sco57
11/21/1925	28Sco40	20Sag33	15Cap45	05Sco17
11/26/1925	03Sag44	25Sag07	20Cap57	08Sco38
12/01/1925	08Sag48	27Sag12	25Cap58	12Sco00
12/06/1925	13Sag52	25Sag18	00Aqu50	15Sco22
12/11/1925	18Sag57	19Sag22	05Aqu28	18Sco45
12/16/1925	24Sag03	13Sag15	09Aqu50	22Sco09
12/21/1925	29Sag08	10Sag55	13Aqu52	25Sco33
12/26/1925	04Cap13	12Sag34	17Aqu30	28Sco58
12/31/1925	09Cap19	16Sag48	20Aqu39	02Sag24
01/05/1926	14Cap25	22Sag27	23Aqu11	05Sag50
01/10/1926	19Cap31	28Sag55	25Aqu00	09Sag18
01/15/1926	24Cap36	05Cap51	25Aqu58	12Sag45
01/20/1926	29Cap42	13Cap09	25Aqu56	16Sag14
01/25/1926	04Aqu47	20Cap42	24Aqu52	19Sag43
01/30/1926	09Aqu52	28Cap33	22Aqu49	23Sag13
02/04/1926	14Aqu56	06Aqu39	20Aqu03	26Sag44
02/09/1926	20Aqu00	15Aqu06	16Aqu57	00Cap15
02/14/1926	25Aqu03	23Aqu51	14Aqu05	03Cap48
02/19/1926	00Pis07	02Pis58	11Aqu53	07Cap20
02/24/1926	05Pis09	12Pis21	10Aqu37	10Cap53
03/01/1926	10Pis10	21Pis46	10Aqu22	14Cap27
03/06/1926	15Pis11	00Ari39	11Aqu06	18Cap01
03/11/1926	20Pis11	08Ari05	12Aqu43	21Cap36
03/16/1926	25Pis10	13Ari02	15Aqu03	25Cap12
03/21/1926	00Ari07	14Ari45	17Aqu59	28Cap48
03/26/1926	05Ari05	13Ari15	21Aqu25	02Aqu24
03/31/1926	10Ari01	09Ari34	25Aqu15	06Aqu00

Date	Sun	Mercury	Venus	Mars
04/05/1926	14Ari57	05Ari36	29Aqu26	09Aqu37
04/10/1926	19Ari52	03Ari04	03Pis53	13Aqu13
04/15/1926	24Ari46	02Ari40	08Pis33	16Aqu51
04/20/1926	29Ari39	04Ari21	13Pis24	20Aqu28
04/25/1926	04Tau31	07Ari46	18Pis25	24Aqu05
04/30/1926	09Tau23	12Ari36	23Pis33	27Aqu42
05/05/1926	14Tau14	18Ari33	28Pis48	01Pis19
05/10/1926	19Tau04	25Ari29	04Ari09	04Pis55
05/15/1926	23Tau54	03Tau19	09Ari34	08Pis30
05/20/1926	28Tau42	12Tau02	15Ari04	12Pis04
05/25/1926	03Gem31	21Tau37	20Ari37	15Pis38
05/30/1926	08Gem19	01Gem58	26Ari15	19Pis10
06/04/1926	13Gem06	12Gem52	01Tau54	22Pis42
06/09/1926	17Gem53	23Gem48	07Tau36	26Pis11
06/14/1926	22Gem40	04Can16	13Tau20	29Pis39
06/19/1926	27Gem26	13Can57	19Tau06	03Ari04
06/24/1926	02Can12	22Can40	24Tau54	06Ari27
06/29/1926	06Can58	00Leo25	00Gem44	09Ari46
07/04/1926	11Can45	07Leo11	06Gem36	13Ari03
07/09/1926	16Can30	12Leo51	12Gem28	16Ari16
07/14/1926	21Can16	17Leo15	18Gem23	19Ari26
07/19/1926	26Can03	20Leo09	24Gem19	22Ari30
07/24/1926	00Leo49	21Leo14	00Can16	25Ari30
07/29/1926	05Leo36	20Leo17	06Can15	28Ari23
08/03/1926	10Leo23	17Leo25	12Can15	01Tau10
08/08/1926	15Leo10	13Leo34	18Can16	03Tau49
08/13/1926	19Leo58	10Leo23	24Can19	06Tau21
08/18/1926	24Leo46	09Leo25	00Leo23	08Tau43
08/23/1926	29Leo36	11Leo29	06Leo28	10Tau54
08/28/1926	04Vir25	16Leo35	12Leo34	12Tau54
09/02/1926	09Vir15	24Leo06	18Leo42	14Tau41
09/07/1926	14Vir06	03Vir03	24Leo51	16Tau13
09/12/1926	18Vir58	12Vir33	01Vir00	17Tau30
09/17/1926	23Vir50	22Vir00	07Vir10	18Tau28
09/22/1926	28Vir43	01Lib08	13Vir22	19Tau07
09/27/1926	03Lib37	09Lib53	19Vir34	19Tau26
10/02/1926	08Lib32	18Lib15	25Vir48	19Tau22
10/07/1926	13Lib28	26Lib15	02Lib01	18Tau57
10/12/1926	18Lib24	03Sco57	08Lib16	18Tau09
10/17/1926	23Lib22	11Sco20	14Lib31	17Tau01
10/22/1926	28Lib20	18Sco24	20Lib46	15Tau36
10/27/1926	03Sco19	25Sco06	27Lib03	13Tau58
11/01/1926	08Sco19	01Sag14	03Sco19	12Tau13
11/06/1926	13Sco19	06Sag30	09Sco35	10Tau29
11/11/1926	18Sco21	10Sag14	15Sco52	08Tau50
11/16/1926	23Sco23	11Sag20	22Sco09	07Tau22
11/21/1926	28Sco26	08Sag31	28Sco26	06Tau10
11/26/1926	03Sag29	02Sag15	04Sag43	05Tau18
12/01/1926	08Sag33	26Sco39	11Sag00	04Tau45
12/06/1926	13Sag37	25Sco16	17Sag18	04Tau32
12/11/1926	18Sag42	27Sco52	23Sag35	04Tau39
12/16/1926	23Sag48	02Sag51	29Sag52	05Tau06
12/21/1926	28Sag53	09Sag05	06Cap09	05Tau49
12/26/1926	03Cap58	15Sag57	12Cap26	06Tau49
12/31/1926	09Cap04	23Sag11	18Cap43	08Tau03

Ephemeris Tables for Sun, Mercury, Venus and Mars

00Date	Sun	Mercury	Venus	Mars
01/05/1927	14Cap10	00Cap39	25Cap00	09Tau30
01/10/1927	19Cap16	08Cap18	01Aqu17	11Tau07
01/15/1927	24Cap22	16Cap07	7Aqu33	12Tau55
01/20/1927	29Cap27	24Cap10	13Aqu49	14Tau51
01/25/1927	04Aqu32	2Aqu27	20Aqu05	16Tau55
01/30/1927	09Aqu37	10Aqu59	26Aqu21	19Tau06
02/04/1927	14Aqu42	19Aqu47	02Pis36	21Tau23
02/09/1927	19Aqu45	28Aqu47	8Pis50	23Tau45
02/14/1927	24Aqu49	07Pis45	15Pis04	26Tau12
02/19/1927	29Aqu52	16Pis07	21Pis16	28Tau43
02/24/1927	04Pis54	22Pis55	27Pis29	01Gem17
03/01/1927	00Pis55	26Pis54	03Ari39	03Gem54
03/06/1927	14Pis56	27Pis09	09Ari50	06Gem34
03/11/1927	19Pis56	23Pis59	15Ari59	09Gem17
03/16/1927	24Pis55	19Pis17	22Ari07	12Gem02
03/21/1927	29Pis54	15Pis28	28Ari14	14Gem49
03/26/1927	04Ari51	13Pis56	04Tau19	17Gem37
03/31/1927	09Ari47	14Pis48	10Tau24	20Gem28
04/05/1927	14Ari43	17Pis37	16Tau27	23Gem19
04/10/1927	19Ari37	21Pis58	22Tau27	26Gem12
04/15/1927	24Ari31	27Pis30	28Tau27	29Gem06
04/20/1927	29Ari25	03Ari59	04Gem24	02Can01
04/25/1927	04Tau17	11Ari17	10Gem19	04Can57
04/30/1927	09Tau09	19Ari22	16Gem12	07Can53
05/05/1927	14Tau00	28Ari12	22Gem03	10Can51
05/10/1927	18Tau50	07Tau47	27Gem51	13Can48
05/15/1927	23Tau40	18Tau06	03Can37	16Can47
05/20/1927	28Tau28	28Tau55	09Can19	19Can46
05/25/1927	03Gem17	09Gem49	14Can58	22Can46
05/30/1927	08Gem04	20Gem17	20Can33	25Can47
06/04/1927	12Gem52	29Gem53	26Can04	28Can48
06/09/1927	17Gem39	08Can25	01Leo30	01Leo50
06/14/1927	22Gem26	15Can49	06Leo49	04Leo52
06/19/1927	27Gem12	22Can03	12Leo03	07Leo55
06/24/1927	01Can58	26Can57	17Leo10	10Leo58
06/29/1927	06Can45	00Leo22	22Leo08	14Leo02
07/04/1927	11Can31	02Leo04	26Leo56	17Leo06
07/09/1927	16Can16	01Leo51	01Vir33	20Leo11
07/14/1927	21Can03	29Can49	05Vir56	23Leo17
07/19/1927	25Can49	26Can36	10Vir03	26Leo23
07/24/1927	00Leo35	23Can28	13Vir49	29Leo30
07/29/1927	05Leo22	21Can49	17Vir12	02Vir37
08/03/1927	10Leo09	22Can31	20Vir07	05Vir45
08/08/1927	14Leo57	25Can54	22Vir27	8Vir54
08/13/1927	19Leo44	01Leo49	24Vir06	12Vir03
08/18/1927	24Leo33	09Leo51	24Vir55	15Vir13
08/23/1927	29Leo21	19Leo12	24Vir49	18Vir23
08/28/1927	04Vir11	29Leo06	23Vir44	21Vir35
09/02/1927	09Vir01	08Vir54	21Vir43	24Vir47
09/07/1927	13Vir52	18Vir20	18Vir59	28Vir00
09/12/1927	18Vir43	27Vir18	15Vir55	01Lib14
09/17/1927	23Vir36	05Lib48	13Vir01	04Lib29
09/22/1927	28Vir29	13Lib52	10Vir42	07Lib45
09/27/1927	03Lib23	21Lib32	09Vir16	11Lib01

Date	Sun	Mercury	Venus	Mars
10/02/1927	08Lib18	28Lib48	08Vir51	14Lib19
10/07/1927	13Lib13	05Sco39	09Vir24	17Lib37
10/12/1927	18Lib10	11Sco59	10Vir51	20Lib57
10/17/1927	23Lib07	17Sco37	13Vir03	24Lib17
10/22/1927	28Lib06	22Sco12	15Vir54	27Lib38
10/27/1927	03Sco04	25Sco04	19Vir16	01Sco00
11/01/1927	08Sco04	25Sco10	23Vir06	04Sco24
11/06/1927	13Sco05	21Sco31	27Vir17	07Sco48
11/11/1927	18Sco06	15Sco10	01Lib47	11Sco14
11/16/1927	23Sco09	10Sco18	06Lib32	14Sco40
11/21/1927	28Sco11	09Sco54	11Lib30	18Sco08
11/26/1927	03Sag15	13Sco22	16Lib39	21Sco37
12/01/1927	08Sag18	19Sco04	21Lib57	25Sco07
12/06/1927	13Sag23	25Sco51	27Lib22	28Sco37
12/11/1927	18Sag28	03Sag07	02Sco55	02Sag09
12/16/1927	23Sag33	10Sag37	08Sco33	05Sag42
12/21/1927	28Sag38	18Sag16	14Sco15	09Sag16
12/26/1927	03Cap44	26Sag00	20Sco03	12Sag52
12/31/1927	08Cap49	03Cap49	25Sco53	16Sag28
01/05/1928	13Cap55	11Cap48	01Sag46	20Sag05
01/10/1928	19Cap01	19Cap55	07Sag43	23Sag43
01/15/1928	24Cap07	28Cap13	13Sag41	27Sag22
01/20/1928	29Cap12	06Aqu42	19Sag41	01Cap03
01/25/1928	04Aqu18	15Aqu18	25Sag43	04Cap44
01/30/1928	09Aqu22	23Aqu46	01Cap46	08Cap26
02/04/1928	14Aqu27	01Pis35	07Cap50	12Cap09
02/09/1928	19Aqu31	07Pis42	13Cap55	15Cap53
02/14/1928	24Aqu34	10Pis41	20Cap01	19Cap38
02/19/1928	29Aqu37	09Pis30	26Cap07	23Cap23
02/24/1928	04Pis40	04Pis56	02Aqu14	27Cap09
02/29/1928	09Pis41	29Aqu47	08Aqu22	00Aqu57
03/05/1928	14Pis42	26Aqu37	14Aqu30	04Aqu44
03/10/1928	19Pis42	26Aqu13	20Aqu37	08Aqu32
03/15/1928	24Pis41	28Aqu14	26Aqu46	12Aqu21
03/20/1928	29Pis39	02Pis00	02Pis55	16Aqu09
03/25/1928	04Ari36	07Pis04	09Pis03	19Aqu59
03/30/1928	09Ari33	13Pis07	15Pis12	23Aqu48
04/04/1928	14Ari28	19Pis57	21Pis21	27Aqu38
04/09/1928	19Ari23	27Pis30	27Pis29	01Pis28
04/14/1928	24Ari18	05Ari42	03Ari37	05Pis19
04/19/1928	29Ari10	14Ari33	09Ari45	09Pis09
04/24/1928	04Tau03	24Ari06	15Ari54	12Pis58
04/29/1928	08Tau55	04Tau16	22Ari01	16Pis47
05/04/1928	14Tau46	14Tau58	28Ari10	20Pis36
05/09/1928	18Tau36	25Tau46	04Tau18	24Pis25
05/14/1928	23Tau25	06Gem09	10Tau26	28Pis12
05/19/1928	28Tau15	15Gem34	16Tau34	01Ari59
05/24/1928	03Gem03	23Gem48	22Tau42	05Ari45
05/29/1928	07Gem51	00Can40	28Tau50	09Ari30
06/03/1928	12Gem38	06Can07	04Gem58	13Ari14
06/08/1928	17Gem25	09Can59	11Gem06	16Ari57
06/13/1928	22Gem12	12Can07	17Gem14	20Ari38
06/18/1928	26Gem58	12Can22	23Gem22	24Ari18
06/23/1928	01Can45	10Can51	29Gem31	27Ari56
06/28/1928	06Can31	08Can08	05Can39	01Tau32

Ephemeris Tables for Sun, Mercury, Venus and Mars

Date	Sun	Mercury	Venus	Mars
07/03/1928	11Can17	05Can17	11Can48	05Tau07
07/08/1928	16Can03	03Can29	17Can57	08Tau39
07/13/1928	20Can49	03Can35	24Can06	12Tau09
07/18/1928	25Can35	05Can55	00Leo15	15Tau36
07/23/1928	00Leo21	10Can28	06Leo25	19Tau00
07/28/1928	05Leo08	17Can09	12Leo34	22Tau22
08/02/1928	09Leo55	25Can36	18Leo44	25Tau41
08/07/1928	14Leo42	05Leo18	24Leo54	28Tau56
08/12/1928	19Leo30	15Leo31	01Vir04	02Gem07
08/17/1928	24Leo18	25Leo40	07Vir14	05Gem15
08/22/1928	29Leo07	05Vir22	13Vir24	08Gem19
08/27/1928	03Vir57	14Vir33	19Vir34	11Gem18
09/01/1928	08Vir47	23Vir12	25Vir45	14Gem12
09/06/1928	13Vir38	01Lib19	01Lib55	17Gem00
09/11/1928	18Vir29	08Lib56	08Lib04	19Gem42
09/16/1928	23Vir21	16Lib04	14Lib14	22Gem18
09/21/1928	28Vir15	22Lib40	20Lib24	24Gem46
09/26/1928	03Lib09	28Lib38	26Lib33	27Gem07
10/01/1928	08Lib03	03Sco43	02Sco43	29Gem19
10/06/1928	12Lib59	07Sco34	08Sco52	01Can21
10/11/1928	17Lib55	09Sco30	15Sco01	03Can12
10/16/1928	22Lib53	08Sco33	21Sco09	04Can51
10/21/1928	27Lib51	04Sco12	27Sco18	06Can17
10/26/1928	02Sco50	28Lib04	03Sag25	07Can28
10/31/1928	07Sco50	24Lib07	09Sag33	08Can22
11/05/1928	12Sco51	24Lib42	15Sag40	08Can59
11/10/1928	17Sco52	29Lib00	21Sag46	09Can16
11/15/1928	22Sco54	05Sco22	27Sag52	09Can13
11/20/1928	27Sco57	12Sco40	03Cap57	08Can48
11/25/1928	03Sag00	20Sco21	10Cap01	08Can01
11/30/1928	08Sag04	28Sco07	16Cap05	06Can54
12/05/1928	13Sag08	5Sag57	22Cap07	05Can27
12/10/1928	18Sag13	13Sag46	28Cap08	03Can45
12/15/1928	23Sag18	21Sag37	04Aqu07	01Can52
12/20/1928	28Sag23	29Sag30	10Aqu05	29Gem54
12/25/1928	03Cap29	07Cap29	16Aqu00	27Gem57
12/30/1928	08Cap34	15Cap33	21Aqu52	26Gem07
01/04/1929	13Cap40	23Cap43	27Aqu42	24Gem30
01/09/1929	18Cap46	01Aqu54	03Pis28	23Gem09
01/14/1929	23Cap52	09Aqu52	09Pis09	22Gem07
01/19/1929	28Cap57	17Aqu04	14Pis46	21Gem25
01/24/1929	04Aqu03	22Aqu25	20Pis16	21Gem03
01/29/1929	09Aqu07	24Aqu23	25Pis40	21Gem01
02/03/1929	14Aqu12	21Aqu52	00Ari56	21Gem18
02/08/1929	19Aqu16	16Aqu17	06Ari03	21Gem51
02/13/1929	24Aqu19	11Aqu12	10Ari59	22Gem40
02/18/1929	29Aqu23	08Aqu58	15Ari42	23Gem44
02/23/1929	04Pis25	09Aqu43	20Ari09	25Gem00
02/28/1929	09Pis27	12Aqu42	24Ari18	26Gem27
03/05/1929	14Pis27	17Aqu13	28Ari04	28Gem04
03/10/1929	19Pis27	22Aqu50	01Tau24	29Gem50
03/15/1929	24Pis26	29Aqu16	04Tau10	01Can44
03/20/1929	29Pis25	06Pis22	06Tau18	03Can45
03/25/1929	04Ari22	14Pis03	07Tau37	05Can51
03/30/1929	09Ari18	22Pis18	08Tau03	08Can04

Date	Sun	Mercury	Venus	Mars
04/04/1929	14Ari14	1Ari07	07Tau28	10Can21
04/09/1929	19Ari09	10Ari33	05Tau52	12Can43
04/14/1929	24Ari03	20Ari34	03Tau24	15Can08
04/19/1929	28Ari57	01Tau03	00Tau22	17Can37
04/24/1929	03Tau49	11Tau40	27Ari16	20Can10
04/29/1929	08Tau40	21Tau52	24Ari34	22Can45
05/04/1929	13Tau31	01Gem03	22Ari40	25Can23
05/09/1929	18Tau22	08Gem49	21Ari45	28Can03
05/14/1929	23Tau12	14Gem58	21Ari48	00Leo46
05/19/1929	28Tau01	19Gem21	22Ari48	03Leo31
05/24/1929	02Gem49	21Gem52	24Ari35	06Leo17
05/29/1929	07Gem37	22Gem24	27Ari03	09Leo06
06/03/1929	12Gem24	21Gem08	00Tau04	11Leo56
06/08/1929	17Gem12	18Gem39	03Tau33	14Leo48
06/13/1929	21Gem58	15Gem57	07Tau24	17Leo41
06/18/1929	26Gem45	14Gem10	11Tau34	20Leo36
06/23/1929	01Can31	14Gem03	15Tau59	23Leo31
06/28/1929	06Can17	15Gem52	20Tau37	26Leo29
07/03/1929	11Can03	19Gem39	25Tau27	29Leo27
07/08/1929	15Can49	25Gem15	00Gem25	02Vir27
07/13/1929	20Can35	02Can33	05Gem31	05Vir29
07/18/1929	25Can21	11Can22	10Gem45	08Vir31
07/23/1929	00Leo07	21Can21	16Gem04	11Vir35
07/28/1929	04Leo54	01Leo51	21Gem29	14Vir40
08/02/1929	09Leo41	12Leo16	26Gem58	17Vir46
08/07/1929	14Leo28	22Leo15	02Can32	20Vir54
08/12/1929	19Leo16	01Vir37	08Can09	24Vir02
08/17/1929	24Leo04	10Vir22	13Can50	27Vir12
08/22/1929	28Leo53	18Vir31	19Can34	00Lib23
08/27/1929	03Vir43	26Vir06	25Can22	03Lib35
09/01/1929	08Vir33	03Lib04	01Leo12	06Lib49
09/06/1929	13Vir24	09Lib23	07Leo05	10Lib04
09/11/1929	18Vir15	14Lib55	13Leo01	13Lib19
09/16/1929	23Vir07	19Lib24	18Leo58	16Lib37
09/21/1929	28Vir00	22Lib25	24Leo58	19Lib55
09/26/1929	02Lib54	23Lib19	01Vir00	23Lib16
10/01/1929	07Lib49	21Lib22	07Vir04	26Lib37
10/06/1929	12Lib45	16Lib33	13Vir10	00Sco00
10/11/1929	17Lib41	10Lib55	19Vir17	03Sco24
10/16/1929	22Lib39	08Lib04	25Vir25	06Sco49
10/21/1929	27Lib36	09Lib38	01Lib36	10Sco15
10/26/1929	02Sco36	14Lib42	07Lib46	13Sco43
10/31/1929	07Sco35	21Lib42	13Lib59	17Sco13
11/05/1929	12Sco36	29Lib30	20Lib12	20Sco43
11/10/1929	17Sco37	07Sco34	26Lib26	24Sco15
11/15/1929	22Sco39	15Sco39	02Sco41	27Sco49
11/20/1929	27Sco42	23Sco39	08Sco57	01Sag24
11/25/1929	02Sag45	01Sag35	15Sco12	05Sag00
11/30/1929	07Sag49	09Sag27	21Sco28	08Sag37
12/05/1929	12Sag53	17Sag17	27Sco45	12Sag15
12/10/1929	17Sag58	25Sag07	04Sag02	15Sag55
12/15/1929	23Sag03	03Cap03	10Sag19	19Sag37
12/20/1929	28Sag09	10Cap49	16Sag36	23Sag19
12/25/1929	03Cap14	18Cap35	22Sag54	27Sag03
12/30/1929	08Cap20	26Cap00	29Sag11	00Cap47

Ephemeris Tables for Sun, Mercury, Venus and Mars

Date	Sun	Mercury	Venus	Mars
01/04/1930	13Cap25	02Aqu33	05Cap28	04Cap33
01/09/1930	18Cap31	07Aqu07	11Cap46	08Cap20
01/14/1930	23Cap37	08Aqu03	18Cap03	12Cap08
01/19/1930	28Cap42	04Aqu22	24Cap20	15Cap57
01/24/1930	03Aqu48	28Cap09	00Aqu37	19Cap46
01/29/1930	08Aqu52	23Cap30	06Aqu54	23Cap37
02/03/1930	13Aqu57	22Cap18	13Aqu10	27Cap28
02/08/1930	19Aqu01	24Cap07	19Aqu27	01Aqu21
02/13/1930	24Aqu04	27Cap57	25Aqu43	05Aqu13
02/18/1930	29Aqu08	03Aqu06	02Pis00	09Aqu06
02/23/1930	04Pis10	09Aqu09	08Pis15	13Aqu00
02/28/1930	09Pis12	15Aqu52	14Pis30	16Aqu54
03/05/1930	14Pis13	23Aqu08	20Pis45	20Aqu48
03/10/1930	19Pis13	00Pis54	26Pis59	24Aqu43
03/15/1930	24Pis12	09Pis09	03Ari12	28Aqu39
03/20/1930	29Pis10	17Pis54	09Ari25	02Pis33
03/25/1930	04Ari07	27Pis10	15Ari37	06Pis28
03/30/1930	09Ari04	06Ari57	21Ari49	10Pis22
04/04/1930	14Ari00	17Ari10	28Ari00	14Pis17
04/09/1930	18Ari55	27Ari33	04Tau11	18Pis11
04/14/1930	23Ari49	7Tau29	10Tau21	22Pis04
04/19/1930	28Ari42	16Tau19	16Tau30	25Pis58
04/24/1930	03Tau35	23Tau30	22Tau38	29Pis50
04/29/1930	08Tau27	28Tau42	28Tau45	03Ari41
05/04/1930	13Tau18	01Gem45	04Gem52	07Ari32
05/09/1930	18Tau08	02Gem35	10Gem58	11Ari22
05/14/1930	22Tau58	01Gem24	17Gem03	15Ari11
05/19/1930	27Tau46	28Tau52	23Gem07	19Ari00
05/24/1930	02Gem35	26Tau05	29Gem10	22Ari46
05/29/1930	07Gem23	24Tau12	05Can13	26Ari32
06/03/1930	12Gem10	23Tau54	11Can14	00Tau16
06/08/1930	16Gem58	25Tau29	17Can14	04Tau00
06/13/1930	21Gem44	28Tau50	23Can13	07Tau41
06/18/1930	26Gem31	03Gem48	29Can11	11Tau21
06/23/1930	01Can17	10Gem15	05Leo07	15Tau00
06/28/1930	06Can03	18Gem05	11Leo03	18Tau37
07/03/1930	10Can49	27Gem12	16Leo56	22Tau12
07/08/1930	15Can35	07Can22	22Leo48	25Tau45
07/13/1930	20Can21	18Can04	28Leo37	29Tau16
07/18/1930	25Can07	28Can44	04Vir25	02Gem46
07/23/1930	29Can54	08Leo55	10Vir10	06Gem14
07/28/1930	04Leo40	18Leo28	15Vir53	09Gem39
08/02/1930	09Leo27	27Leo18	21Vir33	13Gem03
08/07/1930	14Leo15	05Vir27	27Vir10	16Gem24
08/12/1930	19Leo03	12Vir55	02Lib43	19Gem42
08/17/1930	23Leo51	19Vir41	08Lib13	22Gem58
08/22/1930	28Leo39	25Vir40	13Lib38	26Gem12
08/27/1930	03Vir29	00Lib40	18Lib58	29Gem23
09/01/1930	08Vir19	04Lib27	24Lib12	02Can31
09/06/1930	13Vir09	06Lib33	29Lib19	05Can36
09/11/1930	18Vir01	06Lib22	04Sco18	08Can38
09/16/1930	22Vir53	03Lib29	09Sco08	11Can37
09/21/1930	27Vir46	28Vir28	13Sco46	14Can31
09/26/1930	02Lib40	23Vir44	18Sco12	17Can22

Date	Sun	Mercury	Venus	Mars
10/01/1930	07Lib35	22Vir07	22Sco21	20Can09
10/06/1930	12Lib30	24Vir38	26Sco10	22Can51
10/11/1930	17Lib27	00Lib25	29Sco36	25Can28
10/16/1930	22Lib24	08Lib00	02Sag33	28Can00
10/21/1930	27Lib22	16Lib19	04Sag54	00Leo25
10/26/1930	02Sco21	24Lib47	06Sag32	02Leo45
10/31/1930	07Sco21	03Sco10	07Sag19	04Leo57
11/05/1930	12Sco21	11Sco22	07Sag09	07Leo01
11/10/1930	17Sco22	19Sco24	05Sag58	08Leo57
11/15/1930	22Sco24	27Sco18	03Sag52	10Leo42
11/20/1930	27Sco27	05Sag06	01Sag05	12Leo18
11/25/1930	02Sag30	12Sag48	28Sco04	13Leo40
11/30/1930	07Sag34	20Sag26	25Sco19	14Leo50
12/05/1930	12Sag39	27Sag58	23Sco17	15Leo45
12/10/1930	17Sag43	05Cap18	22Sco12	16Leo24
12/15/1930	22Sag48	12Cap10	22Sco08	16Leo45
12/20/1930	27Sag54	18Cap01	23Sco03	16Leo47
12/25/1930	02Cap59	21Cap43	24Sco49	16Leo30
12/30/1930	08Cap05	21Cap39	27Sco20	15Leo51
01/04/1931	13Cap11	17Cap00	00Sag27	14Leo52
01/09/1931	18Cap16	10Cap31	04Sag03	13Leo34
01/14/1931	23Cap22	06Cap33	08Sag04	11Leo59
01/19/1931	28Cap28	06Cap25	12Sag25	10Leo10
01/24/1931	03Aqu33	09Cap11	17Sag01	08Leo13
01/29/1931	08Aqu38	13Cap45	21Sag52	06Leo13
02/03/1931	13Aqu42	19Cap27	26Sag54	04Leo16
02/08/1931	18Aqu46	25Cap52	02Cap04	02Leo27
02/13/1931	23Aqu50	02Aqu49	07Cap23	00Leo51
02/18/1931	28Aqu54	10Aqu13	12Cap48	29Can32
02/23/1931	03Pis55	18Aqu01	18Cap18	28Can31
02/28/1931	08Pis57	26Aqu13	23Cap54	27Can51
03/05/1931	13Pis58	04Pis51	29Cap33	27Can29
03/10/1931	18Pis58	13Pis57	05Aqu15	27Can27
03/15/1931	23Pis57	23Pis29	11Aqu00	27Can43
03/20/1931	28Pis56	03Ari23	16Aqu48	28Can15
03/25/1931	03Ari53	13Ari25	22Aqu37	29Can03
03/30/1931	08Ari49	23Ari02	28Aqu30	00Leo04
04/04/1931	13Ari45	01Tau27	04Pis22	01Leo18
04/09/1931	18Ari40	07Tau55	10Pis17	02Leo43
04/14/1931	23Ari34	11Tau57	16Pis13	04Leo18
04/19/1931	28Ari28	13Tau24	22Pis10	06Leo03
04/24/1931	03Tau21	12Tau24	28Pis07	07Leo54
04/29/1931	08Tau12	09Tau41	04Ari04	09Leo53
05/04/1931	13Tau03	06Tau31	10Ari04	11Leo58
05/09/1931	17Tau54	04Tau13	16Ari03	14Leo10
05/14/1931	22Tau43	03Tau37	22Ari03	16Leo26
05/19/1931	27Tau33	04Tau54	28Ari04	18Leo48
05/24/1931	02Gem21	07Tau56	04Tau05	21Leo13
05/29/1931	07Gem09	12Tau30	10Tau07	23Leo43
06/03/1931	11Gem57	18Tau24	16Tau09	26Leo16
06/08/1931	16Gem43	25Tau30	22Tau11	28Leo53
06/13/1931	21Gem30	03Gem45	28Tau14	01Vir33
06/18/1931	26Gem17	13Gem06	04Gem18	04Vir15
06/23/1931	01Can03	23Gem22	10Gem21	07Vir01
06/28/1931	05Can49	04Can12	16Gem25	09Vir49

Ephemeris Tables for Sun, Mercury, Venus and Mars

Date	Sun	Mercury	Venus	Mars
07/03/1931	10Can35	15Can03	22Gem31	12Vir40
07/08/1931	15Can21	25Can25	28Gem36	15Vir33
07/13/1931	20Can07	05Leo04	04Can42	18Vir28
07/18/1931	24Can54	13Leo57	10Can49	21Vir25
07/23/1931	29Can40	22Leo03	16Can56	24Vir25
07/28/1931	04Leo27	29Leo21	23Can04	27Vir27
08/02/1931	09Leo13	05Vir49	29Can13	00Lib30
08/07/1931	14Leo01	11Vir21	05Leo22	03Lib36
08/12/1931	18Leo48	15Vir43	11Leo31	06Lib43
08/17/1931	23Leo37	18Vir39	17Leo42	09Lib52
08/22/1931	28Leo25	19Vir41	23Leo53	13Lib03
08/27/1931	03Vir15	18Vir24	00Vir04	16Lib16
09/01/1931	08Vir05	14Vir48	06Vir16	19Lib31
09/06/1931	12Vir55	10Vir03	12Vir28	22Lib48
09/11/1931	17Vir47	06Vir31	18Vir42	26Lib06
09/16/1931	22Vir39	06Vir13	24Vir55	29Lib26
09/21/1931	27Vir32	09Vir42	01Lib08	02Sco48
09/26/1931	02Lib26	16Vir09	07Lib22	06Sco11
10/01/1931	07Lib21	24Vir17	13Lib36	09Sco36
10/06/1931	12Lib16	03Lib05	19Lib50	13Sco03
10/11/1931	17Lib12	11Lib57	26Lib04	16Sco31
10/16/1931	22Lib09	20Lib37	02Sco19	20Sco02
10/21/1931	27Lib07	29Lib02	08Sco33	23Sco34
10/26/1931	02Sco06	07Sco12	14Sco48	27Sco07
10/31/1931	07Sco06	15Sco09	21Sco02	00Sag42
11/05/1931	12Sco07	22Sco54	27Sco16	04Sag19
11/10/1931	17Sco08	00Sag29	03Sag31	07Sag57
11/15/1931	22Sco10	07Sag54	09Sag46	11Sag37
11/20/1931	27Sco12	15Sag07	16Sag00	15Sag18
11/25/1931	02Sag16	22Sag01	22Sag15	19Sag01
11/30/1931	07Sag19	28Sag18	28Sag28	22Sag45
12/05/1931	12Sag24	03Cap25	04Cap43	26Sag31
12/10/1931	17Sag28	06Cap15	10Cap57	00Cap18
12/15/1931	22Sag33	05Cap10	17Cap10	04Cap05
12/20/1931	27Sag39	29Sag46	23Cap24	07Cap54
12/25/1931	02Cap45	23Sag20	29Cap36	11Cap45
12/30/1931	07Cap50	20Sag12	05Aqu49	15Cap36
01/04/1932	12Cap56	21Sag06	12Aqu01	19Cap28
01/09/1932	18Cap02	24Sag44	18Aqu12	23Cap21
01/14/1932	23Cap07	29Sag58	24Aqu22	27Cap15
01/19/1932	28Cap13	06Cap07	00Pis32	01Aqu10
01/24/1932	03Aqu18	12Cap52	06Pis40	05Aqu05
01/29/1932	08Aqu23	20Cap02	12Pis47	09Aqu01
02/03/1932	13Aqu28	27Cap31	18Pis52	12Aqu57
02/08/1932	18Aqu31	05Aqu21	24Pis56	16Aqu53
02/13/1932	23Aqu35	13Aqu29	00Ari57	20Aqu50
02/18/1932	28Aqu39	21Aqu58	06Ari57	24Aqu47
02/23/1932	03Pis41	00Pis52	12Ari54	28Aqu45
02/28/1932	08Pis43	10Pis07	18Ari49	02Pis41
03/04/1932	13Pis43	19Pis42	24Ari40	06Pis38
03/09/1932	18Pis43	29Pis21	00Tau28	10Pis34
03/14/1932	23Pis43	08Ari33	06Tau13	14Pis31
03/19/1932	28Pis42	16Ari27	11Tau53	18Pis27
03/24/1932	03Ari39	22Ari05	17Tau29	22Pis22
03/29/1932	08Ari35	24Ari49	22Tau59	26Pis16

Date	Sun	Mercury	Venus	Mars
04/03/1932	13Ari31	24Ari30	28Tau23	00Ari09
04/08/1932	18Ari26	21Ari46	03Gem40	04Ari03
04/13/1932	23Ari21	18Ari03	08Gem50	07Ari55
04/18/1932	28Ari14	15Ari00	13Gem49	11Ari46
04/23/1932	03Tau06	13Ari45	18Gem39	15Ari36
04/28/1932	07Tau58	14Ari33	23Gem16	19Ari26
05/03/1932	12Tau49	17Ari13	27Gem37	23Ari14
05/08/1932	17Tau40	21Ari25	01Can41	27Ari01
05/13/1932	22Tau30	26Ari54	05Can24	00Tau46
05/18/1932	27Tau19	03Tau29	08Can40	04Tau31
05/23/1932	02Gem07	11Tau04	11Can25	08Tau15
05/28/1932	06Gem55	19Tau36	13Can33	11Tau56
06/02/1932	11Gem43	29Tau05	14Can55	15Tau37
06/07/1932	16Gem30	09Gem25	15Can26	19Tau16
06/12/1932	21Gem16	20Gem18	14Can58	22Tau54
06/17/1932	26Gem03	01Can13	13Can31	26Tau30
06/22/1932	00Can49	11Can42	11Can12	00Gem04
06/27/1932	05Can36	21Can25	08Can15	03Gem37
07/02/1932	10Can22	00Leo16	05Can10	07Gem09
07/07/1932	15Can07	08Leo13	02Can22	10Gem39
07/12/1932	19Can54	15Leo15	00Can17	14Gem08
07/17/1932	24Can40	21Leo18	29Gem08	17Gem35
07/22/1932	29Can26	26Leo14	28Gem58	21Gem00
07/27/1932	04Leo13	29Leo48	29Gem44	24Gem24
08/01/1932	09Leo00	01Vir42	01Can19	27Gem46
08/06/1932	13Leo46	01Vir34	03Can37	01Can06
08/11/1932	18Leo34	29Leo16	06Can31	04Can25
08/16/1932	23Leo22	25Leo22	09Can53	07Can42
08/21/1932	28Leo12	21Leo24	13Can39	10Can57
08/26/1932	03Vir01	19Leo19	17Can46	14Can10
08/31/1932	07Vir51	20Leo24	22Can10	17Can22
09/05/1932	12Vir42	24Leo49	26Can48	20Can31
09/10/1932	17Vir33	01Vir52	01Leo39	23Can39
09/15/1932	22Vir25	10Vir31	06Leo39	26Can45
09/20/1932	27Vir18	19Vir45	11Leo49	29Can48
09/25/1932	02Lib12	29Vir00	17Leo07	02Leo49
09/30/1932	07Lib06	07Lib59	22Leo32	05Leo48
10/05/1932	12Lib01	16Lib37	28Leo03	08Leo44
10/10/1932	16Lib58	24Lib55	03Vir40	11Leo37
10/15/1932	21Lib55	02Sco55	09Vir22	14Leo28
10/20/1932	26Lib53	10Sco39	15Vir07	17Leo15
10/25/1932	01Sco52	18Sco07	20Vir57	20Leo00
10/30/1932	06Sco52	25Sco20	26Vir50	22Leo40
11/04/1932	11Sco52	02Sag14	02Lib46	25Leo17
11/09/1932	16Sco53	08Sag40	08Lib46	27Leo49
11/14/1932	21Sco55	14Sag22	14Lib47	00Vir18
11/19/1932	26Sco58	18Sag42	20Lib51	02Vir40
11/24/1932	02Sag01	20Sag35	26Lib57	04Vir58
11/29/1932	07Sag04	18Sag33	03Sco03	07Vir09
12/04/1932	12Sag09	12Sag37	09Sco12	09Vir13
12/09/1932	17Sag13	06Sag31	15Sco22	11Vir10
12/14/1932	22Sag19	04Sag19	21Sco33	12Vir59
12/19/1932	27Sag24	06Sag10	27Sco45	14Vir39
12/24/1932	02Cap30	10Sag36	03Sag57	16Vir07
12/29/1932	07Cap35	16Sag27	10Sag10	17Vir25

Ephemeris Tables for Sun, Mercury, Venus and Mars

Date	Sun	Mercury	Venus	Mars	Date	Sun	Mercury	Venus	Mars
01/03/1933	12Cap41	23Sag03	16Sag24	18Vir30	10/05/1933	11Lib48	28Lib19	23Sco23	27Sco11
01/08/1933	17Cap47	00Cap06	22Sag37	19Vir21	10/10/1933	16Lib43	05Sco40	29Sco12	00Sag43
01/13/1933	22Cap52	07Cap27	28Sag52	19Vir55	10/15/1933	21Lib40	12Sco40	04Sag58	04Sag18
01/18/1933	27Cap58	15Cap01	05Cap06	20Vir14	10/20/1933	26Lib39	19Sco15	10Sag43	07Sag55
01/23/1933	03Aqu03	22Cap51	11Cap21	20Vir14	10/25/1933	01Sco37	25Sco13	16Sag24	11Sag33
01/28/1933	08Aqu08	00Aqu55	17Cap35	19Vir55	10/30/1933	06Sco37	00Sag16	22Sag02	15Sag13
02/02/1933	13Aqu13	09Aqu16	23Cap50	19Vir16	11/04/1933	11Sco37	03Sag46	27Sag36	18Sag55
02/07/1933	18Aqu17	17Aqu55	00Aqu04	18Vir17	11/09/1933	16Sco39	04Sag40	03Cap06	22Sag38
02/12/1933	23Aqu21	26Aqu52	06Aqu19	17Vir00	11/14/1933	21Sco40	01Sag44	08Cap30	26Sag23
02/17/1933	28Aqu24	06Pis06	12Aqu34	15Vir26	11/19/1933	26Sco43	25Sco30	13Cap48	00Cap09
02/22/1933	03Pis27	15Pis19	18Aqu48	13Vir40	11/24/1933	01Sag46	19Sco59	18Cap58	03Cap57
02/27/1933	08Pis28	24Pis03	25Aqu03	11Vir44	11/29/1933	06Sag50	18Sco44	23Cap59	07Cap46
03/04/1933	13Pis29	01Ari21	01Pis18	09Vir46	12/04/1933	11Sag54	21Sco31	28Cap49	11Cap37
03/09/1933	18Pis29	06Ari06	07Pis31	07Vir49	12/09/1933	16Sag59	26Sco42	03Aqu25	15Cap28
03/14/1933	23Pis28	07Ari25	13Pis45	06Vir00	12/14/1933	22Sag04	03Sag07	07Aqu46	19Cap21
03/19/1933	28Pis27	05Ari21	19Pis58	04Vir24	12/19/1933	27Sag09	10Sag08	11Aqu46	23Cap15
03/24/1933	03Ari24	01Ari13	26Pis11	03Vir04	12/24/1933	02Cap15	17Sag28	15Aqu21	27Cap09
03/29/1933	08Ari21	27Pis12	02Ari23	02Vir01	12/29/1933	07Cap21	25Sag00	18Aqu27	01Aqu04
04/03/1933	13Ari17	24Pis55	08Ari36	01Vir19	01/03/1934	12Cap26	02Cap40	20Aqu56	05Aqu00
04/08/1933	18Ari12	24Pis55	14Ari48	00Vir55	01/08/1934	17Cap32	10Cap29	22Aqu41	08Aqu56
04/13/1933	23Ari06	27Pis00	20Ari59	00Vir51	01/13/1934	22Cap37	18Cap29	23Aqu34	12Aqu52
04/18/1933	28Ari00	00Ari45	27Ari10	01Vir06	01/18/1934	27Cap43	26Cap41	23Aqu27	16Aqu49
04/23/1933	02Tau52	05Ari49	03Tau21	01Vir36	01/23/1934	02Aqu48	05Aqu06	22Aqu17	20Aqu46
04/28/1933	07Tau44	11Ari58	09Tau31	02Vir23	01/28/1934	07Aqu54	13Aqu45	20Aqu10	24Aqu44
05/03/1933	12Tau36	19Ari01	15Tau42	03Vir24	02/02/1934	12Aqu58	22Aqu34	17Aqu21	28Aqu42
05/08/1933	17Tau26	26Ari55	21Tau52	04Vir37	02/07/1934	18Aqu02	01Pis21	14Aqu16	02Pis39
05/13/1933	22Tau16	5Tau39	28Tau01	06Vir03	02/12/1934	23Aqu06	9Pis34	11Aqu27	06Pis36
05/18/1933	27Tau04	15Tau12	04Gem10	07Vir39	02/17/1934	28Aqu09	16Pis13	09Aqu18	10Pis32
05/23/1933	01Gem53	25Tau30	10Gem19	09Vir24	02/22/1934	03Pis12	20Pis00	08Aqu09	14Pis28
05/28/1933	06Gem41	06Gem21	16Gem28	11Vir18	02/27/1934	08Pis13	19Pis53	08Aqu00	18Pis24
06/02/1933	11Gem29	17Gem18	22Gem36	13Vir20	03/04/1934	13Pis14	16Pis14	08Aqu49	22Pis19
06/07/1933	16Gem16	27Gem49	28Gem44	15Vir28	03/09/1934	18Pis15	11Pis16	10Aqu30	26Pis13
06/12/1933	21Gem03	07Can31	04Can51	17Vir43	03/14/1934	23Pis14	07Pis33	12Aqu54	00Ari06
06/17/1933	25Gem49	16Can15	10Can59	20Vir04	03/19/1934	28Pis12	06Pis20	15Aqu53	03Ari58
06/22/1933	00Can36	23Can56	17Can06	22Vir31	03/24/1934	03Ari10	07Pis33	19Aqu22	07Ari50
06/27/1933	05Can22	00Leo33	23Can13	25Vir03	03/29/1934	08Ari06	10Pis42	23Aqu15	11Ari41
07/02/1933	10Can07	06Leo00	29Can19	27Vir38	04/03/1934	13Ari03	15Pis18	27Aqu27	15Ari31
07/07/1933	14Can54	10Leo07	05Leo25	00Lib18	04/08/1934	17Ari58	21Pis01	01Pis55	19Ari19
07/12/1933	19Can40	12Leo39	11Leo31	03Lib03	04/13/1934	22Ari52	27Pis37	06Pis37	23Ari07
07/17/1933	24Can26	13Leo19	17Leo36	05Lib51	04/18/1934	27Ari45	04Ari59	11Pis30	26Ari53
07/22/1933	29Can12	11Leo59	23Leo41	08Lib42	04/23/1934	02Tau38	13Ari05	16Pis31	00Tau38
07/27/1933	03Leo58	08Leo59	29Leo46	11Lib37	04/28/1934	07Tau30	21Ari54	21Pis40	04Tau22
08/01/1933	08Leo46	05Leo21	05Vir50	14Lib35	05/03/1934	12Tau21	01Tau25	26Pis57	08Tau04
08/06/1933	13Leo33	02Leo40	11Vir53	17Lib36	05/08/1934	17Tau12	11Tau39	02Ari18	11Tau46
08/11/1933	18Leo21	02Leo40	17Vir56	20Lib40	05/13/1934	22Tau01	22Tau24	07Ari44	15Tau26
08/16/1933	23Leo09	04Leo42	23Vir58	23Lib47	05/18/1934	26Tau51	03Gem17	13Ari14	19Tau04
08/21/1933	27Leo57	09Leo59	29Vir59	26Lib57	05/23/1934	01Gem39	13Gem46	18Ari48	22Tau42
08/26/1933	02Vir47	17Leo36	06Lib00	00Sco09	05/28/1934	06Gem27	23Gem22	24Ari25	26Tau18
08/31/1933	07Vir37	26Leo40	11Lib59	03Sco24					
					06/02/1934	11Gem15	01Can51	00Tau05	29Tau52
09/05/1933	12Vir27	06Vir20	17Lib57	06Sco40	06/07/1934	16Gem02	09Can08	05Tau48	03Gem25
09/10/1933	17Vir19	15Vir57	23Lib55	10Sco00	06/12/1934	20Gem49	15Can08	11Tau32	06Gem57
09/15/1933	22Vir11	25Vir15	29Lib52	13Sco22	06/17/1934	25Gem35	19Can44	17Tau18	10Gem28
09/20/1933	27Vir04	04Lib06	05Sco46	16Sco46	06/22/1934	00Can22	22Can45	23Tau07	13Gem57
09/25/1933	01Lib57	12Lib33	11Sco40	20Sco12	06/27/1934	05Can07	23Can58	28Tau57	17Gem26
09/30/1933	06Lib52	20Lib37	17Sco33	23Sco40					

Ephemeris Tables for Sun, Mercury, Venus and Mars

Date	Sun	Mercury	Venus	Mars	Date	Sun	Mercury	Venus	Mars
07/02/1934	09Can54	23Can18	04Gem48	20Gem52	04/03/1935	12Ari48	21Pis21	14Tau37	17Lib11
07/07/1934	14Can40	20Can59	10Gem42	24Gem18	04/08/1935	17Ari43	29Pis32	20Tau39	15Lib16
07/12/1934	19Can26	17Can51	16Gem36	27Gem42	04/13/1935	22Ari38	08Ari21	26Tau38	13Lib22
07/17/1934	24Can12	15Can10	22Gem32	01Can04	04/18/1935	27Ari31	17Ari48	02Gem36	11Lib33
07/22/1934	28Can58	14Can06	28Gem29	04Can26	04/23/1935	02Tau24	27Ari53	08Gem31	09Lib54
07/27/1934	03Leo45	15Can22	04Can28	07Can46	04/28/1935	07Tau16	08Tau28	14Gem24	08Lib30
08/01/1934	08Leo32	19Can06	10Can28	11Can06	05/03/1935	12Tau07	19Tau12	20Gem15	07Lib24
08/06/1934	13Leo19	25Can13	16Can29	14Can24	05/08/1935	16Tau58	29Tau34	26Gem03	06Lib36
08/11/1934	18Leo07	03Leo19	22Can32	17Can40	05/13/1935	21Tau48	08Gem58	01Can49	06Lib09
08/16/1934	22Leo55	12Leo46	28Can36	20Can56	05/18/1935	26Tau37	17Gem06	07Can31	06Lib01
08/21/1934	27Leo43	22Leo48	04Leo40	24Can10	05/23/1935	01Gem25	23Gem48	13Can09	06Lib13
08/26/1934	02Vir33	02Vir46	10Leo47	27Can23	05/28/1935	06Gem13	28Gem55	18Can45	06Lib43
08/31/1934	07Vir23	12Vir22	16Leo54	00Leo35					
					06/02/1935	11Gem01	02Can22	24Can15	07Lib30
09/05/1934	12Vir13	21Vir27	23Leo03	03Leo46	06/07/1935	15Gem48	03Can58	29Can40	08Lib31
09/10/1934	17Vir04	00Lib02	29Leo12	06Leo55	06/12/1935	20Gem35	03Can41	05Leo00	09Lib47
09/15/1934	21Vir57	08Lib09	05Vir22	10Leo03	06/17/1935	25Gem22	01Can46	10Leo13	11Lib16
09/20/1934	26Vir49	15Lib50	11Vir34	13Leo10	06/22/1935	00Can08	28Gem59	15Leo19	12Lib57
09/25/1934	01Lib43	23Lib04	17Vir46	16Leo15	06/27/1935	04Can54	26Gem27	20Leo17	14Lib48
09/30/1934	06Lib37	29Lib51	23Vir59	19Leo19					
					07/02/1935	09Can40	25Gem15	25Leo04	16Lib48
10/05/1934	11Lib33	06Sco04	00Lib13	22Leo22	07/07/1935	14Can26	25Gem58	29Leo40	18Lib57
10/10/1934	16Lib29	11Sco33	06Lib27	25Leo23	07/12/1935	19Can12	28Gem48	04Vir02	21Lib14
10/15/1934	21Lib27	15Sco55	12Lib42	28Leo23	07/17/1935	23Can58	03Can42	08Vir07	23Lib39
10/20/1934	26Lib24	18Sco31	18Lib57	01Vir21	07/22/1935	28Can45	10Can32	11Vir52	26Lib10
10/25/1934	01Sco23	18Sco24	25Lib13	04Vir17	07/27/1935	03Leo31	19Can04	15Vir13	28Lib47
10/30/1934	06Sco22	14Sco38	01Sco29	07Vir11					
					08/01/1935	08Leo18	28Can50	18Vir06	01Sco30
11/04/1934	11Sco23	08Sco23	07Sco46	10Vir04	08/06/1935	13Leo05	09Leo10	20Vir22	04Sco18
11/09/1934	16Sco24	03Sco40	14Sco02	12Vir54	08/11/1935	17Leo53	19Leo27	21Vir57	07Sco11
11/14/1934	21Sco26	03Sco24	20Sco19	15Vir42	08/16/1935	22Leo41	29Leo19	22Vir43	10Sco09
11/19/1934	26Sco28	07Sco01	26Sco36	18Vir28	08/21/1935	27Leo30	08Vir37	22Vir32	13Sco11
11/24/1934	01Sag31	12Sco55	02Sag53	21Vir11	08/26/1935	02Vir19	17Vir21	21Vir22	16Sco17
11/29/1934	06Sag35	19Sco52	09Sag10	23Vir51	08/31/1935	07Vir09	25Vir31	19Vir17	19Sco27
12/04/1934	11Sag39	27Sco18	15Sag27	26Vir28	09/05/1935	11Vir59	03Lib09	16Vir31	22Sco40
12/09/1934	16Sag44	04Sag55	21Sag45	29Vir02	09/10/1935	16Vir51	10Lib15	13Vir27	25Sco57
12/14/1934	21Sag49	12Sag38	28Sag02	01Lib31	09/15/1935	21Vir42	16Lib46	10Vir34	29Sco17
12/19/1934	26Sag54	20Sag24	04Cap19	03Lib57	09/20/1935	26Vir35	22Lib36	08Vir18	2Sag40
12/24/1934	02Cap00	28Sag13	10Cap36	06Lib19	09/25/1935	01Lib29	27Lib31	06Vir57	6Sag06
12/29/1934	07Cap06	06Cap09	16Cap53	08Lib35	09/30/1935	06Lib24	01Sco08	06Vir36	9Sag35
01/03/1935	12Cap12	14Cap12	23Cap10	10Lib46	10/05/1935	11Lib19	02Sco47	07Vir13	13Sag06
01/08/1935	17Cap17	22Cap24	29Cap27	12Lib50	10/10/1935	16Lib15	01Sco36	08Vir43	16Sag40
01/13/1935	22Cap23	00Aqu45	05Aqu43	14Lib48	10/15/1935	21Lib12	27Lib12	10Vir58	20Sag16
01/18/1935	27Cap28	09Aqu10	11Aqu59	16Lib38	10/20/1935	26Lib10	21Lib13	13Vir51	23Sag54
01/23/1935	02Aqu34	17Aqu27	18Aqu15	18Lib19	10/25/1935	01Sco09	17Lib28	17Vir16	27Sag34
01/28/1935	07Aqu39	25Aqu04	24Aqu30	19Lib51	10/30/1935	06Sco08	18Lib12	21Vir06	01Cap17
02/02/1935	12Aqu43	01Pis02	00Pis46	21Lib12	11/04/1935	11Sco08	22Lib39	25Vir19	05Cap01
02/07/1935	17Aqu48	03Pis49	07Pis00	22Lib22	11/09/1935	16Sco09	29Lib12	29Vir49	08Cap46
02/12/1935	22Aqu51	02Pis19	13Pis14	23Lib18	11/14/1935	21Sco11	06Sco41	04Lib35	12Cap33
02/17/1935	27Aqu55	27Aqu23	19Pis27	24Lib00	11/19/1935	26Sco13	14Sco31	09Lib33	16Cap22
02/22/1935	02Pis57	22Aqu07	25Pis39	24Lib27	11/24/1935	01Sag16	22Sco25	14Lib43	20Cap12
02/27/1935	07Pis59	19Aqu09	01Ari50	24Lib35	11/29/1935	06Sag21	00Sag19	20Lib01	24Cap03
03/04/1935	13Pis00	19Aqu05	08Ari00	24Lib25	12/04/1935	11Sag24	08Sag11	25Lib27	27Cap54
03/09/1935	18Pis00	21Aqu24	14Ari10	23Lib57	12/09/1935	16Sag29	16Sag03	01Sco00	01Aqu47
03/14/1935	23Pis00	25Aqu25	20Ari18	23Lib09	12/14/1935	21Sag34	23Sag55	06Sco38	05Aqu40
03/19/1935	27Pis58	00Pis40	26Ari25	22Lib02	12/19/1935	26Sag39	01Cap49	12Sco21	09Aqu34
03/24/1935	02Ari55	06Pis51	02Tau31	20Lib38	12/24/1935	01Cap45	09Cap48	18Sco09	13Aqu29
03/29/1935	07Ari52	13Pis46	08Tau35	19Lib00	12/29/1935	06Cap51	17Cap49	23Sco59	17Aqu24

Ephemeris Tables for Sun, Mercury, Venus and Mars

Date	Sun	Mercury	Venus	Mars	Date	Sun	Mercury	Venus	Mars
01/03/1936	11Cap57	25Cap50	29Sco53	21Aqu19	10/04/1936	11Lib04	04Lib00	07Sco03	04Vir54
01/08/1936	17Cap03	03Aqu36	05Sag49	25Aqu14	10/09/1936	16Lib00	01Lib24	13Sco11	08Vir00
01/13/1936	22Cap08	10Aqu36	11Sag48	29Aqu10	10/14/1936	20Lib57	03Lib06	19Sco19	11Vir05
01/18/1936	27Cap13	15Aqu47	17Sag48	03Pis04	10/19/1936	25Lib55	08Lib19	25Sco27	14Vir10
01/23/1936	02Aqu19	17Aqu34	23Sag51	06Pis59	10/24/1936	00Sco54	15Lib30	01Sag35	17Vir13
01/28/1936	07Aqu24	14Aqu49	29Sag54	10Pis53	10/29/1936	05Sco54	23Lib30	07Sag42	20Vir16
02/02/1936	12Aqu28	08Aqu59	05Cap58	14Pis47	11/03/1936	10Sco54	01Sco43	13Sag49	23Vir18
02/07/1936	17Aqu33	03Aqu53	12Cap03	18Pis40	11/08/1936	15Sco55	09Sco56	19Sag55	26Vir19
02/12/1936	22Aqu36	01Aqu53	18Cap09	22Pis33	11/13/1936	20Sco57	18Sco02	26Sag01	29Vir19
02/17/1936	27Aqu39	02Aqu55	24Cap16	26Pis25	11/18/1936	25Sco59	26Sco00	02Cap06	02Lib18
02/22/1936	02Pis42	06Aqu10	00Aqu24	00Ari15	11/23/1936	01Sag02	03Sag54	08Cap10	05Lib16
02/27/1936	07Pis44	10Aqu55	06Aqu31	04Ari05	11/28/1936	06Sag06	11Sag43	14Cap13	08Lib13
03/03/1936	12Pis45	16Aqu40	12Aqu39	07Ari54	12/03/1936	11Sag10	19Sag30	20Cap15	11Lib09
03/08/1936	17Pis45	23Aqu11	18Aqu48	11Ari43	12/08/1936	16Sag15	27Sag15	26Cap16	14Lib03
03/13/1936	22Pis45	00Pis20	24Aqu56	15Ari30	12/13/1936	21Sag19	04Cap58	02Aqu15	16Lib56
03/18/1936	27Pis43	08Pis01	01Pis05	19Ari16	12/18/1936	26Sag23	12Cap33	08Aqu12	19Lib47
03/23/1936	02Ari41	16Pis15	07Pis14	23Ari01	12/23/1936	01Cap30	19Cap47	14Aqu07	22Lib36
03/28/1936	07Ari38	25Pis01	13Pis23	26Ari45	12/28/1936	06Cap36	26Cap07	19Aqu59	25Lib24
04/02/1936	12Ari34	04Ari20	19Pis31	00Tau27	01/02/1937	11Cap42	00Aqu30	25Aqu48	28Lib09
04/07/1936	17Ari29	14Ari13	25Pis40	04Tau08	01/07/1937	16Cap48	01Aqu18	01Pis34	00Sco52
04/12/1936	22Ari24	24Ari34	01Ari48	07Tau48	01/12/1937	21Cap53	27Cap26	07Pis15	03Sco33
04/17/1936	27Ari17	05Tau06	07Ari57	11Tau27	01/17/1937	26Cap59	21Cap04	12Pis51	06Sco11
04/22/1936	02Tau10	15Tau15	14Ari06	15Tau04	01/22/1937	02Aqu04	16Cap28	18Pis22	08Sco45
04/27/1936	07Tau02	24Tau22	20Ari14	18Tau41	01/27/1937	07Aqu09	15Cap31	23Pis46	11Sco17
05/02/1936	11Tau53	02Gem01	26Ari22	22Tau16	02/01/1937	12Aqu14	17Cap35	29Pis01	13Sco44
05/07/1936	16Tau43	07Gem54	02Tau31	25Tau50	02/06/1937	17Aqu18	21Cap39	04Ari07	16Sco07
05/12/1936	21Tau34	11Gem53	08Tau39	29Tau22	02/11/1937	22Aqu21	26Cap58	09Ari03	18Sco26
05/17/1936	26Tau23	13Gem50	14Tau47	02Gem54	02/16/1937	27Aqu25	03Aqu09	13Ari45	20Sco40
05/22/1936	01Gem12	13Gem46	20Tau55	06Gem24	02/21/1937	02Pis28	09Aqu56	18Ari11	22Sco48
05/27/1936	06Gem00	12Gem00	27Tau03	09Gem53	02/26/1937	07Pis30	17Aqu14	22Ari19	24Sco49
06/01/1936	10Gem47	09Gem18	03Gem11	13Gem21	03/03/1937	12Pis31	24Aqu59	26Ari04	26Sco43
06/06/1936	15Gem34	06Gem49	09Gem19	16Gem48	03/08/1937	17Pis31	03Pis12	29Ari22	28Sco28
06/11/1936	20Gem21	05Gem32	15Gem27	20Gem13	03/13/1937	22Pis30	11Pis52	2Tau06	00Sag06
06/16/1936	25Gem07	06Gem01	21Gem36	23Gem38	03/18/1937	27Pis29	21Pis02	04Tau11	01Sag32
06/21/1936	29Gem54	08Gem25	27Gem44	27Gem01	03/23/1937	02Ari27	00Ari41	05Tau27	02Sag47
06/26/1936	04Can40	12Gem37	03Can52	00Can24	03/28/1937	07Ari24	10Ari46	05Tau49	03Sag50
07/01/1936	09Can26	18Gem31	10Can01	03Can45	04/02/1937	12Ari19	21Ari00	05Tau09	04Sag39
07/06/1936	14Can12	25Gem58	16Can10	07Can06	04/07/1937	17Ari15	00Tau51	03Tau30	05Sag12
07/11/1936	18Can58	04Can51	22Can19	10Can25	04/12/1937	22Ari09	09Tau37	00Tau58	05Sag28
07/16/1936	23Can45	14Can51	28Can28	13Can43	04/17/1937	27Ari03	16Tau38	27Ari56	05Sag27
07/21/1936	28Can31	25Can25	04Leo37	17Can01	04/22/1937	01Tau56	21Tau30	24Ari50	05Sag07
07/26/1936	03Leo17	05Leo59	10Leo47	20Can18	04/27/1937	06Tau48	24Tau03	22Ari12	04Sag28
07/31/1936	08Leo04	16Leo06	16Leo57	23Can34					
					05/02/1937	11Tau39	24Tau15	20Ari21	03Sag30
08/05/1936	12Leo51	25Leo35	23Leo07	26Can49	05/07/1937	16Tau30	22Tau28	19Ari30	02Sag15
08/10/1936	17Leo39	04Vir25	29Leo16	00Leo04	05/12/1937	21Tau19	19Tau36	19Ari37	00Sag46
08/15/1936	22Leo27	12Vir37	05Vir27	03Leo17	05/17/1937	26Tau09	16Tau53	20Ari41	29Sco06
08/20/1936	27Leo15	20Vir11	11Vir36	6Leo30	05/22/1937	00Gem57	15Tau24	22Ari31	27Sco21
08/25/1936	02Vir05	27Vir07	17Vir46	09Leo42	05/27/1937	05Gem46	15Tau40	25Ari02	25Sco36
08/30/1936	06Vir54	03Lib21	23Vir57	12Leo54					
					06/01/1937	10Gem33	17Tau48	28Ari06	23Sco56
09/04/1936	11Vir45	08Lib43	00Lib06	16Leo04	06/06/1937	15Gem21	21Tau36	01Tau36	22Sco28
09/09/1936	16Vir36	13Lib00	06Lib16	19Leo14	06/11/1937	20Gem07	26Tau55	05Tau29	21Sco14
09/14/1936	21Vir28	15Lib46	12Lib26	22Leo24	06/16/1937	24Gem54	03Gem35	09Tau40	20Sco19
09/19/1936	26Vir21	16Lib22	18Lib35	25Leo32	06/21/1937	29Gem40	11Gem31	14Tau07	19Sco45
09/24/1936	01Lib15	14Lib12	24Lib45	28Leo40	06/26/1937	04Can26	20Gem41	18Tau46	19Sco30
09/29/1936	06Lib09	09Lib21	00Sco54	01Vir48					

Ephemeris Tables for Sun, Mercury, Venus and Mars

Date	Sun	Mercury	Venus	Mars		Date	Sun	Mercury	Venus	Mars
07/01/1937	09Can12	00Can51	23Tau36	19Sco37		04/02/1938	12Ari05	01Tau00	26Ari12	15Tau07
07/06/1937	13Can58	11Can36	28Tau36	20Sco03		04/07/1938	17Ari01	04Tau40	02Tau23	18Tau39
07/11/1937	18Can45	22Can22	03Gem42	20Sco49		04/12/1938	21Ari55	05Tau33	08Tau33	22Tau09
07/16/1937	23Can30	02Leo40	08Gem56	21Sco52		04/17/1938	26Ari49	03Tau55	14Tau42	25Tau39
07/21/1937	28Can17	12Leo19	14Gem16	23Sco10		04/22/1938	01Tau42	00Tau45	20Tau51	29Tau07
07/26/1937	03Leo03	21Leo13	19Gem40	24Sco44		04/27/1938	06Tau34	27Ari30	26Tau58	02Gem34
07/31/1937	07Leo50	29Leo25	25Gem10	26Sco31						
						05/02/1938	11Tau25	25Ari29	03Gem05	06Gem00
08/05/1937	12Leo37	06Vir52	00Can44	28Sco31		05/07/1938	16Tau16	25Ari21	09Gem11	09Gem25
08/10/1937	17Leo25	13Vir34	06Can22	00Sag41		05/12/1938	21Tau06	27Ari09	15Gem16	12Gem50
08/15/1937	22Leo13	19Vir25	12Can03	03Sag01		05/17/1938	25Tau55	00Tau37	21Gem20	16Gem13
08/20/1937	27Leo01	24Vir15	17Can47	05Sag30		05/22/1938	00Gem43	05Tau32	27Gem23	19Gem36
08/25/1937	01Vir51	27Vir47	23Can34	08Sag07		05/27/1938	05Gem31	11Tau40	03Can25	22Gem57
08/30/1937	06Vir40	29Vir34	29Can24	10Sag52						
						06/01/1938	10Gem19	18Tau56	09Can27	26Gem18
09/04/1937	11Vir31	29Vir04	05Leo17	13Sag44		06/06/1938	15Gem07	27Tau16	15Can27	29Gem37
09/09/1937	16Vir22	26Vir00	11Leo12	16Sag42		06/11/1938	19Gem54	06Gem37	21Can26	02Can57
09/14/1937	21Vir14	21Vir06	17Leo10	19Sag45		06/16/1938	24Gem40	16Gem52	27Can24	06Can15
09/19/1937	26Vir07	16Vir42	23Leo10	22Sag54		06/21/1938	29Gem27	27Gem43	03Leo20	09Can33
09/24/1937	01Lib00	15Vir24	29Leo12	26Sag06		06/26/1938	04Can13	08Can37	09Leo15	12Can49
09/29/1937	05Lib55	18Vir05	05Vir15	29Sag24						
						07/01/1938	08Can58	19Can04	15Leo08	16Can06
10/04/1937	10Lib50	24Vir00	11Vir21	02Cap45		07/06/1938	13Can45	28Can49	21Leo00	19Can21
10/09/1937	15Lib46	01Lib46	17Vir27	06Cap10		07/11/1938	18Can30	07Leo45	26Leo49	22Can36
10/14/1937	20Lib43	10Lib15	23Vir36	09Cap37		07/16/1938	23Can17	15Leo51	02Vir37	25Can51
10/19/1937	25Lib41	18Lib54	29Vir46	13Cap08		07/21/1938	28Can03	23Leo06	08Vir22	29Can04
10/24/1937	00Sco39	27Lib24	05Lib57	16Cap42		07/26/1938	02Leo49	29Leo28	14Vir04	02Leo18
10/29/1937	05Sco39	05Sco43	12Lib09	20Cap54		07/31/1938	07Leo36	04Vir49	19Vir44	05Leo31
11/03/1937	10Sco39	13Sco49	18Lib22	23Cap55		08/05/1938	12Leo24	08Vir58	25Vir21	08Leo43
11/08/1937	15Sco40	21Sco45	24Lib36	27Cap34		08/10/1938	17Leo11	11Vir35	00Lib54	11Leo56
11/13/1937	20Sco42	29Sco31	00Sco51	01Aqu15		08/15/1938	21Leo59	12Vir16	06Lib22	15Leo07
11/18/1937	25Sco44	07Sag11	07Sco06	04Aqu58		08/20/1938	26Leo48	10Vir40	11Lib47	18Leo19
11/23/1937	00Sag47	14Sag44	13Sco22	08Aqu42		08/25/1938	01Vir37	07Vir00	17Lib06	21Leo30
11/28/1937	05Sag51	22Sag09	19Sco38	12Aqu27		08/30/1938	06Vir27	02Vir30	22Lib19	24Leo42
12/03/1937	10Sag55	29Sag19	25Sco55	16Aqu12		09/04/1938	11Vir17	29Leo24	27Lib25	27Leo52
12/08/1937	16Sag00	05Cap59	02Sag12	19Aqu58		09/09/1938	16Vir08	29Leo27	02Sco23	01Vir03
12/13/1937	21Sag04	11Cap37	08Sag28	23Aqu45		09/14/1938	21Vir00	03Vir07	07Sco12	04Vir13
12/18/1937	26Sag10	15Cap09	14Sag46	27Aqu32		09/19/1938	25Vir53	09Vir42	11Sco49	07Vir24
12/23/1937	01Cap15	14Cap55	21Sag03	01Pis19		09/24/1938	00Lib46	17Vir59	16Sco12	10Vir33
12/28/1937	06Cap21	10Cap10	27Sag21	05Pis07		09/29/1938	05Lib40	26Vir57	20Sco19	13Vir43
01/02/1938	11Cap27	03Cap37	03Cap38	08Pis54		10/04/1938	10Lib36	05Lib59	24Sco06	16Vir53
01/07/1938	16Cap33	29Sag45	09Cap55	12Pis40		10/09/1938	15Lib31	14Lib49	27Sco29	20Vir03
01/12/1938	21Cap39	29Sag49	16Cap13	16Pis27		10/14/1938	20Lib28	23Lib21	00Sag22	23Vir12
01/17/1938	26Cap44	02Cap49	22Cap30	20Pis13		10/19/1938	25Lib27	01Sco35	02Sag39	26Vir22
01/22/1938	01Aqu49	07Cap36	28Cap47	23Pis59		10/24/1938	00Sco25	09Sco34	04Sag12	29Vir31
01/27/1938	06Aqu54	13Cap27	05Aqu04	27Pis44		10/29/1938	05Sco24	17Sco19	04Sag54	02Lib40
02/01/1938	11Aqu59	19Cap58	11Aqu21	01Ari28		11/03/1938	10Sco24	24Sco52	04Sag38	05Lib49
02/06/1938	17Aqu03	27Cap00	17Aqu37	05Ari11		11/08/1938	15Sco25	02Sag13	03Sag22	08Lib58
02/11/1938	22Aqu07	04Aqu25	23Aqu54	08Ari54		11/13/1938	20Sco27	09Sag19	01Sag10	12Lib07
02/16/1938	27Aqu10	12Aqu12	00Pis10	12Ari36		11/18/1938	25Sco30	16Sag03	28Sco21	15Lib16
02/21/1938	02Pis13	20Aqu21	06Pis26	16Ari16		11/23/1938	00Sag33	22Sag09	25Sco21	18Lib24
02/26/1938	07Pis15	28Aqu55	12Pis41	19Ari57		11/28/1938	05Sag36	27Sag02	22Sco38	21Lib33
03/03/1938	12Pis16	07Pis53	18Pis55	23Ari36		12/03/1938	10Sag40	29Sag39	20Sco40	24Lib41
03/08/1938	17Pis16	17Pis17	25Pis10	27Ari13		12/08/1938	15Sag45	28Sag27	19Sco40	27Lib49
03/13/1938	22Pis16	27Pis03	01Ari23	00Tau51		12/13/1938	20Sag50	22Sag59	19Sco43	00Sco57
03/18/1938	27Pis15	06Ari55	07Ari36	04Tau26		12/18/1938	25Sag55	16Sag33	20Sco43	04Sco04
03/23/1938	02Ari12	16Ari25	13Ari49	08Tau01		12/23/1938	01Cap00	13Sag32	22Sco34	07Sco12
03/28/1938	07Ari09	24Ari43	20Ari01	11Tau34		12/28/1938	06Cap06	14Sag37	25Sco08	10Sco19

Ephemeris Tables for Sun, Mercury, Venus and Mars

Date	Sun	Mercury	Venus	Mars		Date	Sun	Mercury	Venus	Mars
01/02/1939	11Cap12	18Sag29	28Sco18	13Sco25		10/04/1939	10Lib21	19Lib16	18Lib01	04Aqu15
01/07/1939	16Cap18	23Sag55	01Sag57	16Sco31		10/09/1939	15Lib18	27Lib18	24Lib15	06Aqu34
01/12/1939	21Cap24	00Cap13	06Sag00	19Sco37		10/14/1939	20Lib15	05Sco03	00Sco30	09Aqu02
01/17/1939	26Cap29	07Cap04	10Sag22	22Sco42		10/19/1939	25Lib12	12Sco29	06Sco43	11Aqu38
01/22/1939	01Aqu34	14Cap18	15Sag01	25Sco46		10/24/1939	00Sco10	19Sco37	12Sco58	14Aqu21
01/27/1939	06Aqu39	21Cap49	19Sag52	28Sco49		10/29/1939	05Sco10	26Sco25	19Sco12	17Aqu10
02/01/1939	11Aqu44	29Cap36	24Sag55	01Sag52		11/03/1939	10Sco10	02Sag42	25Sco27	20Aqu05
02/06/1939	16Aqu48	07Aqu42	00Cap07	04Sag55		11/08/1939	15Sco11	08Sag12	01Sag42	23Aqu05
02/11/1939	21Aqu52	15Aqu07	05Cap27	07Sag55		11/13/1939	20Sco13	12Sag18	07Sag56	26Aqu09
02/16/1939	26Aqu55	24Aqu52	10Cap52	10Sag55		11/18/1939	25Sco15	13Sag57	14Sag10	29Aqu16
02/21/1939	01Pis58	04Pis00	16Cap24	13Sag54		11/23/1939	00Sag18	11Sag48	20Sag24	02Pis27
02/26/1939	07Pis00	13Pis24	22Cap00	16Sag52		11/28/1939	05Sag21	05Sag51	26Sag38	05Pis40
03/03/1939	12Pis01	22Pis54	27Cap39	19Sag48		12/03/1939	10Sag25	29Sco49	02Cap52	08Pis55
03/08/1939	17Pis02	01Ari57	03Aqu22	22Sag42		12/08/1939	15Sag30	27Sco44	09Cap06	12Pis13
03/13/1939	22Pis01	09Ari43	09Aqu07	25Sag34		12/13/1939	20Sag35	29Sco46	15Cap19	15Pis31
03/18/1939	27Pis00	15Ari09	14Aqu56	28Sag25		12/18/1939	25Sag40	04Sag25	21Cap33	18Pis52
03/23/1939	01Ari57	17Ari30	20Aqu46	01Cap13		12/23/1939	00Cap46	10Sag27	27Cap46	22Pis13
03/28/1939	06Ari55	16Ari37	26Aqu38	03Cap58		12/28/1939	05Cap51	17Sag12	03Aqu58	25Pis36
04/02/1939	11Ari51	13Ari20	02Pis32	06Cap40		01/02/1940	10Cap57	24Sag21	10Aqu10	28Pis59
04/07/1939	16Ari46	09Ari22	08Pis27	09Cap20		01/07/1940	16Cap03	01Cap45	16Aqu21	02Ari22
04/12/1939	21Ari41	06Ari29	14Pis23	11Cap55		01/12/1940	21Cap09	09Cap22	22Aqu31	05Ari46
04/17/1939	26Ari34	05Ari37	20Pis20	14Cap27		01/17/1940	26Cap14	17Cap10	28Aqu41	09Ari10
04/22/1939	01Tau27	06Ari52	26Pis18	16Cap54		01/22/1940	01Aqu19	25Cap12	04Pis49	12Ari35
04/27/1939	06Tau19	09Ari55	02Ari16	19Cap15		01/27/1940	06Aqu25	03Aqu28	10Pis56	16Ari00
05/02/1939	11Tau11	14Ari27	08Ari15	21Cap30		02/01/1940	11Aqu30	12Aqu00	17Pis01	19Ari24
05/07/1939	16Tau01	20Ari10	14Ari15	23Cap38		02/06/1940	16Aqu34	20Aqu49	23Pis05	22Ari48
05/12/1939	20Tau52	26Ari55	20Ari15	25Cap39		02/11/1940	21Aqu37	29Aqu52	29Pis07	26Ari12
05/17/1939	25Tau41	04Tau36	26Ari16	27Cap31		02/16/1940	26Aqu40	08Pis55	05Ari06	29Ari36
05/22/1939	00Gem30	13Tau11	02Tau18	29Cap13		02/21/1940	01Pis43	17Pis29	11Ari03	03Tau00
05/27/1939	05Gem18	22Tau39	08Tau19	00Aqu43		02/26/1940	06Pis46	24Pis39	16Ari58	06Tau22
06/01/1939	10Gem06	02Gem55	14Tau22	02Aqu02		03/02/1940	11Pis47	29Pis12	22Ari50	09Tau45
06/06/1939	14Gem53	13Gem46	20Tau24	03Aqu06		03/07/1940	16Pis47	00Ari07	28Ari38	13Tau07
06/11/1939	19Gem40	24Gem44	26Tau27	03Aqu55		03/12/1940	21Pis47	27Pis33	04Tau22	16Tau28
06/16/1939	24Gem26	05Can17	02Gem31	04Aqu28		03/17/1940	26Pis46	23Pis03	10Tau03	19Tau49
06/21/1939	29Gem12	15Can03	08Gem35	04Aqu42		03/22/1940	01Ari43	18Pis58	15Tau38	23Tau10
06/26/1939	03Can58	23Can55	14Gem39	04Aqu37		03/27/1940	06Ari40	16Pis58	21Tau09	26Tau30
07/01/1939	08Can45	01Leo51	20Gem44	04Aqu14		04/01/1940	11Ari36	17Pis22	26Tau33	29Tau49
07/06/1939	13Can31	08Leo47	26Gem50	03Aqu33		04/06/1940	16Ari32	19Pis49	01Gem49	03Gem07
07/11/1939	18Can17	14Leo40	02Can55	02Aqu36		04/11/1940	21Ari27	23Pis52	06Gem58	06Gem25
07/16/1939	23Can03	19Leo22	09Can03	01Aqu25		04/16/1940	26Ari21	29Pis10	11Gem58	09Gem43
07/21/1939	27Can49	22Leo37	15Can10	00Aqu05		04/21/1940	01Tau13	05Ari28	16Gem47	13Gem00
07/26/1939	02Leo36	24Leo08	21Can18	28Cap43		04/26/1940	06Tau06	12Ari38	21Gem23	16Gem16
07/31/1939	07Leo22	23Leo37	27Can26	27Cap22						
						05/01/1940	10Tau57	20Ari34	25Gem44	19Gem32
08/05/1939	12Leo09	21Leo05	03Leo34	26Cap09		05/06/1940	15Tau48	29Ari18	29Gem46	22Gem48
08/10/1939	16Leo57	17Leo15	09Leo45	25Cap09		05/11/1940	20Tau37	08Tau48	03Can27	26Gem02
08/15/1939	21Leo45	13Leo41	15Leo55	24Cap25		05/16/1940	25Tau27	19Tau02	06Can42	29Gem16
08/20/1939	26Leo34	12Leo08	22Leo06	24Cap00		05/21/1940	00Gem16	29Tau49	09Can25	2Can30
08/25/1939	01Vir23	13Leo36	28Leo17	23Cap56		05/26/1940	05Gem04	10Gem46	11Can31	05Can44
08/30/1939	06Vir13	18Leo13	04Vir28	24Cap12		05/31/1940	09Gem52	21Gem19	12Can51	08Can57
09/04/1939	11Vir03	25Leo23	10Vir40	24Cap49		06/05/1940	14Gem39	01Can03	13Can18	12Can10
09/09/1939	15Vir54	04Vir09	16Vir54	25Cap44		06/10/1940	19Gem26	09Can46	12Can47	15Can22
09/14/1939	20Vir46	13Vir34	23Vir06	26Cap57		06/15/1940	24Gem12	17Can22	11Can16	18Can34
09/19/1939	25Vir39	22Vir59	29Vir19	28Cap26		06/20/1940	28Gem59	23Can49	08Can54	21Can45
09/24/1939	00Lib32	02Lib07	05Lib33	00Aqu10		06/25/1940	03Can45	29Can02	05Can56	24Can57
09/29/1939	05Lib27	10Lib53	11Lib47	02Aqu07		06/30/1940	08Can31	02Leo49	02Can50	28Can08

Ephemeris Tables for Sun, Mercury, Venus and Mars

Date	Sun	Mercury	Venus	Mars
07/05/1940	13Can17	04Leo55	00Can04	01Leo19
07/10/1940	18Can03	05Leo09	28Gem02	04Leo30
07/15/1940	22Can49	03Leo29	26Gem57	07Leo40
07/20/1940	27Can35	00Leo23	26Gem51	10Leo51
07/25/1940	02Leo22	27Can03	27Gem40	14Leo01
07/30/1940	07Leo09	24Can54	29Gem19	17Leo12
08/04/1940	11Leo55	25Can01	01Can39	20Leo22
08/09/1940	16Leo43	27Can52	04Can34	23Leo33
08/14/1940	21Leo31	03Leo22	07Can58	26Leo43
08/19/1940	26Leo20	11Leo05	11Can46	29Leo54
08/24/1940	01Vir09	20Leo16	15Can54	03Vir05
08/29/1940	05Vir58	00Vir04	20Can18	06Vir16
09/03/1940	10Vir49	09Vir52	24Can57	09Vir27
09/08/1940	15Vir40	19Vir18	29Can48	12Vir38
09/13/1940	20Vir32	28Vir18	04Leo49	15Vir50
09/18/1940	25Vir24	06Lib50	09Leo59	19Vir01
09/23/1940	00Lib18	14Lib57	15Leo17	22Vir14
09/28/1940	05Lib12	22Lib39	20Leo42	25Vir27
10/03/1940	10Lib07	00Sco00	26Leo13	28Vir39
10/08/1940	15Lib03	06Sco55	01Vir49	01Lib52
10/13/1940	20Lib00	13Sco23	07Vir31	05Lib06
10/18/1940	24Lib57	19Sco12	13Vir16	08Lib20
10/23/1940	29Lib56	24Sco03	19Vir06	11Lib34
10/28/1940	04Sco55	27Sco18	25Vir00	14Lib49
11/02/1940	09Sco55	27Sco58	00Lib55	18Lib04
11/07/1940	14Sco56	24Sco55	06Lib54	21Lib21
11/12/1940	19Sco58	18Sco44	12Lib56	24Lib37
11/17/1940	25Sco00	13Sco19	19Lib00	27Lib54
11/22/1940	00Sag03	12Sco12	25Lib05	01Sco10
11/27/1940	05Sag07	15Sco09	01Sco12	04Sco28
12/02/1940	10Sag10	20Sco32	07Sco21	07Sco46
12/07/1940	15Sag15	27Sco08	13Sco31	11Sco05
12/12/1940	20Sag20	04Sag18	19Sco42	14Sco24
12/17/1940	25Sag25	11Sag45	25Sco53	17Sco44
12/22/1940	00Cap31	19Sag21	02Sag06	21Sco04
12/27/1940	05Cap37	27Sag03	08Sag19	24Sco25
01/01/1941	10Cap42	04Cap52	13Sag	014Sag33
01/06/1941	15Cap48	12Cap49	20Sag46	01Sag08
01/11/1941	20Cap54	20Cap57	27Sag01	04Sag30
01/16/1941	26Cap00	29Cap16	03Cap15	07Sag52
01/21/1941	01Aqu05	07Aqu46	09Cap30	11Sag16
01/26/1941	06Aqu10	16Aqu25	15Cap45	14Sag39
01/31/1941	11Aqu15	25Aqu00	22Cap00	18Sag03
02/05/1941	16Aqu19	03Pis02	28Cap15	21Sag28
02/10/1941	21Aqu22	09Pis32	4Aqu29	24Sag52
02/15/1941	26Aqu26	13Pis07	10Aqu44	28Sag18
02/20/1941	01Pis29	12Pis40	16Aqu58	01Cap43
02/25/1941	06Pis31	08Pis36	23Aqu13	05Cap09
03/02/1941	11Pis32	03Pis24	29Aqu28	08Cap36
03/07/1941	16Pis33	29Aqu49	05Pis42	12Cap03
03/12/1941	21Pis33	28Aqu55	11Pis56	15Cap30
03/17/1941	26Pis31	00Pis29	18Pis09	18Cap57
03/22/1941	01Ari28	03Pis56	24Pis22	22Cap24
03/27/1941	06Ari26	08Pis46	00Ari34	25Cap51

Date	Sun	Mercury	Venus	Mars
04/01/1941	11Ari22	14Pis37	06Ari47	29Cap18
04/06/1941	16Ari18	21Pis19	12Ari59	02Aqu46
04/11/1941	21Ari12	28Pis45	19Ari11	06Aqu13
04/16/1941	26Ari06	06Ari51	25Ari22	09Aqu40
04/21/1941	00Tau59	15Ari38	01Tau34	13Aqu07
04/26/1941	05Tau51	25Ari06	07Tau44	16Aqu33
05/01/1941	10Tau43	05Tau13	13Tau54	19Aqu59
05/06/1941	15Tau34	15Tau53	20Tau04	23Aqu24
05/11/1941	20Tau24	26Tau44	26Tau14	26Aqu48
05/16/1941	25Tau13	07Gem12	02Gem23	00Pis12
05/21/1941	00Gem01	16Gem48	08Gem32	03Pis34
05/26/1941	04Gem50	25Gem14	14Gem40	06Pis54
05/31/1941	09Gem37	02Can22	20Gem49	10Pis12
06/05/1941	14Gem25	08Can08	26Gem57	13Pis28
06/10/1941	19Gem12	12Can22	03Can04	16Pis41
06/15/1941	23Gem58	14Can57	09Can12	19Pis52
06/20/1941	28Gem45	15Can39	15Can19	22Pis58
06/25/1941	03Can31	14Can32	21Can26	26Pis01
06/30/1941	08Can17	12Can00	27Can32	29Pis00
07/05/1941	13Can03	09Can00	03Leo38	01Ari53
07/10/1941	17Can49	06Can48	09Leo44	04Ari40
07/15/1941	22Can35	06Can22	15Leo49	07Ari21
07/20/1941	27Can22	08Can11	21Leo54	09Ari54
07/25/1941	02Leo08	12Can18	27Leo58	12Ari19
07/30/1941	06Leo55	18Can36	04Vir02	14Ari33
08/04/1941	11Leo42	26Can48	10Vir06	16Ari37
08/09/1941	16Leo30	06Leo19	16Vir08	18Ari28
08/14/1941	21Leo17	16Leo28	22Vir10	20Ari04
08/19/1941	26Leo06	26Leo36	28Vir10	21Ari25
08/24/1941	00Vir55	06Vir21	04Lib11	22Ari30
08/29/1941	05Vir45	15Vir33	10Lib10	23Ari15
09/03/1941	10Vir35	24Vir14	16Lib09	23Ari39
09/08/1941	15Vir26	02Lib25	22Lib06	23Ari42
09/13/1941	20Vir18	10Lib06	28Lib02	23Ari24
09/18/1941	25Vir10	17Lib19	03Sco57	22Ari44
09/23/1941	00Lib04	24Lib01	09Sco50	21Ari45
09/28/1941	04Lib58	00Sco08	15Sco42	20Ari29
10/03/1941	09Lib53	05Sco26	21Sco32	19Ari02
10/08/1941	14Lib49	09Sco34	27Sco20	17Ari28
10/13/1941	19Lib45	11Sco55	03Sag06	15Ari54
10/18/1941	24Lib43	11Sco33	08Sag49	14Ari27
10/23/1941	29Lib42	07Sco43	14Sag31	13Ari11
10/28/1941	04Sco41	01Sco34	20Sag08	12Ari12
11/02/1941	09Sco41	27Lib00	25Sag42	11Ari30
11/07/1941	14Sco42	26Lib52	01Cap10	11Ari09
11/12/1941	19Sco43	00Sco40	06Cap33	11Ari07
11/17/1941	24Sco45	06Sco45	11Cap50	11Ari25
11/22/1941	29Sco48	13Sco54	17Cap00	12Ari02
11/27/1941	04Sag52	21Sco28	21Cap59	12Ari56
12/02/1941	09Sag56	29Sco13	26Cap48	14Ari05
12/07/1941	15Sag00	07Sag00	01Aqu22	15Ari28
12/12/1941	20Sag05	14Sag49	05Aqu41	17Ari04
12/17/1941	25Sag10	22Sag39	09Aqu39	18Ari51
12/22/1941	00Cap16	00Cap33	13Aqu12	20Ari47
12/27/1941	05Cap22	08Cap31	16Aqu15	22Ari52

Ephemeris Tables for Sun, Mercury, Venus and Mars

Date	Sun	Mercury	Venus	Mars	Date	Sun	Mercury	Venus	Mars
01/01/1942	10Cap27	16Cap37	18Aqu40	25Ari04	10/03/1942	09Lib39	24Lib34	28Vir24	10Lib29
01/06/1942	15Cap33	24Cap49	20Aqu21	27Ari23	10/08/1942	14Lib34	20Lib07	4Lib38	13Lib46
01/11/1942	20Cap39	03Aqu04	21Aqu09	29Ari48	10/13/1942	19Lib31	14Lib19	10Lib53	17Lib04
01/16/1942	25Cap45	11Aqu09	20Aqu57	02Tau18	10/18/1942	24Lib28	10Lib48	17Lib08	20Lib22
01/21/1942	00Aqu50	18Aqu35	19Aqu42	04Tau52	10/23/1942	29Lib27	11Lib40	23Lib24	23Lib42
01/26/1942	05Aqu55	24Aqu22	17Aqu30	07Tau30	10/28/1942	04Sco26	16Lib16	29Lib40	27Lib02
01/31/1942	11Aqu00	26Aqu59	14Aqu39	10Tau11					
					11/02/1942	09Sco26	23Lib00	05Sco56	00Sco24
02/05/1942	16Aqu04	25Aqu13	11Aqu34	12Tau55	11/07/1942	14Sco27	00Sco41	12Sco12	03Sco46
02/10/1942	21Aqu08	19Aqu58	08Aqu47	15Tau43	11/12/1942	19Sco28	08Sco40	18Sco29	07Sco09
02/15/1942	26Aqu11	14Aqu37	06Aqu45	18Tau32	11/17/1942	24Sco31	16Sco43	24Sco46	10Sco33
02/20/1942	01Pis15	11Aqu51	05Aqu40	21Tau23	11/22/1942	29Sco34	24Sco42	01Sag03	13Sco58
02/25/1942	06Pis16	12Aqu06	05Aqu37	24Tau16	11/27/1942	04Sag37	02Sag37	07Sag20	17Sco24
03/02/1942	11Pis18	14Aqu42	06Aqu32	27Tau10	12/02/1942	09Sag41	10Sag28	13Sag37	20Sco50
03/07/1942	16Pis18	18Aqu57	8Aqu17	00Gem06	12/07/1942	14Sag46	18Sag19	19Sag54	24Sco18
03/12/1942	21Pis18	24Aqu22	10Aqu45	03Gem03	12/12/1942	19Sag51	26Sag11	26Sag12	27Sco46
03/17/1942	26Pis17	00Pis40	13Aqu48	06Gem01	12/17/1942	24Sag55	04Cap04	02Cap28	01Sag16
03/22/1942	01Ari14	07Pis39	17Aqu19	09Gem00	12/22/1942	00Cap01	11Cap57	08Cap46	04Sag47
03/27/1942	06Ari12	15Pis15	21Aqu13	12Gem00	12/27/1942	05Cap07	19Cap48	15Cap03	08Sag19
04/01/1942	11Ari08	23Pis25	25Aqu28	15Gem00	01/01/1943	10Cap12	27Cap22	21Cap19	11Sag51
04/06/1942	16Ari03	02Ari10	29Aqu58	18Gem01	01/06/1943	15Cap18	04Aqu09	27Cap36	15Sag25
04/11/1942	20Ari58	11Ari33	04Pis41	21Gem03	01/11/1943	20Cap24	09Aqu10	03Aqu52	18Sag59
04/16/1942	25Ari52	21Ari31	09Pis35	24Gem04	01/16/1943	25Cap30	10Aqu48	10Aqu09	22Sag34
04/21/1942	00Tau45	01Tau59	14Pis37	27Gem06	01/21/1943	00Aqu35	07Aqu49	16Aqu25	26Sag10
04/26/1942	05Tau37	12Tau39	19Pis48	0Can09	01/26/1943	05Aqu40	01Aqu47	22Aqu40	29Sag48
					01/31/1943	10Aqu45	26Cap42	28Aqu56	03Cap26
05/01/1942	10Tau29	22Tau58	25Pis05	03Can12					
05/06/1942	15Tau19	02Gem21	00Ari27	06Can15	02/05/1943	15Aqu49	24Cap55	05Pis10	07Cap05
05/11/1942	20Tau09	10Gem22	05Ari53	09Can19	02/10/1943	20Aqu53	26Cap15	11Pis24	10Cap45
05/16/1942	24Tau59	16Gem51	11Ari24	12Can22	02/15/1943	25Aqu57	29Cap45	17Pis37	14Cap25
05/21/1942	29Tau48	21Gem38	16Ari59	15Can27	02/20/1943	01Pis00	04Aqu40	23Pis49	18Cap06
05/26/1942	04Gem36	24Gem36	22Ari36	18Can31	02/25/1943	06Pis02	10Aqu34	00Ari01	21Cap48
05/31/1942	09Gem24	25Gem39	28Ari16	21Can35					
					03/02/1943	11Pis03	17Aqu10	06Ari110	25Cap31
06/05/1942	14Gem11	24Gem48	03Tau59	24Can40	03/07/1943	16Pis04	24Aqu21	12Ari21	29Cap15
06/10/1942	18Gem58	22Gem42	09Tau44	27Can45	03/12/1943	21Pis03	02Pis03	18Ari29	02Aqu58
06/15/1942	23Gem45	19Gem47	15Tau31	00Leo50	03/17/1943	26Pis03	10Pis15	24Ari36	06Aqu43
06/20/1942	28Gem31	17Gem39	21Tau19	03Leo55	03/22/1943	01Ari00	18Pis57	00Tau42	10Aqu28
06/25/1942	03Can17	17Gem03	27Tau10	07Leo01	03/27/1943	05Ari57	28Pis10	06Tau46	14Aqu13
06/30/1942	08Can03	18Gem22	03Gem01	10Leo07					
					04/01/1943	10Ari54	07Ari55	12Tau49	17Aqu59
07/05/1942	12Can49	21Gem42	08Gem55	13Leo13	04/06/1943	15Ari49	18Ari09	18Tau51	21Aqu45
07/10/1942	17Can35	26Gem55	14Gem49	16Leo20	04/11/1943	20Ari44	28Ari33	24Tau50	25Aqu31
07/15/1942	22Can21	3Can55	20Gem45	19Leo27	04/16/1943	25Ari37	08Tau38	00Gem47	29Aqu19
07/20/1942	27Can07	12Can31	26Gem42	22Leo34	04/21/1943	00Tau31	17Tau42	06Gem43	03Pis05
07/25/1942	01Leo54	22Can21	02Can41	25Leo42	04/26/1943	05Tau23	25Tau12	12Gem36	06Pis51
07/30/1942	06Leo41	02Leo46	08Can41	28Leo51					
					05/01/1943	10Tau15	00Gem48	18Gem27	10Pis37
08/04/1942	11Leo28	13Leo12	14Can42	02Vir00	05/06/1943	15Tau06	04Gem20	24Gem15	14Pis23
08/09/1942	16Leo15	23Leo12	20Can45	05Vir09	05/11/1943	19Tau55	05Gem42	00Can00	18Pis09
08/14/1942	21Leo03	02Vir37	26Can48	08Vir18	05/16/1943	24Tau45	05Gem01	05Can42	21Pis54
08/19/1942	25Leo52	11Vir27	02Leo54	11Vir28	05/21/1943	29Tau34	02Gem46	11Can21	25Pis37
08/24/1942	00Vir41	19Vir40	09Leo00	14Vir39	05/26/1943	04Gem22	29Tau57	16Can55	29Pis21
08/29/1942	05Vir30	27Vir19	15Leo06	17Vir51	05/31/1943	09Gem10	27Tau45	22Can26	03Ari03
09/03/1942	10Vir21	04Lib23	21Leo15	21Vir03	06/05/1943	13Gem57	27Tau01	27Can51	06Ari43
09/08/1942	15Vir12	10Lib50	27Leo24	24Vir15	06/10/1943	18Gem44	28Tau07	03Leo10	10Ari24
09/13/1942	20Vir03	16Lib32	03Vir34	27Vir28	06/15/1943	23Gem31	01Gem02	08Leo24	14Ari02
09/18/1942	24Vir52	21Lib16	09Vir45	00Lib42	06/20/1943	28Gem17	05Gem39	13Leo29	17Ari39
09/23/1942	29Vir49	24Lib38	15Vir57	03Lib57	06/25/1943	03Can03	11Gem48	18Leo26	21Ari13
09/28/1942	04Lib43	26Lib00	22Vir10	07Lib13	06/30/1943	07Can49	19Gem23	23Leo13	24Ari46

391

Ephemeris Tables for Sun, Mercury, Venus and Mars

Date	Sun	Mercury	Venus	Mars
07/05/1943	12Can36	28Gem19	27Leo48	28Ari17
07/10/1943	17Can22	08Can21	02Vir09	01Tau45
07/15/1943	22Can07	18Can59	06Vir12	05Tau10
07/20/1943	26Can54	29Can39	09Vir55	08Tau33
07/25/1943	01Leo40	09Leo54	13Vir15	11Tau51
07/30/1943	06Leo27	19Leo30	16Vir04	15Tau07
08/04/1943	11Leo14	28Leo24	18Vir18	18Tau18
08/09/1943	16Leo01	06Vir39	19Vir49	21Tau25
08/14/1943	20Leo49	14Vir13	20Vir30	24Tau28
08/19/1943	25Leo38	21Vir06	20Vir15	27Tau25
08/24/1943	00Vir27	27Vir14	19Vir01	00Gem16
08/29/1943	05Vir16	02Lib28	16Vir52	03Gem01
09/03/1943	10Vir07	06Lib31	14Vir03	05Gem40
09/08/1943	14Vir58	09Lib00	10Vir59	08Gem10
09/13/1943	19Vir49	09Lib18	08Vir08	10Gem32
09/18/1943	24Vir42	06Lib54	05Vir56	12Gem45
09/23/1943	29Vir35	02Lib05	04Vir39	14Gem47
09/28/1943	04Lib29	27Vir00	04Vir22	16Gem37
10/03/1943	09Lib24	24Vir41	05Vir03	18Gem15
10/08/1943	14Lib20	26Vir34	06Vir36	19Gem37
10/13/1943	19Lib16	01Lib55	08Vir54	20Gem44
10/18/1943	24Lib14	09Lib15	11Vir49	21Gem34
10/23/1943	29Lib13	17Lib27	15Vir15	22Gem03
10/28/1943	04Sco12	25Lib51	19Vir07	22Gem13
11/02/1943	09Sco12	4Sco12	23Vir21	22Gem01
11/07/1943	14Sco12	12Sco23	27Vir52	21Gem27
11/12/1943	19Sco14	20Sco26	02Lib39	20Gem31
11/17/1943	24Sco16	28Sco20	07Lib37	19Gem15
11/22/1943	29Sco19	06Sag09	12Lib47	17Gem42
11/27/1943	04Sag22	13Sag53	18Lib06	15Gem55
12/02/1943	09Sag26	21Sag33	23Lib32	14Gem01
12/07/1943	14Sag31	29Sag09	29Lib05	12Gem06
12/12/1943	19Sag36	06Cap34	04Sco43	10Gem16
12/17/1943	24Sag41	13Cap36	10Sco27	08Gem36
12/22/1943	29Sag46	19Cap43	16Sco15	07Gem12
12/27/1943	04Cap52	23Cap55	22Sco06	06Gem07
01/01/1944	09Cap58	24Cap33	28Sco00	05Gem21
01/06/1944	15Cap03	20Cap33	03Sag56	04Gem57
01/11/1944	20Cap09	14Cap04	09Sag55	04Gem52
01/16/1944	25Cap15	09Cap32	15Sag55	05Gem06
01/21/1944	00Aqu20	08Cap48	21Sag58	05Gem38
01/26/1944	05Aqu25	11Cap07	28Sag01	06Gem26
01/31/1944	10Aqu30	15Cap24	4Cap06	07Gem29
02/05/1944	15Aqu34	20Cap54	10Cap12	08Gem45
02/10/1944	20Aqu39	27Cap12	16Cap18	10Gem12
02/15/1944	25Aqu42	04Aqu03	22Cap25	11Gem50
02/20/1944	00Pis44	11Aqu23	28Cap33	13Gem36
02/25/1944	05Pis47	19Aqu07	04Aqu40	15Gem31
03/01/1944	10Pis48	27Aqu17	10Aqu49	17Gem33
03/06/1944	15Pis49	05Pis53	16Aqu57	19Gem41
03/11/1944	20Pis49	14Pis57	23Aqu06	21Gem55
03/16/1944	25Pis48	24Pis28	29Aqu16	24Gem13
03/21/1944	00Ari45	04Ari22	05Pis25	26Gem36
03/26/1944	05Ari44	14Ari28	11Pis34	29Gem03
03/31/1944	10Ari39	24Ari15	17Pis43	01Can34

Date	Sun	Mercury	Venus	Mars
04/05/1944	15Ari35	2Tau54	23Pis52	04Can07
04/10/1944	20Ari30	9Tau45	00Ari00	06Can43
04/15/1944	25Ari24	14Tau18	06Ari09	09Can22
04/20/1944	00Tau16	16Tau18	12Ari18	12Can03
04/25/1944	05Tau09	15Tau52	18Ari26	14Can46
04/30/1944	10Tau00	13Tau31	24Ari35	17Can31
05/05/1944	14Tau51	10Tau24	00Tau43	20Can19
05/10/1944	19Tau42	07Tau50	06Tau52	23Can07
05/15/1944	24Tau31	06Tau47	13Tau00	25Can57
05/20/1944	29Tau20	07Tau37	19Tau08	28Can48
05/25/1944	04Gem08	10Tau15	25Tau16	01Leo41
05/30/1944	08Gem56	14Tau28	01Gem24	04Leo35
06/04/1944	13Gem43	20Tau04	07Gem33	07Leo30
06/09/1944	18Gem30	26Tau57	13Gem40	10Leo26
06/14/1944	23Gem17	05Gem00	19Gem49	13Leo24
06/19/1944	28Gem03	14Gem11	25Gem57	16Leo22
06/24/1944	02Can49	24Gem21	02Can06	19Leo21
06/29/1944	07Can36	05Can07	08Can15	22Leo21
07/04/1944	12Can22	15Can58	14Can24	25Leo22
07/09/1944	17Can07	26Can23	20Can33	28Leo25
07/14/1944	21Can54	06Leo07	26Can42	01Vir28
07/19/1944	26Can40	15Leo06	02Leo51	04Vir32
07/24/1944	01Leo27	23Leo18	09Leo00	07Vir37
07/29/1944	06Leo13	00Vir44	15Leo10	10Vir43
08/03/1944	11Leo00	07Vir21	21Leo19	13Vir50
08/08/1944	15Leo48	13Vir04	27Leo29	16Vir58
08/13/1944	20Leo36	17Vir43	03Vir39	20Vir07
08/18/1944	25Leo24	20Vir59	09Vir49	23Vir18
08/23/1944	00Vir13	22Vir27	15Vir58	26Vir28
08/28/1944	05Vir03	21Vir37	22Vir09	29Vir40
09/02/1944	09Vir52	18Vir22	28Vir18	02Lib54
09/07/1944	14Vir43	13Vir37	04Lib28	06Lib08
09/12/1944	19Vir35	09Vir36	10Lib37	09Lib24
09/17/1944	24Vir28	08Vir38	16Lib46	12Lib40
09/22/1944	29Vir21	11Vir31	22Lib55	15Lib58
09/27/1944	04Lib15	17Vir34	29Lib04	19Lib16
10/02/1944	09Lib10	25Vir29	05Sco13	22Lib37
10/07/1944	14Lib06	04Lib09	11Sco22	25Lib58
10/12/1944	19Lib03	12Lib58	17Sco30	29Lib20
10/17/1944	24Lib00	21Lib37	23Sco37	02Sco43
10/22/1944	28Lib58	00Sco03	29Sco45	06Sco08
10/27/1944	03Sco57	08Sco13	05Sag52	09Sco34
11/01/1944	08Sco57	16Sco10	11Sag58	13Sco01
11/06/1944	13Sco58	23Sco57	18Sag04	16Sco30
11/11/1944	18Sco59	01Sag34	24Sag10	20Sco00
11/16/1944	24Sco01	09Sag03	00Cap14	23Sco31
11/21/1944	29Sco04	16Sag21	06Cap18	27Sco03
11/26/1944	04Sag07	23Sag21	12Cap21	00Sag36
12/01/1944	09Sag12	29Sag49	18Cap23	04Sag11
12/06/1944	14Sag16	05Cap15	24Cap23	07Sag47
12/11/1944	19Sag21	08Cap34	00Aqu22	11Sag24
12/16/1944	24Sag26	08Cap13	06Aqu19	15Sag03
12/21/1944	29Sag31	03Cap21	12Aqu13	18Sag42
12/26/1944	04Cap37	26Sag46	18Aqu06	22Sag22
12/31/1944	09Cap43	22Sag59	23Aqu54	26Sag04

Ephemeris Tables for Sun, Mercury, Venus and Mars

Date	Sun	Mercury	Venus	Mars
01/05/1945	14Cap49	23Sag17	29Aqu40	29Sag47
01/10/1945	19Cap54	26Sag31	05Pis21	03Cap31
01/15/1945	25Cap00	01Cap30	10Pis57	07Cap16
01/20/1945	00Aqu06	07Cap30	16Pis27	11Cap02
01/25/1945	05Aqu11	14Cap08	21Pis51	14Cap49
01/30/1945	10Aqu15	21Cap13	27Pis06	18Cap37
02/04/1945	15Aqu19	28Cap39	02Ari11	22Cap25
02/09/1945	20Aqu24	06Aqu25	07Ari06	26Cap15
02/14/1945	25Aqu27	14Aqu32	11Ari48	00Aqu05
02/19/1945	00Pis30	23Aqu00	16Ari13	03Aqu56
02/24/1945	05Pis33	01Pis52	20Ari20	07Aqu47
03/01/1945	10Pis34	11Pis07	24Ari03	11Aqu39
03/06/1945	15Pis34	20Pis43	27Ari19	15Aqu31
03/11/1945	20Pis34	00Ari27	00Tau01	19Aqu24
03/16/1945	25Pis33	09Ari48	02Tau03	23Aqu18
03/21/1945	00Ari31	18Ari00	03Tau16	27Aqu10
03/26/1945	05Ari28	24Ari05	03Tau34	01Pis04
03/31/1945	10Ari25	27Ari24	02Tau51	04Pis58
04/05/1945	15Ari21	27Ari42	01Tau07	08Pis51
04/10/1945	20Ari15	25Ari28	28Ari32	12Pis44
04/15/1945	25Ari09	21Ari53	25Ari28	16Pis37
04/20/1945	00Tau03	18Ari39	22Ari24	20Pis30
04/25/1945	04Tau55	16Ari58	19Ari48	24Pis21
04/30/1945	09Tau46	17Ari19	18Ari02	28Pis13
05/05/1945	14Tau37	19Ari34	17Ari15	02Ari03
05/10/1945	19Tau27	23Ari26	17Ari27	05Ari53
05/15/1945	24Tau17	28Ari39	18Ari34	09Ari42
05/20/1945	29Tau06	05Tau01	20Ari28	13Ari30
05/25/1945	03Gem54	12Tau25	23Ari01	17Ari18
05/30/1945	08Gem42	20Tau48	26Ari07	21Ari04
06/04/1945	13Gem30	00Gem09	29Ari40	24Ari48
06/09/1945	18Gem16	10Gem22	03Tau34	28Ari32
06/14/1945	23Gem03	21Gem12	07Tau47	02Tau14
06/19/1945	27Gem49	02Can09	12Tau15	05Tau54
06/24/1945	02Can36	12Can42	16Tau55	09Tau33
06/29/1945	07Can22	22Can30	21Tau46	13Tau10
07/04/1945	12Can08	01Leo28	26Tau46	16Tau46
07/09/1945	16Can54	09Leo34	01Gem53	20Tau19
07/14/1945	21Can40	16Leo46	07Gem07	23Tau51
07/19/1945	26Can26	23Leo01	12Gem27	27Tau19
07/24/1945	01Leo13	28Leo11	17Gem52	00Gem47
07/29/1945	05Leo59	02Vir04	23Gem22	04Gem12
08/03/1945	10Leo46	04Vir21	28Gem56	07Gem34
08/08/1945	15Leo34	04Vir40	04Can34	10Gem53
08/13/1945	20Leo22	07Vir46	10Can15	14Gem10
08/18/1945	25Leo10	29Leo03	15Can59	17Gem24
08/23/1945	29Leo59	24Leo51	21Can46	20Gem35
08/28/1945	04Vir48	22Leo13	27Can37	23Gem42
09/02/1945	09Vir39	22Leo40	03Leo29	26Gem46
09/07/1945	14Vir30	26Leo32	09Leo24	29Gem46
09/12/1945	19Vir21	03Vir13	15Leo22	02Can43
09/17/1945	24Vir13	11Vir39	21Leo21	05Can34
09/22/1945	29Vir07	20Vir48	27Leo23	08Can22
09/27/1945	04Lib01	00Lib00	03Vir27	11Can04

Date	Sun	Mercury	Venus	Mars
10/02/1945	08Lib55	08Lib58	09Vir31	13Can40
10/07/1945	13Lib51	17Lib37	15Vir38	16Can11
10/12/1945	18Lib48	25Lib57	21Vir46	18Can35
10/17/1945	23Lib45	03Sco58	27Vir57	20Can51
10/22/1945	28Lib43	11Sco44	04Lib07	23Can00
10/27/1945	03Sco43	19Sco15	10Lib19	24Can59
11/01/1945	08Sco42	26Sco31	16Lib32	26Can49
11/06/1945	13Sco43	03Sag31	22Lib46	28Can27
11/11/1945	18Sco45	10Sag06	29Lib01	29Can54
11/16/1945	23Sco46	16Sag00	05Sco16	01Leo06
11/21/1945	28Sco49	20Sag39	11Sco31	02Leo04
11/26/1945	03Sag53	23Sag04	17Sco48	02Leo45
12/01/1945	08Sag57	21Sag43	24Sco04	03Leo08
12/06/1945	14Sag01	16Sag13	00Sag21	03Leo12
12/11/1945	19Sag06	09Sag49	06Sag38	02Leo55
12/16/1945	24Sag11	06Sag54	12Sag55	02Leo18
12/21/1945	29Sag16	08Sag11	19Sag13	01Leo19
12/26/1945	04Cap22	12Sag15	25Sag30	00Leo01
12/31/1945	09Cap28	17Sag52	01Cap48	28Can26
01/05/1946	14Cap34	24Sag21	08Cap05	26Can37
01/10/1946	19Cap40	01Cap18	14Cap22	24Can40
01/15/1946	24Cap45	08Cap35	20Cap40	22Can40
01/20/1946	29Cap51	16Cap07	26Cap57	20Can43
01/25/1946	04Aqu56	23Cap54	03Aqu14	18Can55
01/30/1946	10Aqu01	01Aqu57	09Aqu31	17Can21
02/04/1946	15Aqu05	10Aqu17	15Aqu48	16Can03
02/09/1946	20Aqu09	18Aqu56	22Aqu04	15Can04
02/14/1946	25Aqu12	27Aqu54	28Aqu21	14Can26
02/19/1946	00Pis16	07Pis09	04Pis36	14Can08
02/24/1946	05Pis18	16Pis28	10Pis52	14Can08
03/01/1946	10Pis19	25Pis22	17Pis06	14Can27
03/06/1946	15Pis20	03Ari00	23Pis21	15Can02
03/11/1946	20Pis19	08Ari15	29Pis34	15Can52
03/16/1946	25Pis19	10Ari13	05Pis48	16Can55
03/21/1946	00Ari16	08Ari48	12Ari00	18Can12
03/26/1946	05Ari14	05Ari00	18Ari12	19Can39
03/31/1946	10Ari10	00Ari52	24Ari24	21Can15
04/05/1946	15Ari06	28Pis12	00Tau34	23Can00
04/10/1946	20Ari01	27Pis43	06Tau45	24Can54
04/15/1946	24Ari55	29Pis23	12Tau54	26Can54
04/20/1946	29Ari48	02Ari48	19Tau03	29Can00
04/25/1946	04Tau41	07Ari37	25Tau10	01Leo12
04/30/1946	09Tau33	13Ari33	01Gem18	03Leo28
05/05/1946	14Tau23	20Ari26	07Gem23	05Leo49
05/10/1946	19Tau13	28Ari11	13Gem28	08Leo15
05/15/1946	24Tau03	06Tau47	19Gem33	10Leo44
05/20/1946	28Tau52	16Tau13	25Gem36	13Leo16
05/25/1946	03Gem40	26Tau27	01Can38	15Leo52
05/30/1946	08Gem28	07Gem15	07Can39	18Leo31
06/04/1946	13Gem16	18Gem13	13Can40	21Leo12
06/09/1946	18Gem03	28Gem49	19Can39	23Leo57
06/14/1946	22Gem49	08Can39	25Can36	26Leo43
06/19/1946	27Gem36	17Can31	01Leo33	29Leo31
06/24/1946	02Can22	25Can23	07Leo27	02Vir22
06/29/1946	07Can08	02Leo13	13Leo20	05Vir15

Ephemeris Tables for Sun, Mercury, Venus and Mars

Date0	Sun	Mercury	Venus	Mars
07/04/1946	11Can54	07Leo55	19Leo12	08Vir09
07/09/1946	16Can40	12Leo21	25Leo01	11Vir06
07/14/1946	21Can26	15Leo15	00Vir48	14Vir04
07/19/1946	26Can12	16Leo21	06Vir33	17Vir04
07/24/1946	00Leo58	15Leo27	12Vir15	20Vir06
07/29/1946	05Leo45	12Leo43	17Vir55	23Vir09
08/03/1946	10Leo33	09Leo00	23Vir31	26Vir14
08/08/1946	15Leo20	05Leo55	29Vir04	29Vir21
08/13/1946	20Leo07	04Leo54	04Lib32	02Lib29
08/18/1946	24Leo56	06Leo47	09Lib55	05Lib39
08/23/1946	29Leo45	11Leo36	15Lib14	08Lib51
08/28/1946	04Vir34	18Leo53	20Lib26	12Lib03
09/02/1946	09Vir25	27Leo46	25Lib31	15Lib18
09/07/1946	14Vir15	07Vir20	00Sco28	18Lib34
09/12/1946	19Vir07	16Vir55	05Sco16	21Lib52
09/17/1946	24Vir00	26Vir13	09Sco51	25Lib11
09/22/1946	28Vir52	05Lib06	14Sco13	28Lib32
09/27/1946	03Lib46	13Lib34	18Sco18	01Sco54
10/02/1946	08Lib41	21Lib40	22Sco03	05Sco18
10/07/1946	13Lib37	29Lib25	25Sco22	08Sco43
10/12/1946	18Lib33	06Sco50	28Sco12	12Sco10
10/17/1946	23Lib31	13Sco55	00Sag24	15Sco39
10/22/1946	28Lib29	20Sco35	01Sag52	19Sco09
10/27/1946	03Sco28	26Sco43	02Sag29	22Sco41
11/01/1946	08Sco28	02Sag01	02Sag07	26Sco15
11/06/1946	13Sco28	05Sag53	00Sag43	29Sco49
11/11/1946	18Sco30	07Sag19	28Sco29	03Sag25
11/16/1946	23Sco32	05Sag02	25Sco36	07Sag03
11/21/1946	28Sco35	29Sco06	22Sco36	10Sag42
11/26/1946	03Sag38	23Sco09	19Sco58	14Sag22
12/01/1946	08Sag42	21Sco10	18Sco05	18Sag04
12/06/1946	13Sag46	23Sco23	17Sco11	21Sag47
12/11/1946	18Sag51	28Sco15	17Sco19	25Sag31
12/16/1946	23Sag57	04Sag28	18Sco24	29Sag18
12/21/1946	29Sag02	11Sag22	20Sco19	03Cap04
12/26/1946	04Cap07	18Sag37	22Sco56	06Cap52
12/31/1946	09Cap13	26Sag06	26Sco09	10Cap42
01/05/1947	14Cap19	03Cap44	29Sco51	14Cap31
01/10/1947	19Cap25	11Cap32	03Sag55	18Cap23
01/15/1947	24Cap30	19Cap31	08Sag20	22Cap15
01/20/1947	29Cap36	27Cap43	13Sag00	26Cap07
01/25/1947	04Aqu41	06Aqu08	17Sag53	00Aqu01
01/30/1947	09Aqu46	14Aqu48	22Sag57	03Aqu55
02/04/1947	14Aqu50	23Aqu40	28Sag10	07Aqu50
02/09/1947	19Aqu54	02Pis33	03Cap30	11Aqu45
02/14/1947	24Aqu58	10Pis57	08Cap57	15Aqu41
02/19/1947	00Pis01	17Pis58	14Cap28	19Aqu37
02/24/1947	05Pis03	22Pis19	20Cap05	23Aqu33
03/01/1947	10Pis04	22Pis54	25Cap45	27Aqu30
03/06/1947	15Pis06	19Pis51	01Aqu29	01Pis27
03/11/1947	20Pis05	14Pis59	07Aqu15	05Pis23
03/16/1947	25Pis04	10Pis57	13Aqu04	09Pis19
03/21/1947	00Ari02	09Pis14	18Aqu54	13Pis15
03/26/1947	05Ari00	10Pis01	24Aqu47	17Pis10
03/31/1947	09Ari56	12Pis48	00Pis42	21Pis05

Date	Sun	Mercury	Venus	Mars
04/05/1947	14Ari52	17Pis07	06Pis37	25Pis00
04/10/1947	19Ari47	22Pis37	12Pis33	28Pis54
04/15/1947	24Ari41	29Pis04	18Pis31	02Ari46
04/20/1947	29Ari34	06Ari18	24Pis29	06Ari38
04/25/1947	04Tau27	14Ari17	00Ari27	10Ari30
04/30/1947	09Tau18	23Ari00	06Ari27	14Ari20
05/05/1947	14Tau09	02Tau26	12Ari27	18Ari10
05/10/1947	19Tau00	12Tau36	18Ari27	21Ari58
05/15/1947	23Tau49	23Tau19	24Ari29	25Ari45
05/20/1947	28Tau38	04Gem13	00Tau30	29Ari31
05/25/1947	03Gem27	14Gem48	06Tau32	03Tau16
05/30/1947	08Gem14	24Gem33	12Tau34	07Tau00
06/04/1947	13Gem01	03Can13	18Tau37	10Tau42
06/09/1947	17Gem49	10Can43	24Tau40	14Tau22
06/14/1947	22Gem36	17Can00	00Gem44	18Tau02
06/19/1947	27Gem22	21Can55	06Gem48	21Tau40
06/24/1947	02Can08	25Can19	12Gem53	25Tau16
06/29/1947	06Can54	26Can59	18Gem58	28Tau51
07/04/1947	11Can40	26Can45	25Gem03	02Gem24
07/09/1947	16Can26	24Can45	01Can09	05Gem55
07/14/1947	21Can12	21Can39	07Can16	09Gem24
07/19/1947	25Can58	18Can40	13Can23	12Gem52
07/24/1947	00Leo45	17Can06	19Can31	16Gem19
07/29/1947	05Leo31	17Can48	25Can39	19Gem43
08/03/1947	10Leo18	21Can03	01Leo48	23Gem06
08/08/1947	15Leo06	26Can45	07Leo57	26Gem26
08/13/1947	19Leo54	04Leo33	14Leo07	29Gem45
08/18/1947	24Leo42	13Leo50	20Leo18	03Can01
08/23/1947	29Leo31	23Leo46	26Leo29	06Can16
08/28/1947	04Vir21	03Vir43	02Vir41	09Can29
09/02/1947	09Vir10	13Vir19	08Vir53	12Can39
09/07/1947	14Vir01	22Vir27	15Vir05	15Can47
09/12/1947	18Vir53	01Lib04	21Vir18	18Can53
09/17/1947	23Vir45	09Lib14	27Vir31	21Can56
09/22/1947	28Vir38	16Lib58	03Lib45	24Can57
09/27/1947	03Lib32	24Lib17	09Lib58	27Can54
10/02/1947	08Lib27	01Sco09	16Lib12	00Leo49
10/07/1947	13Lib23	07Sco30	22Lib26	03Leo40
10/12/1947	18Lib19	13Sco10	28Lib40	06Leo28
10/17/1947	23Lib16	17Sco48	04Sco54	09Leo12
10/22/1947	28Lib15	20Sco48	11Sco09	11Leo53
10/27/1947	03Sco13	21Sco13	17Sco23	14Leo29
11/01/1947	08Sco13	18Sco03	23Sco37	17Leo00
11/06/1947	13Sco14	11Sco57	29Sco52	19Leo27
11/11/1947	18Sco15	06Sco40	06Sag06	21Leo47
11/16/1947	23Sco18	05Sco40	12Sag20	24Leo01
11/21/1947	28Sco20	08Sco47	18Sag34	26Leo09
11/26/1947	03Sag24	14Sco22	24Sag48	28Leo09
12/01/1947	08Sag27	21Sco09	01Cap02	00Vir00
12/06/1947	13Sag31	28Sco28	07Cap15	01Vir42
12/11/1947	18Sag36	06Sag03	13Cap29	03Vir14
12/16/1947	23Sag42	13Sag42	19Cap42	04Vir34
12/21/1947	28Sag47	21Sag27	25Cap55	05Vir41
12/26/1947	03Cap52	29Sag16	02Aqu07	06Vir34
12/31/1947	08Cap58	07Cap12	08Aqu19	07Vir12

Ephemeris Tables for Sun, Mercury, Venus and Mars

Date	Sun	Mercury	Venus	Mars	Date	Sun	Mercury	Venus	Mars
01/05/1948	14Cap04	15Cap15	14Aqu30	07Vir33	10/01/1948	08Lib13	03Sco12	24Leo22	18Sco54
01/10/1948	19Cap10	23Cap27	20Aqu40	07Vir34	10/06/1948	13Lib08	05Sco16	29Leo59	22Sco24
01/15/1948	24Cap15	01Aqu49	26Aqu49	07Vir17	10/11/1948	18Lib05	04Sco39	05Vir40	25Sco55
01/20/1948	29Cap21	10Aqu18	02Pis58	06Vir40	10/16/1948	23Lib02	00Sco43	11Vir26	29Sco28
01/25/1948	04Aqu26	18Aqu41	09Pis05	05Vir43	10/21/1948	28Lib00	24Lib42	17Vir15	03Sag04
01/30/1948	09Aqu31	26Aqu31	15Pis10	04Vir27	10/26/1948	02Sco59	20Lib20	23Vir09	06Sag40
					10/31/1948	07Sco59	20Lib21	29Vir04	10Sag19
02/04/1948	14Aqu36	02Pis52	21Pis14	02Vir53					
02/09/1948	19Aqu40	06Pis17	27Pis16	01Vir07	11/05/1948	13Sco00	24Lib18	05Lib03	13Sag59
02/14/1948	24Aqu43	05Pis31	03Ari15	29Leo11	11/10/1948	18Sco01	00Sco34	11Lib04	17Sag41
02/19/1948	29Aqu46	01Pis04	09Ari13	27Leo12	11/15/1948	23Sco03	07Sco54	17Lib08	21Sag25
02/24/1948	04Pis49	25Aqu42	15Ari07	25Leo15	11/20/1948	28Sco06	15Sco39	23Lib14	25Sag10
02/29/1948	09Pis50	22Aqu15	20Ari59	23Leo24	11/25/1948	03Sag09	23Sco30	29Lib21	28Sag56
					11/30/1948	08Sag13	01Sag22	05Sco30	02Cap43
03/05/1948	14Pis51	21Aqu40	26Ari47	21Leo46					
03/10/1948	19Pis51	23Aqu33	02Tau32	20Leo24	12/05/1948	13Sag17	09Sag13	11Sco39	06Cap33
03/15/1948	24Pis50	27Aqu16	08Tau12	19Leo21	12/10/1948	18Sag22	17Sag04	17Sco50	10Cap22
03/20/1948	29Pis48	02Pis19	13Tau48	18Leo36	12/15/1948	23Sag27	24Sag57	24Sco02	14Cap14
03/25/1948	04Ari45	08Pis19	19Tau18	18Leo12	12/20/1948	28Sag32	02Cap52	00Sag15	18Cap06
03/30/1948	09Ari42	15Pis06	24Tau42	18Leo06	12/25/1948	03Cap38	10Cap52	06Sag28	22Cap00
					12/30/1948	08Cap43	18Cap56	12Sag41	25Cap54
04/04/1948	14Ari37	22Pis34	29Tau58	18Leo19					
04/09/1948	19Ari33	00Ari40	05Gem07	18Leo48	01/04/1949	13Cap49	27Cap01	18Sag55	29Cap49
04/14/1948	24Ari27	09Ari25	10Gem06	19Leo33	01/09/1949	18Cap55	04Aqu54	25Sag10	03Aqu44
04/19/1948	29Ari20	18Ari48	14Gem55	20Leo32	01/14/1949	24Cap01	12Aqu08	01Cap25	07Aqu40
04/24/1948	04Tau12	28Ari50	19Gem30	21Leo44	01/19/1949	29Cap06	17Aqu45	07Cap39	11Aqu37
04/29/1948	09Tau04	09Tau24	23Gem50	23Leo07	01/24/1949	04Aqu11	20Aqu12	13Cap54	15Aqu34
					01/29/1949	09Aqu16	18Aqu10	20Cap09	19Aqu31
05/04/1948	13Tau55	20Tau10	27Gem52	24Leo42					
05/09/1948	18Tau45	00Gem38	01Can31	26Leo24	02/03/1949	14Aqu21	12Aqu39	26Cap24	23Aqu28
05/14/1948	23Tau35	10Gem13	04Can45	28Leo16	02/08/1949	19Aqu25	07Aqu15	02Aqu39	27Aqu25
05/19/1948	28Tau24	18Gem34	07Can26	00Vir15	02/13/1949	24Aqu28	04Aqu41	08Aqu54	01Pis24
05/24/1948	03Gem12	25Gem33	09Can28	02Vir21	02/18/1949	29Aqu31	05Aqu13	15Aqu09	05Pis21
05/29/1948	08Gem00	01Can01	10Can46	04Vir33	02/23/1949	04Pis34	08Aqu07	21Aqu24	09Pis18
					02/28/1949	09Pis36	12Aqu35	27Aqu38	13Pis14
06/03/1948	12Gem48	04Can52	11Can09	06Vir51					
06/08/1948	17Gem35	06Can56	10Can34	09Vir15	03/05/1949	14Pis36	18Aqu10	03Pis52	17Pis10
06/13/1948	22Gem22	07Can07	09Can00	11Vir42	03/10/1949	19Pis36	24Aqu33	10Pis07	21Pis06
06/18/1948	27Gem08	05Can33	06Can35	14Vir15	03/15/1949	24Pis36	01Pis36	16Pis20	25Pis00
06/23/1948	01Can54	02Can52	03Can36	16Vir51	03/20/1949	29Pis34	09Pis12	22Pis34	28Pis55
06/28/1948	06Can40	00Can07	00Can29	19Vir31	03/25/1949	04Ari31	17Pis21	28Pis46	02Ari48
					03/30/1949	09Ari27	26Pis04	04Ari59	06Ari40
07/03/1948	11Can27	28Gem28	27Gem46	22Vir14					
07/08/1948	16Can12	28Gem39	25Gem48	25Vir01	04/04/1949	14Ari24	05Ari20	11Ari11	10Ari31
07/13/1948	20Can58	01Can00	24Gem47	27Vir51	04/09/1949	19Ari18	15Ari11	17Ari23	14Ari22
07/18/1948	25Can45	05Can29	24Gem44	00Lib45	04/14/1949	24Ari12	25Ari31	23Ari34	18Ari12
07/23/1948	00Leo31	11Can58	25Gem37	03Lib40	04/19/1949	29Ari06	06Tau06	29Ari46	22Ari00
07/28/1948	05Leo18	20Can15	27Gem18	06Lib39	04/24/1949	03Tau58	16Tau22	05Tau57	25Ari47
					04/29/1949	08Tau50	25Tau42	12Tau07	29Ari33
08/02/1948	10Leo04	29Can51	29Gem41	09Lib40					
08/07/1948	14Leo52	10Leo07	02Can37	12Lib44	05/04/1949	13Tau41	03Gem37	18Tau17	03Tau18
08/12/1948	19Leo40	20Leo23	06Can03	15Lib50	05/09/1949	18Tau31	09Gem51	24Tau27	07Tau01
08/17/1948	24Leo28	00Vir16	09Can52	18Lib59	05/14/1949	23Tau21	14Gem16	00Gem36	10Tau43
08/22/1948	29Leo17	09Vir37	14Can01	22Lib10	05/19/1949	28Tau10	16Gem42	06Gem45	14Tau25
08/27/1948	04Vir06	18Vir24	18Can26	25Lib23	05/24/1949	02Gem58	17Gem09	12Gem54	18Tau04
					05/29/1949	07Gem46	15Gem46	19Gem02	21Tau42
09/01/1948	08Vir57	26Vir37	23Can06	28Lib38					
09/06/1948	13Vir47	04Lib20	27Can57	01Sco56	06/03/1949	12Gem34	13Gem13	25Gem10	25Tau19
09/11/1948	18Vir39	11Lib31	02Leo58	05Sco15	06/08/1949	17Gem21	10Gem34	01Can18	28Tau55
09/16/1948	23Vir31	18Lib10	08Leo08	08Sco37	06/13/1949	22Gem08	08Gem54	07Can25	02Gem28
09/21/1948	28Vir24	24Lib09	13Leo27	12Sco01	06/18/1949	26Gem54	08Gem54	13Can32	06Gem01
09/26/1948	03Lib18	29Lib17	18Leo51	15Sco27	06/23/1949	01Can40	10Gem50	19Can39	09Gem33
					06/28/1949	06Can27	14Gem37	25Can45	13Gem03

Ephemeris Tables for Sun, Mercury, Venus and Mars

Date	Sun	Mercury	Venus	Mars	Date	Sun	Mercury	Venus	Mars
07/03/1949	11Can12	20Gem09	01Leo51	16Gem31	04/04/1950	14Ari09	22Ari01	28Aqu01	27Vir23
07/08/1949	15Can59	27Gem19	07Leo57	19Gem58	04/09/1950	19Ari04	02Tau01	02Pis45	25Vir45
07/13/1949	20Can45	06Can00	14Leo02	23Gem24	04/14/1950	23Ari58	11Tau00	07Pis40	24Vir22
07/18/1949	25Can31	15Can51	20Leo07	26Gem48	04/19/1950	28Ari52	18Tau22	12Pis44	23Vir18
07/23/1949	00Leo17	26Can21	26Leo11	00Can11	04/24/1950	03Tau44	23Tau40	17Pis55	22Vir32
07/28/1949	05Leo04	06Leo54	02Vir15	03Can33	04/29/1950	08Tau36	26Tau44	23Pis13	22Vir06
08/02/1949	09Leo51	17Leo03	08Vir18	06Can52	05/04/1950	13Tau27	27Tau29	28Pis36	22Vir00
08/07/1949	14Leo38	26Leo36	14Vir20	10Can11	05/09/1950	18Tau18	26Tau10	04Ari03	22Vir12
08/12/1949	19Leo26	05Vir30	20Vir22	13Can28	05/14/1950	23Tau07	23Tau31	09Ari34	22Vir42
08/17/1949	24Leo14	13Vir46	26Vir22	16Can45	05/19/1950	27Tau56	20Tau41	15Ari09	23Vir28
08/22/1949	29Leo03	21Vir26	02Lib22	19Can59	05/24/1950	02Gem45	18Tau50	20Ari47	24Vir29
08/27/1949	03Vir52	28Vir28	08Lib22	23Can12	05/29/1950	07Gem33	18Tau39	26Ari28	25Vir43
09/01/1949	08Vir42	04Lib50	14Lib19	26Can24	06/03/1950	12Gem20	20Tau19	02Tau11	27Vir10
09/06/1949	13Vir33	10Lib24	20Lib16	29Can34	06/08/1950	17Gem07	23Tau44	07Tau56	28Vir48
09/11/1949	18Vir25	14Lib57	26Lib12	02Leo42	06/13/1950	21Gem54	28Tau42	13Tau43	00Lib36
09/16/1949	23Vir17	18Lib03	02Sco06	05Leo49	06/18/1950	26Gem40	05Gem06	19Tau32	02Lib33
09/21/1949	28Vir10	19Lib07	08Sco00	08Leo55	06/23/1950	01Can27	12Gem49	25Tau22	04Lib39
09/26/1949	03Lib04	17Lib27	13Sco51	11Leo58	06/28/1950	06Can13	21Gem48	01Gem14	06Lib52
10/01/1949	07Lib58	12Lib57	19Sco40	15Leo01	07/03/1950	10Can58	01Can50	07Gem07	09Lib12
10/06/1949	12Lib54	07Lib22	25Sco28	18Leo01	07/08/1950	15Can45	12Can31	13Gem02	11Lib38
10/11/1949	17Lib50	04Lib06	01Sag14	21Leo00	07/13/1950	20Can31	23Can17	18Gem58	14Lib10
10/16/1949	22Lib48	05Lib08	06Sag57	23Leo55	07/18/1950	25Can17	03Leo39	24Gem56	16Lib48
10/21/1949	27Lib46	09Lib52	12Sag37	26Leo50	07/23/1950	00Leo03	13Leo21	00Can54	19Lib31
10/26/1949	02Sco45	16Lib47	18Sag13	29Leo42	07/28/1950	04Leo50	22Leo21	06Can54	22Lib18
10/31/1949	07Sco44	24Lib39	23Sag46	02Vir31					
					08/02/1950	09Leo37	00Vir37	12Can55	25Lib09
11/05/1949	12Sco45	02Sco49	29Sag14	05Vir18	08/07/1950	14Leo24	08Vir11	18Can58	28Lib05
11/10/1949	17Sco46	10Sco59	04Cap37	08Vir02	08/12/1950	19Leo12	15Vir01	25Can01	01Sco05
11/15/1949	22Sco48	19Sco04	09Cap52	10Vir43	08/17/1950	24Leo00	21Vir03	01Leo06	04Sco09
11/20/1949	27Sco51	27Sco02	15Cap01	13Vir21	08/22/1950	28Leo49	26Vir06	07Leo12	07Sco15
11/25/1949	02Sag54	04Sag55	20Cap00	15Vir55	08/27/1950	03Vir39	29Vir56	13Leo19	10Sco25
11/30/1949	07Sag58	12Sag45	24Cap46	18Vir25					
					09/01/1950	08Vir28	02Lib07	19Leo27	13Sco39
12/05/1949	13Sag02	20Sag33	29Cap20	20Vir51	09/06/1950	13Vir19	02Lib06	25Leo36	16Sco55
12/10/1949	18Sag07	28Sag21	03Aqu37	23Vir12	09/11/1950	18Vir10	29Vir28	01Vir46	20Sco14
12/15/1949	23Sag12	06Cap07	07Aqu33	25Vir28	09/16/1950	23Vir03	24Vir42	07Vir57	23Sco36
12/20/1949	28Sag17	13Cap48	11Aqu03	27Vir39	09/21/1950	27Vir55	19Vir56	14Vir09	27Sco01
12/25/1949	03Cap23	21Cap10	14Aqu03	29Vir42	09/26/1950	02Lib49	17Vir57	20Vir22	00Sag28
12/30/1949	08Cap28	27Cap45	16Aqu25	01Lib39					
					10/01/1950	07Lib44	20Vir00	26Vir35	03Sag58
01/04/1950	13Cap34	02Aqu35	18Aqu01	03Lib28	10/06/1950	12Lib40	25Vir29	02Lib49	07Sag30
01/09/1950	18Cap40	04Aqu03	18Aqu43	05Lib07	10/11/1950	17Lib36	03Lib00	09Lib04	11Sag04
01/14/1950	23Cap46	00Aqu54	18Aqu26	06Lib37	10/16/1950	22Lib33	11Lib22	15Lib19	14Sag40
01/19/1950	28Cap52	24Cap41	17Aqu06	07Lib56	10/21/1950	27Lib31	19Lib57	21Lib34	18Sag19
01/24/1950	03Aqu57	19Cap37	14Aqu51	09Lib03	10/26/1950	02Sco30	28Lib25	27Lib50	21Sag59
01/29/1950	09Aqu01	18Cap03	11Aqu56	09Lib56	10/31/1950	07Sco30	06Sco43	04Sco06	25Sag42
02/03/1950	14Aqu06	19Cap39	08Aqu52	10Lib34	11/05/1950	12Sco30	14Sco50	10Sco23	29Sag25
02/08/1950	19Aqu10	23Cap24	06Aqu09	10Lib57	11/10/1950	17Sco31	22Sco46	16Sco39	03Cap11
02/13/1950	24Aqu13	28Cap31	04Aqu11	11Lib01	11/15/1950	22Sco33	00Sag34	22Sco56	06Cap58
02/18/1950	29Aqu17	04Aqu32	03Aqu1	10Lib46	11/20/1950	27Sco36	08Sag16	29Sco13	10Cap46
02/23/1950	04Pis19	11Aqu13	03Aqu15	10Lib13	11/25/1950	02Sag39	15Sag52	05Sag30	14Cap36
02/28/1950	09Pis21	18Aqu26	04Aqu15	09Lib20	11/30/1950	07Sag43	23Sag20	11Sag47	18Cap27
03/05/1950	14Pis22	26Aqu07	06Aqu04	08Lib08	12/05/1950	12Sag47	00Cap36	18Sag04	22Cap19
03/10/1950	19Pis22	04Pis17	08Aqu36	06Lib39	12/10/1950	17Sag52	07Cap27	24Sag21	26Cap12
03/15/1950	24Pis21	12Pis54	11Aqu42	04Lib57	12/15/1950	22Sag57	13Cap21	00Cap39	00Aqu06
03/20/1950	29Pis19	22Pis03	15Aqu16	03Lib04	12/20/1950	28Sag03	17Cap21	06Cap55	04Aqu01
03/25/1950	04Ari16	01Ari40	19Aqu13	01Lib08	12/25/1950	03Cap08	17Cap50	13Cap12	07Aqu56
03/30/1950	09Ari13	11Ari44	23Aqu29	29Vir12	12/30/1950	08Cap14	13Cap42	19Cap29	11Aqu51

Ephemeris Tables for Sun, Mercury, Venus and Mars

Date	Sun	Mercury	Venus	Mars
01/04/1951	13Cap19	07Cap08	25Cap46	15Aqu48
01/09/1951	18Cap25	02Cap40	02Aqu03	19Aqu43
01/14/1951	23Cap31	02Cap09	08Aqu18	23Aqu40
01/19/1951	28Cap36	04Cap43	14Aqu34	27Aqu36
01/24/1951	03Aqu42	09Cap13	20Aqu50	01Pis33
01/29/1951	08Aqu46	14Cap53	27Aqu05	05Pis29
02/03/1951	13Aqu51	21Cap17	03Pis20	09Pis25
02/08/1951	18Aqu55	28Cap13	09Pis34	13Pis20
02/13/1951	23Aqu59	05Aqu34	15Pis48	17Pis15
02/18/1951	29Aqu03	13Aqu18	22Pis00	21Pis09
02/23/1951	04Pis04	21Aqu25	28Pis12	25Pis02
02/28/1951	09Pis06	29Aqu57	04Ari21	28Pis55
03/05/1951	14Pis07	08Pis53	10Ari31	02Ari46
03/10/1951	19Pis07	18Pis16	16Ari40	06Ari37
03/15/1951	24Pis06	28Pis03	22Ari47	10Ari27
03/20/1951	29Pis05	07Ari59	28Ari53	14Ari16
03/25/1951	04Ari02	17Ari37	04Tau57	18Ari03
03/30/1951	08Ari59	26Ari12	11Tau00	21Ari50
04/04/1951	13Ari55	02Tau52	17Tau01	25Ari36
04/09/1951	18Ari49	07Tau04	23Tau01	29Ari19
04/14/1951	23Ari44	08Tau33	28Tau59	03Tau03
04/19/1951	28Ari37	07Tau28	04Gem54	06Tau45
04/24/1951	03Tau30	04Tau36	10Gem48	10Tau25
04/29/1951	08Tau22	01Tau18	16Gem39	14Tau04
05/04/1951	13Tau13	28Ari58	22Gem27	17Tau42
05/09/1951	18Tau03	28Ari22	28Gem12	21Tau19
05/14/1951	22Tau53	29Ari43	03Can54	24Tau54
05/19/1951	27Tau42	02Tau49	09Can33	28Tau28
05/24/1951	02Gem31	07Tau25	15Can07	02Gem01
05/29/1951	07Gem18	13Tau18	20Can37	05Gem33
06/03/1951	12Gem06	20Tau21	26Can02	09Gem03
06/08/1951	16Gem53	28Tau29	01Leo21	12Gem33
06/13/1951	21Gem40	07Gem41	06Leo34	16Gem00
06/18/1951	26Gem27	17Gem50	11Leo39	19Gem27
06/23/1951	01Can13	28Gem37	16Leo35	22Gem52
06/28/1951	05Can59	09Can31	21Leo21	26Gem17
07/03/1951	10Can45	20Can03	25Leo55	29Gem40
07/08/1951	15Can31	29Can52	00Vir15	03Can03
07/13/1951	20Can17	08Leo54	04Vir17	06Can24
07/18/1951	25Can03	17Leo07	07Vir58	09Can43
07/23/1951	29Can49	24Leo31	11Vir16	13Can03
07/28/1951	04Leo36	01Vir04	14Vir03	16Can21
08/02/1951	09Leo23	06Vir38	16Vir14	19Can38
08/07/1951	14Leo10	11Vir03	17Vir42	22Can54
08/12/1951	18Leo58	14Vir02	18Vir18	26Can09
08/17/1951	23Leo46	15Vir09	17Vir59	29Can23
08/22/1951	28Leo35	14Vir01	16Vir40	02Leo36
08/27/1951	03Vir24	10Vir37	14Vir27	05Leo49
09/01/1951	08Vir15	06Vir03	11Vir36	09Leo00
09/06/1951	13Vir05	02Vir26	08Vir32	12Leo11
09/11/1951	17Vir57	01Vir51	05Vir43	15Leo21
09/16/1951	22Vir49	04Vir56	03Vir34	18Leo29
09/21/1951	27Vir42	11Vir06	02Vir21	21Leo37
09/26/1951	02Lib35	19Vir10	02Vir08	24Leo44

Date	Sun	Mercury	Venus	Mars
10/01/1951	07Lib30	28Vir01	02Vir54	27Leo50
10/06/1951	12Lib25	07Lib00	04Vir30	00Vir55
10/11/1951	17Lib22	15Lib49	06Vir49	03Vir59
10/16/1951	22Lib19	24Lib21	09Vir47	07Vir02
10/21/1951	27Lib17	02Sco36	13Vir15	10Vir04
10/26/1951	02Sco16	10Sco36	17Vir08	13Vir05
10/31/1951	07Sco15	18Sco23	21Vir22	16Vir04
11/05/1951	12Sco16	25Sco58	25Vir55	19Vir03
11/10/1951	17Sco17	03Sag22	00Lib42	22Vir00
11/15/1951	22Sco19	10Sag33	05Lib41	24Vir55
11/20/1951	27Sco21	17Sag24	10Lib51	27Vir50
11/25/1951	02Sag24	23Sag42	16Lib10	00Lib43
11/30/1951	07Sag28	28Sag53	21Lib37	03Lib33
12/05/1951	12Sag33	02Cap00	27Lib10	06Lib22
12/10/1951	17Sag37	01Cap30	02Sco49	09Lib09
12/15/1951	22Sag42	26Sag35	08Sco33	11Lib54
12/20/1951	27Sag48	19Sag58	14Sco21	14Lib36
12/25/1951	02Cap53	16Sag16	20Sco12	17Lib16
12/30/1951	07Cap59	16Sag46	26Sco06	19Lib52
01/04/1952	13Cap05	20Sag14	02Sag03	22Lib26
01/09/1952	18Cap10	25Sag25	08Sag02	24Lib56
01/14/1952	23Cap16	01Cap34	14Sag03	27Lib22
01/19/1952	28Cap22	08Cap19	20Sag05	29Lib43
01/24/1952	03Aqu27	15Cap27	26Sag09	02Sco00
01/29/1952	08Aqu32	22Cap55	02Cap14	04Sco12
02/03/1952	13Aqu36	00Aqu41	08Cap20	06Sco18
02/08/1952	18Aqu40	08Aqu45	14Cap27	08Sco16
02/13/1952	23Aqu44	17Aqu09	20Cap34	10Sco08
02/18/1952	28Aqu48	25Aqu53	26Cap42	11Sco51
02/23/1952	03Pis50	05Pis00	02Aqu50	13Sco25
02/28/1952	08Pis52	14Pis26	08Aqu58	14Sco48
03/04/1952	13Pis52	24Pis00	15Aqu07	16Sco00
03/09/1952	18Pis52	03Ari13	21Aqu16	17Sco00
03/14/1952	23Pis52	11Ari17	27Aqu25	17Sco45
03/19/1952	28Pis51	17Ari11	03Pis35	18Sco14
03/24/1952	03Ari48	20Ari08	09Pis45	18Sco26
03/29/1952	08Ari45	19Ari54	15Pis54	18Sco21
04/03/1952	13Ari40	17Ari04	22Pis03	17Sco55
04/08/1952	18Ari36	13Ari10	28Pis12	17Sco12
04/13/1952	23Ari30	10Ari00	04Ari21	16Sco09
04/18/1952	28Ari24	08Ari42	10Ari30	14Sco49
04/23/1952	03Tau16	09Ari30	16Ari39	13Sco15
04/28/1952	08Tau07	12Ari10	22Ari47	11Sco31
05/03/1952	12Tau59	16Ari23	28Ari56	09Sco40
05/08/1952	17Tau49	21Ari52	05Tau04	07Sco51
05/13/1952	22Tau39	28Ari25	11Tau13	06Sco06
05/18/1952	27Tau28	05Tau55	17Tau21	04Sco33
05/23/1952	02Gem17	14Tau21	23Tau30	03Sco13
05/28/1952	07Gem05	23Tau42	29Tau37	02Sco12
06/02/1952	11Gem52	03Gem52	05Gem46	01Sco31
06/07/1952	16Gem39	14Gem41	11Gem54	01Sco10
06/12/1952	21Gem26	25Gem40	18Gem03	01Sco10
06/17/1952	26Gem13	06Can16	24Gem11	01Sco29
06/22/1952	00Can59	16Can09	00Can19	02Sco07
06/27/1952	05Can45	25Can09	06Can28	03Sco01

Ephemeris Tables for Sun, Mercury, Venus and Mars

Date	Sun	Mercury	Venus	Mars
07/02/1952	10Can31	03Leo13	12Can37	04Sco12
07/07/1952	15Can17	10Leo21	18Can46	05Sco38
07/12/1952	20Can03	16Leo27	24Can55	07Sco16
07/17/1952	24Can49	21Leo24	01Leo04	09Sco07
07/22/1952	29Can36	25Leo00	07Leo13	11Sco09
07/27/1952	04Leo22	26Leo55	13Leo22	13Sco20
08/01/1952	09Leo09	26Leo52	19Leo32	15Sco40
08/06/1952	13Leo57	24Leo41	25Leo42	18Sco09
08/11/1952	18Leo44	20Leo57	01Vir51	20Sco45
08/16/1952	23Leo32	17Leo06	08Vir01	23Sco28
08/21/1952	28Leo21	14Leo58	14Vir11	26Sco18
08/26/1952	03Vir10	15Leo49	20Vir21	29Sco13
08/31/1952	08Vir00	19Leo55	26Vir30	02Sag13
09/05/1952	12Vir51	26Leo43	02Lib39	05Sag19
09/10/1952	17Vir42	05Vir17	08Lib49	08Sag28
09/15/1952	22Vir34	14Vir36	14Lib58	11Sag43
09/20/1952	27Vir27	23Vir59	21Lib07	15Sag01
09/25/1952	02Lib21	03Lib06	27Lib16	18Sag22
09/30/1952	07Lib16	11Lib52	03Sco24	21Sag48
10/05/1952	12Lib11	20Lib17	09Sco32	25Sag16
10/10/1952	17Lib07	28Lib21	15Sco40	28Sag47
10/15/1952	22Lib04	06Sco08	21Sco48	02Cap21
10/20/1952	27Lib03	13Sco37	27Sco55	05Cap57
10/25/1952	02Sco01	20Sco50	04Sag01	09Cap35
10/30/1952	07Sco01	27Sco43	10Sag07	13Cap16
11/04/1952	12Sco01	04Sag09	16Sag13	16Cap58
11/09/1952	17Sco02	09Sag51	22Sag19	20Cap42
11/14/1952	22Sco04	14Sag17	28Sag23	24Cap27
11/19/1952	27Sco07	16Sag28	04Cap27	28Cap14
11/24/1952	02Sag10	15Sag00	10Cap29	02Aqu01
11/29/1952	07Sag13	09Sag28	16Cap30	05Aqu51
12/04/1952	12Sag18	03Sag06	22Cap31	09Aqu40
12/09/1952	17Sag22	00Sag18	28Cap29	13Aqu30
12/14/1952	22Sag27	01Sag46	04Aqu26	17Aqu21
12/19/1952	27Sag33	06Sag03	10Aqu20	21Aqu14
12/24/1952	02Cap39	11Sag51	16Aqu12	25Aqu04
12/29/1952	07Cap44	18Sag28	22Aqu00	28Aqu55
01/03/1953	12Cap50	25Sag32	27Aqu46	02Pis47
01/08/1953	17Cap55	02Cap53	03Pis27	06Pis38
01/13/1953	23Cap01	10Cap27	09Pis03	10Pis29
01/18/1953	28Cap07	18Cap15	14Pis32	14Pis19
01/23/1953	03Aqu12	26Cap15	19Pis55	18Pis10
01/28/1953	08Aqu17	04Aqu30	25Pis10	21Pis59
02/02/1953	13Aqu22	13Aqu02	00Ari15	25Pis48
02/07/1953	18Aqu26	21Aqu51	05Ari09	29Pis36
02/12/1953	23Aqu30	00Pis56	09Ari50	03Ari22
02/17/1953	28Aqu33	10Pis04	14Ari15	07Ari09
02/22/1953	03Pis36	18Pis49	18Ari20	10Ari54
02/27/1953	08Pis37	26Pis19	22Ari02	14Ari39
03/04/1953	13Pis38	01Ari22	25Ari16	18Ari22
03/09/1953	18Pis38	02Ari59	27Ari56	22Ari04
03/14/1953	23Pis37	01Ari02	29Ari55	25Ari46
03/19/1953	28Pis36	26Pis48	01Tau04	29Ari25
03/24/1953	03Ari33	22Pis34	01Tau18	03Tau04
03/29/1953	08Ari30	20Pis07	00Tau31	06Tau42

Date	Sun	Mercury	Venus	Mars
04/03/1953	13Ari26	20Pis02	28Ari43	10Tau19
04/08/1953	18Ari21	22Pis06	26Ari06	13Tau54
04/13/1953	23Ari15	25Pis50	23Ari01	17Tau28
04/18/1953	28Ari09	00Ari53	19Ari57	21Tau02
04/23/1953	03Tau02	07Ari00	17Ari25	24Tau34
04/28/1953	07Tau54	14Ari00	15Ari42	28Tau04
05/03/1953	12Tau45	21Ari49	15Ari00	01Gem34
05/08/1953	17Tau35	00Tau25	15Ari16	05Gem03
05/13/1953	22Tau25	90Tau49	16Ari27	08Gem30
05/18/1953	27Tau14	19Tau59	18Ari25	11Gem57
05/23/1953	02Gem03	00Gem45	21Ari01	15Gem22
05/28/1953	06Gem51	11Gem42	24Ari09	18Gem46
06/02/1953	11Gem39	22Gem20	27Ari44	22Gem10
06/07/1953	16Gem25	02Can12	01Tau40	25Gem32
06/12/1953	21Gem12	11Can04	05Tau54	28Gem54
06/17/1953	25Gem59	18Can52	10Tau22	02Can14
06/22/1953	00Can45	25Can33	15Tau04	05Can34
06/27/1953	05Can31	01Leo01	19Tau55	08Can52
07/02/1953	10Can17	05Leo09	24Tau55	12Can11
07/07/1953	15Can03	07Leo40	00Gem04	15Can28
07/12/1953	19Can49	08Leo21	05Gem18	18Can45
07/17/1953	24Can36	07Leo04	10Gem39	22Can01
07/22/1953	29Can22	04Leo09	16Gem04	25Can16
07/27/1953	04Leo09	00Leo40	21Gem34	28Can30
08/01/1953	08Leo55	28Can05	27Gem08	01Leo45
08/06/1953	13Leo42	27Can38	02Can46	04Leo58
08/11/1953	18Leo30	29Can56	08Can27	08Leo11
08/16/1953	23Leo18	04Leo58	14Can12	11Leo24
08/21/1953	28Leo07	12Leo22	19Can59	14Leo35
08/26/1953	02Vir57	21Leo21	25Can49	17Leo47
08/31/1953	07Vir46	01Vir04	01Leo41	20Leo58
09/05/1953	12Vir37	10Vir50	07Leo36	24Leo09
09/10/1953	17Vir28	20Vir16	13Leo34	27Leo19
09/15/1953	22Vir20	29Vir18	19Leo33	00Vir28
09/20/1953	27Vir13	07Lib51	25Leo34	03Vir38
09/25/1953	02Lib07	16Lib01	01Vir37	06Vir47
09/30/1953	07Lib01	23Lib46	07Vir43	09Vir56
10/05/1953	11Lib57	01Sco10	13Vir49	13Vir04
10/10/1953	16Lib53	08Sco11	19Vir57	16Vir13
10/15/1953	21Lib50	14Sco45	26Vir07	19Vir21
10/20/1953	26Lib48	20Sco44	02Lib18	22Vir28
10/25/1953	01Sco46	25Sco49	08Lib30	25Vir35
10/30/1953	06Sco46	29Sco27	14Lib42	28Vir42
11/04/1953	11Sco46	00Sag39	20Lib56	01Lib48
11/09/1953	16Sco48	28Sco15	27Lib10	04Lib54
11/14/1953	21Sco49	22Sco20	03Sco25	08Lib00
11/19/1953	26Sco52	16Sco28	09Sco41	11Lib05
11/24/1953	01Sag55	14Sco37	15Sco57	14Lib10
11/29/1953	06Sag59	17Sco00	22Sco14	17Lib14
12/04/1953	12Sag03	22Sco03	28Sco31	20Lib18
12/09/1953	17Sag08	28Sco28	04Sag48	23Lib21
12/14/1953	22Sag13	05Sag31	11Sag05	26Lib23
12/19/1953	27Sag18	12Sag53	17Sag22	29Lib25
12/24/1953	02Cap24	20Sag26	23Sag40	02Sco25
12/29/1953	07Cap29	28Sag07	29Sag57	05Sco25

Ephemeris Tables for Sun, Mercury, Venus and Mars

Date	Sun	Mercury	Venus	Mars
01/03/1954	12Cap35	5Cap55	06Cap15	08Sco25
01/08/1954	17Cap41	13Cap51	12Cap32	11Sco22
01/13/1954	22Cap46	21Cap58	18Cap49	14Sco19
01/18/1954	27Cap52	00Aqu18	25Cap07	17Sco15
01/23/1954	02Aqu57	08Aqu50	01Aqu24	20Sco09
01/28/1954	08Aqu02	17Aqu31	07Aqu41	23Sco02
02/02/1954	13Aqu07	26Aqu12	13Aqu58	25Sco53
02/07/1954	18Aqu11	04Pis26	20Aqu14	28Sco42
02/12/1954	23Aqu15	11Pis18	26Aqu30	01Sag30
02/17/1954	28Aqu18	15Pis28	02Pis46	04Sag15
02/22/1954	03Pis21	15Pis44	09Pis02	06Sag57
02/27/1954	08Pis22	12Pis13	15Pis17	09Sag36
03/04/1954	13Pis23	07Pis05	21Pis31	12Sag13
03/09/1954	18Pis24	03Pis06	27Pis46	14Sag45
03/14/1954	23Pis23	01Pis42	03Ari59	17Sag15
03/19/1954	28Pis21	02Pis50	10Ari12	19Sag39
03/24/1954	03Ari19	05Pis56	16Ari24	21Sag59
03/29/1954	08Ari16	10Pis30	22Ari36	24Sag13
04/03/1954	13Ari12	16Pis10	28Ari46	26Sag22
04/08/1954	18Ari07	22Pis44	04Tau57	28Sag23
04/13/1954	23Ari01	00Ari02	11Tau06	00Cap17
04/18/1954	27Ari55	08Ari02	17Tau15	02Cap02
04/23/1954	02Tau48	16Ari43	23Tau22	03Cap37
04/28/1954	07Tau39	26Ari06	29Tau30	05Cap01
05/03/1954	12Tau31	06Tau10	05Gem36	06Cap13
05/08/1954	17Tau21	16Tau49	11Gem41	07Cap11
05/13/1954	22Tau11	27Tau41	17Gem45	07Cap54
05/18/1954	27Tau00	08Gem15	23Gem49	08Cap21
05/23/1954	01Gem49	18Gem00	29Gem51	08Cap30
05/28/1954	06Gem37	26Gem38	05Can52	08Cap20
06/02/1954	11Gem24	04Can01	11Can52	07Cap51
06/07/1954	16Gem12	10Can04	17Can51	07Cap04
06/12/1954	20Gem58	14Can40	23Can49	06Cap01
06/17/1954	25Gem45	17Can39	29Can45	04Cap43
06/22/1954	00Can31	18Can49	05Leo40	03Cap16
06/27/1954	05Can18	18Can07	11Leo33	01Cap43
07/02/1954	10Can03	15Can49	17Leo24	00Cap11
07/07/1954	14Can49	12Can47	23Leo13	28Sag46
07/12/1954	19Can36	10Can14	29Leo00	27Sag31
07/17/1954	24Can22	09Can17	04Vir45	26Sag33
07/22/1954	29Can08	10Can33	10Vir27	25Sag54
07/27/1954	03Leo55	14Can12	16Vir06	25Sag34
08/01/1954	08Leo41	20Can06	21Vir41	25Sag36
08/06/1954	13Leo28	28Can01	27Vir13	25Sag58
08/11/1954	18Leo16	07Leo22	02Lib41	26Sag42
08/16/1954	23Leo04	17Leo27	08Lib04	27Sag43
08/21/1954	27Leo53	27Leo33	13Lib22	29Sag01
08/26/1954	02Vir42	07Vir18	18Lib34	00Cap36
08/31/1954	07Vir32	16Vir33	23Lib38	02Cap25
09/05/1954	12Vir23	25Vir16	28Lib34	04Cap27
09/10/1954	17Vir14	03Lib30	03Sco19	06Cap40
09/15/1954	22Vir06	11Lib15	07Sco54	09Cap04
09/20/1954	26Vir59	18Lib33	12Sco13	11Cap37
09/25/1954	01Lib52	25Lib21	16Sco16	14Cap18
09/30/1954	06Lib47	01Sco36	19Sco58	17Cap07

Date	Sun	Mercury	Venus	Mars
10/05/1954	11Lib42	07Sco05	23Sco15	20Cap02
10/10/1954	16Lib39	11Sco31	26Sco01	23Cap03
10/15/1954	21Lib36	14Sco16	28Sco09	26Cap09
10/20/1954	26Lib33	14Sco27	29Sco33	29Cap19
10/25/1954	01Sco32	11Sco09	00Sag03	02Aqu34
10/30/1954	06Sco31	05Sco07	29Sco35	05Aqu52
11/04/1954	11Sco32	00Sco00	28Sco07	09Aqu13
11/09/1954	16Sco33	29Lib08	25Sco47	12Aqu37
11/14/1954	21Sco34	02Sco24	22Sco53	16Aqu04
11/19/1954	26Sco37	08Sco10	19Sco54	19Aqu32
11/24/1954	01Sag40	15Sco09	17Sco19	23Aqu02
11/29/1954	06Sag44	22Sco38	15Sco31	26Aqu33
12/04/1954	11Sag48	00Sag19	14Sco42	00Pis07
12/09/1954	16Sag53	08Sag04	14Sco55	03Pis40
12/14/1954	21Sag58	15Sag51	16Sco06	07Pis15
12/19/1954	27Sag03	23Sag41	18Sco04	10Pis49
12/24/1954	02Cap09	01Cap34	20Sco45	14Pis25
12/29/1954	07Cap14	09Cap34	24Sco01	18Pis00
01/03/1955	12Cap20	17Cap41	27Sco45	21Pis36
01/08/1955	17Cap26	25Cap55	01Sag52	25Pis11
01/13/1955	22Cap31	04Aqu13	06Sag18	28Pis46
01/18/1955	27Cap37	12Aqu25	10Sag59	02Ari21
01/23/1955	02Aqu42	20Aqu03	15Sag54	05Ari56
01/28/1955	07Aqu48	26Aqu14	20Sag58	09Ari30
02/02/1955	12Aqu52	29Aqu29	26Sag12	13Ari04
02/07/1955	17Aqu56	28Aqu27	01Cap23	16Ari37
02/12/1955	23Aqu00	23Aqu39	07Cap01	20Ari10
02/17/1955	28Aqu03	18Aqu07	12Cap34	23Ari42
02/22/1955	03Pis06	14Aqu51	18Cap11	27Ari13
02/27/1955	08Pis07	14Aqu34	23Cap52	00Tau44
03/04/1955	13Pis09	16Aqu47	29Cap36	04Tau14
03/09/1955	18Pis09	20Aqu45	05Aqu22	07Tau43
03/14/1955	23Pis09	25Aqu57	11Aqu12	11Tau11
03/19/1955	28Pis07	02Pis06	17Aqu03	14Tau39
03/24/1955	03Ari04	08Pis58	22Aqu56	18Tau05
03/29/1955	08Ari01	16Pis28	28Aqu51	21Tau30
04/03/1955	12Ari57	24Pis33	04Pis46	24Tau55
04/08/1955	17Ari52	03Ari15	10Pis43	28Tau19
04/13/1955	22Ari47	12Ari33	16Pis41	01Gem42
04/18/1955	27Ari40	22Ari28	22Pis40	05Gem05
04/23/1955	02Tau33	02Tau55	28Pis39	08Gem27
04/28/1955	07Tau25	13Tau37	04Ari38	11Gem47
05/03/1955	12Tau16	24Tau03	10Ari39	15Gem07
05/08/1955	17Tau07	03Gem36	16Ari40	18Gem27
05/13/1955	21Tau57	11Gem53	22Ari41	21Gem45
05/18/1955	26Tau46	18Gem40	28Ari43	25Gem03
05/23/1955	01Gem35	23Gem49	04Tau45	28Gem20
05/28/1955	06Gem23	27Gem13	10Tau48	01Can37
06/02/1955	11Gem10	28Gem45	16Tau51	04Can52
06/07/1955	15Gem58	28Gem22	22Tau54	08Can08
06/12/1955	20Gem45	26Gem24	28Tau57	11Can23
06/17/1955	25Gem31	23Gem09	05Gem01	14Can37
06/22/1955	00Can18	21Gem13	11Gem06	17Can51
06/27/1955	05Can04	20Gem09	17Gem11	21Can04

Ephemeris Tables for Sun, Mercury, Venus and Mars

Date	Sun	Mercury	Venus	Mars		Date	Sun	Mercury	Venus	Mars
07/02/1955	09Can50	20Gem58	23Gem16	24Can18		04/02/1956	12Ari43	08Ari54	28Tau07	21Cap58
07/07/1955	14Can36	23Gem50	29Gem22	27Can30		04/07/1956	17Ari38	19Ari06	03Gem15	25Cap12
07/12/1955	19Can22	28Gem40	05Can29	00Leo43		04/12/1956	22Ari33	29Ari33	08Gem15	28Cap25
07/17/1955	24Can08	05Can21	11Can36	03Leo55		04/17/1956	27Ari27	09Tau45	13Gem02	01Aqu37
07/22/1955	28Can54	13Can43	17Can44	07Leo07		04/22/1956	02Tau19	19Tau02	17Gem37	04Aqu48
07/27/1955	03Leo40	23Can22	23Can52	10Leo18		04/27/1956	07Tau11	26Tau49	21Gem56	07Aqu57
08/01/1955	08Leo28	03Leo43	00Leo01	13Leo30		05/02/1956	12Tau03	02Gem49	25Gem57	11Aqu05
08/06/1955	13Leo15	14Leo08	06Leo10	16Leo41		05/07/1956	16Tau53	06Gem49	29Gem36	14Aqu10
08/11/1955	18Leo03	24Leo10	12Leo20	19Leo52		05/12/1956	21Tau43	08Gem42	02Can47	17Aqu14
08/16/1955	22Leo51	03Vir38	18Leo31	23Leo03		05/17/1956	26Tau32	08Gem31	05Can26	20Aqu15
08/21/1955	27Leo39	12Vir30	24Leo42	26Leo14		05/22/1956	01Gem21	06Gem37	07Can26	23Aqu13
08/26/1955	02Vir28	20Vir47	00Vir53	29Leo25		05/27/1956	06Gem09	03Gem52	08Can40	26Aqu09
08/31/1955	07Vir18	28Vir31	07Vir05	02Vir36						
						06/01/1956	10Gem57	01Gem25	09Can00	29Aqu00
09/05/1955	12Vir09	05Lib41	13Vir17	05Vir46		06/06/1956	15Gem44	00Gem15	08Can21	01Pis46
09/10/1955	17Vir00	12Lib15	19Vir30	08Vir58		06/11/1956	20Gem31	00Gem52	06Can44	04Pis28
09/15/1955	21Vir52	18Lib07	25Vir43	12Vir09		06/16/1956	25Gem18	03Gem21	04Can16	07Pis03
09/20/1955	26Vir45	23Lib04	01Lib57	15Vir20		06/21/1956	00Can03	07Gem34	01Can15	09Pis32
09/25/1955	01Lib39	26Lib45	08Lib10	18Vir31		06/26/1956	04Can49	13Gem24	28Gem10	11Pis53
09/30/1955	06Lib33	28Lib34	14Lib24	21Vir43						
						07/01/1956	09Can36	20Gem44	25Gem30	14Pis05
10/05/1955	11Lib28	27Lib41	20Lib37	24Vir54		07/06/1956	14Can22	29Gem27	23Gem34	16Pis07
10/10/1955	16Lib24	23Lib39	26Lib51	28Vir06		07/11/1956	19Can08	09Can21	22Gem37	17Pis58
10/15/1955	21Lib21	17Lib48	03Sco05	01Lib18		07/16/1956	23Can54	19Can55	22Gem38	19Pis36
10/20/1955	26Lib19	13Lib39	09Sco19	04Lib30		07/21/1956	28Can40	00Leo34	23Gem33	21Pis00
10/25/1955	01Sco18	13Lib48	15Sco33	07Lib43		07/26/1956	03Leo27	10Leo51	25Gem18	22Pis08
10/30/1955	06Sco17	17Lib54	21Sco48	10Lib55		07/31/1956	08Leo13	20Leo30	27Gem43	22Pis58
11/04/1955	11Sco18	24Lib21	28Sco02	14Lib09		08/05/1956	13Leo01	29Leo30	00Can42	23Pis29
11/09/1955	16Sco18	01Sco52	04Sag16	17Lib22		08/10/1956	17Leo48	07Vir49	04Can08	23Pis40
11/14/1955	21Sco20	09Sco48	10Sag30	20Lib35		08/15/1956	22Leo36	15Vir29	07Can58	23Pis31
11/19/1955	26Sco22	17Sco47	16Sag44	23Lib49		08/20/1956	27Leo25	22Vir29	12Can08	23Pis02
11/24/1955	01Sag25	25Sco44	22Sag58	27Lib03		08/25/1956	02Vir14	28Vir46	16Can34	22Pis14
11/29/1955	06Sag30	03Sag39	29Sag12	00Sco18		08/30/1956	07Vir04	04Lib12	21Can14	21Pis10
12/04/1955	11Sag33	11Sag31	05Cap25	93Sco32		09/04/1956	11Vir55	08Lib31	26Can06	19Pis55
12/09/1955	16Sag38	19Sag22	11Cap38	96Sco46		09/09/1956	16Vir46	11Lib22	01Leo07	18Pis33
12/14/1955	21Sag43	27Sag14	17Cap51	10Sco02		09/14/1956	21Vir38	12Lib08	06Leo18	17Pis10
12/19/1955	26Sag48	05Cap09	24Cap04	13Sco17		09/19/1956	26Vir31	10Lib13	11Leo36	15Pis54
12/24/1955	01Cap54	13Cap05	00Aqu16	16Sco33		09/24/1956	01Lib24	05Lib41	17Leo01	14Pis48
12/29/1955	07Cap00	21Cap00	06Aqu27	19Sco48		09/29/1956	06Lib19	00Lib21	22Leo33	13Pis57
01/03/1956	12Cap05	28Cap41	12Aqu39	23Sco04		10/04/1956	11Lib13	27Vir22	28Leo09	13Pis24
01/08/1956	17Cap11	05Aqu43	18Aqu49	26Sco21		10/09/1956	16Lib10	28Vir34	03Vir50	13Pis10
01/13/1956	22Cap17	11Aqu09	24Aqu58	29Sco37		10/14/1956	21Lib07	03Lib27	09Vir36	13Pis16
01/18/1956	27Cap22	13Aqu26	01Pis07	02Sag54		10/19/1956	26Lib04	10Lib32	15Vir25	13Pis42
01/23/1956	02Aqu28	11Aqu12	07Pis13	06Sag10		10/24/1956	01Sco03	18Lib36	21Vir18	14Pis26
01/28/1956	07Aqu33	05Aqu27	13Pis19	09Sag27		10/29/1956	06Sco03	26Lib55	27Vir14	15Pis28
02/02/1956	12Aqu37	00Aqu00	19Pis23	12Sag43		11/03/1956	11Sco03	05Sco14	03Lib12	16Pis45
02/07/1956	17Aqu42	27Cap38	25Pis25	16Sag00		11/08/1956	16Sco04	13Sco25	09Lib14	18Pis15
02/12/1956	22Aqu45	28Cap28	01Ari24	19Sag18		11/13/1956	21Sco06	21Sco27	15Lib17	19Pis59
02/17/1956	27Aqu49	01Aqu37	07Ari22	22Sag34		11/18/1956	26Sco08	29Sco22	21Lib22	21Pis54
02/22/1956	02Pis51	06Aqu18	13Ari16	25Sag51		11/23/1956	01Sag11	07Sag11	27Lib30	23Pis58
02/27/1956	07Pis53	12Aqu01	19Ari08	29Sag08		11/28/1956	06Sag15	14Sag57	03Sco38	26Pis12
03/03/1956	12Pis54	18Aqu30	24Ari57	02Cap25		12/03/1956	11Sag19	22Sag39	09Sco48	28Pis33
03/08/1956	17Pis54	25Aqu36	00Tau41	05Cap42		12/08/1956	16Sag23	00Cap18	15Sco59	01Ari00
03/13/1956	22Pis54	03Pis13	06Tau21	08Cap58		12/13/1956	21Sag28	07Cap49	22Sco10	03Ari33
03/18/1956	27Pis52	11Pis21	11Tau57	12Cap13		12/18/1956	26Sag34	15Cap00	28Sco23	06Ari12
03/23/1956	02Ari50	19Pis59	17Tau27	15Cap29		12/23/1956	01Cap39	21Cap22	04Sag36	08Ari55
03/28/1956	07Ari47	29Pis10	22Tau51	18Cap44		12/28/1956	06Cap45	26Cap01	10Sag50	11Ari42

Ephemeris Tables for Sun, Mercury, Venus and Mars

Date	Sun	Mercury	Venus	Mars	Date	Sun	Mercury	Venus	Mars
01/02/1957	11Cap51	27Cap20	17Sag04	14Ari31	10/04/1957	10Lib59	26Vir42	23Sco37	06Lib42
01/07/1957	16Cap56	24Cap01	23Sag19	17Ari25	10/09/1957	15Lib55	05Lib15	29Sco22	09Lib57
01/12/1957	22Cap02	17Cap40	29Sag34	20Ari21	10/14/1957	20Lib52	14Lib00	05Sag04	13Lib13
01/17/1957	27Cap07	12Cap37	05Cap49	23Ari18	10/19/1957	25Lib50	22Lib39	10Sag43	16Lib30
01/22/1957	02Aqu13	11Cap17	12Cap04	26Ari18	10/24/1957	00Sco49	01Sco03	16Sag19	19Lib48
01/27/1957	07Aqu18	13Cap09	18Cap19	29Ari19	10/29/1957	05Sco48	09Sco14	21Sag51	23Lib06
02/01/1957	12Aqu22	17Cap07	24Cap34	02Tau22	11/03/1957	10Sco48	17Sco13	27Sag19	26Lib25
02/06/1957	17Aqu27	22Cap24	00Aqu49	05Tau26	11/08/1957	15Sco49	25Sco00	02Cap40	29Lib45
02/11/1957	22Aqu30	28Cap33	07Aqu04	08Tau31	11/13/1957	20Sco51	02Sag40	07Cap55	03Sco06
02/16/1957	27Aqu33	05Aqu19	13Aqu19	11Tau37	11/18/1957	25Sco53	10Sag12	13Cap02	06Sco27
02/21/1957	02Pis37	12Aqu34	19Aqu34	14Tau43	11/23/1957	00Sag56	17Sag33	18Cap00	09Sco49
02/26/1957	07Pis39	20Aqu15	25Aqu48	17Tau50	11/28/1957	06Sag00	24Sag40	22Cap45	13Sco12
03/03/1957	12Pis40	28Aqu22	02Pis03	20Tau58	12/03/1957	11Sag04	01Cap18	27Cap17	16Sco36
03/08/1957	17Pis40	06Pis55	08Pis18	24Tau06	12/08/1957	16Sag09	07Cap00	01Aqu32	20Sco00
03/13/1957	22Pis39	15Pis57	14Pis31	27Tau13	12/13/1957	21Sag13	10Cap48	05Aqu25	23Sco25
03/18/1957	27Pis38	25Pis27	20Pis45	00Gem22	12/18/1957	26Sag19	11Cap08	08Aqu53	26Sco51
03/23/1957	02Ari36	05Ari22	26Pis58	03Gem30	12/23/1957	01Cap24	06Cap55	11Aqu50	00Sag18
03/28/1957	07Ari33	15Ari31	03Ari10	06Gem39	12/28/1957	06Cap30	00Cap16	14Aqu08	03Sag46
04/02/1957	12Ari29	25Ari24	09Ari23	09Gem48	01/02/1958	11Cap36	25Sag52	15Aqu40	07Sag15
04/07/1957	17Ari24	04Tau19	15Ari35	12Gem56	01/07/1958	16Cap42	25Sag33	16Aqu17	10Sag44
04/12/1957	22Ari18	11Tau31	21Ari46	16Gem05	01/12/1958	21Cap47	28Sag22	16Aqu54	14Sag14
04/17/1957	27Ari12	16Tau31	27Ari58	19Gem13	01/17/1958	26Cap52	03Cap04	14Aqu28	17Sag45
04/22/1957	02Tau05	19Tau05	04Tau09	22Gem22	01/22/1958	01Aqu58	08Cap54	12Aqu09	21Sag16
04/27/1957	06Tau57	19Tau12	10Tau19	25Gem30	01/27/1958	07Aqu03	15Cap25	09Aqu13	24Sag49
05/02/1957	11Tau48	17Tau18	16Tau30	28Gem39	02/01/1958	12Aqu08	22Cap25	06Aqu10	28Sag22
05/07/1957	16Tau39	14Tau18	22Tau40	01Can47	02/06/1958	17Aqu12	29Cap48	03Aqu30	01Cap57
05/12/1957	21Tau29	11Tau32	28Tau49	04Can55	02/11/1958	22Aqu16	07Aqu31	01Aqu37	05Cap31
05/17/1957	26Tau18	10Tau04	04Gem58	08Can04	02/16/1958	27Aqu19	15Aqu36	00Aqu45	09Cap07
05/22/1957	01Gem07	10Tau26	11Gem07	11Can12	02/21/1958	02Pis22	24Aqu01	00Aqu53	12Cap43
05/27/1957	05Gem55	12Tau39	17Gem15	14Can19	02/26/1958	07Pis24	02Pis52	01Aqu58	16Cap20
06/01/1957	10Gem43	16Tau30	23Gem23	17Can28	03/03/1958	12Pis25	12Pis07	03Aqu52	19Cap57
06/06/1957	15Gem30	21Tau49	29Gem31	20Can36	03/08/1958	17Pis25	21Pis43	06Aqu27	23Cap36
06/11/1957	20Gem17	28Tau25	05Can38	23Can43	03/13/1958	22Pis25	01Ari31	09Aqu36	27Cap14
06/16/1957	25Gem03	06Gem16	11Can45	26Can51	03/18/1958	27Pis24	11Ari01	13Aqu13	00Aqu54
06/21/1957	29Gem50	15Gem16	17Can52	29Can59	03/23/1958	02Ari21	19Ari29	17Aqu12	04Aqu33
06/26/1957	04Can36	25Gem19	23Can58	03Leo07	03/28/1958	07Ari18	26Ari00	21Aqu30	08Aqu13
07/01/1957	09Can22	06Can02	00Leo04	06Leo15	04/02/1958	12Ari15	29Ari51	26Aqu03	11Aqu54
07/06/1957	14Can08	16Can53	06Leo10	09Leo24	04/07/1958	17Ari10	00Tau47	00Pis49	15Aqu34
07/11/1957	18Can54	27Can21	12Leo15	12Leo32	04/12/1958	22Ari04	29Ari04	05Pis45	19Aqu15
07/16/1957	23Can40	07Leo09	18Leo19	15Leo40	04/17/1958	26Ari58	25Ari45	10Pis50	22Aqu56
07/21/1957	28Can27	16Leo13	24Leo24	18Leo49	04/22/1958	01Tau51	22Ari22	16Pis02	26Aqu37
07/26/1957	03Leo13	24Leo32	00Vir27	21Leo58	04/27/1958	06Tau43	20Ari18	21Pis21	00Pis19
07/31/1957	08Leo00	02Vir05	06Vir30	25Leo07					
					05/02/1958	11Tau34	20Ari11	26Pis44	04Pis00
08/05/1957	12Leo47	08Vir51	12Vir32	28Leo16	05/07/1958	16Tau25	22Ari01	02Ari12	07Pis40
08/10/1957	17Leo34	14Vir46	18Vir34	01Vir26	05/12/1958	21Tau15	25Ari32	07Ari44	11Pis21
08/15/1957	22Leo22	19Vir39	24Vir34	04Vir36	05/17/1958	26Tau04	00Tau28	13Ari19	15Pis00
08/20/1957	27Leo11	23Vir13	00Lib34	07Vir46	05/22/1958	00Gem53	06Tau35	18Ari58	18Pis39
08/25/1957	02Vir00	25Vir05	06Lib33	10Vir57	05/27/1958	05Gem41	13Tau47	24Ari39	22Pis17
08/30/1957	06Vir50	24Vir45	12Lib31	14Vir09					
					06/01/1958	10Gem29	22Tau00	00Tau22	25Pis54
09/04/1957	11Vir40	21Vir55	18Lib27	17Vir20	06/06/1958	15Gem16	01Gem13	06Tau08	29Pis29
09/09/1957	16Vir31	17Vir13	24Lib22	20Vir33	06/11/1958	20Gem03	11Gem20	11Tau55	03Ari02
09/14/1957	21Vir24	12Vir48	00Sco16	23Vir45	06/16/1958	24Gem49	22Gem07	17Tau45	06Ari35
09/19/1957	26Vir16	11Vir10	06Sco09	26Vir58	06/21/1958	29Gem36	03Can04	23Tau35	10Ari05
09/24/1957	01Lib10	13Vir25	12Sco00	00Lib12	06/26/1958	04Can22	13Can40	29Tau27	13Ari33
09/29/1957	06Lib04	19Vir02	17Sco49	03Lib27					

Ephemeris Tables for Sun, Mercury, Venus and Mars

Date	Sun	Mercury	Venus	Mars	Date	Sun	Mercury	Venus	Mars
07/01/1958	09Can08	23Can34	05Gem21	16Ari58	04/02/1959	12Ari00	04Ari36	15Tau13	25Gem36
07/06/1958	13Can54	02Leo39	11Gem15	20Ari21	04/07/1959	16Ari55	01Ari34	21Tau13	28Gem22
07/11/1958	18Can40	10Leo52	17Gem12	23Ari41	04/12/1959	21Ari50	00Ari39	27Tau10	01Can10
07/16/1958	23Can26	18Leo13	23Gem09	26Ari57	04/17/1959	26Ari44	01Ari52	03Gem06	04Can00
07/21/1958	28Can13	24Leo40	29Gem07	00Tau09	04/22/1959	01Tau37	04Ari56	08Gem59	06Can51
07/26/1958	02Leo59	00Vir04	05Can07	03Tau16	04/27/1959	06Tau29	09Ari28	14Gem50	09Can42
07/31/1958	07Leo46	04Vir15	11Can09	06Tau19					
					05/02/1959	11Tau21	15Ari10	20Gem39	12Can36
08/05/1958	12Leo33	06Vir55	17Can11	09Tau16	05/07/1959	16Tau11	21Ari52	26Gem24	15Can30
08/10/1958	17Leo21	07Vir40	23Can15	12Tau07	05/12/1959	21Tau01	29Ari28	02Can06	18Can25
08/15/1958	22Leo09	06Vir12	29Can19	14Tau50	05/17/1959	25Tau50	07Tau57	07Can44	21Can21
08/20/1958	26Leo57	02Vir43	05Leo25	17Tau29	05/22/1959	00Gem39	17Tau16	13Can18	24Can18
08/25/1958	01Vir46	28Leo21	11Leo31	19Tau57	05/27/1959	05Gem27	27Tau24	18Can48	27Can16
08/30/1958	06Vir36	25Leo13	17Leo39	22Tau16					
					06/01/1959	10Gem15	08Gem10	24Can13	00Leo14
09/04/1958	11Vir27	25Leo01	23Leo48	24Tau25	06/06/1959	15Gem02	19Gem09	29Can31	03Leo13
09/09/1958	16Vir18	28Leo19	29Leo58	26Tau22	06/11/1959	19Gem49	29Gem49	04Leo44	06Leo13
09/14/1958	21Vir10	04Vir37	06Vir09	28Tau05	06/16/1959	24Gem36	09Can45	09Leo48	09Leo14
09/19/1958	26Vir02	12Vir49	12Vir21	29Tau34	06/21/1959	29Gem22	18Can46	14Leo44	12Leo15
09/24/1958	00Lib55	21Vir51	18Vir33	00Gem48	06/26/1959	04Can08	26Can48	19Leo29	15Leo18
09/29/1958	05Lib50	01Lib00	24Vir46	01Gem42					
					07/01/1959	08Can54	03Leo49	24Leo02	18Leo21
10/04/1958	10Lib45	09Lib58	01Lib00	02Gem18	07/06/1959	13Can40	09Leo46	28Leo21	21Leo24
10/09/1958	15Lib41	18Lib37	07Lib15	02Gem33	07/11/1959	18Can27	14Leo29	02Vir22	24Leo28
10/14/1958	20Lib38	26Lib58	13Lib30	02Gem26	07/16/1959	23Can12	17Leo45	06Vir02	27Leo33
10/19/1958	25Lib36	05Sco01	19Lib45	01Gem57	07/21/1959	27Can59	19Leo17	09Vir17	00Vir39
10/24/1958	00Sco34	12Sco48	26Lib01	01Gem05	07/26/1959	02Leo45	18Leo49	12Vir01	03Vir45
10/29/1958	05Sco33	20Sco22	02Sco17	29Tau54	07/31/1959	07Leo32	16Leo24	14Vir10	06Vir52
11/03/1958	10Sco34	27Sco42	08Sco33	28Tau25	08/05/1959	12Leo19	12Leo43	15Vir34	10Vir00
11/08/1958	15Sco34	04Sag46	14Sco49	26Tau43	08/10/1959	17Leo07	09Leo16	16Vir06	13Vir09
11/13/1958	20Sco36	11Sag28	21Sco06	24Tau54	08/15/1959	21Leo55	07Leo41	15Vir42	16Vir18
11/18/1958	25Sco39	17Sag34	27Sco23	23Tau05	08/20/1959	26Leo43	08Leo58	14Vir18	19Vir28
11/23/1958	00Sag42	22Sag33	03Sag40	21Tau21	08/25/1959	01Vir32	13Leo17	12Vir03	22Vir39
11/28/1958	05Sag45	25Sag27	09Sag57	19Tau48	08/30/1959	06Vir22	20Leo13	09Vir10	25Vir51
12/03/1958	10Sag49	24Sag48	16Sag14	18Tau31	09/04/1959	11Vir12	28Leo53	06Vir06	29Vir04
12/08/1958	15Sag54	19Sag49	22Sag31	17Tau33	09/09/1959	16Vir04	08Vir21	03Vir19	02Lib18
12/13/1958	20Sag58	13Sag12	28Sag48	16Tau55	09/14/1959	20Vir55	17Vir54	01Vir13	05Lib33
12/18/1958	26Sag04	09Sag36	05Cap05	16Tau37	09/19/1959	25Vir48	27Vir12	00Vir04	08Lib48
12/23/1958	01Cap09	10Sag17	11Cap22	16Tau40	09/24/1959	00Lib41	06Lib06	29Leo55	12Lib04
12/28/1958	06Cap15	13Sag58	17Cap39	17Tau01	09/29/1959	05Lib36	14Lib36	00Vir44	15Lib22
01/02/1959	11Cap21	19Sag21	23Cap55	17Tau40	10/04/1959	10Lib31	22Lib43	02Vir23	18Lib41
01/07/1959	16Cap27	25Sag40	00Aqu12	18Tau35	10/09/1959	15Lib27	00Sco30	04Vir46	22Lib00
01/12/1959	21Cap32	02Cap31	06Aqu28	19Tau45	10/14/1959	20Lib24	07Sco59	07Vir45	25Lib21
01/17/1959	26Cap38	09Cap44	12Aqu44	21Tau07	10/19/1959	25Lib21	15Sco08	11Vir15	28Lib43
01/22/1959	01Aqu43	17Cap13	19Aqu00	22Tau40	10/24/1959	00Sco19	21Sco55	15Vir10	02Sco06
01/27/1959	06Aqu48	24Cap59	25Aqu15	24Tau24	10/29/1959	05Sco19	28Sco12	19Vir25	05Sco30
02/01/1959	11Aqu53	03Aqu00	01Pis30	26Tau16	11/03/1959	10Sco19	03Sag42	23Vir58	08Sco55
02/06/1959	16Aqu57	11Aqu19	07Pis44	28Tau16	11/08/1959	15Sco20	07Sag55	28Vir46	12Sco21
02/11/1959	22Aqu01	19Aqu57	13Pis57	00Gem24	11/13/1959	20Sco21	09Sag52	03Lib45	15Sco48
02/16/1959	27Aqu04	28Aqu56	20Pis10	02Gem37	11/18/1959	25Sco24	08Sag15	08Lib56	19Sco17
02/21/1959	02Pis07	08Pis12	26Pis22	04Gem56	11/23/1959	00Sag42	02Sag42	14Lib15	22Sco46
02/26/1959	07Pis09	17Pis35	02Ari32	07Gem19	11/28/1959	05Sag30	26Sco24	19Lib42	26Sco18
03/03/1959	12Pis10	26Pis39	08Ari42	09Gem46	12/03/1959	10Sag34	23Sco42	25Lib16	29Sco49
03/08/1959	17Pis10	04Ari35	14Ari50	12Gem18	12/08/1959	15Sag39	25Sco21	00Sco55	03Sag22
03/13/1959	22Pis10	10Ari19	20Ari58	14Gem52	12/13/1959	20Sag44	29Sco50	06Sco39	06Sag57
03/18/1959	27Pis09	12Ari55	27Ari04	17Gem30	12/18/1959	25Sag49	05Sag50	12Sco27	10Sag31
03/23/1959	02Ari07	12Ari07	03Tau09	20Gem10	12/23/1959	00Cap54	12Sag36	18Sco18	14Sag08
03/28/1959	07Ari04	08Ari45	09Tau12	22Gem52	12/28/1959	06Cap00	19Sag47	24Sco13	17Sag45

Ephemeris Tables for Sun, Mercury, Venus and Mars

Date	Sun	Mercury	Venus	Mars	Date	Sun	Mercury	Venus	Mars
01/02/1960	11Cap06	27Sag12	0Sag10	21Sag24	10/03/1960	10Lib16	02Sco26	07Sco43	06Can01
01/07/1960	16Cap12	04Cap49	06Sag09	25Sag04	10/08/1960	15Lib12	08Sco54	13Sco51	08Can13
01/12/1960	21Cap18	12Cap35	12Sag10	28Sag44	10/13/1960	20Lib09	14Sco43	19Sco58	10Can16
01/17/1960	26Cap23	20Cap33	18Sag13	02Cap26	10/18/1960	25Lib07	19Sco37	26Sco04	12Can08
01/22/1960	01Aqu28	28Cap44	24Sag17	06Cap09	10/23/1960	00Sco05	23Sco00	02Sag11	13Can49
01/27/1960	06Aqu33	07Aqu10	00Cap22	09Cap52	10/28/1960	05Sco04	23Sco58	08Sag17	15Can18
02/01/1960	11Aqu38	15Aqu51	06Cap28	13Cap37	11/02/1960	10Sco04	21Sco24	14Sag22	16Can32
02/06/1960	16Aqu42	24Aqu45	12Cap35	17Cap22	11/07/1960	15Sco05	15Sco32	20Sag27	17Can31
02/11/1960	21Aqu46	03Pis43	18Cap43	21Cap09	11/12/1960	20Sco07	09Sco48	26Sag31	18Can12
02/16/1960	26Aqu49	12Pis17	24Cap51	24Cap55	11/17/1960	25Sco09	08Sco03	02Cap35	18Can36
02/21/1960	01Pis53	19Pis38	00Aqu59	28Cap43	11/22/1960	00Sag12	10Sco37	08Cap37	18Can39
02/26/1960	06Pis55	24Pis31	07Aqu08	02Aqu32	11/27/1960	05Sag16	15Sco52	14Cap39	18Can21
03/02/1960	11Pis56	25Pis48	13Aqu17	06Aqu21	12/02/1960	10Sag19	22Sco27	20Cap38	17Can41
03/07/1960	16Pis56	23Pis22	19Aqu26	10Aqu10	12/07/1960	15Sag24	29Sco40	26Cap36	16Can40
03/12/1960	21Pis56	18Pis43	25Aqu36	14Aqu01	12/12/1960	20Sag29	07Sag10	02Aqu33	15Can20
03/17/1960	26Pis55	14Pis27	01Pis46	17Aqu51	12/17/1960	25Sag34	14Sag48	08Aqu27	13Can43
03/22/1960	01Ari52	12Pis16	07Pis55	21Aqu42	12/22/1960	00Cap40	22Sag30	14Aqu18	11Can52
03/27/1960	06Ari49	12Pis34	14Pis05	25Aqu33	12/27/1960	05Cap45	00Cap19	20Aqu06	09Can55
04/01/1960	11Ari46	14Pis58	20Pis14	29Aqu25	01/01/1961	10Cap51	08Cap13	25Aqu51	07Can56
04/06/1960	16Ari41	19Pis00	26Pis24	03Pis16	01/06/1961	15Cap57	16Cap16	01Pis32	06Can02
04/11/1960	21Ari36	24Pis17	02Ari33	07Pis08	01/11/1961	21Cap03	24Cap30	07Pis07	04Can18
04/16/1960	26Ari30	00Ari32	08Ari42	10Pis59	01/16/1961	26Cap08	02Aqu54	12Pis37	02Can48
04/21/1960	01Tau22	07Ari38	14Ari51	14Pis50	01/21/1961	01Aqu13	11Aqu25	18Pis00	01Can36
04/26/1960	06Tau15	15Ari30	21Ari00	18Pis40	01/26/1961	06Aqu19	19Aqu54	23Pis14	00Can44
					01/31/1961	11Aqu24	27Aqu57	28Pis19	00Can12
05/01/1960	11Tau06	24Ari06	27Ari09	22Pis31					
05/06/1960	15Tau57	03Tau28	03Tau17	26Pis21	02/05/1961	16Aqu28	04Pis39	03Ari12	00Can00
05/11/1960	20Tau47	13Tau33	09Tau25	00Ari09	02/10/1961	21Aqu31	08Pis39	07Ari52	00Can07
05/16/1960	25Tau36	24Tau14	15Tau34	03Ari58	02/15/1961	26Aqu35	08Pis37	12Ari16	00Can32
05/21/1960	00Gem25	05Gem10	21Tau42	07Ari45	02/20/1961	01Pis38	04Pis42	16Ari20	01Can13
05/26/1960	05Gem13	15Gem49	27Tau51	11Ari31	02/25/1961	06Pis40	29Aqu19	20Ari00	02Can09
05/31/1960	10Gem01	25Gem42	03Gem59	15Ari17					
					03/02/1961	11Pis41	25Aqu27	23Ari13	03Can18
06/05/1960	14Gem48	04Can33	10Gem07	19Ari01	03/07/1961	16Pis42	24Aqu21	25Ari50	04Can38
06/10/1960	19Gem35	12Can16	16Gem16	22Ari44	03/12/1961	21Pis41	25Aqu49	27Ari46	06Can10
06/15/1960	24Gem22	18Can47	22Gem24	26Ari26	03/17/1961	26Pis40	29Aqu13	28Ari52	07Can50
06/20/1960	29Gem08	24Can01	28Gem33	00Tau06	03/22/1961	01Ari38	04Pis00	29Ari01	09Can39
06/25/1960	03Can55	27Can47	04Can42	03Tau44	03/27/1961	06Ari35	09Pis49	28Ari11	11Can36
06/30/1960	08Can40	29Can52	10Can50	07Tau21					
					04/01/1961	11Ari31	16Pis28	26Ari19	13Can39
07/05/1960	13Can27	00Leo06	16Can59	10Tau55	04/06/1961	16Ari27	23Pis50	23Ari38	15Can48
07/10/1960	18Can13	28Can26	23Can07	14Tau27	04/11/1961	21Ari22	01Ari51	20Ari33	18Can01
07/15/1960	22Can59	25Can27	29Can17	17Tau57	04/16/1961	26Ari15	10Ari30	17Ari31	20Can20
07/20/1960	27Can45	22Can15	5Leo26	21Tau25	04/21/1961	01Tau09	19Ari49	15Ari01	22Can43
07/25/1960	02Leo31	20Can12	11Leo36	24Tau50	04/26/1961	06Tau01	29Ari48	13Ari22	25Can10
07/30/1960	07Leo18	20Can20	17Leo45	28Tau13					
					05/01/1961	10Tau52	10Tau19	12Ari45	27Can40
08/04/1960	12Leo05	23Can03	23Leo54	01Gem33	05/06/1961	15Tau43	21Tau07	13Ari06	00Leo14
08/09/1960	16Leo53	28Can20	00Vir04	04Gem49	05/11/1961	20Tau33	01Gem41	14Ari21	02Leo51
08/14/1960	21Leo41	05Leo49	06Vir13	08Gem02	05/16/1961	25Tau22	11Gem25	16Ari21	05Leo30
08/19/1960	26Leo29	14Leo55	12Vir23	11Gem12	05/21/1961	00Gem11	20Gem00	19Ari00	08Leo11
08/24/1960	01Vir18	24Leo46	18Vir33	14Gem18	05/26/1961	05Gem00	27Gem15	22Ari10	10Leo55
08/29/1960	06Vir08	04Vir41	24Vir42	17Gem19	05/31/1961	09Gem47	03Can02	25Ari47	13Leo40
09/03/1960	10Vir58	14Vir18	00Lib51	20Gem16	06/05/1961	14Gem34	07Can16	29Ari45	16Leo28
09/08/1960	15Vir49	23Vir26	07Lib00	23Gem09	06/10/1961	19Gem22	09Can48	04Tau00	19Leo18
09/13/1960	20Vir41	02Lib06	13Lib09	25Gem55	06/15/1961	24Gem08	10Can25	08Tau30	22Leo09
09/18/1960	25Vir34	10Lib18	19Lib18	28Gem37	06/20/1961	28Gem54	09Can15	13Tau12	25Leo03
09/23/1960	00Lib27	18Lib06	25Lib27	01Can12	06/25/1961	03Can40	06Can45	18Tau04	27Leo57
09/28/1960	05Lib21	25Lib28	01Sco35	03Can40	06/30/1961	08Can27	03Can51	23Tau06	00Vir53

Ephemeris Tables for Sun, Mercury, Venus and Mars

Date	Sun	Mercury	Venus	Mars
07/05/1961	13Can13	01Can48	28Tau15	03Vir51
07/10/1961	17Can58	01Can28	03Gem30	06Vir50
07/15/1961	22Can45	03Can18	08Gem50	09Vir51
07/20/1961	27Can31	07Can20	14Gem16	12Vir53
07/25/1961	02Leo18	13Can28	19Gem46	15Vir57
07/30/1961	07Leo04	21Can28	25Gem21	19Vir01
08/04/1961	11Leo51	00Leo54	00Can58	22Vir07
08/09/1961	16Leo39	11Leo04	06Can40	25Vir15
08/14/1961	21Leo27	21Leo19	12Can24	28Vir24
08/19/1961	26Leo15	01Vir14	18Can11	01Lib34
08/24/1961	01Vir04	10Vir37	24Can01	04Lib46
08/29/1961	05Vir54	19Vir26	29Can54	07Lib59
09/03/1961	10Vir45	27Vir43	05Leo48	11Lib13
09/08/1961	15Vir36	05Lib30	11Leo46	14Lib28
09/13/1961	20Vir27	12Lib46	17Leo45	17Lib46
09/18/1961	25Vir19	19Lib31	23Leo46	21Lib04
09/23/1961	00Lib13	25Lib39	29Leo49	24Lib24
09/28/1961	05Lib07	00Sco59	05Vir54	27Lib45
10/03/1961	10Lib02	05Sco11	12Vir00	01Sco08
10/08/1961	14Lib58	07Sco41	18Vir08	04Sco32
10/13/1961	19Lib55	07Sco36	24Vir18	07Sco57
10/18/1961	24Lib52	04Sco11	00Lib28	11Sco24
10/23/1961	29Lib51	28Lib15	06Lib40	14Sco52
10/28/1961	04Sco50	23Lib19	12Lib52	18Sco22
11/02/1961	09Sco50	22Lib35	19Lib06	21Sco53
11/07/1961	14Sco51	26Lib01	25Lib21	25Sco26
11/12/1961	19Sco52	01Sco58	01Sco36	29Sco00
11/17/1961	24Sco54	09Sco08	07Sco51	02Sag35
11/22/1961	29Sco57	16Sco47	14Sco07	06Sag12
11/27/1961	05Sag01	24Sco36	20Sco24	09Sag50
12/02/1961	10Sag05	02Sag26	26Sco40	13Sag29
12/07/1961	15Sag09	10Sag16	02Sag58	17Sag10
12/12/1961	20Sag14	18Sag06	09Sag15	20Sag52
12/17/1961	25Sag19	25Sag59	15Sag32	24Sag35
12/22/1961	00Cap25	03Cap55	21Sag49	28Sag19
12/27/1961	05Cap31	11Cap56	28Sag07	02Cap05
01/01/1962	10Cap36	20Cap03	04Cap24	05Cap52
01/06/1962	15Cap42	28Cap10	10Cap42	09Cap39
01/11/1962	20Cap48	06Aqu11	17Cap00	13Cap28
01/16/1962	25Cap54	13Aqu37	23Cap16	17Cap18
01/21/1962	00Aqu59	19Aqu47	29Cap34	21Cap09
01/26/1962	06Aqu04	22Aqu42	05Aqu51	25Cap00
01/31/1962	11Aqu09	21Aqu25	12Aqu07	28Cap52
02/05/1962	16Aqu13	16Aqu20	18Aqu24	02Aqu45
02/10/1962	21Aqu17	10Aqu42	24Aqu40	06Aqu39
02/15/1962	26Aqu20	07Aqu36	00Pis57	10Aqu33
02/20/1962	01Pis24	07Aqu37	07Pis13	14Aqu27
02/25/1962	06Pis25	10Aqu07	13Pis28	18Aqu22
03/02/1962	11Pis27	14Aqu19	19Pis42	22Aqu18
03/07/1962	16Pis27	19Aqu42	25Pis57	26Aqu13
03/12/1962	21Pis27	25Aqu57	02Ari10	00Pis09
03/17/1962	26Pis26	02Pis52	08Ari23	04Pis04
03/22/1962	01Ari24	10Pis24	14Ari36	08Pis00
03/27/1962	06Ari21	18Pis28	20Ari47	11Pis55
04/01/1962	11Ari17	27Pis07	26Ari58	15Pis49
04/06/1962	16Ari13	06Ari20	03Tau09	19Pis44
04/11/1962	21Ari07	16Ari09	09Tau18	23Pis38
04/16/1962	26Ari01	26Ari28	15Tau27	27Pis31
04/21/1962	00Tau54	07Tau04	21Tau35	01Ari24
04/26/1962	05Tau46	17Tau27	27Tau42	05Ari16
05/01/1962	10Tau38	26Tau58	03Gem48	09Ari07
05/06/1962	15Tau29	05Gem09	09Gem54	12Ari57
05/11/1962	20Tau19	11Gem44	15Gem58	16Ari46
05/16/1962	25Tau09	16Gem33	22Gem01	20Ari35
05/21/1962	29Tau57	19Gem28	28Gem04	24Ari22
05/26/1962	04Gem45	20Gem24	04Can05	28Ari08
05/31/1962	09Gem33	19Gem27	10Can05	01Tau52
06/05/1962	14Gem21	17Gem07	16Can04	05Tau36
06/10/1962	19Gem07	14Gem23	22Can01	09Tau18
06/15/1962	23Gem54	12Gem22	27Can57	12Tau58
06/20/1962	28Gem40	11Gem58	03Leo52	16Tau37
06/25/1962	03Can27	13Gem19	09Leo45	20Tau15
06/30/1962	08Can13	16Gem41	15Leo36	23Tau51
07/05/1962	12Can59	21Gem51	21Leo25	27Tau25
07/10/1962	17Can45	28Gem44	27Leo12	00Gem57
07/15/1962	22Can31	07Can10	02Vir56	04Gem27
07/20/1962	27Can17	16Can51	08Vir38	07Gem56
07/25/1962	02Leo04	27Can18	14Vir16	11Gem22
07/30/1962	06Leo51	07Leo49	19Vir52	14Gem47
08/04/1962	11Leo37	18Leo00	25Vir24	18Gem10
08/09/1962	16Leo25	27Leo36	00Lib51	21Gem30
08/14/1962	21Leo13	06Vir33	06Lib13	24Gem48
08/19/1962	26Leo01	14Vir54	11Lib30	28Gem04
08/24/1962	00Vir51	22Vir39	16Lib41	01Can18
08/29/1962	05Vir40	29Vir48	21Lib44	04Can29
09/03/1962	10Vir30	6Lib17	26Lib39	07Can37
09/08/1962	15Vir21	12Lib02	01Sco24	10Can43
09/13/1962	20Vir13	16Lib48	05Sco56	13Can45
09/18/1962	25Vir06	20Lib14	10Sco14	16Can45
09/23/1962	29Vir59	21Lib45	14Sco15	19Can41
09/28/1962	04Lib53	20Lib37	17Sco54	22Can34
10/03/1962	09Lib48	16Lib30	21Sco08	25Can22
10/08/1962	14Lib44	10Lib49	23Sco51	28Can07
10/13/1962	19Lib40	06Lib56	25Sco54	00Leo48
10/18/1962	24Lib38	07Lib15	27Sco12	03Leo24
10/23/1962	29Lib36	11Lib30	27Sco37	05Leo54
10/28/1962	04Sco35	18Lib07	27Sco04	08Leo18
11/02/1962	09Sco36	25Lib49	25Sco31	10Leo37
11/07/1962	14Sco36	03Sco54	23Sco05	12Leo48
11/12/1962	19Sco37	12Sco03	20Sco09	14Leo52
11/17/1962	24Sco40	20Sco06	17Sco12	16Leo47
11/22/1962	29Sco43	28Sco04	14Sco39	18Leo33
11/27/1962	04Sag46	05Sag57	12Sco56	20Leo07
12/02/1962	09Sag50	13Sag48	12Sco13	21Leo31
12/07/1962	14Sag54	21Sag37	12Sco31	22Leo42
12/12/1962	19Sag59	29Sag26	13Sco46	23Leo38
12/17/1962	25Sag40	07Cap15	15Sco50	24Leo19
12/22/1962	00Cap10	15Cap00	18Sco34	24Leo42
12/27/1962	05Cap16	22Cap31	21Sco53	24Leo47

Ephemeris Tables for Sun, Mercury, Venus and Mars

Date	Sun	Mercury	Venus	Mars
01/01/1963	10Cap21	29Cap20	25Sco39	24Leo32
01/06/1963	15Cap27	04Aqu34	29Sco48	23Leo57
01/11/1963	20Cap33	06Aqu42	04Sag16	23Leo02
01/16/1963	25Cap39	04Aqu16	08Sag58	21Leo47
01/21/1963	00Aqu44	28Cap20	13Sag54	20Leo15
01/26/1963	05Aqu49	22Cap52	19Sag00	18Leo28
01/31/1963	10Aqu54	20Cap42	24Sag15	16Leo33
02/05/1963	15Aqu58	21Cap49	29Sag37	14Leo33
02/10/1963	21Aqu02	25Cap13	05Cap05	12Leo35
02/15/1963	26Aqu05	00Aqu06	10Cap39	10Leo44
02/20/1963	01Pis09	05Aqu57	16Cap16	09Leo04
02/25/1963	06Pis11	12Aqu31	21Cap58	07Leo42
03/02/1963	11Pis12	19Aqu39	27Cap43	06Leo37
03/07/1963	16Pis13	27Aqu16	03Aqu30	05Leo52
03/12/1963	21Pis12	05Pis22	09Aqu19	05Leo27
03/17/1963	26Pis12	13Pis57	15Aqu12	05Leo20
03/22/1963	01Ari09	23Pis02	21Aqu04	05Leo31
03/27/1963	06Ari06	02Ari38	27Aqu00	06Leo01
04/01/1963	11Ari03	12Ari42	02Pis56	06Leo45
04/06/1963	15Ari58	23Ari02	08Pis53	07Leo43
04/11/1963	20Ari53	03Tau09	14Pis52	08Leo55
04/16/1963	25Ari47	12Tau21	20Pis51	10Leo17
04/21/1963	00Tau40	20Tau02	26Pis50	11Leo50
04/26/1963	05Tau33	25Tau45	02Ari49	13Leo32
05/01/1963	10Tau24	29Tau18	08Ari50	15Leo22
05/06/1963	15Tau15	00Gem36	14Ari51	17Leo20
05/11/1963	20Tau05	29Tau47	20Ari53	19Leo25
05/16/1963	24Tau54	27Tau25	26Ari55	21Leo35
05/21/1963	29Tau43	24Tau32	02Tau57	23Leo51
05/26/1963	04Gem31	22Tau22	09Tau00	26Leo12
05/31/1963	09Gem19	21Tau45	15Tau03	28Leo37
06/05/1963	14Gem07	22Tau56	21Tau07	01Vir07
06/10/1963	18Gem54	25Tau56	27Tau10	03Vir40
06/15/1963	23Gem40	00Gem33	03Gem15	06Vir18
06/20/1963	28Gem27	06Gem40	09Gem19	08Vir58
06/25/1963	03Can13	14Gem09	15Gem24	11Vir42
06/30/1963	07Can59	22Gem55	21Gem30	14Vir28
07/05/1963	12Can45	02Can49	27Gem36	17Vir17
07/10/1963	17Can31	13Can27	03Can43	20Vir09
07/15/1963	22Can17	24Can12	09Can49	23Vir03
07/20/1963	27Can03	04Leo36	15Can57	26Vir00
07/25/1963	01Leo50	14Leo22	22Can05	29Vir00
07/30/1963	06Leo37	23Leo27	28Can14	02Lib01
08/04/1963	11Leo24	01Vir48	04Leo23	05Lib04
08/09/1963	16Leo11	09Vir28	10Leo33	08Lib10
08/14/1963	20Leo59	16Vir26	16Leo43	11Lib18
08/19/1963	25Leo47	22Vir37	22Leo54	14Lib27
08/24/1963	00Vir36	27Vir54	29Leo06	17Lib39
08/29/1963	05Vir26	02Lib01	05Vir17	20Lib52
09/03/1963	10Vir16	04Lib34	11Vir29	24Lib08
09/08/1963	15Vir07	05Lib01	17Vir42	27Lib25
09/13/1963	19Vir59	02Lib52	23Vir55	00Sco45
09/18/1963	24Vir51	28Vir19	00Lib08	04Sco06
09/23/1963	29Vir45	23Vir16	06Lib21	07Sco29
09/28/1963	04Lib39	20Vir36	12Lib35	10Sco54

Date	Sun	Mercury	Venus	Mars
10/03/1963	09Lib34	22Vir00	18Lib48	14Sco21
10/08/1963	14Lib30	27Vir01	25Lib02	17Sco49
10/13/1963	19Lib26	04Lib16	01Sco16	21Sco19
10/18/1963	24Lib24	12Lib30	07Sco30	24Sco51
10/23/1963	29Lib22	21Lib00	13Sco44	28Sco24
10/28/1963	04Sco21	29Lib27	19Sco58	02Sag00
11/02/1963	09Sco21	07Sco45	26Sco12	05Sag36
11/07/1963	14Sco22	15Sco51	02Sag26	09Sag15
11/12/1963	19Sco23	23Sco49	08Sag40	12Sag55
11/17/1963	24Sco25	01Sag37	14Sag54	16Sag36
11/22/1963	29Sco28	09Sag21	21Sag07	20Sag19
11/27/1963	04Sag31	16Sag58	27Sag21	24Sag04
12/02/1963	09Sag36	24Sag31	03Cap34	27Sag50
12/07/1963	14Sag40	01Cap52	09Cap47	01Cap37
12/12/1963	19Sag45	08Cap52	16Cap00	05Cap25
12/17/1963	24Sag50	15Cap01	22Cap13	09Cap15
12/22/1963	29Sag55	19Cap28	28Cap25	13Cap06
12/27/1963	05Cap01	20Cap38	04Aqu36	16Cap57
01/01/1964	10Cap07	17Cap12	10Aqu48	20Cap50
01/06/1964	15Cap12	10Cap43	16Aqu57	24Cap43
01/11/1964	20Cap18	05Cap43	23Aqu07	28Cap38
01/16/1964	25Cap24	04Cap34	29Aqu15	02Aqu33
01/21/1964	00Aqu29	06Cap41	05Pis22	06Aqu28
01/26/1964	05Aqu34	10Cap53	11Pis28	10Aqu25
01/31/1964	10Aqu39	16Cap21	17Pis32	14Aqu21
02/05/1964	15Aqu43	22Cap37	23Pis34	18Aqu18
02/10/1964	20Aqu47	29Cap27	29Pis34	22Aqu15
02/15/1964	25Aqu51	06Aqu43	05Ari31	26Aqu12
02/20/1964	00Pis54	14Aqu25	11Ari25	00Pis10
02/25/1964	05Pis56	22Aqu29	17Ari17	04Pis07
03/01/1964	10Pis58	00Pis59	23Ari06	08Pis04
03/06/1964	15Pis58	09Pis54	28Ari50	12Pis01
03/11/1964	20Pis58	19Pis16	04Tau30	15Pis57
03/16/1964	25Pis57	29Pis03	10Tau06	19Pis52
03/21/1964	00Ari56	09Ari01	15Tau36	23Pis48
03/26/1964	05Ari52	18Ari48	20Tau59	27Pis42
03/31/1964	10Ari48	27Ari37	26Tau16	01Ari35
04/05/1964	15Ari44	04Tau40	01Gem24	05Ari28
04/10/1964	20Ari39	09Tau22	06Gem22	09Ari21
04/15/1964	25Ari33	11Tau25	11Gem10	13Ari12
04/20/1964	00Tau26	10Tau54	15Gem44	17Ari01
04/25/1964	05Tau18	08Tau25	20Gem03	20Ari51
04/30/1964	10Tau10	05Tau09	24Gem01	24Ari39
05/05/1964	15Tau01	02Tau32	27Gem39	28Ari25
05/10/1964	19Tau51	01Tau31	00Can49	02Tau11
05/15/1964	24Tau40	02Tau25	03Can26	05Tau55
05/20/1964	29Tau30	05Tau07	05Can24	09Tau38
05/25/1964	04Gem18	09Tau22	06Can34	13Tau19
05/30/1964	09Gem06	14Tau59	06Can51	17Tau00
06/04/1964	13Gem53	21Tau48	06Can09	20Tau39
06/09/1964	18Gem40	29Tau45	04Can28	24Tau16
06/14/1964	23Gem27	08Gem47	01Can56	27Tau52
06/19/1964	28Gem13	18Gem49	28Gem54	01Gem27
06/24/1964	02Can59	29Gem32	25Gem50	05Gem00
06/29/1964	07Can45	10Can27	23Gem11	08Gem31

405

Ephemeris Tables for Sun, Mercury, Venus and Mars

Date	Sun	Mercury	Venus	Mars		Date	Sun	Mercury	Venus	Mars
07/04/1964	12Can31	21Can00	21Gem19	12Gem01		04/05/1965	15Ari30	20Ari43	13Ari46	10Vir03
07/09/1964	17Can17	00Leo55	20Gem26	15Gem30		04/10/1965	20Ari25	17Ari00	19Ari59	09Vir17
07/14/1964	22Can03	10Leo03	20Gem31	18Gem57		04/15/1965	25Ari19	13Ari37	26Ari10	08Vir51
07/19/1964	26Can49	18Leo22	21Gem30	22Gem23		04/20/1965	00Tau12	11Ari52	02Tau21	08Vir43
07/24/1964	01Leo36	25Leo54	23Gem17	25Gem47		04/25/1965	05Tau04	12Ari13	08Tau32	08Vir55
07/29/1964	06Leo22	02Vir36	25Gem45	29Gem09		04/30/1965	09Tau56	14Ari30	14Tau42	09Vir23
08/03/1964	11Leo10	08Vir23	28Gem45	02Can30		05/05/1965	14Tau47	18Ari23	20Tau52	10Vir07
08/08/1964	15Leo57	13Vir04	02Can14	05Can50		05/10/1965	19Tau37	23Ari36	27Tau02	11Vir06
08/13/1964	20Leo45	16Vir22	06Can05	09Can07		05/15/1965	24Tau27	29Ari56	03Gem11	12Vir19
08/18/1964	25Leo33	17Vir54	10Can15	12Can24		05/20/1965	29Tau15	07Tau16	09Gem20	13Vir43
08/23/1964	00Vir22	17Vir14	14Can43	15Can38		05/25/1965	04Gem04	15Tau33	15Gem28	15Vir18
08/28/1964	05Vir12	14Vir12	19Can23	18Can51		05/30/1965	08Gem52	24Tau45	21Gem36	17Vir04
09/02/1964	10Vir02	09Vir38	24Can15	22Can02		06/04/1965	13Gem39	04Gem51	27Gem44	18Vir57
09/07/1964	14Vir53	05Vir36	29Can17	25Can12		06/09/1965	18Gem26	15Gem36	03Can51	20Vir59
09/12/1964	19Vir45	04Vir20	04Leo28	28Can19		06/14/1965	23Gem13	26Gem34	09Can58	23Vir09
09/17/1964	24Vir37	06Vir49	09Leo46	01Leo24		06/19/1965	27Gem59	07Can15	16Can05	25Vir24
09/22/1964	29Vir30	12Vir33	15Leo11	04Leo28		06/24/1965	02Can45	17Can14	22Can11	27Vir46
09/27/1964	04Lib24	20Vir22	20Leo42	07Leo30		06/29/1965	07Can31	26Can21	28Can17	00Lib13
10/02/1964	09Lib19	29Vir06	26Leo19	10Leo29		07/04/1965	12Can18	04Leo33	04Leo22	02Lib46
10/07/1964	14Lib15	08Lib02	02Vir00	13Leo26		07/09/1965	17Can03	11Leo51	10Leo27	05Lib24
10/12/1964	19Lib12	16Lib49	07Vir45	16Leo21		07/14/1965	21Can49	18Leo09	16Leo32	08Lib06
10/17/1964	24Lib09	25Lib21	13Vir34	19Leo13		07/19/1965	26Can36	23Leo22	22Leo36	10Lib52
10/22/1964	29Lib07	03Sco37	19Vir27	22Leo02		07/24/1965	01Leo22	27Leo18	28Leo40	13Lib42
10/27/1964	04Sco06	11Sco38	25Vir23	24Leo49		07/29/1965	06Leo09	29Leo36	04Vir42	16Lib36
11/01/1964	09Sco06	19Sco27	01Lib22	27Leo32		08/03/1965	10Leo56	29Leo59	10Vir44	19Lib33
11/06/1964	14Sco07	27Sco04	07Lib23	00Vir12		08/08/1965	15Leo43	28Leo13	16Vir46	22Lib34
11/11/1964	19Sco09	04Sag31	13Lib27	02Vir48		08/13/1965	20Leo31	24Leo39	22Vir46	25Lib37
11/16/1964	24Sco10	11Sag46	19Lib31	05Vir19		08/18/1965	25Leo19	20Leo34	28Vir45	28Lib44
11/21/1964	29Sco13	18Sag44	25Lib39	07Vir47		08/23/1965	00Vir08	17Leo55	04Lib44	01Sco54
11/26/1964	04Sag16	25Sag12	01Sco47	10Vir10		08/28/1965	04Vir58	18Leo09	10Lib42	05Sco06
12/01/1964	09Sag21	00Cap40	07Sco57	12Vir27		09/02/1965	09Vir48	21Leo42	16Lib38	08Sco21
12/06/1964	14Sag25	04Cap15	14Sco07	14Vir39		09/07/1965	14Vir39	28Leo07	22Lib33	11Sco39
12/11/1964	19Sag30	04Cap27	20Sco19	16Vir43		09/12/1965	19Vir31	06Vir27	28Lib27	15Sco00
12/16/1964	24Sag35	00Cap07	26Sco32	18Vir40		09/17/1965	24Vir23	15Vir38	04Sco19	18Sco22
12/21/1964	29Sag40	23Sag27	2Sag45	20Vir30		09/22/1965	29Vir16	24Vir58	10Sco10	21Sco48
12/26/1964	04Cap46	19Sag07	08Sag59	22Vir10		09/27/1965	04Lib10	04Lib06	15Sco58	25Sco15
12/31/1964	09Cap52	19Sag00	15Sag13	23Vir40						
						10/02/1965	09Lib05	12Lib52	21Sco45	28Sco45
01/05/1965	14Cap57	22Sag02	21Sag28	25Vir00		10/07/1965	14Lib01	21Lib18	27Sco30	02Sag16
01/10/1965	20Cap03	26Sag57	27Sag43	26Vir06		10/12/1965	18Lib57	29Lib24	03Sag12	05Sag50
01/15/1965	25Cap09	02Cap57	03Cap58	26Vir59		10/17/1965	23Lib54	07Sco13	08Sag50	09Sag26
01/20/1965	00Aqu15	09Cap34	10Cap13	27Vir37		10/22/1965	28Lib53	14Sco45	14Sag25	13Sag04
01/25/1965	05Aqu19	16Cap39	16Cap28	27Vir58		10/27/1965	03Sco52	22Sco01	19Sag57	16Sag43
01/30/1965	10Aqu24	24Cap03	22Cap43	28Vir01						
						11/01/1965	08Sco52	28Sco59	25Sag23	20Sag25
02/04/1965	15Aqu28	01Aqu46	28Cap59	27Vir46		11/06/1965	13Sco52	05Sag33	00Cap43	24Sag09
02/09/1965	20Aqu33	09Aqu48	05Aqu14	27Vir11		11/11/1965	18Sco54	11Sag27	05Cap58	27Sag53
02/14/1965	25Aqu36	18Aqu10	11Aqu29	26Vir16		11/16/1965	23Sco56	16Sag12	11Cap03	01Cap39
02/19/1965	00Pis39	26Aqu54	17Aqu44	25Vir03		11/21/1965	28Sco58	18Sag52	15Cap59	05Cap27
02/24/1965	05Pis41	06Pis00	23Aqu58	23Vir33		11/26/1965	04Sag02	18Sag04	20Cap43	09Cap16
03/01/1965	10Pis43	15Pis27	00Pis14	21Vir49		12/01/1965	09Sag06	13Sag03	25Cap14	13Cap06
03/06/1965	15Pis43	25Pis05	06Pis28	19Vir55		12/06/1965	14Sag10	06Sag28	29Cap27	16Cap58
03/11/1965	20Pis43	04Ari27	12Pis42	17Vir57		12/11/1965	19Sag15	02Sag58	03Aqu18	20Cap51
03/16/1965	25Pis42	12Ari47	18Pis56	16Vir00		12/16/1965	24Sag20	03Sag49	06Aqu43	24Cap44
03/21/1965	00Ari40	19Ari08	25Pis09	14Vir10		12/21/1965	29Sag25	07Sag43	09Aqu36	28Cap38
03/26/1965	05Ari37	22Ari39	01Ari22	12Vir32		12/26/1965	04Cap31	13Sag18	11Aqu51	02Aqu33
03/31/1965	10Ari34	23Ari03	07Ari34	11Vir09		12/31/1965	09Cap37	19Sag46	13Aqu18	06Aqu29

Ephemeris Tables for Sun, Mercury, Venus and Mars

Date	Sun	Mercury	Venus	Mars
01/05/1966	14Cap43	26Sag44	13Aqu50	10Aqu25
01/10/1966	19Cap49	04Cap02	13Aqu22	14Aqu22
01/15/1966	24Cap54	11Cap33	11Aqu51	18Aqu19
01/20/1966	00Aqu00	19Cap18	09Aqu27	22Aqu15
01/25/1966	05Aqu04	27Cap17	06Aqu29	26Aqu13
01/30/1966	10Aqu10	05Aqu31	03Aqu27	00Pis10
02/04/1966	15Aqu14	14Aqu03	00Aqu50	04Pis07
02/09/1966	20Aqu18	22Aqu53	29Cap03	08Pis04
02/14/1966	25Aqu21	02Pis00	28Cap17	12Pis00
02/19/1966	00Pis25	11Pis12	28Cap31	15Pis55
02/24/1966	05Pis27	20Pis06	29Cap41	19Pis51
03/01/1966	10Pis28	27Pis55	01Aqu39	23Pis45
03/06/1966	15Pis29	03Ari27	04Aqu18	27Pis39
03/11/1966	20Pis28	05Ari43	07Aqu30	01Ari31
03/16/1966	25Pis28	04Ari25	11Aqu09	05Ari24
03/21/1966	00Ari25	00Ari34	15Aqu11	09Ari15
03/26/1966	05Ari23	26Pis13	19Aqu31	13Ari05
03/31/1966	10Ari20	23Pis23	24Aqu06	16Ari54
04/05/1966	15Ari15	22Pis50	28Aqu53	20Ari42
04/10/1966	20Ari10	24Pis28	03Pis50	24Ari28
04/15/1966	25Ari04	27Pis52	08Pis56	28Ari15
04/20/1966	29Ari58	02Ari16	14Pis09	01Tau59
04/25/1966	04Tau50	08Ari34	19Pis28	05Tau42
04/30/1966	09Tau42	15Ari24	24Pis53	09Tau24
05/05/1966	14Tau33	23Ari05	00Ari21	13Tau04
05/10/1966	19Tau23	01Tau34	05Ari54	16Tau44
05/15/1966	24Tau12	10Tau52	11Ari30	20Tau22
05/20/1966	29Tau01	20Tau57	17Ari09	23Tau58
05/25/1966	03Gem50	01Gem39	22Ari51	27Tau34
05/30/1966	08Gem37	12Gem37	28Ari34	01Gem08
06/04/1966	13Gem25	23Gem19	04Tau20	04Gem40
06/09/1966	18Gem12	03Can18	10Tau07	08Gem12
06/14/1966	22Gem59	12Can20	15Tau57	11Gem42
06/19/1966	27Gem45	20Can19	21Tau48	15Gem11
06/24/1966	02Can31	27Can13	27Tau40	18Gem39
06/29/1966	07Can18	02Leo57	03Gem34	22Gem05
07/04/1966	12Can04	07Leo24	09Gem29	25Gem30
07/09/1966	16Can49	10Leo18	15Gem25	28Gem54
07/14/1966	21Can36	11Leo25	21Gem22	02Can17
07/19/1966	26Can22	10Leo33	27Gem21	05Can38
07/24/1966	01Leo08	07Leo55	03Can21	08Can58
07/29/1966	05Leo55	04Leo21	09Can22	12Can18
08/03/1966	10Leo42	01Leo22	15Can24	15Can36
08/08/1966	15Leo29	00Leo21	21Can27	18Can53
08/13/1966	20Leo17	02Leo04	27Can32	22Can09
08/18/1966	25Leo06	06Leo39	03Leo37	25Can24
08/23/1966	29Leo54	13Leo41	09Leo44	28Can37
08/28/1966	04Vir44	22Leo28	15Leo52	01Leo49
09/02/1966	09Vir34	02Vir04	22Leo00	05Leo01
09/07/1966	14Vir25	11Vir48	28Leo10	08Leo11
09/12/1966	19Vir16	21Vir15	04Vir21	11Leo21
09/17/1966	24Vir09	00Lib17	10Vir33	14Leo28
09/22/1966	29Vir02	08Lib52	16Vir45	17Leo35
09/27/1966	03Lib56	17Lib04	22Vir58	20Leo41

Date	Sun	Mercury	Venus	Mars
10/02/1966	08Lib51	24Lib52	29Vir12	23Leo45
10/07/1966	13Lib46	02Sco20	05Lib25	26Leo48
10/12/1966	18Lib43	09Sco25	11Lib40	29Leo51
10/17/1966	23Lib40	16Sco06	17Lib55	02Vir51
10/22/1966	28Lib38	22Sco14	24Lib11	05Vir50
10/27/1966	03Sco37	27Sco33	00Sco27	08Vir47
11/01/1966	08Sco37	01Sag31	06Sco43	11Vir43
11/06/1966	13Sco37	03Sag15	13Sco00	14Vir37
11/11/1966	18Sco39	01Sag28	19Sco16	17Vir30
11/16/1966	23Sco41	25Sco56	25Sco33	20Vir20
11/21/1966	28Sco44	19Sco43	01Sag50	23Vir09
11/26/1966	03Sag47	17Sco07	08Sag07	25Vir55
12/01/1966	08Sag51	18Sco56	14Sag24	28Vir38
12/06/1966	13Sag55	23Sco37	20Sag41	01Lib19
12/11/1966	19Sag00	29Sco49	26Sag58	03Lib57
12/16/1966	24Sag05	06Sag45	03Cap15	06Lib32
12/21/1966	29Sag10	14Sag03	09Cap32	09Lib03
12/26/1966	04Cap16	21Sag33	15Cap49	11Lib30
12/31/1966	09Cap22	29Sag11	22Cap05	13Lib53
01/05/1967	14Cap28	06Cap58	28Cap22	16Lib12
01/10/1967	19Cap33	14Cap54	04Aqu38	18Lib25
01/15/1967	24Cap39	23Cap01	10Aqu54	20Lib31
01/20/1967	29Cap45	01Aqu20	17Aqu09	22Lib32
01/25/1967	04Aqu49	09Aqu53	23Aqu24	24Lib25
01/30/1967	09Aqu55	18Aqu37	29Aqu40	26Lib11
02/04/1967	14Aqu59	27Aqu22	05Pis54	27Lib47
02/09/1967	20Aqu03	05Pis47	12Pis07	29Lib13
02/14/1967	25Aqu07	12Pis59	18Pis20	00Sco28
02/19/1967	00Pis10	17Pis42	24Pis32	01Sco31
02/24/1967	05Pis12	18Pis40	00Ari42	02Sco20
03/01/1967	10Pis13	15Pis47	06Ari52	02Sco53
03/06/1967	15Pis15	10Pis48	13Ari01	03Sco10
03/11/1967	20Pis15	06Pis31	19Ari09	03Sco09
03/16/1967	25Pis13	04Pis37	25Ari15	02Sco49
03/21/1967	00Ari11	05Pis16	01Tau19	02Sco10
03/26/1967	05Ari09	08Pis01	07Tau23	01Sco12
03/31/1967	10Ari06	12Pis19	13Tau24	29Lib56
04/05/1967	15Ari01	17Pis46	19Tau24	28Lib24
04/10/1967	19Ari56	24Pis10	25Tau22	26Lib40
04/15/1967	24Ari50	01Ari21	01Gem18	24Lib49
04/20/1967	29Ari43	09Ari14	07Gem11	22Lib54
04/25/1967	04Tau36	17Ari50	13Gem02	21Lib04
04/30/1967	09Tau28	27Ari08	18Gem50	19Lib22
05/05/1967	14Tau18	07Tau08	24Gem35	17Lib53
05/10/1967	19Tau09	17Tau44	00Can17	16Lib40
05/15/1967	23Tau58	28Tau37	05Can55	15Lib47
05/20/1967	28Tau48	09Gem16	11Can30	15Lib13
05/25/1967	03Gem36	19Gem10	16Can59	15Lib00
05/30/1967	08Gem24	28Gem00	22Can24	15Lib06
06/04/1967	13Gem11	05Can36	27Can42	15Lib31
06/09/1967	17Gem58	11Can55	02Leo54	16Lib13
06/14/1967	22Gem45	16Can52	07Leo58	17Lib12
06/19/1967	27Gem31	20Can15	12Leo53	18Lib25
06/24/1967	02Can18	21Can52	17Leo37	19Lib51
06/29/1967	07Can04	21Can36	22Leo10	21Lib30

Ephemeris Tables for Sun, Mercury, Venus and Mars

Date	Sun	Mercury	Venus	Mars		Date	Sun	Mercury	Venus	Mars
07/04/1967	11Can50	19Can36	26Leo27	23Lib21		04/04/1968	14Ari47	25Pis43	24Pis35	05Tau31
07/09/1967	16Can36	16Can36	00Vir27	25Lib21		04/09/1968	19Ari42	04Ari19	00Ari44	09Tau10
07/14/1967	21Can22	13Can46	04Vir05	27Lib30		04/14/1968	24Ari36	13Ari34	06Ari53	12Tau48
07/19/1967	26Can08	12Can18	07Vir18	29Lib48		04/19/1968	29Ari29	23Ari26	13Ari03	16Tau24
07/24/1967	00Leo55	13Can01	10Vir00	02Sco13		04/24/1968	04Tau22	03Tau52	19Ari12	20Tau00
07/29/1967	05Leo41	16Can10	12Vir05	04Sco45		04/29/1968	09Tau13	14Tau35	25Ari21	23Tau34
08/03/1967	10Leo28	21Can40	13Vir25	07Sco24		05/04/1968	14Tau04	25Tau06	01Tau30	27Tau06
08/08/1967	15Leo15	29Can17	13Vir54	10Sco09		05/09/1968	18Tau55	04Gem49	07Tau38	00Gem38
08/13/1967	20Leo03	08Leo27	13Vir26	12Sco59		05/14/1968	23Tau45	13Gem21	13Tau47	04Gem09
08/18/1967	24Leo52	18Leo25	11Vir58	15Sco54		05/19/1968	28Tau34	20Gem25	19Tau55	07Gem38
08/23/1967	29Leo40	28Leo30	09Vir39	18Sco54		05/24/1968	03Gem22	25Gem55	26Tau04	11Gem06
08/28/1967	04Vir30	08Vir15	06Vir43	21Sco58		05/29/1968	08Gem10	29Gem45	02Gem12	14Gem33
09/02/1967	09Vir20	17Vir33	03Vir39	25Sco07		06/03/1968	12Gem57	01Can45	08Gem21	17Gem59
09/07/1967	14Vir11	26Vir18	00Vir53	28Sco20		06/08/1968	17Gem44	01Can50	14Gem29	21Gem24
09/12/1967	19Vir02	04Lib34	28Leo52	01Sag36		06/13/1968	22Gem31	00Can12	20Gem37	24Gem48
09/17/1967	23Vir54	12Lib23	27Leo48	04Sag56		06/18/1968	27Gem18	27Gem32	26Gem46	28Gem10
09/22/1967	28Vir48	19Lib45	27Leo44	08Sag19		06/23/1968	02Can04	24Gem53	02Can55	01Can33
09/27/1967	03Lib42	26Lib39	28Leo36	11Sag45		06/28/1968	06Can50	23Gem22	09Can03	04Can53
10/02/1967	08Lib36	03Sco01	00Vir18	15Sag13		07/03/1968	11Can36	23Gem41	15Can12	08Can13
10/07/1967	13Lib32	08Sco42	02Vir43	18Sag45		07/08/1968	16Can22	26Gem03	21Can21	11Can32
10/12/1967	18Lib28	13Sco23	05Vir45	22Sag19		07/13/1968	21Can08	00Can28	27Can30	14Can50
10/17/1967	23Lib25	16Sco31	09Vir15	25Sag55		07/18/1968	25Can54	06Can49	03Leo39	18Can07
10/22/1967	28Lib24	17Sco13	13Vir11	29Sag34		07/23/1968	00Leo40	14Can55	09Leo48	21Can24
10/27/1967	03Sco22	14Sco31	17Vir28	03Cap15		07/28/1968	05Leo27	24Can24	15Leo58	24Can40
11/01/1967	08Sco22	08Sco42	22Vir01	06Cap57		08/02/1968	10Leo15	04Leo40	22Leo07	27Can55
11/06/1967	13Sco23	03Sco07	26Vir50	10Cap42		08/07/1968	15Leo01	15Leo04	28Leo16	01Leo09
11/11/1967	18Sco24	01Sco30	01Lib50	14Cap28		08/12/1968	19Leo49	25Leo07	04Vir26	04Leo23
11/16/1967	23Sco27	04Sco13	07Lib01	18Cap15		08/17/1968	24Leo38	04Vir37	10Vir36	07Leo36
11/21/1967	28Sco29	09Sco39	12Lib21	22Cap04		08/22/1968	29Leo27	13Vir33	16Vir45	10Leo48
11/26/1967	03Sag33	16Sco26	17Lib48	25Cap54		08/27/1968	04Vir16	21Vir54	22Vir54	14Leo00
12/01/1967	08Sag36	23Sco49	23Lib21	29Cap44		09/01/1968	09Vir06	29Vir42	29Vir03	17Leo11
12/06/1967	13Sag40	01Sag26	29Lib01	03Aqu36		09/06/1968	13Vir57	06Lib57	05Lib12	20Leo22
12/11/1967	18Sag45	09Sag09	04Sco45	07Aqu28		09/11/1968	18Vir48	13Lib38	11Lib21	23Leo31
12/16/1967	23Sag51	16Sag55	10Sco33	11Aqu21		09/16/1968	23Vir40	19Lib39	17Lib30	26Leo41
12/21/1967	28Sag56	24Sag43	16Sco25	15Aqu15		09/21/1968	28Vir33	24Lib49	23Lib38	29Leo49
12/26/1967	04Cap01	02Cap37	22Sco19	19Aqu09		09/26/1968	03Lib27	28Lib48	29Lib46	02Vir58
12/31/1967	09Cap07	10Cap36	28Sco16	23Aqu03						
01/05/1968	14Cap13	18Cap44	04Sag16	26Aqu57		10/01/1968	08Lib22	01Sco01	05Sco54	06Vir06
01/10/1968	19Cap19	27Cap00	10Sag18	00Pis51		10/06/1968	13Lib18	00Sco42	12Sco01	09Vir13
01/15/1968	24Cap24	05Aqu21	16Sag21	04Pis45		10/11/1968	18Lib14	27Lib09	18Sco08	12Vir19
01/20/1968	29Cap30	13Aqu39	22Sag25	08Pis39		10/16/1968	23Lib11	21Lib19	24Sco15	15Vir25
01/25/1968	04Aqu35	21Aqu30	28Sag30	12Pis32		10/21/1968	28Lib09	16Lib37	00Sag21	18Vir31
01/30/1968	09Aqu40	28Aqu01	04Cap36	16Pis25		10/26/1968	03Sco09	16Lib02	06Sag27	21Vir35
						10/31/1968	08Sco08	19Lib36	12Sag32	24Vir39
02/04/1968	14Aqu44	01Pis51	10Cap43	20Pis17		11/05/1968	13Sco09	25Lib45	18Sag36	27Vir43
02/09/1968	19Aqu48	01Pis34	16Cap51	24Pis08		11/10/1968	18Sco10	03Sco06	24Sag40	00Lib46
02/14/1968	24Aqu52	27Aqu17	23Cap00	27Pis59		11/15/1968	23Sco12	10Sco55	00Cap43	03Lib48
02/19/1968	29Aqu55	21Aqu42	29Cap08	01Ari48		11/20/1968	28Sco14	18Sco52	06Cap45	06Lib48
02/24/1968	04Pis58	17Aqu57	05Aqu18	05Ari37		11/25/1968	03Sag18	26Sco48	12Cap46	09Lib49
02/29/1968	09Pis59	17Aqu10	11Aqu27	09Ari25		11/30/1968	08Sag22	04Sag41	18Cap46	12Lib48
03/05/1968	15Pis00	18Aqu57	17Aqu36	13Ari12		12/05/1968	13Sag25	12Sag33	24Cap43	15Lib46
03/10/1968	20Pis00	22Aqu36	23Aqu46	16Ari58		12/10/1968	18Sag30	20Sag24	00Aqu39	18Lib43
03/15/1968	24Pis59	27Aqu35	29Aqu56	20Ari43		12/15/1968	23Sag36	28Sag16	06Aqu33	21Lib40
03/20/1968	29Pis57	03Pis34	06Pis06	24Ari27		12/20/1968	28Sag41	06Cap13	12Aqu24	24Lib34
03/25/1968	04Ari54	10Pis18	12Pis15	28Ari09		12/25/1968	03Cap46	14Cap12	18Aqu12	27Lib28
03/30/1968	09Ari51	17Pis42	18Pis25	01Tau51		12/30/1968	08Cap52	22Cap10	23Aqu57	00Sco19

Ephemeris Tables for Sun, Mercury, Venus and Mars

Date	Sun	Mercury	Venus	Mars
01/04/1969	13Cap58	29Cap59	29Aqu37	03Sco10
01/09/1969	19Cap04	07Aqu13	05Pis13	05Sco58
01/14/1969	24Cap10	13Aqu03	10Pis42	08Sco44
01/19/1969	29Cap15	15Aqu57	16Pis04	11Sco28
01/24/1969	04Aqu20	14Aqu28	21Pis18	14Sco10
01/29/1969	09Aqu25	09Aqu06	26Pis22	16Sco49
02/03/1969	14Aqu30	03Aqu24	01Ari15	19Sco25
02/08/1969	19Aqu34	00Aqu28	05Ari54	21Sco57
02/13/1969	24Aqu37	00Aqu48	10Ari17	24Sco26
02/18/1969	29Aqu40	03Aqu33	14Ari19	26Sco51
02/23/1969	04Pis43	07Aqu58	17Ari58	29Sco11
02/28/1969	09Pis45	13Aqu31	21Ari09	01Sag27
03/05/1969	14Pis45	19Aqu52	23Ari44	03Sag36
03/10/1969	19Pis45	26Aqu51	25Ari37	05Sag39
03/15/1969	24Pis45	04Pis24	26Ari39	07Sag35
03/20/1969	29Pis43	12Pis27	26Ari45	09Sag23
03/25/1969	04Ari40	21Pis03	25Ari48	11Sag02
03/30/1969	09Ari37	00Ari10	23Ari54	12Sag31
04/04/1969	14Ari33	09Ari51	21Ari10	13Sag49
04/09/1969	19Ari28	20Ari03	18Ari05	14Sag55
04/14/1969	24Ari22	00Tau33	15Ari04	15Sag46
04/19/1969	29Ari15	10Tau51	12Ari37	16Sag22
04/24/1969	04Tau07	20Tau19	11Ari03	16Sag42
04/29/1969	09Tau00	28Tau24	10Ari30	16Sag43
05/04/1969	13Tau51	04Gem45	10Ari55	16Sag27
05/09/1969	18Tau41	09Gem11	12Ari14	15Sag51
05/14/1969	23Tau30	11Gem34	14Ari18	14Sag57
05/19/1969	28Tau19	11Gem54	17Ari00	13Sag45
05/24/1969	03Gem08	10Gem24	20Ari12	12Sag19
05/29/1969	07Gem55	07Gem47	23Ari50	10Sag43
06/03/1969	12Gem43	05Gem10	27Ari50	09Sag01
06/08/1969	17Gem30	03Gem36	02Tau07	07Sag20
06/13/1969	22Gem17	03Gem43	06Tau37	05Sag45
06/18/1969	27Gem04	05Gem45	11Tau21	04Sag21
06/23/1969	01Can50	09Gem34	16Tau14	03Sag12
06/28/1969	06Can36	15Gem04	21Tau16	02Sag21
07/03/1969	11Can22	22Gem07	26Tau25	01Sag51
07/08/1969	16Can08	00Can37	01Gem40	01Sag42
07/13/1969	20Can54	10Can21	07Gem02	01Sag53
07/18/1969	25Can40	20Can51	12Gem28	02Sag25
07/23/1969	00Leo27	01Leo29	17Gem58	03Sag16
07/28/1969	05Leo13	11Leo48	23Gem33	04Sag24
08/02/1969	10Leo00	21Leo31	29Gem11	05Sag48
08/07/1969	14Leo48	00Vir34	04Can52	07Sag27
08/12/1969	19Leo36	08Vir58	10Can36	09Sag20
08/17/1969	24Leo24	16Vir43	16Can24	11Sag24
08/22/1969	29Leo12	23Vir51	22Can13	13Sag40
08/27/1969	04Vir01	00Lib16	28Can06	16Sag05
09/01/1969	08Vir52	05Lib52	04Leo00	18Sag39
09/06/1969	13Vir43	10Lib27	09Leo57	21Sag21
09/11/1969	18Vir34	13Lib38	15Leo57	24Sag10
09/16/1969	23Vir26	14Lib51	21Leo58	27Sag07
09/21/1969	28Vir19	13Lib27	28Leo00	00Cap09
09/26/1969	03Lib13	09Lib16	04Vir05	03Cap16

Date	Sun	Mercury	Venus	Mars
10/01/1969	08Lib08	03Lib47	10Vir12	06Cap28
10/06/1969	13Lib03	00Lib10	16Vir19	09Cap44
10/11/1969	18Lib00	00Lib41	22Vir28	13Cap04
10/16/1969	22Lib57	05Lib04	28Vir39	16Cap28
10/21/1969	27Lib55	11Lib51	04Lib50	19Cap55
10/26/1969	02Sco54	19Lib45	11Lib03	23Cap25
10/31/1969	07Sco54	28Lib00	17Lib16	26Cap57
11/05/1969	12Sco54	06Sco16	23Lib30	00Aqu31
11/10/1969	17Sco55	14Sco27	29Lib45	04Aqu07
11/15/1969	22Sco57	22Sco28	06Sco01	07Aqu45
11/20/1969	28Sco00	00Sag24	12Sco17	11Aqu25
11/25/1969	03Sag03	08Sag13	18Sco33	15Aqu06
11/30/1969	08Sag07	16Sag00	24Sco50	18Aqu47
12/05/1969	13Sag11	23Sag45	01Sag07	22Aqu29
12/10/1969	18Sag16	01Cap27	07Sag24	26Aqu12
12/15/1969	23Sag21	09Cap03	13Sag42	29Aqu57
12/20/1969	28Sag27	16Cap22	19Sag59	03Pis40
12/25/1969	03Cap31	22Cap58	26Sag16	07Pis24
12/30/1969	08Cap37	28Cap01	02Cap34	11Pis08
01/04/1970	13Cap43	00Aqu00	08Cap52	14Pis52
01/09/1970	18Cap49	27Cap25	15Cap09	18Pis35
01/14/1970	23Cap55	21Cap18	21Cap27	22Pis18
01/19/1970	29Cap00	15Cap49	27Cap44	26Pis01
01/24/1970	04Aqu06	13Cap51	04Aqu01	29Pis43
01/29/1970	09Aqu10	15Cap14	10Aqu18	03Ari24
02/03/1970	14Aqu15	18Cap52	16Aqu34	07Ari05
02/08/1970	19Aqu19	23Cap57	22Aqu51	10Ari45
02/13/1970	24Aqu22	29Cap56	29Aqu07	14Ari24
02/18/1970	29Aqu26	06Aqu36	05Pis23	18Ari03
02/23/1970	04Pis28	13Aqu45	11Pis39	21Ari40
02/28/1970	09Pis30	21Aqu23	17Pis54	25Ari17
03/05/1970	14Pis31	29Aqu27	24Pis08	28Ari53
03/10/1970	19Pis31	07Pis58	00Ari21	02Tau27
03/15/1970	24Pis30	16Pis57	06Ari34	06Tau01
03/20/1970	29Pis28	26Pis25	12Ari46	09Tau34
03/25/1970	04Ari25	06Ari21	18Ari58	13Tau06
03/30/1970	09Ari22	16Ari32	25Ari10	16Tau36
04/04/1970	14Ari18	26Ari32	01Tau21	20Tau06
04/09/1970	19Ari13	05Tau40	07Tau30	23Tau34
04/14/1970	24Ari07	13Tau13	13Tau39	27Tau03
04/19/1970	29Ari01	18Tau39	19Tau47	00Gem29
04/24/1970	03Tau54	21Tau45	25Tau54	03Gem55
04/29/1970	08Tau45	22Tau26	02Gem01	07Gem19
05/04/1970	13Tau36	21Tau00	08Gem06	10Gem43
05/09/1970	18Tau27	18Tau12	14Gem10	14Gem06
05/14/1970	23Tau16	15Tau19	20Gem14	17Gem28
05/19/1970	28Tau06	13Tau30	26Gem16	20Gem49
05/24/1970	02Gem54	13Tau24	02Can18	24Gem10
05/29/1970	07Gem42	15Tau09	08Can18	27Gem29
06/03/1970	12Gem30	18Tau37	14Can16	00Can48
06/08/1970	17Gem17	23Tau36	20Can14	04Can06
06/13/1970	22Gem04	29Tau57	26Can10	07Can24
06/18/1970	26Gem50	07Gem34	02Leo04	10Can40
06/23/1970	01Can36	16Gem24	07Leo57	13Can56
06/28/1970	06Can22	26Gem19	13Leo48	17Can12

409

Ephemeris Tables for Sun, Mercury, Venus and Mars

Date	Sun	Mercury	Venus	Mars
07/03/1970	11Can09	06Can57	19Leo37	20Can27
07/08/1970	15Can54	17Can48	25Leo24	23Can41
07/13/1970	20Can40	28Can18	01Vir08	26Can55
07/18/1970	25Can27	08Leo11	06Vir49	00Leo09
07/23/1970	00Leo13	17Leo20	12Vir28	03Leo21
07/28/1970	05Leo00	25Leo44	18Vir03	06Leo34
08/02/1970	09Leo46	03Vir24	23Vir34	09Leo46
08/07/1970	14Leo34	10Vir19	29Vir00	12Leo58
08/12/1970	19Leo21	16Vir24	04Lib22	16Leo10
08/17/1970	24Leo10	21Vir30	09Lib39	19Leo22
08/22/1970	28Leo58	25Vir23	14Lib48	22Leo33
08/27/1970	03Vir48	27Vir39	19Lib51	25Leo44
09/01/1970	08Vir38	27Vir46	24Lib45	28Leo55
09/06/1970	13Vir28	25Vir22	29Lib28	02Vir06
09/11/1970	18Vir20	20Vir50	03Sco58	05Vir16
09/16/1970	23Vir12	16Vir06	08Sco15	08Vir27
09/21/1970	28Vir05	13Vir48	12Sco13	11Vir37
09/26/1970	02Lib59	15Vir24	15Sco50	14Vir48
10/01/1970	07Lib54	20Vir33	19Sco00	17Vir58
10/06/1970	12Lib49	27Vir57	21Sco39	21Vir09
10/11/1970	17Lib45	06Lib22	23Sco39	24Vir19
10/16/1970	22Lib42	15Lib03	24Sco52	27Vir29
10/21/1970	27Lib40	23Lib40	25Sco11	00Lib40
10/26/1970	02Sco39	02Sco04	24Sco32	03Lib50
10/31/1970	07Sco39	10Sco15	22Sco52	07Lib01
11/05/1970	12Sco40	18Sco15	20Sco25	10Lib11
11/10/1970	17Sco40	26Sco04	17Sco27	13Lib22
11/15/1970	22Sco43	03Sag45	14Sco29	16Lib32
11/20/1970	27Sco45	11Sag19	12Sco01	19Lib43
11/25/1970	02Sag48	18Sag44	10Sco24	22Lib54
11/30/1970	07Sag52	25Sag57	09Sco46	26Lib04
12/05/1970	12Sag56	02Cap45	10Sco10	29Lib15
12/10/1970	18Sag01	08Cap42	11Sco29	02Sco25
12/15/1970	23Sag06	12Cap56	13Sco36	05Sco36
12/20/1970	28Sag12	13Cap57	16Sco25	08Sco46
12/25/1970	03Cap17	10Cap23	19Sco45	11Sco56
12/30/1970	08Cap23	03Cap50	23Sco34	15Sco06
01/04/1971	13Cap28	28Sag53	27Sco45	18Sco16
01/09/1971	18Cap34	27Sag55	02Sag14	21Sco26
01/14/1971	23Cap40	00Cap16	06Sag58	24Sco36
01/19/1971	28Cap45	04Cap42	11Sag25	27Sco45
01/24/1971	03Aqu51	10Cap19	17Sag02	00Sag54
01/29/1971	08Aqu55	16Cap43	22Sag18	04Sag03
02/03/1971	14Aqu00	23Cap37	27Sag41	07Sag10
02/08/1971	19Aqu04	00Aqu57	03Cap10	10Sag18
02/13/1971	24Aqu08	08Aqu37	08Cap44	13Sag25
02/18/1971	29Aqu11	16Aqu39	14Cap22	16Sag32
02/23/1971	04Pis13	25Aqu04	20Cap04	19Sag37
02/28/1971	09Pis15	03Pis53	25Cap49	22Sag42
03/05/1971	14Pis16	13Pis07	01Aqu37	25Sag46
03/10/1971	19Pis16	22Pis44	07Aqu28	28Sag49
03/15/1971	24Pis16	02Ari34	13Aqu19	01Cap51
03/20/1971	29Pis14	12Ari13	19Aqu13	04Cap52
03/25/1971	04Ari11	20Ari55	25Aqu09	07Cap51
03/30/1971	09Ari08	27Ari49	01Pis06	10Cap48

Date	Sun	Mercury	Venus	Mars
04/04/1971	14Ari04	02Tau12	07Pis03	13Cap43
04/09/1971	18Ari59	03Tau45	13Pis01	16Cap36
04/14/1971	23Ari54	02Tau36	19Pis01	19Cap27
04/19/1971	28Ari46	29Ari35	25Pis01	22Cap15
04/24/1971	03Tau39	26Ari08	01Ari01	25Cap00
04/29/1971	08Tau31	23Ari45	07Ari02	27Cap42
05/04/1971	13Tau22	23Ari11	13Ari03	00Aqu19
05/09/1971	18Tau13	24Ari35	19Ari06	02Aqu51
05/14/1971	23Tau03	27Ari43	25Ari07	05Aqu19
05/19/1971	27Tau52	02Tau20	01Tau10	07Aqu40
05/24/1971	02Gem40	08Tau13	07Tau13	09Aqu55
05/29/1971	07Gem28	15Tau12	13Tau16	12Aqu03
06/03/1971	12Gem16	23Tau15	19Tau20	14Aqu01
06/08/1971	17Gem03	02Gem18	25Tau24	15Aqu49
06/13/1971	21Gem49	12Gem19	01Gem28	17Aqu26
06/18/1971	26Gem36	23Gem01	07Gem33	18Aqu51
06/23/1971	01Can22	03Can58	13Gem38	20Aqu01
06/28/1971	06Can09	14Can37	19Gem43	20Aqu56
07/03/1971	10Can54	24Can37	25Gem49	21Aqu34
07/08/1971	15Can40	03Leo49	01Can56	21Aqu54
07/13/1971	20Can27	12Leo09	08Can03	21Aqu55
07/18/1971	25Can13	19Leo39	14Can10	21Aqu36
07/23/1971	29Can59	26Leo16	20Can18	20Aqu59
07/28/1971	04Leo46	01Vir54	26Can27	20Aqu06
08/02/1971	09Leo33	06Vir21	02Leo36	18Aqu59
08/07/1971	14Leo20	09Vir22	08Leo46	17Aqu43
08/12/1971	19Leo07	10Vir33	14Leo56	16Aqu24
08/17/1971	23Leo56	09Vir33	21Leo07	15Aqu06
08/22/1971	28Leo45	06Vir21	27Leo18	13Aqu57
08/27/1971	03Vir34	01Vir57	03Vir30	13Aqu00
09/01/1971	08Vir24	28Leo19	09Vir42	12Aqu18
09/06/1971	13Vir15	27Leo28	15Vir54	11Aqu56
09/11/1971	18Vir06	00Vir12	22Vir06	11Aqu54
09/16/1971	22Vir58	06Vir04	28Vir19	12Aqu12
09/21/1971	27Vir51	14Vir01	04Lib33	12Aqu49
09/26/1971	02Lib45	22Vir55	10Lib46	13Aqu46
10/01/1971	07Lib39	02Lib01	17Lib00	14Aqu59
10/06/1971	12Lib34	10Lib58	23Lib13	16Aqu28
10/11/1971	17Lib31	19Lib37	29Lib27	18Aqu11
10/16/1971	22Lib28	27Lib59	05Sco41	20Aqu06
10/21/1971	27Lib26	06Sco03	11Sco55	22Aqu13
10/26/1971	02Sco25	13Sco52	18Sco09	24Aqu30
10/31/1971	07Sco24	21Sco28	24Sco22	26Aqu55
11/05/1971	12Sco25	28Sco51	00Sag36	29Aqu28
11/10/1971	17Sco26	06Sag00	06Sag50	02Pis08
11/15/1971	22Sco28	12Sag49	13Sag03	04Pis53
11/20/1971	27Sco30	19Sag06	19Sag17	07Pis43
11/25/1971	02Sag33	24Sag21	25Sag30	10Pis39
11/30/1971	07Sag37	27Sag43	01Cap43	13Pis37
12/05/1971	12Sag42	27Sag45	07Cap57	16Pis39
12/10/1971	17Sag46	23Sag22	14Cap10	19Pis44
12/15/1971	22Sag51	16Sag40	20Cap22	22Pis52
12/20/1971	27Sag57	12Sag25	26Cap34	26Pis01
12/25/1971	03Cap02	12Sag28	02Aqu45	29Pis12
12/30/1971	08Cap07	15Sag44	08Aqu56	02Ari25

Ephemeris Tables for Sun, Mercury, Venus and Mars

Date	Sun	Mercury	Venus	Mars		Date	Sun	Mercury	Venus	Mars
01/04/1972	13Cap13	20Sag51	15Aqu06	05Ari39		10/05/1972	12Lib20	23Lib46	00Vir10	02Lib55
01/09/1972	18Cap19	27Sag00	21Aqu15	08Ari54		10/10/1972	17Lib16	01Sco36	05Vir55	06Lib10
01/14/1972	23Cap25	03Cap45	27Aqu24	12Ari10		10/15/1972	22Lib13	09Sco07	11Vir44	09Lib24
01/19/1972	28Cap31	10Cap54	03Pis31	15Ari27		10/20/1972	27Lib12	16Sco20	17Vir37	12Lib39
01/24/1972	03Aqu36	18Cap20	09Pis37	18Ari44		10/25/1972	02Sco10	23Sco12	23Vir33	15Lib55
01/29/1972	08Aqu41	26Cap03	15Pis40	22Ari01		10/30/1972	07Sco10	29Sco37	29Vir31	19Lib12
02/03/1972	13Aqu45	04Aqu03	21Pis43	25Ari19		11/04/1972	12Sco10	05Sag20	05Lib32	22Lib28
02/08/1972	18Aqu49	12Aqu21	27Pis43	28Ari37		11/09/1972	17Sco11	09Sag52	11Lib35	25Lib45
02/13/1972	23Aqu53	20Aqu58	03Ari39	01Tau55		11/14/1972	22Sco13	12Sag18	17Lib40	29Lib03
02/18/1972	28Aqu57	29Aqu57	09Ari34	05Tau13		11/19/1972	27Sco16	11Sag21	23Lib48	02Sco22
02/23/1972	03Pis59	09Pis13	15Ari26	08Tau31		11/24/1972	02Sag19	06Sag18	29Lib55	05Sco41
02/28/1972	09Pis01	18Pis41	21Ari15	11Tau49		11/29/1972	07Sag22	29Sco45	06Sco05	09Sco01
03/04/1972	14Pis01	27Pis54	26Ari59	15Tau07		12/04/1972	12Sag27	26Sco21	12Sco16	12Sco21
03/09/1972	19Pis01	06Ari06	02Tau39	18Tau24		12/09/1972	17Sag31	27Sco22	18Sco28	15Sco42
03/14/1972	24Pis01	12Ari16	08Tau15	21Tau42		12/14/1972	22Sag36	01Sag28	24Sco41	19Sco04
03/19/1972	29Pis00	15Ari29	13Tau45	24Tau58		12/19/1972	27Sag42	07Sag15	00Sag54	22Sco26
03/24/1972	03Ari57	15Ari21	19Tau08	28Tau15		12/24/1972	02Cap47	13Sag52	07Sag08	25Sco49
03/29/1972	08Ari54	12Ari28	24Tau24	01Gem31		12/29/1972	07Cap53	20Sag58	13Sag22	29Sco12
04/03/1972	13Ari49	08Ari24	29Tau32	04Gem46		01/03/1973	12Cap59	28Sag20	19Sag37	02Sag36
04/08/1972	18Ari45	05Ari04	04Gem31	08Gem01		01/08/1973	18Cap04	05Cap54	25Sag52	06Sag01
04/13/1972	23Ari39	03Ari42	09Gem17	11Gem16		01/13/1973	23Cap10	13Cap39	02Cap07	09Sag26
04/18/1972	28Ari33	04Ari28	13Gem51	14Gem30		01/18/1973	28Cap16	21Cap36	08Cap22	12Sag52
04/23/1972	03Tau25	07Ari09	18Gem08	17Gem45		01/23/1973	03Aqu21	29Cap46	14Cap38	16Sag19
04/28/1972	08Tau17	11Ari22	22Gem07	20Gem58		01/28/1973	08Aqu26	08Aqu12	20Cap53	19Sag46
05/03/1972	13Tau08	16Ari51	25Gem43	24Gem11		02/02/1973	13Aqu30	16Aqu53	27Cap09	23Sag13
05/08/1972	17Tau59	23Ari21	28Gem51	27Gem24		02/07/1973	18Aqu34	25Aqu49	03Aqu24	26Sag42
05/13/1972	22Tau49	00Tau48	01Can26	00Can36		02/12/1973	23Aqu38	04Pis51	09Aqu39	00Cap10
05/18/1972	27Tau37	09Tau07	03Can21	03Can48		02/17/1973	28Aqu42	13Pis36	15Aqu54	03Cap40
05/23/1972	02Gem26	18Tau19	04Can28	07Can00		02/22/1973	03Pis44	21Pis15	22Aqu09	07Cap10
05/28/1972	07Gem14	28Tau22	04Can42	10Can12		02/27/1973	08Pis46	26Pis38	28Aqu24	10Cap40
06/02/1972	12Gem02	09Gem05	03Can56	13Can23		03/04/1973	13Pis47	28Pis36	04Pis39	14Cap11
06/07/1972	16Gem49	20Gem04	02Can11	16Can34		03/09/1973	18Pis47	26Pis48	10Pis53	17Cap43
06/12/1972	21Gem36	00Can48	29Gem37	19Can45		03/14/1973	23Pis46	22Pis29	17Pis07	21Cap15
06/17/1972	26Gem22	10Can50	26Gem34	22Can55		03/19/1973	28Pis45	18Pis02	23Pis21	24Cap46
06/22/1972	01Can09	19Can59	23Gem31	26Can05		03/24/1973	03Ari42	15Pis24	29Pis34	28Cap19
06/27/1972	05Can55	28Can10	20Gem55	29Can15		03/29/1973	08Ari39	15Pis14	05Ari46	01Aqu52
07/02/1972	10Can40	05Leo23	19Gem06	02Leo25		04/03/1973	13Ari36	17Pis14	11Ari59	05Aqu25
07/07/1972	15Can27	11Leo33	18Gem16	05Leo35		04/08/1973	18Ari30	20Pis57	18Ari11	08Aqu58
07/12/1972	20Can13	16Leo33	18Gem25	08Leo45		04/13/1973	23Ari25	26Pis00	24Ari22	12Aqu31
07/17/1972	24Can59	20Leo09	19Gem27	11Leo55		04/18/1973	28Ari18	02Ari03	00Tau34	16Aqu04
07/22/1972	29Can45	22Leo06	21Gem17	15Leo05		04/23/1973	03Tau11	09Ari00	06Tau45	19Aqu37
07/27/1972	04Leo32	22Leo04	23Gem46	18Leo15		04/28/1973	08Tau03	16Ari45	12Tau55	23Aqu09
08/01/1972	09Leo19	20Leo00	26Gem49	21Leo25		05/03/1973	12Tau54	25Ari15	19Tau05	26Aqu42
08/06/1972	14Leo06	16Leo25	00Can19	24Leo35		05/08/1973	17Tau45	04Tau30	25Tau15	00Pis14
08/11/1972	18Leo54	12Leo42	04Can12	27Leo45		05/13/1973	22Tau34	14Tau31	01Gem24	03Pis45
08/16/1972	23Leo42	10Leo34	08Can24	00Vir55		05/18/1973	27Tau24	25Tau09	07Gem33	07Pis15
08/21/1972	28Leo30	11Leo15	12Can51	04Vir06		05/23/1973	02Gem12	06Gem06	13Gem42	10Pis45
08/26/1972	03Vir20	15Leo03	17Can32	07Vir17		05/28/1973	07Gem00	16Gem49	19Gem49	14Pis13
08/31/1972	08Vir10	21Leo36	22Can24	10Vir28						
						06/02/1973	11Gem48	26Gem49	25Gem57	17Pis39
09/05/1972	13Vir00	00Vir02	27Can27	13Vir39		06/07/1973	16Gem35	05Can51	02Can04	21Pis04
09/10/1972	17Vir52	09Vir23	02Leo37	16Vir51		06/12/1973	21Gem22	13Can45	08Can12	24Pis27
09/15/1972	22Vir44	18Vir54	07Leo56	20Vir03		06/17/1973	26Gem08	20Can31	14Can18	27Pis47
09/20/1972	27Vir37	28Vir10	13Leo21	23Vir16		06/22/1973	00Can55	26Can02	20Can24	01Ari04
09/25/1972	02Lib30	07Lib06	18Leo52	26Vir28		06/27/1973	05Can41	00Leo09	26Can30	04Ari18
09/30/1972	07Lib25	15Lib37	24Leo28	29Vir42						

Ephemeris Tables for Sun, Mercury, Venus and Mars

Date	Sun	Mercury	Venus	Mars		Date	Sun	Mercury	Venus	Mars
07/02/1973	10Can27	02Leo39	02Leo36	07Ari28		04/03/1974	13Ari21	17Pis52	26Aqu56	20Gem03
07/07/1973	15Can13	03Leo19	08Leo40	10Ari35		04/08/1974	18Ari16	25Pis07	01Pis55	22Gem59
07/12/1973	19Can59	02Leo04	14Leo45	13Ari37		04/13/1974	23Ari10	03Ari01	07Pis02	25Gem56
07/17/1973	24Can45	29Can15	20Leo49	16Ari34		04/18/1974	28Ari04	11Ari36	12Pis16	28Gem54
07/22/1973	29Can31	25Can54	26Leo52	19Ari24		04/23/1974	02Tau57	20Ari50	17Pis36	01Can53
07/27/1973	04Leo18	23Can25	02Vir54	22Ari08		04/28/1974	07Tau49	00Tau45	23Pis01	04Can52
08/01/1973	09Leo05	22Can58	08Vir57	24Ari45		05/03/1974	12Tau40	11Tau15	28Pis31	07Can52
08/06/1973	13Leo52	25Can09	14Vir57	27Ari12		05/08/1974	17Tau31	22Tau04	04Ari04	10Can52
08/11/1973	18Leo40	29Can58	20Vir58	29Ari30		05/13/1974	22Tau21	02Gem42	09Ari40	13Can53
08/16/1973	23Leo28	07Leo09	26Vir57	01Tau37		05/18/1974	27Tau10	12Gem37	15Ari20	16Can54
08/21/1973	28Leo16	16Leo01	02Lib55	03Tau32		05/23/1974	01Gem58	21Gem23	21Ari01	19Can56
08/26/1973	03Vir06	25Leo45	08Lib52	05Tau13		05/28/1974	06Gem46	28Gem52	26Ari46	22Can58
08/31/1973	07Vir55	05Vir39	14Lib49	06Tau39		06/02/1974	11Gem34	04Can58	02Tau32	26Can01
09/05/1973	12Vir46	15Vir15	20Lib43	07Tau47		06/07/1974	16Gem21	09Can34	08Tau20	29Can04
09/10/1973	17Vir37	24Vir25	26Lib37	08Tau37		06/12/1974	21Gem08	12Can31	14Tau09	02Leo07
09/15/1973	22Vir30	03Lib07	02Sco29	09Tau07		06/17/1974	25Gem55	13Can38	20Tau01	05Leo10
09/20/1973	27Vir22	11Lib22	08Sco19	09Tau15		06/22/1974	00Can41	12Can52	25Tau53	08Leo15
09/25/1973	02Lib16	19Lib13	14Sco07	09Tau01		06/27/1974	05Can27	10Can36	01Gem47	11Leo19
09/30/1973	07Lib11	26Lib39	19Sco54	8Tau26		07/02/1974	10Can13	07Can37	07Gem42	14Leo24
10/05/1973	12Lib06	03Sco41	25Sco37	07Tau30		07/07/1974	14Can59	05Can13	13Gem38	17Leo30
10/10/1973	17Lib02	10Sco16	01Sag18	06Tau15		07/12/1974	19Can45	04Can23	19Gem36	20Leo36
10/15/1973	21Lib59	16Sco15	06Sag57	04Tau46		07/17/1974	24Can31	05Can42	25Gem34	23Leo42
10/20/1973	26Lib57	21Sco22	12Sag31	03Tau08		07/22/1974	29Can18	09Can16	01Can34	26Leo49
10/25/1973	01Sco55	25Sco07	18Sag01	01Tau27		07/27/1974	04Leo04	15Can01	07Can35	29Leo57
10/30/1973	06Sco55	26Sco36	23Sag27	29Ari50		08/01/1974	08Leo51	22Can43	13Can37	03Vir04
11/04/1973	11Sco55	24Sco39	28Sag47	28Ari22		08/06/1974	13Leo38	01Leo58	19Can40	06Vir13
11/09/1973	16Sco57	19Sco07	04Cap00	27Ari08		08/11/1974	18Leo26	12Leo02	24Can45	09Vir22
11/14/1973	21Sco58	13Sco01	09Cap04	26Ari12		08/16/1974	23Leo14	22Leo16	01Leo50	12Vir32
11/19/1973	27Sco01	10Sco33	13Cap59	25Ari35		08/21/1974	28Leo03	02Vir11	07Leo57	15Vir42
11/24/1973	02Sag04	12Sco31	18Cap42	25Ari19		08/26/1974	02Vir52	11Vir36	14Leo04	18Vir54
11/29/1973	07Sag08	17Sco24	23Cap10	25Ari23		08/31/1974	07Vir42	20Vir28	20Leo13	22Vir05
12/04/1973	12Sag12	23Sco47	27Cap21	25Ari46		09/05/1974	12Vir32	28Vir48	26Leo22	25Vir18
12/09/1973	17Sag16	00Sag53	01Aqu10	26Ari28		09/10/1974	17Vir24	06Lib39	02Vir33	28Vir31
12/14/1973	22Sag22	08Sag18	04Aqu33	27Ari25		09/15/1974	22Vir16	14Lib00	08Vir44	01Lib45
12/19/1973	27Sag27	15Sag53	07Aqu22	28Ari37		09/20/1974	27Vir08	20Lib51	14Vir56	05Lib00
12/24/1973	02Cap33	23Sag34	09Aqu33	00Tau03		09/25/1974	02Lib02	27Lib06	21Vir09	08Lib15
12/29/1973	07Cap38	01Cap21	10Aqu55	01Tau40		09/30/1974	06Lib57	02Sco38	27Vir23	11Lib31
01/03/1974	12Cap44	09Cap16	11Aqu22	03Tau27		10/05/1974	11Lib52	07Sco06	03Lib37	14Lib49
01/08/1974	17Cap49	17Cap19	10Aqu48	05Tau24		10/10/1974	16Lib48	09Sco59	09Lib51	18Lib07
01/13/1974	22Cap55	25Cap33	09Aqu12	07Tau28		10/15/1974	21Lib45	10Sco27	16Lib07	21Lib26
01/18/1974	28Cap01	03Aqu57	06Aqu43	09Tau40		10/20/1974	26Lib43	07Sco34	22Lib22	24Lib46
01/23/1974	03Aqu06	12Aqu31	03Aqu45	11Tau58		10/25/1974	01Sco42	01Sco49	28Lib38	28Lib07
01/28/1974	08Aqu11	21Aqu06	00Aqu44	14Tau21		10/30/1974	06Sco41	26Lib25	04Sco54	01Sco29
02/02/1974	13Aqu16	29Aqu19	28Cap13	16Tau49		11/04/1974	11Sco41	24Lib57	11Sco10	04Sco52
02/07/1974	18Aqu19	06Pis21	26Cap30	19Tau21		11/09/1974	16Sco42	27Lib48	17Sco27	08Sco16
02/12/1974	23Aqu24	10Pis54	25Cap50	21Tau57		11/14/1974	21Sco44	03Sco25	23Sco43	11Sco41
02/17/1974	28Aqu27	11Pis36	26Cap09	24Tau36		11/19/1974	26Sco46	10Sco24	00Sag00	15Sco07
02/22/1974	03Pis30	08Pis17	27Cap24	27Tau18		11/24/1974	01Sag49	17Sco57	06Sag17	18Sco33
02/27/1974	08Pis31	03Pis00	29Cap27	00Gem03		11/29/1974	06Sag53	25Sco42	12Sag34	22Sco01
03/04/1974	13Pis33	28Aqu46	02Aqu10	02Gem49		12/04/1974	11Sag57	03Sag30	18Sag51	25Sco30
03/09/1974	18Pis33	27Aqu09	05Aqu25	05Gem37		12/09/1974	17Sag02	11Sag19	25Sag08	29Sco00
03/14/1974	23Pis32	28Aqu10	09Aqu06	08Gem28		12/14/1974	22Sag07	19Sag09	01Cap25	02Sag31
03/19/1974	28Pis31	01Pis12	13Aqu10	11Gem20		12/19/1974	27Sag12	27Sag01	07Cap42	06Sag03
03/24/1974	03Ari28	05Pis44	17Aqu32	14Gem13		12/24/1974	02Cap18	04Cap57	13Cap58	09Sag36
03/29/1974	08Ari25	11Pis22	22Aqu08	17Gem07		12/29/1974	07Cap23	12Cap59	20Cap15	13Sag10

Ephemeris Tables for Sun, Mercury, Venus and Mars

Date	Sun	Mercury	Venus	Mars
01/03/1975	12Cap29	21Cap07	26Cap31	16Sag45
01/08/1975	17Cap35	29Cap19	02Aqu48	20Sag21
01/13/1975	22Cap40	07Aqu26	09Aqu03	23Sag58
01/18/1975	27Cap46	15Aqu04	15Aqu19	27Sag36
01/23/1975	02Aqu51	21Aqu25	21Aqu34	01Cap15
01/28/1975	07Aqu57	25Aqu06	27Aqu49	04Cap55
02/02/1975	13Aqu01	24Aqu34	04Pis04	08Cap36
02/07/1975	18Aqu05	19Aqu58	10Pis17	12Cap18
02/12/1975	23Aqu09	14Aqu14	16Pis30	16Cap00
02/17/1975	28Aqu12	10Aqu37	22Pis42	19Cap43
02/22/1975	03Pis15	10Aqu07	28Pis53	23Cap28
02/27/1975	08Pis16	12Aqu12	05Ari03	27Cap12
03/04/1975	13Pis18	16Aqu06	11Ari12	00Aqu58
03/09/1975	18Pis18	21Aqu16	17Ari19	04Aqu44
03/14/1975	23Pis18	27Aqu22	23Ari25	08Aqu30
03/19/1975	28Pis16	04Pis11	29Ari30	12Aqu18
03/24/1975	03Ari13	11Pis37	05Tau34	16Aqu05
03/29/1975	08Ari10	19Pis37	11Tau36	19Aqu53
04/03/1975	13Ari07	28Pis12	17Tau36	23Aqu41
04/08/1975	18Ari02	07Ari21	23Tau33	27Aqu30
04/13/1975	22Ari56	17Ari07	29Tau29	01Pis19
04/18/1975	27Ari50	27Ari25	05Gem22	05Pis07
04/23/1975	02Tau43	08Tau03	11Gem13	08Pis55
04/28/1975	07Tau34	18Tau31	17Gem01	12Pis44
05/03/1975	12Tau26	28Tau12	22Gem47	16Pis32
05/08/1975	17Tau16	06Gem38	28Gem28	20Pis19
05/13/1975	22Tau06	13Gem31	04Can07	24Pis06
05/18/1975	26Tau55	18Gem43	09Can41	27Pis52
05/23/1975	01Gem45	22Gem06	15Can10	01Ari37
05/28/1975	06Gem33	23Gem32	20Can34	05Ari22
06/02/1975	11Gem20	23Gem03	25Can52	09Ari06
06/07/1975	16Gem07	21Gem01	01Leo04	12Ari48
06/12/1975	20Gem54	18Gem16	06Leo07	16Ari30
06/17/1975	25Gem40	15Gem56	11Leo02	20Ari09
06/22/1975	00Can27	15Gem00	15Leo46	23Ari47
06/27/1975	05Can13	15Gem56	20Leo17	27Ari23
07/02/1975	09Can59	18Gem49	24Leo33	00Tau57
07/07/1975	14Can45	23Gem37	28Leo31	04Tau29
07/12/1975	19Can31	00Can11	02Vir09	07Tau59
07/17/1975	24Can18	08Can22	05Vir19	11Tau26
07/22/1975	29Can04	17Can54	07Vir59	14Tau50
07/27/1975	03Leo50	28Can15	10Vir00	18Tau12
08/01/1975	08Leo37	08Leo45	11Vir17	21Tau29
08/06/1975	13Leo24	18Leo57	11Vir42	24Tau43
08/11/1975	18Leo12	28Leo36	11Vir08	27Tau54
08/16/1975	23Leo00	07Vir37	09Vir37	01Gem00
08/21/1975	27Leo49	16Vir01	07Vir13	04Gem02
08/26/1975	02Vir38	23Vir51	04Vir17	06Gem58
08/31/1975	07Vir27	01Lib05	01Vir12	09Gem50
09/05/1975	12Vir18	07Lib42	28Leo31	12Gem35
09/10/1975	17Vir09	13Lib36	26Leo32	15Gem14
09/15/1975	22Vir01	18Lib36	25Leo33	17Gem45
09/20/1975	26Vir54	22Lib21	25Leo32	20Gem09
09/25/1975	01Lib48	24Lib18	26Leo28	22Gem23
09/30/1975	06Lib42	23Lib41	28Leo13	24Gem28

Date	Sun	Mercury	Venus	Mars
10/05/1975	11Lib37	20Lib01	00Vir41	26Gem21
10/10/1975	16Lib33	14Lib20	03Vir44	28Gem03
10/15/1975	21Lib30	09Lib52	07Vir16	29Gem31
10/20/1975	26Lib28	09Lib28	11Vir13	0Can44
10/25/1975	01Sco27	13Lib10	15Vir31	01Can41
10/30/1975	06Sco26	19Lib29	20Vir05	02Can19
11/04/1975	11Sco27	27Lib02	24Vir54	02Can38
11/09/1975	16Sco27	05Sco01	29Vir55	02Can36
11/14/1975	21Sco29	13Sco07	05Lib06	02Can12
11/19/1975	26Sco31	21Sco09	10Lib26	01Can27
11/24/1975	01Sag34	29Sco06	15Lib54	00Can20
11/29/1975	06Sag38	06Sag59	21Lib27	28Gem54
12/04/1975	11Sag42	14Sag49	27Lib07	27Gem13
12/09/1975	16Sag47	22Sag40	02Sco51	25Gem21
12/14/1975	21Sag52	00Cap31	08Sco39	23Gem24
12/19/1975	26Sag57	08Cap22	14Sco31	21Gem28
12/24/1975	02Cap03	16Cap12	20Sco26	19Gem40
12/29/1975	07Cap09	23Cap49	26Sco24	18Gem04
01/03/1976	12Cap14	00Aqu52	02Sag24	16Gem45
01/08/1976	17Cap20	06Aqu29	08Sag25	15Gem45
01/13/1976	22Cap25	09Aqu14	14Sag28	15Gem05
01/18/1976	27Cap31	07Aqu34	20Sag33	14Gem46
01/23/1976	02Aqu37	01Aqu59	26Sag38	14Gem46
01/28/1976	07Aqu42	26Cap12	02Cap45	15Gem06
02/02/1976	12Aqu46	23Cap28	08Cap52	15Gem41
02/07/1976	17Aqu51	24Cap03	15Cap00	16Gem33
02/12/1976	22Aqu54	27Cap05	21Cap09	17Gem39
02/17/1976	27Aqu58	01Aqu43	27Cap18	18Gem57
02/22/1976	03Pis00	07Aqu24	03Aqu27	20Gem25
02/27/1976	08Pis02	13Aqu51	09Aqu36	22Gem05
03/03/1976	13Pis03	20Aqu53	15Aqu46	23Gem52
03/08/1976	18Pis03	28Aqu26	21Aqu56	25Gem48
03/13/1976	23Pis03	06Pis28	28Aqu07	27Gem50
03/18/1976	28Pis02	15Pis00	04Pis16	29Gem58
03/23/1976	02Ari59	24Pis03	10Pis27	02Can12
03/28/1976	07Ari56	03Ari37	16Pis36	04Can31
04/02/1976	12Ari52	13Ari40	22Pis46	06Can54
04/07/1976	17Ari48	24Ari02	28Pis56	09Can21
04/12/1976	22Ari42	04Tau15	05Ari05	11Can51
04/17/1976	27Ari36	13Tau40	11Ari15	14Can24
04/22/1976	02Tau28	21Tau37	17Ari24	17Can00
04/27/1976	07Tau21	27Tau45	23Ari33	19Can39
05/02/1976	12Tau12	01Gem46	29Ari42	22Can20
05/07/1976	17Tau03	03Gem36	05Tau51	25Can03
05/12/1976	21Tau52	03Gem18	12Tau00	27Can48
05/17/1976	26Tau42	01Gem15	18Tau09	00Leo35
05/22/1976	01Gem30	28Tau27	24Tau17	03Leo24
05/27/1976	06Gem18	26Tau01	00Gem25	06Leo13
06/01/1976	11Gem06	24Tau57	06Gem34	09Leo05
06/06/1976	15Gem54	25Tau40	12Gem42	11Leo58
06/11/1976	20Gem40	28Tau14	18Gem51	14Leo52
06/16/1976	25Gem27	02Gem30	25Gem00	17Leo48
06/21/1976	00Can13	08Gem17	01Can08	20Leo45
06/26/1976	05Can00	15Gem31	07Can16	23Leo43

Ephemeris Tables for Sun, Mercury, Venus and Mars

Date	Sun	Mercury	Venus	Mars
07/01/1976	09Can45	24Gem05	13Can25	26Leo43
07/06/1976	14Can31	03Can50	19Can34	29Leo43
07/11/1976	19Can17	14Can22	25Can43	02Vir45
07/16/1976	24Can04	25Can07	01Leo52	05Vir47
07/21/1976	28Can50	05Leo33	08Leo01	08Vir51
07/26/1976	03Leo36	15Leo22	14Leo10	11Vir55
07/31/1976	08Leo23	24Leo31	20Leo20	15Vir01
08/05/1976	13Leo10	02Vir58	26Leo29	18Vir09
08/10/1976	17Leo58	10Vir45	02Vir39	21Vir17
08/15/1976	22Leo46	17Vir49	08Vir48	24Vir26
08/20/1976	27Leo34	24Vir10	14Vir57	27Vir37
08/25/1976	02Vir24	29Vir38	21Vir06	00Lib48
08/30/1976	07Vir13	04Lib01	27Vir15	04Lib01
10/04/1976	11Lib23	24Vir05	10Sco12	27Lib04
10/09/1976	16Lib19	28Vir37	16Sco18	00Sco27
10/14/1976	21Lib16	05Lib34	22Sco25	03Sco50
10/19/1976	26Lib13	13Lib39	28Sco31	07Sco15
10/24/1976	01Sco12	22Lib04	04Sag36	10Sco42
10/29/1976	06Sco12	00Sco30	10Sag41	14Sco09
11/03/1976	11Sco12	08Sco46	16Sag45	17Sco39
11/08/1976	16Sco13	16Sco53	22Sag49	21Sco09
11/13/1976	21Sco15	24Sco50	28Sag51	24Sco40
11/18/1976	26Sco17	02Sag40	04Cap53	28Sco13
11/23/1976	01Sag20	10Sag24	10Cap54	01Sag48
11/28/1976	06Sag24	18Sag04	16Cap53	05Sag23
12/03/1976	11Sag27	25Sag40	22Cap51	09Sag00
12/08/1976	16Sag32	03Cap07	28Cap46	12Sag37
12/13/1976	21Sag37	10Cap15	04Aqu40	16Sag17
12/18/1976	26Sag42	16Cap39	10Aqu31	19Sag57
12/23/1976	01Cap48	21Cap30	16Aqu18	23Sag39
12/28/1976	06Cap54	23Cap18	22Aqu03	27Sag22
01/02/1977	11Cap59	20Cap35	27Aqu43	01Cap06
01/07/1977	17Cap05	14Cap20	03Pis18	04Cap51
01/12/1977	22Cap10	08Cap52	08Pis46	08Cap37
01/17/1977	27Cap16	07Cap06	14Pis08	12Cap24
01/22/1977	02Aqu22	08Cap43	19Pis22	16Cap12
01/27/1977	07Aqu27	12Cap36	24Pis25	20Cap01
02/01/1977	12Aqu31	17Cap51	29Pis18	23Cap51
02/06/1977	17Aqu36	23Cap58	03Ari55	27Cap41
02/11/1977	22Aqu39	00Aqu42	08Ari18	01Aqu33
02/16/1977	27Aqu43	07Aqu55	12Ari19	05Aqu24
02/21/1977	02Pis46	15Aqu32	15Ari57	09Aqu17
02/26/1977	07Pis48	23Aqu33	19Ari05	13Aqu10
03/03/1977	12Pis49	02Pis01	21Ari37	17Aqu03
03/08/1977	17Pis49	10Pis54	23Ari27	20Aqu57
03/13/1977	22Pis49	20Pis15	24Ari26	24Aqu51
03/18/1977	27Pis47	00Ari01	24Ari26	28Aqu46
03/23/1977	02Ari45	10Ari03	23Ari27	02Pis40
03/28/1977	07Ari42	19Ari57	21Ari28	06Pis34
09/04/1976	12Vir04	06Lib55	03Lib24	07Lib15
09/09/1976	16Vir55	07Lib50	09Lib32	10Lib30
09/14/1976	21Vir47	06Lib10	15Lib41	13Lib46
09/19/1976	26Vir40	01Lib55	21Lib49	17Lib04
09/24/1976	01Lib34	26Vir40	27Lib57	20Lib22
09/29/1976	06Lib28	23Vir23	04Sco04	23Lib43

Date	Sun	Mercury	Venus	Mars
04/02/1977	12Ari38	29Ari00	18Ari43	10Pis28
04/07/1977	17Ari33	06Tau24	15Ari34	14Pis22
04/12/1977	22Ari28	11Tau34	12Ari36	18Pis15
04/17/1977	27Ari21	14Tau10	10Ari13	22Pis09
04/22/1977	02Tau15	14Tau15	08Ari44	26Pis01
04/27/1977	07Tau06	12Tau10	08Ari15	29Pis54
05/02/1977	11Tau58	09Tau03	08Ari45	03Ari44
05/07/1977	16Tau49	06Tau13	10Ari07	07Ari35
05/12/1977	21Tau39	04Tau48	12Ari14	11Ari24
05/17/1977	26Tau28	05Tau13	14Ari58	15Ari13
05/22/1977	01Gem16	07Tau30	18Ari14	19Ari01
05/27/1977	06Gem04	11Tau24	21Ari54	22Ari48
06/01/1977	10Gem52	16Tau43	25Ari55	26Ari33
06/06/1977	15Gem39	23Tau17	00Tau13	00Tau17
06/11/1977	20Gem27	01Gem02	04Tau45	04Tau00
06/16/1977	25Gem13	09Gem54	09Tau30	07Tau41
06/21/1977	29Gem59	19Gem48	14Tau24	11Tau21
06/26/1977	04Can45	00Can27	19Tau26	14Tau58
07/01/1977	09Can31	11Can21	24Tau36	18Tau35
07/06/1977	14Can18	21Can58	29Tau52	22Tau09
07/11/1977	19Can04	01Leo57	05Gem13	25Tau42
07/16/1977	23Can49	11Leo10	10Gem40	29Tau13
07/21/1977	28Can36	19Leo36	16Gem10	02Gem41
07/26/1977	03Leo22	27Leo16	21Gem45	06Gem08
07/31/1977	08Leo09	04Vir07	27Gem23	09Gem32
08/05/1977	12Leo57	10Vir04	03Can04	12Gem54
08/10/1977	17Leo44	15Vir00	08Can49	16Gem13
08/15/1977	22Leo32	18Vir38	14Can36	19Gem30
08/20/1977	27Leo21	20Vir34	20Can26	22Gem45
08/25/1977	02Vir10	20Vir21	26Can18	25Gem55
08/30/1977	07Vir00	17Vir44	02Leo13	29Gem04
09/04/1977	11Vir50	13Vir15	08Leo10	02Can09
09/09/1977	16Vir41	08Vir51	14Leo09	05Can11
09/14/1977	21Vir33	06Vir56	20Leo09	08Can09
09/19/1977	26Vir25	08Vir47	26Leo12	11Can03
09/24/1977	01Lib19	14Vir04	02Vir16	13Can52
09/29/1977	06Lib13	21Vir37	08Vir22	16Can38
10/04/1977	11Lib09	00Lib12	14Vir30	19Can18
10/09/1977	16Lib04	09Lib04	20Vir39	21Can53
10/14/1977	21Lib01	17Lib50	26Vir49	24Can22
10/19/1977	25Lib59	26Lib22	03Lib01	26Can45
10/24/1977	00Sco58	04Sco38	09Lib13	29Can01
10/29/1977	05Sco57	12Sco40	15Lib27	01Leo09
11/03/1977	10Sco57	20Sco30	21Lib41	03Leo08
11/08/1977	15Sco58	28Sco09	27Lib55	04Leo57
11/13/1977	21Sco00	05Sag39	04Sco11	06Leo36
11/18/1977	26Sco02	12Sag58	10Sco27	08Leo03
11/23/1977	01Sag05	20Sag03	16Sco43	09Leo18
11/28/1977	06Sag09	26Sag39	23Sco00	10Leo17
12/03/1977	11Sag13	02Cap24	29Sco16	11Leo01
12/08/1977	16Sag17	06Cap25	05Sag34	11Leo27
12/13/1977	21Sag22	07Cap16	11Sag51	11Leo34
12/18/1977	26Sag28	03Cap37	18Sag09	11Leo21
12/23/1977	01Cap33	27Sag00	24Sag26	10Leo48
12/28/1977	06Cap39	22Sag06	00Cap44	09Leo53

Ephemeris Tables for Sun, Mercury, Venus and Mars

Date	Sun	Mercury	Venus	Mars
01/02/1978	11Cap45	21Sag19	07Cap01	08Leo39
01/07/1978	16Cap50	23Sag54	13Cap19	07Leo08
01/12/1978	21Cap56	28Sag32	19Cap36	05Leo22
01/17/1978	27Cap01	04Cap21	25Cap54	03Leo25
01/22/1978	02Aqu07	10Cap51	02Aqu11	01Leo25
01/27/1978	07Aqu12	17Cap50	08Aqu28	29Can27
02/01/1978	12Aqu16	25Cap12	14Aqu44	27Can37
02/06/1978	17Aqu21	02Aqu52	21Aqu01	25Can58
02/11/1978	22Aqu25	10Aqu51	27Aqu17	24Can36
02/16/1978	27Aqu28	19Aqu12	03Pis34	23Can31
02/21/1978	02Pis31	27Aqu55	09Pis49	22Can47
02/26/1978	07Pis33	07Pis01	16Pis04	22Can22
03/03/1978	12Pis34	16Pis28	22Pis18	22Can18
03/08/1978	17Pis34	26Pis09	28Pis33	22Can30
03/13/1978	22Pis34	05Ari39	04Ari45	23Can00
03/18/1978	27Pis33	14Ari15	10Ari58	23Can46
03/23/1978	02Ari30	20Ari59	17Ari10	24Can45
03/28/1978	07Ari27	25Ari04	23Ari21	25Can57
04/02/1978	12Ari24	26Ari06	29Ari32	27Can21
04/07/1978	17Ari19	24Ari19	05Tau42	28Can54
04/12/1978	22Ari13	20Ari50	11Tau51	00Leo36
04/17/1978	27Ari07	17Ari19	18Tau00	02Leo27
04/22/1978	02Tau00	15Ari11	24Tau07	04Leo25
04/27/1978	06Tau52	15Ari04	00Gem13	06Leo29
05/02/1978	11Tau44	16Ari55	06Gem19	08Leo39
05/07/1978	16Tau34	20Ari28	12Gem23	10Leo55
05/12/1978	21Tau24	25Ari24	18Gem27	13Leo15
05/17/1978	26Tau14	01Tau31	24Gem29	15Leo39
05/22/1978	01Gem03	08Tau39	00Can30	18Leo07
05/27/1978	05Gem51	16Tau46	06Can30	20Leo40
06/01/1978	10Gem38	25Tau51	12Can29	23Leo15
06/06/1978	15Gem25	05Gem49	18Can27	25Leo54
06/11/1978	20Gem13	16Gem31	24Can22	28Leo35
06/16/1978	24Gem59	27Gem29	00Leo17	01Vir19
06/21/1978	29Gem46	08Can13	06Leo10	04Vir06
06/26/1978	04Can31	18Can17	12Leo00	06Vir55
07/01/1978	09Can18	27Can31	17Leo49	09Vir46
07/06/1978	14Can04	05Leo52	23Leo36	12Vir40
07/11/1978	18Can50	13Leo19	29Leo19	15Vir35
07/16/1978	23Can36	19Leo49	05Vir00	18Vir33
07/21/1978	28Can22	25Leo16	10Vir39	21Vir33
07/26/1978	03Leo09	29Leo29	16Vir13	24Vir34
07/31/1978	07Leo55	02Vir10	21Vir44	27Vir37
08/05/1978	12Leo43	03Vir00	27Vir10	00Lib42
08/10/1978	17Leo30	01Vir39	02Lib31	03Lib49
08/15/1978	22Leo18	28Leo19	07Lib47	06Lib58
08/20/1978	27Leo07	24Leo09	12Lib56	10Lib08
08/25/1978	01Vir56	20Leo59	17Lib57	13Lib20
08/30/1978	06Vir45	20Leo34	22Lib49	16Lib34
09/04/1978	11Vir36	23Leo33	27Lib31	19Lib49
09/09/1978	16Vir27	29Leo33	02Sco01	23Lib06
09/14/1978	21Vir19	07Vir37	06Sco15	26Lib25
09/19/1978	26Vir12	16Vir42	10Sco12	29Lib46
09/24/1978	01Lib05	25Vir58	13Sco46	03Sco08
09/29/1978	05Lib59	05Lib05	16Sco54	06Sco31

Date	Sun	Mercury	Venus	Mars
10/04/1978	10Lib54	13Lib52	19Sco28	09Sco57
10/09/1978	15Lib51	22Lib19	21Sco24	13Sco24
10/14/1978	20Lib47	00Sco26	22Sco31	16Sco52
10/19/1978	25Lib45	08Sco17	22Sco46	20Sco23
10/24/1978	00Sco43	15Sco51	22Sco00	23Sco55
10/29/1978	05Sco43	23Sco12	20Sco16	27Sco28
11/03/1978	10Sco43	00Sag15	17Sco45	01Sag03
11/08/1978	15Sco43	06Sag55	14Sco45	04Sag39
11/13/1978	20Sco45	13Sag00	11Sco49	08Sag18
11/18/1978	25Sco48	18Sag03	09Sco25	11Sag57
11/23/1978	00Sag51	21Sag11	07Sco51	15Sag38
11/28/1978	05Sag54	21Sag03	07Sco19	19Sag20
12/03/1978	10Sag58	16Sag36	07Sco48	23Sag04
12/08/1978	16Sag03	09Sag55	09Sco12	26Sag49
12/13/1978	21Sag07	05Sag46	11Sco24	00Cap35
12/18/1978	26Sag13	05Sag58	14Sco15	04Cap23
12/23/1978	01Cap18	09Sag27	17Sco39	08Cap12
12/28/1978	06Cap24	14Sag46	21Sco29	12Cap01
01/02/1979	11Cap30	21Sag05	25Sco42	15Cap52
01/07/1979	16Cap36	27Sag58	00Sag12	19Cap44
01/12/1979	21Cap41	05Cap10	04Sag58	23Cap36
01/17/1979	26Cap46	12Cap39	09Sag56	27Cap30
01/22/1979	01Aqu52	20Cap22	15Sag04	01Aqu24
01/27/1979	06Aqu57	28Cap19	20Sag21	05Aqu19
02/01/1979	12Aqu02	06Aqu33	25Sag44	09Aqu14
02/06/1979	17Aqu06	15Aqu04	01Cap14	13Aqu10
02/11/1979	22Aqu10	23Aqu54	06Cap49	17Aqu06
02/16/1979	27Aqu13	03Pis02	12Cap28	21Aqu03
02/21/1979	02Pis16	12Pis19	18Cap10	25Aqu00
02/26/1979	07Pis18	21Pis22	23Cap56	28Aqu57
03/03/1979	12Pis19	29Pis27	29Cap45	02Pis54
03/08/1979	17Pis19	05Ari27	05Aqu35	06Pis50
03/13/1979	22Pis19	08Ari21	11Aqu28	10Pis46
03/18/1979	27Pis18	07Ari42	17Aqu22	14Pis42
03/23/1979	02Ari16	04Ari16	23Aqu18	18Pis38
03/28/1979	07Ari13	29Pis58	29Aqu15	22Pis33
04/02/1979	12Ari09	26Pis45	05Pis13	26Pis28
04/07/1979	17Ari04	25Pis44	11Pis12	00Ari21
04/12/1979	22Ari00	26Pis56	17Pis12	04Ari14
04/17/1979	26Ari53	29Pis59	23Pis12	08Ari06
04/22/1979	01Tau46	04Ari30	29Pis13	11Ari58
04/27/1979	06Tau38	10Ari11	05Ari13	15Ari48
05/02/1979	11Tau30	16Ari51	11Ari15	19Ari37
05/07/1979	16Tau21	24Ari22	17Ari17	23Ari26
05/12/1979	21Tau10	02Tau45	23Ari19	27Ari13
05/17/1979	26Tau00	11Tau55	29Ari22	00Tau59
05/22/1979	00Gem48	21Tau55	05Tau25	04Tau44
05/27/1979	05Gem37	02Gem34	11Tau29	08Tau27
06/01/1979	10Gem24	13Gem33	17Tau33	12Tau09
06/06/1979	15Gem12	24Gem19	23Tau37	15Tau50
06/11/1979	19Gem58	04Can24	29Tau42	19Tau29
06/16/1979	24Gem45	13Can34	05Gem46	23Tau07
06/21/1979	29Gem32	21Can43	11Gem51	26Tau43
06/26/1979	04Can18	28Can49	17Gem57	00Gem18

Ephemeris Tables for Sun, Mercury, Venus and Mars

Date	Sun	Mercury	Venus	Mars	Date	Sun	Mercury	Venus	Mars
07/01/1979	09Can04	04Leo49	24Gem03	03Gem51	04/01/1980	11Ari55	14Pis10	27Tau40	26Leo01
07/06/1979	13Can50	09Leo33	00Can09	07Gem22	04/06/1980	16Ari50	19Pis25	02Gem38	25Leo52
07/11/1979	18Can36	12Leo50	06Can16	10Gem52	04/11/1980	21Ari45	25Pis39	07Gem24	26Leo02
07/16/1979	23Can22	14Leo23	12Can24	14Gem21	04/16/1980	26Ari39	02Ari41	11Gem57	26Leo28
07/21/1979	28Can09	13Leo57	18Can32	17Gem48	04/21/1980	01Tau32	10Ari27	16Gem14	27Leo12
07/26/1979	02Leo55	11Leo36	24Can40	21Gem12	04/26/1980	06Tau24	18Ari57	20Gem12	28Leo08
07/31/1979	07Leo42	08Leo04	00Leo49	24Gem36					
					05/01/1980	11Tau15	28Ari10	23Gem46	29Leo19
08/05/1979	12Leo28	04Leo45	06Leo59	27Gem57	05/06/1980	16Tau06	08Tau06	26Gem52	00Vir40
08/10/1979	17Leo16	03Leo10	13Leo09	01Can17	05/11/1980	20Tau57	18Tau39	29Gem25	02Vir13
08/15/1979	22Leo04	04Leo18	19Leo19	04Can35	05/16/1980	25Tau46	29Tau33	01Can18	03Vir56
08/20/1979	26Leo52	08Leo22	25Leo30	07Can51	05/21/1980	00Gem34	10Gem16	02Can22	05Vir47
08/25/1979	01Vir42	15Leo03	01Vir42	11Can05	05/26/1980	05Gem23	20Gem18	02Can32	07Vir46
08/30/1979	06Vir31	23Leo36	07Vir54	14Can18	05/31/1980	10Gem10	29Gem18	01Can42	09Vir52
09/04/1979	11Vir22	03Vir06	14Vir06	17Can28	06/05/1980	14Gem58	07Can08	29Gem54	12Vir04
09/09/1979	16Vir13	12Vir46	20Vir18	20Can36	06/10/1980	19Gem45	13Can43	27Gem18	14Vir22
09/14/1979	21Vir05	21Vir13	26Vir31	23Can42	06/15/1980	24Gem31	18Can58	24Gem13	16Vir46
09/19/1979	25Vir58	01Lib16	02Lib45	26Can45	06/20/1980	29Gem18	22Can43	21Gem12	19Vir15
09/24/1979	00Lib51	09Lib53	08Lib57	29Can46	06/25/1980	04Can04	24Can46	18Gem36	21Vir48
09/29/1979	05Lib45	18Lib06	15Lib10	02Leo45	06/30/1980	08Can50	24Can58	16Gem54	24Vir25
10/04/1979	10Lib40	25Lib58	21Lib24	05Leo40	07/05/1980	13Can36	23Can19	16Gem06	27Vir07
10/09/1979	15Lib36	03Sco28	27Lib38	08Leo33	07/10/1980	18Can22	20Can25	16Gem19	29Vir52
10/14/1979	20Lib33	10Sco38	03Sco52	11Leo23	07/15/1980	23Can08	17Can21	17Gem24	02Lib41
10/19/1979	25Lib30	17Sco25	10Sco05	14Leo09	07/20/1980	27Can55	15Can26	19Gem18	05Lib33
10/24/1979	00Sco28	23Sco42	16Sco19	16Leo52	07/25/1980	02Leo41	15Can35	21Gem49	08Lib28
10/29/1979	05Sco28	29Sco13	22Sco33	19Leo31	07/30/1980	07Leo28	18Can13	24Gem53	11Lib26
11/03/1979	10Sco28	03Sag31	28Sco46	22Leo06	08/04/1980	12Leo15	23Can18	28Gem25	14Lib27
11/08/1979	15Sco29	05Sag43	05Sag00	24Leo37	08/09/1980	17Leo03	00Leo36	02Can19	17Lib30
11/13/1979	20Sco30	04Sag35	11Sag13	27Leo02	08/14/1980	21Leo50	09Leo32	06Can31	20Lib37
11/18/1979	25Sco33	29Sco31	17Sag27	29Leo22	08/19/1980	26Leo39	19Leo24	10Can59	23Lib45
11/23/1979	00Sag36	23Sco03	23Sag40	01Vir36	08/24/1980	01Vir28	29Leo27	15Can40	26Lib57
11/28/1979	05Sag39	19Sco45	29Sag53	03Vir43	08/29/1980	06Vir18	09Vir13	20Can34	00Sco10
12/03/1979	10Sag43	20Sco56	06Cap06	05Vir43	09/03/1980	11Vir07	18Vir31	25Can36	03Sco27
12/08/1979	15Sag48	25Sco14	12Cap19	07Vir34	09/08/1980	15Vir58	27Vir19	00Leo48	06Sco45
12/13/1979	20Sag52	01Sag12	18Cap31	09Vir16	09/13/1980	20Vir51	05Lib39	06Leo06	10Sco06
12/18/1979	25Sag58	08Sag00	24Cap43	10Vir49	09/18/1980	25Vir43	13Lib31	11Leo31	13Sco28
12/23/1979	01Cap03	15Sag13	00Aqu54	12Vir10	09/23/1980	00Lib36	20Lib57	17Leo03	16Sco54
12/28/1979	06Cap09	22Sag39	07Aqu05	13Vir19	09/28/1980	05Lib31	27Lib56	22Leo39	20Sco21
01/02/1980	11Cap15	00Cap16	13Aqu15	14Vir13	10/03/1980	10Lib25	04Sco25	28Leo20	23Sco49
01/07/1980	16Cap21	08Cap01	19Aqu24	14Vir52	10/08/1980	15Lib22	10Sco16	04Vir05	27Sco21
01/12/1980	21Cap27	15Cap56	25Aqu33	15Vir15	10/13/1980	20Lib18	15Sco11	09Vir54	00Sag54
01/17/1980	26Cap32	24Cap03	01Pis40	15Vir20	10/18/1980	25Lib16	18Sco41	15Vir46	04Sag28
01/22/1980	01Aqu37	02Aqu22	07Pis45	15Vir05	10/23/1980	00Sco14	19Sco54	21Vir42	08Sag05
01/27/1980	06Aqu42	10Aqu56	13Pis49	14Vir31	10/28/1980	05Sco13	17Sco47	27Vir40	11Sag43
02/01/1980	11Aqu47	19Aqu42	19Pis51	13Vir37	11/02/1980	10Sco13	12Sco18	03Lib41	15Sag24
02/06/1980	16Aqu51	28Aqu33	25Pis51	12Vir24	11/07/1980	15Sco14	06Sco19	09Lib44	19Sag06
02/11/1980	21Aqu55	07Pis06	01Ari48	10Vir54	11/12/1980	20Sco16	03Sco58	15Lib49	22Sag49
02/16/1980	26Aqu58	14Pis36	07Ari43	09Vir09	11/17/1980	25Sco18	06Sco06	21Lib57	26Sag34
02/21/1980	02Pis02	19Pis50	13Ari35	07Vir15	11/22/1980	00Sag21	11Sco10	28Lib04	00Cap21
02/26/1980	07Pis04	21Pis30	19Ari24	05Vir16	11/27/1980	05Sag25	17Sco45	04Sco14	04Cap08
03/02/1980	12Pis05	19Pis15	25Ari08	03Vir19	12/02/1980	10Sag28	25Sco00	10Sco25	07Cap57
03/07/1980	17Pis06	14Pis32	00Tau48	01Vir27	12/07/1980	15Sag33	02Sag34	16Sco37	11Cap48
03/12/1980	22Pis05	10Pis00	06Tau24	29Leo48	12/12/1980	20Sag38	10Sag13	22Sco50	15Cap39
03/17/1980	27Pis04	07Pis38	11Tau53	28Leo23	12/17/1980	25Sag43	17Sag58	29Sco03	19Cap32
03/22/1980	02Ari01	07Pis49	17Tau16	27Leo16	12/22/1980	00Cap49	25Sag46	05Sag17	23Cap25
03/27/1980	06Ari58	10Pis10	22Tau33	26Leo28	12/27/1980	05Cap54	03Cap39	11Sag31	27Cap19

416

Ephemeris Tables for Sun, Mercury, Venus and Mars

Date	Sun	Mercury	Venus	Mars
01/01/1981	11Cap00	11Cap38	17Sag46	01Aqu15
01/06/1981	16Cap06	19Cap47	24Sag01	05Aqu10
01/11/1981	21Cap12	28Cap04	00Cap16	09Aqu06
01/16/1981	26Cap17	06Aqu28	06Cap31	13Aqu03
01/21/1981	01Aqu22	14Aqu52	12Cap48	17Aqu00
01/26/1981	06Aqu27	22Aqu52	19Cap03	20Aqu57
01/31/1981	11Aqu33	29Aqu45	25Cap18	24Aqu55
02/05/1981	16Aqu37	04Pis07	01Aqu34	28Aqu53
02/10/1981	21Aqu40	04Pis34	07Aqu49	02Pis50
02/15/1981	26Aqu43	00Pis53	14Aqu04	06Pis47
02/20/1981	01Pis47	25Aqu21	20Aqu19	10Pis44
02/25/1981	06Pis49	21Aqu11	26Aqu34	14Pis40
03/02/1981	11Pis50	19Aqu51	02Pis49	18Pis36
03/07/1981	16Pis51	21Aqu12	09Pis04	22Pis31
03/12/1981	21Pis51	24Aqu31	15Pis18	26Pis26
03/17/1981	26Pis49	29Aqu16	21Pis32	00Ari19
03/22/1981	01Ari47	05Pis03	27Pis45	04Ari12
03/27/1981	06Ari44	11Pis40	03Ari58	08Ari04
04/01/1981	11Ari40	18Pis57	10Ari10	11Ari55
04/06/1981	16Ari36	26Pis52	16Ari23	15Ari45
04/11/1981	21Ari31	05Ari25	22Ari34	19Ari34
04/16/1981	26Ari25	14Ari35	28Ari46	23Ari22
04/21/1981	01Tau18	24Ari24	04Tau57	27Ari09
04/26/1981	06Tau10	04Tau48	11Tau07	00Tau54
05/01/1981	11Tau01	15Tau32	17Tau18	04Tau39
05/06/1981	15Tau52	26Tau08	23Tau27	08Tau22
05/11/1981	20Tau42	06Gem01	29Tau37	12Tau04
05/16/1981	25Tau31	14Gem45	05Gem46	15Tau44
05/21/1981	00Gem21	22Gem06	11Gem54	19Tau23
05/26/1981	05Gem09	27Gem56	18Gem03	23Tau01
05/31/1981	09Gem57	02Can10	24Gem10	26Tau37
06/05/1981	14Gem44	04Can37	00Can18	00Gem12
06/10/1981	19Gem31	05Can10	06Can24	03Gem46
06/15/1981	24Gem18	03Can57	12Can31	07Gem18
06/20/1981	29Gem04	01Can25	18Can37	10Gem49
06/25/1981	03Can50	28Gem37	24Can43	14Gem18
06/30/1981	08Can36	26Gem42	00Leo48	17Gem47
07/05/1981	13Can22	26Gem30	06Leo53	21Gem13
07/10/1981	18Can09	28Gem22	12Leo58	24Gem39
07/15/1981	22Can54	02Can21	19Leo01	28Gem03
07/20/1981	27Can40	08Can21	25Leo04	01Can27
07/25/1981	02Leo27	16Can10	01Vir07	04Can48
07/30/1981	07Leo14	25Can28	07Vir09	08Can09
08/04/1981	12Leo01	05Leo37	13Vir09	11Can27
08/09/1981	16Leo48	16Leo00	19Vir10	14Can45
08/14/1981	21Leo36	26Leo04	25Vir09	18Can01
08/19/1981	26Leo25	05Vir37	01Lib07	21Can17
08/24/1981	01Vir14	14Vir35	07Lib04	24Can31
08/29/1981	06Vir03	22Vir59	13Lib00	27Can43
09/03/1981	10Vir54	00Lib51	18Lib54	00Leo54
09/08/1981	15Vir45	08Lib12	24Lib47	04Leo04
09/13/1981	20Vir36	15Lib00	00Sco39	07Leo13
09/18/1981	25Vir29	21Lib09	06Sco28	10Leo19
09/23/1981	00Lib22	26Lib31	12Sco16	13Leo25
09/28/1981	05Lib16	00Sco47	18Sco02	16Leo29

Date	Sun	Mercury	Venus	Mars
10/03/1981	10Lib12	03Sco24	23Sco45	19Leo32
10/08/1981	15Lib07	03Sco35	29Sco26	22Leo33
10/13/1981	20Lib04	00Sco34	05Sag03	25Leo32
10/18/1981	25Lib01	24Lib53	10Sag37	28Leo29
10/23/1981	00Sco00	19Lib41	16Sag07	01Vir25
10/28/1981	04Sco59	18Lib22	21Sag31	04Vir18
11/02/1981	09Sco59	21Lib22	26Sag51	07Vir10
11/07/1981	15Sco00	27Lib10	02Cap02	09Vir58
11/12/1981	20Sco01	04Sco21	07Cap06	12Vir45
11/17/1981	25Sco04	12Sco04	11Cap59	15Vir29
11/22/1981	00Sag06	19Sco57	16Cap40	18Vir10
11/27/1981	05Sag10	27Sco51	21Cap07	20Vir48
12/02/1981	10Sag13	05Sag43	25Cap15	23Vir22
12/07/1981	15Sag18	13Sag35	29Cap02	25Vir53
12/12/1981	20Sag23	21Sag26	02Aqu22	28Vir19
12/17/1981	25Sag28	29Sag20	05Aqu09	00Lib42
12/22/1981	00Cap34	07Cap16	07Aqu14	02Lib58
12/27/1981	05Cap39	15Cap18	08Aqu31	05Lib10
01/01/1982	10Cap45	23Cap20	08Aqu54	07Lib15
01/06/1982	15Cap51	01Aqu15	08Aqu13	09Lib14
01/11/1982	20Cap57	08Aqu41	06Aqu33	11Lib04
01/16/1982	26Cap03	14Aqu51	04Aqu01	12Lib47
01/21/1982	01Aqu08	18Aqu22	01Aqu01	14Lib19
01/26/1982	06Aqu13	17Aqu37	28Cap01	15Lib42
01/31/1982	11Aqu17	12Aqu46	25Cap33	16Lib52
02/05/1982	16Aqu22	06Aqu53	23Cap58	17Lib49
02/10/1982	21Aqu25	03Aqu25	23Cap22	18Lib33
02/15/1982	26Aqu29	03Aqu12	23Cap48	19Lib00
02/20/1982	01Pis32	05Aqu34	25Cap08	19Lib10
02/25/1982	06Pis34	09Aqu42	27Cap15	19Lib02
03/02/1982	11Pis36	15Aqu03	00Aqu01	18Lib34
03/07/1982	16Pis36	21Aqu15	03Aqu19	17Lib48
03/12/1982	21Pis36	28Aqu08	07Aqu03	16Lib41
03/17/1982	26Pis35	05Pis36	11Aqu09	15Lib18
03/22/1982	01Ari33	13Pis34	15Aqu33	13Lib40
03/27/1982	06Ari30	22Pis06	20Aqu10	11Lib51
04/01/1982	11Ari27	01Ari10	25Aqu00	09Lib56
04/06/1982	16Ari22	10Ari50	00Pis00	08Lib01
04/11/1982	21Ari16	21Ari01	05Pis08	06Lib10
04/16/1982	26Ari10	01Tau31	10Pis22	04Lib30
04/21/1982	01Tau04	11Tau55	15Pis44	03Lib03
04/26/1982	05Tau56	21Tau34	21Pis10	01Lib53
05/01/1982	10Tau47	29Tau54	26Pis40	01Lib03
05/06/1982	15Tau38	06Gem36	02Ari13	00Lib33
05/11/1982	20Tau28	11Gem27	07Ari51	00Lib22
05/16/1982	25Tau18	14Gem20	13Ari30	00Lib30
05/21/1982	00Gem06	15Gem10	19Ari13	00Lib57
05/26/1982	04Gem55	14Gem06	24Ari57	01Lib40
05/31/1982	09Gem43	11Gem43	00Tau44	02Lib39
06/05/1982	14Gem30	09Gem00	06Tau32	03Lib51
06/10/1982	19Gem17	07Gem04	12Tau22	05Lib17
06/15/1982	24Gem04	06Gem43	18Tau13	06Lib54
06/20/1982	28Gem50	08Gem15	24Tau06	08Lib42
06/25/1982	03Can36	11Gem38	00Gem00	10Lib39
06/30/1982	08Can22	16Gem47	05Gem55	12Lib45

417

Ephemeris Tables for Sun, Mercury, Venus and Mars

Date	Sun	Mercury	Venus	Mars		Date	Sun	Mercury	Venus	Mars
07/05/1982	13Can09	23Gem33	11Gem51	14Lib58		04/01/1983	11Ari12	17Ari32	15Tau46	26Ari58
07/10/1982	17Can55	01Can49	17Gem49	17Lib19		04/06/1983	16Ari07	27Ari39	21Tau45	00Tau42
07/15/1982	22Can40	11Can22	23Gem48	19Lib47		04/11/1983	21Ari02	07Tau00	27Tau40	04Tau24
07/20/1982	27Can27	21Can47	29Gem47	22Lib21		04/16/1983	25Ari56	14Tau51	03Gem34	08Tau05
07/25/1982	02Leo13	02Leo24	05Can48	25Lib00		04/21/1983	00Tau49	20Tau42	09Gem25	11Tau45
07/30/1982	07Leo00	12Leo45	11Can50	27Lib45		04/26/1983	05Tau42	24Tau19	15Gem13	15Tau23
08/04/1982	11Leo47	22Leo31	17Can54	00Sco34		05/01/1983	10Tau33	25Tau33	20Gem58	19Tau00
08/09/1982	16Leo34	01Vir37	23Can58	03Sco28		05/06/1983	15Tau24	24Tau36	26Gem40	22Tau36
08/14/1982	21Leo22	10Vir06	00Leo03	06Sco27		05/11/1983	20Tau15	22Tau06	02Can18	26Tau10
08/19/1982	26Leo11	17Vir57	06Leo09	09Sco29		05/16/1983	25Tau04	19Tau09	07Can52	29Tau43
08/24/1982	01Vir00	25Vir10	12Leo16	12Sco35		05/21/1983	29Tau53	17Tau00	13Can21	03Gem16
08/29/1982	05Vir49	01Lib43	18Leo25	15Sco45		05/26/1983	04Gem41	16Tau27	18Can45	06Gem46
						05/31/1983	09Gem29	17Tau45	24Can03	10Gem16
09/03/1982	10Vir40	07Lib30	24Leo35	18Sco58						
09/08/1982	15Vir31	12Lib19	00Vir45	22Sco15		06/05/1983	14Gem16	20Tau49	29Can14	13Gem45
09/13/1982	20Vir22	15Lib49	06Vir56	25Sco34		06/10/1983	19Gem03	25Tau28	04Leo17	17Gem12
09/18/1982	25Vir15	17Lib28	13Vir08	28Sco57		06/15/1983	23Gem50	01Gem32	09Leo11	20Gem38
09/23/1982	00Lib08	16Lib35	19Vir21	02Sag22		06/20/1983	28Gem36	08Gem55	13Leo54	24Gem03
09/28/1982	05Lib02	12Lib48	25Vir34	05Sag49		06/25/1983	03Can22	17Gem33	18Leo24	27Gem27
						06/30/1983	08Can09	27Gem19	22Leo39	00Can50
10/03/1982	09Lib57	07Lib16	01Lib48	09Sag20						
10/08/1982	14Lib53	03Lib05	08Lib03	12Sag53		07/05/1983	12Can55	07Can52	26Leo36	04Can12
10/13/1982	19Lib50	02Lib54	14Lib18	16Sag28		07/10/1983	17Can40	18Can42	00Vir11	07Can32
10/18/1982	24Lib47	06Lib44	20Lib33	20Sag06		07/15/1983	22Can27	29Can15	03Vir21	10Can52
10/23/1982	29Lib45	13Lib12	26Lib48	23Sag45		07/20/1983	27Can13	09Leo12	05Vir57	14Can11
10/28/1982	04Sco45	20Lib56	03Sco04	27Sag26		07/25/1983	02Leo00	18Leo25	07Vir56	17Can29
						07/30/1983	06Leo46	26Leo55	09Vir09	20Can46
11/02/1982	09Sco45	29Lib06	09Sco21	01Cap09						
11/07/1982	14Sco45	07Sco20	15Sco37	04Cap54		08/04/1983	11Leo33	04Vir42	09Vir30	24Can02
11/12/1982	19Sco46	15Sco28	21Sco54	08Cap40		08/09/1983	16Leo21	11Vir45	08Vir52	27Can17
11/17/1982	24Sco49	23Sco30	28Sco10	12Cap28		08/14/1983	21Leo09	17Vir59	07Vir16	00Leo31
11/22/1982	29Sco51	01Sag25	04Sag27	16Cap18		08/19/1983	25Leo57	23Vir18	04Vir50	03Leo45
11/27/1982	04Sag55	09Sag16	10Sag44	20Cap08		08/24/1983	00Vir46	27Vir28	01Vir52	06Leo58
						08/29/1983	05Vir36	00Lib06	28Leo49	10Leo09
12/02/1982	09Sag59	17Sag04	17Sag01	24Cap00						
12/07/1982	15Sag03	24Sag50	23Sag18	27Cap52		09/03/1983	10Vir25	00Lib41	26Leo08	13Leo21
12/12/1982	20Sag09	02Cap35	29Sag34	01Aqu45		09/08/1983	15Vir16	28Vir45	24Leo14	16Leo31
12/17/1982	25Sag13	10Cap15	05Cap51	05Aqu39		09/13/1983	20Vir08	24Vir28	23Leo18	19Leo40
12/22/1982	00Cap19	17Cap42	12Cap08	09Aqu34		09/18/1983	25Vir01	19Vir28	23Leo21	22Leo49
12/27/1982	05Cap24	24Cap31	18Cap25	13Aqu29		09/23/1983	29Vir54	16Vir32	24Leo20	25Leo57
						09/28/1983	04Lib48	17Vir29	26Leo09	29Leo04
01/01/1983	10Cap30	29Cap57	24Cap41	17Aqu24						
01/06/1983	15Cap36	02Aqu33	00Aqu57	21Aqu20		10/03/1983	09Lib43	22Vir08	28Leo39	02Vir10
01/11/1983	20Cap42	00Aqu42	07Aqu13	25Aqu16		10/08/1983	14Lib39	29Vir14	01Vir43	05Vir16
01/16/1983	25Cap47	24Cap57	13Aqu28	29Aqu12		10/13/1983	19Lib35	07Lib30	05Vir18	08Vir21
01/21/1983	00Aqu53	19Cap08	19Aqu44	03Pis07		10/18/1983	24Lib33	16Lib07	09Vir16	11Vir25
01/26/1983	05Aqu58	16Cap33	25Aqu59	07Pis03		10/23/1983	29Lib31	24Lib42	13Vir34	14Vir27
01/31/1983	11Aqu03	17Cap25	02Pis13	10Pis58		10/28/1983	04Sco30	03Sco05	18Vir09	17Vir30
02/05/1983	16Aqu07	20Cap42	08Pis27	14Pis52		11/02/1983	09Sco30	11Sco16	22Vir58	20Vir30
02/10/1983	21Aqu11	25Cap31	14Pis40	18Pis46		11/07/1983	14Sco30	19Sco16	28Vir00	23Vir30
02/15/1983	26Aqu15	01Aqu21	20Pis52	22Pis40		11/12/1983	19Sco32	27Sco07	03Lib11	26Vir30
02/20/1983	01Pis17	07Aqu53	27Pis03	26Pis32		11/17/1983	24Sco34	04Sag49	08Lib31	29Vir27
02/25/1983	06Pis19	14Aqu58	03Ari13	00Ari24		11/22/1983	29Sco37	12Sag25	13Lib59	02Lib24
						11/27/1983	04Sag40	19Sag54	19Lib33	05Lib19
03/02/1983	11Pis21	22Aqu31	09Ari22	04Ari15						
03/07/1983	16Pis22	00Pis33	15Ari30	08Ari04		12/02/1983	09Sag44	27Sag12	25Lib13	08Lib12
03/12/1983	21Pis22	09Pis01	21Ari36	11Ari54		12/07/1983	14Sag48	04Cap09	00Sco57	11Lib04
03/17/1983	26Pis21	17Pis57	27Ari41	15Ari41		12/12/1983	19Sag54	10Cap21	06Sco46	13Lib55
03/22/1983	01Ari18	27Pis25	03Tau45	19Ari28		12/17/1983	24Sag58	14Cap59	12Sco38	16Lib43
03/27/1983	06Ari15	07Ari19	09Tau46	23Ari14		12/22/1983	00Cap04	16Cap38	18Sco33	19Lib30
						12/27/1983	05Cap10	13Cap47	24Sco30	22Lib14

Ephemeris Tables for Sun, Mercury, Venus and Mars

Date	Sun	Mercury	Venus	Mars
01/01/1984	10Cap15	07Cap26	00Sag30	24Lib55
01/06/1984	15Cap21	02Cap00	06Sag32	27Lib34
01/11/1984	20Cap27	00Cap24	12Sag36	00Sco11
01/16/1984	25Cap33	02Cap16	18Sag40	02Sco44
01/21/1984	00Aqu38	06Cap21	24Sag46	05Sco13
01/26/1984	05Aqu43	11Cap48	00Cap53	07Sco39
01/31/1984	10Aqu48	18Cap03	07Cap00	10Sco00
02/05/1984	15Aqu52	24Cap52	13Cap09	12Sco16
02/10/1984	20Aqu56	02Aqu06	19Cap17	14Sco27
02/15/1984	26Aqu00	09Aqu44	25Cap27	16Sco31
02/20/1984	01Pis03	17Aqu43	01Aqu36	18Sco29
02/25/1984	06Pis05	26Aqu06	07Aqu46	20Sco19
03/01/1984	11Pis06	04Pis54	13Aqu56	22Sco01
03/06/1984	16Pis07	14Pis07	20Aqu06	23Sco34
03/11/1984	21Pis07	23Pis44	26Aqu16	24Sco55
03/16/1984	26Pis06	03Ari37	02Pis27	26Sco06
03/21/1984	01Ari04	13Ari22	08Pis37	27Sco02
03/26/1984	06Ari01	22Ari18	14Pis48	27Sco45
03/31/1984	10Ari57	29Ari34	20Pis58	28Sco11
04/05/1984	15Ari53	04Tau27	27Pis07	28Sco20
04/10/1984	20Ari48	06Tau36	03Ari17	28Sco10
04/15/1984	25Ari42	06Tau01	09Ari27	27Sco43
04/20/1984	00Tau35	03Tau23	15Ari36	26Sco55
04/25/1984	05Tau27	00Tau00	21Ari45	25Sco50
04/30/1984	10Tau19	27Ari18	27Ari54	24Sco28
05/05/1984	15Tau10	26Ari18	04Tau04	22Sco52
05/10/1984	20Tau00	27Ari14	10Tau12	21Sco08
05/15/1984	24Tau50	29Ari59	16Tau21	19Sco20
05/20/1984	29Tau39	04Tau16	22Tau30	17Sco33
05/25/1984	04Gem27	09Tau53	28Tau39	15Sco54
05/30/1984	09Gem15	16Tau39	04Gem47	14Sco27
06/04/1984	14Gem03	24Tau31	10Gem55	13Sco16
06/09/1984	18Gem49	03Gem25	17Gem04	12Sco24
06/14/1984	23Gem36	13Gem18	23Gem13	11Sco52
06/19/1984	28Gem22	23Gem57	29Gem21	11Sco40
06/24/1984	03Can09	04Can52	05Can30	11Sco50
06/29/1984	07Can55	15Can35	11Can39	12Sco19
07/04/1984	12Can41	25Can40	17Can48	13Sco06
07/09/1984	17Can27	04Leo57	23Can56	14Sco10
07/14/1984	22Can13	13Leo24	00Leo05	15Sco30
07/19/1984	26Can59	21Leo02	06Leo14	17Sco04
07/24/1984	01Leo45	27Leo49	12Leo24	18Sco50
07/29/1984	06Leo32	03Vir39	18Leo32	20Sco49
08/03/1984	11Leo19	08Vir22	24Leo42	22Sco58
08/08/1984	16Leo07	11Vir43	00Vir51	25Sco17
08/13/1984	20Leo54	13Vir19	07Vir00	27Sco45
08/18/1984	25Leo43	12Vir46	13Vir09	00Sag21
08/23/1984	00Vir31	09Vir56	19Vir18	03Sag04
08/28/1984	05Vir21	05Vir33	25Vir27	05Sag54
09/02/1984	10Vir12	01Vir32	01Lib36	08Sag49
09/07/1984	15Vir02	00Vir02	07Lib44	11Sag51
09/12/1984	19Vir54	02Vir09	13Lib52	14Sag57
09/17/1984	24Vir46	07Vir34	20Lib00	18Sag08
09/22/1984	29Vir39	15Vir14	26Lib08	21Sag24
09/27/1984	04Lib33	24Vir00	02Sco15	24Sag43

Date	Sun	Mercury	Venus	Mars
10/02/1984	09Lib28	03Lib03	08Sco22	28Sag06
10/07/1984	14Lib24	11Lib58	14Sco28	01Cap33
10/12/1984	19Lib21	20Lib38	20Sco35	05Cap02
10/17/1984	24Lib18	29Lib00	26Sco40	08Cap34
10/22/1984	29Lib16	07Sco04	02Sag46	12Cap09
10/27/1984	04Sco16	14Sco55	08Sag51	15Cap46
11/01/1984	09Sco15	22Sco33	14Sag54	19Cap25
11/06/1984	14Sco16	00Sag00	20Sag58	23Cap06
11/11/1984	19Sco18	07Sag13	27Sag00	26Cap49
11/16/1984	24Sco20	14Sag09	03Cap01	00Aqu33
11/21/1984	29Sco22	20Sag35	09Cap01	04Aqu18
11/26/1984	04Sag25	26Sag07	15Cap00	08Aqu04
12/01/1984	09Sag30	29Sag55	20Cap58	11Aqu52
12/06/1984	14Sag34	00Cap35	26Cap53	15Aqu40
12/11/1984	19Sag39	26Sag51	02Aqu46	19Aqu28
12/16/1984	24Sag43	20Sag12	08Aqu37	23Aqu17
12/21/1984	29Sag49	15Sag22	14Aqu24	27Aqu07
12/26/1984	04Cap55	14Sag45	20Aqu08	00Pis57
12/31/1984	10Cap00	17Sag34	25Aqu48	04Pis46
01/05/1985	15Cap06	22Sag24	01Pis22	08Pis35
01/10/1985	20Cap12	28Sag22	06Pis51	12Pis24
01/15/1985	25Cap18	05Cap01	12Pis12	16Pis12
01/20/1985	00Aqu23	12Cap04	17Pis25	20Pis00
01/25/1985	05Aqu28	19Cap28	22Pis28	23Pis48
01/30/1985	10Aqu33	27Cap09	27Pis20	27Pis34
02/04/1985	15Aqu37	05Aqu06	01Ari57	01Ari20
02/09/1985	20Aqu41	13Aqu22	06Ari17	05Ari06
02/14/1985	25Aqu45	21Aqu59	10Ari18	08Ari50
02/19/1985	00Pis48	00Pis58	13Ari54	12Ari34
02/24/1985	05Pis51	10Pis15	17Ari00	16Ari16
03/01/1985	10Pis52	19Pis46	19Ari30	19Ari58
03/06/1985	15Pis52	29Pis06	21Ari16	23Ari39
03/11/1985	20Pis52	07Ari34	22Ari12	27Ari18
03/16/1985	25Pis51	14Ari09	22Ari08	00Tau57
03/21/1985	00Ari49	17Ari57	21Ari03	04Tau34
03/26/1985	05Ari46	18Ari28	19Ari00	08Tau10
03/31/1985	10Ari43	16Ari06	16Ari13	11Tau45
04/05/1985	15Ari39	12Ari12	13Ari05	15Tau19
04/10/1985	20Ari34	08Ari40	10Ari08	18Tau52
04/15/1985	25Ari28	06Ari51	07Ari49	22Tau24
04/20/1985	00Tau21	07Ari10	06Ari24	25Tau54
04/25/1985	05Tau13	09Ari27	06Ari00	29Tau24
04/30/1985	10Tau05	13Ari22	06Ari34	02Gem52
05/05/1985	14Tau57	18Ari35	08Ari01	06Gem19
05/10/1985	19Tau46	24Ari53	10Ari11	09Gem46
05/15/1985	24Tau36	02Tau09	12Ari58	13Gem11
05/20/1985	29Tau25	10Tau20	16Ari15	16Gem35
05/25/1985	04Gem13	19Tau24	19Ari58	19Gem58
05/30/1985	09Gem01	29Tau21	24Ari00	23Gem21
06/04/1985	13Gem48	10Gem00	28Ari19	26Gem42
06/09/1985	18Gem36	20Gem59	02Tau53	00Can03
06/14/1985	23Gem22	01Can46	07Tau38	03Can22
06/19/1985	28Gem09	11Can54	12Tau33	06Can42
06/24/1985	02Can55	21Can10	17Tau36	10Can00
06/29/1985	07Can41	29Can31	22Tau46	13Can17

Ephemeris Tables for Sun, Mercury, Venus and Mars

Date	Sun	Mercury	Venus	Mars
07/04/1985	12Can27	06Leo54	28Tau03	16Can34
07/09/1985	17Can13	13Leo16	03Gem25	19Can50
07/14/1985	21Can59	18Leo31	08Gem52	23Can06
07/19/1985	26Can45	22Leo27	14Gem22	26Can20
07/24/1985	01Leo32	24Leo48	19Gem57	29Can34
07/29/1985	06Leo18	25Leo13	25Gem36	02Leo48
08/03/1985	11Leo06	23Leo33	01Can17	06Leo01
08/08/1985	15Leo52	20Leo09	07Can01	09Leo14
08/13/1985	20Leo41	16Leo13	12Can49	12Leo27
08/18/1985	25Leo29	13Leo35	18Can39	15Leo39
08/23/1985	00Vir18	13Leo37	24Can30	18Leo50
08/28/1985	05Vir07	16Leo53	00Leo25	22Leo01
09/02/1985	09Vir58	23Leo01	06Leo22	25Leo12
09/07/1985	14Vir48	01Vir12	12Leo21	28Leo23
09/12/1985	19Vir40	10Vir25	18Leo21	01Vir33
09/17/1985	24Vir32	19Vir53	24Leo24	04Vir43
09/22/1985	29Vir25	29Vir09	00Vir28	07Vir53
09/27/1985	04Lib19	08Lib05	06Vir34	11Vir03
10/02/1985	09Lib14	16Lib37	12Vir41	14Vir12
10/07/1985	14Lib10	24Lib48	18Vir50	17Vir21
10/12/1985	19Lib06	02Sco40	25Vir00	20Vir30
10/17/1985	24Lib04	10Sco15	01Lib11	23Vir39
10/22/1985	29Lib02	17Sco31	07Lib24	26Vir47
10/27/1985	04Sco01	24Sco29	13Lib37	29Vir55
11/01/1985	09Sco01	01Sag01	19Lib51	03Lib03
11/06/1985	14Sco01	06Sag55	26Lib06	06Lib11
11/11/1985	19Sco03	11Sag45	02Sco21	09Lib19
11/16/1985	24Sco05	14Sag40	08Sco37	12Lib26
11/21/1985	29Sco07	14Sag20	14Sco53	15Lib33
11/26/1985	04Sag10	09Sag51	21Sco10	18Lib40
12/01/1985	09Sag15	03Sag12	27Sco27	21Lib46
12/06/1985	14Sag19	29Sco07	03Sag43	24Lib52
12/11/1985	19Sag24	29Sco30	10Sag01	27Lib58
12/16/1985	24Sag29	03Sag11	16Sag19	01Sco03
12/21/1985	29Sag34	08Sag42	22Sag36	04Sco08
12/26/1985	04Cap40	15Sag10	28Sag54	07Sco12
12/31/1985	09Cap46	22Sag10	05Cap11	10Sco16
01/05/1986	14Cap51	29Sag28	11Cap28	13Sco19
01/10/1986	19Cap57	06Cap59	17Cap46	16Sco21
01/15/1986	25Cap03	14Cap43	24Cap04	19Sco23
01/20/1986	00Aqu09	22Cap38	00Aqu21	22Sco24
01/25/1986	05Aqu13	00Aqu48	06Aqu37	25Sco23
01/30/1986	10Aqu18	09Aqu13	12Aqu54	28Sco21
02/04/1986	15Aqu23	17Aqu55	19Aqu11	01Sag19
02/09/1986	20Aqu27	26Aqu53	25Aqu27	04Sag15
02/14/1986	25Aqu30	05Pis59	01Pis44	07Sag09
02/19/1986	00Pis34	14Pis51	08Pis00	10Sag03
02/24/1986	05Pis36	22Pis48	14Pis15	12Sag54
03/01/1986	10Pis37	28Pis39	20Pis29	15Sag43
03/06/1986	15Pis38	01Ari15	26Pis43	18Sag30
03/11/1986	20Pis38	00Ari08	02Ari57	21Sag14
03/16/1986	25Pis37	26Pis13	09Ari09	23Sag55
03/21/1986	00Ari35	21Pis42	15Ari21	26Sag34
03/26/1986	05Ari32	18Pis39	21Ari33	29Sag09
03/31/1986	10Ari29	18Pis00	27Ari44	01Cap40

Date	Sun	Mercury	Venus	Mars
04/05/1986	15Ari24	19Pis35	03Tau54	04Cap07
04/10/1986	20Ari19	22Pis58	10Tau03	06Cap29
04/15/1986	25Ari13	27Pis45	16Tau12	08Cap46
04/20/1986	00Tau07	03Ari37	22Tau19	10Cap55
04/25/1986	04Tau59	10Ari24	28Tau25	12Cap59
04/30/1986	09Tau51	18Ari01	04Gem31	14Cap54
05/05/1986	14Tau42	26Ari24	10Gem36	16Cap40
05/10/1986	19Tau32	05Tau33	16Gem39	18Cap16
05/15/1986	24Tau22	15Tau29	22Gem42	19Cap41
05/20/1986	29Tau11	26Tau04	28Gem43	20Cap53
05/25/1986	04Gem00	07Gem01	04Can43	21Cap51
05/30/1986	08Gem47	17Gem48	10Can42	22Cap33
06/04/1986	13Gem34	27Gem55	16Can39	22Cap59
06/09/1986	18Gem22	07Can06	22Can35	23Cap06
06/14/1986	23Gem08	15Can12	28Can30	22Cap55
06/19/1986	27Gem55	22Can11	04Leo22	22Cap25
06/24/1986	02Can41	27Can58	10Leo12	21Cap37
06/29/1986	07Can27	02Leo24	16Leo01	20Cap34
07/04/1986	12Can13	05Leo18	21Leo47	19Cap18
07/09/1986	16Can59	06Leo25	27Leo31	17Cap53
07/14/1986	21Can45	05Leo34	03Vir12	16Cap26
07/19/1986	26Can31	03Leo01	08Vir49	15Cap01
07/24/1986	01Leo18	29Can36	14Vir24	13Cap46
07/29/1986	06Leo04	26Can44	19Vir54	12Cap43
08/03/1986	10Leo52	25Can44	25Vir19	11Cap57
08/08/1986	15Leo39	27Can21	00Lib40	11Cap31
08/13/1986	20Leo27	01Leo42	05Lib55	11Cap27
08/18/1986	25Leo15	08Leo30	11Lib03	11Cap40
08/23/1986	00Vir04	17Leo09	16Lib04	12Cap16
08/28/1986	04Vir53	26Leo46	20Lib55	13Cap11
09/02/1986	09Vir43	06Vir37	25Lib36	14Cap23
09/07/1986	14Vir34	16Vir13	00Sco04	15Cap52
09/12/1986	19Vir26	25Vir24	04Sco16	17Cap36
09/17/1986	24Vir18	04Lib08	08Sco10	19Cap34
09/22/1986	29Vir12	12Lib26	11Sco42	21Cap43
09/27/1986	04Lib06	20Lib19	14Sco46	24Cap03
10/02/1986	09Lib00	27Lib48	17Sco17	26Cap32
10/07/1986	13Lib55	04Sco55	19Sco08	29Cap10
10/12/1986	18Lib52	11Sco37	20Sco12	01Aqu55
10/17/1986	23Lib49	17Sco45	20Sco19	04Aqu46
10/22/1986	28Lib48	23Sco05	19Sco29	07Aqu43
10/27/1986	03Sco46	27Sco09	17Sco39	10Aqu46
11/01/1986	08Sco46	29Sco07	15Sco02	13Aqu53
11/06/1986	13Sco46	27Sco48	12Sco02	17Aqu04
11/11/1986	18Sco48	22Sco43	09Sco08	20Aqu18
11/16/1986	23Sco50	16Sco21	06Sco47	23Aqu34
11/21/1986	28Sco53	13Sco10	05Sco21	26Aqu54
11/26/1986	03Sag56	14Sco30	04Sco55	00Pis16
12/01/1986	09Sag00	18Sco59	05Sco28	03Pis40
12/06/1986	14Sag04	25Sco09	06Sco56	07Pis05
12/11/1986	19Sag09	02Sag07	09Sco11	10Pis31
12/16/1986	24Sag14	09Sag27	12Sco06	13Pis58
12/21/1986	29Sag20	16Sag59	15Sco22	17Pis27
12/26/1986	04Cap25	24Sag38	19Sco24	20Pis55
12/31/1986	09Cap31	02Cap24	23Sco39	24Pis24

Ephemeris Tables for Sun, Mercury, Venus and Mars

Date	Sun	Mercury	Venus	Mars	Date	Sun	Mercury	Venus	Mars
01/05/1987	14Cap37	10Cap18	28Sco11	27Pis54	10/02/1987	08Lib45	04Sco14	19Lib36	25Vir57
01/10/1987	19Cap42	18Cap21	02Sag58	01Ari23	10/07/1987	13Lib41	08Sco57	25Lib49	29Vir10
01/15/1987	24Cap48	26Cap35	07Sag57	04Ari52	10/12/1987	18Lib37	12Sco12	02Sco03	02Lib22
01/20/1987	29Cap54	05Aqu01	13Sag06	08Ari22	10/17/1987	23Lib34	13Sco10	08Sco16	05Lib36
01/25/1987	04Aqu58	13Aqu37	18Sag23	11Ari52	10/22/1987	28Lib33	10Sco54	14Sco30	08Lib49
01/30/1987	10Aqu03	22Aqu16	23Sag48	15Ari21	10/27/1987	03Sco32	05Sco24	20Sco43	12Lib03
02/04/1987	15Aqu08	00Pis39	29Sag18	18Ari50	11/01/1987	08Sco31	29Lib37	26Sco57	15Lib17
02/09/1987	20Aqu12	07Pis59	04Cap54	22Ari18	11/06/1987	13Sco32	27Lib24	03Sag10	18Lib31
02/14/1987	25Aqu15	13Pis03	10Cap33	25Ari46	11/11/1987	18Sco33	29Lib39	09Sag24	21Lib46
02/19/1987	00Pis19	14Pis27	16Cap16	29Ari13	11/16/1987	23Sco36	04Sco55	15Sag37	25Lib01
02/24/1987	05Pis21	11Pis48	22Cap03	02Tau40	11/21/1987	28Sco38	11Sco41	21Sag50	28Lib17
					11/26/1987	03Sag42	19Sco07	28Sag03	01Sco33
03/01/1987	10Pis22	06Pis43	27Cap52	06Tau07					
03/06/1987	15Pis24	02Pis10	03Aqu43	09Tau33	12/01/1987	08Sag45	26Sco49	04Cap16	04Sco49
03/11/1987	20Pis24	00Pis04	09Aqu36	12Tau57	12/06/1987	13Sag49	04Sag34	10Cap28	08Sco06
03/16/1987	25Pis22	00Pis36	15Aqu31	16Tau22	12/11/1987	18Sag54	12Sag22	16Cap40	11Sco23
03/21/1987	00Ari20	03Pis16	21Aqu27	19Tau45	12/16/1987	23Sag59	20Sag11	22Cap52	14Sco40
03/26/1987	05Ari18	07Pis32	27Aqu24	23Tau09	12/21/1987	29Sag04	28Sag03	29Cap03	17Sco58
03/31/1987	10Ari14	12Pis58	03Pis23	26Tau31	12/26/1987	04Cap10	06Cap00	05Aqu14	21Sco17
					12/31/1987	09Cap16	14Cap03	11Aqu24	24Sco36
04/05/1987	15Ari10	19Pis19	09Pis22	29Tau52					
04/10/1987	20Ari05	26Pis25	15Pis22	03Gem13	01/05/1988	14Cap22	22Cap13	17Aqu33	27Sco55
04/15/1987	25Ari00	04Ari14	21Pis23	06Gem33	01/10/1988	19Cap28	00Aqu27	23Aqu41	01Sag14
04/20/1987	29Ari53	12Ari42	27Pis24	09Gem52	01/15/1988	24Cap33	08Aqu40	29Aqu48	04Sag34
04/25/1987	04Tau45	21Ari52	03Ari25	13Gem11	01/20/1988	29Cap39	16Aqu28	05Pis54	07Sag54
04/30/1987	09Tau37	01Tau43	09Ari27	16Gem30	01/25/1988	04Aqu44	23Aqu09	11Pis58	11Sag15
					01/30/1988	09Aqu49	27Aqu22	18Pis00	14Sag36
05/05/1987	14Tau28	12Tau11	15Ari29	19Gem47					
05/10/1987	19Tau18	23Tau01	21Ari32	23Gem04	02/04/1988	14Aqu53	27Aqu36	24Pis00	17Sag57
05/15/1987	24Tau08	03Gem43	27Ari35	26Gem20	02/09/1988	19Aqu57	23Aqu35	29Pis57	21Sag18
05/20/1987	28Tau57	13Gem45	03Tau39	29Gem36	02/14/1988	25Aqu01	17Aqu51	05Ari52	24Sag40
05/25/1987	03Gem45	22Gem43	09Tau42	02Can51	02/19/1988	00Pis04	13Aqu45	11Ari44	28Sag01
05/30/1987	08Gem33	00Can27	15Tau46	06Can06	02/24/1988	05Pis06	12Aqu43	17Ari32	01Cap24
					02/29/1988	10Pis08	14Aqu21	23Ari17	04Cap46
06/04/1987	13Gem21	06Can50	21Tau50	09Can19					
06/09/1987	18Gem08	11Can47	27Tau55	12Can33	03/05/1988	15Pis09	17Aqu57	28Ari57	08Cap08
06/14/1987	22Gem54	15Can08	04Gem00	15Can46	03/10/1988	20Pis09	22Aqu54	04Tau32	11Cap31
06/19/1987	27Gem41	16Can42	10Gem04	18Can59	03/15/1988	25Pis08	28Aqu49	10Tau02	14Cap53
06/24/1987	02Can27	16Can24	16Gem10	22Can12	03/20/1988	00Ari06	05Pis31	15Tau25	18Cap16
06/29/1987	07Can13	14Can25	22Gem16	25Can24	03/25/1988	05Ari03	12Pis51	20Tau41	21Cap38
					03/30/1988	10Ari00	20Pis46	25Tau48	25Cap00
07/04/1987	12Can00	11Can28	28Gem23	28Can36					
07/09/1987	16Can45	08Can45	04Can30	01Leo48	04/04/1988	14Ari56	29Pis16	00Gem45	28Cap22
07/14/1987	21Can31	07Can25	10Can37	04Leo58	04/09/1988	19Ari51	08Ari22	05Gem31	01Aqu45
07/19/1987	26Can18	08Can11	16Can45	08Leo10	04/14/1988	24Ari45	18Ari05	10Gem04	05Aqu06
07/24/1987	01Leo04	11Can16	22Can53	11Leo21	04/19/1988	29Ari39	28Ari22	14Gem19	08Aqu27
07/29/1987	05Leo51	16Can37	29Can02	14Leo32	04/24/1988	04Tau31	09Tau00	18Gem16	11Aqu47
					04/29/1988	09Tau23	19Tau33	21Gem49	15Aqu06
08/03/1987	10Leo38	24Can01	05Leo12	17Leo43					
08/08/1987	15Leo25	03Leo03	11Leo22	20Leo54	05/04/1988	14Tau14	29Tau25	24Gem54	18Aqu24
08/13/1987	20Leo13	13Leo01	17Leo32	24Leo04	05/09/1988	19Tau04	08Gem04	27Gem25	21Aqu42
08/18/1987	25Leo01	23Leo13	23Leo43	27Leo15	05/14/1988	23Tau54	15Gem15	29Gem14	24Aqu57
08/23/1987	29Leo50	03Vir09	29Leo54	00Vir26	05/19/1988	28Tau43	20Gem49	00Can16	28Aqu12
08/28/1987	04Vir39	12Vir35	06Vir06	03Vir37	05/24/1988	03Gem31	24Gem37	00Can21	01Pis24
					05/29/1988	08Gem19	26Gem33	29Gem28	04Pis33
09/02/1987	09Vir29	21Vir29	12Vir18	06Vir48					
09/07/1987	14Vir20	29Vir53	18Vir30	09Vir59	06/03/1988	13Gem07	26Gem32	27Gem37	07Pis40
09/12/1987	19Vir12	07Lib47	24Vir43	13Vir10	06/08/1988	17Gem54	24Gem51	24Gem59	10Pis44
09/17/1987	24Vir04	15Lib12	00Lib56	16Vir22	06/13/1988	22Gem41	22Gem09	21Gem53	13Pis44
09/22/1987	28Vir57	22Lib09	07Lib09	19Vir33	06/18/1988	27Gem27	19Gem37	18Gem52	16Pis40
09/27/1987	03Lib51	28Lib32	13Lib22	22Vir45	06/23/1988	02Can13	18Gem12	16Gem20	19Pis31
					06/28/1988	07Can00	18Gem39	14Gem40	22Pis16

Ephemeris Tables for Sun, Mercury, Venus and Mars

Date	Sun	Mercury	Venus	Mars	Date	Sun	Mercury	Venus	Mars
07/03/1988	11Can46	21Gem04	13Gem57	24Pis55	04/04/1989	14Ari42	14Ari38	14Ari34	14Gem46
07/08/1988	16Can31	25Gem27	14Gem13	27Pis28	04/09/1989	19Ari37	25Ari01	20Ari46	17Gem51
07/13/1988	21Can18	01Can41	15Gem22	29Pis51	04/14/1989	24Ari31	05Tau19	26Ari58	20Gem56
07/18/1988	26Can04	09Can37	17Gem18	02Ari04	04/19/1989	29Ari24	14Tau55	03Tau09	24Gem01
07/23/1988	00Leo51	18Can57	19Gem51	04Ari09	04/24/1989	04Tau17	23Tau10	09Tau20	27Gem06
07/28/1988	05Leo37	29Can12	22Gem57	06Ari00	04/29/1989	09Tau09	29Tau39	15Tau30	00Can12
08/02/1988	10Leo24	09Leo41	26Gem31	07Ari38	05/04/1989	14Tau00	04Gem08	21Tau40	03Can17
08/07/1988	15Leo11	19Leo54	00Can25	09Ari01	05/09/1989	18Tau50	06Gem28	27Tau49	06Can23
08/12/1988	19Leo59	29Leo35	04Can39	10Ari07	05/14/1989	23Tau40	06Gem41	03Gem58	09Can28
08/17/1988	24Leo47	08Vir39	09Can08	10Ari54	05/19/1989	28Tau29	05Gem03	10Gem07	12Can34
08/22/1988	29Leo36	17Vir07	13Can50	11Ari22	05/24/1989	03Gem17	02Gem22	16Gem15	15Can40
08/27/1988	04Vir25	25Vir01	18Can43	11Ari28	05/29/1989	08Gem06	29Tau45	22Gem24	18Can46
09/01/1988	09Vir16	02Lib22	23Can46	11Ari14	06/03/1989	12Gem53	28Tau16	28Gem31	21Can52
09/06/1988	14Vir06	09Lib06	28Can58	10Ari39	06/08/1989	17Gem40	28Tau31	04Can37	24Can58
09/11/1988	18Vir58	15Lib09	04Leo16	09Ari45	06/13/1989	22Gem27	00Gem38	10Can45	28Can05
09/16/1988	23Vir49	20Lib21	09Leo42	08Ari34	06/18/1989	27Gem13	04Gem30	16Can51	01Leo12
09/21/1988	28Vir43	24Lib24	15Leo13	07Ari12	06/23/1989	02Can00	09Gem57	22Can56	04Leo18
09/26/1988	03Lib37	26Lib45	20Leo49	05Ari44	06/28/1989	06Can46	16Gem55	29Can01	07Leo25
10/01/1988	08Lib31	26Lib40	26Leo30	04Ari16	07/03/1989	11Can32	25Gem16	05Leo06	10Leo32
10/06/1988	13Lib27	23Lib28	02Vir15	02Ari54	07/08/1989	16Can18	04Can52	11Leo10	13Leo39
10/11/1988	18Lib23	17Lib53	08Vir04	01Ari43	07/13/1989	21Can04	15Can18	17Leo14	16Leo47
10/16/1988	23Lib21	12Lib55	13Vir56	00Ari49	07/18/1989	25Can50	26Can01	23Leo17	19Leo55
10/21/1988	28Lib19	11Lib48	19Vir52	00Ari12	07/23/1989	00Leo36	06Leo29	29Leo19	23Leo03
10/26/1988	03Sco18	14Lib56	25Vir50	29Pis55	07/28/1989	05Leo23	16Leo22	05Vir21	26Leo11
10/31/1988	08Sco17	20Lib54	01Lib51	29Pis58					
					08/02/1989	10Leo10	25Leo35	11Vir22	29Leo20
11/05/1988	13Sco18	28Lib15	07Lib54	00Ari20	08/07/1989	14Leo57	04Vir07	17Vir21	02Vir29
11/10/1988	18Sco19	06Sco09	13Lib59	01Ari01	08/12/1989	19Leo45	11Vir59	23Vir21	05Vir39
11/15/1988	23Sco21	14Sco11	20Lib05	01Ari59	08/17/1989	24Leo33	19Vir11	29Vir18	08Vir49
11/20/1988	28Sco24	22Sco11	26Lib14	03Ari13	08/22/1989	29Leo22	25Vir40	05Lib15	12Vir00
11/25/1988	03Sag27	00Sag07	02Sco23	04Ari40	08/27/1989	04Vir12	01Lib19	11Lib10	15Vir10
11/30/1988	08Sag30	08Sag01	08Sco34	06Ari19					
					09/01/1989	09Vir01	05Lib57	17Lib05	18Vir22
12/05/1988	13Sag35	15Sag52	14Sco46	08Ari10	09/06/1989	13Vir52	09Lib12	22Lib58	21Vir34
12/10/1988	18Sag39	23Sag43	20Sco58	10Ari10	09/11/1989	18Vir43	10Lib33	28Lib48	24Vir46
12/15/1988	23Sag44	01Cap35	27Sco12	12Ari19	09/16/1989	23Vir36	09Lib23	04Sco38	28Vir00
12/20/1988	28Sag50	09Cap29	03Sag26	14Ari36	09/21/1989	28Vir28	05Lib29	10Sco25	01Lib14
12/25/1988	03Cap56	17Cap22	09Sag40	16Ari58	09/26/1989	03Lib22	00Lib09	16Sco10	04Lib28
12/30/1988	09Cap01	25Cap06	15Sag55	19Ari27					
					10/01/1989	08Lib17	26Vir16	21Sco54	07Lib43
01/04/1989	14Cap07	02Aqu21	22Sag10	22Ari01	10/06/1989	13Lib12	26Vir16	27Sco33	11Lib00
01/09/1989	19Cap13	08Aqu19	28Sag25	24Ari39	10/11/1989	18Lib09	00Lib16	03Sag10	14Lib16
01/14/1989	24Cap18	11Aqu39	04Cap41	27Ari21	10/16/1989	23Lib06	06Lib54	08Sag43	17Lib34
01/19/1989	29Cap24	10Aqu45	10Cap57	00Tau06	10/21/1989	28Lib04	14Lib48	14Sag12	20Lib52
01/24/1989	04Aqu29	05Aqu39	17Cap13	02Tau54	10/26/1989	03Sco03	23Lib10	19Sag36	24Lib11
01/29/1989	09Aqu34	29Cap39	23Cap28	05Tau44	10/31/1989	08Sco02	01Sco32	24Sag53	27Lib31
02/03/1989	14Aqu39	26Cap20	29Cap43	08Tau37	11/05/1989	13Sco03	09Sco48	00Cap04	00Sco51
02/08/1989	19Aqu43	26Cap24	05Aqu59	11Tau32	11/10/1989	18Sco04	17Sco54	05Cap06	04Sco13
02/13/1989	24Aqu46	29Cap02	12Aqu15	14Tau28	11/15/1989	23Sco06	25Sco52	09Cap58	07Sco36
02/18/1989	29Aqu49	03Aqu24	18Aqu30	17Tau26	11/20/1989	28Sco09	03Sag43	14Cap38	10Sco58
02/23/1989	04Pis52	08Aqu54	24Aqu45	20Tau25	11/25/1989	03Sag12	11Sag28	19Cap03	14Sco22
02/28/1989	09Pis54	15Aqu12	01Pis00	23Tau25	11/30/1989	08Sag16	19Sag10	23Cap10	17Sco48
03/05/1989	14Pis54	22Aqu08	07Pis15	26Tau27	12/05/1989	13Sag20	26Sag49	26Cap54	21Sco13
03/10/1989	19Pis55	29Aqu37	13Pis29	29Tau29	12/10/1989	18Sag25	04Cap21	00Aqu10	24Sco40
03/15/1989	24Pis54	07Pis36	19Pis43	02Gem31	12/15/1989	23Sag30	11Cap36	02Aqu53	28Sco07
03/20/1989	29Pis52	16Pis03	25Pis57	05Gem34	12/20/1989	28Sag35	18Cap13	04Aqu55	01Sag36
03/25/1989	04Ari49	25Pis04	02Ari09	08Gem38	12/25/1989	03Cap40	23Cap27	06Aqu08	05Sag06
03/30/1989	09Ari46	04Ari35	08Ari22	11Gem42	12/30/1989	08Cap46	25Cap52	06Aqu24	08Sag36

Ephemeris Tables for Sun, Mercury, Venus and Mars

Date	Sun	Mercury	Venus	Mars
01/04/1990	13Cap52	23Cap54	05Aqu38	12Sag07
01/09/1990	18Cap58	17Cap59	03Aqu52	15Sag39
01/14/1990	24Cap04	12Cap09	01Aqu18	19Sag12
01/19/1990	29Cap09	09Cap43	28Cap15	22Sag46
01/24/1990	04Aqu14	10Cap50	25Cap18	26Sag21
01/29/1990	09Aqu19	14Cap22	22Cap55	29Sag56
02/03/1990	14Aqu24	19Cap23	21Cap25	03Cap33
02/08/1990	19Aqu28	25Cap22	20Cap55	07Cap10
02/13/1990	24Aqu31	01Aqu59	21Cap26	10Cap48
02/18/1990	29Aqu35	09Aqu07	22Cap52	14Cap27
02/23/1990	04Pis37	16Aqu40	25Cap03	18Cap06
02/28/1990	09Pis39	24Aqu39	27Cap52	21Cap46
03/05/1990	14Pis40	03Pis03	01Aqu13	25Cap27
03/10/1990	19Pis40	11Pis55	05Aqu01	29Cap09
03/15/1990	24Pis39	21Pis14	09Aqu09	02Aqu51
03/20/1990	29Pis37	01Ari00	13Aqu33	06Aqu33
03/25/1990	04Ari34	11Ari04	18Aqu13	10Aqu16
03/30/1990	09Ari31	21Ari04	23Aqu04	14Aqu00
04/04/1990	14Ari27	00Tau19	28Aqu05	17Aqu43
04/09/1990	19Ari22	08Tau03	03Pis14	21Aqu27
04/14/1990	24Ari16	13Tau39	08Pis30	25Aqu12
04/19/1990	29Ari10	16Tau49	13Pis51	28Aqu57
04/24/1990	04Tau03	17Tau27	19Pis18	02Pis40
04/29/1990	08Tau55	15Tau52	24Pis49	06Pis25
05/04/1990	13Tau46	12Tau57	00Ari22	10Pis09
05/09/1990	18Tau36	09Tau57	06Ari00	13Pis52
05/14/1990	23Tau26	08Tau10	11Ari41	17Pis36
05/19/1990	28Tau15	08Tau09	17Ari24	21Pis18
05/24/1990	03Gem03	09Tau58	23Ari09	25Pis00
05/29/1990	07Gem52	13Tau30	28Ari55	28Pis40
06/03/1990	12Gem39	18Tau31	04Tau44	02Ari20
06/08/1990	17Gem26	24Tau49	10Tau34	05Ari58
06/13/1990	22Gem13	02Gem21	16Tau26	09Ari36
06/18/1990	27Gem00	11Gem03	22Tau18	13Ari11
06/23/1990	01Can46	20Gem48	28Tau13	16Ari44
06/28/1990	06Can31	01Can22	04Gem08	20Ari16
07/03/1990	11Can18	12Can15	10Gem04	23Ari45
07/08/1990	16Can04	22Can54	16Gem02	27Ari12
07/13/1990	20Can50	02Leo58	22Gem01	00Tau35
07/18/1990	25Can36	12Leo16	28Gem01	03Tau55
07/23/1990	00Leo22	20Leo48	04Can01	07Tau13
07/28/1990	05Leo09	28Leo35	10Can03	10Tau25
08/02/1990	09Leo56	05Vir34	16Can06	13Tau34
08/07/1990	14Leo43	11Vir43	22Can11	16Tau39
08/12/1990	19Leo31	16Vir52	28Can16	19Tau37
08/17/1990	24Leo19	20Vir48	04Leo22	22Tau31
08/22/1990	29Leo08	23Vir08	10Leo30	25Tau18
08/27/1990	03Vir57	23Vir22	16Leo37	27Tau57
09/01/1990	08Vir48	21Vir11	22Leo47	00Gem30
09/06/1990	13Vir38	16Vir53	28Leo57	02Gem52
09/11/1990	18Vir30	12Vir12	05Vir08	05Gem06
09/16/1990	23Vir21	09Vir39	11Vir20	07Gem09
09/21/1990	28Vir15	10Vir51	17Vir33	09Gem00
09/26/1990	03Lib08	15Vir38	23Vir45	10Gem38

Date	Sun	Mercury	Venus	Mars
10/01/1990	08Lib03	22Vir53	29Vir59	12Gem01
10/06/1990	12Lib58	01Lib19	06Lib13	13Gem07
10/11/1990	17Lib54	10Lib07	12Lib28	13Gem55
10/16/1990	22Lib51	18Lib51	18Lib43	14Gem25
10/21/1990	27Lib49	27Lib22	24Lib59	14Gem33
10/26/1990	02Sco48	05Sco39	01Sco15	14Gem19
10/31/1990	07Sco48	13Sco41	07Sco31	13Gem43
11/05/1990	12Sco49	21Sco33	13Sco48	12Gem45
11/10/1990	17Sco49	29Sco14	20Sco04	11Gem27
11/15/1990	22Sco51	06Sag47	26Sco21	09Gem52
11/20/1990	27Sco54	14Sag10	02Sag37	08Gem06
11/25/1990	02Sag57	21Sag19	08Sag54	06Gem13
11/30/1990	08Sag01	28Sag05	15Sag11	04Gem21
12/05/1990	13Sag05	04Cap04	21Sag27	02Gem35
12/10/1990	18Sag10	08Cap29	27Sag45	01Gem00
12/15/1990	23Sag15	09Cap58	04Cap01	29Tau43
12/20/1990	28Sag20	07Cap01	10Cap18	28Tau43
12/25/1990	03Cap25	00Cap35	16Cap34	28Tau04
12/30/1990	08Cap31	25Sag10	22Cap51	27Tau46
01/04/1991	13Cap37	23Sag45	29Cap07	27Tau48
01/09/1991	18Cap43	25Sag51	05Aqu23	28Tau08
01/14/1991	23Cap49	00Cap10	11Aqu39	28Tau46
01/19/1991	28Cap54	05Cap46	17Aqu54	29Tau40
01/24/1991	04Aqu00	12Cap09	24Aqu09	00Gem48
01/29/1991	09Aqu04	19Cap03	00Pis24	02Gem08
02/03/1991	14Aqu09	26Cap20	06Pis37	03Gem40
02/08/1991	19Aqu13	03Aqu58	12Pis50	05Gem22
02/13/1991	24Aqu16	11Aqu55	19Pis02	07Gem13
02/18/1991	29Aqu20	20Aqu14	25Pis13	09Gem11
02/23/1991	04Pis22	28Aqu55	01Ari23	11Gem16
02/28/1991	09Pis24	08Pis01	07Ari33	13Gem27
03/05/1991	14Pis25	17Pis29	13Ari40	15Gem44
03/10/1991	19Pis25	27Pis12	19Ari47	18Gem05
03/15/1991	24Pis24	06Ari48	25Ari52	20Gem31
03/20/1991	29Pis23	15Ari39	01Tau56	23Gem00
03/25/1991	04Ari20	22Ari46	07Tau57	25Gem33
03/30/1991	09Ari17	27Ari22	13Tau57	28Gem08
04/04/1991	14Ari13	29Ari00	19Tau55	00Can46
04/09/1991	19Ari08	27Ari49	25Tau52	03Can27
04/14/1991	24Ari03	24Ari39	01Gem45	06Can10
04/19/1991	28Ari06	21Ari06	07Gem36	08Can54
04/24/1991	03Tau48	18Ari36	13Gem24	11Can41
04/29/1991	08Tau40	18Ari01	19Gem10	14Can29
05/04/1991	13Tau32	19Ari27	24Gem51	17Can18
05/09/1991	18Tau22	22Ari37	00Can29	20Can09
05/14/1991	23Tau12	27Ari16	06Can03	23Can01
05/19/1991	28Tau01	03Tau08	11Can32	25Can55
05/24/1991	02Gem49	10Tau04	16Can56	28Can49
05/29/1991	07Gem37	18Tau01	22Can13	01Leo45
06/03/1991	12Gem25	26Tau57	27Can24	04Leo41
06/08/1991	17Gem12	06Gem49	02Leo27	07Leo39
06/13/1991	21Gem59	17Gem25	07Leo20	10Leo37
06/18/1991	26Gem46	28Gem24	12Leo02	13Leo36
06/23/1991	01Can32	09Can10	16Leo31	16Leo36
06/28/1991	06Can18	19Can19	20Leo45	19Leo37

423

Ephemeris Tables for Sun, Mercury, Venus and Mars

Date	Sun	Mercury	Venus	Mars
07/03/1991	11Can04	28Can40	24Leo41	22Leo39
07/08/1991	15Can50	07Leo09	28Leo15	25Leo42
07/13/1991	20Can36	14Leo44	01Vir21	28Leo45
07/18/1991	25Can22	21Leo25	03Vir55	01Vir49
07/23/1991	00Leo09	27Leo06	05Vir52	04Vir55
07/28/1991	04Leo55	01Vir36	07Vir01	08Vir01
08/02/1991	09Leo42	04Vir39	07Vir17	11Vir08
08/07/1991	14Leo30	05Vir54	06Vir37	14Vir16
08/12/1991	19Leo17	05Vir00	04Vir57	17Vir24
08/17/1991	24Leo06	01Vir58	02Vir27	20Vir34
08/22/1991	28Leo54	27Leo45	29Leo26	23Vir45
08/27/1991	03Vir43	24Leo09	26Leo24	26Vir56
09/01/1991	08Vir33	23Leo06	23Leo46	00Lib09
09/06/1991	13Vir24	25Leo29	21Leo55	03Lib22
09/11/1991	18Vir15	01Vir02	21Leo03	06Lib37
09/16/1991	23Vir07	08Vir50	21Leo10	09Lib52
09/21/1991	28Vir00	17Vir46	22Leo13	13Lib09
09/26/1991	02Lib54	26Vir59	24Leo04	16Lib27
10/01/1991	07Lib48	06Lib05	26Leo37	19Lib45
10/06/1991	12Lib44	14Lib52	29Leo43	23Lib05
10/11/1991	17Lib40	23Lib20	03Vir19	26Lib26
10/16/1991	22Lib37	01Sco28	07Vir18	29Lib48
10/21/1991	27Lib35	09Sco21	11Vir37	03Sco12
10/26/1991	02Sco34	16Sco58	16Vir14	06Sco36
10/31/1991	07Sco33	24Sco21	21Vir03	10Sco01
11/05/1991	12Sco34	01Sag28	26Vir05	13Sco28
11/10/1991	17Sco35	08Sag16	01Lib17	16Sco57
11/15/1991	22Sco37	14Sag31	06Lib37	20Sco25
11/20/1991	27Sco39	19Sag50	12Lib05	23Sco56
11/25/1991	02Sag42	23Sag24	17Lib39	27Sco27
11/30/1991	07Sag46	23Sag55	23Lib19	01Sag00
12/05/1991	12Sag50	20Sag06	29Lib04	04Sag34
12/10/1991	17Sag55	13Sag27	04Sco52	08Sag10
12/15/1991	23Sag00	08Sag40	10Sco45	11Sag46
12/20/1991	28Sag06	08Sag13	16Sco40	15Sag24
12/25/1991	03Cap11	11Sag15	22Sco37	19Sag02
12/30/1991	08Cap17	16Sag18	28Sco37	22Sag42
01/04/1992	13Cap22	22Sag25	04Sag40	26Sag22
01/09/1992	18Cap28	29Sag12	10Sag43	00Cap04
01/14/1992	23Cap34	06Cap21	16Sag48	03Cap48
01/19/1992	28Cap39	13Cap46	22Sag54	07Cap31
01/24/1992	03Aqu45	21Cap27	29Sag01	11Cap16
01/29/1992	08Aqu49	29Cap22	05Cap09	15Cap03
02/03/1992	13Aqu54	07Aqu35	11Cap17	18Cap49
02/08/1992	18Aqu58	16Aqu06	17Cap26	22Cap37
02/13/1992	24Aqu01	24Aqu55	23Cap36	26Cap25
02/18/1992	29Aqu05	04Pis04	29Cap45	00Aqu15
02/23/1992	04Pis08	13Pis24	05Aqu55	04Aqu04
02/28/1992	09Pis10	22Pis35	12Aqu06	07Aqu55
03/04/1992	14Pis10	00Ari54	18Aqu16	11Aqu46
03/09/1992	19Pis11	07Ari21	24Aqu27	15Aqu37
03/14/1992	24Pis10	10Ari51	00Pis37	19Aqu29
03/19/1992	29Pis09	10Ari53	06Pis48	23Aqu21
03/24/1992	04Ari06	07Ari57	12Pis58	27Aqu13
03/29/1992	09Ari03	03Ari43	19Pis09	01Pis07

Date	Sun	Mercury	Venus	Mars
04/03/1992	13Ari59	00Ari14	25Pis19	05Pis00
04/08/1992	18Ari54	28Pis46	01Ari28	08Pis52
04/13/1992	23Ari48	29Pis30	07Ari39	12Pis44
04/18/1992	28Ari42	02Ari10	13Ari48	16Pis36
04/23/1992	03Tau34	06Ari24	19Ari58	20Pis28
04/28/1992	08Tau27	11Ari51	26Ari07	24Pis19
05/03/1992	13Tau18	18Ari19	02Tau16	28Pis10
05/08/1992	18Tau08	25Ari42	08Tau25	02Ari00
05/13/1992	22Tau58	03Tau56	14Tau34	05Ari49
05/18/1992	27Tau47	13Tau00	20Tau43	09Ari37
05/23/1992	02Gem36	22Tau54	26Tau52	13Ari25
05/28/1992	07Gem24	03Gem30	03Gem00	17Ari12
06/02/1992	12Gem11	14Gem27	09Gem09	20Ari57
06/07/1992	16Gem58	25Gem17	15Gem18	24Ari41
06/12/1992	21Gem45	05Can28	21Gem26	28Ari24
06/17/1992	26Gem31	14Can46	27Gem34	02Tau05
06/22/1992	01Can18	23Can06	03Can43	05Tau45
06/27/1992	06Can04	00Leo23	09Can52	09Tau23
07/02/1992	10Can51	06Leo37	16Can01	12Tau59
07/07/1992	15Can36	11Leo38	22Can09	16Tau33
07/12/1992	20Can22	15Leo15	28Can18	20Tau05
07/17/1992	25Can09	17Leo13	04Leo27	23Tau36
07/22/1992	29Can55	17Leo13	10Leo36	27Tau03
07/27/1992	04Leo41	15Leo16	16Leo45	00Gem28
08/01/1992	09Leo28	11Leo48	22Leo54	03Gem51
08/06/1992	14Leo15	08Leo13	29Leo03	07Gem11
08/11/1992	19Leo03	06Leo06	05Vir12	10Gem28
08/16/1992	23Leo51	06Leo39	11Vir21	13Gem42
08/21/1992	28Leo40	10Leo11	17Vir30	16Gem53
08/26/1992	03Vir30	16Leo28	23Vir39	20Gem00
08/31/1992	08Vir19	24Leo46	29Vir47	23Gem04
09/05/1992	13Vir10	04Vir07	05Lib55	26Gem03
09/10/1992	18Vir01	13Vir45	12Lib04	28Gem59
09/15/1992	22Vir53	23Vir12	18Lib11	01Can49
09/20/1992	27Vir46	02Lib15	24Lib19	04Can35
09/25/1992	02Lib40	10Lib54	00Sco26	07Can15
09/30/1992	07Lib34	19Lib09	06Sco33	09Can49
10/05/1992	12Lib30	27Lib03	12Sco39	12Can16
10/10/1992	17Lib25	04Sco36	18Sco45	14Can36
10/15/1992	22Lib22	11Sco50	24Sco51	16Can48
10/20/1992	27Lib21	18Sco42	00Sag55	18Can51
10/25/1992	02Sco19	25Sco07	07Sag00	20Can44
10/30/1992	07Sco19	00Sag50	13Sag03	22Can27
11/04/1992	12Sco19	05Sag27	19Sag06	23Can57
11/09/1992	17Sco20	08Sag07	25Sag09	25Can13
11/14/1992	22Sco22	07Sag36	01Cap09	26Can15
11/19/1992	27Sco25	03Sag05	07Cap09	27Can00
11/24/1992	02Sag28	26Sco29	13Cap08	27Can28
11/29/1992	07Sag31	22Sco30	19Cap05	27Can36
12/04/1992	12Sag36	23Sco01	25Cap00	27Can23
12/09/1992	17Sag40	26Sco54	00Aqu53	26Can49
12/14/1992	22Sag46	02Sag38	06Aqu43	25Can55
12/19/1992	27Sag51	09Sag16	12Aqu30	24Can40
12/24/1992	02Cap56	16Sag24	18Aqu13	23Can07
12/29/1992	08Cap02	23Sag46	23Aqu52	21Can21

Ephemeris Tables for Sun, Mercury, Venus and Mars

Date	Sun	Mercury	Venus	Mars
01/03/1993	13Cap07	01Cap21	29Aqu27	19Can25
01/08/1993	18Cap13	09Cap04	04Pis55	17Can25
01/13/1993	23Cap19	16Cap58	10Pis16	15Can27
01/18/1993	28Cap24	25Cap04	15Pis28	13Can39
01/23/1993	03Aqu30	03Aqu24	20Pis31	12Can03
01/28/1993	08Aqu34	11Aqu58	25Pis22	10Can43
02/02/1993	13Aqu39	20Aqu46	29Pis58	09Can43
02/07/1993	18Aqu43	29Aqu41	04Ari18	09Can03
02/12/1993	23Aqu47	08Pis23	08Ari16	08Can42
02/17/1993	28Aqu51	16Pis10	11Ari51	08Can40
02/22/1993	03Pis54	21Pis52	14Ari55	08Can58
02/27/1993	08Pis55	24Pis12	17Ari22	09Can32
03/04/1993	13Pis56	22Pis39	19Ari06	10Can21
03/09/1993	18Pis56	18Pis16	19Ari57	11Can24
03/14/1993	23Pis56	13Pis36	19Ari51	12Can39
03/19/1993	28Pis54	10Pis46	18Ari41	14Can06
03/24/1993	03Ari51	10Pis28	16Ari33	15Can42
03/29/1993	08Ari48	12Pis25	13Ari43	17Can27
04/03/1993	13Ari45	16Pis07	10Ari36	19Can19
04/08/1993	18Ari40	21Pis07	07Ari40	21Can19
04/13/1993	23Ari34	27Pis10	05Ari25	23Can25
04/18/1993	28Ari28	04Ari03	04Ari04	25Can37
04/23/1993	03Tau20	11Ari42	03Ari45	27Can53
04/28/1993	08Tau12	20Ari06	04Ari24	00Leo14
05/03/1993	13Tau04	29Ari13	05Ari54	02Leo39
05/08/1993	17Tau54	09Tau04	08Ari07	05Leo08
05/13/1993	22Tau43	19Tau34	10Ari57	07Leo40
05/18/1993	27Tau33	00Gem28	14Ari17	10Leo15
05/23/1993	02Gem22	11Gem16	18Ari01	12Leo53
05/28/1993	07Gem10	21Gem25	22Ari06	15Leo34
06/02/1993	11Gem57	00Can35	26Ari26	18Leo17
06/07/1993	16Gem45	08Can37	01Tau01	21Leo03
06/12/1993	21Gem31	15Can27	05Tau46	23Leo50
06/17/1993	26Gem18	21Can00	10Tau42	26Leo40
06/22/1993	01Can04	25Can07	15Tau46	29Leo31
06/27/1993	05Can51	27Can36	20Tau57	02Vir25
07/02/1993	10Can36	28Can13	26Tau14	05Vir20
07/07/1993	15Can22	26Can58	01Gem36	08Vir16
07/12/1993	20Can09	24Can14	07Gem03	11Vir15
07/17/1993	24Can55	21Can01	12Gem34	14Vir15
07/22/1993	29Can41	18Can39	18Gem09	17Vir17
07/27/1993	04Leo28	18Can16	23Gem48	20Vir20
08/01/1993	09Leo15	20Can22	29Gem30	23Vir25
08/06/1993	14Leo01	25Can00	05Can14	26Vir31
08/11/1993	18Leo49	01Leo56	11Can01	29Vir39
08/16/1993	23Leo37	10Leo40	16Can51	02Lib48
08/21/1993	28Leo26	20Leo24	22Can43	05Lib59
08/26/1993	03Vir15	00Vir25	28Can37	09Lib11
08/31/1993	08Vir05	10Vir10	04Leo34	12Lib25
09/05/1993	12Vir56	19Vir30	10Leo33	15Lib40
09/10/1993	17Vir47	28Vir20	16Leo33	18Lib57
09/15/1993	22Vir39	06Lib42	22Leo36	22Lib15
09/20/1993	27Vir32	14Lib37	28Leo40	25Lib34
09/25/1993	02Lib25	22Lib07	04Vir45	28Lib55
09/30/1993	07Lib20	29Lib12	10Vir52	02Sco18

Date	Sun	Mercury	Venus	Mars
10/05/1993	12Lib15	05Sco48	17Vir01	05Sco42
10/10/1993	17Lib12	11Sco47	23Vir11	09Sco07
10/15/1993	22Lib09	16Sco56	29Vir22	12Sco34
10/20/1993	27Lib06	20Sco46	05Lib34	16Sco03
10/25/1993	02Sco05	22Sco29	11Lib47	19Sco33
10/30/1993	07Sco04	20Sco58	18Lib01	23Sco04
11/04/1993	12Sco05	15Sco52	24Lib16	26Sco37
11/09/1993	17Sco06	09Sco38	00Sco31	00Sag12
11/14/1993	22Sco07	06Sco34	06Sco46	03Sag48
11/19/1993	27Sco10	08Sco03	13Sco03	07Sag24
11/24/1993	02Sag13	12Sco43	19Sco19	11Sag03
11/29/1993	07Sag16	19Sco05	25Sco36	14Sag43
12/04/1993	12Sag21	26Sco13	01Sag53	18Sag25
12/09/1993	17Sag25	03Sag42	08Sag10	22Sag07
12/14/1993	22Sag30	11Sag19	14Sag28	25Sag51
12/19/1993	27Sag36	19Sag01	20Sag45	29Sag36
12/24/1993	02Cap41	26Sag48	27Sag03	03Cap22
12/29/1993	07Cap47	04Cap41	03Cap21	07Cap10
01/03/1994	12Cap52	12Cap40	09Cap38	10Cap59
01/08/1994	17Cap58	20Cap49	15Cap56	14Cap48
01/13/1994	23Cap04	29Cap07	22Cap13	18Cap39
01/18/1994	28Cap10	07Aqu34	28Cap30	22Cap30
01/23/1994	03Aqu15	16Aqu03	04Aqu48	26Cap22
01/28/1994	08Aqu20	24Aqu13	11Aqu04	00Aqu16
02/02/1994	13Aqu25	01Pis24	17Aqu21	04Aqu09
02/07/1994	18Aqu29	06Pis18	23Aqu37	08Aqu04
02/12/1994	23Aqu33	07Pis28	29Aqu54	11Aqu58
02/17/1994	28Aqu36	04Pis25	06Pis10	15Aqu54
02/22/1994	03Pis39	29Aqu02	12Pis25	19Aqu49
02/27/1994	08Pis40	24Aqu29	18Pis40	23Aqu45
03/04/1994	13Pis41	22Aqu39	24Pis54	27Aqu42
03/09/1994	18Pis41	23Aqu31	01Ari07	01Pis37
03/14/1994	23Pis41	26Aqu30	07Ari21	05Pis33
03/19/1994	28Pis40	01Pis00	13Ari33	09Pis29
03/24/1994	03Ari37	06Pis36	19Ari45	13Pis25
03/29/1994	08Ari34	13Pis03	25Ari55	17Pis20
04/03/1994	13Ari30	20Pis14	02Tau06	21Pis15
04/08/1994	18Ari25	28Pis03	08Tau15	25Pis09
04/13/1994	23Ari19	06Ari31	14Tau24	29Pis03
04/18/1994	28Ari13	15Ari37	20Tau31	02Ari55
04/23/1994	03Tau06	25Ari22	26Tau37	06Ari48
04/28/1994	07Tau58	05Tau44	02Gem43	10Ari39
05/03/1994	12Tau49	16Tau28	08Gem48	14Ari30
05/08/1994	17Tau40	27Tau09	14Gem52	18Ari19
05/13/1994	22Tau30	07Gem11	20Gem54	22Ari07
05/18/1994	27Tau19	16Gem07	26Gem55	25Ari55
05/23/1994	02Gem08	23Gem43	02Can56	29Ari40
05/28/1994	06Gem55	29Gem52	08Can54	03Tau25
06/02/1994	11Gem43	04Can28	14Can52	07Tau09
06/07/1994	16Gem31	07Can22	20Can48	10Tau51
06/12/1994	21Gem17	08Can24	26Can42	14Tau31
06/17/1994	26Gem04	07Can34	02Leo34	18Tau11
06/22/1994	00Can51	05Can18	08Leo25	21Tau48
06/27/1994	05Can36	02Can25	14Leo13	25Tau24

Ephemeris Tables for Sun, Mercury, Venus and Mars

Date	Sun	Mercury	Venus	Mars	Date	Sun	Mercury	Venus	Mars
07/02/1994	10Can22	00Can08	19Leo59	28Tau59	04/03/1995	13Ari16	02Ari12	07Pis32	13Leo43
07/07/1994	15Can09	29Gem26	25Leo42	02Gem32	04/08/1995	18Ari11	11Ari49	13Pis33	14Leo24
07/12/1994	19Can55	00Can48	01Vir23	06Gem03	04/13/1995	23Ari06	21Ari58	19Pis33	15Leo19
07/17/1994	24Can41	04Can19	07Vir00	09Gem32	04/18/1995	27Ari59	02Tau29	25Pis35	16Leo29
07/22/1994	29Can27	09Can56	12Vir34	13Gem00	04/23/1995	02Tau52	12Tau58	01Ari36	17Leo49
07/27/1994	04Leo14	17Can28	18Vir04	16Gem25	04/28/1995	07Tau44	22Tau47	07Ari39	19Leo21
08/01/1994	09Leo01	26Can33	23Vir30	19Gem49	05/03/1995	12Tau35	01Gem22	13Ari41	21Leo01
08/06/1994	13Leo48	06Leo36	28Vir49	23Gem10	05/08/1995	17Tau26	08Gem23	19Ari44	22Leo51
08/11/1994	18Leo36	16Leo56	04Lib04	26Gem30	05/13/1995	22Tau16	13Gem38	25Ari48	24Leo47
08/16/1994	23Leo24	27Leo01	09Lib11	29Gem48	05/18/1995	27Tau05	16Gem58	01Tau51	26Leo51
08/21/1994	28Leo12	06Vir36	14Lib10	03Can03	05/23/1995	01Gem54	18Gem19	07Tau55	29Leo01
08/26/1994	03Vir01	15Vir37	19Lib01	06Can16	05/28/1995	06Gem42	17Gem43	13Tau59	01Vir17
08/31/1994	07Vir51	24Vir04	23Lib40	09Can28					
					06/02/1995	11Gem30	15Gem36	20Tau03	03Vir38
09/05/1994	12Vir42	02Lib00	28Lib06	12Can36	06/07/1995	16Gem17	12Gem51	26Tau08	06Vir03
09/10/1994	17Vir33	09Lib26	02Sco17	15Can42	06/12/1995	21Gem04	10Gem37	02Gem13	08Vir33
09/15/1994	22Vir25	16Lib19	06Sco09	18Can45	06/17/1995	25Gem50	09Gem48	08Gem18	11Vir07
09/20/1994	27Vir18	22Lib37	09Sco37	21Can46	06/22/1995	00Can36	10Gem51	14Gem24	13Vir45
09/25/1994	02Lib11	28Lib10	12Sco39	24Can43	06/27/1995	05Can23	13Gem48	20Gem30	16Vir27
09/30/1994	07Lib06	02Sco41	15Sco06	27Can37					
					07/02/1995	10Can09	18Gem34	26Gem36	19Vir11
10/05/1994	12Lib01	05Sco41	16Sco53	00Leo28	07/07/1995	14Can55	25Gem01	02Can43	21Vir59
10/10/1994	16Lib57	06Sco22	17Sco51	03Leo15	07/12/1995	19Can41	03Can03	08Can51	24Vir49
10/15/1994	21Lib54	03Sco55	17Sco54	05Leo58	07/17/1995	24Can27	12Can26	14Can58	27Vir43
10/20/1994	26Lib52	28Lib28	16Sco57	08Leo37	07/22/1995	29Can13	22Can44	21Can07	00Lib39
10/25/1994	01Sco51	22Lib52	15Sco02	11Leo11	07/27/1995	04Leo00	03Leo19	27Can15	03Lib37
10/30/1994	06Sco50	20Lib49	12Sco23	13Leo40					
					08/01/1995	08Leo46	13Leo41	03Leo24	06Lib39
11/04/1994	11Sco50	23Lib13	09Sco21	16Leo04	08/06/1995	13Leo34	23Leo30	09Leo34	09Lib42
11/09/1994	16Sco51	28Lib39	06Sco29	18Leo21	08/11/1995	18Leo21	02Vir40	15Leo45	12Lib48
11/14/1994	21Sco53	05Sco37	04Sco13	20Leo31	08/16/1995	23Leo10	11Vir13	21Leo55	15Lib55
11/19/1994	26Sco55	13Sco13	02Sco50	22Leo34	08/21/1995	27Leo58	19Vir09	28Leo07	19Lib06
11/24/1994	01Sag58	21Sco03	02Sco29	24Leo30	08/26/1995	02Vir48	26Vir28	04Vir18	22Lib18
11/29/1994	07Sag02	28Sco55	03Sco09	26Leo15	08/31/1995	07Vir37	03Lib08	10Vir30	25Lib33
12/04/1994	12Sag06	06Sag46	04Sco40	27Leo51	09/05/1995	12Vir28	09Lib05	16Vir42	28Lib49
12/09/1994	17Sag10	14Sag37	06Sco59	29Leo15	09/10/1995	17Vir19	14Lib07	22Vir55	02Sco07
12/14/1994	22Sag16	22Sag28	09Sco56	00Vir27	09/15/1995	22Vir10	17Lib55	29Vir07	05Sco28
12/19/1994	27Sag21	00Cap22	13Sco25	01Vir24	09/20/1995	27Vir04	20Lib00	05Lib21	08Sco50
12/24/1994	02Cap27	08Cap20	17Sco20	02Vir06	09/25/1995	01Lib57	19Lib37	11Lib33	12Sco14
12/29/1994	07Cap32	16Cap22	21Sco36	02Vir31	09/30/1995	06Lib51	16Lib18	17Lib47	15Sco40
01/03/1995	12Cap38	24Cap28	26Sco10	02Vir39	10/05/1995	11Lib46	10Lib49	24Lib00	19Sco09
01/08/1995	17Cap43	02Aqu30	00Sag58	02Vir27	10/10/1995	16Lib43	06Lib07	00Sco13	22Sco39
01/13/1995	22Cap49	10Aqu07	05Sag58	01Vir54	10/15/1995	21Lib40	05Lib12	06Sco27	26Sco10
01/18/1995	27Cap55	16Aqu36	11Sag08	01Vir02	10/20/1995	26Lib37	08Lib28	12Sco40	29Sco43
01/23/1995	03Aqu00	20Aqu40	16Sag20	29Leo50	10/25/1995	01Sco36	14Lib36	18Sco54	03Sag19
01/28/1995	08Aqu06	20Aqu41	21Sag52	28Leo21	10/30/1995	06Sco35	22Lib09	25Sco07	06Sag55
02/02/1995	13Aqu10	16Aqu22	27Sag22	26Leo37	11/04/1995	11Sco36	00Sco13	01Sag21	10Sag34
02/07/1995	18Aqu14	10Aqu27	02Cap58	24Leo43	11/09/1995	16Sco36	08Sco24	07Sag33	14Sag15
02/12/1995	23Aqu18	06Aqu28	08Cap39	22Leo44	11/14/1995	21Sco38	16Sco31	13Sag46	17Sag56
02/17/1995	28Aqu21	05Aqu43	14Cap23	20Leo45	11/19/1995	26Sco40	24Sco32	20Sag00	21Sag40
02/22/1995	03Pis24	07Aqu39	20Cap09	18Leo53	11/24/1995	01Sag43	02Sag27	26Sag12	25Sag24
02/27/1995	08Pis25	11Aqu29	25Cap59	17Leo12	11/29/1995	06Sag47	10Sag18	02Cap25	29Sag11
03/04/1995	13Pis27	16Aqu37	01Aqu51	15Leo45	12/04/1995	11Sag51	18Sag07	08Cap37	02Cap58
03/09/1995	18Pis27	22Aqu40	07Aqu44	14Leo37	12/09/1995	16Sag56	25Sag55	14Cap49	06Cap47
03/14/1995	23Pis27	29Aqu27	13Aqu39	13Leo48	12/14/1995	22Sag01	03Cap42	21Cap01	10Cap37
03/19/1995	28Pis25	06Pis48	19Aqu36	13Leo19	12/19/1995	27Sag06	11Cap27	27Cap12	14Cap28
03/24/1995	03Ari22	14Pis43	25Aqu33	13Leo09	12/24/1995	02Cap12	19Cap00	03Aqu22	18Cap20
03/29/1995	08Ari20	23Pis11	01Pis33	13Leo16	12/29/1995	07Cap17	26Cap01	09Aqu33	22Cap13

Ephemeris Tables for Sun, Mercury, Venus and Mars

Date	Sun	Mercury	Venus	Mars
01/03/1996	12Cap23	01Aqu48	15Aqu42	26Cap07
01/08/1996	17Cap29	04Aqu59	21Aqu49	00Aqu01
01/13/1996	22Cap34	03Aqu54	27Aqu57	03Aqu57
01/18/1996	27Cap40	28Cap36	04Pis03	07Aqu53
01/23/1996	02Aqu45	22Cap32	10Pis06	11Aqu49
01/28/1996	07Aqu51	19Cap21	16Pis09	15Aqu46
02/02/1996	12Aqu55	19Cap40	22Pis09	19Aqu43
02/07/1996	17Aqu59	22Cap34	28Pis06	23Aqu40
02/12/1996	23Aqu03	27Cap09	04Ari00	27Aqu37
02/17/1996	28Aqu07	02Aqu48	09Ari52	01Pis36
02/22/1996	03Pis09	09Aqu13	15Ari40	05Pis33
02/27/1996	08Pis11	16Aqu12	21Ari25	09Pis30
03/03/1996	13Pis12	23Aqu42	27Ari06	13Pis27
03/08/1996	18Pis13	01Pis39	02Tau41	17Pis22
03/13/1996	23Pis12	10Pis04	08Tau10	21Pis18
03/18/1996	28Pis11	18Pis58	13Tau33	25Pis13
03/23/1996	03Ari08	28Pis24	18Tau49	29Pis07
03/28/1996	08Ari05	08Ari17	23Tau56	03Ari00
04/02/1996	13Ari01	18Ari32	28Tau53	06Ari53
04/07/1996	17Ari57	28Ari45	03Gem39	10Ari45
04/12/1996	22Ari51	08Tau16	08Gem10	14Ari36
04/17/1996	27Ari45	16Tau25	12Gem25	18Ari26
04/22/1996	02Tau37	22Tau40	16Gem20	22Ari15
04/27/1996	07Tau30	26Tau45	19Gem52	26Ari02
05/02/1996	12Tau21	28Tau33	22Gem55	29Ari48
05/07/1996	17Tau12	28Tau07	25Gem24	03Tau34
05/12/1996	22Tau02	25Tau57	27Gem11	07Tau18
05/17/1996	26Tau51	23Tau04	28Gem10	11Tau00
05/22/1996	01Gem40	20Tau38	28Gem12	14Tau42
05/27/1996	06Gem28	19Tau39	27Gem15	18Tau21
06/01/1996	11Gem16	20Tau29	25Gem21	22Tau00
06/06/1996	16Gem03	23Tau06	22Gem37	25Tau37
06/11/1996	20Gem50	27Tau24	19Gem33	29Tau13
06/16/1996	25Gem36	03Gem10	16Gem32	02Gem47
06/21/1996	00Can22	10Gem18	14Gem03	06Gem20
06/26/1996	05Can09	18Gem45	12Gem26	09Gem51
07/01/1996	09Can55	28Gem21	11Gem47	13Gem21
07/06/1996	14Can41	08Can49	12Gem07	16Gem50
07/11/1996	19Can27	19Can37	13Gem19	20Gem17
07/16/1996	24Can13	00Leo11	15Gem17	23Gem43
07/21/1996	29Can00	10Leo12	17Gem53	27Gem07
07/26/1996	03Leo46	19Leo30	21Gem02	00Can30
07/31/1996	08Leo33	28Leo05	24Gem36	03Can51
08/05/1996	13Leo20	05Vir57	28Gem32	07Can11
08/10/1996	18Leo07	13Vir07	02Can47	10Can30
08/15/1996	22Leo55	19Vir31	07Can17	13Can46
08/20/1996	27Leo45	25Vir03	12Can00	17Can01
08/25/1996	02Vir33	29Vir28	16Can53	20Can16
08/30/1996	07Vir23	02Lib27	21Can56	23Can28
09/04/1996	12Vir13	03Lib29	27Can08	26Can39
09/09/1996	17Vir05	02Lib03	02Leo27	29Can48
09/14/1996	21Vir57	28Vir04	07Leo52	02Leo55
09/19/1996	26Vir49	22Vir55	13Leo23	06Leo01
09/24/1996	01Lib43	19Vir24	19Leo00	09Leo04
09/29/1996	06Lib37	19Vir39	24Leo40	12Leo06

Date	Sun	Mercury	Venus	Mars
10/04/1996	11Lib32	23Vir46	00Vir25	15Leo07
10/09/1996	16Lib28	00Lib33	06Vir14	18Leo04
10/14/1996	21Lib25	08Lib39	12Vir06	21Leo00
10/19/1996	26Lib23	17Lib11	18Vir01	23Leo54
10/24/1996	01Sco21	25Lib43	24Vir00	26Leo45
10/29/1996	06Sco21	04Sco06	00Lib00	29Leo33
11/03/1996	11Sco21	12Sco17	06Lib03	02Vir19
11/08/1996	16Sco22	20Sco18	12Lib08	05Vir01
11/13/1996	21Sco24	28Sco09	18Lib15	07Vir40
11/18/1996	26Sco26	05Sag54	24Lib23	10Vir16
11/23/1996	01Sag29	13Sag31	00Sco33	12Vir48
11/28/1996	06Sag32	21Sag04	06Sco43	15Vir15
12/03/1996	11Sag36	28Sag27	12Sco55	17Vir38
12/08/1996	16Sag41	05Cap31	19Sco07	19Vir55
12/13/1996	21Sag46	11Cap56	25Sco21	22Vir07
12/18/1996	26Sag51	16Cap57	01Sag35	24Vir13
12/23/1996	01Cap57	19Cap13	07Sag49	26Vir11
12/28/1996	07Cap02	17Cap07	14Sag04	28Vir01
01/02/1997	12Cap09	11Cap04	20Sag19	29Vir43
01/07/1997	17Cap13	05Cap13	26Sag34	01Lib15
01/12/1997	22Cap19	02Cap58	02Cap50	02Lib36
01/17/1997	27Cap25	04Cap19	09Cap06	03Lib45
01/22/1997	02Aqu30	08Cap05	15Cap22	04Lib41
01/27/1997	07Aqu36	13Cap18	21Cap38	05Lib22
02/01/1997	12Aqu40	19Cap24	27Cap53	05Lib47
02/06/1997	17Aqu45	26Cap07	04Aqu09	05Lib54
02/11/1997	22Aqu48	03Aqu17	10Aqu24	05Lib43
02/16/1997	27Aqu52	10Aqu51	16Aqu40	05Lib12
02/21/1997	02Pis54	18Aqu48	22Aqu55	04Lib22
02/26/1997	07Pis56	27Aqu08	29Aqu10	03Lib13
03/03/1997	12Pis57	05Pis54	05Pis25	01Lib47
03/08/1997	17Pis58	15Pis06	11Pis40	00Lib06
03/13/1997	22Pis58	24Pis44	17Pis54	28Vir14
03/18/1997	27Pis56	04Ari38	24Pis07	26Vir18
03/23/1997	02Ari54	14Ari30	00Ari21	24Vir21
03/28/1997	07Ari51	23Ari39	06Ari33	22Vir29
04/02/1997	12Ari47	01Tau15	12Ari46	20Vir49
04/07/1997	17Ari42	06Tau37	18Ari58	19Vir23
04/12/1997	22Ari37	09Tau19	25Ari10	18Vir14
04/17/1997	27Ari31	09Tau20	01Tau22	17Vir24
04/22/1997	02Tau24	07Tau09	07Tau33	16Vir54
04/27/1997	07Tau16	03Tau52	13Tau43	16Vir43
05/02/1997	12Tau07	00Tau57	19Tau53	16Vir52
05/07/1997	16Tau58	29Ari33	26Tau03	17Vir17
05/12/1997	21Tau48	00Tau01	02Gem12	18Vir00
05/17/1997	26Tau37	02Tau21	08Gem20	18Vir57
05/22/1997	01Gem26	06Tau18	14Gem28	20Vir08
05/27/1997	06Gem14	11Tau37	20Gem36	21Vir31
06/01/1997	11Gem02	18Tau09	26Gem44	23Vir06
06/06/1997	15Gem49	25Tau49	02Can51	24Vir50
06/11/1997	20Gem36	04Gem33	08Can57	26Vir44
06/16/1997	25Gem23	14Gem18	15Can04	28Vir46
06/21/1997	00Can09	24Gem52	21Can09	00Lib56
06/26/1997	04Can55	05Can47	27Can14	03Lib13

Ephemeris Tables for Sun, Mercury, Venus and Mars

Date	Sun	Mercury	Venus	Mars
07/01/1997	09Can41	16Can31	03Leo19	05Lib36
07/06/1997	14Can27	26Can40	09Leo23	08Lib04
07/11/1997	19Can13	06Leo03	15Leo27	10Lib39
07/16/1997	23Can59	14Leo37	21Leo30	13Lib18
07/21/1997	28Can46	22Leo24	27Leo32	16Lib02
07/26/1997	03Leo32	29Leo19	03Vir33	18Lib50
07/31/1997	08Leo19	05Vir21	09Vir34	21Lib42
08/05/1997	13Leo06	10Vir19	15Vir34	24Lib39
08/10/1997	17Leo54	13Vir59	21Vir32	27Lib39
08/15/1997	22Leo42	15Vir59	27Vir30	00Sco42
08/20/1997	27Leo30	15Vir54	03Lib26	03Sco48
08/25/1997	02Vir19	13Vir28	09Lib22	06Sco58
08/30/1997	07Vir09	09Vir12	15Lib16	10Sco10
09/04/1997	12Vir00	04Vir50	21Lib08	13Sco26
09/09/1997	16Vir51	02Vir43	26Lib58	16Sco45
09/14/1997	21Vir42	04Vir11	02Sco48	20Sco06
09/19/1997	26Vir35	09Vir07	08Sco34	23Sco29
09/24/1997	01Lib29	16Vir30	14Sco19	26Sco55
09/29/1997	06Lib23	25Vir07	20Sco01	00Sag24
10/04/1997	11Lib18	04Lib05	25Sco41	03Sag55
10/09/1997	16Lib14	12Lib59	01Sag17	07Sag28
10/14/1997	21Lib11	21Lib38	06Sag49	11Sag03
10/19/1997	26Lib09	00Sco00	12Sag18	14Sag40
10/24/1997	01Sco07	08Sco06	17Sag40	18Sag19
10/29/1997	06Sco06	15Sco59	22Sag57	22Sag00
11/03/1997	11Sco06	23Sco39	28Sag06	25Sag43
11/08/1997	16Sco07	01Sag09	03Cap07	29Sag27
11/13/1997	21Sco09	08Sag25	07Cap58	03Cap13
11/18/1997	26Sco11	15Sag27	12Cap36	07Cap01
11/23/1997	01Sag14	22Sag02	16Cap59	10Cap49
11/28/1997	06Sag17	27Sag48	21Cap03	14Cap39
12/03/1997	11Sag22	02Cap01	24Cap45	18Cap31
12/08/1997	16Sag26	03Cap19	27Cap58	22Cap23
12/13/1997	21Sag31	00Cap16	00Aqu38	26Cap16
12/18/1997	26Sag36	23Sag48	02Aqu36	00Aqu10
12/23/1997	01Cap42	18Sag25	03Aqu44	04Aqu06
12/28/1997	06Cap48	17Sag08	03Aqu54	08Aqu01
01/02/1998	11Cap54	19Sag28	03Aqu03	11Aqu57
01/07/1998	16Cap59	24Sag00	01Aqu11	15Aqu53
01/12/1998	22Cap05	29Sag47	28Cap33	19Aqu50
01/17/1998	27Cap10	06Cap18	25Cap30	23Aqu46
01/22/1998	02Aqu16	13Cap16	22Cap36	27Aqu44
01/27/1998	07Aqu21	20Cap36	20Cap18	01Pis40
02/01/1998	12Aqu25	28Cap14	18Cap53	05Pis37
02/06/1998	17Aqu30	06Aqu09	18Cap28	09Pis33
02/11/1998	22Aqu33	14Aqu25	19Cap05	13Pis28
02/16/1998	27Aqu36	23Aqu00	20Cap35	17Pis24
02/21/1998	02Pis40	01Pis58	22Cap51	21Pis18
02/26/1998	07Pis42	11Pis16	25Cap44	25Pis12
03/03/1998	12Pis43	20Pis49	29Cap08	29Pis06
03/08/1998	17Pis43	00Ari16	02Aqu58	02Ari57
03/13/1998	22Pis43	08Ari59	07Aqu07	06Ari49
03/18/1998	27Pis42	15Ari58	11Aqu34	10Ari40
03/23/1998	02Ari39	20Ari18	16Aqu15	14Ari29
03/28/1998	07Ari36	21Ari28	21Aqu07	18Ari17

Date	Sun	Mercury	Venus	Mars
04/02/1998	12Ari33	19Ari40	26Aqu09	22Ari04
04/07/1998	17Ari28	16Ari02	01Pis20	25Ari51
04/12/1998	22Ari22	12Ari21	06Pis36	29Ari36
04/17/1998	27Ari16	10Ari07	11Pis59	03Tau19
04/22/1998	02Tau10	10Ari00	17Pis27	07Tau02
04/27/1998	07Tau01	11Ari52	22Pis58	10Tau43
05/02/1998	11Tau53	15Ari25	28Pis33	14Tau22
05/07/1998	16Tau44	20Ari22	04Ari10	18Tau01
05/12/1998	21Tau34	26Ari27	09Ari51	21Tau39
05/17/1998	26Tau23	03Tau32	15Ari34	25Tau15
05/22/1998	01Gem12	11Tau34	21Ari19	28Tau49
05/27/1998	06Gem00	20Tau30	27Ari07	02Gem23
06/01/1998	10Gem48	00Gem21	02Tau56	05Gem55
06/06/1998	15Gem35	10Gem55	08Tau46	09Gem26
06/11/1998	20Gem22	21Gem53	14Tau38	12Gem55
06/16/1998	25Gem09	02Can43	20Tau31	16Gem24
06/21/1998	29Gem55	12Can57	26Tau26	19Gem51
06/26/1998	04Can42	22Can21	02Gem21	23Gem17
07/01/1998	09Can27	00Leo49	08Gem18	26Gem42
07/06/1998	14Can13	08Leo22	14Gem15	00Can05
07/11/1998	19Can00	14Leo57	20Gem14	03Can28
07/16/1998	23Can46	20Leo26	26Gem14	06Can49
07/21/1998	28Can32	24Leo40	02Can15	10Can09
07/26/1998	03Leo18	27Leo24	08Can16	13Can28
07/31/1998	08Leo05	28Leo15	14Can19	16Can46
08/05/1998	12Leo52	27Leo00	20Can24	20Can03
08/10/1998	17Leo39	23Leo49	26Can29	23Can19
08/15/1998	22Leo28	19Leo48	02Leo35	26Can34
08/20/1998	27Leo16	16Leo40	08Leo42	29Can48
08/25/1998	02Vir06	16Leo07	14Leo50	03Leo01
08/30/1998	06Vir55	18Leo47	21Leo00	06Leo13
09/04/1998	11Vir45	24Leo30	27Leo09	09Leo24
09/09/1998	16Vir37	02Vir25	03Vir09	12Leo34
09/14/1998	21Vir28	11Vir30	09Vir32	15Leo43
09/19/1998	26Vir21	20Vir53	15Vir44	18Leo51
09/24/1998	01Lib15	00Lib09	21Vir57	21Leo58
09/29/1998	06Lib09	09Lib04	28Vir10	25Leo04
10/04/1998	11Lib04	17Lib37	04Lib25	28Leo09
10/09/1998	16Lib00	25Lib50	10Lib39	01Vir13
10/14/1998	20Lib57	03Sco45	16Lib55	04Vir16
10/19/1998	25Lib54	11Sco21	23Lib10	07Vir16
10/24/1998	00Sco52	18Sco42	29Lib25	10Vir17
10/29/1998	05Sco51	25Sco43	05Sco42	13Vir16
11/03/1998	10Sco52	02Sag23	11Sco58	16Vir13
11/08/1998	15Sco52	08Sag28	18Sco14	19Vir09
11/13/1998	20Sco54	13Sag34	24Sco31	22Vir03
11/18/1998	25Sco57	16Sag55	00Sag47	24Vir56
11/23/1998	01Sag00	17Sag13	07Sag04	27Vir47
11/28/1998	06Sag03	13Sag21	13Sag21	00Lib36
12/03/1998	11Sag07	06Sag43	19Sag37	03Lib23
12/08/1998	16Sag12	02Sag00	25Sag54	06Lib07
12/13/1998	21Sag16	01Sag43	02Cap11	08Lib49
12/18/1998	26Sag22	04Sag56	08Cap27	11Lib28
12/23/1998	01Cap27	10Sag11	14Cap44	14Lib05
12/28/1998	06Cap33	16Sag30	21Cap00	16Lib37

Ephemeris Tables for Sun, Mercury, Venus and Mars

Date	Sun	Mercury	Venus	Mars
01/02/1999	11Cap39	23Sag24	27Cap16	19Lib07
01/07/1999	16Cap44	00Cap37	03Aqu32	21Lib32
01/12/1999	21Cap50	08Cap06	09Aqu48	23Lib53
01/17/1999	26Cap55	15Cap47	16Aqu03	26Lib09
01/22/1999	02Aqu01	23Cap40	22Aqu18	28Lib19
01/27/1999	07Aqu06	01Aqu49	28Aqu33	00Sco24
02/01/1999	12Aqu10	10Aqu15	04Pis47	02Sco21
02/06/1999	17Aqu15	18Aqu57	11Pis00	04Sco11
02/11/1999	22Aqu19	27Aqu56	17Pis12	05Sco53
02/16/1999	27Aqu22	07Pis05	23Pis24	07Sco25
02/21/1999	02Pis25	16Pis06	29Pis34	08Sco46
02/26/1999	07Pis27	24Pis17	05Ari43	09Sco56
03/03/1999	12Pis28	00Ari34	11Ari51	10Sco52
03/08/1999	17Pis29	03Ari48	17Ari57	11Sco35
03/13/1999	22Pis28	03Ari22	24Ari03	12Sco01
03/18/1999	27Pis27	29Pis55	00Tau06	12Sco10
03/23/1999	02Ari25	25Pis24	06Tau09	12Sco01
03/28/1999	07Ari22	22Pis01	12Tau09	11Sco33
04/02/1999	12Ari18	20Pis54	18Tau07	10Sco46
04/07/1999	17Ari14	22Pis02	24Tau03	09Sco40
04/12/1999	22Ari09	25Pis04	29Tau57	08Sco17
04/17/1999	27Ari03	29Pis34	05Gem48	06Sco40
04/22/1999	01Tau55	05Ari14	11Gem36	04Sco54
04/27/1999	06Tau48	11Ari51	17Gem21	03Sco02
05/02/1999	11Tau39	19Ari19	23Gem03	01Sco10
05/07/1999	16Tau30	27Ari34	28Gem40	29Lib25
05/12/1999	21Tau19	06Tau37	04Can14	27Lib51
05/17/1999	26Tau09	16Tau27	09Can43	26Lib31
05/22/1999	00Gem58	27Tau00	15Can06	25Lib30
05/27/1999	05Gem46	07Gem56	20Can24	24Lib49
06/01/1999	10Gem34	18Gem46	25Can34	24Lib28
06/06/1999	15Gem21	29Gem00	00Leo36	24Lib27
06/11/1999	20Gem09	08Can20	05Leo29	24Lib45
06/16/1999	24Gem55	16Can36	10Leo10	25Lib22
06/21/1999	29Gem42	23Can48	14Leo39	26Lib16
06/26/1999	04Can27	29Can50	18Leo52	27Lib25

Date	Sun	Mercury	Venus	Mars
07/01/1999	09Can13	04Leo36	22Leo45	28Lib49
07/06/1999	14Can00	07Leo52	26Leo18	00Sco25
07/11/1999	18Can46	09Leo24	29Leo22	02Sco14
07/16/1999	23Can31	08Leo58	01Vir54	04Sco13
07/21/1999	28Can18	06Leo45	03Vir47	06Sco22
07/26/1999	03Leo04	03Leo20	04Vir52	08Sco40
07/31/1999	07Leo51	00Leo08	05Vir05	11Sco05
08/05/1999	12Leo39	28Can37	04Vir20	13Sco39
08/10/1999	17Leo26	29Can38	02Vir36	16Sco19
08/15/1999	22Leo14	03Leo29	00Vir03	19Sco04
08/20/1999	27Leo03	09Leo55	27Leo03	21Sco57
08/25/1999	01Vir51	18Leo18	23Leo58	24Sco54
08/30/1999	06Vir41	27Leo48	21Leo25	27Sco56
09/04/1999	11Vir31	07Vir34	19Leo37	01Sag03
09/09/1999	16Vir22	17Vir12	18Leo51	04Sag14
09/14/1999	21Vir14	26Vir24	19Leo01	07Sag29
09/19/1999	26Vir07	05Lib08	20Leo07	10Sag48
09/24/1999	01Lib00	13Lib28	22Leo01	14Sag10
09/29/1999	05Lib54	21Lib24	24Leo36	17Sag36
10/04/1999	10Lib49	28Lib57	27Leo43	21Sag04
10/09/1999	15Lib45	06Sco09	01Vir21	24Sag35
10/14/1999	20Lib42	12Sco55	05Vir21	28Sag09
10/19/1999	25Lib39	19Sco12	09Vir41	01Cap45
10/24/1999	00Sco38	24Sco45	14Vir18	05Cap24
10/29/1999	05Sco37	29Sco07	19Vir08	09Cap04
11/03/1999	10Sco37	01Sag33	24Vir10	12Cap47
11/08/1999	15Sco38	00Sag52	29Vir22	16Cap31
11/13/1999	20Sco40	26Sco16	04Lib43	20Cap16
11/18/1999	25Sco42	19Sco45	10Lib11	24Cap04
11/23/1999	00Sag45	15Sco53	15Lib45	27Cap52
11/28/1999	05Sag48	16Sco34	21Lib25	01Aqu42
12/03/1999	10Sag52	20Sco38	27Lib10	05Aqu32
12/08/1999	15Sag57	26Sco33	02Sco59	09Aqu23
12/13/1999	21Sag01	03Sag22	08Sco51	13Aqu15
12/18/1999	26Sag07	10Sag37	14Sco46	17Aqu07
12/23/1999	01Cap12	18Sag06	20Sco45	20Aqu59
12/28/1999	06Cap18	25Sag43	26Sco45	24Aqu52

Ephemeris Tables for Jupiter, Saturn, Uranus, Neptune, and Pluto

Date	Jupiter	Saturn	Uranus	Neptune	Pluto
01/01/1900	01Sag13	27Sag46	10Sag10	25Gem12	15Gem13
01/16/1900	04Sag00	29Sag28	10Sag57	24Gem48	14Gem58
01/31/1900	06Sag26	01Cap03	11Sag36	24Gem30	14Gem48
02/15/1900	08Sag25	02Cap25	12Sag05	24Gem18	14Gem42
03/02/1900	09Sag52	03Cap33	12Sag23	24Gem12	14Gem40
03/17/1900	10Sag41	04Cap24	12Sag29	24Gem15	14Gem44
04/01/1900	10Sag49	04Cap53	12Sag24	24Gem24	14Gem52
04/16/1900	10Sag15	05Cap01	12Sag07	24Gem41	15Gem04
05/01/1900	09Sag04	04Cap47	11Sag40	25Gem04	15Gem21
05/16/1900	07Sag24	04Cap12	11Sag08	25Gem32	15Gem40
05/31/1900	05Sag31	03Cap22	10Sag31	26Gem03	16Gem00
06/15/1900	03Sag42	02Cap20	09Sag55	26Gem36	16Gem21
06/30/1900	02Sag13	01Cap14	09Sag21	27Gem10	16Gem41
07/15/1900	01Sag17	00Cap11	08Sag54	27Gem42	17Gem00
07/30/1900	01Sag00	29Sag19	08Sag35	28Gem11	17Gem16
08/14/1900	01Sag25	28Sag43	08Sag27	28Gem36	17Gem28
08/29/1900	02Sag28	28Sag26	08Sag31	28Gem56	17Gem36
09/13/1900	04Sag07	28Sag31	08Sag45	29Gem09	17Gem40
09/28/1900	06Sag15	28Sag58	09Sag11	29Gem15	17Gem39
10/13/1900	08Sag49	29Sag45	09Sag47	29Gem13	17Gem33
10/28/1900	11Sag42	00Cap51	10Sag31	29Gem04	17Gem23
11/12/1900	14Sag50	02Cap11	11Sag21	28Gem49	17Gem09
11/27/1900	18Sag08	03Cap44	12Sag15	28Gem28	16Gem53
12/12/1900	21Sag31	05Cap25	13Sag09	28Gem03	16Gem36
12/27/1900	24Sag56	07Cap10	14Sag03	27Gem38	16Gem19
01/11/1901	28Sag18	08Cap56	14Sag53	27Gem14	16Gem04
01/26/1901	01Cap30	10Cap38	15Sag37	26Gem53	15Gem51
02/10/1901	04Cap30	12Cap13	16Sag12	26Gem37	15Gem43
02/25/1901	07Cap10	13Cap38	16Sag37	26Gem28	15Gem40
03/12/1901	09Cap28	14Cap48	16Sag51	26Gem27	15Gem41
03/27/1901	11Cap15	15Cap40	16Sag53	26Gem33	15Gem48
04/11/1901	12Cap28	16Cap12	16Sag43	26Gem46	15Gem58
04/26/1901	13Cap01	16Cap22	16Sag24	27Gem06	16Gem13
05/11/1901	12Cap52	16Cap11	15Sag55	27Gem32	16Gem31
05/26/1901	12Cap02	15Cap39	15Sag21	28Gem01	16Gem51
06/10/1901	10Cap37	14Cap51	14Sag43	28Gem34	17Gem12
06/25/1901	08Cap49	13Cap50	14Sag07	29Gem07	17Gem33
07/10/1901	06Cap55	12Cap44	13Sag36	29Gem40	17Gem52
07/25/1901	05Cap12	11Cap40	13Sag12	00Can11	18Gem09
08/09/1901	03Cap55	10Cap46	12Sag57	00Can39	18Gem24
08/24/1901	03Cap16	10Cap07	12Sag52	01Can01	18Gem34
09/08/1901	03Cap20	09Cap48	13Sag00	01Can18	18Gem39
09/23/1901	04Cap05	09Cap51	13Sag18	01Can27	18Gem40
10/08/1901	05Cap29	10Cap15	13Sag48	01Can29	18Gem36
10/23/1901	07Cap27	11Cap00	14Sag27	01Can24	18Gem28
11/07/1901	09Cap54	12Cap04	15Sag12	01Can12	18Gem15
11/22/1901	12Cap44	13Cap23	16Sag04	00Can53	18Gem00
12/07/1901	15Cap52	14Cap55	16Sag58	00Can30	17Gem43
12/22/1901	19Cap12	16Cap36	17Sag53	00Can05	17Gem25
01/06/1902	22Cap40	18Cap21	18Sag45	29Gem40	17Gem09
01/21/1902	26Cap12	20Cap07	19Sag33	29Gem17	16Gem56
02/05/1902	29Cap42	21Cap50	20Sag14	28Gem58	16Gem46
02/20/1902	03Aqu06	23Cap27	20Sag46	28Gem46	16Gem40
03/07/1902	06Aqu19	24Cap52	21Sag07	28Gem40	16Gem40
03/22/1902	09Aqu18	26Cap04	21Sag16	28Gem43	16Gem44

Ephemeris Tables for Jupiter, Saturn, Uranus, Neptune, and Pluto

Date	Jupiter	Saturn	Uranus	Neptune	Pluto
04/06/1902	11Aqu55	26Cap59	21Sag14	28Gem53	16Gem54
04/21/1902	14Aqu07	27Cap34	21Sag00	29Gem10	17Gem07
05/06/1902	15Aqu48	27Cap47	20Sag37	29Gem33	17Gem24
05/21/1902	16Aqu52	27Cap39	20Sag06	00Can00	17Gem43
06/05/1902	17Aqu15	27Cap10	19Sag31	00Can31	18Gem03
06/20/1902	16Aqu55	26Cap23	18Sag54	01Can04	18Gem24
07/05/1902	15Aqu55	25Cap24	18Sag19	01Can38	18Gem44
07/20/1902	14Aqu22	24Cap18	17Sag50	02Can10	19Gem03
08/04/1902	12Aqu28	23Cap13	17Sag28	02Can39	19Gem18
08/19/1902	10Aqu34	22Cap17	17Sag17	03Can04	19Gem30
09/03/1902	08Aqu55	21Cap36	17Sag17	03Can24	19Gem38
09/18/1902	07Aqu49	21Cap14	17Sag28	03Can37	19Gem41
10/03/1902	07Aqu25	21Cap13	17Sag51	03Can43	19Gem39
10/18/1902	07Aqu44	21Cap35	18Sag24	03Can42	19Gem32
11/02/1902	08Aqu46	22Cap18	19Sag05	03Can33	19Gem21
11/17/1902	10Aqu28	23Cap20	19Sag53	03Can17	19Gem07
12/02/1902	12Aqu42	24Cap39	20Sag45	02Can56	18Gem51
12/17/1902	15Aqu24	26Cap10	21Sag40	02Can32	18Gem33
01/01/1903	18Aqu27	27Cap50	22Sag34	02Can06	18Gem16
01/16/1903	21Aqu46	29Cap36	23Sag25	01Can42	18Gem01
01/31/1903	25Aqu15	01Aqu22	24Sag10	01Can21	17Gem49
02/15/1903	28Aqu51	03Aqu07	24Sag48	01Can06	17Gem42
03/02/1903	02Pis27	04Aqu45	25Sag16	00Can57	17Gem40
03/17/1903	06Pis01	06Aqu12	25Sag33	00Can55	17Gem42
04/01/1903	09Pis27	07Aqu26	25Sag38	01Can01	17Gem49
04/16/1903	12Pis40	08Aqu24	25Sag31	01Can15	18Gem01
05/01/1903	15Pis39	09Aqu01	25Sag14	01Can34	18Gem16
05/16/1903	18Pis15	09Aqu18	24Sag48	02Can00	18Gem34
05/31/1903	20Pis24	09Aqu13	24Sag15	02Can30	18Gem55
06/15/1903	22Pis01	08Aqu47	23Sag39	03Can02	19Gem16
06/30/1903	23Pis01	08Aqu02	23Sag03	03Can36	19Gem36
07/15/1903	23Pis19	07Aqu04	22Sag30	04Can09	19Gem55
07/30/1903	22Pis53	05Aqu58	22Sag03	04Can39	20Gem13
08/14/1903	21Pis46	04Aqu53	21Sag45	05Can07	20Gem26
08/29/1903	20Pis06	03Aqu55	21Sag37	05Can30	20Gem36
09/13/1903	18Pis09	03Aqu11	21Sag41	05Can46	20Gem41
09/28/1903	16Pis14	02Aqu46	21Sag57	05Can55	20Gem41
10/13/1903	14Pis40	02Aqu42	22Sag22	05Can57	20Gem36
10/28/1903	13Pis41	03Aqu01	22Sag58	05Can52	20Gem27
11/12/1903	13Pis27	03Aqu42	23Sag42	05Can40	20Gem14
11/27/1903	13Pis58	04Aqu43	24Sag32	05Can21	19Gem58
12/12/1903	15Pis13	06Aqu00	25Sag25	04Can58	19Gem41
12/27/1903	17Pis06	07Aqu31	26Sag20	04Can33	19Gem24
01/11/1904	19Pis31	09Aqu12	27Sag13	04Can08	19Gem07
01/26/1904	22Pis22	10Aqu57	28Sag01	03Can45	18Gem54
02/10/1904	25Pis32	12Aqu45	28Sag44	03Can27	18Gem45
02/25/1904	28Pis56	14Aqu30	29Sag18	03Can14	18Gem40
03/11/1904	02Ari28	16Aqu10	29Sag42	03Can09	18Gem41
03/26/1904	06Ari06	17Aqu39	29Sag55	03Can11	18Gem46
04/10/1904	09Ari43	18Aqu56	29Sag56	03Can21	18Gem56
04/25/1904	13Ari16	19Aqu57	29Sag45	03Can38	19Gem10
05/10/1904	16Ari42	20Aqu37	29Sag25	04Can01	19Gem27
05/25/1904	19Ari54	20Aqu58	28Sag56	04Can28	19Gem47
06/09/1904	22Ari49	20Aqu57	28Sag22	05Can00	20Gem07
06/24/1904	25Ari24	20Aqu33	27Sag45	05Can33	20Gem28

Ephemeris Tables for Jupiter, Saturn, Uranus, Neptune, and Pluto

Date	Jupiter	Saturn	Uranus	Neptune	Pluto
07/09/1904	27Ari30	19Aqu51	27Sag10	06Can06	20Gem49
07/24/1904	29Ari04	18Aqu54	26Sag39	06Can38	21Gem07
08/08/1904	00Tau00	17Aqu49	26Sag15	07Can07	21Gem22
08/23/1904	00Tau12	16Aqu42	26Sag01	07Can33	21Gem33
09/07/1904	29Ari40	15Aqu42	25Sag57	07Can52	21Gem40
09/22/1904	28Ari27	14Aqu55	26Sag05	08Can06	21Gem42
10/07/1904	26Ari41	14Aqu27	26Sag24	08Can12	21Gem40
10/22/1904	24Ari41	14Aqu21	26Sag54	08Can10	21Gem32
11/06/1904	22Ari46	14Aqu37	27Sag33	08Can01	21Gem21
11/21/1904	21Ari15	15Aqu16	28Sag18	07Can45	21Gem06
12/06/1904	20Ari24	16Aqu15	29Sag10	07Can24	20Gem49
12/21/1904	20Ari18	17Aqu31	00Cap03	07Can00	20Gem31
01/05/1905	20Ari58	19Aqu01	00Cap57	06Can34	20Gem15
01/20/1905	22Ari22	20Aqu42	01Cap49	06Can10	20Gem00
02/04/1905	24Ari22	22Aqu28	02Cap36	05Can49	19Gem49
02/19/1905	26Ari52	24Aqu16	03Cap15	05Can34	19Gem43
03/06/1905	29Ari45	26Aqu03	03Cap46	05Can25	19Gem41
03/21/1905	02Tau56	27Aqu45	04Cap06	05Can23	19Gem44
04/05/1905	06Tau19	29Aqu17	04Cap14	05Can30	19Gem52
04/20/1905	09Tau51	00Pis37	04Cap10	05Can43	20Gem04
05/05/1905	13Tau25	01Pis40	03Cap57	06Can03	20Gem21
05/20/1905	16Tau58	02Pis26	03Cap33	06Can28	20Gem39
06/04/1905	20Tau27	02Pis50	03Cap02	06Can58	21Gem00
06/19/1905	23Tau47	02Pis52	02Cap27	07Can30	21Gem21
07/04/1905	26Tau54	02Pis33	01Cap50	08Can03	21Gem42
07/19/1905	29Tau45	01Pis54	01Cap16	08Can36	22Gem01
08/03/1905	02Gem12	00Pis59	00Cap47	09Can07	22Gem17
08/18/1905	04Gem12	29Aqu54	00Cap27	09Can34	22Gem30
09/02/1905	05Gem37	28Aqu46	00Cap16	09Can57	22Gem39
09/17/1905	06Gem24	27Aqu44	00Cap16	10Can14	22Gem43
10/02/1905	06Gem26	26Aqu54	00Cap28	10Can24	22Gem43
10/17/1905	05Gem43	26Aqu22	00Cap51	10Can25	22Gem37
11/01/1905	04Gem21	26Aqu12	01Cap24	10Can20	22Gem27
11/16/1905	02Gem29	26Aqu26	02Cap06	10Can07	22Gem13
12/01/1905	00Gem27	27Aqu02	02Cap54	09Can49	21Gem57
12/16/1905	28Tau36	28Aqu00	03Cap46	09Can26	21Gem40
12/31/1905	27Tau13	29Aqu15	04Cap40	09Can01	21Gem22
01/15/1906	26Tau31	00Pis44	05Cap33	08Can36	21Gem07
01/30/1906	26Tau36	02Pis24	06Cap23	08Can13	20Gem54
02/14/1906	27Tau25	04Pis11	07Cap07	07Can55	20Gem46
03/01/1906	28Tau55	06Pis00	07Cap43	07Can42	20Gem42
03/16/1906	00Gem58	07Pis49	08Cap10	07Can37	20Gem43
03/31/1906	03Gem30	09Pis32	08Cap25	07Can39	20Gem49
04/15/1906	06Gem22	11Pis07	08Cap30	07Can49	21Gem00
04/30/1906	09Gem30	12Pis30	08Cap22	08Can06	21Gem15
05/15/1906	12Gem49	13Pis37	08Cap04	08Can28	21Gem33
05/30/1906	16Gem15	14Pis27	07Cap38	08Can56	21Gem52
06/14/1906	19Gem43	14Pis55	07Cap06	09Can27	22Gem13
06/29/1906	23Gem09	15Pis03	06Cap30	10Can00	22Gem34
07/14/1906	26Gem30	14Pis47	05Cap54	10Can34	22Gem54
07/29/1906	29Gem42	14Pis11	05Cap21	11Can06	23Gem12
08/13/1906	02Can40	13Pis18	04Cap55	11Can35	23Gem27
08/28/1906	05Can21	12Pis13	04Cap37	12Can00	23Gem37
09/12/1906	07Can37	11Pis05	04Cap31	12Can20	23Gem44
09/27/1906	09Can23	10Pis01	04Cap35	12Can33	23Gem45

Ephemeris Tables for Jupiter, Saturn, Uranus, Neptune, and Pluto

Date	Jupiter	Saturn	Uranus	Neptune	Pluto
10/12/1906	10Can34	09Pis08	04Cap51	12Can39	23Gem42
10/27/1906	11Can03	08Pis33	05Cap18	12Can37	23Gem33
11/11/1906	10Can48	08Pis19	05Cap54	12Can28	23Gem21
11/26/1906	09Can49	08Pis29	06Cap38	12Can13	23Gem06
12/11/1906	08Can15	09Pis03	07Cap27	11Can52	22Gem49
12/26/1906	06Can18	09Pis58	08Cap21	11Can27	22Gem31
01/10/1907	04Can18	11Pis11	09Cap14	11Can02	22Gem15
01/25/1907	02Can35	12Pis40	10Cap06	10Can38	22Gem01
02/09/1907	01Can27	14Pis19	10Cap54	10Can17	21Gem50
02/24/1907	01Can00	16Pis07	11Cap36	10Can01	21Gem44
03/11/1907	01Can18	17Pis57	12Cap08	09Can52	21Gem43
03/26/1907	02Can18	19Pis47	12Cap31	09Can51	21Gem48
04/10/1907	03Can55	21Pis33	12Cap42	09Can57	21Gem56
04/25/1907	06Can02	23Pis10	12Cap42	10Can10	22Gem09
05/10/1907	08Can34	24Pis37	12Cap31	10Can30	22Gem26
05/25/1907	11Can25	25Pis49	12Cap10	10Can56	22Gem45
06/09/1907	14Can31	26Pis43	11Cap41	11Can25	23Gem06
06/24/1907	17Can45	27Pis16	11Cap07	11Can57	23Gem27
07/09/1907	21Can05	27Pis28	10Cap30	12Can31	23Gem48
07/24/1907	24Can26	27Pis18	09Cap55	13Can04	24Gem07
08/08/1907	27Can45	26Pis46	09Cap25	13Can35	24Gem23
08/23/1907	00Leo57	25Pis55	09Cap01	14Can02	24Gem36
09/07/1907	03Leo59	24Pis52	08Cap48	14Can25	24Gem43
09/22/1907	06Leo46	23Pis43	08Cap45	14Can42	24Gem47
10/07/1907	09Leo12	22Pis36	08Cap54	14Can51	24Gem46
10/22/1907	11Leo12	21Pis40	09Cap13	14Can53	24Gem39
11/06/1907	12Leo39	21Pis00	09Cap43	14Can48	24Gem28
11/21/1907	13Leo27	20Pis43	10Cap23	14Can35	24Gem15
12/06/1907	13Leo33	20Pis49	11Cap09	14Can16	23Gem58
12/21/1907	12Leo55	21Pis19	12Cap00	13Can54	23Gem40
01/05/1908	11Leo37	22Pis12	12Cap54	13Can28	23Gem23
01/20/1908	09Leo50	23Pis23	13Cap47	13Can03	23Gem08
02/04/1908	07Leo51	24Pis51	14Cap37	12Can40	22Gem56
02/19/1908	05Leo59	26Pis30	15Cap22	12Can22	22Gem48
03/05/1908	04Leo33	28Pis17	16Cap01	12Can10	22Gem45
03/20/1908	03Leo43	00Ari08	16Cap30	12Can04	22Gem47
04/04/1908	03Leo36	01Ari59	16Cap48	12Can07	22Gem54
04/19/1908	04Leo11	03Ari47	16Cap55	12Can17	23Gem05
05/04/1908	05Leo24	05Ari28	16Cap51	12Can34	23Gem21
05/19/1908	07Leo10	06Ari58	16Cap36	12Can56	23Gem39
06/03/1908	09Leo24	08Ari15	16Cap12	13Can24	23Gem59
06/18/1908	12Leo00	09Ari14	15Cap41	13Can55	24Gem21
07/03/1908	14Leo52	09Ari54	15Cap06	14Can28	24Gem42
07/18/1908	17Leo56	10Ari11	14Cap30	15Can01	25Gem01
08/02/1908	21Leo08	10Ari06	13Cap56	15Can33	25Gem19
08/17/1908	24Leo24	09Ari38	13Cap28	16Can03	25Gem33
09/01/1908	27Leo40	08Ari51	13Cap08	16Can28	25Gem43
09/16/1908	00Vir52	07Ari49	12Cap58	16Can48	25Gem49
10/01/1908	03Vir55	06Ari39	13Cap00	17Can01	25Gem49
10/16/1908	06Vir46	05Ari30	13Cap12	17Can07	25Gem45
10/31/1908	09Vir19	04Ari31	13Cap36	17Can05	25Gem36
11/15/1908	11Vir28	03Ari47	14Cap09	16Can56	25Gem23
11/30/1908	13Vir06	03Ari25	14Cap51	16Can40	25Gem07
12/15/1908	14Vir09	03Ari27	15Cap39	16Can19	24Gem50
12/30/1908	14Vir31	03Ari53	16Cap31	15Can55	24Gem33

Ephemeris Tables for Jupiter, Saturn, Uranus, Neptune, and Pluto

Date	Jupiter	Saturn	Uranus	Neptune	Pluto
01/14/1909	14Vir09	04Ari42	17Cap25	15Can30	24Gem16
01/29/1909	13Vir07	05Ari51	18Cap17	15Can05	24Gem03
02/13/1909	11Vir31	07Ari17	19Cap06	14Can45	23Gem53
02/28/1909	09Vir36	08Ari55	19Cap49	14Can29	23Gem48
03/15/1909	07Vir42	10Ari43	20Cap23	14Can20	23Gem48
03/30/1909	06Vir04	12Ari35	20Cap48	14Can19	23Gem52
04/14/1909	04Vir58	14Ari28	21Cap03	14Can25	24Gem02
04/29/1909	04Vir32	16Ari18	21Cap06	14Can38	24Gem16
05/14/1909	04Vir46	18Ari02	20Cap57	14Can58	24Gem33
05/29/1909	05Vir40	19Ari36	20Cap39	15Can23	24Gem53
06/13/1909	07Vir09	20Ari58	20Cap12	15Can52	25Gem14
06/28/1909	09Vir07	22Ari02	19Cap39	16Can25	25Gem35
07/13/1909	11Vir30	22Ari48	19Cap03	16Can58	25Gem55
07/28/1909	14Vir12	23Ari11	18Cap28	17Can31	26Gem14
08/12/1909	17Vir08	23Ari12	17Cap56	18Can02	26Gem30
08/27/1909	20Vir15	22Ari49	17Cap31	18Can30	26Gem42
09/11/1909	23Vir27	22Ari06	17Cap14	18Can52	26Gem49
09/26/1909	26Vir42	21Ari06	17Cap08	19Can09	26Gem52
10/11/1909	29Vir54	19Ari57	17Cap13	19Can18	26Gem50
10/26/1909	03Lib00	18Ari46	17Cap30	19Can21	26Gem43
11/10/1909	05Lib55	17Ari43	17Cap58	19Can15	26Gem31
11/25/1909	08Lib34	16Ari55	18Cap34	19Can02	26Gem17
12/10/1909	10Lib51	16Ari28	19Cap19	18Can44	26Gem00
12/25/1909	12Lib39	16Ari25	20Cap09	18Can21	25Gem42
01/09/1910	13Lib54	16Ari46	21Cap01	17Can55	25Gem25
01/24/1910	14Lib30	17Ari32	21Cap54	17Can31	25Gem10
02/08/1910	14Lib24	18Ari38	22Cap45	17Can08	24Gem59
02/23/1910	13Lib35	20Ari01	23Cap32	16Can49	24Gem52
03/10/1910	12Lib11	21Ari39	24Cap12	16Can37	24Gem49
03/25/1910	10Lib23	23Ari25	24Cap43	16Can32	24Gem52
04/09/1910	08Lib28	25Ari18	25Cap04	16Can34	25Gem00
04/24/1910	06Lib43	27Ari12	25Cap14	16Can44	25Gem12
05/09/1910	05Lib25	29Ari04	25Cap13	17Can01	25Gem28
05/24/1910	04Lib43	00Tau52	25Cap01	17Can24	25Gem47
06/08/1910	04Lib40	02Tau30	24Cap39	17Can51	26Gem07
06/23/1910	05Lib18	03Tau56	24Cap10	18Can22	26Gem29
07/08/1910	06Lib32	05Tau06	23Cap36	18Can55	26Gem50
07/23/1910	08Lib18	05Tau58	23Cap00	19Can28	27Gem10
08/07/1910	10Lib30	06Tau28	22Cap25	20Can00	27Gem27
08/22/1910	13Lib04	06Tau36	21Cap55	20Can30	27Gem40
09/06/1910	15Lib55	06Tau19	21Cap33	20Can55	27Gem50
09/21/1910	18Lib59	05Tau40	21Cap20	21Can15	27Gem55
10/06/1910	22Lib10	04Tau43	21Cap18	21Can28	27Gem55
10/21/1910	25Lib25	03Tau35	21Cap28	21Can34	27Gem50
11/05/1910	28Lib40	02Tau23	21Cap48	21Can32	27Gem40
11/20/1910	01Sco51	01Tau16	22Cap19	21Can23	27Gem27
12/05/1910	04Sco52	00Tau24	22Cap59	21Can07	27Gem10
12/20/1910	07Sco37	29Ari51	23Cap46	20Can46	26Gem52
01/04/1911	10Sco03	29Ari43	24Cap36	20Can22	26Gem35
01/19/1911	12Sco03	29Ari59	25Cap30	19Can57	26Gem19
02/03/1911	13Sco31	00Tau40	26Cap22	19Can33	26Gem06
02/18/1911	14Sco22	01Tau42	27Cap12	19Can12	25Gem57
03/05/1911	14Sco31	03Tau03	27Cap55	18Can56	25Gem52
03/20/1911	13Sco59	04Tau37	28Cap32	18Can48	25Gem53
04/04/1911	12Sco48	06Tau23	29Cap00	18Can46	25Gem59

Ephemeris Tables for Jupiter, Saturn, Uranus, Neptune, and Pluto

Date	Jupiter	Saturn	Uranus	Neptune	Pluto
04/19/1911	11Sco09	08Tau16	29Cap16	18Can52	26Gem09
05/04/1911	09Sco15	10Tau11	29Cap22	19Can05	26Gem24
05/19/1911	07Sco25	12Tau05	29Cap17	19Can25	26Gem42
06/03/1911	05Sco56	13Tau55	29Cap01	19Can50	27Gem02
06/18/1911	04Sco58	15Tau37	28Cap37	20Can19	27Gem23
07/03/1911	04Sco40	17Tau09	28Cap05	20Can52	27Gem45
07/18/1911	05Sco01	18Tau25	27Cap30	21Can25	28Gem05
08/02/1911	06Sco02	19Tau23	26Cap54	21Can58	28Gem24
08/17/1911	07Sco36	20Tau00	26Cap21	22Can29	28Gem39
09/01/1911	09Sco40	20Tau14	25Cap54	22Can57	28Gem50
09/16/1911	12Sco09	20Tau04	25Cap34	23Can19	28Gem57
10/01/1911	14Sco56	19Tau31	25Cap26	23Can36	28Gem59
10/16/1911	17Sco58	18Tau39	25Cap28	23Can45	28Gem56
10/31/1911	21Sco11	17Tau32	25Cap42	23Can48	28Gem48
11/15/1911	24Sco29	16Tau19	26Cap06	23Can42	28Gem36
11/30/1911	27Sco49	15Tau10	26Cap41	23Can29	28Gem21
12/15/1911	01Sag05	14Tau12	27Cap23	23Can10	28Gem04
12/30/1911	04Sag14	13Tau34	28Cap12	22Can48	27Gem46
01/14/1912	07Sag10	13Tau19	29Cap03	22Can22	27Gem29
01/29/1912	09Sag47	13Tau30	29Cap56	21Can58	27Gem15
02/13/1912	12Sag01	14Tau05	00Aqu48	21Can35	27Gem03
02/28/1912	13Sag45	15Tau03	01Aqu35	21Can16	26Gem57
03/14/1912	14Sag54	16Tau19	02Aqu16	21Can04	26Gem55
03/29/1912	15Sag23	17Tau52	02Aqu50	20Can59	26Gem59
04/13/1912	15Sag10	19Tau36	03Aqu13	21Can01	27Gem08
04/28/1912	14Sag17	21Tau27	03Aqu26	21Can11	27Gem21
05/13/1912	12Sag50	23Tau23	03Aqu28	21Can28	27Gem37
05/28/1912	11Sag01	25Tau19	03Aqu18	21Can51	27Gem57
06/12/1912	09Sag08	27Tau12	02Aqu59	22Can18	28Gem18
06/27/1912	07Sag27	28Tau57	02Aqu32	22Can49	28Gem39
07/12/1912	06Sag13	00Gem33	01Aqu59	23Can22	29Gem00
07/27/1912	05Sag36	01Gem55	01Aqu23	23Can55	29Gem20
08/11/1912	05Sag40	03Gem00	00Aqu48	24Can27	29Gem37
08/26/1912	06Sag24	03Gem44	00Aqu16	24Can57	29Gem50
09/10/1912	07Sag46	04Gem06	29Cap52	25Can22	29Gem59
09/25/1912	09Sag41	04Gem03	29Cap37	25Can42	00Can03
10/10/1912	12Sag03	03Gem36	29Cap32	25Can55	00Can02
10/25/1912	14Sag48	02Gem48	29Cap39	26Can01	29Gem56
11/09/1912	17Sag50	01Gem44	29Cap56	25Can59	29Gem46
11/24/1912	21Sag05	00Gem31	00Aqu25	25Can50	29Gem31
12/09/1912	24Sag27	29Tau19	01Aqu02	25Can34	29Gem15
12/24/1912	27Sag53	28Tau18	01Aqu47	25Can13	28Gem57
01/08/1913	01Cap17	27Tau33	02Aqu37	24Can49	28Gem39
01/23/1913	04Cap36	27Tau12	03Aqu29	24Can23	28Gem24
02/07/1913	07Cap43	27Tau16	04Aqu21	23Can59	28Gem11
02/22/1913	10Cap35	27Tau45	05Aqu12	23Can39	28Gem03
03/09/1913	13Cap06	28Tau37	05Aqu57	23Can23	27Gem59
03/24/1913	15Cap09	29Tau49	06Aqu35	23Can14	28Gem01
04/08/1913	16Cap41	01Gem19	07Aqu05	23Can13	28Gem07
04/23/1913	17Cap36	03Gem00	07Aqu24	23Can19	28Gem19
05/08/1913	17Cap49	04Gem51	07Aqu33	23Can32	28Gem34
05/23/1913	17Cap21	06Gem46	07Aqu30	23Can52	28Gem52
06/07/1913	16Cap13	08Gem42	07Aqu17	24Can17	29Gem13
06/22/1913	14Cap35	10Gem37	06Aqu55	24Can46	29Gem34
07/07/1913	12Cap42	12Gem26	06Aqu25	25Can18	29Gem56

Ephemeris Tables for Jupiter, Saturn, Uranus, Neptune, and Pluto

Date	Jupiter	Saturn	Uranus	Neptune	Pluto
07/22/1913	10Cap51	14Gem06	05Aqu51	25Can52	00Can16
08/06/1913	09Cap18	15Gem33	05Aqu15	26Can25	00Can34
08/21/1913	08Cap19	16Gem45	04Aqu41	26Can55	00Can49
09/05/1913	08Cap00	17Gem36	04Aqu12	27Can23	01Can00
09/20/1913	08Cap24	18Gem05	03Aqu50	27Can46	01Can06
10/05/1913	09Cap29	18Gem10	03Aqu39	28Can03	01Can07
10/20/1913	11Cap11	17Gem50	03Aqu38	28Can12	01Can04
11/04/1913	13Cap24	17Gem07	03Aqu49	28Can14	00Can55
11/19/1913	16Cap04	16Gem07	04Aqu11	28Can09	00Can42
12/04/1913	19Cap04	14Gem55	04Aqu43	27Can56	00Can27
12/19/1913	22Cap19	13Gem42	05Aqu23	27Can37	00Can09
01/03/1914	25Cap45	12Gem36	06Aqu10	27Can14	29Gem51
01/18/1914	29Cap16	11Gem46	07Aqu01	26Can49	29Gem34
02/02/1914	02Aqu48	11Gem18	07Aqu53	26Can24	29Gem20
02/17/1914	06Aqu16	11Gem15	08Aqu45	26Can01	29Gem10
03/04/1914	09Aqu36	11Gem37	09Aqu33	25Can43	29Gem04
03/19/1914	12Aqu44	12Gem24	10Aqu16	25Can31	29Gem04
04/03/1914	15Aqu34	13Gem30	10Aqu51	25Can26	29Gem08
04/18/1914	18Aqu00	14Gem55	11Aqu17	25Can28	29Gem18
05/03/1914	19Aqu59	16Gem33	11Aqu33	25Can38	29Gem31
05/18/1914	21Aqu24	18Gem21	11Aqu37	25Can55	29Gem48
06/02/1914	22Aqu10	20Gem16	11Aqu30	26Can17	00Can08
06/17/1914	22Aqu13	22Gem13	11Aqu13	26Can45	00Can30
07/02/1914	21Aqu35	24Gem09	10Aqu48	27Can15	00Can51
07/17/1914	20Aqu18	26Gem01	10Aqu16	27Can48	01Can12
08/01/1914	18Aqu33	27Gem44	09Aqu41	28Can22	01Can31
08/16/1914	16Aqu37	29Gem16	09Aqu06	28Can54	01Can48
08/31/1914	14Aqu47	00Can33	08Aqu33	29Can23	02Can01
09/15/1914	13Aqu22	01Can31	08Aqu07	29Can48	02Can09
09/30/1914	12Aqu34	02Can08	07Aqu49	00Leo08	02Can12
10/15/1914	12Aqu30	02Can21	07Aqu41	00Leo21	02Can11
10/30/1914	13Aqu10	02Can08	07Aqu45	00Leo27	02Can04
11/14/1914	14Aqu32	01Can31	08Aqu00	00Leo25	01Can53
11/29/1914	16Aqu30	00Can36	08Aqu25	00Leo16	01Can38
12/14/1914	18Aqu58	29Gem26	09Aqu01	00Leo00	01Can21
12/29/1914	21Aqu52	28Gem12	09Aqu44	29Can39	01Can03
01/13/1915	25Aqu03	27Gem03	10Aqu32	29Can15	00Can46
01/28/1915	28Aqu28	26Gem07	11Aqu24	28Can49	00Can30
02/12/1915	02Pis01	25Gem33	12Aqu16	28Can25	00Can18
02/27/1915	05Pis39	25Gem22	13Aqu07	28Can05	00Can10
03/14/1915	09Pis14	25Gem37	13Aqu53	27Can49	00Can08
03/29/1915	12Pis45	26Gem17	14Aqu33	27Can41	00Can10
04/13/1915	16Pis06	27Gem18	15Aqu05	27Can39	00Can18
04/28/1915	19Pis14	28Gem37	15Aqu27	27Can45	00Can30
05/13/1915	22Pis03	00Can12	15Aqu38	27Can58	00Can45
05/28/1915	24Pis28	01Can57	15Aqu39	28Can18	01Can04
06/12/1915	26Pis24	03Can49	15Aqu28	28Can43	01Can25
06/27/1915	27Pis45	05Can46	15Aqu08	29Can13	01Can47
07/12/1915	28Pis26	07Can43	14Aqu40	29Can45	02Can09
07/27/1915	28Pis24	09Can36	14Aqu06	00Leo18	02Can29
08/11/1915	27Pis39	11Can23	13Aqu31	00Leo51	02Can47
08/26/1915	26Pis16	13Can00	12Aqu56	01Leo22	03Can01
09/10/1915	24Pis26	14Can22	12Aqu25	01Leo49	03Can12
09/25/1915	22Pis27	15Can26	12Aqu01	02Leo12	03Can17
10/10/1915	20Pis39	16Can10	11Aqu48	02Leo29	03Can18

Ephemeris Tables for Jupiter, Saturn, Uranus, Neptune, and Pluto

Date	Jupiter	Saturn	Uranus	Neptune	Pluto
10/25/1915	19Pis19	16Can30	11Aqu44	02Leo39	03Can13
11/09/1915	18Pis40	16Can24	11Aqu52	02Leo40	03Can04
11/24/1915	18Pis46	15Can55	12Aqu11	02Leo35	02Can50
12/09/1915	19Pis39	15Can04	12Aqu40	02Leo22	02Can34
12/24/1915	21Pis12	13Can57	13Aqu19	02Leo03	02Can16
01/08/1916	23Pis21	12Can43	14Aqu04	01Leo40	01Can58
01/23/1916	25Pis58	11Can32	14Aqu54	01Leo15	01Can42
02/07/1916	28Pis59	10Can32	15Aqu46	00Leo51	01Can28
02/22/1916	02Ari15	09Can51	16Aqu38	00Leo28	01Can18
03/08/1916	05Ari44	09Can34	17Aqu27	00Leo10	01Can13
03/23/1916	09Ari19	09Can41	18Aqu11	29Can58	01Can13
04/07/1916	12Ari57	10Can13	18Aqu48	29Can52	01Can19
04/22/1916	16Ari33	11Can07	19Aqu16	29Can55	01Can29
05/07/1916	20Ari02	12Can21	19Aqu34	00Leo04	01Can43
05/22/1916	23Ari22	13Can51	19Aqu41	00Leo21	02Can01
06/06/1916	26Ari27	15Can32	19Aqu37	00Leo43	02Can22
06/21/1916	29Ari13	17Can22	19Aqu23	01Leo11	02Can43
07/06/1916	01Tau36	19Can18	19Aqu00	01Leo42	03Can05
07/21/1916	03Tau28	21Can15	18Aqu30	02Leo15	03Can26
08/05/1916	04Tau45	23Can09	17Aqu55	02Leo48	03Can45
08/20/1916	05Tau21	24Can58	17Aqu19	03Leo20	04Can01
09/04/1916	05Tau13	26Can38	16Aqu45	03Leo49	04Can13
09/19/1916	04Tau22	28Can05	16Aqu17	04Leo15	04Can21
10/04/1916	02Tau52	29Can15	15Aqu57	04Leo34	04Can24
10/19/1916	00Tau57	00Leo05	15Aqu46	04Leo48	04Can21
11/03/1916	28Ari57	00Leo32	15Aqu48	04Leo54	04Can14
11/18/1916	27Ari10	00Leo34	16Aqu00	04Leo52	04Can02
12/03/1916	25Ari57	00Leo11	16Aqu23	04Leo42	03Can47
12/18/1916	25Ari25	29Can25	16Aqu56	04Leo27	03Can30
01/02/1917	25Ari41	28Can22	17Aqu37	04Leo06	03Can12
01/17/1917	26Ari42	27Can10	18Aqu24	03Leo41	02Can54
02/01/1917	28Ari22	25Can57	19Aqu15	03Leo16	02Can39
02/16/1917	00Tau37	24Can54	20Aqu07	02Leo52	02Can27
03/03/1917	03Tau18	24Can07	20Aqu58	02Leo31	02Can21
03/18/1917	06Tau19	23Can43	21Aqu45	02Leo16	02Can18
04/02/1917	09Tau36	23Can43	22Aqu27	02Leo07	02Can22
04/17/1917	13Tau03	24Can07	23Aqu00	02Leo06	02Can30
05/02/1917	16Tau35	24Can54	23Aqu25	02Leo12	02Can43
05/17/1917	20Tau09	26Can02	23Aqu39	02Leo25	02Can59
06/01/1917	23Tau40	27Can26	23Aqu42	02Leo45	03Can19
06/16/1917	27Tau04	29Can04	23Aqu34	03Leo10	03Can40
07/01/1917	00Gem19	00Leo51	23Aqu16	03Leo39	04Can02
07/16/1917	03Gem18	02Leo44	22Aqu50	04Leo11	04Can24
07/31/1917	05Gem58	04Leo40	22Aqu18	04Leo44	04Can44
08/15/1917	08Gem13	06Leo35	21Aqu42	05Leo17	05Can01
08/30/1917	09Gem57	08Leo26	21Aqu07	05Leo48	05Can15
09/14/1917	11Gem04	10Leo08	20Aqu35	06Leo16	05Can25
09/29/1917	11Gem30	11Leo39	20Aqu09	06Leo39	05Can30
10/14/1917	11Gem11	12Leo54	19Aqu52	06Leo55	05Can30
10/29/1917	10Gem09	13Leo50	19Aqu46	07Leo04	05Can24
11/13/1917	08Gem30	14Leo23	19Aqu52	07Leo06	05Can14
11/28/1917	06Gem31	14Leo32	20Aqu08	07Leo01	05Can00
12/13/1917	04Gem31	14Leo15	20Aqu35	06Leo48	04Can43
12/28/1917	02Gem52	13Leo36	21Aqu12	06Leo29	04Can25

Ephemeris Tables for Jupiter, Saturn, Uranus, Neptune, and Pluto

Date	Jupiter	Saturn	Uranus	Neptune	Pluto
01/12/1918	01Gem48	12Leo37	21Aqu55	06Leo06	04Can07
01/27/1918	01Gem28	11Leo27	22Aqu44	05Leo41	03Can51
02/11/1918	01Gem54	10Leo13	23Aqu36	05Leo16	03Can38
02/26/1918	03Gem02	09Leo07	24Aqu27	04Leo54	03Can29
03/13/1918	04Gem48	08Leo15	25Aqu17	04Leo36	03Can25
03/28/1918	07Gem04	07Leo45	26Aqu02	04Leo24	03Can26
04/12/1918	09Gem46	07Leo37	26Aqu40	04Leo18	03Can32
04/27/1918	12Gem45	07Leo54	27Aqu11	04Leo21	03Can43
05/12/1918	15Gem58	08Leo34	27Aqu31	04Leo30	03Can58
05/27/1918	19Gem20	09Leo36	27Aqu42	04Leo47	04Can16
06/11/1918	22Gem46	10Leo54	27Aqu40	05Leo09	04Can37
06/26/1918	26Gem13	12Leo27	27Aqu28	05Leo37	04Can59
07/11/1918	29Gem36	14Leo10	27Aqu07	06Leo07	05Can21
07/26/1918	02Can53	16Leo01	26Aqu38	06Leo40	05Can42
08/10/1918	05Can58	17Leo56	26Aqu04	07Leo13	06Can01
08/25/1918	08Can48	19Leo51	25Aqu29	07Leo46	06Can17
09/09/1918	11Can17	21Leo42	24Aqu54	08Leo15	06Can28
09/24/1918	13Can19	23Leo27	24Aqu25	08Leo40	06Can36
10/09/1918	14Can48	25Leo00	24Aqu02	09Leo00	06Can37
10/24/1918	15Can39	26Leo19	23Aqu49	09Leo13	06Can34
11/08/1918	15Can46	27Leo20	23Aqu47	09Leo19	06Can26
11/23/1918	15Can10	27Leo59	23Aqu57	09Leo18	06Can13
12/08/1918	13Can52	28Leo14	24Aqu17	09Leo08	05Can58
12/23/1918	12Can04	28Leo04	24Aqu48	08Leo52	05Can40
01/07/1919	10Can03	27Leo30	25Aqu27	08Leo31	05Can22
01/22/1919	08Can09	26Leo36	26Aqu13	08Leo07	05Can04
02/06/1919	06Can42	25Leo28	27Aqu03	07Leo42	04Can50
02/21/1919	05Can54	24Leo15	27Aqu55	07Leo18	04Can39
03/08/1919	05Can48	23Leo07	28Aqu47	06Leo57	04Can33
03/23/1919	06Can27	22Leo12	29Aqu35	06Leo42	04Can31
04/07/1919	07Can45	21Leo34	00Pis18	06Leo33	04Can36
04/22/1919	09Can37	21Leo21	00Pis53	06Leo31	04Can45
05/07/1919	11Can57	21Leo30	01Pis20	06Leo37	04Can58
05/22/1919	14Can37	22Leo04	01Pis36	06Leo51	05Can15
06/06/1919	17Can35	22Leo58	01Pis42	07Leo10	05Can35
06/21/1919	20Can45	24Leo11	01Pis37	07Leo36	05Can57
07/06/1919	24Can01	25Leo39	01Pis21	08Leo04	06Can19
07/21/1919	27Can22	27Leo19	00Pis57	08Leo37	06Can40
08/05/1919	00Leo42	29Leo07	00Pis26	09Leo10	07Can01
08/20/1919	03Leo57	01Vir00	29Aqu51	09Leo43	07Can18
09/04/1919	07Leo04	02Vir54	29Aqu15	10Leo14	07Can31
09/19/1919	09Leo59	04Vir45	28Aqu42	10Leo42	07Can40
10/04/1919	12Leo36	06Vir31	28Aqu15	11Leo04	07Can45
10/19/1919	14Leo49	08Vir07	27Aqu56	11Leo21	07Can44
11/03/1919	16Leo33	09Vir29	27Aqu47	11Leo30	07Can37
11/18/1919	17Leo40	10Vir34	27Aqu49	11Leo32	07Can27
12/03/1919	18Leo08	11Vir18	28Aqu03	11Leo26	07Can12
12/18/1919	17Leo51	11Vir38	28Aqu28	11Leo13	06Can55
01/02/1920	16Leo52	11Vir34	29Aqu02	10Leo55	06Can37
01/17/1920	15Leo18	11Vir05	29Aqu44	10Leo32	06Can19
02/01/1920	13Leo22	10Vir16	00Pis32	10Leo07	06Can03
02/16/1920	11Leo25	09Vir11	01Pis23	09Leo42	05Can50
03/02/1920	09Leo44	08Vir00	02Pis15	09Leo19	05Can42
03/17/1920	08Leo35	06Vir50	03Pis04	09Leo01	05Can39
04/01/1920	08Leo06	05Vir51	03Pis51	08Leo49	05Can40

Ephemeris Tables for Jupiter, Saturn, Uranus, Neptune, and Pluto

Date	Jupiter	Saturn	Uranus	Neptune	Pluto
04/16/1920	08Leo21	05Vir10	04Pis31	08Leo44	05Can47
05/01/1920	09Leo15	04Vir49	05Pis03	08Leo46	05Can59
05/16/1920	10Leo45	04Vir53	05Pis26	08Leo56	06Can15
05/31/1920	12Leo45	05Vir19	05Pis39	09Leo13	06Can34
06/15/1920	15Leo09	06Vir07	05Pis40	09Leo35	06Can55
06/30/1920	17Leo53	07Vir15	05Pis31	10Leo02	07Can17
07/15/1920	20Leo51	08Vir37	05Pis12	10Leo33	07Can39
07/30/1920	24Leo00	10Vir13	04Pis45	11Leo06	08Can00
08/14/1920	27Leo13	11Vir58	04Pis12	11Leo39	08Can19
08/29/1920	00Vir30	13Vir49	03Pis36	12Leo12	08Can34
09/13/1920	03Vir44	15Vir42	03Pis01	12Leo41	08Can45
09/28/1920	06Vir52	17Vir33	02Pis30	13Leo06	08Can52
10/13/1920	09Vir49	19Vir19	02Pis06	13Leo26	08Can53
10/28/1920	12Vir31	20Vir57	01Pis50	13Leo39	08Can49
11/12/1920	14Vir52	22Vir22	01Pis45	13Leo45	08Can40
11/27/1920	16Vir46	23Vir30	01Pis52	13Leo43	08Can27
12/12/1920	18Vir07	24Vir18	02Pis10	13Leo33	08Can10
12/27/1920	18Vir49	24Vir43	02Pis39	13Leo18	07Can52
01/11/1921	18Vir49	24Vir44	03Pis16	12Leo57	07Can34
01/26/1921	18Vir06	24Vir20	04Pis01	12Leo32	07Can17
02/10/1921	16Vir45	23Vir35	04Pis50	12Leo07	07Can03
02/25/1921	14Vir57	22Vir34	05Pis41	11Leo43	06Can52
03/12/1921	13Vir00	21Vir24	06Pis33	11Leo22	06Can47
03/27/1921	11Vir13	20Vir15	07Pis21	11Leo07	06Can46
04/11/1921	09Vir50	19Vir13	08Pis05	10Leo58	06Can51
04/26/1921	09Vir04	18Vir27	08Pis43	10Leo57	07Can01
05/11/1921	08Vir58	18Vir02	09Pis11	11Leo03	07Can16
05/26/1921	09Vir33	17Vir59	09Pis30	11Leo16	07Can33
06/10/1921	10Vir45	18Vir19	09Pis39	11Leo36	07Can54
06/25/1921	12Vir29	19Vir01	09Pis36	12Leo01	08Can16
07/10/1921	14Vir40	20Vir03	09Pis23	12Leo30	08Can39
07/25/1921	17Vir13	21Vir21	09Pis01	13Leo02	09Can00
08/09/1921	20Vir02	22Vir52	08Pis31	13Leo35	09Can20
08/24/1921	23Vir04	24Vir34	07Pis57	14Leo08	09Can37
09/08/1921	26Vir14	26Vir22	07Pis21	14Leo39	09Can50
09/23/1921	29Vir28	28Vir14	06Pis47	15Leo07	09Can58
10/08/1921	02Lib42	00Lib05	06Pis18	15Leo30	10Can02
10/23/1921	05Lib52	01Lib52	05Pis57	15Leo46	10Can00
11/07/1921	08Lib53	03Lib30	05Pis45	15Leo55	09Can53
11/22/1921	11Lib40	04Lib57	05Pis45	15Leo57	09Can42
12/07/1921	14Lib08	06Lib08	05Pis56	15Leo52	09Can27
12/22/1921	16Lib12	07Lib00	06Pis18	15Leo39	09Can09
01/06/1922	17Lib43	07Lib29	06Pis51	15Leo20	08Can51
01/21/1922	18Lib39	07Lib34	07Pis31	14Leo57	08Can33
02/05/1922	18Lib52	07Lib15	08Pis18	14Leo32	08Can17
02/20/1922	18Lib24	06Lib34	09Pis07	14Leo07	08Can05
03/07/1922	17Lib16	05Lib37	09Pis59	13Leo45	07Can57
03/22/1922	15Lib39	04Lib29	10Pis49	13Leo27	07Can54
04/06/1922	13Lib45	03Lib19	11Pis37	13Leo15	07Can57
04/21/1922	11Lib53	02Lib16	12Pis18	13Leo10	08Can05
05/06/1922	10Lib21	01Lib27	12Pis52	13Leo12	08Can18
05/21/1922	09Lib20	00Lib57	13Pis18	13Leo21	08Can34
06/05/1922	08Lib58	00Lib48	13Pis33	13Leo38	08Can54
06/20/1922	09Lib16	01Lib03	13Pis37	14Leo00	09Can15
07/05/1922	10Lib12	01Lib39	13Pis30	14Leo28	09Can37

Ephemeris Tables for Jupiter, Saturn, Uranus, Neptune, and Pluto

Date	Jupiter	Saturn	Uranus	Neptune	Pluto
07/20/1922	11Lib43	02Lib36	13Pis13	14Leo58	10Can00
08/04/1922	13Lib43	03Lib49	12Pis48	15Leo31	10Can21
08/19/1922	16Lib07	05Lib16	12Pis16	16Leo04	10Can39
09/03/1922	18Lib51	06Lib55	11Pis42	16Leo37	10Can54
09/18/1922	21Lib49	08Lib41	11Pis06	17Leo06	11Can05
10/03/1922	24Lib57	10Lib31	10Pis33	17Leo31	11Can10
10/18/1922	28Lib12	12Lib21	10Pis07	17Leo51	11Can11
11/02/1922	01Sco27	14Lib08	09Pis49	18Leo04	11Can06
11/17/1922	04Sco41	15Lib48	09Pis42	18Leo10	10Can57
12/02/1922	07Sco47	17Lib16	09Pis46	18Leo08	10Can43
12/17/1922	10Sco41	18Lib29	10Pis01	17Leo58	10Can26
01/01/1923	13Sco18	19Lib23	10Pis28	17Leo42	10Can07
01/16/1923	15Sco31	19Lib56	11Pis03	17Leo21	09Can49
01/31/1923	17Sco15	20Lib05	11Pis46	16Leo57	09Can33
02/15/1923	18Sco25	19Lib51	12Pis34	16Leo32	09Can18
03/02/1923	18Sco55	19Lib14	13Pis25	16Leo08	09Can09
03/17/1923	18Sco43	18Lib19	14Pis16	15Leo48	09Can04
04/01/1923	17Sco50	17Lib14	15Pis06	15Leo33	09Can04
04/16/1923	16Sco24	16Lib04	15Pis51	15Leo24	09Can10
05/01/1923	14Sco35	15Lib00	16Pis30	15Leo22	09Can21
05/16/1923	12Sco42	14Lib08	17Pis01	15Leo28	09Can36
05/31/1923	11Sco00	13Lib34	17Pis22	15Leo42	09Can54
06/15/1923	09Sco45	13Lib21	17Pis33	16Leo01	10Can15
06/30/1923	09Sco07	13Lib30	17Pis33	16Leo26	10Can37
07/15/1923	09Sco09	14Lib01	17Pis23	16Leo55	11Can00
07/30/1923	09Sco51	14Lib52	17Pis03	17Leo27	11Can22
08/14/1923	11Sco09	16Lib02	16Pis34	18Leo00	11Can42
08/29/1923	12Sco59	17Lib26	16Pis01	18Leo33	11Can58
09/13/1923	15Sco16	19Lib01	15Pis25	19Leo04	12Can11
09/28/1923	17Sco55	20Lib45	14Pis51	19Leo32	12Can19
10/13/1923	20Sco52	22Lib34	14Pis20	19Leo54	12Can22
10/28/1923	24Sco00	24Lib23	13Pis57	20Leo11	12Can19
11/12/1923	27Sco17	26Lib09	13Pis43	20Leo21	12Can11
11/27/1923	00Sag37	27Lib49	13Pis40	20Leo22	11Can59
12/12/1923	03Sag56	29Lib19	13Pis48	20Leo16	11Can43
12/27/1923	07Sag10	00Sco34	14Pis08	20Leo03	11Can25
01/11/1924	10Sag13	01Sco30	14Pis38	19Leo45	11Can07
01/26/1924	13Sag00	02Sco06	15Pis17	19Leo22	10Can49
02/10/1924	15Sag27	02Sco19	16Pis02	18Leo57	10Can34
02/25/1924	17Sag26	02Sco08	16Pis51	18Leo32	10Can22
03/11/1924	18Sag54	01Sco35	17Pis43	18Leo10	10Can15
03/26/1924	19Sag43	00Sco44	18Pis34	17Leo52	10Can13
04/10/1924	19Sag52	29Lib40	19Pis22	17Leo40	10Can16
04/25/1924	19Sag19	28Lib32	20Pis04	17Leo34	10Can25
05/10/1924	18Sag07	27Lib27	20Pis40	17Leo37	10Can39
05/25/1924	16Sag28	26Lib33	21Pis08	17Leo46	10Can56
06/09/1924	14Sag35	25Lib55	21Pis25	18Leo03	11Can16
06/24/1924	12Sag45	25Lib37	21Pis32	18Leo25	11Can38
07/09/1924	11Sag16	25Lib42	21Pis28	18Leo52	12Can01
07/24/1924	10Sag20	26Lib09	21Pis14	19Leo23	12Can23
08/08/1924	10Sag03	26Lib55	20Pis51	19Leo56	12Can44
08/23/1924	10Sag28	28Lib01	20Pis20	20Leo29	13Can02
09/07/1924	11Sag31	29Lib21	19Pis45	21Leo01	13Can16
09/22/1924	13Sag11	00Sco54	19Pis10	21Leo31	13Can27
10/07/1924	15Sag21	02Sco36	18Pis36	21Leo56	13Can32

Ephemeris Tables for Jupiter, Saturn, Uranus, Neptune, and Pluto

Date	Jupiter	Saturn	Uranus	Neptune	Pluto
10/22/1924	17Sag55	04Sco22	18Pis08	22Leo16	13Can31
11/06/1924	20Sag50	06Sco11	17Pis48	22Leo29	13Can26
11/21/1924	24Sag00	07Sco57	17Pis38	22Leo34	13Can16
12/06/1924	27Sag19	09Sco37	17Pis39	22Leo33	13Can01
12/21/1924	00Cap45	11Sco07	17Pis52	22Leo23	12Can44
01/05/1925	04Cap11	12Sco24	18Pis16	22Leo07	12Can25
01/20/1925	07Cap33	13Sco23	18Pis50	21Leo46	12Can07
02/04/1925	10Cap48	14Sco01	19Pis31	21Leo22	11Can50
02/19/1925	13Cap48	14Sco17	20Pis18	20Leo57	11Can37
03/06/1925	16Cap31	14Sco10	21Pis09	20Leo33	11Can28
03/21/1925	18Cap49	13Sco40	22Pis00	20Leo12	11Can24
04/05/1925	20Cap39	12Sco52	22Pis50	19Leo57	11Can25
04/20/1925	21Cap53	11Sco51	23Pis36	19Leo49	11Can31
05/05/1925	22Cap28	10Sco43	24Pis17	19Leo47	11Can43
05/20/1925	22Cap22	09Sco37	24Pis49	19Leo53	11Can58
06/04/1925	21Cap33	08Sco42	25Pis13	20Leo06	12Can18
06/19/1925	20Cap10	08Sco01	25Pis27	20Leo26	12Can39
07/04/1925	18Cap22	07Sco39	25Pis30	20Leo51	13Can02
07/19/1925	16Cap27	07Sco40	25Pis22	21Leo20	13Can25
08/03/1925	14Cap43	08Sco02	25Pis04	21Leo52	13Can46
08/18/1925	13Cap25	08Sco45	24Pis37	22Leo25	14Can06
09/02/1925	12Cap45	09Sco46	24Pis05	22Leo58	14Can22
09/17/1925	12Cap48	11Sco04	23Pis29	23Leo29	14Can34
10/02/1925	13Cap32	12Sco34	22Pis54	23Leo57	14Can42
10/17/1925	14Cap56	14Sco14	22Pis22	24Leo19	14Can44
11/01/1925	16Cap55	16Sco00	21Pis57	24Leo36	14Can40
11/16/1925	19Cap22	17Sco48	21Pis40	24Leo45	14Can32
12/01/1925	22Cap13	19Sco33	21Pis35	24Leo47	14Can19
12/16/1925	25Cap22	21Sco13	21Pis40	24Leo41	14Can03
12/31/1925	28Cap43	22Sco45	21Pis58	24Leo28	13Can45
01/15/1926	02Aqu13	24Sco02	22Pis26	24Leo09	13Can26
01/30/1926	05Aqu46	25Sco03	23Pis03	23Leo46	13Can08
02/14/1926	09Aqu17	25Sco43	23Pis46	23Leo21	12Can53
03/01/1926	12Aqu43	26Sco02	24Pis35	22Leo57	12Can42
03/16/1926	15Aqu58	25Sco58	25Pis26	22Leo34	12Can36
03/31/1926	18Aqu58	25Sco31	26Pis17	22Leo16	12Can34
04/15/1926	21Aqu37	24Sco46	27Pis06	22Leo04	12Can39
04/30/1926	23Aqu52	23Sco46	27Pis50	22Leo00	12Can48
05/15/1926	25Aqu36	22Sco40	28Pis28	22Leo01	13Can03
05/30/1926	26Aqu43	21Sco34	28Pis58	22Leo11	13Can20
06/14/1926	27Aqu10	20Sco37	29Pis18	22Leo28	13Can41
06/29/1926	26Aqu54	19Sco54	29Pis27	22Leo50	14Can03
07/14/1926	25Aqu56	19Sco29	29Pis25	23Leo17	14Can27
07/29/1926	24Aqu24	19Sco25	29Pis14	23Leo48	14Can49
08/13/1926	22Aqu31	19Sco44	28Pis52	24Leo21	15Can10
08/28/1926	20Aqu36	20Sco23	28Pis24	24Leo54	15Can28
09/12/1926	18Aqu55	21Sco22	27Pis49	25Leo26	15Can42
09/27/1926	17Aqu47	22Sco36	27Pis13	25Leo55	15Can51
10/12/1926	17Aqu19	24Sco04	26Pis39	26Leo21	15Can56
10/27/1926	17Aqu37	25Sco42	26Pis09	26Leo40	15Can55
11/11/1926	18Aqu37	27Sco27	25Pis47	26Leo54	15Can48
11/26/1926	20Aqu18	29Sco14	25Pis34	26Leo59	15Can37
12/11/1926	22Aqu32	01Sag00	25Pis33	26Leo57	15Can22
12/26/1926	25Aqu13	02Sag40	25Pis44	26Leo48	15Can04

Ephemeris Tables for Jupiter, Saturn, Uranus, Neptune, and Pluto

Date	Jupiter	Saturn	Uranus	Neptune	Pluto
01/10/1927	28Aqu17	04Sag12	26Pis05	26Leo31	14Can46
01/25/1927	01Pis36	05Sag30	26Pis37	26Leo10	14Can27
02/09/1927	05Pis06	06Sag33	27Pis16	25Leo46	14Can11
02/24/1927	08Pis42	07Sag15	28Pis03	25Leo21	13Can58
03/11/1927	12Pis18	07Sag37	28Pis52	24Leo57	13Can49
03/26/1927	15Pis52	07Sag35	29Pis43	24Leo37	13Can46
04/10/1927	19Pis20	07Sag12	00Ari33	24Leo22	13Can48
04/25/1927	22Pis35	06Sag29	01Ari21	24Leo13	13Can55
05/10/1927	25Pis35	05Sag31	02Ari03	24Leo12	14Can08
05/25/1927	28Pis13	04Sag27	02Ari37	24Leo18	14Can24
06/09/1927	00Ari25	03Sag21	03Ari04	24Leo31	14Can44
06/24/1927	02Ari06	02Sag21	03Ari20	24Leo50	15Can06
07/09/1927	03Ari10	01Sag36	03Ari25	25Leo15	15Can29
07/24/1927	03Ari31	01Sag08	03Ari20	25Leo44	15Can52
08/08/1927	03Ari10	01Sag01	03Ari04	26Leo16	16Can13
08/23/1927	02Ari06	01Sag16	02Ari39	26Leo49	16Can33
09/07/1927	00Ari28	01Sag52	02Ari08	27Leo22	16Can49
09/22/1927	28Pis31	02Sag48	01Ari33	27Leo54	17Can01
10/07/1927	26Pis34	04Sag00	00Ari57	28Leo21	17Can07
10/22/1927	24Pis57	05Sag26	00Ari24	28Leo43	17Can09
11/06/1927	23Pis55	07Sag03	29Pis57	29Leo00	17Can05
11/21/1927	23Pis38	08Sag46	29Pis39	29Leo09	16Can55
12/06/1927	24Pis07	10Sag33	29Pis31	29Leo11	16Can42
12/21/1927	25Pis19	12Sag18	29Pis34	29Leo05	16Can25
01/05/1928	27Pis10	13Sag59	29Pis49	28Leo52	16Can07
01/20/1928	29Pis33	15Sag31	00Ari13	28Leo33	15Can48
02/04/1928	02Ari22	16Sag52	00Ari49	28Leo10	15Can30
02/19/1928	05Ari31	17Sag55	01Ari31	27Leo45	15Can16
03/05/1928	08Ari54	18Sag40	02Ari19	27Leo21	15Can05
03/20/1928	12Ari27	19Sag03	03Ari09	26Leo58	15Can00
04/04/1928	16Ari03	19Sag04	04Ari01	26Leo40	14Can59
04/19/1928	19Ari40	18Sag44	04Ari50	26Leo29	15Can04
05/04/1928	23Ari13	18Sag04	05Ari36	26Leo24	15Can15
05/19/1928	26Ari39	17Sag09	06Ari15	26Leo26	15Can29
06/03/1928	29Ari52	16Sag04	06Ari47	26Leo36	15Can48
06/18/1928	02Tau49	14Sag58	07Ari09	26Leo52	16Can09
07/03/1928	05Tau25	13Sag58	07Ari21	27Leo14	16Can32
07/18/1928	07Tau34	13Sag10	07Ari23	27Leo42	16Can55
08/02/1928	09Tau10	12Sag39	07Ari13	28Leo12	17Can18
08/17/1928	10Tau09	12Sag30	06Ari54	28Leo45	17Can39
09/01/1928	10Tau25	12Sag41	06Ari27	29Leo18	17Can56
09/16/1928	09Tau57	13Sag15	05Ari54	29Leo51	18Can10
10/01/1928	08Tau45	14Sag07	05Ari18	00Vir20	18Can19
10/16/1928	07Tau01	15Sag18	04Ari42	00Vir45	18Can23
10/31/1928	05Tau01	16Sag42	04Ari11	01Vir05	18Can21
11/15/1928	03Tau05	18Sag17	03Ari46	01Vir18	18Can14
11/30/1928	01Tau32	20Sag00	03Ari32	01Vir23	18Can02
12/15/1928	00Tau37	21Sag46	03Ari28	01Vir21	17Can46
12/30/1928	00Tau28	23Sag31	03Ari36	01Vir12	17Can28
01/14/1929	01Tau06	25Sag13	03Ari55	00Vir55	17Can09
01/29/1929	02Tau26	26Sag46	04Ari24	00Vir34	16Can51
02/13/1929	04Tau23	28Sag07	05Ari03	00Vir10	16Can35
02/28/1929	06Tau50	29Sag12	05Ari47	29Leo45	16Can22
03/15/1929	09Tau42	29Sag59	06Ari36	29Leo21	16Can15
03/30/1929	12Tau50	00Cap25	07Ari27	29Leo01	16Can12

Ephemeris Tables for Jupiter, Saturn, Uranus, Neptune, and Pluto

Date	Jupiter	Saturn	Uranus	Neptune	Pluto
04/14/1929	16Tau12	00Cap29	08Ari18	28Leo46	16Can15
04/29/1929	19Tau41	00Cap11	09Ari07	28Leo37	16Can23
05/14/1929	23Tau13	29Sag33	09Ari50	28Leo36	16Can36
05/29/1929	26Tau46	28Sag40	10Ari27	28Leo42	16Can53
06/13/1929	00Gem14	27Sag37	10Ari55	28Leo55	17Can13
06/28/1929	03Gem34	26Sag31	11Ari14	29Leo15	17Can36
07/13/1929	06Gem41	25Sag29	11Ari22	29Leo39	17Can59
07/28/1929	09Gem32	24Sag39	11Ari19	00Vir09	18Can22
08/12/1929	12Gem00	24Sag06	11Ari06	00Vir40	18Can44
08/27/1929	14Gem01	23Sag53	10Ari43	01Vir13	19Can03
09/11/1929	15Gem28	24Sag02	10Ari13	01Vir46	19Can19
09/26/1929	16Gem16	24Sag33	09Ari39	02Vir18	19Can30
10/11/1929	16Gem21	25Sag23	09Ari03	02Vir45	19Can36
10/26/1929	15Gem40	26Sag31	08Ari28	03Vir08	19Can37
11/10/1929	14Gem19	27Sag54	07Ari59	03Vir24	19Can32
11/25/1929	12Gem28	29Sag29	07Ari38	03Vir33	19Can22
12/10/1929	10Gem26	01Cap11	07Ari28	03Vir35	19Can08
12/25/1929	08Gem34	02Cap57	07Ari28	03Vir29	18Can51
01/09/1930	07Gem09	04Cap42	07Ari40	03Vir16	18Can32
01/24/1930	06Gem26	06Cap24	08Ari04	02Vir57	18Can13
02/08/1930	06Gem28	07Cap58	08Ari37	02Vir34	17Can55
02/23/1930	07Gem14	09Cap20	09Ari18	02Vir09	17Can41
03/10/1930	08Gem41	10Cap27	10Ari04	01Vir45	17Can31
03/25/1930	10Gem42	11Cap16	10Ari55	01Vir22	17Can26
04/09/1930	13Gem10	11Cap45	11Ari46	01Vir04	17Can27
04/24/1930	16Gem00	11Cap52	12Ari36	00Vir53	17Can33
05/09/1930	19Gem06	11Cap36	13Ari23	00Vir48	17Can44
05/24/1930	22Gem23	11Cap01	14Ari04	00Vir50	17Can59
06/08/1930	25Gem46	10Cap10	14Ari38	01Vir00	18Can18
06/23/1930	29Gem13	09Cap07	15Ari03	01Vir16	18Can40
07/08/1930	02Can38	08Cap01	15Ari18	01Vir38	19Can03
07/23/1930	05Can58	06Cap59	15Ari22	02Vir06	19Can27
08/07/1930	09Can09	06Cap07	15Ari15	02Vir36	19Can50
08/22/1930	12Can07	05Cap31	14Ari58	03Vir09	20Can10
09/06/1930	14Can47	05Cap16	14Ari32	03Vir42	20Can28
09/21/1930	17Can03	05Cap22	14Ari00	04Vir15	20Can41
10/06/1930	18Can49	05Cap49	13Ari24	04Vir44	20Can50
10/21/1930	20Can00	06Cap38	12Ari48	05Vir09	20Can53
11/05/1930	20Can30	07Cap45	12Ari15	05Vir29	20Can51
11/20/1930	20Can15	09Cap06	11Ari49	05Vir42	20Can43
12/05/1930	19Can17	10Cap40	11Ari32	05Vir47	20Can30
12/20/1930	17Can42	12Cap21	11Ari25	05Vir45	20Can14
01/04/1931	15Can45	14Cap07	11Ari31	05Vir35	19Can55
01/19/1931	13Can46	15Cap53	11Ari48	05Vir19	19Can36
02/03/1931	12Can04	17Cap36	12Ari15	04Vir58	19Can18
02/18/1931	10Can54	19Cap10	12Ari51	04Vir34	19Can02
03/05/1931	10Can27	20Cap34	13Ari34	04Vir09	18Can50
03/20/1931	10Can43	21Cap43	14Ari23	03Vir45	18Can43
04/04/1931	11Can42	22Cap35	15Ari14	03Vir25	18Can41
04/19/1931	13Can16	23Cap06	16Ari05	03Vir10	18Can45
05/04/1931	15Can22	23Cap16	16Ari54	03Vir01	18Can53
05/19/1931	17Can52	23Cap04	17Ari39	03Vir00	19Can07
06/03/1931	20Can41	22Cap31	18Ari18	03Vir06	19Can25
06/18/1931	23Can44	21Cap42	18Ari48	03Vir19	19Can46
07/03/1931	26Can57	20Cap40	19Ari10	03Vir38	20Can09

Ephemeris Tables for Jupiter, Saturn, Uranus, Neptune, and Pluto

Date	Jupiter	Saturn	Uranus	Neptune	Pluto
07/18/1931	00Leo15	19Cap34	19Ari21	04Vir03	20Can33
08/02/1931	03Leo36	18Cap30	19Ari20	04Vir32	20Can56
08/17/1931	06Leo53	17Cap36	19Ari09	05Vir04	21Can18
09/01/1931	10Leo04	16Cap58	18Ari49	05Vir37	21Can37
09/16/1931	13Leo06	16Cap40	18Ari21	06Vir10	21Can52
10/01/1931	15Leo51	16Cap43	17Ari46	06Vir42	22Can03
10/16/1931	18Leo16	17Cap09	17Ari10	07Vir09	22Can09
10/31/1931	20Leo15	17Cap55	16Ari35	07Vir31	22Can09
11/15/1931	21Leo42	19Cap00	16Ari04	07Vir48	22Can03
11/30/1931	22Leo29	20Cap21	15Ari41	07Vir57	21Can52
12/15/1931	22Leo34	21Cap54	15Ari28	07Vir59	21Can37
12/30/1931	21Leo55	23Cap35	15Ari26	07Vir52	21Can19
01/14/1932	20Leo37	25Cap21	15Ari36	07Vir40	21Can00
01/29/1932	18Leo50	27Cap07	15Ari57	07Vir21	20Can42
02/13/1932	16Leo51	28Cap51	16Ari28	06Vir58	20Can24
02/28/1932	15Leo00	00Aqu27	17Ari07	06Vir33	20Can10
03/14/1932	13Leo34	01Aqu52	17Ari52	06Vir08	20Can01
03/29/1932	12Leo45	03Aqu04	18Ari42	05Vir46	19Can57
04/13/1932	12Leo37	03Aqu58	19Ari34	05Vir28	19Can58
04/28/1932	13Leo12	04Aqu32	20Ari24	05Vir16	20Can04
05/13/1932	14Leo24	04Aqu45	21Ari12	05Vir12	20Can16
05/28/1932	16Leo10	04Aqu36	21Ari55	05Vir14	20Can33
06/12/1932	18Leo22	04Aqu06	22Ari31	05Vir24	20Can52
06/27/1932	20Leo57	03Aqu18	22Ari58	05Vir40	21Can15
07/12/1932	23Leo48	02Aqu18	23Ari16	06Vir02	21Can39
07/27/1932	26Leo51	01Aqu12	23Ari22	06Vir29	22Can03
08/11/1932	00Vir02	00Aqu07	23Ari18	07Vir00	22Can25
08/26/1932	03Vir18	29Cap11	23Ari04	07Vir33	22Can46
09/10/1932	06Vir33	28Cap30	22Ari40	08Vir06	23Can03
09/25/1932	09Vir44	28Cap09	22Ari09	08Vir38	23Can16
10/10/1932	12Vir47	28Cap09	21Ari33	09Vir07	23Can24
10/25/1932	15Vir37	28Cap33	20Ari57	09Vir33	23Can27
11/09/1932	18Vir09	29Cap17	20Ari23	09Vir52	23Can23
11/24/1932	20Vir16	00Aqu20	19Ari55	10Vir05	23Can15
12/09/1932	21Vir54	01Aqu40	19Ari36	10Vir10	23Can01
12/24/1932	22Vir55	03Aqu12	19Ari26	10Vir08	22Can45
01/08/1933	23Vir15	04Aqu54	19Ari29	09Vir58	22Can26
01/23/1933	22Vir52	06Aqu40	19Ari43	09Vir42	22Can06
02/07/1933	21Vir49	08Aqu27	20Ari08	09Vir21	21Can48
02/22/1933	20Vir12	10Aqu12	20Ari42	08Vir57	21Can33
03/09/1933	18Vir18	11Aqu49	21Ari24	08Vir32	21Can21
03/24/1933	16Vir24	13Aqu17	22Ari12	08Vir09	21Can15
04/08/1933	14Vir48	14Aqu31	23Ari03	07Vir48	21Can13
04/23/1933	13Vir43	15Aqu28	23Ari54	07Vir33	21Can18
05/08/1933	13Vir17	16Aqu05	24Ari44	07Vir25	21Can27
05/23/1933	13Vir32	16Aqu21	25Ari30	07Vir24	21Can42
06/07/1933	14Vir26	16Aqu16	26Ari11	07Vir30	22Can00
06/22/1933	15Vir55	15Aqu49	26Ari43	07Vir42	22Can22
07/07/1933	17Vir53	15Aqu03	27Ari07	08Vir02	22Can45
07/22/1933	20Vir15	14Aqu04	27Ari21	08Vir27	23Can09
08/06/1933	22Vir57	12Aqu58	27Ari24	08Vir56	23Can33
08/21/1933	25Vir53	11Aqu52	27Ari16	09Vir28	23Can55
09/05/1933	29Vir00	10Aqu55	26Ari57	10Vir01	24Can14
09/20/1933	02Lib12	10Aqu11	26Ari30	10Vir34	24Can29
10/05/1933	05Lib27	09Aqu46	25Ari57	11Vir05	24Can39

Ephemeris Tables for Jupiter, Saturn, Uranus, Neptune, and Pluto

Date	Jupiter	Saturn	Uranus	Neptune	Pluto
10/20/1933	08Lib39	09Aqu44	25Ari21	11Vir33	24Can44
11/04/1933	11Lib45	10Aqu04	24Ari45	11Vir55	24Can43
11/19/1933	14Lib40	10Aqu47	24Ari13	12Vir12	24Can37
12/04/1933	17Lib18	11Aqu49	23Ari48	12Vir21	24Can26
12/19/1933	19Lib34	13Aqu07	23Ari32	12Vir22	24Can10
01/03/1934	21Lib21	14Aqu39	23Ari27	12Vir16	23Can52
01/18/1934	22Lib34	16Aqu21	23Ari34	12Vir03	23Can33
02/02/1934	23Lib09	18Aqu07	23Ari53	11Vir44	23Can13
02/17/1934	23Lib01	19Aqu55	24Ari22	11Vir21	22Can57
03/04/1934	22Lib12	21Aqu41	24Ari59	10Vir56	22Can43
03/19/1934	20Lib47	23Aqu21	25Ari43	10Vir31	22Can34
04/03/1934	18Lib59	24Aqu51	26Ari33	10Vir09	22Can31
04/18/1934	17Lib04	26Aqu07	27Ari24	09Vir52	22Can33
05/03/1934	15Lib21	27Aqu07	28Ari15	09Vir40	22Can40
05/18/1934	14Lib03	27Aqu49	29Ari04	09Vir35	22Can53
06/02/1934	13Lib22	28Aqu09	29Ari48	09Vir37	23Can10
06/17/1934	13Lib20	28Aqu07	00Tau27	09Vir47	23Can30
07/02/1934	13Lib58	27Aqu44	00Tau56	10Vir03	23Can53
07/17/1934	15Lib13	27Aqu01	01Tau16	10Vir25	24Can17
08/01/1934	17Lib00	26Aqu03	01Tau26	10Vir52	24Can41
08/16/1934	19Lib12	24Aqu57	01Tau25	11Vir23	25Can04
08/31/1934	21Lib47	23Aqu50	01Tau13	11Vir56	25Can25
09/15/1934	24Lib39	22Aqu50	00Tau51	12Vir29	25Can42
09/30/1934	27Lib43	22Aqu03	00Tau21	13Vir01	25Can54
10/15/1934	00Sco55	21Aqu36	29Ari46	13Vir31	26Can02
10/30/1934	04Sco12	21Aqu30	29Ari10	13Vir56	26Can04
11/14/1934	07Sco27	21Aqu48	28Ari34	14Vir16	26Can00
11/29/1934	10Sco38	22Aqu28	28Ari04	14Vir28	25Can51
12/14/1934	13Sco39	23Aqu28	27Ari43	14Vir34	25Can36
12/29/1934	16Sco25	24Aqu45	27Ari31	14Vir31	25Can19
01/13/1935	18Sco50	26Aqu16	27Ari31	14Vir22	25Can00
01/28/1935	20Sco49	27Aqu58	27Ari42	14Vir06	24Can40
02/12/1935	22Sco17	29Aqu45	28Ari05	13Vir44	24Can22
02/27/1935	23Sco07	01Pis34	28Ari37	13Vir20	24Can07
03/14/1935	23Sco15	03Pis22	29Ari18	12Vir55	23Can56
03/29/1935	22Sco42	05Pis04	00Tau04	12Vir31	23Can50
04/13/1935	21Sco31	06Pis36	00Tau55	12Vir12	23Can49
04/28/1935	19Sco52	07Pis56	01Tau46	11Vir57	23Can55
05/13/1935	17Sco58	09Pis00	02Tau37	11Vir48	24Can05
05/28/1935	16Sco09	09Pis45	03Tau25	11Vir47	24Can21
06/12/1935	14Sco40	10Pis09	04Tau07	11Vir53	24Can40
06/27/1935	13Sco42	10Pis12	04Tau42	12Vir06	25Can02
07/12/1935	13Sco25	09Pis52	05Tau09	12Vir25	25Can25
07/27/1935	13Sco48	09Pis12	05Tau25	12Vir50	25Can50
08/11/1935	14Sco48	08Pis17	05Tau31	13Vir19	26Can14
08/26/1935	16Sco24	07Pis12	05Tau25	13Vir51	26Can36
09/10/1935	18Sco29	06Pis03	05Tau09	14Vir24	26Can55
09/25/1935	20Sco58	05Pis01	04Tau44	14Vir57	27Can09
10/10/1935	23Sco47	04Pis11	04Tau12	15Vir28	27Can19
10/25/1935	26Sco51	03Pis40	03Tau36	15Vir56	27Can24
11/09/1935	00Sag05	03Pis31	03Tau00	16Vir18	27Can22
11/24/1935	03Sag25	03Pis45	02Tau26	16Vir34	27Can15
12/09/1935	06Sag45	04Pis22	01Tau58	16Vir44	27Can03
12/24/1935	10Sag03	05Pis21	01Tau40	16Vir45	26Can47

Ephemeris Tables for Jupiter, Saturn, Uranus, Neptune, and Pluto

Date	Jupiter	Saturn	Uranus	Neptune	Pluto
01/08/1936	13Sag12	06Pis37	01Tau33	16Vir39	26Can28
01/23/1936	16Sag09	08Pis07	01Tau37	16Vir26	26Can09
02/07/1936	18Sag47	09Pis48	01Tau53	16Vir07	25Can49
02/22/1936	21Sag01	11Pis36	02Tau20	15Vir44	25Can33
03/08/1936	22Sag45	13Pis26	02Tau55	15Vir19	25Can19
03/23/1936	23Sag55	15Pis15	03Tau39	14Vir55	25Can12
04/07/1936	24Sag25	16Pis59	04Tau27	14Vir33	25Can09
04/22/1936	24Sag13	18Pis34	05Tau18	14Vir15	25Can11
05/07/1936	23Sag20	19Pis58	06Tau10	14Vir03	25Can19
05/22/1936	21Sag53	21Pis06	07Tau00	13Vir58	25Can33
06/06/1936	20Sag05	21Pis55	07Tau46	14Vir01	25Can51
06/21/1936	18Sag11	22Pis25	08Tau25	14Vir10	26Can12
07/06/1936	16Sag30	22Pis31	08Tau58	14Vir26	26Can35
07/21/1936	15Sag16	22Pis16	09Tau21	14Vir49	27Can00
08/05/1936	14Sag39	21Pis40	09Tau33	15Vir16	27Can24
08/20/1936	14Sag42	20Pis47	09Tau35	15Vir46	27Can47
09/04/1936	15Sag27	19Pis42	09Tau25	16Vir19	28Can07
09/19/1936	16Sag50	18Pis33	09Tau06	16Vir52	28Can24
10/04/1936	18Sag46	17Pis28	08Tau37	17Vir25	28Can37
10/19/1936	21Sag09	16Pis36	08Tau03	17Vir54	28Can43
11/03/1936	23Sag55	16Pis00	07Tau27	18Vir19	28Can45
11/18/1936	26Sag59	15Pis47	06Tau51	18Vir39	28Can40
12/03/1936	00Cap15	15Pis58	06Tau19	18Vir52	28Can30
12/18/1936	03Cap39	16Pis32	05Tau55	18Vir57	28Can16
01/02/1937	07Cap06	17Pis28	05Tau40	18Vir54	27Can58
01/17/1937	10Cap32	18Pis42	05Tau37	18Vir45	27Can38
02/01/1937	13Cap52	20Pis12	05Tau46	18Vir28	27Can18
02/16/1937	17Cap01	21Pis52	06Tau07	18Vir07	27Can00
03/03/1937	19Cap54	23Pis40	06Tau37	17Vir43	26Can45
03/18/1937	22Cap27	25Pis31	07Tau16	17Vir18	26Can35
04/02/1937	24Cap32	27Pis22	08Tau01	16Vir55	26Can30
04/17/1937	26Cap06	29Pis09	08Tau51	16Vir34	26Can30
05/02/1937	27Cap03	00Ari46	09Tau43	16Vir20	26Can36
05/17/1937	27Cap18	02Ari13	10Tau34	16Vir12	26Can47
06/01/1937	26Cap52	03Ari26	11Tau23	16Vir10	27Can03
06/16/1937	25Cap46	04Ari21	12Tau07	16Vir16	27Can23
07/01/1937	24Cap09	04Ari55	12Tau45	16Vir29	27Can46
07/16/1937	22Cap15	05Ari08	13Tau13	16Vir48	28Can10
07/31/1937	20Cap23	04Ari57	13Tau33	17Vir13	28Can35
08/15/1937	18Cap49	04Ari25	13Tau41	17Vir42	28Can59
08/30/1937	17Cap49	03Ari35	13Tau39	18Vir14	29Can21
09/14/1937	17Cap28	02Ari31	13Tau25	18Vir47	29Can39
09/29/1937	17Cap52	01Ari22	13Tau02	19Vir20	29Can54
10/14/1937	18Cap57	00Ari15	12Tau31	19Vir51	00Leo03
10/29/1937	20Cap39	29Pis19	11Tau56	20Vir19	00Leo07
11/13/1937	22Cap53	28Pis39	11Tau19	20Vir42	00Leo05
11/28/1937	25Cap33	28Pis22	10Tau44	20Vir58	29Can57
12/13/1937	28Cap34	28Pis28	10Tau15	21Vir07	29Can45
12/28/1937	01Aqu51	28Pis59	09Tau54	21Vir08	29Can28
01/12/1938	05Aqu18	29Pis52	09Tau44	21Vir01	29Can09
01/27/1938	08Aqu50	01Ari04	09Tau45	20Vir48	28Can49
02/11/1938	12Aqu24	02Ari32	09Tau58	20Vir30	28Can30
02/26/1938	15Aqu54	04Ari12	10Tau23	20Vir07	28Can13
03/13/1938	19Aqu15	06Ari00	10Tau57	19Vir42	28Can00
03/28/1938	22Aqu25	07Ari52	11Tau39	19Vir17	27Can53

447

Ephemeris Tables for Jupiter, Saturn, Uranus, Neptune, and Pluto

Date	Jupiter	Saturn	Uranus	Neptune	Pluto
04/12/1938	25Aqu16	09Ari44	12Tau26	18Vir55	27Can51
04/27/1938	27Aqu46	11Ari33	13Tau16	18Vir38	27Can54
05/12/1938	29Aqu48	13Ari15	14Tau09	18Vir26	28Can03
05/27/1938	01Pis16	14Ari45	15Tau00	18Vir21	28Can17
06/11/1938	02Pis06	16Ari03	15Tau47	18Vir24	28Can36
06/26/1938	02Pis13	17Ari03	16Tau29	18Vir33	28Can57
07/11/1938	01Pis38	17Ari43	17Tau03	18Vir49	29Can21
07/26/1938	00Pis24	18Ari01	17Tau29	19Vir12	29Can46
08/10/1938	28Aqu40	17Ari57	17Tau45	19Vir39	00Leo11
08/25/1938	26Aqu42	17Ari30	17Tau49	20Vir09	00Leo34
09/09/1938	24Aqu51	16Ari43	17Tau42	20Vir42	00Leo55
09/24/1938	23Aqu24	15Ari40	17Tau25	21Vir15	01Leo11
10/09/1938	22Aqu33	14Ari31	16Tau59	21Vir48	01Leo23
10/24/1938	22Aqu27	13Ari22	16Tau26	22Vir17	01Leo30
11/08/1938	23Aqu05	12Ari22	15Tau49	22Vir42	01Leo30
11/23/1938	24Aqu25	11Ari38	15Tau12	23Vir02	01Leo25
12/08/1938	26Aqu22	11Ari16	14Tau39	23Vir15	01Leo14
12/23/1938	28Aqu51	11Ari18	14Tau13	23Vir19	00Leo59
01/07/1939	01Pis44	11Ari44	13Tau56	23Vir17	00Leo40
01/22/1939	04Pis56	12Ari33	13Tau50	23Vir07	00Leo21
02/06/1939	08Pis21	13Ari43	13Tau56	22Vir51	00Leo01
02/21/1939	11Pis55	15Ari09	14Tau14	22Vir30	29Can43
03/08/1939	15Pis32	16Ari48	14Tau42	22Vir06	29Can28
03/23/1939	19Pis09	18Ari36	15Tau19	21Vir40	29Can18
04/07/1939	22Pis40	20Ari28	16Tau03	21Vir17	29Can13
04/22/1939	26Pis03	22Ari22	16Tau52	20Vir57	29Can15
05/07/1939	29Pis12	24Ari13	17Tau44	20Vir43	29Can21
05/22/1939	02Ari03	25Ari58	18Tau36	20Vir34	29Can33
06/06/1939	04Ari30	27Ari33	19Tau25	20Vir33	29Can50
06/21/1939	06Ari30	28Ari55	20Tau12	20Vir39	00Leo10
07/06/1939	07Ari55	00Tau01	20Tau51	20Vir52	00Leo34
07/21/1939	08Ari40	00Tau48	21Tau23	21Vir11	00Leo58
08/05/1939	08Ari43	01Tau12	21Tau45	21Vir36	01Leo24
08/20/1939	08Ari01	01Tau13	21Tau57	22Vir05	01Leo48
09/04/1939	06Ari41	00Tau52	21Tau57	22Vir37	02Leo10
09/19/1939	04Ari52	00Tau09	21Tau46	23Vir10	02Leo28
10/04/1939	02Ari52	29Ari10	21Tau25	23Vir43	02Leo43
10/19/1939	01Ari01	28Ari00	20Tau56	24Vir14	02Leo52
11/03/1939	29Pis39	26Ari49	20Tau21	24Vir42	02Leo55
11/18/1939	28Pis57	25Ari46	19Tau44	25Vir04	02Leo52
12/03/1939	29Pis00	24Ari57	19Tau08	25Vir20	02Leo44
12/18/1939	29Pis49	24Ari30	18Tau37	25Vir29	02Leo30
01/02/1940	01Ari20	24Ari27	18Tau14	25Vir30	02Leo13
01/17/1940	03Ari27	24Ari48	18Tau01	25Vir24	01Leo54
02/01/1940	06Ari03	25Ari33	18Tau00	25Vir11	01Leo33
02/16/1940	09Ari02	26Ari39	18Tau10	24Vir52	01Leo15
03/02/1940	12Ari18	28Ari03	18Tau32	24Vir29	00Leo58
03/17/1940	15Ari45	29Ari40	19Tau04	24Vir04	00Leo46
04/01/1940	19Ari20	01Tau27	19Tau43	23Vir40	00Leo39
04/16/1940	22Ari57	03Tau20	20Tau30	23Vir18	00Leo37
05/01/1940	26Ari33	05Tau15	21Tau21	23Vir00	00Leo41
05/16/1940	00Tau03	07Tau07	22Tau12	22Vir49	00Leo51
05/31/1940	03Tau22	08Tau55	23Tau04	22Vir44	01Leo06
06/15/1940	06Tau29	10Tau35	23Tau53	22Vir46	01Leo25
06/30/1940	09Tau17	12Tau02	24Tau37	22Vir55	01Leo48

Ephemeris Tables for Jupiter, Saturn, Uranus, Neptune, and Pluto

Date	Jupiter	Saturn	Uranus	Neptune	Pluto
07/15/1940	11Tau42	13Tau13	25Tau14	23Vir12	02Leo12
07/30/1940	13Tau37	14Tau07	25Tau42	23Vir34	02Leo37
08/14/1940	14Tau57	14Tau38	26Tau01	24Vir01	03Leo03
08/29/1940	15Tau36	14Tau46	26Tau09	24Vir32	03Leo25
09/13/1940	15Tau32	14Tau31	26Tau05	25Vir04	03Leo46
09/28/1940	14Tau43	13Tau54	25Tau50	25Vir38	04Leo03
10/13/1940	13Tau16	12Tau57	25Tau26	26Vir10	04Leo14
10/28/1940	11Tau22	11Tau49	24Tau54	26Vir40	04Leo20
11/12/1940	09Tau21	10Tau36	24Tau18	27Vir05	04Leo20
11/27/1940	07Tau32	09Tau30	23Tau40	27Vir24	04Leo14
12/12/1940	06Tau15	08Tau36	23Tau06	27Vir37	04Leo03
12/27/1940	05Tau41	08Tau03	22Tau37	27Vir42	03Leo47
01/11/1941	05Tau54	07Tau54	22Tau18	27Vir39	03Leo28
01/26/1941	06Tau51	08Tau10	22Tau09	27Vir30	03Leo07
02/10/1941	08Tau28	08Tau50	22Tau12	27Vir13	02Leo48
02/25/1941	10Tau40	09Tau52	22Tau27	26Vir52	02Leo30
03/12/1941	13Tau18	11Tau12	22Tau52	26Vir28	02Leo16
03/27/1941	16Tau18	12Tau47	23Tau28	26Vir03	02Leo06
04/11/1941	19Tau32	14Tau33	24Tau10	25Vir40	02Leo02
04/26/1941	22Tau59	16Tau25	24Tau59	25Vir20	02Leo04
05/11/1941	26Tau27	18Tau21	25Tau50	25Vir05	02Leo11
05/26/1941	29Tau59	20Tau16	26Tau43	24Vir57	02Leo24
06/10/1941	03Gem30	22Tau06	27Tau34	24Vir55	02Leo42
06/25/1941	06Gem54	23Tau49	28Tau21	25Vir01	03Leo03
07/10/1941	10Gem07	25Tau22	29Tau03	25Vir14	03Leo27
07/25/1941	13Gem07	26Tau39	29Tau37	25Vir34	03Leo52
08/09/1941	15Gem48	27Tau39	00Gem02	25Vir58	04Leo18
08/24/1941	18Gem03	28Tau17	00Gem17	26Vir27	04Leo42
09/08/1941	19Gem49	28Tau33	00Gem21	27Vir00	05Leo04
09/23/1941	20Gem58	28Tau24	00Gem13	27Vir33	05Leo22
10/08/1941	21Gem25	27Tau52	29Tau54	28Vir06	05Leo36
10/23/1941	21Gem08	27Tau00	29Tau27	28Vir37	05Leo45
11/07/1941	20Gem07	25Tau54	28Tau53	29Vir04	05Leo48
11/22/1941	18Gem30	24Tau41	28Tau16	29Vir27	05Leo44
12/07/1941	16Gem31	23Tau31	27Tau39	29Vir43	05Leo35
12/22/1941	14Gem32	22Tau33	27Tau06	29Vir52	05Leo21
01/06/1942	12Gem51	21Tau54	26Tau40	29Vir53	05Leo03
01/21/1942	11Gem45	21Tau39	26Tau25	29Vir46	04Leo43
02/05/1942	11Gem22	21Tau48	26Tau21	29Vir33	04Leo23
02/20/1942	11Gem45	22Tau22	26Tau28	29Vir14	04Leo04
03/07/1942	12Gem51	23Tau19	26Tau47	28Vir51	03Leo48
03/22/1942	14Gem34	24Tau36	27Tau16	28Vir27	03Leo36
04/06/1942	16Gem48	26Tau08	27Tau55	28Vir02	03Leo29
04/21/1942	19Gem26	27Tau51	28Tau40	27Vir40	03Leo28
05/06/1942	22Gem23	29Tau43	29Tau30	27Vir23	03Leo33
05/21/1942	25Gem33	01Gem39	00Gem22	27Vir11	03Leo44
06/05/1942	28Gem53	03Gem34	01Gem14	27Vir06	04Leo00
06/20/1942	02Can17	05Gem28	02Gem04	27Vir09	04Leo19
07/05/1942	05Can42	07Gem15	02Gem50	27Vir18	04Leo42
07/20/1942	09Can04	08Gem51	03Gem30	27Vir34	05Leo07
08/04/1942	12Can20	10Gem14	04Gem01	27Vir57	05Leo33
08/19/1942	15Can25	11Gem20	04Gem22	28Vir24	05Leo58
09/03/1942	18Can13	12Gem06	04Gem33	28Vir54	06Leo22
09/18/1942	20Can42	12Gem29	04Gem33	29Vir27	06Leo42
10/03/1942	22Can43	12Gem28	04Gem21	00Lib01	06Leo58

449

Ephemeris Tables for Jupiter, Saturn, Uranus, Neptune, and Pluto

Date	Jupiter	Saturn	Uranus	Neptune	Pluto
10/18/1942	24Can13	12Gem02	03Gem59	00Lib33	07Leo10
11/02/1942	25Can04	11Gem15	03Gem28	01Lib02	07Leo15
11/17/1942	25Can11	10Gem11	02Gem53	01Lib27	07Leo15
12/02/1942	24Can34	08Gem59	02Gem15	01Lib47	07Leo08
12/17/1942	23Can17	07Gem47	01Gem39	01Lib59	06Leo56
01/01/1943	21Can29	06Gem45	01Gem09	02Lib04	06Leo39
01/16/1943	19Can29	06Gem00	00Gem46	02Lib01	06Leo20
01/31/1943	17Can36	05Gem37	00Gem35	01Lib52	06Leo00
02/15/1943	16Can08	05Gem40	00Gem35	01Lib35	05Leo40
03/02/1943	15Can19	06Gem08	00Gem47	01Lib14	05Leo22
03/17/1943	15Can12	07Gem00	01Gem10	00Lib50	05Leo08
04/01/1943	15Can49	08Gem11	01Gem43	00Lib25	04Leo59
04/16/1943	17Can06	09Gem39	02Gem24	00Lib02	04Leo55
05/01/1943	18Can55	11Gem20	03Gem12	29Vir42	04Leo58
05/16/1943	21Can13	13Gem10	04Gem03	29Vir27	05Leo06
05/31/1943	23Can52	15Gem05	04Gem55	29Vir19	05Leo19
06/15/1943	26Can48	17Gem01	05Gem47	29Vir18	05Leo38
06/30/1943	29Can55	18Gem57	06Gem36	29Vir24	06Leo00
07/15/1943	03Leo10	20Gem46	07Gem20	29Vir36	06Leo24
07/30/1943	06Leo28	22Gem27	07Gem57	29Vir56	06Leo50
08/14/1943	09Leo47	23Gem55	08Gem25	00Lib21	07Leo16
08/29/1943	13Leo01	25Gem07	08Gem43	00Lib50	07Leo40
09/13/1943	16Leo07	26Gem00	08Gem50	01Lib22	08Leo03
09/28/1943	19Leo01	26Gem31	08Gem45	01Lib55	08Leo21
10/13/1943	21Leo36	26Gem37	08Gem30	02Lib28	08Leo34
10/28/1943	23Leo48	26Gem18	08Gem04	02Lib59	08Leo43
11/12/1943	25Leo31	25Gem37	07Gem31	03Lib27	08Leo45
11/27/1943	26Leo37	24Gem37	06Gem54	03Lib49	08Leo41
12/12/1943	27Leo03	23Gem25	06Gem16	04Lib05	08Leo31
12/27/1943	26Leo45	22Gem12	05Gem42	04Lib14	08Leo16
01/11/1944	25Leo45	21Gem06	05Gem15	04Lib15	07Leo58
01/26/1944	24Leo10	20Gem15	04Gem56	04Lib09	07Leo38
02/10/1944	22Leo16	19Gem46	04Gem48	03Lib55	07Leo18
02/25/1944	20Leo19	19Gem42	04Gem53	03Lib36	06Leo58
03/11/1944	18Leo39	20Gem03	05Gem09	03Lib13	06Leo42
03/26/1944	17Leo31	20Gem48	05Gem36	02Lib48	06Leo31
04/10/1944	17Leo03	21Gem54	06Gem13	02Lib24	06Leo25
04/25/1944	17Leo16	23Gem18	06Gem57	02Lib03	06Leo25
05/10/1944	18Leo10	24Gem55	07Gem45	01Lib45	06Leo30
05/25/1944	19Leo39	26Gem42	08Gem37	01Lib33	06Leo42
06/09/1944	21Leo38	28Gem36	09Gem30	01Lib28	06Leo58
06/24/1944	24Leo01	00Can33	10Gem21	01Lib31	07Leo19
07/09/1944	26Leo44	02Can29	11Gem09	01Lib40	07Leo42
07/24/1944	29Leo42	04Can21	11Gem51	01Lib57	08Leo08
08/08/1944	02Vir49	06Can05	12Gem25	02Lib19	08Leo34
08/23/1944	06Vir02	07Can38	12Gem50	02Lib46	09Leo00
09/07/1944	09Vir17	08Can56	13Gem04	03Lib16	09Leo23
09/22/1944	12Vir30	09Can55	13Gem07	03Lib49	09Leo43
10/07/1944	15Vir37	10Can33	12Gem58	04Lib23	10Leo00
10/22/1944	18Vir34	10Can47	12Gem39	04Lib55	10Leo10
11/06/1944	21Vir15	10Can36	12Gem10	05Lib25	10Leo15
11/21/1944	23Vir34	10Can00	11Gem35	05Lib49	10Leo14
12/06/1944	25Vir27	09Can05	10Gem57	06Lib09	10Leo07
12/21/1944	26Vir45	07Can55	10Gem20	06Lib21	09Leo54

Ephemeris Tables for Jupiter, Saturn, Uranus, Neptune, and Pluto

Date	Jupiter	Saturn	Uranus	Neptune	Pluto
01/05/1945	27Vir25	06Can42	09Gem48	06Lib27	09Leo37
01/20/1945	27Vir23	05Can33	09Gem23	06Lib24	09Leo18
02/04/1945	26Vir38	04Can37	09Gem09	06Lib13	08Leo57
02/19/1945	25Vir16	04Can01	09Gem06	05Lib57	08Leo37
03/06/1945	23Vir28	03Can50	09Gem15	05Lib36	08Leo19
03/21/1945	21Vir32	04Can03	09Gem35	05Lib12	08Leo06
04/05/1945	19Vir45	04Can41	10Gem06	04Lib47	07Leo57
04/20/1945	18Vir24	05Can41	10Gem45	04Lib24	07Leo54
05/05/1945	17Vir39	06Can59	11Gem31	04Lib04	07Leo57
05/20/1945	17Vir34	08Can32	12Gem21	03Lib49	08Leo06
06/04/1945	18Vir10	10Can16	13Gem14	03Lib41	08Leo21
06/19/1945	19Vir22	12Can09	14Gem07	03Lib40	08Leo39
07/04/1945	21Vir06	14Can04	14Gem57	03Lib46	09Leo02
07/19/1945	23Vir18	16Can01	15Gem43	03Lib58	09Leo27
08/03/1945	25Vir50	17Can55	16Gem23	04Lib18	09Leo54
08/18/1945	28Vir40	19Can42	16Gem54	04Lib43	10Leo19
09/02/1945	01Lib42	21Can18	17Gem15	05Lib12	10Leo45
09/17/1945	04Lib52	22Can42	17Gem25	05Lib44	11Leo07
10/02/1945	08Lib06	23Can47	17Gem24	06Lib17	11Leo25
10/17/1945	11Lib19	24Can31	17Gem11	06Lib51	11Leo39
11/01/1945	14Lib29	24Can52	16Gem48	07Lib21	11Leo46
11/16/1945	17Lib30	24Can48	16Gem17	07Lib49	11Leo48
12/01/1945	20Lib16	24Can19	15Gem40	08Lib11	11Leo43
12/16/1945	22Lib43	23Can29	15Gem02	08Lib27	11Leo33
12/31/1945	24Lib45	22Can23	14Gem26	08Lib36	11Leo18
01/15/1946	26Lib15	21Can10	13Gem56	08Lib37	10Leo59
01/30/1946	27Lib09	19Can58	13Gem35	08Lib30	10Leo38
02/14/1946	27Lib21	18Can58	13Gem24	08Lib17	10Leo18
03/01/1946	26Lib51	18Can16	13Gem26	07Lib58	09Leo58
03/16/1946	25Lib42	17Can58	13Gem39	07Lib35	09Leo43
03/31/1946	24Lib03	18Can04	14Gem03	07Lib10	09Leo31
04/15/1946	22Lib09	18Can34	14Gem37	06Lib46	09Leo26
04/30/1946	20Lib19	19Can27	15Gem19	06Lib24	09Leo27
05/15/1946	18Lib47	20Can40	16Gem08	06Lib07	09Leo33
05/30/1946	17Lib48	22Can08	17Gem00	05Lib55	09Leo45
06/14/1946	17Lib27	23Can48	17Gem52	05Lib51	10Leo02
06/29/1946	17Lib46	25Can37	18Gem45	05Lib53	10Leo23
07/14/1946	18Lib44	27Can32	19Gem34	06Lib02	10Leo48
07/29/1946	20Lib16	29Can28	20Gem18	06Lib19	11Leo13
08/13/1946	22Lib16	01Leo23	20Gem55	06Lib41	11Leo40
08/28/1946	24Lib42	03Leo12	21Gem24	07Lib08	12Leo06
09/12/1946	27Lib27	04Leo52	21Gem41	07Lib39	12Leo30
09/27/1946	00Sco25	06Leo19	21Gem47	08Lib12	12Leo51
10/12/1946	03Sco35	07Leo30	21Gem42	08Lib45	13Leo06
10/27/1946	06Sco50	08Leo21	21Gem25	09Lib17	13Leo17
11/11/1946	10Sco07	08Leo48	20Gem58	09Lib47	13Leo21
11/26/1946	13Sco21	08Leo51	20Gem25	10Lib12	13Leo19
12/11/1946	16Sco28	08Leo29	19Gem47	10Lib31	13Leo12
12/26/1946	19Sco22	07Leo44	19Gem09	10Lib43	12Leo58
01/10/1947	21Sco58	06Leo42	18Gem35	10Lib48	12Leo41
01/25/1947	24Sco11	05Leo30	18Gem07	10Lib45	12Leo21
02/09/1947	25Sco55	04Leo17	17Gem50	10Lib35	12Leo00
02/24/1947	27Sco03	03Leo13	17Gem44	10Lib19	11Leo40
03/11/1947	27Sco33	02Leo26	17Gem49	09Lib58	11Leo22
03/26/1947	27Sco19	02Leo01	18Gem07	09Lib33	11Leo09

Ephemeris Tables for Jupiter, Saturn, Uranus, Neptune, and Pluto

Date	Jupiter	Saturn	Uranus	Neptune	Pluto
04/10/1947	26Sco26	02Leo00	18Gem35	09Lib09	11Leo00
04/25/1947	24Sco59	02Leo22	19Gem13	08Lib46	10Leo58
05/10/1947	23Sco10	03Leo09	19Gem57	08Lib26	11Leo02
05/25/1947	21Sco17	04Leo15	20Gem47	08Lib12	11Leo12
06/09/1947	19Sco36	05Leo37	21Gem40	08Lib03	11Leo27
06/24/1947	18Sco22	07Leo14	22Gem33	08Lib01	11Leo46
07/09/1947	17Sco45	09Leo00	23Gem25	08Lib07	12Leo10
07/24/1947	17Sco48	10Leo52	24Gem13	08Lib21	12Leo36
08/08/1947	18Sco31	12Leo48	24Gem55	08Lib40	13Leo02
08/23/1947	19Sco50	14Leo42	25Gem29	09Lib05	13Leo29
09/07/1947	21Sco42	16Leo33	25Gem54	09Lib34	13Leo54
09/22/1947	24Sco01	18Leo15	26Gem07	10Lib06	14Leo16
10/07/1947	26Sco42	19Leo46	26Gem09	10Lib39	14Leo34
10/22/1947	29Sco40	21Leo01	26Gem00	11Lib12	14Leo48
11/06/1947	02Sag51	21Leo57	25Gem39	11Lib43	14Leo55
11/21/1947	06Sag09	22Leo31	25Gem10	12Lib11	14Leo56
12/06/1947	09Sag30	22Leo40	24Gem34	12Lib33	14Leo51
12/21/1947	12Sag51	22Leo24	23Gem55	12Lib49	14Leo40
01/05/1948	16Sag06	21Leo45	23Gem19	12Lib58	14Leo24
01/20/1948	19Sag10	20Leo46	22Gem46	12Lib58	14Leo05
02/04/1948	21Sag58	19Leo37	22Gem22	12Lib52	13Leo44
02/19/1948	24Sag26	18Leo24	22Gem09	12Lib39	13Leo23
03/05/1948	26Sag27	17Leo18	22Gem07	12Lib19	13Leo04
03/20/1948	27Sag54	16Leo26	22Gem17	11Lib57	12Leo48
04/04/1948	28Sag45	15Leo54	22Gem39	11Lib32	12Leo38
04/19/1948	28Sag54	15Leo46	23Gem10	11Lib08	12Leo33
05/04/1948	28Sag22	16Leo02	23Gem51	10Lib46	12Leo34
05/19/1948	27Sag12	16Leo40	24Gem37	10Lib29	12Leo41
06/03/1948	25Sag32	17Leo40	25Gem28	10Lib17	12Leo54
06/18/1948	23Sag39	18Leo58	26Gem22	10Lib12	13Leo12
07/03/1948	21Sag49	20Leo29	27Gem15	10Lib15	13Leo34
07/18/1948	20Sag19	22Leo12	28Gem06	10Lib24	13Leo58
08/02/1948	19Sag22	24Leo02	28Gem52	10Lib40	14Leo25
08/17/1948	19Sag06	25Leo55	29Gem32	11Lib03	14Leo52
09/01/1948	19Sag31	27Leo50	00Can03	11Lib30	15Leo19
09/16/1948	20Sag36	29Leo41	00Can24	12Lib01	15Leo43
10/01/1948	22Sag16	01Vir25	00Can34	12Lib34	16Leo03
10/16/1948	24Sag27	02Vir58	00Can31	13Lib07	16Leo19
10/31/1948	27Sag04	04Vir18	00Can18	13Lib39	16Leo29
11/15/1948	00Cap01	05Vir18	29Gem54	14Lib09	16Leo33
11/30/1948	03Cap12	05Vir57	29Gem22	14Lib34	16Leo31
12/15/1948	06Cap34	06Vir12	28Gem45	14Lib53	16Leo22
12/30/1948	10Cap01	06Vir01	28Gem06	15Lib05	16Leo09
01/14/1949	13Cap30	05Vir28	27Gem31	15Lib10	15Leo51
01/29/1949	16Cap54	04Vir34	27Gem01	15Lib07	15Leo30
02/13/1949	20Cap10	03Vir27	26Gem40	14Lib57	15Leo09
02/28/1949	23Cap13	02Vir15	26Gem31	14Lib40	14Leo48
03/15/1949	25Cap58	01Vir07	26Gem33	14Lib19	14Leo31
03/30/1949	28Cap19	00Vir11	26Gem48	13Lib55	14Leo18
04/14/1949	00Aqu11	29Leo34	27Gem13	13Lib30	14Leo10
04/29/1949	01Aqu28	29Leo19	27Gem48	13Lib07	14Leo08
05/14/1949	02Aqu06	29Leo28	28Gem31	12Lib48	14Leo13
05/29/1949	02Aqu03	00Vir00	29Gem19	12Lib33	14Leo23
06/13/1949	01Aqu16	00Vir54	00Can12	12Lib25	14Leo39
06/28/1949	29Cap55	02Vir05	01Can06	12Lib24	14Leo59

Ephemeris Tables for Jupiter, Saturn, Uranus, Neptune, and Pluto

Date	Jupiter	Saturn	Uranus	Neptune	Pluto
07/13/1949	28Cap07	03Vir32	01Can58	12Lib30	15Leo23
07/28/1949	26Cap12	05Vir11	02Can48	12Lib42	15Leo49
08/12/1949	24Cap27	06Vir58	03Can33	13Lib02	16Leo17
08/27/1949	23Cap07	08Vir50	04Can10	13Lib27	16Leo44
09/11/1949	22Cap25	10Vir43	04Can38	13Lib56	17Leo09
09/26/1949	22Cap25	12Vir34	04Can55	14Lib28	17Leo32
10/11/1949	23Cap10	14Vir19	05Can01	15Lib01	17Leo50
10/26/1949	24Cap34	15Vir55	04Can55	15Lib34	18Leo03
11/10/1949	26Cap33	17Vir17	04Can37	16Lib06	18Leo10
11/25/1949	29Cap01	18Vir21	04Can10	16Lib33	18Leo11
12/10/1949	01Aqu54	19Vir04	03Can36	16Lib55	18Leo05
12/25/1949	05Aqu04	19Vir25	02Can57	17Lib11	17Leo54
01/09/1950	08Aqu27	19Vir20	02Can19	17Lib19	17Leo37
01/24/1950	11Aqu58	18Vir51	01Can45	17Lib20	17Leo18
02/08/1950	15Aqu33	18Vir02	01Can18	17Lib13	16Leo56
02/23/1950	19Aqu06	16Vir58	01Can01	17Lib00	16Leo35
03/10/1950	22Aqu33	15Vir47	00Can56	16Lib41	16Leo16
03/25/1950	25Aqu51	14Vir38	01Can03	16Lib18	16Leo01
04/09/1950	28Aqu54	13Vir39	01Can21	15Lib54	15Leo50
04/24/1950	01Pis37	12Vir57	01Can51	15Lib30	15Leo46
05/09/1950	03Pis55	12Vir37	02Can28	15Lib08	15Leo47
05/24/1950	05Pis43	12Vir39	03Can14	14Lib51	15Leo55
06/08/1950	06Pis55	13Vir05	04Can04	14Lib39	16Leo09
06/23/1950	07Pis26	13Vir52	04Can58	14Lib34	16Leo27
07/08/1950	07Pis15	14Vir58	05Can52	14Lib36	16Leo50
07/23/1950	06Pis21	16Vir21	06Can44	14Lib46	17Leo15
08/07/1950	04Pis51	17Vir55	07Can33	15Lib02	17Leo43
08/22/1950	02Pis59	19Vir39	08Can15	15Lib24	18Leo10
09/06/1950	01Pis02	21Vir29	08Can49	15Lib52	18Leo37
09/21/1950	29Aqu19	23Vir21	09Can13	16Lib22	19Leo01
10/06/1950	28Aqu07	25Vir12	09Can27	16Lib55	19Leo22
10/21/1950	27Aqu36	26Vir58	09Can28	17Lib29	19Leo37
11/05/1950	27Aqu51	28Vir35	09Can18	18Lib01	19Leo48
11/20/1950	28Aqu49	29Vir59	08Can57	18Lib31	19Leo51
12/05/1950	00Pis28	01Lib06	08Can27	18Lib55	19Leo48
12/20/1950	02Pis41	01Lib54	07Can51	19Lib15	19Leo39
01/04/1951	05Pis22	02Lib18	07Can12	19Lib27	19Leo25
01/19/1951	08Pis25	02Lib18	06Can34	19Lib31	19Leo06
02/03/1951	11Pis44	01Lib54	06Can03	19Lib28	18Leo45
02/18/1951	15Pis14	01Lib09	05Can39	19Lib18	18Leo24
03/05/1951	18Pis50	00Lib08	05Can26	19Lib01	18Leo03
03/20/1951	22Pis28	28Vir59	05Can25	18Lib40	17Leo46
04/04/1951	26Pis03	27Vir49	05Can36	18Lib16	17Leo33
04/19/1951	29Pis32	26Vir48	05Can58	17Lib52	17Leo26
05/04/1951	02Ari49	26Vir03	06Can31	17Lib29	17Leo25
05/19/1951	05Ari51	25Vir37	07Can12	17Lib09	17Leo30
06/03/1951	08Ari33	25Vir34	08Can00	16Lib55	17Leo41
06/18/1951	10Ari49	25Vir54	08Can51	16Lib46	17Leo57
07/03/1951	12Ari34	26Vir35	09Can45	16Lib45	18Leo18
07/18/1951	13Ari43	27Vir36	10Can39	16Lib51	18Leo43
08/02/1951	14Ari10	28Vir53	11Can31	17Lib04	19Leo10
08/17/1951	13Ari53	00Lib24	12Can18	17Lib24	19Leo38
09/01/1951	12Ari53	02Lib05	12Can57	17Lib48	20Leo06
09/16/1951	11Ari18	03Lib53	13Can29	18Lib18	20Leo31
10/01/1951	09Ari22	05Lib43	13Can49	18Lib49	20Leo54

Ephemeris Tables for Jupiter, Saturn, Uranus, Neptune, and Pluto

Date	Jupiter	Saturn	Uranus	Neptune	Pluto
10/16/1951	07Ari23	07Lib34	13Can59	19Lib23	21Leo12
10/31/1951	05Ari43	09Lib20	13Can57	19Lib56	21Leo25
11/15/1951	04Ari37	10Lib58	13Can42	20Lib27	21Leo31
11/30/1951	04Ari15	12Lib24	13Can18	20Lib55	21Leo32
12/15/1951	04Ari39	13Lib33	12Can45	21Lib16	21Leo25
12/30/1951	05Ari48	14Lib24	12Can07	21Lib33	21Leo13
01/14/1952	07Ari36	14Lib52	11Can28	21Lib41	20Leo57
01/29/1952	09Ari56	14Lib57	10Can52	21Lib42	20Leo36
02/13/1952	12Ari43	14Lib37	10Can23	21Lib35	20Leo15
02/28/1952	15Ari50	13Lib56	10Can03	21Lib21	19Leo54
03/14/1952	19Ari12	12Lib58	09Can54	21Lib02	19Leo34
03/29/1952	22Ari43	11Lib51	09Can57	20Lib39	19Leo19
04/13/1952	26Ari18	10Lib41	10Can12	20Lib15	19Leo09
04/28/1952	29Ari55	09Lib39	10Can39	19Lib51	19Leo05
05/13/1952	03Tau28	08Lib50	11Can15	19Lib29	19Leo07
05/28/1952	06Tau54	08Lib20	11Can58	19Lib12	19Leo16
06/12/1952	10Tau08	08Lib12	12Can48	19Lib00	19Leo30
06/27/1952	13Tau06	08Lib26	13Can40	18Lib55	19Leo49
07/12/1952	15Tau44	09Lib02	14Can35	18Lib58	20Leo12
07/27/1952	17Tau56	09Lib58	15Can28	19Lib07	20Leo39
08/11/1952	19Tau36	11Lib11	16Can19	19Lib24	21Leo07
08/26/1952	20Tau39	12Lib38	17Can04	19Lib46	21Leo35
09/10/1952	20Tau59	14Lib16	17Can41	20Lib13	22Leo02
09/25/1952	20Tau34	16Lib01	18Can09	20Lib44	22Leo26
10/10/1952	19Tau27	17Lib51	18Can27	21Lib17	22Leo47
10/25/1952	17Tau45	19Lib40	18Can31	21Lib51	23Leo03
11/09/1952	15Tau45	21Lib26	18Can25	22Lib23	23Leo12
11/24/1952	13Tau47	23Lib04	18Can07	22Lib52	23Leo16
12/09/1952	12Tau11	24Lib32	17Can39	23Lib17	23Leo12
12/24/1952	11Tau13	25Lib43	17Can04	23Lib36	23Leo03
01/08/1953	10Tau59	26Lib37	16Can25	23Lib48	22Leo48
01/23/1953	11Tau32	27Lib08	15Can47	23Lib53	22Leo29
02/07/1953	12Tau48	27Lib16	15Can13	23Lib50	22Leo07
02/22/1953	14Tau41	27Lib01	14Can46	23Lib39	21Leo46
03/09/1953	17Tau05	26Lib24	14Can30	23Lib23	21Leo25
03/24/1953	19Tau52	25Lib29	14Can25	23Lib02	21Leo08
04/08/1953	22Tau58	24Lib23	14Can33	22Lib38	20Leo55
04/23/1953	26Tau17	23Lib15	14Can52	22Lib13	20Leo48
05/08/1953	29Tau44	22Lib11	15Can22	21Lib50	20Leo48
05/23/1953	03Gem15	21Lib19	16Can01	21Lib31	20Leo54
06/07/1953	06Gem45	20Lib46	16Can46	21Lib16	21Leo05
06/22/1953	10Gem12	20Lib33	17Can38	21Lib08	21Leo22
07/07/1953	13Gem31	20Lib42	18Can31	21Lib07	21Leo44
07/22/1953	16Gem39	21Lib13	19Can26	21Lib13	22Leo09
08/06/1953	19Gem29	22Lib05	20Can19	21Lib25	22Leo37
08/21/1953	21Gem58	23Lib14	21Can08	21Lib45	23Leo06
09/05/1953	24Gem00	24Lib37	21Can51	22Lib10	23Leo33
09/20/1953	25Gem29	26Lib13	22Can25	22Lib39	24Leo00
10/05/1953	26Gem19	27Lib56	22Can50	23Lib11	24Leo22
10/20/1953	26Gem25	29Lib44	23Can03	23Lib45	24Leo40
11/04/1953	25Gem47	01Sco33	23Can04	24Lib18	24Leo53
11/19/1953	24Gem27	03Sco18	22Can54	24Lib49	25Leo00
12/04/1953	22Gem38	04Sco57	22Can32	25Lib16	25Leo00
12/19/1953	20Gem36	06Sco25	22Can01	25Lib38	24Leo53

Ephemeris Tables for Jupiter, Saturn, Uranus, Neptune, and Pluto

Date	Jupiter	Saturn	Uranus	Neptune	Pluto
01/03/1954	18Gem43	07Sco39	21Can24	25Lib54	24Leo40
01/18/1954	17Gem17	08Sco34	20Can45	26Lib02	24Leo23
02/02/1954	16Gem31	09Sco09	20Can08	26Lib03	24Leo02
02/17/1954	16Gem30	09Sco19	19Can36	25Lib56	23Leo40
03/04/1954	17Gem13	09Sco07	19Can13	25Lib42	23Leo19
03/19/1954	18Gem36	08Sco34	19Can01	25Lib24	23Leo00
04/03/1954	20Gem33	07Sco42	19Can00	25Lib01	22Leo45
04/18/1954	22Gem58	06Sco39	19Can12	24Lib36	22Leo35
05/03/1954	25Gem45	05Sco31	19Can35	24Lib12	22Leo31
05/18/1954	28Gem48	04Sco27	20Can08	23Lib51	22Leo34
06/02/1954	02Can01	03Sco33	20Can49	23Lib33	22Leo43
06/17/1954	05Can22	02Sco56	21Can37	23Lib22	22Leo58
07/02/1954	08Can46	02Sco39	22Can30	23Lib17	23Leo18
07/17/1954	12Can10	02Sco44	23Can25	23Lib19	23Leo42
08/01/1954	15Can28	03Sco11	24Can19	23Lib29	24Leo09
08/16/1954	18Can39	03Sco58	25Can11	23Lib45	24Leo37
08/31/1954	21Can35	05Sco03	25Can58	24Lib07	25Leo06
09/15/1954	24Can14	06Sco24	26Can39	24Lib35	25Leo33
09/30/1954	26Can30	07Sco57	27Can10	25Lib06	25Leo58
10/15/1954	28Can15	09Sco38	27Can31	25Lib39	26Leo19
10/30/1954	29Can26	11Sco25	27Can41	26Lib12	26Leo34
11/14/1954	29Can55	13Sco12	27Can38	26Lib45	26Leo44
11/29/1954	29Can40	14Sco58	27Can23	27Lib14	26Leo47
12/14/1954	28Can43	16Sco37	26Can58	27Lib39	26Leo43
12/29/1954	27Can09	18Sco06	26Can24	27Lib58	26Leo33
01/13/1955	25Can13	19Sco21	25Can46	28Lib10	26Leo18
01/28/1955	23Can13	20Sco18	25Can07	28Lib14	25Leo58
02/12/1955	21Can31	20Sco55	24Can31	28Lib11	25Leo37
02/27/1955	20Can21	21Sco09	24Can03	28Lib01	25Leo15
03/14/1955	19Can53	21Sco00	23Can43	27Lib44	24Leo54
03/29/1955	20Can07	20Sco30	23Can34	27Lib23	24Leo37
04/13/1955	21Can04	19Sco41	23Can38	26Lib59	24Leo25
04/28/1955	22Can36	18Sco39	23Can54	26Lib34	24Leo18
05/13/1955	24Can39	17Sco33	24Can21	26Lib12	24Leo18
05/28/1955	27Can07	16Sco27	24Can57	25Lib52	24Leo24
06/12/1955	29Can54	15Sco32	25Can41	25Lib37	24Leo36
06/27/1955	02Leo55	14Sco52	26Can31	25Lib29	24Leo54
07/12/1955	06Leo06	14Sco32	27Can24	25Lib28	25Leo16
07/27/1955	09Leo22	14Sco33	28Can19	25Lib34	25Leo42
08/11/1955	12Leo40	14Sco56	29Can13	25Lib47	26Leo10
08/26/1955	15Leo57	15Sco39	00Leo04	26Lib06	26Leo40
09/10/1955	19Leo07	16Sco42	00Leo50	26Lib31	27Leo08
09/25/1955	22Leo07	17Sco59	01Leo28	27Lib01	27Leo34
10/10/1955	24Leo51	19Sco30	01Leo56	27Lib33	27Leo58
10/25/1955	27Leo15	21Sco09	02Leo13	28Lib06	28Leo16
11/09/1955	29Leo12	22Sco54	02Leo18	28Lib39	28Leo29
11/24/1955	00Vir36	24Sco42	02Leo12	29Lib10	28Leo35
12/09/1955	01Vir22	26Sco27	01Leo52	29Lib38	28Leo34
12/24/1955	01Vir26	28Sco06	01Leo24	00Sco00	28Leo27
01/08/1956	00Vir46	29Sco36	00Leo49	00Sco15	28Leo14
01/23/1956	29Leo27	00Sag52	00Leo10	00Sco24	27Leo57
02/07/1956	27Leo40	01Sag51	29Can31	00Sco24	27Leo35
02/22/1956	25Leo42	02Sag30	28Can58	00Sco17	27Leo13
03/08/1956	23Leo51	02Sag47	28Can31	00Sco04	26Leo51
03/23/1956	22Leo27	02Sag41	28Can16	29Lib45	26Leo32

Ephemeris Tables for Jupiter, Saturn, Uranus, Neptune, and Pluto

Date	Jupiter	Saturn	Uranus	Neptune	Pluto
04/07/1956	21Leo38	02Sag13	28Can11	29Lib22	26Leo18
04/22/1956	21Leo31	01Sag27	28Can19	28Lib57	26Leo08
05/07/1956	22Leo04	00Sag28	28Can39	28Lib33	26Leo04
05/22/1956	23Leo16	29Sco22	29Can09	28Lib12	26Leo08
06/06/1956	25Leo01	28Sco16	29Can48	27Lib55	26Leo18
06/21/1956	27Leo12	27Sco19	00Leo34	27Lib43	26Leo33
07/06/1956	29Leo46	26Sco37	01Leo26	27Lib39	26Leo54
07/21/1956	02Vir36	26Sco13	02Leo21	27Lib41	27Leo18
08/05/1956	05Vir38	26Sco11	03Leo16	27Lib50	27Leo46
08/20/1956	08Vir48	26Sco30	04Leo09	28Lib07	28Leo15
09/04/1956	12Vir03	27Sco10	04Leo59	28Lib29	28Leo44
09/19/1956	15Vir17	28Sco10	05Leo42	28Lib56	29Leo12
10/04/1956	18Vir27	29Sco25	06Leo17	29Lib27	29Leo37
10/19/1956	21Vir30	00Sag54	06Leo42	00Sco00	29Leo58
11/03/1956	24Vir18	02Sag31	06Leo55	00Sco34	00Vir13
11/18/1956	26Vir49	04Sag16	06Leo57	01Sco06	00Vir23
12/03/1956	28Vir54	06Sag03	06Leo45	01Sco36	00Vir26
12/18/1956	00Lib30	07Sag48	06Leo23	02Sco00	00Vir22
01/02/1957	01Lib29	09Sag27	05Leo51	02Sco19	00Vir12
01/17/1957	01Lib47	10Sag57	05Leo14	02Sco31	29Leo55
02/01/1957	01Lib22	12Sag15	04Leo35	02Sco36	29Leo36
02/16/1957	00Lib17	13Sag15	03Leo58	02Sco32	29Leo13
03/03/1957	28Vir40	13Sag56	03Leo26	02Sco22	28Leo51
03/18/1957	26Vir46	14Sag16	03Leo03	02Sco05	28Leo30
04/02/1957	24Vir52	14Sag13	02Leo51	01Sco44	28Leo13
04/17/1957	23Vir18	13Sag48	02Leo51	01Sco20	28Leo01
05/02/1957	22Vir14	13Sag04	03Leo03	00Sco56	27Leo55
05/17/1957	21Vir49	12Sag07	03Leo26	00Sco33	27Leo55
06/01/1957	22Vir06	11Sag01	04Leo00	00Sco13	28Leo01
06/16/1957	23Vir00	09Sag56	04Leo42	29Lib59	28Leo15
07/01/1957	24Vir29	08Sag58	05Leo30	29Lib51	28Leo33
07/16/1957	26Vir28	08Sag13	06Leo23	29Lib49	28Leo56
07/31/1957	28Vir50	07Sag46	07Leo18	29Lib55	29Leo23
08/15/1957	01Lib32	07Sag41	08Leo13	00Sco08	29Leo52
08/30/1957	04Lib28	07Sag57	09Leo06	00Sco28	00Vir21
09/14/1957	07Lib35	08Sag34	09Leo54	00Sco53	00Vir50
09/29/1957	10Lib48	09Sag31	10Leo35	01Sco22	01Vir17
10/14/1957	14Lib03	10Sag44	11Leo07	01Sco54	01Vir40
10/29/1957	17Lib15	12Sag10	11Leo28	02Sco28	01Vir59
11/13/1957	20Lib21	13Sag48	11Leo37	03Sco01	02Vir12
11/28/1957	23Lib15	15Sag31	11Leo34	03Sco32	02Vir18
12/13/1957	25Lib52	17Sag17	11Leo19	03Sco59	02Vir17
12/28/1957	28Lib07	19Sag02	10Leo53	04Sco21	02Vir09
01/12/1958	29Lib53	20Sag42	10Leo19	04Sco37	01Vir56
01/27/1958	01Sco04	22Sag13	09Leo41	04Sco45	01Vir37
02/11/1958	01Sco37	23Sag31	09Leo02	04Sco45	01Vir16
02/26/1958	01Sco27	24Sag33	08Leo27	04Sco39	00Vir54
03/13/1958	00Sco36	25Sag16	07Leo57	04Sco25	00Vir31
03/28/1958	29Lib11	25Sag39	07Leo38	04Sco06	00Vir12
04/12/1958	27Lib22	25Sag38	07Leo30	03Sco43	29Leo58
04/27/1958	25Lib28	25Sag16	07Leo34	03Sco18	29Leo48
05/12/1958	23Lib46	24Sag35	07Leo49	02Sco54	29Leo45
05/27/1958	22Lib30	23Sag39	08Leo16	02Sco33	29Leo49
06/11/1958	21Lib49	22Sag35	08Leo53	02Sco16	29Leo59
06/26/1958	21Lib49	21Sag30	09Leo37	02Sco04	00Vir15

Ephemeris Tables for Jupiter, Saturn, Uranus, Neptune, and Pluto

Date	Jupiter	Saturn	Uranus	Neptune	Pluto
07/11/1958	22Lib28	20Sag30	10Leo28	02Sco00	00Vir37
07/26/1958	23Lib45	19Sag43	11Leo22	02Sco02	01Vir02
08/10/1958	25Lib32	19Sag14	12Leo18	02Sco12	01Vir30
08/25/1958	27Lib46	19Sag06	13Leo12	02Sco28	02Vir00
09/09/1958	00Sco22	19Sag19	14Leo04	02Sco50	02Vir30
09/24/1958	03Sco16	19Sag53	14Leo50	03Sco18	02Vir58
10/09/1958	06Sco21	20Sag47	15Leo28	03Sco49	03Vir24
10/24/1958	09Sco34	21Sag58	15Leo57	04Sco22	03Vir45
11/08/1958	12Sco52	23Sag24	16Leo15	04Sco55	04Vir00
11/23/1958	16Sco09	24Sag59	16Leo19	05Sco28	04Vir10
12/08/1958	19Sco20	26Sag42	16Leo12	05Sco57	04Vir12
12/23/1958	22Sco21	28Sag28	15Leo53	06Sco22	04Vir08
01/07/1959	25Sco07	00Cap13	15Leo24	06Sco40	03Vir57
01/22/1959	27Sco33	01Cap54	14Leo48	06Sco52	03Vir41
02/06/1959	29Sco32	03Cap25	14Leo09	06Sco57	03Vir21
02/21/1959	00Sag59	04Cap45	13Leo31	06Sco54	02Vir58
03/08/1959	01Sag48	05Cap49	12Leo57	06Sco43	02Vir35
03/23/1959	01Sag57	06Cap34	12Leo31	06Sco26	02Vir15
04/07/1959	01Sag22	06Cap58	12Leo15	06Sco05	01Vir57
04/22/1959	00Sag11	07Cap01	12Leo11	05Sco41	01Vir45
05/07/1959	28Sco31	06Cap42	12Leo19	05Sco17	01Vir39
05/22/1959	26Sco38	06Cap03	12Leo39	04Sco54	01Vir40
06/06/1959	24Sco49	05Cap09	13Leo09	04Sco34	01Vir47
06/21/1959	23Sco20	04Cap06	13Leo49	04Sco20	02Vir01
07/06/1959	22Sco24	03Cap00	14Leo36	04Sco12	02Vir19
07/21/1959	22Sco07	01Cap59	15Leo28	04Sco10	02Vir43
08/05/1959	22Sco30	01Cap10	16Leo22	04Sco16	03Vir11
08/20/1959	23Sco33	00Cap39	17Leo18	04Sco30	03Vir40
09/04/1959	25Sco09	00Cap27	18Leo12	04Sco49	04Vir10
09/19/1959	27Sco16	00Cap37	19Leo03	05Sco14	04Vir40
10/04/1959	29Sco48	01Cap09	19Leo46	05Sco43	05Vir07
10/19/1959	02Sag39	02Cap01	20Leo22	06Sco16	05Vir31
11/03/1959	05Sag44	03Cap10	20Leo47	06Sco49	05Vir49
11/18/1959	09Sag00	04Cap34	21Leo00	07Sco22	06Vir02
12/03/1959	12Sag22	06Cap10	21Leo01	07Sco54	06Vir08
12/18/1959	15Sag45	07Cap52	20Leo50	08Sco21	06Vir07
01/02/1960	19Sag04	09Cap37	20Leo27	08Sco43	05Vir59
01/17/1960	22Sag15	11Cap23	19Leo55	08Sco58	05Vir45
02/01/1960	25Sag12	13Cap04	19Leo18	09Sco06	05Vir27
02/16/1960	27Sag52	14Cap37	18Leo39	09Sco06	05Vir04
03/02/1960	00Cap07	15Cap58	18Leo02	09Sco00	04Vir42
03/17/1960	01Cap53	17Cap04	17Leo30	08Sco46	04Vir19
04/01/1960	03Cap04	17Cap52	17Leo07	08Sco27	04Vir00
04/16/1960	03Cap35	18Cap19	16Leo55	08Sco04	03Vir46
05/01/1960	03Cap24	18Cap24	16Leo55	07Sco40	03Vir37
05/16/1960	02Cap33	18Cap07	17Leo07	07Sco16	03Vir34
05/31/1960	01Cap07	17Leo31	17Leo31	06Sco54	03Vir38
06/15/1960	29Sag18	16Cap39	18Leo04	06Sco37	03Vir49
06/30/1960	27Sag24	15Cap36	18Leo46	06Sco25	04Vir06
07/15/1960	25Sag42	14Cap30	19Leo35	06Sco21	04Vir27
07/30/1960	24Sag27	13Cap28	20Leo28	06Sco23	04Vir54
08/14/1960	23Sag49	12Cap38	21Leo24	06Sco33	05Vir22
08/29/1960	23Sag53	12Cap03	22Leo20	06Sco49	05Vir52
09/13/1960	24Sag39	11Cap49	23Leo13	07Sco12	06Vir23
09/28/1960	26Sag02	11Cap57	24Leo01	07Sco39	06Vir52

Ephemeris Tables for Jupiter, Saturn, Uranus, Neptune, and Pluto

Date	Jupiter	Saturn	Uranus	Neptune	Pluto
10/13/1960	27Sag59	12Cap26	24Leo43	08Sco10	07Vir18
10/28/1960	00Cap24	13Cap16	25Leo15	08Sco43	07Vir39
11/12/1960	03Cap13	14Cap24	25Leo37	09Sco17	07Vir55
11/27/1960	06Cap18	15Cap47	25Leo46	09Sco49	08Vir04
12/12/1960	09Cap37	17Cap21	25Leo43	10Sco18	08Vir07
12/27/1960	13Cap03	19Cap03	25Leo27	10Sco43	08Vir02
01/11/1961	16Cap32	20Cap49	25Leo01	11Sco02	07Vir51
01/26/1961	20Cap00	22Cap35	24Leo28	11Sco13	07Vir34
02/10/1961	23Cap22	24Cap17	23Leo49	11Sco18	07Vir13
02/25/1961	26Cap33	25Cap51	23Leo10	11Sco15	06Vir51
03/12/1961	29Cap29	27Cap14	22Leo34	11Sco04	06Vir28
03/27/1961	02Aqu04	28Cap22	22Leo06	10Sco47	06Vir07
04/11/1961	04Aqu12	29Cap12	21Leo46	10Sco26	05Vir49
04/26/1961	05Aqu49	29Cap42	21Leo38	10Sco03	05Vir37
05/11/1961	06Aqu49	29Cap50	21Leo42	09Sco38	05Vir32
05/26/1961	07Aqu09	29Cap37	21Leo58	09Sco15	05Vir33
06/10/1961	06Aqu45	29Cap03	22Leo25	08Sco55	05Vir40
06/25/1961	05Aqu42	28Cap13	23Leo01	08Sco41	05Vir54
07/10/1961	04Aqu07	27Cap11	23Leo46	08Sco33	06Vir14
07/25/1961	02Aqu13	26Cap05	24Leo37	08Sco32	06Vir39
08/09/1961	00Aqu20	25Cap02	25Leo31	08Sco38	07Vir06
08/24/1961	28Cap44	24Cap09	26Leo27	08Sco51	07Vir36
09/08/1961	27Cap41	23Cap32	27Leo22	09Sco10	08Vir07
09/23/1961	27Cap19	23Cap15	28Leo15	09Sco36	08Vir37
10/08/1961	27Cap40	23Cap19	29Leo01	10Sco05	09Vir05
10/23/1961	28Cap44	23Cap47	29Leo40	10Sco37	09Vir29
11/07/1961	00Aqu26	24Cap34	00Vir09	11Sco11	09Vir48
11/22/1961	02Aqu40	25Cap41	00Vir27	11Sco44	10Vir01
12/07/1961	05Aqu22	27Cap03	00Vir31	12Sco15	10Vir07
12/22/1961	08Aqu24	28Cap37	00Vir24	12Sco42	10Vir06
01/06/1962	11Aqu42	00Aqu19	00Vir05	13Sco04	09Vir57
01/21/1962	15Aqu10	02Aqu05	29Leo36	13Sco19	09Vir43
02/05/1962	18Aqu45	03Aqu52	29Leo00	13Sco27	09Vir24
02/20/1962	22Aqu19	05Aqu35	28Leo21	13Sco28	09Vir01
03/07/1962	25Aqu51	07Aqu10	27Leo43	13Sco21	08Vir38
03/22/1962	29Aqu16	08Aqu36	27Leo09	13Sco07	08Vir16
04/06/1962	02Pis28	09Aqu46	26Leo43	12Sco48	07Vir57
04/21/1962	05Pis22	10Aqu39	26Leo27	12Sco25	07Vir42
05/06/1962	07Pis55	11Aqu12	26Leo23	12Sco01	07Vir33
05/21/1962	10Pis01	11Aqu23	26Leo31	11Sco37	07Vir31
06/05/1962	11Pis34	11Aqu13	26Leo50	11Sco15	07Vir35
06/20/1962	12Pis28	10Aqu42	27Leo21	10Sco58	07Vir46
07/05/1962	12Pis41	09Aqu54	28Leo00	10Sco47	08Vir04
07/20/1962	12Pis10	08Aqu53	28Leo47	10Sco42	08Vir26
08/04/1962	11Pis00	07Aqu47	29Leo39	10Sco45	08Vir52
08/19/1962	09Pis18	06Aqu42	00Vir34	10Sco54	09Vir22
09/03/1962	07Pis21	05Aqu47	01Vir31	11Sco10	09Vir53
09/18/1962	05Pis27	05Aqu07	02Vir25	11Sco33	10Vir24
10/03/1962	03Pis56	04Aqu48	03Vir16	12Sco00	10Vir54
10/18/1962	03Pis02	04Aqu49	04Vir01	12Sco31	11Vir19
11/02/1962	02Pis52	05Aqu14	04Vir36	13Sco04	11Vir42
11/17/1962	03Pis27	06Aqu00	05Vir02	13Sco38	11Vir58
12/02/1962	04Pis45	07Aqu05	05Vir15	14Sco10	12Vir07
12/17/1962	06Pis40	08Aqu26	05Vir16	14Sco40	12Vir09

Ephemeris Tables for Jupiter, Saturn, Uranus, Neptune, and Pluto

Date	Jupiter	Saturn	Uranus	Neptune	Pluto
01/01/1963	09Pis07	10Aqu00	05Vir05	15Sco04	12Vir04
01/16/1963	11Pis59	11Aqu42	04Vir42	15Sco23	11Vir53
01/31/1963	15Pis10	13Aqu28	04Vir10	15Sco35	11Vir36
02/15/1963	18Pis35	15Aqu16	03Vir33	15Sco39	11Vir15
03/02/1963	22Aqu09	17Aqu00	02Vir54	15Sco36	10Vir51
03/17/1963	25Pis46	18Aqu37	02Vir16	15Sco25	10Vir28
04/01/1963	29Pis24	20Aqu04	01Vir45	15Sco08	10Vir07
04/16/1963	02Ari55	21Aqu18	01Vir22	14Sco47	09Vir50
05/01/1963	06Ari19	22Aqu14	01Vir10	14Sco24	09Vir38
05/16/1963	09Ari31	22Aqu51	01Vir10	13Sco59	09Vir33
05/31/1963	12Ari24	23Aqu06	01Vir22	13Sco36	09Vir34
06/15/1963	14Ari55	22Aqu59	01Vir45	13Sco17	09Vir42
06/30/1963	16Ari59	22Aqu31	02Vir18	13Sco03	09Vir56
07/15/1963	18Ari28	21Aqu45	03Vir00	12Sco54	10Vir16
07/30/1963	19Ari19	20Aqu46	03Vir49	12Sco53	10Vir42
08/14/1963	19Ari27	19Aqu39	04Vir43	12Sco59	11Vir10
08/29/1963	18Ari50	18Aqu33	05Vir39	13Sco12	11Vir40
09/13/1963	17Ari33	17Aqu36	06Vir35	13Sco31	12Vir12
09/28/1963	15Ari46	16Aqu53	07Vir29	13Sco57	12Vir43
10/13/1963	13Ari46	16Aqu30	08Vir18	14Sco26	13Vir11
10/28/1963	11Ari53	16Aqu29	09Vir00	14Sco58	13Vir36
11/12/1963	10Ari26	16Aqu51	09Vir33	15Sco32	13Vir55
11/27/1963	09Ari39	17Aqu35	09Vir54	16Sco06	14Vir07
12/12/1963	09Ari38	18Aqu39	10Vir03	16Sco36	14Vir13
12/27/1963	10Ari22	19Aqu58	10Vir00	17Sco04	14Vir12
01/11/1964	11Ari50	21Aqu31	09Vir45	17Sco25	14Vir03
01/26/1964	13Ari53	23Aqu13	09Vir19	17Sco40	13Vir49
02/10/1964	16Ari26	25Aqu01	08Vir45	17Sco48	13Vir30
02/25/1964	19Ari22	26Aqu49	08Vir06	17Sco49	13Vir07
03/11/1964	22Ari36	28Aqu36	07Vir27	17Sco42	12Vir43
03/26/1964	26Ari02	00Pis15	06Vir52	17Sco28	12Vir21
04/10/1964	29Ari35	01Pis45	06Vir23	17Sco09	12Vir01
04/25/1964	03Tau11	03Pis01	06Vir03	16Sco46	11Vir46
05/10/1964	06Tau46	04Pis01	05Vir55	16Sco22	11Vir38
05/25/1964	10Tau15	04Pis42	05Vir58	15Sco58	11Vir36
06/09/1964	13Tau36	05Pis01	06Vir14	15Sco36	11Vir40
06/24/1964	16Tau43	04Pis58	06Vir41	15Sco19	11Vir52
07/09/1964	19Tau32	04Pis34	07Vir18	15Sco08	12Vir10
07/24/1964	21Tau58	03Pis50	08Vir02	15Sco03	12Vir33
08/08/1964	23Tau56	02Pis52	08Vir53	15Sco06	13Vir00
08/23/1964	25Tau19	01Pis46	09Vir48	15Sco15	13Vir30
09/07/1964	26Tau03	00Pis39	10Vir44	15Sco31	14Vir01
09/22/1964	26Tau02	29Aqu39	11Vir40	15Sco54	14Vir33
10/07/1964	25Tau16	28Aqu53	12Vir33	16Sco22	15Vir03
10/22/1964	23Tau52	28Aqu26	13Vir19	16Sco53	15Vir30
11/06/1964	21Tau59	28Aqu22	13Vir58	17Sco26	15Vir52
11/21/1964	19Tau57	28Aqu41	14Vir28	18Sco00	16Vir08
12/06/1964	18Tau07	29Aqu22	14Vir46	18Sco32	16Vir18
12/21/1964	16Tau47	00Pis24	14Vir51	19Sco01	16Vir20
01/05/1965	16Tau09	01Pis43	14Vir43	19Sco26	16Vir15
01/20/1965	16Tau17	03Pis16	14Vir24	19Sco45	16Vir03
02/04/1965	17Tau10	04Pis58	13Vir55	19Sco56	15Vir46
02/19/1965	18Tau43	06Pis46	13Vir19	20Sco00	15Vir24
03/06/1965	20Tau51	08Pis35	12Vir40	19Sco57	15Vir01
03/21/1965	23Tau25	10Pis23	12Vir02	19Sco46	14Vir37

Ephemeris Tables for Jupiter, Saturn, Uranus, Neptune, and Pluto

Date	Jupiter	Saturn	Uranus	Neptune	Pluto
04/05/1965	26Tau21	12Pis05	11Vir28	19Sco30	14Vir16
04/20/1965	29Tau33	13Pis37	11Vir02	19Sco08	13Vir59
05/05/1965	02Gem55	14Pis57	10Vir46	18Sco45	13Vir47
05/20/1965	06Gem23	16Pis01	10Vir42	18Sco20	13Vir42
06/04/1965	09Gem53	16Pis46	10Vir49	17Sco57	13Vir43
06/19/1965	13Gem21	17Pis10	11Vir09	17Sco38	13Vir51
07/04/1965	16Gem44	17Pis11	11Vir39	17Sco24	14Vir06
07/19/1965	19Gem57	16Pis51	12Vir18	17Sco15	14Vir27
08/03/1965	22Gem56	16Pis10	13Vir05	17Sco14	14Vir52
08/18/1965	25Gem37	15Pis14	13Vir57	17Sco20	15Vir22
09/02/1965	27Gem53	14Pis08	14Vir53	17Sco33	15Vir53
09/17/1965	29Gem39	13Pis00	15Vir49	17Sco53	16Vir25
10/02/1965	00Can49	11Pis57	16Vir45	18Sco18	16Vir56
10/17/1965	01Can18	11Pis08	17Vir36	18Sco48	17Vir25
11/01/1965	01Can03	10Pis37	18Vir21	19Sco20	17Vir50
11/16/1965	00Can03	10Pis30	18Vir57	19Sco54	18Vir09
12/01/1965	28Gem27	10Pis45	19Vir22	20Sco27	18Vir22
12/16/1965	26Gem30	11Pis24	19Vir36	20Sco58	18Vir28
12/31/1965	24Gem30	12Pis24	19Vir37	21Sco25	18Vir27
01/15/1966	22Gem48	13Pis42	19Vir25	21Sco46	18Vir18
01/30/1966	21Gem40	15Pis13	19Vir03	22Sco02	18Vir03
02/14/1966	21Gem15	16Pis55	18Vir31	22Sco10	17Vir43
03/01/1966	21Gem35	18Pis43	17Vir54	22Sco10	17Vir21
03/16/1966	22Gem37	20Pis34	17Vir15	22Sco03	16Vir57
03/31/1966	24Gem17	22Pis24	16Vir37	21Sco49	16Vir34
04/15/1966	26Gem28	24Pis08	16Vir06	21Sco30	16Vir15
04/30/1966	29Gem03	25Pis43	15Vir43	21Sco07	16Vir00
05/15/1966	01Can57	27Pis07	15Vir31	20Sco43	15Vir51
05/30/1966	05Can04	28Pis15	15Vir30	20Sco19	15Vir49
06/14/1966	08Can21	29Pis05	15Vir42	19Sco58	15Vir54
06/29/1966	11Can43	29Pis34	16Vir04	19Sco40	16Vir06
07/14/1966	15Can06	29Pis41	16Vir38	19Sco29	16Vir24
07/29/1966	18Can27	29Pis25	17Vir20	19Sco24	16Vir48
08/13/1966	21Can41	28Pis48	18Vir09	19Sco27	17Vir15
08/28/1966	24Can44	27Pis54	19Vir03	19Sco36	17Vir46
09/12/1966	27Can32	26Pis49	19Vir59	19Sco53	18Vir18
09/27/1966	00Leo00	25Pis40	20Vir55	20Sco16	18Vir51
10/12/1966	02Leo00	24Pis34	21Vir49	20Sco43	19Vir21
10/27/1966	03Leo28	23Pis42	22Vir39	21Sco14	19Vir48
11/11/1966	04Leo19	23Pis07	23Vir21	21Sco48	20Vir10
11/26/1966	04Leo26	22Pis55	23Vir54	22Sco21	20Vir27
12/11/1966	03Leo49	23Pis07	24Vir16	22Sco54	20Vir37
12/26/1966	02Leo31	23Pis42	24Vir25	23Sco23	20Vir39
01/10/1967	00Leo44	24Pis40	24Vir22	23Sco47	20Vir34
01/25/1967	28Can44	25Pis55	24Vir06	24Sco06	20Vir22
02/09/1967	26Can51	27Pis26	23Vir40	24Sco17	20Vir04
02/24/1967	25Can24	29Pis07	23Vir07	24Sco21	19Vir43
03/11/1967	24Can34	00Ari56	22Vir28	24Sco18	19Vir19
03/26/1967	24Can27	02Ari48	21Vir49	24Sco07	18Vir55
04/10/1967	25Can03	04Ari39	21Vir14	23Sco51	18Vir34
04/25/1967	26Can18	06Ari26	20Vir45	23Sco29	18Vir16
05/10/1967	28Can06	08Ari04	20Vir25	23Sco06	18Vir04
05/25/1967	00Leo21	09Ari32	20Vir17	22Sco41	17Vir59
06/09/1967	02Leo58	10Ari45	20Vir20	22Sco18	18Vir00
06/24/1967	05Leo51	11Ari40	20Vir36	21Sco59	18Vir09

Ephemeris Tables for Jupiter, Saturn, Uranus, Neptune, and Pluto

Date	Jupiter	Saturn	Uranus	Neptune	Pluto
07/09/1967	08Leo57	12Ari15	21Vir01	21Sco45	18Vir24
07/24/1967	12Leo10	12Ari27	21Vir38	21Sco37	18Vir45
08/08/1967	15Leo28	12Ari17	22Vir22	21Sco36	19Vir12
08/23/1967	18Leo45	11Ari45	23Vir13	21Sco42	19Vir41
09/07/1967	21Leo58	10Ari53	24Vir08	21Sco55	20Vir13
09/22/1967	25Leo03	09Ari49	25Vir04	22Sco14	20Vir46
10/07/1967	27Leo55	08Ari39	26Vir01	22Sco39	21Vir18
10/22/1967	00Vir30	07Ari31	26Vir54	23Sco09	21Vir47
11/06/1967	02Vir40	06Ari34	27Vir41	23Sco42	22Vir12
11/21/1967	04Vir21	05Ari55	28Vir20	24Sco15	22Vir32
12/06/1967	05Vir25	05Ari39	28Vir49	24Sco48	22Vir46
12/21/1967	05Vir49	05Ari46	29Vir07	25Sco19	22Vir52
01/05/1968	05Vir30	06Ari18	29Vir13	25Sco46	22Vir50
01/20/1968	04Vir29	07Ari12	29Vir05	26Sco08	22Vir42
02/04/1968	02Vir54	08Ari25	28Vir46	26Sco23	22Vir26
02/19/1968	00Vir59	09Ari55	28Vir17	26Sco31	22Vir06
03/05/1968	29Leo03	11Ari36	27Vir42	26Sco31	21Vir43
03/20/1968	27Leo24	13Ari24	27Vir03	26Sco24	21Vir19
04/04/1968	26Leo17	15Ari17	26Vir25	26Sco10	20Vir56
04/19/1968	25Leo49	17Ari10	25Vir51	25Sco51	20Vir36
05/04/1968	26Leo04	19Ari00	25Vir25	25Sco28	20Vir21
05/19/1968	26Leo57	20Ari42	25Vir09	25Sco04	20Vir13
06/03/1968	28Leo26	22Ari13	25Vir04	24Sco40	20Vir10
06/18/1968	00Vir24	23Ari31	25Vir11	24Sco19	20Vir16
07/03/1968	02Vir47	24Ari32	25Vir30	24Sco02	20Vir28
07/18/1968	05Vir30	25Ari13	26Vir00	23Sco51	20Vir46
08/02/1968	08Vir26	25Ari31	26Vir39	23Sco46	21Vir10
08/17/1968	11Vir33	25Ari27	27Vir25	23Sco48	21Vir39
09/01/1968	14Vir45	25Ari00	28Vir18	23Sco58	22Vir10
09/16/1968	18Vir00	24Ari12	29Vir13	24Sco14	22Vir43
10/01/1968	21Vir13	23Ari10	00Lib10	24Sco37	23Vir16
10/16/1968	24Vir19	21Ari59	01Lib06	25Sco04	23Vir47
10/31/1968	27Vir15	20Ari49	01Lib57	25Sco36	24Vir15
11/15/1968	29Vir55	19Ari49	02Lib42	26Sco09	24Vir37
11/30/1968	02Lib13	19Ari05	03Lib18	26Sco43	24Vir54
12/15/1968	04Lib04	18Ari43	03Lib44	27Sco15	25Vir04
12/30/1968	05Lib21	18Ari46	03Lib58	27Sco44	25Vir06
01/14/1969	05Lib59	19Ari13	03Lib58	28Sco09	25Vir01
01/29/1969	05Lib55	20Ari03	03Lib47	28Sco27	24Vir49
02/13/1969	05Lib09	21Ari14	03Lib25	28Sco39	24Vir31
02/28/1969	03Lib45	22Ari41	02Lib53	28Sco43	24Vir09
03/15/1969	01Lib58	24Ari21	02Lib16	28Sco39	23Vir45
03/30/1969	00Lib02	26Ari09	01Lib37	28Sco28	23Vir21
04/14/1969	28Vir16	28Ari03	01Lib00	28Sco12	23Vir00
04/29/1969	26Vir57	29Ari57	00Lib28	27Sco51	22Vir42
05/14/1969	26Vir13	01Tau48	00Lib06	27Sco27	22Vir30
05/29/1969	26Vir09	03Tau34	29Vir53	27Sco03	22Vir25
06/13/1969	26Vir45	05Tau10	29Vir52	26Sco40	22Vir26
06/28/1969	27Vir58	06Tau33	00Lib03	26Sco20	22Vir35
07/13/1969	29Vir43	07Tau40	00Lib25	26Sco06	22Vir51
07/28/1969	01Lib54	08Tau27	00Lib58	25Sco58	23Vir12
08/12/1969	04Lib28	08Tau52	01Lib40	25Sco57	23Vir39
08/27/1969	07Lib18	08Tau54	02Lib29	26Sco03	24Vir09
09/11/1969	10Lib20	08Tau33	03Lib23	26Sco16	24Vir42
09/26/1969	13Lib31	07Tau49	04Lib19	26Sco36	25Vir15

Ephemeris Tables for Jupiter, Saturn, Uranus, Neptune, and Pluto

Date	Jupiter	Saturn	Uranus	Neptune	Pluto
10/11/1969	16Lib45	06Tau49	05Lib16	27Sco01	25Vir47
10/26/1969	20Lib00	05Tau40	06Lib10	27Sco31	26Vir17
11/10/1969	23Lib10	04Tau28	07Lib00	28Sco03	26Vir43
11/25/1969	26Lib10	03Tau24	07Lib42	28Sco37	27Vir03
12/10/1969	28Lib57	02Tau35	08Lib15	29Sco10	27Vir17
12/25/1969	01Sco23	02Tau07	08Lib37	29Sco41	27Vir23
01/09/1970	03Sco24	02Tau04	08Lib46	00Sag08	27Vir22
01/24/1970	04Sco53	02Tau27	08Lib43	00Sag30	27Vir13
02/08/1970	05Sco45	03Tau12	08Lib27	00Sag45	26Vir57
02/23/1970	05Sco56	04Tau19	08Lib01	00Sag52	26Vir37
03/10/1970	05Sco25	05Tau43	07Lib28	00Sag52	26Vir14
03/25/1970	04Sco15	07Tau21	06Lib50	00Sag45	25Vir49
04/09/1970	02Sco36	09Tau09	06Lib12	00Sag31	25Vir26
04/24/1970	00Sco43	11Tau02	05Lib36	00Sag12	25Vir06
05/09/1970	28Lib52	12Tau58	05Lib07	29Sco49	24Vir51
05/24/1970	27Lib22	14Tau52	04Lib47	29Sco25	24Vir42
06/08/1970	26Lib24	16Tau40	04Lib39	29Sco01	24Vir40
06/23/1970	26Lib03	18Tau21	04Lib41	28Sco40	24Vir46
07/08/1970	26Lib24	19Tau49	04Lib56	28Sco23	24Vir58
07/23/1970	27Lib22	21Tau01	05Lib22	28Sco12	25Vir17
08/07/1970	28Lib55	21Tau55	05Lib58	28Sco07	25Vir42
08/22/1970	00Sco58	22Tau28	06Lib42	28Sco09	26Vir10
09/06/1970	03Sco24	22Tau36	07Lib33	28Sco19	26Vir42
09/21/1970	06Sco10	22Tau21	08Lib28	28Sco36	27Vir15
10/06/1970	09Sco11	21Tau43	09Lib24	28Sco58	27Vir49
10/21/1970	12Sco22	20Tau47	10Lib20	29Sco26	28Vir21
11/05/1970	15Sco39	19Tau38	11Lib13	29Sco57	28Vir49
11/20/1970	18Sco57	18Tau25	12Lib01	00Sag31	29Vir12
12/05/1970	22Sco12	17Tau18	12Lib40	01Sag04	29Vir30
12/20/1970	25Sco19	16Tau24	13Lib09	01Sag37	29Vir39
01/04/1971	28Sco14	15Tau51	13Lib27	02Sag06	29Vir42
01/19/1971	00Sag51	15Tau42	13Lib33	02Sag30	29Vir37
02/03/1971	03Sag04	15Tau58	13Lib25	02Sag49	29Vir25
02/18/1971	04Sag48	16Tau38	13Lib06	03Sag00	29Vir07
03/05/1971	05Sag57	17Tau40	12Lib37	03Sag04	28Vir45
03/20/1971	06Sag26	19Tau01	12Lib02	03Sag00	28Vir20
04/04/1971	06Sag13	20Tau36	11Lib24	02Sag49	27Vir56
04/19/1971	05Sag20	22Tau22	10Lib45	02Sag33	27Vir34
05/04/1971	03Sag52	24Tau15	10Lib12	02Sag12	27Vir16
05/19/1971	02Sag04	26Tau12	09Lib46	01Sag48	27Vir04
06/03/1971	00Sag11	28Tau07	09Lib30	01Sag24	26Vir58
06/18/1971	28Sco30	29Tau58	09Lib24	01Sag01	27Vir00
07/03/1971	27Sco16	01Gem42	09Lib31	00Sag42	27Vir09
07/18/1971	26Sco39	03Gem15	09Lib49	00Sag27	27Vir25
08/02/1971	26Sco42	04Gem34	10Lib19	00Sag19	27Vir47
08/17/1971	27Sco25	05Gem34	10Lib58	00Sag18	28Vir14
09/01/1971	28Sco46	06Gem14	11Lib44	00Sag24	28Vir45
09/16/1971	00Sag39	06Gem31	12Lib36	00Sag37	29Vir18
10/01/1971	03Sag00	06Gem22	13Lib32	00Sag57	29Vir52
10/16/1971	05Sag42	05Gem51	14Lib28	01Sag22	00Lib25
10/31/1971	08Sag42	04Gem58	15Lib24	01Sag52	00Lib55
11/15/1971	11Sag55	03Gem52	16Lib15	02Sag25	01Lib21
11/30/1971	15Sag15	02Gem39	17Lib00	02Sag58	01Lib42
12/15/1971	18Sag39	01Gem28	17Lib36	03Sag31	01Lib56
12/30/1971	22Sag01	00Gem30	18Lib02	04Sag03	02Lib02

Ephemeris Tables for Jupiter, Saturn, Uranus, Neptune, and Pluto

Date	Jupiter	Saturn	Uranus	Neptune	Pluto
01/14/1972	25Sag17	29Tau50	18Lib16	04Sag30	02Lib01
01/29/1972	28Sag23	29Tau34	18Lib16	04Sag51	01Lib52
02/13/1972	01Cap13	29Tau44	18Lib05	05Sag06	01Lib37
02/28/1972	03Cap42	00Gem18	17Lib43	05Sag13	01Lib16
03/14/1972	05Cap44	01Gem15	17Lib12	05Sag13	00Lib53
03/29/1972	07Cap14	02Gem31	16Lib35	05Sag06	00Lib28
04/13/1972	08Cap06	04Gem03	15Lib56	04Sag52	00Lib05
04/28/1972	08Cap18	05Gem47	15Lib19	04Sag33	29Vir45
05/13/1972	07Cap47	07Gem39	14Lib48	04Sag10	29Vir30
05/28/1972	06Cap37	09Gem35	14Lib25	03Sag46	29Vir21
06/12/1972	04Cap59	11Gem31	14Lib12	03Sag22	29Vir18
06/27/1972	03Cap06	13Gem25	14Lib11	03Sag01	29Vir24
07/12/1972	01Cap15	15Gem13	14Lib21	02Sag45	29Vir36
07/27/1972	29Sag44	16Gem50	14Lib43	02Sag33	29Vir55
08/11/1972	28Sag46	18Gem15	15Lib16	02Sag28	00Lib20
08/26/1972	28Sag28	19Gem21	15Lib57	02Sag31	00Lib49
09/10/1972	28Sag53	20Gem08	16Lib46	02Sag40	01Lib22
09/25/1972	29Sag58	20Gem32	17Lib39	02Sag57	01Lib55
10/10/1972	01Cap39	20Gem31	18Lib36	03Sag20	02Lib30
10/25/1972	03Cap51	20Gem07	19Lib32	03Sag48	03Lib01
11/09/1972	06Cap30	19Gem19	20Lib26	04Sag19	03Lib30
11/24/1972	09Cap28	18Gem16	21Lib16	04Sag52	03Lib54
12/09/1972	12Cap41	17Gem03	21Lib58	05Sag26	04Lib12
12/24/1972	16Cap04	15Gem51	22Lib31	05Sag58	04Lib22
01/08/1973	19Cap34	14Gem48	22Lib52	06Sag27	04Lib25
01/23/1973	23Cap04	14Gem02	23Lib01	06Sag52	04Lib20
02/07/1973	26Cap30	13Gem39	22Lib58	07Sag10	04Lib08
02/22/1973	29Cap48	13Gem42	22Lib43	07Sag21	03Lib50
03/09/1973	02Aqu54	14Gem10	22Lib18	07Sag25	03Lib27
03/24/1973	05Aqu40	15Gem01	21Lib44	07Sag21	03Lib03
04/08/1973	08Aqu04	16Gem12	21Lib07	07Sag10	02Lib39
04/23/1973	09Aqu59	17Gem39	20Lib28	06Sag54	02Lib16
05/08/1973	11Aqu20	19Gem20	19Lib53	06Sag33	01Lib58
05/23/1973	12Aqu02	21Gem10	19Lib24	06Sag09	01Lib46
06/07/1973	12Aqu01	23Gem05	19Lib04	05Sag45	01Lib40
06/22/1973	11Aqu19	25Gem03	18Lib55	05Sag22	01Lib42
07/07/1973	10Aqu00	26Gem58	18Lib58	05Sag03	01Lib51
07/22/1973	08Aqu13	28Gem48	19Lib12	04Sag49	02Lib07
08/06/1973	06Aqu18	00Can30	19Lib37	04Sag40	02Lib29
08/21/1973	04Aqu30	01Can58	20Lib13	04Sag39	02Lib57
09/05/1973	03Aqu08	03Can12	20Lib57	04Sag45	03Lib28
09/20/1973	02Aqu23	04Can06	21Lib47	04Sag58	04Lib01
10/05/1973	02Aqu21	04Can37	22Lib42	05Sag19	04Lib36
10/20/1973	03Aqu04	04Can44	23Lib39	05Sag44	05Lib09
11/04/1973	04Aqu27	04Can26	24Lib34	06Sag14	05Lib40
11/19/1973	06Aqu25	03Can45	25Lib27	06Sag46	06Lib07
12/04/1973	08Aqu54	02Can45	26Lib14	07Sag20	06Lib28
12/19/1973	11Aqu46	01Can33	26Lib54	07Sag54	06Lib42
01/03/1974	14Aqu57	00Can19	27Lib22	08Sag24	06Lib49
01/18/1974	18Aqu21	29Gem13	27Lib40	08Sag51	06Lib48
02/02/1974	21Aqu54	28Gem22	27Lib45	09Sag13	06Lib39
02/17/1974	25Aqu29	27Gem52	27Lib38	09Sag27	06Lib24
03/04/1974	29Aqu04	27Gem48	27Lib19	09Sag35	06Lib03
03/19/1974	02Pis34	28Gem08	26Lib51	09Sag35	05Lib40
04/03/1974	05Pis53	28Gem52	26Lib15	09Sag28	05Lib15

Ephemeris Tables for Jupiter, Saturn, Uranus, Neptune, and Pluto

Date	Jupiter	Saturn	Uranus	Neptune	Pluto
04/18/1974	08Pis58	29Gem58	25Lib37	09Sag14	04Lib51
05/03/1974	11Pis44	01Can21	25Lib00	08Sag55	04Lib31
05/18/1974	14Pis05	02Can57	24Lib26	08Sag32	04Lib15
06/02/1974	15Pis57	04Can45	24Lib00	08Sag08	04Lib06
06/17/1974	17Pis13	06Can39	23Lib43	07Sag44	04Lib04
07/02/1974	17Pis49	08Can35	23Lib38	07Sag23	04Lib09
07/17/1974	17Pis42	10Can31	23Lib45	07Sag06	04Lib22
08/01/1974	16Pis53	12Can24	24Lib03	06Sag54	04Lib41
08/16/1974	15Pis26	14Can09	24Lib31	06Sag49	05Lib06
08/31/1974	13Pis35	15Can42	25Lib10	06Sag52	05Lib36
09/15/1974	11Pis37	17Can01	25Lib56	07Sag02	06Lib09
09/30/1974	09Pis51	18Can01	26Lib48	07Sag19	06Lib43
10/15/1974	08Pis36	18Can39	27Lib43	07Sag42	07Lib17
10/30/1974	08Pis01	18Can54	28Lib40	08Sag09	07Lib50
11/14/1974	08Pis12	18Can43	29Lib35	08Sag40	08Lib19
11/29/1974	09Pis07	18Can08	00Sco26	09Sag14	08Lib43
12/14/1974	10Pis43	17Can13	01Sco11	09Sag48	09Lib02
12/29/1974	12Pis54	16Can04	01Sco47	10Sag20	09Lib13
01/13/1975	15Pis34	14Can50	02Sco12	10Sag49	09Lib15
01/28/1975	18Pis36	13Can40	02Sco25	11Sag13	09Lib10
02/12/1975	21Pis54	12Can45	02Sco26	11Sag32	08Lib58
02/27/1975	25Pis24	12Can09	02Sco15	11Sag43	08Lib40
03/14/1975	29Pis00	11Can57	01Sco52	11Sag46	08Lib18
03/29/1975	02Ari37	12Can09	01Sco22	11Sag43	07Lib53
04/13/1975	06Ari12	12Can46	00Sco45	11Sag32	07Lib28
04/28/1975	09Ari42	13Can45	00Sco07	11Sag15	07Lib06
05/13/1975	13Ari00	15Can03	29Lib30	10Sag54	06Lib48
05/28/1975	16Ari04	16Can35	28Lib59	10Sag31	06Lib36
06/12/1975	18Ari48	18Can19	28Lib36	10Sag07	06Lib30
06/27/1975	21Ari07	20Can10	28Lib23	09Sag44	06Lib31
07/12/1975	22Ari56	22Can06	28Lib21	09Sag24	06Lib40
07/27/1975	24Ari09	24Can03	28Lib31	09Sag10	06Lib56
08/11/1975	24Ari40	25Can56	28Lib53	09Sag02	07Lib18
08/26/1975	24Ari28	27Can43	29Lib25	09Sag01	07Lib46
09/10/1975	23Ari32	29Can21	00Sco06	09Sag07	08Lib18
09/25/1975	22Ari00	00Leo44	00Sco55	09Sag20	08Lib51
10/10/1975	20Ari04	01Leo50	01Sco48	09Sag40	09Lib26
10/25/1975	18Ari04	02Leo35	02Sco44	10Sag06	10Lib00
11/09/1975	16Ari21	02Leo57	03Sco40	10Sag36	10Lib32
11/24/1975	15Ari11	02Leo52	04Sco34	11Sag08	10Lib59
12/09/1975	14Ari45	02Leo24	05Sco23	11Sag42	11Lib21
12/24/1975	15Ari04	01Leo34	06Sco05	12Sag15	11Lib36
01/08/1976	16Ari09	00Leo28	06Sco37	12Sag46	11Lib43
01/23/1976	17Ari54	29Can15	06Sco58	13Sag13	11Lib42
02/07/1976	20Ari12	28Can04	07Sco08	13Sag34	11Lib33
02/22/1976	22Ari55	27Can04	07Sco04	13Sag49	11Lib18
03/08/1976	26Ari00	26Can22	06Sco49	13Sag57	10Lib57
03/23/1976	29Ari19	26Can03	06Sco24	13Sag57	10Lib33
04/07/1976	02Tau49	26Can08	05Sco51	13Sag49	10Lib09
04/22/1976	06Tau23	26Can37	05Sco13	13Sag35	09Lib45
05/07/1976	09Tau58	27Can30	04Sco36	13Sag16	09Lib24
05/22/1976	13Tau30	28Can41	04Sco00	12Sag54	09Lib08
06/06/1976	16Tau55	00Leo08	03Sco31	12Sag30	08Lib59
06/21/1976	20Tau10	01Leo48	03Sco12	12Sag06	08Lib57
07/06/1976	23Tau09	03Leo37	03Sco02	11Sag45	09Lib01

Ephemeris Tables for Jupiter, Saturn, Uranus, Neptune, and Pluto

Date	Jupiter	Saturn	Uranus	Neptune	Pluto
07/21/1976	25Tau48	05Leo31	03Sco04	11Sag27	09Lib14
08/05/1976	28Tau01	07Leo27	03Sco18	11Sag16	09Lib33
08/20/1976	29Tau43	09Leo21	03Sco43	11Sag11	09Lib58
09/04/1976	00Gem49	11Leo10	04Sco19	11Sag14	10Lib28
09/19/1976	01Gem12	12Leo50	05Sco02	11Sag24	11Lib01
10/04/1976	00Gem50	14Leo18	05Sco52	11Sag40	11Lib36
10/19/1976	29Tau45	15Leo28	06Sco47	12Sag03	12Lib12
11/03/1976	28Tau05	16Leo19	07Sco43	12Sag31	12Lib45
11/18/1976	26Tau05	16Leo47	08Sco39	13Sag03	13Lib15
12/03/1976	24Tau06	16Leo50	09Sco31	13Sag36	13Lib39
12/18/1976	22Tau28	16Leo28	10Sco18	14Sag10	13Lib58
01/02/1977	21Tau27	15Leo43	10Sco57	14Sag42	14Lib09
01/17/1977	21Tau10	14Leo42	11Sco25	15Sag11	14Lib12
02/01/1977	21Tau40	13Leo30	11Sco42	15Sag36	14Lib07
02/16/1977	22Tau52	12Leo18	11Sco47	15Sag54	13Lib55
03/03/1977	24Tau42	11Leo14	11Sco40	16Sag04	13Lib37
03/18/1977	27Tau02	10Leo27	11Sco21	16Sag08	13Lib15
04/02/1977	29Tau46	10Leo01	10Sco52	16Sag04	12Lib51
04/17/1977	02Gem49	09Leo59	10Sco18	15Sag54	12Lib25
05/02/1977	06Gem05	10Leo21	09Sco40	15Sag37	12Lib03
05/17/1977	09Gem30	11Leo06	09Sco03	15Sag16	11Lib44
06/01/1977	12Gem58	12Leo12	08Sco30	14Sag52	11Lib31
06/16/1977	16Gem27	13Leo33	08Sco04	14Sag28	11Lib25
07/01/1977	19Gem52	15Leo09	07Sco47	14Sag06	11Lib27
07/16/1977	23Gem10	16Leo54	07Sco42	13Sag46	11Lib36
07/31/1977	26Gem17	18Leo46	07Sco48	13Sag31	11Lib51
08/15/1977	29Gem07	20Leo41	08Sco05	13Sag24	12Lib14
08/30/1977	01Can36	22Leo35	08Sco34	13Sag22	12Lib42
09/14/1977	03Can39	24Leo25	09Sco12	13Sag28	13Lib13
09/29/1977	05Can07	26Leo07	09Sco58	13Sag42	13Lib48
10/14/1977	05Can58	27Leo38	10Sco49	14Sag02	14Lib23
10/29/1977	06Can06	28Leo53	11Sco45	14Sag27	14Lib58
11/13/1977	05Can28	29Leo49	12Sco40	14Sag57	15Lib30
11/28/1977	04Can09	00Vir22	13Sco36	15Sag30	15Lib57
12/13/1977	02Can21	00Vir31	14Sco26	16Sag04	16Lib19
12/28/1977	00Can19	00Vir16	15Sco10	16Sag37	16Lib34
01/12/1978	28Gem26	29Leo37	15Sco46	17Sag08	16Lib42
01/27/1978	26Gem59	28Leo39	16Sco10	17Sag35	16Lib42
02/11/1978	26Gem11	27Leo30	16Sco23	17Sag56	16Lib33
02/26/1978	26Gem08	26Leo18	16Sco24	18Sag11	16Lib18
03/13/1978	26Gem49	25Leo12	16Sco12	18Sag18	15Lib58
03/28/1978	28Gem09	24Leo19	15Sco50	18Sag18	15Lib34
04/12/1978	00Can04	23Leo48	15Sco19	18Sag11	15Lib09
04/27/1978	02Can27	23Leo39	14Sco43	17Sag57	14Lib45
05/12/1978	05Can10	23Leo54	14Sco06	17Sag38	14Lib24
05/27/1978	08Can10	24Leo33	13Sco29	17Sag15	14Lib07
06/11/1978	11Can22	25Leo31	12Sco58	16Sag51	13Lib58
06/26/1978	14Can42	26Leo48	12Sco35	16Sag27	13Lib55
07/11/1978	18Can04	28Leo18	12Sco22	16Sag06	14Lib00
07/26/1978	21Can25	00Vir00	12Sco20	15Sag49	14Lib12
08/10/1978	24Can42	01Vir49	12Sco30	15Sag37	14Lib32
08/25/1978	27Can51	03Vir42	12Sco51	15Sag33	14Lib57
09/09/1978	00Leo47	05Vir36	13Sco23	15Sag36	15Lib27
09/24/1978	03Leo25	07Vir27	14Sco04	15Sag45	16Lib00
10/09/1978	05Leo39	09Vir10	14Sco52	16Sag02	16Lib36

Ephemeris Tables for Jupiter, Saturn, Uranus, Neptune, and Pluto

Date	Jupiter	Saturn	Uranus	Neptune	Pluto
10/24/1978	07Leo24	10Vir43	15Sco45	16Sag25	17Lib11
11/08/1978	08Leo34	12Vir01	16Sco40	16Sag53	17Lib45
11/23/1978	09Leo03	13Vir01	17Sco37	17Sag25	18Lib15
12/08/1978	08Leo47	13Vir40	18Sco30	17Sag58	18Lib40
12/23/1978	07Leo49	13Vir55	19Sco19	18Sag32	19Lib00
01/07/1979	06Leo15	13Vir45	20Sco00	19Sag04	19Lib11
01/22/1979	04Leo19	13Vir11	20Sco31	19Sag33	19Lib15
02/06/1979	02Leo21	12Vir18	20Sco52	19Sag57	19Lib10
02/21/1979	00Leo39	11Vir11	21Sco01	20Sag15	18Lib58
03/08/1979	29Can30	09Vir59	20Sco57	20Sag27	18Lib40
03/23/1979	29Can01	08Vir52	20Sco42	20Sag30	18Lib18
04/07/1979	29Can15	07Vir56	20Sco16	20Sag26	17Lib53
04/22/1979	00Leo10	07Vir19	19Sco44	20Sag15	17Lib28
05/07/1979	01Leo42	07Vir04	19Sco07	19Sag59	17Lib06
05/22/1979	03Leo43	07Vir13	18Sco29	19Sag38	16Lib46
06/06/1979	06Leo09	07Vir44	17Sco55	19Sag14	16Lib33
06/21/1979	08Leo54	08Vir37	17Sco26	18Sag50	16Lib27
07/06/1979	11Leo54	09Vir48	17Sco06	18Sag27	16Lib28
07/21/1979	15Leo03	11Vir13	16Sco57	18Sag08	16Lib37
08/05/1979	18Leo19	12Vir51	16Sco59	17Sag54	16Lib52
08/20/1979	21Leo36	14Vir38	17Sco12	17Sag45	17Lib15
09/04/1979	24Leo51	16Vir29	17Sco37	17Sag44	17Lib43
09/19/1979	28Leo00	18Vir22	18Sco12	17Sag51	18Lib15
10/04/1979	00Vir59	20Vir12	18Sco55	18Sag04	18Lib49
10/19/1979	03Vir42	21Vir57	19Sco45	18Sag24	19Lib25
11/03/1979	06Vir05	23Vir31	20Sco39	18Sag49	20Lib00
11/18/1979	08Vir01	24Vir52	21Sco35	19Sag19	20Lib33
12/03/1979	09Vir24	25Vir56	22Sco30	19Sag52	21Lib01
12/18/1979	10Vir08	26Vir39	23Sco22	20Sag26	21Lib24
01/02/1980	10Vir10	26Vir58	24Sco09	21Sag00	21Lib39
01/17/1980	09Vir28	26Vir54	24Sco46	21Sag30	21Lib47
02/01/1980	08Vir09	26Vir25	25Sco15	21Sag57	21Lib46
02/16/1980	06Vir22	25Vir36	25Sco31	22Sag18	21Lib39
03/02/1980	04Vir24	24Vir32	25Sco35	22Sag33	21Lib24
03/17/1980	02Vir35	23Vir21	25Sco27	22Sag40	21Lib03
04/01/1980	01Vir11	22Vir13	25Sco09	22Sag40	20Lib39
04/16/1980	00Vir24	21Vir15	24Sco40	22Sag33	20Lib14
05/01/1980	00Vir17	20Vir33	24Sco06	22Sag19	19Lib49
05/16/1980	00Vir51	20Vir13	23Sco28	22Sag00	19Lib28
05/31/1980	02Vir03	20Vir15	22Sco52	21Sag37	19Lib12
06/15/1980	03Vir47	20Vir40	22Sco19	21Sag13	19Lib02
06/30/1980	05Vir58	21Vir27	21Sco53	20Sag49	18Lib59
07/15/1980	08Vir31	22Vir33	21Sco37	20Sag28	19Lib04
07/30/1980	11Vir21	23Vir54	21Sco31	20Sag11	19Lib16
08/14/1980	14Vir22	25Vir28	21Sco37	20Sag00	19Lib35
08/29/1980	17Vir33	27Vir12	21Sco54	19Sag55	20Lib00
09/13/1980	20Vir47	29Vir00	22Sco22	19Sag57	20Lib30
09/28/1980	24Vir01	00Lib52	23Sco00	20Sag07	21Lib04
10/13/1980	27Vir11	02Lib42	23Sco46	20Sag24	21Lib40
10/28/1980	00Lib13	04Lib27	24Sco37	20Sag47	22Lib15
11/12/1980	03Lib01	06Lib03	25Sco32	21Sag15	22Lib49
11/27/1980	05Lib30	07Lib26	26Sco28	21Sag47	23Lib21
12/12/1980	07Lib35	08Lib33	27Sco22	22Sag21	23Lib46
12/27/1980	09Lib09	09Lib19	28Sco12	22Sag54	24Lib06

Ephemeris Tables for Jupiter, Saturn, Uranus, Neptune, and Pluto

Date	Jupiter	Saturn	Uranus	Neptune	Pluto
01/11/1981	10Lib06	09Lib43	28Sco55	23Sag27	24Lib18
01/26/1981	10Lib23	09Lib42	29Sco30	23Sag55	24Lib22
02/10/1981	09Lib57	09Lib18	29Sco54	24Sag19	24Lib18
02/25/1981	08Lib50	08Lib33	00Sag06	24Sag37	24Lib06
03/12/1981	07Lib13	07Lib32	00Sag06	24Sag48	23Lib48
03/27/1981	05Lib19	06Lib24	29Sco54	24Sag52	23Lib26
04/11/1981	03Lib27	05Lib15	29Sco32	24Sag48	23Lib01
04/26/1981	01Lib52	04Lib15	29Sco02	24Sag37	22Lib36
05/11/1981	00Lib50	03Lib30	28Sco26	24Sag21	22Lib13
05/26/1981	00Lib27	03Lib04	27Sco49	24Sag00	21Lib54
06/10/1981	00Lib43	03Lib01	27Sco13	23Sag36	21Lib40
06/25/1981	01Lib39	03Lib21	26Sco42	23Sag12	21Lib33
07/10/1981	03Lib09	04Lib01	26Sco19	22Sag49	21Lib34
07/25/1981	05Lib07	05Lib02	26Sco06	22Sag30	21Lib42
08/09/1981	07Lib31	06Lib19	26Sco04	22Sag15	21Lib58
08/24/1981	10Lib13	07Lib49	26Sco15	22Sag07	22Lib20
09/08/1981	13Lib10	09Lib30	26Sco36	22Sag06	22Lib48
09/23/1981	16Lib18	11Lib16	27Sco07	22Sag12	23Lib20
10/08/1981	19Lib31	13Lib07	27Sco48	22Sag26	23Lib55
10/23/1981	22Lib46	14Lib56	28Sco36	22Sag46	24Lib31
11/07/1981	25Lib59	16Lib42	29Sco28	23Sag12	25Lib06
11/22/1981	29Lib05	18Lib18	00Sag24	23Sag42	25Lib39
12/07/1981	02Sco00	19Lib43	01Sag19	24Sag15	26Lib08
12/22/1981	04Sco36	20Lib52	02Sag12	24Sag49	26Lib31
01/06/1982	06Sco51	21Lib41	02Sag59	25Sag22	26Lib47
01/21/1982	08Sco36	22Lib09	03Sag40	25Sag52	26Lib55
02/05/1982	09Sco46	22Lib12	04Sag10	26Sag19	26Lib55
02/20/1982	10Sco18	21Lib52	04Sag30	26Sag40	26Lib48
03/07/1982	10Sco07	21Lib10	04Sag38	26Sag55	26Lib33
03/22/1982	09Sco16	20Lib13	04Sag34	27Sag02	26Lib13
04/06/1982	07Sco49	19Lib06	04Sag18	27Sag02	25Lib49
04/21/1982	06Sco01	17Lib57	03Sag53	26Sag55	25Lib24
05/06/1982	04Sco07	16Lib55	03Sag21	26Sag40	24Lib59
05/21/1982	02Sco25	16Lib07	02Sag44	26Sag22	24Lib37
06/05/1982	01Sco10	15Lib38	02Sag07	25Sag59	24Lib21
06/20/1982	00Sco30	15Lib30	01Sag33	25Sag35	24Lib10
07/05/1982	00Sco31	15Lib44	01Sag04	25Sag11	24Lib07
07/20/1982	01Sco12	16Lib20	00Sag45	24Sag50	24Lib12
08/04/1982	02Sco28	17Lib16	00Sag36	24Sag33	24Lib24
08/19/1982	04Sco17	18Lib29	00Sag37	24Sag21	24Lib43
09/03/1982	06Sco33	19Lib55	00Sag51	24Sag17	25Lib07
09/18/1982	09Sco10	21Lib33	01Sag16	24Sag19	25Lib38
10/03/1982	12Sco04	23Lib18	01Sag51	24Sag30	26Lib12
10/18/1982	15Sco11	25Lib07	02Sag34	24Sag46	26Lib48
11/02/1982	18Sco26	26Lib56	03Sag24	25Sag09	27Lib24
11/17/1982	21Sco44	28Lib41	04Sag17	25Sag37	27Lib58
12/02/1982	25Sco02	00Sco18	05Sag13	26Sag09	28Lib29
12/17/1982	28Sco14	01Sco45	06Sag07	26Sag43	28Lib55
01/01/1983	01Sag16	02Sco55	06Sag58	27Sag16	29Lib15
01/16/1983	04Sag03	03Sco47	07Sag43	27Sag49	29Lib28
01/31/1983	06Sag29	04Sco17	08Sag21	28Sag18	29Lib32
02/15/1983	08Sag28	04Sco24	08Sag48	28Sag42	29Lib28
03/02/1983	09Sag55	04Sco08	09Sag03	29Sag00	29Lib17
03/17/1983	10Sag45	03Sco30	09Sag07	29Sag10	29Lib00
04/01/1983	10Sag53	02Sco36	08Sag58	29Sag14	28Lib37

Ephemeris Tables for Jupiter, Saturn, Uranus, Neptune, and Pluto

Date	Jupiter	Saturn	Uranus	Neptune	Pluto
04/16/1983	10Sag19	01Sco30	08Sag39	29Sag10	28Lib12
05/01/1983	09Sag08	00Sco22	08Sag12	29Sag00	27Lib47
05/16/1983	07Sag28	29Lib19	07Sag37	28Sag43	27Lib24
05/31/1983	05Sag36	28Lib28	07Sag00	28Sag22	27Lib04
06/15/1983	03Sag46	27Lib55	06Sag24	27Sag58	26Lib51
06/30/1983	02Sag17	27Lib43	05Sag52	27Sag34	26Lib43
07/15/1983	01Sag21	27Lib53	05Sag26	27Sag11	26Lib44
07/30/1983	01Sag04	28Lib24	05Sag10	26Sag52	26Lib52
08/14/1983	01Sag28	29Lib16	05Sag04	26Sag37	27Lib07
08/29/1983	02Sag30	00Sco25	05Sag10	26Sag30	27Lib29
09/13/1983	04Sag09	01Sco48	05Sag28	26Sag28	27Lib57
09/28/1983	06Sag16	03Sco24	05Sag56	26Sag34	28Lib29
10/13/1983	08Sag49	05Sco06	06Sag34	26Sag48	29Lib04
10/28/1983	11Sag42	06Sco54	07Sag19	27Sag08	29Lib40
11/12/1983	14Sag49	08Sco42	08Sag10	27Sag34	00Sco16
11/27/1983	18Sag07	10Sco27	09Sag05	28Sag04	00Sco49
12/12/1983	21Sag30	12Sco05	10Sag00	28Sag37	01Sco18
12/27/1983	24Sag54	13Sco32	10Sag54	29Sag11	01Sco42
01/11/1984	28Sag15	14Sco44	11Sag43	29Sag44	01Sco58
01/26/1984	01Cap27	15Sco38	12Sag25	00Cap15	02Sco07
02/10/1984	04Cap26	16Sco11	12Sag58	00Cap42	02Sco07
02/25/1984	07Cap06	16Sco21	13Sag21	01Cap03	02Sco00
03/11/1984	09Cap23	16Sco09	13Sag33	01Cap18	01Sco45
03/26/1984	11Cap10	15Sco34	13Sag32	01Cap25	01Sco25
04/10/1984	12Cap22	14Sco42	13Sag20	01Cap24	01Sco01
04/25/1984	12Cap55	13Sco39	12Sag58	01Cap17	00Sco36
05/10/1984	12Cap46	12Sco31	12Sag27	01Cap03	00Sco12
05/25/1984	11Cap56	11Sco28	11Sag52	00Cap44	29Lib50
06/09/1984	10Cap31	10Sco35	11Sag15	00Cap21	29Lib33
06/24/1984	08Cap43	09Sco58	10Sag40	29Sag57	29Lib22
07/09/1984	06Cap49	09Sco42	10Sag09	29Sag33	29Lib19
07/24/1984	05Cap06	09Sco48	09Sag46	29Sag12	29Lib22
08/08/1984	03Cap49	10Sco15	09Sag34	28Sag55	29Lib34
08/23/1984	03Cap11	11Sco03	09Sag33	28Sag44	29Lib53
09/07/1984	03Cap14	12Sco08	09Sag42	28Sag39	00Sco18
09/22/1984	03Cap59	13Sco29	10Sag04	28Sag42	00Sco48
10/07/1984	05Cap22	15Sco02	10Sag35	28Sag52	01Sco22
10/22/1984	07Cap21	16Sco43	11Sag16	29Sag09	01Sco57
11/06/1984	09Cap46	18Sco30	12Sag03	29Sag32	02Sco34
11/21/1984	12Cap36	20Sco17	12Sag55	00Cap00	03Sco09
12/06/1984	15Cap43	22Sco01	13Sag51	00Cap31	03Sco40
12/21/1984	19Cap03	23Sco40	14Sag45	01Cap06	04Sco07
01/05/1985	22Cap30	25Sco07	15Sag37	01Cap39	04Sco27
01/20/1985	26Cap01	26Sco21	16Sag24	02Cap12	04Sco40
02/04/1985	29Cap30	27Sco17	17Sag03	02Cap40	04Sco45
02/19/1985	02Aqu54	27Sco52	17Sag33	03Cap04	04Sco41
03/06/1985	06Aqu07	28Sco06	17Sag52	03Cap22	04Sco30
03/21/1985	09Aqu04	27Sco56	17Sag58	03Cap33	04Sco13
04/05/1985	11Aqu41	27Sco25	17Sag54	03Cap37	03Sco51
04/20/1985	13Aqu52	26Sco36	17Sag38	03Cap33	03Sco26
05/05/1985	15Aqu32	25Sco34	17Sag13	03Cap22	03Sco01
05/20/1985	16Aqu35	24Sco27	16Sag40	03Cap05	02Sco37
06/04/1985	16Aqu57	23Sco23	16Sag04	02Cap44	02Sco18
06/19/1985	16Aqu37	22Sco28	15Sag27	02Cap21	02Sco03
07/04/1985	15Aqu36	21Sco49	14Sag54	01Cap57	01Sco56

Ephemeris Tables for Jupiter, Saturn, Uranus, Neptune, and Pluto

Date	Jupiter	Saturn	Uranus	Neptune	Pluto
07/19/1985	14Aqu02	21Sco29	14Sag26	01Cap34	01Sco56
08/03/1985	12Aqu09	21Sco31	14Sag07	01Cap14	02Sco03
08/18/1985	10Aqu15	21Sco55	13Sag58	01Cap00	02Sco18
09/02/1985	08Aqu37	22Sco39	14Sag00	00Cap52	02Sco40
09/17/1985	07Aqu31	23Sco41	14Sag14	00Cap51	03Sco08
10/02/1985	07Aqu07	25Sco00	14Sag39	00Cap57	03Sco40
10/17/1985	07Aqu27	26Sco30	15Sag13	01Cap10	04Sco15
11/01/1985	08Aqu30	28Sco10	15Sag57	01Cap31	04Sco51
11/16/1985	10Aqu10	29Sco55	16Sag46	01Cap57	05Sco27
12/01/1985	12Aqu25	01Sag42	17Sag39	02Cap27	06Sco00
12/16/1985	15Aqu06	03Sag27	18Sag34	03Cap00	06Sco30
12/31/1985	18Aqu09	05Sag06	19Sag28	03Cap34	06Sco54
01/15/1986	21Aqu27	06Sag34	20Sag18	04Cap07	07Sco10
01/30/1986	24Aqu57	07Sag49	21Sag02	04Cap38	07Sco19
02/14/1986	28Aqu32	08Sag46	21Sag38	05Cap04	07Sco21
03/01/1986	02Pis08	09Sag24	22Sag04	05Cap25	07Sco13
03/16/1986	05Pis41	09Sag40	22Sag19	05Cap40	07Sco00
03/31/1986	09Pis06	09Sag33	22Sag21	05Cap47	06Sco40
04/15/1986	12Pis19	09Sag04	22Sag12	05Cap47	06Sco16
04/30/1986	15Pis16	08Sag18	21Sag53	05Cap39	05Sco51
05/15/1986	17Pis52	07Sag18	21Sag25	05Cap25	05Sco26
05/30/1986	20Pis00	06Sag12	20Sag51	05Cap06	05Sco04
06/14/1986	21Pis36	05Sag07	20Sag15	04Cap44	04Sco47
06/29/1986	22Pis35	04Sag11	19Sag39	04Cap19	04Sco36
07/14/1986	22Pis52	03Sag30	19Sag07	03Cap56	04Sco31
07/29/1986	22Pis25	03Sag07	18Sag42	03Cap34	04Sco35
08/13/1986	21Pis16	03Sag05	18Sag26	03Cap18	04Sco46
08/28/1986	19Pis36	03Sag25	18Sag21	03Cap06	05Sco04
09/12/1986	17Pis39	04Sag06	18Sag27	03Cap01	05Sco29
09/27/1986	15Pis44	05Sag06	18Sag45	03Cap04	05Sco59
10/12/1986	14Pis11	06Sag22	19Sag13	03Cap14	06Sco33
10/27/1986	13Pis13	07Sag51	19Sag51	03Cap31	07Sco09
11/11/1986	13Pis00	09Sag29	20Sag36	03Cap54	07Sco45
11/26/1986	13Pis32	11Sag13	21Sag27	04Cap22	08Sco20
12/11/1986	14Pis48	13Sag00	22Sag21	04Cap54	08Sco52
12/26/1986	16Pis42	14Sag45	23Sag16	05Cap28	09Sco19
01/10/1987	19Pis07	16Sag24	24Sag09	06Cap02	09Sco39
01/25/1987	21Pis58	17Sag53	24Sag57	06Cap34	09Sco52
02/09/1987	25Pis09	19Sag09	25Sag37	07Cap03	09Sco58
02/24/1987	28Pis33	20Sag09	26Sag10	07Cap27	09Sco55
03/11/1987	02Ari05	20Sag49	26Sag31	07Cap45	09Sco44
03/26/1987	05Ari42	21Sag07	26Sag42	07Cap56	09Sco27
04/10/1987	09Ari19	21Sag03	26Sag40	07Cap59	09Sco06
04/25/1987	12Ari52	20Sag37	26Sag28	07Cap55	08Sco41
05/10/1987	16Ari18	19Sag52	26Sag05	07Cap45	08Sco16
05/25/1987	19Ari30	18Sag55	25Sag35	07Cap28	07Sco52
06/09/1987	22Ari25	17Sag49	25Sag00	07Cap07	07Sco32
06/24/1987	24Ari58	16Sag44	24Sag23	06Cap43	07Sco18
07/09/1987	27Ari04	15Sag46	23Sag48	06Cap19	07Sco09
07/24/1987	28Ari37	15Sag03	23Sag19	05Cap56	07Sco09
08/08/1987	29Ari31	14Sag37	22Sag57	05Cap37	07Sco16
08/23/1987	29Ari42	14Sag32	22Sag44	05Cap22	07Sco31
09/07/1987	29Ari09	14Sag49	22Sag43	05Cap14	07Sco52
09/22/1987	27Ari55	15Sag27	22Sag54	05Cap13	08Sco19
10/07/1987	26Ari09	16Sag25	23Sag15	05Cap19	08Sco51

Ephemeris Tables for Jupiter, Saturn, Uranus, Neptune, and Pluto

Date	Jupiter	Saturn	Uranus	Neptune	Pluto
10/22/1987	24Ari09	17Sag39	23Sag47	05Cap33	09Sco27
11/06/1987	22Ari14	19Sag06	24Sag28	05Cap54	10Sco03
11/21/1987	20Ari45	20Sag43	25Sag15	06Cap19	10Sco39
12/06/1987	19Ari54	22Sag27	26Sag07	06Cap50	11Sco12
12/21/1987	19Ari49	24Sag13	27Sag01	07Cap23	11Sco42
01/05/1988	20Ari31	25Sag58	27Sag55	07Cap57	12Sco06
01/20/1988	21Ari55	27Sag37	28Sag46	08Cap30	12Sco23
02/04/1988	23Ari57	29Sag08	29Sag32	09Cap01	12Sco33
02/19/1988	26Ari27	00Cap25	00Cap10	09Cap27	12Sco34
03/05/1988	29Ari21	01Cap27	00Cap39	09Cap48	12Sco27
03/20/1988	02Tau33	02Cap09	00Cap56	10Cap03	12Sco13
04/04/1988	05Tau57	02Cap29	01Cap02	10Cap10	11Sco54
04/19/1988	09Tau28	02Cap28	00Cap57	10Cap10	11Sco31
05/04/1988	13Tau03	02Cap05	00Cap40	10Cap02	11Sco06
05/19/1988	16Tau37	01Cap23	00Cap15	09Cap48	10Sco40
06/03/1988	20Tau06	00Cap27	29Sag42	09Cap29	10Sco19
06/18/1988	23Tau26	29Sag22	29Sag06	09Cap07	10Sco01
07/03/1988	26Tau34	28Sag16	28Sag30	08Cap42	09Sco49
07/18/1988	29Tau24	27Sag18	27Sag57	08Cap19	09Sco45
08/02/1988	01Gem51	26Sag31	27Sag30	07Cap57	09Sco48
08/17/1988	03Gem51	26Sag03	27Sag11	07Cap40	09Sco59
09/01/1988	05Gem16	25Sag55	27Sag02	07Cap29	10Sco16
09/16/1988	06Gem01	26Sag09	27Sag05	07Cap24	10Sco41
10/01/1988	06Gem03	26Sag45	27Sag19	07Cap27	11Sco11
10/16/1988	05Gem20	27Sag40	27Sag45	07Cap37	11Sco45
10/31/1988	03Gem57	28Sag52	28Sag20	07Cap54	12Sco20
11/15/1988	02Gem04	00Cap18	29Sag03	08Cap18	12Sco57
11/30/1988	00Gem03	01Cap55	29Sag52	08Cap46	13Sco31
12/15/1988	28Tau12	03Cap38	00Cap45	09Cap18	14Sco03
12/30/1988	26Tau49	05Cap24	01Cap40	09Cap51	14Sco31
01/14/1989	26Tau09	07Cap09	02Cap33	10Cap25	14Sco51
01/29/1989	26Tau14	08Cap49	03Cap22	10Cap57	15Sco05
02/13/1989	27Tau04	10Cap21	04Cap04	11Cap26	15Sco10
02/28/1989	28Tau35	11Cap40	04Cap39	11Cap50	15Sco08
03/15/1989	00Gem39	12Cap43	05Cap04	12Cap08	14Sco58
03/30/1989	03Gem12	13Cap27	05Cap17	12Cap19	14Sco41
04/14/1989	06Gem04	13Cap50	05Cap19	12Cap22	14Sco19
04/29/1989	09Gem13	13Cap52	05Cap09	12Cap18	13Sco55
05/14/1989	12Gem33	13Cap31	04Cap49	12Cap07	13Sco30
05/29/1989	16Gem00	12Cap52	04Cap21	11Cap51	13Sco06
06/13/1989	19Gem28	11Cap57	03Cap48	11Cap30	12Sco46
06/28/1989	22Gem55	10Cap54	03Cap11	11Cap06	12Sco31
07/13/1989	26Gem17	09Cap48	02Cap36	10Cap42	12Sco23
07/28/1989	29Gem29	08Cap47	02Cap04	10Cap19	12Sco22
08/12/1989	02Can28	07Cap58	01Cap40	10Cap00	12Sco28
08/27/1989	05Can08	07Cap28	01Cap24	09Cap45	12Sco43
09/11/1989	07Can25	07Cap17	01Cap20	09Cap37	13Sco04
09/26/1989	09Can11	07Cap28	01Cap27	09Cap36	13Sco31
10/11/1989	10Can22	08Cap01	01Cap45	09Cap42	14Sco03
10/26/1989	10Can51	08Cap55	02Cap14	09Cap56	14Sco37
11/10/1989	10Can36	10Cap05	02Cap52	10Cap16	15Sco13
11/25/1989	09Can37	11Cap30	03Cap37	10Cap43	15Sco49
12/10/1989	08Can03	13Cap06	04Cap28	11Cap13	16Sco23
12/25/1989	06Can05	14Cap49	05Cap22	11Cap46	16Sco53

Ephemeris Tables for Jupiter, Saturn, Uranus, Neptune, and Pluto

Date	Jupiter	Saturn	Uranus	Neptune	Pluto
01/09/1990	04Can05	16Cap36	06Cap16	12Cap20	17Sco18
01/24/1990	02Can23	18Cap21	07Cap07	12Cap53	17Sco35
02/08/1990	01Can14	20Cap02	07Cap54	13Cap24	17Sco45
02/23/1990	00Can48	21Cap34	08Cap34	13Cap51	17Sco46
03/10/1990	01Can06	22Cap55	09Cap05	14Cap12	17Sco40
03/25/1990	02Can07	24Cap00	09Cap25	14Cap26	17Sco27
04/09/1990	03Can45	24Cap47	09Cap34	14Cap33	17Sco07
04/24/1990	05Can52	25Cap13	09Cap32	14Cap33	16Sco44
05/09/1990	08Can25	25Cap18	09Cap19	14Cap25	16Sco19
05/24/1990	11Can17	25Cap00	08Cap56	14Cap11	15Sco54
06/08/1990	14Can23	24Cap23	08Cap25	13Cap52	15Sco32
06/23/1990	17Can38	23Cap30	07Cap51	13Cap30	15Sco15
07/08/1990	20Can58	22Cap27	07Cap14	13Cap06	15Sco03
07/23/1990	24Can20	21Cap21	06Cap40	12Cap42	14Sco58
08/07/1990	27Can40	20Cap19	06Cap10	12Cap21	15Sco00
08/22/1990	00Leo52	19Cap28	05Cap49	12Cap03	15Sco10
09/06/1990	03Leo55	18Cap55	05Cap37	11Cap52	15Sco28
09/21/1990	06Leo42	18Cap41	05Cap37	11Cap47	15Sco52
10/06/1990	09Leo09	18Cap50	05Cap48	11Cap50	16Sco21
10/21/1990	11Leo09	19Cap21	06Cap10	12Cap00	16Sco55
11/05/1990	12Leo36	20Cap12	06Cap43	12Cap17	17Sco30
11/20/1990	13Leo25	21Cap21	07Cap24	12Cap40	18Sco07
12/05/1990	13Leo32	22Cap45	08Cap11	13Cap09	18Sco42
12/20/1990	12Leo54	24Cap21	09Cap03	13Cap41	19Sco13
01/04/1991	11Leo36	26Cap03	09Cap57	14Cap15	19Sco41
01/19/1991	09Leo49	27Cap50	10Cap50	14Cap49	20Sco02
02/03/1991	07Leo50	29Cap36	11Cap40	15Cap21	20Sco16
02/18/1991	05Leo58	01Aqu18	12Cap24	15Cap49	20Sco22
03/05/1991	04Leo31	02Aqu52	13Cap01	16Cap13	20Sco19
03/20/1991	03Leo42	04Aqu15	13Cap28	16Cap31	20Sco10
04/04/1991	03Leo34	05Aqu22	13Cap44	16Cap42	19Sco54
04/19/1991	04Leo09	06Aqu12	13Cap49	16Cap45	19Sco32
05/04/1991	05Leo22	06Aqu41	13Cap42	16Cap42	19Sco08
05/19/1991	07Leo09	06Aqu48	13Cap25	16Cap30	18Sco43
06/03/1991	09Leo23	06Aqu34	13Cap00	16Cap14	18Sco19
06/18/1991	11Leo59	06Aqu00	12Cap27	15Cap53	17Sco58
07/03/1991	14Leo51	05Aqu09	11Cap51	15Cap29	17Sco43
07/18/1991	17Leo56	04Aqu06	11Cap16	15Cap05	17Sco35
08/02/1991	21Leo08	03Aqu00	10Cap43	14Cap42	17Sco33
08/17/1991	24Leo25	01Aqu57	10Cap16	14Cap23	17Sco40
09/01/1991	27Leo41	01Aqu04	09Cap58	14Cap09	17Sco54
09/16/1991	00Vir53	00Aqu27	09Cap51	14Cap00	18Sco14
10/01/1991	03Vir57	00Aqu11	09Cap54	13Cap59	18Sco40
10/16/1991	06Vir49	00Aqu17	10Cap09	14Cap06	19Sco12
10/31/1991	09Vir22	00Aqu45	10Cap35	14Cap19	19Sco46
11/15/1991	11Vir31	01Aqu34	11Cap10	14Cap40	20Sco23
11/30/1991	13Vir10	02Aqu42	11Cap54	15Cap06	20Sco58
12/15/1991	14Vir14	04Aqu06	12Cap43	15Cap36	21Sco33
12/30/1991	14Vir37	05Aqu40	13Cap36	16Cap09	22Sco02
01/14/1992	14Vir16	07Aqu23	14Cap30	16Cap43	22Sco27
01/29/1992	13Vir13	09Aqu10	15Cap22	17Cap17	22Sco44
02/13/1992	11Vir38	10Aqu57	16Cap09	17Cap48	22Sco54
02/28/1992	09Vir43	12Aqu40	16Cap51	18Cap14	22Sco56
03/14/1992	07Vir48	14Aqu16	17Cap24	18Cap35	22Sco51
03/29/1992	06Vir10	15Aqu41	17Cap47	18Cap49	22Sco37

Ephemeris Tables for Jupiter, Saturn, Uranus, Neptune, and Pluto

Date	Jupiter	Saturn	Uranus	Neptune	Pluto
04/13/1992	05Vir04	16Aqu51	18Cap00	18Cap56	22Sco18
04/28/1992	04Vir37	17Aqu44	18Cap00	18Cap56	21Sco55
05/13/1992	04Vir52	18Aqu16	17Cap49	18Cap48	21Sco31
05/28/1992	05Vir45	18Aqu27	17Cap29	18Cap34	21Sco06
06/12/1992	07Vir13	18Aqu16	17Cap01	18Cap16	20Sco43
06/27/1992	09Vir12	17Aqu45	16Cap27	17Cap53	20Sco25
07/12/1992	11Vir34	16Aqu56	15Cap51	17Cap29	20Sco13
07/27/1992	14Vir16	15Aqu55	15Cap16	17Cap05	20Sco08
08/11/1992	17Vir12	14Aqu48	14Cap45	16Cap44	20Sco10
08/26/1992	20Vir19	13Aqu43	14Cap21	16Cap27	20Sco20
09/10/1992	23Vir31	12Aqu48	14Cap07	16Cap15	20Sco37
09/25/1992	26Vir46	12Aqu09	14Cap03	16Cap10	21Sco01
10/10/1992	29Vir58	11Aqu49	14Cap11	16Cap13	21Sco30
10/25/1992	03Lib05	11Aqu52	14Cap30	16Cap24	22Sco03
11/09/1992	06Lib00	12Aqu18	15Cap00	16Cap40	22Sco38
11/24/1992	08Lib39	13Aqu06	15Cap38	17Cap04	23Sco15
12/09/1992	10Lib57	14Aqu12	16Cap24	17Cap33	23Sco49
12/24/1992	12Lib46	15Aqu34	17Cap15	18Cap04	24Sco21
01/08/1993	14Lib01	17Aqu09	18Cap07	18Cap39	24Sco49
01/23/1993	14Lib38	18Aqu52	19Cap01	19Cap12	25Sco10
02/07/1993	14Lib32	20Aqu39	19Cap51	19Cap45	25Sco24
02/22/1993	13Lib44	22Aqu27	20Cap37	20Cap13	25Sco30
03/09/1993	12Lib21	24Aqu12	21Cap15	20Cap37	25Sco28
03/24/1993	10Lib33	25Aqu50	21Cap45	20Cap55	25Sco19
04/08/1993	08Lib37	27Aqu17	22Cap04	21Cap06	25Sco03
04/23/1993	06Lib53	28Aqu31	22Cap12	21Cap09	24Sco42
05/08/1993	05Lib34	29Aqu27	22Cap08	21Cap05	24Sco18
05/23/1993	04Lib51	00Pis03	21Cap54	20Cap54	23Sco53
06/07/1993	04Lib48	00Pis18	21Cap30	20Cap37	23Sco29
06/22/1993	05Lib25	00Pis11	21Cap00	20Cap16	23Sco09
07/07/1993	06Lib39	29Aqu43	20Cap25	19Cap53	22Sco53
07/22/1993	08Lib24	28Aqu56	19Cap49	19Cap28	22Sco44
08/06/1993	10Lib36	27Aqu56	19Cap15	19Cap06	22Sco42
08/21/1993	13Lib10	26Aqu49	18Cap46	18Cap46	22Sco48
09/05/1993	16Lib00	25Aqu42	18Cap26	18Cap32	23Sco01
09/20/1993	19Lib03	24Aqu45	18Cap15	18Cap24	23Sco22
10/05/1993	22Lib15	24Aqu02	18Cap16	18Cap23	23Sco48
10/20/1993	25Lib30	23Aqu40	18Cap28	18Cap29	24Sco19
11/04/1993	28Lib45	23Aqu40	18Cap51	18Cap43	24Sco53
11/19/1993	01Sco55	24Aqu03	19Cap24	19Cap04	25Sco29
12/04/1993	04Sco55	24Aqu48	20Cap05	19Cap30	26Sco04
12/19/1993	07Sco42	25Aqu52	20Cap52	20Cap00	26Sco39
01/03/1994	10Sco07	27Aqu13	21Cap44	20Cap33	27Sco08
01/18/1994	12Sco07	28Aqu48	22Cap37	21Cap07	27Sco33
02/02/1994	13Sco36	00Pis31	23Cap30	21Cap40	27Sco51
02/17/1994	14Sco27	02Pis19	24Cap18	22Cap11	28Sco01
03/04/1994	14Sco37	04Pis09	25Cap01	22Cap37	28Sco03
03/19/1994	14Sco05	05Pis55	25Cap37	22Cap58	27Sco57
04/03/1994	12Sco55	07Pis35	26Cap02	23Cap13	27Sco45
04/18/1994	11Sco15	09Pis05	26Cap17	23Cap20	27Sco26
05/03/1994	09Sco22	10Pis22	26Cap21	23Cap19	27Sco04
05/18/1994	07Sco32	11Pis22	26Cap13	23Cap12	26Sco39
06/02/1994	06Sco02	12Pis03	25Cap55	22Cap58	26Sco15
06/17/1994	05Sco04	12Pis22	25Cap29	22Cap39	25Sco52
07/02/1994	04Sco45	12Pis19	24Cap57	22Cap17	25Sco34

472

Ephemeris Tables for Jupiter, Saturn, Uranus, Neptune, and Pluto

Date	Jupiter	Saturn	Uranus	Neptune	Pluto
07/17/1994	05Sco06	11Pis54	24Cap21	21Cap52	25Sco21
08/01/1994	06Sco06	11Pis10	23Cap45	21Cap29	25Sco16
08/16/1994	07Sco40	10Pis12	23Cap13	21Cap07	25Sco17
08/31/1994	09Sco43	09Pis05	22Cap48	20Cap50	25Sco27
09/15/1994	12Sco11	07Pis58	22Cap30	20Cap39	25Sco43
09/30/1994	14Sco58	06Pis57	22Cap24	20Cap34	26Sco06
10/15/1994	18Sco00	06Pis12	22Cap28	20Cap37	26Sco35
10/30/1994	21Sco12	05Pis45	22Cap44	20Cap47	27Sco07
11/14/1994	24Sco30	05Pis42	23Cap11	21Cap04	27Sco43
11/29/1994	27Sco49	06Pis01	23Cap47	21Cap28	28Sco19
12/14/1994	01Sag05	06Pis44	24Cap31	21Cap57	28Sco54
12/29/1994	04Sag13	07Pis47	25Cap20	22Cap28	29Sco25
01/13/1995	07Sag09	09Pis07	26Cap13	23Cap03	29Sco53
01/28/1995	09Sag46	10Pis40	27Cap06	23Cap36	00Sag14
02/12/1995	12Sag00	12Pis24	27Cap57	24Cap09	00Sag28
02/27/1995	13Sag43	14Pis12	28Cap43	24Cap37	00Sag34
03/14/1995	14Sag52	16Pis03	29Cap24	25Cap01	00Sag33
03/29/1995	15Sag21	17Pis51	29Cap55	25Cap19	00Sag24
04/13/1995	15Sag09	19Pis33	00Aqu17	25Cap30	00Sag08
04/28/1995	14Sag16	21Pis07	00Aqu27	25Cap33	29Sco48
05/13/1995	12Sag49	22Pis27	00Aqu27	25Cap29	29Sco24
05/28/1995	11Sag00	23Pis31	00Aqu15	25Cap18	28Sco59
06/12/1995	09Sag07	24Pis16	29Cap54	25Cap01	28Sco36
06/27/1995	07Sag26	24Pis41	29Cap25	24Cap40	28Sco15
07/12/1995	06Sag12	24Pis43	28Cap52	24Cap17	27Sco59
07/27/1995	05Sag35	24Pis22	28Cap16	23Cap52	27Sco50
08/11/1995	05Sag39	23Pis42	27Cap41	23Cap30	27Sco48
08/26/1995	06Sag22	22Pis45	27Cap11	23Cap10	27Sco53
09/10/1995	07Sag44	21Pis39	26Cap48	22Cap55	28Sco06
09/25/1995	09Sag38	20Pis30	26Cap34	22Cap48	28Sco25
10/10/1995	12Sag00	19Pis27	26Cap32	22Cap46	28Sco51
10/25/1995	14Sag44	18Pis37	26Cap41	22Cap53	29Sco22
11/09/1995	17Sag45	18Pis07	27Cap01	23Cap07	29Sco56
11/24/1995	21Sag00	18Pis00	27Cap31	23Cap28	00Sag31
12/09/1995	24Sag21	18Pis16	28Cap10	23Cap54	01Sag07
12/24/1995	27Sag46	18Pis56	28Cap57	24Cap24	01Sag40
01/08/1996	01Cap10	19Pis57	29Cap47	24Cap58	02Sag10
01/23/1996	04Cap28	21Pis15	00Aqu40	25Cap31	02Sag34
02/07/1996	07Cap35	22Pis48	01Aqu32	26Cap05	02Sag52
02/22/1996	10Cap26	24Pis30	02Aqu22	26Cap36	03Sag03
03/08/1996	12Cap57	26Pis19	03Aqu06	27Cap02	03Sag06
03/23/1996	15Cap00	28Pis11	03Aqu43	27Cap22	03Sag00
04/07/1996	16Cap31	00Ari01	04Aqu11	27Cap37	02Sag48
04/22/1996	17Cap25	01Ari44	04Aqu28	27Cap44	02Sag30
05/07/1996	17Cap38	03Ari22	04Aqu35	27Cap43	02Sag07
05/22/1996	17Cap09	04Ari46	04Aqu30	27Cap36	01Sag43
06/06/1996	16Cap01	05Ari55	04Aqu15	27Cap22	01Sag18
06/21/1996	14Cap23	06Ari46	03Aqu51	27Cap03	00Sag56
07/06/1996	12Cap30	07Ari15	03Aqu20	26Cap41	00Sag38
07/21/1996	10Cap39	07Ari23	02Aqu45	26Cap16	00Sag25
08/05/1996	09Cap07	07Ari07	02Aqu09	25Cap53	00Sag19
08/20/1996	08Cap07	06Ari31	01Aqu36	25Cap31	00Sag21
09/04/1996	07Cap49	05Ari37	01Aqu08	25Cap14	00Sag29
09/19/1996	08Cap13	04Ari31	00Aqu49	25Cap03	00Sag45
10/04/1996	09Cap18	03Ari21	00Aqu39	24Cap58	01Sag08

Ephemeris Tables for Jupiter, Saturn, Uranus, Neptune, and Pluto

Date	Jupiter	Saturn	Uranus	Neptune	Pluto
10/19/1996	11Cap00	02Ari16	00Aqu41	25Cap01	01Sag36
11/03/1996	13Cap13	01Ari22	00Aqu54	25Cap11	02Sag09
11/18/1996	15Cap52	00Ari48	01Aqu18	25Cap28	02Sag43
12/03/1996	18Cap51	00Ari36	01Aqu52	25Cap52	03Sag19
12/18/1996	22Cap06	00Ari48	02Aqu33	26Cap21	03Sag54
01/02/1997	25Cap31	01Ari24	03Aqu21	26Cap53	04Sag25
01/17/1997	29Cap02	02Ari22	04Aqu13	27Cap27	04Sag52
02/01/1997	02Aqu33	03Ari39	05Aqu06	28Cap01	05Sag13
02/16/1997	06Aqu01	05Ari10	05Aqu57	28Cap33	05Sag28
03/03/1997	09Aqu21	06Ari52	06Aqu45	29Cap01	05Sag34
03/18/1997	12Aqu28	08Ari42	07Aqu26	29Cap25	05Sag33
04/02/1997	15Aqu17	10Ari34	08Aqu00	29Cap43	05Sag24
04/17/1997	17Aqu43	12Ari26	08Aqu24	29Cap54	05Sag09
05/02/1997	19Aqu40	14Ari13	08Aqu37	29Cap57	04Sag49
05/17/1997	21Aqu04	15Ari54	08Aqu40	29Cap53	04Sag25
06/01/1997	21Aqu49	17Ari22	08Aqu31	29Cap42	04Sag01
06/16/1997	21Aqu52	18Ari36	08Aqu12	29Cap25	03Sag37
07/01/1997	21Aqu13	19Ari32	07Aqu45	29Cap04	03Sag16
07/16/1997	19Aqu55	20Ari07	07Aqu13	28Cap41	03Sag01
07/31/1997	18Aqu10	20Ari21	06Aqu37	28Cap17	02Sag51
08/15/1997	16Aqu13	20Ari11	06Aqu02	27Cap54	02Sag49
08/30/1997	14Aqu24	19Ari39	05Aqu30	27Cap34	02Sag54
09/14/1997	13Aqu00	18Ari48	05Aqu06	27Cap20	03Sag06
09/29/1997	12Aqu13	17Ari44	04Aqu49	27Cap12	03Sag25
10/14/1997	12Aqu09	16Ari33	04Aqu44	27Cap11	03Sag51
10/29/1997	12Aqu50	15Ari25	04Aqu50	27Cap18	04Sag21
11/13/1997	14Aqu12	14Ari28	05Aqu07	27Cap31	04Sag54
11/28/1997	16Aqu10	13Ari49	05Aqu35	27Cap52	05Sag30
12/13/1997	18Aqu39	13Ari32	06Aqu12	28Cap18	06Sag04
12/28/1997	21Aqu32	13Ari40	06Aqu56	28Cap49	06Sag38
01/12/1998	24Aqu43	14Ari12	07Aqu45	29Cap22	07Sag07
01/27/1998	28Aqu09	15Ari06	08Aqu37	29Cap56	07Sag32
02/11/1998	01Pis42	16Ari19	09Aqu30	00Aqu30	07Sag49
02/26/1998	05Pis18	17Ari49	10Aqu20	01Aqu00	08Sag00
03/13/1998	08Pis54	19Ari31	11Aqu06	01Aqu27	08Sag03
03/28/1998	12Pis24	21Ari20	11Aqu44	01Aqu47	07Sag58
04/12/1998	15Pis45	23Ari13	12Aqu14	02Aqu01	07Sag46
04/27/1998	18Pis52	25Ari07	12Aqu34	02Aqu09	07Sag28
05/12/1998	21Pis40	26Ari57	12Aqu43	02Aqu08	07Sag06
05/27/1998	24Pis04	28Ari40	12Aqu42	02Aqu01	06Sag42
06/11/1998	26Pis00	00Tau13	12Aqu29	01Aqu47	06Sag18
06/26/1998	27Pis20	01Tau32	12Aqu07	01Aqu28	05Sag55
07/11/1998	28Pis00	02Tau34	11Aqu38	01Aqu06	05Sag37
07/26/1998	27Pis57	03Tau16	11Aqu04	00Aqu41	05Sag24
08/10/1998	27Pis11	03Tau36	10Aqu28	00Aqu18	05Sag18
08/25/1998	25Pis47	03Tau32	09Aqu54	29Cap56	05Sag19
09/09/1998	23Pis57	03Tau06	09Aqu25	29Cap39	05Sag27
09/24/1998	21Pis58	02Tau19	09Aqu03	29Cap27	05Sag43
10/09/1998	20Pis10	01Tau16	08Aqu51	29Cap22	06Sag05
10/24/1998	18Pis51	00Tau06	08Aqu49	29Cap25	06Sag33
11/08/1998	18Pis13	28Ari55	08Aqu59	29Cap36	07Sag04
11/23/1998	18Pis21	27Ari54	09Aqu21	29Cap53	07Sag39
12/08/1998	19Pis14	27Ari10	09Aqu52	00Aqu17	08Sag14
12/23/1998	20Pis48	26Ari48	10Aqu32	00Aqu46	08Sag49

Ephemeris Tables for Jupiter, Saturn, Uranus, Neptune, and Pluto

Date	Jupiter	Saturn	Uranus	Neptune	Pluto
01/07/1999	22Pis57	26Ari50	11Aqu18	01Aqu18	09Sag20
01/22/1999	25Pis36	27Ari17	12Aqu09	01Aqu52	09Sag47
02/06/1999	28Pis36	28Ari07	13Aqu01	02Aqu25	10Sag08
02/21/1999	01Ari54	29Ari18	13Aqu53	02Aqu58	10Sag22
03/08/1999	05Ari22	00Tau45	14Aqu41	03Aqu26	10Sag29
03/23/1999	08Ari58	02Tau25	15Aqu24	03Aqu50	10Sag28
04/07/1999	12Ari36	04Tau14	16Aqu00	04Aqu07	10Sag19
04/22/1999	16Ari12	06Tau07	16Aqu26	04Aqu18	10Sag04
05/07/1999	19Ari41	08Tau02	16Aqu42	04Aqu22	09Sag45
05/22/1999	23Ari01	09Tau55	16Aqu48	04Aqu18	09Sag21
06/06/1999	26Ari06	11Tau41	16Aqu42	04Aqu07	08Sag57
06/21/1999	28Ari52	13Tau18	16Aqu25	03Aqu51	08Sag33
07/06/1999	01Tau13	14Tau43	16Aqu00	03Aqu30	08Sag13
07/21/1999	03Tau06	15Tau51	15Aqu29	03Aqu06	07Sag57
08/05/1999	04Tau22	16Tau39	14Aqu54	02Aqu42	07Sag47
08/20/1999	04Tau57	17Tau06	14Aqu18	02Aqu19	07Sag45
09/04/1999	04Tau48	17Tau09	13Aqu46	01Aqu59	07Sag49
09/19/1999	03Tau55	16Tau49	13Aqu19	01Aqu45	08Sag01
10/04/1999	02Tau25	16Tau06	13Aqu00	01Aqu36	08Sag20
10/19/1999	00Tau30	15Tau07	12Aqu52	01Aqu36	08Sag45
11/03/1999	28Ari30	13Tau57	12Aqu55	01Aqu42	09Sag15
11/18/1999	26Ari44	12Tau45	13Aqu09	01Aqu56	09Sag48
12/03/1999	25Ari31	11Tau40	13Aqu34	02Aqu17	10Sag22
12/18/1999	25Ari01	10Tau51	14Aqu09	02Aqu43	10Sag57

Ephemeris Tables for the Nodes

Date	Node	Date	Node	Date	Node	Date	Node
01/01/1900	19Sag08	07/01/1912	17Ari27	01/01/1925	15Leo36	07/01/1937	13Sag56
04/1/01900	14Sag22	10/01/1912	12Ari34	04/01/1925	10Leo50	10/01/1937	09Sag04
07/01/1900	09Sag33			07/01/1925	06Leo01		
10/01/1900	04Sag41	01/01/1913	07Ari42	10/01/1925	01Leo09	01/01/1938	04Sag11
		04/01/1913	02Ari56			04/01/1938	29Sco25
01/01/1901	29Sco48	07/01/1913	28Pis07	01/01/1926	26Can16	07/01/1938	24Sco36
04/01/1901	25Sco02	10/01/1913	23Pis15	04/01/1926	21Can31	10/01/1938	19Sco44
07/01/1901	20Sco13			07/01/1926	16Can41		
10/01/1901	15Sco21	01/01/1914	18Pis23	10/01/1926	11Can49	01/01/1939	14Sco51
		04/01/1914	13Pis37			04/01/1939	10Sco05
01/01/1902	10Sco29	07/01/1914	08Pis48	01/01/1927	06Can57	07/01/1939	05Sco16
04/01/1902	05Sco43	10/01/1914	03Pis55	04/01/1927	02Can11	10/01/1939	00Sco24
07/01/1902	00Sco53			07/01/1927	27Gem22		
10/01/1902	26Lib01	01/01/1915	29Aqu03	10/01/1927	22Gem29	01/01/1940	25Lib32
		04/01/1915	24Aqu17			04/01/1940	20Lib43
01/01/1903	21Lib09	07/01/1915	19Aqu28	01/01/1928	17Gem37	07/01/1940	15Lib53
04/01/1903	16Lib23	10/01/1915	14Aqu36	04/01/1928	12Gem48	10/01/1940	11Lib01
07/01/1903	11Lib34			07/01/1928	07Gem59		
10/01/1903	06Lib41	01/01/1916	09Aqu43	10/01/1928	03Gem07	01/01/1941	06Lib09
		04/01/1916	04Aqu54			04/01/1941	01Lib23
01/01/1904	01Lib49	07/01/1916	00Aqu05	01/01/1929	28Tau14	07/01/1941	26Vir34
04/01/1904	27Vir00	10/01/1916	25Cap13	04/01/1929	23Tau28	10/01/1941	21Vir41
07/01/1904	22Vir11			07/01/1929	18Tau39		
10/01/1904	17Vir18	01/01/1917	20Cap21	10/01/1929	13Tau47	01/01/1942	16Vir49
		04/01/1917	15Cap35			04/01/1942	12Vir03
01/01/1905	12Vir26	07/01/1917	10Cap46	01/01/1930	08Tau55	07/01/1942	07Vir14
04/01/1905	07Vir40	10/01/1917	05Cap53	04/01/1930	04Tau09	10/01/1942	02Vir21
07/01/1905	02Vir51			07/01/1930	29Ari20		
10/01/1905	27Leo59	01/01/1918	01Cap01	10/01/1930	24Ari27	01/01/1943	27Leo29
		04/01/1918	26Sag15			04/01/1943	22Leo43
01/01/1906	23Leo06	07/01/1918	21Sag26	01/01/1931	19Ari35	07/01/1943	17Leo54
04/01/1906	18Leo20	10/01/1918	16Sag34	04/01/1931	14Ari49	10/01/1943	13Leo02
07/01/1906	13Leo31			07/01/1931	10Ari00		
10/01/1906	08Leo39	01/01/1919	11Sag41	10/01/1931	05Ari08	01/01/1944	08Leo09
		04/01/1919	06Sag55			04/01/1944	03Leo20
01/01/1907	03Leo47	07/01/1919	02Sag06	01/01/1932	00Ari15	07/01/1944	28Can31
04/01/1907	29Can01	10/01/1919	27Sco14	04/01/1932	25Pis26	10/01/1944	23Can39
07/01/1907	24Can11			07/01/1932	20Pis37		
10/01/1907	19Can19	01/01/1920	22Sco21	10/01/1932	15Pis45	01/01/1945	18Can46
		04/01/1920	17Sco32			04/01/1945	14Can01
01/01/1908	14Can27	07/01/1920	12Sco43	01/01/1933	10Pis53	07/01/1945	09Can11
04/01/1908	09Can38	10/01/1920	07Sco51	04/01/1933	06Pis07	10/01/1945	04Can19
07/01/1908	04Can49			07/01/1933	01Pis18		
10/01/1908	29Gem56	01/01/1921	02Sco59	10/01/1933	26Aqu25	01/01/1946	29Gem27
		04/01/1921	28Lib13			04/01/1946	24Gem41
01/01/1909	25Gem04	07/01/1921	23Lib23	01/01/1934	21Aqu33	07/01/1946	19Gem52
04/01/1909	20Gem18	10/01/1921	18Lib31	04/01/1934	16Aqu47	10/01/1946	14Gem59
07/01/1909	15Gem29			07/01/1934	11Aqu58		
10/01/1909	10Gem37	01/01/1922	13Lib39	10/01/1934	07Aqu06	01/01/1947	10Gem07
		04/01/1922	08Lib53			04/01/1947	05Gem21
01/01/1910	05Gem44	07/01/1922	04Lib04	01/01/1935	02Aqu13	07/01/1947	00Gem32
04/01/1910	00Gem58	10/01/1922	29Vir11	04/01/1935	27Cap27	10/01/1947	25Tau40
07/01/1910	26Tau09			07/01/1935	22Cap38		
10/01/1910	21Tau17	01/01/1923	24Vir19	10/01/1935	17Cap46	01/01/1948	20Tau47
		04/01/1923	19Vir33			04/01/1948	15Tau40
01/01/1911	16Tau25	07/01/1923	14Vir44	01/01/1936	12Cap54	07/01/1948	11Tau09
04/01/1911	11Tau39	10/01/1923	09Vir52	04/01/1936	08Cap05	10/01/1948	06Tau17
07/01/1911	06Tau50			07/01/1936	03Cap16		
10/01/1911	01Tau57	01/01/1924	04Vir59	10/01/1936	28Sag23	01/01/1949	01Tau25
		04/01/1924	00Vir10			04/01/1949	26Ari39
01/01/1912	27Ari05	07/01/1924	25Leo21	01/01/1937	23Sag31	07/01/1949	21Ari50
04/01/1912	22Ari16	10/01/1924	20Leo29	04/01/1937	18Sag45	10/01/1949	16Ari57

Ephemeris Tables for the Nodes

Date	Node	Date	Node	Date	Node	Date	Node
01/01/1950	12Ari05	07/01/1962	10Leo24	01/01/1975	08Sag34	07/01/1987	06Ari53
04/01/1950	07Ari19	10/01/1962	05Leo32	04/01/1975	03Sag48	10/01/1987	02Ari01
07/01/1950	02Ari30			07/01/1975	28Sco59		
10/01/1950	27Pis38	01/01/1963	00Leo39	10/01/1975	24Sco07	01/01/1988	27Pis08
		04/01/1963	25Can53			04/01/1988	22Pis19
01/01/1951	22Pis45	07/01/1963	21Can04	01/01/1976	19Sco14	07/01/1988	17Pis30
04/01/1951	18Pis00	10/01/1963	16Can12	04/01/1976	14Sco25	10/01/1988	12Pis38
07/01/1951	13Pis10			07/01/1976	09Sco36		
10/01/1951	08Pis18	01/01/1964	11Can20	10/01/1976	04Sco44	01/01/1989	07Pis46
		04/01/1964	06Can31			04/01/1989	03Pis00
01/01/1952	03Pis26	07/01/1964	01Can41	01/01/1977	29Lib51	07/01/1989	28Aqu11
04/01/1952	28Aqu37	10/01/1964	26Gem49	04/01/1977	25Lib05	10/01/1989	23Aqu18
07/01/1952	23Aqu48			07/01/1977	20Lib16		
10/01/1952	18Aqu56	01/01/1965	21Gem57	10/01/1977	15Lib24	01/01/1990	18Aqu26
		04/01/1965	17Gem11			04/01/1990	13Aqu40
01/01/1953	14Aqu03	07/01/1965	12Gem22	01/01/1978	10Lib32	07/01/1990	08Aqu51
04/01/1953	09Aqu17	10/01/1965	07Gem29	04/01/1978	05Lib46	10/01/1990	03Aqu59
07/01/1953	04Aqu28			07/01/1978	00Lib57		
10/01/1953	29Cap36	01/01/1966	02Gem37	10/01/1978	26Vir04	01/01/1991	29Cap07
		04/01/1966	27Tau51			04/01/1991	24Cap20
01/01/1954	24Cap43	07/01/1966	23Tau02	01/01/1979	21Vir12	07/01/1991	19Cap31
04/01/1954	19Cap57	10/01/1966	18Tau10	04/01/1979	16Vir26	10/01/1991	14Cap39
07/01/1954	15Cap08			07/01/1979	11Vir37		
10/01/1954	10Cap16	01/01/1967	13Tau17	10/01/1979	06Vir44	01/01/1992	09Cap47
		04/01/1967	08Tau31			04/01/1992	04Cap58
01/01/1955	05Cap24	07/01/1967	03Tau42	01/01/1980	01Vir52	07/01/1992	00Cap08
04/01/1955	00Cap38	10/01/1967	28Ari50	04/01/1980	27Leo03	10/01/1992	25Sag16
07/01/1955	25Sag49			07/01/1980	22Leo14		
10/01/1955	20Sag56	01/01/1968	23Ari58	10/01/1980	17Leo21	01/01/1993	20Sag24
		04/01/1968	19Ari09			04/01/1993	15Sag38
01/01/1956	16Sag04	07/01/1968	14Ari20	01/01/1981	12Leo29	07/01/1993	10Sag49
04/01/1956	11Sag15	10/01/1968	09Ari27	04/01/1981	07Leo43	10/01/1993	05Sag56
07/01/1956	06Sag26			07/01/1981	02Leo54		
10/01/1956	01Sag34	01/01/1969	04Ari35	10/01/1981	28Can02	01/01/1994	01Sag04
		04/01/1969	29Pis49			04/01/1994	26Sco18
01/01/1957	26Sco41	07/01/1969	25Pis00	01/01/1982	23Can09	07/01/1994	21Sco29
04/01/1957	21Sco55	10/01/1969	20Pis08	04/01/1982	18Can23	10/01/1994	16Sco37
07/01/1957	17Sco06			07/01/1982	13Can34		
10/01/1957	12Sco14	01/01/1970	15Pis16	10/01/1982	08Can42	01/01/1995	11Sco44
		04/01/1970	10Pis30			04/01/1995	06Sco58
01/01/1958	07Sco21	07/01/1970	05Pis40	01/01/1983	03Can50	07/01/1995	02Sco09
04/01/1958	02Sco35	10/01/1970	00Pis48	04/01/1983	29Gem04	10/01/1995	27Lib17
07/01/1958	27Lib46			07/01/1983	24Gem15		
10/01/1958	22Lib54	01/01/1971	25Aqu56	10/01/1983	19Gem22	01/01/1996	22Lib25
		04/01/1971	21Aqu10			04/01/1996	17Lib35
01/01/1959	18Lib02	07/01/1971	16Aqu21	01/01/1984	14Gem30	07/01/1996	12Lib46
04/01/1959	13Lib16	10/01/1971	11Aqu290	04/01/1984	09Gem41	10/01/1996	07Lib54
07/01/1959	08Lib27			07/01/1984	04Gem52		
10/01/1959	03Lib34	01/01/1972	06Aqu36	10/01/1984	29Tau59	01/01/1997	03Lib02
		04/01/1972	01Aqu47			04/01/1997	28Vir16
01/01/1960	28Vir42	07/01/1972	26Cap58	01/01/1985	25Tau07	07/01/1997	23Vir27
04/01/1960	23Vir53	10/01/1972	22Cap06	04/01/1985	20Tau21	10/01/1997	18Vir34
07/01/1960	19Vir04			07/01/1985	15Tau32		
10/01/1960	14Vir11	01/01/1973	17Cap13	10/01/1985	10Tau40	01/01/1998	13Vir42
		04/01/1973	12Cap28			04/01/1998	08Vir56
01/01/1961	09Vir19	07/01/1973	07Cap38	01/01/1986	05Tau48	07/01/1998	04Vir07
04/01/1961	04Vir33	10/01/1973	02Cap46	04/01/1986	01Tau02	10/01/1998	29Leo14
07/01/1961	29Leo44			07/01/1986	26Ari13		
10/01/1961	24Leo51	01/01/1974	27Sag54	10/01/1986	21Ari20	01/01/1999	24Leo22
		04/01/1974	23Sag08			04/01/1999	19Leo36
01/01/1962	19Leo59	07/01/1974	18Sag19	01/01/1987	16Ari28	07/01/1999	14Leo47
04/01/1962	15Leo13	10/01/1974	13Sag26	04/01/1987	11Ari42	10/01/1999	09Leo55

Ephemeris Tables for the Moon

Date	Moon	Date	Moon	Date	Moon	Date	Moon
01/03/1900	08Aqu57	05/01/1900	10Gem42	09/02/1900	11Sag30	01/02/1901	09Gem24
01/05/1900	08Pis27	05/03/1900	07Can22	09/04/1900	07Cap31	01/04/1901	07Can04
01/07/1900	07Ari13	05/05/1900	02Leo32	09/06/1900	05Aqu27	01/06/1901	03Leo51
01/09/1900	04Tau49	05/07/1900	26Leo42	09/08/1900	05Pis10	01/08/1901	29Leo27
01/11/1900	01Gem16	05/09/1900	20Vir29	09/10/1900	05Ari41	01/10/1901	23Vir57
01/13/1900	26Gem48	05/11/1900	14Lib25	09/12/1900	05Tau39	01/12/1901	17Lib45
01/15/1900	21Can36	05/13/1900	08Sco54	09/14/1900	04Gem04	01/14/1901	11Sco28
01/17/1900	15Leo51	05/15/1900	04Sag12	09/16/1900	00Can43	01/16/1901	05Sag49
01/19/1900	09Vir41	05/17/1900	00Cap21	09/18/1900	26Can03	01/18/1901	01Cap22
01/21/1900	03Lib25	05/19/1900	27Cap24	09/20/1900	20Leo31	01/20/1901	28Cap23
01/23/1900	27Lib30	05/21/1900	25Aqu15	09/22/1900	14Vir30	01/22/1901	26Aqu36
01/25/1900	22Sco30	05/23/1900	23Pis47	09/24/1900	08Lib13	01/24/1901	25Pis22
01/27/1900	19Sag04	05/25/1900	22Ari36	09/26/1900	01Sco54	01/26/1901	23Ari57
01/29/1900	17Cap31	05/27/1900	21Tau09	09/28/1900	25Sco52	01/28/1901	21Tau58
01/31/1900	17Aqu28	05/29/1900	18Gem50	09/30/1900	20Sag30	01/30/1901	19Gem23
		05/31/1900	15Can17				
02/02/1900	17Pis47			10/02/1900	16Cap22	02/01/1901	16Can11
02/04/1900	17Ari12	06/02/1900	10Leo27	10/04/1900	14Aqu01	02/03/1901	12Leo16
02/06/1900	15Tau01	06/04/1900	04Vir41	10/06/1900	13Pis28	02/05/1901	07Vir30
02/08/1900	11Gem12	06/06/1900	28Vir30	10/08/1900	13Ari56	02/07/1901	01Lib52
02/10/1900	06Can14	06/08/1900	22Lib30	10/10/1900	14Tau09	02/09/1901	25Lib37
02/12/1900	00Leo35	06/10/1900	17Sco12	10/12/1900	12Gem57	02/11/1901	19Sco16
02/14/1900	24Leo33	06/12/1900	12Sag58	10/14/1900	09Can54	02/13/1901	13Sag33
02/16/1900	18Vir19	06/14/1900	09Cap55	10/16/1900	05Leo14	02/15/1901	09Cap09
02/18/1900	12Lib07	06/16/1900	07Aqu49	10/18/1900	29Leo33	02/17/1901	06Aqu31
02/20/1900	06Sco13	06/18/1900	06Pis15	10/20/1900	23Vir22	02/19/1901	05Pis28
02/22/1900	01Sag06	06/20/1900	04Ari45	10/22/1900	17Lib04	02/21/1901	05Ari06
02/24/1900	27Sag22	06/22/1900	02Tau58	10/24/1900	10Sco55	02/23/1901	04Tau24
02/26/1900	25Cap34	06/24/1900	00Gem38	10/26/1900	05Sag10	02/25/1901	02Gem40
02/28/1900	25Aqu30	06/26/1900	27Gem32	10/28/1900	00Cap06	02/27/1901	29Gem47
		06/28/1900	23Can29	10/30/1900	26Cap05		
		06/30/1900	18Leo28				
03/02/1900	26Pis10			11/01/1900	23Aqu27	03/01/1901	25Can57
03/04/1900	26Ari06	07/02/1900	12Vir39	11/03/1900	22Pis19	03/03/1901	21Leo22
03/06/1900	24Tau19	07/04/1900	06Lib26	11/05/1900	22Ari11	03/05/1901	16Vir05
03/08/1900	20Gem38	07/06/1900	00Sco24	11/07/1900	22Tau06	03/07/1901	10Lib10
03/10/1900	15Can32	07/08/1900	25Sco10	11/09/1900	21Gem00	03/09/1901	03Sco51
03/12/1900	09Leo39	07/10/1900	21Sag16	11/11/1900	18Can13	03/11/1901	27Sco30
03/14/1900	03Vir25	07/12/1900	18Cap52	11/13/1900	13Leo46	03/13/1901	21Sag42
03/16/1900	27Vir11	07/14/1900	17Aqu40	11/15/1900	08Vir07	03/15/1901	17Cap10
03/18/1900	21Lib09	07/16/1900	16Pis54	11/17/1900	01Lib53	03/17/1901	14Aqu29
03/20/1900	15Sco29	07/18/1900	15Ari43	11/19/1900	25Lib37	03/19/1901	13Pis39
03/22/1900	10Sag30	07/20/1900	13Tau40	11/21/1900	19Sco42	03/21/1901	13Ari50
03/24/1900	06Cap40	07/22/1900	10Gem40	11/23/1900	14Sag26	03/23/1901	13Tau51
03/26/1900	04Aqu28	07/24/1900	06Can49	11/25/1900	09Cap58	03/25/1901	12Gem39
03/28/1900	03Pis57	07/26/1900	02Leo11	11/27/1900	06Aqu25	03/27/1901	09Can54
03/30/1900	04Ari18	07/28/1900	26Leo48	11/29/1900	03Pis51	03/29/1901	05Leo49
		07/30/1900	20Vir50			03/31/1901	00Vir46
04/01/1900	04Tau16			12/01/1900	02Ari10		
04/03/1900	02Gem44	08/01/1900	14Lib33	12/03/1900	01Tau12	04/02/1901	25Vir03
04/05/1900	29Gem18	08/03/1900	08Sco27	12/05/1900	00Gem19	04/04/1901	18Lib52
04/07/1900	24Can18	08/05/1900	03Sag09	12/07/1900	28Gem48	04/06/1901	12Sco28
04/09/1900	18Leo24	08/07/1900	29Sag18	12/09/1900	26Can00	04/08/1901	06Sag13
04/11/1900	12Vir08	08/09/1900	27Cap16	12/11/1900	21Leo42	04/10/1901	00Cap30
04/13/1900	05Lib58	08/11/1900	26Aqu45	12/13/1900	16Vir10	04/12/1901	25Cap53
04/15/1900	00Sco10	08/13/1900	26Pis46	12/15/1900	09Lib57	04/14/1901	22Aqu57
04/17/1900	24Sco57	08/15/1900	26Ari09	12/17/1900	03Sco42	04/16/1901	21Pis52
04/19/1900	20Sag25	08/17/1900	24Tau12	12/19/1900	27Sco59	04/18/1901	22Ari02
04/21/1900	16Cap50	08/19/1900	20Gem51	12/21/1900	23Sag13	04/20/1901	22Tau20
04/23/1900	14Aqu28	08/21/1900	16Can27	12/23/1900	19Cap33	04/22/1901	21Gem39
04/25/1900	13Pis22	08/23/1900	11Leo17	12/25/1900	16Aqu49	04/24/1901	19Can16
04/27/1900	13Ari00	08/25/1900	05Vir33	12/27/1900	14Pis43	04/26/1901	15Leo15
04/29/1900	12Tau25	08/27/1900	29Vir23	12/29/1900	12Ari56	04/28/1901	10Vir01
		08/29/1900	23Lib03	12/31/1900	11Tau15	04/30/1901	04Lib01
		08/31/1900	16Sco54				

Ephemeris Tables for the Moon

Date	Moon	Date	Moon	Date	Moon	Date	Moon
05/02/1901	27Lib41	09/01/1901	14Ari04	01/01/1902	08Lib15	05/01/1902	16Aqu27
05/04/1901	21Sco19	09/03/1901	13Tau02	01/03/1902	02Sco13	05/03/1902	12Pis32
05/06/1901	15Sag17	09/05/1901	11Gem24	01/05/1902	25Sco46	05/05/1902	10Ari19
05/08/1901	09Cap52	09/07/1901	09Can00	01/07/1902	19Sag32	05/07/1902	09Tau42
05/10/1901	05Aqu25	09/09/1901	05Leo49	01/09/1902	13Cap55	05/09/1902	09Gem51
05/12/1901	02Pis19	09/11/1901	01Vir51	01/11/1902	09Aqu07	05/11/1902	09Can40
05/14/1901	00Ari45	09/13/1901	26Vir59	01/13/1902	05Pis07	05/13/1902	08Leo12
05/16/1901	00Tau27	09/15/1901	21Lib17	01/15/1902	01Ari51	05/15/1902	05Vir09
05/18/1901	00Gem33	09/17/1901	15Sco00	01/17/1902	29Ari21	05/17/1902	00Lib40
05/20/1901	29Gem57	09/19/1901	08Sag36	01/19/1902	27Tau42	05/19/1902	25Lib13
05/22/1901	27Can52	09/21/1901	02Cap41	01/21/1902	26Gem45	05/21/1902	19Sco10
05/24/1901	24Leo02	09/23/1901	27Cap57	01/23/1902	25Can51	05/23/1902	12Sag50
05/26/1901	18Vir48	09/25/1901	24Aqu54	01/25/1902	24Leo08	05/25/1902	06Cap32
05/28/1901	12Lib43	09/27/1901	23Pis33	01/27/1902	20Vir55	05/27/1902	00Aqu35
05/30/1901	06Sco20	09/29/1901	23Ari15	01/29/1902	16Lib08	05/29/1902	25Aqu19
				01/31/1902	10Sco11	05/31/1902	21Pis14
06/01/1901	00Sag07	10/01/1901	22Tau59				
06/03/1901	24Sag27	10/03/1901	21Gem52	02/02/1902	03Sag48	06/02/1902	18Ari45
06/05/1901	19Cap32	10/05/1901	19Can29	02/04/1902	27Sag39	06/04/1902	17Tau58
06/07/1901	15Aqu32	10/07/1901	15Leo02	02/06/1902	22Cap21	06/06/1902	18Gem17
06/09/1901	12Pis33	10/09/1901	11Vir16	02/08/1902	18Aqu07	06/08/1902	18Can31
06/11/1901	10Ari37	10/11/1901	05Lib52	02/10/1902	14Pis55	06/10/1902	17Leo29
06/13/1901	09Tau38	10/13/1901	29Lib49	02/12/1902	12Ari22	06/12/1902	14Vir36
06/15/1901	09Gem05	10/15/1901	23Sco25	02/14/1902	10Tau14	06/14/1902	10Lib01
06/17/1901	08Can09	10/17/1901	17Sag02	02/16/1902	08Gem23	06/16/1902	04Sco10
06/19/1901	06Leo00	10/19/1901	11Cap07	02/18/1902	06Can42	06/18/1902	28Sco03
06/21/1901	02Vir16	10/21/1901	06Aqu15	02/20/1902	04Leo53	06/20/1902	21Sag42
06/23/1901	27Vir06	10/23/1901	03Pis00	02/22/1902	02Vir24	06/22/1902	15Cap33
06/25/1901	21Lib01	10/25/1901	01Ari33	02/24/1902	28Vir46	06/24/1902	09Aqu51
06/27/1901	14Sco39	10/27/1901	01Tau30	02/26/1902	23Lib52	06/26/1902	04Pis50
06/29/1901	08Sag38	10/29/1901	01Gem50	02/28/1902	17Sco57	06/28/1902	00Ari43
		10/31/1901	01Can22			06/30/1902	27Ari58
07/01/1901	03Cap23			03/02/1902	11Sag36		
07/03/1901	29Cap07	11/02/1901	29Can22	03/04/1902	05Cap30	07/02/1902	26Tau46
07/05/1901	25Aqu48	11/04/1901	25Leo42	03/06/1902	00Aqu19	07/04/1902	26Gem46
07/07/1901	23Pis16	11/06/1901	20Vir43	03/08/1902	26Aqu29	07/06/1902	26Can57
07/09/1901	21Ari16	11/08/1901	14Lib54	03/10/1902	23Pis57	07/08/1902	26Leo03
07/11/1901	19Tau44	11/10/1901	08Sco36	03/12/1902	22Ari18	07/10/1902	23Vir19
07/13/1901	18Gem24	11/12/1901	02Sag10	03/14/1902	20Tau56	07/12/1902	18Lib48
07/15/1901	16Can45	11/14/1901	25Sag55	03/16/1902	19Gem23	07/14/1902	13Sco03
07/17/1901	14Leo12	11/16/1901	20Cap09	03/18/1902	17Can24	07/16/1902	06Sag45
07/19/1901	10Vir18	11/18/1901	15Aqu16	03/20/1902	14Leo48	07/18/1902	00Cap27
07/21/1901	05Lib06	11/20/1901	11Pis43	03/22/1902	11Vir25	07/20/1902	24Cap34
07/23/1901	29Lib00	11/22/1901	09Ari49	03/24/1902	07Lib07	07/22/1902	19Aqu16
07/25/1901	22Sco40	11/24/1901	09Tau20	03/26/1902	01Sco50	07/24/1902	14Pis41
07/27/1901	16Sag47	11/26/1901	09Gem52	03/28/1902	25Sco51	07/26/1902	10Ari52
07/29/1901	11Cap54	11/28/1901	09Can49	03/30/1902	19Sag31	07/28/1902	08Tau04
07/31/1901	08Aqu17	11/30/1901	08Leo16			07/30/1902	06Gem27
				04/01/1902	13Cap25		
08/02/1901	05Pis48	12/02/1901	04Vir50	04/03/1902	08Aqu12	08/01/1902	05Can49
08/04/1901	03Ari57	12/04/1901	29Vir48	04/05/1902	04Pis27	08/03/1902	05Leo27
08/06/1901	02Tau16	12/06/1901	23Lib46	04/07/1902	02Ari16	08/05/1902	04Vir16
08/08/1901	00Gem30	12/08/1901	17Sco21	04/09/1902	01Tau20	08/07/1902	01Lib30
08/10/1901	28Gem28	12/10/1901	10Sag59	04/11/1902	00Gem51	08/09/1902	27Lib03
08/12/1901	26Can00	12/12/1901	05Cap00	04/13/1902	29Gem57	08/11/1902	21Sco20
08/14/1901	22Leo46	12/14/1901	29Cap38	04/15/1902	28Can06	08/13/1902	15Sag04
08/16/1901	18Vir28	12/16/1901	25Aqu02	04/17/1902	25Leo05	08/15/1902	08Cap53
08/18/1901	13Lib04	12/18/1901	21Pis25	04/19/1902	21Vir01	08/17/1902	03Aqu16
08/20/1901	06Sco54	12/20/1901	19Ari03	04/21/1902	16Lib02	08/19/1902	28Aqu28
08/22/1901	00Sag33	12/22/1901	18Tau01	04/23/1902	10Sco20	08/21/1902	24Pis30
08/24/1901	24Sag42	12/24/1901	17Gem54	04/25/1902	04Sag09	08/23/1902	21Ari17
08/26/1901	20Cap00	12/26/1901	17Can42	04/27/1902	27Sag49	08/25/1902	18Tau46
08/28/1901	16Aqu51	12/28/1901	16Leo19	04/29/1902	21Cap44	08/27/1902	16Gem58
08/30/1901	15Pis05	12/30/1901	13Vir09			08/29/1902	15Can42
						08/31/1902	14Leo30

Ephemeris Tables for the Moon

Date	Moon	Date	Moon	Date	Moon	Date	Moon
09/02/1902	12Vir38	01/02/1903	20Aqu18	05/02/1903	16Can49	09/01/1903	07Cap20
09/04/1902	09Lib31	01/04/1903	14Pis44	05/04/1903	15Leo21	09/03/1903	01Aqu06
09/06/1902	04Sco58	01/06/1903	10Ari01	05/06/1903	13Vir08	09/05/1903	24Aqu55
09/08/1902	29Sco17	01/08/1903	06Tau44	05/08/1903	10Lib06	09/07/1903	19Pis07
09/10/1902	23Sag03	01/10/1903	05Gem19	05/10/1903	06Sco13	09/09/1903	13Ari54
09/12/1902	16Cap56	01/12/1903	05Can27	05/12/1903	01Sag33	09/11/1903	09Tau29
09/14/1902	11Aqu30	01/14/1903	06Leo03	05/14/1903	26Sag06	09/13/1903	06Gem05
09/16/1902	07Pis07	01/16/1903	05Vir42	05/16/1903	20Cap04	09/15/1903	03Can51
09/18/1902	03Ari49	01/18/1903	03Lib30	05/18/1903	13Aqu50	09/17/1903	02Leo45
09/20/1902	01Tau26	01/20/1903	29Lib21	05/20/1903	07Pis57	09/19/1903	02Vir15
09/22/1902	29Tau36	01/22/1903	23Sco52	05/22/1903	03Ari00	09/21/1903	01Lib31
09/24/1902	27Gem59	01/24/1903	17Sag42	05/24/1903	29Ari37	09/23/1903	29Lib41
09/26/1902	26Can19	01/26/1903	11Cap24	05/26/1903	27Tau54	09/25/1903	26Sco19
09/28/1902	24Leo16	01/28/1903	05Aqu16	05/28/1903	27Gem24	09/27/1903	21Sag28
09/30/1902	21Vir30	01/30/1903	29Aqu32	05/30/1903	27Can06	09/29/1903	15Cap38
10/02/1902	17Lib45	02/01/1903	24Pis18	06/01/1903	26Leo02	10/01/1903	09Aqu23
10/04/1902	12Sco54	02/03/1903	19Ari49	06/03/1903	23Vir40	10/03/1903	03Pis18
10/06/1902	07Sag10	02/05/1903	16Tau27	06/05/1903	20Lib06	10/05/1903	27Pis49
10/08/1902	00Cap56	02/07/1903	14Gem33	06/07/1903	15Sco36	10/07/1903	23Ari11
10/10/1902	24Cap47	02/09/1903	14Can01	06/09/1903	10Sag23	10/09/1903	19Tau30
10/12/1902	19Aqu21	02/11/1903	14Leo06	06/11/1903	04Cap37	10/11/1903	16Gem42
10/14/1902	15Pis09	02/13/1903	13Vir34	06/13/1903	28Cap28	10/13/1903	14Can37
10/16/1902	12Ari21	02/15/1903	11Lib29	06/15/1903	22Aqu12	10/15/1903	13Leo03
10/18/1902	10Tau48	02/17/1903	07Sco36	06/17/1903	16Pis16	10/17/1903	11Vir41
10/20/1902	09Gem54	02/19/1903	02Sag16	06/19/1903	11Ari13	10/19/1903	10Lib05
10/22/1902	08Can53	02/21/1903	26Sag09	06/21/1903	07Tau46	10/21/1903	07Sco43
10/24/1902	07Leo12	02/23/1903	19Cap52	06/23/1903	06Gem13	10/23/1903	04Sag11
10/26/1902	04Vir33	02/25/1903	13Aqu54	06/25/1903	06Can11	10/25/1903	29Sag22
10/28/1902	00Lib57	02/27/1903	08Pis32	06/27/1903	06Leo31	10/27/1903	23Cap33
10/30/1902	26Lib28			06/29/1903	05Vir58	10/29/1903	17Aqu18
		03/01/1903	03Ari52			10/31/1903	11Pis14
11/01/1902	21Sco11	03/03/1903	00Tau00	07/01/1903	03Lib47		
11/03/1902	15Sag16	03/05/1903	26Tau58	07/03/1903	00Sco01	11/02/1903	05Ari57
11/05/1902	09Cap00	03/07/1903	24Gem55	07/05/1903	25Sco07	11/04/1903	01Tau52
11/07/1902	02Aqu48	03/09/1903	23Can43	07/07/1903	19Sag31	11/06/1903	29Tau02
11/09/1902	27Aqu14	03/11/1903	22Leo53	07/09/1903	13Cap29	11/08/1903	27Gem08
11/11/1902	22Pis54	03/13/1903	21Vir38	07/11/1903	07Aqu13	11/10/1903	25Can36
11/13/1902	20Ari14	03/15/1903	19Lib15	07/13/1903	01Pis00	11/12/1903	23Leo58
11/15/1902	19Tau13	03/17/1903	15Sco22	07/15/1903	25Pis06	11/14/1903	21Vir57
11/17/1902	19Gem10	03/19/1903	10Sag12	07/17/1903	20Ari03	11/16/1903	19Lib27
11/19/1902	19Can00	03/21/1903	04Cap11	07/19/1903	16Tau26	11/18/1903	16Sco17
11/21/1902	17Leo42	03/23/1903	27Cap57	07/21/1903	14Gem43	11/20/1903	12Sag16
11/23/1902	14Vir53	03/25/1903	22Aqu06	07/23/1903	14Can39	11/22/1903	07Cap16
11/25/1902	10Lib43	03/27/1903	17Pis03	07/25/1903	15Leo12	11/24/1903	01Aqu25
11/27/1902	05Sco37	03/29/1903	13Ari00	07/27/1903	15Vir00	11/26/1903	25Aqu06
11/29/1902	29Sco54	03/31/1903	09Tau56	07/29/1903	13Lib07	11/28/1903	18Pis58
				07/31/1903	09Sco27	11/30/1903	13Ari41
12/01/1902	23Sag47	04/02/1903	07Gem40				
12/03/1902	17Cap30	04/04/1903	05Can54	08/02/1903	04Sag25	12/02/1903	09Tau52
12/05/1902	11Aqu18	04/06/1903	04Leo21	08/04/1903	28Sag36	12/04/1903	07Gem43
12/07/1902	05Pis39	04/08/1903	02Vir40	08/06/1903	22Cap24	12/06/1903	06Can45
12/09/1902	01Ari02	04/10/1903	00Lib28	08/08/1903	16Aqu09	12/08/1903	06Leo05
12/11/1902	28Ari07	04/12/1903	27Lib23	08/10/1903	10Pis04	12/10/1903	04Vir51
12/13/1902	27Tau06	04/14/1903	23Sco13	08/12/1903	04Ari24	12/12/1903	02Lib39
12/15/1902	27Gem28	04/16/1903	18Sag00	08/14/1903	29Ari31	12/14/1903	29Lib28
12/17/1902	27Can57	04/18/1903	12Cap03	08/16/1903	25Tau52	12/16/1903	25Sco32
12/19/1902	27Leo15	04/20/1903	05Aqu50	08/18/1903	23Gem51	12/18/1903	20Sag54
12/21/1902	24Vir40	04/22/1903	00Pis00	08/20/1903	23Can20	12/20/1903	15Cap32
12/23/1902	20Lib21	04/24/1903	25Pis05	08/22/1903	23Leo34	12/22/1903	09Aqu31
12/25/1902	14Sco54	04/26/1903	21Ari30	08/24/1903	23Vir21	12/24/1903	03Pis09
12/27/1902	08Sag52	04/28/1903	19Tau15	08/26/1903	21Lib40	12/26/1903	26Pis55
12/29/1902	02Cap36	04/30/1903	17Gem55	08/28/1903	18Sco12	12/28/1903	21Ari30
12/31/1902	26Cap21			08/30/1903	13Sag13	12/30/1903	17Tau37

Ephemeris Tables for the Moon

Date	Moon	Date	Moon	Date	Moon	Date	Moon
01/01/1904	15Gem41	05/02/1904	14Sag15	09/01/1904	19Tau31	01/01/1905	17Sco16
01/03/1904	15Can19	05/04/1904	10Cap03	09/03/1904	15Gem04	01/03/1905	14Sag42
01/05/1904	15Leo29	05/06/1904	04Aqu36	09/05/1904	12Can13	01/05/1905	11Cap21
01/07/1904	14Vir57	05/08/1904	28Aqu24	09/07/1904	11Leo04	01/07/1905	06Aqu58
01/09/1904	13Lib01	05/10/1904	22Pis06	09/09/1904	11Vir10	01/09/1905	01Pis32
01/11/1904	09Sco39	05/12/1904	16Ari21	09/11/1904	11Lib28	01/11/1905	25Pis21
01/13/1904	05Sag13	05/14/1904	11Tau38	09/13/1904	10Sco46	01/13/1905	18Ari57
01/15/1904	00Cap01	05/16/1904	08Gem06	09/15/1904	08Sag25	01/15/1905	13Tau04
01/17/1904	24Cap15	05/18/1904	05Can34	09/17/1904	04Cap22	01/17/1905	08Gem21
01/19/1904	18Aqu02	05/20/1904	03Leo37	09/19/1904	29Cap01	01/19/1905	05Can11
01/21/1904	11Pis39	05/22/1904	01Vir52	09/21/1904	22Aqu55	01/21/1905	03Leo28
01/23/1904	05Ari24	05/24/1904	00Lib07	09/23/1904	16Pis32	01/23/1905	02Vir34
01/25/1904	29Ari54	05/26/1904	28Lib11	09/25/1904	10Ari12	01/25/1905	01Lib42
01/27/1904	25Tau48	05/28/1904	25Sco46	09/27/1904	04Tau15	01/27/1905	00Sco13
01/29/1904	23Gem38	05/30/1904	22Sag28	09/29/1904	28Tau57	01/29/1905	27Sco52
01/31/1904	23Can17					01/31/1905	24Sag36
		06/01/1904	18Cap02	10/01/1904	24Gem36		
02/02/1904	23Leo49	06/03/1904	12Aqu30	10/03/1904	21Can30	02/02/1905	20Cap28
02/04/1904	23Vir53	06/05/1904	06Pis17	10/05/1904	19Leo51	02/04/1905	15Aqu27
02/06/1904	22Lib30	06/07/1904	00Ari00	10/07/1904	19Vir29	02/06/1905	09Pis42
02/08/1904	19Sco21	06/09/1904	24Ari21	10/09/1904	19Lib35	02/08/1905	03Ari24
02/10/1904	14Sag46	06/11/1904	19Tau57	10/11/1904	19Sco04	02/10/1905	27Ari01
02/12/1904	09Cap15	06/13/1904	17Gem03	10/13/1904	17Sag00	02/12/1905	21Tau05
02/14/1904	03Aqu10	06/15/1904	15Can21	10/15/1904	13Cap07	02/14/1905	16Gem13
02/16/1904	26Aqu49	06/17/1904	14Leo10	10/17/1904	07Aqu45	02/16/1905	12Can58
02/18/1904	20Pis29	06/19/1904	12Vir50	10/19/1904	01Pis33	02/18/1905	11Leo28
02/20/1904	14Ari26	06/21/1904	10Lib57	10/21/1904	25Pis08	02/20/1905	11Vir12
02/22/1904	09Tau04	06/23/1904	08Sco26	10/23/1904	18Ari59	02/22/1905	11Lib10
02/24/1904	04Gem53	06/25/1904	05Sag15	10/25/1904	13Tau27	02/24/1905	10Sco23
02/26/1904	02Can21	06/27/1904	01Cap16	10/27/1904	08Gem41	02/26/1905	08Sag15
02/28/1904	01Leo31	06/29/1904	26Cap21	10/29/1904	04Can45	02/28/1905	04Cap40
				10/31/1904	01Leo40		
03/01/1904	01Vir46	07/01/1904	20Aqu35			03/02/1905	29Cap57
03/03/1904	01Lib57	07/03/1904	14Pis18	11/02/1904	29Leo36	03/04/1905	24Aqu24
03/05/1904	00Sco57	07/05/1904	07Ari59	11/04/1904	28Vir30	03/06/1905	18Pis18
03/07/1904	28Sco12	07/07/1904	02Tau21	11/06/1904	27Lib56	03/08/1905	11Ari55
03/09/1904	23Sag46	07/09/1904	28Tau03	11/08/1904	27Sco04	03/10/1905	05Tau35
03/11/1904	18Cap10	07/11/1904	25Gem28	11/10/1904	24Sag59	03/12/1905	29Tau42
03/13/1904	11Aqu57	07/13/1904	24Can22	11/12/1904	21Cap13	03/14/1905	24Gem42
03/15/1904	05Pis34	07/15/1904	23Leo58	11/14/1904	15Aqu55	03/16/1905	21Can10
03/17/1904	29Pis24	07/17/1904	23Vir16	11/16/1904	09Pis43	03/18/1905	19Leo25
03/19/1904	23Ari43	07/19/1904	21Lib37	11/18/1904	03Ari19	03/20/1905	19Vir13
03/21/1904	18Tau48	07/21/1904	18Sco52	11/20/1904	27Ari23	03/22/1905	19Lib40
03/23/1904	14Gem51	07/23/1904	15Sag06	11/22/1904	22Tau18	03/24/1905	19Sco31
03/25/1904	12Can07	07/25/1904	10Cap28	11/24/1904	18Gem13	03/26/1905	17Sag49
03/27/1904	10Leo42	07/27/1904	05Aqu04	11/26/1904	15Can00	03/28/1905	14Cap19
03/29/1904	10Vir13	07/29/1904	29Aqu01	11/28/1904	12Leo23	03/30/1905	09Aqu21
03/31/1904	09Lib57	07/31/1904	22Pis38	11/30/1904	10Vir15		
						04/01/1905	03Pis28
04/02/1904	08Sco53	08/02/1904	16Ari19	12/02/1904	08Lib33	04/03/1905	27Pis08
04/04/1904	06Sag19	08/04/1904	10Tau40	12/04/1904	07Sco07	04/05/1905	20Ari43
04/06/1904	02Cap07	08/06/1904	06Gem18	12/06/1904	05Sag28	04/07/1905	14Tau34
04/08/1904	26Cap36	08/08/1904	03Can41	12/08/1904	02Cap55	04/09/1905	08Gem54
04/10/1904	20Aqu21	08/10/1904	02Leo47	12/10/1904	29Cap00	04/11/1905	04Can00
04/12/1904	14Pis00	08/12/1904	02Vir52	12/12/1904	23Aqu43	04/13/1905	00Leo15
04/14/1904	08Ari03	08/14/1904	02Lib49	12/14/1904	17Pis33	04/15/1905	28Leo04
04/16/1904	02Tau52	08/16/1904	01Sco40	12/16/1904	11Ari10	04/17/1905	27Vir28
04/18/1904	28Tau37	08/18/1904	29Sco00	12/18/1904	05Tau19	04/19/1905	27Lib48
04/20/1904	25Gem16	08/20/1904	24Sag56	12/20/1904	00Gem33	04/21/1905	27Sco52
04/22/1904	22Can45	08/22/1904	19Cap50	12/22/1904	27Gem05	04/23/1905	26Sag31
04/24/1904	20Leo57	08/24/1904	14Aqu01	12/24/1904	24Can42	04/25/1905	23Cap14
04/26/1904	19Vir43	08/26/1904	07Pis45	12/26/1904	22Leo54	04/27/1905	18Aqu16
04/28/1904	18Lib36	08/28/1904	01Ari19	12/28/1904	21Vir13	04/29/1905	12Pis18
04/30/1904	17Sco00	08/30/1904	25Ari06	12/30/1904	19Lib22		

Ephemeris Tables for the Moon

Date	Moon	Date	Moon	Date	Moon	Date	Moon
05/01/1905	05Ari52	09/02/1905	20Lib03	01/02/1906	09Ari53	05/02/1906	19Leo31
05/03/1905	29Ari34	09/04/1905	19Sco16	01/04/1906	03Tau39	05/04/1906	16Vir27
05/05/1905	23Tau41	09/06/1905	17Sag25	01/06/1906	27Tau29	05/06/1906	15Lib21
05/07/1905	18Gem25	09/08/1905	14Cap18	01/08/1906	21Gem52	05/08/1906	15Sco41
05/09/1905	13Can53	09/10/1905	10Aqu03	01/10/1906	17Can06	05/10/1906	16Sag12
05/11/1905	10Leo15	09/12/1905	04Pis58	01/12/1906	13Leo11	05/12/1906	15Cap34
05/13/1905	07Vir46	09/14/1905	29Pis13	01/14/1906	10Vir04	05/14/1906	13Aqu06
05/15/1905	06Lib36	09/16/1905	23Ari02	01/16/1906	07Lib39	05/16/1906	08Pis55
05/17/1905	06Sco22	09/18/1905	16Tau45	01/18/1906	05Sco50	05/18/1906	03Moo36
05/19/1905	06Sag05	09/20/1905	10Gem43	01/20/1906	04Sag25	05/20/1906	27Ari37
05/21/1905	04Cap40	09/22/1905	05Can27	01/22/1906	02Cap57	05/22/1906	21Tau22
05/23/1905	01Aqu30	09/24/1905	01Leo31	01/24/1906	00Aqu53	05/24/1906	15Gem06
05/25/1905	26Aqu39	09/26/1905	29Leo20	01/26/1906	27Aqu43	05/26/1906	09Can03
05/27/1905	20Pis42	09/28/1905	28Vir48	01/28/1906	23Pis15	05/28/1906	03Leo29
05/29/1905	14Ari19	09/30/1905	29Lib07	01/30/1906	17Ari40	05/30/1906	28Leo49
05/31/1905	08Tau10						
		10/02/1905	29Sco02	02/01/1906	11Tau30	06/01/1906	25Vir34
06/02/1905	02Gem37	10/04/1905	27Sag32	02/03/1906	05Gem21	06/03/1906	24Lib07
06/04/1905	27Gem52	10/06/1905	24Cap18	02/05/1906	29Gem48	06/05/1906	24Sco08
06/06/1905	23Can56	10/08/1905	19Aqu39	02/07/1906	25Can20	06/07/1906	24Sag34
06/08/1905	20Leo44	10/10/1905	14Pis06	02/09/1906	22Leo06	06/09/1906	24Cap06
06/10/1905	18Vir19	10/12/1905	08Ari01	02/11/1906	19Vir54	06/11/1906	21Aqu52
06/12/1905	16Lib45	10/14/1905	01Tau45	02/13/1906	18Lib20	06/13/1906	17Pis52
06/14/1905	15Sco46	10/16/1905	25Tau31	02/15/1906	16Sco54	06/15/1906	12Ari32
06/16/1905	14Sag45	10/18/1905	19Gem34	02/17/1906	15Sag10	06/17/1906	06Tau29
06/18/1905	12Cap51	10/20/1905	14Can16	02/19/1906	12Cap52	06/19/1906	00Gem13
06/20/1905	09Aqu28	10/22/1905	10Leo06	02/21/1906	09Aqu51	06/21/1906	24Gem03
06/22/1905	04Pis38	10/24/1905	07Vir36	02/23/1906	05Pis58	06/23/1906	18Can16
06/24/1905	28Pis44	10/26/1905	06Lib54	02/25/1906	01Moo10	06/25/1906	13Leo06
06/26/1905	22Ari26	10/28/1905	07Sco24	02/27/1906	25Ari31	06/27/1906	08Vir45
06/28/1905	16Tau24	10/30/1905	07Sag45			06/29/1906	05Lib35
06/30/1905	11Gem09			03/01/1906	19Tau21		
07/02/1905	06Can55	11/01/1905	06Cap42	03/03/1906	13Gem10	07/01/1906	03Sco48
07/04/1905	03Leo42	11/03/1905	03Aqu40	03/05/1906	07Can33	07/03/1906	03Sag12
07/06/1905	01Vir13	11/05/1905	28Aqu56	03/07/1906	03Leo07	07/05/1906	03Cap02
07/08/1905	29Vir16	11/07/1905	23Pis08	03/09/1906	00Vir16	07/07/1906	02Aqu16
07/10/1905	27Lib36	11/09/1905	16Ari54	03/11/1906	28Vir52	07/09/1906	00Pis04
07/12/1905	26Sco01	11/11/1905	10Tau37	03/13/1906	28Lib16	07/11/1906	26Pis13
07/14/1905	24Sag07	11/13/1905	04Gem33	03/15/1906	27Sco34	07/13/1906	20Ari58
07/16/1905	21Cap26	11/15/1905	28Gem52	03/17/1906	26Sag00	07/15/1906	14Tau57
07/18/1905	17Aqu35	11/17/1905	23Can45	03/19/1906	23Cap16	07/17/1906	08Gem43
07/20/1905	12Pis33	11/19/1905	19Leo33	03/21/1906	19Aqu31	07/19/1906	02Can43
07/22/1905	06Ari37	11/21/1905	16Vir43	03/23/1906	14Pis55	07/21/1906	27Can18
07/24/1905	00Tau22	11/23/1905	15Lib31	03/25/1906	09Ari37	07/23/1906	22Leo42
07/26/1905	24Tau24	11/25/1905	15Sco34	03/27/1906	03Tau46	07/25/1906	18Vir59
07/28/1905	19Gem17	11/27/1905	15Sag48	03/29/1906	27Tau33	07/27/1906	16Lib12
07/30/1905	15Can25	11/29/1905	14Cap54	03/31/1906	21Gem19	07/29/1906	14Sco18
						07/31/1906	13Sag06
08/01/1905	12Leo51	12/01/1905	12Aqu09	04/02/1906	15Can35		
08/03/1905	11Vir14	12/03/1905	07Pis34	04/04/1906	11Leo01	08/02/1906	12Cap06
08/05/1905	10Lib00	12/05/1905	01Moo47	04/06/1906	08Vir10	08/04/1906	10Aqu38
08/07/1905	08Sco38	12/07/1905	25Ari30	04/08/1906	07Lib09	08/06/1906	08Pis06
08/09/1905	06Sag44	12/09/1905	19Tau16	04/10/1906	07Sco17	08/08/1906	04Moo12
08/11/1905	04Cap05	12/11/1905	13Gem27	04/12/1906	07Sag21	08/10/1906	29Ari01
08/13/1905	00Aqu33	12/13/1905	08Can12	04/14/1906	06Cap14	08/12/1906	23Tau03
08/15/1905	26Aqu04	12/15/1905	03Leo35	04/16/1906	03Aqu31	08/14/1906	16Gem49
08/17/1905	20Pis42	12/17/1905	29Leo44	04/18/1906	29Aqu29	08/16/1906	10Can57
08/19/1905	14Ari40	12/19/1905	26Vir52	04/20/1906	24Pis16	08/18/1906	05Leo54
08/21/1905	08Tau24	12/21/1905	25Lib10	04/22/1906	18Ari33	08/20/1906	01Vir56
08/23/1905	02Gem24	12/23/1905	24Sco27	04/24/1906	12Tau20	08/22/1906	29Vir03
08/25/1905	27Gem15	12/25/1905	23Sag58	04/26/1906	06Gem11	08/24/1906	26Lib58
08/27/1905	23Can28	12/27/1905	22Cap43	04/28/1906	29Gem59	08/26/1906	25Sco19
08/29/1905	21Leo18	12/29/1905	19Aqu57	04/30/1906	24Can14	08/28/1906	23Sag44
08/31/1905	20Vir25	12/31/1905	15Pis33			08/30/1906	21Cap54

Ephemeris Tables for the Moon

Date	Moon	Date	Moon	Date	Moon	Date	Moon
09/01/1906	19Aqu33	01/01/1907	28Can45	05/01/1907	24Sag31	09/02/1907	09Can09
09/03/1906	16Pis24	01/03/1907	23Leo07	05/03/1907	23Cap25	09/04/1907	02Leo49
09/05/1906	12Ari12	01/05/1907	18Vir17	05/05/1907	21Aqu21	09/06/1907	26Leo58
09/07/1906	06Tau57	01/07/1907	14Lib36	05/07/1907	18Pis18	09/08/1907	21Vir56
09/09/1906	00Gem57	01/09/1907	12Sco24	05/09/1907	14Ari23	09/10/1907	17Lib50
09/11/1906	24Gem42	01/11/1907	11Sag40	05/11/1907	09Tau40	09/12/1907	14Sco34
09/13/1906	18Can51	01/13/1907	11Cap43	05/13/1907	04Gem12	09/14/1907	12Sag03
09/15/1906	14Leo00	01/15/1907	11Aqu28	05/15/1907	28Gem06	09/16/1907	10Cap12
09/17/1906	10Vir33	01/17/1907	09Pis57	05/17/1907	21Can42	09/18/1907	08Aqu54
09/19/1906	08Lib29	01/19/1907	06Moo42	05/19/1907	15Leo28	09/20/1907	07Pis47
09/21/1906	07Sco19	01/21/1907	01Tau52	05/21/1907	10Vir05	09/22/1907	06Ari10
09/23/1906	06Sag16	01/23/1907	25Tau59	05/23/1907	06Lib12	09/24/1907	03Tau22
09/25/1906	04Cap40	01/25/1907	19Gem40	05/25/1907	04Sco10	09/26/1907	29Tau04
09/27/1906	02Aqu18	01/27/1907	13Can25	05/27/1907	03Sag42	09/28/1907	23Gem28
09/29/1906	29Aqu08	01/29/1907	07Leo37	05/29/1907	03Cap48	09/30/1907	17Can10
		01/31/1907	02Vir32	05/31/1907	03Aqu21		
10/01/1906	25Pis14					10/02/1907	10Leo53
10/03/1906	20Ari33	02/02/1907	28Vir16	06/02/1907	01Pis38	10/04/1907	05Vir16
10/05/1906	15Tau04	02/04/1907	24Lib56	06/04/1907	28Pis29	10/06/1907	00Lib45
10/07/1906	08Gem58	02/06/1907	22Sco36	06/06/1907	24Ari09	10/08/1907	27Lib23
10/09/1906	02Can40	02/08/1907	21Sag10	06/08/1907	18Tau57	10/10/1907	24Sco55
10/11/1906	26Can43	02/10/1907	20Cap21	06/10/1907	13Gem03	10/12/1907	22Sag55
10/13/1906	21Leo49	02/12/1907	19Aqu27	06/12/1907	06Can45	10/14/1907	21Cap04
10/15/1906	18Vir34	02/14/1907	17Pis43	06/14/1907	00Leo18	10/16/1907	19Aqu15
10/17/1906	17Lib05	02/16/1907	14Ari33	06/16/1907	24Leo09	10/18/1907	17Pis18
10/19/1906	16Sco46	02/18/1907	09Tau52	06/18/1907	18Vir47	10/20/1907	14Ari52
10/21/1906	16Sag30	02/20/1907	04Gem05	06/20/1907	14Lib46	10/22/1907	11Tau31
10/23/1906	15Cap19	02/22/1907	27Gem46	06/22/1907	12Sco33	10/24/1907	06Gem57
10/25/1906	12Aqu48	02/24/1907	21Can35	06/24/1907	12Sag01	10/26/1907	01Can18
10/27/1906	09Pis06	02/26/1907	16Leo04	06/26/1907	12Cap22	10/28/1907	24Can59
10/29/1906	04Moo33	02/28/1907	11Vir34	06/28/1907	12Aqu23	10/30/1907	18Leo42
10/31/1906	29Ari20			06/30/1907	11Pis06		
		03/02/1907	08Lib07	07/02/1907	08Ari08	11/01/1907	13Vir09
11/02/1906	23Tau33	03/04/1907	05Sco31	07/04/1907	03Tau40	11/03/1907	08Lib55
11/04/1906	17Gem21	03/06/1907	03Sag28	07/06/1907	28Tau10	11/05/1907	06Sco09
11/06/1906	10Can59	03/08/1907	01Cap43	07/08/1907	22Gem01	11/07/1907	04Sag32
11/08/1906	04Leo57	03/10/1907	00Aqu05	07/10/1907	15Can35	11/09/1907	03Cap22
11/10/1906	29Leo54	03/12/1907	28Aqu17	07/12/1907	09Leo13	11/11/1907	02Aqu00
11/12/1906	26Vir31	03/14/1907	25Pis52	07/14/1907	03Vir17	11/13/1907	00Pis06
11/14/1906	25Lib07	03/16/1907	22Ari24	07/16/1907	28Vir07	11/15/1907	27Pis31
11/16/1906	25Sco13	03/18/1907	17Tau41	07/18/1907	24Lib06	11/17/1907	24Ari14
11/18/1906	25Sag37	03/20/1907	11Gem55	07/20/1907	21Sco34	11/19/1907	20Tau09
11/20/1906	25Cap03	03/22/1907	05Can36	07/22/1907	20Sag37	11/21/1907	15Gem07
11/22/1906	22Aqu48	03/24/1907	29Can26	07/24/1907	20Cap41	11/23/1907	09Can16
11/24/1906	18Pis59	03/26/1907	24Leo05	07/26/1907	20Aqu46	11/25/1907	02Leo55
11/26/1906	14Ari02	03/28/1907	20Vir02	07/28/1907	19Pis47	11/27/1907	26Leo36
11/28/1906	08Tau25	03/30/1907	17Lib22	07/30/1907	17Ari04	11/29/1907	20Vir59
11/30/1906	02Gem21						
		04/01/1907	15Sco42	08/01/1907	12Tau40	12/01/1907	16Lib43
12/02/1906	26Gem03	04/03/1907	14Sag19	08/03/1907	07Gem03	12/03/1907	14Sco10
12/04/1906	19Can45	04/05/1907	12Cap43	08/05/1907	00Can46	12/05/1907	13Sag07
12/06/1906	13Leo48	04/07/1907	10Aqu38	08/07/1907	24Can21	12/07/1907	12Cap48
12/08/1906	08Vir42	04/09/1907	08Pis02	08/09/1907	18Leo13	12/09/1907	12Aqu15
12/10/1906	05Lib04	04/11/1907	04Ari48	08/11/1907	12Vir40	12/11/1907	10Pis42
12/12/1906	03Sco19	04/13/1907	00Tau44	08/13/1907	07Lib55	12/13/1907	07Ari55
12/14/1906	03Sag13	04/15/1907	25Tau43	08/15/1907	04Sco07	12/15/1907	04Tau03
12/16/1906	03Cap46	04/17/1907	19Gem50	08/17/1907	01Sag27	12/17/1907	29Tau16
12/18/1906	03Aqu37	04/19/1907	13Can29	08/19/1907	29Sag57	12/19/1907	23Gem43
12/20/1906	01Pis51	04/21/1907	07Leo17	08/21/1907	29Cap23	12/21/1907	17Can37
12/22/1906	28Pis16	04/23/1907	01Vir57	08/23/1907	29Aqu040	12/23/1907	11Leo13
12/24/1906	23Ari15	04/25/1907	28Vir06	08/25/1907	27Pis58	12/25/1907	04Vir56
12/26/1906	17Tau24	04/27/1907	25Lib57	08/27/1907	25Ari22	12/27/1907	29Vir15
12/28/1906	11Gem09	04/29/1907	25Sco04	08/29/1907	21Tau05	12/29/1907	24Lib47
12/30/1906	04Can51			08/31/1907	15Gem28	12/31/1907	22Sco01

Ephemeris Tables for the Moon

Date	Moon	Date	Moon	Date	Moon	Date	Moon
01/02/1908	21Sag01	05/01/1908	21Tau19	09/02/1908	23Sco06	01/02/1909	22Tau51
01/04/1908	21Cap10	05/03/1908	17Gem17	09/04/1908	19Sag22	01/04/1909	19Gem06
01/06/1908	21Aqu19	05/05/1908	12Can00	09/06/1908	17Cap13	01/06/1909	14Can30
01/08/1908	20Pis26	05/07/1908	05Leo54	09/08/1908	16Aqu42	01/08/1909	09Leo10
01/10/1908	17Ari54	05/09/1908	29Leo37	09/10/1908	17Pis07	01/10/1909	03Vir13
01/12/1908	13Tau49	05/11/1908	23Vir48	09/12/1908	17Ari10	01/12/1909	26Vir58
01/14/1908	08Gem34	05/13/1908	19Lib00	09/14/1908	15Tau42	01/14/1909	20Lib52
01/16/1908	02Can36	05/15/1908	15Sco29	09/16/1908	12Gem15	01/16/1909	15Sco31
01/18/1908	26Can18	05/17/1908	13Sag06	09/18/1908	07Can10	01/18/1909	11Sag34
01/20/1908	19Leo55	05/19/1908	11Cap25	09/20/1908	01Leo08	01/20/1909	09Cap22
01/22/1908	13Vir47	05/21/1908	09Aqu57	09/22/1908	24Leo47	01/22/1909	08Aqu40
01/24/1908	08Lib13	05/23/1908	08Pis21	09/24/1908	18Vir34	01/24/1909	08Pis39
01/26/1908	03Sco37	05/25/1908	06Ari19	09/26/1908	12Lib46	01/26/1909	08Ari06
01/28/1908	00Sag29	05/27/1908	03Tau40	09/28/1908	07Sco33	01/28/1909	06Tau18
01/30/1908	29Sag03	05/29/1908	00Gem06	09/30/1908	02Sag59	01/30/1909	03Gem04
		05/31/1908	25Gem31				
02/01/1908	29Cap03			10/02/1908	29Sag20	02/01/1909	28Gem39
02/03/1908	29Aqu30	06/02/1908	20Can00	10/04/1908	26Cap54	02/03/1909	23Can28
02/05/1908	29Pis06	06/04/1908	13Leo51	10/06/1908	25Aqu48	02/05/1909	17Leo44
02/07/1908	26Ari59	06/06/1908	07Vir35	10/08/1908	25Pis37	02/07/1909	11Vir38
02/09/1908	23Tau01	06/08/1908	01Lib46	10/10/1908	25Ari18	02/09/1909	05Lib22
02/11/1908	17Gem37	06/10/1908	27Lib01	10/12/1908	23Tau46	02/11/1909	29Lib16
02/13/1908	11Can27	06/12/1908	23Sco44	10/14/1908	20Gem28	02/13/1909	23Sco47
02/15/1908	05Leo01	06/14/1908	21Sag54	10/16/1908	15Can30	02/15/1909	19Sag35
02/17/1908	28Leo46	06/16/1908	21Cap03	10/18/1908	09Leo30	02/17/1909	17Cap13
02/19/1908	22Vir57	06/18/1908	20Aqu23	10/20/1908	03Vir12	02/19/1909	16Aqu43
02/21/1908	17Lib45	06/20/1908	19Pis10	10/22/1908	27Vir07	02/21/1909	17Pis14
02/23/1908	13Sco19	06/22/1908	16Ari58	10/24/1908	21Lib40	02/23/1909	17Ari23
02/25/1908	09Sag59	06/24/1908	13Tau42	10/26/1908	16Sco58	02/25/1909	16Tau04
02/27/1908	08Cap01	06/26/1908	09Gem24	10/28/1908	13Sag02	02/27/1909	12Gem54
02/29/1908	07Aqu25	06/28/1908	04Can14	10/30/1908	09Cap51		
		06/30/1908	28Can23			03/01/1909	08Can14
03/02/1908	07Pis30			11/01/1908	07Aqu27	03/03/1909	02Leo40
03/04/1908	07Ari06	07/02/1908	22Leo07	11/03/1908	05Pis54	03/05/1909	26Leo38
03/06/1908	05Tau13	07/04/1908	15Vir51	11/05/1908	04Ari52	03/07/1909	20Vir25
03/08/1908	01Gem28	07/06/1908	10Lib00	11/07/1908	03Tau44	03/09/1909	14Lib12
03/10/1908	26Gem09	07/08/1908	05Sco09	11/09/1908	01Gem42	03/11/1909	08Sco13
03/12/1908	19Can57	07/10/1908	01Sag49	11/11/1908	28Gem14	03/13/1909	02Sag48
03/14/1908	13Leo33	07/12/1908	00Cap12	11/13/1908	23Can21	03/15/1909	28Sag27
03/16/1908	07Vir28	07/14/1908	29Cap55	11/15/1908	17Leo27	03/17/1909	25Cap45
03/18/1908	02Lib03	07/16/1908	00Pis00	11/17/1908	11Vir11	03/19/1909	24Aqu55
03/20/1908	27Lib24	07/18/1908	29Pis22	11/19/1908	05Lib11	03/21/1909	25Pis22
03/22/1908	23Sco30	07/20/1908	27Ari18	11/21/1908	29Lib58	03/23/1909	25Ari45
03/24/1908	20Sag22	07/22/1908	23Tau43	11/23/1908	25Sco48	03/25/1909	24Tau49
03/26/1908	18Cap09	07/24/1908	18Gem54	11/25/1908	22Sag39	03/27/1909	21Gem56
03/28/1908	16Aqu52	07/26/1908	13Can16	11/27/1908	20Cap17	03/29/1909	17Can21
03/30/1908	16Pis11	07/28/1908	07Leo07	11/29/1908	18Aqu25	03/31/1909	11Leo41
		07/30/1908	00Vir46				
04/01/1908	15Ari13	08/01/1908	24Vir32	12/01/1908	16Pis46	04/02/1909	05Vir31
04/03/1908	13Tau07	08/03/1908	18Lib43	12/03/1908	15Ari02	04/04/1909	29Vir15
04/05/1908	09Gem24	08/05/1908	13Sco48	12/05/1908	12Tau55	04/06/1909	23Lib11
04/07/1908	04Can10	08/07/1908	10Sag14	12/07/1908	10Gem02	04/08/1909	17Sco30
04/09/1908	28Can03	08/09/1908	08Cap27	12/09/1908	06Can07	04/10/1909	12Sag24
04/11/1908	21Leo42	08/11/1908	08Aqu16	12/11/1908	01Leo06	04/12/1909	08Cap12
04/13/1908	15Vir48	08/13/1908	08Pis48	12/13/1908	25Leo14	04/14/1909	05Aqu19
04/15/1908	10Lib45	08/15/1908	08Ari40	12/15/1908	18Vir59	04/16/1909	04Pis01
04/17/1908	06Sco43	08/17/1908	06Tau56	12/17/1908	12Lib57	04/18/1909	03Ari52
04/19/1908	03Sag34	08/19/1908	03Gem19	12/19/1908	07Sco46	04/20/1909	03Tau54
04/21/1908	01Cap03	08/21/1908	28Gem15	12/21/1908	03Sag52	04/22/1909	02Gem55
04/23/1908	29Cap01	08/23/1908	22Can19	12/23/1908	01Cap24	04/24/1909	00Can13
04/25/1908	27Aqu22	08/25/1908	16Leo01	12/25/1908	29Cap59	04/26/1909	25Can50
04/27/1908	25Pis53	08/27/1908	09Vir42	12/27/1908	29Aqu01	04/28/1909	20Leo15
04/29/1908	24Ari03	08/29/1908	03Lib36	12/29/1908	27Pis46	04/30/1909	14Vir04
		08/31/1908	27Lib59	12/31/1908	25Ari45		

Ephemeris Tables for the Moon

Date	Moon	Date	Moon	Date	Moon	Date	Moon
05/02/1909	07Lib51	09/01/1909	26Pis37	01/01/1910	17Vir38	05/01/1910	27Cap26
05/04/1909	01Sco59	09/03/1909	26Ari39	01/03/1910	11Lib37	05/03/1910	23Aqu47
05/06/1909	26Sco43	09/05/1909	25Tau25	01/05/1910	05Sco17	05/05/1910	21Pis52
05/08/1909	22Sag10	09/07/1909	22Gem35	01/07/1910	29Sco19	05/07/1910	21Ari28
05/10/1909	18Cap30	09/09/1909	18Can24	01/09/1910	24Sag18	05/09/1910	21Tau47
05/12/1909	15Aqu48	09/11/1909	13Leo18	01/11/1910	20Cap30	05/11/1910	21Gem38
05/14/1909	14Pis09	09/13/1909	07Vir36	01/13/1910	17Aqu51	05/13/1910	20Can03
05/16/1909	13Ari16	09/15/1909	01Lib29	01/15/1910	15Pis59	05/15/1910	16Leo44
05/18/1909	12Tau30	09/17/1909	25Lib09	01/17/1910	14Ari19	05/17/1910	11Vir55
05/20/1909	11Gem00	09/19/1909	18Sco53	01/19/1910	12Tau31	05/19/1910	06Lib06
05/22/1909	08Can10	09/21/1909	13Sag08	01/21/1910	10Gem26	05/21/1910	29Lib48
05/24/1909	03Leo51	09/23/1909	08Cap30	01/23/1910	07Can55	05/23/1910	23Sco25
05/26/1909	28Leo22	09/25/1909	05Aqu36	01/25/1910	04Leo45	05/25/1910	17Sag20
05/28/1909	22Vir15	09/27/1909	04Pis38	01/27/1910	00Vir37	05/27/1910	11Cap51
05/30/1909	16Lib06	09/29/1909	05Ari01	01/29/1910	25Vir25	05/29/1910	07Aqu12
				01/31/1910	19Lib24	05/31/1910	03Pis39
06/01/1909	10Sco25	10/01/1909	05Tau28				
06/03/1909	05Sag34	10/03/1909	04Gem43	02/02/1910	13Sco03	06/02/1910	01Ari23
06/05/1909	01Cap42	10/05/1909	02Can09	02/04/1910	07Sag03	06/04/1910	00Tau25
06/07/1909	28Cap48	10/07/1909	27Can56	02/06/1910	02Cap07	06/06/1910	00Gem12
06/09/1909	26Aqu39	10/09/1909	22Leo36	02/08/1910	28Cap44	06/08/1910	29Gem49
06/11/1909	25Pis02	10/11/1909	16Vir37	02/10/1910	26Aqu53	06/10/1910	28Can21
06/13/1909	23Ari34	10/13/1909	10Lib22	02/12/1910	25Pis57	06/12/1910	25Leo12
06/15/1909	21Tau54	10/15/1909	04Sco03	02/14/1910	25Ari01	06/14/1910	20Vir28
06/17/1909	19Gem35	10/17/1909	27Sco58	02/16/1910	23Tau25	06/16/1910	14Lib39
06/19/1909	16Can16	10/19/1909	22Sag24	02/18/1910	20Gem57	06/18/1910	08Sco18
06/21/1909	11Leo48	10/21/1909	17Cap47	02/20/1910	17Can42	06/20/1910	02Sag01
06/23/1909	06Vir18	10/23/1909	14Aqu38	02/22/1910	13Leo45	06/22/1910	26Sag16
06/25/1909	00Lib12	10/25/1909	13Pis15	02/24/1910	09Vir03	06/24/1910	21Cap18
06/27/1909	24Lib03	10/27/1909	13Ari13	02/26/1910	03Lib33	06/26/1910	17Aqu15
06/29/1909	18Sco28	10/29/1909	13Tau34	02/28/1910	27Lib25	06/28/1910	14Pis06
		10/31/1909	13Gem02			06/30/1910	11Ari47
07/01/1909	13Sag56			03/02/1910	21Sco01		
07/03/1909	10Cap43	11/02/1909	10Can49	03/04/1910	14Sag57	07/02/1910	10Tau17
07/05/1909	08Aqu42	11/04/1909	06Leo49	03/06/1910	09Cap57	07/04/1910	09Gem19
07/07/1909	07Pis22	11/06/1909	01Vir28	03/08/1910	06Aqu37	07/06/1910	08Can19
07/09/1909	06Ari06	11/08/1909	25Vir24	03/10/1910	05Pis09	07/08/1910	06Leo30
07/11/1909	04Tau22	11/10/1909	19Lib04	03/12/1910	04Ari54	07/10/1910	03Vir18
07/13/1909	01Gem59	11/12/1909	12Sco54	03/14/1910	04Tau47	07/12/1910	28Vir36
07/15/1909	28Gem50	11/14/1909	07Sag09	03/16/1910	03Gem46	07/14/1910	22Lib46
07/17/1909	24Can51	11/16/1909	02Cap01	03/18/1910	01Can24	07/16/1910	16Sco27
07/19/1909	20Leo00	11/18/1909	27Cap46	03/20/1910	27Can48	07/18/1910	10Sag18
07/21/1909	14Vir21	11/20/1909	24Aqu38	03/22/1910	23Leo16	07/20/1910	04Cap51
07/23/1909	08Lib12	11/22/1909	22Pis46	03/24/1910	18Vir00	07/22/1910	00Aqu28
07/25/1909	02Sco00	11/24/1909	22Ari00	03/26/1910	12Lib08	07/24/1910	27Aqu11
07/27/1909	26Sco22	11/26/1909	21Tau40	03/28/1910	05Sco51	07/26/1910	24Pis42
07/29/1909	21Sag57	11/28/1909	20Gem51	03/30/1910	29Sco28	07/28/1910	22Ari41
07/31/1909	19Cap10	11/30/1909	18Can43			07/30/1910	20Tau56
				04/01/1910	23Sag25		
08/02/1909	17Aqu54	12/02/1909	14Leo58	04/03/1910	18Cap18	08/01/1910	19Gem16
08/04/1909	17Pis27	12/04/1909	09Vir46	04/05/1910	14Aqu49	08/03/1910	17Can27
08/06/1909	16Ari47	12/06/1909	03Lib43	04/07/1910	13Pis15	08/05/1910	15Leo00
08/08/1909	15Tau10	12/08/1909	27Lib23	04/09/1910	13Ari11	08/07/1910	11Vir25
08/10/1909	12Gem22	12/10/1909	21Sco21	04/11/1910	13Tau33	08/09/1910	06Lib34
08/12/1909	08Can33	12/12/1909	16Sag00	04/13/1910	13Gem07	08/11/1910	00Sco42
08/14/1909	03Leo56	12/14/1909	11Cap23	04/15/1910	11Can10	08/13/1910	24Sco21
08/16/1909	28Leo38	12/16/1909	08Aqu01	04/17/1910	07Leo36	08/15/1910	18Sag15
08/18/1909	22Vir45	12/18/1909	05Pis19	04/19/1910	02Vir48	08/17/1910	13Cap01
08/20/1909	16Lib28	12/20/1909	03Ari18	04/21/1910	27Vir09	08/19/1910	09Aqu08
08/22/1909	10Sco13	12/22/1909	01Tau49	04/23/1910	21Lib00	08/21/1910	06Pis35
08/24/1909	04Sag30	12/24/1909	00Gem33	04/25/1910	14Sco36	08/23/1910	04Ari55
08/26/1909	00Cap00	12/26/1909	28Gem58	04/27/1910	08Sag19	08/25/1910	03Tau33
08/28/1909	27Cap17	12/28/1909	26Can30	04/29/1910	02Cap27	08/27/1910	01Gem55
08/30/1909	26Aqu24	12/30/1909	22Leo43			08/29/1910	29Gem51
						08/31/1910	27Can17

Ephemeris Tables for the Moon

Date	Moon	Date	Moon	Date	Moon	Date	Moon
09/02/1910	24Leo01	01/02/1911	01Aqu32	05/02/1911	00Can33	09/01/1911	16Sag51
09/04/1910	19Vir52	01/04/1911	26Aqu52	05/04/1911	29Can19	09/03/1911	10Cap36
09/06/1910	14Lib41	01/06/1911	23Pis01	05/06/1911	26Leo46	09/05/1911	04Aqu48
09/08/1910	08Sco40	01/08/1911	20Ari07	05/08/1911	22Vir54	09/07/1911	29Aqu51
09/10/1910	02Sag16	01/10/1911	18Tau21	05/10/1911	17Lib59	09/09/1911	25Pis51
09/12/1910	26Sag08	01/12/1911	17Gem37	05/12/1911	12Sco19	09/11/1911	22Ari42
09/14/1910	20Cap57	01/14/1911	17Can16	05/14/1911	06Sag10	09/13/1911	20Tau14
09/16/1910	17Aqu15	01/16/1911	16Leo18	05/16/1911	29Sag50	09/15/1911	18Gem18
09/18/1910	15Pis13	01/18/1911	13Vir50	05/18/1911	23Cap39	09/17/1911	16Can44
09/20/1910	14Ari20	01/20/1911	09Lib36	05/20/1911	18Aqu01	09/19/1911	15Leo15
09/22/1910	13Tau45	01/22/1911	03Sco57	05/22/1911	13Pis29	09/21/1911	13Vir18
09/24/1910	12Gem39	01/24/1911	27Sco36	05/24/1911	10Ari30	09/23/1911	10Lib22
09/26/1910	10Can34	01/26/1911	21Sag15	05/26/1911	09Tau17	09/25/1911	06Sco11
09/28/1910	07Leo30	01/28/1911	15Cap29	05/28/1911	09Gem21	09/27/1911	00Sag49
09/30/1910	03Vir33	01/30/1911	10Aqu36	05/30/1911	09Can39	09/29/1911	24Sag44
10/02/1910	28Vir44	02/01/1911	06Pis39	06/01/1911	08Leo58	10/01/1911	18Cap30
10/04/1910	23Lib07	02/03/1911	03Ari25	06/03/1911	06Vir36	10/03/1911	12Aqu45
10/06/1910	16Sco55	02/05/1911	00Tau48	06/05/1911	02Lib34	10/05/1911	08Pis02
10/08/1910	10Sag29	02/07/1911	28Tau47	06/07/1911	27Lib18	10/07/1911	04Ari32
10/10/1910	04Cap18	02/09/1911	27Gem19	06/09/1911	21Sco18	10/09/1911	02Tau12
10/12/1910	29Cap01	02/11/1911	26Can06	06/11/1911	14Sag59	10/11/1911	00Gem37
10/14/1910	25Aqu13	02/13/1911	24Leo25	06/13/1911	08Cap40	10/13/1911	29Gem16
10/16/1910	23Pis16	02/15/1911	21Vir37	06/15/1911	02Aqu38	10/15/1911	27Can42
10/18/1910	22Ari48	02/17/1911	17Lib19	06/17/1911	27Aqu10	10/17/1911	25Leo36
10/20/1910	22Tau55	02/19/1911	11Sco46	06/19/1911	20Ari32	10/19/1911	22Vir44
10/22/1910	22Gem31	02/21/1911	05Sag28	06/21/1911	19Ari22	10/21/1911	19Lib01
10/24/1910	20Can50	02/23/1911	29Sag11	06/23/1911	17Tau49	10/23/1911	14Sco19
10/26/1910	17Leo40	02/25/1911	23Cap35	06/25/1911	17Gem44	10/25/1911	08Sag48
10/28/1910	13Vir14	02/27/1911	19Aqu06	06/27/1911	18Can09	10/27/1911	02Cap39
10/30/1910	07Lib52			06/29/1911	17Leo48	10/29/1911	26Cap24
		03/01/1911	15Pis49			10/31/1911	20Aqu34
11/01/1910	01Sco53	03/03/1911	13Ari27	07/01/1911	15Vir42		
11/03/1910	25Sco31	03/05/1911	11Tau33	07/03/1911	11Lib43	11/02/1911	15Pis49
11/05/1910	19Sag06	03/07/1911	09Gem46	07/05/1911	06Sco19	11/04/1911	12Ari31
11/07/1910	12Cap59	03/09/1911	07Can58	07/07/1911	00Sag10	11/06/1911	10Tau48
11/09/1910	07Aqu40	03/11/1911	05Leo55	07/09/1911	23Sag49	11/08/1911	10Gem08
11/11/1910	03Pis39	03/13/1911	03Vir20	07/11/1911	17Cap37	11/10/1911	09Can40
11/13/1910	01Ari21	03/15/1911	29Vir49	07/13/1911	11Aqu53	11/12/1911	08Leo30
11/15/1910	00Tau44	03/17/1911	25Lib12	07/15/1911	06Pis46	11/14/1911	06Vir11
11/17/1910	01Gem07	03/19/1911	19Sco33	07/17/1911	02Ari24	11/16/1911	02Lib40
11/19/1910	01Can17	03/21/1911	13Sag17	07/19/1911	29Ari06	11/18/1911	28Lib11
11/21/1910	00Leo09	03/23/1911	07Cap01	07/21/1911	27Tau10	11/20/1911	22Sco57
11/23/1910	27Leo14	03/25/1911	01Aqu27	07/23/1911	26Gem35	11/22/1911	17Sag07
11/25/1910	22Vir40	03/27/1911	27Aqu06	07/25/1911	26Can37	11/24/1911	10Cap54
11/27/1910	17Lib00	03/29/1911	24Pis16	07/27/1911	26Leo08	11/26/1911	04Aqu37
11/29/1910	10Sco44	03/31/1911	22Ari39	07/29/1911	24Vir07	11/28/1911	28Aqu43
				07/31/1911	20Lib14	11/30/1911	23P:is45
12/01/1910	04Sag18	04/02/1911	21Tau39				
12/03/1910	28Sag01	04/04/1911	20Gem33	08/02/1911	14Sco52	12/02/1911	20Ari18
12/05/1910	22Cap10	04/06/1911	18Can52	08/04/1911	08Sag42	12/04/1911	18Tau42
12/07/1910	17Aqu02	04/08/1911	16Leo22	08/06/1911	02Cap24	12/06/1911	18Gem37
12/09/1910	12Pis55	04/10/1911	12Vir59	08/08/1911	26Cap25	12/08/1911	18Can58
12/11/1910	10Ari12	04/12/1911	08Lib42	08/10/1911	21Aqu04	12/10/1911	18Leo29
12/13/1910	09Tau01	04/14/1911	03Sco31	08/12/1911	16Pis28	12/12/1911	16Vir23
12/15/1910	09Gem03	04/16/1911	27Sco38	08/14/1911	12Ari35	12/14/1911	12Lib37
12/17/1910	09Can15	04/18/1911	21Sag21	08/16/1911	09Tau31	12/16/1911	07Sco38
12/19/1910	08Leo28	04/20/1911	15Cap06	08/18/1911	07Gem25	12/18/1911	01Sag56
12/21/1910	05Vir54	04/22/1911	09Aqu29	08/20/1911	06Can15	12/20/1911	25Sag50
12/23/1910	01Lib29	04/24/1911	05Pis04	08/22/1911	05Leo34	12/22/1911	19Cap34
12/25/1910	25Lib45	04/26/1911	02Ari18	08/24/1911	04Vir30	12/24/1911	13Aqu21
12/27/1910	19Sco22	04/28/1911	01Tau06	08/26/1911	02Lib11	12/26/1911	07Pis27
12/29/1910	12Sag58	04/30/1911	00Gem51	08/28/1911	28Lib17	12/28/1911	02Ari19
12/31/1910	06Cap56			08/30/1911	22Sco58	12/30/1911	28Ari33

Ephemeris Tables for the Moon

Date	Moon	Date	Moon	Date	Moon	Date	Moon
01/01/1912	26Tau40	05/02/1912	24Sco27	09/01/1912	01Tau24	01/01/1913	01Sco12
01/03/1912	26Gem34	05/04/1912	19Sag28	09/03/1912	27Tau21	01/03/1913	27Sco18
01/05/1912	27Can15	05/06/1912	13Cap42	09/05/1912	24Gem39	01/05/1913	22Sag39
01/07/1912	27Leo19	05/08/1912	07Aqu31	09/07/1912	23Can25	01/07/1913	17Cap19
01/09/1912	25Vir39	05/10/1912	01Pis27	09/09/1912	23Leo12	01/09/1913	11Aqu24
01/11/1912	22Lib02	05/12/1912	26Pis07	09/11/1912	23Vir04	01/11/1913	05Pis06
01/13/1912	16Sco55	05/14/1912	22Ari05	09/13/1912	21Lib57	01/13/1913	28Pis42
01/15/1912	10Sag58	05/16/1912	19Tau36	09/15/1912	19Sco10	01/15/1913	22Ari51
01/17/1912	04Cap42	05/18/1912	18Gem22	09/17/1912	14Sag46	01/17/1913	18Tau15
01/19/1912	28Cap27	05/20/1912	17Can40	09/19/1912	09Cap11	01/19/1913	15Gem30
01/21/1912	22Aqu24	05/22/1912	16Leo37	09/21/1912	03Aqu01	01/21/1913	14Can39
01/23/1912	16Pis45	05/24/1912	14Vir41	09/23/1912	26Aqu47	01/23/1913	14Leo57
01/25/1912	11Ari43	05/26/1912	11Lib43	09/25/1912	20Pis55	01/25/1913	15Vir05
01/27/1912	07Tau49	05/28/1912	07Sco51	09/27/1912	15Ari40	01/27/1913	14Lib00
01/29/1912	05Gem30	05/30/1912	03Sag12	09/29/1912	11Tau14	01/29/1913	11Sco16
01/31/1912	04Can52					01/31/1913	07Sag09
		06/01/1912	27Sag50	10/01/1912	07Gem42		
02/02/1912	05Leo15	06/03/1912	21Cap54	10/03/1912	05Can07	02/02/1913	02Cap03
02/04/1912	05Vir20	06/05/1912	15Aqu40	10/05/1912	03Leo28	02/04/1913	26Cap18
02/06/1912	03Lib57	06/07/1912	09Pis34	10/07/1912	02Vir28	02/06/1913	20Aqu07
02/08/1912	00Sco36	06/09/1912	04Ari09	10/09/1912	01Lib33	02/08/1913	13Pis45
02/10/1912	25Sco38	06/11/1912	00Tau07	10/11/1912	29Lib57	02/10/1913	07Ari26
02/12/1912	19Sag41	06/13/1912	27Tau52	10/13/1912	27Sco06	02/12/1913	01Tau38
02/14/1912	13Cap22	06/15/1912	27Gem15	10/15/1912	22Sag47	02/14/1913	26Tau54
02/16/1912	07Aqu12	06/17/1912	27Can19	10/17/1912	17Cap16	02/16/1913	23Gem51
02/18/1912	01Pis25	06/19/1912	26Leo53	10/19/1912	11Aqu06	02/18/1913	22Can42
02/20/1912	26Pis11	06/21/1912	25Vir08	10/21/1912	04Pis54	02/20/1913	22Leo55
02/22/1912	21Ari39	06/23/1912	21Lib54	10/23/1912	29Pis14	02/22/1913	23Vir22
02/24/1912	17Tau58	06/25/1912	17Sco32	10/25/1912	24Ari28	02/24/1913	22Lib48
02/26/1912	15Gem28	06/27/1912	12Sag22	10/27/1912	20Tau46	02/26/1913	20Sco31
02/28/1912	14Can14	06/29/1912	06Cap38	10/29/1912	18Gem04	02/28/1913	16Sag31
				10/31/1912	16Can01		
03/01/1912	13Leo49	07/01/1912	00Aqu30			03/02/1913	11Cap16
03/03/1912	13Vir19	07/03/1912	24Aqu13	11/02/1912	14Leo18	03/04/1913	05Aqu17
03/05/1912	11Lib44	07/05/1912	18Pis07	11/04/1912	12Vir38	03/06/1913	28Aqu57
03/07/1912	08Sco31	07/07/1912	12Ari39	11/06/1912	10Lib46	03/08/1913	22Pis36
03/09/1912	03Sag45	07/09/1912	08Tau30	11/08/1912	08Sco22	03/10/1913	16Ari31
03/11/1912	27Sag55	07/11/1912	06Gem11	11/10/1912	05Sag04	03/12/1913	11Tau01
03/13/1912	21Cap39	07/13/1912	05Can42	11/12/1912	00Cap37	03/14/1913	06Gem27
03/15/1912	15Aqu33	07/15/1912	06Leo11	11/14/1912	25Cap07	03/16/1913	03Can13
03/17/1912	10Pis03	07/17/1912	06Vir16	11/16/1912	18Aqu56	03/18/1913	01Leo32
03/19/1912	05Ari21	07/19/1912	04Lib52	11/18/1912	12Pis42	03/20/1913	01Vir11
03/21/1912	01Tau31	07/21/1912	01Sco42	11/20/1912	07Ari03	03/22/1913	01Lib20
03/23/1912	28Tau30	07/23/1912	27Sco06	11/22/1912	02Tau36	03/24/1913	00Sco51
03/25/1912	26Gem16	07/25/1912	21Sag37	11/24/1912	29Tau36	03/26/1913	28Sco52
03/27/1912	24Can41	07/27/1912	15Cap37	11/26/1912	27Gem49	03/28/1913	25Sag10
03/29/1912	23Leo27	07/29/1912	09Aqu22	11/28/1912	26Can39	03/30/1913	20Cap00
03/31/1912	22Vir00	07/31/1912	03Pis07	11/30/1912	25Leo19		
						04/01/1913	13Aqu56
04/02/1912	19Lib45	08/02/1912	27Pis08	12/02/1912	23Vir24	04/03/1913	07Pis34
04/04/1912	16Sco17	08/04/1912	21Ari46	12/04/1912	20Lib48	04/05/1913	01Ari19
04/06/1912	11Sag32	08/06/1912	17Tau33	12/06/1912	17Sco31	04/07/1913	25Ari36
04/08/1912	05Cap48	08/08/1912	15Gem00	12/08/1912	13Sag33	04/09/1913	20Tau39
04/10/1912	29Cap36	08/10/1912	14Can15	12/10/1912	08Cap43	04/11/1913	16Gem34
04/12/1912	23Aqu33	08/12/1912	14Leo37	12/12/1912	03Aqu04	04/13/1913	13Can30
04/14/1912	18Pis13	08/14/1912	14Vir51	12/14/1912	26Aqu49	04/15/1913	11Leo29
04/16/1912	13Ari57	08/16/1912	13Lib45	12/16/1912	20Pis30	04/17/1913	10Vir24
04/18/1912	10Tau52	08/18/1912	10Sco49	12/18/1912	14Ari45	04/19/1913	09Lib47
04/20/1912	08Gem46	08/20/1912	06Sag15	12/20/1912	10Tau19	04/21/1913	08Sco51
04/22/1912	07Can12	08/22/1912	00Cap38	12/22/1912	07Gem40	04/23/1913	06Sag49
04/24/1912	05Leo42	08/24/1912	24Cap30	12/24/1912	06Can37	04/25/1913	03Cap14
04/26/1912	03Vir55	08/26/1912	18Aqu14	12/26/1912	06Leo21	04/27/1913	28Cap11
04/28/1912	01Lib34	08/28/1912	12Pis08	12/28/1912	05Vir46	04/29/1913	22Aqu09
04/30/1912	28Lib28	08/30/1912	06Ari26	12/30/1912	04Lib06		

Ephemeris Tables for the Moon

Date	Moon	Date	Moon	Date	Moon	Date	Moon
05/01/1913	15Pis48	09/02/1913	02Lib39	01/02/1914	19Pis10	05/02/1914	01Leo42
05/03/1913	09Ari43	09/04/1913	02Sco13	01/04/1914	12Ari47	05/04/1914	28Leo48
05/05/1913	04Tau24	09/06/1913	00Sag17	01/06/1914	06Tau39	05/06/1914	27Vir25
05/07/1913	00Gem05	09/08/1913	26Sag44	01/08/1914	01Gem27	05/08/1914	27Lib17
05/09/1913	26Gem46	09/10/1913	21Cap52	01/10/1914	27Gem38	05/10/1914	27Sco28
05/11/1913	24Can14	09/12/1913	16Aqu07	01/12/1914	25Can10	05/12/1914	26Sag43
05/13/1913	22Leo15	09/14/1913	09Pis52	01/14/1914	23Leo37	05/14/1914	24Cap13
05/15/1913	20Vir39	09/16/1913	03Ari27	01/16/1914	22Vir19	05/16/1914	19Aqu53
05/17/1913	19Lib12	09/18/1913	27Ari12	01/18/1914	20Lib46	05/18/1914	14Pis14
05/19/1913	17Sco28	09/20/1913	21Tau27	01/20/1914	18Sco42	05/20/1914	07Ari55
05/21/1913	14Sag57	09/22/1913	16Gem34	01/22/1914	16Sag02	05/22/1914	01Tau33
05/23/1913	11Cap10	09/24/1913	12Can59	01/24/1914	12Cap38	05/24/1914	25Tau36
05/25/1913	06Aqu06	09/26/1913	11Leo01	01/26/1914	08Aqu20	05/26/1914	20Gem17
05/27/1913	00Pis06	09/28/1913	10Vir34	01/28/1914	03Pis05	05/28/1914	15Can42
05/29/1913	23Pis46	09/30/1913	10Lib52	01/30/1914	27Pis04	05/30/1914	11Leo55
05/31/1913	17Ari47						
		10/02/1913	10Sco45	02/01/1914	20Ari40	06/01/1914	09Vir02
06/02/1913	12Tau46	10/04/1913	09Sag13	02/03/1914	14Tau30	06/03/1914	07Lib15
06/04/1913	09Gem04	10/06/1913	05Cap52	02/05/1914	09Gem13	06/05/1914	06Sco28
06/06/1913	06Can34	10/08/1913	00Aqu56	02/07/1914	05Can25	06/07/1914	06Sag01
06/08/1913	04Leo49	10/10/1913	24Aqu59	02/09/1914	03Leo18	06/09/1914	04Cap54
06/10/1913	03Vir15	10/12/1913	18Pis37	02/11/1914	02Vir28	06/11/1914	02Aqu19
06/12/1913	01Lib30	10/14/1913	12Ari16	02/13/1914	02Lib04	06/13/1914	28Aqu03
06/14/1913	29Lib25	10/16/1913	06Tau17	02/15/1914	01Sco14	06/15/1914	22Pis27
06/16/1913	26Sco53	10/18/1913	00Gem55	02/17/1914	29Sco23	06/17/1914	16Ari10
06/18/1913	23Sag38	10/20/1913	26Gem21	02/19/1914	26Sag21	06/19/1914	09Tau56
06/20/1913	19Cap24	10/22/1913	22Can46	02/21/1914	22Cap15	06/21/1914	04Gem14
06/22/1913	14Aqu06	10/24/1913	20Leo25	02/23/1914	17Aqu16	06/23/1914	29Gem23
06/24/1913	08Pis02	10/26/1913	19Vir19	02/25/1914	11Pis33	06/25/1914	25Can27
06/26/1913	01Ari40	10/28/1913	19Lib05	02/27/1914	05Ari20	06/27/1914	22Leo17
06/28/1913	25Ari43	10/30/1913	18Sco47			06/29/1914	19Vir47
06/30/1913	20Tau52			03/01/1914	28Ari57		
07/02/1913	17Gem33	11/01/1913	17Sag23	03/03/1914	22Tau48	07/01/1914	17Lib55
07/04/1913	15Can43	11/03/1913	14Cap15	03/05/1914	17Gem25	07/03/1914	16Sco34
07/06/1913	14Leo48	11/05/1913	09Aqu24	03/07/1914	13Can24	07/05/1914	15Sag17
07/08/1913	13Vir54	11/07/1913	03Pis26	03/09/1914	11Leo09	07/07/1914	13Cap26
07/10/1913	12Lib22	11/09/1913	27Pis01	03/11/1914	10Vir33	07/09/1914	10Aqu24
07/12/1913	10Sco01	11/11/1913	20Ari47	03/13/1914	10Lib46	07/11/1914	05Pis58
07/14/1913	06Sag51	11/13/1913	15Tau10	03/15/1914	10Sco43	07/13/1914	00Ari22
07/16/1913	02Cap52	11/15/1913	10Gem23	03/17/1914	09Sag22	07/15/1914	24Ari09
07/18/1913	28Cap03	11/17/1913	06Can26	03/19/1914	06Cap23	07/17/1914	18Tau00
07/20/1913	22Aqu24	11/19/1913	03Leo13	03/21/1914	01Aqu57	07/19/1914	12Gem28
07/22/1913	16Pis11	11/21/1913	00Vir46	03/23/1914	26Aqu28	07/21/1914	08Can00
07/24/1913	09Ari47	11/23/1913	29Vir06	03/25/1914	20Pis24	07/23/1914	04Leo42
07/26/1913	03Tau49	11/25/1913	28Lib02	03/27/1914	14Ari01	07/25/1914	02Vir19
07/28/1913	28Tau57	11/27/1913	27Sco03	03/29/1914	07Tau40	07/27/1914	00Lib32
07/30/1913	25Gem43	11/29/1913	25Sag18	03/31/1914	01Gem39	07/29/1914	28Lib58
						07/31/1914	27Sco18
08/01/1913	24Can15	12/01/1913	22Cap06	04/02/1914	26Gem19		
08/03/1913	23Leo55	12/03/1913	17Aqu21	04/04/1914	22Can06	08/02/1914	25Sag16
08/05/1913	23Vir45	12/05/1913	11Pis25	04/06/1914	19Leo30	08/04/1914	22Cap32
08/07/1913	22Lib44	12/07/1913	05Ari01	04/08/1914	18Vir37	08/06/1914	18Aqu48
08/09/1913	20Sco27	12/09/1913	28Ari52	04/10/1914	18Lib55	08/08/1914	14Pis01
08/11/1913	16Sag57	12/11/1913	23Tau34	04/12/1914	19Sco15	08/10/1914	08Ari18
08/13/1913	12Cap24	12/13/1913	19Gem22	04/14/1914	18Sag24	08/12/1914	02Tau05
08/15/1913	07Aqu03	12/15/1913	16Can12	04/16/1914	15Cap41	08/14/1914	25Tau56
08/17/1913	01Pis03	12/17/1913	13Leo45	04/18/1914	11Aqu13	08/16/1914	20Gem27
08/19/1913	24Pis42	12/19/1913	11Vir40	04/20/1914	05Pis34	08/18/1914	16Can08
08/21/1913	18Ari18	12/21/1913	09Lib47	04/22/1914	29Pis17	08/20/1914	13Leo16
08/23/1913	12Tau22	12/23/1913	08Sco01	04/24/1914	22Ari51	08/22/1914	11Vir39
08/25/1913	07Gem25	12/25/1913	06Sag07	04/26/1914	16Tau39	08/24/1914	10Lib45
08/27/1913	04Can03	12/27/1913	03Cap36	04/28/1914	10Gem56	08/26/1914	09Sco48
08/29/1913	02Leo28	12/29/1913	29Cap59	04/30/1914	05Can51	08/28/1914	08Sag12
08/31/1913	02Vir21	12/31/1913	25Aqu05			08/30/1914	05Cap40

Ephemeris Tables for the Moon

Date	Moon	Date	Moon	Date	Moon	Date	Moon
09/01/1914	02Aqu08	01/01/1915	09Can50	05/01/1915	07Sag11	09/02/1915	18Gem30
09/03/1914	27Aqu41	01/03/1915	05Leo15	05/03/1915	06Cap51	09/04/1915	12Can25
09/05/1914	22Pis25	01/05/1915	01Vir24	05/05/1915	04Aqu53	09/06/1915	07Leo06
09/07/1914	16Ari29	01/07/1915	28Vir21	05/07/1915	01Pis14	09/08/1915	02Vir55
09/09/1914	10Tau14	01/09/1915	26Lib12	05/09/1915	26Pis20	09/10/1915	00Lib00
09/11/1914	04Gem03	01/11/1915	24Sco54	05/11/1915	20Ari40	09/12/1915	28Lib04
09/13/1914	28Gem28	01/13/1915	24Sag01	05/13/1915	14Tau35	09/14/1915	26Sco37
09/15/1914	24Can05	01/15/1915	22Cap47	05/15/1915	08Gem19	09/16/1915	25Sag06
09/17/1914	21Leo19	01/17/1915	20Aqu25	05/17/1915	02Can04	09/18/1915	23Cap10
09/19/1914	20Vir10	01/19/1915	16Pis34	05/19/1915	26Can10	09/20/1915	20Aqu40
09/21/1914	20Lib04	01/21/1915	11Ari22	05/21/1915	21Leo01	09/22/1915	17Pis29
09/23/1914	19Sco54	01/23/1915	05Tau19	05/23/1915	17Vir13	09/24/1915	13Ari27
09/25/1914	18Sag42	01/25/1915	29Tau04	05/25/1915	15Lib16	09/26/1915	08Tau27
09/27/1914	16Cap00	01/27/1915	23Gem15	05/27/1915	15Sco04	09/28/1915	02Gem38
09/29/1914	11Aqu57	01/29/1915	18Can15	05/29/1915	15Sag40	09/30/1915	26Gem22
		01/31/1915	14Leo16	05/31/1915	15Cap40		
10/01/1914	06Pis54					10/02/1915	20Can15
10/03/1914	01Ari11	02/02/1915	11Vir16	06/02/1915	14Aqu02	10/04/1915	14Leo57
10/05/1914	25Ari03	02/04/1915	08Lib59	06/04/1915	10Pis32	10/06/1915	11Vir01
10/07/1914	18Tau46	02/06/1915	07Sco11	06/06/1915	05Ari34	10/08/1915	08Lib45
10/09/1914	12Gem36	02/08/1915	05Sag34	06/08/1915	29Ari45	10/10/1915	07Sco43
10/11/1914	06Can58	02/10/1915	03Cap50	06/10/1915	23Tau31	10/12/1915	07Sag06
10/13/1914	02Leo22	02/12/1915	01Aqu37	06/12/1915	17Gem15	10/14/1915	05Cap59
10/15/1914	29Leo23	02/14/1915	28Aqu32	06/14/1915	11Can09	10/16/1915	03Aqu52
10/17/1914	28Vir15	02/16/1915	24Pis21	06/16/1915	05Leo31	10/18/1915	00Pis45
10/19/1914	28Lib29	02/18/1915	19Ari06	06/18/1915	00Vir35	10/20/1915	26Pis48
10/21/1914	28Sco55	02/20/1915	13Tau07	06/20/1915	26Vir49	10/22/1915	22Ari09
10/23/1914	28Sag16	02/22/1915	06Gem53	06/22/1915	24Lib35	10/24/1915	16Tau48
10/25/1914	25Cap48	02/24/1915	01Can01	06/24/1915	23Sco55	10/26/1915	10Gem49
10/27/1914	21Aqu34	02/26/1915	26Can07	06/26/1915	24Sag06	10/28/1915	04Can29
10/29/1914	16Pis10	02/28/1915	22Leo34	06/28/1915	23Cap58	10/30/1915	28Can16
10/31/1914	10Ari08			06/30/1915	22Aqu27		
		03/02/1915	20Vir21	07/02/1915	19Pis09	11/01/1915	22Leo51
11/02/1914	03Tau52	03/04/1915	19Lib04	07/04/1915	14Ari17	11/03/1915	18Vir53
11/04/1914	27Tau37	03/06/1915	18Sco01	07/06/1915	08Tau27	11/05/1915	16Lib49
11/06/1914	21Gem38	03/08/1915	16Sag34	07/08/1915	02Gem13	11/07/1915	16Sco23
11/08/1914	16Can06	03/10/1915	14Cap21	07/10/1915	26Gem01	11/09/1915	16Sag34
11/10/1914	11Leo25	03/12/1915	11Aqu16	07/12/1915	20Can12	11/11/1915	16Cap07
11/12/1914	08Vir07	03/14/1915	07Pis22	07/14/1915	14Leo58	11/13/1915	14Aqu15
11/14/1914	06Lib34	03/16/1915	02Ari38	07/16/1915	10Vir33	11/15/1915	10Pis55
11/16/1914	06Sco35	03/18/1915	27Ari09	07/18/1915	07Lib06	11/17/1915	06Ari27
11/18/1914	07Sag08	03/20/1915	21Tau07	07/20/1915	04Sco48	11/19/1915	01Tau16
11/20/1914	06Cap49	03/22/1915	14Gem51	07/22/1915	03Sag36	11/21/1915	25Tau31
11/22/1914	04Aqu40	03/24/1915	08Can54	07/24/1915	03Cap03	11/23/1915	19Gem21
11/24/1914	00Pis36	03/26/1915	03Leo54	07/26/1915	02Aqu18	11/25/1915	13Can00
11/26/1914	25Pis07	03/28/1915	00Vir26	07/28/1915	00Pis32	11/27/1915	06Leo48
11/28/1914	18Ari57	03/30/1915	28Vir42	07/30/1915	27Pis15	11/29/1915	01Vir16
11/30/1914	12Tau38						
		04/01/1915	28Lib15	08/01/1915	22Ari30	12/01/1915	27Vir06
12/02/1914	06Gem32	04/03/1915	28Sco05	08/03/1915	16Tau43	12/03/1915	24Lib51
12/04/1914	00Can51	04/05/1915	27Sag09	08/05/1915	10Gem31	12/05/1915	24Sco25
12/06/1914	25Can42	04/07/1915	24Cap54	08/07/1915	04Can25	12/07/1915	24Sag57
12/08/1914	21Leo15	04/09/1915	21Aqu20	08/09/1915	28Can54	12/09/1915	25Cap05
12/10/1914	17Vir50	04/11/1915	16Pis47	08/11/1915	24Leo13	12/11/1915	23Aqu44
12/12/1914	15Lib51	04/13/1915	11Ari30	08/13/1915	20Vir30	12/13/1915	20Pis36
12/14/1914	15Sco13	04/15/1915	05Tau41	08/15/1915	17Lib42	12/15/1915	16Ari00
12/16/1914	15Sag14	04/17/1915	29Tau31	08/17/1915	15Sco39	12/17/1915	10Tau28
12/18/1914	14Cap43	04/19/1915	23Gem14	08/19/1915	14Sag06	12/19/1915	04Gem25
12/20/1914	12Aqu42	04/21/1915	17Can15	08/21/1915	12Cap45	12/21/1915	28Gem08
12/22/1914	08Pis51	04/23/1915	12Leo06	08/23/1915	11Aqu08	12/23/1915	21Can51
12/24/1914	03Ari30	04/25/1915	08Vir29	08/25/1915	08Pis45	12/25/1915	15Leo50
12/26/1914	27Ari21	04/27/1915	06Lib48	08/27/1915	05Ari13	12/27/1915	10Vir27
12/28/1914	21Tau04	04/29/1915	06Sco43	08/29/1915	00Tau26	12/29/1915	06Lib11
12/30/1914	15Gem07			08/31/1915	24Tau42	12/31/1915	03Sco33

Ephemeris Tables for the Moon

Date	Moon	Date	Moon	Date	Moon	Date	Moon
01/02/1916	02Sag39	05/01/1916	02Tau13	09/02/1916	05Sco50	01/02/1917	05Tau54
01/04/1916	02Cap54	05/03/1916	27Tau19	09/04/1916	02Sag49	01/04/1917	01Gem12
01/06/1916	03Aqu07	05/05/1916	21Gem35	09/06/1916	00Cap45	01/06/1917	25Gem41
01/08/1916	02Pis09	05/07/1916	15Can18	09/08/1916	29Cap36	01/08/1917	19Can37
01/10/1916	29Pis24	05/09/1916	08Leo57	09/10/1916	28Aqu57	01/10/1917	13Leo15
01/12/1916	24Ari57	05/11/1916	03Vir12	09/12/1916	28Pis01	01/12/1917	06Vir55
01/14/1916	19Tau22	05/13/1916	28Vir45	09/14/1916	25Ari58	01/14/1917	00Lib58
01/16/1916	13Gem10	05/15/1916	26Lib03	09/16/1916	22Tau18	01/16/1917	25Lib57
01/18/1916	06Can50	05/17/1916	24Sco57	09/18/1916	17Gem07	01/18/1917	22Sco21
01/20/1916	00Leo43	05/19/1916	24Sag42	09/20/1916	10Can58	01/20/1917	20Sag33
01/22/1916	25Leo05	05/21/1916	24Cap12	09/22/1916	04Leo36	01/22/1917	20Cap18
01/24/1916	20Vir08	05/23/1916	22Aqu43	09/24/1916	28Leo36	01/24/1917	20Aqu45
01/26/1916	16Lib08	05/25/1916	20Pis01	09/26/1916	23Vir26	01/26/1917	20Pis37
01/28/1916	13Sco20	05/27/1916	16Ari13	09/28/1916	19Lib18	01/28/1917	18Ari57
01/30/1916	11Sag50	05/29/1916	11Tau34	09/30/1916	16Sco05	01/30/1917	15Tau30
		05/31/1916	06Gem08				
02/01/1916	11Cap19			10/02/1916	13Sag33	02/01/1917	10Gem35
02/03/1916	11Aqu00	06/02/1916	00Can06	10/04/1916	11Cap28	02/03/1917	04Can42
02/05/1916	09Pis57	06/04/1916	23Can43	10/06/1916	09Aqu47	02/05/1917	28Can24
02/07/1916	07Ari24	06/06/1916	17Leo22	10/08/1916	08Pis19	02/07/1917	22Leo00
02/09/1916	03Tau13	06/08/1916	11Vir36	10/10/1916	06Ari36	02/09/1917	15Vir51
02/11/1916	27Tau43	06/10/1916	07Lib03	10/12/1916	04Tau03	02/11/1917	10Lib10
02/13/1916	21Gem30	06/12/1916	04Sco16	10/14/1916	00Gem11	02/13/1917	05Sco15
02/15/1916	15Can11	06/14/1916	03Sag18	10/16/1916	24Gem59	02/15/1917	01Sag26
02/17/1916	09Leo17	06/16/1916	03Cap25	10/18/1916	18Can51	02/17/1917	29Sag09
02/19/1916	04Vir07	06/18/1916	03Aqu31	10/20/1916	12Leo29	02/19/1917	28Cap25
02/21/1916	29Vir52	06/20/1916	02Pis33	10/22/1916	06Vir35	02/21/1917	28Aqu42
02/23/1916	26Lib31	06/22/1916	00Ari02	10/24/1916	01Lib45	02/23/1917	28Pis46
02/25/1916	23Sco58	06/24/1916	26Ari04	10/26/1916	28Lib13	02/25/1917	27Ari30
02/27/1916	22Sag07	06/26/1916	21Tau00	10/28/1916	25Sco51	02/27/1917	24Tau19
02/29/1916	20Cap48	06/28/1916	15Gem11	10/30/1916	24Sag05		
		06/30/1916	08Can54			03/01/1917	19Gem27
03/02/1916	19Aqu36			11/01/1916	22Cap27	03/03/1917	13Can28
03/04/1916	17Pis56	07/02/1916	02Leo27	11/03/1916	20Aqu37	03/05/1917	07Leo04
03/06/1916	15Ari11	07/04/1916	26Leo12	11/05/1916	18Pis30	03/07/1917	00Vir45
03/08/1916	11Tau04	07/06/1916	20Vir33	11/07/1916	15Ari54	03/09/1917	24Vir52
03/10/1916	05Gem39	07/08/1916	16Lib00	11/09/1916	12Tau35	03/11/1917	19Lib39
03/12/1916	29Gem27	07/10/1916	13Sco00	11/11/1916	08Gem15	03/13/1917	15Sco08
03/14/1916	23Can09	07/12/1916	11Sag44	11/13/1916	02Can51	03/15/1917	11Sag27
03/16/1916	17Leo24	07/14/1916	11Cap46	11/15/1916	26Can41	03/17/1917	08Cap52
03/18/1916	12Vir40	07/16/1916	12Aqu05	11/17/1916	20Leo18	03/19/1917	07Aqu31
03/20/1916	09Lib10	07/18/1916	11Pis31	11/19/1916	14Vir22	03/21/1917	07Pis08
03/22/1916	06Sco42	07/20/1916	09Ari19	11/21/1916	09Lib36	03/23/1917	06Ari49
03/24/1916	04Sag49	07/22/1916	05Tau25	11/23/1916	06Sco23	03/25/1917	05Tau29
03/26/1916	03Cap05	07/24/1916	00Gem11	11/25/1916	04Sag40	03/27/1917	02Gem26
03/28/1916	01Aqu16	07/26/1916	24Gem09	11/27/1916	03Cap48	03/29/1917	27Gem42
03/30/1916	29Aqu13	07/28/1916	17Can45	11/29/1916	02Aqu57	03/31/1917	21Can46
		07/30/1916	11Leo22				
04/01/1916	26Pis42	08/01/1916	05Vir22	12/01/1916	01Pis29	04/02/1917	15Leo24
04/03/1916	23Ari22	08/03/1916	00Lib02	12/03/1916	29Pis06	04/04/1917	09Vir12
04/05/1916	18Tau58	08/05/1916	25Lib39	12/05/1916	25Ari49	04/06/1917	03Lib40
04/07/1916	13Gem29	08/07/1916	22Sco31	12/07/1916	21Tau43	04/08/1917	28Lib58
04/09/1916	07Can17	08/09/1916	20Sag48	12/09/1916	16Gem45	04/10/1917	25Sco06
04/11/1916	00Leo58	08/11/1916	20Cap19	12/11/1916	11Can01	04/12/1917	21Sag57
04/13/1916	25Leo15	08/13/1916	20Aqu21	12/13/1916	04Leo46	04/14/1917	19Cap29
04/15/1916	20Vir46	08/15/1916	19Pis51	12/15/1916	28Leo22	04/16/1917	17Aqu45
04/17/1916	17Lib49	08/17/1916	17Ari52	12/17/1916	22Vir23	04/18/1917	16Pis37
04/19/1916	16Sco12	08/19/1916	14Tau09	12/19/1916	17Lib28	04/20/1917	15Ari28
04/21/1916	15Sag11	08/21/1916	08Gem54	12/21/1916	14Sco12	04/22/1917	13Tau35
04/23/1916	13Cap58	08/23/1916	02Can46	12/23/1916	12Sag40	04/24/1917	10Gem19
04/25/1916	12Aqu08	08/25/1916	26Can22	12/25/1916	12Cap24	04/26/1917	05Can34
04/27/1916	09Pis34	08/27/1916	20Leo10	12/27/1916	12Aqu23	04/28/1917	29Can43
04/29/1916	06Ari16	08/29/1916	14Vir33	12/29/1916	11Pis36	04/30/1917	23Leo24
		08/31/1916	09Lib45	12/31/1916	09Ari27		

Ephemeris Tables for the Moon

Date	Moon	Date	Moon	Date	Moon	Date	Moon
05/02/1917	17Vir19	09/01/1917	08Pis10	01/01/1918	26Leo49	05/01/1918	09Cap57
05/04/1917	12Lib01	09/03/1917	08Ari31	01/03/1918	20Vir30	05/03/1918	06Aqu39
05/06/1917	07Sco49	09/05/1917	07Tau37	01/05/1918	14Lib26	05/05/1918	04Pis40
05/08/1917	04Sag40	09/07/1917	04Gem46	01/07/1918	08Sco49	05/07/1918	03Ari54
05/10/1917	02Cap19	09/09/1917	00Can10	01/09/1918	04Sag22	05/09/1918	03Tau39
05/12/1917	00Aqu23	09/11/1917	24Can25	01/11/1918	01Cap28	05/11/1918	02Gem55
05/14/1917	28Aqu42	09/13/1917	18Leo09	01/13/1918	00Aqu03	05/13/1918	00Can49
05/16/1917	27Pis01	09/15/1917	11Vir49	01/15/1918	29Aqu27	05/15/1918	27Can03
05/18/1917	25Ari00	09/17/1917	05Lib43	01/17/1918	28Pis45	05/17/1918	21Leo54
05/20/1917	22Tau17	09/19/1917	00Sco01	01/19/1918	27Ari12	05/19/1918	15Vir55
05/22/1917	18Gem28	09/21/1917	24Sco57	01/21/1918	24Tau30	05/21/1918	09Lib41
05/24/1917	13Can28	09/23/1917	20Sag46	01/23/1918	20Gem45	05/23/1918	03Sco42
05/26/1917	07Leo35	09/25/1917	17Cap54	01/25/1918	16Can09	05/25/1918	28Sco20
05/28/1917	01Vir18	09/27/1917	16Aqu35	01/27/1918	10Leo51	05/27/1918	23Sag46
05/30/1917	25Vir15	09/29/1917	16Pis33	01/29/1918	05Vir01	05/29/1918	20Cap06
				01/31/1918	28Vir48	05/31/1918	17Aqu17
06/01/1917	20Lib03	10/01/1917	16Ari45				
06/03/1917	16Sco09	10/03/1917	15Tau57	02/02/1918	22Lib34	06/02/1918	15Pis20
06/05/1917	13Sag36	10/05/1917	13Gem18	02/04/1918	16Sco49	06/04/1918	14Ari01
06/07/1917	12Cap05	10/07/1917	08Can48	02/06/1918	12Sag11	06/06/1918	12Tau55
06/09/1917	10Aqu58	10/09/1917	03Leo03	02/08/1918	09Cap14	06/08/1918	11Gem24
06/11/1917	09Pis41	10/11/1917	26Leo46	02/10/1918	08Aqu08	06/10/1918	08Can51
06/13/1917	07Ari48	10/13/1917	20Vir31	02/12/1918	08Pis15	06/12/1918	05Leo00
06/15/1917	05Tau09	10/15/1917	14Lib39	02/14/1918	08Ari22	06/14/1918	29Leo53
06/17/1917	01Gem36	10/17/1917	09Sco24	02/16/1918	07Tau22	06/16/1918	23Vir57
06/19/1917	27Gem06	10/19/1917	04Sag49	02/18/1918	04Gem43	06/18/1918	17Lib45
06/21/1917	21Can43	10/21/1917	00Cap59	02/20/1918	00Can35	06/20/1918	11Sco52
06/23/1917	15Leo40	10/23/1917	28Cap06	02/22/1918	25Can27	06/22/1918	06Sag48
06/25/1917	09Vir22	10/25/1917	26Aqu22	02/24/1918	19Leo44	06/24/1918	02Cap50
06/27/1917	03Lib19	10/27/1917	25Pis36	02/26/1918	13Vir39	06/26/1918	29Cap58
06/29/1917	28Lib04	10/29/1917	25Ari06	02/28/1918	07Lib24	06/28/1918	27Aqu57
		10/31/1917	23Tau54			06/30/1918	26Pis22
07/01/1917	24Sco12			03/02/1918	01Sco14		
07/03/1917	21Sag58	11/02/1917	21Gem12	03/04/1918	25Sco28	07/02/1918	24Ari49
07/05/1917	21Cap04	11/04/1917	16Can50	03/06/1918	20Sag39	07/04/1918	22Tau59
07/07/1917	20Aqu47	11/06/1917	11Leo12	03/08/1918	17Cap25	07/06/1918	20Gem34
07/09/1917	20Pis09	11/08/1917	04Vir57	03/10/1918	16Aqu09	07/08/1918	17Can20
07/11/1917	18Ari27	11/10/1917	28Vir46	03/12/1918	16Pis25	07/10/1918	13Leo06
07/13/1917	15Tau27	11/12/1917	23Lib09	03/14/1918	17Ari00	07/12/1918	07Vir51
07/15/1917	11Gem16	11/14/1917	18Sco21	03/16/1918	16Tau31	07/14/1918	01Lib54
07/17/1917	06Can09	11/16/1917	14Sag27	03/18/1918	14Gem11	07/16/1918	25Lib40
07/19/1917	00Leo21	11/18/1917	11Cap20	03/20/1918	10Can04	07/18/1918	19Sco48
07/21/1917	24Leo08	11/20/1917	08Aqu54	03/22/1918	04Leo43	07/20/1918	14Sag52
07/23/1917	17Vir48	11/22/1917	07Pis03	03/24/1918	28Leo45	07/22/1918	11Cap20
07/25/1917	11Lib45	11/24/1917	05Ari36	03/26/1918	22Vir31	07/24/1918	09Aqu15
07/27/1917	06Sco27	11/26/1917	04Tau10	03/28/1918	16Lib18	07/26/1918	08Pis08
07/29/1917	02Sag25	11/28/1917	02Gem09	03/30/1918	10Sco18	07/28/1918	07Ari13
07/31/1917	00Cap07	11/30/1917	29Gem00			07/30/1918	05Tau48
				04/01/1918	04Sag44		
08/02/1917	29Cap28	12/02/1917	24Can33	04/03/1918	29Sag59	08/01/1918	03Gem31
08/04/1917	29Aqu46	12/04/1917	19Leo00	04/05/1918	26Cap33	08/03/1918	00Can21
08/06/1917	29Pis47	12/06/1917	12Vir48	04/07/1918	24Aqu52	08/05/1918	26Can22
08/08/1917	28Ari28	12/08/1917	06Lib38	04/09/1918	24Pis45	08/07/1918	21Leo36
08/10/1917	25Tau27	12/10/1917	01Sco06	04/11/1918	25Ari10	08/09/1918	16Vir06
08/12/1917	20Gem54	12/12/1917	26Sco37	04/13/1918	24Tau49	08/11/1918	10Lib01
08/14/1917	15Can22	12/14/1917	23Sag22	04/15/1918	22Gem46	08/13/1918	03Sco44
08/16/1917	09Leo15	12/16/1917	21Cap10	04/17/1918	18Can52	08/15/1918	27Sco46
08/18/1917	02Vir55	12/18/1917	19Aqu34	04/19/1918	13Leo34	08/17/1918	22Sag49
08/20/1917	26Vir38	12/20/1917	18Pis06	04/21/1918	07Vir33	08/19/1918	19Cap26
08/22/1917	20Lib42	12/22/1917	16Ari22	04/23/1918	01Lib16	08/21/1918	17Aqu50
08/24/1917	15Sco24	12/24/1917	14Tau06	04/25/1918	25Lib09	08/23/1918	17Pis31
08/26/1917	11Sag12	12/26/1917	11Gem06	04/27/1918	19Sco27	08/25/1918	17Ari22
08/28/1917	08Cap36	12/28/1917	07Can15	04/29/1918	14Sag19	08/27/1918	16Tau24
08/30/1917	07Aqu46	12/30/1917	02Leo27			08/29/1918	14Gem01
						08/31/1918	10Can23

Ephemeris Tables for the Moon

Date	Moon	Date	Moon	Date	Moon	Date	Moon
09/02/1918	05Leo48	01/02/1919	12Cap51	05/02/1919	13Gem04	09/01/1919	26Sco04
09/04/1918	00Vir33	01/04/1919	09Aqu21	05/04/1919	11Can54	09/03/1919	19Sag47
09/06/1918	24Vir43	01/06/1919	06Pis44	05/06/1919	09Leo03	09/05/1919	14Cap10
09/08/1918	18Lib30	01/08/1919	04Ari40	05/08/1919	04Vir41	09/07/1919	09Aqu52
09/10/1918	12Sco09	01/10/1919	02Tau55	05/10/1919	29Vir14	09/09/1919	07Pis04
09/12/1918	06Sag08	01/12/1919	01Gem16	05/12/1919	23Lib07	09/11/1919	05Ari30
09/14/1918	01Cap03	01/14/1919	29Gem27	05/14/1919	16Sco45	09/13/1919	04Tau27
09/16/1918	27Cap33	01/16/1919	27Can01	05/16/1919	10Sag25	09/15/1919	03Gem12
09/18/1918	26Aqu01	01/18/1919	23Leo35	05/18/1919	04Cap29	09/17/1919	01Can21
09/20/1918	26Pis05	01/20/1919	18Vir55	05/20/1919	29Cap15	09/19/1919	28Can47
09/22/1918	26Ari33	01/22/1919	13Lib11	05/22/1919	25Aqu07	09/21/1919	25Leo29
09/24/1918	26Tau06	01/24/1919	06Sco54	05/24/1919	22Pis26	09/23/1919	21Vir22
09/26/1918	24Gem00	01/26/1919	00Sag42	05/26/1919	21Ari18	09/25/1919	16Lib19
09/28/1918	20Can15	01/28/1919	25Sag18	05/28/1919	21Tau15	09/27/1919	10Sco28
09/30/1918	15Leo20	01/30/1919	21Cap12	05/30/1919	21Gem18	09/29/1919	04Sag06
10/02/1918	09Vir41	02/01/1919	18Aqu30	06/01/1919	20Can24	10/01/1919	27Sag46
10/04/1918	03Lib36	02/03/1919	16Pis50	06/03/1919	17Leo49	10/03/1919	22Cap06
10/06/1918	27Lib17	02/05/1919	15Ari30	06/05/1919	13Vir34	10/05/1919	17Aqu47
10/08/1918	21Sco00	02/07/1919	13Tau55	06/07/1919	08Lib03	10/07/1919	15Pis13
10/10/1918	15Sag03	02/09/1919	11Gem49	06/09/1919	01Sco51	10/09/1919	14Ari10
10/12/1918	09Cap55	02/11/1919	09Can09	06/11/1919	25Sco27	10/11/1919	13Tau55
10/14/1918	06Aqu13	02/13/1919	05Leo53	06/13/1919	19Sag19	10/13/1919	13Gem25
10/16/1918	04Pis25	02/15/1919	01Vir50	06/15/1919	13Cap46	10/15/1919	11Can56
10/18/1918	04Ari16	02/17/1919	26Vir52	06/17/1919	09Aqu02	10/17/1919	09Leo12
10/20/1918	04Tau49	02/19/1919	21Lib04	06/19/1919	05Pis15	10/19/1919	05Vir22
10/22/1918	04Gem45	02/21/1919	14Sco45	06/21/1919	02Ari30	10/21/1919	00Lib35
10/24/1918	03Can04	02/23/1919	08Sag29	06/23/1919	00Tau54	10/23/1919	25Lib03
10/26/1918	29Can31	02/25/1919	03Cap03	06/25/1919	00Gem10	10/25/1919	18Sco54
10/28/1918	24Leo33	02/27/1919	29Cap06	06/27/1919	29Gem42	10/27/1919	12Sag28
10/30/1918	18Vir42			06/29/1919	28Can34	10/29/1919	06Cap09
		03/01/1919	26Aqu52			10/31/1919	00Aqu26
11/01/1918	12Lib27	03/03/1919	26Pis01	07/01/1919	26Leo04		
11/03/1918	06Sco09	03/05/1919	25Ari34	07/03/1919	21Vir54	11/02/1919	25Aqu57
11/05/1918	00Sag03	03/07/1919	24Tau34	07/05/1919	16Lib25	11/04/1919	23Pis11
11/07/1918	24Sag24	03/09/1919	22Gem31	07/07/1919	10Sco10	11/06/1919	22Ari10
11/09/1918	19Cap31	03/11/1919	19Can24	07/09/1919	03Sag52	11/08/1919	22Tau19
11/11/1918	15Aqu48	03/13/1919	15Leo27	07/11/1919	27Sag58	11/10/1919	22Gem31
11/13/1918	13Pis36	03/15/1919	10Vir45	07/13/1919	22Cap55	11/12/1919	21Can39
11/15/1918	12Ari49	03/17/1919	05Lib20	07/15/1919	18Aqu50	11/14/1919	19Leo12
11/17/1918	12Tau54	03/19/1919	29Lib18	07/17/1919	15Pis40	11/16/1919	15Vir09
11/19/1918	12Gem42	03/21/1919	22Sco55	07/19/1919	13Ari12	11/18/1919	09Lib56
11/21/1918	11Can12	03/23/1919	16Sag39	07/21/1919	11Tau21	11/20/1919	03Sco58
11/23/1918	07Leo59	03/25/1919	11Cap08	07/23/1919	09Gem57	11/22/1919	27Sco38
11/25/1918	03Vir10	03/27/1919	07Aqu04	07/25/1919	08Can42	11/24/1919	21Sag13
11/27/1918	27Vir18	03/29/1919	04Pis54	07/27/1919	06Leo59	11/26/1919	15Cap02
11/29/1918	21Lib00	03/31/1919	04Ari24	07/29/1919	04Vir10	11/28/1919	09Aqu25
				07/31/1919	29Vir55	11/30/1919	04Pis50
12/01/1918	14Sco45	04/02/1919	04Tau36				
12/03/1918	08Sag57	04/04/1919	04Gem18	08/02/1919	24Lib25	12/02/1919	01Ari41
12/05/1918	03Cap50	04/06/1919	02Can40	08/04/1919	18Sco12	12/04/1919	00Tau15
12/07/1918	29Cap31	04/08/1919	29Can32	08/06/1919	11Sag55	12/06/1919	00Gem14
12/09/1918	26Aqu09	04/10/1919	25Leo13	08/08/1919	06Cap15	12/08/1919	00Can39
12/11/1918	23Pis48	04/12/1919	20Vir01	08/10/1919	01Aqu39	12/10/1919	00Leo19
12/13/1918	22Ari22	04/14/1919	14Lib12	08/12/1919	28Aqu18	12/12/1919	28Leo16
12/15/1918	21Tau34	04/16/1919	07Sco56	08/14/1919	25Pis54	12/14/1919	24Vir22
12/17/1918	20Gem40	04/18/1919	01Sag32	08/16/1919	24Ari03	12/16/1919	19Lib00
12/19/1918	18Can57	04/20/1919	25Sag22	08/18/1919	22Tau18	12/18/1919	12Sco49
12/21/1918	15Leo48	04/22/1919	19Cap52	08/20/1919	20Gem30	12/20/1919	06Sag23
12/23/1918	11Vir10	04/24/1919	15Aqu40	08/22/1919	18Can27	12/22/1919	00Cap05
12/25/1918	05Lib24	04/26/1919	13Pis16	08/24/1919	15Leo56	12/24/1919	24Cap12
12/27/1918	29Lib06	04/28/1919	12Ari36	08/26/1919	12Vir32	12/26/1919	18Aqu58
12/29/1918	22Sco55	04/30/1919	12Tau56	08/28/1919	07Lib58	12/28/1919	14Pis33
12/31/1918	17Sag24			08/30/1919	02Sco21	12/30/1919	11Ari11

Ephemeris Tables for the Moon

Date	Moon	Date	Moon	Date	Moon	Date	Moon
01/01/1920	09Tau12	05/02/1920	05Sco19	09/01/1920	14Ari13	01/01/1921	14Lib18
01/03/1920	08Gem33	05/04/1920	29Sco31	09/03/1920	11Tau06	01/03/1921	09Sco39
01/05/1920	08Can35	05/06/1920	23Sag16	09/05/1920	08Gem43	01/05/1921	04Sag02
01/07/1920	08Leo13	05/08/1920	16Cap58	09/07/1920	07Can06	01/07/1921	27Sag56
01/09/1920	06Vir27	05/10/1920	11Aqu03	09/09/1920	06Leo00	01/09/1921	21Cap40
01/11/1920	02Lib46	05/12/1920	06Pis06	09/11/1920	04Vir48	01/11/1921	15Aqu27
01/13/1920	27Lib30	05/14/1920	02Ari35	09/13/1920	02Lib45	01/13/1921	09Pis28
01/15/1920	21Sco18	05/16/1920	00Tau50	09/15/1920	29Lib17	01/15/1921	04Ari01
01/17/1920	14Sag52	05/18/1920	00Gem28	09/17/1920	24Sco25	01/17/1921	29Ari36
01/19/1920	08Cap43	05/20/1920	00Can36	09/19/1920	18Sag31	01/19/1921	26Tau49
01/21/1920	03Aqu16	05/22/1920	00Leo06	09/21/1920	12Cap16	01/21/1921	25Gem54
01/23/1920	28Aqu37	05/24/1920	28Leo12	09/23/1920	06Aqu16	01/23/1921	26Can20
01/25/1920	24Pis43	05/26/1920	24Vir43	09/25/1920	01Pis04	01/25/1921	26Leo49
01/27/1920	21Ari35	05/28/1920	20Lib00	09/27/1920	26Pis55	01/27/1921	26Vir02
01/29/1920	19Tau18	05/30/1920	14Sco23	09/29/1920	23Ari48	01/29/1921	23Lib16
01/31/1920	17Gem55					01/31/1921	18Sco43
		06/01/1920	08Sag15	10/01/1920	21Tau29		
02/02/1920	17Can09	06/03/1920	01Cap55	10/03/1920	19Gem40	02/02/1921	13Sag01
02/04/1920	16Leo13	06/05/1920	25Cap41	10/05/1920	18Can02	02/04/1921	06Cap47
02/06/1920	14Vir13	06/07/1920	19Aqu52	10/07/1920	16Leo19	02/06/1921	00Aqu30
02/08/1920	10Lib37	06/09/1920	14Pis51	10/09/1920	14Vir13	02/08/1921	24Aqu25
02/10/1920	05Sco28	06/11/1920	11Ari09	10/11/1920	11Lib18	02/10/1921	18Pis45
02/12/1920	29Sco20	06/13/1920	09Tau09	10/13/1920	07Sco21	02/12/1921	13Ari38
02/14/1920	22Sag56	06/15/1920	08Gem48	10/15/1920	02Sag16	02/14/1921	09Tau22
02/16/1920	16Cap58	06/17/1920	09Can14	10/17/1920	26Sag23	02/16/1921	06Gem21
02/18/1920	11Aqu53	06/19/1920	09Leo13	10/19/1920	20Cap07	02/18/1921	04Can54
02/20/1920	07Pis52	06/21/1920	07Vir39	10/21/1920	14Aqu06	02/20/1921	04Leo41
02/22/1920	04Ari45	06/23/1920	04Lib15	10/23/1920	08Pis57	02/22/1921	04Vir47
02/24/1920	02Tau15	06/25/1920	29Lib18	10/25/1920	05Ari03	02/24/1921	03Lib57
02/26/1920	00Gem09	06/27/1920	23Sco26	10/27/1920	02Tau34	02/26/1921	01Sco25
02/28/1920	28Gem24	06/29/1920	17Sag08	10/29/1920	01Gem11	02/28/1921	27Sco05
				10/31/1920	00Can14		
03/01/1920	26Can49	07/01/1920	10Cap49			03/02/1921	21Sag30
03/03/1920	24Leo58	07/03/1920	04Aqu44	11/02/1920	29Can01	03/04/1921	15Cap18
03/05/1920	22Vir19	07/05/1920	29Aqu09	11/04/1920	27Leo05	03/06/1921	09Aqu03
03/07/1920	18Lib24	07/07/1920	24Pis18	11/06/1920	24Vir14	03/08/1921	03Pis11
03/09/1920	13Sco13	07/09/1920	20Ari29	11/08/1920	20Lib28	03/10/1921	27Pis55
03/11/1920	07Sag07	07/11/1920	18Tau10	11/10/1920	15Sco50	03/12/1921	23Ari23
03/13/1920	00Cap47	07/13/1920	17Gem25	11/12/1920	10Sag26	03/14/1921	19Tau38
03/15/1920	24Cap52	07/15/1920	17Can40	11/14/1920	04Cap25	03/16/1921	16Gem50
03/17/1920	20Aqu00	07/17/1920	17Leo42	11/16/1920	28Cap09	03/18/1921	15Can02
03/19/1920	16Pis28	07/19/1920	16Vir22	11/18/1920	22Aqu03	03/20/1921	14Leo04
03/21/1920	14Ari07	07/21/1920	13Lib06	11/20/1920	16Pis45	03/22/1921	13Vir18
03/23/1920	12Tau29	07/23/1920	08Sco10	11/22/1920	12Ari47	03/24/1921	11Lib54
03/25/1920	11Gem02	07/25/1920	02Sag12	11/24/1920	10Tau34	03/26/1921	09Sco10
03/27/1920	09Can23	07/27/1920	25Sag52	11/26/1920	09Gem52	03/28/1921	04Sag57
03/29/1920	07Leo18	07/29/1920	19Cap39	11/28/1920	09Can50	03/30/1921	29Sag30
03/31/1920	04Vir36	07/31/1920	13Aqu51	11/30/1920	09Leo22		
						04/01/1921	23Cap23
04/02/1920	01Lib06	08/02/1920	08Pis42	12/02/1920	07Vir39	04/03/1921	17Aqu12
04/04/1920	26Lib36	08/04/1920	04Ari12	12/04/1920	04Lib28	04/05/1921	11Pis30
04/06/1920	21Sco08	08/06/1920	00Tau35	12/06/1920	00Sco04	04/07/1921	06Ari37
04/08/1920	15Sag01	08/08/1920	28Tau04	12/08/1920	24Sco50	04/09/1921	02Tau46
04/10/1920	08Cap41	08/10/1920	26Gem49	12/10/1920	19Sag01	04/11/1921	29Tau51
04/12/1920	02Aqu46	08/12/1920	26Can27	12/12/1920	12Cap53	04/13/1921	27Gem39
04/14/1920	27Aqu55	08/14/1920	26Leo04	12/14/1920	06Aqu35	04/15/1921	25Can58
04/16/1920	24Pis33	08/16/1920	24Vir34	12/16/1920	00Pis29	04/17/1921	24Leo28
04/18/1920	22Ari41	08/18/1920	21Lib21	12/18/1920	25Pis01	04/19/1921	22Vir46
04/20/1920	21Tau52	08/20/1920	16Sco29	12/20/1920	20Ari47	04/21/1921	20Lib27
04/22/1920	21Gem16	08/22/1920	10Sag33	12/22/1920	18Tau22	04/23/1921	17Sco11
04/24/1920	20Can06	08/24/1920	04Cap15	12/24/1920	17Gem50	04/25/1921	12Sag46
04/26/1920	17Leo57	08/26/1920	28Cap10	12/26/1920	18Can21	04/27/1921	07Cap21
04/28/1920	14Vir43	08/28/1920	22Aqu43	12/28/1920	18Leo36	04/29/1921	01Aqu16
04/30/1920	10Lib27	08/30/1920	18Pis04	12/30/1920	17Vir23		

Ephemeris Tables for the Moon

Date	Moon	Date	Moon	Date	Moon	Date	Moon
05/01/1921	25Aqu06	09/02/1921	14Vir24	01/02/1922	28Aqu39	05/02/1922	15Can04
05/03/1921	19Pis27	09/04/1921	13Lib54	01/04/1922	22Pis15	05/04/1922	12Leo43
05/05/1921	14Ari50	09/06/1921	11Sco44	01/06/1922	16Ari09	05/06/1922	11Vir08
05/07/1921	11Tau33	09/08/1921	07Sag48	01/08/1922	11Tau04	05/08/1922	10Lib04
05/09/1921	09Gem30	09/10/1921	02Cap31	01/10/1922	07Gem42	05/10/1922	08Sco59
05/11/1921	08Can12	09/12/1921	26Cap30	01/12/1922	06Can12	05/12/1922	07Sag13
05/13/1921	07Leo00	09/14/1921	20Aqu14	01/14/1922	06Leo03	05/14/1922	04Cap08
05/15/1921	05Vir21	09/16/1921	14Pis07	01/16/1922	06Vir03	05/16/1922	29Cap36
05/17/1921	02Lib58	09/18/1921	08Ari24	01/18/1922	05Lib08	05/18/1922	23Aqu52
05/19/1921	29Lib48	09/20/1921	03Tau18	01/20/1922	02Sco47	05/20/1922	17Pis34
05/21/1921	25Sco48	09/22/1921	29Tau04	01/22/1922	29Sco09	05/22/1922	11Ari21
05/23/1921	20Sag58	09/24/1921	25Gem55	01/24/1922	24Sag33	05/24/1922	05Tau48
05/25/1921	15Cap23	09/26/1921	24Can00	01/26/1922	19Cap15	05/26/1922	01Gem21
05/27/1921	09Aqu16	09/28/1921	23Leo11	01/28/1922	13Aqu22	05/28/1922	28Gem02
05/29/1921	03Pis04	09/30/1921	22Vir48	01/30/1922	07Pis06	05/30/1922	25Can36
05/31/1921	27Pis22						
		10/02/1921	21Lib57	02/01/1922	00Ari40	06/01/1922	23Leo39
06/02/1921	22Ari48	10/04/1921	19Sco46	02/03/1922	24Ari34	06/03/1922	21Vir55
06/04/1921	19Tau51	10/06/1921	16Sag01	02/05/1922	19Tau22	06/05/1922	20Lib11
06/06/1921	18Gem28	10/08/1921	10Cap51	02/07/1922	15Gem46	06/07/1922	18Sco16
06/08/1921	18Can03	10/10/1921	04Aqu49	02/09/1922	14Can08	06/09/1922	15Sag46
06/10/1921	17Leo33	10/12/1921	28Aqu34	02/11/1922	14Leo07	06/11/1922	12Cap16
06/12/1921	16Vir06	10/14/1921	22Pis35	02/13/1922	14Vir37	06/13/1922	07Aqu31
06/14/1921	13Lib25	10/16/1921	17Ari15	02/15/1922	14Lib19	06/15/1922	01Pis46
06/16/1921	09Sco37	10/18/1921	12Tau48	02/17/1922	12Sco28	06/17/1922	25Pis28
06/18/1921	04Sag59	10/20/1921	09Gem16	02/19/1922	08Sag54	06/19/1922	19Ari17
06/20/1921	29Sag41	10/22/1921	06Can35	02/21/1922	04Cap04	06/21/1922	13Tau55
06/22/1921	23Cap49	10/24/1921	04Leo38	02/23/1922	28Cap24	06/23/1922	09Gem54
06/24/1921	17Aqu36	10/26/1921	03Vir10	02/25/1922	22Aqu14	06/25/1922	07Can17
06/26/1921	11Pis23	10/28/1921	01Lib53	02/27/1922	15Pis52	06/27/1922	05Leo40
06/28/1921	05Ari36	10/30/1921	00Sco14			06/29/1922	04Vir25
06/30/1921	00Tau57			03/01/1922	09Ari33		
		11/01/1921	27Sco41	03/03/1922	03Tau36	07/01/1922	02Lib54
07/02/1921	28Tau01	11/03/1921	23Sag52	03/05/1922	28Tau29	07/03/1922	00Sco52
07/04/1921	26Gem57	11/05/1921	18Cap45	03/07/1922	24Gem41	07/05/1922	28Sco16
07/06/1921	27Can06	11/07/1921	12Aqu46	03/09/1922	22Can39	07/07/1922	24Sag59
07/08/1921	27Leo15	11/09/1921	06Pis30	03/11/1922	22Leo13	07/09/1922	20Cap50
07/10/1921	26Vir13	11/11/1921	00Ari34	03/13/1922	22Vir37	07/11/1922	15Aqu44
07/12/1921	23Lib33	11/13/1921	25Ari32	03/15/1922	22Lib34	07/13/1922	09Pis49
07/14/1921	19Sco28	11/15/1921	21Tau44	03/17/1922	21Sco08	07/15/1922	03Ari27
07/16/1921	14Sag24	11/17/1921	19Gem06	03/19/1922	17Sag55	07/17/1922	27Ari15
07/18/1921	08Cap42	11/19/1921	17Can15	03/21/1922	13Cap07	07/19/1922	21Tau56
07/20/1921	02Aqu36	11/21/1921	15Leo40	03/23/1922	07Aqu19	07/21/1922	18Gem04
07/22/1921	26Aqu19	11/23/1921	13Vir56	03/25/1922	01Pis01	07/23/1922	15Can54
07/24/1921	20Pis07	11/25/1921	11Lib50	03/27/1922	24Pis39	07/25/1922	15Leo00
07/26/1921	14Ari22	11/27/1921	09Sco16	03/29/1922	18Ari32	07/27/1922	14Vir31
07/28/1921	09Tau39	11/29/1921	06Sag00	03/31/1922	13Tau00	07/29/1922	13Lib32
07/30/1921	06Gem33					07/31/1922	11Sco34
		12/01/1921	01Cap49	04/02/1922	08Gem15		
08/01/1921	05Can21	12/03/1921	26Cap36	04/04/1922	04Can35	08/02/1922	08Sag34
08/03/1921	05Leo37	12/05/1921	20Aqu36	04/06/1922	02Leo13	08/04/1922	04Cap37
08/05/1921	06Vir06	12/07/1921	14Pis15	04/08/1922	01Vir09	08/06/1922	29Cap51
08/07/1921	05Lib28	12/09/1921	08Ari16	04/10/1922	00Lib53	08/08/1922	24Aqu17
08/09/1921	03Sco03	12/11/1921	03Tau19	04/12/1922	00Sco33	08/10/1922	18Pis09
08/11/1921	28Sco57	12/13/1921	29Tau55	04/14/1922	29Sco10	08/12/1922	11Ari43
08/13/1921	23Sag40	12/15/1921	28Gem04	04/16/1922	26Sag10	08/14/1922	05Tau32
08/15/1921	17Cap45	12/17/1921	27Can11	04/18/1922	21Cap34	08/16/1922	00Gem09
08/17/1921	11Aqu31	12/19/1921	26Leo21	04/20/1922	15Aqu48	08/18/1922	26Gem14
08/19/1921	05Pis16	12/21/1921	24Vir50	04/22/1922	09Pis29	08/20/1922	24Can07
08/21/1921	29Pis15	12/23/1921	22Lib22	04/24/1922	03Ari10	08/22/1922	23Leo34
08/23/1921	23Ari41	12/25/1921	19Sco03	04/26/1922	27Ari22	08/24/1922	23Vir41
08/25/1921	19Tau03	12/27/1921	15Sag02	04/28/1922	22Tau21	08/26/1922	23Lib21
08/27/1921	15Gem48	12/29/1921	10Cap16	04/30/1922	18Gem15	08/28/1922	21Sco46
08/29/1921	14Can15	12/31/1921	04Aqu46			08/30/1922	18Sag41
08/31/1921	14Leo06						

Ephemeris Tables for the Moon

Date	Moon	Date	Moon	Date	Moon	Date	Moon
09/01/1922	14Cap21	01/01/1923	20Gem16	05/01/1923	18Sco42	09/02/1923	27Tau36
09/03/1922	09Aqu04	01/03/1923	17Can03	05/03/1923	18Sag28	09/04/1923	21Gem46
09/05/1922	03Pis08	01/05/1923	14Leo46	05/05/1923	16Cap36	09/06/1923	16Can56
09/07/1922	26Pis48	01/07/1923	12Vir57	05/07/1923	12Aqu49	09/08/1923	13Leo34
09/09/1922	20Ari23	01/09/1923	11Lib10	05/09/1923	07Pis32	09/10/1923	11Vir45
09/11/1922	14Tau16	01/11/1923	09Sco18	05/11/1923	01Ari23	09/12/1923	11Lib02
09/13/1922	08Gem55	01/13/1923	07Sag10	05/13/1923	24Ari57	09/14/1923	10Sco33
09/15/1922	04Can52	01/15/1923	04Cap32	05/15/1923	18Tau43	09/16/1923	09Sag29
09/17/1922	02Leo28	01/17/1923	01Aqu01	05/17/1923	12Gem57	09/18/1923	07Cap17
09/19/1922	01Vir46	01/19/1923	26Aqu24	05/19/1923	07Can48	09/20/1923	03Aqu52
09/21/1922	02Lib03	01/21/1923	20Pis45	05/21/1923	03Leo25	09/22/1923	29Aqu27
09/23/1922	02Sco12	01/23/1923	14Ari27	05/23/1923	00Vir03	09/24/1923	24Pis13
09/25/1922	01Sag05	01/25/1923	08Tau09	05/25/1923	27Vir57	09/26/1923	18Ari23
09/27/1922	28Sag14	01/27/1923	02Gem30	05/27/1923	27Lib10	09/28/1923	12Tau10
09/29/1922	23Cap46	01/29/1923	28Gem09	05/29/1923	27Sco07	09/30/1923	05Gem54
		01/31/1923	25Can21	05/31/1923	26Sag42		
10/01/1922	18Aqu12					10/02/1923	00Can00
10/03/1922	12Pis00	02/02/1923	23Leo51	06/02/1923	24Cap52	10/04/1923	25Can01
10/05/1922	05Ari35	02/04/1923	22Vir55	06/04/1923	21Aqu12	10/06/1923	21Leo32
10/07/1922	29Ari18	02/06/1923	21Lib53	06/06/1923	15Pis59	10/08/1923	19Vir49
10/09/1922	23Tau28	02/08/1923	20Sco10	06/08/1923	09Ari51	10/10/1923	19Lib36
10/11/1922	18Gem21	02/10/1923	17Sag37	06/10/1923	03Tau29	10/12/1923	19Sco54
10/13/1922	14Can15	02/12/1923	14Cap12	06/12/1923	27Tau27	10/14/1923	19Sag28
10/15/1922	11Leo31	02/14/1923	09Aqu54	06/14/1923	22Gem03	10/16/1923	17Cap29
10/17/1922	10Vir18	02/16/1923	04Pis45	06/16/1923	17Can26	10/18/1923	13Aqu49
10/19/1922	10Lib13	02/18/1923	28Pis50	06/18/1923	13Leo37	10/20/1923	08Pis55
10/21/1922	10Sco19	02/20/1923	22Ari30	06/20/1923	10Vir33	10/22/1923	03Ari13
10/23/1922	09Sag30	02/22/1923	16Tau10	06/22/1923	08Lib21	10/24/1923	27Ari07
10/25/1922	06Cap57	02/24/1923	10Gem28	06/24/1923	07Sco03	10/26/1923	20Tau51
10/27/1922	02Aqu36	02/26/1923	05Can59	06/26/1923	06Sag15	10/28/1923	14Gem38
10/29/1922	26Aqu57	02/28/1923	03Leo12	06/28/1923	05Cap10	10/30/1923	08Can48
10/31/1922	20Pis38			06/30/1923	02Aqu58		
		03/02/1923	02Vir02			11/01/1923	03Leo42
11/02/1922	14Ari13	03/04/1923	01Lib53	07/02/1923	29Aqu13	11/03/1923	29Leo55
11/04/1922	08Tau12	03/06/1923	01Sco40	07/04/1923	24Pis01	11/05/1923	27Vir56
11/06/1922	02Gem48	03/08/1923	00Sag31	07/06/1923	17Ari57	11/07/1923	27Lib42
11/08/1922	28Gem10	03/10/1923	28Sag00	07/08/1923	11Tau39	11/09/1923	28Sco18
11/10/1922	24Can23	03/12/1923	24Cap09	07/10/1923	05Gem48	11/11/1923	28Sag22
11/12/1922	21Leo31	03/14/1923	19Aqu13	07/12/1923	00Can45	11/13/1923	26Cap48
11/14/1922	19Vir44	03/16/1923	13Pis33	07/14/1923	26Can45	11/15/1923	23Aqu15
11/16/1922	18Lib55	03/18/1923	07Ari21	07/16/1923	23Leo07	11/17/1923	18Pis10
11/18/1922	18Sco28	03/20/1923	00Tau58	07/18/1923	21Vir13	11/19/1923	12Ari13
11/20/1922	17Sag25	03/22/1923	24Tau43	07/20/1923	19Lib18	11/21/1923	05Tau58
11/22/1922	14Cap58	03/24/1923	19Gem00	07/22/1923	17Sco43	11/23/1923	29Tau43
11/24/1922	10Aqu46	03/26/1923	14Can21	07/24/1923	16Sag10	11/25/1923	23Gem42
11/26/1922	05Pis10	03/28/1923	11Leo16	07/26/1923	14Cap13	11/27/1923	18Can06
11/28/1922	28Pis50	03/30/1923	10Vir00	07/28/1923	11Aqu19	11/29/1923	13Leo09
11/30/1922	22Ari30			07/30/1923	07Pis12		
		04/01/1923	10Lib04	08/01/1923	01Ari55	12/01/1923	09Vir13
12/02/1922	16Tau43	04/03/1923	10Sco27	08/03/1923	25Ari52	12/03/1923	06Lib49
12/04/1922	11Gem51	04/05/1923	09Sag55	08/05/1923	19Tau37	12/05/1923	06Sco04
12/06/1922	07Can56	04/07/1923	07Cap43	08/07/1923	13Gem49	12/07/1923	06Sag22
12/08/1922	04Leo47	04/09/1923	03Aqu48	08/09/1923	09Can00	12/09/1923	06Cap28
12/10/1922	02Vir13	04/11/1923	28Aqu34	08/11/1923	05Leo27	12/11/1923	05Aqu08
12/12/1922	00Lib12	04/13/1923	22Pis33	08/13/1923	03Vir05	12/13/1923	01Pis51
12/14/1922	28Lib39	04/15/1923	16Ari10	08/15/1923	01Lib31	12/15/1923	26Pis53
12/16/1922	27Sco19	04/17/1923	09Tau48	08/17/1923	00Sco13	12/17/1923	20Ari54
12/18/1922	25Sag36	04/19/1923	03Gem43	08/19/1923	28Sco42	12/19/1923	14Tau36
12/20/1922	22Cap48	04/21/1923	28Gem12	08/21/1923	26Sag40	12/21/1923	08Gem26
12/22/1922	18Aqu32	04/23/1923	23Can33	08/23/1923	23Cap52	12/23/1923	02Can43
12/24/1922	12Pis59	04/25/1923	20Leo12	08/25/1923	20Aqu09	12/25/1923	27Can34
12/26/1922	06Ari41	04/27/1923	18Vir29	08/27/1923	15Pis31	12/27/1923	23Leo03
12/28/1922	00Tau20	04/29/1923	18Lib16	08/29/1923	09Ari58	12/29/1923	19Vir22
12/30/1922	24Tau45			08/31/1923	03Tau51	12/31/1923	16Lib46

Ephemeris Tables for the Moon

Date	Moon	Date	Moon	Date	Moon	Date	Moon
01/02/1924	15Sco27	05/01/1924	13Ari31	09/02/1924	19Lib03	01/02/1925	17Ari44
01/04/1924	14Sag57	05/03/1924	07Tau43	09/04/1924	17Sco02	01/04/1925	12Tau29
01/06/1924	14Cap27	05/05/1924	01Gem34	09/06/1924	15Sag24	01/06/1925	06Gem30
01/08/1924	12Aqu54	05/07/1924	25Gem17	09/08/1924	13Cap47	01/08/1925	00Can13
01/10/1924	09Pis44	05/09/1924	19Can09	09/10/1924	11Aqu56	01/10/1925	23Can55
01/12/1924	04Ari57	05/11/1924	13Leo36	09/12/1924	09Pis31	01/12/1925	17Leo54
01/14/1924	29Ari05	05/13/1924	09Vir17	09/14/1924	06Ari11	01/14/1925	12Vir22
01/16/1924	22Tau49	05/15/1924	06Lib46	09/16/1924	01Tau45	01/16/1925	07Lib45
01/18/1924	16Gem45	05/17/1924	06Sco09	09/18/1924	26Tau18	01/18/1925	04Sco26
01/20/1924	11Can16	05/19/1924	06Sag40	09/20/1924	20Gem09	01/20/1925	02Sag40
01/22/1924	06Leo40	05/21/1924	06Cap57	09/22/1924	13Can57	01/22/1925	02Cap16
01/24/1924	02Vir53	05/23/1924	05Aqu48	09/24/1924	08Leo18	01/24/1925	02Aqu25
01/26/1924	29Vir52	05/25/1924	02Pis49	09/26/1924	03Vir46	01/26/1925	01Pis58
01/28/1924	27Lib34	05/27/1924	28Pis18	09/28/1924	00Lib39	01/28/1925	00Ari01
01/30/1924	25Sco54	05/29/1924	22Ari47	09/30/1924	28Lib48	01/30/1925	26Ari19
		05/31/1924	16Tau45				
02/01/1924	24Sag35			10/02/1924	27Sco39	02/01/1925	21Tau10
02/03/1924	23Cap07	06/02/1924	10Gem80	10/04/1924	26Sag25	02/03/1925	15Gem07
02/05/1924	20Aqu53	06/04/1924	04Can14	10/06/1924	24Cap37	02/05/1925	08Can46
02/07/1924	17Pis25	06/06/1924	28Can14	10/08/1924	22Aqu04	02/07/1925	02Leo35
02/09/1924	12Ari40	06/08/1924	22Leo49	10/10/1924	18Pis48	02/09/1925	26Leo54
02/11/1924	06Tau55	06/10/1924	18Vir28	10/12/1924	14Ari46	02/11/1925	21Vir57
02/13/1924	00Gem42	06/12/1924	15Lib43	10/14/1924	09Tau57	02/13/1925	17Lib51
02/15/1924	24Gem37	06/14/1924	14Sco46	10/16/1924	04Gem19	02/15/1925	14Sco44
02/17/1924	19Can19	06/16/1924	15Sag05	10/18/1924	28Gem07	02/17/1925	12Sag38
02/19/1924	15Leo06	06/18/1924	15Cap24	10/20/1924	21Can51	02/19/1925	11Cap28
02/21/1924	12Vir04	06/20/1924	14Aqu30	10/22/1924	16Leo06	02/21/1925	10Aqu47
02/23/1924	10Lib00	06/22/1924	11Pis46	10/24/1924	11Vir35	02/23/1925	09Pis50
02/25/1924	08Sco27	06/24/1924	07Ari20	10/26/1924	08Lib49	02/25/1925	07Ari48
02/27/1924	06Sag56	06/26/1924	01Tau46	10/28/1924	07Sco40	02/27/1925	04Tau16
02/29/1924	05Cap06	06/28/1924	25Tau38	10/30/1924	07Sag24		
		06/30/1924	19Gem21			03/01/1925	29Tau15
03/02/1924	02Aqu43			11/01/1924	06Cap54	03/03/1925	23Gem16
03/04/1924	29Aqu34	07/02/1924	13Can14	11/03/1924	05Aqu19	03/05/1925	16Can55
03/06/1924	25Pis33	07/04/1924	07Leo33	11/05/1924	02Pis28	03/07/1925	10Leo50
03/08/1924	20Ari32	07/06/1924	02Vir29	11/07/1924	28Pis34	03/09/1925	05Vir33
03/10/1924	14Tau45	07/08/1924	28Vir23	11/09/1924	23Ari54	03/11/1925	01Lib15
03/12/1924	08Gem32	07/10/1924	25Lib34	11/11/1924	18Tau35	03/13/1925	27Lib57
03/14/1924	02Can26	07/12/1924	24Sco12	11/13/1924	12Gem42	03/15/1925	25Sco26
03/16/1924	27Can04	07/14/1924	23Sag53	11/15/1924	06Can25	03/17/1925	23Sag27
03/18/1924	23Leo01	07/16/1924	23Cap45	11/17/1924	00Leo06	03/19/1925	21Cap46
03/20/1924	20Vir31	07/18/1924	22Aqu42	11/19/1924	24Leo14	03/21/1925	20Aqu12
03/22/1924	19Lib20	07/20/1924	20Pis04	11/21/1924	19Vir34	03/23/1925	18Pis24
03/24/1924	18Sco42	07/22/1924	15Ari47	11/23/1924	16Lib42	03/25/1925	15Ari50
03/26/1924	17Sag46	07/24/1924	10Tau17	11/25/1924	15Sco47	03/27/1925	12Tau05
03/28/1924	15Cap54	07/26/1924	04Gem09	11/27/1924	16Sag04	03/29/1925	07Gem05
03/30/1924	12Aqu55	07/28/1924	27Gem55	11/29/1924	16Cap16	03/31/1925	01Can07
		07/30/1924	22Can01				
04/01/1924	09Pis01	08/01/1924	16Leo45	12/01/1924	15Aqu14	04/02/1925	24Can46
04/03/1924	04Ari17	08/03/1924	12Vir17	12/03/1924	12Pis32	04/04/1925	18Leo45
04/05/1924	28Ari54	08/05/1924	08Lib44	12/05/1924	08Ari24	04/06/1925	13Vir42
04/07/1924	22Tau56	08/07/1924	06Sco09	12/07/1924	03Tau16	04/08/1925	09Lib59
04/09/1924	16Gem42	08/09/1924	04Sag28	12/09/1924	27Tau33	04/10/1925	07Sco31
04/11/1924	10Can31	08/11/1924	03Cap27	12/11/1924	21Gem25	04/12/1925	05Sag53
04/13/1924	05Leo03	08/13/1924	02Aqu29	12/13/1924	15Can06	04/14/1925	04Cap25
04/15/1924	00Vir54	08/15/1924	00Pis53	12/15/1924	08Leo49	04/16/1925	02Aqu42
04/17/1924	28Vir33	08/17/1924	28Pis03	12/17/1924	03Vir01	04/18/1925	00Pis32
04/19/1924	27Lib53	08/19/1924	23Ari49	12/19/1924	28Vir13	04/20/1925	27Pis53
04/21/1924	28Sco03	08/21/1924	18Tau22	12/21/1924	25Lib04	04/22/1925	24Ari32
04/23/1924	27Sag49	08/23/1924	12Gem16	12/23/1924	23Sco51	04/24/1925	20Tau18
04/25/1924	26Cap15	08/25/1924	06Can05	12/25/1924	24Sag04	04/26/1925	15Gem04
04/27/1924	23Aqu08	08/27/1924	00Leo22	12/27/1924	24Cap33	04/28/1925	09Can01
04/29/1924	18Pis45	08/29/1924	25Leo33	12/29/1924	24Aqu01	04/30/1925	02Leo39
		08/31/1924	21Vir48	12/31/1924	21Pis45		

Ephemeris Tables for the Moon

Date	Moon	Date	Moon	Date	Moon	Date	Moon
05/02/1925	26Leo37	09/01/1925	20Aqu02	01/01/1926	06Leo42	05/01/1926	23Sag25
05/04/1925	21Vir38	09/03/1925	19Pis41	01/03/1926	00Vir18	05/03/1926	20Cap58
05/06/1925	18Lib13	09/05/1925	18Ari18	01/05/1926	24Vir06	05/05/1926	19Aqu01
05/08/1925	16Sco24	09/07/1925	15Tau15	01/07/1926	18Lib40	05/07/1926	17Pis31
05/10/1925	15Sag36	09/09/1925	10Gem33	01/09/1926	14Sco36	05/09/1926	16Ari06
05/12/1925	14Cap54	09/11/1925	04Can40	01/11/1926	12Sag19	05/11/1926	14Tau12
05/14/1925	13Aqu30	09/13/1925	28Can17	01/13/1926	11Cap42	05/13/1926	11Gem12
05/16/1925	11Pis11	09/15/1925	22Leo00	01/15/1926	11Aqu55	05/15/1926	06Can51
05/18/1925	07Ari56	09/17/1925	16Vir20	01/17/1926	11Pis52	05/17/1926	01Leo19
05/20/1925	03Tau54	09/19/1925	11Lib28	01/19/1926	10Ari32	05/19/1926	25Leo07
05/22/1925	29Tau03	09/21/1925	07Sco31	01/21/1926	07Tau34	05/21/1926	18Vir53
05/24/1925	23Gem27	09/23/1925	04Sag22	01/23/1926	03Gem10	05/23/1926	13Lib18
05/26/1925	17Can13	09/25/1925	01Cap59	01/25/1926	27Gem43	05/25/1926	08Sco48
05/28/1925	10Leo49	09/27/1925	00Aqu19	01/27/1926	21Can40	05/27/1926	05Sag32
05/30/1925	04Vir45	09/29/1925	29Aqu13	01/29/1926	15Leo19	05/29/1926	03Cap16
				01/31/1926	08Vir59	05/31/1926	01Aqu35
06/01/1925	29Vir43	10/01/1925	28Pis09				
06/03/1925	26Lib20	10/03/1925	26Ari22	02/02/1926	02Lib57	06/02/1926	00Pis03
06/05/1925	24Sco46	10/05/1925	23Tau14	02/04/1926	27Lib34	06/04/1926	28Pis22
06/07/1925	24Sag30	10/07/1925	18Gem33	02/06/1926	23Sco17	06/06/1926	26Ari17
06/09/1925	24Cap29	10/09/1925	12Can42	02/08/1926	20Sag36	06/08/1926	23Tau30
06/11/1925	23Aqu41	10/11/1925	06Leo19	02/10/1926	19Cap38	06/10/1926	19Gem45
06/13/1925	21Pis33	10/13/1925	00Vir09	02/12/1926	19Aqu52	06/12/1926	14Can58
06/15/1925	18Ari04	10/15/1925	24Vir46	02/14/1926	20Pis13	06/14/1926	09Leo16
06/17/1925	13Tau32	10/17/1925	20Lib30	02/16/1926	19Ari25	06/16/1926	03Vir03
06/19/1925	08Gem11	10/19/1925	17Sco19	02/18/1926	16Tau49	06/18/1926	26Vir51
06/21/1925	02Can11	10/21/1925	14Sag55	02/20/1926	12Gem24	06/20/1926	21Lib16
06/23/1925	25Can49	10/23/1925	12Cap53	02/22/1926	06Can46	06/22/1926	16Sco53
06/25/1925	19Leo24	10/25/1925	11Aqu03	02/24/1926	00Leo29	06/24/1926	13Sag58
06/27/1925	13Vir23	10/27/1925	09Pis16	02/26/1926	24Leo05	06/26/1926	12Cap24
06/29/1925	08Lib20	10/29/1925	07Ari19	02/28/1926	17Vir54	06/28/1926	11Aqu34
		10/31/1925	04Tau47			06/30/1926	10Pis45
07/01/1925	04Sco48			03/02/1926	12Lib12		
07/03/1925	03Sag05	11/02/1925	01Gem13	03/04/1926	07Sco07	07/02/1926	09Ari14
07/05/1925	02Cap54	11/04/1925	26Gem22	03/06/1926	02Sag54	07/04/1926	06Tau47
07/07/1925	03Aqu15	11/06/1925	20Can30	03/08/1926	29Sag54	07/06/1926	03Gem17
07/09/1925	02Pis58	11/08/1925	14Leo08	03/10/1926	28Cap22	07/08/1926	28Gem49
07/11/1925	01Ari13	11/10/1925	07Vir58	03/12/1926	28Aqu06	07/10/1926	23Can31
07/13/1925	27Ari47	11/12/1925	02Lib43	03/14/1926	28Pis14	07/12/1926	17Leo33
07/15/1925	23Tau02	11/14/1925	28Lib49	03/16/1926	27Ari34	07/14/1926	11Vir16
07/17/1925	17Gem19	11/16/1925	26Sco21	03/18/1926	25Tau12	07/16/1926	05Lib03
07/19/1925	11Can05	11/18/1925	24Sag50	03/20/1926	20Gem58	07/18/1926	29Lib26
07/21/1925	04Leo38	11/20/1925	23Cap34	03/22/1926	15Can21	07/20/1926	24Sco57
07/23/1925	28Leo20	11/22/1925	22Aqu01	03/24/1926	09Leo02	07/22/1926	22Sag05
07/25/1925	22Vir31	11/24/1925	19Pis57	03/26/1926	02Vir40	07/24/1926	20Cap51
07/27/1925	17Lib36	11/26/1925	17Ari15	03/28/1926	26Vir43	07/26/1926	20Aqu43
07/29/1925	13Sco57	11/28/1925	13Tau52	03/30/1926	21Lib26	07/28/1926	20Pis39
07/31/1925	11Sag54	11/30/1925	09Gem37			07/30/1926	19Ari38
				04/01/1926	16Sco55		
08/02/1925	11Cap20	12/02/1925	04Can25	04/03/1926	13Sag09	08/01/1926	17Tau07
08/04/1925	11Aqu34	12/04/1925	28Can25	04/05/1926	10Cap12	08/03/1926	13Gem12
08/06/1925	11Pis30	12/06/1925	22Leo01	04/07/1926	08Aqu15	08/05/1926	08Can09
08/08/1925	10Ari04	12/08/1925	15Vir49	04/09/1926	07Pis17	08/07/1926	02Leo24
08/10/1925	06Tau52	12/10/1925	10Lib30	04/11/1926	06Ari43	08/09/1926	26Leo13
08/12/1925	02Gem04	12/12/1925	06Sco39	04/13/1926	05Tau36	08/11/1926	19Vir52
08/14/1925	26Gem13	12/14/1925	04Sag31	04/15/1926	03Gem08	08/13/1926	13Lib42
08/16/1925	19Can51	12/16/1925	03Cap42	04/17/1926	28Gem58	08/15/1926	08Sco04
08/18/1925	13Leo28	12/18/1925	03Aqu19	04/19/1926	23Can27	08/17/1926	03Sag27
08/20/1925	07Vir25	12/20/1925	02Pis30	04/21/1926	17Leo12	08/19/1926	00Cap21
08/22/1925	02Lib01	12/22/1925	00Ari36	04/23/1926	10Vir55	08/21/1926	29Cap04
08/24/1925	27Lib26	12/24/1925	27Ari33	04/25/1926	05Lib11	08/23/1926	29Aqu12
08/26/1925	23Sco53	12/26/1925	23Tau29	04/27/1926	00Sco22	08/25/1926	29Pis41
08/28/1925	21Sag31	12/28/1925	18Gem33	04/29/1926	26Sco30	08/27/1926	29Ari09
08/30/1925	20Cap22	12/30/1925	12Can52			08/29/1926	26Tau52
						08/31/1926	22Gem48

Ephemeris Tables for the Moon

Date	Moon	Date	Moon	Date	Moon	Date	Moon
09/02/1926	17Can27	01/02/1927	23Sag50	05/02/1927	24Tau35	09/01/1927	05Sco37
09/04/1926	11Leo25	01/04/1927	21Cap36	05/04/1927	23Gem11	09/03/1927	29Sco26
09/06/1926	05Vir06	01/06/1927	20Aqu16	05/06/1927	20Can01	09/05/1927	23Sag57
09/08/1926	28Vir48	01/08/1927	19Pis13	05/08/1927	15Leo15	09/07/1927	19Cap54
09/10/1926	22Lib47	01/10/1927	17Ari46	05/10/1927	09Vir27	09/09/1927	17Aqu42
09/12/1926	17Sco17	01/12/1927	15Tau34	05/12/1927	03Lib15	09/11/1927	17Pis13
09/14/1926	12Sag37	01/14/1927	12Gem30	05/14/1927	27Lib04	09/13/1927	17Ari25
09/16/1926	09Cap16	01/16/1927	08Can36	05/16/1927	21Sco18	09/15/1927	17Tau08
09/18/1926	07Aqu37	01/18/1927	03Leo54	05/18/1927	16Sag08	09/17/1927	15Gem27
09/20/1926	07Pis31	01/20/1927	28Leo25	05/20/1927	11Cap43	09/19/1927	12Can12
09/22/1926	08Ari01	01/22/1927	22Vir22	05/22/1927	08Aqu13	09/21/1927	07Leo46
09/24/1926	07Tau46	01/24/1927	16Lib07	05/24/1927	05Pis49	09/23/1927	02Vir32
09/26/1926	05Gem46	01/26/1927	10Sco090	05/26/1927	04Ari27	09/25/1927	26Vir46
09/28/1926	01Can49	01/28/1927	05Sag07	05/28/1927	03Tau46	09/27/1927	20Lib34
09/30/1926	26Can24	01/30/1927	01Cap35	05/30/1927	02Gem59	09/29/1927	14Sco13
10/02/1926	20Leo15	02/01/1927	29Cap47	06/01/1927	01Can13	10/01/1927	08Sag02
10/04/1926	13Vir54	02/03/1927	29Aqu19	06/03/1927	28Can01	10/03/1927	02Cap29
10/06/1926	07Lib45	02/05/1927	29Pis10	06/05/1927	23Leo21	10/05/1927	28Cap16
10/08/1926	02Sco03	02/07/1927	28Ari19	06/07/1927	17Vir39	10/07/1927	25Aqu54
10/10/1926	26Sco54	02/09/1927	26Tau06	06/09/1927	11Lib28	10/09/1927	25Pis25
10/12/1926	22Sag30	02/11/1927	22Gem34	06/11/1927	05Sco22	10/11/1927	25Ari57
10/14/1926	19Cap06	02/13/1927	17Can59	06/13/1927	29Sco51	10/13/1927	26Tau10
10/16/1926	17Aqu03	02/15/1927	12Leo42	06/15/1927	25Sag12	10/15/1927	24Gem56
10/18/1926	16Pis20	02/17/1927	06Vir54	06/17/1927	21Cap31	10/17/1927	21Can52
10/20/1926	16Ari18	02/19/1927	00Lib45	06/19/1927	18Aqu45	10/19/1927	17Leo18
10/22/1926	15Tau50	02/21/1927	24Lib30	06/21/1927	16Pis43	10/21/1927	11Vir46
10/24/1926	13Gem54	02/23/1927	18Sco28	06/23/1927	15Ari09	10/23/1927	05Lib44
10/26/1926	10Can06	02/25/1927	13Sag16	06/25/1927	13Tau45	10/25/1927	29Lib27
10/28/1926	04Leo48	02/27/1927	09Cap30	06/27/1927	12Gem03	10/27/1927	23Sco08
10/30/1926	28Leo39			06/29/1927	09Can36	10/29/1927	17Sag07
		03/01/1927	07Aqu40			10/31/1927	11Cap42
11/01/1926	22Vir21	03/03/1927	07Pis33	07/01/1927	06Leo03		
11/03/1926	16Lib24	03/05/1927	08Ari03	07/03/1927	01Vir19	11/02/1927	07Aqu24
11/05/1926	11Sco04	03/07/1927	07Tau51	07/05/1927	25Vir36	11/04/1927	04Pis43
11/07/1926	06Sag31	03/09/1927	06Gem01	07/07/1927	19Lib27	11/06/1927	03Ari46
11/09/1926	02Cap41	03/11/1927	02Can25	07/09/1927	13Sco22	11/08/1927	04Tau03
11/11/1926	29Cap37	03/13/1927	27Can30	07/11/1927	08Sag01	11/10/1927	04Gem18
11/13/1926	27Aqu25	03/15/1927	21Leo49	07/13/1927	03Cap47	11/12/1927	03Can24
11/15/1926	26Pis07	03/17/1927	15Vir44	07/15/1927	00Aqu51	11/14/1927	00Leo40
11/17/1926	25Ari12	03/19/1927	09Lib31	07/17/1927	28Aqu58	11/16/1927	26Leo16
11/19/1926	24Tau00	03/21/1927	03Sco18	07/19/1927	27Pis37	11/18/1927	20Vir42
11/21/1926	21Gem42	03/23/1927	27Sco25	07/21/1927	26Ari12	11/20/1927	14Lib30
11/23/1926	17Can54	03/25/1927	22Sag12	07/23/1927	24Tau20	11/22/1927	08Sco10
11/25/1926	12Leo42	03/27/1927	18Cap13	07/25/1927	21Gem50	11/24/1927	02Sag03
11/27/1926	06Vir39	03/29/1927	16Aqu04	07/27/1927	18Can34	11/26/1927	26Sag24
11/29/1926	00Lib22	03/31/1927	15Pis43	07/29/1927	14Leo27	11/28/1927	21Cap24
				07/31/1927	09Vir25	11/30/1927	17Aqu22
12/01/1926	24Lib31	04/02/1927	16Ari18				
12/03/1926	19Sco32	04/04/1927	16Tau27	08/02/1927	03Lib37	12/02/1927	14Pis33
12/05/1926	15Sag34	04/06/1927	14Gem58	08/04/1927	27Lib24	12/04/1927	13Ari01
12/07/1926	12Cap33	04/08/1927	11Can36	08/06/1927	21Sco16	12/06/1927	12Tau31
12/09/1926	10Aqu15	04/10/1927	06Leo40	08/08/1927	15Sag55	12/08/1927	12Gem13
12/11/1926	08Pis25	04/12/1927	00Vir51	08/10/1927	11Cap55	12/10/1927	11Can12
12/13/1926	06Ari46	04/14/1927	24Vir37	08/12/1927	09Aqu31	12/12/1927	08Leo40
12/15/1926	05Tau03	04/16/1927	18Lib23	08/14/1927	08Pis30	12/14/1927	04Vir31
12/17/1926	02Gem52	04/18/1927	12Sco22	08/16/1927	07Ari58	12/16/1927	29Vir03
12/19/1926	29Gem49	04/20/1927	06Sag45	08/18/1927	07Tau03	12/18/1927	22Lib51
12/21/1926	25Can39	04/22/1927	01Cap48	08/20/1927	05Gem05	12/20/1927	16Sco33
12/23/1926	20Leo26	04/24/1927	27Cap53	08/22/1927	02Can01	12/22/1927	10Sag37
12/25/1926	14Vir25	04/26/1927	25Aqu28	08/24/1927	28Can03	12/24/1927	05Cap26
12/27/1926	08Lib10	04/28/1927	24Pis35	08/26/1927	23Leo19	12/26/1927	01Aqu09
12/29/1926	02Sco18	04/30/1927	24Ari40	08/28/1927	17Vir55	12/28/1927	27Aqu45
12/31/1926	27Sco24			08/30/1927	11Lib55	12/30/1927	25Pis12

Ephemeris Tables for the Moon

Date	Moon	Date	Moon	Date	Moon	Date	Moon
01/01/1928	23Ari19	05/02/1928	16Lib18	09/01/1928	26Pis48	01/01/1929	25Vir38
01/03/1928	22Tau00	05/04/1928	10Sco04	09/03/1928	25Ari10	01/03/1929	20Lib49
01/05/1928	20Gem47	05/06/1928	03Sag40	09/05/1928	23Tau39	01/05/1929	14Sco50
01/07/1928	19Can07	05/08/1928	27Sag25	09/07/1928	21Gem55	01/07/1929	08Sag25
01/09/1928	16Leo25	05/10/1928	21Cap43	09/09/1928	19Can45	01/09/1929	02Cap03
01/11/1928	12Vir18	05/12/1928	17Aqu01	09/11/1928	17Leo07	01/11/1929	26Cap09
01/13/1928	06Lib57	05/14/1928	13Pis50	09/13/1928	13Vir45	01/13/1929	20Aqu54
01/15/1928	00Sco46	05/16/1928	12Ari23	09/15/1928	09Lib23	01/15/1929	16Pis21
01/17/1928	24Sco28	05/18/1928	12Tau19	09/17/1928	03Sco59	01/17/1929	12Ari40
01/19/1928	18Sag40	05/20/1928	12Gem38	09/19/1928	27Sco50	01/19/1929	10Tau02
01/21/1928	13Cap55	05/22/1928	12Can09	09/21/1928	21Sag27	01/21/1929	08Gem37
01/23/1928	10Aqu22	05/24/1928	10Leo07	09/23/1928	15Cap28	01/23/1929	08Can10
01/25/1928	07Pis53	05/26/1928	06Vir19	09/25/1928	10Aqu39	01/25/1929	07Leo50
01/27/1928	06Ari00	05/28/1928	01Lib13	09/27/1928	07Pis24	01/27/1929	06Vir35
01/29/1928	04Tau17	05/30/1928	25Lib14	09/29/1928	05Ari40	01/29/1929	03Lib40
01/31/1928	02Gem27					01/31/1929	29Lib01
		06/01/1928	18Sco52	10/01/1928	04Tau53		
02/02/1928	00Can21	06/03/1928	12Sag31	10/03/1928	04Gem08	02/02/1929	23Sco06
02/04/1928	27Can48	06/05/1928	06Cap32	10/05/1928	02Can44	02/04/1929	16Sag42
02/06/1928	24Leo30	06/07/1928	01Aqu12	10/07/1928	00Leo24	02/06/1929	10Cap27
02/08/1928	20Vir07	06/09/1928	26Aqu46	10/09/1928	27Leo08	02/08/1929	04Aqu51
02/10/1928	14Lib43	06/11/1928	23Pis33	10/11/1928	23Vir00	02/10/1929	00Pis10
02/12/1928	08Sco33	06/13/1928	21Ari41	10/13/1928	18Lib03	02/12/1929	26Pis18
02/14/1928	02Sag13	06/15/1928	21Tau02	10/15/1928	12Sco19	02/14/1929	23Ari10
02/16/1928	26Sag26	06/17/1928	20Gem57	10/17/1928	06Sag01	02/16/1929	20Tau39
02/18/1928	21Cap51	06/19/1928	20Can25	10/19/1928	29Sag35	02/18/1929	18Gem49
02/20/1928	18Aqu51	06/21/1928	18Leo32	10/21/1928	23Cap34	02/20/1929	17Can34
02/22/1928	17Pis14	06/23/1928	14Vir57	10/23/1928	18Aqu37	02/22/1929	16Leo24
02/24/1928	16Ari17	06/25/1928	09Lib51	10/25/1928	15Pis19	02/24/1929	14Vir34
02/26/1928	15Tau08	06/27/1928	03Sco48	10/27/1928	13Ari47	02/26/1929	11Lib25
02/28/1928	13Gem19	06/29/1928	27Sco25	10/29/1928	13Tau33	02/28/1929	06Sco47
				10/31/1928	13Gem34		
03/01/1928	10Can42	07/01/1928	21Sag15			03/02/1929	00Sag58
03/03/1928	07Leo20	07/03/1928	15Cap37	11/02/1928	12Can51	03/04/1929	24Sag37
03/05/1928	03Vir17	07/05/1928	10Aqu50	11/04/1928	10Leo43	03/06/1929	18Cap27
03/07/1928	28Vir25	07/07/1928	06Pis57	11/06/1928	07Vir13	03/08/1929	13Aqu05
03/09/1928	22Lib46	07/09/1928	03Ari57	11/08/1928	02Lib33	03/10/1929	08Pis53
03/11/1928	16Sco33	07/11/1928	01Tau52	11/10/1928	27Lib03	03/12/1929	05Ari46
03/13/1928	10Sag10	07/13/1928	00Gem36	11/12/1928	20Sco57	03/14/1929	03Tau27
03/15/1928	04Cap19	07/15/1928	29Gem47	11/14/1928	14Sag33	03/16/1929	01Gem33
03/17/1928	29Cap42	07/17/1928	28Can45	11/16/1928	08Cap10	03/18/1929	29Gem45
03/19/1928	26Aqu52	07/19/1928	26Leo40	11/18/1928	02Aqu11	03/20/1929	27Can58
03/21/1928	25Pis46	07/21/1928	23Vir06	11/20/1928	27Aqu08	03/22/1929	25Leo55
03/23/1928	25Ari34	07/23/1928	18Lib01	11/22/1928	23Pis34	03/24/1929	23Vir13
03/25/1928	25Tau13	07/25/1928	12Sco00	11/24/1928	21Ari44	03/26/1929	19Lib28
03/27/1928	23Gem48	07/27/1928	05Sag38	11/26/1928	21Tau30	03/28/1929	14Sco36
03/29/1928	21Can06	07/29/1928	29Sag36	11/28/1928	21Gem57	03/30/1929	08Sag46
03/31/1928	17Leo17	07/31/1928	24Cap24	11/30/1928	21Can51		
						04/01/1929	02Cap27
04/02/1928	12Vir37	08/02/1928	20Aqu15	12/02/1928	20Leo14	04/03/1929	26Cap19
04/04/1928	07Lib14	08/04/1928	17Pis07	12/04/1928	16Vir50	04/05/1929	21Aqu00
04/06/1928	01Sco16	08/06/1928	14Ari40	12/06/1928	11Lib57	04/07/1929	17Pis02
04/08/1928	24Sco56	08/08/1928	12Tau42	12/08/1928	06Sco05	04/09/1929	14Ari29
04/10/1928	18Sag34	08/10/1928	11Gem00	12/10/1928	29Sco46	04/11/1929	13Tau00
04/12/1928	12Cap42	08/12/1928	09Can25	12/12/1928	23Sag20	04/13/1929	11Gem57
04/14/1928	07Aqu58	08/14/1928	07Leo36	12/14/1928	17Cap07	04/15/1929	10Can40
04/16/1928	05Pis01	08/16/1928	04Vir58	12/16/1928	11Aqu24	04/17/1929	08Leo48
04/18/1928	03Ari54	08/18/1928	01Lib07	12/18/1928	06Pis27	04/19/1929	06Vir08
04/20/1928	04Tau04	08/20/1928	25Lib58	12/20/1928	02Ari39	04/21/1929	02Lib36
04/22/1928	04Gem16	08/22/1928	19Sco54	12/22/1928	00Tau19	04/23/1929	28Lib09
04/24/1928	03Can25	08/24/1928	13Sag34	12/24/1928	29Tau35	04/25/1929	22Sco48
04/26/1928	01Leo01	08/26/1928	07Cap37	12/26/1928	29Gem49	04/27/1929	16Sag49
04/28/1928	27Leo06	08/28/1928	02Aqu43	12/28/1928	29Can55	04/29/1929	10Cap29
04/30/1928	22Vir04	08/30/1928	29Aqu09	12/30/1928	28Leo44		

Ephemeris Tables for the Moon

Date	Moon	Date	Moon	Date	Moon	Date	Moon
05/01/1929	04Aqu22	09/02/1929	26Leo04	01/02/1930	08Aqu39	05/02/1930	28Gem53
05/03/1929	29Aqu01	09/04/1929	24Vir49	01/04/1930	02Pis28	05/04/1930	27Can18
05/05/1929	25Pis02	09/06/1929	22Lib10	01/06/1930	26Pis41	05/06/1930	25Leo46
05/07/1929	22Ari40	09/08/1929	17Sco52	01/08/1930	21Ari50	05/08/1930	23Vir55
05/09/1929	21Tau44	09/10/1929	12Sag15	01/10/1930	18Tau31	05/10/1930	21Lib28
05/11/1929	21Gem30	09/12/1929	06Cap03	01/12/1930	17Gem12	05/12/1930	18Sco15
05/13/1929	20Can57	09/14/1929	29Cap51	01/14/1930	17Can27	05/14/1930	14Sag01
05/15/1929	19Leo22	09/16/1929	24Aqu13	01/16/1930	18Leo06	05/16/1930	08Cap52
05/17/1929	16Vir28	09/18/1929	19Pis28	01/18/1930	17Vir45	05/18/1930	02Aqu560
05/19/1929	12Lib20	09/20/1929	15Ari37	01/20/1930	15Lib32	05/20/1930	26Aqu45
05/21/1929	07Sco16	09/22/1929	12Tau35	01/22/1930	11Sco28	05/22/1930	20Pis49
05/23/1929	01Sag29	09/24/1929	10Gem11	01/24/1930	06Sag05	05/24/1930	15Ari46
05/25/1929	25Sag17	09/26/1929	08Can20	01/26/1930	00Cap03	05/26/1930	12Tau07
05/27/1929	18Cap57	09/28/1929	06Leo52	01/28/1930	23Cap47	05/28/1930	09Gem56
05/29/1929	12Aqu52	09/30/1929	05Vir24	01/30/1930	17Aqu33	05/30/1930	08Can50
05/31/1929	07Pis29						
		10/02/1929	03Lib20	02/01/1930	11Pis33	06/01/1930	08Leo01
06/02/1929	03Ari18	10/04/1929	00Sco10	02/03/1930	05Ari58	06/03/1930	06Vir44
06/04/1929	00Tau49	10/06/1929	25Sco42	02/05/1930	01Tau09	06/05/1930	04Lib33
06/06/1929	00Gem01	10/08/1929	20Sag07	02/07/1930	27Tau37	06/07/1930	01Sco23
06/08/1929	00Can16	10/10/1929	13Cap56	02/09/1930	25Gem48	06/09/1930	27Sco23
06/10/1929	00Leo20	10/12/1929	07Aqu45	02/11/1930	25Can36	06/11/1930	22Sag36
06/12/1929	29Leo13	10/14/1929	02Pis15	02/13/1930	26Leo04	06/13/1930	17Cap08
06/14/1929	26Vir22	10/16/1929	27Pis47	02/15/1930	25Vir54	06/15/1930	11Aqu06
06/16/1929	21Lib58	10/18/1929	24Ari34	02/17/1930	24Lib00	06/17/1930	04Pis51
06/18/1929	16Sco30	10/20/1929	22Tau23	02/19/1930	20Sco10	06/19/1930	28Pis51
06/20/1929	10Sag24	10/22/1929	20Gem49	02/21/1930	14Sag54	06/21/1930	23Ari46
06/22/1929	04Cap04	10/24/1929	19Can23	02/23/1930	08Cap48	06/23/1930	20Tau12
06/24/1929	27Cap48	10/26/1929	17Leo40	02/25/1930	02Aqu30	06/25/1930	18Gem20
06/26/1929	21Aqu52	10/28/1929	15Vir27	02/27/1930	26Aqu22	06/27/1930	18Can02
06/28/1929	16Pis34	10/30/1929	12Lib28			06/29/1930	18Leo00
06/30/1929	12Ari18			03/01/1930	20Pis40		
		11/01/1929	08Sco34	03/03/1930	15Ari32	07/01/1930	17Vir10
07/02/1929	09Tau31	11/03/1929	03Sag43	03/05/1930	11Tau08	07/03/1930	15Lib01
07/04/1929	08Gem27	11/05/1929	28Sag01	03/07/1930	07Gem43	07/05/1930	11Sco27
07/06/1929	08Can40	11/07/1929	21Cap49	03/09/1930	05Can34	07/07/1930	06Sag54
07/08/1929	09Leo01	11/09/1929	15Aqu36	03/11/1930	04Leo41	07/09/1930	01Cap37
07/10/1929	08Vir14	11/11/1929	10Pis01	03/13/1930	04Vir25	07/11/1930	25Cap49
07/12/1929	05Lib36	11/13/1929	05Ari36	03/15/1930	03Lib48	07/13/1930	19Aqu39
07/14/1929	01Sco09	11/15/1929	02Tau42	03/17/1930	01Sco50	07/15/1930	13Pis22
07/16/1929	25Sco31	11/17/1929	01Gem16	03/19/1930	28Sco12	07/17/1930	07Ari21
07/18/1929	19Sag16	11/19/1929	00Can39	03/21/1930	23Sag06	07/19/1930	02Tau10
07/20/1929	12Cap56	11/21/1929	00Leo00	03/23/1930	17Cap06	07/21/1930	28Tau29
07/22/1929	06Aqu49	11/23/1929	28Leo31	03/25/1930	10Aqu51	07/23/1930	26Gem45
07/24/1929	01Pis11	11/25/1929	25Vir54	03/27/1930	04Pis51	07/25/1930	26Can37
07/26/1929	26Pis10	11/27/1929	22Lib09	03/29/1930	29Pis29	07/27/1930	27Leo07
07/28/1929	22Ari00	11/29/1929	17Sco31	03/31/1930	24Ari55	07/29/1930	26Vir49
07/30/1929	19Tau03					07/31/1930	24Lib54
08/01/1929	17Gem34	12/01/1929	12Sag10	04/02/1930	21Tau13		
08/03/1929	17Can19	12/03/1929	06Cap15	04/04/1930	18Gem21	08/02/1930	21Sco17
08/05/1929	17Leo25	12/05/1929	00Aqu01	04/06/1930	16Can16	08/04/1930	16Sag25
08/07/1929	16Vir38	12/07/1929	23Aqu46	04/08/1930	14Leo52	08/06/1930	10Cap49
08/09/1929	14Lib07	12/09/1929	18Pis02	04/10/1930	13Vir43	08/08/1930	04Aqu45
08/11/1929	09Sco46	12/11/1929	13Ari24	04/12/1930	12Lib13	08/10/1930	28Aqu29
08/13/1929	04Sag06	12/13/1929	10Tau26	04/14/1930	09Sco46	08/12/1930	22Pis14
08/15/1929	27Sag52	12/15/1929	09Gem18	04/16/1930	05Sag59	08/14/1930	16Ari20
08/17/1929	21Cap34	12/17/1929	09Can24	04/18/1930	00Cap57	08/16/1930	11Tau10
08/19/1929	15Aqu44	12/19/1929	09Leo36	04/20/1930	25Cap03	08/18/1930	07Gem23
08/21/1929	10Pis31	12/21/1929	08Vir42	04/22/1930	18Aqu50	08/20/1930	05Can22
08/23/1929	06Ari01	12/23/1929	06Lib06	04/24/1930	12Pis55	08/22/1930	05Leo04
08/25/1929	02Tau15	12/25/1929	02Sco01	04/26/1930	07Ari47	08/24/1930	05Vir34
08/27/1929	29Tau23	12/27/1929	26Sco50	04/28/1930	03Tau48	08/26/1930	05Lib32
08/29/1929	27Gem34	12/29/1929	21Sag03	04/30/1930	00Gem54	08/28/1930	03Sco57
08/31/1929	26Can39	12/31/1929	14Cap55			08/30/1930	00Sag31

Ephemeris Tables for the Moon

Date	Moon	Date	Moon	Date	Moon	Date	Moon
09/01/1930	25Sag36	01/01/1931	00Gem13	05/01/1931	00Sco21	09/02/1931	07Tau26
09/03/1930	19Cap49	01/03/1931	28Gem00	05/03/1931	29Sco16	09/04/1931	01Gem42
09/05/1930	13Aqu37	01/05/1931	27Can12	0505/1931	26Sag52	09/06/1931	27Gem07
09/07/1930	07Pis22	01/07/1931	26Leo51	05/07/1931	22Cap52	09/08/1931	24Can15
09/09/1930	01Ari18	01/09/1931	25Vir57	05/09/1931	17Aqu30	09/10/1931	23Leo07
09/11/1930	25Ari42	01/11/1931	23Lib56	05/11/1931	11Pis20	09/12/1931	23Vir12
09/13/1930	20Tau50	01/13/1931	20Sco47	05/13/1931	04Ari59	09/14/1931	23Lib23
09/15/1930	17Gem04	01/15/1931	16Sag44	05/15/1931	29Ari01	09/16/1931	22Sco35
09/17/1930	14Can48	01/17/1931	11Cap59	05/17/1931	23Tau55	09/18/1931	20Sag12
09/19/1930	13Leo56	01/19/1931	06Aqu33	05/19/1931	19Gem47	09/20/1931	16Cap14
09/21/1930	13Vir56	01/21/1931	00Pis31	05/21/1931	16Can37	09/22/1931	11Aqu07
09/23/1930	13Lib41	01/23/1931	24Pis10	05/23/1931	14Leo10	09/24/1931	05Pis14
09/25/1930	12Sco12	01/25/1931	17Ari50	05/25/1931	12Vir18	09/26/1931	28Pis56
09/27/1930	09Sag00	01/27/1931	12Tau14	05/27/1931	10Lib50	09/28/1931	22Ari31
09/29/1930	04Cap13	01/29/1931	08Gem05	05/29/1931	09Sco27	09/30/1931	16Tau19
		01/31/1931	05Can51	05/31/1931	07Sag42		
10/01/1930	28Cap25					10/02/1931	10Gem45
10/03/1930	22Aqu09	02/02/1931	05Leo24	06/02/1931	04Cap55	10/04/1931	06Can08
10/05/1930	15Pis59	02/04/1931	05Vir43	06/04/1931	00Aqu50	10/06/1931	02Leo58
10/07/1930	10Ari13	02/06/1931	05Lib33	06/06/1931	25Aqu28	10/08/1931	01Vir28
10/09/1930	05Tau06	02/08/1931	04Sco00	06/08/1931	19Pis18	10/10/1931	01Lib21
10/11/1930	00Gem49	02/10/1931	00Sag54	06/10/1931	13Ari00	10/12/1931	01Sco41
10/13/1930	27Gem27	02/12/1931	26Sag31	06/12/1931	07Tau12	10/14/1931	01Sag18
10/15/1930	25Can06	02/14/1931	21Cap16	06/14/1931	02Gem30	10/16/1931	29Sag17
10/17/1930	23Leo41	02/16/1931	15Aqu25	06/16/1931	29Gem03	10/18/1931	25Cap27
10/19/1930	22Vir51	02/18/1931	09Pis11	06/18/1931	26Can43	10/20/1931	20Aqu12
10/21/1930	21Lib55	02/20/1931	02Ari46	06/20/1931	24Leo58	10/22/1931	14Pis04
10/23/1930	20Sco06	02/22/1931	26Ari32	06/22/1931	23Vir18	10/24/1931	07Ari40
10/25/1930	16Sag56	02/24/1931	20Tau57	06/24/1931	21Lib30	10/26/1931	01Tau22
10/27/1930	12Cap16	02/26/1931	16Gem37	06/26/1931	19Sco24	10/28/1931	25Tau30
10/29/1930	06Aqu32	02/28/1931	14Can04	06/28/1931	16Sag48	10/30/1931	20Gem16
10/31/1930	00Pis17			06/30/1931	13Cap24		
		03/02/1931	13Leo24			11/01/1931	15Can52
11/02/1930	24Pis09	03/04/1931	13Vir48	07/02/1931	08Aqu56	11/03/1931	12Leo34
11/04/1930	18Ari39	03/06/1931	14Lib04	07/04/1931	03Pis26	11/05/1931	10Vir35
11/06/1930	14Tau06	03/08/1931	13Sco04	07/06/1931	27Pis13	11/07/1931	09Lib49
11/08/1930	10Gem37	03/10/1931	10Sag17	07/08/1931	20Ari54	11/09/1931	09Sco46
11/10/1930	08Can00	03/12/1931	05Cap56	07/10/1931	15Tau10	11/11/1931	09Sag20
11/12/1930	06Leo01	03/14/1931	00Aqu28	07/12/1931	10Gem42	11/13/1931	07Cap32
11/14/1930	04Vir19	03/16/1931	24Aqu22	07/14/1931	07Can46	11/15/1931	03Aqu55
11/16/1930	02Lib40	03/18/1931	17Pis59	07/16/1931	06Leo11	11/17/1931	28Aqu43
11/18/1930	00Sco48	03/20/1931	11Ari39	07/18/1931	05Vir14	11/19/1931	22Pis33
11/20/1930	28Sco17	03/22/1931	05Tau40	07/20/1931	04Lib07	11/21/1931	16Ari07
11/22/1930	24Sag47	03/24/1931	00Gem21	07/22/1931	02Sco22	11/23/1931	10Tau00
11/24/1930	20Cap05	03/26/1931	26Gem04	07/24/1931	29Sco49	11/25/1931	04Gem32
11/26/1930	14Aqu22	03/28/1931	23Can15	07/26/1931	26Sag31	11/27/1931	29Gem55
11/28/1930	08Pis07	03/30/1931	22Leo01	07/28/1931	22Cap25	11/29/1931	26Can04
11/30/1930	01Ari55			07/30/1931	17Aqu25		
		04/01/1931	21Vir56	08/01/1931	11Pis38	12/01/1931	23Leo00
12/02/1930	26Ari33	04/03/1931	22Lib04	08/03/1931	05Ari18	12/03/1931	20Vir43
12/04/1930	22Tau25	04/05/1931	21Sco17	08/05/1931	28Ari58	12/05/1931	19Lib16
12/06/1930	19Gem43	04/07/1931	18Sag51	08/07/1931	23Tau13	12/07/1931	18Sco24
12/08/1930	18Can05	04/09/1931	14Cap42	08/09/1931	18Gem46	12/09/1931	17Sag23
12/10/1930	16Leo50	04/11/1931	09Aqu15	08/11/1931	16Can02	12/11/1931	15Cap22
12/12/1930	15Vir20	04/13/1931	03Pis03	08/13/1931	14Leo54	12/13/1931	11Aqu49
12/14/1930	13Lib14	04/15/1931	26Pis39	08/15/1931	14Vir40	12/15/1931	06Pis42
12/16/1930	10Sco32	04/17/1931	20Ari29	08/17/1931	14Lib15	12/17/1931	00Ari34
12/18/1930	07Sag10	04/19/1931	14Tau54	08/19/1931	12Sco52	12/19/1931	24Ari09
12/20/1930	03Cap05	04/21/1931	10Gem06	08/21/1931	10Sag15	12/21/1931	18Tau10
12/22/1930	28Cap06	04/23/1931	06Can15	08/23/1931	06Cap28	12/23/1931	13Gem06
12/24/1930	22Aqu16	04/25/1931	03Leo24	08/25/1931	01Aqu45	12/25/1931	09Can08
12/26/1930	15Pis58	04/27/1931	01Vir42	08/27/1931	26Aqu15	12/27/1931	06Leo06
12/28/1930	09Ari42	04/29/1931	00Lib53	08/29/1931	20Pis10	12/29/1931	03Vir39
12/30/1930	04Tau13			08/31/1931	13Ari45	12/31/1931	01Lib35

Ephemeris Tables for the Moon

Date	Moon	Date	Moon	Date	Moon	Date	Moon
01/02/1932	29Lib45	05/01/1932	24Pis40	09/02/1932	02Lib05	01/02/1933	28Pis19
01/04/1932	28Sco04	05/03/1932	18Ari20	09/04/1932	01Sco10	01/04/1933	22Ari42
01/06/1932	26Sag09	05/05/1932	11Tau56	09/06/1932	00Sag00	01/06/1933	16Tau28
01/08/1932	23Cap29	05/07/1932	05Gem49	09/08/1932	28Sag10	01/08/1933	10Gem14
01/10/1932	19Aqu36	05/09/1932	00Can12	09/10/1932	25Cap24	01/10/1933	04Can26
01/12/1932	14Pis25	05/11/1932	25Can18	09/12/1932	21Aqu42	01/12/1933	29Can14
01/14/1932	08Ari19	05/13/1932	21Leo05	09/14/1932	17Pis06	01/14/1933	24Leo46
01/16/1932	01Tau55	05/15/1932	18Vir56	09/16/1932	11Ari40	01/16/1933	21Vir02
01/18/1932	26Tau00	05/17/1932	18Lib01	09/18/1932	05Tau40	01/18/1933	18Lib09
01/20/1932	21Gem07	05/19/1932	18Sco08	09/20/1932	29Tau23	01/20/1933	16Sco15
01/22/1932	17Can36	05/21/1932	18Sag14	09/22/1932	23Gem18	01/22/1933	15Sag12
01/24/1932	15Leo21	05/23/1932	17Cap04	09/24/1932	17Can58	01/24/1933	14Cap24
01/26/1932	13Vir49	05/25/1932	14Aqu04	09/26/1932	14Leo00	01/26/1933	13Aqu00
01/28/1932	12Lib25	05/27/1932	09Pis18	09/28/1932	11Vir39	01/28/1933	10Pis21
01/30/1932	10Sco42	05/29/1932	03Ari24	09/30/1932	10Lib51	01/30/1933	06Ari06
		05/31/1932	27Ari01				
02/01/1932	08Sag33			10/02/1932	10Sco46	02/01/1933	00Tau39
02/03/1932	05Cap48	06/02/1932	20Tau43	10/04/1932	10Sag20	02/03/1933	24Tau30
02/05/1932	02Aqu15	06/04/1932	14Gem53	10/06/1932	08Cap43	02/05/1933	18Gem18
02/07/1932	27Aqu47	06/06/1932	09Can42	10/08/1932	05Aqu39	02/07/1933	12Can37
02/09/1932	22Pis21	06/08/1932	05Leo15	10/10/1932	01Pis20	02/09/1933	07Leo49
02/11/1932	16Ari11	06/10/1932	01Vir37	10/12/1932	26Pis07	02/11/1933	04Vir03
02/13/1932	09Tau48	06/12/1932	29Vir01	10/14/1932	20Ari19	02/13/1933	01Lib09
02/15/1932	03Gem48	06/14/1932	27Lib35	10/16/1932	14Tau10	02/15/1933	28Lib57
02/17/1932	28Gem52	06/16/1932	27Sco04	10/18/1932	07Gem52	02/17/1933	27Sco12
02/19/1932	25Can30	06/18/1932	26Sag38	10/20/1932	01Can48	02/19/1933	25Sag37
02/21/1932	23Leo43	06/20/1932	25Cap15	10/22/1932	26Can21	02/21/1933	23Cap53
02/23/1932	23Vir00	06/22/1932	22Aqu12	10/24/1932	22Leo07	02/23/1933	21Aqu33
02/25/1932	22Lib30	06/24/1932	17Pis31	10/26/1932	19Vir38	02/25/1933	18Pis17
02/27/1932	21Sco22	06/26/1932	11Ari49	10/28/1932	18Lib57	02/27/1933	13Ari51
02/29/1932	19Sag13	06/28/1932	05Tau21	10/30/1932	19Sco23		
		06/30/1932	29Tau12			03/01/1933	08Tau25
03/02/1932	15Cap57			11/01/1932	19Sag37	03/03/1933	02Gem19
03/04/1932	11Aqu39	07/02/1932	23Gem41	11/03/1932	18Cap30	03/05/1933	26Gem07
03/06/1932	06Pis32	07/04/1932	19Can01	11/05/1932	15Aqu29	03/07/1933	20Can27
03/08/1932	00Ari42	07/06/1932	15Leo11	11/07/1932	10Pis55	03/09/1933	15Leo50
03/10/1932	24Ari25	07/08/1932	12Vir07	11/09/1932	05Ari18	03/11/1933	12Vir36
03/12/1932	18Tau04	07/10/1932	09Lib45	11/11/1932	29Ari12	03/13/1933	10Lib36
03/14/1932	12Gem03	07/12/1932	08Sco03	11/13/1932	22Tau57	03/15/1933	09Sco21
03/16/1932	06Can59	07/14/1932	06Sag51	11/15/1932	16Gem44	03/17/1933	08Sag11
03/18/1932	03Leo24	07/16/1932	05Cap36	11/17/1932	10Can48	03/19/1933	06Cap32
03/20/1932	01Vir38	07/18/1932	03Aqu34	11/19/1932	05Leo24	03/21/1933	04Aqu09
03/22/1932	01Lib18	07/20/1932	00Pis13	11/21/1932	01Vir01	03/23/1933	00Pis56
03/24/1932	01Sco31	07/22/1932	25Pis28	11/23/1932	28Vir09	03/25/1933	26Pis54
03/26/1932	01Sag08	07/24/1932	19Ari38	11/25/1932	27Lib07	03/27/1933	22Ari02
03/28/1932	29Sag20	07/26/1932	13Tau22	11/27/1932	27Sco27	03/29/1933	16Tau25
03/30/1932	25Cap58	07/28/1932	07Gem20	11/29/1932	27Sag55	03/31/1933	10Gem17
		07/30/1932	02Can02				
04/01/1932	21Aqu14	08/01/1932	27Can51	12/01/1932	27Cap11	04/02/1933	04Can03
04/03/1932	15Pis38	08/03/1932	24Leo42	12/03/1932	24Aqu30	04/04/1933	28Can18
04/05/1932	09Ari28	08/05/1932	22Vir27	12/05/1932	19Pis58	04/06/1933	23Leo39
04/07/1932	03Tau04	08/07/1932	20Lib39	12/07/1932	14Ari16	04/08/1933	20Vir37
04/09/1932	26Tau47	08/09/1932	19Sco03	12/09/1932	08Tau01	04/10/1933	19Lib15
04/11/1932	20Gem53	08/11/1932	17Sag22	12/11/1932	01Gem45	04/12/1933	18Sco53
04/13/1932	15Can47	08/13/1932	15Cap15	12/13/1932	25Gem43	04/14/1933	18Sag32
04/15/1932	11Leo57	08/15/1932	12Aqu22	12/15/1932	20Can06	04/16/1933	17Cap14
04/17/1932	09Vir51	08/17/1932	08Pis27	12/17/1932	15Leo03	04/18/1933	14Aqu38
04/19/1932	09Lib24	08/19/1932	03Ari25	12/19/1932	10Vir46	04/20/1933	10Pis49
04/21/1932	09Sco50	08/21/1932	27Ari32	12/21/1932	07Lib41	04/22/1933	06Ari07
04/23/1932	09Sag57	08/23/1932	21Tau18	12/23/1932	06Sco06	04/24/1933	00Tau45
04/25/1932	08Cap36	08/25/1932	15Gem16	12/25/1932	05Sag50	04/26/1933	24Tau51
04/27/1932	05Aqu22	08/27/1932	10Can01	12/27/1932	05Cap54	04/28/1933	18Gem39
04/29/1932	00Pis33	08/29/1932	06Leo04	12/29/1932	05Aqu07	04/30/1933	12Can23
		08/31/1932	03Vir31	12/31/1932	02Pis38		

Ephemeris Tables for the Moon

Date	Moon	Date	Moon	Date	Moon	Date	Moon
05/02/1933	06Leo34	09/01/1933	02Aqu58	01/01/1934	17Can12	05/01/1934	06Sag34
05/04/1933	01Vir46	09/03/1933	01Pis19	01/03/1934	10Leo55	05/03/1934	05Cap27
05/06/1933	28Vir39	09/05/1933	28Pis44	01/05/1934	05Vir00	05/05/1934	04Aqu03
05/08/1933	27Lib28	09/07/1933	24Ari55	01/07/1934	29Vir48	05/07/1934	02Pis02
05/10/1933	27Sco37	09/09/1933	19Tau53	01/09/1934	25Lib56	05/09/1934	29Pis21
05/12/1933	27Sag57	09/11/1933	13Gem57	01/11/1934	23Sco47	05/11/1934	25Ari57
05/14/1933	27Cap10	09/13/1933	07Can43	01/13/1934	23Sag19	05/13/1934	21Tau46
05/16/1933	24Aqu42	09/15/1933	01Leo46	01/15/1934	23Cap43	05/15/1934	16Gem40
05/18/1933	20Pis42	09/17/1933	26Leo42	01/17/1934	23Aqu43	05/17/1934	10Can48
05/20/1933	15Ari34	09/19/1933	22Vir48	01/19/1934	22Pis19	05/19/1934	04Leo27
05/22/1933	09Tau50	09/21/1933	20Lib06	01/21/1934	19Ari05	05/21/1934	28Leo12
05/24/1933	03Gem42	09/23/1933	18Sco16	01/23/1934	14Tau18	05/23/1934	22Vir44
05/26/1933	27Gem25	09/25/1933	16Sag45	01/25/1934	08Gem31	05/25/1934	18Lib43
05/28/1933	21Can12	09/27/1933	15Cap06	01/27/1934	02Can15	05/27/1934	16Sco28
05/30/1933	15Leo25	09/29/1933	13Aqu04	01/29/1934	25Can56	05/29/1934	15Sag37
				01/31/1934	19Leo52	05/31/1934	15Cap19
06/01/1933	10Vir34	10/01/1933	10Pis31				
06/03/1933	07Lib15	10/03/1933	07Ari13	02/02/1934	14Vir21	06/02/1934	14Aqu31
06/05/1933	05Sco52	10/05/1933	03Tau00	02/04/1934	09Lib34	06/04/1934	12Pis41
06/07/1933	06Sag01	10/07/1933	27Tau49	02/06/1934	05Sco49	06/06/1934	09Ari42
06/09/1933	06Cap36	10/09/1933	21Gem50	02/08/1934	03Sag22	06/08/1934	05Tau43
06/11/1933	06Aqu12	10/11/1933	15Can34	02/10/1934	02Cap12	06/10/1934	00Gem55
06/13/1933	04Pis01	10/13/1933	09Leo34	02/12/1934	01Aqu54	06/12/1934	25Gem21
06/15/1933	00Ari04	10/15/1933	04Vir35	02/14/1934	01Pis33	06/14/1934	19Can13
06/17/1933	24Ari49	10/17/1933	01Lib04	02/16/1934	00Ari13	06/16/1934	12Leo48
06/19/1933	18Tau53	10/19/1933	29Lib07	02/18/1934	27Ari14	06/18/1934	06Vir32
06/21/1933	12Gem37	10/21/1933	28Sco13	02/20/1934	22Tau40	06/20/1934	01Lib03
06/23/1933	06Can22	10/23/1933	27Sag27	02/22/1934	16Gem56	06/22/1934	26Lib57
06/25/1933	00Leo21	10/25/1933	26Cap01	02/24/1934	10Can37	06/24/1934	24Sco42
06/27/1933	24Leo48	10/27/1933	23Aqu37	02/26/1934	04Leo21	06/26/1934	24Sag06
06/29/1933	20Vir06	10/29/1933	20Pis21	02/28/1934	28Leo34	06/28/1934	24Cap18
07/01/1933	16Lib42	10/31/1933	16Ari18			06/30/1934	24Aqu07
07/03/1933	14Sco58			03/02/1934	23Vir36		
07/05/1933	14Sag41	11/02/1933	11Tau31	03/04/1934	19Lib31	07/02/1934	22Pis43
07/07/1933	14Cap58	11/04/1933	06Gem03	03/06/1934	16Sco18	07/04/1934	19Ari46
07/09/1933	14Aqu35	11/06/1933	29Gem57	03/08/1934	13Sag55	07/06/1934	15Tau30
07/11/1933	12Pis35	11/08/1933	23Can36	03/10/1934	12Cap14	07/08/1934	10Gem15
07/13/1933	08Ari49	11/10/1933	17Leo31	03/12/1934	11Aqu04	07/10/1934	04Can19
07/15/1933	03Tau37	11/12/1933	12Vir24	03/14/1934	09Pis55	07/12/1934	27Can58
07/17/1933	27Tau39	11/14/1933	08Lib56	03/16/1934	08Ari06	07/14/1934	21Leo31
07/19/1933	21Gem23	11/16/1933	07Sco21	03/18/1934	05Tau04	07/16/1934	15Vir22
07/21/1933	15Can13	11/18/1933	07Sag09	03/20/1934	00Gem34	07/18/1934	09Lib57
07/23/1933	09Leo30	11/20/1933	07Cap11	03/22/1934	24Gem55	07/20/1934	05Sco46
07/25/1933	04Vir23	11/22/1933	06Aqu21	03/24/1934	18Can37	07/22/1934	03Sag15
07/27/1933	00Lib08	11/24/1933	04Pis04	03/26/1934	12Leo24	07/24/1934	02Cap27
07/29/1933	26Lib55	11/26/1933	00Ari25	03/28/1934	06Vir50	07/26/1934	02Aqu42
07/31/1933	24Sco58	11/28/1933	25Ari47	03/30/1934	02Lib22	07/28/1934	02Pis54
		11/30/1933	20Tau29			07/30/1934	01Ari54
08/02/1933	24Sag04			04/01/1934	29Lib06		
08/04/1933	23Cap38	12/02/1933	14Gem40	04/03/1934	26Sco43	08/01/1934	29Ari13
08/06/1933	22Aqu46	12/04/1933	08Can25	04/05/1934	24Sag50	08/03/1934	24Tau54
08/08/1933	20Pis40	12/06/1933	02Leo04	04/07/1934	23Cap04	08/05/1934	19Gem24
08/10/1933	16Ari59	12/08/1933	25Leo58	04/09/1934	21Aqu16	08/07/1934	13Can14
08/12/1933	11Tau55	12/10/1933	20Vir42	04/11/1934	19Pis14	08/09/1934	06Leo48
08/14/1933	05Gem58	12/12/1933	17Lib01	04/13/1934	16Ari38	08/11/1934	00Vir29
08/16/1933	29Gem44	12/14/1933	15Sco17	04/15/1934	13Tau07	08/13/1934	24Vir34
08/18/1933	23Can43	12/16/1933	15Sag14	04/17/1934	08Gem27	08/15/1934	19Lib26
08/20/1933	18Leo22	12/18/1933	15Cap47	04/19/1934	02Can45	08/17/1934	15Sco19
08/22/1933	13Vir51	12/20/1933	15Aqu33	04/21/1934	26Can27	08/19/1934	12Sag33
08/24/1933	10Lib18	12/22/1933	13Pis43	04/23/1934	20Leo13	08/21/1934	11Cap15
08/26/1933	07Sco37	12/24/1933	10Ari08	04/25/1934	14Vir48	08/23/1934	11Aqu04
08/28/1933	05Sag42	12/26/1933	05Tau17	04/27/1934	10Lib40	08/25/1934	11Pis08
08/30/1933	04Cap16	12/28/1933	29Tau37	04/29/1934	08Sco04	08/27/1934	10Ari19
		12/30/1933	23Gem30			08/29/1934	07Tau54
						08/31/1934	03Gem43

Ephemeris Tables for the Moon

Date	Moon	Date	Moon	Date	Moon	Date	Moon
09/02/1934	28Gem09	01/02/1935	04Sag22	05/02/1935	05Tau50	09/01/1935	15Lib47
09/04/1934	21Can53	01/04/1935	03Cap13	05/04/1935	03Gem42	09/03/1935	09Sco56
09/06/1934	15Leo28	01/06/1935	03Aqu04	05/06/1935	00Can03	09/05/1935	04Sag51
09/08/1934	09Vir23	01/08/1935	02Pis53	05/08/1935	24Can58	09/07/1935	01Cap02
09/10/1934	03Lib55	01/10/1935	01Ari44	05/10/1935	18Leo56	09/09/1935	28Cap57
09/12/1934	29Lib16	01/12/1935	29Ari112	05/12/1935	12Vir37	09/11/1935	28Aqu34
09/14/1934	25Sco31	01/14/1935	25Tau21	05/14/1935	06Lib41	09/13/1935	29Pis07
09/16/1934	22Sag42	01/16/1935	20Gem28	05/16/1935	01Sco37	09/15/1935	29Ari16
09/18/1934	20Cap55	01/18/1935	14Can49	05/18/1935	27Sco39	09/17/1935	27Tau49
09/20/1934	20Aqu010	01/20/1935	08Leo41	05/20/1935	24Sag38	09/19/1935	24Gem27
09/22/1934	19Pis30	01/22/1935	02Vir17	05/22/1935	22Cap19	09/21/1935	19Can27
09/24/1934	18Ari26	01/24/1935	26Vir01	05/24/1935	20Aqu25	09/23/1935	13Leo32
09/26/1934	16Tau00	01/26/1935	20Lib15	05/26/1935	18Pis45	09/25/1935	07Vir13
09/28/1934	11Gem55	01/28/1935	15Sco33	05/28/1935	17Ari06	09/27/1935	00Lib55
09/30/1934	06Can24	01/30/1935	12Sag24	05/30/1935	15Tau04	09/29/1935	24Lib54
10/02/1934	00Leo07	02/01/1935	11Cap03	06/01/1935	12Gem10	10/01/1935	19Sco18
10/04/1934	23Leo46	02/03/1935	11Aqu06	06/03/1935	08Can04	10/03/1935	14Sag22
10/06/1934	17Vir57	02/05/1935	11Pis30	06/05/1935	02Leo51	10/05/1935	10Cap27
10/08/1934	13Lib00	02/07/1935	11Ari01	06/07/1935	26Leo48	10/07/1935	08Aqu00
10/10/1934	09Sco03	02/09/1935	08Tau51	06/09/1935	20Vir31	10/09/1935	07Pis09
10/12/1934	05Sag56	02/11/1935	04Gem59	06/11/1935	14Lib39	10/11/1935	07Ari22
10/14/1934	03Cap26	02/13/1935	29Gem47	06/13/1935	09Sco45	10/13/1935	07Tau28
10/16/1934	01Aqu27	02/15/1935	23Can46	06/15/1935	06Sag12	10/15/1935	06Gem14
10/18/1934	29Aqu54	02/17/1935	17Leo26	06/17/1935	03Cap53	10/17/1935	03Can04
10/20/1934	28Pis31	02/19/1935	11Vir04	06/19/1935	02Aqu25	10/19/1935	28Can10
10/22/1934	26Ari46	02/21/1935	05Lib00	06/21/1935	01Pis13	10/21/1935	22Leo13
10/24/1934	23Tau58	02/23/1935	29Lib28	06/23/1935	29Pis46	10/23/1935	15Vir54
10/26/1934	19Gem46	02/25/1935	24Sco44	06/25/1935	27Ari45	10/25/1935	09Lib41
10/28/1934	14Can16	02/27/1935	21Sag18	06/27/1935	24Tau55	10/27/1935	03Sco57
10/30/1934	08Leo01			06/29/1935	21Gem13	10/29/1935	28Sco47
		03/01/1935	19Cap28			10/31/1935	24Sag19
11/01/1934	01Vir42	03/03/1935	19Aqu08	07/01/1935	16Can33		
11/03/1934	26Vir00	03/05/1935	19Pis31	07/03/1935	10Leo59	11/02/1935	20Cap38
11/05/1934	21Lib28	03/07/1935	19Ari21	07/05/1935	04Vir52	11/04/1935	18Aqu01
11/07/1934	18Sco13	03/09/1935	17Tau36	07/07/1935	28Vir34	11/06/1935	16Pis38
11/09/1934	15Sag58	03/11/1935	13Gem55	07/09/1935	22Lib41	11/08/1935	16Ari06
11/11/1934	14Cap10	03/13/1935	08Can41	07/11/1935	17Sco46	11/10/1935	15Tau37
11/13/1934	12Aqu27	03/15/1935	02Leo32	07/13/1935	14Sag19	11/12/1935	14Gem07
11/15/1934	10Pis34	03/17/1935	26Leo08	07/15/1935	12Cap27	11/14/1935	11Can01
11/17/1934	08Ari23	03/19/1935	19Vir54	07/17/1935	11Aqu43	11/16/1935	06Leo15
11/19/1934	05Tau45	03/21/1935	14Lib08	07/19/1935	11Pis22	11/18/1935	00Vir24
11/21/1934	02Gem16	03/23/1935	09Sco02	07/21/1935	10Ari25	11/20/1935	24Vir07
11/23/1934	27Gem42	03/25/1935	04Sag39	07/23/1935	08Tau22	11/22/1935	18Lib01
11/25/1934	22Can05	03/27/1935	01Cap12	07/25/1935	05Gem04	11/24/1935	12Sco34
11/27/1934	15Leo48	03/29/1935	28Cap57	07/27/1935	00Can40	11/26/1935	07Sag57
11/29/1934	09Vir29	03/31/1935	28Aqu00	07/29/1935	25Can25	11/28/1935	04Cap10
				07/31/1935	19Leo31	11/30/1935	01Aqu09
12/01/1934	03Lib47	04/02/1935	27Pis49				
12/03/1934	29Lib24	04/04/1935	27Ari23	08/02/1935	13Vir15	12/02/1935	28Aqu48
12/05/1934	26Sco33	04/06/1935	25Tau40	08/04/1935	06Lib57	12/04/1935	27Pis06
12/07/1934	25Sag04	04/08/1935	22Gem09	08/06/1935	01Sco02	12/06/1935	25Ari46
12/09/1934	24Cap11	04/10/1935	17Can01	08/08/1935	26Sco02	12/08/1935	24Tau19
12/11/1934	23Aqu08	04/12/1935	10Leo55	08/10/1935	22Sag27	12/10/1935	22Gem08
12/13/1934	21Pis26	04/14/1935	04Vir32	08/12/1935	20Cap37	12/12/1935	18Can44
12/15/1934	18Ari49	04/16/1935	28Vir28	08/14/1935	20Aqu19	12/14/1935	14Leo00
12/17/1934	15Tau25	04/18/1935	23Lib05	08/16/1935	20Pis37	12/16/1935	08Vir13
12/19/1934	11Gem09	04/20/1935	18Sco33	08/18/1935	20Ari18	12/18/1935	02Lib00
12/21/1934	06Can03	04/22/1935	14Sag47	08/20/1935	18Tau31	12/20/1935	25Lib55
12/23/1934	00Leo11	04/24/1935	11Cap45	08/22/1935	15Gem03	12/22/1935	20Sco36
12/25/1934	23Leo51	04/26/1935	09Aqu27	08/24/1935	10Can12	12/24/1935	16Sag23
12/27/1934	17Vir30	04/28/1935	07Pis58	08/26/1935	04Leo31	12/26/1935	13Cap21
12/29/1934	11Lib43	04/30/1935	07Ari00	08/28/1935	28Leo21	12/28/1935	11Aqu16
12/31/1934	07Sco12			08/30/1935	22Vir01	12/30/1935	09Pis40

Ephemeris Tables for the Moon

Date	Moon	Date	Moon	Date	Moon	Date	Moon
01/01/1936	08Ari07	05/02/1936	26Vir40	09/01/1936	08Pis28	01/01/1937	05Vir31
01/03/1936	06Tau18	05/04/1936	20Lib25	09/03/1936	08Ari14	01/03/1937	00Lib33
01/05/1936	03Gem56	05/06/1936	14Sco21	09/05/1936	07Tau53	01/05/1937	24Lib34
01/07/1936	00Can49	05/08/1936	08Sag43	09/07/1936	06Gem29	01/07/1937	18Sco14
01/09/1936	26Can48	05/10/1936	03Cap42	09/09/1936	03Can45	01/09/1937	12Sag09
01/11/1936	21Leo49	05/12/1936	29Cap33	09/11/1936	29Can52	01/11/1937	06Cap50
01/13/1936	16Vir01	05/14/1936	26Aqu34	09/13/1936	25Leo10	01/13/1937	02Aqu30
01/15/1936	09Lib49	05/16/1936	24Pis59	09/15/1936	19Vir48	01/15/1937	29Aqu10
01/17/1936	03Sco40	05/18/1936	24Ari31	09/17/1936	13Lib52	01/17/1937	26Pis38
01/19/1936	28Sco19	05/20/1936	24Tau19	09/19/1936	07Sco36	01/19/1937	24Ari38
01/21/1936	24Sag13	05/22/1936	23Gem21	09/21/1936	01Sag16	01/21/1937	22Tau57
01/23/1936	21Cap42	05/24/1936	20Can48	09/23/1936	25Sag26	01/23/1937	21Gem21
01/25/1936	20Aqu28	05/26/1936	16Leo39	09/25/1936	20Cap42	01/25/1937	19Can31
01/27/1936	19Pis51	05/28/1936	11Vir13	09/27/1936	17Aqu45	01/27/1937	16Leo57
01/29/1936	18Ari55	05/30/1936	05Lib07	09/29/1936	16Pis44	01/29/1937	13Vir16
01/31/1936	17Tau04					01/31/1937	08Lib19
		06/01/1936	28Lib54	10/01/1936	16Ari59		
02/02/1936	14Gem08	06/03/1936	23Sco01	10/03/1936	17Tau17	02/02/1937	02Sco24
02/04/1936	10Can13	06/05/1936	17Sag48	10/05/1936	16Gem23	02/04/1937	26Sco03
02/06/1936	05Leo30	06/07/1936	13Cap24	10/07/1936	13Can48	02/06/1937	20Sag00
02/08/1936	00Vir06	06/09/1936	09Aqu51	10/09/1936	09Leo42	02/08/1937	14Cap52
02/10/1936	24Vir10	06/11/1936	07Pis14	10/11/1936	04Vir34	02/10/1937	11Aqu05
02/12/1936	17Lib56	06/13/1936	05Ari28	10/13/1936	28Vir51	02/12/1937	08Pis38
02/14/1936	11Sco46	06/15/1936	04Tau20	10/15/1936	22Lib42	02/14/1937	07Ari00
02/16/1936	06Sag13	06/17/1936	03Gem17	10/17/1936	16Sco21	02/16/1937	05Tau35
02/18/1936	01Cap59	06/19/1936	01Can38	10/19/1936	10Sag04	02/18/1937	03Gem52
02/20/1936	29Cap31	06/21/1936	28Can49	10/21/1936	04Cap16	02/20/1937	01Can39
02/22/1936	28Aqu49	06/23/1936	24Leo37	10/23/1936	29Cap26	02/22/1937	28Can57
02/24/1936	29Pis00	06/25/1936	19Vir16	10/25/1936	26Aqu13	02/24/1937	25Leo35
02/26/1936	28Ari51	06/27/1936	13Lib11	10/27/1936	24Pis57	02/26/1937	21Vir23
02/28/1936	27Tau24	06/29/1936	07Sco01	10/29/1936	25Ari07	02/28/1937	16Lib13
				10/31/1936	25Tau40		
03/01/1936	24Gem19	07/01/1936	01Sag18			03/02/1937	10Sco14
03/03/1936	19Can56	07/03/1936	26Sag28	11/02/1936	25Gem13	03/04/1937	03Sag53
03/05/1936	14Leo40	07/05/1936	22Cap43	11/04/1936	23Can01	03/06/1937	27Sag45
03/07/1936	08Vir52	07/07/1936	20Aqu00	11/06/1936	19Leo03	03/08/1937	22Cap40
03/09/1936	02Lib45	07/09/1936	18Pis03	11/08/1936	13Vir48	03/10/1937	19Aqu08
03/11/1936	26Lib31	07/11/1936	16Ari28	11/10/1936	07Lib49	03/12/1937	17Pis18
03/13/1936	20Sco24	07/13/1936	14Tau54	11/12/1936	01Sco31	03/14/1937	16Ari33
03/15/1936	14Sag47	07/15/1936	13Gem01	11/14/1936	25Sco14	03/16/1937	15Tau55
03/17/1936	10Cap20	07/17/1936	10Can31	11/16/1936	19Sag11	03/18/1937	14Gem38
03/19/1936	07Aqu37	07/19/1936	07Leo07	11/18/1936	13Cap40	03/20/1937	12Can17
03/21/1936	06Pis52	07/21/1936	02Vir39	11/20/1936	09Aqu00	03/22/1937	09Leo01
03/23/1936	07Ari21	07/23/1936	27Vir13	11/22/1936	05Pis38	03/24/1937	04Vir55
03/25/1936	07Tau43	07/25/1936	21Lib07	11/24/1936	03Ari51	03/26/1937	00Lib07
03/27/1936	06Gem46	07/27/1936	14Sco56	11/26/1936	03Tau26	03/28/1937	24Lib34
03/29/1936	03Can54	07/29/1936	09Sag16	11/28/1936	03Gem37	03/30/1937	18Sco25
03/31/1936	29Can26	07/31/1936	04Cap39	11/30/1936	03Can12		
						04/01/1937	12Sag01
04/02/1936	23Leo54	08/02/1936	01Aqu28	12/02/1936	01Leo18	04/03/1937	05Cap53
04/04/1936	17Vir52	08/04/1936	29Aqu37	12/04/1936	27Leo37	04/05/1937	00Aqu41
04/06/1936	11Lib37	08/06/1936	28Pis33	12/06/1936	22Vir28	04/07/1937	27Aqu06
04/08/1936	05Sco25	08/08/1936	27Ari28	12/08/1936	16Lib27	04/09/1937	25Pis26
04/10/1936	29Sco28	08/10/1936	25Tau48	12/10/1936	10Sco06	04/11/1937	25Ari12
04/12/1936	24Sag02	08/12/1936	23Gem19	12/12/1936	03Sag55	04/13/1937	25Tau17
04/14/1936	19Cap34	08/14/1936	20Can00	12/14/1936	28Sag14	04/15/1937	24Gem37
04/16/1936	16Aqu35	08/16/1936	15Leo54	12/16/1936	23Cap41	04/17/1937	22Can33
04/18/1936	15Pis27	08/18/1936	11Vir00	12/18/1936	19Aqu06	04/19/1937	19Leo07
04/20/1936	15Ari37	08/20/1936	05Lib22	12/20/1936	15Pis55	04/21/1937	14Vir36
04/22/1936	15Tau59	08/22/1936	29Lib12	12/22/1936	13Ari49	04/23/1937	09Lib15
04/24/1936	15Gem15	08/24/1936	22Sco56	12/24/1936	12Tau39	04/25/1937	03Sco19
04/26/1936	12Can40	08/26/1936	17Sag10	12/26/1936	11Gem59	04/27/1937	27Sco00
04/28/1936	08Leo20	08/28/1936	12Cap35	12/28/1936	11Can03	04/29/1937	20Sag37
04/30/1936	02Vir49	08/30/1936	09Aqu41	12/30/1936	09Leo02		

Ephemeris Tables for the Moon

Date	Moon	Date	Moon	Date	Moon	Date	Moon
05/01/1937	14Cap33	09/02/1937	08Leo28	01/02/1938	19Cap11	05/02/1938	12Gem21
05/03/1937	09Aqu21	09/04/1937	05Vir52	01/04/1938	13Aqu25	05/04/1938	11Can36
05/05/1937	05Pis37	09/06/1937	02Lib15	01/06/1938	08Pis20	05/06/1938	10Leo12
05/07/1937	03Ari43	09/08/1937	27Lib26	01/08/1938	04Ari06	05/08/1938	07Vir46
05/09/1937	03Tau26	09/10/1937	21Sco36	01/10/1938	01Tau04	05/10/1938	04Lib18
05/11/1937	03Gem49	09/12/1937	15Sag14	01/12/1938	29Tau30	05/12/1938	29Lib52
05/13/1937	03Can39	09/14/1937	09Cap04	01/14/1938	29Gem09	05/14/1938	24Sco36
05/15/1937	02Leo01	09/16/1937	03Aqu45	01/16/1938	29Can17	05/16/1938	18Sag40
05/17/1937	28Leo44	09/18/1937	29Aqu49	01/18/1938	28Leo40	05/18/1938	12Cap23
05/19/1937	24Vir03	09/20/1937	27Pis21	01/20/1938	26Vir25	05/20/1938	06Aqu09
05/21/1937	18Lib24	09/22/1937	25Ari52	01/22/1938	22Lib16	05/22/1938	00Pis27
05/23/1937	12Sco13	09/24/1937	24Tau44	01/24/1938	16Sco42	05/24/1938	25Pis51
05/25/1937	05Sag48	09/26/1937	23Gem17	01/26/1938	10Sag22	05/26/1938	22Ari48
05/27/1937	29Sag32	09/28/1937	21Can15	01/28/1938	03Cap58	05/28/1938	21Tau27
05/29/1937	23Cap43	09/30/1937	18Leo33	01/30/1938	27Cap58	05/30/1938	21Gem16
05/31/1937	18Aqu42						
		10/02/1937	15Vir07	02/01/1938	22Aqu39	06/01/1938	21Can16
06/02/1937	14Pis56	10/04/1937	10Lib52	02/03/1938	18Pis08	06/03/1938	20Leo23
06/04/1937	12Ari40	10/06/1937	05Sco37	02/05/1938	14Ari20	06/05/1938	18Vir02
06/06/1937	11Tau58	10/08/1937	29Sco37	02/07/1938	11Tau22	06/07/1938	14Lib14
06/08/1937	12Gem06	10/10/1937	23Sag13	02/09/1938	09Gem21	06/09/1938	09Sco16
06/10/1937	12Can01	10/12/1937	17Cap00	02/11/1938	08Can15	06/11/1938	03Sag33
06/12/1937	10Leo42	10/14/1937	11Aqu37	02/13/1938	07Leo38	06/13/1938	27Sag21
06/14/1937	07Vir39	10/16/1937	07Pis45	02/15/1938	06Vir34	06/15/1938	21Cap01
06/16/1937	03Lib00	10/18/1937	05Ari36	02/17/1938	04Lib14	06/17/1938	14Aqu51
06/18/1937	27Lib15	10/20/1937	04Tau47	02/19/1938	00Sco12	06/19/1938	09Pis12
06/20/1937	20Sco56	10/22/1937	04Gem29	02/21/1938	24Sco43	06/21/1938	04Ari28
06/22/1937	14Sag34	10/24/1937	03Can43	02/23/1938	18Sag28	06/23/1938	01Tau12
06/24/1937	08Cap33	10/26/1937	01Leo54	02/25/1938	12Cap07	06/25/1938	29Tau44
06/26/1937	03Aqu09	10/28/1937	28Leo53	02/27/1938	06Aqu20	06/27/1938	29Gem43
06/28/1937	28Aqu34	10/30/1937	24Vir49			06/29/1938	00Leo09
06/30/1937	25Pis01			03/01/1938	01Pis28		
		11/01/1937	19Lib53	03/03/1938	27Pis38	07/01/1938	29Leo45
07/02/1937	22Ari33	11/03/1937	14Sco12	03/05/1938	24Ari36	07/03/1938	27Vir40
07/04/1937	21Tau16	11/05/1937	07Sag59	03/07/1938	22Tau08	07/05/1938	23Lib48
07/06/1937	20Gem48	11/07/1937	01Cap31	03/09/1938	20Gem07	07/07/1938	18Sco33
07/08/1937	20Can18	11/09/1937	25Cap18	03/11/1938	18Can28	07/09/1938	12Sag32
07/10/1937	18Leo56	11/11/1937	19Aqu51	03/13/1938	16Leo58	07/11/1938	06Cap13
07/12/1937	15Vir59	11/13/1937	15Pis46	03/15/1938	15Vir04	07/13/1938	29Cap55
07/14/1937	11Lib25	11/15/1937	13Ari30	03/17/1938	12Lib10	07/15/1938	23Aqu57
07/16/1937	05Sco39	11/17/1937	12Tau52	03/19/1938	07Sco58	07/17/1938	18Pis29
07/18/1937	29Sco20	11/19/1937	13Gem07	03/21/1938	02Sag30	07/19/1938	13Ari49
07/20/1937	23Sag04	11/21/1937	13Can06	03/23/1938	26Sag18	07/21/1938	10Tau24
07/22/1937	17Cap21	11/23/1937	11Leo49	03/25/1938	20Cap00	07/23/1938	08Gem32
07/24/1937	12Aqu29	11/25/1937	08Vir54	03/27/1938	14Aqu19	07/25/1938	08Can12
07/26/1937	08Pis34	11/27/1937	04Lib31	03/29/1938	09Pis45	07/27/1938	08Leo34
07/28/1937	05Ari31	11/29/1937	29Lib06	03/31/1938	06Ari28	07/29/1938	08Vir22
07/30/1937	03Tau09					07/31/1938	06Lib31
		12/01/1937	23Sco01	04/02/1938	04Tau16		
08/01/1937	01Gem28	12/03/1937	16Sag40	04/04/1938	02Gem38	08/02/1938	02Sco45
08/03/1937	00Can15	12/05/1937	10Cap16	04/06/1938	01Can06	08/04/1938	27Sco27
08/05/1937	29Can02	12/07/1937	04Aqu10	04/08/1938	29Can21	08/06/1938	21Sag20
08/07/1937	27Leo10	12/09/1937	28Aqu46	04/10/1938	27Leo13	08/08/1938	15Cap00
08/09/1937	24Vir03	12/11/1937	24Pis30	04/12/1938	24Vir26	08/10/1938	08Aqu51
08/11/1937	19Lib27	12/13/1937	21Ari47	04/14/1938	20Lib43	08/12/1938	03Pis10
08/13/1937	13Sco42	12/15/1937	20Tau48	04/16/1938	16Sco01	08/14/1938	28Pis07
08/15/1937	07Sag22	12/17/1937	21Gem03	04/18/1938	10Sag23	08/16/1938	23Ari45
08/17/1937	01Cap12	12/19/1937	21Can25	04/20/1938	04Cap11	08/18/1938	20Tau22
08/19/1937	25Cap45	12/21/1937	20Leo40	04/22/1938	27Cap55	08/20/1938	18Gem12
08/21/1937	21Aqu27	12/23/1937	18Vir07	04/24/1938	22Aqu13	08/22/1938	17Can19
08/23/1937	18Pis18	12/25/1937	13Lib46	04/26/1938	17Pis43	08/24/1938	17Leo09
08/25/1937	15Ari59	12/27/1937	08Sco09	04/28/1938	14Ari43	08/26/1938	16Vir39
08/27/1937	14Tau06	12/29/1937	01Sag51	04/30/1938	13Tau08	08/28/1938	14Lib45
08/29/1937	12Gem19	12/31/1937	25Sag25			08/30/1938	11Sco03
08/31/1937	10Can31						

Ephemeris Tables for the Moon

Date	Moon	Date	Moon	Date	Moon	Date	Moon
09/01/1938	05Sag50	01/01/1939	10Tau40	05/01/1939	12Lib54	09/02/1939	18Ari24
09/03/1938	29Sag44	01/03/1939	08Gem47	05/03/1939	10Sco27	09/04/1939	13Tau00
09/05/1938	23Cap27	01/05/1939	08Can37	05/05/1939	06Sag57	09/06/1939	08Gem41
09/07/1938	17Aqu27	01/07/1939	09Leo11	05/07/1939	02Cap16	09/08/1939	05Can53
09/09/1938	12Pis11	01/09/1939	09Vir05	05/09/1939	26Cap39	09/10/1939	04Leo48
09/11/1938	07Ari41	01/11/1939	07Lib22	05/11/1939	20Aqu30	09/12/1939	04Vir57
09/13/1938	03Tau55	01/13/1939	03Sco49	05/13/1939	14Pis24	09/14/1939	05Lib12
09/15/1938	00Gem54	01/15/1939	28Sco52	05/15/1939	08Ari58	09/16/1939	04Sco19
09/17/1938	28Gem42	01/17/1939	23Sag09	05/17/1939	04Tau39	09/18/1939	01Sag39
09/19/1938	27Can19	01/19/1939	17Cap01	05/19/1939	01Gem40	09/20/1939	27Sag18
09/21/1938	26Leo21	01/21/1939	10Aqu44	05/21/1939	29Gem46	09/22/1939	21Cap46
09/23/1938	25Vir05	01/23/1939	04Pis32	05/23/1939	28Can27	09/24/1939	15Aqu39
09/25/1938	22Lib46	01/25/1939	28Pis38	05/25/1939	27Leo08	09/26/1939	09Pis23
09/27/1938	18Sco58	01/27/1939	23Ari22	05/27/1939	25Vir19	09/28/1939	03Ari18
09/29/1938	13Sag48	01/29/1939	19Tau19	05/29/1939	22Lib48	09/30/1939	27Ari41
		01/31/1939	17Gem03	05/31/1939	19Sco30		
10/01/1938	07Cap45					10/02/1939	22Tau43
10/03/1938	01Aqu29	02/02/1939	16Can37	06/02/1939	15Sag24	10/04/1939	18Gem40
10/05/1938	25Aqu38	02/04/1939	17Leo15	06/04/1939	10Cap25	10/06/1939	15Can49
10/07/1938	20Pis40	02/06/1939	17Vir30	06/06/1939	04Aqu40	10/08/1939	14Leo16
10/09/1938	16Ari45	02/08/1939	16Lib12	06/08/1939	28Aqu29	10/10/1939	13Vir43
10/11/1938	13Tau45	02/10/1939	12Sco55	06/10/1939	22Pis21	10/12/1939	13Lib23
10/13/1938	11Gem31	02/12/1939	08Sag00	06/12/1939	16Ari54	10/14/1939	12Sco18
10/15/1938	09Can42	02/14/1939	02Cap09	06/14/1939	12Tau43	10/16/1939	09Sag45
10/17/1938	08Leo05	02/16/1939	25Cap51	06/16/1939	10Gem10	10/18/1939	05Cap36
10/19/1938	06Vir21	02/18/1939	19Aqu36	06/18/1939	09Can05	10/20/1939	00Aqu09
10/21/1938	04Lib09	02/20/1939	13Pis35	06/20/1939	08Leo38	10/22/1939	24Aqu00
10/23/1938	01Sco05	02/22/1939	07Ari59	06/22/1939	07Vir52	10/24/1939	17Pis46
10/25/1938	26Sco54	02/24/1939	03Tau00	06/24/1939	06Lib04	10/26/1939	11Ari52
10/27/1938	21Sag36	02/26/1939	28Tau58	06/26/1939	03Sco05	10/28/1939	06Tau43
10/29/1938	15Cap34	02/28/1939	26Gem23	06/28/1939	29Sco07	10/30/1939	02Gem26
10/31/1938	09Aqu19			06/30/1939	24Sag22		
		03/02/1939	25Can22	07/02/1939	18Cap58		
11/02/1938	03Pis30	03/04/1939	25Leo27			11/01/1939	29Gem02
11/04/1938	28Pis37	03/06/1939	25Vir26	07/04/1939	13Aqu00	11/03/1939	26Can31
11/06/1938	25Ari03	03/08/1939	24Lib13	07/06/1939	06Pis46	11/05/1939	24Leo41
11/08/1938	22Tau49	03/10/1939	21Sco13	07/08/1939	00Ari35	11/07/1939	23Vir21
11/10/1938	21Gem32	03/12/1939	16Sag30	07/10/1939	25Ari04	11/09/1939	22Lib06
11/12/1938	20Can29	03/14/1939	10Cap41	07/12/1939	20Tau49	11/11/1939	20Sco22
11/14/1938	19Leo04	03/16/1939	04Aqu25	07/14/1939	18Gem24	11/13/1939	17Sag35
11/16/1938	16Vir56	03/18/1939	28Aqu15	07/16/1939	17Can45	11/15/1939	13Cap28
11/18/1938	13Lib53	03/20/1939	22Pis29	07/18/1939	17Leo58	11/17/1939	08Aqu05
11/20/1938	09Sco59	03/22/1939	17Ari18	07/20/1939	17Vir49	11/19/1939	01Pis57
11/22/1938	05Sag12	03/24/1939	12Tau54	07/22/1939	16Lib19	11/21/1939	25Pis42
11/24/1938	29Sag40	03/26/1939	09Gem19	07/24/1939	13Sco14	11/23/1939	19Ari56
11/26/1938	23Cap35	03/28/1939	06Can46	07/26/1939	08Sag53	11/25/1939	15Tau10
11/28/1938	17Aqu18	03/30/1939	05Leo16	07/28/1939	03Cap40	11/27/1939	11Gem37
11/30/1938	11Pis20			07/30/1939	27Cap52	11/29/1939	09Can09
		04/01/1939	04Vir30	08/01/1939	21Aqu43	12/01/1939	07Leo20
12/02/1938	06Ari18	04/03/1939	03Lib45	08/03/1939	15Pis27	12/03/1939	05Vir40
12/04/1938	02Tau48	04/05/1939	02Sco06	08/05/1939	09Ari17	12/05/1939	03Lib52
12/06/1938	00Gem59	04/07/1939	29Sco01	08/07/1939	03Tau43	12/07/1939	01Sco43
12/08/1938	00Can31	04/09/1939	24Sag26	08/09/1939	29Tau24	12/09/1939	29Sco07
12/10/1938	00Leo24	04/11/1939	18Cap46	08/11/1939	26Gem49	12/11/1939	25Sag43
12/12/1938	29Leo36	04/13/1939	12Aqu34	08/13/1939	26Can09	12/13/1939	21Cap19
12/14/1938	27Vir30	04/15/1939	06Pis28	08/15/1939	26Leo34	12/15/1939	15Aqu54
12/16/1938	23Lib58	04/17/1939	00Ari54	08/17/1939	26Vir52	12/17/1939	09Pis45
12/18/1938	19Sco22	04/19/1939	26Ari14	08/19/1939	25Lib46	12/19/1939	03Ari26
12/20/1938	14Sag01	04/21/1939	22Tau34	08/21/1939	22Sco51	12/21/1939	27Ari39
12/22/1938	08Cap10	04/23/1939	19Gem45	08/23/1939	18Sag22	12/23/1939	23Tau03
12/24/1938	01Aqu59	04/25/1939	17Can40	08/25/1939	12Cap52	12/25/1939	20Gem03
12/26/1938	25Aqu42	04/27/1939	16Leo04	08/27/1939	06Aqu52	12/27/1939	18Can26
12/28/1938	19Pis40	04/29/1939	14Vir36	08/29/1939	00Pis37	12/29/1939	17Leo33
12/30/1938	14Ari27			08/31/1939	24Pis22	12/31/1939	16Vir30

Ephemeris Tables for the Moon

Date	Moon	Date	Moon	Date	Moon	Date	Moon
01/02/1940	14Lib44	05/01/1940	05Pis00	09/02/1940	14Vir22	01/02/1941	08Pis00
01/04/1940	12Sco04	05/03/1940	28Pis36	09/04/1940	14Lib25	01/04/1941	02Ari11
01/06/1940	08Sag39	05/05/1940	22Ari21	09/06/1940	13Sco45	01/06/1941	25Ari49
01/08/1940	04Cap31	05/07/1940	16Tau40	09/08/1940	11Sag43	01/08/1941	19Tau37
01/10/1940	29Cap37	05/09/1940	11Gem50	09/10/1940	08Cap17	01/10/1941	14Gem14
01/12/1940	23Aqu59	05/11/1940	07Can55	09/12/1940	03Aqu42	01/12/1941	10Can04
01/14/1940	17Pis45	05/13/1940	04Leo55	09/14/1940	28Aqu16	01/14/1941	07Leo02
01/16/1940	11Ari21	05/15/1940	02Vir46	09/16/1940	22Pis15	01/16/1941	04Vir49
01/18/1940	05Tau27	05/17/1940	01Lib24	09/18/1940	15Ari51	01/18/1941	02Lib55
01/20/1940	00Gem46	05/19/1940	00Sco30	09/20/1940	09Tau28	01/20/1941	01Sco07
01/22/1940	27Gem54	05/21/1940	29Sco24	09/22/1940	03Gem29	01/22/1941	29Sco15
01/24/1940	26Can47	05/23/1940	27Sag22	09/24/1940	28Gem25	01/24/1941	27Sag06
01/26/1940	26Leo43	05/25/1940	23Cap57	09/26/1940	24Can46	01/26/1941	24Cap22
01/28/1940	26Vir30	05/27/1940	19Aqu02	09/28/1940	22Leo52	01/28/1941	20Aqu38
01/30/1940	25Lib12	05/29/1940	13Pis07	09/30/1940	22Vir33	01/30/1941	15Pis48
		05/31/1940	06Ari45				
02/01/1940	22Sco28			10/02/1940	22Lib55	02/01/1941	09Ari56
02/03/1940	18Sag35	06/02/1940	00Tau39	10/04/1940	22Sco49	02/03/1941	03Tau34
02/05/1940	13Cap52	06/04/1940	25Tau19	10/06/1940	21Sag14	02/05/1941	27Tau23
02/07/1940	08Aqu27	06/06/1940	21Gem07	10/08/1940	17Cap54	02/07/1941	22Gem01
02/09/1940	02Pis31	06/08/1940	17Can58	10/10/1940	13Aqu06	02/09/1941	18Can04
02/11/1940	26Pis08	06/10/1940	15Leo36	10/12/1940	07Pis21	02/11/1941	15Leo34
02/13/1940	19Ari45	06/12/1940	13Vir41	10/14/1940	01Ari03	02/13/1941	14Vir12
02/15/1940	13Tau49	06/14/1940	11Lib58	10/16/1940	24Ari37	02/15/1941	13Lib14
02/17/1940	08Gem58	06/16/1940	10Sco19	10/18/1940	18Tau26	02/17/1941	11Sco59
02/19/1940	05Can52	06/18/1940	08Sag22	10/20/1940	12Gem42	02/19/1941	10Sag03
02/21/1940	04Leo44	06/20/1940	05Cap45	10/22/1940	07Can47	02/21/1941	07Cap19
02/23/1940	04Vir58	06/22/1940	02Aqu00	10/24/1940	04Leo00	02/23/1941	03Aqu46
02/25/1940	05Lib20	06/24/1940	26Aqu58	10/26/1940	01Vir39	02/25/1941	29Aqu19
02/27/1940	04Sco37	06/26/1940	21Pis01	10/28/1940	00Lib51	02/27/1941	24Pis00
02/29/1940	02Sag18	06/28/1940	14Ari39	10/30/1940	00Sco59		
		06/30/1940	08Tau39			03/01/1941	17Ari58
03/02/1940	28Sag22			11/01/1940	01Sag00	03/03/1941	11Tau36
03/04/1940	23Cap19	07/02/1940	03Gem36	11/03/1940	29Sag46	03/05/1941	05Gem24
03/06/1940	17Aqu31	07/04/1940	29Gem54	11/05/1940	26Cap45	03/07/1941	29Gem56
03/08/1940	11Pis18	07/06/1940	27Can31	11/07/1940	22Aqu00	03/09/1941	25Can52
03/10/1940	04Ari54	07/08/1940	25Leo58	11/09/1940	16Pis06	03/11/1941	23Leo30
03/12/1940	28Ari37	07/10/1940	24Vir36	11/11/1940	09Ari41	03/13/1941	22Vir40
03/14/1940	22Tau49	07/12/1940	22Lib55	11/13/1940	03Tau20	03/15/1941	22Lib31
03/16/1940	17Gem58	07/14/1940	20Sco46	11/15/1940	27Tau26	03/17/1941	22Sco04
03/18/1940	14Can39	07/16/1940	18Sag06	11/17/1940	22Gem10	03/19/1941	20Sag33
03/20/1940	13Leo06	07/18/1940	14Cap42	11/19/1940	17Can40	03/21/1941	17Cap40
03/22/1940	13Vir02	07/20/1940	10Aqu24	11/21/1940	14Leo04	03/23/1941	13Aqu34
03/24/1940	13Lib26	07/22/1940	05Pis04	11/23/1940	11Vir27	03/25/1941	08Pis28
03/26/1940	13Sco06	07/24/1940	29Pis00	11/25/1940	09Lib59	03/27/1941	02Ari39
03/28/1940	11Sag12	07/26/1940	22Ari36	11/27/1940	09Sco25	03/29/1941	26Ari26
03/30/1940	07Cap30	07/28/1940	16Tau36	11/29/1940	09Sag00	03/31/1941	20Tau03
		07/30/1940	11Gem37				
04/01/1940	02Aqu24	08/01/1940	08Can12	12/01/1940	07Cap44	04/02/1941	13Gem54
04/03/1940	26Aqu26	08/03/1940	06Leo24	12/03/1940	04Aqu49	04/04/1941	08Can24
04/05/1940	20Pis06	08/05/1940	05Vir36	12/05/1940	00Pis13	04/06/1941	04Leo07
04/07/1940	13Ari45	08/07/1940	04Lib58	12/07/1940	24Pis20	04/08/1941	01Vir33
04/09/1940	07Tau43	08/09/1940	03Sco42	12/09/1940	17Ari56	04/10/1941	00Lib42
04/11/1940	02Gem18	08/11/1940	01Sag25	12/11/1940	11Tau41	04/12/1941	00Sco57
04/13/1940	27Gem46	08/13/1940	28Sag13	12/13/1940	06Gem07	04/14/1941	01Sag09
04/15/1940	24Can25	08/15/1940	24Cap07	12/15/1940	01Can25	04/16/1941	00Cap12
04/17/1940	22Leo25	08/17/1940	19Aqu12	12/17/1940	27Can38	04/18/1941	27Cap30
04/19/1940	21Vir42	08/19/1940	13Pis30	12/19/1940	24Leo34	04/20/1941	23Aqu12
04/21/1940	21Lib36	08/21/1940	07Ari15	12/21/1940	22Vir05	04/22/1941	17Pis45
04/23/1940	21Sco07	08/23/1940	00Tau51	12/23/1940	20Lib11	04/24/1941	11Ari36
04/25/1940	19Sag22	08/25/1940	24Tau47	12/25/1940	18Sco49	04/26/1941	05Tau13
04/27/1940	15Cap55	08/27/1940	19Gem46	12/27/1940	17Sag34	04/28/1941	28Tau54
04/29/1940	10Aqu57	08/29/1940	16Can19	12/29/1940	15Cap44	04/30/1941	22Gem55
		08/31/1940	14Leo40	12/31/1940	12Aqu35		

Ephemeris Tables for the Moon

Date	Moon	Date	Moon	Date	Moon	Date	Moon
05/02/1941	17Can34	09/01/1941	16Cap34	01/01/1942	27Gem37	05/01/1942	18Sco40
05/04/1941	13Leo12	09/03/1941	13Aqu37	01/03/1942	21Can59	05/03/1942	18Sag45
05/06/1941	10Vir17	09/05/1941	09Pis45	01/05/1942	16Leo55	05/05/1942	18Cap10
05/08/1941	09Lib03	09/07/1941	04Ari55	01/07/1942	12Vir33	05/07/1942	16Aqu10
05/10/1941	09Sco10	09/09/1941	29Ari13	01/09/1942	09Lib04	05/09/1942	12Pis42
05/12/1941	09Sag33	09/11/1941	23Tau03	01/11/1942	06Sco48	05/11/1942	08Ari05
05/14/1941	08Cap58	09/13/1941	16Gem50	01/13/1942	05Sag49	05/13/1942	02Tau44
05/16/1941	06Aqu33	09/15/1941	11Can12	01/15/1942	05Cap30	05/15/1942	26Tau53
05/18/1941	02Pis18	09/17/1941	06Leo43	01/17/1942	04Aqu54	05/17/1942	20Gem41
05/20/1941	26Pis44	09/19/1941	03Vir46	01/19/1942	03Pis01	05/19/1942	14Can25
05/22/1941	20Ari27	09/21/1941	02Lib14	01/21/1942	29Pis24	05/21/1942	08Leo22
05/24/1941	14Tau04	09/23/1941	01Sco35	01/23/1942	24Ari16	05/23/1942	03Vir04
05/26/1941	07Gem52	09/25/1941	00Sag58	01/25/1942	18Tau15	05/25/1942	29Vir13
05/28/1941	02Can13	09/27/1941	29Sag34	01/27/1942	11Gem58	05/27/1942	27Lib15
05/30/1941	27Can13	09/29/1941	27Cap04	01/29/1942	06Can00	05/29/1942	27Sco03
				01/31/1942	00Leo43	05/31/1942	27Sag37
06/01/1941	23Leo02	10/01/1941	23Aqu24				
06/03/1941	19Vir57	10/03/1941	18Pis48	02/02/1942	26Leo14	06/02/1942	27Cap33
06/05/1941	18Lib16	10/05/1941	13Ari28	02/04/1942	22Vir35	06/04/1942	25Aqu54
06/07/1941	17Sco52	10/07/1941	07Tau32	02/06/1942	19Lib40	06/06/1942	22Pis25
06/09/1941	17Sag55	10/09/1941	01Gem17	02/08/1942	17Sco31	06/08/1942	17Ari37
06/11/1941	17Cap15	10/11/1941	25Gem03	02/10/1942	16Sag01	06/10/1942	11Tau57
06/13/1941	14Aqu55	10/13/1941	19Can21	02/12/1942	14Cap48	06/12/1942	05Gem52
06/15/1941	10Pis47	10/15/1941	14Leo43	02/14/1942	13Aqu16	06/14/1942	29Gem34
06/17/1941	05Ari15	10/17/1941	11Vir40	02/16/1942	10Pis50	06/16/1942	23Can20
06/19/1941	28Ari59	10/19/1941	10Lib25	02/18/1942	07Ari05	06/18/1942	17Leo26
06/21/1941	22Tau39	10/21/1941	10Sco25	02/20/1942	02Tau04	06/20/1942	12Vir13
06/23/1941	16Gem45	10/23/1941	10Sag36	02/22/1942	26Tau08	06/22/1942	08Lib15
06/25/1941	11Can30	10/25/1941	09Cap45	02/24/1942	19Gem54	06/24/1942	06Sco01
06/27/1941	07Leo02	10/27/1941	07Aqu16	02/26/1942	13Can57	06/26/1942	05Sag34
06/29/1941	03Vir17	10/29/1941	03Pis16	02/28/1942	08Leo53	06/28/1942	06Cap03
		10/31/1941	28Pis08			06/30/1942	06Aqu09
07/01/1941	00Lib25			03/02/1942	04Vir55		
07/03/1941	28Lib28	11/02/1941	22Ari21	03/04/1942	02Lib04	07/02/1942	04Pis46
07/05/1941	27Sco27	11/04/1941	16Tau13	03/06/1942	00Sco06	07/04/1942	01Ari31
07/07/1941	26Sag45	11/06/1941	09Gem56	03/08/1942	28Sco31	07/06/1942	26Ari43
07/09/1941	25Cap32	11/08/1941	03Can46	03/10/1942	26Sag58	07/08/1942	20Tau59
07/11/1941	23Aqu00	11/10/1941	28Can03	03/12/1942	25Cap03	07/10/1942	14Gem45
07/13/1941	18Pis50	11/12/1941	23Leo13	03/14/1942	22Aqu34	07/12/1942	08Can29
07/15/1941	13Ari20	11/14/1941	19Vir52	03/16/1942	19Pis19	07/14/1942	02Leo25
07/17/1941	07Tau09	11/16/1941	18Lib25	03/18/1942	15Ari04	07/16/1942	26Leo49
07/19/1941	00Gem55	11/18/1941	18Sco33	03/20/1942	09Tau53	07/18/1942	21Vir56
07/21/1941	25Gem14	11/20/1941	19Sag10	03/22/1942	03Gem57	07/20/1942	18Lib06
07/23/1941	20Can25	11/22/1941	18Cap52	03/24/1942	27Gem44	07/22/1942	15Sco42
07/25/1941	16Leo33	11/24/1941	16Aqu44	03/26/1942	21Can46	07/24/1942	14Sag43
07/27/1941	13Vir33	11/26/1941	12Pis44	03/28/1942	16Leo42	07/26/1942	14Cap37
07/29/1941	11Lib12	11/28/1941	07Ari22	03/30/1942	13Vir00	07/28/1942	14Aqu24
07/31/1941	09Sco22	11/30/1941	01Tau18			07/30/1942	13Pis01
				04/01/1942	10Lib49		
08/02/1941	07Sag50	12/02/1941	25Tau02	04/03/1942	09Sco48	08/01/1942	09Ari55
08/04/1941	06Cap21	12/04/1941	18Gem50	04/05/1942	09Sag04	08/03/1942	05Tau16
08/06/1941	04Aqu17	12/06/1941	12Can53	04/07/1942	07Cap52	08/05/1942	29Tau32
08/08/1941	01Pis11	12/08/1941	07Leo21	04/09/1942	05Aqu43	08/07/1942	23Gem19
08/10/1941	26Pis46	12/10/1941	02Vir34	04/11/1942	02Pis34	08/09/1942	17Can08
08/12/1941	21Ari14	12/12/1941	28Vir58	04/13/1942	28Pis31	08/11/1942	11Leo20
08/14/1941	15Tau05	12/14/1941	27Lib04	04/15/1942	23Ari40	08/13/1942	06Vir12
08/16/1941	08Gem54	12/16/1941	26Sco45	04/17/1942	18Tau09	08/15/1942	01Lib54
08/18/1941	03Can18	12/18/1941	27Sag10	04/19/1942	12Gem06	08/17/1942	28Lib30
08/20/1941	28Can46	12/20/1941	27Cap02	04/21/1942	05Can51	08/19/1942	26Sco09
08/22/1941	25Leo30	12/22/1941	25Aqu12	04/23/1942	29Can48	08/21/1942	24Sag43
08/24/1941	23Vir18	12/24/1941	21Pis27	04/25/1942	24Leo36	08/23/1942	23Cap51
08/26/1941	21Lib46	12/26/1941	16Ari06	04/27/1942	20Vir55	08/25/1942	22Aqu52
08/28/1941	20Sco22	12/28/1941	10Tau01	04/29/1942	19Lib02	08/27/1942	21Pis06
08/30/1941	18Sag44	12/30/1941	03Gem43			08/29/1942	17Ari55
						08/31/1942	13Tau20

Ephemeris Tables for the Moon

Date	Moon	Date	Moon	Date	Moon	Date	Moon
09/02/1942	07Gem41	01/02/1943	15Sco15	05/02/1943	17Ari45	09/01/1943	26Vir39
09/04/1942	01Can28	01/04/1943	14Sag30	05/04/1943	14Tau17	09/03/1943	21Lib23
09/06/1942	25Can22	01/06/1943	14Cap54	05/06/1943	09Gem49	09/05/1943	17Sco00
09/08/1942	19Leo49	01/08/1943	15Aqu15	05/08/1943	04Can21	09/07/1943	13Sag43
09/10/1942	15Vir12	01/10/1943	14Pis16	05/10/1943	28Can12	09/09/1943	11Cap42
09/12/1942	11Lib40	01/12/1943	11Ari31	05/12/1943	21Leo52	09/11/1943	10Aqu52
09/14/1942	09Sco03	01/14/1943	07Tau08	05/14/1943	16Vir01	09/13/1943	10Pis45
09/16/1942	07Sag04	01/16/1943	01Gem40	05/16/1943	11Lib25	09/15/1943	10Ari15
09/18/1942	05Cap27	01/18/1943	25Gem36	05/18/1943	08Sco25	09/17/1943	08Tau31
09/20/1942	03Aqu52	01/20/1943	19Can16	05/20/1943	06Sag54	09/19/1943	05Gem01
09/22/1942	02Pis01	01/22/1943	13Leo00	05/22/1943	06Cap05	09/21/1943	29Gem55
09/24/1942	29Pis28	01/24/1943	07Vir01	05/24/1943	05Aqu09	09/23/1943	23Can49
09/26/1942	25Ari55	01/26/1943	01Lib41	05/26/1943	03Pis31	09/25/1943	17Leo24
09/28/1942	21Tau15	01/28/1943	27Lib20	05/28/1943	00Ari58	09/27/1943	11Vir14
09/30/1942	15Gem35	01/30/1943	24Sco24	05/30/1943	27Ari34	09/29/1943	05Lib42
10/02/1942	09Can22	02/01/1943	23Sag04	06/01/1943	23Tau24	10/01/1943	01Sco02
10/04/1942	03Leo13	02/03/1943	22Cap58	06/03/1943	18Gem25	10/03/1943	27Sco13
10/06/1942	27Leo48	02/05/1943	23Aqu07	06/05/1943	12Can39	10/05/1943	24Sag12
10/08/1942	23Vir36	02/07/1943	22Pis21	06/07/1943	06Leo21	10/07/1943	21Cap56
10/10/1942	20Lib48	02/09/1943	19Ari57	06/09/1943	29Leo58	10/09/1943	20Aqu30
10/12/1942	19Sco07	02/11/1943	15Tau50	06/11/1943	24Vir07	10/11/1943	19Pis35
10/14/1942	17Sag54	02/13/1943	10Gem24	06/13/1943	19Lib30	10/13/1943	18Ari30
10/16/1942	16Cap29	02/15/1943	04Can14	06/15/1943	16Sco36	10/15/1943	16Tau29
10/18/1942	14Aqu30	02/17/1943	27Can52	06/17/1943	15Sag26	10/17/1943	12Gem58
10/20/1942	11Pis49	02/19/1943	21Leo45	06/19/1943	15Cap18	10/19/1943	07Can57
10/22/1942	08Ari26	02/21/1943	16Vir11	06/21/1943	15Aqu03	10/21/1943	01Leo53
10/24/1942	04Tau19	02/23/1943	11Lib24	06/23/1943	13Pis53	10/23/1943	25Leo28
10/26/1942	29Tau19	02/25/1943	07Sco28	06/25/1943	11Ari21	10/25/1943	19Vir27
10/28/1942	23Gem33	02/27/1943	04Sag34	06/27/1943	07Tau36	10/27/1943	14Lib18
10/30/1942	17Can16			06/29/1943	02Gem54	10/29/1943	10Sco18
		03/01/1943	02Cap47			10/31/1943	07Sag15
11/01/1942	11Leo03	03/03/1943	01Aqu52	07/01/1943	27Gem24		
11/03/1942	05Vir34	03/05/1943	01Pis18	07/03/1943	21Can17	11/02/1943	04Cap52
11/05/1942	01Lib28	03/07/1943	00Ari12	07/05/1943	14Leo52	11/04/1943	02Aqu51
11/07/1942	29Lib08	03/09/1943	27Ari49	07/07/1943	08Vir31	11/06/1943	01Pis02
11/09/1942	28Sco15	03/11/1943	23Tau54	07/09/1943	02Lib42	11/08/1943	29Pis19
11/11/1942	27Sag57	03/13/1943	18Gem34	07/11/1943	28Lib01	11/10/1943	27Ari21
11/13/1942	27Cap09	03/15/1943	12Can25	07/13/1943	24Sco58	11/12/1943	24Tau42
11/15/1942	25Aqu11	03/17/1943	06Leo04	07/15/1943	23Sag44	11/14/1943	20Gem51
11/17/1942	22Pis04	03/19/1943	00Vir09	07/17/1943	23Cap49	11/16/1943	15Can45
11/19/1942	18Ari00	03/21/1943	25Vir03	07/19/1943	24Aqu04	11/18/1943	09Leo40
11/21/1942	13Tau15	03/23/1943	20Lib57	07/21/1943	23Pis24	11/20/1943	03Vir16
11/23/1942	07Gem49	03/25/1943	17Sco47	07/23/1943	21Ari09	11/22/1943	27Vir18
11/25/1942	01Can50	03/27/1943	15Sag21	07/25/1943	17Tau21	11/24/1943	22Lib21
11/27/1942	25Can31	03/29/1943	13Cap27	07/27/1943	12Gem19	11/26/1943	18Sco48
11/29/1942	19Leo13	03/31/1943	11Aqu52	07/29/1943	06Can28	11/28/1943	16Sag34
				07/31/1943	00Leo09	11/30/1943	15Cap04
12/01/1942	13Vir37	04/02/1943	10Pis24				
12/03/1942	09Lib21	04/04/1943	08Ari32	08/02/1943	23Leo41	12/02/1943	13Aqu42
12/05/1942	07Sco02	04/06/1943	05Tau46	08/04/1943	17Vir28	12/04/1943	12Pis00
12/07/1942	06Sag31	04/08/1943	01Gem44	08/06/1943	11Lib49	12/06/1943	09Ari46
12/09/1942	06Cap52	04/10/1943	26Gem25	08/08/1943	07Sco10	12/08/1943	07Tau00
12/11/1942	06Aqu46	04/12/1943	20Can18	08/10/1943	03Sag56	12/10/1943	03Gem30
12/13/1942	05Pis16	04/14/1943	14Leo00	08/12/1943	02Cap20	12/12/1943	29Gem04
12/15/1942	02Ari10	04/16/1943	08Vir09	08/14/1943	02Aqu09	12/14/1943	23Can40
12/17/1942	27Ari45	04/18/1943	03Lib23	08/16/1943	02Pis27	12/16/1943	17Leo33
12/19/1942	22Tau29	04/20/1943	29Lib57	08/18/1943	02Ari06	12/18/1943	11Vir08
12/21/1942	16Gem41	04/22/1943	27Sco41	08/20/1943	00Tau13	12/20/1943	05Lib07
12/23/1942	10Can30	04/24/1943	26Sag02	08/22/1943	26Tau31	12/22/1943	00Sco07
12/25/1942	04Leo09	04/26/1943	24Cap28	08/24/1943	21Gem22	12/24/1943	26Sco42
12/27/1942	27Leo55	04/28/1943	22Aqu39	08/26/1943	15Can19	12/26/1943	24Sag55
12/29/1942	22Vir18	04/30/1943	20Pis27	08/28/1943	08Leo55	12/28/1943	24Cap14
12/31/1942	17Lib52			08/30/1943	02Vir34	12/30/1943	23Aqu43

Ephemeris Tables for the Moon

Date	Moon	Date	Moon	Date	Moon	Date	Moon
01/01/1944	22Pis36	05/02/1944	06Vir22	09/01/1944	19Aqu48	01/01/1945	15Leo10
01/03/1944	20Ari25	05/04/1944	00Lib10	09/03/1944	20Pis09	01/03/1945	09Vir43
01/05/1944	17Tau09	05/06/1944	24Lib37	09/05/1944	20Ari26	01/05/1945	03Lib36
01/07/1944	12Gem54	05/08/1944	19Sco58	09/07/1944	19Tau28	01/07/1945	27Lib24
01/09/1944	07Can48	05/10/1944	16Sag16	09/09/1944	16Gem39	01/09/1945	21Sco42
01/11/1944	02Leo01	05/12/1944	13Cap17	09/11/1944	12Can12	01/11/1945	17Sag06
01/13/1944	25Leo46	05/14/1944	10Aqu54	09/13/1944	06Leo36	01/13/1945	13Cap51
01/15/1944	19Vir22	05/16/1944	09Pis06	09/15/1944	00Vir30	01/15/1945	11Aqu49
01/17/1944	13Lib18	05/18/1944	07Ari43	09/17/1944	24Vir11	01/17/1945	10Pis34
01/19/1944	08Sco11	05/20/1944	06Tau22	09/19/1944	17Lib55	01/19/1945	09Ari22
01/21/1944	04Sag34	05/22/1944	04Gem19	09/21/1944	11Sco58	01/21/1945	07Tau43
01/23/1944	02Cap45	05/24/1944	01Can01	09/23/1944	06Sag36	01/23/1945	05Gem21
01/25/1944	02Aqu25	05/26/1944	26Can21	09/25/1944	02Cap13	01/25/1945	02Can09
01/27/1944	02Pis39	05/28/1944	20Leo34	09/27/1944	29Cap18	01/27/1945	28Can06
01/29/1944	02Ari16	05/30/1944	14Vir19	09/29/1944	28Aqu10	01/29/1945	23Leo15
01/31/1944	00Tau30					01/31/1945	17Vir40
		06/01/1944	08Lib13	10/01/1944	28Pis24		
02/02/1944	27Tau08	06/03/1944	02Sco51	10/03/1944	28Ari51	02/02/1945	11Lib33
02/04/1944	22Gem27	06/05/1944	28Sco39	10/05/1944	28Tau14	02/04/1945	05Sco18
02/06/1944	16Can52	06/07/1944	25Sag35	10/07/1944	25Gem40	02/06/1945	29Sco30
02/08/1944	10Leo43	06/09/1944	23Cap24	10/09/1944	21Can15	02/08/1945	24Sag48
02/10/1944	04Vir23	06/11/1944	21Aqu42	10/11/1944	15Leo35	02/10/1945	21Cap43
02/12/1944	28Vir04	06/13/1944	20Pis08	10/13/1944	09Vir19	02/12/1945	20Aqu16
02/14/1944	22Lib08	06/15/1944	18Ari24	10/15/1944	03Lib01	02/14/1945	19Pis55
02/16/1944	17Sco00	06/17/1944	16Tau15	10/17/1944	26Lib55	02/16/1945	19Ari37
02/18/1944	13Sag05	06/19/1944	13Gem19	10/19/1944	21Sco19	02/18/1945	18Tau23
02/20/1944	10Cap52	06/21/1944	09Can22	10/21/1944	16Sag16	02/20/1945	15Gem50
02/22/1944	10Aqu19	06/23/1944	04Leo23	10/23/1944	12Cap03	02/22/1945	12Can00
02/24/1944	10Pis45	06/25/1944	28Leo31	10/25/1944	08Aqu57	02/24/1945	07Leo18
02/26/1944	10Ari53	06/27/1944	22Vir15	10/27/1944	07Pis18	02/26/1945	01Vir55
02/28/1944	09Tau37	06/29/1944	16Lib09	10/29/1944	06Ari57	02/28/1945	26Vir04
				10/31/1944	07Tau00		
03/01/1944	06Gem30	07/01/1944	10Sco51			03/02/1945	19Lib52
03/03/1944	01Can42	07/03/1944	06Sag51	11/02/1944	06Gem16	03/04/1945	13Sco37
03/05/1944	25Can52	07/05/1944	04Cap16	11/04/1944	03Can51	03/06/1945	07Sag45
03/07/1944	19Leo32	07/07/1944	02Aqu52	11/06/1944	29Can38	03/08/1945	02Cap51
03/09/1944	13Vir09	07/09/1944	02Pis01	11/08/1944	24Leo03	03/10/1945	29Cap36
03/11/1944	07Lib04	07/11/1944	01Ari00	11/10/1944	17Vir48	03/12/1945	28Aqu17
03/13/1944	01Sco27	07/13/1944	29Ari15	11/12/1944	11Lib31	03/14/1945	28Pis24
03/15/1944	26Sco33	07/15/1944	26Tau33	11/14/1944	05Sco40	03/16/1945	28Ari48
03/17/1944	22Sag33	07/17/1944	22Gem52	11/16/1944	00Sag31	03/18/1945	28Tau10
03/19/1944	19Cap57	07/19/1944	18Can13	11/18/1944	26Sag03	03/20/1945	25Gem49
03/21/1944	18Aqu52	07/21/1944	12Leo47	11/20/1944	22Cap18	03/22/1945	21Can49
03/23/1944	18Pis52	07/23/1944	06Vir44	11/22/1944	19Aqu25	03/24/1945	16Leo43
03/25/1944	18Ari57	07/25/1944	00Lib25	11/24/1944	17Pis29	03/26/1945	10Vir58
03/27/1944	17Tau54	07/27/1944	24Lib19	11/26/1944	16Ari23	03/28/1945	04Lib50
03/29/1944	15Gem01	07/29/1944	18Sco57	11/28/1944	15Tau35	03/30/1945	28Lib36
03/31/1944	10Can22	07/31/1944	14Sag52	11/30/1944	14Gem15		
						04/01/1945	22Sco26
04/02/1944	04Leo31	08/02/1944	12Cap26	12/02/1944	11Can38	04/03/1945	16Sag39
04/04/1944	28Leo08	08/04/1944	11Aqu34	12/04/1944	07Leo27	04/05/1945	11Cap40
04/06/1944	21Vir49	08/06/1944	11Pis30	12/06/1944	01Vir58	04/07/1945	08Aqu10
04/08/1944	16Lib00	08/08/1944	11Ari12	12/08/1944	25Vir48	04/09/1945	06Pis34
04/10/1944	10Sco52	08/10/1944	09Tau45	12/10/1944	19Lib36	04/11/1945	06Ari36
04/12/1944	06Sag27	08/12/1944	06Gem49	12/12/1944	13Sco55	04/13/1945	07Tau12
04/14/1944	02Cap48	08/14/1944	02Can37	12/14/1944	09Sag08	04/15/1945	06Gem57
04/16/1944	00Aqu07	08/16/1944	27Can24	12/16/1944	05Cap21	04/17/1945	04Can58
04/18/1944	28Aqu31	08/18/1944	21Leo33	12/18/1944	02Aqu26	04/19/1945	01Leo08
04/20/1944	27Pis47	08/20/1944	15Vir18	12/20/1944	00Pis13	04/21/1945	25Leo55
04/22/1944	27Ari16	08/22/1944	09Lib00	12/22/1944	28Pis25	04/23/1945	19Vir58
04/24/1944	25Tau55	08/24/1944	02Sco55	12/24/1944	26Ari48	04/25/1945	13Lib43
04/26/1944	23Gem03	08/26/1944	27Sco28	12/26/1944	25Tau04	04/27/1945	07Sco31
04/28/1944	18Can28	08/28/1944	23Sag12	12/28/1944	22Gem47	04/29/1945	01Sag33
04/30/1944	12Leo40	08/30/1944	20Cap36	12/30/1944	19Can34		

Ephemeris Tables for the Moon

Date	Moon	Date	Moon	Date	Moon	Date	Moon
05/01/1945	26Sag01	09/02/1945	21Can39	01/02/1946	29Sag54	05/02/1946	24Tau55
05/03/1945	21Cap16	09/04/1945	17Leo32	01/04/1946	24Cap52	05/04/1946	24Gem53
05/05/1945	17Aqu42	09/06/1945	12Vir42	01/06/1946	20Aqu44	05/06/1946	23Can36
05/07/1945	15Pis46	09/08/1945	07Lib10	01/08/1946	17Pis31	05/08/1946	20Leo45
05/09/1945	15Ari16	09/10/1945	01Sco04	01/10/1946	15Ari06	05/10/1946	16Vir32
05/11/1945	15Tau30	09/12/1945	24Sco45	01/12/1946	13Tau25	05/12/1946	11Lib19
05/13/1945	15Gem10	09/14/1945	18Sag40	01/14/1946	12Gem13	05/14/1946	05Sco25
05/15/1945	13Can21	09/16/1945	13Cap31	01/16/1946	11Can03	05/16/1946	29Sco08
05/17/1945	09Leo42	09/18/1945	09Aqu57	01/18/1946	09Leo16	05/18/1946	22Sag45
05/19/1945	04Vir35	09/20/1945	08Pis16	01/20/1946	06Vir15	05/20/1946	16Cap35
05/21/1945	28Vir39	09/22/1945	08Ari02	01/22/1946	01Lib49	05/22/1946	11Aqu04
05/23/1945	22Lib24	09/24/1945	08Tau09	01/24/1946	26Lib12	05/24/1946	06Pis44
05/25/1945	16Sco18	09/26/1945	07Gem29	01/26/1946	19Sco55	05/26/1946	04Ari02
05/27/1945	10Sag36	09/28/1945	05Can19	01/28/1946	13Sag42	05/28/1946	03Tau03
05/29/1945	05Cap33	09/30/1945	01Leo44	01/30/1946	08Cap04	05/30/1946	03Gem13
05/31/1945	01Aqu19						
		10/02/1945	27Leo06	02/01/1946	03Aqu35	06/01/1946	03Can27
06/02/1945	28Aqu03	10/04/1945	21Vir46	02/03/1946	00Pis16	06/03/1946	02Leo34
06/04/1945	25Pis56	10/06/1945	15Lib55	02/05/1946	27Pis53	06/05/1946	00Vir02
06/06/1945	24Ari51	10/08/1945	09Sco40	02/07/1946	26Ari00	06/07/1946	25Vir51
06/08/1945	24Tau20	10/10/1945	03Sag17	02/09/1946	24Tau15	06/09/1946	20Lib27
06/10/1945	23Gem27	10/12/1945	27Sag11	02/11/1946	22Gem25	06/11/1946	14Sco20
06/12/1945	21Can23	10/14/1945	21Cap55	02/13/1946	20Can18	06/13/1946	07Sag57
06/14/1945	17Leo47	10/16/1945	18Aqu10	02/15/1946	17Leo42	06/15/1946	01Cap39
06/16/1945	12Vir48	10/18/1945	16Pis22	02/17/1946	14Vir12	06/17/1946	25Cap45
06/18/1945	06Lib55	10/20/1945	16Ari15	02/19/1946	09Lib36	06/19/1946	20Aqu36
06/20/1945	00Sco41	10/22/1945	16Tau50	02/21/1946	03Sco59	06/21/1946	16Pis25
06/22/1945	24Sco41	10/24/1945	16Gem44	02/23/1946	27Sco42	06/23/1946	13Ari33
06/24/1945	19Sag21	10/26/1945	14Can58	02/25/1946	21Sag26	06/25/1946	12Tau06
06/26/1945	14Cap52	10/28/1945	11Leo27	02/27/1946	15Cap54	06/27/1946	11Gem45
06/28/1945	11Aqu21	10/30/1945	06Vir36			06/29/1946	11Can43
06/30/1945	08Pis43			03/01/1946	11Aqu42		
		11/01/1945	00Lib56	03/03/1946	09Pis04	07/01/1946	10Leo55
07/02/1945	06Ari46	11/03/1945	24Lib49	03/05/1946	07Ari34	07/03/1946	08Vir36
07/04/1945	05Tau20	11/05/1945	18Sco30	03/07/1946	06Tau33	07/05/1946	04Lib32
07/06/1945	03Gem58	11/07/1945	12Sag12	03/09/1946	05Gem12	07/07/1946	29Lib08
07/08/1945	02Can13	11/09/1945	06Cap16	03/11/1946	03Can10	07/09/1946	22Sco58
07/10/1945	29Can34	11/11/1945	01Aqu04	03/13/1946	00Leo24	07/11/1946	16Sag34
07/12/1945	25Leo46	11/13/1945	27Aqu08	03/15/1946	26Leo58	07/13/1946	10Cap28
07/14/1945	20Vir45	11/15/1945	24Pis56	03/17/1946	22Vir49	07/15/1946	05Aqu00
07/16/1945	14Lib54	11/17/1945	24Ari27	03/19/1946	17Lib47	07/17/1946	00Pis24
07/18/1945	08Sco41	11/19/1945	24Tau52	03/21/1946	11Sco58	07/19/1946	26Pis40
07/20/1945	02Sag45	11/21/1945	24Gem57	03/23/1946	05Sag39	07/21/1946	23Ari51
07/22/1945	27Sag38	11/23/1945	23Can36	03/25/1946	29Sag21	07/23/1946	22Tau01
07/24/1945	23Cap42	11/25/1945	20Leo24	03/27/1946	23Cap45	07/25/1946	21Gem00
07/26/1945	20Aqu58	11/27/1945	15Vir39	03/29/1946	19Aqu36	07/27/1946	20Can19
07/28/1945	19Pis11	11/29/1945	09Lib51	03/31/1946	17Pis14	07/29/1946	19Leo08
07/30/1945	17Ari48					07/31/1946	16Vir45
		12/01/1945	03Sco34	04/02/1946	16Ari23		
08/01/1945	16Tau17	12/03/1945	27Sco16	04/04/1946	16Tau12	08/02/1946	12Lib46
08/03/1945	14Gem18	12/05/1945	21Sag12	04/06/1946	15Gem31	08/04/1946	07Sco22
08/05/1945	11Can40	12/07/1945	15Cap40	04/08/1946	13Can45	08/06/1946	01Sag10
08/07/1945	08Leo17	12/09/1945	10Aqu50	04/10/1946	10Leo46	08/08/1946	24Sag49
08/09/1945	04Vir01	12/11/1945	07Pis02	04/12/1946	06Vir46	08/10/1946	18Cap58
08/11/1945	28Vir48	12/13/1945	04Ari31	04/14/1946	01Lib59	08/12/1946	13Aqu59
08/13/1945	22Lib51	12/15/1945	03Tau22	04/16/1946	26Lib28	08/14/1946	10Pis03
08/15/1945	16Sco36	12/17/1945	03Gem05	04/18/1946	20Sco23	08/16/1946	07Ari01
08/17/1945	10Sag37	12/19/1945	02Can46	04/20/1946	14Sag00	08/18/1946	04Tau38
08/19/1945	05Cap35	12/21/1945	01Leo28	04/22/1946	07Cap43	08/20/1946	02Gem43
08/21/1945	01Aqu57	12/23/1945	28Leo31	04/24/1946	02Aqu05	08/22/1946	01Can07
08/23/1945	29Aqu57	12/25/1945	24Vir00	04/26/1946	27Aqu48	08/24/1946	29Can37
08/25/1945	29Pis05	12/27/1945	18Lib15	04/28/1946	25Pis22	08/26/1946	27Leo44
08/27/1945	28Ari25	12/29/1945	11Sco58	04/30/1946	24Ari40	08/28/1946	24Vir55
08/29/1945	27Tau11	12/31/1945	05Sag42			08/30/1946	20Lib45
08/31/1945	24Gem54						

Ephemeris Tables for the Moon

Date	Moon	Date	Moon	Date	Moon	Date	Moon
09/01/1946	15Sco18	01/01/1947	22Ari28	05/01/1947	25Vir53	09/02/1947	29Pis58
09/03/1946	09Sag06	01/03/1947	20Tau37	05/03/1947	22Lib12	09/04/1947	25Ari34
09/05/1946	02Cap46	01/05/1947	20Gem16	05/05/1947	17Sco34	09/06/1947	21Tau57
09/07/1946	27Cap04	01/07/1947	20Can36	05/07/1947	12Sag04	09/08/1947	19Gem19
09/09/1946	22Aqu28	01/09/1947	20Leo30	05/09/1947	05Cap59	09/10/1947	17Can48
09/11/1946	19Pis12	01/11/1947	18Vir50	05/11/1947	29Cap40	09/12/1947	17Leo09
09/13/1946	17Ari00	01/13/1947	15Lib15	05/13/1947	23Aqu42	09/14/1947	16Vir36
09/15/1946	15Tau20	01/15/1947	10Sco03	05/15/1947	18Pis40	09/16/1947	15Lib06
09/17/1946	13Gem42	01/17/1947	03Sag54	05/17/1947	15Ari04	09/18/1947	12Sco02
09/19/1946	11Can51	01/19/1947	27Sag28	05/19/1947	13Tau06	09/20/1947	07Sag20
09/21/1946	09Leo40	01/21/1947	21Cap10	05/21/1947	12Gem24	09/22/1947	01Cap30
09/23/1946	06Vir58	01/23/1947	15Aqu24	05/23/1947	12Can04	09/24/1947	25Cap12
09/25/1946	03Lib27	01/25/1947	10Pis14	05/25/1947	11Leo15	09/26/1947	19Aqu08
09/27/1946	28Lib51	01/27/1947	05Ari51	05/27/1947	09Vir19	09/28/1947	13Pis42
09/29/1946	23Sco15	01/29/1947	02Tau23	05/29/1947	06Lib05	09/30/1947	09Ari06
		01/31/1947	00Gem04	05/31/1947	01Sco45		
10/01/1946	16Sag59					10/02/1947	05Tau24
10/03/1946	10Cap37	02/02/1947	29Gem00	06/02/1947	26Sco31	10/04/1947	02Gem25
10/05/1946	04Aqu54	02/04/1947	28Can45	06/04/1947	20Sag38	10/06/1947	00Can07
10/07/1946	00Pis28	02/06/1947	28Leo22	06/06/1947	14Cap24	10/08/1947	28Can24
10/09/1946	27Pis37	02/08/1947	26Vir48	06/08/1947	08Aqu06	10/10/1947	27Leo02
10/11/1946	26Ari09	02/10/1947	23Lib22	06/10/1947	02Pis09	10/12/1947	25Vir34
10/13/1946	25Tau21	02/12/1947	18Sco20	06/12/1947	27Pis02	10/14/1947	23Lib21
10/15/1946	24Gem24	02/14/1947	12Sag13	06/14/1947	23Ari18	10/16/1947	19Sco55
10/17/1946	22Can43	02/16/1947	05Cap49	06/16/1947	21Tau18	10/18/1947	15Sag09
10/19/1946	20Leo09	02/18/1947	29Cap40	06/18/1947	20Gem51	10/20/1947	09Cap22
10/21/1946	16Vir43	02/20/1947	24Aqu15	06/20/1947	21Can07	10/22/1947	03Aqu09
10/23/1946	12Lib27	02/22/1947	19Pis44	06/22/1947	20Leo55	10/24/1947	27Aqu04
10/25/1946	07Sco20	02/24/1947	15Ari59	06/24/1947	19Vir19	10/26/1947	21Pis46
10/27/1946	01Sag27	02/26/1947	12Tau55	06/26/1947	16Lib01	10/28/1947	17Ari35
10/29/1946	25Sag06	02/28/1947	10Gem33	06/28/1947	11Sco18	10/30/1947	14Tau36
10/31/1946	18Cap43			06/30/1947	05Sag39		
		03/02/1947	08Can57	07/02/1947	29Sag30	11/01/1947	12Gem32
11/02/1946	12Aqu54	03/04/1947	07Leo51	07/04/1947	23Cap10	11/03/1947	10Can57
11/04/1946	08Pis22	03/06/1947	06Vir43	07/06/1947	16Aqu55	11/05/1947	09Leo27
11/06/1946	05Ari31	03/08/1947	04Lib39	07/08/1947	11Pis07	11/07/1947	07Vir38
11/08/1946	04Tau22	03/10/1947	01Sco09	07/10/1947	06Ari00	11/09/1947	05Lib18
11/10/1946	04Gem15	03/12/1947	26Sco10	07/12/1947	02Tau07	11/11/1947	02Sco10
11/12/1946	04Can07	03/14/1947	20Sag09	07/14/1947	29Tau49	11/13/1947	28Sco06
11/14/1946	03Leo02	03/16/1947	13Cap46	07/16/1947	29Gem13	11/15/1947	23Sag05
11/16/1946	00Vir32	03/18/1947	07Aqu47	07/18/1947	29Can38	11/17/1947	17Cap14
11/18/1946	26Vir42	03/20/1947	02Pis40	07/20/1947	29Leo48	11/19/1947	10Aqu58
11/20/1946	21Lib49	03/22/1947	28Pis41	07/22/1947	28Vir31	11/21/1947	04Pis52
11/22/1946	16Sco11	03/24/1947	25Ari43	07/24/1947	25Lib21	11/23/1947	29Pis32
11/24/1946	10Sag01	03/26/1947	23Tau26	07/26/1947	20Sco30	11/25/1947	25Ari27
11/26/1946	03Cap34	03/28/1947	21Gem30	07/28/1947	14Sag40	11/27/1947	22Tau57
11/28/1946	27Cap16	03/30/1947	19Can46	07/30/1947	08Cap22	11/29/1947	21Gem43
11/30/1946	21Aqu27						
		04/01/1947	18Leo00	08/01/1947	02Aqu03	12/01/1947	21Can06
12/02/1946	16Pis45	04/03/1947	15Vir55	08/03/1947	26Aqu01	12/03/1947	20Leo15
12/04/1946	13Ari35	04/05/1947	13Lib05	08/05/1947	20Pis30	12/05/1947	18Vir27
12/06/1946	12Tau15	04/07/1947	09Sco06	08/07/1947	15Ari38	12/07/1947	15Lib32
12/08/1946	12Gem19	04/09/1947	03Sag58	08/09/1947	11Tau41	12/09/1947	11Sco36
12/10/1946	12Can43	04/11/1947	27Sag58	08/11/1947	09Gem08	12/11/1947	06Sag51
12/12/1946	12Leo16	04/13/1947	21Cap38	08/13/1947	08Can05	12/13/1947	01Cap25
12/14/1946	10Vir10	04/15/1947	15Aqu40	08/15/1947	08Leo08	12/15/1947	25Cap23
12/16/1946	06Lib21	04/17/1947	10Pis41	08/17/1947	08Vir10	12/17/1947	19Aqu07
12/18/1946	01Sco09	04/19/1947	07Ari01	08/19/1947	07Lib00	12/19/1947	12Pis57
12/20/1946	25Sco10	04/21/1947	04Tau43	08/21/1947	03Sco58	12/21/1947	07Ari26
12/22/1946	18Sag47	04/23/1947	03Gem20	08/23/1947	29Sco12	12/23/1947	03Tau11
12/24/1946	12Cap22	04/25/1947	02Can12	08/25/1947	23Sag18	12/25/1947	00Gem42
12/26/1946	06Aqu15	04/27/1947	00Leo45	08/27/1947	16Cap58	12/27/1947	29Gem58
12/28/1946	00Pis40	04/29/1947	28Leo42	08/29/1947	10Aqu48	12/29/1947	00Leo10
12/30/1946	25Pis56			08/31/1947	05Pis04	12/31/1947	00Vir07

514

Ephemeris Tables for the Moon

Date	Moon	Date	Moon	Date	Moon	Date	Moon
01/02/1948	28Vir44	05/01/1948	14Aqu16	09/02/1948	25Leo58	01/02/1949	17Aqu25
01/04/1948	25Lib43	05/03/1948	08Pis06	09/04/1948	26Vir28	01/04/1949	11Pis27
01/06/1948	21Sco21	05/05/1948	02Ari19	09/06/1948	26Lib04	01/06/1949	05Ari03
01/08/1948	16Sag01	05/07/1948	27Ari26	09/08/1948	23Sco58	01/08/1949	28Ari57
01/10/1948	10Cap10	05/09/1948	23Tau37	09/10/1948	20Sag04	01/10/1949	23Tau48
01/12/1948	04Aqu00	05/11/1948	20Gem55	09/12/1948	14Cap54	01/12/1949	20Gem13
01/14/1948	27Aqu44	05/13/1948	18Can59	09/14/1948	08Aqu58	01/14/1949	18Can24
01/16/1948	21Pis35	05/15/1948	17Leo24	09/16/1948	02Pis44	01/16/1949	17Leo43
01/18/1948	15Ari58	05/17/1948	15Vir49	09/18/1948	26Pis30	01/18/1949	17Vir15
01/20/1948	11Tau28	05/19/1948	13Lib55	09/20/1948	20Ari29	01/20/1949	16Lib01
01/22/1948	08Gem40	05/21/1948	11Sco24	09/22/1948	14Tau58	01/22/1949	13Sco41
01/24/1948	07Can51	05/23/1948	08Sag01	09/24/1948	10Gem19	01/24/1949	10Sag21
01/26/1948	08Leo21	05/25/1948	03Cap36	09/26/1948	06Can55	01/26/1949	06Cap11
01/28/1948	08Vir50	05/27/1948	28Cap13	09/28/1948	05Leo04	01/28/1949	01Aqu18
01/30/1948	08Lib02	05/29/1948	22Aqu11	09/30/1948	04Vir34	01/30/1949	25Aqu45
		05/31/1948	16Pis01				
02/01/1948	05Sco16			10/02/1948	04Lib40	02/01/1949	19Pis38
02/03/1948	00Sag48	06/02/1948	10Ari15	10/04/1948	04Sco14	02/03/1949	13Ari13
02/05/1948	25Sag13	06/04/1948	05Tau31	10/06/1948	02Sag21	02/05/1949	07Tau01
02/07/1948	19Cap08	06/06/1948	02Gem13	10/08/1948	28Sag40	02/07/1949	01Gem43
02/09/1948	12Aqu51	06/08/1948	00Can18	10/10/1948	23Cap34	02/09/1949	28Gem03
02/11/1948	06Pis40	06/10/1948	29Can17	10/12/1948	17Aqu36	02/11/1949	26Can21
02/13/1948	00Ari42	06/12/1948	28Leo18	10/14/1948	11Pis19	02/13/1949	26Leo10
02/15/1948	25Ari13	06/14/1948	26Vir46	10/16/1948	05Ari12	02/15/1949	26Vir24
02/17/1948	20Tau41	06/16/1948	24Lib20	10/18/1948	29Ari31	02/17/1949	25Lib54
02/19/1948	17Gem34	06/18/1948	21Sco03	10/20/1948	24Tau33	02/19/1949	23Sco54
02/21/1948	16Can16	06/20/1948	16Sag55	10/22/1948	20Gem25	02/21/1949	20Sag26
02/23/1948	16Leo24	06/22/1948	12Cap01	10/24/1948	17Can15	02/23/1949	15Cap51
02/25/1948	16Vir53	06/24/1948	06Aqu25	10/26/1948	15Leo09	02/25/1949	10Aqu28
02/27/1948	16Lib20	06/26/1948	00Pis18	10/28/1948	13Vir58	02/27/1949	04Pis33
02/29/1948	13Sco54	06/28/1948	24Pis03	10/30/1948	13Lib16		
		06/30/1948	18Ari15			03/01/1949	28Pis14
03/02/1948	09Sag38			11/01/1948	12Sco15	03/03/1949	21Ari49
03/04/1948	04Cap04	07/02/1948	13Tau31	11/03/1948	10Sag13	03/05/1949	15Tau40
03/06/1948	27Cap55	07/04/1948	10Gem25	11/05/1948	06Cap40	03/07/1949	10Gem21
03/08/1948	21Aqu37	07/06/1948	09Can03	11/07/1948	01Aqu41	03/09/1949	06Can27
03/10/1948	15Pis33	07/08/1948	08Leo48	11/09/1948	25Aqu45	03/11/1949	04Leo28
03/12/1948	09Ari56	07/10/1948	08Vir33	11/11/1948	19Pis28	03/13/1949	04Vir11
03/14/1948	04Tau54	07/12/1948	07Lib22	11/13/1948	13Ari25	03/15/1949	04Lib40
03/16/1948	00Gem41	07/14/1948	04Sco48	11/15/1948	08Tau06	03/17/1949	04Sco40
03/18/1948	27Gem33	07/16/1948	00Sag57	11/17/1948	03Gem47	03/19/1949	03Sag10
03/20/1948	25Can48	07/18/1948	26Sag16	11/19/1948	00Can28	03/21/1949	29Sag57
03/22/1948	25Leo15	07/20/1948	20Cap53	11/21/1948	27Can56	03/23/1949	25Cap16
03/24/1948	25Vir04	07/22/1948	15Aqu01	11/23/1948	26Leo00	03/25/1949	19Aqu38
03/26/1948	24Lib12	07/24/1948	08Pis47	11/25/1948	24Vir20	03/27/1949	13Pis27
03/28/1948	21Sco50	07/26/1948	02Ari30	11/27/1948	22Lib44	03/29/1949	07Ari02
03/30/1948	17Sag47	07/28/1948	26Ari39	11/29/1948	20Sco50	03/31/1949	00Tau44
		07/30/1948	21Tau48				
04/01/1948	12Cap23	08/01/1948	18Gem38	12/01/1948	18Sag12	04/02/1949	24Tau51
04/03/1948	06Aqu17	08/03/1948	17Can24	12/03/1948	14Cap28	04/04/1949	19Gem45
04/05/1948	00Pis03	08/05/1948	17Leo34	12/05/1948	09Aqu30	04/06/1949	15Can48
04/07/1948	24Pis09	08/07/1948	17Vir56	12/07/1948	03Pis36	04/08/1949	13Leo25
04/09/1948	18Ari55	08/09/1948	17Lib12	12/09/1948	27Pis15	04/10/1949	12Vir37
04/11/1948	14Tau30	08/11/1948	14Sco46	12/11/1948	21Ari13	04/12/1949	12Lib45
04/13/1948	10Gem55	08/13/1948	10Sag46	12/13/1948	16Tau07	04/14/1949	12Sco46
04/15/1948	08Can13	08/15/1948	05Cap43	12/15/1948	12Gem20	04/16/1949	11Sag34
04/17/1948	06Leo21	08/17/1948	29Cap58	12/17/1948	09Can52	04/18/1949	08Cap40
04/19/1948	05Vir09	08/19/1948	23Aqu51	12/19/1948	08Leo18	04/20/1949	04Aqu09
04/21/1948	04Lib03	08/21/1948	17Pis35	12/21/1948	06Vir57	04/22/1949	28Aqu27
04/23/1948	02Sco26	08/23/1948	11Ari21	12/23/1948	05Lib16	04/24/1949	22Pis09
04/25/1948	29Sco42	08/25/1948	05Tau35	12/25/1948	03Sco03	04/26/1949	15Ari45
04/27/1948	25Sag37	08/27/1948	00Gem43	12/27/1948	00Sag16	04/28/1949	09Tau41
04/29/1948	20Cap19	08/29/1948	27Gem22	12/29/1948	26Sag50	04/30/1949	04Gem13
		08/31/1948	25Can53	12/31/1948	22Cap36		

Ephemeris Tables for the Moon

Date	Moon	Date	Moon	Date	Moon	Date	Moon
05/02/1949	29Gem37	09/01/1949	29Sag56	01/01/1950	07Gem32	05/01/1950	00Sco15
05/04/1949	25Can57	09/03/1949	25Cap57	01/03/1950	02Can42	05/03/1950	00Sag44
05/06/1949	23Leo25	09/05/1949	21Aqu05	01/05/1950	28Can54	05/05/1950	00Cap30
05/08/1949	22Vir02	09/07/1949	15Pis27	01/07/1950	25Leo57	05/07/1950	28Cap38
05/10/1949	21Lib27	09/09/1949	09Ari15	01/09/1950	23Vir33	05/09/1950	24Aqu57
05/12/1949	20Sco56	09/11/1949	02Tau49	01/11/1950	21Lib31	05/11/1950	19Pis48
05/14/1949	19Sag38	09/13/1949	26Tau36	01/13/1950	19Sco46	05/13/1950	13Ari45
05/16/1949	16Cap49	09/15/1949	21Gem06	01/15/1950	18Sag09	05/15/1950	07Tau22
05/18/1949	12Aqu26	09/17/1949	16Can57	01/17/1950	16Cap12	05/17/1950	01Gem02
05/20/1949	06Pis46	09/19/1949	14Leo34	01/19/1950	13Aqu20	05/19/1950	25Gem01
05/22/1949	00Ari29	09/21/1949	13Vir51	01/21/1950	09Pis09	05/21/1950	19Can31
05/24/1949	24Ari09	09/23/1949	14Lib04	01/23/1950	03Ari41	05/23/1950	14Leo49
05/26/1949	18Tau23	09/25/1949	14Sco03	01/25/1950	27Ari28	05/25/1950	11Vir15
05/28/1949	13Gem27	09/27/1949	12Sag48	01/27/1950	21Tau07	05/27/1950	09Lib15
05/30/1949	09Can30	09/29/1949	09Cap57	01/29/1950	15Gem25	05/29/1950	08Sco45
				01/31/1950	10Can50	05/31/1950	09Sag01
06/01/1949	06Leo28	10/01/1949	05Aqu40				
06/03/1949	04Vir08	10/03/1949	00Pis20	02/02/1950	07Leo37	06/02/1950	08Cap56
06/05/1949	02Lib24	10/05/1949	24Pis19	02/04/1950	05Vir32	06/04/1950	07Aqu18
06/07/1949	01Sco03	10/07/1949	17Ari58	02/06/1950	03Lib58	06/06/1950	03Pis46
06/09/1949	29Sco46	10/09/1949	11Tau34	02/08/1950	02Sco27	06/08/1950	28Pis37
06/11/1949	27Sag54	10/11/1949	05Gem30	02/10/1950	00Sag38	06/10/1950	22Ari30
06/13/1949	24Cap51	10/13/1949	00Can05	02/12/1950	28Sag24	06/12/1950	16Tau08
06/15/1949	20Aqu24	10/15/1949	25Can48	02/14/1950	25Cap33	06/14/1950	09Gem55
06/17/1949	14Pis46	10/17/1949	23Leo05	02/16/1950	21Aqu52	06/16/1950	04Can11
06/19/1949	08Ari30	10/19/1949	22Vir01	02/18/1950	17Pis12	06/18/1950	29Can07
06/21/1949	02Tau16	10/21/1949	22Lib10	02/20/1950	11Ari33	06/20/1950	24Leo48
06/23/1949	26Tau42	10/23/1949	22Sco27	02/22/1950	05Tau19	06/22/1950	21Vir22
06/25/1949	22Gem17	10/25/1949	21Sag42	02/24/1950	28Tau58	06/24/1950	19Lib06
06/27/1949	19Can05	10/27/1949	19Cap12	02/26/1950	23Gem12	06/26/1950	18Sco02
06/29/1949	16Leo51	10/29/1949	14Aqu54	02/28/1950	18Can37	06/28/1950	17Sag44
		10/31/1949	09Pis23			06/30/1950	17Cap15
07/01/1949	15Vir03			03/02/1950	15Leo40		
07/03/1949	13Lib20	11/02/1949	03Ari08	03/04/1950	14Vir10	07/02/1950	15Aqu29
07/05/1949	11Sco31	11/04/1949	26Ari44	03/06/1950	13Lib30	07/04/1950	11Pis59
07/07/1949	09Sag24	11/06/1949	20Tau30	03/08/1950	12Sco49	07/06/1950	06Ari53
07/09/1949	06Cap44	11/08/1949	14Gem43	03/10/1950	11Sag24	07/08/1950	00Tau52
07/11/1949	03Aqu09	11/10/1949	09Can39	03/12/1950	08Cap59	07/10/1950	24Tau33
07/13/1949	28Aqu26	11/12/1949	05Leo28	03/14/1950	05Aqu30	07/12/1950	18Gem31
07/15/1949	22Pis42	11/14/1949	02Vir28	03/16/1950	01Pis03	07/14/1950	13Can09
07/17/1949	16Ari24	11/16/1949	00Lib49	03/18/1950	25Pis47	07/16/1950	08Leo38
07/19/1949	10Tau10	11/18/1949	00Sco25	03/20/1950	19Ari50	07/18/1950	04Vir56
07/21/1949	04Gem43	11/20/1949	00Sag27	03/22/1950	13Tau31	07/20/1950	01Lib57
07/23/1949	00Can39	11/22/1949	29Sag48	03/24/1950	07Gem10	07/22/1950	29Lib44
07/25/1949	28Can04	11/24/1949	27Cap33	03/26/1950	01Can22	07/24/1950	28Sco16
07/27/1949	26Leo37	11/26/1949	23Aqu27	03/28/1950	26Can40	07/26/1950	27Sag12
07/29/1949	25Vir36	11/28/1949	17Pis57	03/30/1950	23Leo34	07/28/1950	25Cap56
07/31/1949	24Lib16	11/30/1949	11Ari37			07/30/1950	23Aqu39
				04/01/1950	22Vir12		
08/02/1949	22Sco18	12/02/1949	05Tau13	04/03/1950	22Lib04	08/01/1950	19Pis57
08/04/1949	19Sag37	12/04/1949	29Tau14	04/05/1950	22Sco11	08/03/1950	14Ari52
08/06/1949	16Cap11	12/06/1949	23Gem56	04/07/1950	21Sag25	08/05/1950	08Tau52
08/08/1949	11Aqu55	12/08/1949	19Can27	04/09/1950	19Cap13	08/07/1950	02Gem36
08/10/1949	06Pis46	12/10/1949	15Leo43	04/11/1950	15Aqu27	08/09/1950	26Gem42
08/12/1949	00Ari49	12/12/1949	12Vir46	04/13/1950	10Pis30	08/11/1950	21Can40
08/14/1949	24Ari25	12/14/1949	10Lib43	04/15/1950	04Ari45	08/13/1950	17Leo41
08/16/1949	18Tau12	12/16/1949	09Sco33	04/17/1950	28Ari31	08/15/1950	14Vir44
08/18/1949	12Gem45	12/18/1949	08Sag49	04/19/1950	22Tau08	08/17/1950	12Lib30
08/20/1949	08Can44	12/20/1949	07Cap42	04/21/1950	15Gem55	08/19/1950	10Sco43
08/22/1949	06Leo26	12/22/1949	05Aqu23	04/23/1950	10Can10	08/21/1950	09Sag07
08/24/1949	05Vir34	12/24/1949	01Pis24	04/25/1950	05Leo22	08/23/1950	07Cap24
08/26/1949	05Lib19	12/26/1949	25Pis58	04/27/1950	01Vir57	08/25/1950	05Aqu13
08/28/1949	04Sco38	12/28/1949	19Ari41	04/29/1950	00Lib21	08/27/1950	02Pis12
08/30/1949	02Sag53	12/30/1949	13Tau19			08/29/1950	28Pis02
						08/31/1950	22Ari48

Ephemeris Tables for the Moon

Date	Arin	Date	Arin	Date	Moon	Date	Moon
09/02/1950	16Tau46	01/02/1951	27Lib40	05/02/1951	00Ari17	09/01/1951	07Vir51
09/04/1950	10Gem31	01/04/1951	26Sco31	05/04/1951	25Ari28	09/03/1951	03Lib30
09/06/1950	04Can37	01/06/1951	26Sag32	05/06/1951	20Tau00	09/05/1951	00Sco06
09/08/1950	29Can42	01/08/1951	26Cap33	05/08/1951	14Gem01	09/07/1951	27Sco33
09/10/1950	26Leo05	01/10/1951	25Aqu24	05/10/1951	07Can47	09/09/1951	25Sag47
09/12/1950	23Vir48	01/12/1951	22Pis25	05/12/1951	01Leo34	09/11/1951	24Cap30
09/14/1950	22Lib30	01/14/1951	17Ari43	05/14/1951	25Leo58	09/13/1951	23Aqu13
09/16/1950	21Sco28	01/16/1951	11Tau52	05/16/1951	21Vir34	09/15/1951	21Pis29
09/18/1950	20Sag08	01/18/1951	05Gem36	05/18/1951	18Lib59	09/17/1951	18Ari40
09/20/1950	18Cap02	01/20/1951	29Gem26	05/20/1951	18Sco15	09/19/1951	14Tau34
09/22/1950	15Aqu06	01/22/1951	23Can43	05/22/1951	18Sag31	09/21/1951	09Gem15
09/24/1950	11Pis15	01/24/1951	18Leo40	05/24/1951	18Cap35	09/23/1951	03Can10
09/26/1950	06Ari28	01/26/1951	14Vir17	05/26/1951	17Aqu19	09/25/1951	26Can57
09/28/1950	00Tau55	01/28/1951	10Lib40	05/28/1951	14Pis24	09/27/1951	21Leo10
09/30/1950	24Tau49	01/30/1951	08Sco03	05/30/1951	10Ari03	09/29/1951	16Vir22
10/02/1950	18Gem34	02/01/1951	06Sag25	06/01/1951	04Tau49	10/01/1951	12Lib42
10/04/1950	12Can38	02/03/1951	05Cap34	06/03/1951	28Tau59	10/03/1951	10Sco11
10/06/1950	07Leo34	02/05/1951	04Aqu46	06/05/1951	22Gem48	10/05/1951	08Sag22
10/08/1950	04Vir01	02/07/1951	03Pis12	06/07/1951	16Can31	10/07/1951	06Cap49
10/10/1950	02Lib06	02/09/1951	00Ari10	06/09/1951	10Leo22	10/09/1951	05Aqu06
10/12/1950	01Sco32	02/11/1951	25Ari36	06/11/1951	04Vir45	10/11/1951	03Pis00
10/14/1950	01Sag23	02/13/1951	19Tau54	06/13/1951	00Lib14	10/13/1951	00Ari22
10/16/1950	00Cap39	02/15/1951	13Gem40	06/15/1951	27Lib28	10/15/1951	26Ari56
10/18/1950	28Cap38	02/17/1951	07Can34	06/17/1951	26Sco37	10/17/1951	22Tau31
10/20/1950	25Aqu12	02/19/1951	02Leo03	06/19/1951	27Sag02	10/19/1951	17Gem09
10/22/1950	20Pis41	02/21/1951	27Leo27	06/21/1951	27Cap27	10/21/1951	11Can02
10/24/1950	15Ari19	02/23/1951	23Vir50	06/23/1951	26Aqu34	10/23/1951	04Leo46
10/26/1950	09Tau28	02/25/1951	21Lib03	06/25/1951	23Pis52	10/25/1951	28Leo58
10/28/1950	03Gem15	02/27/1951	18Sco55	06/27/1951	19Ari30	10/27/1951	24Vir18
10/30/1950	27Gem00			06/29/1951	14Tau03	10/29/1951	21Lib10
		03/01/1951	17Sag13			10/31/1951	19Sco31
11/01/1950	21Can01	03/03/1951	15Cap42	07/01/1951	08Gem01		
11/03/1950	15Leo49	03/05/1951	13Aqu57	07/03/1951	01Can45	11/02/1951	18Sag38
11/05/1950	12Vir01	03/07/1951	11Pis30	07/05/1951	25Can30	11/04/1951	17Cap40
11/07/1950	10Lib01	03/09/1951	07Ari59	07/07/1951	19Leo31	11/06/1951	15Aqu59
11/09/1950	09Sco43	03/11/1951	03Tau19	07/09/1951	14Vir07	11/08/1951	13Pis21
11/11/1950	10Sag14	03/13/1951	27Tau42	07/11/1951	09Lib42	11/10/1951	09Ari55
11/13/1950	10Cap10	03/15/1951	21Gem31	07/13/1951	06Sco45	11/12/1951	05Tau46
11/15/1950	08Aqu32	03/17/1951	15Can24	07/15/1951	05Sag30	11/14/1951	00Gem53
11/17/1950	05Pis04	03/19/1951	09Leo27	07/17/1951	05Cap32	11/16/1951	25Gem16
11/19/1950	00Ari10	03/21/1951	05Vir38	07/19/1951	05Aqu49	11/18/1951	19Can05
11/21/1950	24Ari25	03/23/1951	02Lib41	07/21/1951	05Pis04	11/20/1951	12Leo43
11/23/1950	18Tau18	03/25/1951	00Sco50	07/23/1951	02Ari36	11/22/1951	06Vir48
11/25/1950	12Gem01	03/27/1951	29Sco34	07/25/1951	28Ari21	11/24/1951	02Lib04
11/27/1950	05Can51	03/29/1951	28Sag16	07/27/1951	22Tau54	11/26/1951	29Lib07
11/29/1950	00Leo00	03/31/1951	26Cap29	07/29/1951	16Gem49	11/28/1951	27Sco56
				07/31/1951	10Can31	11/30/1951	27Sag51
12/01/1950	24Leo46	04/02/1951	23Aqu57				
12/03/1950	20Vir43	04/04/1951	20Pis36	08/02/1951	04Leo25	12/02/1951	27Cap41
12/05/1950	18Lib20	04/06/1951	16Ari25	08/04/1951	28Leo48	12/04/1951	26Aqu27
12/07/1950	17Sco47	04/08/1951	11Tau24	08/06/1951	23Vir49	12/06/1951	23Pis45
12/09/1950	18Sag21	04/10/1951	05Gem40	08/08/1951	19Lib46	12/08/1951	19Ari51
12/11/1950	18Cap37	04/12/1951	29Gem28	08/10/1951	16Sco51	12/10/1951	15Tau06
12/13/1950	17Aqu23	04/14/1951	23Can18	08/12/1951	15Sag13	12/12/1951	09Gem42
12/15/1950	14Pis10	04/16/1951	17Leo47	08/14/1951	14Cap36	12/14/1951	03Can48
12/17/1950	09Ari16	04/18/1951	13Vir31	08/16/1951	14Aqu15	12/16/1951	27Can30
12/19/1950	03Tau23	04/20/1951	10Lib54	08/18/1951	13Pis12	12/18/1951	21Leo08
12/21/1950	27Tau07	04/22/1951	09Sco48	08/20/1951	10Ari42	12/20/1951	15Vir10
12/23/1950	20Gem52	04/24/1951	09Sag29	08/22/1951	06Tau39	12/22/1951	10Lib16
12/25/1950	14Can53	04/26/1951	08Cap53	08/24/1951	01Gem16	12/24/1951	07Sco04
12/27/1950	09Leo22	04/28/1951	07Aqu13	08/26/1951	25Gem11	12/26/1951	05Sag51
12/29/1950	04Vir24	04/30/1951	04Pis18	08/28/1951	18Can55	12/28/1951	06Cap06
12/31/1950	00Lib21			08/30/1951	13Leo02	12/30/1951	06Aqu30

Ephemeris Tables for the Moon

Date	Moon	Date	Moon	Date	Moon	Date	Moon
01/01/1952	05Pis54	05/02/1952	15Leo37	09/01/1952	01Aqu49	01/01/1953	25Can18
01/03/1952	03Ari33	05/04/1952	09Vir33	09/03/1952	01Pis53	01/03/1953	19Leo18
01/05/1952	29Ari36	05/06/1952	04Lib24	09/05/1952	01Ari53	01/05/1953	12Vir55
01/07/1952	24Tau32	05/08/1952	00Sco40	09/07/1952	00Tau41	01/07/1953	06Lib41
01/09/1952	18Gem45	05/10/1952	28Sco19	09/09/1952	27Tau46	01/09/1953	01Sco10
01/11/1952	12Can34	05/12/1952	26Sag53	09/11/1952	23Gem09	01/11/1953	27Sco04
01/13/1952	06Leo13	05/14/1952	25Cap40	09/13/1952	17Can21	01/13/1953	24Sag39
01/15/1952	00Vir00	05/16/1952	24Aqu04	09/15/1952	10Leo58	01/15/1953	23Cap49
01/17/1952	24Vir12	05/18/1952	21Pis54	09/17/1952	04Vir35	01/17/1953	23Aqu41
01/19/1952	19Lib16	05/20/1952	19Ari06	09/19/1952	28Vir37	01/19/1953	23Pis16
01/21/1952	15Sco49	05/22/1952	15Tau39	09/21/1952	23Lib18	01/21/1953	21Ari44
01/23/1952	14Sag10	05/24/1952	11Gem19	09/23/1952	18Sco48	01/23/1953	18Tau51
01/25/1952	14Cap04	05/26/1952	06Can01	09/25/1952	15Sag12	01/25/1953	14Gem46
01/27/1952	14Aqu30	05/28/1952	29Can59	09/27/1952	12Cap39	01/27/1953	09Can42
01/29/1952	14Pis13	05/30/1952	23Leo36	09/29/1952	11Aqu10	01/29/1953	03Leo58
01/31/1952	12Ari21					01/31/1953	27Leo45
		06/01/1952	17Vir30	10/01/1952	10Pis32		
02/02/1952	08Tau40	06/03/1952	12Lib22	10/03/1952	10Ari03	02/02/1953	21Vir21
02/04/1952	03Gem36	06/05/1952	08Sco49	10/05/1952	08Tau45	02/04/1953	15Lib10
02/06/1952	27Gem37	06/07/1952	06Sag58	10/07/1952	05Gem56	02/06/1953	09Sco37
02/08/1952	21Can19	06/09/1952	06Cap16	10/09/1952	01Can24	02/08/1953	05Sag15
02/10/1952	15Leo01	06/11/1952	05Aqu50	10/11/1952	25Can36	02/10/1953	02Cap35
02/12/1952	09Vir03	06/13/1952	04Pis44	10/13/1952	19Leo15	02/12/1953	01Aqu42
02/14/1952	03Lib37	06/15/1952	02Ari33	10/15/1952	12Vir58	02/14/1953	01Pis57
02/16/1952	29Lib02	06/17/1952	29Ari21	10/17/1952	07Lib20	02/16/1953	02Ari09
02/18/1952	25Sco36	06/19/1952	25Tau13	10/19/1952	02Sco35	02/18/1953	01Tau16
02/20/1952	23Sag30	06/21/1952	20Gem16	10/21/1952	28Sco46	02/20/1953	28Tau38
02/22/1952	22Cap42	06/23/1952	14Can33	10/23/1952	25Sag46	02/22/1953	24Gem23
02/24/1952	22Aqu32	06/25/1952	08Leo20	10/25/1952	23Cap20	02/24/1953	18Can56
02/26/1952	22Pis04	06/27/1952	01Vir54	10/27/1952	21Aqu27	02/26/1953	12Leo50
02/28/1952	20Ari22	06/29/1952	25Vir48	10/29/1952	20Pis03	02/28/1953	06Vir28
				10/31/1952	18Ari45		
03/01/1952	16Tau58	07/01/1952	20Lib37			03/02/1953	00Lib09
03/03/1952	12Gem02	07/03/1952	17Sco01	11/02/1952	16Tau52	03/04/1953	24Lib09
03/05/1952	06Can04	07/05/1952	15Sag15	11/04/1952	13Gem49	03/06/1953	18Sco45
03/07/1952	29Can45	07/07/1952	14Cap57	11/06/1952	09Can16	03/08/1953	14Sag20
03/09/1952	23Leo33	07/09/1952	15Aqu06	11/08/1952	03Leo30	03/10/1953	11Cap18
03/11/1952	17Vir53	07/11/1952	14Pis35	11/10/1952	27Leo10	03/12/1953	09Aqu56
03/13/1952	13Lib04	07/13/1952	12Ari44	11/12/1952	20Vir56	03/14/1953	09Pis57
03/15/1952	09Sco09	07/15/1952	09Tau25	11/14/1952	15Lib30	03/16/1953	10Ari18
03/17/1952	06Sag06	07/17/1952	04Gem54	11/16/1952	11Sco16	03/18/1953	09Tau49
03/19/1952	03Cap54	07/19/1952	29Gem28	11/18/1952	08Sag13	03/20/1953	07Gem32
03/21/1952	02Aqu25	07/21/1952	23Can24	11/20/1952	06Cap03	03/22/1953	03Can23
03/23/1952	01Pis25	07/23/1952	17Leo01	11/22/1952	04Aqu12	03/24/1953	27Can52
03/25/1952	00Ari15	07/25/1952	10Vir36	11/24/1952	02Pis24	03/26/1953	21Leo37
03/27/1952	28Ari13	07/27/1952	04Lib34	11/26/1952	00Ari28	03/28/1953	15Vir13
03/29/1952	24Tau49	07/29/1952	29Lib26	11/28/1952	28Ari19	03/30/1953	09Lib03
03/31/1952	20Gem01	07/31/1952	25Sco40	11/30/1952	25Tau34		
						04/01/1953	03Sco25
04/02/1952	14Can08	08/02/1952	23Sag41	12/02/1952	21Gem54	04/03/1953	28Sco25
04/04/1952	07Leo48	08/04/1952	23Cap14	12/04/1952	17Can06	04/05/1953	24Sag13
04/06/1952	01Vir40	08/06/1952	23Aqu37	12/06/1952	11Leo17	04/07/1953	21Cap03
04/08/1952	26Vir20	08/08/1952	23Pis35	12/08/1952	04Vir57	04/09/1953	19Aqu10
04/10/1952	22Lib08	08/10/1952	22Ari08	12/10/1952	28Vir42	04/11/1953	18Pis35
04/12/1952	19Sco01	08/12/1952	18Tau57	12/12/1952	23Lib17	04/13/1953	18Ari31
04/14/1952	16Sag43	08/14/1952	14Gem16	12/14/1952	19Sco17	04/15/1953	17Tau54
04/16/1952	14Cap51	08/16/1952	08Can34	12/16/1952	16Sag47	04/17/1953	15Gem44
04/18/1952	13Aqu06	08/18/1952	02Leo18	12/18/1952	15Cap26	04/19/1953	11Can44
04/20/1952	11Pis20	08/20/1952	25Leo51	12/20/1952	14Aqu28	04/21/1953	06Leo18
04/22/1952	09Ari16	08/22/1952	19Vir36	12/22/1952	13Pis15	04/23/1953	00Vir03
04/24/1952	06Tau34	08/24/1952	13Lib50	12/24/1952	11Ari18	04/25/1953	23Vir42
04/26/1952	02Gem49	08/26/1952	08Sco54	12/26/1952	08Tau33	04/27/1953	17Lib45
04/28/1952	27Gem53	08/28/1952	05Sag04	12/28/1952	04Gem59	04/29/1953	12Sco33
04/30/1952	21Can58	08/30/1952	02Cap42	12/30/1952	00Can34		

Ephemeris Tables for the Moon

Date	Moon	Date	Moon	Date	Moon	Date	Moon
05/01/1953	08Sag09	09/02/1953	04Can30	01/02/1954	10Sag09	05/02/1954	06Tau32
05/03/1953	04Cap29	09/04/1953	29Can27	01/04/1954	06Cap12	05/04/1954	06Gem45
05/05/1953	01Aqu34	09/06/1953	23Leo39	01/06/1954	03Aqu22	05/06/1954	05Can31
05/07/1953	29Aqu31	09/08/1953	17Vir26	01/08/1954	01Pis19	05/08/1954	02Leo25
05/09/1953	28Pis17	09/10/1953	11Lib06	01/10/1954	29Pis44	05/10/1954	27Leo44
05/11/1953	27Ari26	09/12/1953	04Sco55	01/12/1954	28Ari08	05/12/1954	22Vir00
05/13/1953	26Tau10	09/14/1953	29Sco13	01/14/1954	26Tau13	05/14/1954	15Lib49
05/15/1953	23Gem43	09/16/1953	24Sag24	01/16/1954	23Gem46	05/16/1954	09Sco34
05/17/1953	19Can41	09/18/1953	21Cap00	01/18/1954	20Can30	05/18/1954	03Sag33
05/19/1953	14Leo18	09/20/1953	19Aqu26	01/20/1954	16Leo19	05/20/1954	28Sag01
05/21/1953	08Vir07	09/22/1953	19Pis27	01/22/1954	11Vir10	05/22/1954	23Cap08
05/23/1953	01Lib51	09/24/1953	20Ari03	01/24/1954	05Lib13	05/24/1954	19Aqu13
05/25/1953	26Lib06	09/26/1953	19Tau50	01/26/1954	28Lib59	05/26/1954	16Pis37
05/27/1953	21Sco17	09/28/1953	17Gem51	01/28/1954	22Sco59	05/28/1954	15Ari26
05/29/1953	17Sag30	09/30/1953	13Can59	01/30/1954	17Sag54	05/30/1954	15Tau15
05/31/1953	14Cap35						
		10/02/1953	08Leo41	02/01/1954	14Cap10	06/01/1954	15Gem00
06/02/1953	12Aqu19	10/04/1953	02Vir37	02/03/1954	11Aqu58	06/03/1954	13Can39
06/04/1953	10Pis27	10/06/1953	26Vir18	02/05/1954	10Pis55	06/05/1954	10Leo43
06/06/1953	08Ari52	10/08/1953	20Lib03	02/07/1954	10Ari12	06/07/1954	06Vir09
06/08/1953	07Tau15	10/10/1953	14Sco04	02/09/1954	09Tau01	06/09/1954	00Lib29
06/10/1953	05Gem07	10/12/1953	08Sag35	02/11/1954	06Gem53	06/11/1954	24Lib19
06/12/1953	02Can01	10/14/1953	03Cap49	02/13/1954	03Can44	06/13/1954	18Sco08
06/14/1953	27Can39	10/16/1953	00Aqu13	02/15/1954	29Can40	06/15/1954	12Sag22
06/16/1953	22Leo10	10/18/1953	28Aqu15	02/17/1954	24Leo51	06/17/1954	07Cap16
06/18/1953	16Vir00	10/20/1953	27Pis49	02/19/1954	19Vir21	06/19/1954	03Aqu00
06/20/1953	09Lib48	10/22/1953	28Ari12	02/21/1954	13Lib19	06/21/1954	29Aqu38
06/22/1953	04Sco09	10/24/1953	28Tau05	02/23/1954	07Sco04	06/23/1954	27Pis20
06/24/1953	29Sco34	10/26/1953	26Gem23	02/25/1954	01Sag00	06/25/1954	25Ari41
06/26/1953	26Sag17	10/28/1953	22Can43	02/27/1954	25Sag44	06/27/1954	24Tau43
06/28/1953	24Cap09	10/30/1953	17Leo27			06/29/1954	23Gem40
06/30/1953	22Aqu42			03/01/1954	21Cap56		
		11/01/1953	11Vir20	03/03/1954	19Aqu57	07/01/1954	21Can49
07/02/1953	21Pis25	11/03/1953	05Lib00	03/05/1954	19Pis33	07/03/1954	18Leo43
07/04/1953	19Ari48	11/05/1953	28Lib53	03/07/1954	19Ari41	07/05/1954	14Vir10
07/06/1953	17Tau39	11/07/1953	23Sco14	03/09/1954	19Tau12	07/07/1954	08Lib34
07/08/1953	14Gem42	11/09/1953	18Sag10	03/11/1954	17Gem17	07/09/1954	02Sco27
07/10/1953	10Can49	11/11/1953	13Cap49	03/13/1954	13Can51	07/11/1954	26Sco19
07/12/1953	5Leo55	11/13/1953	10Aqu20	03/15/1954	09Leo14	07/13/1954	20Sag46
07/14/1953	00Vir14	11/15/1953	08Pis03	03/17/1954	03Vir52	07/15/1954	16Cap09
07/16/1953	24Vir03	11/17/1953	06Ari58	03/19/1954	28Vir02	07/17/1954	12Aqu37
07/18/1953	17Lib49	11/19/1953	06Tau39	03/21/1954	21Lib52	07/19/1954	10Pis03
07/20/1953	12Sco07	11/21/1953	06Gem06	03/23/1954	15Sco37	07/21/1954	08Ari08
07/22/1953	07Sag34	11/23/1953	04Can16	03/25/1954	09Sag34	07/23/1954	06Tau35
07/24/1953	04Cap32	11/25/1953	00Leo42	03/27/1954	04Cap12	07/25/1954	05Gem00
07/26/1953	02Aqu58	11/27/1953	25Leo36	03/29/1954	00Aqu10	07/27/1954	03Can03
07/28/1953	02Pis22	11/29/1953	19Vir34	03/31/1954	28Aqu01	07/29/1954	00Leo26
07/30/1953	01Ari51					07/31/1954	26Leo51
08/01/1953	00Tau35	12/01/1953	13Lib16	04/02/1954	27Pis42	08/02/1954	22Vir09
08/03/1953	28Tau13	12/03/1953	07Sco18	04/04/1954	28Ari15	08/04/1954	16Lib31
08/05/1953	24Gem37	12/05/1953	02Sag00	04/06/1954	28Tau21	08/06/1954	10Sco22
08/07/1953	20Can02	12/07/1953	27Sag32	04/08/1954	26Gem52	08/08/1954	04Sag13
08/09/1953	14Leo38	12/09/1953	23Cap52	04/10/1954	23Can31	08/10/1954	28Sag46
08/11/1953	08Vir40	12/11/1953	20Aqu57	04/12/1954	18Leo43	08/12/1954	24Cap29
08/13/1953	02Lib24	12/13/1953	18Pis45	04/14/1954	13Vir03	08/14/1954	21Aqu40
08/15/1953	26Lib07	12/15/1953	17Ari12	04/16/1954	06Lib58	08/16/1954	20Pis00
08/17/1953	20Sco24	12/17/1953	15Tau58	04/18/1954	00Sco43	08/18/1954	18Ari52
08/19/1953	15Sag42	12/19/1953	14Gem30	04/20/1954	24Sco32	08/18/1954	18Ari52
08/21/1953	12Cap36	12/21/1953	12Can05	04/22/1954	18Sag40	08/20/1954	17Tau38
08/23/1953	11Aqu14	12/23/1953	08Leo24	04/24/1954	13Cap24	08/22/1954	15Gem45
08/25/1953	11Pis11	12/25/1953	03Vir22	04/26/1954	09Aqu17	08/24/1954	13Can04
08/27/1953	11Ari24	12/27/1953	27Vir27	04/28/1954	06Pis49	08/26/1954	09Leo40
08/29/1953	10Tau42	12/29/1953	21Lib10	04/30/1954	06Ari08	08/28/1954	05Vir27
08/31/1953	08Gem24	12/31/1953	15Sco14			08/30/1954	00Lib24

Ephemeris Tables for the Moon

Date	Moon	Date	Moon	Date	Moon	Date	Moon
09/01/1954	24Lib36	01/01/1955	05Ari45	05/01/1955	08Vir38	09/02/1955	11Pis16
09/03/1954	18Sco22	01/03/1955	03Tau54	05/03/1955	03Lib57	09/04/1955	08Ari18
09/05/1954	12Sag10	01/05/1955	03Gem02	05/05/1955	28Lib28	09/06/1955	06Tau01
09/07/1954	06Cap39	01/07/1955	02Can27	05/07/1955	22Sco25	09/08/1955	04Gem06
09/09/1954	02Aqu30	01/09/1955	01Leo22	05/09/1955	16Sag05	09/10/1955	02Can18
09/11/1954	00Pis03	01/11/1955	29Leo02	05/11/1955	09Cap43	09/12/1955	00Leo33
09/13/1954	29Pis10	01/13/1955	25Vir09	05/13/1955	03Aqu49	09/14/1955	28Leo31
09/15/1954	28Ari52	01/15/1955	19Lib52	05/15/1955	28Aqu57	09/16/1955	25Vir45
09/17/1954	28Tau15	01/17/1955	13Sco43	05/17/1955	25Pis48	09/18/1955	21Lib56
09/19/1954	26Gem27	01/19/1955	07Sag24	05/19/1955	24Ari19	09/20/1955	16Sco49
09/21/1954	23Can23	01/21/1955	01Cap27	05/21/1955	24Tau19	09/22/1955	10Sag47
09/23/1954	19Leo20	01/23/1955	26Cap18	05/23/1955	24Gem40	09/24/1955	04Cap25
09/25/1954	14Vir30	01/25/1955	22Aqu10	05/25/1955	24Can07	09/26/1955	28Cap24
09/27/1954	09Lib02	01/27/1955	18Pis59	05/27/1955	22Leo00	09/28/1955	23Aqu24
09/29/1954	03Sco01	01/29/1955	16Ari31	05/29/1955	18Vir17	09/30/1955	19Pis50
		01/31/1955	14Tau35	05/31/1955	13Lib22		
10/01/1954	26Sco42					10/02/1955	17Ari37
10/03/1954	20Sag25	02/02/1955	13Gem01	06/02/1955	07Sco33	10/04/1955	16Tau12
10/05/1954	14Cap47	02/04/1955	11Can28	06/04/1955	01Sag17	10/06/1955	14Gem55
10/07/1954	10Aqu30	02/06/1955	09Leo35	06/06/1955	24Sag54	10/08/1955	13Can18
10/09/1954	08Pis05	02/08/1955	06Vir53	06/08/1955	18Cap40	10/10/1955	11Leo06
10/11/1954	07Ari28	02/10/1955	02Lib54	06/10/1955	13Aqu00	10/12/1955	08Vir17
10/13/1954	07Tau51	02/12/1955	27Lib40	06/12/1955	08Pis15	10/14/1955	04Lib45
10/15/1954	07Gem53	02/14/1955	21Sco34	06/14/1955	04Ari52	10/16/1955	00Sco19
10/17/1954	06Can30	02/16/1955	15Sag15	06/16/1955	03Tau05	10/18/1955	24Sco55
10/19/1954	03Leo27	02/18/1955	09Cap21	06/18/1955	02Gem43	10/20/1955	18Sag44
10/21/1954	29Leo06	02/20/1955	04Aqu31	06/20/1955	02Can58	10/22/1955	12Cap21
10/23/1954	23Vir49	02/22/1955	01Pis04	06/22/1955	02Leo39	10/24/1955	06Aqu17
10/25/1954	17Lib58	02/24/1955	28Pis47	06/24/1955	00Vir52	10/26/1955	01Pis16
10/27/1954	11Sco44	02/26/1955	27Ari09	06/26/1955	27Vir23	10/28/1955	27Pis53
10/29/1954	05Sag25	02/28/1955	25Tau36	06/28/1955	22Lib22	10/30/1955	26Ari03
10/31/1954	29Sag12			06/30/1955	16Sco24		
		03/02/1955	23Gem47	07/02/1955	10Sag01	11/01/1955	25Tau24
11/02/1954	23Cap33	03/04/1955	21Can30	07/04/1955	03Cap43	11/03/1955	24Gem58
11/04/1954	19Aqu06	03/06/1955	18Leo44	07/06/1955	27Cap47	11/05/1955	23Can55
11/06/1954	16Pis24	03/08/1955	15Vir18	07/08/1955	22Aqu31	11/07/1955	21Leo45
11/08/1954	15Ari35	03/10/1955	10Lib54	07/10/1955	18Pis10	11/09/1955	18Vir28
11/10/1954	16Tau02	03/12/1955	05Sco31	07/12/1955	14Ari50	11/11/1955	14Lib12
11/12/1954	16Gem25	03/14/1955	29Sco23	07/14/1955	12Tau43	11/13/1955	09Sco08
11/14/1954	15Can32	03/16/1955	23Sag03	07/16/1955	11Gem45	11/15/1955	03Sag19
11/16/1954	12Leo49	03/18/1955	17Cap08	07/18/1955	11Can28	11/17/1955	27Sag01
11/18/1954	08Vir28	03/20/1955	12Aqu23	07/20/1955	10Leo54	11/19/1955	20Cap37
11/20/1954	02Lib59	03/22/1955	09Pis19	07/22/1955	09Vir10	11/21/1955	14Aqu31
11/22/1954	26Lib54	03/24/1955	07Ari44	07/24/1955	05Lib48	11/23/1955	09Pis21
11/24/1954	20Sco37	03/26/1955	07Tau01	07/26/1955	00Sco50	11/25/1955	05Ari42
11/26/1954	14Sag20	03/28/1955	06Gem12	07/28/1955	24Sco51	11/27/1955	03Tau55
11/28/1954	08Cap19	03/30/1955	04Can37	07/30/1955	18Sag28	11/29/1955	03Gem37
11/30/1954	02Aqu55						
		04/01/1955	02Leo02	08/01/1955	12Cap18	12/01/1955	03Can52
12/02/1954	28Aqu34	04/03/1955	28Leo36	08/03/1955	06Aqu45	12/03/1955	03Leo33
12/04/1954	25Pis38	04/05/1955	24Vir25	08/05/1955	02Pis04	12/05/1955	01Vir49
12/06/1954	24Ari13	04/07/1955	19Lib28	08/07/1955	28Pis21	12/07/1955	28Vir29
12/08/1954	24Tau09	04/09/1955	13Sco46	08/09/1955	25Ari22	12/09/1955	23Lib50
12/10/1954	24Gem19	04/11/1955	07Sag33	08/11/1955	23Tau10	12/11/1955	18Sco14
12/12/1954	23Can37	04/13/1955	01Cap09	08/13/1955	21Gem39	12/13/1955	12Sag05
12/14/1954	21Leo15	04/15/1955	25Cap11	08/15/1955	20Can36	12/15/1955	05Cap40
12/16/1954	17Vir09	04/17/1955	20Aqu22	08/17/1955	19Leo24	12/17/1955	29Cap19
12/18/1954	11Lib43	04/19/1955	17Pis21	08/19/1955	17Vir19	12/19/1955	23Aqu21
12/20/1954	05Sco33	04/21/1955	16Ari04	08/21/1955	13Lib52	12/21/1955	18Pis09
12/22/1954	29Sco13	04/23/1955	15Tau57	08/23/1955	08Sco54	12/23/1955	14Ari16
12/24/1954	23Sag06	04/25/1955	15Gem54	08/25/1955	02Sag55	12/25/1955	12Tau01
12/26/1954	17Cap30	04/27/1955	14Can49	08/27/1955	26Sag33	12/27/1955	11Gem27
12/28/1954	12Aqu39	04/29/1955	12Leo22	08/29/1955	20Cap31	12/29/1955	11Can52
12/30/1954	08Pis43			08/31/1955	15Aqu19	12/31/1955	12Leo05

Ephemeris Tables for the Moon

Date	Moon	Date	Moon	Date	Moon	Date	Moon
01/02/1956	10Vir53	05/01/1956	23Cap21	09/02/1956	07Leo54	01/02/1957	27Cap18
01/04/1956	07Lib49	05/03/1956	17Aqu12	09/04/1956	07Vir53	01/04/1957	21Aqu04
01/06/1956	03Sco06	05/05/1956	11Pis46	09/06/1956	07Lib09	01/06/1957	14Pis49
01/08/1956	27Sco15	05/07/1956	07Ari37	09/08/1956	04Sco48	01/08/1957	08Ari55
01/10/1956	20Sag53	05/09/1956	05Tau00	09/10/1956	00Sag37	01/10/1957	04Tau00
01/12/1956	14Cap28	05/11/1956	03Gem37	09/12/1956	25Sag07	01/12/1957	00Gem42
01/14/1956	08Aqu19	05/13/1956	02Can49	09/14/1956	18Cap54	01/14/1957	29Gem19
01/16/1956	02Pis40	05/15/1956	01Leo51	09/16/1956	12Aqu38	01/16/1957	29Can27
01/18/1956	27Pis45	05/17/1956	00Vir12	09/18/1956	06Pis49	01/18/1957	29Leo55
01/20/1956	23Ari44	05/19/1956	27Vir31	09/20/1956	01Ari40	01/20/1957	29Vir26
01/22/1956	21Tau04	05/21/1956	23Lib51	09/22/1956	27Ari16	01/22/1957	27Lib11
01/24/1956	19Gem54	05/23/1956	19Sco18	09/24/1956	23Tau36	01/24/1957	23Sco13
01/26/1956	19Can51	05/25/1956	13Sag52	09/26/1956	20Gem45	01/26/1957	18Sag03
01/28/1956	19Leo58	05/27/1956	07Cap51	09/28/1956	18Can46	01/28/1957	12Cap16
01/30/1956	19Vir01	05/29/1956	01Aqu32	09/30/1956	17Leo35	01/30/1957	06Aqu06
		05/31/1956	25Aqu24				
02/01/1956	16Lib15			10/02/1956	16Vir44	02/01/1957	29Aqu49
02/03/1956	11Sco42	06/02/1956	19Pis55	10/04/1956	15Lib21	02/03/1957	23Pis40
02/05/1956	05Sag51	06/04/1956	15Ari42	10/06/1956	12Sco43	02/05/1957	17Ari50
02/07/1956	29Sag26	06/06/1956	13Tau08	10/08/1956	08Sag35	02/07/1957	12Tau48
02/09/1956	23Cap03	06/08/1956	12Gem09	10/10/1956	03Cap07	02/09/1957	09Gem10
02/11/1956	17Aqu13	06/10/1956	12Can03	10/12/1956	26Cap55	02/11/1957	07Can28
02/13/1956	12Pis04	06/12/1956	11Leo50	10/14/1956	20Aqu42	02/13/1957	07Leo27
02/15/1956	07Ari38	06/14/1956	10Vir33	10/16/1956	15Pis05	02/15/1957	08Vir07
02/17/1956	04Tau00	06/16/1956	07Lib48	10/18/1956	10Ari19	02/17/1957	08Lib04
02/19/1956	01Gem13	06/18/1956	03Sco40	10/20/1956	06Tau34	02/19/1957	06Sco13
02/21/1956	29Gem29	06/20/1956	28Sco33	10/22/1956	03Gem44	02/21/1957	02Sag26
02/23/1956	28Can41	06/22/1956	22Sag40	10/24/1956	01Can31	02/23/1957	27Sag13
02/25/1956	28Leo08	06/24/1956	16Cap27	10/26/1956	29Can43	02/25/1957	21Cap14
02/27/1956	26Vir52	06/26/1956	10Aqu07	10/28/1956	28Leo07	02/27/1957	14Aqu57
02/29/1956	24Lib07	06/28/1956	04Pis04	10/30/1956	26Vir24		
		06/30/1956	28Pis37			03/01/1957	08Pis42
03/02/1956	19Sco41			11/01/1956	24Lib05	03/03/1957	02Ari46
03/04/1956	13Sag56	07/02/1956	24Ari13	11/03/1956	20Sco49	03/05/1957	27Ari15
03/06/1956	07Cap34	07/04/1956	21Tau27	11/05/1956	16Sag24	03/07/1957	22Tau24
03/08/1956	01Aqu21	07/06/1956	20Gem26	11/07/1956	10Cap54	03/09/1957	18Gem41
03/10/1956	25Aqu45	07/08/1956	20Can39	11/09/1956	04Aqu45	03/11/1957	16Can34
03/12/1956	21Pis06	07/10/1956	20Leo57	11/11/1956	28Aqu33	03/13/1957	16Leo00
03/14/1956	17Ari22	07/12/1956	20Vir08	11/13/1956	22Pis55	03/15/1957	16Vir13
03/16/1956	14Tau26	07/14/1956	17Lib31	11/15/1956	18Ari18	03/17/1957	16Lib03
03/18/1956	12Gem01	07/16/1956	13Sco13	11/17/1956	15Tau04	03/19/1957	14Sco24
03/20/1956	10Can07	07/18/1956	07Sag45	11/19/1956	13Gem06	03/21/1957	10Sag52
03/22/1956	08Leo37	07/20/1956	01Cap39	11/21/1956	11Can50	03/23/1957	05Cap49
03/24/1956	07Vir11	07/22/1956	25Cap18	11/23/1956	10Leo40	03/25/1957	29Cap51
03/26/1956	05Lib10	07/24/1956	19Aqu05	11/25/1956	09Vir04	03/27/1957	23Aqu33
03/28/1956	01Sco59	07/26/1956	13Pis10	11/27/1956	06Lib43	03/29/1957	17Pis25
03/30/1956	27Sco27	07/28/1956	07Ari49	11/29/1956	03Sco31	03/31/1957	11Ari45
		07/30/1956	03Tau25				
04/01/1956	21Sag45	08/01/1956	00Gem25	12/01/1956	29Sco27	04/02/1957	06Tau43
04/03/1956	15Cap27	08/03/1956	29Gem03	12/03/1956	24Sag33	04/04/1957	02Gem25
04/05/1956	09Aqu16	08/05/1956	29Can04	12/05/1956	18Cap54	04/06/1957	29Gem05
04/07/1956	03Pis50	08/07/1956	29Leo28	12/07/1956	12Aqu43	04/08/1957	26Can49
04/09/1956	29Pis37	08/09/1956	28Vir54	12/09/1956	06Pis28	04/10/1957	25Leo36
04/11/1956	26Ari30	08/11/1956	26Lib30	12/11/1956	00Ari41	04/12/1957	25Vir00
04/13/1956	24Tau25	08/13/1956	22Sco14	12/13/1956	26Ari00	04/14/1957	24Lib12
04/15/1956	22Gem45	08/15/1956	16Sag40	12/15/1956	22Tau54	04/16/1957	22Sco15
04/17/1956	21Can07	08/17/1956	10Cap27	12/17/1956	21Gem30	04/18/1957	18Sag46
04/19/1956	19Leo21	08/19/1956	04Aqu07	12/19/1956	21Can07	04/20/1957	13Cap54
04/21/1956	17Vir08	08/21/1956	28Aqu04	12/21/1956	20Leo51	04/22/1957	08Aqu01
04/23/1956	14Lib13	08/23/1956	22Pis30	12/23/1956	19Vir45	04/24/1957	01Pis47
04/25/1956	10Sco21	08/25/1956	17Ari31	12/25/1956	17Lib13	04/26/1957	25Pis45
04/27/1956	05Sag26	08/27/1956	13Tau19	12/27/1956	13Sco25	04/28/1957	20Ari22
04/29/1956	29Sag37	08/29/1956	10Gem19	12/29/1956	08Sag39	04/30/1957	15Tau53
		08/31/1956	08Can26	12/31/1956	03Cap14		

Ephemeris Tables for the Moon

Date	Moon	Date	Moon	Date	Moon	Date	Moon
05/02/1957	12Gem21	09/01/1957	12Sag30	01/01/1958	17Tau06	05/01/1958	12Lib22
05/04/1957	09Can41	09/03/1957	07Cap41	01/03/1958	12Gem52	05/03/1958	12Sco19
05/06/1957	07Leo42	09/05/1957	02Aqu06	01/05/1958	10Can12	05/05/1958	11Sag39
05/08/1957	06Vir10	09/07/1957	26Aqu00	01/07/1958	08Leo47	05/07/1958	09Cap27
05/10/1957	04Lib46	09/09/1957	19Pis43	01/09/1958	07Vir52	05/09/1958	05Aqu33
05/12/1957	03Sco02	09/11/1957	13Ari29	01/11/1958	06Lib36	05/11/1958	00Pis15
05/14/1957	00Sag24	09/13/1957	07Tau36	01/13/1958	04Sco33	05/13/1958	24Pis08
05/16/1957	26Sag39	09/15/1957	02Gem24	01/15/1958	01Sag45	05/15/1958	17Ari43
05/18/1957	21Cap45	09/17/1957	28Gem24	01/17/1958	28Sag13	05/17/1958	11Tau34
05/20/1957	15Aqu57	09/19/1957	26Can06	01/19/1958	23Cap59	05/19/1958	06Gem04
05/22/1957	09Pis45	09/21/1957	25Leo29	01/21/1958	18Aqu59	05/21/1958	01Can23
05/24/1957	03Ari45	09/23/1957	25Vir49	01/23/1958	13Pis11	05/23/1958	27Can37
05/26/1957	28Ari34	09/25/1957	25Lib53	01/25/1958	06Ari51	05/25/1958	24Leo48
05/28/1957	24Tau32	09/27/1957	24Sco35	01/27/1958	00Tau29	05/27/1958	22Vir54
05/30/1957	21Gem46	09/29/1957	21Sag26	01/29/1958	24Tau52	05/29/1958	21Lib46
				01/31/1958	20Gem37	05/31/1958	20Sco58
06/01/1957	20Can00	10/01/1957	16Cap42				
06/03/1957	18Leo40	10/03/1957	11Aqu00	02/02/1958	18Can12	06/02/1958	19Sag48
06/05/1957	17Vir12	10/05/1957	04Pis48	02/04/1958	17Leo27	06/04/1958	17Cap29
06/07/1957	15Lib16	10/07/1957	28Pis30	02/06/1958	17Vir21	06/06/1958	13Aqu38
06/09/1957	12Sco39	10/09/1957	22Ari28	02/08/1958	16Lib49	06/08/1958	08Pis24
06/11/1957	09Sag13	10/11/1957	16Tau58	02/10/1958	15Sco06	06/10/1958	02Ari16
06/13/1957	04Cap56	10/13/1957	12Gem10	02/12/1958	12Sag06	06/12/1958	25Ari55
06/15/1957	29Cap47	10/15/1957	08Can21	02/14/1958	08Cap01	06/14/1958	19Tau58
06/17/1957	23Aqu54	10/17/1957	05Leo51	02/16/1958	03Aqu09	06/16/1958	14Gem55
06/19/1957	17Pis41	10/19/1957	04Vir38	02/18/1958	27Aqu39	06/18/1958	10Can55
06/21/1957	11Ari42	10/21/1957	04Lib18	02/20/1958	21Pis36	06/20/1958	07Leo54
06/23/1957	06Tau31	10/23/1957	03Sco55	02/22/1958	15Ari11	06/22/1958	05Vir37
06/25/1957	02Gem45	10/25/1957	02Sag35	02/24/1958	08Tau51	06/24/1958	03Lib43
06/27/1957	00Can34	10/27/1957	29Sag37	02/26/1958	03Gem09	06/26/1958	02Sco04
06/29/1957	29Can40	10/29/1957	25Cap04	02/28/1958	28Gem43	06/28/1958	00Sag28
		10/31/1957	19Aqu24			06/30/1958	28Sag33
07/01/1957	29Leo08			03/02/1958	26Can08		
07/03/1957	28Vir03	11/02/1957	13Pis09	03/04/1958	25Leo29	07/02/1958	25Cap43
07/05/1957	25Lib57	11/04/1957	06Ari55	03/06/1958	25Vir50	07/04/1958	21Aqu38
07/07/1957	22Sco43	11/06/1957	01Tau13	03/08/1958	25Lib57	07/06/1958	16Pis22
07/09/1957	18Sag36	11/08/1957	26Tau11	03/10/1958	24Sco48	07/08/1958	10Ari13
07/11/1957	13Cap45	11/10/1957	22Gem03	03/12/1958	22Sag01	07/10/1958	03Tau53
07/13/1957	08Aqu15	11/12/1957	18Can48	03/14/1958	17Cap46	07/12/1958	28Tau03
07/15/1957	02Pis12	11/14/1957	16Leo27	03/16/1958	12Aqu31	07/14/1958	23Gem20
07/17/1957	25Pis55	11/16/1957	14Vir46	03/18/1958	06Pis39	07/16/1958	19Can57
07/19/1957	19Ari51	11/18/1957	13Lib34	03/20/1958	00Ari21	07/18/1958	17Leo45
07/21/1957	14Tau36	11/20/1957	12Sco22	03/22/1958	23Ari56	07/20/1958	16Vir14
07/23/1957	10Gem49	11/22/1957	10Sag30	03/24/1958	17Tau43	07/22/1958	14Lib43
07/25/1957	08Can54	11/24/1957	07Cap26	03/26/1958	12Gem07	07/24/1958	12Sco55
07/27/1957	08Leo36	11/26/1957	02Aqu58	03/28/1958	07Can37	07/26/1958	10Sag40
07/29/1957	08Vir46	11/28/1957	27Aqu22	03/30/1958	04Leo45	07/28/1958	07Cap57
07/31/1957	08Lib14	11/30/1957	21Pis07			07/30/1958	04Aqu25
				04/01/1958	03Vir43		
08/02/1957	06Sco18	12/02/1957	14Ari54	04/03/1958	3Lib53	08/01/1958	29Aqu54
08/04/1957	02Sag49	12/04/1957	09Tau21	04/05/1958	04Sco12	08/03/1958	24Pis23
08/06/1957	28Sag13	12/06/1957	04Gem51	04/07/1958	03Sag31	08/05/1958	18Ari10
08/08/1957	22Cap54	12/08/1957	01Can31	04/09/1958	01Cap57	08/07/1958	11Tau49
08/10/1957	17Aqu03	12/10/1957	29Can10	04/11/1958	27Cap01	08/09/1958	06Gem00
08/12/1957	10Pis51	12/12/1957	27Leo21	04/13/1958	21Aqu39	08/11/1958	01Can25
08/14/1957	04Ari32	12/14/1957	25Vir39	04/15/1958	15Pis34	08/13/1958	28Can25
08/16/1957	28Ari29	12/16/1957	23Lib47	04/17/1958	09Ari09	08/15/1958	26Leo53
08/18/1957	23Tau10	12/18/1957	21Sco40	04/19/1958	02Tau49	08/17/1958	26Vir09
08/20/1957	19Gem15	12/20/1957	18Sag58	04/21/1958	26Tau55	08/19/1958	25Lib18
08/22/1957	17Can15	12/22/1957	15Cap25	04/23/1958	21Gem39	08/21/1958	23Sco43
08/24/1957	17Leo00	12/24/1957	10Aqu46	04/25/1958	17Can22	08/23/1958	21Sag13
08/26/1957	17Vir32	12/26/1957	05Pis10	04/27/1958	14Leo21	08/25/1958	17Cap51
08/28/1957	17Lib30	12/28/1957	28Pis54	04/29/1958	12Vir47	08/27/1958	13Aqu35
08/30/1957	15Sco55	12/30/1957	22Ari38			08/29/1958	08Pis30
						08/31/1958	02Ari42

Ephemeris Tables for the Moon

Date	Moon	Date	Moon	Date	Moon	Date	Moon
09/02/1958	26Ari22	01/02/1959	11Lib58	05/02/1959	12Pis31	09/01/1959	18Leo38
09/04/1958	19Tau58	01/04/1959	10Sco15	05/04/1959	06Ari51	09/03/1959	15Vir36
09/06/1958	14Gem08	01/06/1959	09Sag03	05/06/1959	00Tau42	09/05/1959	13Lib30
09/08/1958	09Can30	01/08/1959	07Cap49	05/08/1959	24Tau18	09/07/1959	11Sco57
09/10/1958	06Leo32	01/10/1959	05Aqu47	05/10/1959	18Gem01	09/09/1959	10Sag29
09/12/1958	05Vir18	01/12/1959	02Pis19	05/12/1959	12Can09	09/11/1959	08Cap44
09/14/1958	05Lib10	01/14/1959	27Pis22	05/14/1959	07Leo00	09/13/1959	06Aqu26
09/16/1958	05Sco03	01/16/1959	21Ari22	05/16/1959	02Vir58	09/15/1959	03Pis22
09/18/1958	03Sag59	01/18/1959	14Tau58	05/18/1959	00Lib30	09/17/1959	29Pis19
09/20/1958	01Cap34	01/20/1959	08Gem54	05/20/1959	29Lib46	09/19/1959	24Ari16
09/22/1958	27Cap49	01/22/1959	03Can46	05/22/1959	00Sag06	09/21/1959	18Tau27
09/24/1958	23Aqu01	01/24/1959	29Can53	05/24/1959	00Cap21	09/23/1959	12Gem13
09/26/1958	17Pis26	01/26/1959	27Leo00	05/26/1959	29Cap18	09/25/1959	06Can06
09/28/1958	11Ari19	01/28/1959	24Vir48	05/28/1959	26Aqu21	09/27/1959	00Leo43
09/30/1958	04Tau54	01/30/1959	22Lib54	5/30/1959	21Pis40	09/29/1959	26Leo38
10/02/1958	28Tau33	02/01/1959	21Sco04	06/01/1959	15Ari51	10/01/1959	24Vir02
10/04/1958	22Gem47	02/03/1959	19Sag12	06/03/1959	09Tau32	10/03/1959	22Lib45
10/06/1958	18Can01	02/05/1959	17Cap02	06/05/1959	03Gem09	10/05/1959	22Sco07
10/08/1958	14Leo49	02/07/1959	14Aqu11	06/07/1959	27Gem04	10/07/1959	21Sag16
10/10/1958	13Vir24	02/09/1959	10Pis15	06/09/1959	21Can30	10/09/1959	19Cap34
10/12/1958	13Lib23	02/11/1959	05Ari07	06/11/1959	16Leo40	10/11/1959	16Aqu44
10/14/1958	13Sco44	02/13/1959	29Ari06	06/13/1959	12Vir42	10/13/1959	12Pis54
10/16/1958	13Sag16	02/15/1959	22Tau43	06/15/1959	09Lib58	10/15/1959	08Ari09
10/18/1958	11Cap14	02/17/1959	16Gem41	06/17/1959	08Sco46	10/17/1959	02Tau41
10/20/1958	07Aqu28	02/19/1959	11Can40	06/19/1959	08Sag39	10/19/1959	26Tau42
10/22/1958	02Pis22	02/21/1959	08Leo03	06/21/1959	08Cap41	10/21/1959	20Gem25
10/24/1958	26Pis25	02/23/1959	05Vir49	06/23/1959	07Aqu39	10/23/1959	14Can15
10/26/1958	20Ari06	02/25/1959	04Lib31	06/25/1959	04Pis52	10/25/1959	08Leo45
10/28/1958	13Tau42	02/27/1959	03Sco28	06/27/1959	00Ari16	10/27/1959	04Vir30
10/30/1958	07Gem33			06/29/1959	24Ari27	10/29/1959	01Lib55
		03/01/1959	02Sag01			10/31/1959	01Sco04
11/01/1958	02Can00	03/03/1959	29Sag55	07/01/1959	18Tau08		
11/03/1958	27Can16	03/05/1959	27Cap04	07/03/1959	11Gem52	11/02/1959	01Sag14
11/05/1958	23Leo49	03/07/1959	23Aqu20	07/05/1959	06Can03	11/04/1959	01Cap10
11/07/1958	21Vir55	03/09/1959	18Pis43	07/07/1959	00Leo57	11/06/1959	29Cap53
11/09/1958	21Lib30	03/11/1959	13Ari13	07/09/1959	26Leo36	11/08/1959	26Aqu55
11/11/1958	21Sco46	03/13/1959	07Tau06	07/11/1959	23Vir00	11/10/1959	22Pis38
11/13/1958	21Sag36	03/15/1959	00Gem43	07/13/1959	20Lib19	11/12/1959	17Ari19
11/15/1958	19Cap57	03/17/1959	24Gem39	07/15/1959	18Sco43	11/14/1959	11Tau28
11/17/1958	16Aqu24	03/19/1959	19Can32	07/17/1959	17Sag56	11/16/1959	05Gem18
11/19/1958	11Pis16	03/21/1959	15Leo54	07/19/1959	17Cap16	11/18/1959	29Gem02
11/21/1958	05Ari09	03/23/1959	13Vir56	07/21/1959	15Aqu52	11/20/1959	22Can55
11/23/1958	28Ari45	03/25/1959	13Lib17	07/23/1959	12Pis56	11/22/1959	17Leo21
11/25/1958	22Tau28	03/27/1959	13Sco06	07/25/1959	08Ari22	11/24/1959	12Vir51
11/27/1958	16Gem40	03/29/1959	12Sag21	07/27/1959	02Tau36	11/26/1959	09Lib59
11/29/1958	11Can34	03/31/1959	10Cap27	07/29/1959	26Tau21	11/28/1959	09Sco01
				07/31/1959	20Gem13	11/30/1959	09Sag27
12/01/1958	07Leo12	04/02/1959	07Aqu18				
12/03/1958	03Vir46	04/04/1959	02Pis58	08/02/1959	14Can41	12/02/1959	09Cap56
12/05/1958	01Lib27	04/06/1959	27Pis42	08/04/1959	10Leo05	12/04/1959	09Aqu10
12/07/1958	00Sco19	04/08/1959	21Ari48	08/06/1959	06Vir22	12/06/1959	06Pis30
12/09/1958	29Sco57	04/10/1959	15Tau31	08/08/1959	03Lib27	12/08/1959	02Ari06
12/11/1958	29Sag30	04/12/1959	09Gem10	08/10/1959	01Sco10	12/10/1959	26Ari31
12/13/1958	27Cap55	04/14/1959	03Can07	08/12/1959	29Sco26	12/12/1959	20Tau22
12/15/1958	24Aqu34	04/16/1959	27Can54	08/14/1959	28Sag01	12/14/1959	14Gem08
12/17/1958	19Pis34	04/18/1959	24Leo03	08/16/1959	26Cap31	12/16/1959	07Can57
12/19/1958	13Ari29	04/20/1959	21Vir57	08/18/1959	24Aqu22	12/18/1959	02Leo03
12/21/1958	07Tau03	04/22/1959	21Lib27	08/20/1959	20Pis59	12/20/1959	26Leo39
12/23/1958	00Gem55	04/24/1959	21Sco48	08/22/1959	16Ari15	12/22/1959	22Vir04
12/25/1958	25Gem30	04/26/1959	21Sag45	08/24/1959	10Tau30	12/24/1959	18Lib53
12/27/1958	21Can01	04/28/1959	20Cap18	08/26/1959	04Gem18	12/26/1959	17Sco27
12/29/1958	17Leo20	04/30/1959	17Aqu10	08/28/1959	28Gem13	12/28/1959	17Sag31
12/31/1958	14Vir19			08/30/1959	22Can51	12/30/1959	17Cap58

Ephemeris Tables for the Moon

Date	Moon	Date	Moon	Date	Moon	Date	Moon
01/01/1960	17Aqu27	05/02/1960	25Can03	09/01/1960	15Cap02	01/01/1961	05Can48
01/03/1960	15Pis08	05/04/1960	19Leo10	09/03/1960	14Aqu18	01/03/1961	29Can32
01/05/1960	10Ari52	05/06/1960	14Vir17	09/05/1960	13Pis17	01/05/1961	23Leo12
01/07/1960	05Tau18	05/08/1960	11Lib05	09/07/1960	11Ari12	01/07/1961	17Vir02
01/09/1960	29Tau06	05/10/1960	09Sco38	09/09/1960	07Tau43	01/09/1961	11Lib38
01/11/1960	22Gem51	05/12/1960	09Sag25	09/11/1960	02Gem48	01/11/1961	07Sco41
01/13/1960	16Can50	05/14/1960	09Cap23	09/13/1960	26Gem55	01/13/1961	05Sag34
01/15/1960	11Leo15	05/16/1960	08Aqu23	09/15/1960	20Can42	01/15/1961	05Cap15
01/17/1960	06Vir19	05/18/1960	05Pis57	09/17/1960	14Leo38	01/17/1961	05Aqu47
01/19/1960	02Lib04	05/20/1960	02Ari10	09/19/1960	09Vir16	01/19/1961	05Pis51
01/21/1960	28Lib51	05/22/1960	27Ari25	09/21/1960	04Lib52	01/21/1961	04Ari24
01/23/1960	26Sco57	05/24/1960	21Tau58	09/23/1960	01Sco32	01/23/1961	01Tau09
01/25/1960	26Sag18	05/26/1960	16Gem02	09/25/1960	29Sco01	01/25/1961	26Tau28
01/27/1960	26Cap06	05/28/1960	09Can49	09/27/1960	27Sag07	01/27/1961	20Gem49
01/29/1960	25Aqu17	05/30/1960	03Leo32	09/29/1960	25Cap33	01/29/1961	14Can40
01/31/1960	23Pis00					01/31/1961	08Leo20
		06/01/1960	27Leo37	10/01/1960	23Aqu58		
02/02/1960	18Ari57	06/03/1960	22Vir42	10/03/1960	22Pis03	02/02/1961	02Vir05
02/04/1960	13Tau33	06/05/1960	19Lib19	10/05/1960	19Ari22	02/04/1961	26Vir12
02/06/1960	07Gem24	06/07/1960	17Sco54	10/07/1960	15Tau37	02/06/1961	21Lib01
02/08/1960	01Can10	06/09/1960	17Sag59	10/09/1960	10Gem41	02/08/1961	17Sco01
02/10/1960	25Can19	06/11/1960	18Cap30	10/11/1960	04Can49	02/10/1961	14Sag30
02/12/1960	20Leo09	06/13/1960	18Aqu01	10/13/1960	28Can34	02/12/1961	13Cap36
02/14/1960	15Vir51	06/15/1960	15Pis49	10/15/1960	22Leo02	02/14/1961	13Aqu45
02/16/1960	12Lib15	06/17/1960	11Ari57	10/17/1960	17Vir22	02/16/1961	13Pis47
02/18/1960	09Sco29	06/19/1960	06Tau54	10/19/1960	13Lib29	02/18/1961	12Ari38
02/20/1960	07Sag31	06/21/1960	01Gem07	10/21/1960	10Sco58	02/20/1961	09Tau46
02/22/1960	06Cap13	06/23/1960	24Gem58	10/23/1960	09Sag22	02/22/1961	05Gem16
02/24/1960	05Aqu04	06/25/1960	18Can40	10/25/1960	08Cap04	02/24/1961	29Gem35
02/26/1960	03Pis27	06/27/1960	12Leo28	10/27/1960	06Aqu31	02/26/1961	23Can19
02/28/1960	00Ari46	06/29/1960	06Vir39	10/29/1960	04Pis21	02/28/1961	16Leo59
				10/31/1960	01Ari34		
03/01/1960	26Ari41	07/01/1960	01Lib43			03/02/1961	10Vir57
03/03/1960	21Tau23	07/03/1960	28Lib12	11/02/1960	28Ari07	03/04/1961	05Lib30
03/05/1960	15Gem19	07/05/1960	26Sco31	11/04/1960	23Tau51	03/06/1961	00Sco51
03/07/1960	09Can07	07/07/1960	26Sag27	11/06/1960	18Gem40	03/08/1961	27Sco09
03/09/1960	03Leo21	07/09/1960	27Cap01	11/08/1960	12Can44	03/10/1961	24Sag31
03/11/1960	28Leo29	07/11/1960	26Aqu46	11/10/1960	06Leo25	03/12/1961	23Cap01
03/13/1960	24Vir46	07/13/1960	24Pis52	11/12/1960	00Vir18	03/14/1961	22Aqu21
03/15/1960	22Lib05	07/15/1960	21Ari09	11/14/1960	25Vir07	03/16/1961	21Pis48
03/17/1960	20Sco09	07/17/1960	16Tau03	11/16/1960	21Lib28	03/18/1961	20Ari28
03/19/1960	18Sag36	07/19/1960	10Gem08	11/18/1960	19Sco32	03/20/1961	17Tau43
03/21/1960	16Cap58	07/21/1960	03Can52	11/20/1960	18Sag50	03/22/1961	13Gem26
03/23/1960	15Aqu00	07/23/1960	27Can37	11/22/1960	18Cap23	03/24/1961	07Can50
03/25/1960	12Pis25	07/25/1960	21Leo37	11/24/1960	17Aqu16	03/26/1961	01Leo33
03/27/1960	09Ari01	07/27/1960	16Vir06	11/26/1960	14Pis58	03/28/1961	25Leo16
03/29/1960	04Tau36	07/29/1960	11Lib25	11/28/1960	11Ari36	03/30/1961	19Vir29
03/31/1960	29Tau13	07/31/1960	07Sco55	11/30/1960	07Tau27		
						04/01/1961	14Lib34
04/02/1960	23Gem12	08/02/1960	05Sag55	12/02/1960	02Gem35	04/03/1961	10Sco40
04/04/1960	16Can58	08/04/1960	05Cap19	12/04/1960	27Gem02	04/05/1961	07Sag38
04/06/1960	11Leo10	08/06/1960	04Aqu25	12/06/1960	20Can56	04/07/1961	05Cap18
04/08/1960	06Vir24	08/08/1960	05Pis01	12/08/1960	14Leo36	04/09/1961	03Aqu29
04/10/1960	03Lib05	08/10/1960	03Ari13	12/10/1960	08Vir24	04/11/1961	02Pis04
04/12/1960	01Sco11	08/12/1960	29Ari42	12/12/1960	03Lib03	04/13/1961	00Ari37
04/14/1960	00Sag12	08/14/1960	24Tau39	12/14/1960	29Lib19	04/15/1961	28Ari40
04/16/1960	29Sag22	08/16/1960	18Gem44	12/16/1960	27Sco30	04/17/1961	25Tau39
04/18/1960	27Cap55	08/18/1960	12Can30	12/18/1960	27Sag17	04/19/1961	21Gem17
04/20/1960	25Aqu30	08/20/1960	06Leo21	12/20/1960	27Cap34	04/21/1961	15Can43
04/22/1960	22Pis10	08/22/1960	00Vir40	12/22/1960	27Aqu40	04/23/1961	09Leo28
04/24/1960	17Ari58	08/24/1960	25Vir39	12/24/1960	25Pis10	04/25/1961	03Vir15
04/26/1960	13Tau01	08/26/1960	21Lib31	12/26/1960	21Ari40	04/27/1961	27Vir37
04/28/1960	07Gem23	08/28/1960	18Sco20	12/28/1960	17Tau04	04/29/1961	23Lib08
04/30/1960	01Can18	08/30/1960	16Sag12	12/30/1960	11Gem42		

Ephemeris Tables for the Moon

Date	Moon	Date	Moon	Date	Moon	Date	Moon
05/01/1961	20Sco00	09/02/1961	16Gem03	01/02/1962	19Sco50	05/02/1962	18Ari24
05/03/1961	17Sag50	09/04/1961	10Can37	01/04/1962	16Sag49	05/04/1962	17Tau50
05/05/1961	16Cap09	09/06/1961	04Leo25	01/06/1962	15Cap22	05/06/1962	16Gem10
05/07/1961	14Aqu29	09/08/1961	27Leo58	01/08/1962	14Aqu44	05/08/1962	12Can49
05/09/1961	12Pis37	09/10/1961	21Vir42	01/10/1962	14Pis04	05/10/1962	07Leo52
05/11/1961	10Ari23	09/12/1961	15Lib52	01/12/1962	12Ari39	05/12/1962	01Vir52
05/13/1961	07Tau36	09/14/1961	10Sco46	01/14/1962	10Tau11	05/14/1962	25Vir31
05/15/1961	04Gem00	09/16/1961	06Sag38	01/16/1962	06Gem41	05/16/1962	19Lib28
05/17/1961	29Gem19	09/18/1961	03Cap38	01/18/1962	02Can15	05/18/1962	14Sco06
05/19/1961	23Can38	09/20/1961	01Aqu59	01/20/1962	27Can03	05/20/1962	09Sag38
05/21/1961	17Leo21	09/22/1961	01Pis28	01/22/1962	21Leo09	05/22/1962	06Cap01
05/23/1961	11Vir06	09/24/1961	01Ari27	01/24/1962	14Vir49	05/24/1962	03Aqu08
05/25/1961	05Lib33	09/26/1961	00Tau46	01/26/1962	08Lib29	05/26/1962	00Pis51
05/27/1961	01Sco19	09/28/1961	28Tau36	01/28/1962	02Sco36	05/28/1962	29Pis16
05/29/1961	28Sco44	09/30/1961	24Gem38	01/30/1962	27Sco48	05/30/1962	28Ari02
05/31/1961	27Sag22						
		10/02/1961	19Can12	02/01/1962	24Sag38	06/01/1962	26Tau39
06/02/1961	26Cap29	10/04/1961	12Leo56	02/03/1962	23Cap16	06/03/1962	24Gem24
06/04/1961	25Aqu19	10/06/1961	06Vir31	02/05/1962	23Aqu09	06/05/1962	20Can46
06/06/1961	23Pis27	10/08/1961	00Lib28	02/07/1962	23Pis16	06/07/1962	15Leo47
06/08/1961	20Ari43	10/10/1961	25Lib07	02/09/1962	22Ari34	06/09/1962	09Vir49
06/10/1961	17Tau13	10/12/1961	20Sco35	02/11/1962	20Tau22	06/11/1962	03Lib32
06/12/1961	12Gem56	10/14/1961	16Sag54	02/13/1962	16Gem38	06/13/1962	27Lib36
06/14/1961	07Can45	10/16/1961	14Cap01	02/15/1962	11Can43	06/15/1962	22Sco29
06/16/1961	01Leo49	10/18/1961	11Aqu58	02/17/1962	06Leo00	06/17/1962	18Sag31
06/18/1961	25Leo28	10/20/1961	10Pis45	02/19/1962	29Leo48	06/19/1962	15Cap37
06/20/1961	19Vir11	10/22/1961	10Ari00	02/21/1962	23Vir25	06/21/1962	13Aqu31
06/22/1961	13Lib36	10/24/1961	08Tau51	02/23/1962	17Lib11	06/23/1962	11Pis48
06/24/1961	09Sco24	10/26/1961	06Gem31	02/25/1962	11Sco24	06/25/1962	10Ari11
06/26/1961	07Sag01	10/28/1961	02Can38	02/27/1962	06Sag30	06/27/1962	08Tau28
06/28/1961	06Cap09	10/30/1961	27Can16			06/29/1962	06Gem12
06/30/1961	06Aqu00			03/01/1962	03Cap01		
		11/01/1961	21Leo01	03/03/1962	01Aqu17	07/01/1962	03Can07
07/02/1961	05Pis33	11/03/1961	14Vir39	03/05/1962	01Pis07	07/03/1962	28Can57
07/04/1961	03Ari57	11/05/1961	08Lib48	03/07/1962	01Ari34	07/05/1962	23Leo45
07/06/1961	01Tau04	11/07/1961	03Sco54	03/09/1962	01Tau25	07/07/1962	17Vir45
07/08/1961	27Tau05	11/09/1961	00Sag05	03/11/1962	29Tau39	07/09/1962	11Lib28
07/10/1961	22Gem14	11/11/1961	27Sag10	03/13/1962	26Gem02	07/11/1962	05Sco33
07/12/1961	16Can36	11/13/1961	24Cap48	03/15/1962	20Can58	07/13/1962	00Sag32
07/14/1961	10Leo24	11/15/1961	22Aqu46	03/17/1962	14Leo58	07/15/1962	26Sag52
07/16/1961	03Vir58	11/17/1961	21Pis01	03/19/1962	08Vir36	07/17/1962	24Cap36
07/18/1961	27Vir41	11/19/1961	19Ari22	03/21/1962	02Lib13	07/19/1962	23Aqu19
07/20/1961	22Lib06	11/21/1961	17Tau24	03/23/1962	26Lib14	07/21/1962	22Pis24
07/22/1961	17Sco48	11/23/1961	14Gem33	03/25/1962	20Sco44	07/23/1962	21Ari09
07/24/1961	15Sag18	11/25/1961	10Can27	03/27/1962	16Sag00	07/25/1962	19Tau11
07/26/1961	14Cap30	11/27/1961	05Leo03	03/29/1962	12Cap21	07/27/1962	16Gem16
07/28/1961	14Aqu43	11/29/1961	28Leo48	03/31/1962	10Aqu10	07/29/1962	12Can24
07/30/1961	14Pis48					07/31/1962	07Leo38
		12/01/1961	22Vir29	04/02/1962	09Pis28		
08/01/1961	13Ari42	12/03/1961	16Lib42	04/04/1962	09Ari40	08/02/1962	02Vir01
08/03/1961	10Tau59	12/05/1961	12Sco04	04/06/1962	09Tau36	08/04/1962	25Vir53
08/05/1961	06Gem48	12/07/1961	08Sag50	04/08/1962	08Gem07	08/06/1962	19Lib34
08/07/1961	01Can33	12/09/1961	06Cap46	04/10/1962	04Can43	08/08/1962	13Sco39
08/09/1961	25Can33	12/11/1961	05Aqu15	04/12/1962	29Can40	08/10/1962	08Sag34
08/11/1961	19Leo10	12/13/1961	03Pis44	04/14/1962	23Leo37	08/12/1962	04Cap54
08/13/1961	12Vir46	12/15/1961	01Ari55	04/16/1962	17Vir12	08/14/1962	02Aqu55
08/15/1961	06Lib38	12/17/1961	29Ari37	04/18/1962	10Lib59	08/16/1962	02Pis19
08/17/1961	01Sco10	12/19/1961	26Tau45	04/20/1962	05Sco19	08/18/1962	02Ari12
08/19/1961	26Sco50	12/21/1961	23Gem06	04/22/1962	00Sag18	08/20/1962	01Tau34
08/21/1961	24Sag03	12/23/1961	18Can29	04/24/1962	25Sag59	08/22/1962	29Tau44
08/23/1961	22Cap55	12/25/1961	12Leo54	04/26/1962	22Cap33	08/24/1962	26Gem27
08/25/1961	22Aqu59	12/27/1961	06Vir39	04/28/1962	20Aqu08	08/26/1962	21Can57
08/27/1961	23Pis17	12/29/1961	00Lib19	04/30/1962	18Pis51	08/28/1962	16Leo37
08/29/1961	22Ari34	12/31/1961	24Lib27			08/30/1962	10Vir41
08/31/1961	20Tau10						

Ephemeris Tables for the Moon

Date	Moon	Date	Moon	Date	Moon	Date	Moon
09/01/1962	04Lib24	01/01/1963	20Pis10	05/01/1963	20Leo33	09/02/1963	22Aqu06
09/03/1962	28Lib06	01/03/1963	18Ari25	05/03/1963	15Vir07	09/04/1963	20Pis23
09/05/1962	22Sco08	01/05/1963	16Tau51	05/05/1963	09Lib06	09/06/1963	19Ari35
09/07/1962	16Sag56	01/07/1963	15Gem07	05/07/1963	02Sco51	09/08/1963	18Tau46
09/09/1962	13Cap04	01/09/1963	12Can43	05/09/1963	26Sco38	09/10/1963	17Gem12
09/11/1962	11Aqu01	01/11/1963	09Leo15	05/11/1963	20Sag44	09/12/1963	14Can42
09/13/1962	10Pis38	01/13/1963	04Vir37	05/13/1963	15Cap20	09/14/1963	11Leo15
09/15/1962	11Ari04	01/15/1963	28Vir59	05/15/1963	10Aqu48	09/16/1963	07Vir01
09/17/1962	11Tau04	01/17/1963	22Lib47	05/17/1963	07Pis40	09/18/1963	02Lib04
09/19/1962	09Gem37	01/19/1963	16Sco38	05/19/1963	06Ari12	09/20/1963	26Lib25
09/21/1962	06Can18	01/21/1963	11Sag11	05/21/1963	06Tau04	09/22/1963	20Sco13
09/23/1962	01Leo28	01/23/1963	06Cap52	05/23/1963	06Gem18	09/24/1963	13Sag54
09/25/1962	25Leo46	01/25/1963	03Aqu53	05/25/1963	05Can42	09/26/1963	08Cap00
09/27/1962	19Vir34	01/27/1963	02Pis03	05/27/1963	03Leo22	09/28/1963	03Aqu12
09/29/1962	13Lib15	01/29/1963	00Ari45	05/29/1963	29Leo16	09/30/1963	00Pis07
		01/31/1963	29Ari26	05/31/1963	23Vir54		
10/01/1962	07Sco03					10/02/1963	28Pis56
10/03/1962	01Sag11	02/02/1963	27Tau37	06/02/1963	17Lib49	10/04/1963	28Ari49
10/05/1962	26Sag00	02/04/1963	25Gem07	06/04/1963	11Sco34	10/06/1963	28Tau45
10/07/1962	21Cap55	02/06/1963	21Can47	06/06/1963	05Sag30	10/08/1963	27Gem39
10/09/1962	19Aqu30	02/08/1963	17Leo37	06/08/1963	29Sag56	10/10/1963	25Can06
10/11/1962	18Pis51	02/10/1963	12Vir37	06/10/1963	25Cap00	10/12/1963	21Leo13
10/13/1962	19Ari18	02/12/1963	06Lib53	06/12/1963	20Aqu55	10/14/1963	16Vir24
10/15/1962	19Tau39	02/14/1963	00Sco42	06/14/1963	17Pis56	10/16/1963	10Lib58
10/17/1962	18Gem32	02/16/1963	24Sco30	06/16/1963	16Ari09	10/18/1963	05Sco03
10/19/1962	15Can24	02/18/1963	18Sag59	06/18/1963	15Tau22	10/20/1963	28Sco45
10/21/1962	10Leo34	02/20/1963	14Cap36	06/20/1963	14Gem54	10/22/1963	22Sag23
10/23/1962	04Vir43	02/22/1963	11Aqu50	06/22/1963	13Can51	10/24/1963	16Cap26
10/25/1962	28Vir25	02/24/1963	10Pis49	06/24/1963	11Leo25	10/26/1963	11Aqu29
10/27/1962	22Lib07	02/26/1963	10Ari29	06/26/1963	07Vir26	10/28/1963	08Pis13
10/29/1962	16Sco09	02/28/1963	09Tau56	06/28/1963	02Lib11	10/30/1963	06Ari57
10/31/1962	10Sag36			06/30/1963	26Lib09		
		03/02/1963	08Gem20			11/01/1963	07Tau09
11/02/1962	05Cap40	03/04/1963	05Can27	07/02/1963	19Sco55	11/03/1963	07Gem39
11/04/1962	01Aqu37	03/06/1963	01Leo27	07/04/1963	14Sag02	11/05/1963	07Can07
11/06/1962	28Aqu55	03/08/1963	26Leo36	07/06/1963	08Cap51	11/07/1963	04Leo52
11/08/1962	27Pis43	03/10/1963	21Vir10	07/08/1963	04Aqu33	11/09/1963	00Vir56
11/10/1962	27Ari37	03/12/1963	15Lib13	07/10/1963	01Pis10	11/11/1963	25Vir51
11/12/1962	27Tau40	03/14/1963	08Sco58	07/12/1963	28Pis42	11/13/1963	20Lib06
11/14/1962	26Gem36	03/16/1963	02Sag48	07/14/1963	26Ari52	11/15/1963	13Sco53
11/16/1962	23Can42	03/18/1963	27Sag06	07/16/1963	25Tau31	11/17/1963	07Sag32
11/18/1962	19Leo02	03/20/1963	22Cap35	07/18/1963	24Gem12	11/19/1963	01Cap16
11/20/1962	13Vir14	03/22/1963	19Aqu49	07/20/1963	22Can23	11/21/1963	25Cap28
11/22/1962	06Lib54	03/24/1963	18Pis59	07/22/1963	19Leo31	11/23/1963	20Aqu31
11/24/1962	00Sco42	03/26/1963	19Ari15	07/24/1963	15Vir24	11/25/1963	17Pis00
11/26/1962	25Sco01	03/28/1963	19Tau26	07/26/1963	10Lib09	11/27/1963	15Ari19
11/28/1962	19Sag57	03/30/1963	18Gem21	07/28/1963	04Sco08	11/29/1963	15Tau13
11/30/1962	15Cap35			07/30/1963	27Sco55		
		04/01/1963	15Can31	08/01/1963	22Sag08	12/01/1963	15Gem42
12/02/1962	11Aqu58	04/03/1963	11Leo12	08/03/1963	17Cap19	12/03/1963	15Can29
12/04/1962	09Pis18	04/05/1963	05Vir55	08/05/1963	13Aqu39	12/05/1963	13Leo40
12/06/1962	07Ari36	04/07/1963	00Lib06	08/07/1963	11Pis06	12/07/1963	10Vir00
12/08/1962	06Tau43	04/09/1963	23Lib57	08/09/1963	09Ari24	12/09/1963	04Lib55
12/10/1962	05Gem59	04/11/1963	17Sco41	08/11/1963	07Tau56	12/11/1963	28Lib58
12/12/1962	04Can26	04/13/1963	11Sag36	08/13/1963	06Gem18	12/13/1963	22Sco39
12/14/1962	01Leo27	04/15/1963	05Cap57	08/15/1963	04Can15	12/15/1963	16Sag21
12/16/1962	26Leo55	04/17/1963	01Aqu16	08/17/1963	01Leo31	12/17/1963	10Cap21
12/18/1962	21Vir13	04/19/1963	28Aqu16	08/19/1963	28Leo01	12/19/1963	04Aqu55
12/20/1962	14Lib58	04/21/1963	27Pis15	08/21/1963	23Vir32	12/21/1963	00Pis16
12/22/1962	08Sco50	04/23/1963	27Ari33	08/23/1963	18Lib09	12/23/1963	26Pis49
12/24/1962	03Sag22	04/25/1963	28Tau03	08/25/1963	12Sco04	12/25/1963	24Ari40
12/26/1962	28Sag45	04/27/1963	27Gem22	08/27/1963	05Sag49	12/27/1963	23Tau50
12/28/1962	25Cap07	04/29/1963	24Can49	08/29/1963	00Cap02	12/29/1963	23Gem43
12/30/1962	22Aqu21			08/31/1963	25Cap19	12/31/1963	23Can15

Ephemeris Tables for the Moon

Date	Moon	Date	Moon	Date	Moon	Date	Moon
01/02/1964	21Leo37	05/01/1964	03Cap06	09/02/1964	21Can16	01/02/1965	07Cap49
01/04/1964	18Vir16	05/03/1964	26Cap54	09/04/1964	19Leo49	01/04/1965	01Aqu26
01/06/1964	13Lib21	05/05/1964	21Aqu36	09/06/1964	17Vir54	01/06/1965	25Aqu23
01/08/1964	07Sco25	05/07/1964	17Pis47	09/08/1964	14Lib48	01/08/1965	19Pis58
01/10/1964	01Sag04	05/09/1964	15Ari50	09/10/1964	10Sco17	01/10/1965	15Ari29
01/12/1964	24Sag52	05/11/1964	15Tau31	09/12/1964	04Sag36	01/12/1965	12Tau25
01/14/1964	19Cap13	05/13/1964	15Gem43	09/14/1964	28Sag16	01/14/1965	11Gem00
01/16/1964	14Aqu21	05/15/1964	15Can21	09/16/1964	22Cap03	01/16/1965	11Can00
01/18/1964	10Pis22	05/17/1964	13Leo37	09/18/1964	16Aqu33	01/18/1965	11Leo24
01/20/1964	07Ari16	05/19/1964	10Vir25	09/20/1964	12Pis18	01/20/1965	10Vir57
01/22/1964	05Tau02	05/21/1964	05Lib55	09/22/1964	09Ari16	01/22/1965	08Lib49
01/24/1964	03Gem33	05/23/1964	00Sco33	09/24/1964	07Tau09	01/24/1965	04Sco45
01/26/1964	02Can30	05/25/1964	24Sco34	09/26/1964	05Gem27	01/26/1965	29Sco13
01/28/1964	01Leo22	05/27/1964	18Sag12	09/28/1964	03Can43	01/28/1965	22Sag56
01/30/1964	29Leo22	05/29/1964	11Cap49	09/30/1964	01Leo48	01/30/1965	16Cap31
		05/31/1964	05Aqu45				
02/01/1964	26Vir02			10/02/1964	29Leo34	02/01/1965	10Aqu19
02/03/1964	21Lib14	06/02/1964	00Pis31	10/04/1964	26Vir49	02/03/1965	04Pis39
02/05/1964	15Sco25	06/04/1964	26Pis39	10/06/1964	23Lib05	02/05/1965	29Pis38
02/07/1964	09Sag04	06/06/1964	24Ari22	10/08/1964	18Sco16	02/07/1965	25Ari24
02/09/1964	02Cap55	06/08/1964	23Tau49	10/10/1964	12Sag30	02/09/1965	22Tau10
02/11/1964	27Cap34	06/10/1964	24Gem08	10/12/1964	06Cap07	02/11/1965	20Gem13
02/13/1964	23Aqu18	06/12/1964	24Can08	10/14/1964	29Cap52	02/13/1965	19Can31
02/15/1964	20Pis10	06/14/1964	22Leo49	10/16/1964	24Aqu25	02/15/1965	19Leo25
02/17/1964	17Ari52	06/16/1964	19Vir48	10/18/1964	20Pis24	02/17/1965	18Vir51
02/19/1964	16Tau00	06/18/1964	15Lib15	10/20/1964	17Ari53	02/19/1965	16Lib51
02/21/1964	14Gem13	06/20/1964	09Sco37	10/22/1964	16Tau35	02/21/1965	12Sco58
02/23/1964	12Can23	06/22/1964	03Sag27	10/24/1964	15Gem44	02/23/1965	07Sag34
02/25/1964	10Leo18	06/24/1964	27Sag02	10/26/1964	14Can33	02/25/1965	01Cap21
02/27/1964	07Vir35	06/26/1964	20Cap46	10/28/1964	12Leo37	02/27/1965	24Cap57
02/29/1964	03Lib53	06/28/1964	15Aqu02	10/30/1964	09Vir51		
		06/30/1964	10Pis03			03/01/1965	18Aqu55
03/02/1964	29Lib01			11/01/1964	06Lib18	03/03/1965	13Pis41
03/04/1964	23Sco12	07/02/1964	06Ari10	11/03/1964	01Sco52	03/05/1965	09Ari18
03/06/1964	16Sag52	07/04/1964	03Tau40	11/05/1964	26Sco35	03/07/1965	05Tau39
03/08/1964	10Cap42	07/06/1964	02Gem38	11/07/1964	20Sag36	03/09/1965	02Gem43
03/10/1964	05Aqu29	07/08/1964	02Can32	11/09/1964	14Cap10	03/11/1965	00Can33
03/12/1964	01Pis39	07/10/1964	02Leo27	11/11/1964	07Aqu52	03/13/1965	29Can10
03/14/1964	29Pis17	07/12/1964	01Vir20	11/13/1964	02Pis20	03/15/1965	28Leo15
03/16/1964	27Ari53	07/14/1964	28Vir31	11/15/1964	28Pis17	03/17/1965	27Vir01
03/18/1964	26Tau45	07/16/1964	24Lib03	11/17/1964	25Ari51	03/19/1965	24Lib41
03/20/1964	25Gem12	07/18/1964	18Sco21	11/19/1964	25Tau01	03/21/1965	20Sco48
03/22/1964	22Can59	07/20/1964	12Sag04	11/21/1964	24Gem57	03/23/1965	15Sag28
03/24/1964	20Leo09	07/22/1964	05Cap42	11/23/1964	24Can34	03/25/1965	09Cap19
03/26/1964	16Vir37	07/24/1964	29Cap42	11/25/1964	23Leo04	03/27/1965	02Aqu58
03/28/1964	12Lib18	07/26/1964	24Aqu26	11/27/1964	20Vir13	03/29/1965	27Aqu09
03/30/1964	07Sco07	07/28/1964	19Pis58	11/29/1964	16Lib07	03/31/1965	22Pis16
		07/30/1964	16Ari24				
04/01/1964	01Sag09	08/01/1964	13Tau48	12/01/1964	11Sco04	04/02/1965	18Ari32
04/03/1964	24Sag46	08/03/1964	12Gem17	12/03/1964	05Sag18	04/04/1965	15Tau39
04/05/1964	18Cap36	08/05/1964	11Can30	12/05/1964	29Sag04	04/06/1965	13Gem23
04/07/1964	13Aqu21	08/07/1964	10Leo51	12/07/1964	22Cap37	04/08/1965	11Can31
04/09/1964	09Pis37	08/09/1964	09Vir31	12/09/1964	16Aqu22	04/10/1965	09Leo48
04/11/1964	07Ari39	08/11/1964	06Lib44	12/11/1964	10Pis48	04/12/1965	08Vir05
04/13/1964	07Tau03	08/13/1964	02Sco19	12/13/1964	06Ari25	04/14/1965	05Lib57
04/15/1964	06Gem43	08/15/1964	26Sco37	12/15/1964	03Tau45	04/16/1965	02Sco55
04/17/1964	05Can43	08/17/1964	20Sag20	12/17/1964	02Gem51	04/18/1965	28Sco40
04/19/1964	03Leo36	08/19/1964	14Cap03	12/19/1964	03Can09	04/20/1965	23Sag16
04/21/1964	00Vir23	08/21/1964	08Aqu22	12/21/1964	03Leo25	04/22/1965	17Cap09
04/23/1964	26Vir14	08/23/1964	03Pis37	12/23/1964	02Vir33	04/24/1965	10Aqu52
04/25/1964	21Lib18	08/25/1964	29Pis53	12/25/1964	29Vir59	04/26/1965	05Pis06
04/27/1964	15Sco41	08/27/1964	26Ari54	12/27/1964	25Lib45	04/28/1965	00Ari25
04/29/1964	09Sag30	08/29/1964	24Tau34	12/29/1964	20Sco19	04/30/1965	27Ari06
		08/31/1964	22Gem46	12/31/1964	14Sag12		

Ephemeris Tables for the Moon

Date	Moon	Date	Moon	Date	Moon	Date	Moon
05/02/1965	25Tau00	09/01/1965	23Sco41	01/01/1966	26Ari54	05/01/1966	25Vir28
05/04/1965	23Gem36	09/03/1965	18Sag31	01/03/1966	23Tau06	05/03/1966	24Lib24
05/06/1965	22Can21	09/05/1965	12Cap27	01/05/1966	21Gem05	05/05/1966	22Sco36
05/08/1965	20Leo46	09/07/1965	06Aqu09	01/07/1966	20Can39	05/07/1966	19Sag37
05/10/1965	18Vir34	09/09/1965	00Pis01	01/09/1966	20Leo52	05/09/1966	15Cap11
05/12/1965	15Lib40	09/11/1965	24Pis24	01/11/1966	20Vir29	05/11/1966	09Aqu39
05/14/1965	11Sco48	09/13/1965	19Ari24	01/13/1966	18Lib39	05/13/1966	03Pis29
05/16/1965	06Sag59	09/15/1965	15Tau07	01/15/1966	15Sco14	05/15/1966	27Pis23
05/18/1965	01Cap20	09/17/1965	11Gem40	01/17/1966	10Sag38	05/17/1966	21Ari46
05/20/1965	25Cap09	09/19/1965	09Can19	01/19/1966	05Cap12	05/19/1966	17Tau06
05/22/1965	18Aqu53	09/21/1965	08Leo10	01/21/1966	29Cap16	05/21/1966	13Gem32
05/24/1965	13Pis07	09/23/1965	07Vir43	01/23/1966	23Aqu06	05/23/1966	10Can57
05/26/1965	08Ari25	09/25/1965	07Lib05	01/25/1966	16Pis49	05/25/1966	09Leo03
05/28/1965	05Tau15	09/27/1965	05Sco18	01/27/1966	10Ari45	05/27/1966	07Vir31
05/30/1965	03Gem37	09/29/1965	01Sag46	01/29/1966	05Tau20	05/29/1966	05Lib55
				01/31/1966	01Gem15	05/31/1966	03Sco57
06/01/1965	03Can01	10/01/1965	26Sag42				
06/03/1965	02Leo34	10/03/1965	20Cap40	02/02/1966	29Gem00	06/02/1966	01Sag19
06/05/1965	01Vir26	10/05/1965	14Aqu25	02/04/1966	28Can36	06/04/1966	27Sag45
06/07/1965	29Vir09	10/07/1965	08Pis28	02/06/1966	29Leo15	06/06/1966	23Cap06
06/09/1965	25Lib40	10/09/1965	03Ari10	02/08/1966	29Vir28	06/08/1966	17Aqu32
06/11/1965	21Sco07	10/11/1965	28Ari46	02/10/1966	28Lib08	06/10/1966	11Pis27
06/13/1965	15Sag45	10/13/1965	25Tau10	02/12/1966	24Sco52	06/12/1966	05Ari18
06/15/1965	09Cap46	10/15/1965	22Gem16	02/14/1966	20Sag04	06/14/1966	29Ari45
06/17/1965	03Aqu32	10/17/1965	20Can04	02/16/1966	14Cap21	06/16/1966	25Tau20
06/19/1965	27Aqu16	10/19/1965	18Leo30	02/18/1966	08Aqu12	06/18/1966	22Gem24
06/21/1965	21Pis28	10/21/1965	17Vir15	02/20/1966	01Pis58	06/20/1966	20Can42
06/23/1965	16Ari42	10/23/1965	15Lib44	02/22/1966	25Pis45	06/22/1966	19Leo39
06/25/1965	13Tau25	10/25/1965	13Sco20	02/24/1966	19Ari51	06/24/1966	18Vir31
06/27/1965	11Gem52	10/27/1965	09Sag36	02/26/1966	14Tau32	06/26/1966	16Lib45
06/29/1965	11Can42	10/29/1965	04Cap32	02/28/1966	10Gem19	06/28/1966	14Sco07
		10/31/1965	28Cap34			06/30/1966	10Sag40
07/01/1965	11Leo57			03/02/1966	07Can42		
07/03/1965	11Vir22	11/02/1965	22Aqu19	03/04/1966	06Leo53	07/02/1966	06Cap27
07/05/1965	09Lib16	11/04/1965	16Pis25	03/06/1966	07Vir18	07/04/1966	01Aqu25
07/07/1965	05Sco34	11/06/1965	11Ari21	03/08/1966	07Lib38	07/06/1966	25Aqu40
07/09/1965	00Sag34	11/08/1965	07Tau28	03/10/1966	06Sco37	07/08/1966	19Pis30
07/11/1965	24Sag47	11/10/1965	04Gem39	03/12/1966	03Sag40	07/10/1966	13Ari18
07/13/1965	18Cap36	11/12/1965	02Can39	03/14/1966	29Sag00	07/12/1966	07Tau42
07/15/1965	12Aqu15	11/14/1965	01Leo01	03/16/1966	23Cap15	07/14/1966	03Gem22
07/17/1965	06Pis06	11/16/1965	29Leo28	03/18/1966	17Aqu00	07/16/1966	00Can46
07/19/1965	00Ari23	11/18/1965	27Vir34	03/20/1966	10Pis45	07/18/1966	29Can42
07/21/1965	25Ari34	11/20/1965	25Lib07	03/22/1966	04Ari44	07/20/1966	29Leo29
07/23/1965	22Tau04	11/22/1965	21Sco52	03/24/1966	29Ari12	07/22/1966	29Vir01
07/25/1965	20Gem15	11/24/1965	17Sag37	03/26/1966	24Tau19	07/24/1966	27Lib25
07/27/1965	20Can06	11/26/1965	12Cap23	03/28/1966	20Gem16	07/26/1966	24Sco28
07/29/1965	20Leo36	11/28/1965	06Aqu25	03/30/1966	17Can30	07/28/1966	20Sag26
07/31/1965	20Vir27	11/30/1965	00Pis10			07/30/1966	15Cap37
				04/01/1966	16Leo09		
08/02/1965	18Lib39	12/02/1965	24Pis10	04/03/1966	15Vir54	08/01/1966	10Aqu09
08/04/1965	14Sco58	12/04/1965	19Ari05	04/05/1966	15Lib43	08/03/1966	04Pis10
08/06/1965	09Sag47	12/06/1965	15Tau24	04/07/1966	14Sco33	08/05/1966	27Pis55
08/08/1965	03Cap46	12/08/1965	13Gem13	04/09/1966	11Sag45	08/07/1966	21Ari40
08/10/1965	27Cap28	12/10/1965	12Can09	04/11/1966	07Cap17	08/09/1966	16Tau00
08/12/1965	21Aqu12	12/12/1965	11Leo28	04/13/1966	01Aqu39	08/11/1966	11Gem35
08/14/1965	15Pis15	12/14/1965	10Vir23	04/15/1966	25Aqu26	08/13/1966	08Can57
08/16/1965	09Ari47	12/16/1965	08Lib18	04/17/1966	19Pis15	08/15/1966	08Leo10
08/18/1965	05Tau06	12/18/1965	05Sco06	04/19/1966	13Ari28	08/17/1966	08Vir30
08/20/1965	01Gem28	12/20/1965	01Sag03	04/21/1966	08Tau22	08/19/1966	08Lib38
08/22/1965	29Gem20	12/22/1965	26Sag10	04/23/1966	04Gem06	08/21/1966	07Sco24
08/24/1965	28Can46	12/24/1965	20Cap36	04/25/1966	00Can40	08/23/1966	04Sag30
08/26/1965	29Leo00	12/26/1965	14Aqu33	04/27/1966	28Can09	08/25/1966	00Cap13
08/28/1965	28Vir50	12/28/1965	08Pis16	04/29/1966	26Leo30	08/27/1966	24Cap58
08/30/1965	27Lib12	12/30/1965	02Ari10			08/29/1966	19Aqu09
						08/31/1966	12Pis58

Ephemeris Tables for the Moon

Date	Moon	Date	Moon	Date	Moon	Date	Moon
09/02/1966	06Ari40	01/02/1967	26Vir59	05/02/1967	23Aqu31	09/01/1967	28Can47
09/04/1966	00Tau30	01/04/1967	25Lib11	05/04/1967	17Pis36	09/03/1967	26Leo55
09/06/1966	24Tau52	01/06/1967	22Sco52	05/06/1967	11Ari12	09/05/1967	26Vir15
09/08/1966	20Gem21	01/08/1967	20Sag01	05/08/1967	04Tau53	09/07/1967	25Lib52
09/10/1966	17Can30	01/10/1967	16Cap31	05/10/1967	28Tau54	09/09/1967	24Sco54
09/12/1966	16Leo33	01/12/1967	12Aqu06	05/12/1967	23Gem36	09/11/1967	22Sag48
09/14/1966	16Vir53	01/14/1967	06Pis42	05/14/1967	19Can09	09/13/1967	19Cap35
09/16/1966	17Lib18	01/16/1967	00Ari34	05/16/1967	15Leo45	09/15/1967	15Aqu23
09/18/1966	16Sco28	01/18/1967	24Ari13	05/18/1967	13Vir33	09/17/1967	10Pis22
09/20/1966	13Sag50	01/20/1967	18Tau16	05/20/1967	12Lib27	09/19/1967	04Ari36
09/22/1966	09Cap34	01/22/1967	13Gem29	05/22/1967	12Sco04	09/21/1967	28Ari19
09/24/1966	04Aqu07	01/24/1967	10Can22	05/24/1967	11Sag31	09/23/1967	21Tau56
09/26/1966	28Aqu06	01/26/1967	08Leo51	05/26/1967	09Cap53	09/25/1967	15Gem49
09/28/1966	21Pis49	01/28/1967	08Vir13	05/28/1967	06Aqu39	09/27/1967	10Can37
09/30/1966	15Ari37	01/30/1967	07Lib31	05/30/1967	01Pis53	09/29/1967	06Leo53
10/02/1966	09Tau40	02/01/1967	06Sco00	06/01/1967	25Pis59	10/01/1967	05Vir01
10/04/1966	04Gem18	02/03/1967	03Sag24	06/03/1967	19Ari36	10/03/1967	04Lib39
10/06/1966	29Gem54	02/05/1967	29Sag52	06/05/1967	13Tau24	10/05/1967	04Sco52
10/08/1966	26Can51	02/07/1967	25Cap37	06/07/1967	07Gem46	10/07/1967	04Sag33
10/10/1966	25Leo26	02/09/1967	20Aqu38	06/09/1967	03Can01	10/09/1967	02Cap52
10/12/1966	25Vir16	02/11/1967	14Pis57	06/11/1967	29Can14	10/11/1967	29Cap36
10/14/1966	25Lib25	02/13/1967	08Ari42	06/13/1967	26Leo21	10/13/1967	25Aqu00
10/16/1966	24Sco42	02/15/1967	02Tau19	06/15/1967	24Vir09	10/15/1967	19Pis30
10/18/1966	22Sag19	02/17/1967	26Tau16	06/17/1967	22Lib34	10/17/1967	13Ari24
10/20/1966	18Cap15	02/19/1967	21Gem21	06/19/1967	21Sco24	10/19/1967	07Tau00
10/22/1966	12Aqu51	02/21/1967	18Can13	06/21/1967	20Sag07	10/21/1967	00Gem39
10/24/1966	06Pis44	02/23/1967	16Leo57	06/23/1967	18Cap03	10/23/1967	24Gem40
10/26/1966	00Ari27	02/25/1967	16Vir57	06/25/1967	14Aqu42	10/25/1967	19Can28
10/28/1966	24Ari23	02/27/1967	17Lib01	06/27/1967	09Pis54	10/27/1967	15Leo33
10/30/1966	18Tau49			06/29/1967	04Ari01	10/29/1967	13Vir19
		03/01/1967	16Sco06			10/31/1967	12Lib42
11/01/1966	13Gem58	03/03/1967	13Sag40	07/01/1967	27Ari40		
11/03/1966	10Can03	03/05/1967	09Cap54	07/03/1967	21Tau34	11/02/1967	13Sco00
11/05/1966	07Leo06	03/07/1967	05Aqu09	07/05/1967	16Gem15	11/04/1967	13Sag09
11/07/1966	05Vir16	03/09/1967	29Aqu40	07/07/1967	12Can06	11/06/1967	11Cap58
11/09/1966	04Lib21	03/11/1967	23Pis38	07/09/1967	09Leo09	11/08/1967	08Aqu57
11/11/1966	03Sco43	03/13/1967	17Ari15	07/11/1967	06Vir57	11/10/1967	04Pis16
11/13/1966	02Sag35	03/15/1967	10Tau53	07/13/1967	05Lib06	11/12/1967	28Pis31
11/15/1966	00Cap12	03/17/1967	04Gem53	07/15/1967	03Sco21	11/14/1967	22Ari11
11/17/1966	26Cap18	03/19/1967	29Gem52	07/17/1967	01Sag33	11/16/1967	15Tau46
11/19/1966	21Aqu01	03/21/1967	26Can29	07/19/1967	29Sag27	11/18/1967	09Gem38
11/21/1966	14Pis55	03/23/1967	25Leo00	07/21/1967	26Cap40	11/20/1967	03Can59
11/23/1966	08Ari38	03/25/1967	25Vir01	07/23/1967	22Aqu52	11/22/1967	29Can03
11/25/1966	02Tau43	03/27/1967	25Lib31	07/25/1967	17Pis52	11/24/1967	25Leo07
11/27/1966	27Tau36	03/29/1967	25Sco09	07/27/1967	11Ari55	11/26/1967	22Vir27
11/29/1966	23Gem27	03/31/1967	23Sag10	07/29/1967	05Tau34	11/28/1967	21Lib13
				07/31/1967	29Tau31	11/30/1967	21Sco04
12/01/1966	20Can18	04/02/1967	19Cap31				
12/03/1966	17Leo52	04/04/1967	14Aqu34	08/02/1967	24Gem22	12/02/1967	21Sag08
12/05/1966	15Vir58	04/06/1967	08Pis46	08/04/1967	20Can39	12/04/1967	20Cap09
12/07/1966	14Lib25	04/08/1967	02Ari30	08/06/1967	18Leo23	12/06/1967	17Aqu24
12/09/1966	12Sco50	04/10/1967	26Ari06	08/08/1967	17Vir01	12/08/1967	12Pis55
12/11/1966	10Sag52	04/12/1967	19Tau51	08/10/1967	15Lib51	12/10/1967	07Ari06
12/13/1966	08Cap03	04/14/1967	14Gem05	08/12/1967	14Sco19	12/12/1967	00Tau42
12/15/1966	04Aqu04	04/16/1967	09Can13	08/14/1967	12Sag10	12/14/1967	24Tau21
12/17/1966	28Aqu51	04/18/1967	05Leo40	08/16/1967	09Cap22	12/16/1967	18Gem30
12/19/1966	22Pis46	04/20/1967	03Vir46	08/18/1967	05Aqu49	12/18/1967	13Can21
12/21/1966	16Ari27	04/22/1967	03Lib19	08/20/1967	01Pis27	12/20/1967	08Leo58
12/23/1966	10Tau35	04/24/1967	03Sco36	08/22/1967	26Pis05	12/22/1967	05Vir24
12/25/1966	05Gem45	04/26/1967	03Sag23	08/24/1967	19Ari58	12/24/1967	02Lib37
12/27/1966	02Can16	04/28/1967	01Cap46	08/26/1967	13Tau34	12/26/1967	00Sco49
12/29/1966	00Leo01	04/30/1967	28Cap23	08/28/1967	07Gem30	12/28/1967	29Sco54
12/31/1966	28Leo28			08/30/1967	02Can22	12/30/1967	29Sag16

Ephemeris Tables for the Moon

Date	Moon	Date	Moon	Date	Moon	Date	Moon
01/01/1968	28Cap00	05/02/1968	05Can06	09/01/1968	29Sag11	01/01/1969	16Gem10
01/03/1968	25Aqu16	05/04/1968	29Can32	09/03/1968	27Cap28	01/03/1969	09Can58
01/05/1968	20Pis55	05/06/1968	25Leo03	09/05/1968	25Aqu12	01/05/1969	04Leo06
01/07/1968	15Ari09	05/08/1968	22Vir09	09/07/1968	21Pis58	01/07/1969	28Leo37
01/09/1968	08Tau46	05/10/1968	21Lib00	09/09/1968	17Ari33	01/09/1969	23Vir48
01/11/1968	02Gem30	05/12/1968	21Sco10	09/11/1968	12Tau06	01/11/1969	20Lib02
01/13/1968	26Gem56	05/14/1968	21Sag33	09/13/1968	05Gem58	01/13/1969	17Sco47
01/15/1968	22Can19	05/16/1968	20Cap57	09/15/1968	29Gem45	01/15/1969	17Sag04
01/17/1968	18Leo41	05/18/1968	18Aqu33	09/17/1968	24Can06	01/17/1969	17Cap15
01/19/1968	15Vir48	05/20/1968	14Pis24	09/19/1968	19Leo28	01/19/1969	17Aqu08
01/21/1968	13Lib25	05/22/1968	08Ari58	09/21/1968	16Vir10	01/21/1969	15Pis33
01/23/1968	11Sco27	05/24/1968	02Tau50	09/23/1968	14Lib07	01/23/1969	12Ari04
01/25/1968	09Sag49	05/26/1968	26Tau27	09/25/1968	12Sco51	01/25/1969	07Tau00
01/27/1968	08Cap18	05/28/1968	20Gem08	09/27/1968	11Sag42	01/27/1969	01Gem01
01/29/1968	06Aqu15	05/30/1968	14Can13	09/29/1968	10Cap10	01/29/1969	24Gem43
01/31/1968	03Pis07	06/01/1968	08Leo51	10/01/1968	07Aqu54	01/31/1969	18Can37
02/02/1968	28Pis37	06/03/1968	04Vir23	10/03/1968	04Pis46	02/02/1969	13Leo02
02/04/1968	22Ari55	06/05/1968	01Lib15	10/05/1968	00Ari45	02/04/1969	08Vir04
02/06/1968	16Tau36	06/07/1968	29Lib42	10/07/1968	25Ari50	02/06/1969	03Lib48
02/08/1968	10Gem23	06/09/1968	29Sco34	10/09/1968	20Tau10	02/08/1969	00Sco21
02/10/1968	04Can53	06/11/1968	29Sag55	10/11/1968	13Gem59	02/10/1969	28Sco00
02/12/1968	00Leo37	06/13/1968	29Cap31	10/13/1968	07Can44	02/12/1969	26Sag40
02/14/1968	27Leo39	06/15/1968	27Aqu21	10/15/1968	01Leo59	02/14/1969	26Cap01
02/16/1968	25Vir41	06/17/1968	23Pis19	10/17/1968	27Leo17	02/16/1969	25Aqu12
02/18/1968	24Lib05	06/19/1968	17Ari51	10/19/1968	24Vir07	02/18/1969	23Pis19
02/20/1968	22Sco27	06/21/1968	11Tau37	10/21/1968	22Lib37	02/20/1969	19Ari52
02/22/1968	20Sag35	06/23/1968	05Gem15	10/23/1968	22Sco12	02/22/1969	14Tau58
02/24/1968	18Cap16	06/25/1968	29Gem06	10/25/1968	21Sag54	02/24/1969	09Gem07
02/26/1968	15Aqu19	06/27/1968	23Can31	10/27/1968	20Cap48	02/26/1969	02Can51
02/28/1968	11Pis27	06/29/1968	18Leo34	10/29/1968	18Aqu25	02/28/1969	26Can50
03/01/1968	06Ari34	07/01/1968	14Vir23	10/31/1968	14Pis42	03/02/1969	21Leo31
03/03/1968	00Tau45	07/03/1968	11Lib15	11/02/1968	09Ari58	03/04/1969	17Vir06
03/05/1968	24Tau26	07/05/1968	09Sco18	11/04/1968	04Tau33	03/06/1969	13Lib36
03/07/1968	18Gem12	07/07/1968	08Sag36	11/06/1968	28Tau36	03/08/1969	10Sco56
03/09/1968	12Can41	07/09/1968	08Cap29	11/08/1968	22Gem22	03/10/1969	08Sag54
03/11/1968	08Leo30	07/11/1968	07Aqu47	11/10/1968	16Can07	03/12/1969	07Cap17
03/13/1968	05Vir54	07/13/1968	05Pis37	11/12/1968	10Leo17	03/14/1969	05Aqu48
03/15/1968	04Lib37	07/15/1968	01Ari39	11/14/1968	05Vir22	03/16/1969	04Pis03
03/17/1968	03Sco56	07/17/1968	26Ari14	11/16/1968	02Lib00	03/18/1969	01Ari25
03/19/1968	03Sag03	07/19/1968	20Tau03	11/18/1968	00Sco33	03/20/1969	27Ari39
03/21/1968	01Cap24	07/21/1968	13Gem44	11/20/1968	00Sag34	03/22/1969	22Tau46
03/23/1968	28Cap43	07/23/1968	07Can51	11/22/1968	01Cap00	03/24/1969	16Gem57
03/25/1968	25Aqu02	07/25/1968	02Leo39	11/24/1968	00Aqu33	03/26/1969	10Can43
03/27/1968	20Pis24	07/27/1968	28Leo16	11/26/1968	28Aqu26	03/28/1969	04Leo43
03/29/1968	15Ari01	07/29/1968	24Vir39	11/28/1968	24Pis30	03/30/1969	29Leo31
03/31/1968	08Tau58	07/31/1968	21Lib49	11/30/1968	19Ari21	04/01/1969	25Vir30
04/02/1968	02Gem36	08/02/1968	19Sco48	12/02/1968	13Tau33	04/03/1969	22Lib47
04/04/1968	26Gem23	08/04/1968	18Sag31	12/04/1968	07Gem23	04/05/1969	21Sco04
04/06/1968	20Can48	08/06/1968	17Cap37	12/06/1968	01Can07	04/07/1969	19Sag46
04/08/1968	16Leo28	08/08/1968	16Aqu13	12/08/1968	24Can58	04/09/1969	18Cap20
04/10/1968	13Vir50	08/10/1968	13Pis40	12/10/1968	19Leo12	04/11/1969	16Aqu23
04/12/1968	12Lib52	08/12/1968	09Ari34	12/12/1968	14Vir12	04/13/1969	13Pis44
04/14/1968	12Sco51	08/14/1968	04Tau14	12/14/1968	10Lib31	04/15/1969	10Ari15
04/16/1968	12Sag45	08/16/1968	28Tau06	12/16/1968	08Sco41	04/17/1969	05Tau55
04/18/1968	11Cap36	08/18/1968	21Gem52	12/18/1968	08Sag34	04/19/1969	00Gem47
04/20/1968	08Aqu57	08/20/1968	16Can09	12/20/1968	09Cap12	04/21/1969	24Gem54
04/22/1968	04Pis52	08/22/1968	11Leo20	12/22/1968	09Aqu12	04/23/1969	18Can38
04/24/1968	29Pis46	08/24/1968	07Vir34	12/24/1968	07Pis27	04/25/1969	12Leo34
04/26/1968	23Ari52	08/26/1968	04Lib43	12/26/1968	03Ari42	04/27/1969	07Vir22
04/28/1968	17Tau36	08/28/1968	02Sco33	12/28/1968	28Ari28	04/29/1969	03Lib30
04/30/1968	11Gem12	08/30/1968	00Sag47	12/30/1968	22Tau29		

Ephemeris Tables for the Moon

Date	Moon	Date	Moon	Date	Moon	Date	Moon
05/01/1969	01Sco17	09/02/1969	26Tau10	01/02/1970	29Lib57	05/02/1970	01Ari25
05/03/1969	00Sag25	09/04/1969	20Gem33	01/04/1970	27Sco18	05/04/1970	29Ari21
05/05/1969	00Cap00	09/06/1969	14Can21	01/06/1970	26Sag34	05/06/1970	26Tau30
05/07/1969	29Cap06	09/08/1969	08Leo09	01/08/1970	26Cap57	05/08/1970	22Gem28
05/09/1969	27Aqu05	09/10/1969	02Vir21	01/10/1970	27Aqu08	05/10/1970	17Can15
05/11/1969	23Pis55	09/12/1969	27Vir21	01/12/1970	26Pis03	05/12/1970	11Leo11
05/13/1969	19Ari44	09/14/1969	23Lib10	01/14/1970	23Ari15	05/14/1970	04Vir50
05/15/1969	14Tau48	09/16/1969	19Sco54	01/16/1970	18Tau59	05/16/1970	28Vir56
05/17/1969	09Gem15	09/18/1969	17Sag33	01/18/1970	13Gem43	05/18/1970	24Lib09
05/19/1969	03Can12	09/20/1969	15Cap55	01/20/1970	07Can52	05/20/1970	20Sco42
05/21/1969	26Can55	09/22/1969	14Aqu44	01/22/1970	01Leo38	05/22/1970	18Sag34
05/23/1969	20Leo51	09/24/1969	13Pis31	01/24/1970	25Leo17	05/24/1970	17Cap09
05/25/1969	15Vir29	09/26/1969	11Ari37	01/26/1970	19Vir04	05/26/1970	15Aqu49
05/27/1969	11Lib31	09/28/1969	08Tau33	01/28/1970	13Lib26	05/28/1970	14Pis04
05/29/1969	09Sco27	09/30/1969	04Gem07	01/30/1970	08Sco49	05/30/1970	11Ari46
05/31/1969	09Sag05						
		10/02/1969	28Gem34	02/01/1970	05Sag50	06/01/1970	08Tau56
06/02/1969	09Cap22	10/04/1969	22Can22	02/03/1970	04Cap43	06/03/1970	05Gem20
06/04/1969	09Aqu05	10/06/1969	16Leo11	02/05/1970	04Aqu54	06/05/1970	00Can48
06/06/1969	07Pis22	10/08/1969	10Vir36	02/07/1970	05Pis16	06/07/1970	25Can19
06/08/1969	04Ari01	10/10/1969	06Lib03	02/09/1970	04Ari36	06/09/1970	19Leo09
06/10/1969	29Ari25	10/12/1969	02Sco39	02/11/1970	02Tau15	06/11/1970	12Vir47
06/12/1969	24Tau02	10/14/1969	00Sag15	02/13/1970	28Tau10	06/13/1970	06Lib52
06/14/1969	18Gem09	10/16/1969	28Sag30	02/15/1970	22Gem48	06/15/1970	02Sco09
06/16/1969	11Can55	10/18/1969	26Cap52	02/17/1970	16Can45	06/17/1970	29Sco02
06/18/1969	05Leo37	10/20/1969	25Aqu03	02/19/1970	10Leo24	06/19/1970	27Sag30
06/20/1969	29Leo33	10/22/1969	22Pis57	02/21/1970	04Vir07	06/21/1970	26Cap55
06/22/1969	24Vir10	10/24/1969	20Ari13	02/23/1970	28Vir13	06/23/1970	26Aqu13
06/24/1969	20Lib04	10/26/1969	16Tau39	02/25/1970	22Lib57	06/25/1970	24Pis48
06/26/1969	17Sco51	10/28/1969	12Gem01	02/27/1970	18Sco35	06/27/1970	22Ari21
06/28/1969	17Sag28	10/30/1969	06Can26			06/29/1970	18Tau58
06/30/1969	18Cap01			03/01/1970	15Sag27		
		11/01/1969	00Leo13	03/03/1970	13Cap46	07/01/1970	14Gem42
07/02/1969	18Aqu09	11/03/1969	23Leo58	03/05/1970	13Aqu16	07/03/1970	09Can36
07/04/1969	16Pis49	11/05/1969	18Vir25	03/07/1970	13Pis12	07/05/1970	03Leo46
07/06/1969	13Ari34	11/07/1969	14Lib07	03/09/1970	12Ari30	07/07/1970	27Leo27
07/08/1969	08Tau52	11/09/1969	11Sco22	03/11/1970	10Tau25	07/09/1970	21Vir02
07/10/1969	03Gem15	11/11/1969	09Sag54	03/13/1970	06Gem36	07/11/1970	15Lib06
07/12/1969	27Gem09	11/13/1969	09Cap00	03/15/1970	01Can19	07/13/1970	10Sco20
07/14/1969	20Can51	11/15/1969	07Aqu48	03/17/1970	25Can15	07/15/1970	07Sag13
07/16/1969	14Leo37	11/17/1969	05Pis51	03/19/1970	18Leo52	07/17/1970	05Cap54
07/18/1969	08Vir44	11/19/1969	03Ari04	03/21/1970	12Vir45	07/19/1970	05Aqu48
07/20/1969	03Lib30	11/21/1969	29Ari30	03/23/1970	07Lib16	07/21/1970	05Pis48
07/22/1969	29Lib24	11/23/1969	25Tau14	03/25/1970	02Sco36	07/23/1970	04Ari55
07/24/1969	26Sco55	11/25/1969	20Gem13	03/27/1970	28Sco49	07/25/1970	02Tau37
07/26/1969	26Sag10	11/27/1969	14Can29	03/29/1970	25Sag57	07/27/1970	28Tau58
07/28/1969	26Cap27	11/29/1969	08Leo12	03/31/1970	23Cap57	07/29/1970	24Gem13
07/30/1969	26Aqu34					07/31/1970	18Can38
		12/01/1969	01Vir53	04/02/1970	22Aqu42		
08/01/1969	25Pis25	12/03/1969	26Vir13	04/04/1970	21Pis48	08/02/1970	12Leo31
08/03/1969	22Ari25	12/05/1969	21Lib53	04/06/1970	20Ari34	08/04/1970	06Vir05
08/05/1969	17Tau48	12/07/1969	19Sco23	04/08/1970	18Tau17	08/06/1970	29Vir43
08/07/1969	12Gem09	12/09/1969	18Sag33	04/10/1970	14Gem31	08/08/1970	23Lib49
08/09/1969	05Can58	12/11/1969	18Cap31	04/12/1970	09Can22	08/10/1970	19Sco01
08/11/1969	29Can41	12/13/1969	18Aqu03	04/14/1970	03Leo19	08/12/1970	15Sag43
08/13/1969	23Leo37	12/15/1969	16Pis24	04/16/1970	26Leo57	08/14/1970	14Cap12
08/15/1969	18Vir07	12/17/1969	13Ari22	04/18/1970	20Vir58	08/16/1970	14Aqu08
08/17/1969	13Lib17	12/19/1969	09Tau16	04/20/1970	15Lib55	08/18/1970	14Pis30
08/19/1969	09Sco27	12/21/1969	04Gem23	04/22/1970	11Sco55	08/20/1970	14Ari07
08/21/1969	06Sag53	12/23/1969	28Gem54	04/24/1970	08Sag58	08/22/1970	12Tau12
08/23/1969	05Cap36	12/25/1969	22Can54	04/26/1970	06Cap43	08/24/1970	08Gem35
08/25/1969	05Aqu13	12/27/1969	16Leo33	04/28/1970	04Aqu51	08/26/1970	03Can34
08/27/1969	04Pis51	12/29/1969	10Vir13	04/30/1970	03Pis09	08/28/1970	27Can41
08/29/1969	03Ari32	12/31/1969	04Lib28			08/30/1970	21Leo21
08/31/1969	00Tau38						

Ephemeris Tables for the Moon

Date	Moon	Date	Moon	Date	Moon	Date	Moon
09/01/1970	14Vir55	01/01/1971	04Pis45	05/01/1971	01Leo13	09/02/1971	02Aqu54
09/03/1970	08Lib43	01/03/1971	03Ari16	05/03/1971	25Leo29	09/04/1971	01Pis55
09/05/1970	03Sco09	01/05/1971	01Tau07	05/05/1971	19Vir10	09/06/1971	02Ari00
09/07/1970	28Sco25	01/07/1971	28Tau13	05/07/1971	12Lib53	09/08/1971	02Tau04
09/09/1970	24Sag55	01/09/1971	24Gem32	05/09/1971	07Sco04	09/10/1971	00Gem55
09/11/1970	22Cap58	01/11/1971	19Can58	05/11/1971	02Sag00	09/12/1971	28Gem09
09/13/1970	22Aqu30	01/13/1971	14Leo31	05/13/1971	27Sag43	09/14/1971	23Can56
09/15/1970	22Pis43	01/15/1971	08Vir26	05/15/1971	24Cap10	09/16/1971	18Leo39
09/17/1970	22Ari31	01/17/1971	02Lib02	05/17/1971	21Aqu27	09/18/1971	12Vir45
09/19/1970	20Tau56	01/19/1971	25Lib54	05/19/1971	19Pis42	09/20/1971	06Lib30
09/21/1970	17Gem31	01/21/1971	20Sco42	05/21/1971	18Ari42	09/22/1971	00Sco12
09/23/1970	12Can29	01/23/1971	17Sag01	05/23/1971	17Tau56	09/24/1971	24Sco05
09/25/1970	06Leo27	01/25/1971	15Cap03	05/25/1971	16Gem30	09/26/1971	18Sag31
09/27/1970	00Vir03	01/27/1971	14Aqu25	05/27/1971	13Can40	09/28/1971	14Cap02
09/29/1970	23Vir43	01/29/1971	14Pis16	05/29/1971	09Leo14	09/30/1971	11Aqu07
		01/31/1971	13Ari33	05/31/1971	03Vir34		
10/01/1970	17Lib52					10/02/1971	10Pis03
10/03/1970	12Sco43	02/02/1971	11Tau38	06/02/1971	27Vir19	10/04/1971	10Ari24
10/05/1970	08Sag22	02/04/1971	08Gem28	06/04/1971	21Lib07	10/06/1971	10Tau52
10/07/1970	04Cap58	02/06/1971	04Can09	06/06/1971	15Sco34	10/08/1971	10Gem14
10/09/1970	02Aqu40	02/08/1971	28Can55	06/08/1971	10Sag57	10/10/1971	07Can42
10/11/1970	01Pis32	02/10/1971	23Leo04	06/10/1971	07Cap21	10/12/1971	03Leo24
10/13/1970	01Ari05	02/12/1971	16Vir49	06/12/1971	04Aqu31	10/14/1971	27Leo51
10/15/1970	00Tau34	02/14/1971	10Lib26	06/14/1971	02Pis17	10/16/1971	21Vir42
10/17/1970	29Tau01	02/16/1971	04Sco21	06/16/1971	00Ari30	10/18/1971	15Lib24
10/19/1970	25Gem45	02/18/1971	29Sco03	06/18/1971	29Ari00	10/20/1971	09Sco10
10/21/1970	20Can49	02/20/1971	25Sag06	06/20/1971	27Tau24	10/22/1971	03Sag15
10/23/1970	14Leo46	02/22/1971	22Cap55	06/22/1971	25Gem09	10/24/1971	27Sag52
10/25/1970	08Vir22	02/24/1971	22Aqu24	06/24/1971	21Can49	10/26/1971	23Cap21
10/27/1970	02Lib12	02/26/1971	22Pis45	06/26/1971	17Leo10	10/28/1971	20Aqu07
10/29/1970	26Lib43	02/28/1971	22Ari43	06/28/1971	11Vir26	10/30/1971	18Pis37
10/31/1970	22Sco12			06/30/1971	05Lib15		
		03/02/1971	21Tau22	07/02/1971	29Lib07	11/01/1971	18Ari36
11/02/1970	18Sag31	03/04/1971	18Gem19	07/04/1971	23Sco42	11/03/1971	19Tau02
11/04/1970	15Cap33	03/06/1971	13Can42	07/06/1971	19Sag26	11/05/1971	18Gem36
11/06/1970	13Aqu13	03/08/1971	08Leo03	07/08/1971	16Cap25	11/07/1971	16Can21
11/08/1970	11Pis32	03/10/1971	01Vir52	07/10/1971	14Aqu24	11/09/1971	12Leo12
11/10/1970	10Ari16	03/12/1971	25Vir32	07/12/1971	12Pis57	11/11/1971	06Vir39
11/12/1970	09Tau00	03/14/1971	19Lib16	07/14/1971	11Ari33	11/13/1971	00Lib25
11/14/1970	07Gem00	03/16/1971	13Sco22	07/16/1971	09Tau50	11/15/1971	24Lib08
11/16/1970	03Can33	03/18/1971	08Sag10	07/18/1971	07Gem32	11/17/1971	18Sco06
11/18/1970	28Can40	03/20/1971	04Cap02	07/20/1971	04Can27	11/19/1971	12Sag32
11/20/1970	22Leo43	03/22/1971	01Aqu26	07/22/1971	00Leo22	11/21/1971	07Cap33
11/22/1970	16Vir18	03/24/1971	00Pis32	07/24/1971	25Leo19	11/23/1971	03Aqu21
11/24/1970	10Lib13	03/26/1971	00Ari48	07/26/1971	19Vir27	11/25/1971	00Pis07
11/26/1970	05Sco03	03/28/1971	01Tau04	07/28/1971	13Lib15	11/27/1971	28Pis12
11/28/1970	01Sag06	03/30/1971	00Gem08	07/30/1971	07Sco06	11/29/1971	27Ari27
11/30/1970	28Sag13						
		04/01/1971	27Gem21	08/01/1971	01Sag39	12/01/1971	27Tau15
12/02/1970	26Cap03	04/03/1971	22Can46	08/03/1971	27Sag30	12/03/1971	26Gem30
12/04/1970	24Aqu11	04/05/1971	17Leo00	08/05/1971	24Cap50	12/05/1971	24Can16
12/06/1970	22Pis21	04/07/1971	10Vir40	08/07/1971	23Aqu31	12/07/1971	20Leo18
12/08/1970	20Ari25	04/09/1971	04Lib19	08/09/1971	22Pis57	12/09/1971	14Vir53
12/10/1970	18Tau13	04/11/1971	28Lib13	08/11/1971	22Ari13	12/11/1971	08Lib43
12/12/1970	15Gem24	04/13/1971	22Sco42	08/13/1971	20Tau39	12/13/1971	02Sco27
12/14/1970	11Can31	04/15/1971	17Sag52	08/15/1971	17Gem57	12/15/1971	26Sco36
12/16/1970	06Leo27	04/17/1971	13Cap51	08/17/1971	14Can09	12/17/1971	21Sag27
12/18/1970	00Vir27	04/19/1971	11Aqu00	08/19/1971	09Leo23	12/19/1971	17Cap09
12/20/1970	24Vir04	04/21/1971	09Pis35	08/21/1971	03Vir52	12/21/1971	13Aqu34
12/22/1970	17Lib58	04/23/1971	09Ari16	08/23/1971	27Vir48	12/23/1971	10Pis46
12/24/1970	12Sco52	04/25/1971	09Tau15	08/25/1971	21Lib30	12/25/1971	08Ari42
12/26/1970	09Sag16	04/27/1971	08Gem18	08/27/1971	15Sco21	12/27/1971	07Tau21
12/28/1970	07Cap03	04/29/1971	05Can40	08/29/1971	09Sag49	12/29/1971	06Gem13
12/30/1970	05Aqu47			08/31/1971	05Cap33	12/31/1971	04Can39

Ephemeris Tables for the Moon

Date	Moon	Date	Moon	Date	Moon	Date	Moon
01/02/1972	02Leo01	05/01/1972	13Sag40	09/02/1972	05Can39	01/02/1973	18Sag19
01/04/1972	27Leo59	05/03/1972	07Cap52	09/04/1972	02Leo51	01/04/1973	12Cap16
01/06/1972	22Vir42	05/05/1972	02Aqu50	09/06/1972	29Leo18	01/06/1973	06Aqu48
01/08/1972	16Lib37	05/07/1972	29Aqu08	09/08/1972	24Vir58	01/08/1973	02Pis06
01/10/1972	10Sco23	05/09/1972	27Pis16	09/10/1972	19Lib46	01/10/1973	28Pis23
01/12/1972	04Sag36	05/11/1972	26Ari57	09/12/1972	13Sco49	01/12/1973	25Ari39
01/14/1972	29Sag45	05/13/1972	27Tau30	09/14/1972	07Sag33	01/14/1973	24Tau07
01/16/1972	26Cap03	05/15/1972	27Gem24	09/16/1972	01Cap27	01/16/1973	23Gem28
01/18/1972	23Aqu21	05/17/1972	25Can40	09/18/1972	26Cap13	01/18/1973	22Can55
01/20/1972	21Pis22	05/19/1972	22Leo06	09/20/1972	22Aqu28	01/20/1973	21Leo37
01/22/1972	19Ari44	05/21/1972	17Vir03	09/22/1972	20Pis29	01/22/1973	18Vir56
01/24/1972	18Tau07	05/23/1972	11Lib10	09/24/1972	19Ari46	01/24/1973	14Lib42
01/26/1972	16Gem10	05/25/1972	04Sco55	09/26/1972	19Tau25	01/26/1973	09Sco07
01/28/1972	13Can34	05/27/1972	28Sco43	09/28/1972	18Gem28	01/28/1973	02Sag51
01/30/1972	10Leo13	05/29/1972	22Sag46	09/30/1972	16Can17	01/30/1973	26Sag34
		05/31/1972	17Cap19				
02/01/1972	05Vir49			10/02/1972	12Leo57	02/01/1973	20Cap45
02/03/1972	00Lib28	06/02/1972	12Aqu37	10/04/1972	08Vir43	02/03/1973	15Aqu48
02/05/1972	24Lib25	06/04/1972	09Pis00	10/06/1972	03Lib51	02/05/1973	11Pis51
02/07/1972	18Sco11	06/06/1972	06Ari48	10/08/1972	28Lib16	02/07/1973	08Ari48
02/09/1972	12Sag21	06/08/1972	06Tau00	10/10/1972	22Sco09	02/09/1973	06Tau26
02/11/1972	07Cap33	06/10/1972	05Gem59	10/12/1972	15Sag48	02/11/1973	04Gem36
02/13/1972	04Aqu12	06/12/1972	05Can36	10/14/1972	09Cap37	02/13/1973	03Can07
02/15/1972	02Pis17	06/14/1972	03Leo54	10/16/1972	04Aqu15	02/15/1973	01Leo39
02/17/1972	01Ari18	06/16/1972	00Vir30	10/18/1972	00Pis27	02/17/1973	29Leo41
02/19/1972	00Tau27	06/18/1972	25Vir35	10/20/1972	28Pis36	02/19/1973	26Vir42
02/21/1972	29Tau03	06/20/1972	19Lib43	10/22/1972	28Ari18	02/21/1973	22Lib28
02/23/1972	26Gem40	06/22/1972	13Sco28	10/24/1972	28Tau39	02/23/1973	16Sco57
02/25/1972	23Can18	06/24/1972	07Sag23	10/26/1972	28Gem20	02/25/1973	10Sag42
02/27/1972	19Leo09	06/26/1972	01Cap43	10/28/1972	26Can28	02/27/1973	04Cap27
02/29/1972	14Vir10	06/28/1972	26Cap45	10/30/1972	23Leo01		
		06/30/1972	22Aqu39			03/01/1973	28Cap46
03/02/1972	08Lib33			11/01/1972	18Vir24	03/03/1973	24Aqu14
03/04/1972	02Sco30	07/02/1972	19Pis28	11/03/1972	13Lib00	03/05/1973	21Pis01
03/06/1972	26Sco14	07/04/1972	17Ari16	11/05/1972	07Sco04	03/07/1973	18Ari53
03/08/1972	20Sag18	07/06/1972	15Tau58	11/07/1972	00Sag48	03/09/1973	17Tau15
03/10/1972	15Cap22	07/08/1972	15Gem09	11/09/1972	24Sag28	03/11/1973	15Gem37
03/12/1972	12Aqu01	07/10/1972	14Can03	11/11/1972	18Cap19	03/13/1973	13Can42
03/14/1972	10Pis29	07/12/1972	11Leo58	11/13/1972	12Aqu54	03/15/1973	11Leo24
03/16/1972	10Ari15	07/14/1972	08Vir31	11/15/1972	08Pis53	03/17/1973	08Vir34
03/18/1972	10Tau17	07/16/1972	03Lib40	11/17/1972	06Ari42	03/19/1973	04Lib58
03/20/1972	09Gem25	07/18/1972	27Lib51	11/19/1972	06Tau21	03/21/1973	00Sco23
03/22/1972	07Can04	07/20/1972	21Sco38	11/21/1972	06Gem55	03/23/1973	24Sco47
03/24/1972	03Leo18	07/22/1972	15Sag39	11/23/1972	07Can04	03/25/1973	18Sag32
03/26/1972	28Leo33	07/24/1972	10Cap16	11/25/1972	05Leo42	03/27/1973	12Cap14
03/28/1972	23Vir05	07/26/1972	05Aqu51	11/27/1972	02Vir30	03/29/1973	06Aqu34
03/30/1972	17Lib10	07/28/1972	02Pis33	11/29/1972	27Vir48	03/31/1973	02Pis13
		07/30/1972	00Ari04				
04/01/1972	11Sco00			12/01/1972	22Lib09	04/02/1973	29Pis34
04/03/1972	04Sag44	08/01/1972	28Ari13	12/03/1972	15Sco59	04/04/1973	28Ari12
04/05/1972	28Sag47	08/03/1972	26Tau42	12/05/1972	09Sag39	04/06/1973	27Tau26
04/07/1972	23Cap42	08/05/1972	25Gem06	12/07/1972	03Cap24	04/08/1973	26Gem22
04/09/1972	20Aqu10	08/07/1972	23Can07	12/09/1972	27Cap30	04/10/1973	24Can31
04/11/1972	18Pis34	08/09/1972	20Leo22	12/11/1972	22Aqu16	04/12/1973	21Leo45
04/13/1972	18Ari34	08/11/1972	16Vir44	12/13/1972	18Pis13	04/14/1973	18Vir12
04/15/1972	19Tau09	08/13/1972	11Lib37	12/15/1972	15Ari39	04/16/1973	13Lib55
04/17/1972	18Gem49	08/15/1972	05Sco48	12/17/1972	14Tau43	04/18/1973	08Sco48
04/19/1972	16Can48	08/17/1972	29Sco35	12/19/1972	14Gem51	04/20/1973	02Sag58
04/21/1972	13Leo01	08/19/1972	23Sag34	12/21/1972	15Can00	04/22/1973	26Sag38
04/23/1972	08Vir00	08/21/1972	18Cap22	12/23/1972	13Leo55	04/24/1973	20Cap19
04/25/1972	02Lib13	08/23/1972	14Aqu25	12/25/1972	11Vir04	04/26/1973	14Aqu36
04/27/1972	26Lib04	08/25/1972	11Pis54	12/27/1972	06Lib35	04/28/1973	10Pis13
04/29/1972	19Sco49	08/27/1972	10Ari18	12/29/1972	00Sco54	04/30/1973	07Ari39
		08/29/1972	09Tau07	12/31/1972	24Sco39		
		08/31/1972	07Gem43				

Ephemeris Tables for the Moon

Date	Moon	Date	Moon	Date	Moon	Date	Moon
05/02/1973	06Tau45	09/01/1973	03Sco34	01/01/1974	07Ari38	05/01/1974	09Vir22
05/04/1973	06Gem41	09/03/1973	28Sco16	01/03/1974	04Tau07	05/03/1974	07Lib05
05/06/1973	06Can19	09/05/1973	22Sag06	01/05/1974	02Gem24	05/05/1974	04Sco01
05/08/1973	04Leo54	09/07/1973	15Cap45	01/07/1974	02Can13	05/07/1974	29Sco55
05/10/1973	02Vir06	09/09/1973	09Aqu53	01/09/1974	02Leo42	05/09/1974	24Sag48
05/12/1973	28Vir06	09/11/1973	04Pis57	01/11/1974	02Vir38	05/11/1974	18Cap51
05/14/1973	23Lib16	09/13/1973	01Ari07	01/13/1974	00Lib55	05/13/1974	12Aqu33
05/16/1973	17Sco40	09/15/1973	28Ari16	01/15/1974	27Lib22	05/15/1974	06Pis33
05/18/1973	11Sag33	09/17/1973	26Tau01	01/17/1974	22Sco18	05/17/1974	01Ari24
05/20/1973	05Cap08	09/19/1973	24Gem06	01/19/1974	16Sag19	05/19/1974	27Ari37
05/22/1973	28Cap51	09/21/1973	22Can20	01/21/1974	09Cap55	05/21/1974	25Tau18
05/24/1973	23Aqu10	09/23/1973	20Leo37	01/23/1974	03Aqu31	05/23/1974	24Gem04
05/26/1973	18Pis42	09/25/1973	18Vir33	01/25/1974	27Aqu28	05/25/1974	23Can12
05/28/1973	15Ari58	09/27/1973	15Lib38	01/27/1974	21Pis56	05/27/1974	22Leo02
05/30/1973	15Tau02	09/29/1973	11Sco32	01/29/1974	17Ari09	05/29/1974	20Vir07
				01/31/1974	13Tau28	05/31/1974	17Lib15
06/01/1973	15Gem13	10/01/1973	06Sag10				
06/03/1973	15Can22	10/03/1973	29Sag58	02/02/1974	11Gem12	06/02/1974	13Sco24
06/05/1973	14Leo26	10/05/1973	23Cap35	02/04/1974	10Can27	06/04/1974	08Sag39
06/07/1973	11Vir52	10/07/1973	17Aqu49	02/06/1974	10Leo37	06/06/1974	03Cap07
06/09/1973	07Lib47	10/09/1973	13Pis10	02/08/1974	10Vir36	06/08/1974	27Cap00
06/11/1973	02Sco37	10/11/1973	09Ari54	02/10/1974	09Lib14	06/10/1974	20Aqu41
06/13/1973	26Sco42	10/13/1973	07Tau53	02/12/1974	05Sco58	06/12/1974	14Pis42
06/15/1973	20Sag20	10/15/1973	06Gem28	02/14/1974	01Sag01	06/14/1974	09Ari30
06/17/1973	13Cap58	10/17/1973	05Can02	02/16/1974	24Sag56	06/16/1974	05Tau42
06/19/1973	07Aqu50	10/19/1973	03Leo13	02/18/1974	18Cap29	06/18/1974	03Gem34
06/21/1973	02Pis21	10/21/1973	00Vir57	02/20/1974	12Aqu12	06/20/1974	02Can52
06/23/1973	27Pis57	10/23/1973	28Vir03	02/22/1974	06Pis31	06/22/1974	02Leo47
06/25/1973	24Ari57	10/25/1973	24Lib21	02/24/1974	01Ari28	06/24/1974	02Vir17
06/27/1973	23Tau38	10/27/1973	19Sco44	02/26/1974	27Ari10	6/26/1974	00Lib36
06/29/1973	23Gem34	10/29/1973	14Sag07	02/28/1974	23Tau42	06/28/1974	27Lib27
		10/31/1973	07Cap52			06/30/1974	23Sco03
07/01/1973	23Can49			03/02/1974	21Gem10		
07/03/1973	23Leo10	11/02/1973	01Aqu28	03/04/1974	19Can45	07/02/1974	17Sag45
07/05/1973	20Vir55	11/04/1973	25Aqu39	03/06/1974	19Leo10	07/04/1974	11Cap49
07/07/1973	16Lib55	11/06/1973	21Pis00	03/08/1974	18Vir39	07/06/1974	05Aqu33
07/09/1973	11Sco38	11/08/1973	17Ari57	03/10/1974	17Lib06	07/08/1974	29Aqu16
07/11/1973	05Sag31	11/10/1973	16Tau33	03/12/1974	13Sco55	07/10/1974	23Pis19
07/13/1973	29Sag07	11/12/1973	15Gem58	03/14/1974	09Sag05	07/12/1974	18Ari03
07/15/1973	22Cap52	11/14/1973	15Can21	03/16/1974	03Cap06	07/14/1974	14Tau04
07/17/1973	17Aqu03	11/16/1973	14Leo59	03/18/1974	26Cap42	07/16/1974	11Gem50
07/19/1973	11Pis56	11/18/1973	11Vir31	03/20/1974	20Aqu34	07/18/1974	11Can14
07/21/1973	07Ari45	11/20/1973	08Lib01	03/22/1974	15Pis110	07/20/1974	11Leo36
07/23/1973	04Tau45	11/22/1973	03Sco36	03/24/1974	10Ari42	07/22/1974	11Vir40
07/25/1973	03Gem00	11/24/1973	28Sco22	03/26/1974	07Tau07	07/24/1974	10Lib22
07/27/1973	02Can21	11/26/1973	22Sag27	03/28/1974	04Gem15	07/26/1974	07Sco15
07/29/1973	02Leo10	11/28/1973	16Cap06	03/30/1974	01Can56	07/28/1974	02Sag34
07/31/1973	01Vir27	11/30/1973	09Aqu42			07/30/1974	26Sag55
				04/01/1974	00Leo10		
08/02/1973	29Vir19	12/02/1973	03Pis48	04/03/1974	28Leo48	08/01/1974	20Cap44
08/04/1973	25Lib28	12/04/1973	29Pis03	04/05/1974	27Vir25	08/03/1974	14Aqu24
08/06/1973	20Sco10	12/06/1973	25Ari48	04/07/1974	25Lib14	08/05/1974	08Pis12
08/08/1973	14Sag00	12/08/1973	24Tau28	04/09/1974	21Sco45	08/07/1974	02Ari24
08/10/1973	07Cap37	12/10/1973	24Gem23	04/11/1974	16Sag53	08/09/1974	27Ari14
08/12/1973	01Aqu34	12/12/1973	24Can31	04/13/1974	10Cap58	08/11/1974	23Tau07
08/14/1973	26Aqu11	12/14/1973	23Leo52	04/15/1974	04Aqu39	08/13/1974	20Gem36
08/16/1973	21Pis40	12/16/1973	21Vir42	04/17/1974	28Aqu37	08/15/1974	19Can41
08/18/1973	18Ari02	12/18/1973	17Lib59	04/19/1974	23Pis25	08/17/1974	19Leo59
08/20/1973	15Tau14	12/20/1973	13Sco04	04/21/1974	19Ari25	08/19/1974	20Vir16
08/22/1973	13Gem13	12/22/1973	07Sag21	04/23/1974	16Tau33	08/21/1974	19Lib18
08/24/1973	11Can55	12/24/1973	01Cap07	04/25/1974	14Gem31	08/23/1974	16Sco21
08/26/1973	11Leo01	12/26/1973	24Cap42	04/27/1974	12Can48	08/25/1974	11Sag39
08/28/1973	09Vir45	12/28/1973	18Aqu25	04/29/1974	11Leo09	08/27/1974	05Cap51
08/30/1973	07Lib25	12/30/1973	12Pis35			08/29/1974	29Cap33
						08/31/1974	23Aqu16

Ephemeris Tables for the Moon

Date	Moon	Date	Moon	Date	Moon	Date	Moon
09/02/1974	17Pis17	01/02/1975	11Vir13	05/02/1975	03Aqu13	09/01/1975	09Can18
09/04/1974	11Ari48	01/04/1975	09Lib41	05/04/1975	27Aqu14	09/03/1975	07Leo49
09/06/1974	06Tau57	01/06/1975	06Sco52	05/06/1975	21Pis01	09/05/1975	07Vir56
09/08/1974	02Gem57	01/08/1975	02Sag49	05/08/1975	15Ari04	09/07/1975	08Lib25
09/10/1974	00Can11	01/10/1975	27Sag55	05/10/1975	09Tau52	09/09/1975	07Sco59
09/12/1974	28Can49	01/12/1975	22Cap26	05/12/1975	05Gem33	09/11/1975	05Sag52
09/14/1974	28Leo36	01/14/1975	16Aqu26	05/14/1975	02Can09	09/13/1975	02Cap01
09/16/1974	28Vir33	01/16/1975	10Pis10	05/16/1975	29Can37	09/15/1975	26Cap58
09/18/1974	27Lib31	01/18/1975	03Ari56	05/18/1975	27Leo46	09/17/1975	21Aqu13
09/20/1974	24Sco41	01/20/1975	28Ari15	05/20/1975	26Vir21	09/19/1975	15Pis07
09/22/1974	20Sag06	01/22/1975	23Tau42	05/22/1975	25Lib00	09/21/1975	08Ari49
09/24/1974	14Cap21	01/24/1975	20Gem52	05/24/1975	23Sco10	09/23/1975	02Tau35
09/26/1974	08Aqu03	01/26/1975	19Can59	05/26/1975	20Sag21	09/25/1975	26Tau49
09/28/1974	01Pis52	01/28/1975	20Leo18	05/28/1975	16Cap19	09/27/1975	21Gem51
09/30/1974	26Pis11	01/30/1975	20Vir35	05/30/1975	11Aqu10	09/29/1975	18Can16
10/02/1974	21Ari09	02/01/1975	19Lib37	06/01/1975	05Pis13	10/01/1975	16Leo27
10/04/1974	16Tau51	02/03/1975	16Sco53	06/03/1975	29Pis00	10/03/1975	16Vir15
10/06/1974	13Gem18	02/05/1975	12Sag34	06/05/1975	23Ari07	10/05/1975	16Lib42
10/08/1974	10Can37	02/07/1975	07Cap14	06/07/1975	18Tau13	10/07/1975	16Sco30
10/10/1974	08Leo54	02/09/1975	01Aqu21	06/09/1975	14Gem28	10/09/1975	14Sag43
10/12/1974	07Vir56	02/11/1975	25Aqu09	06/11/1975	11Can55	10/11/1975	11Cap05
10/14/1974	07Lib09	02/13/1975	18Pis54	06/13/1975	10Leo13	10/13/1975	06Aqu01
10/16/1974	05Sco34	02/15/1975	12Ari44	06/15/1975	08Vir49	10/15/1975	00Pis09
10/18/1974	02Sag35	02/17/1975	07Tau05	06/17/1975	07Lib15	10/17/1975	23Pis53
10/20/1974	28Sag03	02/19/1975	02Gem21	06/19/1975	05Sco12	10/19/1975	17Ari37
10/22/1974	22Cap22	02/21/1975	29Gem12	06/21/1975	02Sag29	10/21/1975	11Tau40
10/24/1974	16Aqu07	02/23/1975	28Can01	06/23/1975	28Sag57	10/23/1975	06Gem17
10/26/1974	10Pis00	02/25/1975	28Leo21	06/25/1975	24Cap29	10/25/1975	01Can39
10/28/1974	04Ari33	02/27/1975	28Vir57	06/27/1975	19Aqu09	10/27/1975	28Can05
10/30/1974	00Tau00			06/29/1975	13Pis09	10/29/1975	25Leo58
		03/01/1975	28Lib29			10/31/1975	25Vir06
11/01/1974	26Tau24	03/03/1975	26Sco05	07/01/1975	06Ari55		
11/03/1974	23Gem37	03/05/1975	21Sag52	07/03/1975	01Tau03	11/02/1975	24Lib55
11/05/1974	21Can30	03/07/1975	16Cap24	07/05/1975	26Tau13	11/04/1975	24Sco27
11/07/1974	19Leo45	03/09/1975	10Aqu19	07/07/1975	22Gem51	11/06/1975	22Sag46
11/09/1974	18Vir10	03/11/1975	04Pis03	07/09/1975	21Can01	11/08/1975	19Cap23
11/11/1974	16Lib26	03/13/1975	27Pis51	07/11/1975	20Leo14	11/10/1975	14Aqu29
11/13/1974	14Sco00	03/15/1975	21Ari55	07/13/1975	19Vir33	11/12/1975	08Pis36
11/15/1974	10Sag31	03/17/1975	16Tau30	07/15/1975	18Lib09	11/14/1975	02Ari18
11/17/1974	05Cap50	03/19/1975	11Gem53	07/17/1975	15Sco44	11/16/1975	26Ari08
11/19/1974	00Aqu10	03/21/1975	08Can33	07/19/1975	12Sag20	11/18/1975	20Tau30
11/21/1974	23Aqu57	03/23/1975	06Leo56	07/21/1975	08Cap06	11/20/1975	15Gem40
11/23/1974	17Pis49	03/25/1975	06Vir43	07/23/1975	03Aqu07	11/22/1975	11Can42
11/25/1974	12Ari23	03/27/1975	07Lib00	07/25/1975	27Aqu30	11/24/1975	08Leo36
11/27/1974	08Tau06	03/29/1975	06Sco34	07/27/1975	21Pis22	11/26/1975	06Vir24
11/29/1974	05Gem09	03/31/1975	04Sag25	07/29/1975	15Ari05	11/28/1975	04Lib54
				07/31/1975	09Tau10	11/30/1975	03Sco49
12/01/1974	03Can18	04/02/1975	00Cap26				
12/03/1974	02Leo04	04/04/1975	25Cap04	08/02/1975	04Gem16	12/02/1975	02Sag36
12/05/1974	00Vir46	04/06/1975	19Aqu00	08/04/1975	00Can59	12/04/1975	00Cap34
12/07/1974	28Vir58	04/08/1975	12Pis43	08/06/1975	29Can32	12/06/1975	27Cap12
12/09/1974	26Lib30	04/10/1975	06Ari38	08/08/1975	29Leo25	12/08/1975	22Aqu25
12/11/1974	23Sco09	04/12/1975	01Tau04	08/10/1975	29Vir27	12/10/1975	16Pis36
12/13/1974	18Sag56	04/14/1975	26Tau09	08/12/1975	28Lib31	12/12/1975	10Ari16
12/15/1974	13Cap54	04/16/1975	22Gem00	08/14/1975	26Sco07	12/14/1975	04Tau10
12/17/1974	08Aqu06	04/18/1975	18Can52	08/16/1975	22Sag20	12/16/1975	28Tau49
12/19/1974	01Pis52	04/20/1975	16Leo07	08/18/1975	17Cap34	12/18/1975	24Gem35
12/21/1974	25Pis40	04/22/1975	16Vir02	08/20/1975	12Aqu06	12/20/1975	21Can27
12/23/1974	20Ari07	04/24/1975	15Lib33	08/22/1975	06Pis13	12/22/1975	19Leo10
12/25/1974	15Tau48	04/26/1975	14Sco36	08/24/1975	29Pis58	12/24/1975	17Vir21
12/27/1974	13Gem07	04/28/1975	12Sag19	08/26/1975	23Ari39	12/26/1975	15Lib36
12/29/1974	12Can01	04/30/1975	08Cap26	08/28/1975	17Tau43	12/28/1975	13Sco45
12/31/1974	11Leo43			08/30/1975	12Gem43	12/30/1975	11Sag36

Ephemeris Tables for the Moon

Date	Moon	Date	Moon	Date	Moon	Date	Moon
01/01/1976	08Cap48	05/02/1976	16Gem07	09/01/1976	13Sag43	01/01/1977	26Tau10
01/03/1976	05Aqu03	05/04/1976	11Can04	09/03/1976	10Cap58	01/03/1977	20Gem09
01/05/1976	00Pis11	05/06/1976	07Leo04	09/05/1976	07Aqu26	01/05/1977	14Can57
01/07/1976	24Pis23	05/08/1976	04Vir27	09/07/1976	03Pis04	01/07/1977	10Leo37
01/09/1976	18Ari03	05/10/1976	03Lib16	09/09/1976	27Pis48	01/09/1977	07Vir00
01/11/1976	11Tau54	05/12/1976	03Sco07	09/11/1976	21Ari50	01/11/1977	04Lib06
01/13/1976	06Gem39	05/14/1976	03Sag02	09/13/1976	15Tau28	01/13/1977	01Sco52
01/15/1976	02Can47	05/16/1976	02Cap01	09/15/1976	09Gem09	01/15/1977	00Sag26
01/17/1976	00Leo26	05/18/1976	29Cap24	09/17/1976	03Can34	01/17/1977	29Sag22
01/19/1976	29Leo07	05/20/1976	25Aqu04	09/19/1976	29Can21	01/19/1977	28Cap04
01/21/1976	28Vir05	05/22/1976	19Pis30	09/21/1976	26Leo51	01/21/1977	25Aqu49
01/23/1976	26Lib35	05/24/1976	13Ari15	09/23/1976	25Vir58	01/23/1977	21Pis57
01/25/1976	24Sco21	05/26/1976	06Tau50	09/25/1976	25Lib54	01/25/1977	16Ari41
01/27/1976	21Sag25	05/28/1976	00Gem47	09/27/1976	25Sco31	01/27/1977	10Tau31
01/29/1976	17Cap49	05/30/1976	25Gem25	09/29/1976	24Sag06	01/29/1977	04Gem07
01/31/1976	13Aqu28					01/31/1977	28Gem16
		06/01/1976	20Can57	10/01/1976	21Cap16		
02/02/1976	08Pis16	06/03/1976	17Leo22	10/03/1976	17Aqu19	02/02/1977	23Can24
02/04/1976	02Ari19	06/05/1976	14Vir45	10/05/1976	12Pis18	02/04/1977	19Leo42
02/06/1976	25Ari56	06/07/1976	13Lib07	10/07/1976	06Ari36	02/06/1977	16Vir58
02/08/1976	19Tau42	06/09/1976	12Sco13	10/09/1976	00Tau24	02/08/1977	14Lib45
02/10/1976	14Gem23	06/11/1976	11Sag30	10/11/1976	23Tau57	02/10/1977	12Sco50
02/12/1976	10Can36	06/13/1976	10Cap10	10/13/1976	17Gem43	02/12/1977	11Sag03
02/14/1976	08Leo38	06/15/1976	07Aqu30	10/15/1976	12Can05	02/14/1977	09Cap11
02/16/1976	08Vir03	06/17/1976	03Pis16	10/17/1976	07Leo42	02/16/1977	07Aqu00
02/18/1976	07Lib54	06/19/1976	27Pis43	10/19/1976	05Vir00	02/18/1977	04Pis00
02/20/1976	07Sco02	06/21/1976	21Ari27	10/21/1976	04Lib00	02/20/1977	29Pis46
02/22/1976	04Sag57	06/23/1976	15Tau09	10/23/1976	04Sco13	02/22/1977	24Ari24
02/24/1976	01Cap40	06/25/1976	09Gem22	10/25/1976	04Sag28	02/24/1977	18Tau16
02/26/1976	27Cap26	06/27/1976	04Can33	10/27/1976	03Cap35	02/26/1977	11Gem56
02/28/1976	22Aqu28	06/29/1976	00Leo43	10/29/1976	01Aqu04	02/28/1977	06Can04
				10/31/1976	26Aqu55		
03/01/1976	16Pis50	07/01/1976	27Leo49			03/02/1977	01Leo23
03/03/1976	10Ari40	07/03/1976	25Vir33	11/02/1976	21Pis33	03/04/1977	28Leo07
03/05/1976	04Tau15	07/05/1976	23Lib46	11/04/1976	15Ari30	03/06/1977	26Vir05
03/07/1976	28Tau00	07/07/1976	22Sco13	11/06/1976	09Tau08	03/08/1977	24Lib49
03/09/1976	22Gem34	07/09/1976	20Sag42	11/08/1976	02Gem47	03/10/1977	23Sco37
03/11/1976	18Can36	07/11/1976	18Cap41	11/10/1976	26Gem43	03/12/1977	21Sag59
03/13/1976	16Leo34	07/13/1976	15Aqu37	11/12/1976	21Can18	03/14/1977	19Cap46
03/15/1976	16Vir14	07/15/1976	11Pis15	11/14/1976	16Leo52	03/16/1977	16Aqu43
03/17/1976	16Lib39	07/17/1976	05Ari39	11/16/1976	13Vir46	03/18/1977	12Pis53
03/19/1976	16Sco27	07/19/1976	29Ari25	11/18/1976	12Lib20	03/20/1977	08Ari05
03/21/1976	14Sag49	07/21/1976	23Tau07	11/20/1976	12Sco15	03/22/1977	02Tau25
03/23/1976	11Cap39	07/23/1976	17Gem33	11/22/1976	12Sag32	03/24/1977	26Tau13
03/25/1976	07Aqu09	07/25/1976	13Can09	11/24/1976	12Cap05	03/26/1977	19Gem54
03/27/1976	01Pis45	07/27/1976	10Leo04	11/26/1976	09Aqu57	03/28/1977	13Can59
03/29/1976	25Pis45	07/29/1976	07Vir58	11/28/1976	05Pis55	03/30/1977	09Leo13
03/31/1976	19Ari24	07/31/1976	06Lib23	11/30/1976	00Ari28		
						04/01/1977	06Vir02
04/02/1976	12Tau59	08/02/1976	04Sco46	12/02/1976	24Ari12	04/03/1977	04Lib27
04/04/1976	06Gem52	08/04/1976	02Sag52	12/04/1976	17Tau48	04/05/1977	03Sco54
04/06/1976	01Can30	08/06/1976	00Cap37	12/06/1976	11Gem37	04/07/1977	03Sag35
04/08/1976	27Can23	08/08/1976	27Cap49	12/08/1976	05Can55	04/09/1977	02Cap33
04/10/1976	25Leo02	08/10/1976	24Aqu06	12/10/1976	00Leo59	04/11/1977	00Aqu18
04/12/1976	24Vir25	08/12/1976	19Pis22	12/12/1976	26Leo45	04/13/1977	26Aqu51
04/14/1976	24Lib46	08/14/1976	13Ari36	12/14/1976	23Vir31	04/15/1977	22Pis19
04/16/1976	24Sco55	08/16/1976	07Tau18	12/16/1976	21Lib33	04/17/1977	16Ari54
04/18/1976	23Sag46	08/18/1976	01Gem03	12/18/1976	20Sco45	04/19/1977	10Tau55
04/20/1976	20Cap54	08/20/1976	25Gem30	12/20/1976	20Sag36	04/21/1977	04Gem37
04/22/1976	16Aqu24	08/22/1976	21Can21	12/22/1976	19Cap58	04/23/1977	28Gem16
04/24/1976	10Pis49	08/24/1976	18Leo43	12/24/1976	17Aqu59	04/25/1977	22Can25
04/26/1976	04Ari39	08/26/1976	17Vir23	12/26/1976	14Pis12	04/27/1977	17Leo31
04/28/1976	28Ari13	08/28/1976	16Lib39	12/28/1976	08Ari48	04/29/1977	14Vir06
04/30/1976	21Tau56	08/30/1976	15Sco33	12/30/1976	02Tau34		

Ephemeris Tables for the Moon

Date	Moon	Date	Moon	Date	Moon	Date	Moon
05/01/1977	12Lib29	09/02/1977	05Tau42	01/02/1978	11Lib40	05/02/1978	15Pis16
05/03/1977	12Sco16	09/04/1977	29Tau45	01/04/1978	08Sco55	05/04/1978	11Ari45
05/05/1977	12Sag39	09/06/1977	23Gem31	01/06/1978	08Sag00	05/06/1978	07Tau30
05/07/1977	12Cap13	09/08/1977	17Can35	01/08/1978	08Cap21	05/08/1978	02Gem23
05/09/1977	10Aqu16	09/10/1977	12Leo27	01/10/1978	08Aqu41	05/10/1978	26Gem39
05/11/1977	06Pis45	09/12/1977	08Vir30	01/12/1978	07Pis46	05/12/1978	20Can29
05/13/1977	01Ari48	09/14/1977	05Lib41	01/14/1978	04Ari52	05/14/1978	14Leo15
05/15/1977	26Ari00	09/16/1977	03Sco39	01/16/1978	00Tau15	05/16/1978	08Vir36
05/17/1977	19Tau43	09/18/1977	02Sag05	01/18/1978	24Tau27	05/18/1978	04Lib06
05/19/1977	13Gem21	09/20/1977	00Cap33	01/20/1978	18Gem13	05/20/1978	01Sco22
05/21/1977	07Can10	09/22/1977	28Cap42	01/22/1978	11Can59	05/22/1978	00Sag18
05/23/1977	01Leo24	09/24/1977	26Aqu18	01/24/1978	06Leo01	05/24/1978	00Cap09
05/25/1977	26Leo29	09/26/1977	23Pis06	01/26/1978	00Vir34	05/26/1978	29Cap52
05/27/1977	22Vir52	09/28/1977	18Ari52	01/28/1978	25Vir39	05/28/1978	28Aqu29
05/29/1977	20Lib54	09/30/1977	13Tau37	01/30/1978	21Lib36	05/30/1978	25Pis38
05/31/1977	20Sco34						
		10/02/1977	07Gem38	02/01/1978	18Sco44	06/01/1978	21Ari37
06/02/1977	21Sag04	10/04/1977	01Can26	02/03/1978	17Sag13	06/03/1978	16Tau45
06/04/1977	21Cap01	10/06/1977	25Can25	02/05/1978	16Cap51	06/05/1978	11Gem11
06/06/1977	19Aqu28	10/08/1977	20Leo21	02/07/1978	16Aqu42	06/07/1978	05Can12
06/08/1977	16Pis01	10/10/1977	16Vir37	02/09/1978	15Pis35	06/09/1978	28Can57
06/10/1977	10Ari59	10/12/1977	14Lib19	02/11/1978	12Ari51	06/11/1978	22Leo43
06/12/1977	04Tau58	10/14/1977	13Sco13	02/13/1978	08Tau26	06/13/1978	16Vir58
06/14/1977	28Tau34	10/16/1977	12Sag30	02/15/1978	02Gem45	06/15/1978	12Lib24
06/16/1977	22Gem18	10/18/1977	11Cap27	02/17/1978	26Gem33	06/17/1978	09Sco35
06/18/1977	16Can17	10/20/1977	09Aqu27	02/19/1978	20Can22	06/19/1978	08Sag39
06/20/1977	10Leo51	10/22/1977	06Pis22	02/21/1978	14Leo40	06/21/1978	08Cap59
06/22/1977	06Vir10	10/24/1977	02Ari21	02/23/1978	09Vir37	06/23/1978	09Aqu17
06/24/1977	02Lib27	10/26/1977	27Ari28	02/25/1978	05Lib25	06/25/1978	08Pis18
06/26/1977	00Sco10	10/28/1977	21Tau53	02/27/1978	02Sco00	06/27/1978	05Ari37
06/28/1977	29Sco24	10/30/1977	15Gem49			06/29/1978	01Tau21
06/30/1977	29Sag29			03/01/1978	29Sco22		
		11/01/1977	09Can33	03/03/1978	27Sag37	07/01/1978	26Tau07
07/02/1977	29Cap25	11/03/1977	03Leo31	03/05/1978	26Cap28	07/03/1978	20Gem17
07/04/1977	27Aqu57	11/05/1977	28Leo15	03/07/1978	25Aqu21	07/05/1978	14Can03
07/06/1977	24Pis37	11/07/1977	24Vir24	03/09/1978	23Pis36	07/07/1978	07Leo48
07/08/1977	19Ari37	11/09/1977	22Lib20	03/11/1978	20Ari37	07/09/1978	01Vir37
07/10/1977	13Tau35	11/11/1977	21Sco46	03/13/1978	16Tau12	07/11/1978	25Vir56
07/12/1977	07Gem18	11/13/1977	21Sag57	03/15/1978	10Gem40	07/13/1978	21Lib19
07/14/1977	01Can05	11/15/1977	21Cap36	03/17/1978	04Can30	07/15/1978	18Sco18
07/16/1977	25Can23	11/17/1977	19Aqu50	03/19/1978	28Can22	07/17/1978	17Sag10
07/18/1977	20Leo25	11/19/1977	16Pis31	03/21/1978	22Leo47	07/19/1978	17Cap25
07/20/1977	16Vir11	11/21/1977	11Ari55	03/23/1978	18Vir08	07/21/1978	17Aqu54
07/22/1977	12Lib46	11/23/1977	06Tau29	03/25/1978	14Lib40	07/23/1978	17Pis17
07/24/1977	10Sco20	11/25/1977	00Gem35	03/27/1978	12Sco06	07/25/1978	14Ari48
07/26/1977	09Sag02	11/27/1977	24Gem21	03/29/1978	10Sag14	07/27/1978	10Tau39
07/28/1977	08Cap30	11/29/1977	18Can07	03/31/1978	08Cap37	07/29/1978	05Gem18
07/30/1977	07Aqu49					07/31/1978	29Gem16
		12/01/1977	12Leo06	04/02/1978	07Aqu00		
08/01/1977	06Pis07	12/03/1977	06Vir42	04/04/1978	05Pis01	08/02/1978	22Can59
08/03/1977	02Ari45	12/05/1977	02Lib37	04/06/1978	02Ari18	08/04/1978	16Leo46
08/05/1977	27Ari47	12/07/1977	00Sco15	04/08/1978	28Ari42	08/06/1978	10Vir48
08/07/1977	21Tau51	12/09/1977	29Sco44	04/10/1978	24Tau05	08/08/1978	05Lib26
08/09/1977	15Gem34	12/11/1977	00Cap22	04/12/1978	18Gem30	08/10/1978	01Sco00
08/11/1977	09Can30	12/13/1977	00Aqu36	04/14/1978	12Can23	08/12/1978	27Sco51
08/13/1977	04Leo12	12/15/1977	29Aqu21	04/16/1978	06Leo14	08/14/1978	26Sag19
08/15/1977	29Leo44	12/17/1977	26Pis08	04/18/1978	00Vir37	08/16/1978	26Cap03
08/17/1977	26Vir10	12/19/1977	21Ari21	04/20/1978	26Vir12	08/18/1978	26Aqu13
08/19/1977	23Lib21	12/21/1977	15Tau38	04/22/1978	23Lib14	08/20/1978	25Pis33
08/21/1977	21Sco07	12/23/1977	09Gem27	04/24/1978	21Sco32	08/22/1978	23Ari18
08/23/1977	19Sag34	12/25/1977	03Can12	04/26/1978	20Sag36	08/24/1978	19Tau20
08/25/1977	18Cap15	12/27/1977	27Can04	04/28/1978	19Cap33	08/26/1978	13Gem59
08/27/1977	16Aqu45	12/29/1977	21Leo12	04/30/1978	17Aqu54	08/28/1978	07Can56
08/29/1977	14Pis21	12/31/1977	15Vir56			08/30/1978	01Leo37
08/31/1977	10Ari40						

Ephemeris Tables for the Moon

Date	Moon	Date	Moon	Date	Moon	Date	Moon
09/01/1978	25Leo34	01/01/1979	18Aqu12	05/01/1979	10Can48	09/02/1979	14Cap18
09/03/1978	20Vir00	01/03/1979	17Pis21	05/03/1979	04Leo58	09/04/1979	13Aqu37
09/05/1978	15Lib07	01/05/1979	14Ari55	05/05/1979	28Leo40	09/06/1979	13Pis52
09/07/1978	11Sco09	01/07/1979	11Tau08	05/07/1979	22Vir32	09/08/1979	14Ari01
09/09/1978	08Sag13	01/09/1979	06Gem22	05/09/1979	17Lib09	09/10/1979	12Tau55
09/11/1978	06Cap20	01/11/1979	00Can54	05/11/1979	12Sco59	09/12/1979	10Gem00
09/13/1978	05Aqu24	01/13/1979	24Can54	05/13/1979	10Sag00	09/14/1979	05Can28
09/15/1978	04Pis48	01/15/1979	18Leo37	05/15/1979	07Cap55	09/16/1979	29Can48
09/17/1978	03Ari37	01/17/1979	12Vir16	05/17/1979	06Aqu13	09/18/1979	23Leo31
09/19/1978	01Tau16	01/19/1979	06Lib13	05/19/1979	04Pis30	09/20/1979	17Vir03
09/21/1978	27Tau24	01/21/1979	01Sco08	05/21/1979	02Ari35	09/22/1979	10Lib51
09/23/1978	22Gem12	01/23/1979	27Sco38	05/23/1979	00Tau22	09/24/1979	05Sco10
09/25/1978	16Can08	01/25/1979	26Sag01	05/25/1979	27Tau28	09/26/1979	00Sag12
09/27/1978	09Leo51	01/27/1979	26Cap04	05/27/1979	23Gem40	09/28/1979	26Sag18
09/29/1978	03Vir59	01/29/1979	26Aqu33	05/29/1979	18Can45	09/30/1979	23Cap39
		01/31/1979	26Pis17	05/31/1979	12Leo51		
10/01/1978	28Vir48					10/02/1979	22Aqu22
10/03/1978	24Lib37	02/02/1979	24Ari21	06/02/1979	06Vir32	10/04/1979	22Pis10
10/05/1978	21Sco25	02/04/1979	20Tau40	06/04/1979	00Lib25	10/06/1979	22Ari09
10/07/1978	18Sag58	02/06/1979	15Gem43	06/06/1979	25Lib11	10/08/1979	21Tau10
10/09/1978	17Cap09	02/08/1979	09Can57	06/08/1979	21Sco20	10/10/1979	18Gem33
10/11/1978	15Aqu38	02/10/1979	03Leo43	06/10/1979	19Sag03	10/12/1979	14Can06
10/13/1978	14Pis04	02/12/1979	27Leo22	06/12/1979	17Cap49	10/14/1979	08Leo22
10/15/1978	12Ari07	02/14/1979	21Vir11	06/14/1979	16Aqu49	10/16/1979	02Vir02
10/17/1978	09Tau15	02/16/1979	15Lib25	06/16/1979	15Pis27	10/18/1979	25Vir38
10/19/1978	05Gem15	02/18/1979	10Sco27	06/18/1979	13Ari20	10/20/1979	19Lib46
10/21/1978	00Can04	02/20/1979	06Sag47	06/20/1979	10Tau27	10/22/1979	14Sco32
10/23/1978	24Can01	02/22/1979	04Cap46	06/22/1979	06Gem52	10/24/1979	10Sag07
10/25/1978	17Leo48	02/24/1979	04Aqu14	06/24/1979	02Can25	10/26/1979	06Cap35
10/27/1978	11Vir54	02/26/1979	04Pis31	06/26/1979	27Can03	10/28/1979	03Aqu53
10/29/1978	06Lib59	02/28/1979	04Ari22	06/28/1979	21Leo00	10/30/1979	02Pis07
10/31/1978	03Sco26			06/30/1979	14Vir35		
		03/02/1979	02Tau47			11/01/1979	01Ari06
11/02/1978	01Sag08	03/04/1979	29Tau28	07/02/1979	08Lib26	11/03/1979	00Tau25
11/04/1978	29Sag36	03/06/1979	24Gem37	07/04/1979	03Sco12	11/05/1979	29Tau10
11/06/1978	28Cap10	03/08/1979	18Can43	07/06/1979	29Sco27	11/07/1979	26Gem28
11/08/1978	26Aqu27	03/10/1979	12Leo24	07/08/1979	27Sag33	11/09/1979	22Can10
11/10/1978	24Pis12	03/12/1979	06Vir03	07/10/1979	26Cap53	11/11/1979	16Leo30
11/12/1978	21Ari18	03/14/1979	00Lib08	07/12/1979	26Aqu40	11/13/1979	10Vir07
11/14/1978	17Tau45	03/16/1979	24Lib51	07/14/1979	25Pis50	11/15/1979	03Lib51
11/16/1978	13Gem21	03/18/1979	20Sco21	07/16/1979	23Ari54	11/17/1979	28Lib12
11/18/1978	07Can58	03/20/1979	16Sag55	07/18/1979	20Tau45	11/19/1979	23Sco31
11/20/1978	01Leo54	03/22/1979	14Cap34	07/20/1979	16Gem33	11/21/1979	19Sag53
11/22/1978	25Leo35	03/24/1979	13Aqu21	07/22/1979	11Can31	11/23/1979	17Cap03
11/24/1978	19Vir36	03/26/1979	12Pis56	07/24/1979	05Leo46	11/25/1979	14Aqu40
11/26/1978	14Lib47	03/28/1979	12Ari18	07/26/1979	29Leo28	11/27/1979	12Pis44
11/28/1978	11Sco32	03/30/1979	10Tau43	07/28/1979	23Vir02	11/29/1979	11Ari03
11/30/1978	10Sag00			07/30/1979	16Lib54		
		04/01/1979	07Gem33			12/01/1979	09Tau31
12/02/1978	09Cap22	04/03/1979	02Can52	08/01/1979	11Sco34	12/03/1979	07Gem27
12/04/1978	08Aqu42	04/05/1979	27Can03	08/03/1979	07Sag46	12/05/1979	04Can22
12/06/1978	07Pis18	04/07/1979	20Leo40	08/05/1979	05Cap46	12/07/1979	29Can57
12/08/1978	04Ari41	04/09/1979	14Vir28	08/07/1979	05Aqu18	12/09/1979	24Leo16
12/10/1978	01Tau09	04/11/1979	08Lib52	08/09/1979	05Pis36	12/11/1979	17Vir58
12/12/1978	26Tau51	04/13/1979	04Sco07	08/11/1979	05Ari21	12/13/1979	11Lib39
12/14/1978	21Gem54	04/15/1979	00Sag22	08/13/1979	03Tau52	12/15/1979	06Sco09
12/16/1978	16Can15	04/17/1979	27Sag29	08/15/1979	00Gem42	12/17/1979	01Sag52
12/18/1978	10Leo02	04/19/1979	25Cap15	08/17/1979	26Gem11	12/19/1979	28Sag52
12/20/1978	03Vir40	04/21/1979	23Aqu36	08/19/1979	20Can46	12/21/1979	26Cap55
12/22/1978	27Vir38	04/23/1979	22Pis19	08/21/1979	14Leo39	12/23/1979	25Aqu22
12/24/1978	22Lib37	04/25/1979	20Ari55	08/23/1979	08Vir15	12/25/1979	23Pis43
12/26/1978	19Sco22	04/27/1979	18Tau47	08/25/1979	01Lib52	12/27/1979	21Ari47
12/28/1978	18Sag04	04/29/1979	15Gem27	08/27/1979	25Lib49	12/29/1979	19Tau27
12/30/1978	18Cap03			08/29/1979	20Sco36	12/31/1979	16Gem29
				08/31/1979	16Sag36		

Ephemeris Tables for the Moon

Date	Moon	Date	Moon	Date	Moon	Date	Moon
01/02/1980	12Can41	05/01/1980	24Sco39	09/02/1980	19Gem34	01/02/1981	28Sco07
01/04/1980	07Leo52	05/03/1980	19Sag43	09/04/1980	15Can59	01/04/1981	22Sag48
01/06/1980	02Vir07	05/05/1980	15Cap35	09/06/1980	11Leo16	01/06/1981	18Cap25
01/08/1980	25Vir45	05/07/1980	12Aqu22	09/08/1980	05Vir48	01/08/1981	14Aqu54
01/10/1980	19Lib26	05/09/1980	10Pis15	09/10/1980	29Vir49	01/10/1981	12Pis12
01/12/1980	13Sco56	05/11/1980	09Ari20	09/12/1980	23Lib30	01/12/1981	10Ari07
01/14/1980	09Sag40	05/13/1980	09Tau01	09/14/1980	17Sco15	01/14/1981	08Tau25
01/16/1980	07Cap04	05/15/1980	08Gem20	09/16/1980	11Sag26	01/16/1981	06Gem57
01/18/1980	05Aqu50	05/17/1980	06Can18	09/18/1980	06Cap33	01/18/1981	05Can11
01/20/1980	05Pis09	05/19/1980	02Leo28	09/20/1980	03Aqu06	01/20/1981	02Leo36
01/22/1980	04Ari17	05/21/1980	27Leo13	09/22/1980	01Pis33	01/22/1981	28Leo55
01/24/1980	02Tau36	05/23/1980	21Vir03	09/24/1980	01Ari30	01/24/1981	24Vir00
01/26/1980	29Tau52	05/25/1980	14Lib42	09/26/1980	01Tau55	01/26/1981	18Lib12
01/28/1980	26Gem12	05/27/1980	08Sco46	09/28/1980	01Gem35	01/28/1981	11Sco58
01/30/1980	21Can36	05/29/1980	03Sag37	09/30/1980	29Gem36	01/30/1981	05Sag55
		05/31/1980	29Sag19				
02/01/1980	16Leo15			10/02/1980	25Can48	02/01/1981	00Cap45
02/03/1980	10Vir16	06/02/1980	25Cap46	10/04/1980	20Leo43	02/03/1981	26Cap42
02/05/1980	03Lib52	06/04/1980	22Aqu58	10/06/1980	14Vir52	02/05/1981	23Aqu57
02/07/1980	27Lib39	06/06/1980	20Pis54	10/08/1980	08Lib38	02/07/1981	22Pis13
02/09/1980	21Sco58	06/08/1980	19Ari27	10/10/1980	02Sco20	02/09/1981	20Ari55
02/11/1980	17Sag36	06/10/1980	18Tau22	10/12/1980	26Sco09	02/11/1981	19Tau30
02/13/1980	14Cap52	06/12/1980	16Gem57	10/14/1980	20Sag27	02/13/1981	17Gem31
02/15/1980	13Aqu52	06/14/1980	14Can24	10/16/1980	15Cap27	02/15/1981	14Can52
02/17/1980	13Pis54	06/16/1980	10Leo26	10/18/1980	11Aqu43	02/17/1981	11Leo25
02/19/1980	13Ari48	06/18/1980	05Vir09	10/20/1980	09Pis52	02/19/1981	07Vir05
02/21/1980	12Tau42	06/20/1980	29Vir01	10/22/1980	09Ari37	02/21/1981	01Lib57
02/23/1980	10Gem07	06/22/1980	22Lib47	10/24/1980	10Tau15	02/23/1981	26Lib06
02/25/1980	06Can02	06/24/1980	16Sco59	10/26/1980	10Gem16	02/25/1981	19Sco51
02/27/1980	00Leo55	06/26/1980	12Sag09	10/28/1980	08Can39	02/27/1981	13Sag46
02/29/1980	25Leo06	06/28/1980	08Cap27	10/30/1980	05Leo02		
		06/30/1980	05Aqu39			03/01/1981	08Cap28
03/02/1980	18Vir49			11/01/1980	29Leo49	03/03/1981	04Aqu31
03/04/1980	12Lib29	07/02/1980	03Pis39	11/03/1980	23Vir48	03/05/1981	02Pis16
03/06/1980	06Sco19	07/04/1980	01Ari53	11/05/1980	17Lib30	03/07/1981	01Ari22
03/08/1980	00Sag41	07/06/1980	00Tau17	11/07/1980	11Sco14	03/09/1981	01Tau01
03/10/1980	26Sag07	07/08/1980	28Tau31	11/09/1980	05Sag19	03/11/1981	00Gem10
03/12/1980	23Cap04	07/10/1980	26Gem10	11/11/1980	29Sag53	03/13/1981	28Gem12
03/14/1980	21Aqu52	07/12/1980	22Can56	11/13/1980	25Cap04	03/15/1981	25Can04
03/16/1980	21Pis57	07/14/1980	18Leo30	11/15/1980	21Aqu19	03/17/1981	20Leo52
03/18/1980	22Ari20	07/16/1980	13Vir04	11/17/1980	19Pis00	03/19/1981	15Vir56
03/20/1980	21Tau51	07/18/1980	06Lib58	11/19/1980	18Ari11	03/21/1981	10Lib24
03/22/1980	19Gem34	07/20/1980	00Sco42	11/21/1980	18Tau22	03/23/1981	04Sco21
03/24/1980	15Can31	07/22/1980	24Sco59	11/23/1980	18Gem15	03/25/1981	28Sco07
03/26/1980	10Leo07	07/24/1980	20Sag19	11/25/1980	16Can50	03/27/1981	21Sag58
03/28/1980	04Vir01	07/26/1980	16Cap57	11/27/1980	13Leo25	03/29/1981	16Cap32
03/30/1980	27Vir39	07/28/1980	14Aqu56	11/29/1980	08Vir23	03/31/1981	12Aqu28
		07/30/1980	13Pis45				
04/01/1980	21Lib20	08/01/1980	12Ari40	12/01/1980	02Lib23	04/02/1981	10Pis13
04/03/1980	15Sco25	08/03/1980	11Tau15	12/03/1980	26Lib01	04/04/1981	09Ari43
04/05/1980	10Sag04	08/05/1980	09Gem04	12/05/1980	19Sco55	04/06/1981	10Tau05
04/07/1980	05Cap31	08/07/1980	05Can59	12/07/1980	14Sag21	04/08/1981	09Gem55
04/09/1980	02Aqu14	08/09/1980	01Leo55	12/09/1980	09Cap22	04/10/1981	08Can21
04/11/1980	00Pis31	08/11/1980	26Leo56	12/11/1980	05Aqu07	04/12/1981	05Leo07
04/13/1980	00Ari11	08/13/1980	21Vir16	12/13/1980	01Pis39	04/14/1981	00Vir31
04/15/1980	00Tau30	08/15/1980	15Lib03	12/15/1980	29Pis14	04/16/1981	25Vir08
04/17/1980	00Gem11	08/17/1980	08Sco48	12/17/1980	27Ari49	04/18/1981	19Lib15
04/19/1980	28Gem10	08/19/1980	03Sag02	12/19/1980	27Tau07	04/20/1981	13Sco05
04/21/1980	24Can18	08/21/1980	28Sag16	12/21/1980	26Gem21	04/22/1981	06Sag48
04/23/1980	18Leo55	08/23/1980	25Cap03	12/23/1980	24Can34	04/24/1981	00Cap45
04/25/1980	12Vir45	08/25/1980	23Aqu25	12/25/1980	21Leo10	04/26/1981	25Cap19
04/27/1980	06Lib19	08/27/1980	23Pis01	12/27/1980	16Vir19	04/28/1981	21Aqu01
04/29/1980	00Sco12	08/29/1980	22Ari48	12/29/1980	10Lib25	04/30/1981	18Pis35
		08/31/1980	21Tau49	12/31/1980	04Sco10		

Ephemeris Tables for the Moon

Date	Moon	Date	Moon	Date	Moon	Date	Moon
05/02/1981	18Ari00	09/01/1981	13Lib01	01/01/1982	19Pis49	05/01/1982	23Leo24
05/04/1981	18Tau30	09/03/1981	07Sco29	01/03/1982	16Ari36	05/03/1982	19Vir59
05/06/1981	18Gem48	09/05/1981	01Sag17	01/05/1982	14Tau53	05/05/1982	15Lib40
05/08/1981	17Can37	09/07/1981	25Sag03	01/07/1982	14Gem24	05/07/1982	10Sco37
05/10/1981	14Leo32	09/09/1981	19Cap30	01/09/1982	14Can20	05/09/1982	04Sag50
05/12/1981	09Vir55	09/11/1981	15Aqu09	01/11/1982	13Leo43	05/11/1982	28Sag36
05/14/1981	04Lib17	09/13/1981	12Pis21	01/13/1982	11Vir41	05/13/1982	22Cap13
05/16/1981	28Lib12	09/15/1981	10Ari50	01/15/1982	07Lib52	05/15/1982	16Aqu10
05/18/1981	21Sco57	09/17/1981	10Tau01	01/17/1982	02Sco39	05/17/1982	11Pis16
05/20/1981	15Sag45	09/19/1981	09Gem00	01/19/1982	26Sco33	05/19/1982	07Ari55
05/22/1981	09Cap58	09/21/1981	07Can08	01/21/1982	20Sag10	05/21/1982	06Tau28
05/24/1981	04Aqu42	09/23/1981	04Leo24	01/23/1982	14Cap03	05/23/1982	06Gem19
05/26/1981	00Pis30	09/25/1981	01Vir49	01/25/1982	08Aqu31	05/25/1982	06Can27
05/28/1981	27Pis51	09/27/1981	26Vir28	01/27/1982	03Pis52	05/27/1982	05Leo44
05/30/1981	26Ari47	09/29/1981	21Lib25	01/29/1982	00Ari00	05/29/1982	03Vir32
				01/31/1982	27Ari03	05/31/1982	29Vir58
06/01/1981	26Tau58	10/01/1981	15Sco38				
06/03/1981	27Gem06	10/03/1981	09Sag21	02/02/1982	25Tau05	06/02/1982	25Lib16
06/05/1981	26Can04	10/05/1981	03Cap04	02/04/1982	23Gem46	06/04/1982	19Sco43
06/07/1981	23Leo15	10/07/1981	27Cap24	02/06/1982	22Can52	06/06/1982	13Sag39
06/09/1981	18Vir43	10/09/1981	23Aqu00	02/08/1982	21Leo37	06/08/1982	07Cap16
06/11/1981	13Lib07	10/11/1981	20Pis26	02/10/1982	19Vir24	06/10/1982	00Aqu54
06/13/1981	06Sco59	10/13/1981	19Ari31	02/12/1982	15Lib43	06/12/1982	25Aqu00
06/15/1981	00Sag43	10/15/1981	19Tau34	02/14/1982	10Sco36	06/14/1982	20Pis04
06/17/1981	24Sag45	10/17/1981	19Gem13	02/16/1982	04Sag34	06/16/1982	16Ari33
06/19/1981	19Cap16	10/19/1981	17Can42	02/18/1982	28Sag13	06/18/1982	14Tau52
06/21/1981	14Aqu27	10/21/1981	14Leo45	02/20/1982	22Cap12	06/20/1982	14Gem41
06/23/1981	10Pis36	10/23/1981	10Vir37	02/22/1982	17Aqu04	06/22/1982	15Can03
06/25/1981	07Ari52	10/25/1981	05Lib43	02/24/1982	13Pis04	06/24/1982	14Leo43
06/27/1981	06Tau30	10/27/1981	00Sco10	02/26/1982	10Ari04	06/26/1982	12Vir55
06/29/1981	05Gem57	10/29/1981	24Sco09	02/28/1982	07Tau50	06/28/1982	09Lib30
		10/31/1981	17Sag49			06/30/1982	04Sco36
07/01/1981	05Can30			03/02/1982	05Gem58		
07/03/1981	04Leo14	11/02/1981	11Cap28	03/04/1982	04Can12	07/02/1982	28Sco49
07/05/1981	01Vir24	11/04/1981	05Aqu42	03/06/1982	02Leo25	07/04/1982	22Sag32
07/07/1981	27Vir02	11/06/1981	01Pis10	03/08/1982	00Vir16	07/06/1982	16Cap06
07/09/1981	21Lib28	11/08/1981	28Pis30	03/10/1982	27Vir30	07/08/1982	09Aqu56
07/11/1981	15Sco21	11/10/1981	27Ari37	03/12/1982	23Lib31	07/10/1982	04Pis18
07/13/1981	09Sag10	11/12/1981	28Tau03	03/14/1982	18Sco25	07/12/1982	29Pis35
07/15/1981	03Cap23	11/14/1981	28Gem19	03/16/1982	12Sag24	07/14/1982	26Ari01
07/17/1981	28Cap22	11/16/1981	27Can21	03/18/1982	06Cap01	07/16/1982	23Tau55
07/19/1981	24Aqu15	11/18/1981	24Leo37	03/20/1982	00Aqu04	07/18/1982	23Gem16
07/21/1981	21Pis00	11/20/1981	20Vir22	03/22/1982	25Aqu09	07/20/1982	23Can22
07/23/1981	18Ari39	11/22/1981	15Lib04	03/24/1982	21Pis39	07/22/1982	23Leo06
07/25/1981	17Tau01	11/24/1981	09Sco09	03/26/1982	19Ari31	07/24/1982	21Vir36
07/27/1981	15Gem46	11/26/1981	02Sag58	03/28/1982	18Tau09	07/26/1982	18Lib19
07/29/1981	14Can28	11/28/1981	26Sag35	03/30/1982	16Gem52	07/28/1982	13Sco26
07/31/1981	12Leo32	11/30/1981	20Cap24			07/30/1982	07Sag32
				04/01/1982	15Can09		
08/02/1981	09Vir27	12/02/1981	14Aqu43	04/03/1982	12Leo48	08/01/1982	01Cap11
08/04/1981	05Lib00	12/04/1981	10Pis03	04/05/1982	09Vir55	08/03/1982	24Cap53
08/06/1981	29Lib30	12/06/1981	07Ari01	04/07/1982	06Lib17	08/05/1982	18Aqu59
08/08/1981	23Sco24	12/08/1981	05Tau48	04/09/1982	01Sco47	08/07/1982	13Pis51
08/10/1981	17Sag13	12/10/1981	06Gem01	04/11/1982	26Sco25	08/09/1982	09Ari33
08/12/1981	11Cap38	12/12/1981	06Can29	04/13/1982	20Sag19	08/11/1982	06Tau10
08/14/1981	07Aqu03	12/14/1981	05Leo53	04/15/1982	13Cap57	08/13/1982	03Gem53
08/16/1981	03Pis37	12/16/1981	03Vir34	04/17/1982	07Aqu55	08/15/1982	02Can38
08/18/1981	01Ari15	12/18/1981	29Vir30	04/19/1982	03Pis02	08/17/1982	02Leo02
08/20/1981	29Ari34	12/20/1981	24Lib07	04/21/1982	29Pis50	08/19/1982	01Vir25
08/22/1981	28Tau01	12/22/1981	18Sco03	04/23/1982	28Ari10	08/21/1982	29Vir48
08/24/1981	26Gem19	12/24/1981	11Sag43	04/25/1982	27Tau39	08/23/1982	26Lib34
08/26/1981	24Can09	12/26/1981	05Cap28	04/27/1982	27Gem09	08/25/1982	21Sco47
08/28/1981	21Leo21	12/28/1981	29Cap31	04/29/1982	25Can48	08/27/1982	15Sag49
08/30/1981	17Vir43	12/30/1981	24Aqu13			08/29/1982	09Cap31
						08/31/1982	03Aqu18

Ephemeris Tables for the Moon

Date	Moon	Date	Moon	Date	Moon	Date	Moon
09/02/1982	27Aqu48	01/02/1983	24Leo00	05/02/1983	12Cap34	09/01/1983	21Gem22
09/04/1982	23Pis18	01/04/1983	22Vir40	05/04/1983	06Aqu21	09/03/1983	19Can43
09/06/1982	19Ari38	01/06/1983	19Lib38	05/06/1983	00Pis08	09/05/1983	19Leo28
09/08/1982	16Tau48	01/08/1983	15Sco04	05/08/1983	24Pis37	09/07/1983	19Vir50
09/10/1982	14Gem32	01/10/1983	09Sag25	05/10/1983	20Ari13	09/09/1983	19Lib27
09/12/1982	12Can50	01/12/1983	03Cap14	05/12/1983	17Tau15	09/11/1983	17Sco16
09/14/1982	11Leo30	01/14/1983	26Cap51	05/14/1983	15Gem15	09/13/1983	13Sag14
09/16/1982	10Vir05	01/16/1983	20Aqu30	05/16/1983	13Can49	09/15/1983	07Cap46
09/18/1982	07Lib59	01/18/1983	14Pis34	05/18/1983	12Leo31	09/17/1983	01Aqu34
09/20/1982	04Sco36	01/20/1983	09Ari19	05/20/1983	10Vir46	09/19/1983	25Aqu16
09/22/1982	29Sco43	01/22/1983	05Tau10	05/22/1983	08Lib29	09/21/1983	19Pis16
09/24/1982	23Sag48	01/24/1983	02Gem31	05/24/1983	05Sco22	09/23/1983	13Ari43
09/26/1982	17Cap27	01/26/1983	01Can32	05/26/1983	01Sag21	09/25/1983	08Tau51
09/28/1982	11Aqu19	01/28/1983	01Leo51	05/28/1983	26Sag22	09/27/1983	04Gem42
09/30/1982	06Pis09	01/30/1983	02Vir08	05/30/1983	20Cap33	09/29/1983	01Can27
10/02/1982	02Ari10	02/01/1983	01Lib19	06/01/1983	14Aqu19	10/01/1983	29Can27
10/04/1982	29Ari19	02/03/1983	28Lib39	06/03/1983	08Pis09	10/03/1983	28Leo37
10/06/1982	27Tau16	02/05/1983	24Sco06	06/05/1983	02Ari35	10/05/1983	28Vir21
10/08/1982	25Gem27	02/07/1983	18Sag22	06/07/1983	28Ari17	10/07/1983	27Lib33
10/10/1982	23Can43	02/09/1983	11Cap59	06/09/1983	25Tau32	10/09/1983	25Sco19
10/12/1982	21Leo45	02/11/1983	05Aqu34	06/11/1983	24Gem09	10/11/1983	21Sag25
10/14/1982	19Vir31	02/13/1983	29Aqu30	06/13/1983	23Can37	10/13/1983	16Cap01
10/16/1982	16Lib39	02/15/1983	23Pis54	06/15/1983	22Leo59	10/15/1983	09Aqu52
10/18/1982	12Sco42	02/17/1983	19Ari01	06/17/1983	21Vir33	10/17/1983	03Pis39
10/20/1982	07Sag39	02/19/1983	14Tau59	06/19/1983	18Lib56	10/19/1983	27Pis49
10/22/1982	01Cap38	02/21/1983	12Gem02	06/21/1983	15Sco10	10/21/1983	22Ari41
10/24/1982	25Cap15	02/23/1983	10Can30	06/23/1983	10Sag30	10/23/1983	18Tau23
10/26/1982	19Aqu10	02/25/1983	10Leo08	06/25/1983	04Cap59	10/25/1983	14Gem54
10/28/1982	14Pis01	02/27/1983	10Vir04	06/27/1983	28Cap57	10/27/1983	12Can07
10/30/1982	10Ari22			06/29/1983	22Aqu40	10/29/1983	10Leo03
		03/01/1983	09Lib16			10/31/1983	08Vir39
11/01/1982	08Tau12	03/03/1983	06Sco48	07/01/1983	16Pis28		
11/03/1982	06Gem59	03/05/1983	02Sag30	07/03/1983	10Ari55	11/02/1983	07Lib29
11/05/1982	06Can01	03/07/1983	26Sag46	07/05/1983	06Tau30	11/04/1983	05Sco52
11/07/1982	04Leo37	03/09/1983	20Cap26	07/07/1983	03Gem39	11/06/1983	03Sag14
11/09/1982	02Vir27	03/11/1983	14Aqu06	07/09/1983	02Can34	11/08/1983	29Sag12
11/11/1982	29Vir33	03/13/1983	08Pis14	07/11/1983	02Leo33	11/10/1983	23Cap54
11/13/1982	25Lib51	03/15/1983	03Ari09	07/13/1983	02Vir38	11/12/1983	17Aqu46
11/15/1982	21Sco18	03/17/1983	28Ari54	07/15/1983	01Lib40	11/14/1983	11Pis34
11/17/1982	15Sag49	03/19/1983	25Tau19	07/17/1983	29Lib04	11/16/1983	05Ari49
11/19/1982	09Cap42	03/21/1983	22Gem33	07/19/1983	25Sco03	11/18/1983	00Tau59
11/21/1982	03Aqu17	03/23/1983	20Can36	07/21/1983	19Sag49	11/20/1983	27Tau19
11/23/1982	27Aqu06	03/25/1983	19Leo28	07/23/1983	13Cap54	11/22/1983	24Gem41
11/25/1982	21Pis54	03/27/1983	18Vir40	07/25/1983	07Aqu40	11/24/1983	22Can42
11/27/1982	18Ari12	03/29/1983	17Lib17	07/27/1983	01Pis23	11/26/1983	21Leo06
11/29/1982	16Tau14	03/31/1983	14Sco37	07/29/1983	25Pis19	11/28/1983	19Vir28
				07/31/1983	19Ari44	11/30/1983	17Lib29
12/01/1982	15Gem40	04/02/1983	10Sag21				
12/03/1982	15Can33	04/04/1983	04Cap43	08/02/1983	15Tau12	12/02/1983	14Sco57
12/05/1982	14Leo51	04/06/1983	28Cap30	08/04/1983	12Gem10	12/04/1983	11Sag33
12/07/1982	13Vir00	04/08/1983	22Aqu13	08/06/1983	10Can52	12/06/1983	07Cap04
12/09/1982	09Lib47	04/10/1983	16Pis37	08/08/1983	11Leo01	12/08/1983	01Aqu40
12/11/1982	05Sco28	04/12/1983	11Ari56	08/10/1983	11Vir30	12/10/1983	25Aqu34
12/13/1982	00Sag17	04/14/1983	08Tau22	08/12/1983	10Lib56	12/12/1983	19Pis23
12/15/1982	24Sag23	04/16/1983	05Gem36	08/14/1983	08Sco36	12/14/1983	13Ari32
12/17/1982	18Cap08	04/18/1983	03Can21	08/16/1983	04Sag27	12/16/1983	08Tau45
12/19/1982	11Aqu41	04/20/1983	01Leo30	08/18/1983	28Sag58	12/18/1983	05Gem28
12/21/1982	05Pis31	04/22/1983	29Leo54	08/20/1983	22Cap52	12/20/1983	03Can32
12/23/1982	00Ari12	04/24/1983	28Vir12	08/22/1983	16Aqu31	12/22/1983	02Leo36
12/25/1982	26Ari15	04/26/1983	25Lib59	08/24/1983	10Pis19	12/24/1983	01Vir46
12/27/1982	24Tau06	04/28/1983	22Sco43	08/26/1983	04Ari28	12/26/1983	00Lib24
12/29/1982	23Gem33	04/30/1983	18Sag10	08/28/1983	29Ari07	12/28/1983	28Lib04
12/31/1982	23Can57			08/30/1983	24Tau40	12/30/1983	24Sco40

Ephemeris Tables for the Moon

Date	Moon	Date	Moon	Date	Moon	Date	Moon
01/01/1984	20Sag28	05/02/1984	27Tau51	09/01/1984	27Sco27	01/01/1985	05Tau39
01/03/1984	15Cap28	05/04/1984	23Gem43	09/03/1984	24Sag08	01/03/1985	00Gem00
01/05/1984	09Aqu47	05/06/1984	20Can29	09/05/1984	19Cap32	01/05/1985	25Gem26
01/07/1984	03Pis40	05/08/1984	18Leo10	09/07/1984	14Aqu10	01/07/1985	22Can15
01/09/1984	27Pis24	05/10/1984	16Vir43	09/09/1984	08Pis18	01/09/1985	20Leo09
01/11/1984	21Ari26	05/12/1984	15Lib53	09/11/1984	02Ari03	01/11/1985	18Vir34
01/13/1984	16Tau30	05/14/1984	14Sco46	09/13/1984	25Ari45	01/13/1985	17Lib00
01/15/1984	13Gem09	05/16/1984	12Sag47	09/15/1984	19Tau40	01/15/1985	15Sco04
01/17/1984	11Can34	05/18/1984	09Cap26	09/17/1984	14Gem13	01/17/1985	12Sag43
01/19/1984	11Leo22	05/20/1984	04Aqu40	09/19/1984	10Can06	01/19/1985	09Cap47
01/21/1984	11Vir27	05/22/1984	28Aqu56	09/21/1984	07Leo48	01/21/1985	06Aqu09
01/23/1984	10Lib45	05/24/1984	22Pis43	09/23/1984	07Vir18	01/23/1985	01Pis34
01/25/1984	08Sco27	05/26/1984	16Ari40	09/25/1984	07Lib49	01/25/1985	25Pis57
01/27/1984	04Sag43	05/28/1984	11Tau16	09/27/1984	08Sco01	01/27/1985	19Ari43
01/29/1984	29Sag54	05/30/1984	06Gem48	09/29/1984	06Sag44	01/29/1985	13Tau24
01/31/1984	24Cap21					01/31/1985	07Gem40
		06/01/1984	03Can25	10/01/1984	03Cap34		
02/02/1984	18Aqu24	06/03/1984	00Leo58	10/03/1984	28Cap56	02/02/1985	03Can18
02/04/1984	12Pis10	06/05/1984	29Leo07	10/05/1984	23Aqu20	02/04/1985	00Leo33
02/06/1984	05Ari54	06/07/1984	27Vir36	10/07/1984	17Pis12	02/06/1985	29Leo17
02/08/1984	29Ari57	06/09/1984	26Lib01	10/09/1984	10Ari55	02/08/1985	28Vir40
02/10/1984	24Tau47	06/11/1984	23Sco59	10/11/1984	04Tau44	02/10/1985	27Lib41
02/12/1984	21Gem09	06/13/1984	21Sag14	10/13/1984	28Tau51	02/12/1985	25Sco52
02/14/1984	19Can27	06/15/1984	17Cap28	10/15/1984	23Gem39	02/14/1985	23Sag04
02/16/1984	19Leo26	06/17/1984	12Aqu36	10/17/1984	19Can33	02/16/1985	19Cap24
02/18/1984	20Vir08	06/19/1984	06Pis51	10/19/1984	16Leo55	02/18/1985	15Aqu03
02/20/1984	19Lib58	06/21/1984	00Ari40	10/21/1984	15Vir57	02/20/1985	09Pis57
02/22/1984	18Sco04	06/23/1984	24Ari38	10/23/1984	16Lib00	02/22/1985	04Ari08
02/24/1984	14Sag22	06/25/1984	19Tau19	10/25/1984	16Sco06	02/24/1985	27Ari47
02/26/1984	09Cap19	06/27/1984	15Gem16	10/27/1984	15Sag01	02/26/1985	21Tau25
02/28/1984	03Aqu30	06/29/1984	12Can37	10/29/1984	12Cap10	02/28/1985	15Gem39
				10/31/1984	07Aqu45		
03/01/1984	27Aqu16	07/01/1984	11Leo02			03/02/1985	11Can07
03/03/1984	21Pis02	07/03/1984	09Vir57	11/02/1984	02Pis04	03/04/1985	08Leo28
03/05/1984	14Ari52	07/05/1984	08Lib37	11/04/1984	25Pis51	03/06/1985	07Vir37
03/07/1984	09Tau03	07/07/1984	06Sco39	11/06/1984	19Ari34	03/08/1985	07Lib40
03/09/1984	03Gem57	07/09/1984	03Sag54	11/08/1984	13Tau36	03/10/1985	07Sco30
03/11/1984	00Can06	07/11/1984	00Cap19	11/10/1984	08Gem10	03/12/1985	06Sag10
03/13/1984	27Can58	07/13/1984	26Cap00	11/12/1984	03Can27	03/14/1985	03Cap21
03/15/1984	27Leo39	07/15/1984	20Aqu48	11/14/1984	29Can42	03/16/1985	29Cap21
03/17/1984	28Vir13	07/17/1984	14Pis54	11/16/1984	27Leo01	03/18/1985	24Aqu27
03/19/1984	28Lib16	07/19/1984	08Ari43	11/18/1984	25Vir27	03/20/1985	18Pis49
03/21/1984	26Sco46	07/21/1984	02Tau35	11/20/1984	24Lib45	03/22/1985	12Ari43
03/23/1984	23Sag16	07/23/1984	27Tau18	11/22/1984	24Sco11	03/24/1985	06Tau17
03/25/1984	18Cap17	07/25/1984	23Gem21	11/24/1984	22Sag50	03/26/1985	00Gem00
03/27/1984	12Aqu23	07/27/1984	21Can10	11/26/1984	20Cap08	03/28/1985	24Gem10
03/29/1984	06Pis06	07/29/1984	20Leo25	11/28/1984	15Aqu51	03/30/1985	19Can31
03/31/1984	29Pis53	07/31/1984	20Vir07	11/30/1984	10Pis16		
						04/01/1985	16Leo42
04/02/1984	23Ari57	08/02/1984	19Lib19	12/02/1984	04Ari04	04/03/1985	15Vir40
04/04/1984	18Tau30	08/04/1984	17Sco20	12/04/1984	27Ari47	04/05/1985	15Lib57
04/06/1984	13Gem43	08/06/1984	14Sag04	12/06/1984	22Tau04	04/07/1985	16Sco13
04/08/1984	09Can58	08/08/1984	09Cap54	12/08/1984	17Gem07	04/09/1985	15Sag27
04/10/1984	07Leo37	08/10/1984	04Aqu58	12/10/1984	13Can08	04/11/1985	13Cap01
04/12/1984	06Vir39	08/12/1984	29Aqu23	12/12/1984	10Leo09	04/13/1985	08Aqu58
04/14/1984	06Lib36	08/14/1984	23Pis20	12/14/1984	07Vir47	04/15/1985	03Pis49
04/16/1984	06Sco19	08/16/1984	17Ari02	12/16/1984	06Lib00	04/17/1985	27Pis54
04/18/1984	04Sag46	08/18/1984	10Tau52	12/18/1984	04Sco27	04/19/1985	21Ari31
04/20/1984	01Cap31	08/20/1984	05Gem28	12/20/1984	02Sag57	04/21/1985	15Tau08
04/22/1984	26Cap42	08/22/1984	01Can28	12/22/1984	00Cap57	04/23/1985	08Gem58
04/24/1984	20Aqu50	08/24/1984	29Can26	12/24/1984	27Cap54	04/25/1985	03Can21
04/26/1984	14Pis37	08/26/1984	29Leo01	12/26/1984	23Aqu36	04/27/1985	28Can48
04/28/1984	08Ari28	08/28/1984	29Vir24	12/28/1984	18Pis09	04/29/1985	25Leo42
04/30/1984	02Tau47	08/30/1984	29Lib12	12/30/1984	11Ari54		

Ephemeris Tables for the Moon

Date	Moon	Date	Moon	Date	Moon	Date	Moon
05/01/1985	24Vir16	09/02/1985	15Ari19	01/02/1986	25Vir03	05/02/1986	28Aqu39
05/03/1985	24Lib09	09/04/1985	09Tau08	01/04/1986	22Lib31	05/04/1986	24Pis16
05/05/1985	24Sco23	09/06/1985	02Gem43	01/06/1986	21Sco00	05/06/1986	18Ari57
05/07/1985	23Sag57	09/08/1985	26Gem50	01/08/1986	20Sag20	05/08/1986	13Tau00
05/09/1985	21Cap49	09/10/1985	22Can06	01/10/1986	19Cap45	05/10/1986	06Gem40
05/11/1985	18Aqu01	09/12/1985	18Leo57	01/12/1986	18Aqu14	05/12/1986	00Can20
05/13/1985	12Pis49	09/14/1985	17Vir26	01/14/1986	15Pis05	05/14/1986	24Can19
05/15/1985	06Ari42	09/16/1985	16Lib53	01/16/1986	10Ari17	05/16/1986	18Leo57
05/17/1985	00Tau19	09/18/1985	16Sco18	01/18/1986	04Tau20	05/18/1986	14Vir52
05/19/1985	23Tau58	09/20/1985	15Sag01	01/20/1986	27Tau54	05/20/1986	12Lib25
05/21/1985	18Gem07	09/22/1985	12Cap38	01/22/1986	21Gem46	05/22/1986	11Sco45
05/23/1985	12Can59	09/24/1985	09Aqu12	01/24/1986	16Can23	05/24/1986	12Sag06
05/25/1985	08Leo43	09/26/1985	04Pis49	01/26/1986	11Leo57	05/26/1986	12Cap17
05/27/1985	05Vir37	09/28/1985	29Pis39	01/28/1986	08Vir27	05/28/1986	11Aqu15
05/29/1985	03Lib46	09/30/1985	23Ari46	01/30/1986	05Lib38	05/30/1986	08Pis19
05/31/1985	03Sco00						
		10/02/1985	17Tau25	02/01/1986	03Sco16	06/01/1986	03Ari45
06/02/1985	02Sag47	10/04/1985	11Gem01	02/03/1986	01Sag27	06/03/1986	28Ari07
06/04/1985	02Cap04	10/06/1985	05Can07	02/05/1986	29Sag57	06/05/1986	21Tau55
06/06/1985	00Aqu02	10/08/1985	00Leo13	02/07/1986	28Cap27	06/07/1986	15Gem33
06/08/1985	26Aqu22	10/10/1985	27Leo00	02/09/1986	26Aqu17	06/09/1986	09Can16
06/10/1985	21Pis15	10/12/1985	25Vir35	02/11/1986	22Pis50	06/11/1986	03Leo27
06/12/1985	15Ari10	10/14/1985	25Lib25	02/13/1986	18Ari03	06/13/1986	28Leo16
06/14/1985	08Tau45	10/16/1985	25Sco35	02/15/1986	12Tau07	06/15/1986	24Vir04
06/16/1985	02Gem38	10/18/1985	24Sag53	02/17/1986	05Gem46	06/17/1986	21Lib21
06/18/1985	27Gem12	10/20/1985	22Cap46	02/19/1986	29Gem38	06/19/1986	20Sco19
06/20/1985	22Can37	10/22/1985	19Aqu09	02/21/1986	24Can27	06/21/1986	20Sag27
06/22/1985	19Leo01	10/24/1985	14Pis17	02/23/1986	20Leo30	06/23/1986	20Cap48
06/24/1985	16Vir15	10/26/1985	08Ari40	02/25/1986	17Vir43	06/25/1986	19Aqu58
06/26/1985	14Lib11	10/28/1985	02Tau27	02/27/1986	15Lib46	06/27/1986	17Pis15
06/28/1985	12Sco49	10/30/1985	26Tau01			06/29/1986	12Ari45
06/30/1985	11Sag47			03/01/1986	14Sco08		
		11/01/1985	19Gem46	03/03/1986	12Sag25	07/01/1986	07Tau02
07/02/1985	10Cap27	11/03/1985	13Can55	03/05/1986	10Cap30	07/03/1986	00Gem42
07/04/1985	08Aqu10	11/05/1985	09Leo00	03/07/1986	08Aqu09	7/05/1986	24Gem22
07/06/1985	04Pis25	11/07/1985	05Vir27	03/09/1986	05Pis04	07/07/1986	18Can19
07/08/1985	29Pis18	11/09/1985	03Lib41	03/11/1986	01Ari01	07/09/1986	12Leo52
07/10/1985	23Ari13	11/11/1985	03Sco27	03/13/1986	25Ari54	07/11/1986	08Vir01
07/12/1985	16Tau51	11/13/1985	03Sag50	03/15/1986	19Tau55	07/13/1986	04Lib03
07/14/1985	10Gem57	11/15/1985	03Cap43	03/17/1986	13Gem35	07/15/1986	01Sco12
07/16/1985	05Can52	11/17/1985	02Aqu04	03/19/1986	07Can27	07/17/1986	29Sco39
07/18/1985	02Leo00	11/19/1985	28Aqu33	03/21/1986	02Leo18	07/19/1986	29Sag18
07/20/1985	29Leo07	11/21/1985	23Pis33	03/23/1986	28Leo29	07/21/1986	29Cap10
07/22/1985	26Vir58	11/23/1985	17Ari36	03/25/1986	26Vir11	07/23/1986	28Aqu14
07/24/1985	25Lib09	11/25/1985	11Tau12	03/27/1986	25Lib06	07/25/1986	25Pis36
07/26/1985	23Sco23	11/27/1985	04Gem51	03/29/1986	24Sco19	07/27/1986	21Ari09
07/28/1985	21Sag37	11/29/1985	28Gem48	03/31/1986	23Sag13	07/29/1986	15Tau28
07/30/1985	19Cap30					07/31/1986	09Gem12
		12/01/1985	23Can15	04/02/1986	21Cap16		
08/01/1985	16Aqu33	12/03/1985	18Leo30	04/04/1986	18Aqu24	08/02/1986	02Can57
08/03/1985	12Pis30	12/05/1985	14Vir48	04/06/1986	14Pis34	08/04/1986	27Can12
08/05/1985	07Ari15	12/07/1985	12Lib35	04/08/1986	09Ari45	08/06/1986	22Leo10
08/07/1985	01Tau07	12/09/1985	11Sco43	04/10/1986	04Tau13	08/08/1986	17Vir53
08/09/1985	24Tau47	12/11/1985	11Sag49	04/12/1986	28Tau06	08/10/1986	14Lib24
08/11/1985	18Gem55	12/13/1985	11Cap45	04/14/1986	21Gem43	08/12/1986	11Sco44
08/13/1985	14Can06	12/15/1985	10Aqu22	04/16/1986	15Can37	08/14/1986	09Sag57
08/15/1985	10Leo45	12/17/1985	07Pis10	04/18/1986	10Leo21	08/16/1986	08Cap53
08/17/1985	08Vir42	12/19/1985	02Ari13	04/20/1986	06Vir25	08/18/1986	07Aqu59
08/19/1985	07Lib22	12/21/1985	26Ari11	04/22/1986	04Lib15	08/20/1986	06Pis31
08/21/1985	06Sco03	12/23/1985	19Tau46	04/24/1986	03Sco34	08/22/1986	03Ari36
08/23/1985	04Sag18	12/25/1985	13Gem29	04/26/1986	03Sag33	08/24/1986	29Ari10
08/25/1985	02Cap04	12/27/1985	07Can46	04/28/1986	03Cap12	08/26/1986	23Tau32
08/27/1985	29Cap09	12/29/1985	02Leo47	04/30/1986	01Aqu40	08/28/1986	17Gem17
08/29/1985	25Aqu29	12/31/1985	28Leo30			08/30/1986	11Can09
08/31/1985	20Pis54						

Ephemeris Tables for the Moon

Date	Moon	Date	Moon	Date	Moon	Date	Moon
09/01/1986	05Leo36	01/01/1987	00Aqu01	05/01/1987	20Gem06	09/02/1987	26Sag58
09/03/1986	01Vir01	01/03/1987	29Aqu37	05/03/1987	14Can07	09/04/1987	26Cap04
09/05/1986	27Vir27	01/05/1987	27Pis20	05/05/1987	07Leo51	09/06/1987	25Aqu52
09/07/1986	24Lib41	01/07/1987	23Ari09	05/07/1987	01Vir58	09/08/1987	25Pis24
09/09/1986	22Sco34	01/09/1987	17Tau39	05/09/1987	27Vir03	09/10/1987	23Ari48
09/11/1986	20Sag51	01/11/1987	11Gem33	05/11/1987	23Lib34	09/12/1987	20Tau27
09/13/1986	19Cap15	01/13/1987	05Can18	05/13/1987	21Sco44	09/14/1987	15Gem36
09/15/1986	17Aqu34	01/15/1987	29Can06	05/15/1987	21Sag00	09/16/1987	09Can46
09/17/1986	15Pis10	01/17/1987	23Leo16	05/17/1987	20Cap25	09/18/1987	03Leo31
09/19/1986	11Ari40	01/19/1987	17Vir54	05/19/1987	19Aqu14	09/20/1987	27Leo24
09/21/1986	07Tau01	01/21/1987	13Lib15	05/21/1987	16Pis53	09/22/1987	21Vir43
09/23/1986	01Gem23	01/23/1987	09Sco50	05/23/1987	13Ari28	09/24/1987	16Lib51
09/25/1986	25Gem12	01/25/1987	08Sag03	05/25/1987	09Tau11	09/26/1987	12Sco51
09/27/1986	19Can02	01/27/1987	07Cap42	05/27/1987	04Gem07	09/28/1987	09Sag43
09/29/1986	13Leo36	01/29/1987	08Aqu01	05/29/1987	28Gem31	09/30/1987	07Cap32
		01/31/1987	07Pis36	05/31/1987	22Can22		
10/01/1986	09Vir17					10/02/1987	06Aqu06
10/03/1986	06Lib16	02/02/1987	05Ari34	06/02/1987	16Leo06	10/04/1987	05Pis01
10/05/1986	04Sco24	02/04/1987	01Tau38	06/04/1987	10Vir06	10/06/1987	03Ari48
10/07/1986	03Sag08	02/06/1987	26Tau14	06/06/1987	05Lib06	10/08/1987	01Tau44
10/09/1986	01Cap51	02/08/1987	20Gem10	06/08/1987	01Sco39	10/10/1987	28Tau20
10/11/1986	00Aqu09	02/10/1987	13Can52	06/10/1987	00Sag03	10/12/1987	23Gem37
10/13/1986	27Aqu43	02/12/1987	07Leo49	06/12/1987	29Sag56	10/14/1987	17Can50
10/15/1986	24Pis24	02/14/1987	02Vir23	06/14/1987	00Aqu08	10/16/1987	11Leo33
10/17/1986	20Ari13	02/16/1987	27Vir29	06/16/1987	29Aqu25	10/18/1987	05Vir28
10/19/1986	15Tau08	02/18/1987	23Lib22	06/18/1987	27Pis13	10/20/1987	00Lib03
10/21/1986	09Gem24	02/20/1987	20Sco07	06/20/1987	23Ari31	10/22/1987	25Lib48
10/23/1986	03Can09	02/22/1987	18Sag03	06/22/1987	18Tau43	10/24/1987	22Sco35
10/25/1986	26Can57	02/24/1987	17Cap02	06/24/1987	13Gem15	10/26/1987	20Sag19
10/27/1986	21Leo27	02/26/1987	16Aqu29	06/26/1987	07Can18	10/28/1987	18Cap33
10/29/1986	17Vir05	02/28/1987	15Pis33	06/28/1987	01Leo01	10/30/1987	16Aqu51
10/31/1986	14Lib22			06/30/1987	24Leo44		
		03/02/1987	13Ari21			11/01/1987	15Pis03
11/02/1986	13Sco07	03/04/1987	09Tau30	07/02/1987	18Vir45	11/03/1987	12Ari51
11/04/1986	12Sag48	03/06/1987	04Gem19	07/04/1987	13Lib42	11/05/1987	10Tau03
11/06/1986	12Cap20	03/08/1987	28Gem18	07/06/1987	10Sco04	11/07/1987	06Gem19
11/08/1986	10Aqu51	03/10/1987	22Can02	07/08/1987	08Sag23	11/09/1987	01Can26
11/10/1986	08Pis06	03/12/1987	16Leo10	07/10/1987	08Cap26	11/11/1987	25Can39
11/12/1986	04Ari09	03/14/1987	11Vir01	07/12/1987	08Aqu58	11/13/1987	19Leo23
11/14/1986	29Ari14	03/16/1987	06Lib47	07/14/1987	08Pis46	11/15/1987	13Vir13
11/16/1986	23Tau43	03/18/1987	03Sco24	07/16/1987	06Ari52	11/17/1987	07Lib57
11/18/1986	17Gem45	03/20/1987	00Sag48	07/18/1987	03Tau09	11/19/1987	04Sco01
11/20/1986	11Can27	03/22/1987	28Sag56	07/20/1987	28Tau11	11/21/1987	01Sag34
11/22/1986	05Leo16	03/24/1987	27Cap24	07/22/1987	22Gem24	11/23/1987	00Cap16
11/24/1986	29Leo37	03/26/1987	26Aqu00	07/24/1987	16Can15	11/25/1987	29Cap16
11/26/1986	25Vir01	03/28/1987	24Pis08	07/26/1987	09Leo57	11/27/1987	27Aqu52
11/28/1986	22Lib10	03/30/1987	21Ari18	07/28/1987	03Vir43	11/29/1987	25Pis39
11/30/1986	21Sco10			07/30/1987	27Vir57		
		04/01/1987	17Tau18			12/01/1987	22Ari40
12/02/1986	21Sag26	04/03/1987	12Gem06	08/01/1987	22Lib57	12/03/1987	19Tau06
12/04/1986	21Cap42	04/05/1987	06Can10	08/03/1987	19Sco13	12/05/1987	14Gem43
12/06/1986	20Aqu49	04/07/1987	29Can58	08/05/1987	17Sag16	12/07/1987	09Can34
12/08/1986	18Pis10	04/09/1987	24Leo04	08/07/1987	16Cap57	12/09/1987	03Leo39
12/10/1986	13Ari51	04/11/1987	19Vir09	08/09/1987	17Aqu24	12/11/1987	27Leo18
12/12/1986	08Tau33	04/13/1987	15Lib26	08/11/1987	17Pis16	12/13/1987	21Vir05
12/14/1986	02Gem39	04/15/1987	12Sco54	08/13/1987	15Ari37	12/15/1987	15Lib39
12/16/1986	26Gem26	04/17/1987	11Sag15	08/15/1987	12Tau10	12/17/1987	11Sco48
12/18/1986	20Can12	04/19/1987	09Cap55	08/17/1987	07Gem10	12/19/1987	09Sag47
12/20/1986	14Leo05	04/21/1987	08Aqu21	08/19/1987	01Can19	12/21/1987	09Cap10
12/22/1986	08Vir27	04/23/1987	06Pis18	08/21/1987	25Can06	12/23/1987	09Aqu04
12/24/1986	03Lib43	04/25/1987	03Ari32	08/23/1987	18Leo49	12/25/1987	08Pis18
12/26/1986	00Sco28	04/27/1987	29Ari57	08/25/1987	12Vir52	12/27/1987	06Ari12
12/28/1986	29Sco10	04/29/1987	25Tau26	08/27/1987	07Lib27	12/29/1987	02Tau57
12/30/1986	29Sag25			08/29/1987	02Sco46	12/31/1987	28Tau40
				08/31/1987	29Sco13		

Ephemeris Tables for the Moon

Date	Moon	Date	Moon	Date	Moon	Date	Moon
01/02/1988	23Gem42	05/01/1988	05Sco30	09/02/1988	02Gem06	01/02/1989	07Sco21
01/04/1988	18Can05	05/03/1988	01Sag45	09/04/1988	28Gem07	01/04/1989	02Sag34
01/06/1988	12Leo00	05/05/1988	28Sag53	09/06/1988	22Can49	01/06/1989	29Sag17
01/08/1988	05Vir37	05/07/1988	26Cap42	09/08/1988	16Leo46	01/08/1989	27Cap19
01/10/1988	29Vir21	05/09/1988	24Aqu53	09/10/1988	10Vir26	01/10/1989	26Aqu03
01/12/1988	23Lib51	05/11/1988	23Pis13	09/12/1988	04Lib00	01/12/1989	24Pis52
01/14/1988	19Sco48	05/13/1988	21Ari34	09/14/1988	27Lib55	01/14/1989	23Ari14
01/16/1988	17Sag39	05/15/1988	19Tau25	09/16/1988	22Sco25	01/16/1989	20Tau54
01/18/1988	17Cap18	05/17/1988	16Gem22	09/18/1988	17Sag59	01/18/1989	17Gem54
01/20/1988	17Aqu45	05/19/1988	12Can04	09/20/1988	14Cap55	01/20/1989	14Can05
01/22/1988	17Pis38	05/21/1988	06Leo33	09/22/1988	13Aqu24	01/22/1989	09Leo19
01/24/1988	16Ari04	05/23/1988	00Vir24	09/24/1988	13Pis15	01/24/1989	03Vir44
01/26/1988	12Tau52	05/25/1988	24Vir05	09/26/1988	13Ari31	01/26/1989	27Vir33
01/28/1988	08Gem19	05/27/1988	18Lib26	09/28/1988	13Tau03	01/28/1989	21Lib11
01/30/1988	02Can55	05/29/1988	13Sco57	09/30/1988	11Gem00	01/30/1989	15Sco13
		05/31/1988	10Sag49				
02/01/1988	26Can56			10/02/1988	07Can07	02/01/1989	10Sag20
02/03/1988	20Leo43	06/02/1988	08Cap51	10/04/1988	01Leo43	02/03/1989	07Cap09
02/05/1988	14Vir19	06/04/1988	07Aqu22	10/06/1988	25Leo33	02/05/1989	05Aqu31
02/07/1988	08Lib10	06/06/1988	05Pis53	10/08/1988	19Vir08	02/07/1989	05Pis03
02/09/1988	02Sco46	06/08/1988	04Ari01	10/10/1988	12Lib51	02/09/1989	04Ari45
02/11/1988	28Sco31	06/10/1988	01Tau39	10/12/1988	07Sco08	02/11/1989	03Tau41
02/13/1988	26Sag04	06/12/1988	28Tau44	10/14/1988	02Sag05	02/13/1989	01Gem28
02/15/1988	25Cap20	06/14/1988	25Gem01	10/16/1988	27Sag58	02/15/1989	27Gem58
02/17/1988	25Aqu43	06/16/1988	20Can15	10/18/1988	24Cap47	02/17/1989	23Can28
02/19/1988	25Pis57	06/18/1988	14Leo35	10/20/1988	22Aqu49	02/19/1989	18Leo08
02/21/1988	24Ari51	06/20/1988	08Vir19	10/22/1988	21Pis59	02/21/1989	12Vir09
02/23/1988	22Tau00	06/22/1988	02Lib00	10/24/1988	21Ari42	02/23/1989	05Lib52
02/25/1988	17Gem34	06/24/1988	26Lib22	10/26/1988	21Tau06	02/25/1989	29Lib33
02/27/1988	11Can58	06/26/1988	22Sco03	10/28/1988	19Gem09	02/27/1989	23Sco34
02/29/1988	05Leo49	06/28/1988	19Sag22	10/30/1988	15Can24		
		06/30/1988	18Cap04			03/01/1989	18Sag36
03/02/1988	29Leo28			11/01/1988	10Leo07	03/03/1989	15Cap06
03/04/1988	23Vir12	07/02/1988	17Aqu24	11/03/1988	03Vir53	03/05/1989	13Aqu22
03/06/1988	17Lib25	07/04/1988	16Pis34	11/05/1988	27Vir29	03/07/1989	13Pis11
03/08/1988	12Sco19	07/06/1988	14Ari48	11/07/1988	21Lib28	03/09/1989	13Ari31
03/10/1988	08Sag12	07/08/1988	12Tau08	11/09/1988	16Sco09	03/11/1989	13Tau12
03/12/1988	05Cap28	07/10/1988	08Gem34	11/11/1988	11Sag47	03/13/1989	11Gem21
03/14/1988	04Aqu10	07/12/1988	04Can07	11/13/1988	08Cap15	03/15/1989	07Can51
03/16/1988	03Pis58	07/14/1988	28Can54	11/15/1988	05Aqu21	03/17/1989	02Leo58
03/18/1988	03Ari51	07/16/1988	22Leo54	11/17/1988	03Pis11	03/19/1989	27Leo10
03/20/1988	02Tau54	07/18/1988	16Vir32	11/19/1988	01Ari40	03/21/1989	20Vir57
03/22/1988	00Gem22	07/20/1988	10Lib13	11/21/1988	00Tau35	03/23/1989	14Lib36
03/24/1988	26Gem06	07/22/1988	04Sco31	11/23/1988	29Tau16	03/25/1989	08Sco22
03/26/1988	20Can34	07/24/1988	00Sag09	11/25/1988	27Gem00	03/27/1989	02Sag36
03/28/1988	14Leo22	07/26/1988	27Sag34	11/27/1988	23Can15	03/29/1989	27Sag35
03/30/1988	07Vir58	07/28/1988	26Cap36	11/29/1988	18Leo00	03/31/1989	23Cap51
		07/30/1988	26Aqu36				
04/01/1988	01Lib58			12/01/1988	11Vir51	04/02/1989	21Aqu45
04/03/1988	26Lib36	08/01/1988	26Pis24	12/03/1988	05Lib28	04/04/1989	21Pis15
04/05/1988	22Sco07	08/03/1988	25Ari04	12/05/1988	29Lib33	04/06/1989	21Ari40
04/07/1988	18Sag31	08/05/1988	22Tau25	12/07/1988	24Sco39	04/08/1989	21Tau45
04/09/1988	15Cap50	08/07/1988	18Gem28	12/09/1988	20Sag57	04/10/1989	20Gem18
04/11/1988	14Aqu08	08/09/1988	13Can32	12/11/1988	18Cap11	04/12/1989	17Can03
04/13/1988	13Pis05	08/11/1988	07Leo48	12/13/1988	16Aqu03	04/14/1989	12Leo04
04/15/1988	12Ari13	08/13/1988	01Vir35	12/15/1988	14Pis06	04/16/1989	06Vir07
04/17/1988	10Tau52	08/15/1988	25Vir09	12/17/1988	12Ari16	04/18/1989	29Vir43
04/19/1988	08Gem17	08/17/1988	18Lib50	12/19/1988	10Tau24	04/20/1989	23Lib25
04/21/1988	04Can09	08/19/1988	13Sco12	12/21/1988	08Gem10	04/22/1989	17Sco28
04/23/1988	28Can40	08/21/1988	08Sag44	12/23/1988	05Can14	04/24/1989	12Sag01
04/25/1988	22Leo28	08/23/1988	05Cap54	12/25/1988	01Leo04	04/26/1989	07Cap19
04/27/1988	16Vir11	08/25/1988	04Aqu52	12/27/1988	25Leo43	04/28/1989	03Aqu34
04/29/1988	10Lib21	08/27/1988	05Pis03	12/29/1988	19Vir35	04/30/1989	01Pis06
		08/29/1988	05Ari16	12/31/1988	13Lib13		
		08/31/1988	04Tau32				

Ephemeris Tables for the Moon

Date	Moon	Date	Moon	Date	Moon	Date	Moon
05/02/1989	00Ari04	09/01/1989	23Vir05	01/01/1990	03Pis16	05/01/1990	06Leo35
05/04/1989	00Tau03	09/03/1989	16Lib55	01/03/1990	00Ari36	05/03/1990	02Vir27
05/06/1989	29Tau55	09/05/1989	10Sco40	01/05/1990	28Ari45	05/05/1990	27Vir13
05/08/1989	28Gem37	09/07/1989	04Sag36	01/07/1990	27Tau33	05/07/1990	21Lib21
05/10/1989	25Can29	09/09/1989	29Sag22	01/09/1990	26Gem30	05/09/1990	15Sco11
05/12/1989	20Leo36	09/11/1989	25Cap29	01/11/1990	24Can46	05/11/1990	08Sag56
05/14/1989	14Vir39	09/13/1989	23Aqu17	01/13/1990	21Leo51	05/13/1990	02Cap51
05/16/1989	08Lib16	09/15/1989	22Pis42	01/15/1990	17Vir31	05/15/1990	27Cap09
05/18/1989	02Sco07	09/17/1989	22Ari49	01/17/1990	11Lib57	05/17/1990	22Aqu22
05/20/1989	26Sco26	09/19/1989	22Tau34	01/19/1990	05Sco47	05/19/1990	19Pis10
05/22/1989	21Sag28	09/21/1989	21Gem00	01/21/1990	29Sco38	05/21/1990	17Ari45
05/24/1989	17Cap21	09/23/1989	17Can46	01/23/1990	24Sag00	05/23/1990	17Tau53
05/26/1989	13Aqu55	09/25/1989	13Leo15	01/25/1990	19Cap24	05/25/1990	18Gem24
05/28/1989	11Pis27	09/27/1989	07Vir51	01/27/1990	15Aqu52	05/27/1990	17Can54
05/30/1989	09Ari54	09/29/1989	01Lib50	01/29/1990	13Pis22	05/29/1990	15Leo40
				01/31/1990	11Ari24	05/31/1990	11Vir36
06/01/1989	09Tau10	10/01/1989	25Lib36				
06/03/1989	08Gem27	10/03/1989	19Sco19	02/02/1990	09Tau46	06/02/1990	06Lib18
06/05/1989	06Can43	10/05/1989	13Sag16	02/04/1990	08Gem07	06/04/1990	00Sco19
06/07/1989	03Leo30	10/07/1989	07Cap55	02/06/1990	06Can05	06/06/1990	24Sco02
06/09/1989	28Leo42	10/09/1989	03Aqu48	02/08/1990	03Leo27	06/08/1990	17Sag51
06/11/1989	22Vir46	10/11/1989	01Pis25	02/10/1990	29Leo54	06/10/1990	12Cap00
06/13/1989	16Lib30	10/13/1989	00Ari47	02/12/1990	25Vir16	06/12/1990	06Aqu37
06/15/1989	10Sco27	10/15/1989	01Tau16	02/14/1990	19Lib44	06/14/1990	02Pis09
06/17/1989	05Sag04	10/17/1989	01Gem39	02/16/1990	13Sco34	06/16/1990	28Pis57
06/19/1989	00Cap41	10/19/1989	00Can29	02/18/1990	07Sag24	06/18/1990	27Ari06
06/21/1989	27Cap12	10/21/1989	27Can25	02/20/1990	01Cap48	06/20/1990	26Tau42
06/23/1989	24Aqu28	10/23/1989	22Leo43	02/22/1990	27Cap18	06/22/1990	26Gem46
06/25/1989	22Pis17	10/25/1989	16Vir58	02/24/1990	24Aqu20	06/24/1990	26Can10
06/27/1989	20Ari36	10/27/1989	10Lib47	02/26/1990	22Pis37	06/26/1990	24Leo00
06/29/1989	19Tau13	10/29/1989	04Sco27	02/28/1990	21Ari38	06/28/1990	20Vir09
		10/31/1989	28Sco17			06/30/1990	14Lib56
07/01/1989	17Gem36			03/02/1990	20Tau39		
07/03/1989	15Can12	11/02/1989	22Sag28	03/04/1990	19Gem00	07/02/1990	08Sco54
07/05/1989	11Leo34	11/04/1989	17Cap10	03/06/1990	16Can25	07/04/1990	02Sag40
07/07/1989	06Vir36	11/06/1989	12Aqu55	03/08/1990	12Leo53	07/06/1990	26Sag39
07/09/1989	00Lib43	11/08/1989	10Pis10	03/10/1990	08Vir35	07/08/1990	21Cap04
07/11/1989	24Lib29	11/10/1989	09Ari07	03/12/1990	03Lib32	07/10/1990	16Aqu16
07/13/1989	18Sco27	11/12/1989	09Tau25	03/14/1990	27Lib47	07/12/1990	12Pis19
07/15/1989	13Sag19	11/14/1989	09Gem49	03/16/1990	21Sco39	07/14/1990	09Ari18
07/17/1989	09Cap19	11/16/1989	09Can00	03/18/1990	15Sag25	07/16/1990	07Tau24
07/19/1989	06Aqu32	11/18/1989	06Leo12	03/20/1990	09Cap40	07/18/1990	06Gem19
07/21/1989	04Pis39	11/20/1989	01Vir36	03/22/1990	05Aqu07	07/20/1990	05Can39
07/23/1989	03Ari06	11/22/1989	25Vir49	03/24/1990	02Pis15	07/22/1990	04Leo26
07/25/1989	01Tau40	11/24/1989	19Lib31	03/26/1990	01Ari03	07/24/1990	02Vir02
07/27/1989	29Tau51	11/26/1989	13Sco15	03/28/1990	00Tau58	07/26/1990	28Vir16
07/29/1989	27Gem24	11/28/1989	07Sag18	03/30/1990	00Gem45	07/28/1990	23Lib05
07/31/1989	24Can10	11/30/1989	01Cap49			07/30/1990	17Sco07
				04/01/1990	29Gem29		
08/02/1989	19Leo55	12/02/1989	26Cap58	04/03/1990	26Can46	08/01/1990	10Sag52
08/04/1989	14Vir41	12/04/1989	22Aqu55	04/05/1990	22Leo43	08/03/1990	04Cap59
08/06/1989	08Lib41	12/06/1989	19Pis57	04/07/1990	17Vir52	08/05/1990	29Cap50
08/08/1989	02Sco25	12/08/1989	18Ari24	04/09/1990	12Lib18	08/07/1990	25Aqu36
08/10/1989	26Sco26	12/10/1989	18Tau00	04/11/1990	06Sco21	08/09/1990	22Pis27
08/12/1989	21Sag16	12/12/1989	17Gem49	04/13/1990	00Sag05	08/11/1990	20Ari06
08/14/1989	17Cap29	12/14/1989	16Can50	04/15/1990	23Sag53	08/13/1990	18Tau17
08/16/1989	15Aqu12	12/16/1989	14Leo09	04/17/1990	18Cap07	08/15/1990	16Gem48
08/18/1989	14Pis04	12/18/1989	09Vir48	04/19/1990	13Aqu21	08/17/1990	15Can14
08/20/1989	13Ari27	12/20/1989	04Lib07	04/21/1990	10Pis20	08/19/1990	13Leo10
08/22/1989	12Tau30	12/22/1989	27Lib50	04/23/1990	09Ari14	08/21/1990	10Vir16
08/24/1989	10Gem36	12/24/1989	21Sco40	04/25/1990	09Tau30	08/23/1990	06Lib13
08/26/1989	07Can38	12/26/1989	15Sag55	04/27/1990	09Gem54	08/25/1990	01Sco01
08/28/1989	03Leo35	12/28/1989	10Cap57	04/29/1990	09Can09	08/27/1990	25Sco03
08/30/1989	28Leo42	12/30/1989	06Aqu42			08/29/1990	18Sag47
						08/31/1990	12Cap59

Ephemeris Tables for the Moon

Date	Moon	Date	Moon	Date	Moon	Date	Moon
09/02/1990	08Aqu02	01/02/1991	05Leo34	05/02/1991	22Sag07	09/01/1991	05Gem10
09/04/1990	04Pis27	01/04/1991	04Vir05	05/04/1991	15Cap46	09/03/1991	03Can21
09/06/1990	02Ari07	01/06/1991	00Lib46	05/06/1991	09Aqu33	09/05/1991	02Leo16
09/08/1990	00Tau36	01/08/1991	25Lib55	05/08/1991	04Pis10	09/07/1991	01Vir28
09/10/1990	29Tau21	01/10/1991	20Sco03	05/10/1991	00Ari12	09/09/1991	00Lib03
09/12/1990	27Gem42	01/12/1991	13Sag42	05/12/1991	28Ari04	09/11/1991	27Lib24
09/14/1990	25Can29	01/14/1991	07Cap24	05/14/1991	27Tau30	09/13/1991	23Sco07
09/16/1990	22Leo36	01/16/1991	01Aqu28	05/16/1991	27Gem21	09/15/1991	17Sag33
09/18/1990	18Vir56	01/18/1991	26Aqu06	05/18/1991	26Can42	09/17/1991	11Cap16
09/20/1990	14Lib27	01/20/1991	21Pis35	05/20/1991	24Leo52	09/19/1991	04Aqu57
09/22/1990	09Sco05	01/22/1991	18Ari03	05/22/1991	21Vir44	09/21/1991	29Aqu18
09/24/1990	03Sag00	01/24/1991	15Tau41	05/24/1991	17Lib35	09/23/1991	24Pis37
09/26/1990	26Sag42	01/26/1991	14Gem26	05/26/1991	12Sco35	09/25/1991	20Ari58
09/28/1990	20Cap47	01/28/1991	13Can58	05/28/1991	06Sag51	09/27/1991	18Tau13
09/30/1990	15Aqu53	01/30/1991	13Leo24	05/30/1991	00Cap39	09/29/1991	16Gem00
10/02/1990	12Pis36	02/01/1991	11Vir51	06/01/1991	24Cap12	10/01/1991	14Can06
10/04/1990	10Ari58	02/03/1991	08Lib46	06/03/1991	18Aqu01	10/03/1991	12Leo23
10/06/1990	10Tau24	02/05/1991	04Sco09	06/05/1991	12Pis38	10/05/1991	10Vir43
10/08/1990	09Gem52	02/07/1991	28Sco18	06/07/1991	08Ari34	10/07/1991	08Lib37
10/10/1990	08Can33	02/09/1991	21Sag59	06/09/1991	06Tau25	10/09/1991	05Sco28
10/12/1990	06Leo04	02/11/1991	15Cap43	06/11/1991	05Gem51	10/11/1991	01Sag03
10/14/1990	02Vir30	02/13/1991	10Aqu05	06/13/1991	06Can06	10/13/1991	25Sag26
10/16/1990	28Vir10	02/15/1991	05Pis21	06/15/1991	06Leo00	10/15/1991	19Cap07
10/18/1990	23Lib10	02/17/1991	01Ari31	06/17/1991	04Vir37	10/17/1991	12Aqu51
10/20/1990	17Sco27	02/19/1991	28Ari36	06/19/1991	01Lib38	10/19/1991	07Pis18
10/22/1990	11Sag16	02/21/1991	26Tau22	06/21/1991	27Lib13	10/21/1991	02Ari57
10/24/1990	04Cap55	02/23/1991	24Gem38	06/23/1991	21Sco50	10/23/1991	00Tau01
10/26/1990	28Cap51	02/25/1991	23Can17	06/25/1991	15Sag48	10/25/1991	28Tau07
10/28/1990	23Aqu51	02/27/1991	21Leo51	06/27/1991	09Cap24	10/27/1991	26Gem38
10/30/1990	20Pis29			06/29/1991	03Aqu02	10/29/1991	25Can04
		03/01/1991	19Vir48			10/31/1991	23Leo08
11/01/1990	19Ari06	03/03/1991	16Lib31	07/01/1991	27Aqu01		
11/03/1990	19Tau08	03/05/1991	11Sco56	07/03/1991	21Pis44	11/02/1991	20Vir48
11/05/1990	19Gem21	03/07/1991	06Sag12	07/05/1991	17Ari39	11/04/1991	17Lib47
11/07/1990	18Can39	03/09/1991	29Sag52	07/07/1991	15Tau11	11/06/1991	13Sco55
11/09/1990	16Leo18	03/11/1991	23Cap41	07/09/1991	14Gem18	11/08/1991	09Sag08
11/11/1990	12Vir29	03/13/1991	18Aqu16	07/11/1991	14Can28	11/10/1991	03Cap20
11/13/1990	07Lib40	03/15/1991	14Pis00	07/13/1991	14Leo33	11/12/1991	27Cap00
11/15/1990	02Sco11	03/17/1991	11Ari02	07/15/1991	13Vir33	11/14/1991	20Aqu39
11/17/1990	26Sco40	03/19/1991	09Tau00	07/17/1991	10Lib49	11/16/1991	15Pis05
11/19/1990	19Sag52	03/21/1991	07Gem18	07/19/1991	06Sco24	11/18/1991	10Ari51
11/21/1990	13Cap31	03/23/1991	05Can36	07/21/1991	00Sag52	11/20/1991	88Tau13
11/23/1990	07Aqu30	03/25/1991	03Leo38	07/23/1991	24Sag37	11/22/1991	07Gem01
11/25/1990	02Pis21	03/27/1991	01Vir18	07/25/1991	18Cap13	11/24/1991	06Can28
11/27/1990	28Pis51	03/29/1991	28Vir25	07/27/1991	12Aqu00	11/26/1991	05Leo36
11/29/1990	27Ari10	03/31/1991	24Lib37	07/29/1991	06Pis19	11/28/1991	03Vir56
				07/31/1991	01Ari24	11/30/1991	01Lib14
12/01/1990	27Tau10						
12/03/1990	27Gem46	04/02/1991	19Sco51				
12/05/1990	27Can35	04/04/1991	14Sag01	08/02/1991	27Ari27	12/02/1991	27Lib31
12/07/1990	25Leo41	04/06/1991	07Cap40	08/04/1991	24Tau46	12/04/1991	22Sco58
12/09/1990	22Vir03	04/08/1991	01Aqu31	08/06/1991	23Gem24	12/06/1991	17Sag36
12/11/1990	17Lib03	04/10/1991	26Aqu07	08/08/1991	23Can00	12/08/1991	11Cap32
12/13/1990	11Sco18	04/12/1991	22Pis12	08/10/1991	22Leo52	12/10/1991	05Aqu09
12/15/1990	05Sag03	04/14/1991	19Ari48	08/12/1991	21Vir54	12/12/1991	28Aqu48
12/17/1990	28Sag40	04/16/1991	18Tau37	08/14/1991	19Lib18	12/14/1991	23Pis10
12/19/1990	22Cap31	04/16/1991	18Tau37	08/16/1991	15Sco01	12/16/1991	18Ari42
12/21/1990	16Aqu41	04/18/1991	17Gem46	08/18/1991	09Sag26	12/18/1991	16Tau02
12/23/1990	11Pis42	04/20/1991	16Can27	08/20/1991	03Cap07	12/20/1991	15Gem05
12/25/1990	07Ari57	04/22/1991	14Leo22	08/22/1991	26Cap47	12/22/1991	15Can06
12/27/1990	05Tau51	04/24/1991	11Vir28	08/24/1991	20Aqu51	12/24/1991	15Leo07
12/29/1990	05Gem22	04/26/1991	07Lib48	08/26/1991	15Pis40	12/26/1991	14Vir00
12/31/1990	05Can38	04/28/1991	03Sco22	08/28/1991	11Ari17	12/28/1991	11Lib25
		04/30/1991	28Sco07	08/30/1991	07Tau46	12/30/1991	07Sco24

Ephemeris Tables for the Moon

Date	Moon	Date	Moon	Date	Moon	Date	Moon
01/01/1992	02Sag16	05/02/1992	09Tau18	09/01/1992	09Sco30	01/01/1993	14Ari54
01/03/1992	26Sag25	05/04/1992	06Gem37	09/03/1992	06Sag00	01/03/1993	09Tau37
01/05/1992	20Cap10	05/06/1992	04Can36	09/05/1992	00Cap57	01/05/1993	05Gem42
01/07/1992	13Aqu43	05/08/1992	02Leo54	09/07/1992	24Cap59	01/07/1993	03Can24
01/09/1992	07Pis31	05/10/1992	01Vir12	09/09/1992	18Aqu39	01/09/1993	02Leo32
01/11/1992	01Ari51	05/12/1992	29Vir22	09/11/1992	12Pis25	01/11/1993	02Vir13
01/13/1992	27Ari13	05/14/1992	27Lib02	09/13/1992	06Ari30	01/13/1993	01Lib29
01/15/1992	24Tau10	05/16/1992	23Sco48	09/15/1992	01Tau07	01/15/1993	29Lib34
01/17/1992	22Gem55	05/18/1992	19Sag30	09/17/1992	26Tau25	01/17/1993	26Sco25
01/19/1992	23Can03	05/20/1992	14Cap09	09/19/1992	22Gem38	01/19/1993	22Sag13
01/21/1992	23Leo28	05/22/1992	08Aqu01	09/21/1992	20Can18	01/21/1993	17Cap12
01/23/1992	23Vir02	05/24/1992	01Pis47	09/23/1992	19Leo19	01/23/1993	11Aqu36
01/25/1992	20Lib52	05/26/1992	25Pis58	09/25/1992	19Vir20	01/25/1993	05Pis34
01/27/1992	16Sco51	05/28/1992	21Ari07	09/27/1992	19Lib13	01/27/1993	29Pis16
01/29/1992	11Sag30	05/30/1992	17Tau43	09/29/1992	17Sco47	01/29/1993	23Ari07
01/31/1992	05Cap22					01/31/1993	17Tau40
		06/01/1992	15Gem38				
02/02/1992	28Cap55	06/03/1992	14Can31	10/01/1992	14Sag29	02/02/1993	13Gem29
02/04/1992	22Aqu36	06/05/1992	13Leo31	10/03/1992	09Cap28	02/04/1993	11Can13
02/06/1992	16Pis39	06/07/1992	12Vir07	10/05/1992	03Aqu30	02/06/1993	10Leo43
02/08/1992	11Ari12	06/09/1992	10Lib00	10/07/1992	27Aqu12	02/08/1993	11Vir06
02/10/1992	06Tau39	06/11/1992	06Sco57	10/09/1992	21Pis05	02/10/1993	11Lib07
02/12/1992	03Gem16	06/13/1992	02Sag58	10/11/1992	15Ari31	02/12/1993	09Sco38
02/14/1992	01Can28	06/15/1992	28Sag01	10/13/1992	10Tau38	02/14/1993	06Sag30
02/16/1992	01Leo07	06/17/1992	22Cap21	10/15/1992	06Gem25	02/16/1993	01Cap52
02/18/1992	01Vir23	06/19/1992	16Aqu11	10/17/1992	03Can01	02/18/1993	26Cap23
02/20/1992	01Lib12	06/21/1992	09Pis54	10/19/1992	00Leo34	02/20/1993	20Aqu29
02/22/1992	29Lib19	06/23/1992	04Ari03	10/21/1992	29Leo06	02/22/1993	14Pis15
02/24/1992	25Sco34	06/25/1992	29Ari12	10/23/1992	28Vir21	02/24/1993	08Ari00
02/26/1992	20Sag13	06/27/1992	25Tau48	10/25/1992	27Lib30	02/26/1993	01Tau53
02/28/1992	14Cap01	06/29/1992	24Gem06	10/27/1992	25Sco45	02/28/1993	26Tau23
				10/29/1992	22Sag22		
03/01/1992	07Aqu36			10/31/1992	17Cap27		
03/03/1992	01Pis24	07/01/1992	23Can37			03/02/1993	22Gem01
03/05/1992	25Pis49	07/03/1992	23Leo25	11/02/1992	11Aqu36	03/04/1993	19Can23
03/07/1992	20Ari54	07/05/1992	22Vir36	11/04/1992	05Pis19	03/06/1993	18Leo43
03/09/1992	16Tau42	07/07/1992	20Lib31	11/06/1992	29Pis21	03/08/1993	19Vir17
03/11/1992	13Gem25	07/09/1992	17Sco01	11/08/1992	24Ari00	03/10/1993	19Lib42
03/13/1992	11Can13	07/11/1992	12Sag24	11/10/1992	19Tau40	03/12/1993	18Sco43
03/15/1992	10Leo07	07/13/1992	06Cap56	11/12/1992	16Gem15	03/14/1993	15Sag49
03/17/1992	09Vir46	07/15/1992	00Aqu59	11/14/1992	13Can32	03/16/1993	11Cap11
03/19/1992	09Lib09	07/17/1992	24Aqu40	11/16/1992	11Leo27	03/18/1993	05Aqu33
03/21/1992	07Sco13	07/19/1992	18Pis27	11/18/1992	09Vir47	03/20/1993	29Aqu26
03/23/1992	03Sag36	07/21/1992	12Ari37	11/20/1992	08Lib14	03/22/1993	23Pis10
03/25/1992	28Sag22	07/23/1992	07Tau37	11/22/1992	06Sco28	03/24/1993	16Ari57
03/27/1992	22Cap16	07/25/1992	04Gem06	11/24/1992	03Sag54	03/26/1993	11Tau04
03/29/1992	15Aqu52	07/27/1992	02Can18	11/26/1992	00Cap09	03/28/1993	05Gem51
03/31/1992	09Pis51	07/29/1992	02Leo06	11/28/1992	25Cap14	03/30/1993	01Can28
		07/31/1992	02Vir30	11/30/1992	19Aqu24		
04/02/1992	04Ari41					04/01/1993	28Can36
04/04/1992	00Tau22	08/02/1992	02Lib13	12/02/1992	13Pis07	04/03/1993	27Leo27
04/06/1992	26Tau54	08/04/1992	00Sco25	12/04/1992	07Ari07	04/05/1993	27Vir31
04/08/1992	24Gem05	08/06/1992	26Sco50	12/06/1992	01Tau56	04/07/1993	27Lib48
04/10/1992	21Can52	08/08/1992	21Sag50	12/08/1992	27Tau59	04/09/1993	26Sco56
04/12/1992	20Leo19	08/10/1992	16Cap02	12/10/1992	25Gem16	04/11/1993	24Sag18
04/14/1992	19Vir06	08/12/1992	09Aqu49	12/12/1992	23Can33	04/13/1993	19Cap55
04/16/1992	17Lib40	08/14/1992	03Pis30	12/14/1992	22Leo16	04/15/1993	14Aqu16
04/18/1992	15Sco16	08/16/1992	29Pis27	12/16/1992	20Vir49	04/17/1993	08Pis07
04/20/1992	11Sag24	08/18/1992	21Ari40	12/18/1992	18Lib53	04/19/1993	01Ari51
04/22/1992	06Cap14	08/20/1992	16Tau43	12/20/1992	16Sco14	04/21/1993	25Ari51
04/24/1992	00Aqu10	08/22/1992	12Gem57	12/22/1992	12Sag44	04/23/1993	20Tau25
04/26/1992	23Aqu50	08/24/1992	10Can51	12/24/1992	08Cap24	04/25/1993	15Gem35
04/28/1992	17Pis59	08/26/1992	10Leo29	12/26/1992	03Aqu10	04/27/1993	11Can36
04/30/1992	13Ari04	08/28/1992	10Vir56	12/28/1992	27Aqu16	04/29/1993	08Leo47
		08/30/1992	11Lib00	12/30/1992	21Pis01		

Ephemeris Tables for the Moon

Date	Moon	Date	Moon	Date	Moon	Date	Moon
05/01/1993	07Vir12	09/02/1993	25Pis22	01/02/1994	09Vir09	05/02/1994	10Aqu34
05/03/1993	06Lib36	09/04/1993	19Ari031	01/04/1994	07Lib21	05/04/1994	05Pis47
05/05/1993	06Sco09	09/06/1993	12Tau47	01/06/1994	05Sco34	05/06/1994	29Pis59
05/07/1993	04Sag57	09/08/1993	06Gem59	01/08/1994	03Sag45	05/08/1994	23Ari42
05/09/1993	02Cap18	09/10/1993	02Can22	01/10/1994	01Cap31	05/10/1994	17Tau17
05/11/1993	28Cap01	09/12/1993	29Can30	01/12/1994	28Cap38	05/12/1994	11Gem03
05/13/1993	22Aqu33	09/14/1993	28Leo30	01/14/1994	24Aqu42	05/14/1994	05Can22
05/15/1993	16Pis27	09/16/1993	28Vir54	01/16/1994	19Pis33	05/16/1994	00Leo33
05/17/1993	10Ari13	09/18/1993	29Lib12	01/18/1994	13Ari33	05/18/1994	26Leo51
05/19/1993	04Tau26	09/20/1993	28Sco18	01/20/1994	07Tau12	05/20/1994	24Vir40
05/21/1993	29Tau24	09/22/1993	25Sag39	01/22/1994	01Gem12	05/22/1994	23Lib54
05/23/1993	25Gem13	09/24/1993	21Cap28	01/24/1994	26Gem15	05/24/1994	23Sco53
05/25/1993	21Can59	09/26/1993	16Aqu15	01/26/1994	22Can47	05/26/1994	23Sag43
05/27/1993	19Leo33	09/28/1993	10Pis22	01/28/1994	20Leo39	05/28/1994	22Cap18
05/29/1993	17Vir52	09/30/1993	04Ari11	01/30/1994	19Vir25	05/30/1994	19Aqu16
05/31/1993	16Lib36						
		10/02/1993	27Ari54	02/01/1994	18Lib13	06/01/1994	14Pis31
06/02/1993	15Sco14	10/04/1993	21Tau42	02/03/1994	16Sco30	06/03/1994	08Ari42
06/04/1993	13Sag20	10/06/1993	16Gem03	02/05/1994	14Sag08	06/05/1994	02Tau22
06/06/1993	10Cap15	10/08/1993	11Can24	02/07/1994	11Cap04	06/07/1994	25Tau59
06/08/1993	05Aqu57	10/10/1993	08Leo15	02/09/1994	07Aqu27	06/09/1994	20Gem04
06/10/1993	00Pis30	10/12/1993	06Vir57	02/11/1994	02Pis56	06/11/1994	14Can50
06/12/1993	24Pis26	10/14/1993	07Lib06	02/13/1994	27Pis32	06/13/1994	10Leo31
06/14/1993	18Ari16	10/16/1993	07Sco30	02/15/1994	21Ari29	06/15/1994	07Vir09
06/16/1993	12Tau36	10/18/1993	06Sag58	02/17/1994	15Tau03	06/17/1994	04Lib46
06/18/1993	07Gem55	10/20/1993	04Cap41	02/19/1994	09Gem00	06/19/1994	03Sco25
06/20/1993	04Can27	10/22/1993	00Aqu36	02/21/1994	03Can58	06/21/1994	02Sag45
06/22/1993	02Leo03	10/24/1993	25Aqu18	02/23/1994	00Leo40	06/23/1994	02Cap01
06/24/1993	00Vir24	10/26/1993	19Pis14	02/25/1994	29Leo07	06/25/1994	00Aqu27
06/26/1993	28Vir57	10/28/1993	13Ari00	02/27/1994	28Vir40	06/27/1994	27Aqu25
06/28/1993	27Lib16	10/30/1993	06Tau45			06/29/1994	22Pis45
06/30/1993	25Sco09			03/01/1994	28Lib19		
		11/01/1993	00Gem54	03/03/1994	27Sco07	07/01/1994	16Ari57
07/02/1993	22Sag20	11/03/1993	25Gem36	03/05/1994	24Sag40	07/03/1994	10Tau37
07/04/1993	18Cap38	11/05/1993	21Can09	03/07/1994	21Cap12	07/05/1994	04Gem25
07/06/1993	14Aqu00	11/07/1993	17Leo57	03/09/1994	16Aqu51	07/07/1994	28Gem48
07/08/1993	08Pis27	11/09/1993	16Vir09	03/11/1994	11Pis45	07/09/1994	24Can08
07/10/1993	02Ari24	11/11/1993	15Lib37	03/13/1994	06Ari00	07/11/1994	20Leo34
07/12/1993	26Ari10	11/13/1993	15Sco34	03/15/1994	29Ari46	07/13/1994	17Vir44
07/14/1993	20Tau30	11/15/1993	14Sag53	03/17/1994	23Tau18	07/15/1994	15Lib34
07/16/1993	16Gem04	11/17/1993	12Cap49	03/19/1994	17Gem13	07/17/1994	13Sco52
07/18/1993	13Can04	11/19/1993	09Aqu02	03/21/1994	12Can07	07/19/1994	12Sag25
07/20/1993	11Leo31	11/21/1993	03Pis48	03/23/1994	08Leo41	07/21/1994	10Cap57
07/22/1993	10Vir45	11/23/1993	27Pis44	03/25/1994	07Vir08	07/23/1994	08Aqu46
07/24/1993	09Lib49	11/25/1993	21Ari26	03/27/1994	07Lib06	07/25/1994	05Pis27
07/26/1993	08Sco10	11/27/1993	15Tau20	03/29/1994	07Sco23	07/27/1994	00Ari45
07/28/1993	05Sag28	11/29/1993	09Gem52	03/31/1994	06Sag48	07/29/1994	24Ari54
07/30/1993	01Cap55					07/31/1994	18Tau35
		12/01/1993	05Can11	04/02/1994	04Cap45		
08/01/1993	27Cap35	12/03/1993	01Leo22	04/04/1994	01Aqu12	08/02/1994	12Gem27
08/03/1993	22Aqu28	12/05/1993	28Leo25	04/06/1994	26Aqu27	08/04/1994	07Can06
08/05/1993	16Pis44	12/07/1993	26Vir22	04/08/1994	20Pis55	08/06/1994	03Leo04
08/07/1993	10Ari32	12/09/1993	25Lib07	04/10/1994	14Ari48	08/08/1994	00Vir10
08/09/1993	04Tau16	12/11/1993	24Sco09	04/12/1994	08Tau25	08/10/1994	28Vir08
08/11/1993	28Tau33	12/13/1993	22Sag52	04/14/1994	02Gem04	08/12/1994	26Lib29
08/13/1993	24Gem03	12/15/1993	20Cap36	04/16/1994	26Gem03	08/14/1994	24Sco47
08/15/1993	21Can18	12/17/1993	16Aqu52	04/18/1994	21Can00	08/16/1994	22Sag52
08/17/1993	20Leo15	12/19/1993	11Pis48	04/20/1994	17Leo19	08/18/1994	20Cap33
08/19/1993	20Vir13	12/21/1993	05Ari46	04/22/1994	15Vir27	08/20/1994	17Aqu38
08/21/1993	20Lib02	12/23/1993	29Ari25	04/24/1994	15Lib13	08/22/1994	13Pis47
08/23/1993	18Sco38	12/25/1993	23Tau28	04/26/1994	15Sco40	08/24/1994	08Ari45
08/25/1993	15Sag49	12/27/1993	18Gem19	04/28/1994	15Sag33	08/26/1994	02Tau51
08/27/1993	11Cap48	12/29/1993	14Can19	04/30/1994	13Cap54	08/28/1994	26Tau30
08/29/1993	06Aqu52	12/31/1993	11Leo22			08/30/1994	20Gem20
08/31/1993	01Pis22						

Ephemeris Tables for the Moon

Date	Moon	Date	Moon	Date	Moon	Date	Moon
09/01/1994	15Can07	01/01/1995	11Cap12	05/01/1995	00Gem01	09/02/1995	11Sag10
09/03/1994	11Leo21	01/03/1995	10Aqu21	05/03/1995	23Gem42	09/04/1995	09Cap43
09/05/1994	09Vir03	01/05/1995	07Pis56	05/05/1995	17Can28	09/06/1995	08Aqu30
09/07/1994	07Lib54	01/07/1995	03Ari40	05/07/1995	11Leo46	09/08/1995	06Pis57
09/09/1994	06Sco58	01/09/1995	28Ari01	05/09/1995	07Vir15	09/10/1995	04Ari18
09/11/1994	05Sag42	01/11/1995	21Tau38	05/11/1995	04Lib20	09/12/1995	00Tau21
09/13/1994	03Cap35	01/13/1995	15Gem18	05/13/1995	03Sco07	09/14/1995	25Tau03
09/15/1994	00Aqu40	01/15/1995	09Can28	05/15/1995	03Sag10	09/16/1995	19Gem00
09/17/1994	27Aqu03	01/17/1995	04Leo24	05/17/1995	03Cap21	09/18/1995	12Can46
09/19/1994	22Pis29	01/19/1995	00Vir11	05/19/1995	02Aqu32	09/20/1995	06Leo58
09/21/1994	17Ari05	01/21/1995	26Vir42	05/21/1995	00Pis10	09/22/1995	02Vir08
09/23/1994	10Tau57	01/23/1995	23Lib53	05/23/1995	26Pis10	09/24/1995	28Vir24
09/25/1994	04Gem34	01/25/1995	21Sco53	05/25/1995	21Ari03	09/26/1995	25Lib45
09/27/1994	28Gem24	01/27/1995	20Sag39	05/27/1995	15Tau06	09/28/1995	23Sco48
09/29/1994	23Can06	01/29/1995	19Cap42	05/29/1995	08Gem46	09/30/1995	22Sag10
		01/31/1995	18Aqu20	05/31/1995	02Can28		
10/01/1994	19Leo19						
10/03/1994	17Vir18	02/02/1995	15Pis44	06/02/1995	26Can19	10/02/1995	20Cap34
10/05/1994	16Lib39	02/04/1995	11Ari31	06/04/1995	20Leo45	10/04/1995	18Aqu41
10/07/1994	16Sco33	02/06/1995	05Tau55	06/06/1995	16Vir05	10/06/1995	16Pis09
10/09/1994	15Sag55	02/08/1995	29Tau34	06/08/1995	12Lib54	10/08/1995	12Ari46
10/11/1994	14Cap04	02/10/1995	23Gem21	06/10/1995	11Sco28	10/10/1995	08Tau21
10/13/1994	10Aqu57	02/12/1995	17Can40	06/12/1995	11Sag28	10/12/1995	02Gem55
10/15/1994	06Pis43	02/14/1995	13Leo05	06/14/1995	11Cap58	10/14/1995	26Gem51
10/17/1994	01Ari32	02/16/1995	09Vir35	06/16/1995	11Aqu37	10/16/1995	20Can37
10/19/1994	25Ari43	02/18/1995	06Lib53	06/18/1995	09Pis30	10/18/1995	14Leo50
10/21/1994	19Tau27	02/20/1995	04Sco42	06/20/1995	05Ari33	10/20/1995	10Vir01
10/23/1994	13Gem03	02/22/1995	02Sag46	06/22/1995	00Tau12	10/22/1995	06Lib36
10/25/1994	06Can52	02/24/1995	01Cap02	06/24/1995	24Tau03	10/24/1995	04Sco42
10/27/1994	01Leo32	02/26/1995	29Cap16	06/26/1995	17Gem41	10/26/1995	03Sag40
10/29/1994	27Leo33	02/28/1995	26Aqu58	06/28/1995	11Can25	10/28/1995	02Cap52
10/31/1994	25Vir18			06/30/1995	05Leo33	10/30/1995	01Aqu33
		03/02/1995	23Pis45				
11/02/1994	24Lib45	03/04/1995	19Ari16	07/02/1995	00Vir12	11/01/1995	29Aqu15
11/04/1994	25Sco04	03/06/1995	13Tau39	07/04/1995	25Vir42	11/03/1995	25Pis59
11/06/1994	25Sag04	03/08/1995	07Gem24	07/06/1995	22Lib21	11/05/1995	21Ari45
11/08/1994	23Cap47	03/10/1995	01Can09	07/08/1995	20Sco30	11/07/1995	16Tau46
11/10/1994	20Aqu45	03/12/1995	25Can31	07/10/1995	20Sag06	11/09/1995	11Gem07
11/12/1994	16Pis16	03/14/1995	21Leo10	07/12/1995	20Cap23	11/11/1995	04Can57
11/14/1994	10Ari43	03/16/1995	18Vir12	07/14/1995	20Aqu02	11/13/1995	28Can42
11/16/1994	04Tau31	03/18/1995	16Lib22	07/16/1995	18Pis07	11/15/1995	22Leo48
11/18/1994	28Tau09	03/20/1995	15Sco02	07/18/1995	14Ari16	11/17/1995	17Vir49
11/20/1994	21Gem51	03/22/1995	13Sag42	07/20/1995	08Tau54	11/19/1995	14Lib28
11/22/1994	15Can52	03/24/1995	11Cap58	07/22/1995	02Gem45	11/21/1995	12Sco47
11/24/1994	10Leo39	03/26/1995	09Aqu34	07/24/1995	26Gem23	11/23/1995	12Sag31
11/26/1994	06Vir30	03/28/1995	06Pis28	07/26/1995	20Can18	11/25/1995	12Cap34
11/28/1994	03Lib52	03/30/1995	02Ari27	07/28/1995	14Leo46	11/27/1995	11Aqu52
11/30/1994	02Sco50			07/30/1995	09Vir52	11/29/1995	09Pis42
		04/01/1995	27Ari25				
12/02/1994	03Sag01	04/03/1995	21Tau38	08/01/1995	05Lib49	12/01/1995	05Ari59
12/04/1994	03Cap17	04/05/1995	15Gem22	08/03/1995	02Sco33	12/03/1995	01Tau10
12/06/1994	02Aqu25	04/07/1995	09Can05	08/05/1995	00Sag25	12/05/1995	25Tau40
12/08/1994	29Aqu48	04/09/1995	03Leo27	08/07/1995	29Sag27	12/07/1995	19Gem41
12/10/1994	25Pis21	04/11/1995	29Leo02	08/09/1995	29Cap06	12/09/1995	13Can28
12/12/1994	19Ari36	04/13/1995	26Vir16	08/11/1995	28Aqu21	12/11/1995	07Leo15
12/14/1994	13Tau17	04/15/1995	24Lib58	08/13/1995	26Pis14	12/13/1995	01Vir17
12/16/1994	06Gem54	04/17/1995	24Sco29	08/15/1995	22Ari25	12/15/1995	26Vir10
12/18/1994	00Can46	04/19/1995	24Sag01	08/17/1995	17Tau10	12/17/1995	22Lib29
12/20/1994	25Can13	04/21/1995	22Cap37	08/19/1995	11Gem01	12/19/1995	20Sco39
12/22/1994	20Leo20	04/23/1995	20Aqu06	08/21/1995	04Can45	12/21/1995	20Sag34
12/24/1994	16Vir19	04/25/1995	16Pis21	08/23/1995	28Can53	12/23/1995	21Cap09
12/26/1994	13Lib25	04/27/1995	11Ari38	08/25/1995	23Leo43	12/25/1995	21Aqu08
12/28/1994	11Sco46	04/29/1995	06Tau08	08/27/1995	19Vir27	12/27/1995	19Pis19
12/30/1994	11Sag20			08/29/1995	15Lib59	12/29/1995	15Ari37
				08/31/1995	13Sco12	12/31/1995	10Tau36

Ephemeris Tables for the Moon

Date	Moon	Date	Moon	Date	Moon	Date	Moon
01/02/1996	04Gem43	05/01/1996	16Lib04	09/02/1996	13Tau13	01/02/1997	16Lib55
01/04/1996	28Gem33	05/03/1996	13Sco25	09/04/1996	08Gem48	01/04/1997	12Sco21
01/06/1996	22Can16	05/05/1996	11Sag55	09/06/1996	03Can16	01/06/1997	09Sag35
01/08/1996	16Leo10	05/07/1996	10Cap54	09/08/1996	27Can04	01/08/1997	08Cap41
01/10/1996	10Vir25	05/09/1996	09Aqu43	09/10/1996	20Leo49	01/10/1997	08Aqu48
01/12/1996	05Lib17	05/11/1996	07Pis49	09/12/1996	14Vir49	01/12/1997	08Pis41
01/14/1996	01Sco22	05/13/1996	05Ari00	09/14/1996	09Lib20	01/14/1997	07Ari24
01/16/1996	29Sco09	05/15/1996	01Tau23	09/16/1996	04Sco37	01/16/1997	04Tau37
01/18/1996	28Sag39	05/17/1996	26Tau58	09/18/1996	00Sag48	01/18/1997	00Gem32
01/20/1996	29Cap12	05/19/1996	21Gem46	09/20/1996	28Sag07	01/20/1997	25Gem37
01/22/1996	29Aqu22	05/21/1996	15Can52	09/22/1996	26Cap35	01/22/1997	20Can03
01/24/1996	27Pis55	05/23/1996	09Leo36	09/24/1996	25Aqu50	01/24/1997	13Leo58
01/26/1996	24Ari31	05/25/1996	03Vir32	09/26/1996	25Pis16	01/26/1997	07Vir38
01/28/1996	19Tau31	05/27/1996	28Vir07	09/28/1996	23Ari57	01/28/1997	01Lib19
01/30/1996	13Gem33	05/29/1996	24Lib05	09/30/1996	21Tau13	01/30/1997	25Lib29
		05/31/1996	21Sco48				
02/01/1996	07Can18			10/02/1996	16Gem59	02/01/1997	20Sco42
02/03/1996	01Leo06	06/02/1996	20Sag58	10/04/1996	11Can30	02/03/1997	17Sag43
02/05/1996	25Leo15	06/04/1996	20Cap50	10/06/1996	05Leo18	02/05/1997	16Cap40
02/07/1996	19Vir50	06/06/1996	20Aqu13	10/08/1996	29Leo05	02/07/1997	16Aqu54
02/09/1996	15Lib06	06/08/1996	18Pis25	10/10/1996	23Vir19	02/09/1997	17Pis19
02/11/1996	11Sco16	06/10/1996	15Ari17	10/12/1996	18Lib21	02/11/1997	16Ari37
02/13/1996	08Sag43	06/12/1996	11Tau02	10/14/1996	14Sco19	02/13/1997	14Tau10
02/15/1996	07Cap39	06/14/1996	06Gem02	10/16/1996	11Sag15	02/15/1997	10Gem09
02/17/1996	07Aqu32	06/16/1996	00Can26	10/18/1996	08Cap57	02/17/1997	04Can57
02/19/1996	07Pis15	06/18/1996	24Can20	10/20/1996	07Aqu10	02/19/1997	29Can03
02/21/1996	05Ari50	06/20/1996	18Leo03	10/22/1996	05Pis44	02/21/1997	22Leo48
02/23/1996	02Tau36	06/22/1996	11Vir54	10/24/1996	04Ari13	02/23/1997	16Vir25
02/25/1996	27Tau48	06/24/1996	06Lib24	10/26/1996	02Tau09	02/25/1997	10Lib16
02/27/1996	21Gem58	06/26/1996	02Sco16	10/28/1996	29Tau07	02/27/1997	04Sco39
02/29/1996	15Can40	06/28/1996	00Sag00	10/30/1996	24Gem51		
		06/30/1996	29Sag31				
03/02/1996	09Leo37			11/01/1996	19Can22	03/01/1997	29Sco57
03/04/1996	04Vir00	07/02/1996	29Cap54	11/03/1996	13Leo13	03/03/1997	26Sag45
03/06/1996	29Vir05	07/04/1996	29Aqu55	11/05/1996	06Vir57	03/05/1997	25Cap09
03/08/1996	25Lib00	07/06/1996	28Pis27	11/07/1996	01Lib17	03/07/1997	25Aqu00
03/10/1996	21Sco43	07/08/1996	25Ari15	11/09/1996	26Lib43	03/09/1997	25Pis16
03/12/1996	19Sag20	07/10/1996	20Tau45	11/11/1996	23Sco25	03/11/1997	24Ari51
03/14/1996	17Cap46	07/12/1996	15Gem22	11/13/1996	21Sag19	03/13/1997	22Tau51
03/16/1996	16Aqu47	07/14/1996	09Can24	11/15/1996	19Cap45	03/15/1997	19Gem03
03/18/1996	15Pis42	07/16/1996	03Leo11	11/17/1996	18Aqu12	03/17/1997	13Can52
03/20/1996	13Ari41	07/18/1996	26Leo53	11/19/1996	16Pis21	03/19/1997	07Leo51
03/22/1996	10Tau22	07/20/1996	20Vir46	11/21/1996	13Ari59	03/21/1997	01Vir28
03/24/1996	05Gem41	07/22/1996	15Lib19	11/23/1996	11Tau04	03/23/1997	25Vir12
03/26/1996	29Gem55	07/24/1996	11Sco02	11/25/1996	07Gem22	03/25/1997	19Lib23
03/28/1996	23Can43	07/26/1996	08Sag36	11/27/1996	02Can48	03/27/1997	14Sco12
03/30/1996	17Leo40	07/28/1996	07Cap56	11/29/1996	27Can15	03/29/1997	09Sag55
		07/30/1996	08Aqu23			03/31/1997	06Cap44
04/01/1996	12Vir15			12/01/1996	21Leo02	04/02/1997	04Aqu43
04/03/1996	07Lib52	08/01/1996	08Pis43	12/03/1996	14Vir44	04/04/1997	03Pis51
04/05/1996	04Sco30	08/03/1996	07Ari35	12/05/1996	09Lib01	04/06/1997	03Ari28
04/07/1996	02Sag05	08/05/1996	04Tau38	12/07/1996	04Sco32	04/08/1997	02Tau49
04/09/1996	00Cap16	08/07/1996	00Gem04	12/09/1996	01Sag45	04/10/1997	00Gem51
04/11/1996	28Cap40	08/09/1996	24Gem30	12/11/1996	00Cap27	04/12/1997	27Gem15
04/13/1996	27Aqu04	08/11/1996	18Can25	12/13/1996	29Cap49	04/14/1997	22Can15
04/15/1996	24Pis59	08/13/1996	12Leo04	12/15/1996	28Aqu58	04/16/1997	16Leo12
04/17/1996	22Ari11	08/15/1996	05Vir53	12/17/1996	27Pis11	04/18/1997	09Vir51
04/19/1996	18Tau24	08/17/1996	00Lib02	12/19/1996	24Ari22	04/20/1997	03Lib41
04/21/1996	13Gem31	08/19/1996	24Lib46	12/21/1996	20Tau40	04/22/1997	28Lib15
04/23/1996	07Can48	08/21/1996	20Sco37	12/23/1996	16Gem15	04/24/1997	23Sco44
04/25/1996	01Leo35	08/23/1996	17Sag56	12/25/1996	11Can13	04/26/1997	20Sag06
04/27/1996	25Leo31	08/25/1996	16Cap49	12/27/1996	05Leo25	04/28/1997	17Cap21
04/29/1996	20Vir12	08/27/1996	16Aqu52	12/29/1996	29Leo09	04/30/1997	15Aqu17
		08/29/1996	16Pis58	12/31/1996	22Vir48		
		08/31/1996	15Ari56				

Ephemeris Tables for the Moon

Date	Moon	Date	Moon	Date	Moon	Date	Moon
05/02/1997	13Pis46	09/01/1997	03Vir44	01/01/1998	17Aqu01	05/01/1998	18Can07
05/04/1997	12Ari35	09/03/1997	27Vir16	01/03/1998	15Pis24	05/03/1998	13Leo44
05/06/1997	11Tau11	09/05/1997	20Lib54	01/05/1998	13Ari41	05/05/1998	08Vir06
05/08/1997	08Gem51	09/07/1997	15Sco04	01/07/1998	11Tau40	05/07/1998	01Lib49
05/10/1997	05Can13	09/09/1997	10Sag06	01/09/1998	09Gem17	05/09/1998	25Lib25
05/12/1997	00Leo12	09/11/1997	06Cap33	01/11/1998	06Can15	05/11/1998	19Sco25
05/14/1997	24Leo13	09/13/1997	04Aqu43	01/13/1998	02Leo13	05/13/1998	13Sag58
05/16/1997	17Vir51	09/15/1997	04Pis23	01/15/1998	27Leo13	05/15/1998	09Cap13
05/18/1997	11Lib51	09/17/1997	04Ari46	01/17/1998	21Vir16	05/17/1998	05Aqu12
05/20/1997	06Sco46	09/19/1997	04Tau38	01/19/1998	14Lib52	05/19/1998	02Pis15
05/22/1997	02Sag50	09/21/1997	03Gem04	01/21/1998	08Sco43	05/21/1998	00Ari32
05/24/1997	00Cap04	09/23/1997	29Gem43	01/23/1998	03Sag27	05/23/1998	29Ari55
05/26/1997	28Cap02	09/25/1997	24Can46	01/25/1998	29Sag38	05/25/1998	29Tau43
05/28/1997	26Aqu15	09/27/1997	18Leo54	01/27/1998	27Cap21	05/27/1998	28Gem49
05/30/1997	24Pis31	09/29/1997	12Vir33	01/29/1998	26Aqu15	05/29/1998	26Can18
				01/31/1998	25Pis33	05/31/1998	22Leo03
06/01/1997	22Ari38	10/01/1997	06Lib06				
06/03/1997	20Tau21	10/03/1997	29Lib59	02/02/1998	24Ari24	06/02/1998	16Vir25
06/05/1997	17Gem23	10/05/1997	24Sco26	02/04/1998	22Tau27	06/04/1998	10Lib10
06/07/1997	13Can18	10/07/1997	19Sag42	02/06/1998	19Gem33	06/06/1998	03Sco56
06/09/1997	08Leo08	10/09/1997	16Cap01	02/08/1998	15Can41	06/08/1998	28Sco07
06/11/1997	02Vir06	10/11/1997	13Aqu46	02/10/1998	10Leo58	06/10/1998	23Sag10
06/13/1997	25Vir43	10/13/1997	12Pis55	02/12/1998	05Vir29	06/12/1998	18Cap58
06/15/1997	19Lib49	10/15/1997	12Ari54	02/14/1998	29Vir21	06/14/1998	15Aqu31
06/17/1997	14Sco53	10/17/1997	12Tau48	02/16/1998	23Lib00	06/16/1998	12Pis54
06/19/1997	11Sag25	10/19/1997	11Gem29	02/18/1998	16Sco48	06/18/1998	10Ari58
06/21/1997	09Cap24	10/21/1997	08Can19	02/20/1998	11Sag26	06/20/1998	09Tau46
06/23/1997	08Aqu12	10/23/1997	03Leo30	02/22/1998	07Cap28	06/22/1998	08Gem45
06/25/1997	07Pis06	10/25/1997	27Leo33	02/24/1998	05Aqu12	06/24/1998	07Can12
06/27/1997	05Ari27	10/27/1997	21Vir06	02/26/1998	04Pis34	06/26/1998	04Leo22
06/29/1997	03Tau11	10/29/1997	14Lib48	02/28/1998	04Ari34	06/28/1998	00Vir00
		10/31/1997	09Sco02			06/30/1998	24Vir27
07/01/1997	00Gem14			03/02/1998	04Tau16		
07/03/1997	26Gem28	11/02/1997	03Sag57	03/04/1998	02Gem43	07/02/1998	18Lib16
07/05/1997	21Can52	11/04/1997	29Sag43	03/06/1998	29Gem44	07/04/1998	12Sco03
07/07/1997	16Leo22	11/06/1997	26Cap16	03/08/1998	25Can26	07/06/1998	06Sag30
07/09/1997	10Vir09	11/08/1997	23Aqu49	03/10/1998	20Leo06	07/08/1998	01Cap55
07/11/1997	03Lib46	11/10/1997	22Pis18	03/12/1998	14Vir12	07/10/1998	28Cap21
07/13/1997	27Lib48	11/12/1997	21Ari31	03/14/1998	07Lib55	07/12/1998	25Aqu43
07/15/1997	22Sco54	11/14/1997	20Tau55	03/16/1998	01Sco33	07/14/1998	23Pis41
07/17/1997	19Sag39	11/16/1997	19Gem23	03/18/1998	25Sco29	07/16/1998	21Ari56
07/19/1997	18Cap03	11/18/1997	16Can20	03/20/1998	20Sag06	07/18/1998	20Tau22
07/21/1997	17Aqu34	11/20/1997	11Leo35	03/22/1998	15Cap51	07/20/1998	18Gem32
07/23/1997	17Pis12	11/22/1997	05Vir40	03/24/1998	13Aqu19	07/22/1998	16Can09
07/25/1997	16Ari01	11/24/1997	29Vir16	03/26/1998	12Pis32	07/24/1998	12Leo39
07/27/1997	13Tau47	11/26/1997	23Lib03	03/28/1998	12Ari48	07/26/1998	08Vir01
07/29/1997	10Gem21	11/28/1997	17Sco37	03/30/1998	13Tau04	07/28/1998	02Lib23
07/31/1997	06Can00	11/30/1997	13Sag12			07/30/1998	26Lib10
				04/01/1998	12Gem07		
08/02/1997	00Leo49	12/02/1997	09Cap40	04/03/1998	09Can21	08/01/1998	20Sco01
08/04/1997	24Leo54	12/04/1997	06Aqu52	04/05/1998	04Leo52	08/03/1998	14Sag29
08/06/1997	18Vir34	12/06/1997	04Pis36	04/07/1998	29Leo15	08/05/1998	10Cap09
08/08/1997	12Lib07	12/08/1997	02Ari41	04/09/1998	23Vir06	08/07/1998	07Aqu09
08/10/1997	06Sco09	12/10/1997	01Tau10	04/11/1998	16Lib42	08/09/1998	05Pis16
08/12/1997	01Sag13	12/12/1997	29Tau39	04/13/1998	10Sco28	08/11/1998	04Ari04
08/14/1997	27Sag51	12/14/1997	27Gem27	04/15/1998	04Sag39	08/13/1998	02Tau55
08/16/1997	26Cap19	12/16/1997	24Can06	04/17/1998	29Sag25	08/15/1998	01Gem16
08/18/1997	26Aqu12	12/18/1997	19Leo19	04/19/1998	25Cap10	08/17/1998	28Gem54
08/20/1997	26Pis22	12/20/1997	13Vir30	04/21/1998	22Aqu15	08/19/1998	25Can38
08/22/1997	25Ari50	12/22/1997	07Lib05	04/23/1998	21Pis01	08/21/1998	21Leo24
08/24/1997	23Tau51	12/24/1997	00Sco57	04/25/1998	21Ari03	08/23/1998	16Vir18
08/26/1997	20Gem17	12/26/1997	25Sco42	04/27/1998	21Tau18	08/25/1998	10Lib28
08/28/1997	15Can32	12/28/1997	21Sag42	04/29/1998	20Gem37	08/27/1998	04Sco15
08/30/1997	09Leo55	12/30/1997	18Cap58			08/29/1998	28Sco01
						08/31/1998	22Sag28

Ephemeris Tables for the Moon

Date	Moon	Date	Moon	Date	Moon	Date	Moon
09/02/1998	18Cap07	01/02/1999	16Can42	05/02/1999	02Sag10	09/01/1999	19Tau40
09/04/1998	15Aqu18	01/04/1999	14Leo35	05/04/1999	25Sag54	09/03/1999	18Gem06
09/06/1998	14Pis03	01/06/1999	10Vir51	05/06/1999	19Cap57	09/05/1999	16Can18
09/08/1998	13Ari43	01/08/1999	05Lib37	05/08/1999	14Aqu45	09/07/1999	14Leo07
09/10/1998	13Tau17	01/10/1999	29Lib35	05/10/1999	10Pis58	09/09/1999	11Vir13
09/12/1998	11Gem59	01/12/1999	23Sco20	05/12/1999	09Ari01	09/11/1999	07Lib22
09/14/1998	09Can21	01/14/1999	17Sag24	05/14/1999	08Tau52	09/13/1999	02Sco30
09/16/1998	05Leo27	01/16/1999	12Cap16	05/16/1999	09Gem29	09/15/1999	26Sco42
09/18/1998	00Vir35	01/18/1999	08Aqu03	05/18/1999	09Can23	09/17/1999	20Sag28
09/20/1998	24Vir58	01/20/1999	04Pis42	05/20/1999	07Leo41	09/19/1999	14Cap22
09/22/1998	18Lib55	01/22/1999	02Ari03	05/22/1999	04Vir10	09/21/1999	09Aqu02
09/24/1998	12Sco37	01/24/1999	00Tau04	05/24/1999	29Vir13	09/23/1999	05Pis07
09/26/1998	06Sag24	01/26/1999	28Tau31	05/26/1999	23Lib29	09/25/1999	02Ari36
09/28/1998	00Cap48	01/28/1999	27Gem03	05/28/1999	17Sco21	09/27/1999	01Tau15
09/30/1998	26Cap13	01/30/1999	25Can13	05/30/1999	11Sag03	09/29/1999	00Gem24
10/02/1998	23Aqu15	02/01/1999	22Leo30	06/01/1999	04Cap56	10/01/1999	29Gem05
10/04/1998	22Pis10	02/03/1999	18Vir30	06/03/1999	29Cap08	10/03/1999	27Can01
10/06/1998	22Ari22	02/05/1999	13Lib23	06/05/1999	24Aqu06	10/05/1999	24Leo03
10/08/1998	22Tau42	02/07/1999	07Sco25	06/07/1999	20Pis16	10/07/1999	20Vir23
10/10/1998	21Gem54	02/09/1999	01Sag09	06/09/1999	18Ari01	10/09/1999	15Lib58
10/12/1998	19Can23	02/11/1999	25Sag18	06/11/1999	17Tau33	10/11/1999	10Sco43
10/14/1998	15Leo13	02/13/1999	20Cap21	06/13/1999	17Gem51	10/13/1999	04Sag48
10/16/1998	09Vir53	02/15/1999	16Aqu34	06/15/1999	17Can50	10/15/1999	28Sag30
10/18/1998	03Lib58	02/17/1999	14Pis04	06/17/1999	16Leo18	10/17/1999	22Cap16
10/20/1998	27Lib44	02/19/1999	12Ari22	06/19/1999	13Vir00	10/19/1999	16Aqu52
10/22/1998	21Sco24	02/21/1999	11Tau04	06/21/1999	08Lib09	10/21/1999	12Pis58
10/24/1998	15Sag19	02/23/1999	09Gem28	06/23/1999	02Sco19	10/23/1999	10Ari49
10/26/1998	09Cap42	02/25/1999	07Can22	06/25/1999	26Sco07	10/25/1999	10Tau15
10/28/1998	04Aqu57	02/27/1999	04Leo39	06/27/1999	19Sag54	10/27/1999	10Gem13
10/30/1998	01Pis43			06/29/1999	13Cap58	10/29/1999	09Can31
		03/01/1999	01Vir02			10/31/1999	07Leo35
11/01/1998	00Ari17	03/03/1999	26Vir35	07/01/1999	08Aqu36		
11/03/1998	00Tau30	03/05/1999	21Lib15	07/03/1999	03Pis59	11/02/1999	04Vir16
11/05/1998	01Gem06	03/07/1999	15Sco16	07/05/1999	00Ari19	11/04/1999	00Lib02
11/07/1998	00Can45	03/09/1999	09Sag03	07/07/1999	28Ari00	11/06/1999	24Lib59
11/09/1998	28Can37	03/11/1999	03Cap04	07/09/1999	26Tau56	11/08/1999	19Sco22
11/11/1998	24Leo29	03/13/1999	28Cap05	07/11/1999	26Gem36	11/10/1999	13Sag16
11/13/1998	19Vir02	03/15/1999	24Aqu34	07/13/1999	26Can06	11/12/1999	06Cap52
11/15/1998	12Lib55	03/17/1999	22Pis37	07/15/1999	24Leo29	11/14/1999	00Aqu37
11/17/1998	06Sco34	03/19/1999	21Ari53	07/17/1999	21Vir16	11/16/1999	25Aqu03
11/19/1998	00Sag23	03/21/1999	21Tau25	07/19/1999	16Lib30	11/18/1999	20Pis58
11/21/1998	24Sag30	03/23/1999	20Gem16	07/21/1999	10Sco43	11/20/1999	18Ari47
11/23/1998	19Cap09	03/25/1999	18Can01	07/23/1999	04Sag34	11/22/1999	18Tau23
11/25/1998	14Aqu33	03/27/1999	14Leo37	07/25/1999	28Sag25	11/24/1999	18Gem54
11/27/1998	11Pis05	03/29/1999	10Vir18	07/27/1999	22Cap48	11/26/1999	18Can55
11/29/1998	09Ari12	03/31/1999	05Lib14	07/29/1999	17Aqu57	11/28/1999	17Leo24
				07/31/1999	13Pis56	11/30/1999	14Vir13
12/01/1998	08Tau51	04/02/1999	29Lib34				
12/03/1998	09Gem07	04/04/1999	23Sco32	08/02/1999	10Ari52	12/02/1999	09Lib41
12/05/1998	08Can49	04/06/1999	17Sag15	08/04/1999	08Tau39	12/04/1999	04Sco13
12/07/1998	06Leo52	04/08/1999	11Cap15	08/06/1999	07Gem12	12/06/1999	28Sco16
12/09/1998	02Vir58	04/10/1999	06Aqu07	08/08/1999	06Can06	12/08/1999	22Sag00
12/11/1998	27Vir37	04/12/1999	02Pis28	08/10/1999	04Leo45	12/10/1999	15Cap39
12/13/1998	21Lib29	04/14/1999	00Ari45	08/12/1999	02Vir37	12/12/1999	09Aqu29
12/15/1998	15Sco11	04/16/1999	00Tau32	08/14/1999	29Vir15	12/14/1999	04Pis00
12/17/1998	09Sag08	04/18/1999	00Gem49	08/16/1999	24Lib30	12/16/1999	29Pis46
12/19/1998	03Cap39	04/20/1999	00Can19	08/18/1999	18Sco47	12/18/1999	27Ari09
12/21/1998	28Cap49	04/22/1999	28Can13	08/20/1999	12Sag36	12/20/1999	26Tau28
12/23/1998	24Aqu39	04/24/1999	24Leo36	08/22/1999	06Cap33	12/22/1999	26Gem54
12/25/1998	21Pis24	04/26/1999	19Vir51	08/24/1999	01Aqu07	12/24/1999	27Can10
12/27/1998	19Ari14	04/28/1999	14Lib19	08/26/1999	26Aqu48	12/26/1999	26Leo11
12/29/1998	18Tau07	04/30/1999	08Sco25	08/28/1999	23Pis38	12/28/1999	23Vir22
12/31/1998	17Gem37			08/30/1999	21Ari21	12/30/1999	18Lib53

✧ Suggested Reading List ✧

Davison, Ronald C. *Astrology*. New York: Arco Pubishing, 1967.

De Vore, Nicholas. *Encyclopedia of Astrology*. New York: Philosophical Library, Inc., 1958.

Erlewine, Michael and Margaret Erlewine. *Astrophysical Directions*. Big Rapids, MI: Heart Center, 1977.

Evans, C. *The New Waite's Compendium of Natal Astrology*. York Beach, ME: Samuel Weiser, Inc., 1971.

George, Llewellyn. *A to Z Horoscope Maker and Delineator*. St. Paul, MN: Llewellyn Publications, 1981.

Janov, Arthur. *The Primal Scream*. New York: Putnam Pub., 1981.

Jung, Carl Gustav. *Psychology & Religion*. Princeton, NJ: Princeton University Press, 1969.

Liedloff, Jean. *The Continuum Concept*. London: Futura, 1976.

Mayo, Jeff. *Teach Yourself Astrology*. New York: McKay, 1980.

On the following pages you will find listed, with their current prices, some of the books now available on related subjects. Your book dealer stocks most of these and will stock new titles in the Llewellyn series as they become available. We urge your patronage.

TO GET A FREE CATALOG

You are invited to write for our bi-monthly news magazine and catalog, *Llewellyn's New Worlds of Mind and Spirit*. A sample copy is free, and it will continue coming to you at no cost as long as you are an active mail customer. Or you may subscribe for just $10 in the United States and Canada ($20 overseas, first class mail). Many bookstores also have *New Worlds* available to their customers. Ask for it.

In *New Worlds* you will find news and features about new books, tapes and services; announcements of meetings and seminars; helpful articles; author interviews and much more. Write to:

Llewellyn's New Worlds of Mind and Spirit
P.O. Box 64383-594, St. Paul, MN 55164-0383, U.S.A.

TO ORDER BOOKS AND TAPES

If your book store does not carry the titles described on the following pages, you may order them directly from Llewellyn by sending the full price in U.S. funds, plus postage and handling (see below).

Credit card orders: VISA, MasterCard, American Express are accepted. Call toll-free in the USA and Canada at 1-800-THE-MOON.

Special Group Discount: Because there is a great deal of interest in group discussion and study of the subject matter of this book, we offer a 20% quantity discount to group leaders or agents. Our Special Quantity Price for a minimum order of five copies of *Your Planetary Personality* is $79.80 cash-with-order. Include postage and handling charges noted below.

Postage and Handling: Include $4 postage and handling for orders $15 and under; $5 for orders *over* $15. There are no postage and handling charges for orders over $100. Postage and handling rates are subject to change. We ship UPS whenever possible within the continental United States; delivery is guaranteed. Please provide your street address as UPS does not deliver to P.O. boxes. Orders shipped to Alaska, Hawaii, Canada, Mexico and Puerto Rico will be sent via first class mail. Allow 4-6 weeks for delivery. **International orders:** Airmail – add retail price of each book and $5 for each non-book item (audiotapes, etc.); Surface mail – add $1 per item.

Minnesota residents please add 7% sales tax.

Mail orders to:
Llewellyn Worldwide, P.O. Box 64383-594, St. Paul, MN 55164-0383, U.S.A.

For customer service, call (612) 291-1970.

Prices subject to change without notice.

ASTROLOGY FOR THE MILLIONS
by Grant Lewi
First published in 1940, this practical, do-it-yourself textbook has become a classic guide to computing accurate horoscopes quickly. Throughout the years, it has been improved upon since Grant Lewi's death by his astrological proteges and Llewellyn's expert editors. Grant Lewi is astrology's forerunner to the computer, a man who literally brought astrology to everyone. This, the first new edition since 1979, presents updated transits and new, user-friendly tables to the year 2050, including a new sun ephemeris of revolutionary simplicity. It's actually easier to use than a computer! Also added is new information on Pluto and rising signs, and a new foreword by Carl Llewellyn Weschcke and introduction by J. Gordon Melton.

Of course, the original material is still here in Lewi's captivating writing style—all of his insights on transits as a tool for planning the future and making the right decisions. His historical analysis of U.S. presidents has been brought up to date to include George Bush. This new edition also features a special In Memoriam to Lewi that presents his birthchart.

One of the most remarkable astrology books available, *Astrology for the Millions* allows the reader to cast a personal horoscope in 15 minutes, interpret from the readings and project the horoscope into the future to forecast coming planetary influences and develop "a grand strategy for living."
0-87542-438-4, 300 pgs., 6 x 9, softcover   **$12.95**

THE NEW A TO Z HOROSCOPE MAKER AND DELINEATOR
by Llewellyn George
This is a new and totally revised edition of the text used by more American astrologers than any other—135,000 copies sold. Every detail of: How to Cast the Birth Chart—time changes, calculations, aspects & orbs, signs & planetary rulers, parts of fortune, etc.; The Progressed Chart—all the techniques and the major delineations; Transits—how to use them in prediction; also lunations and solar days. Rectification. Locality Charts, a comprehensive Astrological Dictionary and a complete index for easy use. It's an encyclopedia, a textbook, a self–study course and and a dictionary all–in–one!
0–87542–264–0, 600 pgs., 6 x 9, softcover.   **$12.95**

ASTROLOGY FOR BEGINNERS
by William Hewitt
Anyone who is interested in astrology will enjoy *Astrology for Beginners*. This book makes astrology easy and exciting by presenting all of the basics in an orderly sequence while focusing on the natal chart. Llewellyn even includes a coupon for a free computerized natal chart so you can begin interpretations almost immediately without complicated mathematics.

Astrology for Beginners covers all of the basics. Learn exactly what astrology is and how it works. Explore signs, planets, houses and aspects. Learn how to interpret a birth chart. Discover the meaning of transits, predictive astrology and progressions. Determine your horoscope chart in minutes without using math.

Whether you want to practice astrology for a hobby or aspire to become a professional astrologer, *Astrology for Beginners* is the book you need to get started on the right track.
0-87542-307-8, 288 pgs., 5-1/4 x 8, softcover   **$7.95**

THE ASTROLOGY OF THE MACROCOSM
edited by Joan McEvers

The fifth book in Llewellyn's New World Astrology Series, *The Astrology of the Macrocosm* contains charts and articles from some of the world's top astrologers, explaining various mundane, transpersonal, and worldly events through astrology. It will help you gain insights into the global arenas of politics, social organization, and cultural analysis. It is the perfect introduction to understanding the fate of nations, weather patterns, and other global movements.

Featured are noted astrologers Nick Campion, Carolyn W. Casey, Steve Cozzi, Jimm Erickson, Charles Harvey, Jim Lewis, Richard Nolle, Marc Penfield, Nancy Soller and Judy Johns. Topics include ingress charts, cycles, Astro*Carto*Graphy, cultural and mythological evolution, the chart of England, weather forecasting and more. Charts and diagrams expand and illustrate most of the articles.

0-87542-384-1, 480 pgs., 5-1/4 x 8, softcover $14.95

ASTROLOGICAL COUNSELING: The Path to Self-Actualization
edited by Joan McEvers

A very prominent, yet rarely discussed astrological topic, is that of the role between the counselor and the counseled. *Astrological Counseling*, the sixth book in Llewellyn's New World Astrology series, explores the challenges for today's counselors, and gives guidance to those interested in seeking a counselor to help them with their own personal challenges. Editor Joan McEvers has enlisted the help of ten top astrologers to discuss this important subject.

Bill Herbst, Donna Cunningham, Gray Keen, Donald L. Weston, Susan Dearborn Jackson, Ginger Chalford, Maritha Pottenger, David Pond, Doris A. Hebel and Eileen Nauman are this volume's featured astrologers. Their articles cover such topics as co-dependency, psychotherapy, reading the body, healing wounded spirits, personal counseling, business counseling, medical counseling, and more.

There are more people consulting with astrologers than there are devoted astrological students. This book helps both groups understand the needs of the modern counseling client.

0-87542-385-X, 368 pgs., 5-1/4 x 8, softcover $14.95

INTIMATE RELATIONSHIPS
edited by Joan McEvers

Explore the deeper meaning of intimate relationships with the knowledge and expertise of eight renowned astrologers. Dare to look into your own chart and confront your own vulnerabilities. Find the true meaning of love and its place in your life. Gain new insights into the astrology of marriage, dating, affairs and more!

In *Intimate Relationships*, the seventh book in Llewellyn's New World Astrology Series, eight astrologers discuss their views on romance and the horoscope. The roles of Venus and the Moon, as well as the asteroids Sappho, Eros and Amor, are explored in our attitudes and actions toward potential mates. The theory of affinities is also presented wherein we are attracted to someone with similar planetary energies.

Is it a love that will last a lifetime, or mere animal lust that will burn itself out in a few months? The authors of *Intimate Relationships* will help you discover your natal attractions as well as your fatal attractions.

0-87542-386-8, 298 pgs., 6 x 9, softcover $14.95

PLANETS: THE ASTROLOGICAL TOOLS
Edited by Joan McEvers
This is the second in the Llewellyn New World Astrology Series edited by respected astrologer Joan McEvers, who provides a brief factual overview of the planets.

Then take off through the solar system with 10 professional astrologers as they bring their insights to the symbolism and influences of the planets.

- Toni Glover Sedgwick: The Sun as the life force and our ego
- Joanne Wickenburg: The Moon as our emotional signal to change
- Erin Sullivan-Seale: Mercury as the multi-faceted god, followed with an in-depth explanation of its retrogradation
- Robert Glasscock: Venus as your inner value system and relationships
- Johanna Mitchell: Mars as your cooperative, energizing inner warrior
- Don Borkowski: Jupiter as expansion and preservation
- Gina Ceaglio: Saturn as a source of freedom through self-discipline
- Bil Tierney: Uranus as the original, growth-producing planet
- Karma Welch: Neptune as selfless giving and compassionate love
- Joan Negus: Pluto as a powerful personal force

0–87542–381–7, 380 pgs., 5-1/4 x 8, charts, softcover   **$12.95**

THE HOUSES: POWER PLACES OF THE HOROSCOPE
Edited by Joan McEvers
The fourth in Llewellyn's astrology anthology series, this volume explores each house of the natal chart with clarity and understanding, drawing on the knowledge and talents of 11 respected astrologers. Various house systems are briefly described in Joan McEvers' introduction. Learn about house associations and planetary influences upon each house's activities with the following experts.:

- Peter Damian: The First House and the Rising Sun
- Ken Negus: The Seventh House
- Noel Tyl: The Second House and The Eighth House
- Spencer Grendahl: The Third House
- Dona Shaw: The Ninth House
- Gloria Star: The Fourth House
- Marwayne Leipzig: The Tenth House
- Lina Accurso: Exploring Your Fifth House
- Sara Corbin Looms: The Eleventh: House of Tomorrow
- Michael Munkasey: The Sixth House
- Joan McEvers: The Twelfth House: Strength, Peace, Tranquillity

0–87542–383–3, 400 pgs., 5-1/4 x 8, illus., softcover   **$12.95**

COMPUTERIZED ASTROLOGY REPORTS

Simple Natal
Your chart calculated by computer in the Tropical/Placidus House system or the House system of your choice. It has all of the trimmings, including aspects, midpoints, Chiron and a glossary of symbols, plus a free booklet!
APS03-119. . . . . $5.00

Personality Profile Horoscope
Our most popular reading! This ten-part reading gives you a complete look at how the planets affect you. Learn about your general characteristics and life patterns. Look into your imagination and emotional needs. It is an excellent way to become acquainted with astrology and to learn about yourself. Very reasonable price!
APS03-503 . . . . $20.00

Transit Forecasts
These reports keep you abreast of positive trends and challenging periods. Transit Forecasts can be an invaluable aid for timing your actions and decision making. Reports begin the first day of the month you specify.
3-month Transit Forecast : APS03-500 . . . .$12.00
6-month Transit Forecast : APS03-501 . . . .$20.00
1-year Transit Forecast : APS03-502 . . . .$25.00

Life Progressions :
Discover what the future has in store for you! This incredible reading covers a year's time and is designed to complement the Personality Profile Reading. Progressions are a special system with which astrologers map how the "natal you" develops through specified periods of your present and future life, and with this report you can discover the "now you!"
APSO3-507. . . . . $20.00

Personal Relationship Reading
If you've just called it quits on one relationship and know you need to understand more about yourself before you test the waters again, then this is the report for you! This reading will tell you how you approach relationships in general, what kind of people you look for and what kind of people might rub you the wrong way. Important for anyone!
APS03-506. . . . . $20.00

Compatibility Profile
Find out if you really are compatible with your lover, spouse, friend or business partner! This is a great way of getting an in-depth look at your relationship with another person. Find out each person's approach to the relationship. Do you have the same goals? How well do you deal with arguments? Do you have the same values? This service includes planetary placements for both individuals, so send birth data for both and specify the type of relationship (i.e., friends, lovers, etc.). Order today!
APS03-504 . . . . $30.00

Ultimate Astro-Profile
Receive over 40 pages of fascinating, insightful and uncanny descriptions of your innermost qualities and talents. Read about your burn rate (thirst for change). Explore your personal patterns (inside and outside). Examine the particular pattern of your Houses. The Astro-Profile doesn't repeat what you've already learned from other personality profiles, but considers the often neglected natal influence of the lunar nodes, plus much more!
APS03-505 . . . . $40.00

How to Order
1. Fill out this order form.
2. Send form with descriptive letter and main concerns.
3. Use birth certificate for accurate information.
4. Send order by mail; absolutely no phone orders.

NAME OF SERVICE

ORDER NUMBER

Astrological Knowledge: ❑ Novice   ❑ Student   ❑ Advanced

FULL NAME (1ST PERSON)

BIRTH TIME   ❑ am   ❑ pm   DATE   YEAR

BIRTHPLACE – CITY, COUNTY, STATE, COUNTRY

FULL NAME (2ND PERSON)

BIRTH TIME   ❑ am   ❑ pm   DATE   YEAR

BIRTHPLACE – CITY, COUNTY, STATE, COUNTRY

BILLING INFORMATION

NAME

ADDRESS

CITY   STATE   ZIP

DAYTIME PHONE

Make checks or money orders payable to Llewellyn Worldwide.

CHARGE IT!   ❑ VISA   ❑ MASTERCARD   ❑ AMERICAN EXPRESS

CARD #   EXP. DATE

SIGNATURE OF CARDHOLDER

MAIL THIS FORM WITH PAYMENT TO: Llewellyn Personal Services, P.O. Box 64383-307, St. Paul, MN 55164-0383. Allow 4-6 wks. for delivery.

Prices subject to change without notice.